Encyclopedia of World Literature in the 20th Century

Encyclopedia of
in the

REVISED EDITION

IN FOUR VOLUMES
AND
INDEX

World Literature 20th Century

LEONARD S. KLEIN, General Editor

VOLUME 3: L to Q

A Frederick Ungar Book
CONTINUUM • NEW YORK

1989

The Continuum Publishing Company
370 Lexington Avenue
New York, NY 10017

Copyright © 1969, 1971, 1975, 1983
Frederick Ungar Publishing Co., Inc.

Third Printing

Printed in the United States of America
Designed by Patrick Vitacco

Library of Congress Cataloging in Publication Data

Main entry under title:
Encyclopedia of world literature in the 20th century.

    Includes bibliographies.
    1.   Literature, Modern–20th century-Bio-bibli-
ography.   2.   Literature, Modern–20th century-
Dictionaries.   I.   Klein, Leonard S.
PN771.E5   1983   803   81–3357
ISBN 0–8044–3137–X (v. 3)   AACR2

Board of Advisers

Tamas Aczel
UNIVERSITY OF MASSACHUSETTS

Hungarian Literature

Roger M. A. Allen
UNIVERSITY OF PENNSYLVANIA

Arabic Literatures

Edward Allworth
COLUMBIA UNIVERSITY

Non-Slavic Soviet Literatures

Thomas E. Bird
QUEENS COLLEGE

Yiddish, Byelorussian, and Russian Literatures

Carlo Coppola
OAKLAND UNIVERSITY

South Asian Literatures

John M. Echols
CORNELL UNIVERSITY

Southeast Asian Literatures

John H. Ferres
MICHIGAN STATE UNIVERSITY

Commonwealth Literatures

Harold Fisch
BAR-ILAN UNIVERSITY

Israeli Literature

Z. Folejewski
UNIVERSITY OF OTTAWA

Polish Literature

Albert S. Gérard
UNIVERSITÉ DE LIÈGE

African Literatures

Jerry Glenn
UNIVERSITY OF CINCINNATI

German Literature

v

vi

vii

Contributors to Volume 3

Tamas Aczel
Nagy updating

Jaakko A. Ahokas
Manner
Meri

Earl M. Aldrich, Jr.
Peruvian Literature

Roger M. A. Allen
Mahfūz

James J. Alstrum
Lugones
Magic Realism
Neruda
Parra

Benedict R. O'G. Anderson
Pramoedya

Joseph Aquilina
Maltese Literature
Psaila

James B. Atkinson
Mamet

Ehrhard Bahr
Lukács

Maria Němcová Banerjee
Majerová
Nezval
Novomeský

Lowell A. Bangerter
Müller

Chandler B. Beall
Quasimodo

George J. Becker
Postrealism

C. Harold Bedford
Merezhkovsky

E. M. Beekman
Ostaijen
Pillecijn

David F. Beer
La Guma

Janine Beichman
Masaoka

Carl D. Bennett
Pynchon

Alice R. Bensen
Macaulay

Bernard Benstock
O'Brien, F.
O'Casey

Gene M. Bernstein
Lévi-Strauss

CONTRIBUTORS TO VOLUME 3

Jo Brantley Berryman
Lowell, A.
Pound

Konrad Bieber
Prévert

Thomas E. Bird
Lewis, Saunders

Randi Birn
New Novel

Joan Bischoff
Morrison

R. L. Blackmore
Powys, J. C.
Powys, T. F.

Issa J. Boullata
Palestinian Literature
Qabbānī

Anthony Boxill
Lamming
Mittelholzer

B. R. Bradbrook
Machar

Sidney D. Braun
Paulhan

Wilhelm Braun
Musil

Evelyn Bristol
Pilnyak

Barbara J. Bucknall
Leduc

Robert L. Busch
Platonov

Robert L. Calder
Maugham

Rocco Capozzi
Ottieri

Alice-Catherine Carls
Parnicki

Boyd G. Carter
López y Fuentes
Magdaleno
Modernism

Anita Marie Caspary, I. H. M.
Mauriac, F.

Leonard Casper
Philippine Literature

David Castronovo
Mencken

Glenn Clever
Leacock

Carl W. Cobb
Pérez de Ayala

Arthur B. Coffin
Merwin

Carol J. Compton
Lao Literature

Michael G. Cooke
p'Bitek

Henry R. Cooper, Jr.
Przybyszewski

Carlo Coppola
Naidu
Nazrul Islam
Premchand

Jane E. Cottrell
Moravia

Bijay Kumar Das
Mohanty

Andonis Decavalles
Palamas
Prevelakis

Diana Der Hovanessian
Matevossian
Oshagan

Lynn DeVore
Marquand
O'Hara, J.
Purdy

D. J. Dooley
Priestley
Pritchett

Fraser Drew
Masefield

Vytas Dukas
Leonov

Joris Duytschaever
Mulisch

John M. Echols
Perron

Rolfs Ekmanis
Latvian Literature

Ahmet Ö. Evin
Nesin

Marion Faber
Mann, H.

Michel Fabre
Mauritian Literature

Doris V. Falk
O'Neill

John M. Fein
Paz

John H. Ferres
MacLennan
New Zealand Literature

Leland Fetzer
Prishvin

Earl E. Fitz
Lispector
Lobato
Meireles

Jeanne A. Flood
Moore, B.

Zbigniew Folejewski
Polish Literature

Albert M. Forcadas
Pedrolo

Marianne Forssblad
Munk
Panduro

Leonard Fox
North Caucasian Literatures

Wynne Francis
Layton

John Franzosa
Olson

Bernard J. Fridsma, Sr.
Netherlands Literature: Frisian
Literature

Alan Warren Friedman
Miller, H.

Erik Frykman
MacCaig

Steven H. Gale
Pinter

Xenia Gasiorowska
Nałkowska

Janet Powers Gemmill
Malgonkar
Markandaya
Narayan

Albert S. Gérard
Malagasy Literature: In Malagasy
Nigerian Literature

CONTRIBUTORS TO VOLUME 3

Helmut E. Gerber
Moore, G.

George E. Gingras
Péguy

Nancy K. Gish
MacDiarmid

Jerry Glenn
Piontek

Barbara Godard
Nelligan

Itche Goldberg
Manger

Ambrose Gordon
Marechal

Sherrill E. Grace
Lowry

Vernon Gras
Phenomenology and Literature

Charlotte Schiander Gray
Malinovski

Sheldon N. Grebstein
Lewis, Sinclair

Geoffrey Green
Mailer

Robert W. Greene
Ponge

Frederic J. Grover
Montherlant

Yvonne Guers-Villate
Mallet-Joris

Clara Györgyey
Molnár

Igor Hájek
Lustig
Mňačko
Páral

Russell G. Hamilton
Mozambican Literature

John G. Hanna
Morris

John Edward Hardy
Percy
Porter

George Harjan
Parandowski

William E. Harkins
Olesha

Emmanuel Hatzantonis
Levi

Adnan Haydar
Lebanese Literature

Michael Heim
Olbracht

Erich Heller
Mann, T.

James Robert Hewitt
Larbaud
Malraux
Proust

Leah D. Hewitt
Leiris

Charles G. Hill
Pagnol
Queneau

Evelyn J. Hinz
Nin

Edward Hirsch
Lowell, R.
Owen

Keith Hitchins
Mamedkulizade
Moldavian Literature

xii

CONTRIBUTORS TO VOLUME 3

Sona Stephan Hoisington
Paustovsky

Elizabeth Huberman
Muir

Olga Raevsky Hughes
Pasternak

Gaetano A. Iannace
Piccolo

Chidi Ikonné
Maran

A. Illiano
Marinetti
Prisco

Niels Ingwersen
Nexø

Astrid Ivask
Latvian Literature

Raymond Jarvi
Lidman

Nadja Jernakoff
Ostrovsky
Panova

Manly Johnson
Paton

Richard A. Johnson
Powell

Edward T. Jones
Lewis, W.
Myers

Eveline L. Kanes
Morgenstern

Alexander Karanikas
Panayotopoulos

L. Clark Keating
Maurois

Donald Keene
Mishima

Rosemarie Kieffer
Luxembourg Literature

Robert F. Kiernan
McCullers
O'Connor, Flannery

Edmund L. King
Miró

Bettina L. Knapp
Maeterlinck

Stephen W. Kohl
Natsume
Ōe

Egbert Krispyn
Marsman

John R. Krueger
Mongolian Literature

Leo Ou-fan Lee
Lu Hsün

Peter H. Lee
Pak

Vincent B. Leitch
Masing

Sharon L. Leiter
Mandelshtam

Madeline G. Levine
Lechoń
Przyboś

Emanuele Licastro
Pavese

Myron I. Lichtblau
Mallea

Bernth Lindfors
Ngugi
Okara
Okigbo

CONTRIBUTORS TO VOLUME 3

Liu Wu-chi
Liu
Mao Tun

Joyce O. Lowrie
Pieyre de Mandiargues

Torborg Lundell
Lindegren
Lo-Johansson

James Lundquist
London

Gregory Luznycky
Lusatian Literature

William A. Lyell
Lao She

Marvin Magalaner
Mansfield

Nathan K. Mao
Pa Chin

Marzbed Margossian
Matevossian
Oshagan

Jean Marquard
Millin

Wilson Martins
Queiroz

Ben McKulik
MacLeish

A. L. McLeod
McKay

George R. McMurray
Leñero
Marqués
Mexican Literature

Tibor Méray
Nagy

Siegfried Mews
Lenz

Mario B. Mignone
Pratolini

Vasa D. Mihailovich
Popa

Mohd. Taib bin Osman
Malaysian Literature

Charles Molesworth
Plath

Charles Moorman
Lewis, C. S.

Nicholas Moravčevich
Nušić

Patricia Morley
Laurence

Robert K. Morris
Naipaul

Walter D. Morris
Mehren
Norwegian Literature

Mildred Mortimer
Mali Literature

Edward Mullen
Nervo

Antonino Musumeci
Neorealism

Virgil Nemoianu
Lovinescu
Negoiţescu
Petrescu
Popescu
Preda

Susanna S. Nettleton
Qadiriy

Dinh-Hoa Nguyen
Nguyễn
Nhất-Linh

xiv

CONTRIBUTORS TO VOLUME 3

Fred J. Nichols
Leopold
Nijhoff

George W. Nitchie
Moore, M.

Gillian L. G. Noero
Plomer

Patricia W. O'Connor
Martínez Sierra

Vésteinn Ólason
Laxness

Harold Orel
Lindsay
Millay

Eugene Orenstein
Der Nister

María-Luisa Osorio
Matute

Augustus Pallotta
Mastronardi
Piovene

Goffredo Pallucchini
Luzi
Morante

K. Ayyappa Paniker
Menon

Uma Parameswaran
Pacific Islands Literatures

Jan L. Perkowski
Polish Literature: Kashubian Literature

Thomas Amherst Perry
Philippide

Richard F. Peterson
Murphy
O'Brien, E.
O'Connor, Frank

Sandy Petrey
Mauriac, C.

Debra Popkin
Martin du Gard
Oyono

Zephyra Porat
Oz

John Povey
Lesotho Literature
Liberian Literature
Malawian Literature

Richard Priebe
Peters

Peter Prochnik
Nossack

Carl R. Proffer
Nabokov

Phyllis Rackin
Leavis

Olga Ragusa
Pirandello

Aleksis Rannit
Liiv

Robert M. Rehder
Larkin

M. Ricciardelli
Ortese

Friedhelm Rickert
Meyrink
Preradović

J. Thomas Rimer
Mori
Nagai

Hugo Rodríguez-Alcalá
Paraguayan Literature

Sidney Rosenfeld
Polgar

David G. Roskies
Markish

Sven H. Rossel
Paludan
Petersen

Steven J. Rubin
Malamud

Judith Ruderman
Lawrence

Leo D. Rudnytzky
Lusatian Literature

Randolph Runyon
Nizan

Rinaldina Russell
Pascoli

Richard Sáez
Merrill

Mariolina Salvatori
Landolfi

Ivan Sanders
Móricz
Németh
Pilinszky

Hiroaki Sato
Miyazawa

George D. Schade
Quiroga

George O. Schanzer
Mujica Láinez

Paul Schlueter
Lessing
Masters
McCarthy
Pitter

Marshall J. Schneider
Laforet
Pérez Galdós

George C. Schoolfield
Lehtonen
Linna

Kessel Schwartz
Machado
Onetti

Steven Schwartz
O'Hara, F.

Robert H. Scott
Payró

Eric Sellin
Mammeri

Jorge de Sena
Pessoa

Tara Nath Sharma
Nepalese Literature

R. Baird Shuman
Odets

William L. Siemens
Lezama Lima

Rimvydas Šilbajoris
Lithuanian Literature
Mykolaitis

Jan Sjåvik
Øverland

Viktoria Skrupskelis
La Tour du Pin
Michaux

Biljana Šljivić-Šimšić
Lalić
Maksimović
Pavlović

Elton E. Smith
MacNeice

Esther M. G. Smith
Manning

CONTRIBUTORS TO VOLUME 3

Steven P. Sondrup
Lundkvist

Gene Sosin
Okudzhava

Mihai Spariosu
Maniu
Papadat-Bengescu
Pillat

Martin S. Stabb
Martínez Estrada

Juliette R. Stapanian
Mayakovsky

Marie-Georgette Steisel
Ollier
Pinget

Irwin Stern
Martín-Santos
Namora
Pessoa updating
Pires
Portuguese Literature

Norman A. Stillman
Moroccan Literature

David Stouck
Pratt

Philip Stratford
Langevin

Larry ten Harmsel
Lucebert
Nemerov

Anthony R. Terrizzi
Palazzeschi

George Thaniel
Myrivilis
Papadiamantis

Ewa Thompson
Leśmian
Miłosz
Mrożek

Fridrik Thordarson
Ossetic Literature

Lindsey Tucker
Murdoch

Martin Tucker
Mofolo
Mphahlele

Alberta Turner
Levertov

Marie Olesen Urbanski
Oates

Jack A. Vaughn
Miller, A.

Catherine Vera
Mistral

Manindra K. Verma
Nepalese Literature

Reino Virtanen
Leino

Jennifer R. Waelti-Walters
Le Clézio

Clive Wake
Malagasy Literature: In French
Negritude

Lars G. Warme
Martinson

Wayne Warncke
Orwell

Frank J. Warnke
Netherlands Literature: Dutch
Literature

René Wellek
Literary Criticism

Linda Wentink
Pakistani Literature

CONTRIBUTORS TO VOLUME 3

Rebecca J. West
Montale
Pasolini

Raymond L. Williams
Puig

Krishna Winston
Mehring

Howard B. Wolman
Osborne

Rochelle Wright
Lagerkvist
Moberg

Frances Wyers
Ortega y Gasset

Winston Yang
Pa Chin

Ruth B. York
Marcel
Morand

Michael Zand
Lahuti

Abbreviations for Periodicals, Volume 3

AAS	Asian and African Studies	BRMMLA	Rocky Mountain Review of Language and Literature
AAW	Afro-Asian Writing	BUJ	Boston University Journal
AfricaL	Africa (London)	CA	Cuadernos americanos
AfricaR	Africa Report	CALC	Cahiers algériens de littérature comparée
AIPHOS	Annuaire de l'Institut de Philologie et d'Histoire Orientales et Slaves	CanL	Canadian Literature
AL	American Literature	CARHS	Canadian-American Review of Hungarian Studies
ALT	African Literature Today	CarQ	Caribbean Quarterly
ANP	Anales de la narrativa española contemporánea	CAsJ	Central Asiatic Journal
AQ	American Quarterly	CCrit	Comparative Criticism
ArielE	Ariel: A Review of International English Literature	CE	College English
		CELFAN	CELFAN Review
ASch	The American Scholar	CentR	Centennial Review
ASQ	Arab Studies Quarterly	CHA	Cuadernos hispanoamericanos
ASR	American Scandinavian Review	ChiR	Chicago Review
AUB-LLR	Analele Universității, București, Limbă și litereră română	CJIts	Canadian Journal of Italian Studies
AUMLA	Journal of the Australasian Universities Language and Literature Association	CL	Comparative Literature
		CLAJ	College Language Association Journal
BA	Books Abroad	CLQ	Colby Library Quarterly
BAALE	Bulletin of the Association for African Literature in English	CLS	Comparative Literature Studies
BALF	Black American Literature Forum	CMRS	Cahiers du monde russe et soviétique
		CNLR	CNL/Quarterly World Report
BalSt	Balkan Studies	CompD	Comparative Drama
BF	Books from Finland	ComQ	Commonwealth Quarterly
BO	Black Orpheus	ConL	Contemporary Literature

CQ	Cambridge Quarterly	*IBSB*	International P.E.N. Bulletin of Selected Books
CRCL	Canadian Review of Comparative Literature	*IC*	Islamic Culture
CREL	Cahiers roumains d'études littéraires	*IFR*	International Fiction Review
Crit	Critique: Studies in Modern Fiction	*IndSch*	Indian Scholar
		IQ	Italian Quarterly
Critique	Critique: Revue générale des publications françaises et étrangères	*IS*	Italian Studies
		IUR	Irish University Review
		IWT	Indian Writing Today
CritQ	Critical Quarterly	*JARCE*	Journal of the American Research Center in Egypt
CS	Cahiers du Sud	*JATJ*	Journal of the Association of Teachers of Japanese
CSP	Canadian Slavonic Papers		
CSS	Canadian Slavic Studies	*JBalS*	Journal of Baltic Studies
DQ	Denver Quarterly	*JCF*	Journal of Canadian Fiction
DSt	Deutsche Studien	*JCL*	Journal of Commonwealth Literature
DutchS	Dutch Studies		
ECr	L'esprit créateur	*JCLTA*	Journal of the Chinese Language Teachers Association
ECW	Essays on Canadian Writing	*JCS*	Journal of Croatian Studies
EinA	English in Africa	*JEthS*	Journal of Ethnic Studies
Éire	Éire-Ireland	*JJS*	Journal of Japanese Studies
ELit	Études littéraires	*JPalS*	Journal of Palestinian Studies
ES	Engish Studies	*JSoAL*	Journal of South Asian Literature
ESA	English Studies in Africa		
FE	France-Eurafrique	*JSS*	Journal of Semitic Studies
FI	Forum Italicum	*JSSB*	Journal of the Siam Society
FMLS	Forum for Modern Language Studies	*JSSTC*	Journal of Spanish Studies: Twentieth Century
FR	French Review	*JTamS*	Journal of Tamil Studies
FrF	French Forum	*KanQ*	Kansas Quarterly
FS	French Studies	*KFLQ*	Kentucky Foreign Language Quarterly
GL&L	German Life and Letters		
GQ	German Quarterly	*KR*	Kenyon Review
GRM	Germanisch-Romanische Monatsschrift	*KRQ*	Kentucky Romance Quarterly
HC	Hollins Critic	*LAAW*	Lotus: Afro-Asian Writing
Hispano	Hispanófila	*LALR*	Latin American Literary Review
HJAS	Harvard Journal of Asiatic Studies	*LATR*	Latin American Theatre Review
		LBR	Luso-Brazilian Review
HR	Hispanic Review	*LE&W*	Literature East and West
HSS	Harvard Slavic Studies	*LHY*	Literary Half-Yearly
HudR	Hudson Review	*LitR*	Literary Review
HungQ	Hungarian Quarterly	*London*	London Magazine

LQ	Literary Quarterly (Belgrade)	*PMLA*	Publications of the Modern Language Association of America
MD	Modern Drama		
MEF	Middle East Forum	*PolP*	Polish Perspectives
MEJ	Middle East Journal	*PolR*	Polish Review
MES	Middle Eastern Studies	*PPNCFL*	Proceedings of the Pacific Northwest Conference on Foreign Languages
MFS	Modern Fiction Studies		
MHL	Modern Hebrew Literature		
MLF	Modern Language Forum	*PQM*	Pacific Quarterly (Moana)
MLJ	Modern Language Journal	*PR*	Partisan Review
MLN	Modern Language Notes	*PrS*	Prairie Schooner
MLR	Modern Language Review	*PSMLAB*	Pennsylvania State Modern Language Association Bulletin
MLS	Modern Language Studies		
MN	Monumenta Nipponica	*QQ*	Queen's Quarterly
ModA	Modern Age	*RAL*	Research in African Literatures
MPS	Modern Poetry Studies	*RCF*	Review of Contemporary Fiction
MQ	Midwest Quarterly		
MR	Massachusetts Review	*REH*	Revista de estudios hispánicos
MuK	Maske and Kothurn	*REI*	Revue des études italiennes
MW	The Muslim World	*RevB*	Revista bilingüe
NDEJ	Notre Dame English Journal	*RevI*	Revista/Review Interamericana
NER	New England Review	*RI*	Revista iberoamericana
NewS	New Scholar	*RLJ*	Russian Language Journal
NGC	New German Critique	*RLT*	Russian Literature Triquarterly
NHQ	New Hungarian Quarterly	*RLV*	Revue des langues vivantes
NMQ	New Mexico Quarterly	*RNL*	Review of National Literatures
NorS	Northern Studies	*RomN*	Romance Notes
NorthwestR	Northwest Review	*RoR*	Romanian Review
NYLF	New York Literary Forum	*RR*	Romanic Review
NYRB	New York Review of Books	*RRWL*	Renaissance and Renascences in Western Literature
NYTBR	New York Times Book Review		
NYTMag	New York Times Magazine	*RS*	Research Studies
NZSJ	New Zealand Slavonic Journal	*RUO*	Revue de l'Université d'Ottawa
O&C	Œuvres et critiques	*RusL*	Russian Literature
ÖGL	Österreich in Geschichte und Literatur	*RusR*	Russian Review
		SAJL	Studies in American Jewish Literature
OJES	Osmania Journal of English Studies	*SAQ*	South Atlantic Quarterly
		SatR	Saturday Review
OL	Orbis Litterarum	*SBL*	Studies in Black Literature
PA	Présence africaine	*Scan*	Scandinavica
PCL	Perspectives on Contemporary Literature	*SchM*	Schweizer Monatshefte
		SCL	Studies in Canadian Literature
PCP	Pacific Coast Philology	*ScotIR*	Scottish International Review

ScotR	Scottish Review	*SUS*	Susquehanna University Studies
SEEJ	Slavic and East European Journal	*SWR*	Southwest Review
SEER	Slavonic and East European Review	*TAH*	The American Hispanist
		TCL	Twentieth Century Literature
SHEH	Stanford Honors Essays in the Humanities	*TDR*	Tulane Drama Review/The Drama Review
SlavR	Slavic Review	*TkR*	Tamkang Review
SoR	Southern Review	*TLS*	[London] Times Literary Supplement
SoRA	Southern Review (Adelaide, Australia)		
		TQ	Texas Quarterly
SovL	Soviet Literature	*TriQ*	TriQuarterly
SPFA	Bulletin de la Société des Professeurs Français en Amérique	*VQR*	Virginia Quarterly Review
		WAL	Western American Literature
SPHQ	Swedish Pioneer Historical Quarterly	*WB*	Weimarer Beiträge
		WHR	Western Humanities Review
SR	Sewanee Review	*WLT*	World Literature Today
SS	Scandinavian Studies	*WLWE*	World Literature Written in English
SSF	Studies in Short Fiction		
SSl	Scando-Slavica	*WSlA*	Wiener Slawistischer Almanach
SSL	Studies in Scottish Literature	*YFS*	Yale French Studies
SSLit	Soviet Studies in Literature	*YItS*	Yale Italian Studies
SSMLN	Society for the Study of Midwestern Literature Newsletter	*YR*	Yale Review
		Y/T	Yale/Theatre
SuF	Sinn und Form	*ZS*	Zeitschrift für Slawistik

Illustrations

	facing page		facing page
Pär Lagerkvist	76	Sławomir Mrożek	339
D. H. Lawrence	76	Iris Murdoch	339
Halldór Laxness	77	Robert Musil	339
Doris Lessing	77	Vladimir Nabokov	380
Claude Lévi-Strauss	77	V. S. Naipaul	380
Sinclair Lewis	160	Pablo Neruda	381
Väinö Linna	160	Sean O'Casey	381
Robert Lowell	160	Flannery O'Connor	434
György Lukács	161	Eugene O'Neill	434
Maurice Maeterlinck	161	José Ortega y Gasset	435
Norman Mailer	161	George Orwell	435
Bernard Malamud	216	John Osborne	452
André Malraux	216	Kostis Palamas	452
Osip Mandelshtam	217	Pier Paolo Pasolini	453
Thomas Mann	217	Boris Pasternak	453
Roger Martin du Gard	250	Cesare Pavese	496
François Mauriac	250	Octavio Paz	496
Vladimir Mayakovsky	251	Charles Péguy	496
H. L. Mencken	251	Ramón Pérez de Ayala	497
Henri Michaux	251	Benito Pérez Galdós	497
Arthur Miller	278	Harold Pinter	544
Henry Miller	278	Luigi Pirandello	544
Czesław Miłosz	279	Francis Ponge	545
Mishima Yukio	279	Katherine Anne Porter	545
Gabriela Mistral	279	Ezra Pound	613
Henry de Montherlant	338	Marcel Proust	612
Alberto Moravia	338	Salvatore Quasimodo	613
Zsigmond Móricz	338		

Acknowledgments

For permission to reproduce the illustrations in this volume,
the publisher is indebted to the following:

PÄR LAGERKVIST	Bildarchiv Herder, Freiburg im Breisgau
D. H. LAWRENCE	The Viking Press, Inc., N.Y.
HALLDÓR LAXNESS	Suhrkamp Verlag, Frankfurt am Main
DORIS LESSING	Lutfi Özkök, Älvsjö, Sweden
CLAUDE LÉVI-STRAUSS	Jerry Bauer and Harper & Row, Publishers, N.Y.
SINCLAIR LEWIS	Bildarchiv Herder, Freiburg im Breisgau
VÄINÖ LINNA	Consulate General of Finland, N.Y.
ROBERT LOWELL	The New York Times, N.Y.
GYÖRGY LUKÁCS	New York Public Library
MAURICE MAETERLINCK	Süddeutscher Verlag, Munich
NORMAN MAILER	The New York Times, N.Y.
BERNARD MALAMUD	Janna Malamud and Farrar, Straus & Giroux, Inc.
ANDRÉ MALRAUX	Bildarchiv Herder, Freiburg im Breisgau; Wilfried Göpel, Berlin
OSIP MANDELSHTAM	Ardis Publishers
THOMAS MANN	Fritz Eschen, Berlin
ROGER MARTIN DU GARD	French Cultural Services, N.Y.
FRANÇOIS MAURIAC	French Cultural Services, N.Y.
VLADIMIR MAYAKOVSKY	Presseagentur Nowosti, Berlin
H. L. MENCKEN	The Bettman Archive, Inc.
HENRI MICHAUX	Gisèle Freund, Paris
ARTHUR MILLER	German Information Center
HENRY MILLER	Cedric Wright and Grove Press, Inc., N.Y.
CZESŁAW MIŁOSZ	University of California Press
MISHIMA YUKIO	Tamotsu Yato and Alfred A. Knopf, Inc.
GABRIELA MISTRAL	Bildarchiv Herder, Freiburg im Breisgau
HENRY DE MONTHERLANT	Verlag Kiepenheur & Witsch, Cologne
ALBERTO MORAVIA	Istituto Italiano di Cultura, N.Y.
ZSIGMOND MÓRICZ	Imre Kovács
SŁAWOMIR MROŻEK	Grove Press, Inc., N.Y.
IRIS MURDOCH	The Viking Press, Inc., N.Y.
ROBERT MUSIL	Bildarchiv Herder, Freiburg im Breisgau
VLADIMIR NABOKOV	Horst Tappe and Pix, Inc. N.Y.
V. S. NAIPAUL	Lutfi Özkök, Älvsjö, Sweden
PABLO NERUDA	Bertil Dahlgren and Camera Press-Pix, Inc. N.Y.
SEAN O'CASEY	Edizione Paoline, Rome
FLANNERY O'CONNOR	New York Public Library
EUGENE O'NEILL	Bildarchiv Herder, Freiburg im Breisgau
JOSÉ ORTEGA Y GASSET	W. W. Norton & Company, Inc., N.Y.
GEORGE ORWELL	Harcourt Brace Jovanovich, Inc.
JOHN OSBORNE	Mark Gerson
KOSTIS PALAMAS	Edizione Paoline, Rome
PIER PAOLO PASOLINI	Istituto Italiano di Cultura, N.Y.
BORIS PASTERNAK	Harcourt Brace Jovanovich, Inc.

ACKNOWLEDGMENTS

CESARE PAVESE   Farrar, Straus & Giroux, Inc., N.Y.
OCTAVIO PAZ   Grove Press, Inc., N.Y.
CHARLES PÉGUY   Bildarchiv Herder, Freiburg im Breisgau
RAMÓN PÉREZ DE AYALA   The Bettmann Archive, Inc.
BENITO PÉREZ GALDÓS   The Bettmann Archive, Inc.
HAROLD PINTER   The Bettmann Archive, Inc.
LUIGI PIRANDELLO   Bildarchiv Herder, Freiburg im Breisgau
FRANCIS PONGE   Lutfi Özkök, Älvsjö, Sweden
KATHERINE ANNE PORTER   New York Public Library
EZRA POUND   Boris De Rachewiltz and New Directions Publ. Corp., N.Y.
MARCEL PROUST   The Bettmann Archive, Inc.
SALVATORE QUASIMODO   Istituto Italiano di Cultura, N.Y.

Encyclopedia of World Literature
in the 20th Century

LAFORET, Carmen

Spanish novelist and short-story writer, b. 6 Sept. 1921, Barcelona

After growing up in the Canary Islands, L. returned to the Spanish mainland and studied law at the universities of Barcelona and Madrid. She published her first novel, *Nada* (1945; *Nada,* 1958), when she was twenty-four. Since 1963 she has been writing mostly travel pieces, articles, and short stories.

With *Nada,* for which she won the first Nadal Prize, L. brought energy and direction to the post-civil-war novel. This highly successful and widely acclaimed work spoke eloquently for a generation wounded by war and despair. In *Nada* L. portrays the experiences of Andrea, an eighteen-year-old girl, not unlike herself, who has just arrived from the Canary Islands to study at the University of Barcelona. She stays at her grandmother's house, a microcosm of Spain, where she is surrounded by aunts and uncles, inadequate and troubled human beings, who, out of weakness and pain, inexorably destroy each other. At the end of the novel Andrea frees herself from this lugubrious environment by going off with a friend to study in Madrid.

In L.'s next novel, *La isla y los demonios* (1952; the island and the devils), she again portrays the coming to maturity of a young girl and her struggles for liberation. Contrary to what might be expected, L.'s first novel is actually a sequel to the second, for *La isla y los demonios* takes place in the Canary Islands, a few years *before* the time frame of *Nada,* and Marta, its protagonist, is two years younger than Andrea.

L.'s third novel, *La nueva mujer* (1955; the new woman), presents Paulina—a kindred spirit of Andrea and Marta—who struggles with the problems of freeing herself from an impinging society. Toward the end of the novel Paulina has a religious experience, just as L. herself did, and suddenly regains her Catholic faith.

La insolación (1963; sunstroke), the first novel of a planned trilogy that so far has not been completed, also deals with the coming of age of an adolescent. L. recounts three summers in the life of Martín, a sensitive and alienated teenager. At the end of the novel Martín is forced to leave his family and make his own way in the world.

Nada has already secured a place of honor for L. in the history of the post-civil-war novel. It is to be regretted that she has never gone beyond the scope of this book. Nevertheless, she is a fine novelist who has had great success with her character studies and her delicate portrayal of adolescence.

FURTHER WORKS: *La muerta* (1952); *La llamada* (1954); *Gran Canaria* (1961); *Paralelo 35* (1967)

BIBLIOGRAPHY: Coster, C. C., "C. L.: A Tentative Evaluation," *Hispania,* 40 (1957), 187–91; Mulvihill, E. R., and Sánchez, R. G., Introduction to *Nada* (1958), pp. ix–xv; Ullman, P. L., "The Structure of C. L.'s Novels," in Friedman, M., ed., *The Vision Obscured* (1970), pp. 201–19; Illanes Adaro, G., *La novelística de C. L.* (1971); El Saffar, R., "Structural and Thematic Tactics of Suppression in C. L.'s *Nada,*" *Symposium,* 28 (1974), 119–29; Thomas, M., "Symbolic Portals in L.'s *Nada,*" *ANP,* 3 (1978), 57–74; Johnson, R., *C. L.* (1981)

MARSHALL J. SCHNEIDER

LAGERKVIST, Pär

Swedish novelist, short-story writer, poet, and dramatist, b. 23 May 1891, Växjö; d. 11 July 1974, Stockholm

L. grew up in Växjö, the provincial capital of Småland, in southern Sweden. His parents' pietistically inclined religious faith lent an atmosphere of security and calm restraint to his childhood home, evocatively described in the autobiographical novel *Gäst hos verkligheten* (1925; *Guest of Reality,* (1936). As an adolescent L. distanced himself intellectually from the fundamentally conservative milieu by turning to Darwin's theory and to political radicalism. Nevertheless, the conversion was an uneasy one, as L.'s lifelong preoccupation with metaphysical and religious questions attests.

After studying briefly at the University of Uppsala, L. made his literary debut in 1912 (the year of Strindberg's [q.v.] death) with *Människor* (human beings), but he first attracted attention the following year with the theoretical essay "Ordkonst och bildkonst" (verbal art and pictorial art). During a visit to Paris he had become aware of new trends in the visual arts. Proposing that modern literature be revitalized through architecture-like construction analagous to cubism (q.v.), he rejected naturalism in favor of the elevation and simplicity found in Greek tragedy, the Old Testament, and the Icelandic sagas. L.'s search for a new style is apparent in the works that followed: the prose poems of *Motiv* (1913; motifs), the short stories in *Järn och människor* (1914; iron and human beings), and most importantly, the poetry collection *Ångest* (1916; anguish). Often cited as the beginning of poetic modernism (q.v.) in Sweden, this volume, in which startling imagery and a disjointed, expressionistic (q.v.) style communicate the despair and pain brought on by World War I, was his true breakthrough.

L.'s early dramas also demonstrate his interest in aesthetic revolt and renewal. The essay "Modern teater: Synpunkter och angrepp" ("Modern Theatre: Points of View and Attack," 1966), published in the volume titled *Teater* (1918; theater), provides the theoretical program. Ibsen's "five long acts of words, words, words" are characterized as ineffective; L. expresses admiration for medieval drama, the plays of Shakespeare, and the work of Strindberg after the mental crisis of his "Inferno" period, all of which he views as approaching the essence of human experience through allegory and symbolism. The three short expressionistic plays *Den svåra stunden I–III* (1918; *The Difficult Hour I–III,* 1966), published in *Teater,* reveal that L. had learned a great deal from Strindberg's dramatic technique in, for instance, *A Dream Play.*

Den svåra stunden explores different individual responses to death; another play, *Himlens hemlighet* (1919; *The Secret of Heaven,* 1966), poses the question, What is the meaning of life? L. implies that while this issue preoccupies human beings, it is a matter of total indifference to the Almighty. Similarly, in the story "Det eviga leendet" (1920; "The Eternal Smile," 1954), a group of people ask God what His purpose was in creating them. The answer is that He had not meant anything in particular, but merely had done His best. L.'s pessimism is tempered by a note of affirmation: although there may be no intrinsic meaning in life, human beings are capable of creating their own meaning within a circumscribed sphere; they may find happiness through a sense of duty and solidarity with others.

A gradual movement toward the resigned acceptance of humankind's lot, combined with a more straightforward, realistic style, is apparent in the collection *Onda sagor* (1924; evil tales) and in *Gäst hos verkligheten,* which provides a key to L.'s personal and philosophical development. The drama *Han som fick leva om sitt liv* (1928; *The Man Who Lived His Life Over,* 1971) is a step toward a more realistic stage art.

L.'s works of the 1930s and 1940s are dominated by his preoccupation with the nature of evil and the crisis of humanism when confronted with the fascist threat. The theme is established in the poetry collection *Vid lägereld* (1932; at the campfire). The novella *Bödeln* (1933; *The Hangman,* 1936), which L. made into a play, also called *Bödeln* (1934; *The Hangman,* 1966), investigates the universality of evil by comparing and contrasting medieval with modern times. Two other dramas, *Mannen utan själ* (1936; *The Man without a Soul,* 1944) and *Seger i mörkret* (1939; victory in darkness) express faith in the moral superiority and eventual triumph of the humanist tradition, despite the temporary victory of the powers of darkness.

Dvärgen (1944; *The Dwarf,* 1945), L.'s first nonautobiographical novel, considered by many to be his finest work, evinces a direct thematic connection with *Bödeln.* While skillfully creating a pastiche of Renaissance Italy, L. establishes his title character as a universal symbol of the evil forces within every human being—forces that may lie dormant for a while but are certain eventually to surface.

Although L. came late to the novel, that genre dominates his later production. He continued to put questions about the nature of religious faith and the meaning of life. In *Barabbas* (1950; *Barabbas,* 1951), which L. dramatized under the same title in 1953, the

2

protagonist can neither live in accordance with the message of Jesus—"Love one another"—nor reject it out of hand. He wants to believe, but is unable to make the necessary leap of faith. This ambivalence is conveyed through antithetical symbols and images: light and darkness, life and death, love and hate. Similar paradoxes are central to the poetry collection *Aftonland* (1953; *Evening Land,* 1975), in which God is an unseen spear thrower striking down the narrator from behind, and to interlinking novels *Sibyllan* (1956; *The Sibyl,* 1958), *Ahasverus död* (1960; *The Death of Ahasuerus,* 1962), *Pilgrim på havet* (1962; *Pilgrim at Sea,* 1964), and *Det heliga landet* (1964; *The Holy Land,* 1966). The sibyl, chosen as the mouthpiece of Apollo, finds that her encounter with the irrational fills her with terror as well as ecstasy, while Ahasuerus hates the God who has condemned him to wander eternally, only to discover that his very hatred binds him forever to God.

L.'s position in 20th-c. Swedish literature is unusual. His production spans more than half a century and encompasses all major genres and many literary trends. Yet L. has had few imitators and founded no school; his early formalist experiments provided a foundation for later poets to build on, but he remained an isolated individualist. Typical of L.'s reserve is that his only speeches were on the occasion of his election to the Swedish Academy in 1940 and his receiving the Nobel Prize in 1951. L.'s works display a remarkable internal consistency. His prose style is immediately recognizable—simple, unadorned, incorporating forms from the spoken language, and at the same time strangely stylized and impersonal. The tendency toward abstraction in language complements his propensity for timeless themes.

FURTHER WORKS: *Två sagor om livet* (1913); *Sista mänskan* (1917); *Kaos* (1919); *Den lyckliges väg* (1920); *Den osynlige* (1923); *Valda sidor* (1925); *Hjärtats sånger* (1926); *Det besegrade livet* (1927); *Kämpande ande* (1930); *Konungen* (1932; *The King,* 1966); *Skrifter* (3 vols., 1932); *Den knutna näven* (1934); *I den tiden* (1935); *Genius* (1937); *Den befriade människan* (1939); *Sång och strid* (1940); *Dikter* (1941); *Midsommardröm i fattighuset* (1941; *Midsummer Dream in the Workhouse,* 1953); *Hemmet och stjärnan* (1942); *Prosa* (1945); *Dramatik* (1946); *De vises sten* (1947; *The Philosopher's Stone,* 1966); *Låt människan leva* (1949; *Let Man Live,* 1951); *Prosa* (5 vols., 1949); *Dramatik* (3 vols., 1956); *Dikter* (1965); *Prosa* (1966); *Mariamne* (1967; *Herod and Mariamne,* 1968). FURTHER VOLUMES IN ENGLISH: *The Eternal Smile, and Other Stories* (1954); *The Marriage Feast, and Other Stories* (1955); *Modern Theater: Seven Plays and an Essay* (1966); *The Eternal Smile: Three Stories* (1971)

BIBLIOGRAPHY: Buchman, T. R., "P. L. and the Swedish Theatre," *TDR,* 6, 2 (1961), 60–89; Scobbie, I., *P. L.: An Introduction* (1963); Ryberg, A., *P. L. in Translation: A Bibliography* (1964); Swanson, R., "Evil and Love in L.'s Crucifixion Cycle," *SS,* 38 (1966), 302–17; Linnér, S., ed., special L. issue, supplement to *Scan,* 10, 1 (1971); Spector, R. D., *P. L.* (1973); Sjöberg, L., *P. L.* (1976)

ROCHELLE WRIGHT

LA GUMA, Alex

South African novelist and short-story writer (writing in English), b. 20 Feb. 1925, Cape Town

After attending secondary school, L. held a variety of jobs before beginning a career as a journalist. His active opposition to the South African government and its policy of apartheid led to periods of imprisonment, house arrest, and in 1966 exile to England, where he now lives.

L.'s writing frequently stems from personal experience as a black man and reflects his deep opposition to the South African regime. Thus, *A Walk in the Night* (1962), set in the slums of Cape Town, pictures the losing struggle to retain a fundamental humanity in the face of racial oppression. *And a Threefold Cord* (1964) is also based on life in the ghetto, while *The Stone Country* (1967) is inspired by L.'s own imprisonment and is dedicated to "the daily 70,351 prisoners in South African gaols in 1964." L.'s early political activism is reflected in *In the Fog of the Season's End* (1972), a novel based on organizing underground opposition to apartheid.

Thus L.'s literary world grimly mirrors the realities of life for nonwhites in South Africa. Crime and brutality inevitably erupt as people keenly aware of their own powerlessness find themselves in intolerable situations. Little room for sentimentality exists in such a world, yet love and even comedy can occasionally and fleetingly blossom. L. handles his settings concretely and vividly, whether a prison, shantytown, white suburbs, or, as in *Time of the Butcherbird* (1979), a new Bantu homeland to which people have been forcefully removed.

Characters in L.'s fiction are inevitably victims of society. People like Michael Adonis, a "coloured" who unjustly loses his job in *A Walk in the Night,* and Charlie Pauls, who in *And a Threefold Cord* attacks a white policeman, move outside the law because the social structure allows them no other choice. For L., this structure can only produce disease and parasitism, whether in the form of a petty criminal living off shanty people, a tough jailbird off other prisoners, or whites off the rest of the country's population. Given the vicious situation they find themselves in, moral action for L.'s characters becomes defensive, passive, and even perverted, rather than assertive and positive, as might be possible in a freer society.

Since L. is concerned with the enormous direct impact that political and social realities have on the life of his country and its people, it has been argued that his characters become artistically subordinated to the depiction of particular situations. Yet L. cannot be validly accused, as some black South African writers might be, of presenting journalistic fact in the guise of creative literature. Rather, L. comes to his subject with freshness and originality. His description of person and place is graphic, his accurate rendition of various dialects invigorating. He masterfully evokes both mood and atmosphere, and even on occasion finds humor in the midst of pathos; these qualities enable him to make some telling points about the human condition. He is considered by many critics to be one of black South Africa's most significant and successful writers.

FURTHER WORKS: *A Walk in the Night, and Other Stories* (1967); *A Soviet Journey* (1978)

BIBLIOGRAPHY: Rabkin, D., "L. and Reality in South Africa," *JCL,* 8 (1973), 54–61; Wanjala, C. L., "The Face of Injustice: A. L.'s Fiction," in Wanjala, C. L., ed., *Standpoints on African Literature* (1973), pp. 305–22; Asein, S., "The Revolutionary Vision in A. L.'s Novels," *LAAW,* 24–25 (1975), 9–21 (also in *Phylon,* 39 [1978], 74–86); Gakwandi, A., *The Novel and Contemporary Experience in Africa* (1977), pp. 8, 21–26; Wade, M., "Art and Morality in A. L.'s *A Walk in the Night,*" in Parker, K., ed., *The South African Novel in English: Essays in Criticism and Society* (1978), pp. 164–91; Scanlon, P. A., "A. L.'s Novels of Protest: The Growth of the Revolutionary," *Okike,* 16 (1979), 85–93; Moore, G., *Twelve African Writers* (1980), pp. 104–20

DAVID F. BEER

LAHUTI, Abulqasim

Persian and Tajik poet, b. 31 Dec. 1887, Kermanshah, Iran; d. 16 March 1957, Moscow, U.S.S.R.

L. was the son of a minor Sufi (mystical) poet. He went to school in Tehran and participated in the Iranian revolution of 1905–11. After the failure of the revolution, he escaped to Baghdad (1913–15), and after returning to Iran for a while, emigrated to Istanbul (1918–20). In 1921 he led an antigovernment revolt in Tabriz. After its suppression he fled to the Soviet Union. From 1925 to 1931 L. lived in Soviet Tajikistan, where he held high administrative and Party posts. In 1931 he settled in Moscow and in 1934 became one of the secretaries of the Writers Union of the U.S.S.R. His political fortunes began to decline in 1941. From the middle of 1949 the publishing of L.'s works ceased almost completely, to be renewed only in 1954 in order to scotch published rumors in Iran about his alleged defection from Soviet Tajikistan via Afghanistan to Pakistan.

L.'s earliest poems, written at the age of sixteen, were of the Sufi character. In his first revolutionary poems (1907–11) he praised revolution as the real implementation of the spirit of Islam. L.'s main preference during this period was for the classical *ghazal,* a short lyrical or mystical poem, which, however, he filled with political and patriotic content. His finest political *ghazals,* written between 1919 and 1921, formed the main part of his first published book, *La'aliyi lahuti* (1921; divine pearls)—the title is a pun on his name; *lahuti* means "divine."

L.'s almost immediate conversion to communism after his arrival in the U.S.S.R. led his early Soviet poems, such as "Kreml" (1923; the Kremlin), to be suffused with an abstract but sincere exaltation. These poems were written mainly in a classical Persian common to Persians and Tajiks. L.'s poetry of the 1920s and 1930s pictures the Soviet Union in bright and joyous colors, contrasting it with a gloomy non-Soviet world.

During the 1930s L. emerged as one of the main Soviet poet-panegyrists of Stalin, so much so that Stalin once mocked L.'s fawning. Yet although the praise is evidently sincere, the style is dependent on the elaborate Persian classical tradition of panegyrical court poetry.

L.'s main poetic interest in the late 1920s and the 1930s was Tajikistan. The language and style of Tajik poetry at that time were still close to those of classical Persian poetry. In 1940 a special volume of his poems on Tajik topics, *Shi'rhayi tajikistani* (Tajikistani poems), was published; in these he used the Tajik vernacular to a great extent. The most outstanding among them, still regarded as one of the masterpieces of Tajik Soviet poetry, is the epic poem "Taj va bayraq" (1935; crown and banner).

With the outbreak of war with Germany in 1941, L.'s political themes shifted from a contrast of classes—triumphant proletariat and oppressive capitalists—to patriotic ones, juxtaposing the heroic Soviet people, led by Russians, with the satanic Germans.

The late 1940s and 1950s were years of artistic decline for L. Deeply depressed by Party attacks, barred from publication, impoverished, incurably ill, the poet turned his eyes to his native country, writing nostalgic poems about Iran.

Throughout his creative life L. wrote love poems. Although mainly in the classical Persian tradition, they are spontaneous, natural, full of sincere romantic feeling. Many of them became Tajik folk songs.

L.'s influence on the development of Tajik poetry was enormous. He also had a great impact on leftist poetry in Iran in the 1940s, and although almost forgotten again from the 1950s through the 1970s, he was rediscovered once more after the upheaval at the end of the 1970s and recognized as one of the greatest modern Persian poets.

FURTHER WORKS: *Ruba'iyat* (1924); *Inqilabi surkh* (1926); *Hazar misra'* (1935); *Divan* (1939); *Divani ash'ar* (1942); *Asari muntakhab* (1946); *Surudhayi azadi va sulh* (1954); *Muntakhabi az ash'ar* (1954); *Nidayi zindagi* (1956); *Divan* (1957); *Kulliyat* (6 vols., 1960–63); *Kulliyat* (1978); *Divan* (1979)

BIBLIOGRAPHY: Ishaque, M., *Modern Persian Poetry* (1943), pp. 146–48; Munibur Rahman, *Post-Revolution Persian Verse* (1955), pp. 42–51; Alavi, B., *Geschichte und Entwicklung der modernen persischen Literatur* (1964), pp. 105–12; Machalski, F., *La littérature de l'Iran contemporain* (1965), Vol. I, pp. 138–43; Bečka, J., in Rypka, J., et al., *History of Iranian Literature* (1968), pp. 564–66

MICHAEL ZAND

LAK LITERATURE
See North Caucasian Literatures

LALIĆ, Mihailo
Yugoslav novelist and short-story writer (writing in Serbian), b. 14 Oct. 1914, Trepča (near Andrijevica)

In 1933 L. left his native Montenegro to study law in Belgrade. Before World War II he was imprisoned several times for his revolutionary activities. In 1941 he joined the partisans (anti-Fascist, procommunist guerrillas) in Montenegro, was apprehended by the chetniks (anti-Fascist, promonarchist guerrillas) and deported to a camp in Greece, but he escaped in 1943 and rejoined the partisans. He was the director of the Yugoslav news agency for Montenegro from 1944 to 1946, then held various editorial jobs in Belgrade until his retirement in 1965. He has been a member of Serbian Academy of Sciences and Arts since 1964.

The focal point of L.'s fiction is the struggle between the partisans and chetniks in Italian-occupied Montenegro during World War II. Against this background L. explores the eternal conflict between good and evil and analyzes various aspects of human nature in the face of the extreme conditions brought about by the war. L.'s tendency to equate good with the partisans and evil with the chetniks at times adversely affects the universal character of his poetic message. A distinct characteristic of L.'s writing is his striving for perfection, which prompted him to revise some of his best works after their initial publication.

In his best-known novel, *Lelejska gora* (1957; new version, 1962; *The Wailing*

Mountain, 1965), L. explores the horrifying and potentially destructive effects of loneliness and despair on a partisan separated from his unit and pursued by the enemy like a wild animal. The hero, a man of honor and principle, undergoes many trials until he realizes that evil can be defeated only when one confronts it and fights it with its own weapons.

In the novel *Pramen tame* (1970; a patch of darkness), which grew out of a long short story, L. assigned the leading role to a negative hero, Riko Gizdić, a chetnik and a former policeman, a servant of many regimes. Through Riko's story L. traces the development of the chetnik movement in Montenegro and comments on its ideology.

Two later novels, *Ratna sreća* (1973; the luck of war) and *Zatočnici* (1976; champions), are the first two volumes of a planned tetralogy. Both are in the form of the protagonist's memoirs and excerpts from his diary. They span a period of some thirty years, from the Balkan wars (1912) to the early 1940s. Together with the hero, Pejo Grujović, L. ponders the fate of patriotism and the traditional values faced with the ever-growing threats and dilemmas of modern times.

In all his works, L. masterfully integrates descriptions of the rugged but majestic Montenegro countryside and the moods and emotional upheavals of his equally rugged characters. In L.'s view, society is composed of two kinds of human beings: those on the right and those on the wrong side of life. A never-ending struggle between the two antagonistic camps forms the texture of life, in which individual men either "walk tall" or break down, depending on their moral rather than physical strength.

A good stylist, writing in short, often broken sentences that appeal to the contemporary reader, and a master of minute psychological analysis, L. is today one of the most impressive literary figures in Yugoslavia. One thing is certain: L.'s opus will remain a monumental document of the most inhuman, destructive, and tragic period in recent Yugoslav history, during which men were, in L.'s words, "like wolves to one another."

FURTHER WORKS: *Staze slobode* (1948); *Izvidnica* (1948); *Svadba* (1950); *Izabrane pripovetke* (1950); *Tri dana* (1950); *Prvi snijeg* (1951; rev. and enl. ed., 1977); *Osveta martoloza* (1951); *Usput zapisano* (1952); *Na Tari* (1952); *Zlo proljeće* (1953); *Raskid* (1955); *Tajne Bistrih voda* (1955); *Na mjesečini* (1956); *Hajka* (1960); *Gosti* (1967); *Posljednje brdo* (1967); *Sabrana dela M. L.* (10 vols., 1979)

BIBLIOGRAPHY: Hitrec, J., on *The Wailing Mountain, NYTBR,* 18 April 1965, 20–21; Suhadolc, J., on *The Wailing Mountain, SEEJ,* 11 (1967), 234–35; Mihailovich, V. D., on *Posljednje brdo, BA,* 43 (1969), 132; Pribić, N., on *Lelejska gora, BalSt,* 10 (1969), 208–9; Mikašinović, B., on *Pramen tame, BA,* 45 (1971), 542; Protić, P., on *Ratna sreća, BA,* 49 (1975), 157; Eekman, T., *Thirty Years of Yugoslav Literature (1945–1975)* (1978), pp. 126–32

BILJANA ŠLJIVIĆ-ŠIMŠIĆ

LAMMING, George

Barbadian novelist, b. 8 June 1927, Carrington Village

L. has told an interviewer that from his first novel, *In the Castle of My Skin* (1953), to *Natives of My Person* (1972) he was writing the same book. This statement may not do justice to the variety of his work, but all his novels are about departure and return. The roots of this theme are probably in his boyhood, when a scholarship took him from his working-class village to Combermere, a school for middle-class Barbadian boys. The education he received there cut him off from the life of the village, but because of his feelings of guilt that he had betrayed his origins, he has never been at home in the new world that the school opened up to him. His books suggest that from his early teens L. has been an outsider, an exile.

This personal deracination is translated in his fiction into a metaphor for the predicament of West Indians in general, and indeed for the anomie of modern man. In his first novel L. describes the gradual alienation of a growing boy from his community. It ends with his escape into a wider world. In *The Emigrants* (1954) this escape is frustrated when a group of West Indian exiles fail to make the foreignness of London fill the void left by their separation from their native islands.

L.'s four most recent novels are about abortive attempts at returning to the islands. The problems created in the West Indies by the history of slavery and colonialism are fused with the theme of return, for L. describes not only physical journeys back, as in *Of Age and Innocence* (1958) and *Natives of My Person,* but also psychological attempts at plunging into the past to discover the forces that separate modern West Indians from themselves. Novels such as *Of Age and Innocence* and *Season of Adventure* (1960) point out the futility of trying to forge ahead politically without first taking a "backward glance" at one's beginnings.

To emphasize the complexity of his themes and the painfulness of his psychological probing, L. often uses elaborately convoluted plots, the intricacies and coincidences of which are sometimes distracting. Nevertheless, the passion of his commitment to the West Indian peasant and to all working-class people, and the vehemence of his hatred of the exploitation of these people are powerfully conveyed by the flexibility and the eloquence of his prose.

FURTHER WORKS: *The Pleasures of Exile* (1960); *Water with Berries* (1971)

BIBLIOGRAPHY: Morris, M., "The Poet as Novelist: The Novels of G. L.," in James, L., ed., *The Islands in Between* (1968), pp. 73–85; Moore, G., *The Chosen Tongue* (1969), pp. 12–17, 37–42, 49–57; Ramchand, K., *The West Indian Novel and Its Background* (1970), pp. 135–49; Ngugi wa Thiong'o, *Homecoming* (1972), pp. 110–44; Larson, C., *The Novel in the Third World* (1976), pp. 89–107; Petersen, K. H., "Time, Timelessness and the Journey Metaphor in G. L.'s *In the Castle of My Skin* and *Natives of My Person,*" in Niven, A., ed., *The Commonwealth Writer Overseas* (1976), pp. 283–88; Griffiths, G., *A Double Exile: African and West Indian Writing between Two Cultures* (1978), pp. 91–96, 100–104, 135–38

ANTHONY BOXILL

LAMPEDUSA, Giuseppe Tomasi di
See Tomasi di Lampedusa, Giuseppe

LANDOLFI, Tommaso
Italian novelist, short-story writer, essayist, translator, and dramatist, b. 9 Aug. 1908, Pico, Frosinone; d. 7 July 1979, Rome

A graduate in Italian language and literature of the University of Florence, L. came into his own as a strikingly mature writer in the 1930s.

Immediately before World War II he was imprisoned for his anti-Fascist beliefs. His imprisonment, however, did not prevent him from writing for *Letteratura* and *Campo di Marte,* two of the most influential journals of modern writing. After his release from prison, he lived in Rome, but he frequently returned to his hometown.

As a critic and as a translator, L. wrote admirable essays on Russian literature and produced excellent translations from Russian and French. As a creative writer he was haunted throughout his career by the "mania for the impossible in literature." He wanted to obtain "from the written word what the word cannot give": the unattainable reality of the "thing."

The collection of short stories *Dialogo dei massimi sistemi* (1937; dialogue of the highest systems), although an early work, already reveals the abundance of themes—mostly polarities—and of interests running through most of L.'s literary production: cruelty and pity, falsity and truth, death and resurrection, love, sensuality and eroticism, dreams, surrealistic imagery, linguistic parody, and experimentalism. The title story tells of a man who believes he knows the Persian language, but who, instead, invents a new language (false Persian); consequently, he is the only one who can read the work of poetry he has created.

La pietra lunare (1937; the moon stone), considered by most critics L.'s masterpiece, is a romantic, demoniac, magical, and lyrical novel. The enigmatic nature of Gurù, the female protagonist (a soft, tender, and delirious half-human, half-feral being), and the male protagonist's fascination for and repulsion from her, seem to epitomize L.'s contradictory feelings about life.

In *Le due zittelle* (1945; the two spinsters) L. plays lucidly and ironically with the possible resemblances between animal and human psychology. Two spinsters lovingly raise a monkey who at night unleashes itself and goes to the church at a nearby nunnery, where it gorges itself on the sacred hosts and horribly mimics the ritual of the mass. This farcical, humorous story takes a startlingly sinister turn when the half-serious theological discussion on whether the monkey, who has no soul, has sinned, ends with a guilty verdict in an atmosphere reminiscent of witch-hunting.

After 1950 L. moved progressively away from the well-structured story toward more loose and openly autobiographical narratives, as in *Cancroregina* (1950; cancerqueen), *Rien va* (1963; French: nothing goes), and *Racconti impossibili* (1966; impossible tales). In *Cancroregina* a mad scientist, unable to return to earth, remains in orbit and dies in that frightening dimension. Within the paradigm of science fiction, L. reveals his anguished vision of man's existence.

"La muta" (the mute girl), the first tale in *Tre racconti* (1964; three tales), is perhaps the best expression of what L. defined as his "religious, and superstitious, love for and hatred of words." The young mute girl with whom the protagonist falls in love becomes the emblem of unattainable and unbearable purity. The girl's muteness—she is uncontaminated by speech—seems to the protagonist a mark of perfection; thus, he kills her before life can find its ways to corrupt her.

One of the most learned Italian writers of the 20th c., L. was both innovative and traditional in his tastes as well as in his style. His writings bear witness to his knowledge of and love for Dante, the great Russian, French, and German writers of the 19th c., and the new literary experiences of the 20th-c. writers, especially the surrealists (q.v.).

FURTHER WORKS: *Il mar delle blatte, e altre storie* (1939); *La spada* (1942); *Racconto d'autunno* (1947); *La bière du pecheur* (1953); *Il principe infelice* (1954); *Ombre* (1954); *La raganella d'oro* (1954); *Ottavio di Saint-Vincent* (1958); *Mezzacoda* (1958); *Landolfo IV di Benevento* (1959); *Se non la realtà* (1960); *Racconti* (1961); *In società* (1962); *Scene della vita di Cagliostro* (1963); *Un amore del nostro tempo* (1965); *Des mois* (1967); *Un paniere di chiocciole* (1968); *Faust '67* (1969); *Gogol a Roma* (1971); *Viola di morte* (1972); *Del meno* (1978)

BIBLIOGRAPHY: Brew, C. C., "The 'Caterpillar Nature' of Imaginative Experience: A Reading of T. L.'s 'Wedding Night,' " *MLN*, 89 (1974), 110–15

MARIOLINA SALVATORI

LANGEVIN, André

Canadian novelist (writing in French), b. 15 July 1927, Montreal, Que.

L. was orphaned at the age of seven and spent five years in an institution, a bitter experience that marked him deeply. After education in a Montreal classical college he joined the newspaper *Le devoir* as messenger boy and quickly rose through the ranks. A journalist and radio producer by profession, he has written a number of novels that by their stark power and originality have singled him out as one of the most accomplished writers of his generation.

His first novel, *Évadé de la nuit* (1951; escaped from the night), strikes the note of incommunicability and despair that is sounded again and again in his fiction. As he grows up, Jean Cherteffe, an abandoned child, seeks to make contact with others, first with an alcoholic poet, then with a young woman. The poet is past help and commits suicide; Micheline dies in childbirth, and Jean takes his own life in the snow.

This apprentice work was followed by *Poussière sur la ville* (1953; *Dust over the City,* 1955), generally considered to be one of the best French-Canadian novels of the 1950s. To the psychological study of existential solitude in L.'s first novel, *Poussière sur la ville* adds a social dimension. The asbestos-mining town of Macklin provides the narrow conventional background for the unconventional drama of Alain Dubois, a young doctor who arrives with his passionate red-haired bride to set up practice. Madeleine is intemperate, impulsive, inexpressive, and quickly bored. She soon runs through the normal resources of Macklin and takes a lover, a local truckdriver. Caught by his love for his wife but unable to please or reach her, Dubois defies the town's ethics and condones the affair. The people of Macklin take revenge by separating the lovers; Madeleine attempts to shoot her lover but turns the weapon on herself instead. From the complex point of view of the sympathetic but helpless participant, Dubois records the drama in the journal that makes up the novel. The dilemma echoes Camus (q.v.) in the hero's detached suffering, his ambiguous choice, his foiled sense of justice. The style is sparse, nervous, intense, like classical French tragedy, and the winter setting is used with great symbolic effect to underscore the action.

A religious concern is grafted on L.'s fiction in *Le temps des hommes* (1956; the time of men). The orphaned hero, Pierre Dupras, is an ex-priest who has left the seminary in revolt against the senseless death of a child. In the northern wilds he seeks to rejoin the world of men but cannot make contact any

LAO LITERATURE

better than L.'s other heroes, and, like them, he is overwhelmed by the brutality of men and the injustice of God.

Sixteen years elapsed before L.'s next novel, *L'élan d'Amérique* (1972; the American moose). During this time he wrote several plays and television dramas and a few short stories, but although he contributed a regular column on Quebec issues to *Le magazine Maclean* in the 1960s, he lived like a recluse. *L'élan d'Amérique* was heralded as a triumphant return to the mainstream of Quebec fiction. Among other things, it is a political allegory dramatizing in strong lyric images and in a new free style some of the collective traumas of the French-Canadian psyche. The protagonists are Claire Peabody, wife of an American pulp and paper magnate who represents the forces of exploitation; and Antoine, a forest guide who stands for Quebec. Their liaison is symbolized in their reactions to a giant moose that Antoine seeks to protect and Claire wishes to dominate and kill. Antoine finally shoots the animal and sends its head to Claire, who throws the head from her husband's airplane and jumps out after it.

The violence and fantasy of L.'s mature style is captured again in *Une chaîne dans le parc* (1974; *Orphan Street,* 1976), a poetic novel with autobiographical overtones. Set in east-end Montreal in 1944, it traces a few months of relative liberty in the life of an eight-year-old hero between bleak stretches in institutions for unwanted children. It is told from the boy's point of view, and movingly—and sometimes humorously—contrasts the spontaneity of childhood with the cold adult world as Pierrot seeks "to arm himself against the mysteries of life."

Despite the sparseness of his literary production and the darkness of his palette, L.'s seriousness and his intense poetic vision have made him one of the most respected writers of fiction in contemporary Quebec.

FURTHER WORKS: *L'œil du peuple* (1957)

BIBLIOGRAPHY: Marcotte, G., *Une littérature qui se fait* (1962), pp. 51–61; Major, J.-L., *Le roman canadien-français* (1964), pp. 207–30; Bessette, G., *Trois romanciers québécois* (1973), pp. 131–80; special L. issue, *ELit,* 6, 2 (1973); Pascal, G., *La quête de l'identité chez A. L.* (1977)

PHILIP STRATFORD

Lao literature, which had its beginnings in poetry, reached its heights in the 16th and 17th cs. with the production of such epic poems as *Sin Xay* (partial tr., "The Sin Xai," 1967) by Thao Pangkham (fl. 1650). These poems were designed to be sung or chanted to the accompaniment of music. They contained descriptions of landscapes and accounts of love scenes and great battles.

Lao literature in the 20th c. reflects the major political changes during this period. During the first third of the century, when Laos was under French control, the *mohlam,* or traditional singers, continued to create and carry on the traditions of Lao poetry. In the 1930s and 1940s a new era in Lao literature was ushered in by young intellectuals who wrote articles in French about their own culture, language, and religion. Following the publication by Katay Don Sasorith (1904–1959) of *Comment joue-t-on le phaytong?* (1931; *The Game of Phay-Tong,* 1959), a string of articles by Lao authors appeared in French publications. Others who wrote in French included Prince Phetsarath Ratanavongsa (1890–1959), Prince Souphanouvong (b. 1912), Prince Souvannaphouma (b. 1901) and Nhouy Abhay (b. 1909).

With the rise of Lao nationalism in the 1940s, many writers began publishing in prose in their native language. Such important authors as Maha Sila Viravong (b. 1904), Thao Kéne (dates n.a.), Phouvong Phimmasone (b. 1911), and Somchine Pierre Nginn (b. 1892) wrote in Lao. By 1953 the Lao Literary Committee had begun publication of *Wannakhadisan,* a magazine devoted to articles on Lao language and culture.

During the 1940s and 1950s—both before and after independence (1954)—works appeared chronicling political events from the point of view of the Lao, albeit the elite. Prince Phetsarath published an important work in Thai, *Chao Phetsarat: Burut lek haeng Ratcha'anachak Lao* (1956; *Iron Man of Laos: Prince Phetsarath Ratanavongsa,* 1978), which provided a view of the life of a person actively involved in the modern history of Laos.

The publication in Paris of Sisouk Na Champassak's (b. 1928) *Tempête sur le Laos* (1961; *Storm over Laos,* 1961), written from the royalist point of view, added a major work of political journalism to the literature by the Lao elite in the French language.

Phoumi Vongvichit (dates n.a.), as secretary-general of the central committee of the Lao Patriotic Front (a component of the communist Pathet Lao), provided a different view of the political situation in his *Le Laos et la lutte victorieuse du peuple lao contre le néo-colonialisme américain* (1968; *Laos and the Victorious Struggle of the Lao People against United States Neo-colonialism,* 1969).

Much of the poetry composed from the late 1950s to the present reflected Lao political struggles. Poets of the major sides in the fight for Laos—communists, royalists, and neutralists—appealed to the people to join them, frequently referring to Buddhist literature and to Lao myths and legends to support their positions. Poems were also written by Lao in western languages. An interesting collection of poems written in Lao, French, and English by Khamchan Pradith (b. 1930) was called simply *Mes poèmes* (1960; my poems).

A great amount of technical literature in Lao was produced in the 1960s, primarily to support an educational system that was now teaching more subjects in the Lao language. Textbooks were written on agriculture, education, home economics, Lao language and literature, mathematics, and science. And Buddhist works were published by the monks of Vat Phonpranao.

Popular fiction in Lao came into its own in the late 1960s and early 1970s. A group of young writers in the Vientiane area attempted to encourage reading and writing in the Lao language; the major themes of their short stories were love, the trials of war, and Lao nationalism. Much of their writing appeared in two new magazines, *Phay nam* (from June 1972) and *Nang* (from December 1972), the latter a magazine written primarily by and for women. Characteristic of the works of this group is Leng Phouphangeum's (dates n.a.) *Sivit ni khy lakhon kom* (1968; this life is like shadow theater), and Panai (a pseudonym, dates n.a.) and Douangchampa's (a pseudonym, dates n.a.) *Thale sivit* (1971; ocean of life).

At the same time, socialist writers were producing works emphasizing the sufferings and struggles of Lao villagers and guerrillas in the areas of the country controlled by the Lao Patriotic Front. Such writing can be found in the short-story anthology *Kay pa* (1968; *The Wood Grouse,* 1968).

In the late 1970s two major types of publications appeared: (1) works produced in Laos under the new Lao People's Democratic Republic, including collections of short stories such as *Siang oen khong phay* (1978; whose cry for help), and collections of poems in traditional *lam* styles such as *Kon lam pativat* (1977; songs of the revolution); (2) writings by Lao refugees in the countries to which they had moved, including newsletters in Lao and English containing information about life in a new country, and articles written in English or French on Lao culture.

During the 20th c. the major innovation in Lao literature was the introduction and acceptance of the short story; the major theme was the consequences of political disruption of life in Laos.

BIBLIOGRAPHY: Phimmasone, P., "Cours de littérature lao," *Bulletin des Amis du Royaume Lao,* Nos. 4–5 (1971), 5–70; Lafont, P.-B., "La littérature politique lao," in Lafont, P.-B., and Lombard, D., eds., *Littératures contemporaines de l'Asie du sud-est,* Colloque du XXIXe Congrès International des Orientalistes (1974), pp. 40–55; Phinith, S., "Contemporary Lao Literature," *JSSB,* 63 (1975), 239–50; Compton, C. J., *Courting Poetry in Laos: A Textual and Linguistic Analysis,* Northern Illinois University, Center for Southeast Asian Studies Special Report No. 18 (1979); Nguyen N., "Lao Literature through History," in Social Science Committee of Vietnam (Hanoi), *History and Culture of South East Asia: Studies on Laos* (1981), pp. 35–48

CAROL J. COMPTON

LAO SHE

(pseud. of Shu Ch'ing-ch'un) Chinese novelist, short-story writer, and dramatist, b. 3 Feb. 1899, Peking; d. 24 Aug. 1966, Peking

Fatherless since early childhood, L. S. worked his way through Peking Teachers' College. After graduation he managed to support himself and his mother through a series of teaching and administrative posts. In 1924 he went to London, where he taught Chinese at the School of Oriental and African Studies.

While in London, L. S. became a great admirer of Dickens, and in 1926 he wrote his first novel, *Lao Chang te che-hsüeh* (1928; the philosophy of Old Chang), in imitation of

Nicholas Nickleby. It was an immediate success, for in addition to being written in the lively dialect of the Peking streets, this novel was the first to introduce humor into the New Literature movement (launched in 1918). In 1930, with his literary reputation already established, he returned to China, where he continued to teach and began to write short stories.

Renewed exposure to the harsh realities of Chinese society increasingly shifted the emphasis of L. S.'s works. *Mao ch'eng Chi* (1933; *Cat Country,* 1970), is one of the bitterest satires about Chinese society ever written. L. S. considered the novel a failure and soon turned his hand again to humor. The results were the eminently successful *Li-hun* (1933; *The Quest for Love of Lao Lee,* 1948) and *Niu T'ien-tz'u chuan* (1934; *Heavensent,* 1951), which was partly modeled on Fielding's *Tom Jones.*

Lo-t'o hsiang-tzu (1938; *Rickshaw,* 1979; also tr. as *Camel Xiangzi,* 1981) is his best novel. This tragic tale, in which he attempted to show the complete bankruptcy of individualism, traces, without sentimentality, the moral ruin of an honest Peking rickshaw puller brought about by a callous, cruel society. The first American translation of this work, *Rickshaw Boy,* became a best seller shortly after its publication in 1945. This version, however, in which the translator took the liberty of providing the story with a happy ending, was not acceptable to L. S. (He was later to disapprove of the same man's translation of *Li-hun* [*Divorce,* 1948], and commissioned a new translation of the same work, *The Quest for Love of Lao Li.*)

The outbreak of the second Sino-Japanese War (1937–45) radically altered L. S.'s writing. Essentially apolitical (he mistrusted all government officials), in 1938 he was elected head of the Chinese Writers' Anti-Aggression Association, a group formed to pull writers of all political persuasions together in the common cause of the war with Japan. L. S. became a patriotic propagandist and indulged his lifelong interest in popular forms of entertainment by writing ballads, plays, and short skits on wartime themes.

After the war, L. S. published a gigantic novel in three parts, *Ssu-shih t'ung-t'ang* (abridged tr., *The Yellow Storm,* 1951), which deals with life in Peking during the Japanese occupation of Manchuria. The first two parts, *Huang-huo* (bewilderment) and *T'ou-sheng* (ignominy), were published in

1946, while part three, *Chi-huang* (famine), was not published until 1950–51, when it appeared in serialized form. Like his wartime works, this trilogy seems dated because of its emphasis on brave patriots and sniveling collaborationists.

Between 1946 and 1949 L. S. lived in the U.S., having gone there at the invitation of the Department of State. While there, he completed a new novel that was translated and published in 1952 as *The Drum Singers;* the Chinese version of this novel has not yet appeared. When the People's Republic was established in 1949, he returned to China and held a number of important cultural posts. During these years he wrote many propagandistic works, the most successful of which was the play *Lung hsü-kou* (1951; *Dragon Beard Ditch,* 1956).

L. S. had a lifelong interest in the craft of writing. In his early collection of essays *Lao-niu p'o-ch'e* (1939; an old ox and worn-out cart) he explains how he wrote much of his best work. His essays after 1949, however, are less concerned with his own writing than with teaching the craft of writing to a new generation; the most noteworthy of these later essayistic works is *Ch'u-k-'ou ch'eng-chang* (1964; spoken so well it's ready to print).

In 1966, during the Cultural Revolution, L. S. was driven to suicide by the Red Guards. Since the fall of Chiang Ch'ing (guiding hand of the Cultural Revolution) in 1976, L. S. has been officially praised, his early works republished, and his persecutors blamed, although not brought to trial.

L. S. will probably be best remembered for the excellent novels and stories he wrote during the 1920s and 1930s. These works show a warm humanitarian humor, graceful handling of the Peking dialect, deep love for China, and sympathy for the underdog, all of which will assure L. S. international readers for a very long time to come.

FURTHER WORKS: *Chao Tzu-yüeh* (1927); *Erh Ma* (1929; *Ma and Son,* 1980); *Hsiao-p'o te sheng-jih* (1931); *Kan-chi* (1934); *Ying-hai-chi* (1935); *Ko-tsao-chi* (1936); *Chien-pei 'Pien* (1940); *Kuo-chia chih-shang* (1940, with Sung Chih-ti); *Huo-ch'e-chi* (1941); *Wen Po-shih* (1941); *Kuei-ch-ü-lai hsi* (1943); *Ts'an-wu* (1943); *Mien-tzu wen-t'i* (1943); *Chung-lieh t'u* (1943); *Wang-chia Chen* (1943); *Chang Tzu-chung* (1943); *Ta-ti lung-she* (1943); *T'au-li ch'un-feng* (1943);

Shei nsien tao-le Ch'ung-ch'ing (1943); *Huo-tsang* (1944); *Tung-hai pa-shan-chi* (1946); *Wei-shen-chi* (1947); *Fang Chen-chu* (1950); *Pieh mi-hsin* (1951); *Ch-un-hua ch'iu-shih* (1953); *Ho kung-jen t'ung-chih-men t'an hsieh-tso* (1954); *Wu-ming kao-ti yu-le ming* (1954); *Shih-wu kuan* (1956); *Hsi-wang Ch'ang-an* (1956); *Ch'a-kuan* (1957); *Fu-hsing-chi* (1958); *Hung Ta-yüan* (1958); *Ch'üan-chia fu* (1959); *Nü-tien-yüan* (1959); *Pao-ch'uan* (1961); *Ho Chu p'ei* (1962); *Shen-ch'üan* (1963). FURTHER VOLUME IN ENGLISH: *Two Writers and the Cultural Revolution: L. S. and Chen Jo-hsi* (1980)

BIBLIOGRAPHY: Slupski, Z., *The Evolution of a Modern Chinese Writer: An Analysis of L. S.'s Fiction, with Biographical and Bibliographical Appendices* (1966); Boorman, H. L., and Howard, R. C., eds., *Biographical Dictionary of Republican China* (1970), Vol. III, pp. 132–35; Hsia, C. T., *A History of Modern Chinese Fiction: 1917–1957* (1971), pp. 165–88, 366–75, 546–50; Vohra, R., *L. S. and the Chinese Revolution* (1974); Kao, G., ed., *Two Writers and the Cultural Revolution: L. S. and Chen Jo-hsi* (1980), pp. 5–34.

WILLIAM A. LYELL

LARBAUD, Valery

French novelist, poet, short-story writer, critic, and translator, b. 29 Aug. 1881, Vichy; d. 2 Feb. 1957, Vichy

The only son of wealthy parents, L. enjoyed a privileged childhood. Despite delicate health, he traveled in Spain, Italy, Germany, and Russia before he was eighteen. At school near Paris L. had already made many foreign friends. His early education and travels left a cosmopolitan stamp on his writing and his widely varied literary interests.

L.'s first book of poems, *Les portiques* (porticoes), was published in 1896 at his mother's expense. His first translation, of Coleridge's *Rime of the Ancient Mariner,* appeared in 1901, the year he enrolled at the Sorbonne for a program of English/German studies he never completed. A facile linguist with an inquiring critical mind, L. fashioned his own eclectic literary education.

L. was a highly personal writer whose work reflects four spheres of interest: the world of childhood, the feminine mystique, travel, and pursuit of the literary life. His adopted pose, that of cosmopolitan aesthete and vagabond, was emulated by contemporaries. In an era of chauvinism, he pioneered the humanistic concept of pan-European civilization.

Fermina Márquez (1911; Fermina Márquez) records L.'s recollection of school days and adolescent romance. *A. O. Barnabooth, ses œuvres complètes: C'est-à-dire un conte, ses poésies et son journal intime* (1913; poems first pub. as *Poèmes par un riche amateur,* 1908; *Poems of a Multimillionaire,* 1955; journal section tr. as *A. O. Barnabooth, His Diary,* 1924) remains L.'s most discussed work. It is a curious potpourri: a brief tale of Voltairean flavor, a collection of free verse conjuring travel memories, and a diary, all purportedly the work of a young South American millionaire. The poems, published earlier with a mock biography, are to be read as the work of an amateur. The diary, light in tone, poses a moral dilemma: the search for identity. Like André Gide's (q.v.) heroes of that period, Barnabooth pursues an impossible freedom from constraint. Efforts to divest himself of possessions and conventions misfire, revealing the tragicomic complexity of his human fate and his inability to escape from his aristocratic condition. L.'s irony is felt in our last glimpse of Barnabooth, newly married.

Enfantines (1918; childlike tales) contains a half-dozen brief tales centering on childhood dreams and desires, essentially those of girls. They show L.'s gift for portraying poignant emotion with unsentimental sensitivity. Lolita-like teenagers and international show girls alike haunt L.'s reverie, extensions of his fascination with Fermina Márquez. Love for women often mingles with a near-erotic attraction to the life of the great cities.

Although devoted to individuals, and curious about alien cultures and eager to embrace them, L. never felt what we now call social consciousness. Through his translations, prefaces, and critical articles, he introduced a great number of British, American, and Spanish writers to French readers. L. is particularly celebrated for the key role he played in promoting James Joyce's (q.v.) *Ulysses,* even collaborating with the author to supervise the difficult translation.

In 1957, shortly before his death, L. was named one of the ten delegates who represented France at the World's Fair in Brussels. Never a widely popular writer, but rather a modest, discerning presence in the world of letters, L. is esteemed for originality of style and vision, for his incisive critical prowess, and for having helped to introduce cosmopolitanism into French literature.

FURTHER WORKS: *Beauté, mon beau souci* (1920); *Amants, heureux amants* (1921); *Mon plus secret conseil* (1923); *Ce vice impuni, la lecture, domaine anglais* (1925); *Notes sur Maurice Scève* (1926); *Allen* (1927); *Jaune bleu blanc* (1927); *Aux couleurs de Rome* (1931); *Ce vice impuni, la lecture, domaine français* (1941); *Sous l'invocation de Saint Jérôme* (1944); *Francis Jammes–V. L.: Lettres inédites* (1947); *Lettres à André Gide* (1948); *Journal 1912–1935* (1955); *Correspondance V. L. et G. Jean-Aubry 1920–1935* (1971); *Léon-Paul Fargue–V. L.: Correspondance 1910–1946* (1971); *Le cœur de l'Angleterre, suivi de Luis Losada* (1971); *Alfonso Reyes–V. L.: Correspondance 1923–1952* (1972); *V. L.–Marcel Ray: Correspondance* (3 vols., 1979–80)

BIBLIOGRAPHY: Jean-Aubry, G., *V. L., sa vie et son œuvre* (1949); Delvaille, B., *V. L.* (1963); Weissman, F., *L'exotisme de V. L.* (1966); O'Brien, J., *The French Literary Horizon* (1967), pp. 193–208; D'Eaudeville, J., *V. L., européen* (1972); Alajouanine, T., *V. L. sous divers visages* (1973); Brown, J. L., *V. L.* (1981)

JAMES ROBERT HEWITT

LARKIN, Philip
English poet, b. 9 Aug. 1922, Coventry

An only son, L. spent his childhood, which he has referred to as "a forgotten boredom," in Coventry. He attended St. John's College, Oxford, and became a librarian in 1943. Since 1955 he has been the Librarian of the University of Hull.

The North Ship (1945) was L.'s first book of poetry. It is a collection of short lyrics, usually with short lines and carefully worked-out rhyme schemes; only a small number have titles. There is a paucity of adjectives. The poems display a studied plainness, and very few of them depend on visual images or precise observation. For the most part they are sad songs of vague and general emotions.

The influence of the short lyrics of Yeats (q.v.) on the poems of *The North Ship* is very marked. In his introduction to the revised edition (1966), L. states that after having been made vividly aware of Yeats's work in 1943, "I spent the next three years trying to write like Yeats . . . out of infatuation with his music. . . . I used to limber up by turning the pages of the 1933 . . . edition, which stopped at 'Words for Music Perhaps,' and which meant in fact that I never absorbed the harsher last poems." Reading Hardy (q.v.) in 1946, he declares, cured him of his infatuation with Yeats.

L.'s reputation as a poet rests on *The Less Deceived* (1955) and *The Whitsun Weddings* (1964). The poems they contain are more elaborate, richer, and more solid than those in *The North Ship*. L. makes skillful use of the tones and rhythms of ordinary speech; even the most formal poems are slightly colloquial. That they all have titles is indicative of their greater particularity and sharper focus.

When the poems have a definite setting it is the urban, English landscape of the industrial north and Midlands. L. concentrates on the ordinary, dreary, humdrum, and unfashionable. He notes the ambulances, the noisy playgrounds, the drainpipes, and the fire escapes. The people who appear in the poems are provincial, weary, poor, bleak, and dull, unaware of the futility of their lives.

The central preoccupation in L.'s work is with going away from experience. A characteristic situation is for the poet to be looking out of a train window or musing on old photographs. He often declares that he prefers loneliness and celebrates his retreat from life.

That the past is simply and absolutely past is felt as being slightly enigmatic, and this mystery informs some of L.'s best poetry. The poet seems to feel that he cannot mourn for what has happened or for lost possibilities, because nothing has any real meaning. He is filled, nevertheless, with elegiac feelings, and his intelligence is at war with this nostalgia. Any sense of tragedy is both muffled and denied. All passions in L. are mundane and deliberately muted.

The persona who speaks makes a point of his own failures, his selfishness and inability to love, his unadventurous nature, and the emptiness and insignificance of his life—but usually with a wry humor. He is a drab and unrhetorical cousin of T. S. Eliot's (q.v.) J. Alfred Prufrock. Perhaps the best known of L.'s phrases is the poet's ironic description of himself entering a church: "Hatless, I take off/My cycle-clips in awkward reverence." The strength of L.'s poetry is in his capacity for metaphorical statement. This can be seen in such powerful lines as: "Why should I let the toad *work*/Squat on my life?" and "All the unhurried day/Your mind lay open like a drawer of knives."

In recent years the urge to self-limitation appears to have carried L. to the point of not writing much poetry and to keeping his deeper feelings out of the poems he *has* written. He continues in *High Windows* (1974) to be the spectator of his own memories, but the poems are only a repetition of his old forms in which the passion is lost.

The vividness of L.'s perception of everyday English life, his ironic self-awareness, and his technical ability have caused him to be considered one of the best English poets of his generation.

FURTHER WORKS: *Jill* (1946; rev. ed., 1963); *A Girl in Winter* (1947); *All What Jazz? A Record Diary 1961–68* (1970)

BIBLIOGRAPHY: Wain, J., "Engagement or Withdrawal: Some Notes on the Work of P. L.," *CritQ*, 6 (1964), 167–78; Timms, D., *P. L.* (1973); Brownjohn, A., *P. L.* (1975); King, P. R., *Nine Contemporary Poets* (1979), pp. 1–43; Morrison, B., *The Movement* (1980), passim; Bloomfield, B. C., *P. L.: A Bibliography* (1980)

ROBERT M. REHDER

LA TOUR DU PIN, Patrice de

French poet, b. 16 March 1911, Paris; d. 28 Oct. 1975, Paris

L. dedicated his life to poetry. Born into an old, aristocratic family, he grew up at Le Bignon-Mirabeau, a country estate near Paris that was to provide the themes and images of his early poems. L. received a Catholic education at Sainte-Croix in Neuilly-sur-Seine, studied literature at the Sorbonne, and enrolled in the École Libre des Sciences Politiques intending to become a lawyer. Within three years he abandoned law. Alternating between Paris and Le Bignon-Mirabeau, he channeled his energies into writing and drew inspiration from nature, contemporary life, reflection, the Bible, and such masters as Montaigne, Dante, Saint Thomas Aquinas,

Saint John of the Cross, and Rainer Maria Rilke (q.v.).

The high praise accorded L.'s first published work, the romantically elusive, descriptive poem "Les enfants de Septembre" (1931; September's children), prefigured the widespread acclaim for *La quête de joie* (1933; the quest of joy), a collection of serene, predominantly religious lyrics, conceived as part of a monumental investigation of man's spirituality that was to occupy L. for over thirty years. World War II slowed down the project. Drafted into the army and taken prisoner by the Germans, he was repatriated in 1942 and reemerged three years later with the six-hundred-page *Une somme de poésie* (1946; a sum of poetry), which incorporates all previously published poems and builds them into a vast construction centered around L.'s interpretations of spirituality seen both as creativity and transcendence. Man's journey inward, redeemed through the discovery of reality beyond the self, forms the unifying theme of this intricate work. It is held together by prose interludes, by recurrent images, and by protagonists who move through a mythic universe of symbolic objects and occurrences. In *Le second jeu* (1959; the second game), written as Part II of *Une somme de poésie,* self-knowledge is attained and transcended. Man opens up to the created world and in an act of generosity that L. associated with creativity, affirms the efficacy of the community.

With *Le petit théâtre crépusculaire* (1963; the little twilight theater) and *Une lutte pour la vie* (1970; a fight for life), as well as the later *Psaumes de tous les temps* (1974; psalms of all times), L. attempts to fuse poetry with prayer, sometimes with theological statement. Here he achieves the unity of himself before God that he had sought from the beginning.

L.'s verse is lofty, rhythmic, regular, at times oratorical, although free of rigidity. It evidences a control and a consciousness of purpose that suggest the presurrealist manner. Unlike his contemporaries, L. shunned experimentation and sought to integrate the diverse functions of poetry, thus evolving a dense, finely tuned, varied style that ranges from sensual descriptions to direct statements to mythical and symbolic structures. Much of his verse is intelligible. But his later poetry, complex, grounded in religious doctrine, derives from an essentially subjective vision, which in the eyes of some critics is marred by intellectualized detail and obscurity.

FURTHER WORKS: *L'enfer* (1935); *Le lucernaire* (1936); *Le don de la passion* (1937); *Psaumes* (1938); *La vie recluse en poésie* (1938; *The Dedicated Life in Poetry,* 1948); *Les anges* (1939); *Deux chroniques intérieures* (1945); *La Genèse* (1945); *Le jeu du seul* (1946); *Les concerts sur terre* (1946); *Les contes de soi* (1946); *un bestiaire fabuleux* (n.d.); *La contemplation errante* (1948); *Noël des eaux* (1951); *Une pépinière d'arbres de Noël* (1957); *Concert eucharistique* (1972). FURTHER VOLUME IN ENGLISH: *The Dedicated Life in Poetry, and The Correspondence of Laurent de Cayeux* (1948)

BIBLIOGRAPHY: Gros, L. G., *Poètes contemporains* (1944), pp. 11–33; Spender, S., Introduction to L., *The Dedicated Life in Poetry* (1948), pp. viii–xix; Rousselot, J., *Panorama critique des nouveaux poètes français* (1952), pp. 191–98; Reid, J. C., "Poetry and P. de L.," *Renascence,* 7, 1 (1954), 17–29; Brereton, G., *An Introduction to the French Poets* (1956), pp. 282–86; Jans, A., "Où en est P. de L.," *Revue générale belge,* Feb. 1960, 95–103; Kushner, E., *P. de L.* (1961)

VIKTORIA SKRUPSKELIS

LATVIAN LITERATURE

Latvian literature, like the literatures of its two neighbors on the Baltic, Estonia and Lithuania, emerged only in the 19th c. The ground from which Latvian letters sprang had been prepared for centuries by folklore. Tribes speaking Baltic languages had settled near the Baltic Sea during the 2nd millennium B.C. Latvian and Lithuanian are the only surviving languages of this once widespread branch of Indo-European: their folk poetry has preserved many aspects of the common Indo-European heritage.

At the beginning of the 20th c. Latvian literature in the accepted sense of the word was only about half a century old. Since the appearance of the first book printed in Latvian in 1585, there had developed a tradition of religious and didactic writing—the authors being mainly German clergymen—which can hardly be classed as literature. The first literary work of merit is *Dziesmiņas* (1856; little songs), a volume of poetry and translations

by Juris Alunāns (1832–1864). The significant movement of National Awakening (1859–80) laid the foundations for all literary genres except the drama. Although it did not produce a major poet, it created a body of poetry whose orientation toward a national romanticism strengthened pride in the Latvian past and hopes for a free state. During this period, a group of realistic prose writers turned out fine work, although with moralistic overtones, an example of which is the panoramic novel *Mērnieku laiki* (1879; the times of the land surveyors) by the brothers Reinis Kaudzīte (1839–1920) and Matīss Kaudzīte (1848–1926).

The interest in collecting Latvian folklore, under the inspired leadership of Krišjānis Barons (1835–1923), was perhaps the most vital seed planted during this period. The first edition of *Latvju dainas* (Latvian folk songs) appeared in eight volumes from 1894 to 1915.

In 1890 a new two-pronged era set in: neoromanticism and the socialist movement called the New Current, the latter having been prompted into existence by urgent sociopolitical problems (Russification by the tsarist regime was only one of them). The most prominent New Current writers were Jānis Rainis (q.v.) and his wife Aspazija (pseud. of Elza Rozenberga-Pliekšāne, 1868–1943). In the personality and works of Aspazija we witness the interplay of the two movements dominating Latvian literature at the turn of the century. In her early dramatic works and lyrics she attacks social injustice and shows feminist tendencies. Her later writing reveals the true personality of a romantic. Her lasting achievement lies in her "lyrical autobiography," five volumes of verse (1910–33). Rainis, a many-sided and philosophically inclined writer, was conscious heir to the poetic aspirations of the National Awakening in trying to incorporate into his work the spirit and structure of the folk songs.

Jānis Poruks (1871–1911) and Fricis Bārda (1880–1919) were both influenced by German neoromanticism. Poruks is also credited with introducing psychological realism into Latvian literature with his prose works. Rūdolfs Blaumanis (1863–1908) continued the traditions of realism established during the National Awakening but he shifted the focus from the social plane of earlier realists to the human soul and thus gave his dramatic works and stories an ageless quality.

After the unsuccessful revolution of 1905 political hopes were shattered, and a change of pace occurred in Latvian literature. Writers advocated the freeing of literature from subservience to social problems, as well as the right to personal and spontaneous expression, echoing western European developments of "art for art's sake" and symbolism (q.v.). These two literary movements acted only as catalysts. The Latvian adaptation had little in common with either, inclining toward impressionism in vividness of images and stressing lyrical qualities in poetry as well as prose. Thus, a period of lyrical impressionism followed the New Current. It counted among its adherents some of the finest poets in the Latvian language, for example, Kārlis Skalbe (q.v.), a master of succinct lyrical expression and simplicity of form. The spirit and ethos of folklore seem to have been reborn in his deeply national poetry and fairy tales. Impressionism with aestheticist tendencies is found in the sonorous rhythmic patterns of Vilis Plūdonis (pseud. of Vilis Lejnieks, 1874–1940).

One of the finest writers of this period, Anna Brigadere (q.v.), had "a passion for the light, color, and symbolic verities of the folk imagination" (W. K. Matthews). Out of these elements she created fairy-tale plays as well as childhood reminiscences, a genre that, especially with the surge of impressionism after 1905, also engaged the best creative powers of such writers as Jānis Jaunsudrabiņš (1877–1962), Antons Austriņš (1884–1934), and Jānis Akurāters (1876–1937). The glorification of the Latvian farmstead as reflecting in its unchanging ways an eternal order reached its apogee in Edvarts Virza's (q.v.) novel-length prose poem *Straumēni* (1933; the Straumēni homestead). (Even during the political exile of writers following World War II several gems of bucolic evocations have enriched Latvian literature, for instance, the autobiographical novels by the painter Margarita Kovaļevska [b. 1910], which reflect both the colorful earthiness and fantasy-charged atmosphere of a fairy tale.)

Side by side with the discovery of the self and nature through impressionism, realism (often verging on naturalism) remained a powerful means of taking stock of the native land, its history and people. Following in the footsteps of the brothers Kaudzīte and their great novel about the times of the land surveyors in northern Latvia, two 20th-c. novelists put the landscape and past of south-

western Latvia and the capital city, Riga, on the literary map: Augusts Deglavs (1862–1922) with his trilogy *Rīga* (1911–22; Riga) and Jēkabs Janševskis (1865–1931) with *Dzimtene* (1921–24; homeland), also a trilogy. Their earthy style and colorful use of regional dialects engendered a whole school of novelists who attained prominence during the 1930s and continued in the same manner in exile. Prominent among these are Jaunsudrabiņš, Aīda Niedra (1898–1972), Alfrēds Dziļums (1907–1966), and Jānis Klīdzējs (b. 1914).

In the wake of World War I an independent Latvian Democratic Republic was declared and a new period of literature set in, which lasted until 1940. The literary achievement of these twenty-two years is impressive. The first decade of independence was characterized by openness to foreign influences and by an efflorescence of all the arts. French models made themselves felt in the polished prose style of Jānis Ezeriņš (1891–1924). Kārlis Zariņš's (1889–1979) fiction achieved a psychological depth and epical poise between lyricism and realism worthy of the best work of his western European contemporaries. The impact of German expressionism (q.v.), coupled with influences from Russian imagism and futurism (qq.v.), called forth the first truly modern Latvian poets. Pēteris Ērmanis (1893–1969) stands out as a Latvian expressionist, while Aleksandrs Čaks (q.v.) is doubtlessly Latvia's greatest modern poet. A born rebel and keen innovator, Čaks shocked with his first books of poetry, where he discarded rhyme in favor of rhythm and used daring and unexpected images. His best collection, *Iedomu spoguļi* (1938; mirrors of imagination), is one of the finest achievements of Latvian poetry. Not only are his poetic means refreshingly new, but also his world—Riga and its suburbs—had never thus been celebrated in poetry before. Čaks died in Soviet-occupied Latvia at the height of his creative powers after being criticized for being unable to overcome his "bourgeois prejudices."

After the coup d'état of 1934, which brought an authoritarian government to power, instead of an international modernism, a return to indigenous traditions and a glorification of the past became the order of the day. The main figure of this school of poetry was Edvarts Virza. Renewed preoccupation with folklore resulted in experiments with folk-song meter in the poetry of Jānis Me-denis (1903–1961) and a reincarnation of its spirit in the subtly balanced verse of Zinaīda Lazda (1902–1957). In fiction attempts were made to re-create the legendary Latvian past and to reconstruct the ancient religion of the Balts by, among others, Jānis Veselis (1896–1962) and Ilona Leimane (b. 1905). Aleksandrs Grīns (1895–1941) pioneered the novel-legend about the Latvian fight for freedom. Kārlis Zariņš lifted the historical novel onto a higher artistic plane.

During the 1930s, a tendency toward universalism paralleled the national and traditional aspirations, finding expression in the essays of Zenta Mauriņa (1897–1978) and in the short stories and poems of Mirdza Bendrupe (b. 1910), who was greatly influenced by Freud (q.v.) and Oriental mysticism. The work of Ēriks Ādamsons (1907–1947), a major poet and short-story writer, developed during the 1930s in almost direct opposition to national trends. Favoring introspection and refinement rather than focusing on the native soil, he occupies an isolated yet prominent place in Latvian letters.

Toward the end of the 1930s the mores of urban society and the psychology of love gained momentum as literary themes. They were explored and carried over into exile writing in the work of Anšlavs Eglītis (b. 1906), Valdemārs Kārkliņš (1906–1964), and Knuts Lesiņš (b. 1909), the last the author of the short-story collection *Mūžības vīns* (1949; *The Wine of Eternity,* 1957). The only dramatist of note during the 1930s was Mārtiņš Zīverts (q.v.), the author of more than forty plays, in which he experiments both with the form and the subject matter of modern drama, having acquired an especially high degree of perfection in handling dramatic dialogue.

Before going into exile Veronika Strēlerte (pseud. of Rudīte Strēlerte-Johansone, b. 1912) published two collections of verse that established her as the finest artist among a host of Latvian women poets. Her polished, pliant verse lends itself well to intellectual meditation or restrained patriotic feeling. Since 1945 she has published three more poetry volumes. Andrejs Eglītis (b. 1912) gained great popularity with his patriotic verse during the war years and has continued as a national bard in exile, producing more than ten volumes of poetry.

During the German occupation (1941–45) political uncertainty and a violent reaction of disillusionment combined to produce an atmosphere unfavorable to good creative work. Nevertheless, some writers were able to add several works of great merit to Latvian literature.

After the mid-1950s a new generation of poets began to dominate the literary scene in exile. Born during the 1920s and educated in Latvian schools, they brought about a renascence of Latvian poetry by claiming Čaks as their ancestor and incorporating the lesson learned from Western experimental poetry into their work. Among the most original women poets are Velta Sniķere (b. 1920), who continues the traditional dialogue with the language of the folk songs, transposing it into a surrealist (q.v.) key; Astrīde Ivaska (b. 1926), in whose poems life appears vibrant with beauty and mystery; Aina Zemdega (b. 1924), whose emotionally charged images and impressions (mainly of nature) again and again gush forth with all the immediacy and weirdness of a turbulent unconscious; Valda Dreimane (b. 1932), who likes to underscore her Latvian vision by incorporating folklore motifs in her poetry; Velta Toma (b. 1912), whose magic incantations reflect her absorption of the best current poetic developments in her homeland; and Baiba Bičole (b. 1931), who can instantaneously connect the ancient with the immediate, the rational with the irrational, the organic with the inorganic; Aina Kraujiete (b. 1923), whose poetry's most salient feature is its perfect emotional and intellectual balance. Bičole and Kraujiete, as well as Rita Gāle (b. 1925), belonged to the New York group of Latvian poets. Its most outstanding members, however, were Linards Tauns (pseud. of Alfrēds Bērzs, 1922–1963), whose visionary poetry represents the highest achievement to date in Latvian poetry in exile, and Gunars Saliņš (b. 1924), whose mythical poetic imagination ranges in time from ancient Baltic ritual to "happenings" in Greenwich Village, and in space from deep cellars with murals dripping wine, to the tops of Manhattan skyscrapers where cherubs with nylon wings sit inert before sunrise. In Olafs Stumbrs's (b. 1931) poetry exile becomes a metaphor for the poet's fate of loneliness and alienation, whereas Valdis Krāslavietis (pseud. of Valdis Grants, b. 1920) waxes especially indignant at the sterility and aimlessness of exile existence. Juris Kronbergs (b. 1946) was born, brought up, and educated in Sweden. Nevertheless, his idiom is still flexible enough to bend to new sounds, experiences, and expression, and is still absorbent enough to soak up foreign elements without being contaminated.

A breakthrough to modernism in prose among writers in exile began during the 1950s in the novels of Modris Zeberiņš (b. 1923) and Dzintars Sodums (b. 1922); it became an undeniable fact in the work of Guntis Zariņš (1926–1965), who produced six novels in rapid succession, all of which evinced an existentialist (q.v.) point of view and a breathless search for self-identification both as an individual and a Latvian. Ilze Šķipsna (1928–1981) and Andrejs Irbe (b. 1924) center their interest in exploring psychological states and the substratum of dreams and memories in the exile's inner life, which could not be reached by realistic prose writing. The painter Tālivaldis Ķiķauka (b. 1928) leans toward surrealism in his imaginative, exhilarating prose. The prose works of Richards Rīdzinieks (pseud. of Ervins Grīns, 1925–1979) and Aivars Ruņģis (b. 1925) reflect various formalistic and absurdist trends of modern Western literature. Arturs Baumanis's (b. 1905) monumental epic novel *Hernhūtieši* (8 vols., 1976; Herrnhuters), about the Herrnhut religious movement in 18th-c. Livonia, is permeated with earthy humanity. After more than thirty-five years Latvian literature in exile still shows signs of vitality and promise for the future.

Almost immediately after the Red Army entered Latvia in June 1940, official spokesmen declared Soviet Russian literature to be "an absolutely indispensable school for literary development in Latvia," and Latvian writers were urged to strive for the "perfection embodied in the literary experience of the first socialist state, Soviet Russia." The German occupation prevented the Soviet authorities from carrying out these policies immediately. After World War II, however, literary administrators from Moscow resumed their weeding-out process, and Latvian writing was narrowed and reduced to propagandistic functions—with tragic consequences for creativity, for actual works, and for individuals.

Following Stalin's death, especially after the Twentieth Congress of the Communist Party of the Soviet Union in February 1956, a substantial number of those intellectuals who had "taken their own song by the throat" were inspired by the possibility of expressing ideas and sentiments they had long repressed—for example, Ēvalds Vilks (1923–1976), Dagnija Cielava-Zigmonte (b. 1931),

and Jezups Laganovskis (b. 1920). Harijs Heislers (b. 1926) wrote a long poem, *Nepabeigtā dziesma* (1956; *The Unfinished Song*, 1958), perhaps the first work of literature in the entire U.S.S.R. to deal strictly with the theme of banishment to Siberia. Although the literary line hardened after the 1956 "ideological revolt," partly as a consequence of events in Poland and Hungary, and later still more—after the 1968 attempt to "democratize socialism" in Czechoslovakia— some writers found it possible to deal in one way or another with subjects and themes that had been forbidden during the first ten or fifteen postwar years. Several gifted writers endeavored to lead the way toward the revival of literature. Visvaldis Lāms-Eglons (b. 1923), in spite of the obligatory admixture of Socialist Realism (q.v.), succeeded in maintaining a modicum of literary merit and in demonstrating his talent for communicating the atmosphere of a particular time and place, usually his chaos-laden native land during World War II and its aftermath. His many novels, such as *Kāpj dūmu stabi* (1960; smoke is rising), *Visaugstākais amats* (1968; the top post), *Jokdaris un lelle* (1971; a joker and a puppet), and *Mūža gūvums* (1973; *A Life Reviewed*, 1979), combine psychology and social criticism and bring into Latvian fiction complex, unpredictable characters, who are first human beings and only then heroes. The fatuous positive *homo sovieticus* of "socialist" construction and facile happy ending also are completely absent from several other works, for example, the novel *Kailums* (1970; nakedness) by Zigmunds Skujiņš (b. 1926), one of those writers who have been able to straddle the literary fence by writing good literature as easily as sermonizing propaganda pieces. The central theme of several of Regīna Ezera's (b. 1930) works of fiction is the dilemma of sensitive individuals who are isolated and destroyed by the stultification and depravity of the environment. The dominant characteristics of Aivars Kalve (b. 1937), Andris Jakubāns (b. 1941), and Jānis Mauliņš (b. 1933) are indirectly expressed irony, understatement, and an incongruous juxtaposition of situations and characters. Marģeris Zariņš's (b. 1910) narratives often shift spheres of fictional reality in the manner of Pirandello (q.v.). Alberts Bels (b. 1938) in his best novels—*Izmeklētājs* (1967; *The Investigator*, 1980), *Būris* (1972; the cage), and *Saucēja balss* (1973; *The Voice of the Herald*, 1980)—recaptures the spirit of experimentation by using montagelike construction and multidimensional views of events, and by attempting to express illusion, hallucination, and foreboding by syntactical distortions, blurring person and number. Herberts Dorbe (b. 1894), Jānis Kalniņš (b. 1922), Antons Stankevičs (b. 1928), and Saulcerīte Viese (b. 1932) have excelled in the neglected genre of the biographical novel.

The scope of lyrical expression was broadened especially by those poets who entered the literary scene in the 1960s. Vizma Belševica (b. 1931), whose idiosyncratic poems represent perhaps the most important achievement in contemporary Latvian poetry, was silenced by the authorities for almost ten years after the publication of her masterful poem "Indriķa Latvieša piezīmes uz Livonijas hronikas malām" (1969; "The Notations of Henricus de Lettis in the Margins of the Livonian Chronicle," 1970), which renders history with the immediacy of a news broadcast on a current—and personal—crisis. She was partially rehabilitated in the late 1970s. The "Latvian Yevtushenko" (q.v.), Ojārs Vācietis (b. 1933), in quite a few of his poems exalts such abstract terms as "freedom," "justice," "truth," and "human dignity," simultaneously trying to mobilize the conscience of his countrymen against the dry, dehumanizing kind of technology (and ideology).

Especially popular have been the writings of Imants Ziedonis (b. 1933), a prolific, impulsive, impatient and at times even angry poet, author of miniatures ("epiphanies") and travel notes, as well as a skilled translator. Although his poetry is not always free of Party propagandistic appeals, Ziedonis makes a great effort to assert the right of personal freedom, creative freedom, and freedom of thought, and he attempts to resurrect truths and to challenge obliquely the role of the authorities. Māris Čaklais (b. 1940), truly an intellectual poet, whose usually analytical and reflexive, and often difficult, personal, and esoteric poetry is thought out to the smallest detail, repeatedly asserts that "a human being without a past is a human being without a future."

Vitauts Ļūdēns (b. 1937), a master of manipulating language and structure to achieve formal unity and profundity of vision, whether he writes about the Teutonic crusaders in the 13th c., the revolution of 1905, World War I, and the horrors of the last war, or ancient traditions and medieval folklore, always

strives to convey the organic interconnection between historical periods. The answer to the meaning of history lies in the earth, specifically the Latvian soil, also for Jānis Peters (b. 1939), Imants Auziņš (b. 1937), Laima Līvena (b. 1943), and others. Knuts Skujenieks's (b. 1936) short untitled poetic fragments often allude to his sense of oppression at not being allowed to write freely and openly; in the 1960s he was sentenced to seven years in a labor camp for engaging in "anti-Soviet activities."

These well-established poets were joined in the 1970s by several talented newcomers, among them Uldis Bērziņš (b. 1949), Ilze Binde (b. 1941), Leons Briedis (b. 1949), Juris Helds (b. 1942), Viktors Kalniņš (b. 1945), Velga Krile (b. 1945), Hermanis Marģers Majevskis (b. 1951), Māra Misiņa (b. 1949), Aivars Neibarts (b. 1939), and Māra Zālīte (b. 1952). One of the most outstanding newcomers is Jānis Rokpelnis (b. 1945), a master of the paradox, sustained by a truly polyphonic texture with dissonant voices, incongruous word pairs, mocking rhymes, and other sound effects.

Today many Latvian writers are turning away from praise or criticism of the authorities and toward the expression of personal themes. They strive for a culture free from parochialism, one with universal and humanitarian goals, in which there can be creative dialogue between different aesthetic persuasions.

BIBLIOGRAPHY: Virza, E., *La littérature lettonne depuis l'époque de réveil national* (1926); Johansons, A., "Latvian Literature in Exile," *SEER,* 30 (1952), 466–75; Andrups, J., and Kalve, V., *Latvian Literature* (1954); Rubulis, A., and Lahood, M. J., eds., *Latvian Literature* (1964); Rubulis, A., *Baltic Literature* (1970); Andrups, J., "Latvian Literature," in Ivask, I., and Wilpert, G. von, eds., *World Literature since 1945* (1973), pp. 449–55; Ziedonis, A., et al., eds., *Baltic Literature and Linguistics* (1973); Ekmanis, R., *Latvian Literature under the Soviets: 1940–1975* (1978); Ekmanis, R., "Die Literatur in Lettland in den 60er und 70er Jahren," *AB,* 18 (1979), 194–370; Straumanis, A., ed., *Baltic Drama: A Handbook and Bibliography* (1981), pp. 113–380

ASTRID IVASK
ROLFS EKMANIS

LAURENCE, Margaret

Canadian novelist and short-story writer (writing in English), b. 18 July 1926, Neepawa, Man.

L. was born and raised in a small Manitoban town, a locale which has profoundly influenced all of her writing and which became the basis for her fictional Manawaka. She studied English literature at United College, Winnipeg. Her husband's engineering work took the couple to Africa for seven years, to what was then the British Protectorate of Somaliland and to Ghana. Five years in Vancouver were followed by a decade in England. After more than twenty years of traveling, she has returned to settle in Lakefield, a small Ontario town resembling the Neepawa of her youth.

L.'s work may be divided into two parts, by setting. Her African writing is less well known than her Canadian fiction, which is often studied in isolation. The neglect of the African work—a translation of Somali poetry and folktales, *A Tree for Poverty* (1954); a magnificent travel book, *The Prophet's Camel Bell* (1964); a novel set in Accra, *This Side Jordan* (1960); a collection of short stories, *The Tomorrow-Tamer* (1964); and a study of contemporary Nigerian dramatists and novelists, *Long Drums and Cannons* (1968)—is unfortunate, since her Canadian fiction emerges from two streams: the prairie roots, and the self-knowledge and maturity achieved abroad. Africa was the catalyst and crucible for much of L.'s work.

The five Canadian-based novels that make up L.'s Manawaka cycle re-create an entire society and constitute a portrait of human experience. Hagar Shipley, the ninety-year-old heroine of *The Stone Angel* (1964), wrestles with pride, love, and an indomitable lust for life. *The Diviners* (1974) demonstrates, through a middle-aged woman writer's experience and memory, that the past is alive in the present and is constantly being renewed, that it is a living river. The cycle also includes *A Jest of God* (1966), *The Fire-Dwellers* (1969), and *A Bird in the House* (1970).

Travel has played a major role in L.'s life and has provided her with her central metaphor—the psychic journey toward inner freedom and spiritual maturity. Journeying, strangerhood, and exile express (in her phrase) "the pain and interconnectedness of mankind." L.'s recurring themes are roots, ancestors, human complexity, acceptance of the other, and the necessity of growth.

The epic quality of L.'s fiction, and her ability to give symbolic form to social or collective life, has earned her a justified comparison with Tolstoy, while her literary vision of the two-way flow of time places her among philosophical novelists like Marcel Proust (q.v.). Her basic vision is religious, humanistic, and, more recently, increasingly political. Using her prairie region and specific historical issues, L.'s art dramatizes age-old concerns of human dignity and the need for social justice.

FURTHER WORKS: *Jason's Quest* (1970); *Heart of a Stranger* (1976); *The Olden Days Coat* (1979)

BIBLIOGRAPHY: Thomas, C., *M. L.* (1969); Cameron, D., *Conversations with Canadian Novelists,* Vol. I (1973), pp. 96–115; Thomas, C., *The Manawaka World of M. L.* (1975); New, W., ed., *M. L.* (1977); Woodcock, G., "The Human Elements: M. L.'s Fiction," in Helwig, D., *The Human Elements: Critical Essays* (1978), pp. 134–61; special L. issue, *JCS,* 13, 3 (1978); special L. issue, *JCF,* No. 27 (1980); Morley, P., *M. L.* (1981)

PATRICIA MORLEY

LAWRENCE, D(avid) H(erbert)

English novelist, short-story writer, poet, essayist, and dramatist, b. 11 Sept. 1885, Eastwood; d. 30 March 1930, Vence, France

L.'s early life is familiar to many, having been transmuted into the art of *Sons and Lovers* (1913). The coal-mining father, repudiated by his wife and dismissed by his children; the puritanical mother, with social and intellectual aspirations for her children; the artistic son, treasuring but also rebelling against his mother's nurturing, struggling to become an adult—these elements, the core of this novel, are the stuff of his life. His Midlands hometown in Nottinghamshire was a landscape of opposites in close proximity, village streets and coal mines immediately adjacent to lush countryside; the jarring juxtaposition marks L.'s inner landscape as well, a violent stridency alternating with the most exquisite gentleness. Throughout his life, L. railed against the ugliness of industrialization and praised the healing powers of the natural world.

In his youth L. found an intellectual forum in the Congregational Chapel's literary society, the Mechanics' Institute library, and the local socialist movement. He received his formal education in the area schools up through Nottingham University College, where he studied botany and French and trained as a teacher. After graduation in 1908 L. taught grammar school in south London and arrived on the London literary scene, thanks to the encouragement of his long-time sweetheart Jessie Chambers ("Miriam" in *Sons and Lovers*) and the interest of Ford Madox Hueffer (later Ford Madox Ford [q.v.]), editor of the *English Review*. Hueffer found L. a publisher for his first novel, *The White Peacock* (1911), and introduced him to the likes of H. G. Wells, Ezra Pound, and W. B. Yeats (qq.v.). The respiratory illnesses that had plagued L. since birth flared up in 1911 (he attributed this to the death of his mother the year before) and he gave up teaching to devote himself to writing under the editorial mentorship of Edward Garnett (1868–1937). In 1912 L. eloped with the wife of his former college French teacher, Frieda von Richthofen Weekley—several years his elder, daughter of a German baron, and mother of three children. L. was totally unlike Frieda in class, nationality, and temperament and thrived on these differences even as he chafed at them. Throughout his career he portrayed their fiery relationship in many autobiographical poems and stories.

From the first the eroticism of L.'s writings offended polite society. The outbreak of World War I compounded L.'s problems, since he was vociferously opposed to the war and, moreover, had a German wife. L.'s fourth novel, *The Rainbow* (1915), was banned for its alleged obscenity; the banning created further difficulties for him in getting anything published and forced him to rely on the generosity of others. John Middleton Murry (1889–1957) and Katherine Mansfield (q.v.), with whom the Lawrences developed an intense friendship, offered him their various "little magazines" as forums for his work. An important patron was Lady Ottoline Morrell, wife of a Liberal Member of Parliament, to whose home, Garsington Manor, many literati flocked. Through her, L. formed relationships with several people—among them, Aldous Huxley, E. M. Forster (qq.v.), and Bertrand Russell (1872–1970)—whose aid he tried to enlist in the creation of a new, utopian society—a small community to be established outside of England and away from war by those dissatisfied with the status quo.

During the war L. tried to leave England but was not permitted to emigrate until 1919. His years of wandering began: first to Italy and Germany and then to Ceylon, Australia, New Zealand, and, ultimately, North America, beckoned by a New Mexican fan, Mabel Dodge Sterne (later Luhan, 1879–1962), with visions of "primitive" Indians and unsullied landscape. By the 1920s L. was writing and publishing frequently in spite of nagging poor health. He continually wove the ever-changing scenery and events of his life into his fiction. Toward the end of his life he flouted the censors by exhibiting his sexually and religiously provocative paintings and by bringing out in a private edition the very explicit *Lady Chatterley's Lover* (1928; authorized abridged ed., 1932; unexpurgated edition, 1959). Both were seized by the authorities (the novel would not be sold openly in the United States until 1960), and the intransigency of society, as L. saw it, kept his wrath ignited until the last. He died of tuberculosis in southern France in 1930, but his ashes are interred at his ranch outside Taos, New Mexico, where Frieda lived on until her own death in 1956.

L. had an apocalyptic vision of life, formed by his coming of age as the century was newly ended, when old orders—agricultural and rural—were passing away, and by the cataclysm of the Great War. Like Yeats, L. was interested in cycles of death and rebirth: the phoenix was his personal emblem and appears time and again in his literary and pictorial art. L.'s works are characteristically open-ended, with no definitive resolutions to the crises they depict but with the possibility of better worlds ahead. Thus, *Sons and Lovers,* L.'s third and perhaps finest novel, ends with Paul Morel's heading toward the city and a new life, after the death of his mother. As in any novel of development, this hero tries out a variety of relationships and learns from them how to create a future for himself. That future is tentative, but the guiding values are set for Paul as for the writer whose life he mirrors: reverence for nature, faith in the regenerative powers of sex, and respect for the need for separateness in every person.

In *Sons and Lovers* Paul articulates L.'s desire to break through the crust of personality to get at the "protoplasm" beneath. This desire becomes a credo in *The Rainbow*. The title change from *Paul Morel* to *Sons and Lovers* had shown L.'s attempt at seeing the universal significance of individual identities, and the search for universality marks the direction of L.'s career, culminating in fables like *The Man Who Died* (1929; first pub. as *The Escaped Cock*). Although *The Rainbow* is a family saga and novel of development, it is less realistic than symbolistic; that is, it is "about" contrasting forces: the urge toward the earth, darkness, and "blood-consciousness" (L.'s term for an instinctual, nonrational way of knowing) versus the urge toward civilization, light, and mental consciousness. The rainbow symbolizes union-in-polarity, a life firmly earth-centered but reaching toward the sky. Typically, no such union is achieved in the novel, although Ursula Brangwen comes close to knowing how she might attain it.

Ursula's story continues in *Women in Love* (1920), which L. considered a sequel to *The Rainbow* but which can actually stand alone (the two novels began as one, but L. split the work when it became unwieldy). Episodic in nature, *Women in Love* is knit together by recurring motifs and a dancelike pattern of changing partners. As in *The Rainbow*, many scenes are puzzling on surface levels of plausibility and realism but are charged with deep significance: these include Birkin's stoning of the moon and Gerald Crich's fighting with the rabbit. Yet the novel is also filled with the simplest naturalistic touches that anchor it firmly to earth, like Ursula's worry that her fingers are too fat to wear Birkin's rings. The two modes of realism and symbolism exist in a precarious but ultimately successful balance.

Whereas *The Rainbow* is historical, *Women in Love* is eschatological: the pall of war hangs over it, although the exact war is unspecified; instead, there is a pervasive feeling of destruction and doom. L. is commonly known for his depiction of intimate love relationships, but he always related this personal realm to the larger fate of society. His readings in anthropology and history (for instance, Gibbon's *Decline and Fall of the Roman Empire*) add scope to this ambitious novel, which calls for a leader to resurrect modern society from its ashes.

L. was always seeking the utopia that he called "Rananim." In his searches he produced a great deal of travel writing in two genres, novels and travel books; these are stamped with the force of L.'s idiosyncratic and often negative impressions of a particular country, even as they faithfully capture the distinctive qualities of that country. In his so-called "leadership period," in the novels *Aaron's Rod* (1922), *Kangaroo* (1923), and *The Plumed Serpent* (1926), L. recorded his observations of warring political factions in several countries. His tendency toward propagandizing, obvious in *Women in Love*, came to the fore in these novels, which are generally considered L.'s weakest. But the landscape always lives, even when the novel disappoints. And *The Plumed Serpent*, L.'s reinstatement of pre-Aztec gods into the ruling pantheon of modern Mexico, has many devotees because of its color, poetry, and religious intensity.

L. returned to the English countryside that he knew so intimately for his tenth and final novel, *Lady Chatterley's Lover*. The gamekeeper figure of his first novel, *The White Peacock*, occupies center stage in his last one, representing all the life-nurturing qualities that L., as a good romantic, associated with nature and opposed to mechanization and industrialism. The configuration of characters is the familiar Lawrentian triangle, with an earthy, brutish type in rivalry with a thin-blooded prig for the same woman: in this case, Lady Chatterley renounces her upper-class husband to marry his virile employee. L. deliberately attempted to shock society with four-letter words that he hoped would resore it to healthy sexuality; indeed, the novel preaches a gospel of sex, and in spite of the tenderness of the love affair (*Tenderness* was L.'s original choice for a title), the novel is marred by its preachiness.

L. is undoubtedly best known for his novels, in which he cuts a grand, imposing, and often windy figure. His consummate skill at incident or vignette, as evidenced in these novels, helps to explain why many readers prefer his shorter fiction. At their finest, L.'s novellas and short stories combine meticulously accurate social settings with penetrating psychological analyses. They also have a mythological or archetypal richness, sometimes made explicit, as in "Samson and Delilah" (1917), but more often left to reverberate beneath the surface, as in "The

Rocking-Horse Winner" (1926). So the myth of Persephone wedded to the underworld Hades resonates in many stories, among them "The Ladybird" in *The Ladybird* (1923; Am., *The Captain's Doll*), "Fannie and Annie" (1921), and "The Blind Man" (1920).

L.'s poetry also merits attention. *Look! We Have Come Through!* (1917), his third volume, is a coherent group of confessional poems relating the harmony and conflicts of the unfolding relationship between L. and Frieda, or between any two lovers. In *Birds, Beasts and Flowers* (1923), the natural world offers paradigms for human behavior even as the poet celebrates its otherness. In fact, L.'s wonderment at the "foreignness" of all creatures, plant or animal, characterizes his entire canon and marks his reverence for the Unknown.

L. produced a large body of essayistic writing on subjects ranging from psychoanalysis to education, written in a colloquial and vibrant prose style and influenced by his extensive background readings. Especially noteworthy are his analyses of such American writers as Cooper, Hawthorne, Melville, and Poe, which were eventually revised and collected in *Studies in Classic American Literature* (1923). L. finds in this literature a twofold rhythm of disintegration of the old, European mental consciousness and the formation of a new, American passional self. At once impressionistic and persuasive, these essays are of a piece with all L.'s work in that they attempt to reform modern society and to get at the deeper meanings behind the raw data of experience.

In L. the artist and the prophet coexist. Some of L.'s works are damaged by his haranguing tone and protofascist views; L.'s most doctrinal fiction, however, typically contains the opposing viewpoint in the form of a devil's advocate or scoffer, and this viewpoint was in an important sense L.'s own. He was a questioner and doubter. His fiction's open-endedness results in great part from his unwillingness to commit himself fully to any doctrine, especially one that threatens the inviolate self. If at times his works reveal a misanthropy bordering on hysteria, and if his villains are pasteboard characters, still L. produced some of the most humane fiction and some of the most complex characters in modern literature. His greatness arises from his skill at so many literary forms; his intensity of expression; and

his emphases on personal integrity, humankind's capacity for risk-taking intimacies, and the balanced polarity of instinct and reason.

FURTHER WORKS: *The Trespasser* (1912); *Love Poems, and Others* (1913); *The Widowing of Mrs. Holroyd* (1914); *The Prussian Officer, and Other Stories* (1914); *Twilight in Italy* (1916); *Amores* (1916); *New Poems* (1918); *Bay* (1919); *Touch and Go* (1920); *The Lost Girl* (1920); *Movements in European History* (1921, under pseud. Lawrence H. Davison); *Psychoanalysis and the Unconscious* (1921); *Tortoises* (1921); *Sea and Sardinia* (1921); *Fantasia of the Unconscious* (1922); *England, My England, and Other Stories* (1922); *The Boy in the Bush* (1924, with M. L. Skinner); *St. Mawr, together with The Princess* (1925); *Reflections on the Death of a Porcupine, and Other Essays* (1925); *David* (1926); *Sun* (1926; unexpurgated version, 1928); *Glad Ghosts* (1926); *Mornings in Mexico* (1927); *Selected Poems* (1928); *Rawdon's Roof* (1928); *The Woman Who Rode Away* (1928); *Collected Poems* (2 vols., 1928); *Sex Locked Out* (1929); *The Paintings of D. H. L.* (1929); *Pansies* (1929); *My Skirmish with Jolly Roger* (1929); *Pornography and Obscenity* (1929); *Nettles* (1930); *Assorted Articles* (1930); *A Propos of "Lady Chatterley's Lover"* (1930); *The Virgin and the Gipsy* (1930); *Love among the Haystacks, and Other Pieces* (1930); *Apocalypse* (1931); *The Triumph of the Machine* (1931); *Etruscan Places* (1932); *Letters* (1932); *Last Poems* (1932); *The Lovely Lady, and Other Stories* (1933); *We Need One Another* (1933); *The Plays* (1933); *The Tales* (1933); *A Collier's Friday Night* (1934); *A Modern Lover* (1934); *The Spirit of Place* (1935); *Phoenix: The Posthumous Papers of D. H. L.* (1936); *Foreword to "Women in Love"* (1936); *Fire, and Other Poems* (1940); *The First Lady Chatterley* (1944); *Letters to Bertrand Russell* (1948); *A Prelude* (1949); *The Complete Short Stories* (1955); *Eight Letters to Rachel Annand Taylor* (1956); *The Complete Poems* (1957); *The Collected Letters* (1962); *The Symbolic Meaning: The Uncollected Versions of "Studies in Classic American Literature"* (1962); *The Complete Poems* (1964); *The Paintings of D. H. L.* (1964); *The Complete Plays* (1965); *Phoenix II: Uncollected, Unpublished, and Other Prose Works* (1968); *L. in Love: Letters*

From D. H. L. to Louie Burrows (1968); *The Quest For Rananim: D. H. L.'s Letters to S. S. Koteliansky* (1970); *The Centaur Letters* (1970); *Letters to Martin Secker 1911–1930* (1970); *John Thomas and Lady Jane* (1972); *The Escaped Cock* (1973); *Letters to Thomas and Adele Seltzer* (1976); *The Letters* (1979 ff.)

BIBLIOGRAPHY: Carswell, C., *The Savage Pilgrimage* (1932); Lawrence, F., *Not I, but the Wind* (1934); Chambers, J. [E. T.], *D. H. L.: A Personal Record* (1935); Leavis, F. R., *D. H. L.: Novelist* (1955); Spilka, *The Love Ethic of D. H. L.* (1955); Hough, G., *The Dark Sun: A Study of D. H. L.* (1957); Nehls, E., ed., *D. H. L.: A Composite Biography* (3 vols. 1957–59); Vivas, E., *D. H. L.: The Failure and the Triumph of Art* (1960); Beal, A., *D. H. L.* (1961); Widmer, K., *The Art of Perversity: D. H. L.'s Shorter Fictions* (1962); Moynahan, J., *The Deed of Life* (1963); Roberts, F. W., *A Bibliography of D. H. L.* (1963); Daleski, H., *The Forked Flame: A Study of D. H. L.* (1965); Ford, G., *Double Measure: A Study of the Novels and Stories of D. H. L.* (1965); Sagar, K., *The Art of D. H. L.* (1966); Clarke, C., *River of Dissolution: D. H. L. and the Romantic* (1969); Cowan, J., *D. H. L.'s American Journey* (1970); Gilbert, S., *Acts of Attention: The Poems of D. H. L.* (1972); Kermode, F., *D. H. L.* (1973); Sanders, S., *D. H. L.: The World of the Major Novels* (1973); Moore, H., *The Priest of Love: A Life of D. H. L.* (1974); Delany, P., *D. H. L.'s Nightmare: The Writer and His Circle in the Years of the Great War* (1978)

JUDITH RUDERMAN

He harangues us like Carlyle, whom he resembled in many aspects; the artist in him was doubled with the rhetorician. He too sprang from a poverty-cramped, sullen, illiterate fighting-stock; he too was the favored child of a mother who represented in those surroundings a superior and pious refinement; he too was born with a suspicion of any sort of agreement, and with a conviction, often agonized, that everybody must be wrong except himself; he was born too with a faculty for exquisite sympathy for individuals and an almost sadistic relish for the sufferings of people in general . . . ; he too was a humorist whose sense of fun sprang from a constantly tragic sense of life; he too was a prodigious egotist, yet in himself strangely lovable and fascinating, his egotism finding relief in minatory "uplift" diatribes, and showing itself in his intolerance of the smallest self-assertion on the part of others. For L. the egotist, to whom the experience of "love" was the crucial test of individual excellence, egotism, legitimate or illegitimate, in that relation, was a central problem. He too was, in a sense in which that phrase has a meaning apart from accomplishment, "a great man," one whom to be near, whether through his writings, or directly, meant for others an enhancement of life.

Desmond MacCarthy, *Criticism* (1932), p. 248

[A]mong all English novelists, Hardy and L. have the most faithful touch for the things of nature and the greatest evocative genius in bringing them before the imagination. But there are certain definitive differences of attitude. Both Emily Brontë's and Hardy's worlds are dual, and there is no way of bringing the oppositions of the dualism together: on the one side . . . are those attributes of man that we call "human," his reason, his ethical sensibility; and on the other side is "nature"— the elements and the creatures and man's own instinctive life that he shares with the nonhuman creatures. The opposition is resolved only by destruction of the "human": a destruction that is in Emily Brontë profoundly attractive, in Hardy tragic. But L.'s world is multiple rather than dual. Everything in it is a separate and individual "other" . . . ; and there is a creative relationship between people and between people and things so long as this "otherness" is acknowledged. When it is denied—and it is denied when man tries to rationalize nature and society, or when he presumptuously assumes the things of nature to be merely instruments for the expression of himself, or when he attempts to exercise personal possessorship over people—then he destroys his own selfhood and exerts a destructive influence all about him.

Dorothy Van Ghent, *The English Novel: Form and Function* (1953), p. 252

In the relations between man and woman . . . L. called for balance or "polarity," as if between two oppositely charged entities; or he placed the marriage unit itself in balance with the world of purposive activity—so that the protagonists of his novels must also be in tune, as it were, with the world around them. In other words, they must achieve organic being through "an infinity of pure relations" with the living universe: first, with each other, through love; then with other men and women, through friendship and creative labor; and finally even with birds, beasts, and flowers, which play a vital role in all the novels.

Once this is clearly understood, his psychology begins to take on flesh and substance; it falls within a greater and essentially religious scheme of life, and draws its depth and quality from that fact. Indeed, this interpenetration of the greater universe with specific situations, of the "life-force" with a well-developed psychology of life, is the hallmark of Lawrentian fiction. . . .

Mark Spilka, *The Love Ethic of D. H. L.* (1955), pp. 10–11

L. continually enlarges the boundaries of our consciousness, and a judgment of his individual artistic achievement will in the long run probably depend on the extent and the worth of the new territory acquired. Of course with many novelists this kind of inquiry would be pointless. They are concerned with putting in order experiences of a kind we are already quite familiar with. L. (or Dostoevsky or, in his own way, Proust) extends our experience; and to think about a novelist of this kind at once lands us in difficulties. We cannot talk for long about technique, powers of representation or even of moral insight; for we soon find that we are dealing with ideas and mental states that we have never clearly recognized till we meet them in this particular artistic context. Of course we can set L. against traditional moral habits, as Mr. Eliot does . . . ; and of course L. comes out a heretic. To define the limits of his offences against faith and morals may be a useful thing, even highly illuminating. But the net is so wide that the essence of his work simply slips through the mesh, as Mr. Eliot knows well.

Graham Hough, *The Dark Sun: A Study of D. H. L.* (1956), p. 4

Because the form of action in the behavioral sense is easier to perceive than the structure of inward experience, a first reading of L. and even a second or third gives us little more than a chaos of incidents and scenes that, however brilliantly presented, seem to lack formal inter-relationships. But persistent search for the structure of the work is at last rewarded. Synoptically we grasp the pattern of an ordered whole. We notice the first signs of nascent desire turning into clearly directed urge and notice the passional urge seeking satisfaction and succeeding or arriving at frustration; we notice the pattern of attraction and repulsion, the harmony of wills or their clash, and back of these harmonies or conflicts we notice the values that these inward commotions seek to realize and succeed or fail in realizing. And strange as it might seem, since L. is so frequently dismissed as anti-rational, we notice also the growth in wisdom on the part of his characters—or of what L. takes to be wisdom—and the causes for the success or failure of that growth.

Eliseo Vivas, *D. H. L.: The Failure and the Triumph of Art* (1960), pp. 225–26

On one dimension, which *The Rainbow* shares with the novels of Wells and Bennett, Ursula is the ordinary village girl whose struggle to find herself in the modern world is representatively commonplace. On a second dimension, however, a dimension rarely represented at all in the novels of Wells and Bennett, this ordinary girl is likened to a prophet from the Bible whose life-story is told as if it were of mythic or epic-scale significance. . . .

L. once described the Bible as "a great confused novel," and one is tempted, in the fashion of Oscar Wilde, to retort that *The Rainbow* is a great confused bible. The Bible, L. adds, is not a book about God but about man alive. . . .

[T]here is considerable similarity between [James] Joyce's use of Homeric parallels in *Ulysses* and L.'s use of Biblical parallels. Even though the apparent discrepancy between the large-scaled epic heroes and heroines of antiquity and their more ordinary modern-day equivalents is played up by Joyce for effects of comedy that are different from L.'s . . . , the author of *Ulysses* is nevertheless using similar methods for similar ends. Both novelists, dissatisfied with the one-dimensional level of naturalistic fiction, create a second dimension by suggesting, through parallels, that human experience is constant rather than totally chaotic.

George Ford, *Double Measure: A Study of the Novels and Stories of D. H. L.* (1965), pp. 133–34

Homage to the mystery of power . . . is as essential to L.'s extremely Romantic conception of poetry as to the relationship of leader and follower. And such homage necessarily precludes irony, just as the leadership novels precluded any real exploration of the complexities of self-achievement. The profound egalitarianism which, as L. recognized, is an absolute prerequisite of true democracy, permits the sort of relativism that leads to an ironic—Prufrockian—qualification of experience: "Who am I to ask the overwhelming question? Why not so-and-so?" In the aristocratic Lawrentian system, however, both leader and follower must commit themselves, without ironic reservations, to the power both apprehend as mysteriously fluent in the leader. And therefore the world-vision of both is not ironic, like that of most modern, egalitarian men, but anti-ironic, wholly concentrated on the wonder of power. . . .

In a way, then, L.'s bitterness about the war . . . made possible the writing of *Birds, Beasts and Flowers*, and, more, the success of the poems in that volume. His bitterness inspired a temporary but intense misanthropy, resulting in a contempt for the mass of mankind and a belief in the "sacred right" of a specially chosen few to guide the many. Such a leadership obsession, however incompatible with the writing of successful novels, led to the composition of visionary, anti-ironic poetry.

Sandra Gilbert, *Acts of Attention: The Poems of D. H. L.* (1972), pp. 128–29

[L.] was not on the whole sympathetic to, or even very interested in, the avant-garde movements of his time; if we were to try to relate his innovations to those, virtually contemporary, of Hulme in England or Apollinaire in France, we should be struck at once by his apparent isolation, by the way he worked things out for himself. The formative years, for example, of André Breton, can be recounted with reference to large and well-documented movements such as Dada and Surrealism; at a deeper level we could find affinities with L.— for example, in common apocalyptic and occult preoccupations—but L. is always working alone. His relationship to the history of ideas in his time is so far below the surface that to write it would be to engage in very delicate and also very speculative excavations. And this is true of his political as well as of his psychological and aesthetic positions.

Frank Kermode, *D. H. L.* (1973), pp. 25–26

LAXNESS, Halldór
Icelandic novelist, dramatist, essayist, and poet, b. 23 April 1902, Reykjavík

L. grew up in Reykjavík and nearby Mosfellssveit, thus absorbing both urban and rural influences in his youth. He left school early in order to concentrate on writing. After traveling extensively in Europe and North America in the 1920s, he returned to Iceland, where he has since resided, the first man to earn a living as a creative writer in Icelandic.

At seventeen L. published his first novel, *Barn náttúrunnar* (1919; child of nature), and in the same year made his first journey abroad. During the following decade he struggled to develop an understanding of himself and his world, and to forge a personal style. After his first contact with the turbulent cultural life of Europe, he converted to Roman Catholicism; but after a brief novitiate in a monastery in Luxembourg, his interests again became secular.

This period brought forth L.'s first major novel, *Vefarinn mikli frá Kasmír* (1927; the great weaver of Kashmir), a semiautobiographical work that seethes with uncompromising views about the condition of modern man. Its forceful expressionism (q.v.), outspokenness, and utter disregard of stylistic and moral conventions offended and shocked most readers, but won high praise from a minority.

While the protagonist of *Vefarinn mikli frá Kasmír* ends by rejecting the world and turning to God, L. himself went in the oppo-

site direction. Even before he went to North America in 1927, his Catholicism was weakening; direct experiences with American capitalism and its critics (he became personally acquainted with Upton Sinclair [q.v.]) turned him into an ardent socialist. His socialism inspired *Alþýðubókin* (1929; a book for the people), an essay collection written in America but addressed to his countrymen. In it L. declares man to be the only proper human concern, and vows to dedicate his art to the destiny of his people.

During the next twenty years L. published a series of novels in which he depicts, on an epic scale, the struggle of Iceland's poor against the brutalities of nature and social oppression. In this period L. the mature novelist and master of Icelandic prose emerged. His writing combines compassion, humor, and biting social satire.

In *Sjálfstætt fólk* (2 vols., 1934–35; *Independent People,* 1946) the protagonist is a small farmer who, after many years in the service of others, has bought some land and thereby acquired independence in his own eyes and those of society. The story describes his prolonged struggle to retain this independence; this struggle makes virtual slaves of himself and his family, brings sickness and death to two wives in succession, and ends in loss of the farm in the Great Depression. Unbroken, but having achieved a new understanding of himself and society, he prepares himself for another struggle ahead. Although this novel is set in a remote corner of Iceland, it epitomizes the Icelandic farmers' thousand-year battle against nature and exploitation; it is also a parable about Iceland's development as it began to change from a semicolonial peasant society into an independent capitalist state.

The central theme of *Heimsljós* (4 vols., 1937–40; *World Light,* 1969), another important novel of the 1930s, is the function of traditional literary culture in Icelandic life, even among the poorest. The story, set in a small fishing village dominated by a local "tyrant," is about a destitute poet who is torn between the demands made on him by his love of art and beauty on the one hand, and by his hatred of social injustice on the other.

Íslandsklukkan (3 vols., 1943–46; the bell of Iceland), which appeared during the war years, when Iceland finally acquired independence, takes national culture and national destiny as its major themes. This is a historical novel, based on actual events of the early

18th c., the darkest period in Iceland's history. The ineffectual culture of the upper class, personified by the manuscript collector Arnas Arnæus, is contrasted with the more robust lifestyle of the lower classes, in the person of the invincible fisherman Jón Hreggviðsson. *Íslandsklukkan* gives a vivid picture of Icelandic life in the 18th c. Most of the inhabitants are miserable, even destitute, and great parts of the nation's most valued treasure, the Arnæus manuscript collection, go up in flames when Copenhagen is burned. Despite these conditions, there is an obstinate clinging to life, and the vivid hope of better times ahead—no signs of which, however, are to be seen. Here, as everywhere in L.'s social satire, the grimness of life is counterbalanced by deep compassion and refined humor.

In subsequent novels L. has taken his subject matter from Icelandic postwar society as well as the 11th, 19th, and early 20th cs. In the 1950s he gradually abandoned socialism, and his writing took a new direction. In autobiographical works he denounced Soviet communism and ideologies in general. His later novels are characterized by philosophical skepticism, a semimystical faith in life, and an affirmation of simple values of people who, without being selfish, tend their gardens, and look upon the great and the mighty with a condescending pity.

L. has been very prolific. Apart from his novels, he has published numerous plays, short stories, memoirs, and essays, as well as a volume of poetry. He has used a variety of narrative techniques, but has moved steadily in the direction of objective and dramatic presentation of characters and situations. His style is rich, but not easily rendered in other languages. Always unmistakably personal, it grew in complexity and idiosyncrasy during the 1940s and 1950s, but lately he has simplified his style while retaining a subtle irony. With the partial exception of *Vefarinn mikli frá Kasmír*, L. has always chosen realistic themes from Icelandic life; but in his work their meaning transcends geographical and cultural boundaries.

The Nobel Prize for Literature, which he won in 1955, is a token of his international stature.

FURTHER WORKS: *Nokkrar sögur* (1923); *Undir Helgahnúk* (1924); *Kvæðakver* (1930); *Salka Valka* (2 vols., 1931–32; *Salka Valka*, 1936); *Fótatak manna* (1933); *Straumrof*

(1934); *Dagleið á fjöllum* (1937); *Gerska ævintýrið* (1938); *Vettvangur dagsins* (1942); *Sjö töframenn* (1942); *Sjálfsagðir hlutir* (1946); *Atómstöðin* (1948; *The Atom Station*, (1961); *Reisubókarkorn* (1950); *Heiman eg fór* (1952); *Gerpla* (1952; *The Happy Warriors*, 1958); *Silfurtúnglið* (1954); *Dagur í senn* (1955); *Brekkukotsannáll* (1957; *The Fish Can Sing*, 1966); *Gjörníngabók* (1959); *Paradísarheimt* (1960; *Paradise Reclaimed*, 1962); *Strompleikurinn* (1961); *Prjónastofan Sólin* (1962); *Skáldatími* (1963); *Sjöstafakverið* (1964); *Upphaf mannúðarstefnu* (1965); *Dúfnaveislan* (1966); *Íslendíngaspjall* (1967); *Kristnihald undir Jökli* (1968; *Christianity at Glacier*, 1972); *Vínlandspúnktar* (1969); *Innansveitarkronika* (1970); *Yfirskyggðir staðir* (1971); *Guðsgjafaþula* (1972); *Þjóðhátíðarrolla* (1974); *Í túninu heima* (1975); *Úngur eg var* (1976); *Seiseijú, mikil ósköp* (1977); *Sjömeistarasagan* (1978); *Grikklandsárið* (1980); *Við heygarðshornið* (1981)

BIBLIOGRAPHY: Einarsson, S., "A Contemporary Icelandic Author," *Life and Letters Today*, 14, 4 (1936), 23–30; Kötz, G., *Das Problem Dichter und Gesellschaft im Werke von H. K. L.* (1966); Lange, W., "Über H. L.," *GRM*, 14 (1966), 76–89; Hallberg, P., *H. L.* (1971); Wilz, O., "Der Wikingerroman als politische Tendenzschrift: Zu H. L.s *Gerpla*," *Skandinavistik*, 1 (1971), 1–16; special L. issue, *Scan*, 2,1 (1972); Sonderegger, S., "Rede auf H. L.," in *H. L. in St. Gallen* (1974), pp. 9–34; Höskuldsson, S., "Women and Love in the Novels of L.," *NorS*, 6 (1975), 3–20; Pálsson, H., "Beyond the Atom Station," in Höskuldsson, S., ed., *Ideals and Ideologies in Scandinavian Literature* (1975), pp. 317–29

VÉSTEINN ÓLASON

LAYTON, Irving

Canadian poet (writing in English), b. 12 March 1912, Neamtz, Romania

Brought to Canada at the age of one, L. was raised in the Jewish immigrant district of Montreal. After earning a bachelor's degree in agriculture and serving in the Royal Canadian Artillery (1942–43), he studied history and political economy at McGill University, where he earned an M.A. in 1946. During the 1930s L. became known as a fiery Marxist orator, and he thought his career would be as a political analyst of world affairs. By the early 1940s, however, his poetic talent had begun to emerge, and eventually he decided to devote himself to writing poetry, while earning a living through teaching. He became one of the editors of an avant-garde poetry magazine, *First Statement,* and a founding member of Contact Press, a venture promoting contemporary poetry in Canada. In the 1940s and 1950s he published several volumes of poems and short stories that reached a small but appreciative audience.

In 1959 a commercial publisher launched L.'s first sizable collection, *A Red Carpet for the Sun,* with considerable fanfare. During the next decade L. became a controversial public figure in Canada. His dynamic presence on radio, television, and the poetry-reading circuit, and his provocative prefaces and interviews, combined with the sensational aspects of his poetry, served to create a public image of an iconoclast, an irreverent sensualist, and a relentless satirist. Most critics were distracted by this image, but those, like Northrop Frye (q.v.) and George Woodcock (b. 1912), who managed to see beyond it, discovered L. to be an elegant, elegiac poet with an extraordinary range of technical ability and a complex, integrated vision. Others, like William Carlos Williams (q.v.) applauded the candor, vitality, and audacity of the poems.

L.'s oeuvre consists of over thirty volumes, including two collections of prose and several collected or selected editions of verse, the best of the latter to date being *The Darkening Fire* (1975) and *The Unwavering Eye* (1975). Recently retired from his professorship at York University, L. continues to travel widely and is in great demand as a speaker and reader.

L.'s early poetry displayed a Marxist orientation, and to this day he maintains an admiration for Marx the man, and his early writings. But L. was never a doctrinaire Marxist; and, particularly since the early 1950s, his denunciations of Marxism as an ideology, and especially of Russian Communism, have been a persistent strain in his poetry. Since the early 1950s, too, his work has revealed a remarkably strong affinity with Nietzschean thought. In fact, most of L.'s poetry may be read with great profit in a Nietzschean perspective.

L.'s poetry is also marked by an awareness of his Jewish heritage, sharpened in the late 1960s by the Arab-Israeli conflict. Since that time he has become increasingly concerned with Jewish themes—with the Holocaust, with anti-Semitism in the Soviet Union and elsewhere, and particularly with the historical and current relations between Jews and Christians.

In the early 1970s he embarked on a "campaign" to reclaim Jesus for the Jews and to laugh the remnants of "Xianity" out of existence. His concept of the Jew, however— "Someone/who feels himself to be/a stranger/ everywhere/Even in Israel"—merges on the one hand with the figure of the poet-prophet and, on the other, with the Nietzschean superman, the heroic individualist who by self-mastery and creativity learns to extract a tragic joy from existence. This complex figure, in one guise or another, is at the center of L.'s work. Through it he explores the moral, political, and psychological dilemmas of modern man and probes the erotic and demonic depths of the human psyche, not least his own. An unflinching confrontation with reality leads L. to a sardonic view of human nature and a tragic vision of man's cosmic fate. To this he opposes an exuberant celebration of life through the redemptive agencies of imagination and love. ("Whatever else, poetry is freedom," he claims.) This world is hell indeed; but, as opposed to meek and passive acceptance of suffering, L. applauds those who passionately resist evil, despair, and death.

FURTHER WORKS: *Here and Now* (1945); *Now Is the Place* (1948); *The Black Huntsmen* (1951); *Cerberus* (1952, with L. Dudek and R. Souster); *Love the Conqueror Worm* (1953); *In the Midst of My Fever* (1954); *The Long Pea-Shooter* (1954); *The Blue Propeller* (1955); *The Cold Green Element* (1955); *The Bull Calf, and Other Poems* (1956); *Music on a Kazoo* (1956); *The Improved Binoculars* (1956); *A Laughter in the Mind* (1958); *The Swinging Flesh* (1961); *Balls for a One-Armed Juggler* (1963); *The Laughing Rooster* (1964); *Collected Poems* (1965); *Periods of the Moon* (1967); *The Shattered Plinths* (1968); *Selected Poems* (1969); *The Whole Bloody Bird* (1969); *Nail Polish* (1971); *The Collected Poems of I. L.* (1971); *Engagements: The Prose of I. L.* (1972); *Lovers and Lesser Men* (1973); *The Pole-Vaulter* (1974); *Seventy-five Greek Poems* (1974); *For My Brother Jesus* (1976); *The Poems of I. L.* (1977); *Taking Sides* (1977); *The Uncollected Poems of I. L.* (1977); *The Covenant* (1977); *The Tightrope Dancer* (1978); *The Love Po-*

ems of I. L. (1978); *Droppings from Heaven* (1979); *An Unlikely Affair: The I. L.–Dorothy Rath Correspondence* (1980); *For My Neighbours in Hell* (1980); *Europe and Other Bad News* (1981)

BIBLIOGRAPHY: Woodcock, G., "A Grab at Proteus", *CanL,* No. 28 (1966), 5–21; Mandel, E., *I. L.* (1969); Doyle, M., "The Occasion of I. L.," *CanL,* No. 54 (1972), 70–83; Mayne, S., ed., *I. L.: The Poet and His Critics* (1978); Van Wilt, K., "L., Nietzsche and Overcoming," *ECW,* 10 (1978), 19–42; Baker, H., "Jewish Themes in the Works of I. L.," *ECW,* 10 (1978), 43–54; Francis, W., "The Farting Jesus: L. and the Heroic Vitalists," *Contemporary Verse Two,* 3, 3 (1978), 46–51

WYNNE FRANCIS

LEACOCK, Stephen

Canadian short-story writer, novelist, essayist, and political economist (writing in English), b. 30 Dec. 1869, Swanmore, England; d. 28 March 1944, Toronto, Ont.

L.'s upper-middle-class family emigrated when he was six to Canada, where they lived an impoverished farm life in Simcoe County, Ontario. He earned a Ph.D. at the University of Chicago by 1903, and became a professor of economics and political science at McGill University, Montreal, a post he held until his retirement in 1936. A superb raconteur and speaker, he was much in demand for public appearances, and toured the British Empire in this role in 1907–8. L. was also highly regarded as a university teacher and administrator.

L.'s first book, *Elements of Political Science* (1906), long a university textbook, was his best money-maker, but his reputation rests on his works of humor, which constitute the bulk of his output and led to the establishment of the Leacock Society and its Leacock Medal for the best book of humor published in Canada each year. L. published his first book of humor, *Literary Lapses* (1910), at his own expense. A collection of monologues, parodies, and comments on various topics, many of which he developed in later works, it shows that his singular ability to portray universal human imperfection in a way that stirs the reader to both sympathy and laughter matured early and did not appreciably progress; for it contains many

pieces published previously in journals, some of which, for example "My Financial Career" (1895), he never subsequently surpassed.

Sunshine Sketches of a Little Town (1912), a comedy of pastoral sentiment, mirrored so vividly the mores of small-town life that it incensed a generation of the people of its model, Orillia, Ontario, site of L.'s summer home. *Arcadian Adventures with the Idle Rich* (1914) bubbles with fun and ripples with nonsense but also swirls with somber undercurrents of sharp irony and anger as it indicts the self-interest and the focus on money and power of the North American big city. Both works consist of linked stories; lacking the structural unity of novels, they nevertheless cohere because of their unity of tone and purpose. L.'s shorter fiction likewise succeeds more by a convincing creation of atmosphere and social environment than by the usual plot and characterization of the genre.

L. satirizes institutions, types, and patterns of behavior rather than persons. His targets include wealth, church, government, the business world, education, and con artists together with their gullible victims; these subjects reflect his deep concern that socialism, technology, and commercialism would deny human individuality and dignity.

His success as a humorist can be judged by the continued appearance in paperback editions of many works. *Nonsense Novels* (1911) and *Frenzied Fiction* (1918) parody types of popular fiction of the times, for example, the Sherlock Holmes stories; *Moonbeams from the Larger Lunacy* (1915) tackles human follies ranging from prize-novel contests to World War I; *My Discovery of England* (1922), one of his best, and like his best drawn from personal experience, laughs at topics such as Oxford University and the "public speaker."

L. wrote quickly—almost a book a year—with little concern for literary convention, but he is no glib comic, for his humor is balanced by an awareness of the deliberate evil of much human motive and act. His forte is the short impressionistic glimpse of the incongruities in human interaction. His works on the theory of humor, his criticism, and his biographies of humorists lack the imaginative spark of his creative writing, which brought him an international reputation, with translations into many languages, and made him the best-selling humorist writing in English between 1910 and 1925. L. was the successor in North American humor to the Canadian Thomas Chandler Haliburton (1796–1865) and the American Mark Twain; but whereas those reflect respectively the British and the American humorist traditions, L. speaks with a Canadian sensibility and peoples his humorous writings with distinctively Canadian characters.

FURTHER WORKS: *Baldwin, Lafontaine, Hincks: Responsible Government* (1907; rev. ed., *Mackenzie, Baldwin, LaFontaine, Hincks,* 1926); *Greater Canada, An Appeal: Let Us No Longer Be a Colony* (1907); *Behind the Beyond, and Other Contributions to Human Knowledge* (1913); *Laugh with L.* (1913); *Adventures of the Far North: A Chronicle of the Frozen Seas* (1914); *The Dawn of Canadian History: A Chronicle of Aboriginal Canada* (1914); *The Mariner of St. Malo* (1914); *The Methods of Mr. Sellyer* (1914); *The Marionettes' Calendar* (1915); *Marionettes' Engagement Book* (1915); *"Q.": A Farce in One Act* (1915, with B. M. Hastings); *Essays and Literary Studies* (1916); *Further Foolishness* (1916); *The Hohenzollerns in America, with The Boshelviks in Berlin, and Other Impossibilities* (1919); *The Unsolved Riddle of Social Justice* (1920); *Winsome Winnie, and Other New Nonsense Novels* (1920); *College Days* (1923); *Over the Footlights* (1923); *The Garden of Folly* (1924); *The Proper Limitations of State Interference* (1924); *Winnowed Wisdom* (1926); *Short Circuits* (1928); *The Iron Man and the Tin Woman* (1929); *Economic Prosperity in the British Empire* (1930); *The L. Book* (1930); *Wet Wit and Dry Humor, Distilled from the Pages of S. L.* (1931); *Afternoons in Utopia* (1932); *Back to Prosperity* (1932); *The Dry Pickwick, and Other Incongruities* (1932); *Lahontan's Voyages* (1932); *Mark Twain* (1932); *Winsome Winnie: A Romantic Drama* (1932, with V. C. Clinton-Baddeley); *Charles Dickens: His Life and Work* (1933); *S. L.'s Plan to Relieve the Depression* (1933); *The Greatest Pages of Charles Dickens* (1934); *Lincoln Frees the Slaves* (1934); *The Perfect Salesman* (1934); *The Pursuit of Knowledge* (1934); *Humour, Its Theory and Technique* (1935); *Funny Pieces* (1936); *The Gathering Financial Crisis in Canada* (1936); *Hellements of Hickonomics, in Hiccoughs of Verse Done in Our Social Planning Mill* (1936); *The Greatest Pages of American Humour, Selected and Discussed by S. L.*

(1936); *Here Are My Lectures and Stories* (1937); *Humour and Humanity* (1937); *My Discovery of the West* (1937); *Model Memoirs* (1938); *All Right, Mr. Roosevelt* (1939); *Too Much College; or, Education Eating Up Life* (1939); *Laugh Parade* (1940); *Our British Empire: Its Structure, Its History, Its Strength* (1940); *Canada: The Foundation of Its Future* (1941); *Montreal: Seaport and City* (1942; repub. as *L.'s Montreal,* 1948); *My Remarkable Uncle* (1942); *Our Heritage of Liberty: Its Origin, Its Achievement, Its Crisis* (1942); *Happy Stories, Just to Laugh At* (1943); *How to Write* (1943); *"My Old College" 1843–1943* (1943); *Memories of Christmas* (1943); *Canada and the Sea* (1944, with Leslie Roberts, Wallace Ward, and J. A. Morton); *Last Leaves* (1945); *While There Is Time: The Case against Social Catastrophe* (1945); *The Boy I Left behind Me* (1946); *The L. Roundabout* (1946); *The Bodley Head L.* (1957; Can., *The Best of L.*); *The Unicorn L.* (1960); *Caroline's Christmas* (1969); *Hoodoo McFiggin's Christmas* (1970); *Feast of Stephen* (1970); *L.* (1970); *The Social Criticism of S. L.* (1973); *The Penguin S. L.* (1981)

BIBLIOGRAPHY: Curry, R. L., *S. L.: Humorist and Humanist* (1959); Watters, R. E., "A Special Tang: S. L.'s Canadian Humour," *CanL,* 5 (1960), 21–32; Cameron, D. A., *Faces of L.: An Appreciation* (1967); Davies, R., *S. L.* (1970); Kimball, E., *The Man in the Panama Hat: Reminiscences of My Uncle, S. L.* (1970); Legate, D. M., *S. L.* (1970); Clever, G., "L.'s Dunciad," *SCL,* 1 (1976), 238–41

GLENN CLEVER

LEAVIS, F(rank) R(aymond)
English literary critic, b. 16 July 1895, Cambridge; d. 17 April, 1978, Cambridge

L. was educated at Emmanuel College, Cambridge, where he studied history and English. In 1932 he became Director of English Studies at Downing College, and in 1936 he was appointed Assistant Lecturer in the University and a Fellow of Downing. After 1962, when the Downing Fellowship ended, L. was a visiting professor at various British universities.

In 1932 L. helped to found *Scrutiny,* an influential journal of literary criticism, which he edited from 1932 until 1953, when it ceased publication. His wife, Q. D. (Queenie

Dorothy) Leavis (b. 1906), the author of *Fiction and the Reading Public* (1932), collaborated with L. on *Scrutiny* and on a number of books.

L.'s first major publication was *New Bearings in English Poetry: A Study of the Contemporary Situation* (1932). This radical and influential work, which focused on T. S. Eliot, Ezra Pound (qq.v.), and Gerard Manley Hopkins, was instrumental in establishing their reputations and defining their importance as leaders of a contemporary revolution in English poetry against what L. called the "debilitated nineteenth-century tradition."

L.'s next important critical book, *Revaluation: Tradition and Development in English Poetry* (1936), was a collection of essays that had first appeared as a series of articles in *Scrutiny,* but it was also a continuation of the argument L. had begun in *New Bearings in English Poetry.* In *Revaluation* L. turned to earlier poets, from the metaphysical poets (early 17th c.) to the Victorians, to redefine the tradition of English poetry in terms of the qualities he had already praised in Eliot and Hopkins. L.'s revaluation of the English poetic tradition elevated the metaphysical poets and Pope at the expense of Milton, Dryden, and Shelley. Along with T. S. Eliot and the American New Critics, L. helped to create the contemporary taste for metaphysical wit and complexity.

In the 1940s, L. turned his attention from poetry to the novel. Beginning in 1941, he published a series of essays on the novel in *Scrutiny,* which were later collected in *The Great Tradition: George Eliot, Henry James, Joseph Conrad* (1948). L. added an introductory chapter that began with the controversial statement, "The great English novelists are Jane Austen, George Eliot, Henry James and Joseph Conrad." Although L. later enlarged the "great tradition" to some extent, he never wavered in his conviction that the quality that distinguished the writers who belonged to it was "a vital capacity for experience, a kind of reverent openness before life, and a marked moral intensity."

In *The Great Tradition* L. illustrated his thesis with studies of George Eliot, James, and Conrad (qq.v.). He believed that D. H. Lawrence (q.v.) was the 20th-c. heir to the great tradition, but he had already treated Lawrence in an earlier pamphlet, *D. H. Lawrence* (1930), and he would later devote two books to Lawrence—*D. H. Lawrence, Novelist* (1955) and *Thought, Words and Creativity: Art and Thought in Lawrence* (1976). As for Austen, Q. D. Leavis had already produced a series of *Scrutiny* articles on her work. L. did not place Dickens in his great tradition, but he did provide a final chapter on *Hard Times,* which he believed then to be the only one of Dickens's novels that was a "completely serious work of art." L. later revised this estimate, however. In *Dickens, the Novelist* (1970), written in collaboration with Q. D. Leavis, L. argued that Dickens was not only a great novelist but also a "genius of a greater kind" than Henry James.

Both as a critic and as a teacher, L. inspired dedicated disciples; but he also engaged opponents in vehement critical controversies. His passionate advocacy of the literary and moral values he espoused sometimes descended, especially in later years, to the level of strident personal battles with advocates of opposing positions (L.'s attacks on C. P. Snow [q.v.] are probably the most notorious).

The importance of L.'s contribution to 20th-c. criticism cannot be denied. By his lifelong dedication to the principle that literary values cannot be separated from ethical values, his insistence upon the social relevance of literature, and his emphasis on discrimination and evaluation as central critical tasks, L. preserved the tradition of Matthew Arnold of humanistic criticism is a generally antihumanistic age.

FURTHER WORKS: *Mass Civilisation and Minority Culture* (1930); *How to Teach Reading: A Primer for Ezra Pound* (1932); *For Continuity* (1933); *Culture and Environment: The Training of Critical Awareness* (1933, with D. Thompson); *Education and the University: A Sketch for an "English School"* (1943); *The Common Pursuit* (1952); *Two Cultures? The Significance of C. P. Snow* (1962); *Anna Karenina, and Other Essays* (1967); *Lectures in America* (1969, with Q. D. L.); *English Literature in Our Time and the University* (1969); *Nor Shall My Sword: Discourses on Pluralism, Compassion and Social Hope* (1972); *Letters in Criticism* (1974); *The Living Principle: English as a Discipline of Thought* (1975)

BIBLIOGRAPHY: Bentley, E., ed., *The Importance of Scrutiny* (1948); Buckley, V., *Poetry and Morality: Studies on the Criticism of Matthew Arnold, T. S. Eliot, and F. R. L.* (1959), pp. 158–233; Watson, G., *The Liter-*

ary Critics: A Study of English Descriptive Criticism (1964), pp. 205–15 and passim; Wellek, R., "The Literary Criticism of F. R. L.," in Camden, C., ed., *Literary Views: Critical and Historical Essays* (1964), pp. 175–93; Hayman, R., *L.* (1976); Bilan, R. P., *The Literary Criticism of F. R. L.* (1979); Walsh, W., *F. R. L.* (1980)

PHYLLIS RACKIN

LEBANESE LITERATURE

In Arabic

Benefiting from centuries of close contact with Western civilization, Lebanese writers, translators and journalists in the 19th c. were instrumental in bringing about the literary renascence of the Arabs. Yet while the efforts of the key Lebanese figures of this movement aimed mainly at reviving the classical language after a long period of decadence, the work of the writers in the 20th c. concentrated on innovation in the language of prose and poetry and on experimentation in new genres: the novel, the short story and the drama.

Poetry

During the first three decades of the 20th c. a new poetic sensibility was evident in the compositions of Bishārā al-Khūrī (1884?–1968) and Amīn Nakhla (b. 1901) in Lebanon and the Lebanese Khalīl Mutrān (1870–1949) in Egypt. Al-Khūrī's *Dīwān al-hawā wa al-shabāb* (pub. 1953; the divan of love and youth) introduced into Arabic poetry a fresh diction, a music reminiscent of the Andalusian *Muwashshahas* (strophic poems invented in Arab Spain in the late 9th or early 10th c.), and a sincerity of emotion unknown in earlier poetry. In *Dafātir al-ghazal* (1952; notebooks of love poems), Nakhla chose words with a care much like that of the French Parnassian poets, and practiced a method of composition that was to serve as a check on the rampant experiments of succeeding romantic poets. Mutrān's contributions were in the genre of narrative poetry, in his concern for organic unity, and in his experiments in new poetic forms. His *Dīwān al-Khalīl* (1908; the divan of al-Khalīl) was an early source of inspiration for the poets of the time.

Creative activity among Lebanese writers, however, was not confined to the Middle East; oppressive political and social circumstances leading up to and beyond the civil strife of the 1850s had led many prominent Christian families to emigrate, in particular to the Americas. Thus, in the first quarter of the 20th c., the literary activity called *Adab al-Mahjar* (the literature of the Americas) was initiated. The most prominent writers were members of the Society of the Pen, founded in North America by Khalīl (Kahlil) Gibrān (1883–1931) in 1920, and the Lebanese and Syrian members of the Andalusian League, formed in Brazil in 1932. Whereas the Society of the Pen propagated a universal outlook and the creation of a new language capable of changing the whole conception of classical Arabic poetry, the Andalusian League retained the traditional approach and reflected Arab nationalist themes. Besides Gibrān, the most influential writers in the North were Amīn al-Rīhānī (1876–1940) and Mīkhā'īl Na'īma (b. 1889), whose efforts, along with those of Fawzī al-Ma'lūf (1889–1930), Shafīq al-Ma'lūf (b. 1905), and Ilyās Farhāt (b. 1893) of the Andalusian League, established the romantic school in Arabic poetry and had a profound influence on the course of modern Arabic literature.

Gibrān's simple, poetical prose in such works as *Al-'Awāsif* (1920; the tempests), and *Al-Arwāh al-mutamarrida* (1908; *Spirits Rebellious,* 1947) was the first real break from the rhyming prose of the previous centuries. His subjects were no longer those that tradition dictated, and his images and symbols erased life's dualisms and sought the unity of all existence, so aptly portrayed in his long poem *Al-Mawākib* (1919; *The Processions,* 1958) and in his famous writings in English, *The Prophet* (1923), *The Madman* (1918), and *Jesus the Son of Man* (1928). In all his works he embodied his ideas about life and art, setting an example for the writers who succeeded him.

Like Gibrān, Na'īma and al-Rīhānī devoted most of their work to new experiments in language. Although neither of them was a great poet, al-Rīhānī's prose poems in *Al-Rihāniyyāt* (2 vols., 1922–23; the Rīhaniyyāt) and Na'īma's new simple prose in his short-story collection *Kān mā kān* (1937; once upon a time) and his poem "Akhī" (1917; my brother) were powerful examples of the new poetic idiom that Gibrān established.

In South America, aside from Fawzī al-

Ma'lūf's romantic poem '*Ala bisāt al-rīh* (1929; on the magic carpet), which shows clearly the influence of the Society of the Pen, Shafīq al-Mal'lūf's '*Abqar* (1936; the valley of the muses), which explores the use of Arab mythology, and Ilyās Farhāt's original and successful attempt at the allegorical genre in *Ahlām al-rā'ī* (1953; the shepherd's dreams), the rest of the poets retained the style and form of classical Arabic poetry.

In Lebanon, two main schools of poetry—the romantic and the Parnassian-symbolist—emerged between 1930 and 1948. The former, an extension of the North American school, reached full bloom in the works of Ilyās Abū Shabaka (1903–1947), particularly in *Afā'ī al-firdaws* (1938; the serpents of paradise), where his spiritual conflict, intense personal experiences, and religious suffering are vividly depicted.

The Parnassian-symbolist School, headed by Sa'īd 'Aql (b. 1912), was a reaction against the romantic poets' sentimentality and simple common diction and a product of early French symbolist (q.v.) influence. As Sa'īd 'Aql declared in his introduction to *Al-Majdaliyya* (1937; the Magdalene), poetry was primarily music, evoking meaning indirectly through the creation of an aesthetic atmosphere. 'Aql's influence was short-lived because the generation of committed poets that followed him, while drawing inspiration from his polished diction, had little tolerance for his aesthetic concepts.

After 1948, experimentation and innovation proceeded as a dizzying pace. In Beirut, two influential journals, *Al-Ādāb* and *Shi'r*, popularized free verse and the prose poem. The leading poets of the 1950s and 1960s dropped the distinction between poetic and nonpoetic language, changing the theory and practice of Arabic poetry.

Writing in free verse, one of the greatest poets of the century, Khalīl Hāwī (q.v.) succeeded in eliminating the poetry of statement, employed symbols for maximum emotional and intellectual effects, and explored the untapped rhythms of some classical meters. His five *dīwāns* (collections), especially *Bayādir al-jū'* (1965; the threshingfloors of hunger), reflect the angst of an Arab nationalist in a period of Arab defeat. He was killed during the fighting in Lebanon of 1982.

The use of a prose medium in poetry became the preoccupation of the major poets of the 1960s, Adūnīs (q.v.), Unsī al-Hājj (b.

1937), and Yūsuf al-Khāl (b. 1917). Al-Hājj in *Lan* (1959; never), al-Khāl in *Al-Bi'r al-mahjūra* (1958; the forsaken well), and Adūnīs in *Waqt bayn al-ramād wa al-ward* (1970; a time between ashes and roses) and *Mufrad fī sīghat al-jam'* (1975; singular in the form of plural) created a new language, liberating words from their usual meanings.

In their attempts to change the classical idiom, the 20th-c. poets drew upon the highly developed oral and written folk poetry—the verbal duels of Zaghlūl al-Dāmūr (b. 1925), and *Dūlāb* (1957; wheel) and *Laysh* (1964; why) by Michel Trād (b. 1913). Many of the leading poets, including Gibrān, 'Aql, and Hāwī, did in fact compose in the Lebanese dialect, but criticism has only recently started to explore this genre and assess its effects on these poets' works.

Fiction

The novel, short story, and drama are Western literary genres that have no developed prototypes in the Arabic literary tradition. The Lebanese, whose openness to the West predated that of their fellow Arabs, were among the first to introduce these genres into modern Arabic literature.

The early attempts at fiction, dating back to the 1870s, were either translations of and adaptations from European works, or original compositions with undue emphasis on spectacle and bald narrative rather than on plot and character development. Between 1891 and 1914 appeared the twenty-one historical novels of Jurjī Zaydān (1861–1914). These novels cultivated a new readership in the Arab world and revived a consciousness of a glorious past, which had become indistinct during the previous century.

Of more artistic value were the short stories of Kahlīl Gibrān and Mikhāīl Na'īma, who early in the century introduced a realistic trend into Arabic fiction. In his short-story collections '*Arā'is al-murūj* (1906; *Nymphs of the Valley,* 1948) and *Al-Arwāh al-mutamarrida* and in his romantic novel *Al-Ajnihā al-mutakassira* (1912; *The Broken Wings,* 1957), Gibrān attacked outmoded social customs and religious fanaticism, and sought to demolish the causes of man's misery. On the other hand, Na'īma, who was no less concerned about social injustices, exhorted his characters to follow the life of the mystics as a panacea for their dilemmas. His short stories and his novel, *Liqā'* (1946; en-

33

counter), are technically superior to the works of his immediate predecessors.

Realistic and naturalistic fiction finds its best expression in *Al-Raghīf* (1939; the loaf of bread), a novel by Tawfīq 'Awwād (b. 1911), which depicts the horrors of famine during World War I; in 'Awwād's short-story collections *Al-Sabiyy al-a'raj* (1936; the lame boy) and *Qamīs al-sūf* (1964; the woolen shirt), and later on in his excellent novel *Tawāhīn Bayrūt* (1972; *Death in Beirut*, 1972), a psychological study of the problems of contemporary Lebanese society and the choices facing the Lebanese intellectual in his war against traditional values.

Two novels, Mārūn 'Abbūd's (1886–1962) *Fāris Aghā* (1959; Fāris Aghā), a successful caricature of the waning traditional values in Lebanese villages, and Emily Nasralla's (dates n.a.) *Tuyūr aylūl* (1967; September birds), a probing account of the effects of emigration on Lebanese villagers, are cited by critics as the best examples of novels portraying local color and village life.

Fiction of social protest is best exemplified in Laylā Ba'albakki's (b. 1938) novels *Anā ahyā* (1958; I live) and *Al-Āliha al-mamsūkha* (1960; the disfigured gods), and her short story "Safīnat hanān ila al-qamar" (1964; "A Space Ship of Tenderness to the Moon," 1967), which question the traditional subservient role of women in society and call for woman's liberation and sexual freedom.

In the 1960s and 1970s the novel reached a high stage of development in the intellectual works of Yūsuf Habshī al-Ashqar (dates n.a.), *Arba'at afrās humr* (1964; four red horses) and *Lā tanbut judhūr fi al-samā'* (1971; roots do not grow in the sky), and in Halīm Barakāt's (b. 1933) *'Awdat al-tā'ir ilā al-bahr* (1969; *Days of Dust,* 1974), a successful experiment in form, juxtaposing the events of the 1967 Arab-Israeli war and its aftermath with the Book of Genesis, and inciting the Arab intellectual to contemplate the meaning of the Arab nation's defeat.

Drama

Lebanese writers were also pioneers in the development of drama in modern Arabic literature. In 1848 Mārūn al-Naqqāsh (1817–1855) presented to a yet uncritical audience *Al-Bakhīl* (the miser), an adaptation into Arabic verse of Molière's play, marking the first step in a rich tradition of translation and ad-

aptation of European dramas, as well as of original compositions.

By the turn of the century, however, many of the brightest Lebanese actors and playwrights had already left Lebanon for Egypt, where similar developments in drama were taking place. This mass exodus had adverse effects on the Lebanese theater. Although some dramatists had attempted to combine drama as a mode of written literature and drama as theater art, very few successful examples before the late 1950s are recorded.

The period from 1960 until 1974, the date of the beginning of the Lebanese civil war, marked the establishment of numerous theatrical companies with varied artistic orientations.

In general, the modern Lebanese theater in the Arabic language is part of the modern theater in the West in that it freely draws upon Western theatrical techniques. Freeing itself from oratory and melodrama, it succeeds in efficiently utilizing the innovations of leading Western playwrights, actors, directors, and theoreticians.

The first major trend is represented in the productions of the National Theater, founded in 1965 by Hasan 'Alā' al-Dīn (pseud.: Shū Shū, ?–1976). This is the Lebanese boulevard theater, which depends on a central actor, uses the Lebanese dialect and occasional improvisation, and presents political and social problems in a comical fashion.

Concern for form assumes great importance in the plays of Munīr Abū Dibs (b. 1931), founder of the Modern Theater in 1960 and the Beirut School of Modern Theater in 1970. In such plays as *Al-Tūfān* (1970; the deluge) and *Yasū'* (1973; Jesus), voice, lighting, and external form take precedence over content. On the other hand, the work of the Beirut Dramatic Art Workshop, founded in 1968 by Roger 'Assāf (dates n.a.) and Nidāl al-Ashqar (dates n.a.), is less concerned with form and totally dependent on intellectual content, improvisation, and the colloquial idiom.

An excellent example of political theater is Jalāl Khūrī's (dates n.a.) *Juhā fi al-qurā al-amāmiyya* (1971; Juhā in the frontline villages), a successful play in the manner of Brecht (q.v.) that established a great rapport with its audience because it deals with the concerns of the majority of the populace and faithfully comments on their strengths and weaknesses.

Additionally, critics credit Raymond Gebara's (b. 1935) *Li tamut Dasdamūna* (1970; let Desdemona die), Thérèse 'Awwād's (b. 1933) *Al-Bakara* (1973; the pulley), and Ya'qūb Chedrāwī's (dates n.a.) *A'rib mā yalī* (1970; parse the following) with important artistic innovations.

The Lebanese civil war, which has since 1974 tragically undermined most aspects of life in Lebanon, has had amazingly little effect on literary activity. Publishing houses have increased threefold. Among other things, this fact has led to the appearance of works of questionable literary merit. Even so, the period has also witnessed the publication of a number of distinguished works. Among these are Ilyās Khūrī's (b. 1948) experiments in the form of the novel, *Al-Jabal al-saghīr* (1977; the small mountain) and *Al-Wujūh al-baydā'* (1981; white faces); and Roger 'Assāf's play *Hikāyāt 1936* (1979; the stories of 1936), which revives in modern garb the role of the traditional storyteller. These works would seem to confirm that in spite of current adversities, the Lebanese literary tradition will continue to fulfill its central role in the development of modern Arabic literature.

In French

By the end of the 19th c. and the beginning of the 20th, Lebanese literature in French was quite sophisticated even by the French literary standards of the day. Novels by Jacques Tabet (1885–19??)—*L'émancipée* (1911; the emancipated)—and Georges Samné (1877–19??)—*Au pays du Chérif* (1911; in the land of Chérif), written in collaboration with Maurice Barrès (1862–1923); the plays of Chekri Ganem (1861–1929)—*Antar* (1910; Antar), which was performed at the Odéon in Paris—and Michel I. Sursock (dates n.a.)—*Le serment d'un Arabe* (1906; the oath of an Arab); and a large collection of poetic works by Jacques Tabet and others ushered in a period of "revolutionary literature" concentrating on the liberation of Lebanon and the Arab world from Ottoman domination.

During the period of the French Mandate (1920–43), however, literary themes were marked by a strong adherence to Christianity, a philosophical tendency to identify with the Phoenician rather than the Arab past,

and a celebration of the friendship that many Lebanese Christians have always had with France, the "elder sister."

Aside from the influential prose of Michel Chiha (1891–1954), collected and published as *Essais* (2 vols., 1951–52; essays), poetry was the most prevalent literary genre in this period. Notwithstanding similarity in theme, the poetry of Charles Corm (1894–1963) in, for example, *La montagne inspirée* (1934; the inspired mountain), Hector Klat (1888–1976) in *Le cèdre et les lys* (1934; the cedar and the lilies), and Elie Tyane (1885–1957) in *Le château merveilleux* (1934; the enchanted castle) exhibit a rich variety of Oriental imagery and verse forms ranging from the Alexandrine to free verse.

The work of the new generation of writers, from the 1950s to the present, is, strictly speaking, French, both in execution and appeal. The nationalistic and religious themes of the previous generation give way to a universality of vision and a successful attempt to influence the trends and movements of contemporary French literature. As in much of French poetry, a surrealistic (q.v.) trend is evident in the works of Georges Schehadé (b. 1910) and of the younger generation, especially Nadia Tuéni (b. 1935), Hoda Adib (dates n.a.), and Christiane Saleh (dates n.a.). Schehadé's transparent imagery, of which Saint John-Perse (q.v.) spoke highly, Fouad Naffah's (b. 1925) constant search for the powerful word that can change the world, and Salah Stétié's (b. 1928) poetry of ideas have elicited the keen attention of French critics.

Most of the poets of this period also wrote drama and fiction, and a few published in Arabic, but none attained the renown of Schehadé, whose contributions to the avant-garde theater with such plays as *Le voyage* (1961; the voyage) and *L'émigré de Brisbane* (1965; the emigrant from Brisbane) place him side by side with Beckett, Ionesco, Genet, and Adamov (qq.v.).

In the short story and the novel, with the exception of *L'envers de Caïn* (1959; the other side of Cain), a realistic novel by Farjalla Haïk (b. 1909), which shows the novelist's attachment to Lebanon and his concern for his country's social, political, and religious problems, only a few works in French have been produced by Lebanese writers. The recent civil war and the consequent emigration of many young Lebanese to France will no doubt have a positive impact on Lebanese writing in French.

BIBLIOGRAPHY: Sélim, A., *Le bilinguisme arabe-français au Liban* (1962); Khalaf, S., *Littérature libanaise de langue française* (1974); Salamé, G., *Le théâtre politique au Liban* (1974); Badawī, M. M., *A Critical Introduction to Modern Arabic Poetry* (1975); Jayyūsī, S., *Trends and Movements in Modern Arabic Poetry* (1977)

ADNAN HAYDAR

LECHOŃ, Jan

(pseud. of Leszek Serafinowicz) Polish poet and essayist, b. 13 July 1899, Warsaw; d. 8 July 1956, New York, N.Y., U.S.A.

L. was born and educated in Warsaw, at that time a city under Russian domination. The major events in his life were closely linked to his nation's political fortunes. The beginning of his career as a poet (and also its peak) coincided with the euphoric early 1920s, when Poland was rejoicing in its newly regained independence. During the 1930s L. served as cultural attaché at the Polish embassy in Paris; the outbreak of World War II caught him in France. He eventually fled to the U.S., where he remained in exile as an ardent opponent of the Communist Polish government until his death by suicide.

L.'s fame as a poet, and as something of a prodigy, dates from November 1918 and the founding of the literary café Pod Pikadorem. He was one of the Skamander poets, noted as a group for their poetic verve, satirical irreverence, and their closeness to ruling circles. During the 1920s L.'s literary output was divided between highly serious poetry and buoyant satire. He served as editor of the satirical weekly *Cyrulik Warszawski* from 1926 through 1928.

The poems on which L.'s fame rests, published in two slim volumes—*Karmazynowy poemat* (1920; crimson poem) and *Srebrne i czarne* (1924; silver and black)—display his impressive mastery of classical verse forms. They reveal a troubled reaction to the Polish poetic heritage: in tone and style they are clearly linked with the great romantic tradition, but they also express a modern impatience with the constraints of solemn reverence for matters Polish imposed by that tradition. *Srebrne i czarne* adds personal

themes to the public concerns explored in *Karmazynowy poemat*. The personal poems explore with somber dignity the impossibility of finding love and happiness in life. In "Lenistwo" (1924; laziness) L. proclaims: "My body torments me and my soul is repulsive," while in "Spotkanie" (1924; a meeting) Dante's shade confides in him: "There is neither heaven nor earth, no abyss and no hell./ There is only Beatrice. And she does not exist."

L.'s philosophical despair was compounded by severe psychological depression. He suffered from a serious writer's block, overcome in later life only by the powerful urge to lament Poland's fate in World War II. The poems of the 1940s show even greater technical mastery than the early work, and are no longer at odds with the ardent patriotism of the romantics.

L.'s posthumously published diary, which he kept during the 1950s, reveals a lonely hypochondriac, a man of great aesthetic sensibility, struggling desperately to overcome his writer's block. The uncharitable snobbery and fanatical patriotism expressed in the diary seem to be his way of compensating, as it were, for his failure to live up to the brilliant promise of his youthful poetry.

FURTHER WORKS: *Na złotym polu: Zbiorek wierszy* (1913); *Po różnych ścieżkach: Zbiór wierszy* (1914); *Paryż 1919: Wrażenia i wspomnienia* (1919); *Facecje republikańskie* (1919, with Antoni Słonimski); *Rzeczpospolita Babińska: Śpiewy historyczne* (1920); *Pierwsza szopka warszawska* (1922, with A. Słonimski and Julian Tuwim); *Szopka polityczna "Cyrulika Warszawskiego"* (1927, with Marian Hemar, A. Słonimski, and J. Tuwim); *Szopka polityczna 1930* (1930, with M. Hemar, A. Słonimski and J. Tuwim); *Szopka polityczna 1931* (1931, with M. Hemar and J. Tuwim); *Lutnia po Bekwarku* (1942); *O literaturze polskiej* (1942); *Aria z kurantem* (1945); *Historia o jednym chłopczyku i o jednym lotniku* (1946); *Poezje zebrane 1916–1953* (1954); *Aut Caesar aut nihil* (1955); *Mickiewicz* (1955); *Poezje* (1957); *Dziennik* (3 vols., 1967–73)

BIBLIOGRAPHY: Folejewski, Z., "J. L.'s Poetic Work," *PolR*, 1, 4 (1956), 3–7; Miłosz, C., *The History of Polish Literature* (1969), pp. 397–98

MADELINE G. LEVINE

LE CLÉZIO, J(ean) M(arie) G(ustave)
French novelist, b. 13 April 1940, Nice

After receiving degrees in literature from the Institute of Literary Studies in Nice, L. taught at universities in Thailand and Mexico, after which he spent four years in the Panamanian forests with the Embera Indians. Since that time he has lived in France, the U.S., and Mexico.

L. does not write avant-garde literature in the sense that phrase is used by most critics. He is not concerned with form, with the problems pertaining to the text alone, concerns that isolate literature from the world in which it is created. Hence, he is connected to none of the modern movements in French literature. He stands by himself, expressing his anguish and his quest in powerfully lyrical fiction, which breaks the traditional bounds of the novel and creates an epic of consciousness rather than of deeds.

His first novel, *Le procès-verbal* (1963; *The Interrogation,* 1964), for which he was awarded the Théophraste Renaudot Prize, depicts the quest for discovery of both himself and the world by an alienated young man who subsequently flees from both into the security of a mental hospital. This alternation of quest and flight controls the work, and it is not therefore surprising that many of L.'s subsequent novels are conceived in terms of physical or spiritual journeys: *Terra amata* (1968; *Terra Amata,* 1969), *Le livre des fuites* (1969; *The Book of Flights,* 1972), *Voyages de l'autre côté* (1975; journeys to the other side).

Throughout L.'s work his protagonists are dominated by two major influences: the sun and the sea—or occasionally water in some other form. The sun brings understanding of things that are sometimes too painful to withstand; thus, man tries to escape what the light forces him to see. But everything is focused on the sun; for L., all man's thought, and hence the structures he establishes, are created around it, for it is the source of revelation. It is reality. The complementary influence is water, which is the symbol both of woman and of death in *Le procès-verbal* and in *Le déluge* (1968; *The Flood,* 1968).

The other opposites that dominate L.'s work are the city, with its consumer goods, traffic, and noise, and the natural world of insects, plants, quiet, and so forth. All L.'s heroes have a love-hate relationship with the city (also seen as a woman). This theme is most prominent in *La guerre* (1970; *War,* 1973) and *Les géants* (1973; *The Giants,* 1975).

The same themes are taken up again in two volumes of short stories, *La fièvre* (1965; *Fever,* 1966) and *Mondo, et autres histoires* (1978; Mondo, and other stories), and are explored at length in a different way in two philosophical essays, *L'extase matérielle* (1966; the ecstasy of matter) and *L'inconnu sur la terre* (1978; the unknown man on earth).

For L. the world is a mysterious, dangerous, powerful, and wonderful place which man must struggle to understand but from which he is separated by buildings, electricity, technology, cars, words, people—an ever-increasing multitude of man-made objects from which we must escape before we can perceive the aspects of the world that are normally outside the scope of everyday reality. Madness, walking, emotion, drugs, meditation—all can and do serve to break down the barriers that confine our understanding. L. describes them all in such a way that we share every minute particle of his characters' experience: anguish, confusion, and joy. Theirs are the concerns of today—the concerns of people whose world is rapidly deteriorating to an intolerable level. And they seek solutions to this situation.

Such solutions, however, have become less violent during the course of L.'s career. Indeed, in the more recent volumes—*Voyages de l'autre côté, Mondo, et autres histoires, L'inconnu sur la terre*—protagonists flee into the world of the imagination and of children, rejecting utterly the stress of modern life apparent in the earlier works. These last texts are very gentle, yet they cannot be separated from the others because there is a unity of theme throughout L.'s body of work. Indeed, these last three function in an important way both in opposition to and as a complement to the earlier work.

The juxtaposition of alternatives is a technique the author uses at all levels. In particular, one can note the instability of his subject pronouns at all times. Narration moves frequently from "I" to "you" to "he" without any apparent motivation—a technique that both alienates the reader and forces him to share the alienation of narrator and protagonist very intimately. The novels have little or no plot, and in many cases the sections within a book have no apparent order. Usually they are made up of a series of situations that

37

illustrate a given theme from different angles. These can be complementary or contradictory, developing the theme further or offering another possibility, a different interpretation. The effect is that of a number of tableaux rather than of continuous narration. Each book is complete in itself and yet is linked to the worlds of his other books by a system of recurrent detail, repetition of images, new or further treatment of themes and problems. Hence all L.'s writings are woven together into a single growing structure in which each strand reinforces the others, and adds to their combined impact and power.

FURTHER WORKS: *Haï* (1971); *Mydriase* (1973); *Vers les icebergs* (1979); *Désert* (1980); *Trois villes saintes* (1980)

BIBLIOGRAPHY: Lhoste, P., *Conversations avec J. M. G. L.* (1971); Cagnon, M., and Smith, S., "J. M. G. L.: Fiction's Double Bind," in Federman, R., ed., *Surfiction: Fiction Today and Tomorrow* (1975), pp. 215–26; Waelti-Walters, J., *J. M. G. L.* (1977); Le Clézio, M., "L'être sujet/objet: La vision active et passive chez L.," in Cagnon, M., ed., *Éthique et esthétique dans la littérature française du XXᵉ siècle* (1978), pp. 113–21; Oxenhandler, N., "Nihilism in L.'s *La fièvre*," in Tetel, M., ed., *Symbolism and Modern Literature* (1978), pp. 264–73; Smith, S. L., "L.'s Search for Self in a World of Words," *MLS*, 10, 2 (1980), 48–58; Waelti-Walters, J., *Icare; ou, L'évasion impossible: Étude psycho-mystique de l'œuvre de J. M. G. L.* (1981)

JENNIFER R. WAELTI-WALTERS

LEDUC, Violette

French memoirist and novelist, b. 8 April 1907, Arras; d. 28 May 1972, Faucon

L.'s best writings describe her life, which was a stormy one. She was born to an unmarried mother, a servant seduced by the son of the house, and her intense relationship with her mother was repeated in her affairs with women and in her brief marriage. After a variety of vaguely literary but unimportant jobs, she met the writer Maurice Sachs (1906–1945), whom she admired equally for his writing and his homosexuality. He introduced her to the black market during World War II and persuaded her to write her childhood memories. These became *L'asphyxie* (1946; *In the*

Prison of Her Skin, 1970), which was published on the recommendation of Albert Camus (q.v.), after Simone de Beauvoir (q.v.) had read the manuscript. Jean-Paul Sartre (q.v.) also published extracts from her writings in his periodical, *Les temps modernes*, in 1945, 1946, and 1947.

The story of L.'s adulation of Simone de Beauvoir, who treated her with great kindness, is told in *L'affamée* (1948; the starving woman), a semisurrealistic account of L.'s romantic feelings for "her" (unnamed, but obviously Beauvoir), in which factual detail merges into lyrical effusion.

L.'s mind began to give way when she was working on the novel *Ravages* (1955; *Ravages*, 1967), the book that would make her sex life public, albeit in the form of a novel. She had been a difficult person to cope with for some time. Passionate, possessive, full of complaints and appeals for sympathy, constantly in tears, lamenting the size of her nose, paying homage to prominent homosexuals such as Jean Cocteau and Jean Genet (qq.v.), she had been buoyed up by her spontaneity, by the excitement of her emotional involvements, and by considerable resilience. But now she began to feel herself an object of general interest and censure. At the same time, her unfulfilled love for "Jacques," a rich homosexual manufacturer who admired her writing, led her to believe that she was being persecuted by a gang led by "Jacques." She traveled to take her mind off her troubles, and describes her travels in *Trésors à prendre* (1960; treasures within reach).

L. attained international literary renown—and notoriety—with *La bâtarde* (1964; *La Bâtarde*, 1965), which recounts her life up to 1944 and for which Simone de Beauvoir wrote the preface. The success of *La bâtarde* was upheld by *La folie en tête* (1970; *Mad in Pursuit*, 1971), the last volume of her autobiography to appear in her lifetime. The final volume, *La chasse à l'amour* (1973; the hunt for love), appeared posthumously, edited by Simone de Beauvoir. It brings events up to 1964.

These last two volumes contain a truly extraordinary history of paranoia seen from within. It is amazing to think that L. could have written as well as she did when her mind was so disturbed. She was obviously a born writer. Possibly, her paranoia and her writing were forms of the same solipsism. Her psychiatrist considered that her writing was therapeutic. But she did not always write well. Her novellas are curiously insubstantial in spite of a tremendous straining after emotional effect. For instance, *Le taxi* (1971; *The Taxi,* 1972) consists of a lyrical outpouring of desire from a brother and sister copulating in a cab, but it leaves no definite impression behind, and one feels that it comes to an end so soon because L. did not entirely believe in it herself. When she wrote about herself and the people she knew, she wrote at length because this was a subject she really believed in. In her autobiographical writings her surrealistic lyricism conveys an exact impression of the truth of her emotions, and the effect is immediately convincing.

It is sad that she did not have time to describe her last years, which brought her success and relative peace of mind; but her autobiography, as it is, stands as a monument to all those who are insane, ridiculous, ugly, perverse, lonely, despised, and disinherited, all of whom look at us through her eyes and ask us to remember that they are human beings.

FURTHER WORKS: *La vieille fille et le mort; Les boutons dorés* (1958; *The Old Maid and the Dead Man; The Golden Buttons,* in *The Woman with the Little Fox: Three Novellas,* 1966); *La femme au petit renard* (1965; *The Woman with the Little Fox,* 1966); *Thérèse et Isabelle* (1966; *Thérèse and Isabelle,* 1967)

BIBLIOGRAPHY: Beauvoir, S. de, Foreword to *The Golden Buttons* (1961), pp. 5–6; Flanner, J. ("Genêt"), "Letter from Paris," *New Yorker,* 23 Jan. 1965, 108–14; Beauvoir, S. de, Foreword to *La bâtarde* (1965), pp. v–xviii; Haynes, M., on *The Woman with the Little Fox, Nation,* 23 Jan. 1967, 118–20; Brooks, P., on *Mad in Pursuit, NYTBR,* 3 Oct. 1971, 4, 41; Wood, M., on *The Taxi, NYRB,* Aug. 1972, 15–16; Courtivron, I. de, "V. L.'s *L'affamée:* The Courage to Displease," *ECr,* 19, 2 (1979), 95–96

BARBARA J. BUCKNALL

LEHTONEN, Joel

Finnish novelist, short-story writer, essayist, and poet, 27 Nov. 1881, Sääminki; d. 20. Nov. 1934, Huopalahti

Born out of wedlock and abandoned, L. became the ward of a pastor's widow and received a good education; thus, he had a double perspective, as an outcast and as a member of established society, on life in Savo, his native province in eastern Finland. His first notable work was the semiautobiographical *Mataleena* (1905; Magdalene), about his natural mother and his own early life. Sojourns in Switzerland and Italy (1907–8), France (1911–12), and North Africa and Italy again (1914) led to an admiration for French and Italian literatures (he translated Boccaccio, Stendhal, and Anatole France [q.v.]). During this period he wrote the travel stories of *Myrtti ja alppiruusu* (1911; myrtle and rhododendron) and the prose poems, influenced by Baudelaire, of *Punainen mylly* (1913; the red mill). At the same time, L. remained conscious of his roots, returning to Finnish themes (and using Strindberg's [q.v.] informal lyric technique) in the poems of *Rakkaita muistoja* (1911; beloved memories) and its sequel, the rowdy "little epic" on a rustic engagement party, *Markkinoilta* (1912; from the market).

In 1905 L. had bought a cottage and a piece of land near Savonlinna for an improvident half-brother, and spent many of his summers there; a keen observer of the tensions between the backwoods "savages" and their "civilized" town neighbors, L. undertook what he thought would be a "human comedy" for his home region. (He liked to compare Finnish country folk with James Fenimore Cooper's redskins, or the tribes of the Sahara.) The first volume was *Kerran kesällä* (1917; once in summer), about a composer who, returning from abroad, despairingly perceives the changes time has wrought in him and his people; it was followed by *Kuolleet omenapuut* (1918; the dead apple trees), a collection of masterful short stories, many in monologue form, dealing in part with a very recent event, Finland's civil war (January–May 1918). The artistic climax came with *Putkinotko: Kuvaus laiskasta viinarokarista ja tuhmasta herrasta* (2 vols., 1919–20; Putkinotko: an account of a lazy moonshiner and a stupid gentleman), which takes place on a single summer day before the war and minutely depicts the uneasiness of Aapeli Muttinen, a fat and sybaritic bookdealer, who has put his vacation cottage into the care of Juutas Käkriäinen, an obstinate, shiftless, and ignorant tenant farmer. The series—which has a wealth of other memorable characters: a would-be learned barber, a nouveau-riche Swedophile, a lawyer who blindly admires German discipline, and a ludicrous enthusiast of the *Kalevala,* the Finnish national epic—came to an untimely end with the four novellas of *Korpi ja puutarha* (1923; the backwoods and the garden); here we learn that Käkriäinen has been killed "like an animal" in the civil war.

L.'s other work falls into several groups: realistic novels, where he once again considers the immediate prewar days, now against a Helsinki setting—*Sorron lapset* (1923; children of oppression) and *Punainen mies* (1925; the red man); experiments with expressionism (q.v.) and the grotesque—*Rakastunut rampa* (1922; the enamored cripple) and *Sirkus ja pyhimys* (1927; the circus and the saint); idyllic tales and reflections—*Onnen poika* (1925; the happy fellow) and *Lintukoto* (1929; the bird home), a title also referring to an imaginary land of bliss; and sometimes cruel self-analysis: the author's dog is a main character of *Rai Jakkerintytär* (1927; Rai, Jakker's daughter). L.'s pessimism received its last expression in the visionary novel *Henkien taistelu* (1933; the battle of the spirits), where a devil conducts the hero on a tour of the scenes of Finnish corruption; Helsinki—which L. detested—is the setting of the novel's finale. L. took his own life the next year; the revelatory poems of *Hyvästijättö Lintukodolle* (1935; farewell to Lintukoto) appeared posthumously.

Eino Leino (q.v.) compared L. to Strindberg; in many respects, however, he is closer to Knut Hamsun (q.v.)—in his inclination to occasional stylistic and emotional rhapsodies, in his devotion to his own small world, in his sardonic wit, and in his misanthropy. Yet he had a tolerance for human frailty that Hamsun may well have lacked.

FURTHER WORKS: *Perm* (1904); *Paholaisen viulu* (1904); *Villi* (1905); *Tarulinna* (1906); *Ilvolan juttuja* (1910); *Nuoruus* (1911); *Munkki-kammio* (1914); *Puolikuun alla* (1919); *Tähtimantteli* (1920); *Putkinotkon herra: Kirjeitä 1907–1920* (1969)

BIBLIOGRAPHY: Tarkka, P., *Putkinotkon tausta: J. L. henkilöt 1901–1923* (1977), English summary, pp. 488–505; Tarkka, P., "J. L. and Putkinotko," *BF,* 11 (1977), 239–45

GEORGE C. SCHOOLFIELD

LEINO, Eino

(pseud. of Eino Lönnbohm) Finnish poet, dramatist, and journalist, b. 6 July 1878, Paltamo, d. 10 Jan. 1926, Tuusula

L. made his mark early. At sixteen he published a translation of a poem by Johan Ludvig Runeberg (1804–1877), the great Finland-Swedish poet. After starting studies at the University of Helsinki, he joined Helsinki literary and newspaper circles, where his elder brother Kasimir had preceded him. Having published several books of verse, he produced his masterpiece, the first volume of *Helkavirsiä* (1903; *Whitsongs,* 1978). He became an exponent of the neoromantic movement, which was strong in Finland around the turn of the century. Nearly every year until his death he brought out at least one volume, whether poetry, drama, or fiction.

L. was influenced by Goethe, Heine, and Nietzsche, but more deeply by the *Kalevala,* the Finnish national epic. His subjects are nature, love, his native land, and the quest for truth. Composed in the trochaic meter of the *Kalevala,* the ballads of the *Helkavirsiä* are denser in meaning and often more powerful than their model in their impact on the modern reader. L.'s verse is also rich in alliteration, but there is less parallelism than in the *Kalevala.* Several of the ballads present a kind of Faustian hubris, but the protagonists are more violent, more barbaric than Goethe's hero. The God-defying eponymous hero of "Ylermi" (Ylermi) is an example. In "Kouta" (Kouta) a brawny man of Lapland probes for the answer to the riddle of the universe in a supernatural wilderness. In "Tuuri" (Tuuri) the central figure pleads that death might grant him a reprieve. His plea is granted on a sardonic note. Awaking from a night of revelry with some pagan gods, he discovers that his young wife and little son have long since finished their life cycles, leaving him alone. Time has turned out to be relative, in appalling fashion. Nevertheless, the volume expresses a tragic optimism, a willing acceptance of fate, suggestive of Nietzsche's superman. Other ballads lack the metaphysical dimension. For example, "Kimmon kosto" (Kimmo's revenge) and "Räikkö Räähkä" (Räikkö the wretch) present violent episodes in a dim historical past; Räikkö betrays his village and commits suicide in remorse for collaborating with the enemy.

None of L.'s later works was to surpass his achievement in the first *Helkavirsiä*, but he demonstrated his virtuosity in other types of verse. Nor did he limit himself to Finnish themes. His play *Alkibiades* (1909; Alcibiades) his *Bellerophon* (1919; Bellerophon), a story in verse, and his various translations show his broader interests. There is a remarkable play of end rhyme, internal rhyme, and alliteration in his well-known "Nocturne" (nocturne) and in other lyrics of *Talvi-yö* (1905; winter night), as well as in the collection *Halla* (1908; frost). These titles imply a growing disenchantment with life.

His second volume of *Helkavirsiä* (1916; Whitsuntide songs) is more pessimistic and more mystical than the first. "Ukri" (Ukri) of the later volume recalls "Ylermi," indicating the persistence of L.'s preoccupations with philosophical issues. "Auringon hyvästijättö" (the sun's farewell) presents a cosmic vision with erotic overtones. In this, as in some other poems, the symbolism is obscure. An obsession with the self, with failure, and with death marks certain of the later pieces.

After 1910 people felt that L. was wasting his great talents in hackwork and a bohemian existence. The women he had love affairs with included two writers: L. Onerva (Hilja Onerva Lehtinen-Madetoja, 1882–1972) who wrote his biography; and Aino Kallas (q.v.), the noted short-story writer, who tried in vain to persuade him to write a third collection of *helkavirsiä*.

His most notable plays survive because of their lyrical qualities and their folkloric content. A fine early example is *Tuonelan joutsen* (1896; the swan of the land of death). In it Lemminkäinen (a character from the *Kalevala*) seeks to plumb the mystery of existence. Both the swan and the land of Tuonela would appear in other writings of L. He was disappointed in his effort to establish a viable theater with adaptations of the *Kalevala*. As for his many novels, they were no more than potboilers and have fallen into oblivion.

L.'s major achievement remains the ballads of *Helkavirsiä* and the lyrics of *Talvi-yö* and *Halla*. The vigor and richness of the legend poems have not been matched in Finnish literature. His command of the language is outstanding, and he skillfully applied the resources of his folk heritage to poetry for his own time. If he had few followers, his countrymen still honor him along with the

painter Gallen-Kallela and the composer Sibelius, who were also inspired by the *Kalevala*.

FURTHER WORKS: *Maaliskuun lauluja* (1896); *Kangastuksia* (1902); *Simo Hurtta* (1904); *Naamiota* (6 vols., 1905–11); *Suomalaisia kirjailijoita* (1909); *Suomalaisen kirjallisuuden historia* (1910); *Elämän koreus* (1915); *Juhana herttuan ja Catherina Jagellonican lauluja* (1919); *Syreenien Kukkiessa* (1920); *Elämäni kuvakirja* (1925); *Kootut teokset* (16 vols., 1926–30); *Elämän laulu* (1947); *Kirjokeppi* (1949); *Pakinat* (2 vols., 1960); *Kirjeet* (4 vols., 1961–62); *Maailman kirjailijoita* (1978)

BIBLIOGRAPHY: Tompuri, E., ed., *Voices from Finland: An Anthology* (1947), pp. 13–14, 21; Havu, I., *An Introduction to Finnish Literature* (1952), pp. 64–70; Kolehmainen, J. I., *Epic of the North* (1973), pp. 244–58; Ahokas, J., *A History of Finnish Literature* (1973), pp. 147–66; Branch, M., Introduction to E. L., *Whitsongs* (1978), pp. 5–20; Sarajas, A., "E. L.: 1878–1928," *BF,* 12 (1978), 40–46; Schoolfield, G. C., on *Whitsongs, SS,* 52 (1980), 341–44

REINO VIRTANEN

LEIRIS, Michel

French autobiographer, poet, ethnographer, critic, and novelist, b. 20 April 1901, Paris

From an upper-middle-class family, L. began his literary career as a poet and participated in the surrealist (q.v.) movement between 1924 and 1929. In 1929, after a mental crisis and a period of sexual impotence, he underwent psychoanalysis, after which he began a new career in anthropology, participating in an ethnographical expedition to Africa (1931–33). After returning to France, L. formally studied ethnography and later became a curator at the Museum of Man in Paris. In 1937, with writer-friends Georges Bataille (q.v.) and Roger Caillois (1913–1978), he founded the College of Sociology, a group devoted to the study of social structures. He fought in North Africa in 1939 but returned to Paris during the German occupation and began writing his autobiography. During this period he became a friend of Jean-Paul Sartre (q.v.) and other Resistance writers. After the war he traveled to the Antilles, to China, to

Japan, and in the 1960s to Cuba, whose communist revolution he supported. He has continued actively to promote leftist political causes.

L. has long been interested in the relationship of language to dreams and the unconscious. His poetic works, such as those collected in *Mots sans mémoire* (1969; words without memory) and *Haut mal, suivi de Autres lancers* (1969; severe seizure, followed by other throws)—*Haut mal* was first published alone in 1943—and his only novel, *Aurora* (1946; Aurora), show his fascination with word games, with the associative power of language, and with private mythmaking. Writing, for L., is a means to discover how to live more fully. Indeed, one could say that his literary works constitute one long autobiographical search.

In *Miroir de la tauromachie* (1938; mirror of bullfighting) L. sets forth his aesthetic theories, inspired by Baudelaire, and based on the idea of the *corrida*. In the bullfight L. sees the solemnity of ceremony, the courage to face death, the reenactment of myth and of ritual sacrifice, and erotic overtones that must also be intrinsic to art. In *Le ruban au cou d'Olympia* (1981; the ribbon around Olympia's neck) he returns to the subject matter of *Miroir de la tauromachie*. *L'Afrique fântome* (1934; phantom Africa) incorporates L.'s ethnographical concerns into a personal journal of his trip to Africa. In his self-portrait, *L'âge d'homme* (1939; *Manhood*, 1963)—republished in 1946 with an important prefatory essay "De la littérature considerée comme une tauromachie" (published in English as "The Autobiographer as Torero")—he likens the risks of personal confession to those taken by a bullfighter in the ring. His feelings of inadequacy, his obsessions with physical flaws and infirmities, and his sexual fantasies are given poetic dimension through his meditations on the mythic figures of the biblical Judith, the archetypal man-killer, and the legendary Lucrece, the image of the wounded or punished woman.

Biffures (1948; deletions), the first of the four-volume autobiography *La règle du jeu* (the rules of the game), is a masterpiece of the genre in the way it questions both autobiographical works and the very act of writing. It is not a chronology of events; by showing how one word can evoke another and by "crossing out" or "deleting" illusory connections, L. examines the relationships among writing, history, and a mythopoetic vision of personal experience. *Biffures* focuses on his childhood and on language. In the second volume, *Fourbis* (1955; odds and ends), he discusses his preoccupation with death and celebrates loves and friendships, particularly those from the war years. The third volume, *Fibrilles* (1966; fibrils), evokes his trip to China, deals with the question of the need for political commitment, and includes an account of his 1958 suicide attempt. At the end of *Fibrilles* L. renounces what he now realizes to be an impossible project—that of bringing together all the parts of his life into a unified whole. The last volume, *Frêle bruit* (1976; frail noise), composed primarily of short texts, acknowledges the fragmentary quality of life.

L. has also written sensitive works of ethnography and literary and art criticism, especially texts for art books. His *Brisées* (1966; trail markers) contains articles on the work of many of his friends (including Pablo Picasso, Joan Miró, and André Masson), as well as several ethnographical pieces.

FURTHER WORKS: *Simulacres* (1925); *Le point cardinal* (1927); *Tauromachies* (1937); *Glossaire, j'y serre mes gloses* (1939); *Nuits sans nuits* (1945); *André Masson et son univers* (1947, with Georges Limbour; *André Masson and His Universe*, 1947); *La langue secrète de Dogons de Sanga* (1948); *Toro* (1951); *Contacts de civilisations en Martinique et en Guadeloupe* (1955); *Bagatelles végétales* (1956); *balzacs en bas de casse et picassos sans majuscules* (1957); *La possession et ses aspects théâtraux chez les Éthiopiens de Gondar* (1958); *Vivantes cendres, innommées* (1961); *Marrons sculptés pour Miró* (1961); *Grande fuite de neige* (1964); *Afrique noire: La création plastique* (1967, with Jacqueline Delange; *African Art*, 1968); *Cinq études d'ethnologie* (1969); *Fissures* (1970); *Wifredo Lam* (1970); *André Masson: Massacres et autres dessins* (1971); *Francis Bacon; ou, La vérité criante* (1974). FURTHER VOLUME IN ENGLISH: *The Prints of Joan Miró* (1947)

BIBLIOGRAPHY: Mauriac, C., *The New Literature* (1959), pp. 61–73; Nadeau, M., *M. L. et la quadrature du cercle* (1963); Sontag, S., "M. L.'s *Manhood*" (1964), *Against Interpretation* (1966), pp. 61–68; Boyer, A. M., *M. L.* (1974); Mehlman, J., *A Structural Study of Autobiography* (1974), pp. 65–150; Brée,

G., "M. L.: Mazemaker," in Olney, J., ed., *Autobiography: Essays Theoretical and Critical* (1980), pp. 194–206; Hewitt, L. D., "Historical Intervention in L.'s Bif(f)ur(e)s," *FrF,* 7 (1982), 132–45

LEAH D. HEWITT

LEÑERO, Vicente

Mexican novelist, dramatist, short-story writer, and journalist, b. 9 June 1933, Guadalajara

L. grew up in Mexico City and was graduated from the National University in civil engineering. After practicing his profession briefly, he turned to journalism and literature for his livelihood. Modest, unassuming, and deeply religious, L. has remained aloof from the literary circles in the Mexican capital. He is, nevertheless, one of the most admired intellectuals in the country today. In addition to his activities as a novelist and playwright, he has written television scripts and for several years was editor of *Claudia,* a popular women's magazine.

L.'s first novel, *La voz adolorida* (1961; the sorrowful voice), consists of a monologue of the mentally deranged protagonist, who describes his unhappy life prior to his confinement in a mental hospital. His convincing tone and the fluctuations between his moments of sanity and dementia suggest the relativity of both truth and normality. *Los albañiles* (1964; the bricklayers) is L.'s undisputed masterpiece. This novel, which won the prestigious Biblioteca Breve Prize in Spain, has the outward form of a detective story but, symbolically, the investigator's unsuccessful search for the murderer of a night watchman at a building site represents modern man's vain quest for truth. L. utilizes a wide range of avant-garde techniques designed to eliminate the omniscient narrator and create a multidimensional work of art, thus underscoring the complexities of an indecipherable, rapidly changing world. Even more structurally complex, *Estudio Q* (1965; studio Q) satirizes commercial television by portraying an actor who confuses reality with fiction while filming a play based on his biography. *El garabato* (1967; the squiggle) emerges as an antinovel that parodies L.'s preoccupation with the creative process. Like *Los albañiles,* it takes the form of a detective story, but the parallel plots of a critic seeking the solution to a moral dilemma while he

reads a mediocre murder mystery suggest L.'s frustration as a writer and, perhaps, his disillusionment with the novel as a genre.

After finishing *El garabato,* L. discovered a new medium for himself in drama. Although his most successful play is his adaptation of *Los albañiles* (1970), he also initiated documentary theater in Mexico as a kind of educational vehicle. The best examples of this genre are *Pueblo rechazado* (1969; rejected people), the dramatization of the widely publicized controversy over Prior Gregorio Lemercier's introduction of psychoanalysis into a Benedictine monastery to determine aptitudes for the priesthood; and *El juicio* (1972; the trial), a representation of the 1928 trial of the accused assassins of President-elect Alvaro Obregón. The novel *Los periodistas* (1978; the journalists) demonstrates L.'s continued interest in the documentary mode, its subject being a dispute between *Excelsior,* Mexico's most prestigious newspaper, and then-President Luis Echeverría.

Viewed in its entirety, L.'s oeuvre has registered three successive phases: psychological realism, sophisticated avant-gardism, and a scrupulously objective art form. His awesome versatility and acute sensitivity to the complicated realities of today's world make him one of contemporary Latin America's more significant literary voices.

FURTHER WORKS: *La polvareda, y otros cuentos* (1959); *A fuerza de palabras* (1967); *V. L.* (1967); *El derecho de llorar, y otros reportajes* (1968); *La zona rosa, y otros reportajes* (1968); *Compañero* (1970); *La carpa* (perf. 1971, pub. 1974); *Los hijos de Sánchez* (perf. 1972); *Redil de ovejas* (1973); *Viaje a Cuba* (1974); *El evangelio de Lucas Gavilán* (1979); *La mudanza* (1980)

BIBLIOGRAPHY: McMurray, G. R., "The Novels of V. L.," *Crit,* 8, 3 (1966), 55–61; Robles, H. E., "Approximaciones a *Los albañiles* de V. L.," *RI,* 73 (1970), 579–99; Langford, W. M., *The Mexican Novel Comes of Age* (1971), pp. 151–67; Foster, D. W., and Foster, V. R., eds., *Modern Latin American Literature* (1975), Vol. I, pp. 471–77; Grossman, L. S., "*Los albañiles,* Novel and Play: A Two-Time Winner," *LATR,* 9, 2 (1976), 5–12; Grossman, L., "*Redil de ovejas:* A New Novel from L.," *RomN,* 17 (1976), 127–30; Holzaphel, T., "*Pueblo re-*

chazado: Educating the Public through Reportage," *LATR,* 10, 1 (1976), 15–21

GEORGE R. MCMURRAY

LENZ, Siegfried

West German novelist, short-story writer, dramatist, and essayist, b. 17 March 1926, Lyck (now Ełk, Poland)

L., the son of a civil servant, grew up in a small Masurian town in former East Prussia; he served in the German navy during the last years of World War II. After being held as a prisoner of war for a short time by the British, he began studying philosophy as well as German and English literature at the University of Hamburg. In 1948 L. embarked upon a brief journalistic career and eventually became feuilleton editor of the newspaper *Die Welt* (1950–51), a position he relinquished to devote all his time to writing. Although not a party member, L. has been active in election campaigns on behalf of the Social Democratic Party since 1965; in 1970 Günter Grass (q.v.) and L. accompanied Chancellor Willy Brandt to Warsaw for the signing of the treaty that was to effect a rapprochement between the Federal Republic and Poland.

L. became affiliated with Group 47 in the early 1950s; he subsequently fully subscribed to that group's early endeavors to create a literature of political and social concern and commitment. But L.'s four early novels, like many of his early short stories, tend to concentrate on situations of human crisis in which the protagonist is severely tested and inevitably fails. L.'s first novel, *Es waren Habichte in der Luft* (1951; there were hawks in the sky), develops the theme of guilt, frequently encountered in L.'s work, and that of flight—in an overly symbolic fashion. *Duell mit dem Schatten* (1953; duel with a shadow), with its somewhat contrived plot and stylistic infelicities, was considered a failure by L. himself. In *Der Mann im Strom* (1957; the man in the river), the story of an aged diver, and *Brot und Spiele* (1959; bread and games), a sports novel, the respective heroes are doomed to failure; but in both novels, which are set in contemporary Germany, an element of social criticism is to be noticed.

Stadtgespräch (1963; *The Survivor,* 1965), a novel that presumably takes place in Norway during the German occupation in World War II, probes the ethical dilemma that confronts the Resistance leader Daniel when he has to choose between self-sacrifice or sacrificing the lives of innocent hostages. The limited perspective of the narrator, a member of the Resistance, is broadened by discussions among the hostages and the townspeople, who debate the political and moral consequences of Daniel's decision not to surrender. Although L. implicitly endorses the protagonist's choice as necessary for the continuation of the struggle against a dictatorial regime, the lack of a specific historical context and the tendency toward the parabolic diffuse the central moral question and diminish the novel's impact.

In his masterpiece, the novel *Deutschstunde* (1968; *The German Lesson,* 1972), L. avoids the pitfalls of too abstract a presentation and succeeds in capturing the atmosphere and milieu of a specific landscape as well as the character of its people without succumbing to the maudlin sentimentality and provincialism often to be found in the *Heimatroman,* or regional novel. Despite occasional implausibilities that arise from the first-person narrative perspective, the novel is L.'s most significant artistic contribution to the so-called *Vergangenheitsbewältigung,* or coming to terms with Germany's Nazi past, even if the central conflict seems to pale in comparison to the atrocities depicted in Holocaust literature. Required to write an essay on the "Joys of Duty," the narrator, a juvenile delinquent in a reform school, recounts the dogmatic, obsessive, and, ultimately, inhumane dedication to duty of his father, a policeman in Germany's northernmost region of Schleswig-Holstein. The policeman had been charged with enforcing an edict that forbids the artist Max Ludwig Nansen (based, in part, on the expressionist painter Emil Nolde) to engage in painting. The narrator's questioning of perverted concepts of duty that continue to exist emphasizes his precarious position as an outsider. L. inverts the traditional *Bildungsroman* to demonstrate that the vestiges of the Nazi past have not yet vanished.

The novel *Das Vorbild* (1973; *An Exemplary Life,* 1976) also poses a pedagogical problem. Three educators have been asked to select materials suitable for a representative school reader. They largely fail in their search for a both convincing and generally acceptable role model, an exemplary life to be emulated by young people. The discussions about the various suggested models and the educators' own character flaws encourage the reader of the novel to question the former and present propagation of models that may be used to manipulate youthful enthusiasm. The ambiguous outcome and the insufficient relevance of the story finally agreed upon make the novel less successful than its predecessor.

The narrator of the lengthy novel *Heimatmuseum* (1978; *The Heritage: The History of a Detestable Word,* 1981), an accomplished carpet weaver, delves deeply into both his own past and the history of his native Masuria to explain and justify his decision to set fire to the museum that he had laboriously rebuilt in West Germany after World War II. The museum was in danger of being propagandistically exploited by groups laying claim to Germany's lost eastern territories. The novel's detailed descriptions, vivid episodes, charming anecdotes, and memorable if slightly eccentric characters result in a leisurely, digressive style that lends some credence to the claim that L.'s real forte is the short story.

In fact, L.'s mastery of the short story is attested to by four collections in particular: *Jäger des Spotts* (1958; hunter of ridicule), *Das Feuerschiff* (1960; the lightship), *Der Spielverderber* (1965; the spoilsport), and *Einstein überquert die Elbe bei Hamburg* (1975; Einstein crosses the Elbe near Hamburg). In the early stories the influence of Ernest Hemingway (q.v.), whom L. explicitly acknowledged as a model, is quite pronounced. Thus, the plot of "Jäger des Spotts" in general and the protagonist's stoic dignity in the face of defeat in particular recall Hemingway's *The Old Man and the Sea.* But L. soon began to reject Hemingway, whom he faulted for lacking social awareness and historical perspective. L.'s later short stories exhibit a wide thematic range and a great variety of narrative modes that extend from the profoundly serious to the ironic, satiric, and Kafkaesque questioning of the perception of reality. L.'s versatility as a storyteller is also evident in several collections of humorous tales, notably the tribute to his native Masuria, *So zärtlich war Suleyken* (1955; so tender was Suleyken).

Although L. is primarily considered a writer of fiction, a number of radio and stage plays demonstrate his skill as a playwright. *Zeit der Schuldlosen* (1962; time of the innocents) was especially successful in performance. In its parabolic quality and concentration on the extreme situation as a test for human morality, familiar from L.'s early fiction, the play is reminiscent of both Jean-Paul Sartre and Albert Camus (qq.v.).

Like other writers of his generation (for example, Grass), L. is concerned with the consequences of the Nazi past for contemporary West German society. He considers the writer a witness who is called upon to voice his protest in the face of societal inequities by means of his craft—albeit without provocative stridency and within the framework of conventional narrative. L.'s social commitment, then, is tempered by his insight into the frailty of the human condition. This insight also prevents L. from adopting a moralizing tone. L.'s undoubted gifts as a storyteller, combined with his unobtrusive commitment and undiminished literary output will, in all probability, continue to secure him a place of distinction among contemporary German writers.

FURTHER WORKS: *Das Kabinett der Konterbande* (1956); *Das schönste Fest der Welt* (1956); *Wippchens charmante Scharmützel* (1960, with Egon Schramm); *Zeit der Schuldlosen—Zeit der Schuldigen* (1961); *Stimmungen der See* (1962); *Das Gesicht* (1964); *Lehmanns Erzählungen* (1964); *Flug über Land und Meer* (1967, with Dieter Seelmann); *Haussuchung* (1967); *Leute von Hamburg* (1968); *Die Augenbinde; Nicht alle Förster sind froh* (1970); *Beziehungen* (1970); *Lotte soll nicht sterben* (1970); *So war es mit dem Zirkus* (1971); *Der Geist der Mirabelle* (1975); *Wo die Möwen schreien* (1976, with Dieter Seelmann); *Der Verlust* (1981)

BIBLIOGRAPHY: Russ, C. A. H., "The Short Stories of S. L.," *GL&L,* 19 (1965–66), 241–51; Paslick, R. H., "Narrowing the Distance: S. L.'s *Deutschstunde,*" *GQ,* 46 (1973), 210–18; Russ, C., ed., *Der Schriftsteller S. L.* (1973); Elstren, E. N., "How It Seems and How It Is: Marriage in Three Stories by S. L.," *OL,* 29 (1974), 170–79; Russell, P., "S. L.'s *Deutschstunde:* A 'North German' Novel," *GL&L,* 28 (1974–75), 405–18; Wagener, H., *S. L.* (1976); Russell, P., "The 'Lesson' in S. L.'s *Deutschstunde,*" *Seminar,* 13 (1977), 42–54; Murdoch, B., and Read, M., *S. L.* (1978); Gohlmann, S. A., "Making Words Do for Paint: 'Seeing' and Self-Mastery in S. L.'s *The German Lesson,*" *MLS,* 9, 2 (1979), 80–88; Bosmajian, H., "S. L.'s *The German Lesson:* Metaphors of Evil on Narrow Ground," *Metaphors of Evil* (1979), pp.

57–81; Butler, G. P., "Zygmunt's Follies? On S. L.'s *Heimatmuseum*," *GL&L,* 33 (1979–80), 172–78

SIEGFRIED MEWS

LEONOV, Leonid Maximovich
Russian novelist and dramatist, b. 31 May 1899, Polukhino

L., whose father wrote poetry advocating social reforms, graduated from a Moscow secondary school and attended Moscow University, but did not complete his studies. He served briefly in the Red Army during the civil war. His first works show widely different influences, ranging from E. T. A. Hoffmann (1776–1822) in *Derevyannaya koroleva* (1922; the wooden queen) to Oriental poetry in *Tuatamur* (1924; *Tuatamur*, 1935), which is written in poetic prose.

One can safely assume that L. accepted the revolution without understanding the basic tenets of Marxism. Although he attempts to portray the new social order in a favorable light, his heroes are complex and have all the human frailties. They face ethical and moral dilemmas, suffer emotionally, and more than occasionally are victims of social and revolutionary changes. L. tries to understand the revolution from a sociopsychological point of view; there is also a constant antagonism between the old and the new, between the village and the city. L.'s affection for the old and the rural is more than evident: the village people in his works are pure and strong. L. shows that the new roads, factories, and plants disrupt the idyllic countryside and the cherished Russian traditions. Since the conflict between the old and the new is not to be resolved, L., through sometimes obvious or trite symbolism, tries to reconcile the differences between Hegelian *Verstandesmetaphysik* (rationality) and *Vernunftsmetaphysik* (reason). His symbolism is intricate and complex; it constantly oversteps the boundaries of any type of realism, be it social, historical, concrete, or "mature" (*zrely*), as these terms are used by exponents of Socialist Realism (q.v.). Occasionally L. applies the attitudes of the past to contemporary circumstances, as in *Russky les* (1953; *The Russian Forest*, 1958), in which a girl named Polya views Red Square and Lenin's mausoleum in Moscow as national religious shrines, as someone years before might have viewed a church or a tomb of a saint, and thereupon makes a pledge to be a good girl and a communist.

L.'s language differs from that of other Soviet Russian writers in its extreme complexity and subjectivity. He makes extensive use of hyperbole, oxymoron, synesthesia, and other figures of speech, as well as various Dostoevskian devices such as stream of consciousness (q.v.), archaisms, and colloquial neologisms. Indeed, when L. appeared on the literary scene in the early 1920s many critics, including Gorky (q.v.), called him a follower of Dostoevsky.

L.'s first novel, *Barsuki* (1925; *The Badgers*, 1947), which he made into a play with the same title in 1927, is concerned with two Russias—the prerevolutionary merchant Moscow and the Russian village during the revolution. It depicts two antagonistic brothers; Pasha, who later becomes Comrade Anton; and Semyon, who protects the village. The conflict is not resolved at the end of the novel, but L.'s sympathy remains with Semyon. A story within a story in *Barsuki,* "Pro neistovogo Kalafata" (the fierce Kalafat)—usually referred to in English as "The Kalafat Legend"—portrays a tower representing Communism (as well as any bureaucracy) being built higher and higher but at the end remaining at the same level because it is slowly sinking.

In *Vor* (1927; *The Thief,* 1931), whose action takes place in Moscow during the NEP period, L.'s psychological propensities have obvious Dostoevskian roots. Here pessimism is stronger than optimism, and idealism is trampled in the name of the road to Communism. In his next novel, *Doroga na okean* (1935; *Road to the Ocean,* 1944), which was quite controversial, L. tried to create a Communist work in which readers would actively identify themselves, through the author's appeal to their reason, with the march toward the classless society. This novel, dedicated to the whole of mankind, symbolically depicts a river merging with the "Utopian Ocean." L.'s hero, Kurilov, an ideal Communist who espouses the positive and the rational, predicts a bright future. L., however, fails to make Kurilov plausible. Despite authorial attempts to imbue him with a progressive ideology, Kurilov comes off no better than other characters in the novel.

Until 1936 L. had generally been regarded as a leading novelist, but after Gorky's death in that year, the adverse criticism that he received for his novels became unbearable, and he turned to dramatic works. His plays of the 1930s were also severely criticized, but during World War II L. wrote two plays dealing with the German invasion—*Nashestvie* (1943; *The Invasion,* 1944) and *Lyonushka* (1943; Lyonushka)—for which he received a Stalin Prize.

L.'s difficulties began again with his play *Zolotaya kareta* (1946, rev. version, 1955; the golden coach), the composition of which, in several different versions, played a major role in L.'s creative life. The play contrasts the attitudes of the older and younger generations of revolutionary Russia toward love and marriage. The first version was immediately suppressed. The revisions he was forced to make showed L. that ideological uncertainties in depicting contemporary society were not welcome by Party functionaries. Thus, in his long novel *Russky les,* L. avoids contemporary problems. He goes back to 1941–42 and describes the deforestation of Russia and the conflict between Vikhrov, an honest scientist who sincerely loves forests, and his rival Gratsiansky, a pseudoscientist. Although the novel seems primarily to depict the beauty and the usefulness of the forest, the underlying implications are more intricate and more meaningful.

In general, L.'s novels are of a Dostoevskian polyphonic nature. L's preoccupation with the individual, with *chistota* (purity), and with life that is complex, ambivalent, and irrational makes his works distinctive and understandable to a Western reader. Ultimately L. takes a moralist's position.

FURTHER WORKS: *Untilovsk* (1925); *Provintsialnaya istoria* (1927; dramatized 1928); *Usmirenie Badadoshkina* (1928); *Sarancha* (1930); *Sot* (1930; *Soviet River,* 1932); *Skutarevsky* (1932; *Skutarevsky,* 1936); *Volk* (1938); *Polovchanskie sady* (1938; *The Orchards of Polovchansk,* 1946); *Evgenia Ivanovna* (written 1938, pub. 1963); *Obyknovenny chelovek* (1940); *Metel* (1940); *Vzyatie Velikoshumska* (1945; *Chariot of Wrath,* 1946); *Begstvo Mistera Makkinli* (1960); *Teatr: Dramaticheskie proizvedenya, stati rechi* (2 vols., 1960); *Literaturnye vystuplenia* (1966); *Literatura i vremya* (1967); *Sobranie sochineny* (10 vols., 1969–72)

BIBLIOGRAPHY: Simmons, E. J., *Russian Fiction and Soviet Ideology: Introduction to Fedin, L., and Sholokhov* (1958), pp. 89–161; Muchnic, H., *From Gorky to Pasternak* (1961), pp. 276–303; Terras, V., "L. L.'s Novel *The Russian Forest,*" *SEEJ,* 8 (1964), 123–40; Thomson, R. B., "L. L.," *FMLS,* 2 (1966), 264–73; Plank, D. L., "Unconscious Motifs in L. L.'s *The Badgers,*" *SEEJ,* 16 (1972), 19–35; Thomson, R. B., "L.'s Play *Zolotaja kareta,*" *SEEJ,* 16 (1972), 438–48; Harjan, G., *L. L.: A Critical Study* (1979)

VYTAS DUKAS

LEOPOLD, Jan Hendrik

Dutch poet, b. 11 April 1865, 's Hertogenbosch; d. 21 June 1925, Rotterdam

L. studied classical philology at the University of Leiden, where he received his doctorate in 1891, and thereafter taught classical languages in a secondary school in Rotterdam. A shy and introverted man, in the course of his uneventful life he was increasingly isolated by growing deafness. He began to publish his poetry in *De nieuwe gids* in 1893, and continued to publish in that journal. During his lifetime his work was known to a small but select circle of readers; his poetry has subsequently found a much wider audience.

L. offered a highly individual voice to Dutch poetry. More than any other Dutch poet, he profitably absorbed the strong influence of French symbolism (q.v.), especially that of Verlaine. (Another influence on his poetry is Spinoza, in whom he was deeply read.) His lyrics, often individually untitled, create an intensely private universe, suggested rather than described, in which the voice of the persona often addresses a beloved woman, asleep or dead. This poetry creates a realm suggestive of sleep and dreaming, heightened by the subtle musicality of the verse. L. is a master of assonance and enjambment, and can effectively spin out a long sentence through tight rhymed stanzas in a way that intensifies the sense of the transitory that the poetry often expresses. One of his finest poems, with the Greek title "Oinou hena stalagmon" (1910; a drop of wine), uses several complex images—the offering of a drop of wine to the sea as a libation that pervades all the ocean, the fall of an unpicked apple, mentioned in a fragment of Sappho, that moves the universe—to suggest the way an impulse of the mind may move out and pervade the minds of other men. Yet for the most part, this is elusive and meditative poetry, in which the voice of the persona is never answered.

A somewhat different note is heard in the sequence of poems entitled "Oostersch" (Oriental), which first appeared in *Verzen, tweede bundel* (2 vols., 1926; verses, second collection). Beginning in 1904, L. read Persian and Arabic poetry in French and English translations, and produced his own translations (some from the *Rubaiyat* of Omar Khayyam), adaptations, and original poems in the same style. These poems counterpoint his other work: they are sharper, crisper, and more aphoristic. The note of fatalism and disillusionment L. drew from the great Persian poets can be seen as a way of responding to the delicately modulated frustration his other poems express.

Of his longer poems, *Cheops* (1915; Cheops) has been the most discussed. In its stately cadenced verse we are told how the spirit of the Pharaoh joins in his own funeral procession and moves out into the great spaces of the universe, but chooses finally to return to the tomb in the pyramid, there to remain forever. This act of voluntary inwardness can be seen as central to L.'s poetic art.

FURTHER WORKS: *Verzen* (1913); *Nabetrachtingen van een concertganger* (1929); *Verzamelde verzen* (1935); *Verzameld werk* (2 vols., 1951–52). FURTHER VOLUMES IN ENGLISH: *The Flute* (1949); *The Valley of Irdîn* (1957)

BIBLIOGRAPHY: Jalink, J. M., *Eine Studie über Leben und Werk des Dichters J. H. L.* (1949); Meijer, R. P., *Literature of the Low Countries,* new ed. (1978), pp. 271–74

FRED J. NICHOLS

LEŚMIAN, Bolesław

(pseud. of Bolesław Stanisław Lesman) Polish poet and literary critic, b. 22 Jan. 1877, Warsaw; d. 5 Nov. 1937, Warsaw

L.'s paternal ancestors belonged to the small but not negligible group of Polish Jews who assimilated into Polish society to the point of converting to Roman Catholicism. L. spent his youth in Kiev, where he studied law and was profoundly influenced by the surrounding lush Ukrainian countryside. The years 1918–33 he spent in the towns of Hrubieszów

and Zamość, where he worked as a notary public. In 1933 he was elected member of the Polish Academy of Literature.

L. was associated with the movement known as Young Poland, which followed some tenets of symbolism (q.v.), Decadence, and neoromanticism. Like most truly original poets, however, he cannot be easily assigned to the trend to which he nominally belonged. L.'s poetry seems to derive from evenings spent in country meadows and cemeteries. He was a baroque romantic, or an exuberant yet melancholy author of nature poems in which dazzling verbal acrobatics and gentle humor conceal a deeply pessimistic philosophy. His early poems focus on nature, whereas the later ones tend to deal either with love or with death. His essay "Traktat o poezji" (1937; treatise on poetry) is probably the best essay ever written on L.'s own poetry. He defines poetry as a dance that has rebelled against the drabness of life, and he desires poetry to be unconstrained by the conventional meanings of words and by social and political problems.

L.'s approach to nature is unusual among the European poets of his generation. Instead of painting landscapes in verse, as so many lesser modernists have done, he adopts the point of view of animate and inanimate objects. In his poems nature looks at man and not the other way around. In the title poem of *Łąka* (1920; the meadow), a grassy flatland reminds man how he once gave it the name of meadow and how since then it has had an identity of its own.

The rustic landscapes of L.'s youth reappeared in his poetry in the form of monsters and apparitions who rejoice and grieve for reasons that defy human logic. Students of L.'s poetry have pointed out that these creatures derive from Polish folklore but that they are not simply lifted from it. In "Dusiołek" (1920; an untranslatable neologism designating a spirit that strangles men) the downtrodden peasant Bajdała upbraids his worn-out horse and ox for not waking him up when Dusiołek tried to strangle him in his sleep, and then he also upbraids God for creating Dusiołek. This popular ballad exemplifies L.'s talent for describing fantastic yet believable creatures, as well as his poetic habit of talking back to God in a gently humorous fashion.

In *Łąka*, side by side with a cycle of erotic poems, there appears a cycle entitled "Pieśni kalekujące" (lame songs; the word *lame* translates a neologism) describing a hunchback, a man without legs who lusts after a pretty girl, and a mad cobbler. From these poems of compassion there is but a step to the death poems in *Napój cienisty* (1936; shadowy potion), which express the intuition that nothingness, rather than God, awaits man after death.

L.'s creative use of the dialects of Polish surpasses that of any poet that preceded him. He also created scores of neologisms that fit the individual poems so well that they can hardly be used in another context. L.'s verbal inventiveness contrasts sharply with his rigidly traditional versification. His sensitivity to language manifested itself also in the change of his own Germanic-sounding name Lesman to the very Polish-sounding Leśmian.

L.'s literary criticism consists mostly of book reviews published in literary magazines between 1910 and 1937, which were collected in *Szkice literackie* (1959; literary sketches). These short essays rank among the best works of criticism of his generation.

L. has never enjoyed the popularity of a poet whose verse expresses a world view or a message that is easy to identify and accept. His total output is small: three volumes of poetry published in his lifetime, and one published posthumously. His poems are short and generally unconnected with one another, and his poetic world resembles the atmosphere of Rimbaud's "The Drunken Boat," of Velemir Khlebnikov's (q.v.) futurist (q.v.) verse, and of Boris Pasternak's (q.v.) early volume *Sister My Life*. He is an original creator of the "artificial paradises" invoked in the preceding generation by Rimbaud. He is also one of Poland's most "Polish" poets, in the sense that the values of his poetry are locked in the Polish language and so far they have remained, for the most part, out of the reach of translators.

FURTHER WORKS: *Sad rozstajny* (1912); *Klechdy sezamowe* (1913); *Przygody Sindbada Żeglarza* (1913); *Dziejba leśna* (1938); *Wybór poezyj* (1946); *Wiersze wybrane* (1955); *Klechdy polskie* (1956); *Poezje zebrane* (1957); *Utwory rozproszone; Listy* (1962); *Poezje* (1965)

BIBLIOGRAPHY: Pankowski, M., "La révolte de B. L. contre les limites: À propos de son premier receuil *Sad rozstajny*," *AIPHOS*, 15 (1960), 289–318; Pankowski, M., *L.: La révolte d'un poète contre les limites* (1967); Miłosz, C., *The History of Polish Literature* (1969), pp. 347–51; Heller, R. S., *B. L.: The Poet and His Poetry* (1976)

EWA THOMPSON

LESOTHO LITERATURE

Lesotho (formerly Basutoland) is a mountainous independent state surrounded by South Africa. The dominant language is South Sotho. The country is remarkable for its long tradition of printed vernacular literature, uncommon in Africa, where vernaculars are usually associated with oral poetry and storytelling.

Such writing was originally encouraged by missionaries, who, as early as 1841, imported a press to print translations of the Bible (completed 1878) and religious tracts. The literary tradition begins with Azariele Sekese's (1849–1930) collection in South Sotho *Buka ea pokello ea mekhoa ea Basotho le maele le litsome* (1893; new ed., 1907; customs and proverbs of the Basuto). The most important Sotho writer is Thomas Mofolo (q.v.). His series of moralistic historical novels culminated in a genuine masterpiece, *Chaka* (written 1910, pub. 1925; *Chaka the Zulu,* 1931; new tr., 1981), which recounts the life of the great Zulu conqueror as a tragic epic. This work, widely translated, has been called by the scholar Albert S. Gérard the "first major African contribution to world literature." The publication of *Chaka* marked the beginning of modern Lesotho literature.

Another writer of this period was Mofolo's teacher, Everitt Segoete (1858–1923), who wrote a moralistic novel, *Monono ke moholi mouoane* (1910; riches are like mist, vapor). This work has the distinction of originating the most common plot in southern African writing: the trials of an innocent tribal youth encountering the dangers and temptations of Johannesburg. The South African writer Peter Abrahams's (q.v.) *Mine Boy* (1946) is a classic example of the genre, later scornfully called the "Jim goes to the city" theme. It is also the subject of the most famous modern Lesotho novel, Attwell Sidwell Mopeli-Paulus's (1913–1960) *Blanket Boy's Moon* (1953).

During the 1930s most books published were obliged to feature the Christian ethics demanded by the missionaries, but the 1950s brought a new spate of original Lesotho writing.

The past success of vernacular publication and its established readership caused most Lesotho authors to retain their own language rather than explore English. The themes continue to parallel those that commonly inspire other writers in southern Africa. Albert Nqheku's (b. 1912) novel *Tsielala* (1959; silence, please), about Sotho workers in the gold mines, is bitterly outspoken against the racist policies of South Africa. Bennett Khaketla's (b. 1913) novel *Meokho ea thabo* (1951; tears of joy) is about the inevitable clash between the values of the rural tradition and the expectations of the city life of young migrant workers. Since his theme stresses love as a mode of selecting a bride rather than the customary arranged marriage, he presents cultural conflict in sexual as well as political terms. Khaketla and Michael Mohapi (b. 1926) have written in various genres, including drama and poetry.

Kemuele Ntsane (b. 1920) wrote a series of satiric poems that, uncharacteristically for South Sotho verse, attempt rhyme forms. He also wrote four novels, including *Makumane* (1961; tidbits) and *Bao batho* (1968; these people).

Two novels by Mopeli-Paulus—*Blanket Boy's Moon* and *Turn to the Dark* (1956), both based on his own documentary account *Liretlo* (1950; ritual murder)—are the only modern works that have achieved a widespread international readership. They strongly oppose the apartheid system. Their method of creation was unusual: they were told by the author and then written down by sympathetic translators Richard Lanham and Miriam Basner, who produced the admired English versions, to which they may have contributed new material.

The first book written directly in English was *Masilo's Adventures, and Other Stories* (1968) by Benjamin Leshoai (b. 1920). The use of English was justified by the intention to use this book as a school reader, and it is still not certain whether this is the forerunner of the kind of English-language literature that is encountered elsewhere in Africa or whether the vigorous Sotho-language writing will predominate.

BIBLIOGRAPHY: Franz, G. H., "The Literature of Lesotho," *Bantu Studies*, 6 (1930), 45–80; Beuchat, P.-D., *Do the Bantus Have a Literature?* (1963); Mofolo, B., "Poets of Lesotho," *NewA*, 6, 2 (1967), 19–23; Gérard, A. S., *Four African Literatures* (1971), pp. 101–81; Jordan, A. C., *Towards an African Literature* (1973), passim; Maphike, P. R. S., "On the Essay in Southern Sotho," *Limi*, 8 (1980), 35–49; Gérard, A. S., *African Language Literatures* (1981), pp. 190–223

JOHN POVEY

LESSING, Doris

English novelist, short-story writer, and critic, b. 22 Oct. 1919, Kermanshah, Persia

L. was born in Persia, where her father worked for a bank; dissatisfied, he decided to return to England and so transported his family overland through Russia in 1925. While in England he decided to become a farmer in Southern Rhodesia (now Zimbabwe), where she was raised. She attended both public and convent schools until age thirteen, lived on the family farm thereafter, educating herself through voracious reading, and worked as a secretary in Salisbury. Married and divorced twice, she moved to London in 1949. Her one return visit to Rhodesia resulted in an excellent memoir, *Going Home* (1957).

The Grass Is Singing (1950), her first novel, focuses on settlers in Rhodesia: Mary and Dick Turner are impoverished, unhappy, and ill-adjusted to each other and to the terrain. As they sink to a level barely above that of the natives, Mary turns inward and ignores or mistreats their workers. After she taunts their houseboy, he kills her; her emotional instability, isolation, and violation of the whites' "code" of behavior all lead to the murder.

The first four volumes of L.'s five-volume *Bildungsroman, Children of Violence*—*Martha Quest* (1952), *A Proper Marriage* (1954), *A Ripple from the Storm* (1958), and *Landlocked* (1965)—trace the growth of a woman whose life parallels the events of L.'s own. Martha gradually discovers and accepts her sexuality, a more complete understanding of racial tensions and relations, the appeal of communism as a panacea, and the larger world outside Rhodesia. The apocalyptic fifth volume, *The Four-Gated City* (1969), begins with Martha a new immigrant in England and ends in the 1990s with the world annihilated. Especially vivid are the descriptions of the bleak post-World War II years and the powerful, pessimistic closing chapters, in which mankind is described as rushing madly to chaos.

The sequence was interrupted by L.'s masterpiece, one of the most important works of fiction in modern literature. *The Golden Notebook* (1962) is a structurally complex work, again focusing on a woman somewhat similar to L. Anna Freeman Wulf, a writer, suffers from writer's block and schizophrenically fragments her psyche into four notebooks: black (reflecting her African youth and earlier success), red (her time as a communist), yellow (a fictionalized account of an alter ego), and blue (a diary of Anna's "real" life). These are eventually supplanted by a golden notebook, suggesting a harmonious integration of the aspects of her psyche. As part of her therapy, she writes a short, formal novel, *Free Women,* which like the first four notebooks is offered piecemeal throughout *The Golden Notebook.* As L. has repeatedly stated, the meaning of *The Golden Notebook* is in the relation of the parts to each other.

Such a complex work offers endless interpretive possibilities, and some parts seem to contradict others; L. focuses less on the precise ways individual parts are understood and more on Anna's personal hell as she struggles toward mental health. L. probes unceasingly into various forms of commitment, and many readers (both male and female) have found her account of sexual, marital, racial, political, and psychological experiences profoundly influential. Only as Anna rejects experiential and psychic isolation, especially regarding language, and moves toward integration with the larger world, this time using language publicly (that is, in a novel), can she achieve wholeness.

L.'s forays into the apocalyptic continued with *Briefing for a Descent into Hell* (1971), an "inner-space fiction" especially reflecting the thought of psychoanalyst R. D. Laing (b. 1927). L.'s only major work with a male protagonist, *Briefing for a Descent into Hell* concerns Charles Watkins, a Cambridge University classics professor, who takes a symbolic psychic "journey" into possible past existences before he is restored to mental health (through shock treatment) and to mundane reality: he sees himself adrift in the Atlantic following extraterrestrial contact, shipwrecked in the ruins of a prehistoric city,

transported to a conference on Mount Olympus (where gods are "briefed" before descending to hell, that is, earth), and guerrilla fighting in World War II in Yugoslavia.

The Memoirs of a Survivor (1974) is also concerned with catastrophe, in this case in a city (presumably London) following a major war. The protagonist, an unnamed middle-aged woman, is strong, solitary, and suddenly responsible for twelve-year-old Emily. The two subsequent years show Emily maturing dramatically and the protagonist realizing the extent to which civilization has deteriorated; children such as Emily are naturally more flexible than those tied to a memory of what the world had been like, and a new social system based on barter, gang structure, and existence at any cost, even eating corpses, enables the children to survive. Out of such anarchy necessarily comes a new set of rules for order, one wholly divorced from memory of what had existed prior to the war.

In *The Memoirs of a Survivor* L.'s increasing concern with nonrational, intuitive forms of knowledge (influenced by the ideas of Sufism, a mystical branch of Islam, and especially the writings of Idries Shah, b. 1924) leads to a sharp contrast to the external chaos. As the protagonist focuses on a patch of bare wall, she "sees" the vacant flat next door and envisions a series of scenes from her presumed early life, when she too was called Emily. Reconciling such a fantasy life with the external horror is achieved through a symbolic rejection of precataclysmic thinking and behavior, after which the protagonist has a "vision" of an ethereal, transcendent woman who mystically "protects" her and her friends. Her willingness to discard rational, linear thinking in favor of an intuitive, extrasensory awareness enables her to reconcile the mundane and the ideal into a sublime evolutionary stage, far beyond the rational way the world is "normally" perceived.

L. recently began a new radically different series of "space fiction" even further removed from her early realistic fiction: *Canopus in Argos: Archives. Shikasta* (1979), the least compelling because of its lack of character or dialogue, is a didactic and sometimes tedious sequence of reports, documents, and diaries in which various recognizable periods in Earth's history are depicted from an "objective," celestial perspective. L. suggests that galactic empires of good and evil compete for dominance over earth and other worlds, that the "substance-of-we-feeling" (akin to theological grace) has diminished on Earth, and that an emissary is sent to help Earth avoid the conflagration depicted in *The Four-Gated City*. Earth's "last days" are thus described in an allegorical, deterministic narrative in which man moves from catastrophe to catastrophe because he rejects such divine guidance.

The Marriages between Zones Three, Four, and Five (1980), while still allegorical, operates on a far more human, lyrical level. In *Shikasta* L. posits a series of "zones," with the lower numbers the more ethereal and spiritual. Hence a celestial dictum that the queen of Zone Three must marry the king of Zone Four suggests that a relatively peaceful, harmonious society merges with a more warlike, insensate one. The newlyweds must compromise their respective values, and their child brings their two worlds closer. But the king is again ordered to marry, this time to the even more barbaric queen of Zone Five, and the first queen is banished, left to wander ignominiously back to her kingdom and then up toward the heights of Zone Two.

The Sirian Experiments (1981), a midpoint between the didactic collection of documents of *Shikasta* and the emotional richness of *The Marriages between Zones Three, Four, and Five,* focuses on a female member of the celestial powers who is both participant in and observer of events on Earth and other planets. A kind of emotional compromise occurs as she interacts with an even more exalted superior being, thus showing how the cosmic empires' manipulation of events on earth is balanced by the "human" qualities demonstrated by these beings.

The Making of the Representative for Planet 8 (1982), the fourth in the *Canopus* series, is a short novel about the death—through freezing—of an Earth-like planet. As all forms of life on the planet slowly adjust and mutate because of the climatic changes, the Canopean masters take an active role in the inhabitants' preparation for both the planet's extinction and their escape to a more benign world; yet the overlords too are merely pawns in some larger plan for the universe, and as the planet—and all life indigenous to it—expires, we, like the overlords, are left to wonder about justice and mercy. L.'s long afterword both connects her story to the ill-fated Scott expedition to the Antarctic and expounds on nationalism and universal "pro-

cess." Lessing is as concerned with the larger cosmic picture as in the earlier novels in the sequence and as pessimistically apocalyptic in her sense of celestial, transcendent, certain doom.

Even though L.'s form and technique have undergone radical change since her first realistic novels, she continually deals with certain ideas and themes, including psychic wholeness, the importance of nonphysical phenomena, a pessimistic sense of imminent Armageddon, and solitary, driven protagonists controlled by forces and pressures that they neither fully recognize nor understand. Less positive are her sometimes wooden style, repetitious use of similar character types and incidents, her too-obvious symbolism (especially with names), her verbosity and polemicizing, and an endlessly serious, humorless stance as a Cassandra offering prophetic warnings. Yet she is remarkably able to probe into her characters' controlling impulses, to analyze the underlying causes of the malaise infecting the modern world (especially the conflict of the personal with the universal), to offer a successive series of escape routes (which have necessarily changed as she herself has changed), and finally to indict, in a most compelling way, man's incessant surge toward self-destruction.

FURTHER WORKS: *This Was the Old Chief's Country* (1951); *Five: Short Novels* (1953); *Retreat to Innocence* (1956); *The Habit of Loving* (1957); *Fourteen Poems* (1959); *Each His Own Wilderness* (1959); *In Pursuit of the English* (1961); *Play with a Tiger* (1962); *A Man and Two Women* (1963); *African Stories* (1964); *Particularly Cats* (1967); *The Story of a Non-Marrying Man, and Other Stories* (1972); *The Summer before the Dark* (1973); *A Small Personal Voice: Essays, Reviews, and Interviews* (1974); *Collected Stories* (1978)

BIBLIOGRAPHY: Brewster, D., *D. L.* (1965); Schlueter, P., *The Novels of D. L.* (1973); Thorpe, M., *D. L.* (1973); special L. issue, *ConL*, 14, 4 (1973); special L. section, *WLWE*, 12, 2 (1973), 148–206; Spilka, M., "L. and Lawrence: The Battle of the Sexes," *ConL*, 16 (1975), 218–40; Kaplan, S. J., *Feminine Consciousness in the Modern Novel* (1975), pp. 136–72; Rose, E. C., *The Tree Outside the Window: D. L.'s Children of Violence* (1976); Singleton, M. A., *The City and the Veld: The Fiction of D. L.* (1977); Ruben-stein, R., *The Novelistic Vision of D. L.* (1979); special L. issue, *MFS,* 26, 1 (1980); Seligman, D., *D. L.: An Annotated Bibliography of Criticism* (1981)

PAUL SCHLUETER

As in *The Golden Notebook,* mental breakdowns of all kinds are, in part, a response to the politics of the West, the bureaucratization, the incipient fascism, the irrational violence, and to the dehumanized, propaganda- and drug-addicted culture we live in. But for Mrs. L. in 1969, madness is not merely a debilitating affliction or an escape, or even a novelist's tool. Developing particular forms of what Western man calls "madness" may be the only way out of his afflicted culture. Can anything—any persons or organizations—Mrs. L. asks in [*The Four-Gated City*], call a halt to the inevitable destruction to come, given the growth and movement about the earth of mad machines, on the one hand, and the lack of internal human commonsensical and moral controls, on the other? Her answer is unequivocally No. Our dulled apathy to the condition of daily life and to the cries of war signals what Robert Bly has called "the deep longing for death," a suicidal rush to annihilation, as though the half-drugged of us were longing for total immolation, for the relief of the end. Mrs. L., on the contrary, envisions a struggle toward life, through the use of extraordinary sensory powers by intelligence and a moral consciousness.

Florence Howe, on *The Four-Gated City, Nation,* 11 Aug. 1969, 117

The most considerable single work by an English author in the 1960s has been done by D. L., in *The Golden Notebook* (1962). It is a carefully organized but verbose, almost clumsily written novel, and if we were to view it solely as an aesthetic experience, we might lose most of its force. The book's strength lies not in its arrangement of the several notebooks which make up its narrative and certainly not in the purely literary quality of the writing, but in the wide range of Mrs. L.'s interests, and, more specifically, in her attempt to write honestly about women. To be honest about women in the sixties is, for Mrs. L., tantamount to a severe moral commitment, indeed almost a religious function, in some ways a corollary of her political fervor in the fifties.

While the English novel has not lacked female novelists, few indeed—including Virginia Woolf—have tried to indicate what it is like to be a woman: that is, the sense of being an object or thing even in societies whose values are relatively gentle. For her portraits, Mrs. L. has adopted, indirectly, the rather unlikely form of the descent into hell, a mythical pattern characterized by her female protagonists in their relationships with men,

an excellent metaphor for dislocation and fragmentation in the sixties.

Frederick R. Karl, "D. L. in the Sixties: The New Anatomy of Melancholy," *ConL,* 13 (1972), 15

Indeed, what attracts men as well as women to D. L.'s fiction these days, we might conclude, is what attracted them to [D. H.] Lawrence's: namely, an autobiographical intensity by which images of the author's self are put on the line and exploited with an honesty so self-searching and unsparing as to anticipate most of our critical objections to those images: a prophetic arrogance, too, a projected self-importance by which such characters are taken as where we are now or where we should be heading. . . . And finally, there is an immersion through such characters in some regional manifestation of the fate of a whole civilization in decline . . . in which Anna [Wulf] and [Lawrence's Rupert] Birkin [in *Women in Love*] steep themselves each with a fatal yearning, yet which each also struggles to transcend. . . . [B]oth writers have made the same refusal to be cowed by the modern world's absurdities and incomprehensibilities; and surely both demand of readers the same active faith in their audacity and sincerity as pledges to authenticity—with the surprising result that Lawrence . . . and Lessing . . . have found audiences they have themselves helped to create who approach them with just such activated faith.

Mark Spilka, "L. and Lawrence: The Battle of the Sexes," *ConL,* 16 (1975), 221–22

The ideal of the City stands behind everything L. has written, an expression of her firm sense of purpose, put most explicitly in an important essay, "The Small Personal Voice." There she affirms a belief in "committed" literature, in which the writer considers himself/herself "an instrument of change." . . . [T]he Armageddon of technological disaster looms there as well. . . . L. believes that mankind is at a crucial point in history and that artists must paint the possible evil as well as strengthen "a vision of good which may defeat the evil"; that is, art for society's sake. L.'s criteria for art fit her own work. Not simply an artist, she is also critic and prophet, dissecting in minute detail the faults of a society "hypnotized by the idea of Armageddon" and prophesying the calamitous results of those faults. At the same time, she attempts to delineate possible solutions to the world's problems.

Mary Ann Singleton, *The City and the Veld: The Fiction of D. L.* (1977), p. 18

[The] center of L.'s fictional universe is the perceiving mind as it translates the phenomenal world through its own experience. . . . L.'s primary orientation as a writer is thus less an aesthetic than an ideological one. It is not gracefulness of style but a steadily high level of intellectual energy and the provocative framing of ideas, embodied through deeply felt characters experiencing both typical and unconventional life situations, that invigorate her fiction. Her continuing incorporation of a broad spectrum of social concerns ranging from Leftist politics to racial issues, female roles, sexuality, esoteric tradition, science fiction extrapolations, mid-life crises, the various insanities of contemporary life for which madness itself is the most expressive analogy, and a number of others, may obscure the fact that all of these are meaningful within the larger metaphysical coherence of her vision.

Roberta Rubenstein, *The Novelistic Vision of D. L.: Breaking the Forms of Consciousness* (1979), p. 245

In *Martha Quest* we see the adolescent Martha struggling with her dreams of selfhood and having them stunted by a patriarchal society that is so potent even her own mother betrays her. In *A Proper Marriage* we see the young mother Martha trying to overcome the crippling effects of the institution of motherhood, both as it affects her and her daughter. In the final three books of the series . . . we see a maturing woman still haunted by her mother—driven, in fact, to actual illness upon the prospects of a visit from her. We also witness L.'s ultimate solution to the politics of mother-daughter: eliminate the problem altogether by opening humanity's individual psyches to such an extent that no one would be able to control another person, nor would anyone want or feel the need to. . . . In her cataclysmic conclusion to the series, she dramatically predicts that the power plays and oppression characteristics of the nightmare repetition of motherhood can lead not only to alienated women but to the end of the world.

Katherine Fishburn, "The Nightmare Repetition: The Mother-Daughter Conflict in D. L.'s *Children of Violence*," in Cathy N. Davidson and E. M. Brower, eds., *The Lost Tradition: Mothers and Daughters in Literature* (1980), p. 215

The Four-Gated City is a chronicle of change: a chronicle which explores the evolution of human consciousness and its uneasy interrelation to a changing society; a study of the impact of social values on individual lives; and a revelation of the relative fragility of the individual as he confronts powerful social forces with which he ultimately must grapple if he or society is to survive. The ten fragments which make up the futuristic Appendix to the novel purport to have been written after the terrible catastrophe that has ended modern civilization as we know it. The fragments recount both the events leading up to the catastrophe and those that follow. . . . L. affirms that the survival of

modern civilization lies in the nature of human beings and in the relations that individuals make with others. . . . Shortly after the publication of *The Four-Gated City,* L. stated in an interview . . . that one of her main concerns in writing the book was "to reach the youth." . . . For L. hope lies with the seedling-children, with those rare few who, compelled by the life force, will seek a place to grow, send out roots, join with others, and finally build new islands in the sea of chaos that is the modern world. . . . For L. the ultimate question is whether the few can succeed in forming the complex structures necessary for the survival of the many. . . . The Appendix records one possibility for the future; there is still time for a different history.

Melissa G. Walker, "D. L.'s *The Four-Gated City:* Consciousness and Community—A Different History," *SoR,* 17 (1981), 117–20

LEVERTOV, Denise

American poet and essayist, b. 24 Oct. 1923, Ilford, England

L. was born and raised in a suburb of London. The daughter of a scholarly Russian Jewish father who had converted to Christianity and become an Anglican priest and of a Welsh mother, L. never went to school but was educated chiefly at home by her mother, the BBC Schools Programs, and private tutors. After her marriage to an American she emigrated to the U.S. in 1948 and later became a naturalized U.S. citizen. L. taught at a number of American colleges and universities and retired, a full professor, from Tufts University. She also served as poetry editor of *The Nation.* Long a political activist, especially against the Vietnam war, L. gave antiwar readings and helped in student demonstrations for that cause and others around the country.

L.'s poetry, from the first collection in 1946 to her most recent, shows a consistency of theme, tone, and technical control, with only moderate changes in emphasis caused by increasing maturity and concern with social injustice. Her mood is intense, ranging from tenderness to ebullience or outrage. Her subject matter is feminine without being feminist, and ranges from the smallest sensory or personal detail of domestic life to international social and military atrocities, especially those that involve children. Many of the poems concern the creative process. L.'s technique is determined by the strongly emotional impulses that generate her poems. She writes in the rhythms of speech, often excited, impulsive speech, and in open forms that often reflect physical movement; she pays great attention to precise sensory detail, and uses little metaphor, allusion, or other conspicuous rhetorical devices. She employs a significant amount of direct, emotionally charged statement, which tends to make the meanings of her poems more explicit than mysterious or multileveled. At her most successful the poem is a single swift stab of experience that implies felt ideas; at her least successful (most often in the political poems) she can be somewhat sentimental and expository.

L.'s prose analyses of her own creative process, many of them collected in *The Poet in the World* (1973), consistently explain what her poems demonstrate: a reverence for and cultivation of the initial subconscious emotional impulse and a rhythm dependent on "the cadence of the thinking-feeling process." (Although L. has often been classified with Charles Olson [q.v.] and the "Projectivist" or "Black Mountain" poets, she partly rejects that classification, saying, "I've never fully gone along with Charles Olson's idea of the use of the breath.") She also favors a "semiconscious" creation of metaphor from literal details and a use of diction and reference that achieves "a fairly constant balance between the aesthetic and humane needs" of writer and reader, that is, a style neither "elitist" nor "popular." In other words, L. believes that "a poem *is* a sonic, sensuous event and not a statement or a string of ideas." Her best poems are such events. For example, in "The Curve," from *Relearning the Alphabet* (1966), L. describes a literal walk along a railroad track, and by means of sequence, selection of detail, and rhythm makes the experience represent not only the faith-doubt, hope-surprise inherent in taking a walk, but in creating a poem or at the same time discovering even wider universal meanings.

Despite L.'s British origin, she is clearly an American poet. She shares the interest in social action and personal autobiography of her American contemporaries. In technique she favors the William Carlos Williams (q.v.) side of modernism (q.v.), rather than the T. S. Eliot (q.v.) side. What separates her most clearly from other poets who also write direct, intense poems on social and personal

themes, in open forms, is her tone of gladness. Whether disappointed, reflective, or exultant, L.'s poetry is essentially *glad*.

FURTHER WORKS: *The Double Image* (1946); *Here and Now* (1957); *Overland to the Islands* (1958); *5 Poems* (1958); *With Eyes at the Back of Our Heads* (1959); *The Jacob's Ladder* (1961); *O Taste and See* (1964); *City Psalm* (1964); *Poems Concerning the Castle* (1966); *The Sorrow Dance* (1968); *Three Poems* (1968); *A Tree Telling of Orpheus* (1968); *The Cold Spring, and Other Poems* (1968); *A Marigold from North Vietnam* (1968); *In the Night: A Story* (1968); *Embroideries* (1969); *Relearning the Alphabet* (1970); *Summer Poems 1969* (1970); *A New Year's Garland for My Students, MIT 1969–70* (1970); *To Stay Alive* (1971); *Footprints* (1972); *The Freeing of the Dust* (1975); *Life in the Forest* (1978); *Collected Earlier Poems 1940–1960* (1978); *Light Up the Cave* (1981)

BIBLIOGRAPHY: Wagner, L., *D. L.* (1967); Wilson, R. A., *A Bibliography of D. L.* (1972); Mersmann, J., "D. L.: Piercing In," *Out of the Vietnam Vortex* (1974), pp. 77–112; Carruth, H., "L.," *HudR,* 27 (1974), 475–80; Younkins, R., "D. L. and the Hasidic Tradition," *Descant,* 19 (1974), 40–48; Gitzen, J., "From Reverence to Attention: The Poetry of D. L.," *MQ,* 16 (1975), 328–41; Wagner, L., ed., *D. L.: In Her Own Province* (1979)

ALBERTA TURNER

LEVI, Carlo

Italian essayist, novelist, and journalist, b. 29 Nov. 1902, Turin; d. 4 Jan. 1975, Rome

From his earliest formative years, L. came into contact with socialist ideology, and by the time he had completed his university studies in medicine he was an active member of the incipient resistance to Mussolini in Turin. He was arrested in 1934, incarcerated, and then released but placed under house surveillance. A year later, he was rearrested and exiled in two isolated villages of southern Italy, first in Grassano and shortly thereafter in Galliano, in the province of Lucania. Although the distance from his native Turin was great, and even greater in terms of civilization and culture, it was here that the future author found his intellectual, moral, and artistic nourishment. The two years of his banishment were not spent in sterile isolation but in fruitful activity. He continued his creative work as a painter—he already had a certain reputation, having exhibited in Venice—and became the physician to the villagers, sharing their sufferings with a sympathy that grew into a genuine spiritual communion.

These experiences found their expression in 1939 in an essay, *Paura della libertà* (1946; *Of Fear and Freedom,* 1958), which constitutes an impassioned demonstration of the coercive irrationality of dictatorships and an exaltation of the freedom and dignity of the individual. Creatively, these experiences bore their best fruit during the closing days of World War II, when, hiding in a room for several months in order to avoid deportation as a Jew by the retreating Nazis, they resurfaced most vividly, were set down in a short time (December 1943–July 1944), and appeared in print under the title *Cristo si è fermato a Eboli* (1945; *Christ Stopped at Eboli,* 1947). The book became the world's window on southern Italy, brought its author international recognition, and made him one of the leaders of the committed writers of neorealism (q.v.).

In *Cristo si è fermato a Eboli* L. gives an account of his banishment on two levels. On one, he chronicles his personal vicissitudes from the day of his arrival to that of his departure. On another, he records and comments upon the happenings, routine or startling, in the life of the villages. The private and the public dimensions are skillfully interwoven throughout the book and find their fullest convergence toward the latter part, when L. feels and acts like one of the villagers, themselves victims of Fascist oppression. L. provides us, however, with much more than a book of memories. He illustrates the tyranny of the outsiders, mainly the state functionaries, and of their local Fascist allies, the middle class of landowners and professionals, over the downtrodden farmhands, laborers, and shepherds. He gives us a gallery of portraits of individuals (such as the Fascist mayor, the town crier, and the unforgettable Giulia, who had more than a dozen pregnancies with more than a dozen men), or of groups (such as children at play, the villagers witnessing the pig doctor's operations, and the oratorical tournament). He paints colorful landscapes. He describes, always compellingly—at times elaborately, at others succinctly—everyday incidents and exceptional events, celebrations and rituals. These incidents are often endowed with a symbolic and supernal aura. He probes the inner world of the villagers, revealing their rough or gentle traits, their rudimentary but wholesome and sensitive responses to the occurrences of life, their distrust of all authority, political or religious, their continued belief in superstition and their practice of magic. The most impressive features, however, do not stem from L.'s consummate skill as a portraitist or from his perceptiveness as a diagnostician of this rural society, but from his ability to engage the intellectual, moral, and social consciousness of his readers and to make them share his own sympathies and antipathies. He accomplishes this not by the seemingly documentary presentation and the factual glossing of the reality he apprehended, but by his subjective shaping and creative contrivance of it. Hence, although difficult to categorize neatly, the book is a work of conscious literary art, closer to fiction than to document.

A similarly compassionate commitment to the lot of the victims of the impersonal state pervaded L.'s subsequent work as an editor and journalist who contributed to major Italian publications, as a politician who was elected to the senate in 1963 and served until his death, as a painter whose works sought to express arcane reality, and finally as a writer of short essays, novels, and travel accounts. In his literary works, whether fictional or nonfictional, we find a purposiveness similar to that of *Cristo si è fermato a Eboli.* L.'s writing, in fact, was never an evasion but always stemmed from his urgent concern for the political, social, and moral issues in Italy and elsewhere. None of his subsequent works, however, elicited among the readers or the critics the response of *Cristo si è fermato a Eboli.*

L. was not a transcendent writer, but *Cristo si è fermato a Eboli* exercised an enduring influence, thematically as well as formally, on the development of post-World War II Italian fiction. Although the conditions that engendered his masterpiece have changed or are changing, it has not lost any of its broad appeal for its international readership.

FURTHER WORKS: *L'orologio* (1950; *The Watch,* 1951); *Le parole sono pietre: Tre giornate in Sicilia* (1955; *Words Are Stones: Impressions of Sicily,* 1958); *Il futuro ha un cuore antico* (1956); *La doppia notte dei tigli*

(1959; *The Linden Tree,* 1962); *Un volto che ci somiglia: Ritratto d'Italia* (1960); *Tutto il miele è finito* (1960); *Quaderno a cancelli* (1979)

BIBLIOGRAPHY: Rosenberg, H., "Politics as Dancing," *Tradition of the New* (1959), pp. 199–206; Pacifici, S., "The New Writers," *A Guide to Contemporary Italian Literature* (1962), pp. 114–49; Heiney, D., "Emigration Continued: L., Alvaro, and Others," *America in Modern Italian Literature* (1964), pp. 126–45; Pacifici, S., "C. L.: The Essayist as a Novelist," *The Modern Italian Novel: From Pea to Moravia* (1979), pp. 90–98; Catani, R. D., "Structure and Style as Fundamental Expression: The Works of C. L. and Their Poetic Ideology," *Italica,* 56 (1979), 213–29

EMMANUEL HATZANTONIS

LÉVI-STRAUSS, Claude

French anthropologist and sociologist, b. 28 Nov. 1908, Brussels, Belgium

L.-S. was raised in Versailles and attended the University of Paris. He studied philosophy and law but found anthropology and sociology far more appealing. A teaching position at the University of São Paulo, Brazil, enabled him to do research on Brazilian native tribes, after which he taught at the New School for Social Research in New York, where he was influenced by the linguist Roman Jakobson (b. 1896). In the early 1950s L.-S. returned to France and a teaching post at the École Pratique des Hautes Études. Currently he is professor of social anthropology at the Collège de France.

L.-S. was one of an extraordinary group of French intellectuals—which included Jean-Paul Sartre, Simone de Beauvoir (qq.v.), and Maurice Merleau-Ponty (1908–1961)—who studied in Paris during the early 1930s and shaped postwar French intellectual life. His anthropology is similar to Sir James Frazer's (1854–1941) in that he, too, seeks to extrapolate from the specific data of tribal myths universal characteristics of the human mind. As a result, L.-S. has been attacked by traditional functionalist anthropologists and lionized by interdisciplinary thinkers. For much as Marxism is applied in literary, social, economic, and political interpretation, so too L.-S.'s structural anthropology has had its impact on many disciplines, including literary study.

That structural anthropology should have an impact on literary study is not really surprising when it is noted that seeds of structuralism (q.v.) have been traced as far back as Giambattista Vico (1668–1744) and subsequently Samuel Taylor Coleridge (1772–1834) by some scholars, and it is more generally acknowledged to have germinated from the work of the Swiss linguist Ferdinand de Saussure (1857–1913). He demonstrated that words take their meaning as much from their relationships to other words in a given utterance, or what he called *parole,* as they do from any outside referents or universal rules, or what he called *langue.* This view influenced both Russian and American formalist critics, who analyzed works solely on the basis of the internal relationships in a text; L.-S. does likewise, but also insists that the structure of thought underlying the relationships is universal.

This latter point is advanced most boldly by L.-S. in *Le totémisme aujourd'hui* (1962; *Totemism,* 1963) and *La pensée sauvage* (1962; *The Savage Mind,* 1966). Just as Freud (q.v.) had argued that neurotics differ only in degree rather than kind from normal people, L.-S. argues in these books that primitive thought differs only in degree from modern. In other words, the medicine man is as effective within his world as the modern doctor is within his. This view was supported by the child psychologist Jean Piaget's (1896–1981) analogous claims about the child's perception of reality: it, too, is complete unto itself and not merely an incomplete or nascent form of adult perception. Hence, what L.-S. claimed about primitives (and Piaget about children) could also be applied to modern man—that he structures his world into a self-adjusting whole whose parts interrelate in such a way that to modify one modifies the whole.

But L.-S. has been faulted for not attempting to analyze modern, that is, historically conscious, man, and the task has fallen to others, especially poststructuralist and Marxist critics. The latter influenced L.-S.'s view that the necessities of life explain consciousness and ideology, not vice versa. As a result, inherited—or what are claimed to be intrinsic and thus privileged—interpretations of reality have been dismissed as ultimately fascist; that is, a given view of the world controls our own individual perceptions of it, such as the Judeo-Christian belief that man is "fallen." Thus, art must break out of its traditional conventions of genre and style (as much contemporary art in fact does). Or such privileged views must themselves become the subject of analysis, as in the work of Michel Foucault (b. 1926) and Jacques Derrida (b. 1930).

L.-S.'s fascination with underlying structures can be traced back to his early interest in geology, from which he learned that surface configurations could be fully understood only in terms of subsurface structures. In his autobiographical narrative about research on Brazilian tribes, *Tristes tropiques* (1955; *Tristes Tropiques,* 1964), which first gained him attention, L.-S. identified geology as his first love, with Marxism, psychoanalysis, and music as his three mistresses. All four, of course, stress the structural relationships among the given parts of a whole as the parameters by which manifest appearances should be understood.

L.-S. believes that the underlying structure of human thought itself is based on binary opposition. The seminal opposition in anthropology is between nature and culture: man is simultaneously natural (an animal) and cultural (a human being). Such an antinomy is incapable of resolution, or synthesis, and hence L.-S. rejects, especially in the final chapter of *La pensée sauvage,* the privileged position that the dialectical interpretation of history holds in the intellectual community. There can be no working out of a paradox through time. Nor, because the unconscious infrastructure of the mind orders reality for us more than our conscious mind, is man free to choose his fate. In also rejecting the traditional humanist and the existentialist (q.v.) faith in man's freedom of choice, L.-S. rejects too, at least implicitly, the traditional assumption about the autonomy of the artist.

Dismissing individuality, L.-S. argues instead for the universality of human thought across centuries and continents. This timeless and spaceless quality of the basic logic of humans, which by nature is polar, or binary, makes paradox the subject of myth, as well as of music, for both are free of the specific referential qualities that normally circumscribe other modes of discourse. Or conversely, myth and music are the most universal and easily translatable modes of discourse, hence the most representative of the human mind in its essence. The relationships among the various "bundles of relations" (as L.-S. calls the groupings within a whole) that com-

pose a musical score or a myth are what finally determine their "meaning," not the time of composition, the place of composition, or the biography of the composer.

The influence of L.-S.'s structural approach on literary study has been considerable. Traditionally, literary interpretations have been based, like history, on the diachronic unfolding of events (or signifiers in a text)—that is, changes and occurrences over a period of time. L.-S. offers his synchronic approach not as superior to, but as a complement to the diachronic approach because he wants to find and identify what is timeless and spaceless about the human mind, even if it means neglecting the particular details of a text or an author's life.

By way of demonstrating this approach in his own works, after *Le totémisme aujourd'hui* and *La pensée sauvage* L.-S. wrote a four-volume series entitled *Mythologiques,* which translates roughly as "the logic of myths." The first of these four, *Le cru et le cuit* (1964; *The Raw and the Cooked: Introduction to a Science of Mythology I,* 1969), is organized like a musical score, with "Overture," "Theme and Variation," "Sonata," etc. in place of chapters. Throughout the four volumes, as in this one, L.-S. offers a dazzling synthesis of over six hundred myths from North and South American Indian tribes, demonstrating, or rather advocating, the position that they can all be explained in terms of binary opposition and mediation—that is, an accommodation of opposites without resolution—rather than synthesis.

Despite L.-S.'s claims to the contrary, poetry and fiction can be interpreted in a similar manner, particularly when they are decidedly unique in style and/or language and thus as untranslatable into denotative and referential terms as myth or music. What structural analysis should reveal is something quite different from traditional forms of analysis, as is the case with L.-S.'s treatment of the Oedipus myth in "Les structures des mythes" ("The Structural Study of Myth," 1955), published first in English and in French as a chapter in *Anthropologie structurale* (1958; *Structural Anthropology,* 1963). Therein L.-S. rearranges diachronic elements of the plot into a synchronic score, which he interprets as a message about overvaluation and undervaluation of kinship on the one hand, and denial and acceptance of man's autochthonous origin on the other.

Another literary analysis by L.-S. (in conjunction with Jakobson) is "'Les chats' de Charles Baudelaire" (1962; "Charles Baudelaire's 'The Cats,'" 1972). If L.-S.'s reading of the Oedipus myth seems to move too far outside the text in search of universals, this essay moves too far inside its text, breaking the poem down into phonemic units about which Baudelaire could hardly have been conscious. But no matter, as far as L.-S. is concerned, for binary opposition on the linguistic model has been demonstrated even if the authors have had to murder the poem to dissect it (to paraphrase Wordsworth).

Although literary study has now moved into what is known as poststructuralism, structural analyses and analyses of structuralism continue to interest scholars. Questions about the scientific accuracy of basing studies on the model of binary opposition, and about the extent to which the social sciences can or even should contribute to a "science" of literary study testify to the vivifying influence of L.-S.'s structural anthropology on literary study.

FURTHER WORKS: *Les structures élémentaires de la parenté* (1949; *The Elementary Structures of Kinship,* 1969); *Entretiens avec C. L.-S.* (1961; *Conversations with C. L.-S.* (1969); *Mythologiques II: Du miel aux cendres* (1966; *From Honey to Ashes,* 1973); *Mythologiques III: L'origine des manières de table* (1968; *The Origin of Table Manners,* 1978); *Mythologiques IV: L'homme nu* (1971; *The Naked Man, 1981); Anthropologie Structurale II* (1973; *Structural Anthropology II,* 1976); *Myth and Meaning* (1979)

BIBLIOGRAPHY: Hayes, E. N. and Hayes, T., eds. *C. L.-S.: The Anthropologist as Hero* (1970); Leach, E., *C. L.-S.* (1970); Paz, O., *C. L.-S.* (1970); Macksey, R., and Donato, E., eds., *The Languages of Criticism and the Sciences of Man: The Structuralist Controversy* (1970); Bersani, J., "Is There a Science of Literature?" *PR,* 39 (1972), 535–53; Boon, J., *From Symbolism to Structuralism* (1972); Gardner, H., *The Quest for Mind: Piaget, L.-S., and the Structuralist Movement* (1973); Scholes, R., *Structuralism in Literature* (1973); Culler, J., *Structuralist Poetics* (1975); Cook, A., *Myth and Language* (1980)
GENE M. BERNSTEIN

LEWIS, C(live) S(taples)

English novelist, poet, and essayist, b. 29 Nov. 1898, Belfast, Northern Ireland; d. 22 Nov. 1963, Oxford

Born in Ulster, L. was schooled privately and at English schools, and, having served in World War I, was elected in 1925 to a Fellowship at Magdalen College, Oxford, where he had received three First Class degrees. During the 1940s, L. was the center of the "Inklings," an informal Oxford literary group composed of his friends, notably Charles Williams (1886–1945) and J. R. R. Tolkien (q.v.). In 1954 he was elected unanimously to the Cambridge Professorship of Medieval and Renaissance Literature, which he held until shortly before his death in 1963. His marriage at age fifty-seven to an American and her death in 1960 greatly influenced his later work.

As the autobiography of his early life, *Surprised by Joy* (1955), demonstrates, the watershed in L.'s life was his conversion to Christianity in 1929, prior to which he had maintained a dogmatic atheism and had published only two volumes of verse, *Spirits of Bondage* (1919) and *Dymer* (1926), under the name Clive Hamilton. Although the event itself was almost Pauline in its suddenness, it is clear that his thought had been changing for some time under the influence of his close study of 17th-c. poetry, of the Scottish writer George MacDonald's (1824–1905) novel *Phantastes* (which he first read as a boy), and, particularly of his conversations and arguments with his fellow dons, later to be the nucleus of the Inklings, J. R. R. Tolkien, Owen Barfield (b. 1898), Nevill Coghill (1899–1980), and H. V. D. Dyson (1896–1975).

Although L.'s postconversion work falls generally into three broad areas—religion, literary criticism, and fiction—it is underlain by the same conversative antiliberalist, antiscientific, antimodernist values. In *The Pilgrim's Regress* (1933), a thinly disguised allegory of his own conversion, his hero finds that to discover "joy" he must reject all current intellectual fads and retrace his steps until he has rediscovered right reason and the fundamental religion of his childhood; *The Problem of Pain* (1940) advances an almost fundamentalist approach to Scripture and suggests that pain may well be Satan's infecting of God's world; L.'s popular wartime radio talks made use of post-Hegelian logic effectively disguised by common-sense diction and wartime allegory to present the case for nonsectarian Christian orthodoxy based on extranatural reason and moral law; the enormously successful *Screwtape Letters* (1942) presents the same case inversely by means of the letters of an experienced older devil to his nephew busily at work among men; *Miracles* (1947) attempts to prove that reason and the moral law exist independently of the natural world. However, probably because of both growing attacks on his use of dubious logic and his marriage, his later religious works are reflective and personal rather than argumentative and logic-crammed.

L.'s literary criticism likewise opposes classical, traditional, and purely literary values to the "personal heresies" of biographical, psychological, and impressionistic criticism. L. is at his best, however, when synthesizing literary history, as in *The Allegory of Love* (1936), *English Literature in the Sixteenth Century* (1954), and *The Discarded Image* (1964), and considerably less effective when indulging in literary polemics.

L.'s fiction is principally made up of two series of novels: a science-fiction trilogy—*Out of the Silent Planet* (1938), *Perelandra* (1943), and *That Hideous Strength* (1945)—which explores L.'s notions of Earth as cut off by sin from the rest of creation and of the destructive dehumanizing impulses of science; and the hastily written *Chronicles of Narnia—The Lion, the Witch, and the Wardrobe* (1950), *Prince Caspian* (1951), *The Voyage of the Dawn Treaders* (1952), *The Silver Chair* (1953), *The Horse and His Boy* (1954), *The Magician's Nephew* (1955), and *The Last Battle* (1956)—which present basic Christian doctrine and traditional morality by means of children's fiction. L.'s last novel, however, *Till We Have Faces* (1956), shows the same kind of tranquillity that marks all his later work. A retelling of the Cupid and Psyche myth, it suggests that in the end only faith and the bearing of one another's burdens can conquer the false delusions of scientific rationalism.

L.'s religious tracts are widely quoted and admired, largely because they summarize and reinforce the basic tenets of orthodox Christian belief and morality in a time when these values have been largely abandoned. The Narnia books especially are admired for this reason. It is not unfair to say, however, that posterity will probably view his championing of orthodoxy as the least important of his roles and regard his sound literary judgments to be of enduring worth.

FURTHER WORKS: *The Personal Heresy* (1939); *Rehabilitations* (1939); *Broadcast Talks* (1942; Am., *The Case for Christianity*); *A Preface to "Paradise Lost"* (1942); *Christian Behaviour* (1943); *The Abolition of Man* (1943); *Beyond Personality* (1944); *The Great Divorce* (1946); *Arthurian Torso* (1948, with Charles Williams); *Transposition, and Other Addresses* (1949; Am., *The Weight of Glory*); *Mere Christianity* (1952); *Reflections on the Psalms* (1958); *The Four Loves* (1960); *Studies in Words* (1960); *The World's Last Night, and Other Essays* (1960; rev. and expanded ed., 1980); *A Grief Observed* (1961); *An Experiment in Criticism* (1961); *They Asked for a Paper* (1962); *Poems* (1964); *Letters to Malcolm: Chiefly on Prayer* (1964); *Screwtape Proposes a Toast* (1965); *Studies in Medieval and Renaissance Literature* (1966); *Letters of C. S. L.* (1966); *Of Other Worlds* (1966); *Christian Reflections* (1967); *Spenser's Images of Life* (1967); *Letters to an American Lady* (1969); *Narrative Poems* (1969); *Selected Literary Essays* (1969); *Undeceptions* (1971; Am., *God in the Dark*); *Fern-seed and Elephants, and Other Essays in Christianity* (1976); *The Dark Tower, and Other Stories* (1977); *The Joyful Christian: 127 Readings from C. S. L.* (1977); *They Stand Together: The Letters of C. S. L. to Arthur Greeves* (1979); *The Visionary Christian: 131 Readings from C. S. L.* (1981); *On Stories, and Other Essays on Literature* (1982)

BIBLIOGRAPHY: Green, R. L., and Hooper, W., *C. S. L.: A Biography* (1947); Kilby, C., *The Christian World of C. S. L.* (1964); Gibb, J., ed., *Light on C. S. L.* (1965); Gilbert, D., and Kilby, C., *C. S. L.: Images of His World* (1973); Carpenter, H., *The Inklings* (1978); Glover, D. E., *C. S. L.: The Art of Enchantment* (1981); Hannay, M. P., *C. S. L.* (1981)

CHARLES MOORMAN

LEWIS, Saunders

Welsh dramatist, novelist, essayist, critic, and poet (writing in Welsh and English), b. 15 Oct. 1893, Wallasey, England

The son of a minister and his wife, L. was born just over the border from Wales, was raised in Liverpool, and was graduated from the university in that city, where he also pursued graduate work and published a version of his graduate research under the title *A School of Welsh Augustans* (1924). In 1926 he became president of the newly formed Welsh Nationalist Party, which post he held until 1939. In 1936 he was dismissed from his post of lecturer in Welsh at University College, Swansea, for setting fire, with two others, to a weapons and training establishment in the Llyn peninsula. From then until 1951 he lived at Llanfarian, near Aberystwyth, and contributed to various periodicals. From 1952 to 1957 he was lecturer in Welsh at University College of South Wales and Monmouthshire.

L. has been the dominant writer in Wales during the last forty years. His writings include over five hundred brochures and articles devoted to political and social concerns; several volumes of poetry; ten books and numerous articles of literary criticism; and nearly a score of dramatic works, including translations. L. has published in both Welsh and English.

His major novel, *Monica* (1930), is a *roman à thèse* intended to prove "the idea that the value of love lies in itself." L.'s drama can be divided into three types: comedies; historical plays about contemporary Europe; and plays dealing with the Wales of today. Examples of his satirical comedy are two published in one volume: *Eisteddfod Bodran; Gan bwyll* (1952; the Bodran eisteddfod; take it easy). *'Gymerwch chi sigaret?* (1958; have a cigarette?) is about espionage in eastern Europe, and *Brad* (1958; treason) deals with the attempt by German army officers to assassinate Hitler. *Yn y trên* (1965; on the train), is an allegory about present-day Wales, while *Cymru fydd* (1967; the Wales to be) highlights varieties of political opinion in Wales.

A writer of international stature, L. is both the most important literary critic and the paramount dramatist in 20th c. Wales. His criticism is renowned for its precision and historical erudition. Both the scope of his work and the subtle originality of his mind make him a powerful spokesman for the Welsh cause and its tradition. His convictions about the Catholic faith, to which he converted in February 1932, and Welsh nationalism, of which he has been a prophet and molder, provide the dominant motifs of his writing.

FURTHER WORKS: *The Eve of St. John* (1920); *Gwaed yr uchelwyr* (1922); *Williams Pantycelyn* (1927); *Ceiriog: Yr artist yn Philistia, I* (1929); *Ieuan Glan Geirionydd* (1931); *Braslun o hanes llenyddiaeth Gymraeg hyd 1535* (1932); *Daniel Owen; Yr artist yn Philistia, II* (1936); *Buchedd Garmon* (1937); *Is There an Anglo-Welsh Literature?* (1939); *Amlyn ac Amig* (1940); *Byd a betws* (1942); *Ysgrifau dydd Mercher* (1945); *Blodeuwedd* (1948); *Siwan a cherddi eraill* (1955); *Esther: Serch yw'r doctor* (1960); *Merch Gwern Hywel* (1964); *Gramadegau'r penceirddiaid* (1967); *Problemau prifysgol* (1968). FURTHER VOLUME IN ENGLISH: *Presenting S. L.* (1973)

BIBLIOGRAPHY: Edwards, E., "S. L., the Dramatist," *Wales*, 2 (1958), 39; Davies, P., "The Poetry of S. L.," *Poetry Wales*, 1 (1969), 5; "S. L. for a Nobel Prize?" *The Times* (London), 28 Sept. 1970, 2; Thomas, H. B., "A Welsh Prophet," *London Tablet*, 27 Oct. 1973, 1012–14; Jones, A. R., and Thomas, G., eds., *Presenting S. L.* (1973)

THOMAS E. BIRD

LEWIS, Sinclair

American novelist, b. 7 Feb. 1885, Sauk Centre, Minn.; d. 10 Jan. 1951, Rome, Italy

The son of a respected small-town physician, L. was reared in a comfortable, middle-class home. Although he early demonstrated an anguished awareness of his own difference from both his family and his town, L.'s childhood and youth were not marked by overtly traumatic experiences. He earned a B.A. at Yale and spent the next several years in a roving apprenticeship as a journalist, exhibiting a propensity for the travel that was to become a lifelong habit, as well as verbal facility and cleverness in a variety of literary forms. His first novel, *Hike and the Aeroplane*, a boy's adventure tale written under the pseudonym of Tom Graham, appeared in 1912. L.'s success as an editor and as a writer of short stories for popular magazines enabled him to concentrate on the novel, which was his proper mode.

Between 1914 and 1919 L. published five novels. Although now deservedly forgotten except by serious students of L., they at once typify the popular fiction of their time and presage some of the very elements intrinsic to

L.'s later fame: flashes of satire, an eye for significant minutiae to portray character and social scene, an ear for the quirks of American speech, and the use of disguised or projected autobiographical material. Their dominant optimism and romanticism responded to the requirements of the market L. was serving, yet also genuinely represented fundamental strains of L.'s own sensibility. The best of these early novels is *The Job* (1917), a generally realistic account of the life of a working woman in an urban setting. *The Trail of the Hawk* (1917), which treats the development of aviation, and *Free Air* (1919), inspired by a cross-country automobile trip, manifest L.'s shrewd sense for timely topics.

The appearance of *Main Street* (1920) utterly transformed L.'s career and began a decade of productivity and success that has never been surpassed in American letters. *Main Street* articulated the dissatisfaction many intellectuals felt toward American life. It challenged the "happy village" myth and it excoriated jingoistic patriotism, materialism, and conformity. The town of Gopher Prairie that L. portrays in the novel is as narrow, ugly, and mean in its architecture and attitudes as the natural landscape is large and splendid. No reader, native or foreign, could possibly misunderstand the novel's message. It is announced in the preface and repeatedly reiterated in a series of episodes that demonstrate Gopher Prairie's intolerance for any kind of individualism, talent, taste, or beauty.

The novel's tension and interest derives from its ambivalence toward its characters and subject. Carol Kennicott, the heroine, is clearly the author's persona and the main instrument for his exposé of Gopher Prairie's vices. Yet in her impatience, tactlessness, and inconsistency Carol is also something of a fool. Will Kennicott, her husband, embodies many of the town's worst qualities, yet his steadiness, courage, and competence as a country doctor elicit the reader's admiration. Carol's quarrel with the town is counterpointed by her marital conflicts. Thus, the novel's issues are argued simultaneously in two arenas, social and domestic, with only superficially satisfying resolutions.

Although *Main Street* was recognized even by contemporary reviewers as a flawed novel, it assumed a presence that resisted analytical criticism. Like the novels that followed, it

displayed a driving narrative energy, quick turns of plot, a host of vivid, albeit flat, characters, and a wealth of telling detail, which comprise the essence of L.'s method at its best. The writer's voice—shrill and tedious as it often became—was a new phenomenon in American literature. That voice, conveying a peculiarly timely and provocative message, virtually overnight attracted national and international attention, transforming L. into a celebrity.

Main Street was still enjoying considerable attention and lively sales when L. published *Babbitt* (1922) two years later. L. had discovered his true métier, satirical realism, and *Babbitt* represents perhaps the surest and most controlled example of L.'s craftmanship. The scene is now the invented but typical American city of Zenith in the imagined Midwestern state of Winnemac; the novel's protagonist, a middle-class businessman, could easily have been recruited from among Carol Kennicott's adversaries in Gopher Prairie. But Babbitt too is a tantalizingly ambiguous character, at once tyrant and slave, dangerous and pathetic. *Main Street* had culminated the "revolt from the village"; *Babbitt* served as a dramatic illustration of the social theories and criticism of such figures as Thorstein Veblen (1857–1929), Randolph Bourne (1886–1918), and H. L. Mencken (q.v.).

Yet although the novel functions as a vehicle for ideas and a scathingly effective treatment of commercialism and convention—an entire society dominated by the profit motive—it also integrates the universal theme of the corruption of human dreams by the world's demands and time's passage. When Babbitt attempts his middle-age revolt against the forces he has himself created, it is far too late. Too rich, too well-fed, too experienced, and too rational to believe in heaven and hell, not talented or dedicated enough to believe in himself or his work, he can only rely on what his peers and the mass media tell him. Once he learns that they lie, he loses all capacity for faith. Perhaps Babbitt's most tragic fate is that he becomes incapable of responding to pleasure, or indeed to any powerful or authentic feeling, a condition especially ironical in a culture devoted to physical comfort and constantly in search of entertainment. This view of character, achieved in a narrative that records the world's textures, sights, and sounds in overwhelming detail, verges on mythos.

Arrowsmith (1925) is L.'s best novel of his great decade. Although much of the book satirizes various aspects of the medical establishment and again depicts the powers of hypocrisy, mediocrity, and materialism triumphant over rebels and reformers, the novel's impact derives mainly from the vibrancy of its characters and narrative conception rather than from its social revelations. Moreover, the reader is heartened by L.'s unqualified enthusiasm for science, the work's true hero. In *Arrowsmith* there is no confusion about L.'s standards or loyalties. Both the novel's literary quality and affirmative tone were recognized by the award of the Pulitzer Prize, which L. refused with considerable public ado.

The verisimilitude of *Main Street* and *Babbitt* depended upon common experience and acute observation rather than upon some special knowledge. Although *Arrowsmith* was in part inspired by L.'s family background, it also involved intensive research. From this point on in his career L. often employed the methods of the anthropologist or sociologist in writing his novels, exploring such diverse fields as hotel management, penology, and public relations.

Elmer Gantry (1927) capitalized not only upon such deliberately accumulated material but also on a volatile atmosphere in which the Scopes "Monkey Trial" and the lively presence of the evangelists Billy Sunday and Aimee Semple McPherson provided a ready context for the novel's presumably fictional characters and episodes. Inevitably, the book provoked an immediate and thunderous reaction. It is also important as a literary document, for it was the first major American novel to assault virtually the entire institution of formal religion. Yet despite the work's timeliness and the exercise of L.'s furious narrative energy and sardonic humor, *Elmer Gantry* had less impact upon the national consciousness than his previous novels. Its success was almost entirely that of scandal, not art, and such success is intrinsically transient. One of the novel's basic problems is its characterization: L. gives the reader not a single sympathetic major character.

The decade concluded with two more books: *The Man Who Knew Coolidge* (1928) and *Dodsworth* (1929). The first contains no surprises; it is one of Babbitt's speeches multiplied into 275 pages. But it does demon-

strate L.'s extraordinary skill in the mode of the humorous satirical monologue—a skill unsurpassed until Philip Roth's (q.v.) *Portnoy's Complaint*. *Dodsworth*, by contrast, contains relatively little satire or humor. Although L. treats the international theme with considerable intensity, the novel's fundamental concern is the deterioration of a marriage—an obvious projection of L.'s own experience. The novel's "villain," Fran Dodsworth, is a thinly disguised and acidulous portrayal of L.'s first wife, Grace, whom he divorced in 1927, while its most admirable female character, Edith Cortright, is a totally idealized version of the journalist Dorothy Thompson (1894–1961), whom L. married in 1928.

L.'s great decade was culminated by the award of the Nobel Prize for literature in 1930, the first to an American writer. The Nobel Prize also marked the apogee of L.'s prestige and artistic power. Whether because of his own fame, the exhaustion of his artistic resources, or fundamental changes in American society with the onset of the Depression, after 1930 L. moved from the center of attention to its periphery. Although he continued to publish novels at a regular rate for the next twenty years, only occasionally did his novels capture large audiences and excite discussion, as in *It Can't Happen Here* (1935), which portrays a fascist coup d'état in America, and *Kingsblood Royal* (1947), which deals with racial prejudice. Some of his fiction after 1930 attains substantial quality, but too much is bad, spoiled by sentimentality, self-imitation, and self-contradiction.

In retrospect, if L.'s best work of the 1920s falls short of the masterpieces of his contemporaries—for example, Dreiser's (q.v.) *An American Tragedy* and Fitzgerald's (q.v.) *The Great Gatsby*, both published in the same year as *Arrowsmith*—his total contribution to modern American fiction must nevertheless be acknowledged as considerable. His twenty-three novels present a broad spectrum of American locales and professions and comprise a gallery of national types, an American human comedy after the examples of Balzac or Dickens. Indeed, Dickens strongly influenced L., and there are many resemblances between their work. At the very height of L.'s fame as a controversial social critic and realist, James Branch Cabell (1879–1958) shrewdly pointed out that L. was basically a romanticist who invented imaginary lands and populated them with goblins. Because of his unhappy personal life and the sharp decline of his career after winning the Nobel Prize, there is a tendency to view L. as a failure. But this is neither an appropriate nor an accurate judgment. Although his work reveals conflicting impulses—negation versus affirmation, realism versus romance, reportage versus satire—this very ambivalence is also the major reason for L.'s dynamism and appeal. At the end of his life L. is said to have repeated, "I love America—but I don't like it," a remark that conveys the essence of L.'s attitude toward his material. Whatever may be charged of L.'s defects and excesses, it must also be remembered that he worked to the very maximum of his talent, not a credit all modern writers could claim, and that he changed the way Americans think of themselves.

FURTHER WORKS: *Our Mr. Wrenn* (1914); *The Innocents* (1917); *Mantrap* (1926); *Ann Vickers* (1933); *Work of Art* (1934); *Jayhawker* (1935); *Selected Short Stories* (1935); *The Prodigal Parents* (1938); *Bethel Merriday* (1940); *Gideon Planish* (1943); *Cass Timberlane* (1945); *The God-Seeker* (1949); *World So Wide* (1951); *From Main Street to Stockholm: Letters of S. L. 1919–1930* (1952); *The Man from Main Street: A S. L. Reader* (1953)

BIBLIOGRAPHY: Lewis, G. H., *With Love from Gracie* (1955); Schorer, M., *S. L.: An American Life* (1961); Grebstein, S., *S. L.* (1962); Schorer, M., ed., *S. L.: A Collection of Critical Essays* (1962); Sheean, V., *Dorothy and Red* (1963); Dooley, D. J., *The Art of S. L.* (1967); Griffin, R. J., ed., *Interpretations of "Arrowsmith"* (1968); Light, M., ed., *Studies in "Babbitt"* (1971); O'Connor, R., *S. L.* (1971); Lundquist, J., *S. L.* (1973); Light, M., *The Quixotic Vision of S. L.* (1975)

SHELDON N. GREBSTEIN

S. L. has said of himself: "He has only one illusion: that he is not a journalist and 'photographic realist' but a stylist whose chief concerns in writing are warmth and lucidity." Such illusions are not uncommon: the scientist who prides himself on his violin-playing, the statesman who would like to be known as a poet—most men would rather think of themselves as excelling in another activity than that in which they are eminent. L.'s wish need not prevent us from adopting the general view of him, namely, that though he is a "photographic realist" and also, at times, something of a novelist or creative artist, yet after all he is primarily a satirist—unless indeed he is even more interesting as a product than as a critic of American society. Surely no one else serves so well as he to illustrate the relation between literature and a practical world: in such a world he has himself lived all his life, and such a world he portrays and holds up to ridicule and obloquy.

No small part of his effectiveness is due to the amazing skill with which he reproduces his world. His knack for mimicry is unsurpassed. He is a master of that species of art to which belong glass flowers, imitation fruit, Mme. Tussaud's waxworks, and barnyard symphonies, which aims at deceiving the spectator into thinking that the work in question is not an artificial product but the real thing. Of this art Zeuxis, who painted grapes so truly that birds came and pecked at them, is the most eminent practitioner; but L.'s standard is often little short of the Zeuxine.

T. K. Whipple, *Spokesmen* (1928), p. 208

When I re-read L. I am struck by two strong and conflicting impressions. The first impression is one of annoyance. I am annoyed by the shallowness of his writing, by his lists of places seen and things done, by his attempt to capsule whole areas of emotion and render them in a single paragraph of reportorial neighbourliness, by those caricature-characterisations that Alfred Kazin called his "brilliant equivalents" of American people. And yet, for all this initial feeling of annoyance, I come back always to a feeling of sympathy for these grotesque people he created. This second impression is one that leads me to the man himself—I think it is without any intention on L.'s part or any conscious intention on mine—to this cantankerous soul who was driven by the everlasting gospel of work and whose good heart shines through his work. All these books of his reflect back on him, but since he did not consciously intend it, the result is somehow acceptable. I feel that I can agree with Thomas Wolfe when he goes on in that account of L.-McHarg in *You Can't Go Home Again:* "In spite of the brevity of their acquaintance, George had already seen clearly and unmistakably what a good and noble human being McHarg really was. He knew how much integrity and courage and honesty was contained in that tormented tenement of fury and lacerated hurts. Regardless of all that was jangled, snarled, and twisted in his life, regardless of all that had become bitter, harsh, and acrid, McHarg was obviously one of the truly good, the truly high, the truly great people of the world."

Geoffrey Moore, "S. L.: A Lost Romantic," in Carl Bode, ed., *The Young Rebel in American Literature* (1959), pp. 72–73

Perhaps there was too much, and too much in conflict, to have made self-knowledge possible. Not many men are doomed to live with such a mixture of warring qualities as he was. Consider him at any level of conduct—his domestic habits, his social behavior, his character, his thought, his art—always there is the same extraordinary contradiction. Sloppy and compulsively tidy, absurdly gregarious and lonely, quick in enthusiasms and swiftly bored, extravagant and parsimonious, a dude and a bumpkin, a wit and a bore, given to extremities of gaiety and gloom, equally possessed of a talent for the most intensive concentration and for the maddest dishevelment of energies; sweet of temper and virulent, tolerant and abruptly intolerant, generous and selfish, kind and cruel, a great patron and a small tyrant, disliking women even when he thought he most loved them, profane and a puritan, libertine and prude, plagued by self-doubt as he was eaten by arrogance; rebel and conservative, polemicist and escapist, respectful of intellect and suspicious of intellectual pursuits, loving novelty and hating experiment, pathetically trusting in "culture" and narrowly deriding "art"; cosmopolitan and chauvinist, sentimentalist and satirist, romanticist and realist, blessed—or damned—with an extraordinary verbal skill and no style; Carol Kennicott and Doc, her husband; Paul Riesling and George F. Babbitt; Harry Lewis and Dr. E. J. Lewis or Dr. Claude B. Lewis; Harry Lewis and even Fred the miller, who never left home.

One might list these conflicting qualities in opposite columns and suggest that there were two selves in S. L.; but all these qualities existed together and simultaneously in him, and in their infinite, interacting combinations there must have been not two but six or eight or ten or two hundred selves and, because they could never be one, a large hole in the center. When he peered into that, what could we expect him to see?

Mark Schorer, *S. L.: An American Life* (1961), pp. 9–10

L., however, never lost sight of the dream; we have seen that he conjured it up in novels written at every stage of his career. It provided him with the vision of the one Eden of which he could conceive; the one great objective worth striving for, in an otherwise barren world, was an enlightened and prosperous America. Though at times he viewed its prospects pessimistically, his basic outlook was not one of disillusionment, but of romantic optimism. Even in ridiculing this optimism he added a defense of it, so that when he described his own short stories as "so optimistic, so laudatory . . . so certain that large, bulky Americans are going to do something and do it quickly and help the whole world by doing it," he added to the ironic description the thought that perhaps such optimism is an authentic part of American life.

Then he confessed that he himself, though he had been labeled a satirist and a realist, was actually a romantic medievalist of the most incurable sort.

D. J. Dooley, *The Art of S. L.* (1967), p. 259

S. L. possessed the quixotic imagination, and many of his characters, who read, venture, and fancy, as he did, are inheritors of his vision. In him opposing emotions ran deep, yet surfaced quickly. Perhaps volatility goes hand-in-hand with the impulse to create a body of fiction that searches out and breaks stereotypes apart, pillories injustices, and exposes those beliefs we loosely call "myths" about the American way of living and the American character. In L., the classic struggle between illusion and reality is particularly fierce—for L.'s enemies were both the illusions he discovered in the world and the illusions his nature invented. He fought the illusions the world offered and struggled to understand the illusions his mind and emotions brought forth.

As a result, impudence, flamboyance, and audacity, at one extreme, and gloom, despair, and carelessness, at the other, characterize L.'s books. Mark Schorer and others record L.'s exuberant performances, deep angers, rantings, drunkenness, tasteless practical jokes, and contrition—the emotionalism of a distraught quixote who finds outlet in audacious gestures.

L. stubbornly adhered to a few romantic ideas, personified in his books by yearners, rebels, and builders. His central characters are the pioneer, the doctor, the scientist, the businessman, and the feminist. The appeal of his best fiction lies in the opposition between his idealistic protagonists and an array of fools, charlatans, and scoundrels—evangelists, editorialists, pseudo-artists, cultists, and boosters.

Martin Light, *The Quixotic Vision of S. L.* (1975), p. 4

LEWIS, Wyndham
English novelist, satirist, essayist, literary critic, and polemicist, b. 18 Nov. 1882, on his father's yacht off Amherst, N.S., Canada; d. 1 March 1957, London

Son of an American eccentric and English mother whose permanent separation occurred when their only offspring was eleven years old, L. settled with his mother in England, where he attended Rugby and then the Slade School of Art (1898–1901). Despite his father's urgings that L. complete his formal education, ideally at Cornell University, L. preferred what he called the "vaster alma maters of Paris, of Munich," and other European cities in which he lived for eight years prior to his return to England in 1909. During the next decade L. became a revolutionary artist, helping to establish the movement in painting known as Vorticism, a style noted for its angularity derived from machine forms that was meant to avoid what was perceived as the weaknesses in both cubism and futurism (qq.v.), kindred Continental art movements. From 1914 to 1915 L. coedited with Ezra Pound (q.v.) the review *BLAST* (facsimile eds., 2 vols., pub. 1981), in which he began his revolutionary activity in literature as well as in painting. L. saw heavy action during World War I; some of his more extreme political positions later in his life may have been influenced by his traumatic wartime experiences.

Always a writer who assumed numerous literary personae, L. found particularly congenial to his irascible temperament the role of The Enemy, originally the title of a literary review he edited and largely wrote (1927–29). His pose as The Enemy and some ill-advised writings in the early 1930s endorsing elements of fascism brought L. persecution and abuse. Fearing he would be thought disloyal, although he had repudiated much of his earlier profascist writings, L. and his wife left England for the U.S. and finally settled in Canada at the start of World War II. He resided in Toronto, in dire financial straits, for the war's duration. Upon his return to England, L. enjoyed a measure of public success as painter and writer. He wrote art reviews for *The Listener* until the slow-growing brain tumor, which eventually killed him, rendered him blind. Stoic in affliction, L. produced, "substituting dictaphone for typewriter," an impressive quantity of writing in the last years of his life.

L.'s first novel, *Tarr* (1918; rev. ed., 1928), seemed notably experimental both in form and content, based, in part, on application of vorticist thought to fiction with the end of creating through satire or at least irony externalist art—"deadness is the first condition of art: the second is absence of soul, in the human and sentimental sense," as L.'s protagonist, Frederic Tarr, announces. In contrast, the other would-be artist in the novel, the German sculptor and painter Otto Kreisler, usually considered a more fully delineated character than Tarr, is the romantic sentimentalist who succumbs empathetically to the "writhing turbulent mess" of life and love. He detaches himself sufficiently only at the end of the novel to achieve a clean, well-executed suicide. According to L., Kreisler's death is simply a "tragic game," and this approach to mortality and to characters whom L. calls "machines"—puppets, not natures—will figure prominently in L.'s later cultural theorizing and fiction.

L.'s influential work of cultural philosophy, *Time and Western Man* (1927), likewise has relevance to his subsequent narrative techniques; herein he stakes out his position opposite writers like Joyce, Proust, and Virginia Woolf (qq.v.), whose subjectivist interior monologues and stream of consciousness (q.v.), in L.'s opinion, portray the flux of time rather than overcome it, as he desires to do by transforming the temporal into the spatial. In novel writing L. looks to the "Great Without," with his method of external approach. Thus, L. departs radically from the impressionistic aesthetic that has dominated Anglo-American modernism. General critical agreement often supports Hugh Kenner's assessment of *Time and Western Man* as one of the dozen or so most important books of the 20th c.

L.'s most vitriolic satire against Bloomsbury intellectuals as monuments of triviality is found in *The Apes of God* (1930), presented in a distinctive prose style complementing the violent, mechanized existence of Europe between the wars. Many of L.'s crotchets are displayed in this novel in the catalogue of ridiculed persons, objects, and ideas, namely, the cult of the child, burgeoning feminism and homosexuality, militarism, and the pervasive interest within the best circles in the Freudian unconscious. On the surface, the novel resembles those of Aldous Huxley and Evelyn Waugh (qq.v.) at the same period, but L.'s style is his own, inspiring T. S. Eliot (q.v.) to describe L. as the "greatest prose master of style of my generation."

Generally, *The Revenge for Love* (1937) has been judged the finest and most moving of L.'s novels. Openly political in a way reminiscent of Graham Greene's (q.v.) best work, this novel achieves something unusual in L. in the emotional resonance and sympathy for the victims who fall prey to the revenge for love masterminded by the Marxists and opportunists who set the lovers up for violence and death in Spain during the civil war. The distinguished critic Fredric Jameson, in a recent provocative study of L., brilliantly summarizes what he takes to be the source of this novel's greatness, which might be extended to form the foundation of a revisionist revaluation of L.'s canon: "... it is precisely this reality isolation of the intelligentsia of power, it is precisely its blind imprisonment in its own world of words, which is at issue."

L. turned to largely self-critical novels with *The Vulgar Streak* (1941), wrongly neglected, and *Self-Condemned* (1954), based on his years of penurious self-imposed exile in Canada. *Self-Condemned* is a kind of cryptic war novel about how the violent forces of history transform an intellectually active scholar into a displaced person and misanthrope who finds within himself the violence he has opposed in the external world. L.'s rather autobiographical protagonist, René Harding, discovers the terrifying secret of History and ends his career in an academic "cemetery of shells" where "the Faculty had no idea that it was a glacial shell of a man who had come to live among them, mainly because they were themselves unfilled with anything more than a little academic stuffing."

L.'s most ambitious, even gargantuan, work, *The Human Age* (1955), consisting of the revised *The Childermass* (original version pub. 1928), *Monstre Gai,* and *Malign Fiesta,* and a fourth part, *The Trial of Man* (existing only as a synopsis and a draft of a first chapter), has been aptly described by Jameson as "theological science fiction." This truncated tetralogy's most enthusiastic advocate, Martin Seymour-Smith, confidently forecasts that *The Human Age* "will come to be recognized as the greatest single imaginative prose work in English of this century." That hyperbolic prophecy has yet to be fulfilled, but interest in and appreciation of L. have recently been renewed, more widely than before. With the increasing critical and popular validation of the seriousness of fantasy fiction, L.'s novels within the genre should finally find an appreciative audience. *The Human Age* examines the effects of rapid technological and media change upon former innocents, satirizes the welfare state, expresses cautionary fears of the spread of various cults, and, in short, offers a Swiftian gloss on the 20th c., its hell on material earth, and its possible projection into a future heaven where Paradise itself emulates the earth's decline and fall.

L.'s enormous and varied output all bear witness to the author's vigorous intelligence and profound imagination. He had an integrated vision in art and literature that also informed his aesthetic theory and his literary criticism. The precise nature of that vision is only now being clarified. Years ago, when L. was a conspicuously neglected writer, Anthony Burgess (q.v.) noted that L. is too massive a writer to be ignored by posterity. L. must be seen as one of the most prodigiously talented modernists, whose freshness and astringency may deter us from too complete absorption in so-called postmodernism. In ideology L. is admittedly often offensive, especially to the present—sexist, fascist, homophobic, and the like—but his art, as Jameson argues, uses and transcends its ideological raw materials. L. endures as a portraitist of the violence within 20th-c. people and their words, ideas, and actions, and as an augur of the apocalyptic doom of mass civilization bereft of those strong personalities whose will and common decency are necessary to prevent the apocalypse.

FURTHER WORKS: *The Art of Being Ruled* (1926); *The Lion and the Fox: The Role of the Hero in the Plays of Shakespeare* (1927); *The Wild Body: A Soldier of Humour, and Other Stories* (1927); *Paleface: The Philosophy of the "Melting Pot"* (1929); *Satire and Fiction* (1930); *The Diabolical Principle and the Dithyrambic Spectator* (1931); *Hitler* (1931); *The Doom of Youth* (1932); *The Enemy of the Stars* (1932); *Filibusters in Barbary* (1932); *Snooty Baronet* (1932); *One-Way Song* (1933); *Men without Art* (1934); *Left Wings over Europe; or, How to Make a War about Nothing* (1936); *The Roaring Queen* (1936, withdrawn before publication; pub. 1973); *Count Your Dead: They Are Alive! or, A New War in the Making* (1937); *Blasting and Bombardiering* (1937); *The Hitler Cult* (1939); *W. L. the Artist, from "Blast" to Burlington House* (1939); *America, I Presume* (1940); *America and Cosmic Man* (1948); *Rude Assignment: A Narrative of My Career Up to Date* (1950); *Rotting Hill* (1951); *The Writer and the Absolute* (1952); *The Demon of Progress in the Arts* (1954); *The Red Priest* (1956); *The Letters of W. L.* (1964); *W. L.: An Anthology of His Prose* (1969); *W. L. on Art: Collected Writing 1913–1956* (1971); *Unlucky for Pringle: Unpublished and Other Stories* (1973)

BIBLIOGRAPHY: Kenner, H., *W. L.* (1954); Tomlin, E. W. F., *W. L.* (1955); Wagner, G., *W. L.: A Portrait of the Artist as the Enemy* (1957); Holloway, J., "W. L.: The Massacre and the Innocents," *The Charted Mirror* (1960), pp. 118–36; Pritchard, W. H., *W. L.* (1968); special L. triple issue, *Agenda,* 7, 3/ 8, 1 (1969–70); Chapman, R. T., *W. L.: Fiction and Satires* (1973); Materer, T., *W. L. the Novelist* (1976); Russell, J., *Style in Modern British Fiction* (1978), pp. 123–57; Henkle, R. B., "The 'Advertised Self': W. L.'s Satire," *Novel,* 13 (1979), 95–108; Jameson, F., *Fables of Aggression: W. L., the Modernist as Fascist* (1979); Meyers, J., *W. L.: A Revaluation: New Essays* (1980); Meyers, J., *The Enemy: A Biography of W. L.* (1980)

EDWARD T. JONES

W. L. has been seen in these pages as a contemporary neoclassicist, and it is seriously to be doubted that this neoclassical approach is positive, especially if we find it in L. Unwittingly, perhaps, he puts the case against himself: "the romantic traditional outlook . . . results in most men living in an historic past." We are too "historical," he argues; even when we satirize ourselves, we do not satirize what we are, only what we have been. We tend to laugh at the foibles of our past, and so fail to progress. Only the laugher, therefore, lives for only he, the true "person" of L.'s political ideal, sees all satirically, externally, nonromantically, in a perpetual present. Only this man is fully conscious.

This would be all very well, if the exigencies of the present time permitted it. But not only does L.'s critical position bind itself too closely to tradition to allow for the present at all, it also insists on continually assailing the present in a *parti pris* fashion. This insistence on particularities, on assailing our time and not all time, robs his satire of universality. Much of his work is contemporary in allusion, and some of it only contemporary. Is it just possible that L.'s loss in powers of observation may be due to the "apriorist heresy," to his approaching reality subjectively (not to say, romantically), selecting from it data to confirm his theories?

Geoffrey Wagner, *W. L.: A Portrait of the Artist as the Enemy* (1957), pp. 310–11

. . . Most important of all in his life's whole work is his insight into the case of twentieth century man; his unique vision of the watershed, or the abyss, of the present. Most important in his fiction is his capacity to transmit and to intensify both his insight and the judgement that passes insensibly with it, through the total unifying movement of narrative. His ideas were always developing, and his work always had to be exploratory of them. He strained his powers to the uttermost or beyond. He probably wrote too much too carelessly. There are enough bad patches and loose ends, it may be said, to prevent any of his books from

being unreservedly a masterpiece. Yet there is no real doubt by now that W. L. established himself as among the great writers of the century, and among (though not equal to) Yeats, Lawrence, Eliot, and the other geniuses born in the astonishing decade of the 1880s.

John Holloway, "W. L.: The Massacre and the Innocents," *The Charted Mirror* (1960), p. 136

With *Childermass* and *Apes* [*of God*], the air thickens, along with the books, and becomes a good deal harder to breathe freely in. If, as T. S. Eliot has said of his own works, prose may deal with ideals while poetry must deal with actuality, then L.'s "poetry" of the late 1920's is, unlikely as it may at first seem, located in these two novels. Although *Childermass* takes place outside something called the Magnetic City and has been termed a philosophical fantasy, its world is still the "moronic inferno of insipidity and decay" that *Apes* renders and that contradicts whatever Utopian ideas seek to transform it. To distinguish between the critical books and the "creative" ones of these years is, of course, particularly difficult; and Eliot's distinction between prose ideals and poetic actuality must not be taken too rigidly—ideals and actuality are admirably fused in works of his own like *Four Quartets* or *The Three Voices of Poetry*. In L.'s case it is only necessary to mention the gallery of rogues and monsters through which the critical books conduct us to be reminded of how certain effects are absolutely dependent on the writer's power of satirical creation. It is perhaps somewhat harder to see how the novels, preoccupied as they are with the world as a moronic inferno, can express those rational standards and values by which the inferno is satirized and ultimately judged.

William H. Pritchard, *W. L.* (1968), p. 69

L. worked consistently hard to keep his imagination under restraint, and to transform it into polemical energy. He tried to ignore the non-cerebral elements in creativity. Perhaps he was afraid of his imagination in rather the same way as Swift (justifiably) was of his. Certainly the fierce hardness of outline that characterizes his painting and most of his prose may be seen as gaining its firmness from a need to curb and control a violent and wild passionateness of nature. Just as L. obstinately stayed "outside" the literary world, so he kept his intellect obstinately outside the animality and the emotionality of its physical residence. He laughed (brilliantly) at the intellectual implications of Lawrence and his "Dark Gods." But he did not in fact deny his own animality; rather he saw it as comic. What is unique about his writing is its comic objectivity about the existence of physicality; this is not calculated to appeal to a fashionable critic, who is after all concerned mainly to pretend to himself that, humanly he can live with himself while he produces an endless stream of shrill, derived patter. Even less will such (in Lewisian terms) automata feel impelled to examine the nature and quality of the feeling and disturbance and emotion that together made up L.'s imagination.

Martin Seymour-Smith, "W. L. as Imaginative Writer," *Agenda,* 7, 3/8, 1 (1969–70), 10

. . . If L. is judged as a traditional novelist, he may well appear to rank closer to writers such as Ford Madox Ford and E. M. Forster than to greater novelists such as James Joyce or D. H. Lawrence. I doubt that L.'s contribution to the novel will ever be appreciated if one claims, as do . . . most of L.'s defenders to date, that he is the equal of such giants as Pope, Swift, Lawrence, and Joyce.

T. S. Eliot observed that "It may be that the very variety of L.'s achievement, and the fact that so much of it just falls short of perfection, obscures his excellence in each kind." If L. is not to be dismissed as a volcanic but burnt-out genius, his achievement should be studied where it is most vital—in the novel. Once his work as a novelist is singled out from the variety of his other achievements, the unique nature of his art will emerge. L. is generally considered an impersonal and highly innovative writer. Yet his greatest novels reveal that his art is highly personal and traditional. His true esthetic is not found in his idiosyncratic theory of satire but in his relatively conventional and less well-known interpretation of Shakespearean tragedy. L.'s central problem as a novelist was to reconcile his satiric with his tragic vision of the world. . . . L.'s art moves between the poles of satire and tragedy. This dual movement, together with an exploration of both the destructive and creative nature of violence in this war-torn century, characterizes all of L.'s novels.

Timothy Materer, *W. L. the Novelist* (1976), pp. 22–23

Like many geniuses—and L. deserves this title—he was a multifarious man who assumed many roles. The disparate aspects of his character cannot readily be focused in a single convincing image, for the Enemy fought bitterly, yet was also a kindly and courtly friend. Though the words "quarrel" and "attack" have frequently appeared as leitmotifs in this book, they do not represent an entirely negative side of L.'s character. In most of the major disputes . . . he was morally and intellectually right. His attacks on friends like Pound, Joyce and Eliot, though personally offensive, contained penetrating and persuasive literary criticism. He was reckless about libel, but demanded honesty and efficiency from his publishers. His political judgment was seriously defective; but his open and defiant stance on artistic issues was stringent and salutary, and his blasts provided a refreshing change from the mealy-mouthed puffs

that usually passed for serious criticism. Though L. was ungrateful to his patrons, his attitude was often justified by their arrogant condescension. . . .

If L., who wrote 50 books and 360 essays, had not composed political tracts, but had concentrated on perfecting his major works and devoted more time to painting, his reputation would have been much greater. He was one of the most lively and stimulating forces in modern English literature, and deserves recognition not only as a painter and writer, but also as an independent, courageous artist and a "brilliant and original observer" of contemporary society.

Jeffrey Meyers, *The Enemy: A Biography of W. L.* (1980), pp. 330–31

LEZAMA LIMA, José
Cuban poet and novelist, b. 19 Dec. 1910, Havana, d. 9 Aug. 1976, Havana

L. L. studied law at the University of Havana and was active in protests against the dictatorship, but he also studied theology and history, both of which left their mark on his literary work. During the 1930s he began publishing his poetry and immediately achieved considerable success. In 1937 he started the periodical *Verbum,* which served as the organ of the Transcendentalist group of poets, of which he was the founder. Transcendentalism was largely an attempt to go beyond the *costumbrista* tradition, which tended to deal more or less superficially with regional experience. Among other journals he founded was the highly influential *Orígenes* (1944–56), the focus of another group of poets who looked to him for leadership. L. L. held various posts in the Castro government, but his main concern was always his literary work.

This intense, imposing man, living in Havana with his mother and surrounded by his disciples, prevented by asthma from traveling as he would have liked, declared that in the creative words he produces, a man returns to the world as divine essence the air vouchsafed him as breath. Always a lover of conversation, he felt that in each word was to be found "a seed germinated by the union of the stellar and the verbal." His task, as he conceived it, was to invent a poetic reinterpretation of the world. Thus, his work is often hermetic, and he is a prime representative of the so-called neo-Baroque tendency. Many influential Hispanic poets of his era were concerned with rescuing from oblivion the great Spanish poet Luis de Góngora (1561–1627), one of whose major concerns was the use of poetic language to exhaust the possibilities inherent in a subject in order to elevate it from a mundane level to a correspondence with the archetypal. For L. L., it is more a matter of exploring the latent possibilities of language itself in the process of building a meaningful new cosmos.

It is generally agreed that L. L.'s controversial novel *Paradiso* (1966; *Paradiso,* 1974) represents the culmination of his art. Having borrowed the title from Dante, he presents a world that is anything but paradisiacal, and yet, true to his principles, he attempts to elevate his otherwise generally undistinguished characters and their equally homely daily activities to a meaningful level by continually comparing them to the deeds of gods and heroes. The critic Raymond D. Souza has noted that L. L.'s imagery often moves from a square to a circle. In Jungian terms this movement represents the transition from earthly wholeness (the square) to the heavenly sort (the circle). L. L.'s desired world is always one created by poetic language.

Accused of writing pornography, L. L. replied that at its roots his work is essentially an *auto sacramental* (religious play), a dramatic accompaniment to the means of grace. The point at issue is the notorious eighth chapter of *Paradiso,* which appears to be a somewhat obscene apology for homosexuality. This chapter, however, which stands between the two natural divisions of the work and serves as a transition between them, in reality portrays man as recently emerged in the form of undifferentiated unity, able to relate only to himself until the creation of woman. In this poet's novel the reader must avoid superficial judgments, for the work constitutes a search for primordial reality in language. It is a sensorial universe, and within it the fundamental experience is that of language as a creative force.

In the field of recent Spanish American fiction, L. L., along with Guillermo Cabrera Infante (q.v.), has taken the lead in concentrating on the possibilities inherent in language itself. He is viewed not only as Cuba's premier modern poet but as an indispensable link between poetry and the novel.

FURTHER WORKS: *Tratados en La Habana* (1958); *Orbita de L. L.* (1966); *L. L.* (1968); *La expresión americana* (1969); *Posible ima-gen de J. L. L.* (1969); *La cantidad hechizada* (1970); *Esferaimagen* (1970); *Poesía completa* (1970; expanded ed., 1975); *Introducción a los vasos órficos* (1971); *Obras completas* (1975); *Cangrejos y golondrinas* (1977); *Oppiano Licario* (1977); *Cartas* (1978); *Fragmentos a su imán* (1979)

BIBLIOGRAPHY: Simón, P., ed., *Recopilación de textos sobre J. L. L.* (1970); "Focus on *Paradiso,*" special section, *Review,* No. 12 (1974), 4–51; special L. section, *RI,* 41, 92–93 (1975), 465–546; Souza, R. D., *Major Cuban Novelists* (1976), pp. 53–79; Lezama Lima, E., "J. L. L., mi hermano," *RevI,* 8 (1978), 297–304; Ulloa, J. C., ed., *J. L. L.: Textos críticos* (1979)

WILLIAM SIEMENS

LEZGIAN LITERATURE
See North Caucasian Literatures

LIBERIAN LITERATURE

Liberia was founded as a nation in the 19th c. by the U.S. Congress to provide a land for freed black slaves who wished to return to West Africa. Unfortunately, the returnees, called "Americos," became a governing class as cruelly indifferent to the problems of the indigenous Africans as any colonial administration. Years of resentment culminated in a coup d'état in 1980. Restrictive rule did little for development of a significant literature.

The Liberian writing that has been published either has been highly derivative, borrowing outdated diction and form from earlier English poetry, or has drawn on the indigenous storytelling tradition. Little of incisive contemporary value has appeared.

Typical of the earlier style is the work of Roland Tombekai Dempster (1910–1965). His poems *Echoes from a Valley* (1947) and "To Monrovia Old and New" (1958) have a declamatory rhetoric and style that derive little from their supposed occasion and locality.

One unusual earlier work, unfortunately without successors, was the novel *Love in Ebony: A West African Romance* (1932) by Varfelli Karlee (b. 1900). If not of outstanding quality, it did at least deal with the issues of the African people outside the society of the Monrovian elite.

Of those writers closely linked with the oral tradition, Bai Moore (b. 1916) is the most distinguished and the most prolific. After spending time studying in Virginia, he returned to Liberia in 1938 and began to collect folktales and poems, particularly from the Golah society into which he had been born. He translated much of this material and incorporated some of it into his English-language writing. Also drawing on the oral tradition is Wilton Sankawulo (b. 1945), whose stories of the Kpelle tribe, including "The Evil Forest" (1971)—part translations, part adaptations—have been published in *African Arts.*

The problems of a writer in Liberia are exemplified by the experience Bai Moore encountered in publishing his work. His major collection of poetry, *Ebony Dust* (1963), in which he reflects on his travels in Europe, America, and Africa, had to be produced in mimeographed form. His more topical journalistic report on a true event, *Murder in the Cassava Patch* (1968), was distributed by Moore himself, who sold two thousand copies on a street corner in Monrovia. Not until it was selected as a school text were the remaining three thousand copies sold.

Despite obstacles, writers do struggle to find an outlet for their work. Doris Henries (b. 1930) is one of the more active of recent writers. She has not yet prepared a full volume of her own work, but she has been instrumental in publishing some important anthologies of Liberian writing: *Poems of Liberia: 1836–1961* (1966) and *Liberian Folklore* (1966). It must be acknowledged that this country has not yet produced a writer of the stature of those from other West African countries. Perhaps the new political situation will encourage the development of a more vital literature.

BIBLIOGRAPHY: *Liberian Writing: Liberia as Seen by Her Own Writers as Well as by German Authors* (1970); Henries, D., *The Status of Writing in Liberia* (1972); Singler, J. V., "The Role of the State in the Development of Literature: The Liberian Government and Creative Fiction," *RAL,* 11 (1980), 511–28; Gérard, A. S., *African Language Literatures* (1981), pp. 243–46

JOHN POVEY

LIDMAN, Sara

Swedish novelist and journalist, b. 30 Dec. 1923, Missenträsk

L. grew up in the isolated rural environment of Västerbotten, an area in northern Sweden. During adolescence she suffered from tuberculosis, which in 1937 and 1938 necessitated her confinement in a sanatorium at Häällnäs. In 1949 she completed studies in English, French, and education at the University of Uppsala.

In her late twenties L. made a stunning literary debut with a regional novel, *Tjärdalen* (1953; the tar still). Set in a northern Swedish village during the 1930s, *Tjärdalen* is not only a re-creation of the writer's own childhood, through the superbly rendered dialect and sense of place, but also a tightly structured narrative about human guilt and responsibility, with frequent biblical overtones and parallels.

In *Hjortronlandet* (1955; cloudberry land) L. combined remarkable descriptions of the far-northern environment with portrayals of intensely alive, sharply differentiated characters. Again the setting is rural Västerbotten of the 1930s. L.'s focus is on the collective, the outland marsh settlers called *öare.* L.'s strong sense of empathy with these social outcasts enables her to probe, more sharply than in *Tjärdalen,* the issue of responsibility toward those whom society has labeled unfit or incompetent.

During the 1960s L.'s horizons were broadened by trips to South Africa, Rhodesia, and Vietnam. A committed observer of what she considered the exploited and oppressed peoples in these areas of conflict, she gradually abandoned fiction in favor of subjective documentary writing. With books such as *Samtal i Hanoi* (1966; conversations in Hanoi) and *Gruva* (1968; mine), she became an influential voice of the Swedish radical left and thus a molder of Scandinavian political opinion.

L. returned to fiction in the late-1970s, with a trilogy on 19th-c. crofter life: *Din tjänare hör* (1977; your servant hears), *Vredens barn* (1979; children of wrath), and *Nabots sten* (1981; Naboth's stone). Her sweeping and masterful narrative traces the roots of the welfare state, to show how a struggle for physical survival four generations ago has led to an industrial society where adverse conditions have adapted rather than disappeared. The wrath that animates her characters can be traced ultimately to their human needs and their spiritual oppression.

L. has written about the poor in spirit and material possessions, racism in South Africa, the war in Vietnam, and inequality in the Swedish welfare state. Abstract ideologies are, however, secondary to her central subject in one work after another—the human being.

FURTHER WORKS: *Job Klockmakares dotter* (1954); *Aina* (1956); *Regnspiran* (1958; *The Rain Bird,* 1962); *Bära mistel* (1960); *Jag och min son* (1961; rev. ed., 1963); *Med fem diamanter* (1964); *Vänner och u-vänner* (1969); *Marta Marta: En folksaga* (1970); *Fåglarna i Nam Dinh: Artiklar om Vietnam* (1972)

BIBLIOGRAPHY: Gustafson, A., *A History of Swedish Literature* (1961), pp. 559–61; Lundbergh, H., on *The Rain Bird, ASR,* 51, 3 (1963), 315; Borland, H. H., "S. L.'s Progress: A Critical Survey of Six Novels," *SS,* 39 (1967), 97–114; Bäckström, L., "Eyvind Johnson, Per Olof Sundman, and S. L.: An Introduction," *ConL,* 12 (1971), 242–51; Dembo, L. S., "An Interview with S. L.," *ConL,* 12 (1971), 252–57; Lagerlöf, K. E., ed., *Modern Swedish Prose in Translation* (1979), pp. 57–58

RAYMOND JARVI

LIIV, Juhan

Estonian poet, short-story and novella writer, and critic, b. 30 April 1864, Alatskivi; d. 1 Dec. 1913, Kavastu

The son of a poor peasant, L. attended a parish school and then, for only a short time, owing to ill health, a secondary school in Tartu. He subsequently became a journalist. Although he published his first poem in 1885, to earn a living he devoted his time mainly to writing prose. L. won recognition for *Kümme lugu* (1893; ten stories), which was quickly followed by the publication of novellas *Käkimäe kägu* (1893; the Käkimäe cuckoo), *Vari* (1894; the shadow), and *Nõia tütar* (1895; the sorcerer's daughter), all written in a naturalistic, in part sentimental, forceful, and musical style. As a critic he preferred the message of humanitarian ideas

and depth of feeling to a formalist "aesthetic chiseling" of the text.

A straightforward writer in both his objective fiction and his controversial criticism, occasionally a powerful realistic painter of village life, in his poetic work L. stands in the front rank of the experimental poets of northern Europe, yet his lyrical talent was little appreciated until after his death. His extant production consists of some three hundred short poems and epigrams, the best of them written during the period of his acute mental illness from 1893 until his death from tuberculosis in 1913. In 1894, depressed by persecution mania, he burned a great number of his manuscripts, including a complete collection of poems, which, according to some of his contemporaries, was a singular masterpiece. Ill and homeless, L. wandered from place to place, the drama of his life played out on moral, nationalist, mystical, and psychic planes, with him as a soothsayer of repentance, anguish, and humility.

L.'s *Luuletused* (poems), consisting of forty-five verse pieces, appeared first in 1909, then again in 1910, and, with supplementary poems, in 1919 and 1926, each time with texts edited and corrected by Gustav Suits (1883–1956) and Friedebert Tuglas (1886–1971); these editors, despite their high literary culture, introduced an Art Nouveau and impressionistic artiness foreign to L.'s style. The original versions were in many cases destroyed. After he had overcome the influence of late romanticism, L. showed great skill in developing and transforming traditional verse schemes into either dramatic or intimate yet very songlike lines with considerable range of expression, full of symbolic, sometimes mysteriously obscure meaning. L.'s diction, rich with compressed and strange imagery, defies classification because his genius, expressed in seemingly simple and yet often undefinable word-gestures, aspires to more than human significance. His verse is at once nature poetry, philosophical poetry, and civic poetry.

L.'s poems exhibited a new type of form, their "verse-sketchiness" also being a factor in his inventive, "finished-unfinished" approach. L.'s phantasms and bodings, his nonconformist, invigorating spiritual force of heart and soul played an important part in the evolution of 20th-c. Estonian poetry. His highly individual style did not produce direct followers, but indirectly he inspired almost all Estonian poets who came after him. In the Soviet Union, L. is looked upon as a "critical realist," and nearly nothing is said about his figurative as well as politically inspired messianic ideas. Prophetically, L., deploring the loss of Estonian sovereignty in the 13th c., announced the coming of a new Estonian statehood long before anybody thought it could happen.

Throughout L.'s tortured literary career, an unusually sensitive trajectory can be traced. Beginning with the brooding peasants of the work of his early period, he moved toward the emotive intensity of his years of dark derangement, creating, however, during hours of mental lucidity increasingly heavy yet intellectually provocative and ever more sonorous poems of extended clairvoyant power. Although interest in his work has grown since his death, L. still is understood only partially.

FURTHER WORKS: *Kogutud teosed* (8 vols., 1921–35); *Valitud luuletused* (1949)

BIBLIOGRAPHY: Ivask, I., "J. L.: The Somber Forest of the Past," in Kõressaar, V., and Rannit, A., eds., *Estonian Poetry and Language: Studies in Honor of Ants Oras* (1965), pp. 258–62; Jänes, H., *Geschichte der estnischen Literatur* (1965), pp. 64–70; Nirk, E., *Estonian Literature* (1970), pp. 137–40, 390; Terras, V., "J. L.: An Estonian Visionary Poet," in Leitch, V. B., ed., *The Poetry of Estonia: Essays in Comparative Analysis* (1982), pp. 29–47

ALEKSIS RANNIT

LINDEGREN, Erik

Swedish poet, b. 5 Aug. 1910, Luleå; d. 31 May 1968, Stockholm

L. was born and raised in northern Sweden. His family belonged to the small middle class of a mining town. L. studied philosophy and literature at the University of Stockholm but did not graduate, although he continued to study classics, psychology, and religion on his own. He was a literary reviewer for major newspapers and magazines, contributing editor of the leading literary journal, *Bonniers litterära magasin,* and from 1948 to 1950 editor of *Prisma,* an experimental journal of high quality but short life. He was also a member of the Swedish Academy.

L. published poetry in small local papers during his school years. His first collection, *Posthum ungdom* (1935; posthumous youth), is characterized by irony, formal elegance, and conventionality. Present already in this work, however, is what would later become a characteristic feature of L.'s mature poetry: sudden leaps of feeling into moments of ecstasy.

Before publishing his next collection, L. studied contemporary literature, especially French symbolist and surrealist (qq.v.) poetry. In 1942 he published privately a small numbered edition of *Mannen utan väg* (the man without a way), consisting of forty poems in broken sonnet form in which the only thing that remains of the original form is the number of lines. It was first acknowledged more as an admirable experiment than as a finished work of art. Over the years general opinion has changed, and the work is now recognized as sophisticated verse representing the new modernist (q.v.) direction of poetry in Sweden. With grotesque imagery describing anxiety, brutality, and pain, L. advocates stoic acceptance of life's chaotic totality.

His next work, *Sviter* (1947; suites), containing more accessible poetry, immediately inspired a great number of imitators. L.'s fascination with Hamlet (he translated the play in 1967) is reflected in the introductory poem, "Hamlets himmelsfärd" (Hamlet's ascension to heaven), where he describes a Hamlet overwhelmed by his longing for death. The poem sets the tone for many others that deal with death almost lovingly. The musical quality of L.'s poetry is evident particularly in his most anthologized poem, "Arioso" ("Arioso," 1963). *Sviter* also contains a number of prose poems in which L. takes a humorous attitude toward an absurd life. A key word in *Sviter* is "statue," used to connote lifelessness, confinement, or hollowness.

L.'s last work, *Vinteroffer* (1954; winter sacrifice), contains his most personal poetry and deals with loneliness, aging, and death. In the introductory poem, "Ikaros" (Icarus), one of his many classically inspired poems, L. describes a flight toward the limits of ecstasy, where reality is destroyed without creating new reality—a destruction of art and of the artist as well. The key word "statue" is, in *Vinteroffer,* used differently from the way it is used in *Sviter.* Here it signifies a captured movement and feeling, something lasting. Snow and winter here symbolize paralysis and death.

L.'s heritage from his paternal grandfather, a composer and music teacher, is evident from the musical quality and phraseology of L.'s poetry. L. also wrote directly for musical works, such as scenarios for several ballets. He translated Verdi's opera *Un ballo in maschera* (1950) and Mozart's *Don Giovanni* (1961), and wrote the libretto for an opera, *Aniara* (1959; Aniara), based on the work of the contemporary poet Harry Martinson (q.v.).

L. also translated a number of important modern works into Swedish, including several plays by T. S. Eliot (q.v.), fiction by William Faulkner (q.v.), modern French poetry, and Rainer Maria Rilke's (q.v.) *Duinese Elegies*.

L. is one of the most important poets of modern Swedish literature. His masterpiece, *Mannen utan väg*, is one of the leading works of the new modernist movement of the 1940s. *Sviter* is equally important for the poetry of the 1950s. And as a reviewer and translator as well as a poet, L. played a major role in Swedish letters.

FURTHER WORK: *Dikter* (1962)

BIBLIOGRAPHY: Gustafson, A., *A History of Swedish Literature* (1961), pp. 548–51; Ekner, R., "The Artist as the Eye of a Needle," *SS*, 42 (1970), 1–13; Böhm, A., "L.'s *Mannen utan väg* und die Naturwissenschaft," *Scan*, 12 (1973), 37–42; Steene, B., "E. L.: An Assessment," *BA*, 49 (1975), 29–32; Prinz-Påhlson, G., "The Canon of Literary Modernism: A Note on Abstraction in the Poetry of E. L.," *CCrit*, 1 (1979), 155–66
TORBORG LUNDELL

LINDSAY, Vachel
American poet, b. 10 Nov. 1879, Springfield, Ill.; d. 5 Dec. 1931, Springfield, Ill.

L. considered it significant that at birth his face had been covered by a "prophet's veil" (a caul), and indeed he was destined to become a preaching poet. Born into a family of Disciples of Christ, an evangelical sect, he grew up in a city permeated with memories of Lincoln. His primary interests at Hiram College (1897–1900) were oratory and art;

but his odd study habits at the Art Institute of Chicago (1900–1903) and as an intermittent apprentice of the painter Robert Henri in New York (1904–8) lengthened the period of casting about for a career. His mother, opposed to his writing poetry, created a tension that delayed his marrying until 1925, and much of his work shows the effect of an unhealthy loneliness. On walking tours through America he sought to convince listeners of the value of beauty.

His first important poem, "General William Booth Enters into Heaven," was published in *Poetry* magazine in 1913, and launched the new poetry movement more than two decades after Walt Whitman's death. Like many of his later poems, it was elaborately scored for musical instruments, and was set (in L.'s words) "to the tune that is not a tune, but a speech, a refrain used most frequently in the meetings of the [Salvation] Army on any public square to this day." He became a platform poet, declaiming his works at universities and in small towns.

L. wrote several extraordinary poems: "The Eagle That Is Forgotten" (1913), about Peter Altgeld, the reformist Democratic governor of Illinois (1893–97), who after his defeat for reelection became a symbol of martyred liberalism; "The Congo" (1914), a memorial to a Disciple missionary in Africa, which L. subtitled "A Study of the Negro Race"; "Bryan, Bryan, Bryan, Bryan" (1918), about the presidential election campaign of 1896 as seen by an adolescent; and "Abraham Lincoln Walks at Midnight" (1914), a sentimental favorite with the public. To explain his private symbolism, he made a "Map of the Universe," a drawing depicting throne mountains, fallen palaces, and so forth that, as one biographer has noted, was more a map of L.'s mind, theology, theodicy, and cosmology than of the universe. During the 1920s he became increasingly interested in Chinese hieroglyphics (i.e., pictographs), motion pictures, and Jeffersonian democracy.

The writings of H. L. Mencken and Sinclair Lewis (qq.v.), which set the tone for the last decade of L.'s life, were partly responsible for the loss of reader interest in his exuberant, open poetry. Yet L. himself was responsible for many of his problems. He could not evaluate his own work justly, with detachment, and wrote far too much; he was never clear in his own mind just what poetry should do, or what his message was; he remained defiantly ignorant of the technical devices whereby poetry can release meaning with power. He was, nevertheless, far more than a poet of the Jazz Age (a tag that he repudiated). His bardic powers, as well as his vision of the future (*The Golden Book of Springfield,* 1920), confirm Yeats's (q.v.) judgment that this was a poet.

More than half a century has elapsed since L.'s paranoia led to suicide (by drinking Lysol). Current misconceptions about his character and poetical talents may be traced back to Edgar Lee Masters's (q.v.) biography, published shortly after L.'s death, which praised the strongly rhythmical poems at the expense of practically everything else L. wrote. New studies of the final works in his canon, and of the uncompleted manuscripts that he left behind, indicate that he was testing original ideas on religion, music, and Americanism. His writings continue to resist easy categorization. Moreover, his pessimism about this country's direction in the 1920s needs to be stressed; he believed, as the critic Ann Massa has written, in our "perpetual need of Lincolns." In the 1980s such a view may not be dismissed as naïve; like many other opinions held by L., it repays closer examination.

FURTHER WORKS: *The Tramp's Excuse, and Other Poems* (1909); *Rhymes to Be Traded for Bread* (1912); *General William Booth Enters into Heaven, and Other Poems* (1913); *Adventures While Preaching the Gospel of Beauty* (1914); *The Congo, and Other Poems* (1914); *The Art of the Moving Picture* (1915); *A Handy Guide for Beggars* (1916); *The Chinese Nightingale, and Other Poems* (1917); *The Golden Whales of California, and Other Rhymes in the American Language* (1920); *Going-to-the-Sun* (1923); *Going-to-the-Stars* (1926); *The Candle in the Cabin: A Weaving Together of Script and Singing* (1926); *The Litany of Washington Street* (1929); *Every Soul Is a Circus* (1929); *Letters of V. L. to A. Joseph Armstrong* (1940)

BIBLIOGRAPHY: Masters, E. L., *V. L.: A Poet in America* (1935); Harris, M., *City of Discontent* (1952); Ruggles, E., *The West-Going Heart* (1959); Massa, A., *V. L.: Fieldworker for the American Dream* (1970); McInerny, D. Q., "V. L.: A Reappraisal," and Chénetier, M., "V. L.'s American Mythocracy and Some Unpublished Sources," in Hallwas, J. E., and Reader, D. J., eds., *The Vision of This Land: Studies of V. L., Edgar Lee Masters, and Carl Sandburg* (1976), pp. 29–54

HAROLD OREL

LINNA, Väinö

Finnish novelist, b. 20 Dec. 1920, Urjala

L. was the seventh child (of ten) of a country butcher, a man known in his home region for his trusting nature and honesty; these qualities may have led to the collapse of the family finances before the father's death in 1927. After attending public school for six years, L. did odd jobs, was briefly employed as a farmhand and lumberjack, and in 1938 set out for the textile mills of Tampere, capital of L.'s native province of Häme. There he spent his spare time in libraries, discovering, among other things, Jaroslav Hašek's (q.v.) *The Good Soldier Švejk.* Drafted in April 1940, directly after Finland's "Winter War," L. was sent to noncommissioned officers' school, and fought in the "Continuation War" with the Soviet Union until the spring of 1943, when he was posted back to Finland as an instructor.

Following the armistice of September 1944 L. returned to Tampere and continued work in the mills until 1955; however, he had long since decided to become a writer, and in 1947 his novel, *Päämäärä* (the goal) was published. The book was a thinly disguised autobiography. Although overburdened with philosophical reflections, *Päämäärä* was treated kindly by critics, one saying that L. was a diamond in the rough. *Musta rakkaus* (1948; black love), a tale of jealousy and murder set in Tampere, revealed a marked increase in L.'s ability to portray scenes he knew. In 1957 L. brought out a much shortened version of the melodramatic narrative, but has subsequently refused to allow a new printing.

The productivity of the immediate postwar years (in which L. also wrote two unpublished volumes of verse) was succeeded by a period of depression; L. embarked upon a new novel, variously called "The Messiah" or "The Lonely One," about a tubercular factory clerk, but the project was interrupted by an emotional crisis, and was never completed: L. was unwilling to let the torso appear as a "miniature novel."

L. then began a broad epic about the war

of 1941–44; the result was *Tuntematon soti-las* (1954; *The Unknown Soldier,* 1957), and L. suddenly became the most discussed author in Finland. The book follows a single platoon from the summer offensive of 1941 to the capture of Petrozavodsk on Lake Onega, then to the trench warfare in the Svir bridgehead in 1942 and 1943, and to the bloody retreat of 1944. Like Zola in *The Debacle,* L. tries to see the war from the viewpoint of the enlisted man and (much less obviously than Zola) to indicate the larger movements of history; yet the realism of his soldiers' language and behavior, his sometimes biting portraits of individual officers, and an isolated episode about the immorality of a member of the women's auxiliary corps, enraged those Finns who still were determined to regard their army in an idealized light. Shortly, however, thanks in part to Edvin Laine's film version of 1955, *Tuntematon sotilas* became not only a best seller but a national classic: its characters (who speak a variety of Finnish dialects) were familiar to the general public, and its patriotism was no longer impugned but, rather, extolled by readers who saw the novel as an encomium of the Finnish soldier's humor, independence, and unostentatious heroism. There is no question about its popular appeal. Nonetheless, the novel is in fact a complex work of art, which admits a variety of interpretations, not least on the basis of L.'s skillful interpolation of phrases from J. L. Runeberg's (1804–1877) two-part patriotic poem cycle *The Songs of Ensign Stål.* Paradoxically, L. can be taken as a representative of the very Runebergian stoicism and dutifulness he mocks, and which he has disparaged in essays and addresses; unintentionally, he has become Runeberg's substitute as a flatterer of the national ego.

L.'s other masterpiece is the trilogy *Täällä pohjantähden alla* (1959–62; here beneath the north star), the account of a family and its neighbors in a south Finnish hamlet from the 1880s until the middle 1940s. A farm laborer, Jussi Koskela, drains a bog on property belonging to the local parsonage, and comes to regard the land as his own; Jussi's son, Akseli—resentful when a new pastor, bullied by his wife, claims the fields—enters the socialist movement and becomes an officer in the Red Army during Finland's civil war of 1918. Imprisoned and almost executed during the reprisals of the victorious Whites, Akseli eventually buys the plot during the agricultural reforms of the 1920s and ac-

quires a certain prosperity while losing his interest in politics. Of his sons, two are killed in the Winter War, and a third—a main figure in *Tuntematon sotilas*—falls in the retreat of 1944. As the suite ends, Akseli's surviving son is a well-placed farmer, the proud owner of a tractor.

Again, L. has shown himself to be a traditionalist: in his choice of the family novel as his form (used by Zacharias Topelius [1818–1898] for a widely read novella cycle about Finland's history), in his old-fashioned linear narration, in his wealth of memorable characters, in his great set pieces (for example, a roofing bee, the expulsion of a tenant farmer in midwinter, the execution of Red prisoners in 1918, the kidnapping of a Socialist politician by a band of would-be fascists in the early 1930s). Tightly controlling his cast of characters and often viewing them with affectionate humor, L. resembles such masters of the 19th-c. novel as Dickens, Theodor Fontane, and Nikolay Leskov; like L.'s war novel, his trilogy has won a broad readership both because many families in contemporary Finland can see their pasts in it, and because its technique (which has been scorned by some sophisticated critics) places no apparent difficulties in the audience's way. Yet there is much more here than meets the eye: a careful structure, a dialogue filled with hidden subtleties (although he has never written a play, L. has been called a born dramatist), and a constant tension between the author's generous humanism and the ultimate pessimism of his outlook. Save for a volume of essays, *Oheisia* (1967; appended materials), L. has been silent since the trilogy's completion, observing, with characteristic honesty, that he has delivered his message and has nothing more to say.

Aided by the brilliant translations into Swedish of N.-B. Stormbom (L.'s biographer), L.'s work has entered the general literary heritage of the North; it has also attained some popularity in eastern Europe, despite L.'s undoctrinaire political and social attitudes. He is as yet too little known in the English-speaking world.

BIBLIOGRAPHY: Laitinen, K., "V. L. and Veijo Meri: Two Aspects of War," *BA,* 36 (1962), 365–67; Varpio, Y., "V. L.: A Classic in His Own Time," *BF,* 11 (1977), 192–97; Niemi, J., "V. L.: Introduction to 'The Strike,'" *BF,* 14 (1980), 139–45

GEORGE C. SCHOOLFIELD

PÄR LAGERKVIST

D. H. LAWRENCE

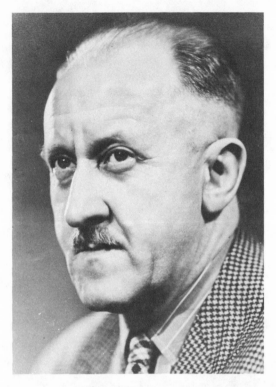

HALLDÓR LAXNESS

DORIS LESSING

CLAUDE LÉVI-STRAUSS

LINS DO RÊGO, José
See Rêgo, José Lins do

LISPECTOR, Clarice
Brazilian novelist and short-story writer, b.
10 Dec. 1925, Chechelnik, Ukraine; d. 9 Dec.
1977, Rio de Janeiro

L. was born while her family was emigrating
from Russia to Brazil. The family settled
first in Recife; in 1937 they moved to Rio de
Janeiro. A precocious child, she first began
to compose stories at the age of six in the
hope of seeing them published in the local
newspapers. L. entered law school in Rio and
took a job as editor at the Agência Nacional,
a news agency, and at the newspaper *A noite*.
While in Rio, L. came to know Lúcio Cardoso (1913–1968), Adonias Filho, (b. 1915),
and Cornélio Pena, (1896–1958), three of the
most innovative and experimental writers of
the time and artists who provided L. with the
kind of criticism and encouragement she
needed. In 1943 L. graduated from Rio's National Faculty of Law, completed her first
novel, *Perto do coração selvagem* (1944; close
to the savage heart), and married a former
classmate. L. and her diplomat husband lived
abroad for many years, including a sojourn
of eight years spent in Washington, D.C. L.
separated from her husband in 1959 and,
with the couple's two children, returned that
same year to live in Rio de Janeiro, her permanent place of residence until her death.

L. first achieved widespread acclaim with
Laços de família (1960; *Family Ties,* 1972), a
collection of introspective, enigmatic short
stories. One of her stories, "Amor"
("Love"), established her as one of the best
writers of short narrative in all of Latin
America. In it the protagonist, Anna, is
jarred out of her sense of security by an unexpected series of epiphanies and crises.
Anna then struggles vainly to balance her
newly discovered self-awareness with her former unthinking complacency, but, unable to
cope with the existential burden of her new,
unsettling consciousness, she finally retreats
into the false security of her earlier routine
existence. Another well-known story in this
collection, "O crime do professor de matemá-
tica" ("The Crime of the Mathematics Professor"), is a sparely written tale of guilt,
obsession, and expiation in which a man attempts to atone for a crime he believes he has
committed.

L.'s major breakthrough as a writer, however, came with the publication of *A maçã no
escuro* (1961; *The Apple in the Dark,* 1967).
Lengthy and complex, this novel is a painstaking study of the birth and abandonment of
a human consciousness. Profoundly symbolic
and mythic, and written in an intense, lyrical
style that recalls that of Djuna Barnes, Virginia Woolf, and Katherine Mansfield
(qq.v.), *A maçã no escuro* is really an ironic
quest novel, one in which the erratic antihero
protagonist ends up by embracing what he
initially abjured. Martim, one of the few
male central characters in L.'s work, is
traced from his first attempt at self-liberation, the commission of a crime, through his
rejection of language on the grounds that it
constitutes a specious, misleading medium of
expression, and, finally, his moving toward a
new apprehension of self, one crowned, ironically, by a contrite acceptance of failure and
a humble desire for reintegration into society. *A maçã no escuro* advances the idea that
while self-awareness is theoretically a worthy
goal, it is difficult to recognize, achieve, and
maintain. Indeed, it may even prove to be
useless or dangerous in a society that stresses
conformity in word and deed, unthinking allegiance to orthodoxy, and programmed behavior.

The themes of isolation, frustration, and
uncertainty, while paramount in this work,
are strongly present in L.'s other fiction as
well, most notably in *A paixão segundo G. H.*
(1964; the passion according to G. H.) and
Água viva (1973; sparkling water). These
novels not only place L. in the mainstream of
20th-c. Western literature but, as Gregory
Rabassa has observed, they also show her to
have much in common with such Spanish
American masters as Julio Cortázar and Gabriel García Márquez (qq.v.).

A member of the revisionist school of writers that emerged in Brazil during the years
immediately following World War II, L. was
instrumental in leading Brazilian fiction
away from the regionalism of the sociologi-
cally oriented northeastern novel of the
1930s. Primarily on the strength of L.'s efforts, Brazilian fiction began to move toward
a more psychological, intellectual, and aesthetic base, one stressing experimentation in
form and aiming thematically at revealing
the universal as it is embedded in the local or
particular. In one sense a continuation of the
"deep regionalism" already initiated by João
Guimarães Rosa (q.v.), L.'s fiction went even

further in internalizing experience, in emphasizing the connection between language and being, between one's sense of identity and one's ability to express it verbally. As such, L. is widely regarded as one of the most important and influential writers of fiction in recent Brazilian literature.

FURTHER WORKS: *O lustre* (1945); *A cidade sitiada* (1948); *Alguns contos* (1952); *A legião estrangeira* (1964); *O mistério do coelho pensante* (1967); *A mulher que matou os peixes* (1968); *Uma aprendizagem; ou, O livro dos prazeres* (1969); *Felicidade clandestina: Contos* (1971); *A imitação da rosa* (1973); *Onde estivestes de noite* (1974); *A via crucis do corpo* (1974); *A vida íntima de Laura* (1974); *De corpo inteiro* (1975); *Visão do esplendor: Impressões leves* (1975); *Para não esquecer* (1978); *Quase de verdade* (1978); *Um sopro de vida* (1978); *A hora da estrela* (1978)

BIBLIOGRAPHY: Bryan, C. D. B., on *The Apple in the Dark, NYTBR,* 3 Sept. 1967, 22–23; Moisés, M., "C. L.: Fiction and Cosmic Vision," *SSF,* 8 (1971), 268–81; Foster, D., and Foster, V., eds., *Modern Latin American Literature* (1975), Vol. II, pp. 484–91; Fitz, E. E., "C. L. and the Lyrical Novel: A Reexamination of *A maçã no escuro," LBR,* 14 (1977), 153–60; Fitz, E. E., "Freedom and Self-Realization: Feminist Characterization in the Fiction of C. L.," *MLS,* 10, 3 (1980), 51–61; Lowe, E., "The Passion according to C. L." (interview), *Review,* No. 24 (1980), 34–37; Patai, D., "C. L. and the Clamor of the Ineffable," *KRQ,* 27 (1980), 133–49

EARL E. FITZ

LITERARY CRITICISM

Both the 18th and 19th cs. have been called "the age of criticism": surely the 20th c. deserves this title with a vengeance. Not only has a veritable spate of criticism descended upon us, but criticism has achieved a new self-consciousness, a much greater public status, and has developed, in recent decades, new methods and new evaluations. Criticism, which even in the later 19th c. was of no more than local significance outside of France and England, has made itself heard in countries that before seemed on the periphery of critical thought: in Italy since Benedetto Croce (q.v.), in Russia, in Spain, and, last but not least, in the United States. Any

survey of 20th c. criticism must take account of this geographical expansion and of the simultaneous revolution of methods. We need some principles of selection among the mountains of printed matter that confront us.

Obviously even today much criticism is being written that is not new in approach: we are surrounded by survivals, leftovers, throwbacks to earlier stages in the history of criticism. Day-to-day book reviewing still mediates between the author and the general public by the well-tried methods of impressionistic description and arbitrary pronouncements of taste. Historical scholarship continues to be of great importance in evaluative criticism. There will always be a place for simple comparisons between literature and life: for the judging of current novels by standards of probability and accuracy of the social situations reflected in them. In all countries there are writers, and often good writers, who practice these methods marked out by 19th c. criticism: impressionistic appreciation, historical explanation, and realistic comparison. Let us recall the charming evocative essays of Virginia Woolf (q.v.), or the nostalgic vignettes of the American past by Van Wyck Brooks (1886–1963), or the mass of social criticism of the recent American novel, and allude to the contribution that historical scholarship has been making toward a better understanding of almost all periods and authors in literary history. But at the risk of some injustice an attempt will be made to sketch out what seem to be the new trends in 20th-c. criticism.

First of all, one is struck by the fact that there are certain international movements in criticism that have transcended the boundaries of any one nation, even though they may have originated in a single nation; that from a very wide perspective a large part of 20th-c. criticism shows a remarkable resemblance of aim and method, even where there are no direct historical or cultural relationships. At the same time, one cannot help observing how ingrained and almost insurmountable national characteristics seem to be: how within the very wide range of Western thought, with cross-currents from Russia to the Americas, from Spain to Scandinavia, the individual nations still tenaciously preserve their own traditions in criticism.

The new trends of criticism, of course, also have roots in the past, are not without antecedents, and are not absolutely original. Still, one can distinguish at least seven general trends that have originated in this century: (1) Marxist criticism; (2) psychoanalytic criticism; (3) myth criticism appealing to the findings of cultural anthropology and the speculations of Carl Jung (q.v.); (4) linguistic and stylistic criticism; (5) a new organistic formalism; (6) what amounts to a new philosophical criticism inspired by existentialism (q.v.) and kindred world views; and (7) the new structuralism (q.v.) and its many variants.

Marxist Criticism

In taste and in theory Marxist criticism has grown out of the realistic criticism of the 19th c. It appeals to a few pronouncements made by Marx and Engels, but as a systematic doctrine it cannot be found before the last decade of the 19th c. In Germany Franz Mehring (1846–1919) and in Russia Georgy Plekhanov (1856–1918) were the first practitioners of Marxist criticism, but they were very unorthodox from the point of view of later Soviet dogma. Mehring combines Marx with Kant and Darwin: he believes, for instance, in a certain autonomy of art and praises Schiller (in a biography: *Schiller,* 1905) for escaping from the sordid realities of his time. In *Lessing-Legende* (1893; Lessing legend) Mehring attacks the academic conceptions of Lessing: he emphasizes his loneliness and opposition to the age of Frederick the Great and analyzes the social conditions of the time. But the method he employs is only vaguely sociological: Mehring had not yet grasped Marxist dialectics. Similarly, Plekhanov draws on Darwin to argue for an innate sense of beauty, and in his discussion of the "art for art's sake" doctrine, in *Isskustvo i obshchestvennaya zhizn* (1912; *Art and Social Life,* 1953), condemns both aestheticism, as the ineffective revolt of the artist against bourgeois civilization, and purely propagandist art.

Marxist criticism as a coherent theory developed only after the victory of the revolution in Russia; Lenin is unsystematic even in his early papers, such as his attempt to make Tolstoy a representative Russian peasant who had not seen the significance of the proletariat. Marxist criticism crystallized into a coherent system only in the 1920s; but even then, in Russia, there were still a good many vacillations, diverse shadings, and compromises allowed. Leon Trotsky (1879–1940), who in *Literatura i revolyutsia* (1924; *Litera-*

ture and Revolution, 1925) sharply attacked formalism, still recognized that art is "a transformation of reality, in accordance with the peculiar laws of art," and Nikolay Bukharin (1888–1938) proposed (at the All-Union Congress of Soviet Writers, 1925) a compromise between Marxism and formalism that would allow formalism at least a subordinate position.

Among the strictly Marxist critics in the 1920s, several groups can be distinguished: those like Vladimir Pereverzev (1882–1968) who were mainly interested in giving a social explanation of literary phenomena in genetic terms; those who saw in Marxism largely a polemical weapon with which they judged all literature according to its immediate usefulness to the Party; and finally subtler critics, such as Alexandr Voronsky (1884–1935), who thought of art largely as "thinking in images," intuitive and unconscious, which only obliquely reflects the processes of society. But by 1932 all debate was suppressed; a uniform creed was devised and imposed and all the later history of Marxist criticism in Russia is really a history of the Party line and its sinuosities.

The term "Socialist Realism" (q.v.) applies to the loose overall theory that asks the writer, on the one hand, to reproduce reality correctly, accurately, to be a realist in the sense of depicting contemporary society with an insight into its structure; and on the other hand, to be a socialist realist, which in practice means that he is not to reproduce reality accurately, but use his art to spread socialism—that is, communism, the Party spirit, and the Party line.

Andrey Zhdanov (1892–1948) proclaimed that Soviet literature cannot be content with "reflecting" or truthfully reporting reality. It must be "instrumental in the ideological molding of the working masses in the spirit of socialism," advice that fitted Stalin's often-quoted saying that writers are "engineers of the human soul." Literature is thus frankly didactic and even idealizing, in the sense that it should show us life not as it is but as it ought to be. Good Marxist theorists understand that art operates with characters and images, actions and feelings. They focus on the concept of type as the bridge between realism and idealization. Type does not mean simply the average, the representative, but also the ideal type, the model, or simply the hero whom the reader is supposed to imitate and follow in actual life.

Georgy Malenkov, then the premier, proclaimed in a speech delivered on October 5, 1952, the "typical, to be the basic sphere of the manifestation of Party spirit in art. The problem of typicalness is always a political problem." The typical allows any and every manipulation of reality that serves the purposes of the Party: one can produce in Russia a simply cartoonlike art, almost in the manner of fairy tales, glorifying the Soviet man, or one can satirize the Russian bourgeoisie and its leftovers. Criticism is almost entirely criticism of the novel and the drama, criticism of characters and types. Authors such as Ilya Ehrenburg and Alexandr Fadeev (qq.v.), however orthodox in their ideology, are taken to task for not depicting reality correctly—for example, for not assigning sufficient weight to the Party or for not depicting certain characters favorably enough. Soviet criticism, especially since World War II, is, besides, highly nationalistic and provincial: foreign influences are minimized or ignored and "comparative literature" was long a blacklisted subject. The general level of artistic and intellectual standards in criticism is extremely low; even the insights of Marxism into social processes and economic motivation are hardly used. Criticism has become an organ of Party discipline.

Marxism spread abroad, especially in the 1920s, and found adherents and followers in most nations. In the United States, F. V. Calverton (1900–1940) and Granville Hicks (1901–1982) were early adherents. Hicks made a systematic though rather innocuous reinterpretation of the history of American literature from a Marxist point of view in *The Great Tradition* (1928), and Bernard Smith (b. 1906) wrote a history of American criticism, *Forces in American Criticism* (1939). The actual Marxist movement in American literary criticism was quite short-lived, but the influence of Marxist ideas extends far beyond the strict Party line writers. It is visible in certain stages of the development of Edmund Wilson (q.v.) and Kenneth Burke (b. 1897), for instance. Recently, more sophisticated versions of Marxism have been propounded in the U.S. Fredric Jameson's (b. 1934) *Marxism and Form* (1971) reports knowledgeably on the German Marxists, on György Lukács (q.v.), and on Jean-Paul Sartre (q.v.), and tries to find a bridge between Marxism and structuralism.

In England Christopher Caudwell (pseud. of Christopher St. John Sprigg, 1907–1937), who was killed in the Spanish Civil War, wrote the outstanding Marxist book *Illusion and Reality* (1937), which draws also on anthropology and psychoanalysis to diagnose the decay of individualistic civilization and the death of false bourgeois freedom. Marxist criticism revived after World War II. The many books by Raymond Williams (b. 1921), such as *Culture and Society 1750–1950* (1958), *The Long Revolution* (1961), and *The Country and the City* (1973), are studies that use literature as documentation for social history seen in terms of the class struggle. More recently, in *Marxism and Literature* (1977), Williams has argued for a version of Marxism that would give up its determinism, the whole assumption that literature reflects reality passively, in favor of an emphasis on human creativity and self-creation. One wonders what remains of Marxism except the hatred for capitalism.

In France the influence of Marxism has been felt even more widely even on thinkers and critics such as Sartre and Roland Barthes (q.v.), who cannot be described as orthodox Marxists. A variation of Marxist criticism was advocated by Lucien Goldmann (1913–1970), who was very close to the young Lukács. He attempted to construe "homologies" rather than prove strict causal relationships between social groups and literary attitudes. In *Le Dieu caché* (1956; *The Hidden God,* 1964) Goldmann linked Racinian tragedy and Pascal's tragic vision with the decay of the *noblesse de robe,* the nobility of lawyers and magistrates deprived of power by the absolute monarchy of Louis XIV. The tragic vision of Jansenism is considered a decisive step beyond the rationalism of Descartes and the empiricism of Hume to the critical philosophy of Kant and the dialectics of Hegel and Marx. In *Pour une sociologie du roman* (1964; *Towards a Sociology of the Novel,* 1975) Goldmann traced the "homology" between the development of 20th-c. capitalism and the novels of André Malraux (q.v.).

Several influential new versions of Marxism applied to literature emerged in the last decades. Roger Garaudy's (b. 1913) *D'un réalisme sans rivages* (1963; of a realism without shores), praised by Louis Aragon (q.v.), argued for replacing the strict requirements of Socialist Realism by a wider conception that would allow the most diverse methods of art as long as the commitment to communism is kept. A new twist to Marxist theory was given by Pierre Macherey (dates n.a.) in *Pour une théorie de la production littéraire* (1970; *A Theory of Literary Production,* 1978). Macherey rejects the neo-Hegelian assumptions of Lukács and suggests that the ideology of a work should be defined rather by its silences, gaps, and absences. The work of art is always incomplete, irregular, decentered, contradictory, and the critic's task is to uncover these inner conflicts.

In Italy, Antonio Gramsci (1891–1937), one of the founders of the Italian Communist Party who spent the last eleven years of his life in a Fascist jail, is revered as the father of Marxist criticism. He was largely a political ideologist, but in his literary studies, collected in *Letteratura e vita nazionale* (1950; literature and national life), he tried to combine a Marxist approach with many motifs derived from the aesthetics of Croce and Francesco De Sanctis (1817–1883). The strange combination of Marxism and Croceanism is his legacy to many recent Italian critics who try to preserve the main doctrines of Croce while abandoning their idealistic basis for dialectical materialism. This is true particularly of Luigi Russo (1892–1962) and the learned literary historian Natalino Sapegno (b. 1901). Quite differently did Galvano della Volpe (1895–1968) attempt to build bridges from Marxism to the most recent semantics. His influential *Critica del gusto* (1960; *Critique of Taste,* 1978), supplemented by many erudite writings on the history of criticism, argues against the whole romantic tradition of imagination and image for an ultimately highly rationalistic reading of literature as truth and "social truth."

In Germany, Marxist criticism was reformulated in the most original ways, in combinations with many other motifs of thought. Marx's early writings, published from manuscripts only in 1935, centering on the concept of alienation, attracted the most attention. The new Marxists analyzed and debated mainly Western modernist literature and rejected the Soviet dogma of Socialist Realism. Walter Benjamin (q.v.) is usually considered a Marxist, although most of his writings on literature predate his conversion to Marxism. He started with erudite works on German romantic criticism and German Baroque tragedy. *Der Ursprung des deutschen Trauerspiels* (1928; *The Origin of German Tragic Drama,* 1977) is, however, deceptively named: instead of the origins of the German tragedy, it studies rather what Benjamin calls the "play of lament" from Shakespeare to the "fate" drama of the German romantics, emphasizing German Baroque tragedy. A new genre, different from tragedy, is defined and its method, allegory, defended. Some of Benjamin's early writings are inspired by a mystical conception of language. An original language to which all languages can be reduced is implied in his essay "Die Aufgabe des Übersetzers" (1923; "The Task of the Translator," 1968). A lengthy and difficult essay, *Goethes "Wahlverwandtschaften"* (1924–25; Goethe's *Elective Affinities*) interprets the death of the heroine, Ottilie, as mythic sacrifice. It was not until 1925 that Benjamin embraced Marxism. His later work centered on the figure of Baudelaire, who becomes for Benjamin the spokesman of the progressive alienation of man in the 19th c. With him the work of art loses its "halo" (*die Aura*) and becomes a commodity, a process described in a famous essay, "Das Kunstwerk im Zeitalter seiner technischen Reproduzierbarkeit" (1936; "The Work of Art in the Age of Mechanical Reproduction," 1968). The fact that works of art can be reproduced freely and thus lose their uniqueness is welcomed as a sign of democratization but also mourned as presaging the imminent death of literature. But other essays, even of his Marxist stage, are only loosely related to his passionate commitment. The cycle of Proust's (q.v.) novels is worked into the general scheme of the decay of the halo. But Kafka (q.v.) is seen as an inventor of parables who combines the "greatest mysteriousness with the greatest simplicity." He harks back to a prehistoric world of German folklore. The famous essay "Der Erzähler: Betrachtungen zum Werk Nikolai Lesskows" (1936; "The Storyteller: Reflections on the Work of Nikolai Leskov," 1968) sketches a history of fiction in social terms, contrasting the storyteller with the novelist, the world of artisans with that of the bourgeoisie. Benjamin was one of the earliest expounders of Bertolt Brecht (q.v.) and wrote perceptively on Karl Kraus (q.v.), but one can hardly speak of a coherent Marxist aesthetic.

Theodor W. Adorno (q.v.), who revived the forgotten Benjamin, was mainly a sociologist, philosopher, and theorist of modern music. But his literary criticism—*Prismen* (1955; *Prisms,* 1967), *Noten zur Literatur* (4 vols., 1958–78; notes on literature)—and *Ästhetische Theorie* (1970; aesthetic theory) show the same synthesis of Marxism, leftist Hegelianism, Freudianism, and a modern sensibility acutely conscious of the crisis of civilization, which constitute the appeal of much of the apocalyptic writings of Marxist prophets of the doom of Western civilization. In Adorno's view, the work of art criticizes reality by the very contradiction between image and external reality.

But by far the most outstanding Marxist critic was György Lukács, not only because he had an extensive knowledge of European literatures and wrote mainly in German (although a Hungarian by birth), but because of the quality and quantity of his production. Lukács began to publish before his conversion to Marxism around 1918: a book in Hungarian on modern drama; a series of sensitive essays, *Die Seele und die Formen* (1911; *Soul and Form,* 1974), and *Die Theorie des Romans* (written 1915, pub. 1920; *The Theory of the Novel,* 1971), which construes a dialectic of literary genres very much in Hegelian terms in which category and history are intrinsically connected. Lukács conceived the novel as reflecting the rise of capitalism, away from the totality of being into social and personal fragmentation. Nostalgically, the modern novel is contrasted with the ancient epic, the totality of life that today no longer exists. The book, written in a precious style, has had, with its emphasis on modern irony and the questing hero, a wide influence and is, in many respects, Lukács's best work anchored in the German aesthetic tradition. Lukács wrote many books after his conversion to Marxism occurred, including numerous political works. Volumes such as *Goethe und seine Zeit* (1947; *Goethe and His Age,* 1969), *Essays über den Realismus* (1948; essays on realism), *Der russische Realismus in der Weltliteratur* (1949; Russian realism in world literature), *Deutsche Realisten des 19. Jahrhunderts* (1951; German realists of the 19th century), and *Der historische Roman* (1955; *The Historical Novel,* 1962) combine a thorough grasp of dialectical materialism and its sources in Hegel with a real knowledge of the main German classics, considerable argumentative skill, and frequent insights into issues that are not purely political. Lukács, in his exposition of the aesthetics of Marx and Engels, manages to approximate it closely to the main tenets of German classicism, with a strong emphasis on what he calls "the great realism." Lukács tries to reinterpret German classicism as a continuation of the Enlightenment and to trace the destruction of Reason

through the 19th c. The results often violate a much more complex reality, but few could deny the illuminative value of seeing Goethe and Schiller, Hölderlin and Heine through the eyes of a consistent Marxist who always looks for progressive elements and emphasizes their social implications.

The writings of Lukács preceding his return from Russia to Hungary in 1945 must be preferred: later he came under strong attack for lack of Marxist orthodoxy, and for a time conformed and indulged in purely "Cold War" polemics against the West, particularly in *Die Zerstörung der Vernunft* (1954; *The Destruction of Reason,* 1981), where Nietzsche and even the philosopher Wilhelm Dilthey (1833–1911) are made out to be protofascists. In 1956 Lukács was for a short time Minister of Education in the Nagy government and, after the suppression of the Hungarian revolt, was deported to Romania. But he was allowed to return after a few months, and, in retirement, wrote the largescale *Die Eigenart des Ästhetischen* (2 vols., 1963; the specific nature of the aesthetic). It combined the main theses of realism—literature as the reflection of reality—with arguments for the specificity of art, an almost Aristotelian emphasis on catharsis, and an incongruous reliance on Pavlovian behaviorist signal systems.

In the satellite countries, Marxism has been imposed as a general creed. It had its early adherents before the Communist takeover, for example, the Czech Bedřich Václavek (1897–1943), a victim of the Nazi terror, who combined the commitment to Marxism with a passionate defense of modernism condemned by Lukács and official Russian literary politics. More recently, there have been other Marxist critics; in Poland, to mention only one, Henryk Markiewicz (b. 1922), and in Yugoslavia the revered Croat novelist and poet Miroslav Krleža (q.v.); within the framework of the Marxist scheme such writers have cultivated acute and sensitive literary criticism. Marxism in criticism has become a genuinely international movement.

Psychoanalytic Criticism

Marxism is often at its best when it serves as a device to expose the latent social and ideological implications of a work of art. Psychoanalysis serves, with its very different individualistic and irrationalistic assumptions, the same general purpose: a reading of literature behind its ostensive façade; an unmasking. Freud (q.v.) himself suggested the leading motifs of psychoanalytical criticism. The artist is a neurotic who by his creative work keeps himself from a crack-up, yet also from any real cure. The poet is a daydreamer who publishes his fantasies and is thus strangely socially validated. These fantasies are to be sought in childhood experiences and complexes, and can be found symbolized in dreams, in myths and fairy tales, and even in jokes. Literature thus contains a rich storehouse of evidence for man's subconscious life, and it is no accident that Freud drew the term Oedipus complex from Sophocles' play, or interpreted *Hamlet* and *The Brothers Karamazov* as allegories of incestual love and hatred.

But in Freud the literary interest is only peripheral, and he himself always recognized that psychoanalysis does not solve the problems of art. His followers, however, have applied his methods systematically to all literature: *Imago* (1912–38) was the organ devoted to these studies, and among Freud's close followers Wilhelm Stekel (1888–1942), Otto Rank (1884–1929), Hanns Sachs (1884–1939), and others demonstrated the theories on an enormous variety of materials. Rank was interested in the interpretation of myths and fairy tales and widened the original, purely individualistic view of literature in the study of the subconscious implications in a work of art, the subconscious drives of a fictional figure, or those to be found in the biography of an author. Literary historians soon profited from psychoanalysis; for example, in 1908 Otokar Fischer (1883–1938) analyzed the dreams of the title character of Gottfried Keller's (1819–1890) *Green Henry.*

Freudian psychoanalysis spread slowly around the world. An English physician, Ernest Jones (1879–1958), who was later to write a comprehensive study of the master, was the first to give "The Oidipus Complex as an Explanation of Hamlet's Mystery" (in *The American Journal of Psychology,* 1910) and developed this thesis in *Essays in Applied Psychoanalysis* (1923) and again in *Hamlet and Oidipus* (1949). An American, Frederick Prescott (1871–1957)—whose series of articles, "Poetry and Dreams," dates back to 1912—in his study *The Poetic Mind* (1922) combined psychoanalytic insights into the nature of dreams with a highly romantic concept of the poetic process. In the United States Freudianism penetrated into strictly

literary criticism after World War I. Conrad Aiken (q.v.), in *Scepticisms* (1919), was an early practitioner, and there is now a mass of psychoanalytical criticism that is not orthodox Freudian but employs the methods of psychoanalysis only occasionally and often loosely: for instance, Kenneth Burke, or Edmund Wilson, who, in the title essay of *The Wound and the Bow* (1941) uses the Philoctetes legend as an allegory for the artist's compensation for his wound; or Joseph Wood Krutch (1893–1970) with his psychoanalytical interpretation of so obvious a subject as Edgar Allan Poe. Lionel Trilling (q.v.), although deeply interested in psychoanalysis, voiced many serious reservations about this method of interpretation.

Psychoanalytical interpretations flourish in biography, not necessarily of literary figures. Much of what has been written on historical figures seems completely unverifiable but when handled with subtlety as, for example, in Leon Edel's (b. 1907) *The Life of Henry James* (5 vols., 1953–72), it can provide insights not only into psychic conflicts but into motivation and choice of themes. Another literary critic with psychoanalytical assumptions, Frederick C. Crews (b. 1933), has written monographs on E. M. Forster (q.v.) and on Hawthorne (*The Sins of the Fathers,* 1966) but later recanted his allegiance to Freudian methods, although only partially (see *Out of My System,* 1975). A new use of psychoanalysis is being propagated by Norman N. Holland (b. 1927) in such books as *The Dynamics of Literary Response* (1968), *Poems in Persons* (1973), and *Five Readers Reading* (1975). Holland investigates with methods for which he claims scientific accuracy the response of readers, which he interprets in terms of their psychic defense mechanisms, conflicts, and associations.

Technical medical analysts have rarely made an impression in literary circles, since they are usually insensitive to texts and artistic values. An exception is Ernst Kris (1900–1957), whose *Psychoanalytic Explorations in Art* (1952) shows a subtle mind conversant both with clinical method and the aesthetics of art.

Psychoanalytical criticism is in evidence in almost all countries this side of the Iron Curtain. Charles Baudoin (1893–1963), a Swiss, in his book *Le symbole chez Verhaeren* (1924; *Psychoanalysis and Aesthetics,* 1924), was an early exponent, while in France, Charles Mauron (1899–1966) was the most widely recognized adherent of the method. His book *Des métaphores obsédantes au mythe personnel* (1963; obsessive metaphors in personal myth) bears the subtitle "Introduction à la psychocritique" (introduction to psychocriticism). But much of Mauron's psychoanalysis shades off into a study of myth. In England, Herbert Read (q.v.), in his *In Defence of Shelley* (1936), gave an analytical interpretation of the poet's behavior, somewhat defeating his avowed apologetic intentions, however, by his frank recital of abnormalities; and John Middleton Murry (1889–1957) interpreted D. H. Lawrence (q.v.) in terms of the Oedipus complex in a biography, *Son of Woman: The Story of D. H. Lawrence* (1931), in which he oddly vacillates between love and hate for his subject.

Myth Criticism

Out of Freudian analysis grew the Jungian version of the subconscious as a collective subconscious that serves as a kind of reservoir of the "archetypal patterns," the primordial images of mankind. Carl Gustav Jung himself was cautious about applying his philosophy to literature; he made many reservations even when he discussed James Joyce's (q.v.) *Ulysses* (1922) or Goethe's *Faust*. But, especially in the Anglo-Saxon world, his caution has been thrown to the winds and a whole group of critics have developed "myth criticism," that is to say, they have tried to discover behind all literature the original myths of mankind: the Divine Father, the Earth Mother, the descent into hell, the purgatorial stair, the sacrificial deaths of the gods, etc. Modern anthropology, since Sir James G. Frazer (1854–1941), author of *The Golden Bough* (1890; rev. ed. 1900), with its new expertise on primitive civilizations, their myths and rituals, from all over the world, and the findings of the so-called Cambridge school—Gilbert Murray (1866–1957), Jane Harrison (1850–1928), and others—which studied Greek religion and the sources of Greek drama in myth, have supplied arguments and materials for this view.

In England, Maud Bodkin (1875–1967), in *Archetypal Patterns in Poetry* (1934), studied *The Ancient Mariner* and *The Waste Land*, for instance, as poems of the rebirth pattern; G. Wilson Knight (b. 1897) and Herbert Read, in their varied careers, have used Jungian concepts; C. Day Lewis (q.v.) ex-

plained poetic imagery (*The Poetic Image*, 1947) in terms of the survival of mythical thinking. In the United States "myth criticism" became a great force in the 1950s; it was offered as the alternative to the New Criticism and will have to be discussed in its place.

These three trends—Marxism, psychoanalysis, myth criticism—are genuinely international ones. The resemblance between all the different movements in individual countries, which, by concentrating upon textual interpretation have reacted against 19th-c. positivism, is, however, only a general one: manifest is the preoccupation with the work of art in the modern world, its meaning and the kind of insight or knowledge it provides; and with the refinement of methods of textual analysis, whether it be focused upon details of verbal texture or upon the underlying structure of ideas. To particularize, we have to distinguish between the different national literatures and their diverse developments.

Italy

The earliest systematic reaction against the conventions of late 19th c. criticism, its antiquarianism, its emphasis on biography, its fragmentation of the work of art, comes from an unexpected quarter—Italy. There Benedetto Croce transformed Italian criticism and, with his *Tesi fondamentali di un'estetica come scienza dell'espressione e linguistica generale* (1902; *Aesthetic as Science of Expression and General Linguistic*, 1909) influenced profoundly the course of criticism almost everywhere in the world. In Germany a school of brilliant scholars in the romance literatures (especially Karl Vossler [1872–1949]) was deeply indebted to him. In England R. G. Collingwood's (1889–1943) *Principles of Art* (1934) could be described as a Crocean aesthetics, and in the United States Joel Elias Spingarn (1875–1939) proclaimed a diluted version of Croce, *The New Criticism*, in 1911.

Croce, in an early booklet, *La critica letteraria* (1894; literary criticism), had attacked the confused state of criticism and had appealed to the model of the great 19th-c. historian of Italian literature Francesco De Sanctis, who then, as a Hegelian, was in eclipse. But only with the founding of the review *La critica* in 1903 did Croce's influence on Italian criticism become decisive. Croce's position, expounded in *Estetica,* had first a negative influence on criticism: his theory of art as intuition, which completely identifies intuition with expression, radically disposed of many traditional problems. Art for Croce is not a physical fact, but purely a matter of mind; it is not pleasure; it is not morality; it is not science, nor is it philosophy. There is no special artistic genius: there is no distinction between form and content. The common view that Croce is a "formalist" or a defender of "art for art's sake" is, however, mistaken. Art does play a role in society and can even be controlled socially, although nothing can touch the artist's original act of intuition. In his practical criticism Croce pays no attention to form in the ordinary sense, but rather to what he calls the "leading sentiment." In Croce's radical monism there is no place for rhetorical categories, for style, for symbol, for genres, even for the distinctions among the arts, since every work of art is a unique, individual intuition-expression. In Croce, the creator, the work, and the auditor are identified. The true reader becomes a poet. Criticism can do little more than remove obstacles to this identification, and pronounce that the identification has been achieved, that a work is art or non-art. Croce's theory hangs together remarkably well and is not open to objections that neglect its basis in an idealistic metaphysics. If we object that Croce neglects medium, or technique, he can answer that "what is external is no longer a work of art."

In the course of his development Croce somewhat modified his position. He came to recognize the universalizing power of art, while still insisting that art does not provide any intellectual knowledge; he retracted the romantic implications of his "expressionism," which seemed to recommend emotion and passion. Rather, he endorsed "classicity," which must not be confused with rhetorical classicism. He also redefined the role of criticism in more intellectual terms: it becomes identified with aesthetics and philosophy. The aim of criticism is the characterization of an individual author, its form is the essay. There is no literary history (except external annals and compendia), since every poet is *sui generis.* Sociological and nationalistic histories of literature as well as the idea of stylistic evolution are dismissed as external.

Croce produced a stream of essays in which he tries to define the true sentiment of each writer discussed and to judge him by his, Croce's, intuitive standard. In his short work *Goethe* (1919; *Goethe,* 1923) he completely divorces man and work from each other. Problems of philosophical truth, biographical correspondence, and intentions are dismissed. Croce can make a selection from Goethe's works and can discuss *Faust* as an album in which Goethe entered his feelings at different times of his life. There is no unity to the two parts. But this is not destructive criticism; rather, Croce argues, it removes an artificially imposed mechanism.

Similarly, in his *La poesia di Dante* (1920; *The Poetry of Dante,* 1922), Croce draws a sharp distinction between the "theological-political romance" and the structure as an abstract scheme, and the poetry that grows around and in it. In a later work, *La poesia* (2 vols., 1935–36; *Poetry and Literature,* 1981), he elaborates with great clarity his distinction between "poetry" and "literature": while "literature" is writing in its civilizing function, involved in society, "poetry" remains unique, immediately accessible intuition-expression. In many other books of essays Croce judges Italian and foreign poets severely. In *Poesia e non poesia* (1923; *European Literature in the Nineteenth Century,* 1924), for instance, Schiller is labeled a philosophical rhetorician, not a poet. Kleist was merely striving by will power to become a poet; but he did not succeed. Walter Scott is only a hero in a history of commerce. Croce's method is particularly well exemplified in *Ariosto, Shakespeare e Corneille* (1920; *Ariosto, Shakespeare, and Corneille,* 1920). Here, the leading sentiment of Ariosto is defined as a desire for cosmic harmony, that of Corneille as the ideal of free will. In practice, his emphasis on the uniqueness of the work of art leads Croce to highly generalized and rather empty definitions.

Croce's taste is very pronounced: he despises the baroque as a form of ugliness and dislikes modern decadence (Gabriele D'Annunzio [q.v.]), symbolism (q.v.), and "pure poetry" à la Paul Valéry (q.v.). In Croce the monistic theory led increasingly to a critical paralysis; his last books are little more than anthologies of passages, with comments on contents and feelings. Croce's great historical learning came increasingly to obscure his criticism. Literary history, psychology, biography, sociology, philosophical interpretation, stylistics, genre criticism—all are ruled out in Croce's scheme. We revert to an intu-

85

itionism which, in practice, is hard to distinguish from impressionism—which isolates appealing passages, or anthologizes arbitrarily from an unargued pronouncement of judgments.

Yet Italian criticism of the last fifty years has been almost completely dominated by Croce. Among his followers there is erudition, there is taste, there is judgment, but, on the other hand, we find no systematic analysis of texts, no *Geistesgeschichte,* no stylistics. Several critical individualities stand out, who differ often in emphasis and taste. One of these is Francesco Flora (1891–1962), author of the five-volume *Storia della letteratura italiana* (1940–42; rev. ed., 1947–49; history of Italian literature), a diffuse, florid, enthusiastic history that combines great erudition with a Crocean emphasis on intuition and individuality (but with a taste very different from Croce's). Flora loved the baroque and the decadent and wrote various books that reveal his sympathy for the viewpoint that sees poetry as metaphor and for the modernist trends, such as futurism and hermeticism (qq.v.), that Croce deprecated. Flora was a colorful, sensual writer engaged in communicating the pleasure and even the voluptuousness of fine poetry, a master of evocation and description rather than a judicial critic.

Attilio Momigliano (1883–1952), although Crocean in many ways, was a sensitive psychologist and impressionistic critic, a delicate reader and interpreter of poetry, subtle, refined, even morbidly so, cautious and scrupulous. His *Storia della letteratura italiana* (1948; history of Italian literature) is a masterpiece of compression and carefully weighted characterization. Momigliano also wrote on Ariosto and, with increasing devotion, repeatedly on Alessandro Manzoni (1785–1873).

Luigi Russo was an ideologist, a theoretician, a brilliant, although violent polemicist who had great social and moral concerns at heart. As a practical critic he was at his best in his books on Giovanni Verga (q.v.) and Machiavelli, rather than with poets in a strict sense. His taste tended to the impersonal and realistic. Still, it is surprising that this orthodox Crocean should have been able to turn to Marxism in his last years.

As theorist and historian of criticism, the most outstanding of the Croceans was Mario Fubini (1900–1977), who wrote a long series of studies on the history of Italian criticism and on Italian literature, mainly of the 18th c. and the romantic movement, and worked toward a solidly founded theory of criticism and literature. *Critica e poesia* (1956; criticism and poetry) shows a slow emancipation from orthodox Croceanism, especially in a learned study of the history of genre theories.

These men illustrate the enormous success Croce had in changing Italian academic scholarship. They are all literary historians, of great erudition, who still remain critics vitally concerned with the judgment of literature.

But the earliest Croceans who plunged into literary life proved unfaithful disciples. Giuseppe Antonio Borgese (1882–1952) started his career with a Crocean work, *Storia della critica romantica in Italia* (1905; history of romantic criticism in Italy), in which he propounded the odd thesis that Italian romanticism is good classicism. More and more, however, Borgese became a declamatory apocalyptic prophet of art as the "transfiguration of man and figuration of God," absorbed in such questions as the meaning of Italian literature in general (which was and is to produce a "sacred, eternal, celestial art"). In later years Borgese (he emigrated to the United States in 1931) devoted his energies to projects for a "World Constitution." Nevertheless, his collection of essays *Poetica dell'unità* (1934; poetics of unity) contains fervent polemics against Croce and his denial of a unified history of poetry, and a sketch of the history of criticism. In general, Borgese held a romantic collectivist view of literature in the Hegelian tradition.

Alfredo Gargiulo (1876–1949), an early collaborator in Croce's *La critica,* also moved away from his master's theories. While his book *D'Annunzio* (1921; D'Annunzio) was a Crocean attempt to distinguish between the maker of naturalistic myths and singer of lyrical landscapes and the decadent *poseur, La letteratura italiana nel Novecento* (1930–33; Italian literature in the twentieth century) shows Gargiulo's taste for symbolism and the Italian hermetic poets (Giuseppe Ungaretti [q.v.] in particular), and many papers on aesthetics, collected in *Scritti di estetica* (1952; writings on aesthetics), argue effectively against several of Croce's central doctrines. Gargiulo developed a theory of "expressive means" that allowed him to reintroduce into aesthetics and literary theory a classification of the arts and concepts of medium and genre dismissed by Croce.

Besides the Crocean tradition, which positively or sometimes polemically at odds with the master has dominated Italian criticism, one can distinguish a second trend that is largely independent of general aesthetics and philosophy and has followed, rather, the tradition of French criticism: the psychological portrait, the close reading and tasting of a text.

Renato Serra (1884–1915), who was killed in World War I, left a few essays, letters, and diaries, which are the earliest examples of what in Italy is called "criticism of the fragment." But Serra was more a moralist, a dreamer and solitary who used criticism as self-examination, than a close student of texts. Textual, stylistic methods were developed in Italy, mainly by Giuseppe de Robertis (1888–1963), who wrote in innumerable, often tiny essays interpreting specific passages of the poets: their sound and sense, associations and implications, which surprisingly enough led him often to final obscurities and gestures toward mysticism.

Among the next generation, Gianfranco Contini (b. 1912) is the best of the close readers. He is linguistically learned and stays away from mysticism. In subject matter his range is wide, writing as he does on the earliest Italian lyricists as well as on the latest, the most opaque, modernists. Two other linguists who developed new divergent methods of stylistic analysis are Giacomo Devoto (1897–1974) and Antonio Pagliaro (1898–1973).

Somewhat apart stand three critics, all close students of American and English literature: Emilio Cecchi (1884–1966), Mario Praz (1896–1982), and Cesare Pavese (q.v.). Cecchi's *Storia della letteratura inglese nel secolo XIX* (1915; history of English literature in the nineteenth century) never progressed beyond the first volume, devoted to the English romantics. Even here he shows his power of evocation and portraiture more in the style of Sainte-Beuve (1804–1869) or Walter Pater (1839–1894) than in the Italian tradition. In his later writings he indulges in a curious sly humor and irony and in personal, often capricious judgments. *Scrittori inglesi e americani* (1946; English and American writers) is a collection of his many essays with an emphasis on what could be called the "dark," irrational, and violent tradition in American and English literature. Cecchi also wrote on many Italian topics as a general essayist.

The starting point of Mario Praz is also English literature. His early book, *Secentismo and marinismo in Inghilterra* (1925; seventeenth-century literary style and Marinism [style of Giambattista Marino, 1569–1625] in England), devoted to Donne and Crashaw, helped to restore the two great English baroque poets to their rightful place. In many other books he studied Italian-English relations (for example, the influence of Machiavelli in England) with acumen and skill. He surveyed English literature in *Storia della letteratura inglese* (1937; history of English literature), which is much more than an excellent textbook. But with *La carne, la morte e il diavolo nella letteratura romantica* (1930; *The Romantic Agony,* 1933) Praz went beyond his specialty to a subtle study of erotic sensibility in all 19th-c. Europe, seen in terms of its sources in the Marquis de Sade and as a part of the general phenomenon of decadence. *La crisi dell'eroe nel romanzo vittoriano* (1952; *The Hero in Eclipse in Victorian Fiction,* 1956) shows a surprising change or broadening of Praz's taste: a sympathy for the idyllic, realistic art of the Biedermeier, which he traces from Dutch genre painting to the novels of Trollope, Thackeray, and George Eliot. Increasingly, in a number of essay collections, Praz tried to use the art of the essayist to define a personal taste and paint his own intellectual portrait. He studies either the psychology of the author, or the sensibility of a time, or the linkage of literature with the plastic arts. He is not so much a day-by-day critic of literature as a scholar-critic, not a theorist but a historian of sensibility and taste.

Pavese, the novelist, as a critic introduced new motifs into Italian literature. Like Cecchi, he was an admirer of American literature, or rather of one strand in it: the mystic, the dark and violent he finds in Melville and Sherwood Anderson (q.v.). But his remarkable diary, *Il mestiere di vivere: Diario 1935–1950* (1951; *The Burning Brand: Diaries 1935–1950,* 1961), revealed a speculative critic of high order concerned with themes usually neglected in Italian criticism: with myth become figure, with time in the novel, and with pervasive imagery similar to that of G. Wilson Knight in England. Pavese called his ideal "rustic classicism," which seems, finally, a primitivistic and naturalistic view in spite of all its sophistication.

But Pavese stands alone. The direction of recent Italian criticism seems unclear except for two facts: the dominance of Croce and Croceanism has waned, and Marxist criticism has found many recruits.

But Italy is today also full of echoes of the other European movements in criticism and aesthetics. Existentialism had wide philosophical repercussions. At least in Enzo Paci (b. 1911) it found a subtle interpreter of literature—of Novalis, Rilke, Dostoevsky, Valéry, and Thomas Mann (q.v.)—discussed in his *Dall'esistenzialismo al realismo* (1958; from existentialism to realism). French structuralism and more recently semiotics (which goes well beyond literary criticism in its claim to encompass all of man's symbol-making activities) have found many adherents: Cesare Segrè (b. 1928) and Umberto Eco (b. 1932) are the outstanding names. Marcello Pagnini (b. 1921), who uses texts from English, excels in structural analyses. Among older critics, Giacomo Debenedetti (1901–1967) has, particularly since his death, emerged as a great figure. His posthumous publications, *Poesia italiana del Novecento* (1974; Italian poetry of the twentieth century), *Verga e il naturalismo* (1976; Verga and naturalism), and *Il romanzo del Novecento* (1971; the twentieth-century novel), have offered support to almost every point of view as he appeals to Henri Bergson (q.v.) and Freud, Husserl and Marx as his spiritual fathers to arrive at a curiously eclectic but often highly perceptive interpretation of 19th- and 20th-c. literature, not just in Italy. Debenedetti illustrates well the Italian situation: criticism there is buffetted by winds of doctrine from almost all sides: east, west, and north.

France

France, around 1900, was the country with the strongest critical tradition. It could look back to Sainte-Beuve and Hippolyte Taine (1828–1893), who had reestablished the leadership of France in criticism during the latter half of the 19th c. In France the divorce between scholarship and criticism never became so acute as in the other countries, and there was then a flourishing "university criticism" that combined erudition with taste, usually of a conservative kind. Ferdinand Brunetière (1849–1906), a doctrinaire upholder of 17th-c. classicism who also propounded a Darwinian theory of the evolution of genres, Émile Faguet (1847–1916), an extremely versatile commentator on all periods

of French literature, and Gustave Lanson (1857–1934), the author of the widely used *Histoire de la littérature française* (1894; history of French literature), were still active and influential in the early 20th c. Besides the historian-critics, the bulk of criticism was impressionist: as a theory, impressionism had been proclaimed by Jules Lemaître (1853–1914) late in the 19th c., but even he, in his later years, embraced a conservative creed that led to his sharp condemnation of Rousseau and all romanticism.

The basically rationalistic, classicist tradition of French criticism continued deep into the 20th c. and had its important revivals. Charles Maurras (1868–1952), the founder of the Action Française, had critical affiliations with the so-called École Romane. He proclaimed Latinity, reason, and conservatism as its standards and condemned the Revolution and romanticism (which strangely enough were conceived as almost identical). Pierre Lasserre (1867–1930), in *Le romantisme français* (1907; French romanticism), attacked romanticism and all its works as a disease due to the "psychopath" Jean-Jacques Rousseau, and (Baron) Ernest Seillière (1866–1955) wrote an unending series of books denouncing romanticism, Germans, and imperialism.

After World War I a purely rationalistic point of view, proclaimed to be particularly French, was restated powerfully in Julien Benda's (1867–1956) *Belphégor* (1919; *Belphégor,* 1929) and in the writings of Henri Massis (1886–1970), who had begun by attacking Lanson and academic criticism and later wrote *La défense de l'Occident* (1925; *The Defence of the West,* 1927), a strident proclamation of Western, Latin values against everything Northern and Eastern. The widely read, largely journalistic critic Paul Souday (1869–1929) can be classed with these defenders of reason, intellectualism, and art as construction, and haters of everything vague, mystical, sentimental, romantic, symbolic, and irrational. Among more recent critics, Ramon Fernandez (1894–1944) was nearest to the conservative classicism of the Action Française. He has on many points striking affinities with T. S. Eliot (q.v.), sharing as he does Eliot's search for objectivity and impersonality. The collection of essays *Messages* (1926; *Messages,* 1927) strongly urges the claim of criticism to yield an "imaginative ontology." The metaphysical problem of being is to be solved in art, although transposed to the plane of imagination. The world of poetry is a world of quality, not a reflection of an author's psyche. Criticism should investigate the philosophical substructure of a work of art and not the biography or psychology of an author or his overt intentions. In an essay on Stendhal, Fernandez shows, for instance, how even so autobiographical an author uses private experiences only as building materials for his books. Unfortunately, Fernandez did not live up to the promise of his early work: in his last books, *Balzac* (1943; Balzac) and *Proust* (1943; Proust), he pursues philosophical themes with some moralistic obtuseness: in Balzac, he argues, intuition, conception, and expression remain unfused. In Proust, there is no way from passive impression to an external world of action, no moral progress.

But clearly the classical, rationalist, and moralist point of view, although important in the academy and in arguments on general culture, lost out to the much more powerful stream of irrationalism that flooded French criticism. One must distinguish among these irrationalisms, however, and must not obscure the strength of the classical tradition in men such as Valéry. One must recognize different strands and chronological groupings. Symbolism might be considered one central critical motif, Bergsonism another, Catholicism a third, within which, however, we must distinguish between mystical thinkers and more rationalistic neo-Thomists.

A fourth definite movement is surrealism (q.v.) and, after World War II, existentialism. Some of these classifications are not clear-cut. A Catholic poet such as Paul Claudel (q.v.) was a symbolist in his poetic theories; the Catholics Charles Péguy (q.v.) and Charles Du Bos (1882–1939) felt the strong impact of Bergson. One can speak today of a Catholic existentialism and the term Bergsonism must not always be interpreted technically; it might be combined with an interest in Freud and find ways to agree with the Church. The situation is extremely fluid, the boundary lines fluctuate. The methods of French criticism of the last fifty years are mostly intuitive and often impressionistic: its form is the essay—so much so that many critics seem never to have written a proper book. The interest in a systematic theory is small, as criticism is conceived as an art and a means of self-expression and self-discovery rather than as a body of knowledge and judgments.

Symbolism as a poetic movement was apparently on the decline since the beginning of the century, although Baudelaire, Mallarmé, and Rimbaud actually determined the course of a modern French poetry and also supplied a body of poetic doctrine. The prolific critic Remy de Gourmont (1858–1915) could be described as a popularizer of the symbolist creed, although Gourmont had nothing of Mallarmé's austerity and has often pronounced tones of elegant fin-de-siècle Decadence. His best books, such as *Le problème du style* (1902; the problem of style), with its advocacy of bright, visual, concrete writing, and his analytical skill in the "disassociation of ideas," provided important suggestions for the imagism (q.v.) of Ezra Pound (q.v.) and the early criticism of T. S. Eliot.

The great poet Claudel, an intensely proselytizing Catholic, formulated a new version of symbolist poetics: image is the essence of poetry. Unlike prose, which gives us knowledge of reality, poetry provides us with an equivalent, or species of reality. The poet does not tell us what a thing is, but what it means, what is its place in the universe, which is a unity, linked by correspondences, surrounding us with "figures of eternity." Claudel's *Art poétique* (1907; *Poetic Art*, 1948) ranges from an immediate vision of God's universe to close prescriptions for the reform of French verse as reflecting the rhythm of the soul, rather than the mind, *anima* rather than *animus*.

A basically symbolist poetics was also formulated by Valéry in writings that in part date back to the 1890s but belong largely to the period between the wars. The five volumes of *Variété* (1924–44; *Variety*, 2 vols., 1927, 1938) especially carried his views on poetry to a wide audience, in a fragmentary fashion. But if we supplement these essays by many other pronouncements in lectures and notebooks, a coherent theory of poetics emerges that is both striking and original. Valéry, more radically than anybody else, asserts a discontinuity between author, work, and reader. He stresses the importance of form divorced from emotion and takes poetry completely out of history into the realm of the absolute. For Valéry, there is first a deep gulf between creative process and work. At times it seems as if Valéry were hardly interested in the work, but only in this process of creation. He did not publish for twenty years and seemed content to analyze the creativity of genius in general. His ideal was the universal man, a Leonardo da Vinci. Later he wrote subtle, introspective descriptions of the process of composing his poems, always citing evidence for the distance between the original idea, the germ that might be, in a word, a rhyme, a line, or a melody, and the finished product. For Valéry poetry is not inspiration, not dream, but a making with a mind wide-awake. Poetry must be impersonal to be perfect. Emotional art, art appealing to sensibility, seems to him always inferior. A poem should aim to be "pure," absolute poetry, free from factual, personal, and emotional admixtures. It cannot be paraphrased, it cannot be translated. It is a tight universe of sound and meaning, so closely interlocked that we cannot distinguish content and form. Poetry exploits the resources of language to the utmost, removing itself from ordinary speech by the use of sound and meter and all the devices of metaphorics. Poetic language is a language within language, language completely formalized. To Valéry poetry is both a calculus, an exercise, even a game, and a song, a chant, an enchantment, a charm. It is figurative and incantatory: a compromise between sound and meaning, which by its conventions, even arbitrary conventions, achieves the ideal work of art, unified, beyond time, absolute. This ideal is realized most fully in Mallarmé and in Valéry's own poetry.

The novel, with its plot complications and irrelevancies, and tragedy, with its appeal to violent emotions, seem to Valéry inferior genres, even not quite art. The novel is historical and hence contingent; it makes claims to truth in relation to an external reality. It can be summarized and easily changed in its details, without damage, as a poem cannot.

Valéry's ideal of poetry is absolute, frozen into the grandeur of pure form. Surprisingly enough, what seems a dense objective structure is to Valéry open to many interpretations. A work of art is essentially ambiguous. "My verses have the meaning that one gives to them," is Valéry's famous paradox, which allows even for "creative misunderstanding." The door seems open for critical caprice and anarchy, but Valéry's own practical criticism—limited in scope mainly to authors such as Mallarmé and Poe, his "pure" poets, or to universal examples of creativity like Goethe and Leonardo da Vinci—preserves an admirable lucidity and balance. It defends a position that seems extreme in its austerity and vulnerable for its discontinuities. But it

has been fruitful in asserting a central concern of modern poetics: the discovery of pure representation, the "unmediated vision," for which two other great poets of the century, Rainer Maria Rilke (q.v.) and Eliot, were also searching. Valéry stands alone in splendid isolation, although the affinities of his theories with Mallarmé's are obvious. In a wide perspective, he could be seen as bringing symbolism back to the classical tradition.

Proust also restated symbolist theory, with important modifications. Although these statements were often disguised in discussions of music and painting, Proust, especially in the last volume—*Le temps retrouvé* (1927; *The Past Recaptured,* 1932)—of his novel cycle *À la recherche du temps perdu* (1913–27; *Remembrance of Things Past,* 1922–32), expounds an aesthetics relevant to literature. The artist is concerned with a knowledge of "essences" recovered by involuntary memory: he fixes the fleeting qualitative side of the world in his own particular singular emotion. Symbolism and Bergsonism are reconciled. Besides, Proust occasionally commented on strictly literary matters: in his introduction to his early translations from John Ruskin (1819–1900), in curious reflections on the style of Flaubert, and in an acid attack on the biographical approach of Sainte-Beuve, *Contre Sainte-Beuve* (1954; *On Art and Literature,* 1958), discovered long after his death.

But the group that assembled around *Nouvelle revue française,* founded by André Gide (q.v.) in 1909, was most influential in defining the new taste of the century. The main contributors can hardly be reduced to a common denominator, but Bergson loomed in the background with his philosophy of flux, of the concrete and the immediate. Gide himself was hardly an important critic, although his published journals are full of literary opinions, and his book *Dostoïevsky* (1923; *Dostoevsky,* 1926) searchingly probes ethical problems. The reigning spirit was Jacques Rivière (1885–1925), who died too soon to fulfill his promise. The early *Études* (1908; studies) show Rivière as the first sensitive expounder of Claudel and Gide. After his return from German captivity in World War I, as editor of *Nouvelle revue française,* he did much to spread the growing fame of Proust. He saw Proust rather as a classicist, that is, a detached observer, and interpreted him also in Freudian terms. But Rivière is not sufficiently described as a psychological critic of considerable finesse and warmth: he is a figure of psychological interest himself, a man who first grappled with religion and then attempted to find himself in a theory of sincerity toward oneself. To him criticism was self-discovery, a way toward a definition of the meaning of life, best exemplified in his essays collected under the title *Nouvelles études* (1927; *The Ideal Reader*, 1960).

Rivière was soon eclipsed by Albert Thibaudet (1874–1936), a voluminous writer who filled the *NRF* with his essays for many years and produced, besides many monographs, an unfinished work, *Histoire de la littérature française* (1937; *French Literature from 1795 to Our Era*, 1967). Thibaudet is somewhat like a modern Sainte-Beuve: he has his versatility and his aversion to clear-cut conclusions and theories. If he has a philosophical outlook, it is that of Bergsonism. He likes to surrender to the flux of impressions, to embrace a literary pantheism. He interpreted, always sympathetically, Mallarmé, Maurice Barrès (1862–1923), Valéry, and Flaubert in separate books. In his *Histoire de la littérature française* he shows his skill in surveying masses: he ranges his authors in a succession of generations and manages to suggest the chain of tradition, the flow of time. Thibaudet is haunted by the vision of a literary landscape, a "Republic of Letters." He evokes the soil, the province, the place of an author. He has a strong feeling and sympathy for regionalism, which is combined with a genuine vision of European solidarity. Sympathy, even at the expense of judgment, is Thibaudet's main trait. He even imitates the style of the writer he discusses, almost compulsively. He seems like a chameleon, elusive, indistinctive. The two books, ostensibly devoted to a theory of criticism, *Physiologie de la critique* (1930; physiology of criticism) and *Réflexions sur la critique* (1939; reflections on criticism), are hardly more than random notes. Nowhere is there an attempt to define a position: it emerges largely by implication, in his admiration for Victor Hugo and Flaubert, in his coolness to Balzac, Alfred de Vigny, and Baudelaire. A final romantic vein seems to prevail.

In his psychological probing, and his impressionistic technique, Charles Du Bos was in his early stages related to Rivière. Du Bos is much more labored, earnest, groping, yet also much wider in range. In contrast to Rivière and Thibaudet, whose horizon was almost exclusively French, Du Bos knew English and German literature well. He wrote extensively on Wordsworth, Shelley, Keats, Browning, and Pater, and produced a full-length psychological study of Byron (*Byron et le besoin de la fatalité*, 1929; *Byron and the Need of Fatality*, 1932). He studied Goethe in detail. In 1927 Du Bos became a convert and then developed a concept of literature which must be described as mystical. His English book, *What Is Literature?* (1938) hinges on key words such as "soul," "light," and "word," leading up to a "beatific vision," an ecstatic communion of the critic with the seers and sages. But this is only Du Bos's last stage: earlier he wrote much on the psychology of writers, the creative process, the concrete detail of a work of art, always with a Bergsonian fear of abstraction, a sense of life that he found also in the complexities of Henry James (q.v.) and Robert Browning. The seven volumes of *Approximations* (1922–37; approximations), which contain some of the most distinguished criticism of the time, are also typical for the course they describe: from a worship of beauty for its own sake to a glorification of God's presence, from the pleasures of sensation to the "essence" embodied in literature.

Du Bos in his concept of poetry is related to the Abbé Henri Bremond (1865–1933), the historian of religious feeling in France, who in *Poésie et prière* (1926; *Prayer and Poetry*, 1927) and *De la poésie pure* (1926; of pure poetry) almost identified poetry with prayer, or rather with mystical exaltation.

But within the Catholic renaissance there was a more intellectual movement, neo-Thomism, Aristotelianism, which found a powerful spokesman in Jacques Maritain (1882–1973). He was the best-known convert (in 1906), the most widely influential Catholic philosopher. Criticism was only one of his many activities. Still, *Art et scolastique* (1920; *Art and Scholasticism*, 1930) and *Situation de la poésie* (1938; *The Situation of Poetry*, 1955) did much to define a neo-Thomist aesthetics. In his later book in English, *Creative Intuition in Art and Poetry* (1953), Maritain moved in the direction of straight mysticism. The argument is still neo-scholastic, but is also Neoplatonist, even visionary. The Thomist concept of making a work of art for human needs is now combined with a belief in free creation, an inner subjectivity. Maritain, the great foe of Cartesian subjectivism, ends with a hymn to intuitive subjectivity, to revelation, even to dark unconscious creation, to mystery and magic. Maritain admires not only English romantic poetry but also surrealism.

Surrealism is the extreme of irrationalism. It grew out of Dadaism and cubism (qq.v.), which found a rather halting theorist in Guillaume Apollinaire (q.v.) just before World War I. But surrealism as a movement is largely due to the organizing and propagandizing zeal of André Breton (q.v.), who composed its first manifesto in 1924. The artist is to reveal the confusion of the world; he is to contribute to the total discredit of what is usually called reality. The poetic state implies a complete renunciation of reason. Automatic writing is its technique, the dream is its model. Complete anarchy and emancipation from reason, God, morality, are proclaimed with flamboyant rhetoric and an air of assurance that suggests the circus barker.

World War II brought a reaction against all theories of pure art, all concepts that suggest the "ivory tower" or civic irresponsibility. The watchword became *la littérature engagée,* as formulated by Jean-Paul Sartre. But Sartre was a philosopher, the main French propounder of existentialism long before the war, and he cannot be described as a simple advocate of the social responsibility of the arts, although he moved more and more in the direction of Marxism. *Qu'est-ce que la littérature?* (1947; *What Is Literature?,* 1949) is actually an impassioned plea for a metaphysical conception of art. The rights of pure poetry are recognized.

Sartre spoke well of the varying relationship between writer and public in history and discussed the American novelists of violence—William Faulkner, John Dos Passos (qq.v.)—in terms of this assertion of human freedom. But imagination is suspect to Sartre—shattered by the first real contact with the absurdity and horror of real existence. The bohemian type of artist is suspect, too. Sartre made a cruel psychoanalytical study, *Baudelaire* (1947; *Baudelaire,* 1949): in spite of all the meanness and rottenness he finds in Baudelaire, he approves his search for "being" rather than mere "existence," his defiance of destiny freely chosen. In a diffuse and turgid book about Jean Genet (q.v.), *Saint-Genet, comédien et martyr* (1952; *Saint-Genet: Actor and Martyr,* 1963), a homosexual thief and convict (as well as playwright) is the subject; Sartre identifies work and author completely and wishes to convince us that good is evil and evil good. The

paradoxes of Sartre's phenomenology cannot, however, succeed in making an author on the margin of literature appear a great writer. Sartre devoted the last years of his life mainly to an enormous biography of Flaubert, *L'idiot de la famille: Gustave Flaubert de 1821 à 1857* (3 vols., 1971–72; Vol. I tr. as *The Family Idiot: Gustave Flaubert, 1821–1857, Vol. I,* 1981), which interprets him mainly in terms of Sartre's own existential psychoanalysis as a representative of the hated French bourgeoisie. Although Sartre claims "empathy," the book is actually a systematic persecution of the man from childhood to the writing of *Madame Bovary,* conceived as the "totalization" of Flaubert's development toward a fusion of his inner experience with contemporary history.

Existentialist assumptions and motifs permeate recent French criticism, which has become increasingly philosophical, metaphysical, and often gropingly obscure as a result. Two outstanding authors—not primarily concerned with literary criticism—defined the new attitude toward art most memorably. André Malraux, in his grand survey of the plastic arts, *Les voix du silence* (1951; *The Voices of Silence,* 1953) makes art appear as man's triumph over destiny. Albert Camus (q.v.), in *L'homme révolté* (1951; *The Rebel,* 1954), sees art as a tool in man's revolt against his human condition, art as conquering even death.

The attitudes, ideas, and methods of these great writers reverberate in more strictly literary and academic criticism. There they combine with suggestions that come from the writings of Gaston Bachelard (1884–1962), a somewhat fantastic philosopher of nature who called his method psychoanalysis, but was, rather, related to Jung. He studied the traditional elements (fire, water, air, earth) in literature and traced the distortions imposed by the imagery of poets in such books as *La psychoanalyse de feu* (1938; *The Psychoanalysis of Fire,* 1964), *L'eau et les rêves* (1942; *Water and Dreams,* 1965), *L'air et les songes* (1943; air and dreams), *La poétique et l'espace* (1958; *The Poetics of Space,* 1964), and *La poétique de la rêverie* (1961; *The Poetics of Reverie,* 1969).

A whole group of French critics can be said to combine existentialist and "myth" interests in order to develop a special method they call *critique de conscience.* They aim less at analysis or judgment of works of art than at the reconstruction of the particular "consciousness" of each writer. Every writer is assumed to live in his peculiar unique world, which has certain interior structures it is the task of the critic to discover. The emphasis on different aspects and the philosophical affiliations of these critics vary. The oldest among them, Marcel Raymond (1897–1981), in his *De Baudelaire au surréalisme* (1935; *From Baudelaire to Surrealism,* 1949), traced the myth of modern poetry to its sources in Baudelaire. Raymond was interested in the claim of poets such as Mallarmé and the surrealists that words are more than symbols, that they can share in the essence of being, that the absolute is somehow incarnated in their work.

In Albert Béguin (1901–1957) the religious motivation is dominant. In his first book, *L'âme romantique et le rêve* (1939; the romantic soul and the dream), he studies German romanticism and the French writers who went the same way—Rousseau, Hugo, Gérard de Nerval (1808–1855)—and he ends with Baudelaire, Rimbaud, Mallarmé, and Proust. Béguin admired German romanticism because it recognized and affirmed the profound resemblance of poetic states and the revelations of a religious order. Romanticism and all poetry is a myth that leads into the dream, the unconscious, and finally into the presence of God. In later writings Béguin became identified with a Catholic mysticism.

Georges Poulet (b. 1902) on the other hand absorbed scholasticism, Descartes, and Bergson, and is primarily interested in the concept and feeling of time in writings and poets. His *Études sur le temps humain* (3 vols., 1949–54; Vol. I tr. as *Studies in Human Time,* 1956; Vol. II, *La distance intérieure* [1952], tr. as *The Interior Distance,* 1959) and *Les métamorphoses du cercle* (1962; *The Metamorphoses of the Circle,* 1967) trace a general history of French thought and feeling in terms of time with unparalleled ingenuity.

Jean-Pierre Richard (b. 1922) is related to Poulet in his method, although *Littérature et sensation* (1954; literature and feeling) and *Poésie et profondeur* (1955; poetry and depth) show his special interest in the perceptual life of the authors (Stendhal, Flaubert, Nerval, Baudelaire, Rimbaud) discussed. We are told, for example, that to Flaubert love is like drowning, or that the lover loses his bones, becomes like plastic paste. Sentences and observations, metaphors and scenes from all books and letters of an author are used indiscriminately to build up a scheme of his mental life, organized by leading motives and obsessions.

Somewhat apart from these critics stands Maurice Blanchot (q.v.), the most difficult and obscure of the group, who in *L'espace littéraire* (1955; the literary space) discusses such topics as "Whether Literature Is Possible" or the "Space of Death," using Kafka, Mallarmé, and Hölderlin as his favorite examples. Blanchot arrives at a strange nihilism: silence is the ultimate significance of literature, the only thing left to express.

Fortunately there are other more articulate and more rational critics in France. All share the general method and philosophical preoccupations, but remain committed to clarity. Claude-Edmonde Magny (?–1966) in *Les sandales d'Empédocle* (1945; the sandals of Empedocles) expounded her philosophical method, which she then applied to Kafka, Charles Morgan (1894–1958), and Sartre lucidly. Gaëtan Picon (1915–1976), in *L'écrivain et son ombre* (1953; the writer and his shadow), began a systematic exposition of a theory of literature that does seem to indicate a return to aesthetic considerations. Obviously the danger of existentialist criticism is its neglect of the work as an aesthetic fact. The work is broken up or ignored in favor of the act of creation and the mind of the poet. Except for recent American attempts to emulate the French method, the gulf between French and Anglo-American criticism has become very deep indeed.

In recent years a group of critics in Paris, usually called French structuralists, has caused a considerable stir. The group is by no means concerned only with literary criticism. An anthropologist (Claude Levi-Strauss, q.v.), a psychoanalyst (Jacques Lacan, 1901–1981), a philosopher (Jacques Derrida, b. 1930), a historian of ideas (Michel Foucault, b. 1926), an interpreter of Marx (Louis Althusser, b. 1918), and a semiologist (A. J. Greimas, b. 1917) play major roles. Even Roland Barthes, primarily a literary critic, could also be classed as a sociologist for his *Mythologies* (1957; *Mythologies,* 1972) and *Système de la mode* (1967; system of fashion) or as a semiologist for his *Éléments de semiologie* (1964; *Elements of Semiology,* 1977). All these critics are deeply influenced by the Swiss linguist Ferdinand de Saussure (1857–1913), whose *Cours de linguistique générale* (1916; *Course in General Linguistics,* 1959) formulated the basic ideas that nourish structuralism, particularly the distinction, within the linguistic sign, between the signifier and the signified, a new terminology for the old distinction between acoustic image and concept. Saussure assumed the complete arbitrariness of the linguistic sign, from which the French new critics draw the conclusion that man is locked in the prison-house of language, that literature has no relation to reality. To speak about literature is to speak about language.

Barthes's first book, *Le degré zéro de l'écriture* (1953; *Writing Degree Zero,* 1968), argues that "the whole of literature, from Flaubert to the present day, has become the problematics of language." The zero style of writing, which he finds in Camus, Blanchot, and Raymond Queneau (q.v.), leads finally to the silence of writing. Literature today has "the very structure of suicide."

The book *Sur Racine* (1963; *On Racine,* 1964) put Barthes at the center of controversy. He was attacked by Raymond Picard (b. 1917), a Racine specialist, in the pamphlet *Nouvelle critique ou nouvelle imposture?* (1965; *New Criticism or New Fraud?,* 1969), which occasioned Barthes's rejoinder *Critique et vérité* (1966; criticism and truth). *Sur Racine,* although generally quoted as the showpiece of structuralist criticism, is mainly psychoanalytical in approach. It is an analysis of Racine's characters and situations. The relationship between the characters is reduced to a double equation: "A has complete power over B. A loves B, who does not love A." This in turn is paralleled in the setting of the plays, where the chamber, in the shadow and silence, the seat of authority, contrasts with the antichamber, where the hero and the heroine are located until they are expelled to die. The same structure is also seen in the implied theology of Racine's plays, in which Barthes sees an identification of God and Father, Blood and Law. Picard rejected Barthes's interpretation as sheer fancy, while Barthes, in his rejoinder, defended the complete liberty of interpretation. "The justification of the critic is not the meaning of the work but the meaning of what he says about it."

Some of Barthes's positions are elaborated in *Essais critiques* (1964; *Critical Essays,* 1972). All writing is narcissistic. Reality is only a pretext. In *S/Z* (1970; *S/Z,* 1974) Barthes interpreted a story by Balzac, *Sarrasine,* very closely, devising a system of five codes, or voices, and arguing again for a distinction between a classical text such as Balzac's as "readable" (*lisible*) against a modern text he considers "*scriptible,*" i.e., when the reader produces the text himself during the act of reading. In *Le plaisir du texte* (1973; *The Pleasure of the Text,* 1975) Barthes exalted the pleasure of literature, which is purely individual and unforeseeable, and surprisingly rejected all claims to establishing a science of literature on the model of linguistics.

This is, however, what several other critics aim at, particularly Tzvetan Todorov (b. 1939), a Bulgarian settled in France. He translated an anthology of the Russian formalists into French, and in *Qu'est-ce le structuralisme?* (1968; what is structuralism?) sketched the outline of a new poetics, a complete system or science of literature. Todorov announces a kind of involution. The aim of poetics "is not so much a better knowledge of the object as the perfecting of scientific discourse." "The object of poetics is precisely its method."

Roman Jakobson (1896–1982), a member of both the Russian formalist group and the Prague Linguistic Circle, provides a personal bridge from Russia via the U.S. to France. His analysis of Baudelaire's *Les chats* (written in collaboration with Claude Lévi-Strauss, published in the review *L'homme,* 1962, and reprinted in *Questions de poétique,* 1973; questions of poetics) uses linguistic categories in order to construe a grammar of poetry: that is, syntactic and morphological correlations and frequencies. He used the same method on poems as diverse as a sonnet of Shakespeare and poems by Dante, Blake, Brecht, and Fernando Pessoa (q.v.). Jakobson is the closest analyst of poetry. Gérard Genette (b. 1930), in *Figures* (3 vols., 1966–72; figures), has most successfully analyzed storytelling and the technique of the novel, using Proust as his prime example.

Today one cannot foretell the positive results of the new structuralism. There is no doubt of the stimulus provided by its close analyses, ingenious analogies, and classifications. But one may question the view that literature is a branch of linguistics and that all reality is linguistic. One may doubt whether literature is a closed system. The consequences of viewing all reality as linguistic are that consciousness and personality are reduced to secondary phenomena. A radical group around the review *Tel Quel* proclaims the death of literature or reduces literature to inconsequential language games. Any humanist will reject these nihilistic and anarchical conclusions.

Spain, Portugal, and Latin America

Spain in the 19th c. had no great critical tradition. The dominant figure who survived into the 20th c., Marcelino Menéndez y Pelayo (1856–1912), was a polyhistor, an enormously productive compiler of histories of literature and ideas, rather than a critic. *Estudios de crítica literaria* (1884–1908; studies in literary criticism) are historical studies rather than criticism. His general outlook is that of Catholic romanticism.

Genuine criticism began in Spain with the "Generation of '98," the group of brilliant writers who—after the catastrophe of the Spanish-American War—began to examine the reasons for the decay of Spain. These Spanish authors were preoccupied with the problem of nationality and only secondarily with strictly literary matters. Cervantes's *Don Quixote* became a national symbol that served as a rallying point for this intensive self-examination. In his *Vida de Don Quijote y Sancho* (1905; *Life of Don Quixote and Sancho,* 1927) Miguel de Unamuno (q.v.) transforms Don Quixote into a saint: the humor of the book is ignored or forgotten. The man Don Quixote steps from the pages as a living being: art and reality are constantly, determinedly confused. Américo Castro (1885–1972) interpreted Cervantes as a Renaissance man, a follower of Erasmus, in *El pensamiento de Cervantes* (1925; the thought of Cervantes), and in *España en su historia* (1948; *The Structure of Spanish History,* 1954) tried to define the Spanish national character in terms of its racial and regional elements. Salvador de Madariaga (1886–1978) also wrote on Don Quixote—*Guía del lector del Quijote* (1926; *Don Quixote: An Introductory Essay in Psychology,* 1935)—and speculated, often in essays first published in English, on Spanish creative genius (*The Genius of Spain,* 1923). The collection of essays *Shelley and Calderón* (1920) contains a remarkable essay on Wordsworth, chiding him for provinciality. Madariaga, who played a role in the League of Nations as ambassador of the Republic, and as professor of Spanish at Oxford, was a type of the new Spanish internationalist: intensely conscious of his nationality, but wide open to the world, anxious to have Spain emerge from its isola-tion and impotence. Madariaga was a convinced liberal. On the opposite end of the political scale, Ramiro de Maeztu (1875–1936) also wrote on Don Quixote—*Don Quijote, Don Juan y la Celestina* (1926; Don Quixote, Don Juan, and La Celestina)—and produced an antidemocratic and antiliberal work, *Defensa de la hispanidad* (1934; defense of hispanism).

These two themes, hispanism and Don Quixote, are also the starting point of the most prominent literary critic Spain has produced: José Ortega y Gasset (q.v.). Ortega was an immensely stimulating, versatile writer on all subjects: history, philosophy, art, and even science, love, pedagogy, and politics. Literary criticism was only a small part of his enormous activity. The early *Meditaciones del Quijote* (1914; *Meditations on Quixote,* 1961) is hardly literary criticism: it is an attack on the surface culture of Mediterranean man in the name of Germanic "profundity." Ortega studied philosophy with Hermann Cohen (1842–1918) in Marburg in 1913–14, and always preserved an intense interest not only in Kant and Kantianism, but in Georg Simmel (1858–1918), Max Scheler (1874–1928), Martin Heidegger (1889–1976), and especially Wilhelm Dilthey, from whom many motifs in his thought are derived.

Two small books by Ortega, both dating from 1925, are literary criticism in a narrow sense. *La deshumanización del arte (The Dehumanization of Art,* 1948) has a somewhat sensational title: Ortega discusses not the dehumanization of art, but rather the retreat of modern art from realism. Ortega sees the common denominator of modern art and literature in the avoidance of living, natural forms, in its ambition for being art and nothing else, with no transcendental claim, and in its essential irony. The builders of modern art are Debussy, Mallarmé, Proust, Picasso, and Pirandello (q.v.). Although the thesis is somewhat overstated and refers particularly to the situation in the early 1920s, Ortega finely characterized the main trend of modernist art as away from personal emotion and toward abstract form. "Poetry has become the higher algebra of metaphors" is Ortega's definition of the aim of Mallarmé and the Spanish symbolists. Quite consistently he helped in the revival of Góngora, the great Spanish baroque poet, with an important essay, "Góngora" (1927; Góngora), in which his poetry (and implicitly all poetry) is defined as circumlocution, as the oblique nam-ing of the taboo. An essay on Mallarmé (1923) defines poetry as a "determined escape from reality," a "keeping silent about the immediate names of things."

In *Ideas sobra la novela* (1925; *Notes on the Novel*, 1948) he applies substantially the same point of view to the modern novel. The novel, with a plot and action, is exhausted as a genre and is being replaced by the "static" novel, which tends not to inspire the reader's immediate interest but requires contemplation induced by its form and structure. The classic examples are Dostoevsky, whom Ortega skillfully defends for his technique and form, and Proust.

The book-length essay that created a sensation in Germany, *Pidiendo un Goethe desde dentro* (1932; "In Search of Goethe from Within," 1949), is not primarily concerned with Goethe's work. It is, rather, an attempt to show that Goethe betrayed his deepest mission by going to Weimar, that classicism, and Goethe's classicism specifically, hides life, as does his optimistic biological philosophy. The real Goethe, the Goethe from within, is a problematic character, constantly fleeing from himself, a habitual deserter of his destiny.

Ortega had a commanding position in Spanish cultural life. All other critics lacked his philosophical clarity and range. They were either impressionists or scholars. Azorín (q.v.) was the best sensitive literary critic of the early group. *Clásicos y modernos* (1913; classics and moderns) and *Los valores literarios* (1913; literary values) are collections in which he tries to define the Spanish literary tradition and to trace the history of the new movement.

Among more recent critics, the sensitive essayist Antonio Marichalar (1893–1973) is concerned largely with French and English literature. Guillermo de Torre (1900–1971) described and criticized avant-garde European literature and later, in exile in Argentina, passionately defended the freedom of the writer. His *Problematica de la literatura* (1951; problematics of literature) was deeply influenced by existentialism; he was disturbed by the problem of the engagement of the writer and the totalitarian attempt to make the writer serve the purpose of the state. The crisis of the concept of literature is de Torre's main theme, which allowed him to survey the contemporary literary situation with a deep social concern that does not lose sight of the nature and freedom of art.

Another development in Spain was a highly competent cultivation of stylistics, in part suggested by German methods, in part drawn from native sources of philology. Ramón Menéndez Pidal (1869–1968) was the teacher of all the younger Spanish literary scholars; he was a great philologist and medievalist whose *La España del Cid* (1929; *The Cid and His Spain,* 1934) is an impressive reconstruction of medieval Spanish civilization. Two younger men, of the same name though not related, stand out: Amado Alonso (1897–1952), who was primarily a philologist but wrote a model study of the Chilean poet Pablo Neruda (q.v.), *Poesía y estilo de Pablo Neruda* (1940; poetry and style of Pablo Neruda); and Dámaso Alonso (q.v.), who started the Góngora revival with his 1927 edition of Góngora's *Soledades* (*The Solitudes,* 1931) and his elaborate study *La lengua poética de Góngora* (1935; the poetic language of Góngora), and who wrote a fine analytical book on Saint John of the Cross, *La poesía de San Juan de la Cruz* (1942; the poetry of Saint John of the Cross), and a large book, *Poesía española: Ensayo de métodos y límites estilísticos* (1950; Spanish poetry: essay on methods and stylistic limits), which contains studies of Garcilaso de la Vega, Fray Luis de León, Saint John of the Cross, Góngora, Lope de Vega, and Quevedo. It succeeds in defining the "uniqueness of the literary object" with flexible interpretative techniques of great sensitivity and learning. Dámaso Alonso sometimes loses sight of the critical ideal and is given to speaking of the "mystery of form" or "expressive intuition." But these vague gestures toward irrationalism rarely damage the mastery of the stylistic analyst, who must surely be one of the best in contemporary criticism, and not only in Spain.

One of Alonso's followers, Carlos Bousoño (b. 1923), has systematized the stylistic approach into a whole theory of literature in *Teoría de la expresión poética* (1952; expanded rev. ed., 1966; theory of poetic expression). In contrast to Alonso, Bousoño concentrates on syntax and vocabulary and makes elaborate analyses, particularly of the symbol and symbolism, which he then develops in *El irracionalismo poético (El símbolo)* (1977; poetic irrationalism [the symbol]).

A Catalan, Eugenio d'Ors (1882–1954), made a deep impression at first by his commentaries (*glosas*), written in Catalan and published under the pseudonym "Xenius," consisting of ironic epigrammatic journalism on almost all subjects. His books on painters (Goya, Cézanne, Picasso, and others) prepared the way for his study (published first in French, *Du baroque,* 1936; in Spanish, *Lo barocco,* 1944; the baroque). Here baroque is conceived as a form of style occurring in all periods of history: Góngora and Richard Wagner, Pope and Vico, Rousseau and El Greco, the Portuguese architecture of the 15th c., and recent poetry are all considered phases of the baroque.

Guillermo Diaz Plaja (b. 1909) is related to d'Ors: he admires him greatly, but goes his own romantic ways. His first book, *Introducción al estudio del romanticismo español* (1935; introduction to the study of Spanish romanticism), was rather derivative, but his essays on the theory of literature, *La ventana del papel* (1939; the paper window); *El espíritu del barocco* (1940; the spirit of the baroque); and his studies of the Spanish lyric and of the prose poem in Spain established him as the most eminent of Spanish literary historians, who manages to combine a strongly personal, often impressionist and irrationalistic criticism with accurate learning. As the editor of the great *Historia general de las literaturas hispánicas* (5 vols., 1949–58; general history of Hispanic literatures) he did not succeed so well as the older Ángel Valbuena Prat (b. 1900), whose *Historia de la literatura española* (3 vols., 1937; history of Spanish literature) is today considered the best history of Spanish literature. Valbuena Prat also wrote an important monograph on Calderón and a basic history of the Spanish theater.

In Portugal, Fidelino de Sousa Figueiredo (1889–1967) was the outstanding figure in literary criticism and history. He wrote a series of immensely learned literary histories and much, mainly psychological, criticism. He drew portraits of many Portuguese authors with great skill and understanding, in, for example, *Estudos da literatura* (5 vols., 1917–50; studies in literature). But he was also deeply concerned with the theory of literature and criticism, with the history of criticism, and with many topics of comparative literature, such as the influence of Shakespeare in Portugal. Figueiredo described his own outlook as that of a militant traditionalism and nationalism: but he did much to free Portuguese intellectual life from provincialism and local complacencies.

Every Latin American country has produced critics and criticism, mainly of the local scene. In Mexico, Alfonso Reyes (q.v.) combined, like Figueiredo, wide-ranging learning with critical insight. Reyes wrote scholarly books on Greek criticism and Roman rhetoric; he early contributed to the revival of interest in Góngora; he showed fine understanding of Mallarmé; and he wrote a sympathetic study of Goethe. In a large theoretical book, *El deslinde* (1944; delimitation), he attempts extremely subtle though excessively scholastic definitions and delimitations that hardly suggest the universality and mobility of his mind. With Reyes, the Spanish culture of the New World has rediscovered its old universal Western spirit.

Jorge Luis Borges (q.v.), the eminent Argentine writer, is also a fine critic and essayist. He ranges widely from Argentine folk literature to old Germanic epics, and judges his Argentine contemporaries with some severity. Ricardo Rojas (1882–1957) was his main rival: his *La literatura argentina* (8 vols., 1924–25; Argentine literature) established his reputation as an essayist.

There are, of course, many literary historians in different countries, among whom Pedro Henriquez Ureña (1884–1946) from the Dominican Republic may be singled out due to the availability of some of his work written in English (*Literary Currents in Hispanic America,* 1945). But Henriquez Ureña wrote most importantly on style and verse—*Seis ensayos en busca de nuestra expresión* (1927; six essays in search of our expression)—and was one of the most distinguished critics of Spanish America. In every country of the New World, the critical spirit is stirring, engaged in a needed examination of local values and in the importation of ideas from all over the world.

Russia and Eastern Europe

Russian criticism has been dominated by Marxism since 1917. But one should realize that early in the century very different points of view prevailed, and that even after 1917 a lively debate raged in Russia and a great diversity of doctrines were propounded. Uniformity was not imposed until about 1932. Russian literary criticism has a special appeal for the student of criticism, independent of the light it may throw on Russian literature itself. More sharply than anywhere in the West, Russian criticism has elaborated three irreconcilable positions: symbolism, formalism, and Marxism.

Symbolism, which came to Russia in the 1890s, adopted there a highly metaphysical and even theological and theosophic doctrine: poetry was thought of as a revelation of a supernatural existence; the poet became a possessor of occult knowledge. Some of the best-known symbolist poets, Konstantin Balmont, Andrey Bely, and Valery Bryusov (qq.v.), wrote criticism that ranges from a vague mysticism to subtle technical investigations of meter and rhyme.

Closely related to the symbolist attitude was the cult and study of Dostoevsky, who was interpreted largely as a religious philosopher. Dmitry Merezhkovsky (q.v.) relentlessly pursued, in his *Tolstoy i Dostoevsky* (1901; *Tolstoy as Man and Artist, with an Essay on Dostoevsky,* 1902), the antithesis between Tolstoy, "the seer of the flesh," and Dostoevsky, "the seer of the spirit," and found antithetical structures, pagan and Christian, everywhere else. Vyacheslav Ivanov (q.v.) interpreted Dostoevsky in a series of essays (1916–17, uncollected in Russian; *Freedom and the Tragic Life: A Study in Dostoevsky,* 1952) as a creator of myths, and his novels as tragedies. Nikolay Berdyaev (1874–1948) studied the world view of Dostoevsky in *Mirosozertzanie Dostoevskogo* (1923; *The World Outlook of Dostoevsky,* 1934) as a philosophy of freedom in which God's existence is justified paradoxically by the existence of evil. These were writers of Russian Orthodox background, who developed their own version of religious philosophy. Two Russian Jews, Mikhail Gershenzon (1869–1925) and Lev Shestov (pseud. of Leo Schwartzmann, 1868–1938), used similar methods to interpret literature with different assumptions; Gershenzon studied the elusive skeptical wisdom of Pushkin in *Mudrost Pushkina* (1919; Pushkin's wisdom), while Shestov searched for an amoral, irrational God and found nihilism everywhere: in Dostoevsky and Tolstoy, in Nietzsche, and Chekhov (q.v.). *Apoteoz bezpochvennosti* (1905; the apotheosis of groundlessness) is the characteristic title of one of his books. Shestov in his late writings published in exile, in French, came very near to existentialism.

Partly in reaction to the mystique of symbolism and the growing power of Marxist criticism, a small but lively and influential group of young scholars, linguists, and literary historians organized a Society for the Study of Poetic Language in 1916, and thus founded what came to be known as the for-

malist movement. They flourished in the turbulent 1920s, but had to conform or were suppressed in the 1930s. They were a short episode in the history of Russian criticism, but their influence spread to Czechoslovakia and Poland and later to the United States.

One must distinguish several stages in the development of Russian formalism: an early stage of extremism that was closely allied with the rising movement of Russian futurism—Velemir Khlebnikov, Vladimir Mayakovsky (qq.v.); a middle period of consolidation and expansion; and a final crisis, breakup, and compromise with Marxism. One must also distinguish among its members: Viktor Shklovsky (b. 1893) was a firebrand, a stimulating gadfly, a crude and shrill publicist, while Boris Eikhenbaum (1886–1959), Roman Jakobson, and Yury Tynyanov (1894–1943) brought a great fund of erudition to their bold speculations. A learned scholar such as Viktor Zhirmunsky (1891–1971), on the other hand, drew ideas from his colleagues and tried to devise combinations with accepted views. Boris Tomashevsky (1886–1957), with his *Teoria literatury* (1905; theory of literature), was rather the popularizer and systematizer of the group.

The formalists, like the futurists, proclaimed poetry to be free creation, its word to be independent of reality, even "beyond sense." They at first denied the social and philosophical content of art and proclaimed its complete indifference, even, to emotions and ideas. In their first stage they were interested in one problem, that of poetic language, which they conceived of as a special language, achieved by a purposeful "deformation" of ordinary language, by what they called "organized violence" committed against it. They studied mainly the sound stratum of language: vowel harmonies, consonant clusters, rhyme, prose rhythm, and meter, drawing heavily on the results of modern linguistics, its concept of the "phoneme" developed by linguists such as Baudoin de Courtenay (1845–1929), Prince Nikolay Trubetskoy (1890–1938), and Roman Jakobson. They devised many technical methods (some even statistical), which can hardly be made comprehensible to someone without a knowledge of Russian. Slowly they saw that they had also to study composition and meaning, and finally that no poetics is complete without aesthetics and history. Shklovsky argued that the purpose of art is to shock us into an awareness of reality and that its main device to achieve this end is "making strange," making us see things from a new and surprising angle.

Another device of art is "putting on the brakes," forcing attention to the rocky road itself. Art is conceived even as a game of solitaire, or as a jigsaw puzzle. The techniques of narration—in folk tales, in the *Arabian Nights,* in the mystery and detective story, or in a novel as contrived as Sterne's *Tristram Shandy*—were analyzed by Shklovsky in *O teorii prozy* (1923; on the theory of prose), always with the emphasis on craft, on the distinction between subject and plot. Another formalist, Boris Eikhenbaum, boldly reinterpreted Gogol's *The Overcoat.* It is not a plea for our common humanity and the little man, as it was understood for a hundred years; it is, rather, a comic, grotesque story displaying the manipulation of the recital, the voice of the narrator. It has nothing to do with realism. Art is thus sharply divorced from life. Roman Jakobson asked: "Why should a poet have more responsibility for a struggle of ideas than for a battle of swords or a duel by pistols?" And he made the striking formulation: "Literary scholarship should investigate what makes literature literary"—that is, its literariness, the devices that make a work of art what it is.

Thus, the formalists rejected all biographical, psychological, and sociological methods as external. They ridiculed old-fashioned literary history as having no real subject matter, limits, or method. They tried to devise instead a historical poetics that would concentrate on the internal evolution of poetry. Poetic schools are considered as changing in a dialectical process of action and reaction, convention and revolt. Conventions wear out: the "automatization" of devices will need a new "actualization." The rise of new genres is seen as a revival of "low" forms, as a needed rebarbarization of literature. Thus, Dostoevsky glorified the sensational French *roman-feuilleton,* and Alexandr Blok (q.v.) raised the gypsy song into the realm of art. The only criterion of value recognized by the formalists is novelty, the success of a work of art in changing the direction of literary evolution.

The parallelism between Russian formalism and similar movements in the West, such as the American New Criticism, is striking, especially in the common preoccupation with the language of poetry. But the Russian

movement seems purely indigenous: some of its forerunners were the comparatist Alexandr Veselovsky (1838–1906), who attempted a historical poetics, and the linguist Alexandr Potebnya (1835–1891). The Russian formalists differed sharply from analogous movements in other countries. They leaned much more heavily on technical linguistics, especially phonemics. They disparaged the role of imagery and symbolism. Their concept of the work of art as a sum of devices was mechanistic. They were positivists, with a scientific ideal of scholarship—technicians who devised ingenious methods of analysis with great clarity. They preserved a strong interest in literary history and historical poetics. But they did not see the crucial problem of evaluation, left as they were with the single criterion of novelty, in the blind alley of relativism.

On many points Russian formalism was greatly improved when it was exported to Poland and Czechoslovakia. In Poland, Manfred Kridl (1882–1957) argued in favor of an "integral method" of literary studies, radically centered on the work of art. A philosopher, Roman Ingarden (1893–1970), writing in German, in *Das literarische Kunstwerk* (1931; new ed., 1960; *The Literary Work of Art,* 1973) applied Husserl's phenomenology to an analysis of the different strata of the work of art and its ontological status. He thus overcame the dichotomy of content and form and grounded the theories of formalism epistemologically. In Czechoslovakia, where Roman Jakobson settled for years, the Prague Linguistic Circle was founded (1926), partly at his instigation, and some of its members devoted themselves to literary theory. Among them Jan Mukařovský (1891–1975) was the outstanding theorist of literature. The Czechs restated Russian formalism, rechristening it "structuralism." Structure is a term like *Gestalt,* which attempts to overcome the dualism of content and form.

While the Czechs adopted the main tenets of Russian formalism, they rejected its positivism—its methods of treating literature as an art entirely determined by language and literary scholarship as almost a branch of linguistics. The Czechs had studied Hegel, Husserl, *Gestalt* psychology, and the philosophy of symbolic forms propounded by Ernst Cassirer (1874–1945). They saw that the meaning of a work of literature is not purely linguistic, that it projects a "world" of motifs, themes, characters, plots, and even ideas. Mukařovský went beyond careful stylistic and semantic analyses to a general theory of aesthetics in which key concepts like function, structure, norm, and value point to an overall goal in a theory of semiology, of meaning in a social and historical context.

But all these promising developments were cut short by World War II and its aftereffects. In Poland and Czechoslovakia, Marxism was imposed after the war: men such as Mukařovský recanted publicly. Others, such as Jakobson and Kridl, emigrated to the United States. Criticism, as an act of understanding and free judgment, is dead behind the Iron Curtain.

In the Soviet Union today a hidebound dogmatic Marxism is firmly entrenched, no doubts about its "correctness" can be voiced, and a standard of judgment is applied very easily, since it is all ready-made and prescribed. Fortunately, there are scholars who try to find a way out of the net, not by revolting against the reigning dogma but by escaping into neutral neighboring disciplines acceptable by their scientific pretensions. Linguistics and semiotics are flourishing and attempt to include literary theory. A whole group of scholars at the University of Tartu in Estonia, headed by Yury Lotman (b. 1922), developed a semiotic scheme that incorporates motifs from the original Russian formalism and the Prague structuralism. Lotman is mainly concerned with a technical analysis of verse, while a younger member of the group, Boris Uspensky (b. 1937), has studied the technique of the novel, particularly what in the West is called the point of view, in *Poetika kompozitsii* (1970; *A Poetics of Composition*, 1973).

The almost miraculous resurrection of Mikhail Bakhtin (1895–1975) has, however, aroused the most attention in the West. In his life he was almost a pariah: he was banished to a remote village on the frontier of Siberia from 1929 to 1936, and only in later years was he allowed to teach in Saransk in Mordvinia. He had to use pseudonyms and work in collaboration. Today N. Voloshinov's books *Froydizm* (1927; *Freudianism,* 1976) and *Marxizm i filosofia yazyka* (1929; *Marxism and the Philosophy of Language,* 1973) and Pavel Medvedev's *Formalny metod v literaturovedeni* (1928; *The Formal Method in Literary Scholarship,* 1978) are ascribed to him. His *Problemy tvorchestva Dostoevskogo* (1929; expanded version, *Prob-*

lemy poetiky Dostoevskogo, 1963; *Problems of Dostoevsky's Poetics,* 1973), his study of Rabelais, *Tvorchestvo Fransua Rable a narodnaya kultura srednevyekovya i renessansa* (written 1940, pub. 1965; *Rabelais and His World,* 1968), and finally a collection of papers, *Voprosy literatury i estetiki* (1975; *The Dialogic Imagination,* 1981) established him as one of the most important literary scholars of this century.

Bakhtin starts out with formalist assumptions, recognizing the specificity of the aesthetic object, but instead of a phenomenology he elaborates a semiotic that by definition is sociological. Man constitutes himself in language from the point of view of another man and thus ultimately from the point of view of a collective, a society. Language is thus dialogue, the word has a "multiple voice." The novel, which is Bakhtin's main concern, is defined as a "consciously structured hybrid of languages." Dialogue is the fundamental form of novelistic discourse, and the elaboration of the voice of the other is for him the leading motif of the history of the novel. He traces this history, with great erudition, through the Middle Ages to the novel of Dostoevsky, which, in his view, as a "polyphonic novel" is radically different from the main tradition of the 18th- and 19th-c. fullfledged novel. Dostoevsky thus has his remote forerunners in the Mennippian satire, in medieval folktales, which in the book on Rabelais are investigated in a context of folk culture, humor, and grotesquerie, a whole strand of human behavior Bakhtin calls "carnivalesque." In the book on Rabelais, the humanist is purposely ignored. In the book on Dostoevsky the religious thinker and prophet is dismissed as Bakhtin concludes that "all points of view are made part of dialogue. There is no final word in the world of Dostoevsky." Although this conclusion seems doubtful, the book has many acute things to say about the hero, the genre, the plot composition, and the verbal style. There is a basic unity to the three books: a vision of man as maker of language in society, a view of the novel beyond the confines of the usual emphasis on the line from Defoe to Proust, and narrative as an all-human indulgence in joyous verbal communication and play.

Germany and Austria

Germany in the latter half of the 18th and early in the 19th c. produced a large body of aesthetic and critical doctrines whose influence was felt throughout the 19th c. The two brothers Schlegel, especially, carried the message of German romanticism all over the Western world. But in the later 19th c. Germany lost its leadership in criticism completely: no single German critic established, even in his own nation, a position remotely comparable to that of Sainte-Beuve or Taine in France, Matthew Arnold in England, De Sanctis in Italy, and Vissarion Grigorevich Belinsky (1811–1848) in Russia. The cleavage between university scholarship and day-by-day reviewing was in Germany greater than elsewhere. Scholarship became purely historical, factual, "objective," and deliberately refrained from judgment and criticism, although it often assumed the standards of value developed by the great German classics. On the other hand, the reviewers became journalists who lost touch with a coherent body of doctrine: either impressionism went rampant or standards of didactic usefulness, mainly based on nationalistic ideals or political attitudes, prevailed. In either case genuine literary criticism was dead.

In the 1880s, however, the movement of naturalism, introduced largely from France, stirred the stagnant waters and aroused violent debates (especially around Ibsen and Zola). Real criticism, in the sense of a definition of a new taste, was produced, even though the theories of naturalism were derivative and often very simplicist in their grasp of the nature of art.

At the dawn of the new century the naturalist movement had run its course; its most important critics had ceased publishing—for example, Otto Brahm (1856–1912), who had fought for Ibsen and Gerhart Hauptmann (q.v.), had become a theatrical manager.

Simultaneous with the rise of German naturalism another reaction had set in against the 19th-c. tradition: that which loosely could be called symbolism. In Germany Stefan George (q.v.) became the leader of a group that exerted great influence on literary taste and criticism. George himself was hardly a literary critic in the strict sense of the word, but his proclamations on the prophetic mission of the artist, of the incantatory power of language, and the need of severe form and unity in a work of poetry, as well as his eulogies of Mallarmé, Verlaine, Jean Paul, and Hölderlin, became the stimulus for the criticism systematized by his circle. George's anthology *Deutsche Dichtung* (3 vols., 1901–

3, ed. with Karl Wolfskehl; German poetry), which, besides single volumes devoted to Goethe and Jean Paul, admitted only a very small selection from nine 19th-c. poets, and George's translations from Dante, Baudelaire, and many recent French and English poets, held up a new ideal of taste that sharply broke with the emotionalism and didacticism of the 19th c.

George's disciples elaborated his hints and dicta into a body of criticism that for the first time, after a long period of relativism, historicism, and philological factualism, asserted a critical creed, proclaimed definite standards, and defined a tradition and taste. Unfortunately, the genuine insights of the school into the nature of poetry are marred by the doctrinaire tone of delivery, the aristocratic pretensions, and the often comically high-pitched, almost oracular solemnity of their pronouncements.

By far the best of George's direct followers was Friedrich Gundolf (1880–1931), while the others, whatever their merits as poets or translators, seem as critics only sectarians. Thus Friedrich Wolters (1876–1930), in his *Stefan George und die Blätter für die Kunst* (1930; Stefan George and the *Blätter für die Kunst* [journal for art]), asserts, at great length, George's claims not only to poetic greatness but to the leadership of the nation and to a religious revelation in George's meeting with Maximin. Other books on George by members of the circle are also written in a tone of adoration for a religious leader; they are saints' lives and acts of the apostles rather than criticism. Gundolf's *George* (1920; George) is no less idolatrous, but succeeds, at least, in concretely describing and analyzing George's poetic achievements.

But the book on George was preceded by Gundolf's best critical work: *Shakespeare und der deutsche Geist* (1911; Shakespeare and the German mind) and *Goethe* (1916; Goethe). These are books nourished by considerable learning, in spite of Gundolf's ostentatious contempt for footnotes and acknowledgements: well-composed, finely phrased books that set, in Germany, new standards of critical judgment and analytical power. The early study of Shakespeare's influence on Germany from the English comedians of the 17th c. to the Schlegels combines criticism of the main German writers with insight into period styles. Gundolf admirably sets forth the distinction between mere borrowings and external parallels on the one hand, and deeper assimilation on the other, and penetratingly analyzes the style of translations and imitations. His harsh judgment of the naturalistic distortions of Shakespeare by the German "Storm and Stress" and of the moralism and rhetoric of Schiller are refreshingly straightforward, even though his own conception of Shakespeare divorces him too sharply from the stage. The concentration on the texts and figures, apart from biographical information and details of literary history, and the cultivated, even precious style of writing were welcome innovations after the spate of colorless books crammed with information but devoid of taste and judgment.

Gundolf's largest book, *Goethe,* shows the same qualities of insight, analytical power, organization, and finished presentation. But while the earlier book was clearly nonbiographical and antipsychological and still remained properly historical, the book on Goethe postulates some obscure synthesis of biography and criticism in a contemplation of the *Gestalt* of Goethe. In this heroically stylized figure no distinction, Gundolf argues, can be made between *Erlebnis* (experience) and work, with the result that the book again confuses life and poetry. Gundolf had studied *Das Erlebnis und die Dichtung* (1905; experience and poetry), a collection of essays, mostly dating from the 19th c., by the great historian of ideas and feelings Wilhelm Dilthey, and had absorbed his philosophy: a version of *Lebensphilosophie,* which Gundolf combined with ideas derived from Bergson. *Leben,* in Dilthey, does not mean life (*bios*), but the total *psyche,* the mental structure that fuses intellect, will, and feeling into one. The function of poetry is seen as an increase of vitality; the main criterion of judgment is emotional sincerity, engagement, personal involvement, presuming an intense *Erlebnis.* In Dilthey, this emotionalism is combined rather incongruously with a view of poetry as expressing a specific *Weltanschauung,* a popular philosophy with relativistic conclusions, as, for Dilthey, there are only three types of *Weltanschauung* (realism, dualistic idealism—what he calls *Idealismus der Freiheit* (idealism of freedom)—and monistic idealism), all illustrated in literature and all ultimately equal as to their claims to truth.

Gundolf, although influenced by Dilthey, never succumbed to the psychologism and relativism of Dilthey. He saved criticism by devising a distinction between *Urerlebnis* and *Bildungserlebnis,* in which the elementary personal experience is preferred to the cultural experience, and by a somewhat parallel scale of the lyrical, symbolical, and allegorical, in which the lyrical (which is not necessarily identical with the traditional genre) precedes the other two categories. The emphasis falls on the personal lyric, but Gundolf argued that the poet experiences differently from the ordinary man, in terms anticipating his creation, forming even while living. Gundolf construed a conflict between Goethe's titanism and eroticism, between work and life, after all. The emphasis on the lyrical, on the *daimon,* which yields fine analyses of the early poetry, and of *Werther,* does not, however, obscure his insight into the structures of Goethe's objective, "symbolic" poetry and into the relation of Goethe's works to tradition and convention. Whatever objections to individual interpretations may be voiced, the book remains an impressive monument. Today we would feel that in spite of many fine discriminations the tone of adoration, the setting up of the pedestal, the arranging of the drapery becomes excessively monotonous. It is hard not to resent the idolatry that changes the eminently humane figure of Goethe into a demonic creator for creation's sake. Real insights are often drowned in a flood of verbiage repeating over and over again the same or similar antitheses.

Even more one-sided is Gundolf's portrait *Heinrich von Kleist* (1922; Heinrich von Kleist), in which Kleist is seen as "a solitary soul without nation and God," as a chaotic, even monstrous genius, great by his defiance of the time, tragic as a symbolic sacrifice. Gundolf's two-volume *Shakespeare: Sein Wesen und Werk* (1928; Shakespeare: his nature and work) is curiously neglected. It suffers from preciosity and monotony, it sees Shakespeare so completely out of the context of the time and the stage that Shakespeare's ethos is falsified; but individual observations show an insight into the poetry and its symbolism, an emphasis on what might be called the baroque in Shakespeare, which was rare at the time. Only the last essays, *Romantiker* (2 vols., 1930–31; romantics), return to more traditional methods of characterization and judgment, which, however, often are excessively unsympathetic to such volatile and elusive figures as Friedrich Schlegel.

Two other members of the George circle wrote significant literary criticism. Ernst

Bertram's (1884–1957) *Nietzsche* (1918; Nietzsche) aroused much adverse comment because of its subtitle, *Versuch einer Mythologie* (attempt at a mythology), and an introduction that boldly proclaimed the aim of the critic to be the creation of a legend, an "image," a myth. But the text of the book does not go all the way into subjectivism. It interprets Nietzsche as a lonely romantic, an ambiguous, contradictory, tortured irrationalist, an "image" that has at least as much justification as more recent attempts, such as that of Walter F. Kaufmann (1921–1980) in *Nietzsche: Philosopher, Psychologist, Antichrist* (1950), to make Nietzsche a reasonable descendant of the Enlightenment.

Max Kommerell (1902–1944), in *Der Dichter als Führer in der deutschen Klassik* (1928; the writer as leader in German classicism), interpreted the whole German classical group in terms of Stefan George's ideals. Klopstock is seen as a disciple of the Greeks, absorbed in antiquity and Platonic friendships, as if he had not been a Christian. Jean Paul is pressed into the Weimar company. Schiller becomes a disciple of Goethe, and Hölderlin is exalted to a national hero, a prophet of a religious regeneration of Germany as a second Greece. The deification of Hölderlin (who, in Dilthey's *Das Erlebnis und die Dichtung,* still appears as a charming, sentimental dreamer) was stimulated by the discovery of Hölderlin's late hymns by another disciple of George's, Norbert von Hellingrath (1888–1916). He prepared a complete new edition and wrote short expositions that found greatness even in the crabbed translations from Pindar and Sophocles and the most baffling fragments from the last stage of Hölderlin's lucid life before madness beclouded his mind. But Kommerell soon broke with George, because he could not accept his intellectual dictatorship, and went his own way. We shall meet him in another context.

George, in his beginnings, attracted the Austrian poet Hugo von Hofmannsthal (q.v.). They shared the opposition to naturalism, the cult of form and word, but they soon drifted apart, because Hofmannsthal would not submit to the "discipline" of the George circle and had other ambitions in the theater and a very different concrete taste in literature. Hofmannsthal is only incidentally a critic; but his early articles written in his precocious youth under the pseudonym "Loris" (1891–97) define a taste that could roughly

be called "decadent" in its love for Swinburne, Pater, and D'Annunzio, and assert the independence of poetry from life and its essence in form and imagery. Later, in many essays, articles, and speeches, Hofmannsthal, often impressionistically and loosely, defined his preferences in literature: for the baroque and romance traditions, for Molière, Hugo, and Balzac, Calderón and the Austrians Franz Grillparzer (1791–1872) and Adalbert Stifter (1805–1868). In literary theory, Hofmannsthal brought out the mystical, Neoplatonic implications of his symbolist aesthetics. The bulk of his later writing on literature moved, however, in generalities of a "political" nature. Thus, in the speech "Das Schrifttum als geistiger Raum der Nation" (1927; writing as a spiritual space of the nation) Hofmannsthal praises tradition against romantic caprice and warns against the worn-out ideals of the *Bildungsphilister* (cultural philistine): a "conservative revolution" is advocated, in which a high ideal of European unity is propped up by a strong consciousness of the role of old Austria as a mediator between North and South, East and West.

With Hofmannsthal two poets were associated in friendship: Rudolf Borchardt (1877–1945) and Rudolf Alexander Schröder (1878–1962). Borchardt, the translator of Dante into a special archaic German, and a learned student of antiquity and Italy, was a passionate, even stridently vociferous asserter of the great tradition. In a postscript to *Ewiger Vorrat deutscher Poesie* (1926; the permanent treasure of German poetry), an anthology of German poetry, he makes short work of the German 19th c. and such established reputations as Heine's, and in eloquent *Reden* (speeches), collected in 1955, he proclaimed his somewhat foggy ideal of a reconciliation of the German and Latin spirits, antiquity and the Middle Ages. But he was at his best in his scattered essays on Pindar and Vergil, Hartmann von Aue and Dante, Lessing, Dante Gabriel Rossetti, Hofmannsthal, and George. In spite of his dogmatic tone, Borchardt was full of sympathy with often very diverse minds, flexible, and even disconcertingly uncritical (for example, his excessive enthusiasm for Edna St. Vincent Millay [q.v.]). His violent criticism of contemporary literature and its commercial aspects, his glorification of the Prussian monarchic tradition, his total condemnation of the 18th c. and the Enlightenment, his panegyric of German romanticism and historicism, his acceptance of Croce's aesthetics, are some of the incongruous elements of his thought, fused only by his powerful temperament and brilliant eloquence.

Compared to Borchardt's violence and eccentricity, Schröder seems a modest, sensible, sober expounder of the great tradition. He is best known for his translations of Homer, Vergil, and Horace. His critical writings, in their smooth eloquence, assert persuasively the mission of the poet as the maker of language, the great comforter for the transience of our existence. The poet, in Schröder's later writings, is more and more identified with the religious leader. Schröder made an intensive study of Protestant hymns and religious poetry, while he clung to a defense of the classical heritage of Europe. Poets like Vergil, Horace, and Racine have found few admirers in modern Germany as sympathetic as Schröder, but Schröder seems less a critic than a scholarly expositor of the classical-Christian heritage.

Also loosely related to this group was Rudolf Kassner (1873–1959), who began with a book of essays, *Die Mystik, die Künstler und das Leben* (1900; mysticism, artists, and life; rev. ed., *Englische Dichter,* 1922; English poets), which combines a taste for the Pre-Raphaelites with a genuine interest in mysticism. William Blake was his early hero. The imagination, which in these essays links the poet and the mystic, becomes, in Kassner's later, mostly philosophical writings, the central concept of a pantheistic world view in which physiognomics, the interpretation of outward physical signs, plays a central role. As a literary critic Kassner remains a symbolist who, however, developed special tastes for authors usually ignored in Germany: Laurence Sterne, whose feeling for time appeals to Kassner; Gogol; De Quincey; and even Thomas Hardy (q.v.). Shakespeare, however, remains the exemplar of the imagination. All authors and all poetry, in the later Kassner, become only specimens to substantiate a philosophy in which oriental and mystical ideas combine to support a revival of a basically romantic view of the imagination: as a "seizure of the thing by the image," a universal system of analogy, of all-in-one. A grandiose attempt is made to abolish the distinctions between sense and spirit, the concrete and the abstract, but literature as such is lost sight of.

Parallel with what could be called the Ger-

man symbolist movement, represented by Stefan George and Hofmannsthal, there arose a new classicism, or rather neoclassicism, which asserted the role of form and tradition, mainly in the drama. Paul Ernst (1866–1933) found, after a youth devoted to naturalism and Marxism, a way to a new, highly intellectual classicism. In *Der Weg zur Form* (1906; the way to form) Ernst pleads for necessity, for fate, for the coercion of form in the drama and the short story, and disparages the novel and all description and psychological analysis. Drama is interpreted as an ethical conflict; tragedy as a joyous recognition of necessity even in the perdition of the hero. An absolute morality is postulated as the basis for a renewal of tragedy. The critical creed, however, remains disconcertingly abstract, and Ernst's many articles on literary figures stay well within the bounds of conventional eclecticism.

In this general tradition of the defense of the cultural values of the German past, two writers might be listed who cultivated the form of the essay. Thomas Mann (q.v.) produced a long series of articles, speeches, lectures, and introductions, which either praise kindred spirits or circle around Mann's problem of the position of the artist in society or probe into the artist's psychology, often by means derived from Freud and Nietzsche. Mann's consciousness—whatever the changes of his political orientation—is definitely conservative, *bürgerlich,* although acutely aware of the limits of the bourgeois tradition. Mann's essays are too autobiographical and too monotonously engaged in developing broad antitheses to be good criticism, aside from the light they throw on Mann's art.

Another general essayist was Josef Hofmiller (1872–1933), whose *Versuche* (1909; attempts) and *Letzte Versuche* (1935; last attempts) are examples of the art of portraiture in the sense of Sainte-Beuve. His outlook was Roman Catholic, his interests widely scattered, his tone is reasonable, his exposition skillful, but the criticism seems often colorless and imperceptive.

The change of taste, the newly acquired sense of form and tradition also influenced academic German scholarship profoundly. A group of Romance scholars, especially, combined scholarship and criticism successfully. Karl Vossler, influenced by Croce's view of language as individual creation, traced the history of the French literary language and wrote a large study of Dante's *Divine Come-*

dy (*Die göttliche Komödie*, 2 vols., 1907–10; *Medieval Culture*, 1929), which is both learnedly historical and critical. He wrote descriptive and analytical monographs on Racine, La Fontaine, Leopardi, Lope de Vega, and the Spanish poetry of solitude.

Ernst Robert Curtius (q.v.) had the most intimate relations with contemporary literature: at first as a critical importer of modern French literature into Germany, and then as a sensitive and often pioneering analyst of Proust, Joyce, and T. S. Eliot, in the collections *Kritische Essays zur europäischen Literatur* (1950; *Essays on European Literature*, 1973) and *Französischer Geist im zwanzigsten Jahrhundert* (1952; the French mind in the twentieth century). In his book *Balzac* (1923; Balzac) he reinterprets the master of realism as a Swedenborgian visionary, and his last and longest book, *Europäische Literatur und lateinisches Mittelalter* (1948; *European Literature and the Latin Middle Ages*, 1953), weighted though it is by immense erudition, aims at a critical point in establishing the unity and continuity of European literature since classical antiquity, not only in its forms and period styles but in its themes and commonplaces (*topoi*). In Curtius a concern for tradition, a feeling for the world of Latinity and for European unity, an admiration for George, Hofmannsthal, and Eliot, combine happily with great historical and rhetorical erudition.

Leo Spitzer (1887–1960) was more of a purely technical student of linguistics and stylistics; but in his wide-ranging studies of literature he developed a method of interpretation treating the word as a sign of the mind and soul that serves genuine critical purposes. Spitzer wrote much on French and Spanish literatures (Racine, Diderot, Voltaire, Proust, Cervantes, Lope de Vega) and later also interpreted poems by Donne and Keats and a story by Poe. Spitzer always worked on a small scale, with a specific text, although he was inspired by a general concept of humanism.

Erich Auerbach (q.v.) also always starts with the stylistic analysis of a text, but in his *Mimesis: Dargestellte Wirklichkeit in der abendländischen Literatur* (1946; *Mimesis: The Representation of Reality in Western Literature*, 1953) he attempts a general history of realism from Homer to Proust. The book combines stylistic analysis of individual passages with literary, social, and intellectual history. Auerbach's concept of realism is very special: it means to him both a concrete insight into social and political reality and an existential sense of reality, understood tragically, as man in solitude facing moral decisions.

Compared to this distinguished group of scholar-critics in the Romance languages, the study of German literature was less affected by the new understanding of form and tradition. Oskar Walzel (1864–1944) was an eminent specialist in the history of ideas, especially of the German romantic movement, before he tried to apply stylistic criteria to literature. He discovered Heinrich Wölfflin's (1864–1945) *Kunstgeschichtliche Grundbegriffe* (1915; *Principles of Art History*, 1932), in which the Swiss art historian expounded a scheme for a definition of the difference between Renaissance and baroque in the plastic arts, and transferred these criteria to literature. Walzel attempted to show, for example, that Shakespeare belongs to the baroque, since his plays are not built in the symmetrical manner found by Wölfflin in pictures of the Renaissance. In a pamphlet, "Wechselseitige Erhellung der Künste" (1917; mutual elucidation of the arts), and in many later writings, Walzel defended the method of transferring criteria developed by art history to literary history and developed devices and stylistic methods of his own. But *Gestalt und Gehalt im Kunstwerk des Dichters* (1923; form and content in the literary work of art) shows that Walzel is rather an eclectic expositor of other people's ideas and opinions than a critic, and his many very valuable, erudite books are strongest when they concern intellectual history. Thus *Grenzen von Poesie und Unpoesie* (1937; limits of poetry and nonpoetry), in spite of its deceptively Crocean title, has nothing to do with criticism: it is a historical study of German romantic aesthetics.

Fritz Strich (1882–1963) showed that the method of Wölfflin's contraries can be applied to German classicism and romanticism. In *Deutsche Klassik und Romantik; oder, Vollendung und Unendlichkeit* (1922; German classicism and romanticism; or, perfection and infinity) Strich shows that the baroque characteristics hold true for romanticism, the Renaissance for classicism. Strich interprets Wölfflin's concepts of closed and open form as analogues to the opposition between the perfect classical form and the open, unfinished, fragmentary and blurred form of romantic poetry expressive of man's

105

longing for the infinite. In detail, Strich is full of subtle remarks and observations, but the general scheme that assumes a sharp division in the general German movement of the late 18th c. will not withstand closer inspection. With Walzel and Strich stylistic analysis clearly passes into intellectual history, which was the preoccupation of most German academic scholars.

We have traced the revival of a sense of tradition and form and the establishment of what could roughly be called the symbolist and formalist point. But German literature soon after 1910 was convulsed by a very different movement: expressionism (q.v.), which corresponds to futurism in Italy and Russia. Expressionism hardly produced criticism, at least in its earlier stages, but only manifestos, declarations, polemics, often vaguely and emotionally phrased: cries, oracular dicta, or mere fancies. Still, expressionism represented an important revolution in taste. Its complete rejection of tradition, its contempt for form, coupled with a rejection of naturalism and impressionism, the proclamation of a return to metaphysics, to an inner world of expression that would not, however, be the psychological analysis of an individual but the cry of a common humanity—all these are critical motifs that were thrown out unsystematically in articles, in *Charon,* in *Der Sturm,* and other short-lived periodicals, or in small booklets like Kasimir Edschmid's (1890–1966) *Über den Expressionismus in der Literatur und die neue Dichtung* (1918; on expressionism in literature and the new poetry). The versatile Austrian critic Hermann Bahr (q.v.), who had written very early his *Die Überwindung des Naturalismus* (1891; the overthrow of naturalism), tried, in his *Expressionismus* (1916; *Expressionism,* 1916), to relate the whole movement to the theory of fine arts and drew on Wilhelm Worringer's (1881–1965) *Abstraktion und Einfühlung* (1911; *Abstraction and Empathy,* 1953), a book that contrasted abstract art, imposing form on nature, with organic art, fusing with the object. Expressionism appears related to Egyptian, Byzantine, Gothic, and baroque art in its rejection of the classical human form. In writers such as Rudolf Pannwitz (1881–1969), Lothar Schreyer (1886–1966), and Carl Sternheim (q.v.) diverse irrationalist ideas are stressed: the vision of the artist and its power, the emancipation of the word, the role of myth in art. The relations to the past, to precursors or supposed precursors such as the rediscovered Georg Büchner (1813–1837), were explored only cursorily.

Among the leading expressionist poets only Gottfried Benn (q.v.) can be said to have practiced criticism with any continuity and coherence. He defined expressionism largely in terms of its destruction of reality and history, of its horrifying experience of the chaos of the world and the decay of values. Benn, who even passed through a period of admiration for Nazism, in later writings found a way to a position that is not very different (in criticism) from Eliot's or Mallarmé's. *Probleme der Lyrik* (1951; problems of poetry) proclaims the ideal of absolute poetry, without belief, without hope, addressed to nobody, made out of words. More sharply than any other German critic, Benn protested against the view that a poem is about feelings and must emanate warmth; he ridicules poems addressed to nature, full of similes starting with the word "like," full of names for colors with a seraphic tone of murmuring fountains, harps, night, and silence. Benn became the most radical critic of the assumptions of the German romantic lyric. He believed in form and reality somehow imposed on the original chaos of the world and ceased to be an expressionist.

While nothing like a coherent theory could come from the deliberately chaotic irrationalism of the expressionists proper, the general influence of expressionist attitudes and vocabulary was widely felt. Theatrical criticism possibly most clearly shows the expressionist mood, even when the critic rejects particular expressionist plays or theories. Alfred Kerr (1867–1948), in hundreds of reviews, written in an affected, clipped style, judged the Berlin stage for years. He outgrew his early naturalistic predilections and moved more and more in the direction of expressionism: his praise of August Strindberg, Frank Wedekind (qq.v.), and Carl Sternheim went with a rejection of everything classical. Kerr was constantly "bored" by Shakespeare and in his introductory pronouncements flaunts the idea (for which he looks in Heine and Oscar Wilde for predecessors) of criticism as art, even superior to creation, as the "eternizing of trash." Bernhard Diebold (1886–1945), in *Anarchie im Drama* (1920; expanded 4th ed., 1928; anarchy in the drama), discusses Georg Kaiser (q.v.), Wedekind, Sternheim, and Strindberg, often very critically, and the many books by Julius Bab (1880–1955) and those of Herbert Ihering (1888–1967) show the same taste: a dissatisfaction with naturalism as a misunderstanding of art, a turn toward experimentalism on the stage, whatever direction it might ultimately take. Although much of this theatrical criticism is necessarily ephemeral, it was the place where criticism as judgment was most alive in Germany.

In style and in his general sense of the world, especially his bitter hatred of commercial civilization, the great Austrian satirist Karl Kraus is related to expressionism. The periodical he wrote singlehandedly, *Die Fackel,* contains much literary criticism, mostly of a polemical sort animated by a fierce ethical pathos against all sham, written in an allusive, witty style that exploits all resources of language. His whole work is permeated by criticism, mostly directed against contemporary Austrian literature and journalism. Neither Arthur Schnitzler nor Franz Werfel (qq.v.) nor Hofmannsthal nor Bahr escaped the spearpoint of this harsh but salutary moralist.

The expressionist movement as a poetic trend was over by about 1920; it had been nourished by the moods of the war and its aftermath. After a few years of comparative normality, criticism was again transformed by an outside factor—the rising tide of Nazism. Nazism defined a literary theory and taste that officially prevailed for the years 1933–45. One must, however, distinguish between two kinds of Nazi criticism: one is primarily racist, biological in its ideology, vaguely realistic, provincial in its taste; the other was, rather, mystical and vaguely philosophical. The first kind wanted *Heimatskunst, Blut und Boden* (national art, blood, and soil); it was idyllic, or pseudoidyllic. Long before World War I, Adolf Bartels (1862–1944) had produced a stream of histories and polemics that interpreted German literature from this point of view and specifically indulged in elaborate attacks on the Jews (and half- and quarter-Jews) in German literature.

A very erudite scholar, Josef Nadler (1884–1963), whose original affiliations were conservative and Catholic, also gave a biological interpretation of German literature. His *Literaturgeschichte der deutschen Stämme und Landschaften* (4 vols., 1922–28; literary history of the German tribes and regions; also pub. in a Nazified ed. as *Literaturgeschichte des deutschen Volkes,* 4 vols., 1938–41; literary history of the German people) was an attempt to write literary history "from below," according to the tribes, districts, and cities, always constructing "tribal souls" of the different regions, professing to read literary traits from the ancestry of the family.

Although much of his biology seems wholly fanciful and his philosophy of German history quite fantastic, Nadler had genuine merits: he revived interest in the submerged and neglected Catholic south, and he had a fine power of racy characterization and sense of locality, which is by no means useless in the study of the frequently very local German literature. In spite of the racist assumptions (and the anti-Semitism and superpatriotism, particularly blatant in the later edition), Nadler represents the curious mixture, common in academic Nazi scholarship, of pseudoscientific biology, old romantic conceptions of the national soul, and even categories derived from *Geistesgeschichte* and the history of artistic styles. Many other German literary historians who joined the Nazi movement and wrote Nazi literary history on a more sophisticated level drew ideas and concepts from almost anywhere: from mysticism and romanticism, from Stefan George and Nietzsche, but capped the ramshackle structure by an overriding concept of German art in which racist assumptions were weirdly amalgamated with philosophical and literary concepts. The special feature of this new literary criticism need hardly be described: the elimination or denigration of Jews, the contortions in fitting inconvenient but unavoidable figures such as Goethe into their pattern, the frantic search for anticipations of Nazi doctrines, the foggy, monotonous jargon, the resentful, nationalist boasting. It is a sorry chapter in the history of German scholarship, only partially excusable on grounds of political pressure.

After the end of World War II, existentialism began to dominate the German intellectual scene. Interpreted, as it popularly is, as a philosophy of despair, of "fear and trembling," of man's exposure in a hostile universe, the reasons for its spread are not far to seek. But the main work by Martin Heidegger, *Sein und Zeit* (1927; *Being and Time,* 1962) dates from an earlier period, and existentialist ideas, in a broad sense, had been familiar to the readers of Dostoevsky and Kafka since the vogue of Kierkegaard in Germany, early in the 1920s. Heidegger's own version of existentialism (as that of Karl Jaspers [1883–1969]) is actually a kind of new humanism, profoundly different from the far more gloomy French school with its dominant concept of absurdity. Heidegger's contribution to literary thinking is that of a vocabulary and an emphasis on some new concepts, such as time and mood, rather than of a strictly aesthetic and critical nature. His writings on aesthetics and his interpretations of Rilke and of Hölderlin are extremely obscure and personal. Beauty is identified with truth, poetry is prophecy.

But more important than these later writings were Heidegger's general ideas: his justification of the neglect of psychology, his dismissal of the whole subject and object relationship that had dominated German thought. Criticism found a new reason (as it found it also in Husserl's phenomenology (see Phenomenology and Literature) to turn to the object itself, and to try to interpret and understand it as such by means that could be called intuitive rather than analytical. In Heidegger's system, moreover, the three dimensions of time—past, present, and future—assume a central importance that helped to focus attention on the concept or feeling for time in literature.

Existentialism thus combined a rejection of the old positivistic factualism with distrust for *Geistesgeschichte,* sociology, and psychology. The newly flourishing textual interpretation in Germany is usually inspired by such philosophical motives. They are prominent in the writings of Max Kommerell after he had left the George circle and struck out on his own. He became adverse to easy generalizations and *Geistesgeschichte* and cultivated what in the United States would be called "close reading." In *Gedanken über Gedichte* (1943; thoughts on poems), which is mainly devoted to subtle interpretations of Goethe's lyrical poetry, the existentialist emphasis on poetry as "self-cognition" (*Selbsterkenntnis*), as the definition of a "mood" (*Stimmung*) is obvious, but it is combined, especially in Kommerell's other writings, with a remarkable grasp of the symbolic and conventional nature of art: with a defense of French tragedy, commedia dell'arte, and Calderón.

Similarly, Emil Staiger (b. 1908) combines a subtle gift of sensitive interpretation with existentialist motifs. In his *Die Zeit als Einbildungskraft des Dichters* (1939; time as the imagination of the poet) he interprets three poems by Brentano, Goethe, and Keller, in contrasts derived from Heidegger's terms. In the introduction all causal and psychological

explanation, even simple description of literature, is rejected in favor of a phenomenology, of interpretation. *Grundbegriffe der Poetik* (1946; principles of poetics) is an attempt to give the three traditional genres (lyric, epic, drama) a new meaning by linking them to the three dimensions of Heidegger's time concept. The lyric is associated with the present; the epic, or rather the epical, with the past; the drama, or rather the dramatic, with the future. The weird scheme is based on an analysis of the German romantic lyric, of Homer, and of some tragedies (Sophocles, Schiller, and Kleist). It revives speculations suggested by Jean Paul and a little-known English 19th-c. critic, E. S. Dallas, but the scheme breaks down, since it has no relation to any historical meaning of the genres. Staiger had to admit that his concept of the tragic had never been purely realized in any work of poetry. In later writings (especially *Goethe,* 3 vols., 1952–56; Goethe) Staiger found a way of combining historical and stylistic methods while still expressing the new existentialist outlook, and in *Die Kunst der Interpretation* (1956; the art of interpretation) he again defended and exemplified his remarkable talent for the "close reading" of German poetry. In *Stilwandel* (1963; changes of style) Staiger collected essays on changes of style, which he interprets purely in terms of the prevailing stylistic situation.

Other critics of the age reflect the turn to the text, combined with existential philosophizing. A collection of interpretations of thirty German poets, *Gedicht und Gedanke* (1942; poem and thought), edited by Heinz Otto Burger, was a sign of the times, and even earlier Johannes Pfeiffer (1902–1970) had written a sensitive introduction to poetry, *Umgang mit Dichtung* (1936; contact with poetry). Pfeiffer's collection of essays *Zwischen Dichtung und Philosophie* (1947; between poetry and philosophy) also propounds the conception that poetry opens the hidden depths of existence. In Hans Hennecke's (dates n.a.) essays, *Dichtung und Dasein* (1950; poetry and being), the existentialist motive is also apparent, but the taste is more eclectic, and much effort goes into rather undiscriminating expositions of American and English authors of the recent past. While Hennecke is definitely a reviewer, a middleman, Otto Friedrich Bollnow (b. 1903) is a philosopher rather than a critic. In his book *Rilke* (1951; Rilke) he interprets, with great acumen, the late poetry in terms of existential philosophy: the uncanniness of the world, the precariousness of human existence, the proximity of death. A later collection of essays, *Unruhe und Geborgenheit* (1953; anxiety and security), points to an escape from existentialism into a new philosophy in which man would find refuge from his anxiety.

Walter Muschg's (1898–1966) *Tragische Literaturgeschichte* (1948; 2nd completely revised ed., 1953; tragic literary history) is also related in mood and interests to the existentialist movement. Muschg, however, criticized Heidegger's interpretations of German poetry very severely. In *Tragische Literaturgeschichte* he treats, in almost encyclopedic fashion, all the sufferings, misfortunes, and tragedies of writers and poets of all times and places, aiming not so much at a sociology of the artist as at a typology of the poet, who may have been magician, seer, singer, juggler, or priest before the modern type was established. Somewhat incongruously, the book attempts, besides, a new theory of genres of the kind envisaged by Staiger: only in Muschg the first person, the poet's "I," is associated with magic, the second with mystical identification with the "Thou," the third with myth and representation. Muschg is acutely aware of what he believes to be the tragedy of German literature: the isolation and final ineffectiveness of its classics. The argument of the book is, however, weakened by its diffuseness and all-inclusive scope. All questions of poetics and literary history are drowned out by the leading theme: a solemn, monotonous dirge over the poet's cruel fate in the world.

Somewhat apart stands Hans Egon Holthusen (b. 1913). He also is deeply influenced by existentialism, but he has found his standard of judgment in Protestant Christianity. In his four books of essays, *Der unbehauste Mensch* (1951; the homeless man), *Ja und Nein* (1954; yes and no), *Das Schöne und das Wahre* (1958; the beautiful and the true), and *Kritisches Verstehen* (1961; critical understanding) he has proved himself a genuine critic, not only an interpreter or historian of poetry. He asserts the necessity of judging, the authority of the critic, which he feels cannot be purely aesthetic. He argues against the usual German prejudice in favor of sentiment and emphasizes the role of language in poetry. The word in poetry does not "mean" anything, but posits reality. It is a reality fraught with the need for decisions and thus

eminently ethical. Holthusen, firmly anchored in his faith, has judged Rilke as a propounder of false ideas (although a great poet), has welcomed the position of the later Eliot, and the passing of what he calls the "zero-point" in recent German literature: its emergence from the depth of despair. Holthusen, in his many fine essays, is not only a literary critic, but a critic of civilization deeply engaged in the present crisis of man, his loss of religion, the dangers of his predicament.

Existentialism strengthened the return to the text, but in the long run, literary values and distinctions between poetry and philosophy tend to disappear in existentialist criticism. Heidegger proclaimed the view that all great works of art say basically the same thing. But individuality and history would disappear if this were true; discrimination and hence criticism would become impossible. Existentialism, in spite of its insights into the human condition, represents an impasse for literary theory and criticism. The structure and form of a work of art are dissolved. We are back again at the identification of art with philosophy, of art with truth, which has been the bane of German criticism since, at least, the time of Schelling and Hegel. While intuitive interpretation in this philosophical sense and *Geistesgeschichte* flourish in Germany, criticism in the sense of judgment by artistic criteria, based on a coherent literary theory, supported by textual analysis, is almost nonexistent.

After existentialism and the ubiquitous Marxism, the most conspicuous new movement in literary theory is *Rezeptionsästhetik,* an aesthetics of the reader's response. Its most prominent advocate, Hans Robert Jauss (b. 1921), whose lecture "Literaturgeschichte als Provokation der Literaturwissenschaft" (1969; "Literary History as a Challenge to Literary Scholarship," 1970) provided the initial stimulus to the movement, has found many adherents and followers. His approach is not merely a demand for a history of readers' reactions, of criticisms, translations, etc., and for a study of readers' expectations and of the reading public; it also assumes a "fusion of horizons," a necessary interplay of text and recipient in which the text is assumed to be transformed by the reader. Jauss argues that the attitude of an author toward the public can be reconstructed not only from addresses to the reader or from external evidence but implicitly through the assumption, for instance, in *Don Quixote,* of a concern for chivalric romances. Jauss has done excellent research in medieval French literature and has exemplified the application of his theory on modern texts such as *Madame Bovary* or Racine's and Goethe's Iphigenia dramas. He had to engage in polemics with Marxism and has developed a whole system of aesthetics, most recently in *Ästhetische Erfahrung und literarische Hermeneutik* (1977; aesthetic experience and literary hermeneutics).

With colleagues at the University of Konstanz he organized regular symposia on poetics and hermeneutics and published voluminous proceedings (there is a selection in English, *New Perspectives in German Literary Criticism,* ed. Richard E. Amacher and Victor Lange, 1979). Among the participants, many of them technical philosophers, Wolfgang Iser's (b. 1926) work is of particular interest, since he writes on English literature. His *Der implizite Leser* (1972; *The Implied Reader,* 1974) traces the history of the English novel from Bunyan's *Pilgrim's Progress* to Joyce, Faulkner, and Beckett, showing how the role of the reader who discovers a new reality through fiction changes in history and how his role in filling out the "spots of indeterminacy" (blank spots in the text, a concept derived from Roman Ingarden) has grown precipitously in modern literature. Iser has developed his point of view in abstract writings collected as *Der Akt des Lesens* (1976; *The Act of Reading,* 1978). While the German approach throws much new light on the history of literature as an institution, it is in constant danger of arriving at a complete historical relativism, the besetting sin of the whole tradition of German historicism.

England and the United States

English and American criticism in the 20th c. have to be considered together, although conditions and developments of imaginative literature have differed widely in the two countries. But in criticism, there was not only the intense interchange of ideas between countries with the same language; the key figures in the renewal of criticism moved from one country to the other and influenced both profoundly. Pound and Eliot were Americans who came to England in 1907 and 1914 respectively, and I. A. Richards (q.v.), a Cambridge don, went to Harvard Universi-

ty in 1931. It is no exaggeration to say that all modern criticism in the English-speaking world is derived from these three critics.

But before their points of view became dominant, much time had elapsed and many various developments had taken place. As these were very different in the two countries, we must deal separately first with pre-Eliotic criticism in England.

In England, around 1900, criticism was at a low ebb. The aesthetic movement was discredited after the trial of Oscar Wilde and survived only in the refined, though erratic essayist Arthur Symons (1865–1945). Very little criticism in the strict sense was produced, although academic literary scholarship with critical pretensions flourished. Several survivors from the 19th c. even wrote their most impressive books. George Saintsbury (1845–1933) wrote *A History of Criticism and Literary Taste in Europe* (3 vols., 1900–1904), a first attempt to map out the whole field from Plato to Pater, *A History of English Prosody* (3 vols., 1906–10), and *A History of English Prose Rhythm* (1912). Saintsbury's last major work, *A History of the French Novel* (2 vols., 1917–19), shows him at his best: directly commenting on books without any need to worry about principles or theories. Saintsbury's standards are impressionistic and vaguely historical. He always celebrates *gusto,* the joy of literature, and carries his enormous reading lightly. He has great merits in boldly surveying wide fields, and he has a taste that is open to the unusual, especially the metaphysical poetry of the 17th c. But he lacks any coherent theory, despises aesthetics, and is often slipshod, jaunty, and violently prejudiced. In contrast to Saintsbury, Sir Edmund Gosse (1849–1928) was almost entirely a portraitist and causerist who in his later years wrote voluminously for the *Sunday Times.* His works of scholarship and biographies are urbane but lack Saintsbury's edge and candor.

William J. Courthope (1842–1917) was the author of a massive *History of English Poetry* (6 vols., 1895–1910), which relates poetry to political and national ideals, with a taste that can be described as neoclassical. Oliver Elton (1861–1945) wrote a monumental work, *Survey of English Literature, 1740–1880* (6 vols., 1912–28), which is always admirably well-informed, firsthand, sane, but critically rather colorless. In philosophical brainwork and subtle analysis A. C. Bradley's (1851–1935) *Shakespearean Tragedy* (1904) superseded earlier criticism of Shakespeare. His concept of Shakespeare, colored by the Hegelian theory of tragedy, and his emphasis on character almost outside and apart from the play have been sharply criticized, but must be recognized as the most coherent and penetrating of their kind. His eloquent statement on "poetry for poetry's sake" (in *Oxford Lectures on Poetry,* 1909) defines an idealistic version of the autonomy of art. W. P. Ker (1855–1923) was primarily a medievalist of wide range who, in his later years, was engaged in a study of poetics and contributed with exceptional learning to a discussion of form, style, and genres, very unusual at that time in English scholarship.

But the most characteristic figures of English academic criticism were Sir Walter Raleigh (1861–1922) and Sir Arthur Quiller-Couch (1863–1944). Raleigh, professor of English literature at Oxford who wrote on Milton, Shakespeare, and Samuel Johnson, always disparaged theory and criticism, and praised empire builders, voyagers, and men of action. The many essays of "Q" are permeated by an even heartier air of manliness and gusto. H. W. Garrod (1878–1960), professor of poetry at Oxford, formulated the prevailing academic attitude when he wrote that criticism is best when "written with the least worry of head, the least disposition to break the heart over ultimate questions." This negative, profoundly skeptical attitude toward criticism was fashionable in England and paralyzed any criticism that went beyond "the art of praise" in rambling, usually whimsical, allusive essays.

A group of writers and intellectuals known as the "Bloomsbury group" was subtler in its tastes and finer in its sensibilities, but did not achieve any break with impressionistic criticism. None of them was primarily a literary critic. Lytton Strachey (1880–1932) started with a short, brilliant book, *Landmarks in French Literature* (1912), and wrote essays that show an exceptional, "un-English" taste in Racine and Pope, but often suffer from his brash wit. Virginia Woolf wrote sensitive, warm, evocative essays that devote attention to questions of the reading public; they are collected in *The Common Reader* (1925) and *The Second Common Reader* (1932). E. M. Forster wrote a sparkling though elementary essay, *Aspects of the Novel* (1927); some of his other essays are collected in *Abinger Harvest* (1936). There were other English essayists—for example, Desmond MacCarthy

(1878–1952), F. L. Lucas (1894–1967), and Cyril Connolly (1903–1974)—who knew how to communicate the pleasures of literature and to share their sensibility. But, in general, whatever the merits of these essayists, English criticism, before the advent of Eliot and Richards, suffered from an almost complete lack of system, method, and theory, or even coherent frame of ideas and, in its taste, propounded little more than diluted romanticism.

American criticism, about 1900, differed sharply from its English counterpart. There was hardly any academic criticism to speak of, as American professors of literature were then philologists, specializing mainly in Anglo-Saxon or Chaucer. There was much impressionistic criticism, best represented by James Huneker (1860–1921), who brought the newest Parisian and German fashions from the Continent and described them in turgid, enthusiastic essays. In the background there loomed Henry James, who had gone to live in England. The *Prefaces* (1907–9) he wrote for the so-called New York edition of his novels were hardly appreciated in their time. They are the finest poetics of the novel—its point of view, its narrative techniques, its implied morality—and the most subtle, possibly oversubtle self-examination of the creative processes of a modern artist. Only Percy Lubbock (1879–1966), an English friend, in his *The Craft of Fiction* (1921), gave currency to James's insights. The *Prefaces* themselves were first made available by R. P. Blackmur (q.v.) in an edition entitled *The Art of the Novel* (1934), with a long analytical introduction.

Against the whole "genteel" tradition of American literature there arose early in the century a critical movement that could be called "radical" and had obvious affinities with the rising American naturalism. Its main spokesman was H. L. Mencken (q.v.), who was professedly a Nietzschean and "aristocrat" in his contempt for the values of a mass civilization, but as a literary critic must be described rather as a propagandist for Theodore Dreiser, Sinclair Lewis (qq.v.), and other new writers—for anybody whom he considered vigorous and alive, capable of breaking with the standards of the past. Mencken, especially as editor of the *American Mercury* (1924–33), fulfilled an important function in the self-criticism of American civilization, but as a literary critic he was a boisterous polemicist of quite erratic taste. He could extol such meretricious authors as Joseph Hergesheimer (1880–1954) or James Branch Cabell (1879–1958) and had little power of characterization and analysis.

Van Wyck Brooks fulfilled a similar function with his early criticism. In many books, especially *America's Coming-of-Age* (1915), Brooks deplored the plight of the artist in America and argued that "our writers who have possessed a vivid personal genius were paralyzed by the want of a social background," because a society whose end is impersonal cannot produce an ideal reflex in literature. In psychological studies of Mark Twain (*The Ordeal of Mark Twain,* 1920) and James (*The Pilgrimage of Henry James,* 1925) Brooks pursued his ideal of a liberal, mature America welcoming the artist and his criticism of American society. Later Brooks turned more and more to an uncritical and even sentimental glorification of American literary history, in a series of books beginning with *The Flowering of New England* (1936). They are little more than nostalgic chronicles. In *The Opinions of Oliver Allston* (1941) Brooks attacked all modern literature as pessimistic and recommended only "primary" writers, producing optimistic literature, "conducive to race-survival." His strange list of cheerful classics includes Tolstoy, Dostoevsky, and Thomas Mann.

A similar point of view was stated even more violently by Bernard De Voto (1897–1955) in *The Literary Fallacy* (1944). World War II changed a liberal critical movement to an uncritical, intolerant, even obscurantist "nativism." The earlier, broader social view of this critical movement was codified for literary history by Vernon L. Parrington (1871–1928), in his *Main Currents of American Thought* (3 vols., 1927–30). Here literature is seen, in terms resembling Taine's, as an expression of national ideals, American literature as the history of Jeffersonian democracy. In Parrington much is done for a history of political ideas, but more "belletristic" writers, such as Poe, Melville, or Henry James, are slighted.

Opposed to this general trend of radicalism was the movement of the American humanists. From various sources (mainly Matthew Arnold and French neoclassicism) they drew a view of literature as a means of personal and social order. They condemned romanticism and all its forms and recommended a literature filled with a sense of balance, ethical restraint, and measure. Paul Elmer More

(1864–1937) collected his essays under the title *Shelburne Essays* (11 vols., 1904–21), to which he added a twelfth volume with the characteristic title *The Demon of the Absolute* (1928). In the early volumes More ranged widely and showed an admirable quality of judicious sympathy that earned him comparisons with Sainte-Beuve. But More's standards became more rigid with time, and the later volumes are all devoted to an attack on aestheticism, naturalism, and modernism in the name of tradition, standards, and a philosophical dualism that rigidly upheld the necessity of an "inner check" in man against all spontaneity and caprice.

More was a learned Greek scholar who wrote in his later years a history of Christian Platonism and embraced High Anglicanism. His friend and ally, Irving Babbitt (1865–1933), differed from him sharply, although he shared his general outlook. Babbitt was a much harder, cruder writer: a violent, pungent polemicist, quite secular in outlook. He was a Stoic with some interest in Buddhism and Confucianism. Babbitt, a Harvard professor of French, attacked the American factualism imported from Germany in *Literature and the American College* (1908). He recommended, with many reservations, the French critics in *The Masters of Modern French Criticism* (1912), especially Ferdinand Brunetière (1849–1906). *Rousseau and Romanticism* (1919) was a powerful antiromantic tract mercilessly ridiculing the romantic worship of genius, passion, and nature, its misconception of man as naturally good. Babbitt's books are filled with a passionate concern for ideas and ethics; they suffer from a lack of aesthetic sensibility, an obtuseness of reading, a harsh and strident manner.

More and Babbitt found several influential adherents, among whom was Norman Foerster (1887–1972). Foerster, who had written well on earlier criticism in *American Criticism* (1929), organized the statements that for a short period (1929–30) attracted wide public attention to the humanist movement. The movement failed for obvious reasons: the social conservatism of the humanists ran counter to the temper of a nation just plunged into the Depression; their rigid moralism violated the nature of literature as an art; and their hostility to the contemporary arts cut them off from literature as a living institution. Still, the humanist movement left an imprint on the American universities. It helped to emancipate literary teaching from the old factualism and spread a concern for ideas and the relation of literature to life. It influenced many critics even when they rejected the creed itself: Eliot, F. O. Matthiessen (1902–1950), Austin Warren (b. 1899), Yvor Winters (q.v.).

But the rejuvenation of criticism came, not only in the United States but also in England, from two Americans: Pound and Eliot. Pound preached "imagism" (q.v.) since about 1912: a simple, colloquial poetry, in rhythms close to those of spoken language, with an eye turned to the object, "austere, direct, free from emotional slither." He had violently reacted against romantic and Victorian taste, but made, at first, little impression beyond a small following, which was joined by Eliot. Eliot had begun to write criticism in 1909, when he was at Harvard, but he established a reputation as a critic only with a collection of essays, *The Sacred Wood* (1920). It was secured, after the great success of *The Waste Land* (1922), with *For Lancelot Andrewes* (1928), which contained, in its preface, the famous declaration that he was "Royalist, Anglo-Catholic and classicist." In the meantime, I. A. Richards's *Principles of Literary Criticism* (1924) had made a profound impact. Richards had an entirely different intellectual background from Eliot, in positivistic psychology and in utilitarianism. Strangely and surprisingly, the doctrines of Eliot and Richards fused in many minds. Eliot and Richards influenced each other. In combination with F. R. Leavis (q.v.) in England, and with Cleanth Brooks (q.v.) in the United States, a body of doctrines evolved that is the core of what is usually called the "New Criticism."

Pound, although highly important as the main instigator of the changes in taste, was himself hardly a critic. He was rather the maker of manifestos, a man who proclaimed his preferences and rankings, but never argued or analyzed as a critic should. Pound's occasional attempts at poetic theory are crude, and his literary history is extremely arbitrary. He had, however, the merit of drawing attention to much poetry that was little known except to specialists: Provençal, very early Italian before Dante, and Chinese. Pound conceived as an ideal of criticism the task "to define the classic." He succeeded in construing a highly selective ancestry for his own poetry and in disparaging everything that did not fit the pattern. According to

Pound, there is nothing in German poetry besides the *Minnesänger* and Heine. There is nothing in French between Villon and the symbolists. In English, Milton is "the most unpleasant poet," a "thorough-going decadent," and among the English 19th-c. poets only Walter Savage Landor and Robert Browning find favor in Pound's eyes. Pound was less interested in prose; he wrote in detail only on James and Joyce. Pound had a personal interest in James's problem of the American expatriate and was one of the first fervent admirers of Joyce. He had the courage of his opinions and the boldness of a specific new taste. But his concept of poetry is very narrow and his idea of tradition is that of an agglomeration of appealing hobbies, unconnected glimpses of most diverse civilizations and styles. He often behaved like a "barbarian in a museum" (Yvor Winters).

T. E. Hulme (1883–1917) is usually coupled with Pound as a precursor of Eliot. He may have influenced Pound in the formulation of the imagist creed. But Eliot never knew Hulme, who was killed in World War I. His writings (with the exception of scattered articles) appeared only in 1924, as *Speculations*. By then Eliot's views were fully established. Hulme has been much overrated; he reflected a new taste and imported new ideas, but he had little to say that is his own. Much of his writing is straight exposition. In his most independent essay, "Romanticism and Classicism," Hulme expounds the antiromanticism of the Action Française. Romanticism is to him the revolution, bourgeois liberalism, "spilt religion," a sentimental trust in human nature. Against this, Hulme pits classicism, which implies a belief in original sin. The contrast is then pinned to the Coleridgean distinction of imagination and fancy. Imagination is romantic, fancy classical. What is needed today is a fanciful, precise, visual poetry. Hulme makes a faltering attempt to claim Coleridge and Bergson for this kind of "classicism," but cannot succeed. He wants an imagist, metaphorical poetry, in free verse. But it is hard to see what all this has to do with Bergson and his romantic philosophy of flux (except the emphasis on the concrete) and how it can be brought in line with admiration for Byzantine mosaics, Egyptian sculpture, and the sculpture of Jacob Epstein. Apparently we have to do with different stages in the development of a young man (the writings on plastic art all date from December 1913 to July

1914) who had a long way to go toward the definition of an original point of view. But he was an important symptom.

Eliot is often similar in taste to Pound. But as a critic he is immeasurably subtler and more profound. Like Pound, Eliot reacted strongly against romanticism and Milton. He exalted Dante, the Jacobean dramatists, the metaphysical poets, and the French symbolists as the bearers of *the* tradition of great poetry. But in Eliot we are confronted not only with a change of taste. The new tradition is defended in terms of a new classicism, of a whole superstructure of ideas that appeals to the Latin and Christian tradition. It is anchored in a theory of poetry that starts with a psychology of poetic creation. Poetry is not the "overflow of powerful feelings," is not the expression of personality, but is an impersonal organization of feelings that demands a "unified sensibility," a collaboration of intellect and feeling in order to find the precise "objective correlative," the symbolic structure of a work of art. Eliot expounded a scheme of the history of English poetry that postulates a "unified sensibility" before the middle of the 17th c., especially in the metaphysical poets, and then traced its "dissociation," in the purely intellectual poetry of the 18th c. and the purely emotional poetry of the 19th. He postulated the need of reintegration, fulfilled in his own poetry (and that of other contemporaries, such as Pound). It is both intellectual and emotional; it concerns the whole man, not only the heart. But while Eliot speaks of unified sensibility, of the fusion of thought and feeling, he still insists that poetry is not knowledge of any kind. The poet is no philosopher or thinker. "Neither Shakespeare nor Dante did any thinking." A poet such as Dante, who has taken over the system of Thomas Aquinas, is preferable, in this respect, to a poet such as Shakespeare, who has picked up ideas from anywhere, or to Goethe, who has construed his own personal philosophy. Eliot, who had earlier defended the "integrity" and autonomy of poetry, came to the recognition of a double standard in criticism: artistic and moral-philosophical-theological. "The 'greatness' of literature," he argued, "cannot be determined solely by literary standards." More and more, Eliot judged works of literature by their conformity to the tradition and to orthodoxy. The distinction between "artness" and "greatness," which again divorces form and content, grew out of Eliot's preoc-

cupation with the question of "belief" in literature. The problem whether the reader should or must share the ideas of an author worried Eliot and Richards greatly.

Eliot took several, often conflicting, positions, at one time arguing that the reader need not agree and later coming to the conclusion that we cannot give poetic assent to anything we consider "incoherent, immature and not founded on the facts of experience" (as the poetry of Shelley appeared to Eliot). But Eliot's criticism was at its best when he could forget about "belief" and the related problem of "sincerity" (how far has the poet to believe the ideas he expresses?) and, rather, analyze the work itself. Eliot constantly stressed the role of language in poetry, which should be "the perfection of common language." Milton's language is condemned as artificial and conventional. Poetry must not lose touch with the living language. Eliot defended what used to be called prosaic poetry such as that of Dryden or Dr. Johnson. But he could think of poetry also as logic of the imagination, a sequence of images or even moments of emotional intensity. Sound and meter seem to him less central, as the "music" of poetry means to him much more than sound-patterns. It is the interplay of sound and meaning and of the secondary meanings. In "music" the poet touches the frontiers of consciousness; yet the poet is not a primitive man, but rather contains all history. Poets are related to their times; they cannot help expressing them, even their chaos, but, on the other hand, poetry is also timeless. There is a final hierarchy of the poets, an ultimate greater or less. There is an interplay between "Tradition and the Individual Talent" (1919). Tradition involves the historical sense and the historical sense to Eliot "involves a perception, not only of the pastness of the past, but of its presence." A poet should write "not merely with his own generation in his bones, but with a feeling that the whole literature of Europe from Homer on has a simultaneous existence and composes a simultaneous order." Tradition is the classical tradition descended from Greece and Rome. Rome (and such a poet as Vergil) is the indispensable link in the chain of tradition. Germany is sometimes excluded from this unity of European culture, defined as both Christian and classical. But in his later years Eliot welcomed Germany back again into the European fold and even recanted his earlier opinion, which excluded Goethe from the great classics, praising his "wisdom" and even his science.

Eliot thus construed the tradition very selectively. It converged on his practice as a poet: the bright visual imagination of Dante, the living speech of the later Shakespeare, of Donne and of Dryden, the dramatic lyricism of Donne, Browning, and Pound, the "wit" and "unified sensibility" of the metaphysical poets, the "irony" of Jules Laforgue (1860–1887), the impersonality of Mallarmé and Valéry. Much of Eliot's impact is due to his practical criticism: to his brief, dogmatic, assertive, but persuasive and subtle essays, which seem often to proceed only by his quoting a few passages and making brief comparisons.

In several lectures (for example, "The Frontiers of Criticism," 1956) Eliot slighted his own criticism, deplored the influence of some catch-phrases derived from it, and detached himself from what he called the "lemon-squeezer school of criticism." From the point of view of literary criticism, Eliot's influence declined in his later years. His interests shifted away from pure criticism, and he was apt to use literature as a document for his jeremiads on the modern world. He finally became committed to a double standard that dissolved the unity of the work of art as well as the sensibility that goes into its making and the critical act itself. But, taken in its early purity, his criticism was the most influential of the century.

Only I. A. Richards can compare with Eliot in influence. Richards differed completely in aim and method, but shared many of Eliot's tastes and, with his practical criticism, helped to define the turn toward an analysis of verbal art that prevails in English and American criticism. But Richards was primarily interested in theory, in the psychic effect of poetry on the mind of its reader. Richards did not recognize a world of aesthetic values and emotions. Rather, the only value of art is the psychic organization it imposes on us, what Richards describes as "the patterning of impulses," the equilibrium of attitudes it induces. The artist is conceived almost as a mental healer, and art as therapy. Richards was not, however, able to describe this effect of art very concretely, although he thought it would replace religion as a social force. He finally had to admit that the desired, balanced poise can be given by "a carpet or a pot, by a gesture as by the Parthenon." It does not ultimately matter

whether we like good or bad poetry, as long as we order our minds. Thus Richards's theory—which is objective and scientific in its pretensions and often appeals to future advances of neurology—ends with critical paralysis: a complete divorce between the poem as an objective structure and the reader's mind.

But fortunately, Richards eluded, in practice, the consequences of his theory and came to grips with specific poetic texts by applying a theory of meaning first developed in *The Meaning of Meaning: A Study of the Influence of Language upon Thought and of the Science of Symbolism* (1923, with C. K. Ogden). In *Principles of Literary Criticism* (1924) Richards analyzed the different components of a work of art in psychological terms, into sensations, images, emotions, attitudes, and suggested standards of evaluation: a grading of poetry in terms of complexity, with a preference for a poetry of "inclusion" (a term derived from George Santayana [q.v.]), a difficult poetry that would resist ironic contemplation. Richards's analysis of meaning, which distinguishes between sense, tone, feeling, and intention, emphasizes the ambiguities of language, the function of metaphor as central to poetry. Later, in *Coleridge on Imagination* (1934), Richards even restated the romantic theory of imagination as fusing and unifying, in which the most disparate elements of the world come together. The affinity with Eliot's "unified sensibility" is obvious; but in Richards, poetry is even more deliberately cut off from all knowledge and even reference. On the basis of a simple dichotomy between intellectual and emotive language, truth is assigned to science, while art can do nothing but arouse emotions, which must, however, be patterned, equipoised, complex, to achieve the purpose of mental ordering. Poetry at most elaborates the myths by which men live, even though these myths may be untrue, may be mere "pseudo-statements" in the light of science.

In his later essays (one collection is *Speculative Instruments,* 1955) Richards gave up his earlier reliance on neurology, but the point of view has remained in substance the same. Richards is primarily a theorist and wrote little on actual texts; but *Practical Criticism* (1929), a book that analyzes the papers of students who were set to discuss a series of poems given to them without the names of the authors, shows Richards's pedagogical talent in the teaching and analyzing of poetry. He distinguishes the various sources of misunderstanding: the difficulty of making out the plain sense of a poem, the lack of sensibility to meter and rhythm, the misinterpretation of figurative language, the critical pitfalls of stock responses, of sentimentality or hardness of heart, of ideological or technical preconceptions. Richards's technique of interpretation analyzes language, but unlike the logical positivists, it favors a great flexibility of vocabulary and trains in distinguishing shades of meaning.

This is the starting point of Richards's most gifted English disciple, William Emerson (q.v.), who, in *Seven Types of Ambiguity* (1930; rev. ed., 1953) developed, in a series of brilliant interpretations of poetic passages, a scheme that allowed him to distinguish types of ambiguity, progressing in complexity, with the increasing distance from the simple statement. Empson draws out implicit meanings, defines by multiple definitions, and pursues to the farthest ends the implications, poetic and social, of difficult, witty, metaphorical poetry. He is not only an analyst but a critic who tries to justify his own taste in poetry and disparages simple romantic emotionalism or vagueness. In his later books Empson combined this method of semantic analysis with ideas drawn from psychoanalysis and Marxism. In *Some Versions of Pastoral* (1935), a term that includes proletarian literature, *Alice in Wonderland* is psychoanalyzed, and Gray's "Elegy Written in a Country Churchyard" is interpreted as a defense of Tory conservatism. In *The Structure of Complex Words* (1951), Empson freed himself from the emotionalism of Richards and developed a concept of meaning that allows for knowledge and reference. He again displayed an amazing ingenuity in verbal analysis and an acute awareness of social implications. Terms such as "wit" or "honest" are analyzed in different contexts, in Pope or Shakespeare.

But Empson often left the realm of literary criticism for a version of lexicography and became more and more enmeshed in a private world of associations and speculations that lose contact with the text and use it only as pretext for his fireworks of wit and recondite ingenuity. His *Milton's God* (1961; rev. ed., 1965) is even further removed from literary criticism. It is an attack on Christianity and, in particular, on the conception of God the Father sacrificing His Son. Milton is praised for his picture of God in *Paradise Lost,* a God who seems to Empson "astonishingly like Uncle Joe Stalin." The poem has "barbaric power" because Milton could express "a downright horrible conception of God."

The impulses emanating from Eliot and Richards were most effectively combined, at least in England, in the work of F. R. Leavis and his disciples grouped around the magazine *Scrutiny* (1932–53). Leavis was a man of strong convictions and harsh polemical manners. In his later years he sharply underlined his disagreement with the later developments of Eliot and Richards. But his starting point is in Eliot's taste and in Richards's technique of analysis. He differed from them mainly by a strongly Arnoldian concern for a moralistic humanism. In *New Bearings in English Poetry* (1932) he criticized Victorian and Georgian poetry, and praised and analyzed the later Yeats, the early Eliot, and the newly discovered Gerard Manley Hopkins (1844–1889), whose poems had been published for the first time in 1918. *Revaluation* (1936) was the first consistent attempt to rewrite the history of English poetry from a 20th-c. point of view. Spenser, Milton, Tennyson, and Swinburne recede into the background; Donne, Pope, Wordsworth, Keats, Hopkins, Yeats, and T. S. Eliot emerge as the carriers of the great tradition.

In contrast to Eliot, Leavis admired Pope much more than Dryden and established his descent from the metaphysical poets. Like Eliot, Leavis disparaged Shelley, "as repetitious, vaporous, monotonously self-regarding, and often emotionally cheap." But he appreciated Wordsworth for his sanity (although he did not share his philosophy) and Keats for his emotional maturity. Similarly, Leavis attempted in *The Great Tradition* (1948) to establish a new selection from the English novel. The 18th-c. novelists and Scott are dismissed, as are Dickens ("a great entertainer"), Thackeray, and Meredith. Only Jane Austen, George Eliot, Henry James, Joseph Conrad (q.v.), and D. H. Lawrence survive. Leavis practiced close reading, a training in sensibility, which has little use for literary history or theory. But "sensibility" with Leavis meant also a sense for tradition, a concern for culture, for humanity. On the one hand, he rejected Marxism, and on the other, the orthodoxy of Eliot. He admired a local culture, the organic community of the English countryside.

Leavis sharply criticized the commercialization and standardization of English literary life and defended the need for tradition, for a social code and order, for "maturity," "sanity," and "discipline." But these terms are purely secular and include the ideals of D. H. Lawrence, whom Leavis interpreted to conform to a healthy tradition (see *D. H. Lawrence, Novelist*, 1955). Leavis's emphasis on the text, and even the texture of words, is often deceptive: his observations on form, technique, and language are often haphazard and arbitrary. Actually he left the verbal surface very quickly in order to define the particular emotions or sentiments an author conveys. He became a social and moral critic, who, however, insisted on the continuity between language and ethics, on the morality of form. Leavis's ultimate value criterion, "Life," remains, however, bafflingly obscure: it means antiaestheticism, realism, optimism, or just courage and devotion in turn, as, on the whole, Leavis as a resolute empiricist left his premises unexamined and displayed a complacent distrust of and even hatred for theory.

In his later writings—*Anna Karenina, and Other Essays* (1967), *English Literature in Our Time and the University* (1969), *Dickens, the Novelist* (1970), *Nor Shall My Sword* (1972), *The Living Principle: English as a Discipline of Thought* (1975)—we can, however, discern a definite shift or even reversal of some of Leavis's positions. Not that he gave up his basic principles; but he distanced himself so completely from T. S. Eliot and embraced D. H. Lawrence and Blake so fervently that one can speak of a conversion to romanticism. He reinstated Dickens as one of the greatest creative writers.

Leavis managed to assemble a group of disciples, of whom many have contributed importantly to the development of English criticism. L. C. Knights (b. 1906), in *Drama and Society in the Age of Jonson* (1937) and in *Explorations* (1947), is mainly concerned with the Elizabethans. Derek Traversi (b. 1912) has interpreted Shakespeare with great sensitivity, especially in *An Approach to Shakespeare* (1938) and *Shakespeare: The Last Phase* (1954). Martin Turnell (b. 1908) has written extensively, although often loosely, on French literature; his *The Classical Moment: Studies in Corneille, Molière, Racine* (1947), *The Novel in France* (1950), *Baudelaire* (1952), and *The Art of French Fiction* (1959), which exalts Stendhal and Proust at the expense of Balzac and Flaubert, are instructive but often diffuse and erratic

books. Mrs. Q. D. Leavis (1906–1981), in *Fiction and the Reading Public* (1932), supplied the arguments for the general view of the decline of modern taste and the shrinking of a cultivated audience. Marius Bewley (1918–1973), an American adherent, studied Hawthorne and Henry James (in *The Complex Fate,* 1952) and the 19th-c. American novel (in *The Eccentric Design,* 1957). The intransigence of the group has diminished its immediate effectiveness; F. R. Leavis did not even recognize parallel efforts elsewhere. But in spite of shortcomings in sympathy, a certain provinciality, and an excessive preoccupation with the pedagogy of literature, Leavis and his group have produced fine practical criticism that has established the new taste and again justified the social role of literature in a minority culture.

Side by side with what could loosely be called Eliotic criticism, a number of English critics were active who could be labeled "neoromantic." They are men who finally appeal to an inner voice, to the subconscious mind, and who think of criticism mainly as a process of self-expression and self-discovery. Still, all have learned from Eliot and would have written quite differently without him as a model.

John Middleton Murry passed through bafflingly diverse stages in his development. He wrote a *Life of Jesus* (1926), as well as *The Necessity of Communism* (1932). Murry, once widely admired, has been losing influence steadily, as his later books are neither good biography nor good criticism, and indulge more and more in private theosophic speculation. But it seems unfair to neglect his early criticism because of the vagaries of his search for God. His book *Dostoevsky* (1916), although often quite mistaken in its interpretations, was an early attempt to see the Russian novelist as a kind of symbolist. *The Problem of Style* (1922) is remarkably similar in outlook to Eliot's early phase, although Eliot is not mentioned. There is the same emphasis on visual imagination, on metaphor as a mode of apprehension, on the transformation of emotion in a work of art which Murry calls "crystallization." His early collection of essays, *Aspects of Literature* (1920), and *Countries of the Mind* (1922), should also be classed with Eliotic criticism. But his *Keats and Shakespeare* (1925) shows a shift: it is a biographical interpretation (often sensitive and moving) of Keats's growth and struggle for maturity, of his "soul-making." The parallel with Shakespeare, however, is forced, and the tone has become fervent and often oracular. *Son of Woman: The Story of D. H. Lawrence* (1931) is a highly personal interpretation of his friend and enemy: it makes Lawrence out a weakling who willed himself into vitality. An arbitrary theosophy invaded the books *William Blake* (1933) and *Shakespeare* (1936), and there is hardly anything to be said for the dull book *Jonathan Swift* (1954).

The same fate seems to have befallen G. Wilson Knight. His early writings, especially *The Wheel of Fire* (1929), elaborate a technique of Shakespeare interpretation by leading images and clusters, by some kind of metaphorical organization. Knight still had contact with the text, a feeling for evidence, although the antithesis, tempest versus music, seems pressed too hard. But Knight's later books show a gradual deterioration of critical intelligence. The same method is applied indiscriminately to all writers: whether Pope or Wordsworth, Milton or Byron. All poetry is reduced to a conveyor of the same mystic message. The allegorical reading of Milton anticipating even details of World War II (with Hitler as Satan) and the interpretation of Byron as "the next Promethean man in Western history after Christ" (in *Byron: The Christian Virtues,* 1952), are so fantastic that they cease to be criticism or scholarship.

By far the best of these neoromantic critics was Sir Herbert Read. He advocated surrealism, psychoanalysis, and the use of the Jungian collective unconscious in literature, but basically kept a central critical insight into organic form. His *Wordsworth* (1930) pressed the theme of Wordsworth's supposed feeling of guilt because of his affair with Annette Vallon very far. In his *In Defence of Shelley* (1936) he attempted a psychoanalysis of Shelley that serves as a rather double-edged apology for his life. But the core of Read's writings is to be found in *Collected Essays on Literary Criticism* (1938) and *The True Voice of Feeling* (1953), in which a theory of organic form, of spontaneity, obscurity, myth, and dream is propounded with constant appeals to the great English romantic poets, particularly Coleridge, in whom Read found anticipations of Freudianism and existentialism. Read shows sensitivity, style, and a theoretical mind. Although he advocated surrender to the "dark unconscious," he did so sanely and clearly. His irrationalism was always tempered by a lively sense of the social role of both the arts and crafts.

F. W. Bateson (1901–1978) stood quite apart from other English critics, playing with gusto the role of a gadfly, of a polemicist who in his periodical, *Essays in Criticism,* argued with almost everybody. Bateson first wrote a short book, *English Poetry and the English Language* (1934); in it he sketched a history of English poetry as completely dependent on changes in the history of language, which alone mediates social influences on literature. A later book, *English Poetry: A Critical Introduction* (1950), rewrites the history of English poetry in terms of the audiences of the different periods. According to Bateson, the audiences are the determining causes of literary change, rather than the economic basis of society. Later Bateson abandoned his emphasis on the continuity between language and literature completely and argued against the use of linguistics in criticism, against the idea of the work of art as an artifact, against formalism, in favor of intention as a standard of judgment, and finally for a judicial criticism that would be both moral and social. *Essays in Critical Dissent* (1972) and *The Scholar-Critic* (1972) are collections of his papers.

Most recently English critics have begun to feel the impact of new speculative developments, particularly in linguistics and semantics. There are now fine technical studies of the language of poetry, such as Christine Brooke-Rose's (q.v.) *A Grammar of Metaphor* (1958) and Winifred Nowottny's (b. 1917) *The Language Poets Use* (1962). David Lodge (b. 1935) has offered "verbal analyses" of the English novel, first in *The Language of Fiction* (1966) and then in *The Modes of Modern Writing* (1977), which sensitively uses Roman Jakobson's dichotomy of metaphor and metonymy to interpret modern novels. Frank Kermode (b. 1919) established his reputation with *Romantic Image* (1957), which argued against the whole tradition of romantic and symbolist poetics, and which saw poems in terms of imagery—concrete, organic, independent of the author's intention, created by an "excluded artist," expressing a truth resistant to rational explanation. Later, in *The Sense of an Ending: Studies in the Theory of Fiction* (1967), Kermode uses existentialist preconceptions of a rationalistic type to set literary fictions, particularly fictions of the Apocalypse, within a general theory of fiction. Kermode also wrote (for example, in *Continuities,* 1968) much about the nature of modernism as apocalyptic, becoming satirical about the new avant-garde, pop and op art, the music of silence, and other recent developments in which "the difference between art and joke is as obscure as that between art and non-art." In contrast, he sets up *The Classic* (1975) which, to be alive, today, has, however, to be accommodated to the modern reader by allegory and prophecy. Kermode shares the concern about the possibility of right reading, about the danger of sheer arbitrariness, and answers it by an appeal to "competence," a linguistic concept that shifts the problem to an elite of experts.

With these few exceptions, English criticism is still traditional, largely concerned with descriptive criticism, with the interpretation of specific texts and with literary history. George Watson (b. 1927), in *The Literary Critics* (1962), argued that it should be so, and he has found much support. John Holloway (b. 1920), the author of *The Victorian Sage* (1953), dismissed all philosophical and aesthetic speculations as abracadabra and pleaded for "calm intelligence, moderation," and "urbanity"; William W. Robson (dates n.a.), who in many ways is near to both Leavis and Bateson in his *Critical Essays* (1966), defended "criticism without principles," since criticism is not a science but a personal encounter with the works. "There is no body of established results which the next critic can build on." It would be the end of all discussion. But Continental ideas and trends have been felt in England increasingly in recent years. George Steiner (q.v.), an American citizen born in Paris, living in Cambridge, England, has become their tireless, eloquent propagator in books such as *Language and Silence* (1967), *Extraterritorial* (1971), *After Babel: Aspects of Language and Translation* (1975), *On Difficulty, and Other Essays* (1978), and *Heidegger* (1978). They are inspired by a strong feeling of the precariousness of traditional literary culture.

Recent American Criticism

Recent American criticism is usually lumped together under the term the "New Criticism," from the title of a book, published in 1941, by John Crowe Ransom (q.v.). It is a misleading term, since it suggests a far greater unity of purpose and doctrine than close examination of recent American critics will reveal. It is hard to find anything in common among all the more important American critics except a reaction against the impressionism or naturalism of the past and a general turn toward a closer analysis of the actual text of a work of art. But even this generalization does not hold good for many critics. It is better to distinguish, at least roughly, two main groups: those who draw on other fields (psychoanalysis, myth, Marxism, semantics) in order to bring their insights to an understanding of literature; and those who have focused single-mindedly on the work of art, have tried to develop techniques of analysis peculiarly suited to poetry, and have defended poetry as a way to a knowledge of concrete reality. The first group of writers tend to become general critics of civilization; the second have concentrated on a modern apology of poetry against science and attempted to define its peculiar nature and function. Only four critics in this second group, Allen Tate, Robert Penn Warren (qq.v.), Ransom, and Cleanth Brooks, the so-called Southern critics, have had close personal relations and form a coherent group unified in its outlook and main preoccupations.

Possibly the best-known American critic (certainly in Europe) is Edmund Wilson, a critic of great versatility and facility who, in turn, applied almost every method to his texts and wrote on almost every subject. He began his career with *Axel's Castle* (1931), a book about the symbolist movement in Western literature, with chapters on Yeats, Valéry, Eliot, Proust, Joyce, and Gertrude Stein (q.v.), and a conclusion that predicted the demise of symbolism in favor of a social collective art. Although Wilson was hostile to aestheticism and decadence, his exposition of the masters of the 20th c. is sympathetic, since on the whole, he aims at conveying enjoyment and envisages rather vaguely a reconciliation of symbolism and naturalism, art and life, criticism and history. His later writings are not unified books (with the exception of an account of socialist and communist theories of history in *To the Finland Station,* 1940), but collections of essays ranging widely over modern literature. The influence of Marxism (always sharply distinguished from Stalinism) is often discernible and, more prominently, the method of psychoanalysis. *The Wound and the Bow* (1941) takes the Philoctetes story as a symbol of the relationship between the artist's wound, his neurosis, and his bow—his art—and shows with great finesse, in studies of Dickens and Kipling (q.v.), that psychoanalytical insight can be joined with literary taste. In all his many collections, from *The Triple Thinkers* (1938) to *The Shores of Light* (1952), Wilson shows his mastery of the form of the essay, his tolerant taste, his skill in exposition, his brilliance of formulation, his secular common sense, and strong social concern.

But Wilson, although highly meritorious in his general effect on a wide reading public, lacked analytical power and suffered from frequent lapses into journalistic indiscriminations and personal idiosyncrasies. With the exception of some original insights into the psychic histories of some of his subjects, Wilson ultimately is a middleman, immensely readable, intelligent, and sensitive, but lacking in a personal center and theory.

Lionel Trilling was also a general critic of civilization rather than strictly a critic of literature. He wrote excellently, with common sense and discrimination, on both Freudianism and the Kinsey Report. He began with a good though diffuse book, *Matthew Arnold* (1939), and collected his essays in *The Liberal Imagination* (1950) and *The Opposing Self* (1955). His chief concern was the relation between literature and politics. Trilling, a convinced liberal (in the American sense), was worried about the gulf between the rationality of his political convictions and the imaginative insights of modern literature. A man of modern sensibility with a taste for Henry James and Forster, to the second of whom he devoted a small book (*E. M. Forster,* 1943; 2nd rev. ed., 1965), and a dislike for naturalism, he was only able to state his problem, but could not solve it in his own terms precisely because he believed that ideas are emotions and that politics permeates literature. He finally had to come to recognize the "fortuitous and gratuitous nature of art, how it exists beyond the reach of the will alone." His fine essay on Keats shows his increasing feeling for selves conceived in opposition to general culture, for the alienation of the artist as a necessary device of his self-realization.

A similar combination of modern literary sensibility and social concern permeates the work of F. O. Matthiessen, except that his development went in the opposite direction from Trilling's. He began (after some academic research) with a sympathetic interpretation, *The Achievement of T. S. Eliot*

(1935), and then produced *The American Renaissance* (1941), a long, careful study of Emerson, Thoreau, Hawthorne, Melville, and Whitman. It combines an Eliotic concern for language and diction, for symbolism and myth, with a fervent belief in the possibilities of democracy in America. Two books on Henry James pursue the old aesthetic interests, while many articles (some collected in *The Responsibilities of the Critic,* 1952) and a book (*Theodore Dreiser,* 1951) show increasingly a change of taste in the direction of realism and an overwhelming, passionately earnest concern with the social duties of the critic, in a Marxism reconciled with Christianity.

Kenneth Burke attempts the most ambitious scheme of recent American criticism: he combines the method of Marxism, psychoanalysis, and anthropology with semantics, in order to devise a system of human behavior and motivation that uses literature only as a starting point or illustration. Burke is rightly admired for the uncanny quickness of his mind, his astonishing originality in making connections, his dialectical skill, and his terminological inventiveness. He has influenced recent criticism by his special terms and mannerisms. But judged as literary criticism, much of his work is irrelevant, and literature, more and more, is even violated and distorted in his work to serve quite extrinsic arguments and purposes.

Burke was still primarily a literary critic in *Counter-Statement* (1931), a collection of essays that contains, for instance, a brilliant comparison of Gide and Thomas Mann. But with *Permanence and Change* (1935) and *Attitudes toward History* (1937), he began to indulge in speculations on psychology and history and to discuss literature only in the sense that, with him, life is a poem and all men are poets. *The Philosophy of Literary Form* (1941) ostensibly returns to literature. It develops a "dialectical" or "dramatic" criticism interpreting poetry as a series of "strategies for the encompassing of situations," in practice as an act of the poet's personal purification. For example, Coleridge's *Rime of the Ancient Mariner* is elaborately interpreted as "a ritual for the redemption of his drug." Similarly, in *A Grammar of Motives* (1945), Keats's "Ode on a Grecian Urn" is read in terms of the identity of love and death, of capitalist individualism and Keats's tubercular fever, in almost complete disregard of the text. *A Grammar of Motives* is the first part of a trilogy (of which the second part, *A Rhetoric of Motives,* was published in 1950; the third part, *A Symbolic of Motives,* has not been finished) in which Burke attempts to construe a whole philosophy of meaning, human behavior, and action. Five terms—act, scene, agent, agency, and purpose—are used as main categories: literary illustrations abound, but the center of the whole project is elsewhere. All distinctions between life and literature, language and action disappear in Burke's theory.

Burke has increasingly lost any sense for the integrity of a work of art, the relevance of an observation or bright idea to a text. He has become imprisoned in a private world of terms and concepts, often so weirdly in opposition to ordinary usage that his speculations seem to evolve in a void. A system that plans to embrace all life ends as a baffling phantasmagoria of "strategies," categories, "charts," and "situations."

In Burke the expansion of criticism has reached its extreme limit. At the opposite pole is the group of "Southern critics," Ransom, Tate, Brooks, and Warren, who have concentrated on a close study of poetic texts and a modern apology for poetry. But it would be a mistake to think of them as aesthetes or even formalists, since their concern with poetry has social and even religious implications: they have defended Southern conservatism and have seen—as Leavis did in England—the evils of urbanization and commercialization, the need for a healthy society that alone can produce vital literature. But the Southern critics have kept their concept of culture separate from their literary criticism, since they understand that art is an autonomous realm and that poetry has its own peculiar function.

Although the theories of the Southern critics could be described as a fusion of those of Eliot and I. A. Richards, they differ from them importantly in having broken with their emotionalism. They recognize that poetry is not merely emotive language, but conveys a kind of knowledge, a particular kind of concrete presentational knowledge. Thus, the analysis of a work of art has to proceed from objectively recognizable factors of the work itself rather than from the reader's responses. Ransom, the oldest of the group, an eminent poet himself, developed the view (in *The World's Body,* 1938) that poetry conveys a sense of the particularity of the world. "As science more and more completely reduces the world to its types and forms, art, replying, must invest it again with the body." But purely physical or imagist poetry is only a first stage. "Platonic" poetry, poetry merely disguising or allegorizing truths, is bad. True poetry is like the "metaphysical" poetry of the 17th c., a new perception of the world, a new awareness of its realness, conveyed mainly by extended metaphor and pervasive symbolism. Ransom emphasized the "texture" of poetry, its seemingly irrelevant detail, although he upheld the need of an overall "structure" (a logical content). In practice, he was often, with his insistence on "texture," in danger of reintroducing the old dichotomy of form and content. In *The New Criticism* (1941) Ransom discussed Richards, Eliot, and Yvor Winters with many reservations and concluded by asking for an "ontological" critic who would treat an order of existence not created in scientific discourse. Ransom drew from Charles W. Morris (b. 1901), a logical positivist, the term "icon" to suggest the symbol in art, and, in a later paper (in *Poems and Essays,* 1955), used the Hegelian term, the "concrete universal," in an attempt to recognize the universalizing power of art while preserving the emphasis on the concrete, on metaphor, and its references to nature.

Allen Tate, like Ransom, was preoccupied with a defense of poetry against science. Science gives us abstraction, poetry concreteness, science partial knowledge, poetry complete knowledge. "Poetry alone gathers up the diverse departments of the intellect into a humane and living whole." Abstraction, mere idea, violates art. Good poetry proceeds from a union of intellect and feeling, or rather from a "tension." Tate elaborated his concept of poetry in several collections of essays, on which *On the Limits of Poetry* (1948) and *The Man of Letters in the Modern World* (1955) are the most inclusive.

Tate consistently rejected the attempt of Richards to make poetry a kind of therapy or make it take the place of religion. He sharply attacked both the scientific and the emotionally romantic view. Scientism, positivism, includes for Tate also historicism, the preoccupation with externals of the conventional literary scholar and any purely sociological approach. But literature is not taken out of society: on the contrary, Tate was deeply worried by the decay of an organic society and a religious world view, which alone, to his mind, could support a living tradition of art. Paradoxically, Tate, however, admired poetry most when it reflects the dissolution of tradition without losing its grasp of it. His essays on Poe, Emily Dickinson, T. S. Eliot, and Yeats show how these poets found personal substitutes for the old myths and symbols, while his discussion of Hart Crane (q.v.), a personal friend, serves to show the failure of the modern artist who has not found support in tradition.

Tate wrote widely, as a reviewer, mainly on modern poetry, but his interests broadened gradually to include, for instance, Dante. He became a convert to Roman Catholicism, and his later writings indicate an increasing skepticism as to the role of poetry and criticism in the modern world. Compared to the urbane, ironical, restrained Ransom, Tate was a passionate, even violent, and often polemical and personal writer.

Cleanth Brooks has been described as the systematizer and technician of the New Criticism. He has, no doubt, a sweet reasonableness and a gift for pedagogy and conciliatory formulation. His textbook, written in collaboration with Robert Penn Warren, *Understanding Poetry* (1938), has done more than any other single book to make the techniques of the New Criticism available in the classrooms of American colleges and universities and to present the techniques of analysis as something to be learned and imitated. But Brooks is not merely a popularizer and codifier. He has his own personal theory. He has taken the terminology of Richards, deprived it of its psychologistic presuppositions, and transformed it into a remarkably clear system. It allows him to analyze poems as structures of tensions: in practice, of paradoxes and ironies.

Paradox and irony, with Brooks, are terms used very broadly. Irony is not the opposite of an overt statement, but "a general term for the kind of qualification which the various elements in a context receive from the context." It indicates the recognition of incongruities, the ambiguity, the union of opposites that Brooks finds in all good, that is, complex poetry. Poetry must be ironic in the sense of being able to withstand ironic contemplation. The method, no doubt, works best when applied to Donne or Shakespeare, Eliot or Yeats, but in *The Well Wrought Urn* (1947), a collection of analyses of poems. Brooks showed that even Wordsworth and Tennyson, Gray and Pope yield to this kind

of technique. The whole theory emphasizes the contextual unity of the poem, its wholeness, its organism, while it allows a close analysis of its linguistic devices.

While Brooks is usually content to confine himself to his specialty—a masterly analysis of hidden meanings and relationships in metaphors and key words—he is also a critic, since his scheme permits him definite value judgments. Poets are ranked in terms of their success in resolving patterns of tensions, and the history of English poetry is seen in a new perspective. In *Modern Poetry and the Tradition* (1939) the romantic and Victorian ages appear as periods of decline compared to the 17th c., the greatest age of English poetry, while our own century appears as one of the revival of a properly "ironical," "tough," and complex poetry, as we find it in the later Yeats or Eliot. Brooks convincingly attacked what he calls "the heresy of paraphrase," that is, all attempts to reduce a poem to its prose content, and he has defended critical absolutism: the need of judgment against the excesses of relativism.

In *William Faulkner: The Yoknapatawpha Country* (1963) Brooks changed his method strikingly: he patiently examines the social picture, the intellectual and religious implications, and the themes and characters of Faulkner's main novels. The "formalistic" preoccupation has disappeared as is also obvious from a serious series of published lectures, *The Hidden God: Studies in Hemingway, Faulkner, Yeats, Eliot, and Warren* (1963), which announces its main topic in the title.

The fourth of the Southern critics, Robert Penn Warren, a fine novelist and poet, has published only one volume of collected criticism, *Selected Essays* (1958). The essay "Pure and Impure Poetry" states the argument for inclusive, complex, difficult (though impure) poetry memorably, and his essays on Hemingway, Thomas Wolfe (qq.v.), and Faulkner, and on Coleridge's *Rime of the Ancient Mariner* show his skill in symbolist interpretation, which widens into a study of the imagination and its role in the modern world.

Among the critics who cannot be called Southern, R. P. Blackmur was nearest to the general outlook of the Southern group. He was, in contrast to them, strongly influenced by Kenneth Burke and later in his career expressed dissatisfaction with their concentration on "close reading." Blackmur himself started as an extremely subtle, refined, elusive analyst, mainly of modern American poetry and Henry James. He was closely concerned with language and words, diction, imagery, rhyme and meter, and later tried to systematize his practice in a general theory of "language as gesture." "Gesture," which for Blackmur was basic to all the arts, is a term combining symbol and expression: a "cumulus of meaning" achieved by all the devices of poetry—punning, rhyme, meter, tropes. Criticism is defined as the "formal discourse of an amateur"—amateur in the sense of lover of poetry. Sympathy, identification, is required, and any external methodologies—Freudianism, Marxism, semantics—are rejected.

Increasingly, Blackmur felt the narrowness of the techniques of the New Criticism and saw that literature should, after all, be judged as a moral act in society. His perspective widened to include Dostoevsky and Tolstoy; in method, he adopted economic and psychoanalytical ideas. But in theoretical reflections he seemed not to have reached any clarity or system of his own. His essays, collected in *Language as Gesture* (1952), and *The Lion and the Honeycomb* (1955), often show a disconcerting loss of contact with the text and a random experimentation with new sets of terms and contraries: symbol, myth, form, "rational imagination," even behavior. Blackmur—just because of his great talent, versatility, and subtlety—illustrates the predicament of much recent American criticism: its involvement in a private world of concepts, feelings, and terms, groping toward a general philosophy of life on the occasion of literature, and a distrust of inherited and traditional methods that leads to reliance on purely personal perceptions and combinations. In some of Blackmur's essays the privacy of terms and feelings reached a stage of fuzziness: his supersubtlety stylistically reminds one of the last stage of Henry James, but has, in Blackmur, become so completely divorced from traditional procedures that it seems impossible to keep any interest in the solution of the riddles propounded.

While Blackmur moved into an opaque world of private ruminations, Yvor Winters could be called a lucid rationalist—a rationalist with a vengeance. Throughout his critical writings, collected under the titles *In Defence of Reason* (1947), *The Function of Criticism* (1957), *On Modern Poets* (1957), and *Forms of Discovery* (1967), Winters per-

secuted obscurantism and irrationalism, and bluntly stated that poetry is good only insofar as a poem makes a defensible rational statement about a given experience. Winters believed in absolute moral truths, and even in the moral content of poetry. He acidly and often vehemently attacked obscurity in modern poetry and despised the whole of the romantic tradition of spontaneous emotional expression. Poe is to Winters a bad poet and writer. Emerson, Hawthorne, and Whitman seem to him hopelessly self-indulgent, and Eliot and Ransom are both included in *The Anatomy of Nonsense* (1943). Winters admired an obscure transcendentalist poet, Jones Very (1813–1880), much more than Emerson, put Robert Bridges (1844–1930) and Sturge Moore (1870–1944) above Yeats and Eliot, and praised many minor poets. He could be easily dismissed as a crotchety doctrinaire, as a moralist similar to the new humanists.

But despite his moralism and rationalism, Winters was a "new critic," a man of modern sensibility, a fine analyst of poetry and fiction who understood that "poetic morality and poetic feelings are inseparable; feelings and technique, structure, are inseparable." Form is to him the decisive part of the moral content. He devised elaborate classifications of poetic structures and described the effects of meter well. He raised questions about the ontological status of poetry and argued against many of the theories of Eliot and Ransom. But the excessively dogmatic manner that hides a very personal and even eccentric sensibility vitiated Winters's effectiveness, which might have been very salutary as a counterweight against the irrationalism of the time. He remained alone on the fringes of the movement.

The main movement of the New Criticism reached a point of exhaustion in the 1960s. Although externally the movement was very successful in penetrating into the universities and monopolizing the critical journals, a state of stagnation set in: many imitators applied the method mechanically and unimaginatively. On some points the movement was not able to go beyond its initial narrow circle: the selection of European writers who have attracted the attention of the critics was oddly narrow and subject to the distortion of very local and temporary perspective. On the whole, the historical perspective of most critics remained very short. Literary history is still beyond the ken of the New Criticism.

Also, the relations to modern linguistics and aesthetics remain unexplored. Much of the study of style, diction, and meter remains dilettantish; and aesthetics, while discussed in practice continually, remains without a sure philosophical foundation. Still, there were some hopeful signs of consolidation and expansion. William K. Wimsatt (1907–1975) in *The Verbal Icon* (1953) made an attempt to consolidate and expand the teachings of the New Criticism. He brilliantly argued against the fallacious tendency of criticism to trust the intention of the author and criticized I. A. Richards for his reliance on the emotion affecting the reader. In his epilogue to *Literary Criticism: A Short History* (1957, with Cleanth Brooks) Wimsatt made the clearest and most persuasive statement of a theory of literature that allows him to keep all three poles of literary theory: the mimetic, the emotive, and the expressionistic. The symbol, the concrete universal, remains the center of poetic theory, but ways are found to keep the relationship of poetry to morals and society intact.

The New Criticism, as a movement, has run its course. It immeasurably raised the level of awareness and sophistication in American criticism. It developed ingenious new methods of an analysis of poetry and its devices: imagery and symbol. It defined a new taste averse to the romantic tradition. It supplied an important apology of poetry in a world dominated by science. But it was unable to go successfully beyond its rather narrow confines, and it did not escape the dangers of ossification and institutionalization.

Several attempts have been made to replace the New Criticism. Among these the so-called Chicago Aristotelianism was the most distinct and most clearly organized. A group of scholars from the University of Chicago, headed by R. S. Crane (1886–1967), published a 650-page volume, *Critics and Criticism* (1952), which is, in part, devoted to very learned studies in the history of criticism and in part defends a view of literature sharply critical of the basic assumptions of the New Criticism. The role of language, metaphor, and symbol is minimized and all emphasis is put on plot and structure: Aristotle's *Poetics* serves as an inspiration for the terminology and the general scheme. In *The Languages of Criticism and the Structure of Poetry* (1953), Crane scored many polemical points against the hunters of paradoxes, sym-

bols, and myths. But he and his followers (the most concretely critical is Elder Olson [b. 1909]) are unable to offer any positive remedies beyond the most arid classifications of hero-types, plot structures, and genres. With them, genre theory reaches more than neoclassical rigidity: for instance, Dante's *Divine Comedy* is classified as didactic and not as mimetic or symbolic. The armature of scholarship, especially imposing in the writings of the philosopher Richard McKeon (b. 1900), hides insensitivity to literary values: the professed "pluralism" and interest in the "pleasure" of literature disguises a lack of critical standards. These scholars want to arrive at them by a foolproof, mechanical way, resuscitating an Aristotelianism quite inadequate to the problems of modern literature. The whole enterprise seems an ultra-academic exercise destined to wither on the vine.

Much more successful, diverse, and stimulating was the myth criticism which, under the influence of Frazer and Jung, arose as a reaction to the New Criticism. It flourished in England and France, but in the United States it assumed a particular vitality, as it was able to absorb many of the achievements of the New Criticism, at least with its best practitioners. Myth appealed to many because it allows the discussions of themes and types, usually considered part of the "content" and thus not quite respectable to formalist critics. Huck Finn floating down the Mississippi with Jim is a "myth," and so is any truth that is generally accepted by society. "Myth" can be simply another name for ideology, *Weltanschauung*. Richard Chase (1914–1962), in *Quest for Myth* (1949), identifies all good, sublime literature with myth. But more accurately and usefully, myth means a system of archetypes recoverable in rituals and tales, or a scheme of metaphors, symbols, and gods created by a poet such as Blake or Yeats.

Among the American myth-critics we must, however, make distinctions. There are allegorizers, who find the story of redemption throughout Shakespeare or discover Swedenborgianism in the novels of Henry James. There are those who expound the private mythologies of Blake, Shelley, or Yeats as gospel truths. But there are others who are genuine literary critics. Francis Fergusson (b. 1904), in *The Idea of a Theater* (1949), uses the results of the Cambridge school to consider the theater of all ages, from Sophocles to T. S. Eliot, as ritual. Philip Wheelwright

(1901–1969), in *The Burning Fountain* (1954), combines myth interest with semantics, and studies also, in a later book, *Metaphor and Reality* (1962), the sequence from literal meaning through metaphor and symbol to myth. Northrop Frye (q.v.), a Canadian, in his *Anatomy of Criticism* (1957), combines, rather, myth criticism with an attempt at an all-embracing theory of literature that is mainly a theory of genres. Frye devises an intricate scheme of modes, symbols, myths, and genres for which the Jungian archetype is the basic assumption. There are four main genres: comedy, romance, tragedy, and satire; these correspond to the four seasons: spring, summer, autumn, and winter, the rhythm of nature. The most surprising confrontations are made and the most extravagant claims for the method are put forward. Literature "imitates the total dream of man," and criticism will "reforge the links between creation and knowledge, art and science, myth and concept." Frye draws freely on the whole range of literature and interprets often sensitively and wittily (see also his *Fables of Identity: Studies in Poetic Mythology,* 1963), but he wants to discard all distinctions between good and bad works of art and ceases then to be a critic.

A recent trend of American criticism is existentialism. It hardly can be described as dependent on Heidegger or Sartre. It is rather a vocabulary, a mood, or it can be "phenomenology," an attempt at reconstructing the author's "consciousness," his relation to time and space, nature and society, in the manner of French critics such as Georges Poulet or Jean-Pierre Richard. Geoffrey Hartman (b. 1929), in his *Unmediated Vision* (1954) and *Wordsworth* (1964), traces a dialectic of perception and consciousness, and J. Hillis Miller's (b. 1928) books—*Charles Dickens: The World of His Novels* (1959), *The Disappearance of God: Five Nineteenth-Century Writers* (1963), and *Poets of Reality: Six Twentieth-Century Writers* (1965)—analyze the interior landscape or the presumed personal world of each author with great subtlety. The theme of loneliness and despair informs Murray Krieger's (b. 1923) *The Tragic Vision* (1960), in which the tragic hero (or rather "visionary") is the man of the "sickness unto death," the new nihilist. Krieger discusses Kafka, Camus, Thomas Mann, Dostoevsky, and Melville. It is in the nature of the method that the individual work of art as an aesthetic structure is ig-nored and that the critic aims at discovering, rather, some inner world behind the text. The method fits the concerns of our time for answers to the ultimate questions and the interest in the personal approach of great writers to the "human condition," but the traditional issues of art and criticism are slighted.

In the last decade a group of scholars, often misleadingly referred to as the Yale School, have taken up the motifs of structuralism and theories of the French philosopher Jacques Derrida to engage in what he and they call "deconstruction." Usually Harold Bloom (b. 1930) is associated with the group, although his writings follow a quite different track. After several books of interpretations of romantic poetry—*Shelley's Mythmaking* (1959), *The Visionary Company: A Reading of English Romantic Poetry* (1961), *Blake's Apocalypse* (1963), and *Yeats* (1970), Bloom has developed a concept of the history of poetry, first expounded in *The Anxiety of Influence* (1973) and elaborated in *A Map of Misreading* (1975), *Kabbalah and Criticism* (1975), and *Poetry and Repression* (1976). Bloom interprets the history of English and American poetry from Milton to Wallace Stevens (q.v.) on the analogy of Freud's "family romance." The "strong" poet revolts against his predecessors, since he cannot endure "the burden of the past" (the phrase used in the title of a book devoted to the romantic poets, *The Burden of the Past and the English Poets* [1970], by Walter Jackson Bate [b. 1918]). Bloom invents odd names—Clinamen, Tessera, Kenosis, Daemonization, Askesis, and Apophrades—to categorize the diverse strategies by which a new poet tries to cope with the "anxiety of influence." All these strategies involve inevitably a misreading or "misprision" of the prior poet. Bloom's theory is basically Freudian, but his concept of misreading links him to his colleagues (J. Hillis Miller, Geoffrey Hartman, Paul de Man [b. 1919]) who have come to completely skeptical conclusions about the very possibility of interpretation, criticism, and the notion of literature. This radical questioning of all traditional assumptions finds its support in some pronouncements of Nietzsche and in the whole long history of suspicion that many poets, critics, and philosophers have voiced against language and its ability to represent reality, to convey any truth, and to express what will forever remain ineffable.

Jacques Derrida and his followers assume that we are firmly locked within a prison-house of language, that words refer only to other words, that a text has no stable identity, origin, or end. The obvious fact that a word is not the thing signified is made to yield the view that all literature is about literature, is self-reflexive, is a mere web of "intertextuality." The difference between criticism and creative literature is denied, criticism in the old sense of evaluation is rejected, and the very concept of art dissolved in favor of the single concept of "text," or "writing," which is supposed to have preceded speaking. What remains is a concern for "rhetoric," which is not used in the old sense of the art of persuasion but as a system of tropes or figuration. It leads to reliance on etymology, in practice to punning and verbal games suggestive of the etymologizing of Heidegger, Joyce's *Finnegans Wake,* and even Dada.

Paul de Man interprets and explains modern critics in the collection *Blindness and Insight* (1971), which contains a discussion of Derrida's views of Rousseau, and in *Allegories of Reading* (1979) gives subtle and, one would assume, correct or at least plausible interpretations of Rilke, Proust, Nietzsche, and Rousseau that focus on the rhetorical or figural potentialities of language. The term "allegory" in the title, used in the sense of speaking "otherwise than one seems to speak," protects the claim for uncertainty and arbitrariness of his readings, although the distinctions and judgments made in the essays are those any traditional critic could have made.

The limitations of the New Criticism are stressed in the recent work of Geoffrey Hartman, especially in *Beyond Formalism* (1970), *The Fate of Reading* (1975), and *Criticism in the Wilderness* (1980). They display his historical learning and sensitivity but more and more embrace a new kind of creative criticism in which the priority of literary text over literary-critical text is challenged in favor of a new hybrid between criticism, inventive, witty word games, and abstract philosophizing.

These new theories, of course, have been criticized and rejected by many. Other points of view and older concepts are being defended. Gerald Graff (b. 1937), in *Literature against Itself* (1979), has surveyed the scene with a jaundiced eye, looking with disfavor even on the New Criticism as preparing the

way for the aberrations of the last decade. Wayne C. Booth (b. 1921), the author of an acute book on the novel that challenged the Jamesian ideal of the absent author, *The Rhetoric of Fiction* (1961), has expounded a concept of pluralism in *Critical Understanding* (1979). It allows him, after admitting the partial truths of the theories of R. S. Crane, Kenneth Burke, and M. H. Abrams (b. 1912), a learned historian of criticism and ideas, to return to a concept of understanding that is not very different from that of the great tradition of hermeneutics descended from Friedrich Schleiermacher (1768–1834) and Dilthey. He calls it "overstanding," pleading for tolerance and sympathy for different viewpoints.

Thirty years ago there was hardly any interest in literary theory in the United States. Today there is a plethora of books that discuss the main issues of the theory of interpretation or the concept of literature and criticism from often contradictory points of view. E. D. Hirsch's (b. 1928) *Validity in Interpretation* (1967) attempts to reassert objective criticism relying on the intention of the author by drawing on the whole history of hermeneutics. His *The Aims of Interpretation* (1976) forcefully restates the arguments against antirationalism and extreme relativism. Murray Krieger has given us a *summa* of his views in *Theory of Criticism* (1976), where he elaborates and defends a scheme not too far removed from the New Criticism while making concessions to several new trends. Krieger calls it a poetics of "presence," since he wants to preserve the literary object in the context of culture without dissolving it into man's general symbol-making activity.

French structuralism has excited the most interest. There is a good expository book by Robert Scholes (b. 1929), *Structuralism in Literature* (1974), which is, however, marred by a sentimental conclusion claiming that "marriage is a sacrament of structuralism." Jonathan Culler's (b. 1944) *Structuralist Poetics* (1975), equally informative as an exposition of Continental theories, soberly proposes a concept of "literary competence" on the analogy of Noam Chomsky's (b. 1928) linguistic "competence." Fredric Jameson's *The Prison-House of Language: A Critical Account of Structuralism and Russian Formalism* (1972) is written from a strict Marxist point of view.

One has the impression that critical languages have become so diversified and mutually exclusive, held often only by small groups, that a fruitful interchange of views has become all but impossible. Grant Webster (b. 1933), in a retrospective book, *The Republic of Letters* (1979), devoted to the New Criticism and the so-called New York intellectuals (Edmund Wilson, Lionel Trilling, et al.), adapted the thesis of Thomas S. Kuhn's (b. 1922) *The Structure of Scientific Revolutions* (1962) to argue that critical theories develop and die without any communication with preceding or succeeding rival theories he calls "charters." The end of criticism as a continuing discipline is adumbrated in this and the not so dissimilar attempt of the "deconstructionists." They all testify to the atomization of our civilization, to the breakdown of communication and thus of meaningful discourse.

Looking back at these new trends one is struck by their (however different) preoccupation with language, with the indifference to old problems of literary criticism such as the relation between art and reality and art and morals. Also, the concern for evaluation, for the distinction between art and non-art has diminished, as it has in the practice of modern art. Theory of literature is often absorbed in general linguistics or subordinated to semiotics. A gain in insight into many problems of technique and verbal surface seems often bought at the expense of generally human concerns. "Dehumanization" seems not too hasty a generalization about the newest developments in literary criticism.

BIBLIOGRAPHY: **General.** Wellek, R., *Concepts of Criticism* (1963); Wellek, R., *Discriminations: Further Concepts of Criticism* (1970); Fokkema, D. W., and Kunne-Ibsch, E., *Theories of Literature in the Twentieth Century: Structuralism, Marxism, Aesthetics of Reception, Semiotics* (1977); Magliola, R. R., *Phenomenology and Literature* (1977); Suleiman, S. R., and Crosman, I., eds., *The Reader in the Text: Essays on Audience and Interpretation* (1980); Hernadi, P., ed., *What Is Criticism?* (1981); Juhl, P. D., *Interpretation: An Essay in the Philosophy of Literary Criticism* (1981); Tompkins, J. P., ed., *Reader-Response Criticism: From Formalism to Post-Structuralism* (1981); Wellek, R., *Four Critics: Croce, Valéry, Lukács, Ingarden* (1981); Wellek, R., *The Attack on Literature, and Other Essays* (1982). **Marxist Criticism.** Demetz, P., *Marx, Engels, and the Poets* (1967); Baxandall, L., *Marxism and Aesthetics: A Bibliography* (1968); Solomon, M., ed., *Marxism and Art: Essays Classic and Contemporary* (1973); Jameson, F., *Marxism and Form: Twentieth-Century Dialectical Theories of Literature* (1974); Eagleton, T., *Criticism and Ideology* (1976); Eagleton, T., *Marxism and Literary Criticism* (1976); Williams, R., *Marxism and Literature* (1977); Bisztray, G., *Marxist Models of Literary Realism* (1978). **Psychoanalytic Criticism.** Hoffman, F. J., *Freudianism and the Literary Mind* (1945); Trilling, L., "Freud and Literature," *The Liberal Imagination* (1950), pp. 34–57; Fraiberg, L., *Psychoanalysis and American Literary Criticism* (1960); Crews, F., ed., *Psychoanalysis and the Literary Process* (1970); Spector, J. J., *The Aesthetics of Freud* (1972); Kaplan, M., and Kloss, R., *The Unspoken Motive: A Guide to Psychoanalytic Literary Criticism* (1973); Strelka, J. P., ed., *Literary Criticism and Psychology* (1976); Orlando, F., *Toward a Freudian Theory of Literature* (1979). **Myth Criticism.** Philipson, M., *Outline of a Jungian Aesthetics* (1963); Vickery, J. B., ed., *Myth and Literature* (1966); Righter, W., *Myth and Literature* (1975); Strelka, J. P., ed., *Literary Criticism and Myth* (1980). **Structuralism, Semiotics, Deconstruction.** Ehrmann, J., *Structuralism* (1966); Macksey, R., and Donato, E., *The Languages of Criticism and the Sciences of Man: The Structuralist Controversy* (1970); Jameson, F., *The Prison-House of Language: A Critical Account of Structuralism and Russian Formalism* (1972); Broekman, J. M., *Structuralism: Moscow–Prague–Paris* (1974); Scholes, R., *Structuralism in Literature* (1974); Culler, J., *Structurealist Poetics* (1975); Hawkes, T., *Structuralism and Semiotics* (1977); Sturrock, J., *Structuralism and Since: From Lévi-Strauss to Derrida* (1979); Harari, J. V., *Textual Strategies: Perspectives in Post-Structuralist Criticism* (1979); Kurzweil, E., *The Age of Structuralism* (1980); Culler, J., *The Pursuit of Signs: Semiotics, Literature, Deconstruction* (1981); Strickland, G., *Structuralism or Criticism?* (1981); Hartman, G. H., *Saving the Text: Literature, Derrida, Philosophy* (1981); Scholes, R., *Semiotics and Interpretation* (1982); Seung, T. K., *Structuralism and Hermeneutics* (1982); Norris, C., *Deconstruction: Theory and Practice* (1982). **Italy.** Gorlier, C., "Contemporary Italian Literary Criticism," *LitR*, 3 (1959), 163–69; Scaglione, A., "Literary Criticism in Postwar

Italy," *IQ,* 4, 13–14 (1960), 27–38. **France.** Girard, R., "Existentialism and Literary Criticism," *YFS,* 16 (1955–56), 45–52; LeSage, L., *The French New Criticism: An Introduction and a Sampler* (1967); Fowlie, W., *The French Critic, 1549–1967* (1968); Lawall, S., *Critics of Consciousness* (1968); Simon, J. K., ed., *Modern French Criticism: From Proust and Valéry to Structuralism* (1972); Doubrovsky, S., *The New Criticism in France* (1973). **Russia.** Hankin, R. M., "Postwar Soviet Ideology and Literary Scholarship," in Simmons, E. J., ed., *Through the Glass of Soviet Literature* (1953), pp. 244–89; Erlich, V., *Russian Formalism: History, Doctrine* (1955); Erlich, V., "Social and Aesthetic Criteria in Soviet Russian Criticism," in Simmons, E. J., ed., *Continuity and Change in Russian and Soviet Thought* (1955), pp. 398–416; Ermolaev, H., *Soviet Literary Theories, 1917–34: The Genesis of Socialist Realism* (1963); Pomorska, K., *Russian Formalist Theory and Its Poetic Ambiance* (1968); Bann, S., and Bowlt, J. E., *Russian Formalism* (1973); Erlich, V., *Twentieth Century Russian Literary Criticism* (1975). **Czechoslovakia.** Wellek, R., "Modern Czech Criticism and Literary Scholarship," *HSS,* 2 (1954), 343–58; Wellek, R., "Recent Czech Literary History and Criticism," *Essays on Czech Literature* (1963), pp. 194–205; Garvin, P. L., ed., *A Prague School Reader on Esthetics, Literary Structure, and Style* (1964); Matejka, J., ed., *Sound, Sign and Meaning: Quinquagenary of the Prague Linguistic Circle* (1976); Steiner, P., ed., *The Prague School: Selected Writings 1929–1946* (1982). **Germany and Austria.** Bruford, W. H., *Literary Interpretation in Germany* (1952); Amacher, R. E., and Lange, V., eds., *New Perspectives in German Literary Criticism* (1979). **England and the United States.** Williams, O., *Contemporary Criticism of Literature* (1925); Smith, B., *Forces in American Criticism* (1939); Hyman, S. E., *The Armed Vision: A Study in the Methods of Modern Literary Criticism* (1948); O'Connor, W. V., *An Age of Criticism: 1900–1950* (1952); Stovall, F., ed., *The Development of American Criticism* (1955); Krieger, M., *The New Apologists for Poetry* (1956); Pritchard, J. P., *Criticism in America* (1956); Wimsatt, W. K., and Brooks, C., *Literary Criticism: A Short History* (1957); Leary, L., *Contemporary Literary Scholarship* (1958); Watson, G., *The Literary Critics* (1962); Sutton, W., *Modern American Criti-* *cism* (1963); Bradbury, M., *Contemporary Criticism,* Stratford-upon-Avon Studies 12 (1970); Graff, G., *Poetic Statement and Critical Dogma* (1970); Miller, D. M., *The Net of Hephaestus: A Study of Modern Criticism and Metaphysical Metaphor* (1971); Borklund, E., *Contemporary Literary Critics* (1977); Graff, G., *Literature against Itself* (1979); Webster, G., *The Republic of Letters: A History of Postwar American Literary Opinion* (1979); Lentricchia, F., *After the New Criticism* (1980); Hartman, G., *Criticism in the Wilderness* (1980); Raval, S., *Metacriticism* (1981)

RENÉ WELLEK

For the contributions of the author of this article to literary criticism, please see separate entry.—Ed.

LITHUANIAN LITERATURE

The Lithuanians, an ancient people, speaking one of the oldest Indo-European languages, have nevertheless lacked, for most of their long history, a written literature of their own. Powerful neighbors, constantly pressing them from the south and the east against the Baltic Sea, have forced the Lithuanians to spend their best energies in the struggle for survival. Under those conditions, the literary genius of the nation was preserved in its rich and ancient folklore. The Lithuanian folk song (those that survived long enough to be recorded) concerns itself with the lyrical expression of an intimate relationship between man and nature, and with a lucid, restrained statement of man's basically tragic situation in a world ruled by sorrow and death.

The first important work of written literature came, in the middle of the 18th c., from the pen of Kristijonas Donelaitis (1714–1780), a Protestant clergyman in East Prussia. His rural epic *Metai* (written c. 1765–75, pub. 1818; *The Seasons,* 1967) describes the daily life of the Lithuanian peasant as he plods the treadmill of time toward the hoped-for eternity in which his plain country virtue is to meet its just reward. In vigorous, earthy language Donelaitis exhorts his countrymen to resist both the oppression and the corrupt enticements coming from the alien culture of the German overlords.

The first significant writers in Lithuania proper—Simanas Daukantas (1793–1864), Simanas Stanevičius (1799–1848), and Motiejus Valančius (1801–1875)—were stimulated by the winds of romantic nationalism blowing from western Europe. Their desire was to arouse Lithuanian self-respect and to encourage allegiance to the country's indigenous cultural values.

Somewhat aloof from these stood the lonely, talented figure of Antanas Baranauskas (1835–1902), who achieved fame with his one major work, *Ankyščių šilesis* (1860–61; the pine grove of Anykščiai), a long lyrical poem in melodious syllabic verse that sings of the past glories of a wooded spot near his home.

The groundswell of romantic nationalism produced intensified resistance against the russification policies of the tsarist regime, which in 1865 had gone so far as to proclaim a ban against Lithuanian books printed in the Latin alphabet. The lifting of the ban in 1904 released the creative energies of a large number of writers whose works established a solid foundation for the further growth of Lithuanian literature.

By far the best of the romantic poets was Maironis (pseud. of Jonas Mačiulevičius-Mačiulis, 1862–1932). His emotionally intense patriotic poems raised Lithuanian poetic diction and prosody to a new dimension. Using the language firmly, he demonstrated sure handling of the syllabo-tonic meters and great sensitivity to the nuances of relationship between rhythm, emotion, and idea. In prose, the major writer of the period was Juozas Tumas-Vaižgantas (1869–1933), who wrote chatty, colorful tales about the emerging national consciousness in the life of the Lithuanian countryside.

Their works, as well as those of Marija Pečkauskaitė-Šatrijos Ragana (1878–1933), Julija Žymantienė-Žimaitė (1845–1921), and Antanas Žukauskas-Vienuolis (1882–1958), spanned a period of crucial changes in Lithuanian history, extending from the 1905 revolution in Russia, through World War I, to the establishment of an independent Lithuanian state in 1918. Vienuolis, in fact, lived to see his country occupied by the Germans in 1940 and to become one of the Party-controlled writers in Lithuania under Soviet rule.

Vincas Krėvė (q.v.), however, chose self-exile when the Soviet armies returned to Lithuania in 1944. A prolific and complex writer, he distinguished himself in several genres. Nostalgia for Lithuanian antiquity inspired him to write *Dainavos šalies senų žmonių padavimai* (1912; tales of the old folk of Dainava), a series of highly stylized legends dealing with heroes of times past. Present-day Lithuania led him to write realistic stories about villagers, living in close intimacy with nature, who possessed, in the author's eyes, the indefinable, deep strength that had sustained his people through countless ages. This same power figures prominently in his plays *Šarūnas* (1911; Šarūnas) and *Skirgaila* (1925; Skirgaila), which deal with crucial moments in Lithuanian history. And in a biblical epic, *Dangaus ir žemės sūnūs* (2 vols., 1949, 1963; the sons of heaven and earth), he pursued his search for the secret of human fortitude to a confrontation between man and God.

The development of poetry after Maironis went in the direction of symbolism (q.v.). Jurgis Baltrušaitis (1873–1944), most of whose poetry was written in Russian, was himself a prominent member of the circle of Russian symbolists. His Lithuanian poems have the same austere clarity of vision and ascetic restraint as his Russian ones, but they also provide a rich interplay among three different language strata, consisting of Lithuanian equivalents to the Russian symbolist vocabulary, highly idiosyncratic personal linguistic constructs, and down-to-earth peasant vocabulary. In both languages, he contemplates man's relationship to eternity on the same terms.

Balys Sruoga (1896–1947), who experimented vigorously with verse forms, succeeded in combining the symbolist outlook with the imagery and diction of the Lithuanian folk song. In his verse drama Sruoga returned to classical order and clarity developing, as in the play *Milžino paunksmė* (1930; shadow of the giant), philosophical portrayals of historical figures in an atmosphere of lyrical contemplation.

Faustas Kirša (1891–1964) and Vincas Mykolaitis (q.v.) followed the Western trends of symbolism, particularly the French. They remained, however, intimately bound to the indigenous traditions, to the Lithuanian manner of translating reality into metaphor and symbol as it had developed in folklore.

Mykolaitis became widely known for his quasi-autobiographical novel *Altorių šešėly* (1933; in the shadow of the altars), in which the hero is a young priest who tries in vain to come to terms with an evanescent image of God. Mykolaitis made a similarly unsuccessful effort to meet the requirements of Socialist Realism (q.v.) under Soviet occupation with the novel *Sukilėliai* (1957; the rebels), dealing with the Polish-Lithuanian uprising against the Russians in 1863.

The literary traditions of Lithuania Minor (East Prussia), begun so well with Donelaitis, were continued by Vilius Storasta-Vydūnas (1868–1953) and by Ieva Simonaitytė (b. 1897). The most philosophical of Lithuanian authors, Storasta-Vydūnas constantly sought, in his many plays and other writings, to understand the ultimate meaning of man's existence in terms of mystical images of "eternal light," which is the unending principle of life and the spark of divinity in man. Simonaitytė, in her novel *Aukštujų Šimonių likimas* (1935; the destiny of the Simonys of Aukštujai), depicted the gradual disappearance of the Lithuanian ethnic minority in East Prussia during the course of centuries, under the influx of German colonists.

In the 1920s the influence of Russian futurism (q.v.) and western European expressionism (q.v.) manifested itself in the "Four Winds" movement, so called after the title of a literary periodical edited by Kazys Binkis (1893–1942). The movement's manifesto contains all the brash statements that were so dear to the futurists: the worship of the machine age; the desire to forge and hammer out poetry like iron by an effort of rational will; contempt for "insipid romantics" and "starry-eyed symbolists." Nevertheless, Binkis's own verse remained light and lyrical in essence, since Lithuania—a land of quiet lakes and green meadows—did not offer the industrial realities necessary for the development of truly dynamic futurism. Other important members of the movement were Juozas Petrėnas-Tarulis (1896–1980) and Teofilis Tilvytis (1904–1969).

The second important literary movement of the 1920s was called the "Third Front." Third Front writers were leftists who were interested in fighting social and economic injustice and who were committed to the budding Lithuanian proletariat and to the peasantry. The most important poet in this group was Salomėja Neris (1904–1945), although her deeply lyrical, and feminine poetry, vibrant with warm personal feeling, transcended the outlines of any particular ideology. Petras Cvirka (1909–1947) wrote novels of social satire directed against the ruling Lithuanian bourgeoisie, in which he glorified the honest work of simple peasants. The literary critic Kostas Korsakas (b. 1909) and the poet Antanas Venclova (b. 1906) also played a significant role in this movement.

Korsakas, Cvirka, Venclova, Neris, and Tilvytis were later to form the nucleus of those who produced the Soviet Lithuanian literature that emerged in the aftermath of World War II.

In the 1930s Lithuanian literature came of age in the sense that art itself, as an embodiment of a personal vision of reality, became the object of primary concern. Bernardas Brazdžionis (b. 1907) believed that reality was permeated and made meaningful by the hidden presence of God. The frequent biblical references in his works create a feeling not only of Christian devotion, but also of a romantic longing for some dimly perceived, intensely desired, ultimate home for the soul. He treats nature, both in broad outlines and in minute details, as a stage setting for his poetic drama of life as a holy pilgrimage toward death. This mood is especially strengthened by Brazdžionis's skillful handling of rhythm and syntax, and by his fine sensitivity to the musical qualities of words.

The poetry of Jonas Aistis (q.v.) broke new ground in the uses of poetic language. Skillfully combining plain everyday language with highly refined literary formulas, he created an intoxicating effect of a still raw, but already inspired, reality, quivering on the verge of poetic fulfillment. Much of his work consists of an intense confrontation with the values and possibilities of art itself, conveyed sometimes directly in its own terms and sometimes through poetic formulations of the themes of love, patriotism, painful human solitude, and his closeness to the Lithuanian landscape.

Other significant poets of the same time were Antanas Miškinis (b. 1905), who used the language and lyrical texture of the native folk songs to perfect a poetry of highly personal lyricism, and Kazys Boruta (1905–1965), a poet who asserted the spirit of freedom and of individual human dignity.

The prose writers in this period were strongly influenced by impressionism, especially of the Scandinavian variety. Although Ignas Šeinius (1889–1959) was to spend much of his life in Sweden, the imprint of such authors as Knut Hamsun (q.v.) can already be seen in his best work, the novella *Kuprelis* (1913; the hunchback), which was written before he left Lithuania. The story tells about a gifted, physically disfigured dreamer who is doomed to vegetate in the provinces. The double psychological tension of the story consists of the desire for personal happiness and the deformity that prevents it on the one hand, and intellectual yearning versus gray reality on the other.

Antanas Vaičiulaitis (q.v.) established his reputation with the novel *Valentina* (1936; Valentina); in which delicate shades of feeling in the soul of a man possessed by love are carefully integrated with summer light and evening shadow, cricket song and sudden storms, in a manner reminiscent of the French impressionist painters. Vaičiulaitis is also known for his stories of country life and for his fairy tales.

Jurgis Savickis (1890–1952) belongs among the better Lithuanian prose stylists. His outstanding qualities are brevity, precision, and a certain dry, elegant irony of understatement that he uses when describing situations fraught with possible tragic meanings. The main theme of his short stories appears to be the blindness of small men—the careerist, the bourgeois, the semi-intellectual—to the immensity of the life passing them by. Savickis spent considerable time in western Europe, in the Lithuanian diplomatic service, and had good opportunities for observing the human comedy of petty ambitions and moral inadequacies, both at home and abroad.

Other significant prose writers are Juozas Grušas (q.v.) and Jurgis Jankus (b. 1906), as well as Liudas Dovydėnas (b. 1906). Grušas, who still lives in Soviet-occupied Lithuania, has recently shown himself a gifted playwright. He has written historical plays as well as plays that approach the modern concept of the Theater of the Absurd (q.v.). Dovydėnas, author of the prize-winning novel *Broliai Domeikos* (1936; *The Brothers Domeika,* 1976), is a close and loving observer of Lithuanian country life.

The events of World War II and their consequences for the Lithuanian people—the German occupation, the return of the Soviets in 1944—resulted in splitting the literary community into two parts. Some writers remained in Lithuania and submitted to Communist Party dictates in art, while others withdrew to the West and were confronted with the variety, and perhaps confusion, of the literary trends prevailing there. The older writer, finding himself sometimes unable to comprehend the intellectual and artistic challenge implicit in the tragedy of his exile, often withdrew into reminiscences of home, or else allowed his bitter patriotic fervor to shape the purposes of his art.

New developments came from a generation of younger writers who, because they were only beginning to emerge by 1944, were sufficiently flexible to be able to respond to the new experiences of spiritual and artistic life that the West offered. Paradoxically, the primary source of their new inspiration must be sought still in Lithuania, in the person of Vytautas Mačernis (1920–1945). He was a gifted existentialist (q.v.) poet whose poetic visions stimulated his friends to seek new relationships between themselves, art, and reality.

The young exiles gathered around the periodical *Literatūros lankai,* which was started in Buenos Aires in 1952. Their guiding spirit at the beginning was the poet Juozas Kėkštas (1915–1981), who died in Poland. Another poet, Kazys Bradūnas (b. 1917), contributed a good deal to organizing the movement, which was to call itself the "Earth" collective.

Bradūnas's early verse was permeated with direct existential pain, born of a physical sense of loss, of sudden alienation in a strange country. Later Bradūnas deepened and at the same time sublimated his sorrow by reconstructing a Lithuanian mythology of those who lived and died on Lithuanian soil through countless ages, thus performing an unending sacrifice before the living presence of God, whether He be understood in pantheistic, pagan terms, or as the Christian God of later generations.

Alfonsas Nyka-Niliūnas (b. 1920) achieved a breakthrough in Lithuanian literary criticism by demanding that the vague, impressionistic approaches of the past be replaced by informed, systematic, and lucid literary analysis. His main contribution to the literature of exile, however, is in his poetry. Niliūnas is a highly complex, searching poet, capable of transforming philosophical quest into intense lyrical emotion, of integrating his own visions with the creative efforts of all mankind by means of subtly interconnected systems of symbolic and intellectual references. His basic position is existentialist: the recognition of reality, especially for an exile, is equivalent to the understanding of alienation.

Closely connected with the "Earth" collective were some prose writers, notably Algirdas Landsbergis (b. 1924) and Antanas Škėma (1911–1961). Landsbergis's first novel, *Kelionė* (1954; the journey), re-created the experience of war and exile on a plane on which chronological time sequence is replaced by an inner continuum of thought and feeling, as if a new mosaic were to be created from the broken pieces of reality destroyed by World War II. Landsbergis also writes short stories and plays in which his satirical intelligence is directed at the sometimes tragic inadequacies of man. One of his better-known plays is *Penki stulpai turgaus aikšteje* (1966; *Five Posts in the Market Place,* 1968).

Antanas Škėma, in his novel *Balta drobulė* (1958; the white shroud) and in a number of short stories and plays, depicts the condition of man as that of being in exile, since the logical inevitabilities that rule the universe do not provide for the principle of life, much less for the irrational urge of creativity that constitutes the divine spark of man. Therefore, the more perfect an organism, the greater is its suffering, and in man the supreme qualities of mind fulfill themselves in supreme agony. Škėma's works often contain cruel, even melodramatic, situations centered around the conflict between freedom and tyranny.

Other significant novelists are Aloyzas Baronas (1917–1980), a prolific writer of quixotic, paradoxical works that investigate man's basic values against the background of ashes left by the holocaust of World War II, and Vincas Ramonas (b. 1905), whose *Kryžiai* (1947; the crosses) depicts the traumatic encounter between the peasants of independent Lithuania and the invading Soviet ideology, borne on the backs of tanks.

Marius Katiliškis (1915–1981), in such novels as *Užuovėja* (1952; the wind shelter) and *Miškais ateina ruduo* (1957; autumn comes through the forests), evokes Lithuania in all its elemental power and shows how the people who inhabit it must live in an indissoluble bond with the soil, as if they were mere configurations upon the surface of continuing life. Then it comes as a special shock to realize that the impossible *has* happened; that these people have actually been separated from their soil; that they have become exiles, groping in vain for some meaning to their lives.

Pulgis Andriušis (1907–1976) re-creates the atmosphere of the Lithuanian countryside in lush, ornate prose, exploiting to the fullest all the resources of the language to spin a web of enchanting memory.

In drama, the exile Kostas Ostrauskas (b. 1926) has written absurdist plays. His main attention is focused upon death as an unimaginable, yet inevitable, final event in the life of both body and mind. Since no rational dialogue is possible between man's intelligence and the incomprehensible void facing it, absurdity must necessarily be the overwhelming presence in any drama purporting to depict the human condition. In such plays as *Pypkė* (1954; *The Pipe,* 1963) and *Duobkasiai* (1967; *The Gravediggers,* 1967) Ostrauskas calls for defiant reassertion of life in the face of death, even if such an act remains ultimately meaningless.

Similarly, death dominates the poetry of Algimantas Mackus (1932–1964). In his work, the condition of exile necessitates a reversal of all the meanings and values of conventional poetic language that are based upon the consciousness that an artist is at home in the world. Mackus was developing a systematic reconstruction of all basic metaphorical and semantic connotations in poetic imagery, assigning the meaning of death to terms that ordinarily mean life. The result is a shattering picture of reality as a visible expression of the ultimate void. In this context Mackus placed the specific events, feelings, and beliefs of the Lithuanian exiles. The result is an image of a deathbound community of lost men in a universe that cannot contain any meaning. Yet, in the very clarity of his dark vision, Mackus managed to lend a tragic dignity to the stature of man.

Perhaps the greatest, and certainly the most complex and subtle Lithuanian poet is Henrikas Radauskas (q.v.). He cannot be readily identified with any trends and movements, whether in independent Lithuania or in exile. The theme of Radauskas's poetry is ultimately art itself, whereas exile, death, nature, history, and the mythological and metaphysical aspects of man's experience constitute the component elements of an aesthetic entity called a poem—a thing of noble beauty, aloof from the lesser passions and accomplishments of man.

Another outstanding poet is Tomas Venclova (b. 1937), son of Antanas Venclova (see above), who has recently left the Soviet Union to live in the U.S. His "arid" poetry, without any surface emotionalism or "beautiful language," presents complex verbal structures of high intellectual order, full of very intricate, subtle and infinitely evocative interrelationships among all aspects of human experience in history and in art. In his work one hears echoes of Russian Acmeists and of recent "underground" Russian poets, for example, Joseph Brodsky (q.v.), as well as of "intellectual" Western poets, such as T. S. Eliot and Ezra Pound (qq.v.).

The literature of Soviet-occupied Lithuania was for a long time at a low point. "Inspiration" came from the desk drawer of a Communist Party bureaucrat; questions of style and technique became subordinate to the ideological requirements of socialist realism. Only in recent years, particularly after de-Stalinization, have new talents come forward, replacing the submissive and often quite mediocre older writers.

Among the ground-breaking poetic talents is Eduardas Mieželaitis (b. 1919), winner of the All-Union Lenin Prize in Literature. In his work, attempts to convey personal experience are combined with an interest in experimenting with florid poetic diction and baroque form.

Justinas Marcinkevičius (b. 1930) searches among the ruins of sorrows long endured for the promise of the future in his own soul and in that of his people, notably in his narrative poem *Kraujas ir pelenai* (1960; blood and ashes), which describes the total destruction of a Lithuanian village by the Nazis during World War II. His historical trilogy—*Mindaugas* (1968; Mindaugas), *Katedra* (1971; the cathedral), and *Mažvydas* (1976; Mažvydas)—focuses on outstanding figures in Lithuanian history in an attempt to depict the moral crucibles of the nation, its resilience under oppression, and its determined search for a cultural and moral identity across the centuries leading toward the modern age.

Judita Vaičiūnaitė (b. 1937) and Janina Degutytė (b. 1928) are young poets of genuine artistic gifts. Sigitas Geda (b. 1943) is a subtle poet of nature and of the soul, whose word-magic is permeated with symbolic references ranging from ancient myth to medieval symbolism. Mykolas Sluckis (b. 1929), Jonas Avyžius (b. 1922), Romualdas Granauskas (b. 1939), and Juozas Aputis (b. 1936) are talented writers of fiction notable especially for their bold experimentation with modern stylistic and psychological devices. Kazys Saja (b. 1932) has been successfully searching for new creative modes in the theater.

Lithuanian literature continues to develop in spite of the contingencies of exile or the difficulties caused by Soviet occupation.

BIBLIOGRAPHY: Engert, H., *Aus litauischer Dichtung* (1935); Mauclère, J., *Panorama de la littérature lithuanienne contemporaine* (1938); Jungfer, V., *Litauen: Antlitz eines Volkes* (1948); Landsbergis, A., Introduction to Landsbergis, A., and Mills, C., eds., *The Green Oak* (1962), pp. 9–21; Rubulis, A., *Baltic Literature* (1970), pp. 163–212; Šilbajoris, R., *Perfection of Exile: Fourteen Contemporary Lithuanian Writers* (1970); Šilbajoris, R., "Lithuanian Literature," in Ivask, I., and Wilpert, G. von, eds., *World Literature since 1945* (1973), pp. 456–61; Ziedonis, A., et al., eds., *Baltic Literature and Linguistics* (1973); Šilbajoris, R., Foreword to Zdanys, J., ed., *Selected Postwar Lithuanian Poetry* (1978), pp. 7–12; Šilbajoris, R., Introduction to Skrupskelis, A., ed., *Lithuanian Writers in the West: An Anthology* (1979), pp. 16–19; Straumanis, A., ed., *Baltic Drama: A Handbook and Bibliography* (1981), pp. 381–560

RIMVYDAS ŠILBAJORIS

LIU Ya-tzu

Chinese poet and historian, b. 28 May 1887, Wu-chiang, Kiangsu Province; d. 21 June 1958, Peking

Born of a landholding gentry-scholar family, L. early imbibed revolutionary ideas prevalent among Chinese youth at the turn of the century. In 1906, while in Shanghai, he joined Sun Yat-sen's China Alliance and wrote inflammatory essays and poems to advocate the overthrow of the Manchu regime. His major activity in this period was the founding (1909) of the Southern Society, which grew under his leadership into a large literary organization with over one thousand members. As a veteran Kuomintang member, he made occasional forays into the political arena in the 1910s and 1920s, but fared better as writer and scholar. He was director of the Gazetteer Bureau of the Shanghai Municipality (1932–37) and supervised the publication of a series of its yearbooks and historical studies. He withdrew from active life during the Sino-Japanese War, but political differences with the Kuomintang faction under Chiang Kai-shek led to L.'s dismissal from the party (1941) and to his subsequent support of the Communist cause. He was invited to Peking by Mao Tse-tung after the Communist victory in 1949 and held various offices in the new regime until his death nine years later.

L. left to posterity a large legacy of poetic

133

works written in the classical style, in which he showed great skill and expertise, even though it was his contention that the future belonged to the new vernacular poetry of the May Fourth era (see Chinese Literature). For almost fifty years—from his first published poems (in *Kiangsu,* a Tokyo-based Chinese periodical) in 1903 to his last poems, written in 1951—he cultivated the poetic art with devotion and diligence. His verses contain fresh ideas and powerful, overflowing emotions that best express the aspirations and ideals of the Chinese revolution. He was also adept at extempore pieces compiled for his many friends on various occasions. Whether occasional or topical, his poems abound in historical and classical allusions that bear witness to his erudition.

L. was dedicated to the memories of his friends. He not only wrote essays and poems to them, but also collected and published their writings after their deaths. Among the works he edited were those of early revolutionary martyrs. L.'s great effort, however, was directed toward the collection of Su Man-shu's (q.v.) literary remains and biographical materials, which he published in five volumes: *Man-shu ch'üan-chi* (1928–31; Man-shu's complete works). Indefatigable in his research, L. succeeded in disentangling the confused threads of his friend's life in a series of new studies. The same interest led to his compilation of *Nan-shê chi-lüeh* (1940; a short account of the Southern Society). Its title notwithstanding, the book is a comprehensive record of the activities of the Southern Society (1909–24) with a complete listing of its members. In another volume, *Huai-chiu chi* (1947; essays in remembrance of old times and friends), L. wrote fondly on some of his friends as well as on topics of current and historical interest.

During the first years of his self-imposed seclusion in Japanese-occupied Shanghai (1937–40) L. started his most ambitious project, on the history of Southern Ming (covering two decades of the mid-17th c. during which the Ming loyalists rallied in south China against the conquering Manchus), which he continued when he moved to Hong Kong (1940–41). Although the work was disrupted by the Japanese occupation of the island after Pearl Harbor and L.'s subsequent flight to the Chinese hinterland, he was able to complete and publish several articles on the subject. The entire work, however, was left unfinished.

The life and thought of L., poet and scholar, was affected by the major political upheavals of his time. Impelled by an inborn patriotism and strong ideological conviction, he plunged, if only for short periods, into the maelstroms. Using his unique experiences reinforced by ardent feelings, he created a new type of revolutionary heroic verse unsurpassed by his contemporaries. Discarding the hackneyed, pedantic classical clichés, he rescued Chinese poetry from degeneration by infusing it with a vigorous spirit and strong individualism. Not an innovator, he was rather a master of age-old poetic conventions, which he artfully transformed into new modes and into a powerful vehicle for the communication of patriotic sentiments.

L.'s influence was widespread. He was beloved of younger writers, to whom he was especially considerate and helpful, and by whom he was acclaimed modern China's great poet.

FURTHER WORKS: *Ch'eng-fu chi* (1928); *L. Y. shih-tz'u hsüan* (1959)

BIBLIOGRAPHY: Boorman, H. L., ed., *Biographical Dictionary of Republican China* (1967), Vol. II, pp. 421–23; Liu Wu-chi, *Su Man-shu* (1972), pp. 68–82

LIU WU-CHI

LOBATO, Monteiro
Brazilian short-story writer and essayist, b. 18 April 1882, Taubaté; d. 4 July 1948, São Paulo

A practicing lawyer in the state of São Paulo, where he was born, L. eventually turned to farming, an occupation that, in 1914, prompted him to write a now famous letter to the newspaper *O Estado de São Paulo* in which he decried the "slash and burn" technique then so widely practiced in Brazilian agriculture. The vigorous, forthright style of that letter, and of his subsequent articles, along with his firsthand knowledge of the life of the backlander, quickly won L. a host of admirers and supporters.

Turning from nonfiction to fiction, L. wrote *Urupês* (1918; Urupês), a collection of stories and sketches that dealt realistically and often pessimistically with life as it was really lived by Brazil's uneducated and exploited rural poor. L. later became instrumental in the development of Brazil's publishing industry and even began his own, ill-fated company. Although negatively disposed toward the basic principles of modernism (q.v.), L. nevertheless published through his company the work of many of that movement's leading writers.

Urupês, with its fresh, distinctly Brazilian language and its iconoclastic treatment of an old but hitherto artificially rendered theme, the lives of Brazil's hinterland populace, was, ironically, cited by Oswald de Andrade (q.v.), modernism's enfant terrible, as the true genesis of the modernist movement in Brazil, despite the fact that L.'s critical and aesthetic views were not consonant with modernist orthodoxy. Jeca Tatu, the backward, disease-ridden, and chronically abused central character of the *Urupês* stories, and a literary figure destined to become immortalized as a national type, is never depicted in a romantic or idealized fashion. By means of a realistic style, one characterized by an often fatalistic human, colorful language, and biting irony, L. portrays Jeca Tatu and his kind more as pathetic victims of an indifferent society rather than as quaintly comical rustics. This theme links *Urupês* directly with two other classic works of Brazilian literature, Euclides da Cunha's (1866–1909) *Os sertões* (1902; *Rebellion in the Backlands,* 1944) and Graciliano Ramos's (q.v.) *Barren Lives.*

Believing that only by properly educating its youth could any society expect to progress and prosper, and therefore judging children's literature to be the most important and worthwhile aspect of his work, L. often commented that he wished the whole of his career had been devoted to it. His story "Lúcia; ou, A menina de narizinho arrebitado" (1921; Lúcia; or, the girl with the turned-up little nose) still ranks among the best loved and most widely read of all children's stories in Brazil.

A true patriot who argued for a renovation of his country's political processes, a firm believer in the positive aspects of material progress, and an enthusiastic advocate of all things authentically Brazilian, L. was an indefatigable idealist, innovator, and reformer. He believed in the greatness of Brazil's future, but he insisted always on a sober, honest assessment of its faults as well as its merits. L. is remembered today chiefly as the first Brazilian writer to deal honestly and truthfully with the poverty-plagued lives of Brazil's rural masses.

FURTHER WORKS: *Problema vital* (1918); *Cidades mortas* (1919); *Idéias de Jeca Tatu* (1919); *Negrinha* (1920); *A onda verde* (1921); *O Saci* (1921); *Fábulas* (1922); *O Marquês de Rabicó* (1922); *O macaco que se fez homem* (1923); *Mundo da lua* (1923); *A caçada da onça* (1924); *O choque das raças; ou, O presidente negro* (1926); *Mr. Slang e o Brasil* (1927); *América* (1931); *O ferro* (1931); *Novas reinações de Narizinho* (1932); *Viagem ao céu* (1932); *As caçadas do Pedrinho* (1933); *História do mundo para as crianças* (1933); *Na antevéspera* (1933); *Emília no país da gramática* (1934); *Aritmética da Emília* (1935); *Contos leves* (1935); *Contos pesados* (1935); *Geografia de Dona Benta* (1935); *O escândalo do petróleo* (1936); *Memórias de Emília* (1936); *Histórias da tia Nastácia* (1937); *O poço do visconde* (1937); *Serões de Dona Benta* (1937); *O minotauro* (1939); *O picapau amarelo* (1939); *A chave do tamanho* (1942); *Urupês, outros contos e coisas* (1943); *Os doze trabalhos de Hércules* (1944); *A barca de Gleyre: Quarenta anos de correspondência literária entre M. L. e Godofredo Rangel* (2 vols., 1944–46); *Prefácios e entrevistas* (1946); *Urupês: Contos: Notas biográficas e críticas* (1946); *Obras completas* (30 vols., 1946–47). FURTHER VOLUME IN ENGLISH: *Brazilian Short Stories* (1925)

BIBLIOGRAPHY: Brown, T., Jr., "Idea and Plot in the Stories of M. L.," *BRMMLA,* 27 (1973), 174–80; Foster, D., and Foster, V., eds., *Modern Latin American Literature* (1975), Vol. I, pp. 491–96; Brown, T., Jr., "The Poetic World of M. L.," *LBR,* 14 (1977), 230–35

EARL E. FITZ

LO-JOHANSSON, Ivar

Swedish novelist, short-story writer, and poet, b. 21 Feb. 1901, Ösmo

L.-J.'s parents originally belonged to the lowest of the farmworker class, the *statare,* whose lot first improved in 1945, thanks in part to L.-J., whose writing had exposed their extreme poverty and misery. At the time of L.-J.'s birth, however, they were poor crofters. L.-J. left school at the age of eleven, and aside from two winter sessions at a school in 1917 and 1920, he is self-educated. He moved to Stockholm and worked in a number of odd jobs while studying on his own, especially languages. In 1925 he left Sweden and lived for the next four years on the Continent and in England.

In 1927 L.-J. published the first of a series of travel books, *Vagabondliv i Frankrike* (vagabond life in France), in which he combines a traveler's observations with comments on society. After his only collection of poetry, *Ur klyvnadens tid* (1931; from the time of division), came his first novel, *Måna är död* (1932; Måna is dead), about a young man torn between a woman's erotic attraction and his work.

The novel *Godnatt, jord* (1933; goodnight, earth) and three collections of short stories, *Statarna* (2 vols., 1936–37; the *statare*) and *Jordproletärer* (1941, proletarians of the earth) constitute L.'s great epic about the people among whom he grew up. These are also works of cultural history, describing an environment that up to the time had not been treated in fiction. *Godnatt, jord* portrays, with both tenderness and a feeling for the beauty of nature, a young man's struggle for freedom in an oppressive social environment. Also belonging to this group of works is *Traktorn* (1943; the tractor), which with its many characters but no main protagonist, except for the machine, conforms to the ideal of a collective novel.

Like *Godnatt, jord,* the novel *Kungsgatan* (1935; King's Street) has been made into a film. Dealing with a farm boy's experiences in a big city, it created a sensation for its frank descriptions of prostitution and venereal disease. Another work that has been filmed is *Bara en mor* (1939; only a mother), one of L.-J.'s finest novels, about a young woman from the *statare* class who swims nude alone in a lonely lake on a hot summer day and is ostracized, regarded as a loose woman. In despair she marries an irresponsible man, works hard, and dies young. In this work L.-J. sides with the individual against the collective, whose narrow-minded moralism destroys the life of an innocent woman.

L.-J.'s next major group of works was a suite of autobiographical novels in which he combined the personal and the societal in a way characteristic of his sense of man as a historical figure. The first, *Analfabeten* (1951; the illiterate man), is a loving portrayal of his father. In *Gårdfariehandlaren* (1953; the country peddler), *Socialisten* (1958; the socialist), and *Proletärförfattaren* (1960; the proletarian writer) he describes his past with both a nostalgic and a satiric tone.

L.-J. often writes about love, sex, and other forces that drive man to actions beyond reason and will. Such vices and sins are exposed in a sequence of short-story collections, many with historical settings, called *Passionssviten* (1968–72; the suite of passions), comprising seven books, among them *Girigbukarna* (1969; the misers), *Vällustingarna* (1970; the lechers), and *Lögnhalsarna* (1971; the liars). Most recently L.-J. has begun a series of memoirs: *Pubertet* (1978; puberty), for which he won the Nordic Council Literary Prize in 1979, *Asfalt* (1979; asphalt), and *Att skriva en roman* (1981; to write a novel).

L.-J. is without doubt one of the major 20th-c. Swedish writers. He is outstanding as a writer of short stories although some critics see him as uneven in that respect. He has created some of the most important and impressive novels in Swedish literature. Few writers match him in descriptions of sensual and erotic elements in life. He has an unusual sense of humor and a deep feeling for man's existential loneliness as well as an admirable talent for integrating contemporary man with history.

FURTHER WORKS: *Kolet i våld* (1928); *Ett lag historier* (1928); *Nerstigen i dödsriket* (1929); *Zigenare* (1929); *Mina städers ansikten* (1930); *Jag tvivlar på idrotten* (1931); *Statarklassen i Sverige* (1939); *Geniet* (1947); *Ålderdom* (1949); *Okänt Paris* (1954); *Stockholmaren* (1954); *Journalisten* (1956); *Författaren* (1957); *Soldaten* (1959); *Lyckan* (1962); *Astronomens hus* (1966); *Elektra: Kvinna år 2070* (1967); *Passionerna* (1968); *Martyrerna* (1968); *Karriäristerna* (1969); *Vishetslärarna* (1972); *Statarskolan i litteraturen* (1972); *Ordets makt* (1973); *Nunnan i Vadstena* (1973); *Furstarna* (1974); *Lastbara berättelser* (1974); *Dagar och dagsverken* (1975)

BIBLIOGRAPHY: Mennie, D. M., "I. L.-J.'s *Vagabondliv i Frankrike:* A Re-evaluation," in Dubois, E. T., et al., eds., *Essays Presented to C. M. Girdlestone* (1960), pp. 219–28; Gustafson, A., *A History of Swedish Literature* (1961), pp. 515–19; Bougnet, P., "I. L.-J. et l'épopée des ouvriers agricoles suédois," *LanM,* 63 (1969), 685–92; Paulsson, J.-A. "I. L.-J.: Crusader for Social Justice," *ASR* 59 (1971), 21–31

TORBORG LUNDELL

LONDON, Jack

American novelist and short-story writer, b. 12 Jan. 1876, San Francisco, Cal.; d. 22 Nov. 1916, Glen Ellen, Cal.

L.'s origins are somewhat obscure. He was probably the illegitimate son of "Professor" W. H. Chaney, a wandering intellectual who claimed all knowledge as his specialty (and who later denied being L.'s father) and Flora Wellman, an unstable woman devoted to spiritualism and astrology. L.'s surname was given him by John London, who married L.'s mother eight months after L. was born.

L. grew up on the San Francisco waterfront, went to sea in the early 1890s, and took part in the Alaskan gold rush in 1896. He read widely as a child, and his later adventures prompted him to try his hand at writing. His short stories about life in the Yukon found a ready audience. His first book, the collection *The Son of the Wolf* (1900), was followed by almost fifty others over the next twenty years.

Despite the wealth he earned from his writing, L. became an earnest socialist, combining Marxism with Herbert Spencer's (1820–1903) theory of evolutionary progress and Nietzsche's idea of the superman. One of the works that best presents L.'s social theory is *The Iron Heel* (1908), a prophetic novel set seven hundred years in the future when fascism has triumphed and must be overthrown by L.'s protagonist. Even though most of L.'s writing rings with high adventure, it is often marred by his persistence in illustrating his social and political beliefs.

There is a sameness about L.'s novels, yet most of them remain surprisingly readable. Three are especially memorable.

The Call of the Wild (1903) is one of the most popular books ever written in the U.S. Buck, a giant pet dog, is stolen in California and shipped to the Yukon; as a sled dog, he acts out the theory of survival of the fittest. He is rescued from a succession of evil masters by the kind and admirable John Thornton. After Thornton is killed by Indians, Buck, his survival instincts now fully awakened, responds to the call of the wild and runs off to lead a wolf pack.

The Sea-Wolf (1904) further reveals L.'s fascination with wild impulses and the demands of survival. Wolf Larsen is the brutal, cynically intelligent captain of a sealing schooner, which picks up two refugees off a shipwreck, Humphrey Van Weyden and Maude Brewster. People of culture, they offer strong contrasts to the roughness of Larsen. Humphrey and Maude, pressed into service, escape from the evil captain, who is determined to assault Maude sexually, but end up stranded on a small Arctic island. Weeks later, the wreck of the schooner, with Larsen aboard, washes up. Larsen soon after dies of a brain tumor, and the two castaways are rescued. *The Sea Wolf* is full of strangely unnatural dialogue, but the characterization of Larsen, along with the descriptions of the Arctic Ocean, combine to provide a powerful effect.

Martin Eden (1909) is L.'s most ambitious novel and one of his most significantly autobiographical. Eden, an uneducated, rough outsider, like L. himself, aspires to money and status through writing. He is drawn to Ruth Morse, a woman who has everything he thinks he wants a wife to have—beauty, wealth, charm. But Eden, who finds himself suddenly successful, becomes disillusioned over the meaninglessness and conformity his good fortune has brought him. He has long been a Nietzschean, but he begins to despair of any hope for valid societal change through Nietzsche's philosophy or anyone else's. His destiny is apparent: he commits suicide. (It is widely assumed that L.'s death was also a suicide.)

Some readers find L. at his best as a short-story writer. Many of his stories are too contrived, but a few, notably "To Build a Fire" (1902) and "The White Silence" (1899), are graphic and intensely suspenseful.

The limitations of L. as a writer are considerable, stemming mainly from the haste with which he wrote and his belief that ideas are more important than style. But his influence, both because of the daring way he lived and because he drew most of his story material from the world of he-men, has been considerable on such writers as Ernest Hemingway, Jack Kerouac (qq.v.), and Robert Ruark (1915–1965).

FURTHER WORKS: *The God of His Fathers* (1901); *Children of the Frost* (1902); *The Cruise of the Dazzler* (1902); *A Daughter of the Snows* (1902); *The Kempton-Wace Letters* (1903, with Ann Strunsky); *The People of the Abyss* (1903); *The Faith of Men* (1904); *The Game* (1905); *Tales of the Fish Patrol* (1905); *War of the Classes* (1905); *Moon-Face, and Other Stories* (1906); *Scorn of Women* (1906); *White Fang* (1906); *Before*

Adam (1907); Love of Life, and Other Stories (1907); *The Road* (1907); *Burning Daylight* (1910); *Lost Face* (1910); *Revolution, and Other Essays* (1910); *Theft: A Play in Four Acts* (1910); *Adventure* (1911); *The Cruise of the Snark* (1911); *South Sea Tales* (1911); *When God Laughs, and Other Stories* (1911); *The House of Pride, and Other Tales of Hawaii* (1912); *Smoke Bellew* (1912); *A Son of the Sun* (1912); *The Abysmal Brute* (1913); *John Barleycorn* (1913); *The Night-Born* (1913); *The Valley of the Moon* (1913); *The Mutiny of the Elsinore* (1914); *The Strength of the Strong* (1914); *The Scarlet Plague* (1915); *The Star Rover* (1915); *The Acorn-Planter: A California Forest Play* (1916); *The Little Lady of the Big House* (1916); *The Turtles of Tasman* (1916); *The Human Drift* (1917); *Jerry of the Islands* (1917); *Michael, Brother of Jerry* (1917); *The Red One* (1918); *On the Makaloa Mat* (1919); *Hearts of Three* (1920); *Dutch Courage, and Other Stories* (1922); *The Assassination Bureau, Ltd.* (1963); *Letters from J. L.* (1965); *J. L. Reports* (1970); *Daughters of the Rich* (1971); *J. L.'s Articles and Short Stories for the (Oakland) High School Aegis* (1971); *Gold* (1972)

BIBLIOGRAPHY: Walker, F., *J. L. and the Klondike: The Genesis of an American Writer* (1966); Labor, E., *J. L.* (1974); McClintock, J. L., *White Logic: J. L.'s Short Stories* (1976); Barltrop, R., *J. L.: The Man, the Writer, the Rebel* (1976); special L. centennial tribute, *MFS*, 22, 1 (1976–77); Sherman, J. R., *J. L.: A Reference Guide* (1977); Sinclair, A., *Jack: A Biography of J. L.* (1977)

JAMES LUNDQUIST

LÓPEZ Y FUENTES, Gregorio

Mexican novelist, short-story writer, journalist, folklorist, and poet, b. 17 Nov. 1897, Huasteca; d. 11 Dec. 1966, Mexico City

After attending school in the state of Veracruz, L. y F. enrolled in a teachers' college in Mexico City, where he began his literary career with contributions to the review *Nosotros*. His first book, *La siringa de cristal* (1914; the crystal flute), was a collection of poems written within the orbit of modernism (q.v.). In 1914 he was sent to Veracruz with other students to oppose U.S. occupation of the city. He sided with Venustiano Carranza

against Pancho Villa when their differences developed into military conflict. L. y F. published twelve novels, a book of short stories, and two volumes of poetry; there are many articles, stories, and sketches still uncollected in book form. As a journalist he contributed to *El universal ilustrado* and was director of *El universal* and *El gráfico*.

L. y F.'s principal novels deal with aspects of the Mexican revolution, with unassimilated and exploited groups of Indians, and with rural life, which he knew well as the son of a rancher and owner of a country store. *Campamento* (1931; bivouac) depicts an overnight encampment of soldiers of the revolution. *Tierra* (1932; land) dramatizes episodes in the life of Emiliano Zapata and his supporters between 1910 and 1920. *El indio* (1935; *El Indio,* 1937), awarded the National Prize for Literature in 1935, is the most famous and internationally known of L. y F.'s novels. In a series of selectively pertinent episodes without a structured plot, the author relates the customs, superstitions, problems, and areas of internal, external, and personal conflict of a group of Mexican Indians on the eve of the revolution in 1910.

L. y F.'s use of types rather than characters, of groups rather than individuals, of details, incidents, and episodes rather than plots, of folklore, proverbs, and popular speech rather than contrived literary language, was distinctively innovative. Using these techniques, he achieved an intensity in his fiction that has a strong emotional impact on the reader.

FURTHER WORKS: *Claros de selva* (1922); *El vagabundo* (1922); *El alma del poblacho* (1922); *Mi general* (1934); *Arrieros* (1937); *Huasteca* (1939); *Cuentos campesinos de México* (1940); *Acomodaticio* (1943); *Los peregrinos inmóviles* (1944); *Entresuelo* (1948); *Milpa, potrero y monte* (1950)

BIBLIOGRAPHY: Morton, R. F., *Los novelistas de la revolución mexicana* (1949), pp. 95–115; González, M. P., *Trayectoria de la novela en México* (1951), pp. 249–67; Carter, B., "The Mexican Novel at Mid-Century," *PrS,* 28 (1954), 147–50; Mate, H. E., "Social Aspects of Novels by L. y F. and Ciro Alegría," *Hispania,* 39 (1956), 287–92; Brushwood, J. S., *Mexico in Its Novel* (1970), pp. 209–11, 215–17, 231–32

BOYD G. CARTER

LOVINESCU, Eugen
Romanian critic and essayist, b. 31 Oct. 1881, Fălticeni; d. 16 July 1943, Bucharest

L. was the son of a high-school teacher. He studied Latin at the University of Bucharest, graduating in 1903, and earned a doctorate in 1909 from the University of Paris. For most of his life L. taught at prestigious secondary schools in Ploieşti, Iaşi, and Bucharest. He published in most of the literary journals of the day, brought out his own journal, *Sburătorul* (1919–22, 1926–27), and presided over a highly influential literary circle that advocated Western and democratic ideas and encouraged a modernist literature, oriented toward the cultural needs of the urban population. For this activity, as well as for his support of groups who were discriminated against (women, Jews), L. was repeatedly attacked by fascist and right-wing authorities.

L.'s central work, *Istoria literaturii române contemporane* (6 vols., 1926–29; a history of contemporary Romanian literature), strongly attacks the neoromantic traditionalism and rural glorification that characterized part of the Romanian literature of the day. He praises technical sophistication, psychological analysis, and urban subjects. Many of the best writers of the interwar period, like Ion Barbu, Camil Petrescu, and Hortensia Papadat-Bengescu (qq.v.), were launched by L. He provided an ideological and sociological statement of his position in *Istoria civilizaţiei române moderne* (3 vols., 1924–25; a history of modern Romanian civilization), in which he makes a forceful case for a liberal, Western-oriented development as the only hope for Romania. In both works he presents the theory of "synchronicity," the need for smaller countries to catch up with present trends in the West, rather than plod slowly through all phases of a previous development. Toward the end of his life L. wrote a cycle of critical works devoted to the Junimea, or Youth group (to which most of the great names of the 19th-c. Romanian literary revival were connected), in which he tries to describe the dialectics of ideological progress and conservation; the implication is that extreme nationalist and fascist trends should not be admitted as partners in civilized discourse.

L. was a consummate master of the polemical essay and the descriptive portrait of a writer's physical appearance; many of his most readable pages are to be found in his memoirs and his incidental criticism. His novels—some rather autobiographical, others in the historical genre—did not enjoy much success with the public. His translations from classical Latin and French and his Latin textbooks were widely used in high schools.

FURTHER WORKS: *Paşi pe nisip* (1906); *J. J. Weiss et son œuvre littéraire* (1909); *Les voyageurs français en Grèce au XIXe siècle* (1909); *Critice* (10 vols., 1909–29); *Gr. Alexandrescu* (1910); *Scenete şi fantezii* (1911); *Costache Negruzzi* (1913); *Aripa morţei* (1913); *Pagini de război* (1918); *In cumpăna vremii* (1919); *Lulu* (1920); *Gh. Asachi* (1921); *Viaţa dublă* (1927); *Memorii* (3 vols., 1930–37); *Bizu* (1932); *Firu-n patru* (1934); *Bălăuca* (1935); *Mite* (1935); *Diana* (1936); *Mili* (1937); *T. Maiorescu* (2 vols., 1940); *Aquaforte* (1941); *P. P. Carp, critic literar şi literat* (1942); *Antologia ideologiei junimiste* (1942); *T. Maiorescu şi contemporanii lui* (2 vols., 1943–44); *Titu Maiorescu şi posteritatea lui critică* (1943); *Antologia scriitorilor ocazionali* (1943)

BIBLIOGRAPHY: Munteano, B., *Modern Romanian Literature* (1939), pp. 168–70; Nemoianu, V., "Variable Sociopolitical Functions of Aesthetic Doctrine: L. vs. Western Aestheticism," in Jowitt, K., ed., *Social Change in Romania, 1860–1940: A Debate on Development in a European Nation* (1978), pp. 174–207

VIRGIL NEMOIANU

LOWELL, Amy
American poet, biographer, and literary critic, b. 9 Feb. 1874, Brookline, Mass.; d. 12 May 1925, Brookline, Mass.

Born into a distinguished Boston family, L. was a cousin of James Russell Lowell (1819–1891) and a sister of Abbott Lawrence Lowell (1855–1916), the noted astronomer. Although she was widely traveled, her childhood home, Sevenels, remained the center for her many literary and social activities.

Her dedication to poetry came late; her first volume of verse was published in 1912. In London in 1913 she met Ezra Pound (q.v.) and the writers associated with imagism (q.v.). Adopting imagist techniques, L. promoted the movement in the U.S. From 1915 to 1917 she edited an annual anthology, *Some Imagist Poets,* which included the work of D. H. Lawrence, Hilda Doolittle (qq.v.), Richard Aldington (1892–1962), and John Gould Fletcher (1886–1950).

The title of her first book of poetry, *A Dome of Many-Coloured Glass* (1912), is a phrase from "Adonais," Shelley's elegy for Keats. Although conventional and sentimental, the volume reveals many of L.'s persistent themes: childhood memories, romantic longings, celebration of the natural world. It also reveals her admiration of Keats, a lifelong interest that resulted in her final work and possibly most significant contribution to literature, the massive and painstakingly detailed two-volume biography, *John Keats* (1925).

Her second book of verse, *Sword Blades and Poppy Seeds* (1914), helped to establish her in the U.S. as a controversial experimentalist in the new poetry. She promoted and publicized modernist verse, and attracted the attention of a wide audience. She used free-verse techniques, what she called "unrhymed cadence," and created "polyphonic prose," prose-poems of varied rhythms and sound patterns. Believing that poetry should be heard, she emphasized verbal effects in her verse; and in numerous poetry readings, she presented her work as performance art. Many of her poems were frankly erotic; she sought complete freedom in the choice of subject matter. She claimed that "the true test of poetry is sincerity and vitality," and her verse is often intense and dramatic. It can also seem excessively self-indulgent and merely histrionic. A recurring theme is the desire for romantic fulfillment.

Visual images predominate in her verse; L. juxtaposes clear and vivid images in order to create striking metaphors. Her sensuous and impressionistic descriptions are often celebrations of physical beauty; the natural world is animated with movement and emotion. The "white mares of the moon" rear in the night sky; fish ponds in moonlight become shimmering dragons. Fanciful, wistful, luminous, her poetry expresses her restless energy, her luxuriant imagination.

What's O'Clock (1925), a collection of lyrics published posthumously, won the Pulitzer Prize. L. was often more imitative than original, more conservative than radical, more romantic than modern. Yet she helped to create a climate in the U.S. in which artistic experimentation could flourish. Her verse

can be faulted for its superficiality; D. H. Lawrence described it as "pure sensation *without concepts.*" L. is often credited with having talents that are more political than poetic. Nevertheless, she remains a significant presence in modern American literature, a productive force encouraging emancipated and vigorous writing.

FURTHER WORKS: *Six French Poets* (1915); *Men, Women, and Ghosts* (1916); *Tendencies in Modern American Poetry* (1917); *Can Grande's Castle* (1918); *Pictures of the Floating World* (1919); *Fir-Flower Tablets* (1920, with Florence Ayscough); *Legends* (1921); *A Critical Fable* (1922); *East Wind* (1926); *The Madonna of Carthagena* (1927); *Ballads for Sale* (1927); *Selected Poems* (1928); *Poets and Poetry* (1930); *Complete Poetical Works* (1955)

BIBLIOGRAPHY: Damon, S. F., *A, L.: A Chronicle* (1936); Greenslet, F., *The Lowells and Their Seven Worlds* (1946); Gregory, H., *A. L.: Portrait of the Poet in Her Time* (1958); Gould, J., *The World of A. L. and the Imagist Movement* (1975); Heymann, C. D., *American Aristocracy: The Lives and Times of James Russell, Amy and Robert Lowell* (1980), pp. 157–279

JO BRANTLEY BERRYMAN

LOWELL, Robert
American poet, b. 1 March 1917, Boston, Mass.; d. 12 Sept. 1977, New York, N.Y.

L. was born to an outwardly conventional, patrician New England family. Without the means to maintain their social position, however, the family was racked by internal tensions, and L. had a moody, turbulent childhood. He spent six uncomfortable years at St. Mark's School, where he studied with the poet Richard Eberhart (b. 1904) and began writing poetry, and then two years at Harvard, where he immersed himself in English literature. Then he made an abrupt break with his milieu by transferring to Kenyon College to study with John Crowe Ransom (q.v.). The fierce radical impulse in his life led L. to a passionate, although ultimately temporary, conversion to Roman Catholicism, followed by his six-month imprisonment as a conscientious objector during World War II. Thereafter, L.'s personal history was always entangled with national history. His subsequent private life was characterized by a succession of mental breakdowns, hospitalizations, and recoveries, and three literary marriages—to Jean Stafford (1915–1979), Elizabeth Hardwick (b. 1916), and Caroline Blackwood (b. 1931). He taught at the University of Iowa, Boston University, and Harvard, and over the years made a number of widely publicized political gestures (the most famous of which was his refusal in 1965 to attend the White House Festival of the Arts because of opposition to the Vietnam war). L.'s poems charted the contours of his own agonized life with ever-increasing directness and candor, and when he died of heart failure at the age of sixty, he left behind a creative output that had uniquely fused the private and public realms of his experience.

L.'s first book, *Land of Unlikeness* (1944), established him as a passionate, rebellious American literary presence. In his introduction to the volume Allen Tate (q.v.) noted the willed intricate formalism of L.'s poems and the consciously Catholic nature of his aesthetics and his symbolism. L. derived his title, and his inscription for the book, from Saint Bernard's idea that "as the soul is unlike God, so too it is unlike itself," dwelling in the "land of unlikeness." L. rewrote and reprinted ten of the poems in the Pulitzer Prize-winning *Lord Weary's Castle* (1946). These harsh, alliterative, and difficult early poems are heavily freighted with Christian symbolism, juxtaposing the world of grace to the secular culture of the urban wasteland. Poems like "Christmas Eve under Hooker's Statue" and "The Quaker Graveyard in Nantucket" stand as didactic indictments of American imperialism and materialism, in particular attacking the capitalist/Puritan heritage of New England. L.'s apocalyptic renunciations of a world that "out-Herods Herod" ("The Holy Innocents") provide a scathing critique of American ambition and culture.

L.'s next book, *The Mills of the Kavanaughs* (1951), reflects the defects and marks the crisis of his early style. The long narrative monologues at the book's core are burdened by obscure allusions, a wrenching formalism, and a false rhetorical style. L.'s turn to Robert Frost (q.v.) and Robert Browning as models demonstrated a new interest in plot and character, but the poems' ambitions were undermined by their willful difficulty. Ironically, the book's most successful poems are translations: a pastiche from Vergil and an adaptation from Franz Werfel (q.v.). This crisis in L.'s career was both formal and religious, and thereafter he published no new book for eight years as he sought a new language and a new subject matter.

Life Studies (1959) was the major breakthrough and remains his most accomplished and influential book. The poems dispense with the symbolism and formal rigidity of the earlier work, speaking in a more intimate personal and public manner. The prose of Chekhov (q.v.) and Flaubert, as well as William Carlos Williams's (q.v.) poetry, served as models for this flexible new style. The core of the book is composed of a long prose memoir, "91 Revere Street," and fifteen unsparingly personal poems about L.'s family and himself. These family and self-portraits are so unrelentingly and dramatically honest that the critic M. L. Rosenthal termed them "confessional poetry." The satiric prose autobiography unveils the milieu of L.'s childhood, characterizing his father as weak and ineffectual and his mother as cold, shrill, and domineering. With a delicate blend of love, disgust, and wit, the related sequence of poems moves from L.'s childhood to his middle years, exposing private humiliations and treating his own bouts with mental illness with psychological frankness. In placing the unmasked personality of the poet at the center of his volume L. deeply affected the direction of American postwar poetry. In *For the Union Dead* (1964) he continued in the confessional mode, but extended the range of his poems to include public themes.

L.'s historical imagination also led him to translating European poets. In *Imitations* (1961), which he called "a book of versions and free translations," he adapted and re-created a small anthology of poetry ranging from Homer to Boris Pasternak (q.v.). The book shows him assimilating a range of dark and disparate voices into his own native idiom, and often the poems read as L. originals (hence his borrowing from Dryden the idea of translation as "imitation"). L.'s translations of Racine's *Phaedra* (1961) and Aeschylus' *Prometheus Bound* (1969) and *The Oresteia* (1978) also show him freely adapting and absorbing those two to his own model. By his vast effort of translation L. tried to create for himself a viable European tradition. And always this European tradition pointed back to the New World. For exam-

141

ple, the theme of Rome, the greatness and horror of her empire, threads together L.'s translations of Horace, Juvenal, Dante, Quevedo, and Góngora in *Near the Ocean* (1967), but that imperial story also represents a parable for America.

L.'s trilogy of one-act plays, *The Old Glory* (1964), reflects his deep preoccupation with the dilemmas of the American past. The plays, unified by the emblem of the flag, dramatize the idealism and violence of the American character at three different historical stages. The first play, *Endecott and the Red Cross,* based on Hawthorne's story "The Maypole of Merrymount," evokes a gentle Puritan forced into bloodshed because of religious expediency. The second, *My Kinsman, Major Molineux,* a dramatization of Hawthorne's story, treats the American revolution in its darkest, most violent aspect. The third and strongest play, *Benito Cereno,* based on Melville's haunting novella of the same title, attacks the problem of race (and, implicitly, American foreign policy) through the story of a slave revolt. These plays dramatize the moral forces and contradictions at the heart of American history.

L.'s most extensive late work was his series of unrhymed blank verse sonnets. The original *Notebook 1967–1968* (1969) began as a verse diary, but outgrew its initial format and reappeared, heavily revised and expanded, in 1970 as *Notebook*. The loose sonnet form marks L.'s attempt to combine his formal and informal modes while meditating on both private and public themes. The scheme of *Notebook*—which he considered a single poem, intuitive in arrangement and jagged in pattern—follows the arc of the seasons. Diary entries, historical meditations, contemporary events, letters, and soliloquies were all poured into this open framework. At their weakest the sonnets read as undigested fragments; at their strongest they chart a rich autobiographical history. L. himself remained dissatisfied with the coherence of the sonnets and felt compelled continually to revise them. Three years later they again reappeared, radically metamorphosed into three new books. *History* (1973) re-creates a host of historical figures from biblical times to the present day, including a striking series of verse portraits of other writers. *For Lizzie and Harriet* (1973) contained no new poems, but reworked and regrouped poems dealing with L.'s second wife and his daughter. *The Dolphin* (1973) details L.'s move to England

as he left one wife for another. The domestic plot of his subsequent marriage and the birth of his son suggests his deep compulsion to rewrite his own story. The unsparing self-revelations continue the personal mode of *Life Studies*. In L.'s final book of poems, *Day by Day* (1977), he at last abandoned the sonnet form for an irregular free verse but continued his struggle to record honestly and accurately his painful domestic history.

L.'s collected works passionately embody his own turbulent life history. At the same time they show a firm critical insight into the political and historical nature of his own era. He is the most central American poet of the postwar generation.

FURTHER WORKS: *The Voyage, and Other Versions of Poems by Baudelaire* (1968); *Selected Poems* (1976)

BIBLIOGRAPHY: Jarrell, R., *Poetry and the Age* (1953), pp. 208–19; Mazzaro, J., *The Achievement of R. L.: 1939–1959* (1960); Staples, H. B., *R. L.: The First Twenty Years* (1962); Mazzaro, J., *The Poetic Themes of R. L.* (1965); Rosenthal, M. L., *The New Poets: American and British Poetry since World War II* (1967), pp. 25–78; Parkinson, T., ed., *R. L.: A Collection of Critical Essays* (1968); Boyers, R., and London, M., eds., *R. L.: A Portrait of the Artist in His Time* (1970); Williamson, A., *Pity the Monsters: The Political Vision of R. L.* (1974); Yenser, S., *Circle to Circle: The Poetry of R. L.* (1975); Axelrod, S. G., *R. L.: Life and Art* (1978); Fein, R. J., *R. L.,* 2nd ed. (1979); Vendler, H., *Part of Nature, Part of Us: Modern American Poets* (1980), pp. 125–73

EDWARD HIRSCH

Underneath all these poems "there is one story and one story only"; when this essential theme or subject is understood, the unity of attitudes and judgments underlying the variety of the poems becomes startlingly explicit. The poems understand the world as a sort of conflict of opposites. In this struggle one opposite is that cake of custom in which all of us lie embedded like lungfish—the stasis or inertia of the stubborn self, the obstinate persistence in evil that is damnation. Into this realm of necessity the poems push everything that is closed, turned inward, incestuous, that blinds or binds: the Old Law, imperialism, militarism, capitalism, Calvinism, Authority, the Father, the "proper Bostonians," the rich who will "do everything for the poor except get off their backs." But struggling within this like leaven, falling to it like light, is everything that is free or open, that grows or is willing to change: here is the generosity or openness or willingness that is itself salvation; here is "accessibility to experience"; this is the realm of freedom, of the Grace that has replaced the Law, of the perfect liberator whom the poet calls Christ.

Consequently the poems can have two possible movements or organizations: they can move from what is closed to what is open, or from what is open to what is closed.

Randall Jarrell, *Poetry and the Age* (1953), pp. 208–9

What seems to be happening in *The Mills of the Kavanaughs* is that L., having mastered the traditional forms, is engaging in a search for a more individualized style. That is to say, reacting against the conventional, he is preoccupied with setting for himself increasingly difficult formal problems to solve. The direction that his ingenuity takes at this point is towards more and more complicated rhyme schemes combined, as in "Thanksgiving's Over," with a fantastically elaborate metrical pattern. This poem is almost unintelligible, partly because of the very odd religious symbolism involved, but more importantly because in this poem, L. has reached the point where decadence begins—where considerations of style and form become so obsessive as to obscure meaning and intention.

"Thanksgiving's Over" is the last poem in *The Mills of the Kavanaughs,* and it marks the climax of L.'s preoccupation with form for its own sake. In *Life Studies,* published after an interval of eight years, the structure of his poetry is much looser than anything written earlier. Just as the sense of strain, conflict and rebellion is markedly reduced as L. tends towards an acceptance of reality, so the rigidity of his early period gives way to a more informal, even casual blend of free verse and occasional rhyme. To be sure, there are a few reminders of his old contention with the order of things in such poems as "Beyond the Alps" and "Skunk Hour"; significantly, it is these poems that bear the closest resemblance on a formal level to his earlier work.

In its broadest outlines, then, the curve of L.'s development as a poet in his first two decades is from a posture of rebellion towards a position of acceptance. And the parallel tendency away from his initial formalism towards relative flexibility is not the paradox it seems, but a function of his poetic needs.

Hugh B. Staples, *R. L.: The First Twenty Years* (1962), pp. 20–21

[In *Life Studies*] the poet who emerged in 1944 as "consciously a Catholic poet" can no longer find souls to be saved. What had been L.'s religious view has turned into a soulless world of conformity. In the process, Conrad Aiken's hopes that L. might "expand his range" and try things of a "non-religious sort" have been fulfilled. R. P. Blackmur's objections to the "fractious vindictiveness" and the "nearly blasphemous" nature of the character portrayals have been resolved by their removal from his writing. However, man caught in the network of society is treated as vindictively as he was when caught in the lockstep of time. That later one is as materially destroyed as the other was spiritually. Nevertheless, in an age which likes to separate its religion from its art, the technical accomplishments of *Life Studies* may far outweigh the loss of the Christian experience.

Jerome Mazzaro, *The Poetic Themes of R. L.* (1965), pp. 118–19

. . . For L. the process of "recasting and clarification" has continued beyond *Life Studies. Life Studies* was the most remarkable poetic sequence to appear since Hart Crane's *The Bridge* and William Carlos Williams's *Paterson.* It may well stand as L.'s chief accomplishment. At the same time, it presented L. himself so vulnerably and humiliatingly that only his extraordinary gifts enabled him to transcend the hysteria behind it. The transcendence made for a revolutionary achievement, but of a sort that can never be repeated by the same poet. In *For the Union Dead,* we are shown that for L. at least there is a further way, closer to the "main stream." To maintain indefinitely the violent pace of *Life Studies* would be to cultivate a poetry that not only repeated itself but also fed on, and encouraged, suicidal madness. Instead, beyond a certain point at least, L. has been working free of the intolerable burden of his self-laceration. The problem is to hold on meanwhile to what he has gained in poetic conception (the painfully alert sensibility alive to the pressure of its own anxieties and those of the age) and in its embodiment in a brilliantly improvised formal technique.

M. L. Rosenthal, *The New Poets: American and British Poetry since World War II* (1967), p. 76

L. as much as any current poet deserves systematic study in universities. He is entwined in the great moral issues of our age with compelling fullness, reacting against the savagery and barbarism of great and small wars, apprehending passionately the solitude and waste of the individual caught in a world that, in Rilke's phrase, has "fallen into the hands of men." He is in effect the poetic conscience tormented by its perception of reality and its imagination of possibilities in this most terrible of centuries, once spoken of with unconscious irony as The American Century. And he sees this century within the total web of the past and as a trouble to be seen in the major languages of the world. He is neither a temporal nor a spatial provincial. American historical life is seen as an experienced whole, and the ancestral voices of his poetry are familial, of New England, and at the same time universal spirits. His work is not national in any sense, but local and international, representing his identity as a New England writer and his obligations as a member of the international poetic community. It would be too much to ask that he embrace Oriental culture; his only provincialism resides in his faithfully European affections, and surely the legacy of Western Europe is rich—and relevant—enough to engage the energies of a lifetime.

Thomas Parkinson, "Introduction: R. L. and the Uses of Modern Poetry in the University," in Thomas Parkinson, ed., *R. L.: A Collection of Critical Essays* (1968), p. 8

All of L.'s work since *Life Studies* might be seen as an attempt to find a center for his enormously complex and self-divided personality in the act of finding a totally adequate language. Such a language would have to be at once deep and spontaneous enough to reach the innermost recesses of feeling, and versatile enough to catch all responses to the outside. The sense that, if one could find this central point, one could move the world, is not unique to L.; it is there in every poet who undertakes such a quest for the absolute language, even if he merely wishes to move the world into his poems. But in L.'s case, the claim is more serious, more philosophical, than in most, due to the movement of his work toward microcosmic-macrocosmic orderings, his psychoanalytic view of history.

Alan Williamson, *Pity the Monsters: The Political Vision of R. L.* (1974), p. 215

... By including versions of poems from all of L.'s preceding volumes (except the first, much of which was incorporated in the second), *History* testifies to and helps to establish a contextual relationship among all of these volumes that is comparable to the relationships among the poems within one of them. The book is a synecdoche for L.'s work: what his poetry is to history, *History* is to his poetry. More than this, it is L.'s most ambitious attempt to date to discover the whole of his life—which is to say its shape as well as much of its data—in a part of it.

If it still risks being lost, as one of its sections implies the *Cantos* risk being lost, "in the rock-slide of history," *History* certainly better fits the conception of a book that is "one poem" than had either of the *Notebooks*. A troubling and troubled work, which takes chances that most of us did not even know could be taken, it nevertheless reassures us that L. has not lost touch with the formal desiderata of poetry, just as he has not lost touch

with his earliest work. Perhaps there is little need to worry that he will ever do so. The principle that accounts for the nature of his development so far and betokens that of his future development also provides for the preservation of the shaping spirit.

Stephen Yenser, *Circle to Circle: The Poetry of R. L.* (1975), pp. 10–11

Although the style of L.'s art changed radically over the years, its essentially experiential character remained constant. "The thread that strings it together," he remarked, "is my autobiography"; "what made the earlier poems valuable seems to be some recording of experience and that seems to be what makes the later ones." "Experience" does not mean only what "happened" to L., for that formulation would place too much emphasis on an active but unilateral environment, and would reduce the experiencer's mind to the passive role of a transmitting lens. The mind itself is active, trembling to "caress the light." "Experience" more truly means the sum of the relations and interactions between psyche and environment. It grows from the Cartesian dualism of inner and outer, but through its interpenetrating energies abolishes the dualism. Just as experience mediates between self and world, partaking of both, so L.'s poems mediate between himself and his world, and between his personal history and that of his readers. His poems are structures of experience. They both record his life and assume a life of their own; and as they transform the poet's life into the autonomous life of art, they reenter his life by clarifying and completing it.

Steven Gould Axelrod, *R. L.: Life and Art* (1978), pp. 4–5

LOWRY, Malcolm

English novelist, b. 28 July 1909, Liscard; d. 27 June 1957, Ripe

L.'s father was a successful Liverpool businessman, and L., the youngest of four brothers, in many ways rejected his conservative family. Before studying English at Cambridge (1929–32), L. worked for six months on a ship sailing to the Far East, and this voyage inspired his first novel, *Ultramarine* (1933). After Cambridge, L. traveled to the U.S. and Mexico before moving, in 1939, to British Columbia, Canada, where he spent the next fourteen, highly productive years of his life. L. was deeply attached to his home in British Columbia and thought of himself as Canadian. Leaving this home in 1954 to travel to Europe contributed to his alcoholic breakdown and early death.

Because L. was a decidedly autobiographical writer, his chief theme is man's search for a physical and spiritual home. A master of English prose, he used language with astonishing dexterity and baroque richness. He believed, moreover, that art should imitate the movement of life and, like Marcel Proust (q.v.), he planned to write a masterwork, entitled *The Voyage That Never Ends,* which would comprise each of his novels in sequence. L. died before completing the sequence; therefore, he is best known for his masterpiece, *Under the Volcano* (1947).

Under the Volcano, which took ten years to write, portrays the problems of human communication—conjugal, fraternal, and national—within a story of the personal disintegration of its hero, Geoffrey Firmin. The novel embraces other themes as well, but the most significant theme is the treatment of spiritual apathy, for one level of this complex work is an allegory of the Garden of Eden and of man's fall from Grace. Set in Mexico on the November Day of the Dead, and in 1938, on the eve of World War II, the novel recounts the last day in the life of Firmin, an alcoholic former British consul, and his estranged wife, Yvonne. Through deft use of allusion and symbol, as well as an evocative richness of language reminiscent of Renaissance drama and poetry, L. transforms his hero's sordid story into a prophetic image of human destruction. Firmin is Adam, Prometheus, or Faust, and thus an embodiment of the ambition yet defeat of the human spirit. The key motif of the book is the phrase *"No se puede vivir sin amar"* (one cannot live without loving), which points to modern man's failure on the personal, political, and spiritual levels of life. L. began *Under the Volcano* with Dante's *Inferno* in mind, and although the structure outgrew this model, the novel remains a compelling vision of hell.

Two other works published posthumously are of particular note. *October Ferry to Gabriola* (1970), his only novel set entirely in British Columbia, describes the protagonist's love for his spectacular mountain-and-sea home, which he must leave, as Adam must leave Eden. The hero achieves a vision of hope and reaffirmation, however, thereby allowing L. to speak of *October Ferry to Gabriola* as an *Under the Volcano* "in reverse." *Hear Us O Lord from Heaven Thy Dwelling Place* (1961), a fascinating collection of interrelated short stories, involves another symbolic voyage and celebrates man's discovery of his home—once again in British Columbia. The last story of the collection, "The Forest Path to the Spring," offers a further dramatization of L.'s great theme—the ceaseless struggle of the human spirit in search of light or a home. Unlike the dark vision of *Under the Volcano,* this story marks a lyrical affirmation of L.'s faith in man.

Despite the unfinished state of much of L.'s work, L. must be considered one of the major writers in English of this century; *Under the Volcano* is an undisputed masterpiece, on a level with the novels of D. H. Lawrence, James Joyce, and John Fowles (qq.v.).

FURTHER WORKS: *Selected Poems* (1962); *Selected Letters* (1965); *Lunar Caustic* (1968); *Dark as the Grave wherein My Friend Is Laid* (1968)

BIBLIOGRAPHY: Epstein, P., *The Private Labyrinth of M. L.* (1969); Day, D., *M. L.: A Biography* (1973); Bradbrook, M. C., *M. L.: His Art and Early Life* (1974); Markson, D., *M. L.'s Volcano: Myth, Symbol, Meaning* (1978); New, W., ed., *M. L.: A Reference Guide* (1978); Smith, A., ed., *The Art of M. L.* (1978); Cross, R., *M. L.: A Preface to His Fiction* (1980); Wood, B., ed., *M. L.: The Writer and His Critics* (1980); Grace, S. E., *The Voyage That Never Ends: M. L.'s Fiction* (1982)

SHERRILL E. GRACE

LOZI LITERATURE
See Zambian Literature

LU HSÜN

(pseud. of Chou Shu-jen) Chinese short-story writer, essayist, critic, translator, and literary theorist, b. 25 Sept. 1881, Shaoshing, Chekiang Province; d. 19 Oct. 1936, Shanghai

Born into the gentry class, rapidly declining under the Ching (Manchu) dynasty, L. H. was brought up in the twilight of a vanishing way of life. He received a traditional education before he enrolled in new-style schools in Nanking. He was sent to Japan in 1902 on a government scholarship to study medicine, but in 1905 he abruptly terminated his medical studies and decided to devote his full energies to literary endeavors. He wanted to explore the Chinese national character through his writing. After a decade of constant failure following his return to China in 1909, he was finally catapulted to literary renown in 1918 with the short story "K'uang-jen jih-chi" (1918; "The Diary of a Madman," 1941), published in *Hsin ch'ing-nien,* the journal that initiated the intellectual revolution in China known as the New Culture Movement. The work has been called China's first modern story because of its use of the vernacular and its highly subjective, devastating critique of traditional culture.

Two collections of short stories followed: *Na han* (1923; *Call to Arms,* 1981) and *P'ang huang* (1926; *Wandering,* 1981)—published together in English as *The Complete Stories of Lu Xun* (1981). Between 1918 and 1936, the year he died, he also wrote sixteen volumes of essays, a collection each of personal reminiscences, prose poetry, and historical tales, some sixty classical-style poems, half a dozen volumes of scholarly research (mainly on Chinese fiction), and numerous translations of Russian, eastern European, and Japanese writers.

In 1928 L. H. settled in Shanghai, where he became the doyen of literati. Having witnessed the vicissitudes of the Chinese political situation, he turned increasingly leftist and was a founding member of the League of Left-Wing Writers in 1930. While sympathetic to the underground Chinese Communist Party, he was never a Party member. He eventually became embroiled in the internecine squabbles on the leftist front and died a tormented and alienated man. After his death, however, he was deified by Mao Tse-tung as China's greatest "writer, thinker, and revolutionist" and enjoyed a renown comparable to Mao's.

L. H.'s works have often been read as scathing critiques of Chinese society and culture. His sardonic, satirical essays have been seen as effective weapons with which he launched attacks on enemies of all hues. Privately, however, he was seized with periodic spells of spiritual nihilism and seemed unable to shake off the inner ghosts of his traditional past. Thus, some of his literary works, particularly his later fiction and prose poetry, reveal a subtle lyricism and a philosophical

depth unparalled in modern Chinese literature.

L. H. is known in the West chiefly for his short stories, which have been translated into more than a dozen languages. In them he succeeded brilliantly in rendering a multifaceted portrait of Chinese people caught in all their tribulations. Aside from his first modern story, "K'uang-jen jih-chi," his most celebrated story, both in China and abroad, is "Ah Q cheng-chuan" (1921; "The True Story of Ah Q," 1926), a satirical "biography" of an ignorant village laborer who experiences, with an utter lack of self-awareness, a series of humiliations and finally dies a victim of the chaos of the Republican revolution of 1911. Comparable in cultural significance to Cervantes's Don Quixote, L. H.'s Ah Q stands as a personification of the negative traits of the Chinese national character.

Less allegorical and more realistic and moving are such well-known stories as "Kung I-chi" (1919; "Kung I-chi," 1932), "Ku-hsiang" (1921; "My Native Town," 1935), "Chu-fu" (1924; "The New Year Blessing," 1936), and "Fei-tsao" (1924; "The Cake of Soap," 1941), in all of which the hypocrisy and insensitivity of upper-class intellectuals are contrasted with the suffering of the lower-class people. Nonetheless, L. H.'s own profound ambivalence toward his countrymen and his sophistication as an artist infused his stories with layers of ambiguity in both characterization and narrative technique, which defy easy ideological analysis. In most of his stories there can be found a metaphysical level, centering on an alienated loner besieged and persecuted by an uncomprehending crowd. Thus, the "philosophical" messages of L. H.'s works are much less positive than they are perceived to be in the numerous eulogistic biographies, monographs, and articles that have poured out continually from his Chinese adulators. This introspective, almost tragic, side of L. H.'s works, ignored by his admirers in China, is notably present in his classical-style poetry, his prose poetry collection *Yeh-ts'ao* (1927; *Wild Grass,* 1974), and some of his early essays.

Despite these darker and apolitical aspects of L. H.'s art and psyche, his name has been constantly used in successive political campaigns by the Chinese Communists since 1949, including the Cultural Revolution, in which his reputation remained unscathed, although his numerous disciples, friends, and scholars were purged. L. H. is still modern China's most admired and respected writer.

FURTHER WORKS: *L. H. ch'uan-chi* (20 vols., 1938); *L. H. ch'uan-chi pu-i* (2 vols., 1946, 1952); *L. H. shu-chien* (2 vols., 1952). FURTHER VOLUMES IN ENGLISH: *Ah Q and Others* (1941); *Selected Works of L. H.* (4 vols., 1956–57); *Selected Stories of L. H.* (1960)

BIBLIOGRAPHY: Huang S., *L. H. and the New Culture Movement of Modern China* (1957); Hsia, C. T., *A History of Modern Chinese Fiction* (1961), pp. 28–54; Hsia, T. A., *The Gate of Darkness* (1968), pp. 101–62; Hanan, P. "The Technique of L. H.'s Fiction," *HJAS,* 34 (1974), 53–95; Lyell, W. A., *L. H.'s Vision of Reality* (1976); Lee, L. O., "Genesis of a Writer: Notes on Lu Xun's Educational Experience," Mills, H. C., "Lu Xun: Literature and Revolution—from Mara to Marx," Doleželová-Velingerová, M., "Lu Xun's 'Medicine,'" in Goldman, M., ed., *Modern Chinese Literature in the May Fourth Era* (1977), pp. 161–232; Semanov, V. I., *L. H. and His Predecessors* (1980)

LEO OU-FAN LEE

LUANDINO VIEIRA, José
See Vieira, José Luandino

LUCEBERT
(pseud. of Lubertus Jacobus Swaanswijk) Dutch poet, b. 15 Feb. 1924, Amsterdam

L. was raised by his strict Calvinist grandmother on a farm near Amsterdam. His early schooling in Amsterdam was interrupted by World War II, when he was conscripted into forced labor by the occupying German army. Arrested on suspicion of sabotage, he was later released and spent the remaining years of the war in underground activities. After the war L. studied German romanticism and philosophy. He is a prolific painter, whose work has been widely exhibited in British and continental galleries.

Shortly after the liberation in 1945, L. associated himself with radical political and artistic groups in the Netherlands. One such group of artists, both painters and writers, began to react against what they considered unconscionable provincialism in Holland.

Known as "De Vijftigers" (the generation of the 1950s), they incorporated various current "isms" into an invigorating, albeit somewhat formless, body of protest. An early member of De Vijftigers, L. played a crucial role in developing the concept of language as physical form—employing wordplay neologisms, typographical tricks—which continues to be characteristic of the poetic avant-garde in the Netherlands. Because of L.'s skill as painter and poet, the amalgamation of the two forms met with considerable success.

In 1952 L. published five books of poetry: *Apocrief* (apocryphal), *De analfabetische naam* (the illiterate name), *De welbespraakte slaap* (the eloquent sleep), *De getekende naam* (the signed name), and *De amsterdamse school* (the Amsterdam school). These books were intended as a protest against the condition of art in the postwar society. It seems as if L. offered, in these early works, the principle of disruption as his supreme credo. There are times, as in the title poem of *9000 jakhalzen zwemmen naar Boston* (1950; 9000 jackals are swimming to Boston), when he breaks up his own vision with conflicting images and words. L. learned, however, the virtue of control, the ability to organize his insight around a particular set of metaphors.

By the time of the publication of *Val voor vliegengod* (1959; trap for the lord of the flies), L., altering the emphasis of his concerns, had turned his attention to mankind's search for enduring beauty. The problems of society became, in a sense, the problems of aesthetics; where once L. showed beasts at large in society, he now detected the "lord of the flies" within each human breast as well.

Throughout the 1960s and 1970s L. devoted most of his time to painting. Although *Gedichten 1948–1963* (1965; poems 1948–1963) brought him recognition as one of the most important Dutch poets of the 20th c., he has published few books of verse since. His poems have been translated into sixteen languages, however, some fifty of them have been set to music and recorded, and adaptations of his work are regularly performed on Dutch television and radio and on the stage.

The variorum edition of L.'s poetry, *Verzamelde gedichten* (1974; collected poems), illustrated by the author, reveals a skillful practitioner of two complementary art forms. He is able to develop powerful images of the beautiful and the grotesque (concepts he finds inseparable) by combining language and line, word and color, to dissolve their apparent differences in one encompassing vision.

FURTHER WORKS: *Triangel in de jungel* (1951); *De dieren der democratie* (1951); *Van de afgrond en de luchtmens* (1953); *Alfabel* (1955); *Amulet* (1957); *Mooi uitzicht & andere kurioziteiten* (1963); *Poezie is kinderspel* (1968); *Drie lagen diep* (1969); *... en morgen de hele wereld* (1973); *Oogsten in de dwaaltuin* (1981). FURTHER VOLUME IN ENGLISH: *The Tired Lovers They Are Machines* (1973)

BIBLIOGRAPHY: Snapper, J., *Post-War Dutch Literature: A Harp Full of Nails* (1972), passim

LARRY TEN HARMSEL

LUGONES, Leopoldo

Argentine poet, short-story writer, essayist, and historian, b. 13 June 1874, Villa de María del Río Seco; d. 18 Feb. 1938, Isla del Tigre

L. was Argentina's most important lyric poet of the early 20th c. He left his native province of Córdoba in 1893 and moved to Buenos Aires. Once in the capital, L. befriended Rubén Darío (q.v.) and became Argentina's premier modernist (q.v.) poet, but he had to support himself through bureaucratic posts in the national government. L. became the director of the library of the National Council of Education after 1914 and was the Argentine representative to the Committee on Intellectual Cooperation of the League of Nations. In 1926 he won the National Prize for Literature. Turning from the socialism of his youth to advocacy of ultraconservative nationalism, he became alienated from many of his former friends. As his isolation from the Argentine intelligentsia grew, disillusionment led to emotional depression and finally suicide in 1938.

Although L.'s poetry and prose evolved gradually, there are several constant themes: love and feminine sensuality; the celebration of natural beauty in vivid landscape descriptions and a metaphysical concern about organic processes; increasing nationalism and a search for Argentine identity; a preoccupation with death linked to love; and the poet's original treatment of the symbolic imagery associated with the moon.

L. began the modernist phase of his work with *Las montañas del oro* (1897; the mountains of gold), which was influenced by French symbolism (q.v.) and represented an elaborate experiment with visual imagery, rhyme, and meter (especially free verse). Although *Los crepúsculos del jardín* (1905; the garden twilights) is generally considered to be L.'s most typically modernist book, his exceptional talents as a creator of metaphor and as a musical poet attuned to the subtle nuances and interplay of sound and meaning first emerge here. By filtering emotions through the eyes of a distant poetic speaker or by using natural landscapes as contrasting backgrounds rather than projections of the emotional stress felt by his characters, L. avoids maudlin sentimentality.

Most critics consider *Lunario sentimental* (1909; sentimental phases of the moon) L.'s masterpiece because its original metaphors, phantasmagoric imagery, and ironic tone anticipate facets of the vanguardist poetry of the next decade. Jorge Luis Borges (q.v.) and the *Martinfierrista* group would later praise L.'s use of metaphor in this book as a direct influence on their own poetry, although they rejected his insistence on rhyme. This book also signals the culmination of L.'s youthful modernist verse. The moon is the central motif of the book, which is a potpourri of verse, one-act plays in verse and prose, prose poems, and lyrical short stories.

Odas seculares (1910; secular odes) initiated L.'s postmodernist poetry. The book's epic vision of Argentina's past, its flora and fauna, its mountains and streams, its major cities and national heroes (especially, the Argentine gaucho), commemorate the nation's centennial. "A los ganados y las mieses" (to the cattle and grainfields) stands out for its distinctive metaphors but lies within the tradition inaugurated by the Venezuelan Andrés Bello (1781–1865), in which South America's agriculture is extolled. Some of L.'s best love poetry is found in *El libro fiel* (1912; the faithful book), where L. provides an essentially romantic but philosophical view of conjugal love presented in a nostalgic tone of poignant tenderness. L. also employs popular verse forms like ballads or the Argentine *vidalita* (a sentimental folk song).

In *El libro de los paisajes* (1917; the book of landscapes), L. strips his verse of all vestiges of the exotic themes and settings common in modernist poetry to focus his attention on the flora and fauna of the region around Buenos Aires. L.'s interest in musical composition is reflected here by the use of onomatopeia, euphony, and alliteration. Many poems are modeled on symphonic forms and the orchestral tonality and range of classical musical instruments.

L.'s later poetry was of uneven quality but continued to evolve toward autobiographical lyricism in *Poemas solariegos* (1927; ancestral poems) and narrative verse in his glorification of the national spirit and past incarnated by the gaucho in the posthumously published *Romances del río seco* (1938; ballads of the dry river).

This last collection was an attempt to apply his theories of gaucho songs and verse, theories that are contained in his most important collection of essays, *El payador* (1916; the minstrel cowboy). L.'s prose includes both historical and cultural essays, but he is probably most remembered for some of his short stories. In *La guerra gaucha* (1905; the gaucho war), the narrative focus of these historical vignettes is overshadowed by a proliferation of rhetorical adornments and poetic imagery. *Las fuerzas extrañas* (1906; the strange forces) is L.'s most important contribution to fiction because it introduced science fiction to Argentine literature and surely influenced the fantastic stories of Adolfo Bioy-Casares (q.v.) and Borges.

L. was much more than the leading Argentine disciple of Darío's modernism. An indisputable master of metaphor and visual imagery, he was an original precursor of the essential elements of vanguardist poetry and contemporary prose in Latin America.

FURTHER WORKS: *El imperio jesuítico* (1904); *Piedras liminares* (1910); *Historia de Sarmiento* (1911); *Las horas doradas* (1922); *Estudios helénicos* (1923); *Cuentos fatales* (1924); *El ángel de la sombra* (1926); *La grande Argentina* (1930); *Poesías completas* (1948); *Obras en prosa* (1962)

BIBLIOGRAPHY: Borges, J. L., *L.* (1955); Moreno, J. C., "Silence in the Poetry of L. L.," *Hispania,* 46 (1963), 760–63; Ashhurst, A. W., Scari, R. M., et al., *Homenaje a L. L. (1874–1938)* (1964); Sola González, A., "Las *Odas seculares* de L. L.," *RI,* 32 (1966), 23–51; Martínez Estrada, E., *L. L.: Retrato sin retocar* (1968); Omil, A., *L. L.: Poesía y prosa* (1968); Mudrovic, M., "The Speaker's Position in Some Poems of Machado and L.," *KRQ,* 27 (1980), 281–88

JAMES J. ALSTRUM

LUKÁCS, György

(also known as Georg Lukács) Hungarian literary historian, critic, and philosopher (writing in Hungarian and German), b. 13 April 1885, Budapest; d. 4 June 1971, Budapest

L. was born into a wealthy Jewish family. He was a student of neo-Kantianism, and from the very first combined philosophical studies with a great interest in literature and sociology. L. studied at the universities of Budapest and Berlin. Georg Simmel (1858–1918) and Max Weber (1864–1920) were his teachers and models. After travels in Italy, he lived in Heidelberg (1912–16), where he belonged to the Max Weber circle. The publication of a collection of his essays, *Die Seele und die Formen* (1911; *Soul and Form,* 1974), established L. as a critic of international reputation.

In 1917 L. returned to Budapest, joined the Communist Party, and became people's commissar for public education in the short-lived government of the Hungarian Communist republic of 1919. After its overthrow by Horthy, L. was forced to flee to Austria, settling in Vienna.

When, in 1923, L. published *Geschichte und Klassenbewußtsein* (*History and Class Consciousness,* 1971), the Communist International charged him with "revisionism," a term that was to haunt him for the rest of his life. When a similar charge was brought against him in 1929, he withdrew from politics. From 1931 to 1933 he lived in Berlin. At the advent of Hitler he emigrated to the Soviet Union, where he worked at the Philosophical Institute of the Academy of Sciences, laying the foundations for his major works.

In 1945, at the end of World War II, L. returned to Budapest after twenty-five years of exile. He became a member of the national assembly of Hungary, which was then ruled by a postwar coalition government. He was also appointed a member of the presidium of the Hungarian Academy of Sciences and professor of aesthetics and cultural history at the University of Budapest. In 1948 the Hungarian Communist Party, although a minority, gained power and, in 1949, proclaimed

Hungary a People's Republic. In the following period, in which Hungary aligned itself with the Soviet bloc, renewed accusations of revisionism caused L. again to withdraw from political life. When, in October 1956, a popular anti-Communist revolt broke out, a new coalition government under Imre Nagy declared Hungary neutral and withdrew from the Warsaw Pact. It was in this short-lived coalition government that L. served as minister of culture. Soon, however, Soviet troops suppressed the rebellion, and L. was deported to Romania. In 1957 he was allowed to return to Budapest, and with his brief political career over, he devoted himself until his death to his studies in aesthetics and ethics. L.'s death was for the most part ignored by the Communist press of eastern Europe, although he was buried in Budapest with all due Party honors.

As a literary scholar and critic, L. was primarily concerned with the historical, political, and social dynamics of a work of art. Art to L. was not simply a political tool or social documentation. In fact, he stressed the originality and freedom of the artist's imagination. He pointed out how artistic imagination reflects the reality of the historical process, elevating events and circumstances that may appear devoid of meaning to the level of symbolic significance. The outstanding feature of L.'s aesthetics is that art has the function of "a seeing, hearing, and feeling organon of humanity—of humanity in every human being." Art, therefore, plays a most important role in the development of man's consciousness of humanity; it forms an integral part of the process of freeing mankind from its state of alienation.

L.'s approach to literature was philosophical, his vision of history, Marxist, and his aesthetics, Hegelian. Hegel is the most relevant in the sense that L. adopted his view of the historical development of form in art. From Hegel and Marx L. evolved his own philosophy of history, which was formulated in *Geschichte und Klassenbewußtsein* in 1923. A major work in Marxist philosophy, this book is the integration of Marx's interpretation of history—a chronicle of man's emancipation from the class struggle—with Hegel's concept of totality. Its particular significance lies in the fact that L. had in it visualized the matrix from which his literary criticism could be evolved.

In *Die Theorie des Romans* (completed 1916, pub. 1920; *The Theory of the Novel,* 1971), which marked L.'s transition from neo-Kantianism to Hegelianism, L. related the genres of epic and novel to Western intellectual history. Epic poetry, he maintained, expressed a sense of the "extensive totality of life," as experienced in Greece at the dawn of history. The novel is regarded as "an expression of the transcendental homelessness" of modern man, its development being paralleled by the decline of religious faith and the rise of scientific ideology. *Die Theorie des Romans* was L.'s first step in formulating his theory that artistic forms can be perceived in terms of historical development.

It was after L.'s emigration to the Soviet Union that the doctrine of Socialist Realism (q.v.) was officially proclaimed. Under the ideological umbrella of this doctrine L. began to develop his own theory of the "great realism." Basing his theory on Lenin's epistemology in *Materialism and Empiriocritism* (1908), which posits a "real world" that is independent of the mind, L. considered art a special form of reflecting "reality that exists independently of our consciousness." The work of art, however, does not mirror reality directly, but only indirectly. Works of art that reflect reality directly were condemned by L. as "naturalistic," while those that are too far removed from reality were denounced as "formalistic." This aesthetic theory became the basis of L.'s literary criticism for the following years. His "great realism" differs from Socialist Realism in paying more attention to the classical heritage and in deemphasizing the importance of adhering to the Party line in literary works. L.'s literary taste gravitated to the writers of the 18th and 19th cs., however bourgeois they may have been, and he always opposed mere propaganda literature, an attitude for which he was to be attacked by the Party in the late 1950s.

During the 1930s L. participated in the discussion on the origins and goals of German expressionism (q.v.) that was published in the exile journal *Das Wort* and that was to become one of the most important debates in the history of Marxist aesthetics. The two major antagonists, Bertolt Brecht (q.v.) and L., both vigorously opposed fascism. Brecht maintained that Communist writers must break radically with traditional forms and that they must utilize modern techniques. L. sought to employ the liberal and humanist traditions of bourgeois art as allies against fascism, condemning at the same time modern art as decadent or formalist. Thus L. denounced James Joyce, John Dos Passos, and Alfred Döblin (qq.v.) for their formalism, while praising Maxim Gorky, Romain Rolland, and Thomas and Heinrich Mann (qq.v.) for their realism.

In *Der historische Roman* (Russian, 1937; German, 1955; *The Historical Novel,* 1962) L. cited the historical novel, as represented by Sir Walter Scott, Balzac, and Tolstoy as the prime example of realist literature, since this type of narrative demonstrates not only the effect of historical reality upon literature but also the interrelationship of economic and social developments with literature and art. The integrity of the genre, threatened by the romanticists and the bourgeois writers after the revolution of 1848, is reestablished by Anatole France, Stefan Zweig, Lion Feuchtwanger (qq.v.), Roman Rolland, and Henrich Mann.

L.'s studies in European realism are characterized by questions such as "Balzac or Flaubert?" and "Tolstoy or Dostoevsky?" Making the representation of reality the criterion for his judgment, L. decided in favor of Balzac and Tolstoy. Balzac exemplifies Friedrich Engels's idea of "the triumph of realism," that is to say, a great writer cannot but portray reality, even if such reality conflicts with his ideology. In the case of Flaubert, L. is critical of the writer's preoccupation with literature as "a revelation of the inner life."

Thomas Mann, for L., is one of the great realists, "the last great bourgeois writer" and representative of German humanism. In his *Thomas Mann* (1949; *Essays on Thomas Mann,* 1964), L. traced Mann's brand of realism back to Goethe. Demonstrating in his studies—*Skizze einer Geschichte der neueren deutschen Literatur* (1953; an outline of the history of modern German literature) and *Die Zerstörung der Vernunft* (1954; the destruction of reason)—the interrelationship between political and intellectual history in German literature and philosophy, L. pointed out a progressive and a suppressive trend within German culture—rationalism and humanism as represented by Lessing, Goethe, Hegel, Heine, Marx, and Thomas Mann on the one hand, and irrationalism and barbarism as represented by the romanticists Richard Wagner and Nietzsche on the other. In these studies L. attempted to analyze the German catastrophe of 1933–45 while also formulating designs for a better future.

The last phase of L.'s writings is characterized by his opposition to manifestations of Stalinism in literature, such as the mandatory expression of Socialist Realism and political control of the artist in general. He energetically fought the "expedient character" of Stalinist theories of art, working for what he called the "liquidation of Stalinism in literature."

During these last years, he also adopted Aristotelian concepts in place of Lenin's theory of reflection. *Die Eigenart des Ästhetischen* (2 vols., 1963; the specific nature of the aesthetic), which forms part of a projected magnum opus of his later years, introduces Aristotle's definition of art as mimesis (imitation), stressing the anthropomorphic, evocative, and cathartic character of art.

Although *Zur Ontologie des gesellschaftlichen Seins* (3 vols., 1971–73; on the ontology of social existence; Vol. 1, *Marx's Basic Ontological Principles,* 1978), the first Marxist ontology written since Marx, was completed, a planned work on ethics had only been begun at his death.

World literature in Goethe's sense was always L.'s preoccupation. As one of the most important and thought-provoking Marxist theoreticians of literature and aesthetics, L. influenced decisively the philosophical writings of Ernst Bloch (1885–1977), Herbert Marcuse (1898–1979), Jean-Paul Sartre (q.v.), and Maurice Merleau-Ponty (1908–1961), among others, as well as Karl Mannheim's (1893–1947) sociology of knowledge and the literary criticism of Walter Benjamin (q.v.), Lucien Goldmann (1913–1970), and Ernst Fischer (1899–1972). Any formalist or structuralist (q.v.) school of literary criticism cannot fail to benefit from the historical perspective L. brought to the understanding of literature.

FURTHER WORKS: *Lenin: Studie über den Zusammenhang seiner Gedanken* (1924; *Lenin: A Study on the Unity of His Thought,* 1971); *Moses Hess und die Probleme der idealistischen Dialektik* (1926); *Goethe und seine Zeit* (1947; *Goethe and His Age,* 1969); *Der junge Hegel* (1948; *The Young Hegel,* 1976); *Essays über den Realismus* (1948); *Schicksalswende: Beiträge zu einer neuen deutschen Ideologie* (1948); *Karl Marx und Friedrich Engels als Literaturhistoriker*

(1948); *Der russische Realismus in der Weltliteratur* (1949; partial tr. in *Studies in European Realism,* 1964); *Deutsche Realisten des 19. Jahrhunderts* (1951); *Balzac und der französische Realismus* (1952; partial tr. in *Studies in European Realism,* 1964); *Beiträge zur Geschichte der Ästhetik* (1954); *Probleme des Realismus* (1955); *Wider den mißverstandenen Realismus* (1958; *Realism in Our Time: Literature and the Class Struggle,* 1964); *Schriften zur Literatursoziologie* (1961); *Werke: Gesamtausgabe* (17 vols., 1962–81); *Von Nietzsche zu Hitler; oder, Der Irrationalismus und die deutsche Politik* (1966); *Schriften zur Ideologie und Politik* (1967); *Ausgewählte Schriften* (4 vols., 1967–70); *Über die Besonderheit als Kategorie der Ästhetik* (1967); *Gespräche mit G. L.: Hans Heinz Holz, Leo Kofler, Wolfgang Abendroth Pinkus:* (1967; *Conversations with L.,* 1975); *Solschenizyn* (1970; *Solzhenitsyn,* 1971); *Heidelberger Philosophie der Kunst: 1912–1914* (1974); *Heidelberger Ästhetik: 1916–1918* (1975); *Politische Aufsätze* (3 vols., 1975–77); *Entwicklungsgeschichte des modernen Dramas* (1981); *Gelebtes Leben: Eine Autobiographie im Dialog* (1981). FURTHER VOLUMES IN ENGLISH: *Writer and Critic, and Other Essays* (1970); *Political Writings: 1919–1929* (1972); *Marxism and Human Liberation: Essays on History, Culture and Revolution* (1973); *Essays on Realism* (1980)

BIBLIOGRAPHY: Demetz, P., "G. L. as a Theoretician of Literature," *Marx, Engels and the Poets: Origins of Marxist Literary Criticism,* rev. ed. (1967), pp. 199–227; Sontag, S., "The Literary Criticism of G. L.," *Against Interpretation* (1969), pp. 90–99; Lichtheim, G., *G. L.* (1970); Parkinson, G. H. R., ed., *G. L.: The Man, His Work and His Ideas* (1970); Jameson, F., "The Case for G. L.," *Marxism and Form: Twentieth Century Dialectical Theories of Literature* (1971); Bahr, E., and Kunzer, R. G., *G. L.* (1972); Mészáros, I., *L.'s Concept of Dialectic, with Biography, Bibliography and Documents* (1972); Királyfalvi, B., *The Aesthetics of G. L.* (1975); Arato, A., and Breines, P., *The Young L. and the Origins of Western Marxism* (1979); Miles, D. H., "Portrait of the Marxist as a Young Hegelian: L.'s Theory of the Novel," *PMLA,* 94 (1979), 22–35; Löwy, M., *G. L.: From Romanticism to Bolshevism* (1979); Fekete, É., and Karádi, E., eds., *G. L.: Sein Leben in Bildern, Selbstzeugnissen und Dokumenten* (1981); Tar, J. M., *Thomas Mann und G. L.* (1982)

EHRHARD BAHR

G. L. is probably the only Communist philosopher and literary critic in East Europe who still has the power to interest and to teach many readers in the West. This is due entirely to his intellectual gifts and to the systematically moral vision of history that he has retained as a writer despite his many servilities to Stalin and the betrayals of his own intellectual standards that he has in times past committed as a Communist leader. L. owes his reputation entirely to the logical skill and intellectual vision with which, as a thinker rather than as a "party intellectual," he has sought to illuminate the deepest aspects of Marxism. He gives the impression that no other Communist philosopher has done for some time—that despite official avowals and mechanical formulas, here is an individual thinker who is fascinated by and thoroughly committed to Marxism as a philosophy, and who uses it for the intellectual pleasure and moral satisfaction that it gives him. Yet unlike the really noble figures in the early days of Communist history like Rosa Luxemburg, and brilliant writers like Leon Trotsky, who were truly revolutionary intellectuals . . . L. is actually a more "bourgeois" and academic humanist—who because of his inner detachment can stimulate and provoke us by his insights into a text and his formulations of an esthetic issue.

Alfred Kazin, Introduction to G. L., *Studies in European Realism* (1964), p. v

L. strikes me as seeing through to the very bones and muscles and working organs of the literary tradition where most critics are content to describe its skin; and what enables him to get this depth is his historical sense. In this he brings to literary studies something they have been short of for generations. . . .

The philosophy that underlies his own interpretations of literary history springs from the historical materialism of Marx. . . . The test of making it one's own is how one applies it, or (to come closer to the critical act itself) not how one "applies" it but rather, temporarily ceasing to be aware of Marx's idea, how one goes to work among literature; manages to find, say, family likenesses between works, or main lines of growth inside a trend, or equivalences between a trend or an individual work and things in the main life of an epoch; and *then,* this specifically critical task being done, one may recognize afresh and claim to have confirmed the deep large anterior idea: it is indeed the case at point after point that social being determines consciousness. . . .

The question is: how does the critic find or

identify the social equivalent among the mass of possibles? and, once found, what sort of value can it confer on the work of art? To put the question in terms purely of evaluation ... , how is the critic to distinguish between an intelligent conception of an epoch which, however, remains artistically inert and a work which is fully alive and effective in its own medium and thereby succeeds in having, as counterpart to its theme, a social equivalent which is historically important? That this is what L. is committed to finding, and evaluating, shows through in many of his theoretical asides.

David Craig, "L.'s Views on How History Moulds Literature," in G. H. R. Parkinson, ed., *G. L.: The Man, His Work and His Ideas* (1970), pp. 191–95

G. L. stands as a lone and splendid tower amidst the gray landscape of eastern European and Communist intellectual life.... No contemporary Western critic, with the possible exception of Croce, has brought to bear on literary problems a philosophic equipment of comparable authority. In no one since Sainte-Beuve has the sense of history, the feeling for the rootedness of the imagination in time and in place, been as solid and acute....

... In his works two beliefs are incarnate. First, that literary criticism is not a luxury, that is not what the subtlest of American critics has called "a discourse for amateurs." But that it is, on the contrary, a central and militant force toward shaping men's lives. Secondly, L. affirms that the work of the critic is neither subjective nor uncertain. The truth of judgment can be verified.

... L. has put forward a solution to the twofold dilemma of the modern critic. As a Marxist, he discerns in literature the action of economic, social, and political forces. This action follows on certain laws of historical necessity. To L. criticism is a science even before it is an art.... Secondly, he has given his writing an intense immediacy. It is rooted in the political struggles and social circumstances of the time. His writings on literature ... are instruments of combat.... L.'s arguments are relevant to issues that are central in our lives. His critiques are not a mere echo to literature. Even where it is sectarian and polemic, a book by L. has a curious nobility. It possesses what Matthew Arnold called "high seriousness."

George Steiner, "Marxism and the Literary Critic" and "G. L. and His Devil's Pact," *Language and Silence: Essays on Language, Literatures and the Inhuman* (1970), pp. 311, 327–28, 330

L., as a thoroughgoing Hegelian idealist, may err in the *Theory of the Novel* in the direction of ... "surplus metaphysics," but he still ranks, together

with Benjamin, Adorno, and Auerbach, as one of our major critics and theoreticians in the German idealist tradition. Perhaps one of the best ways to assess his achievement is to refer to Isaiah Berlin's famous study of Tolstoy, *The Hedgehog and the Fox,* in which he sets up a typology whereby the hedgehog "knows one big thing" and the fox "knows many things." Tolstoy himself, as Berlin points out, was obviously a fox, but a fox who constantly strove (and failed) to become a hedgehog—particularly in the chapters on the philosophy of history in *War and Peace.* L., by contrast, like so many other thinkers in the Hegelian tradition, was the complete hedgehog—yet a hedgehog who tried, again and again, and without success, to become a political fox (cf. his would-be conversion to Marxism-Leninism in 1918). Whereas Tolstoy's genius lay in fastening on the infinite variety of the world and perceiving how "each given object is uniquely different from all others," L.'s talents lay in the opposite direction: he had the ability, which Tolstoy constantly longed for but never acquired, of relating everything in the world to a central, all embracing system, to a "universal explanatory principle," in Berlin's words, one that could perceive, "in the apparent variety of the bits and pieces which compose the furniture of the world," a deep and underlying unity.

David H. Miles, "Portrait of the Marxist as a Young Hegelian: L.'s *Theory of the Novel,*" *PMLA,* 94 (1979), 32–33

With universities and students at or close to the center, a New Left social movement spread across the Western world and parts of the rest of the globe in the late 1960s.... In it the young L.'s ideas found their first extensive audience. It was not the audience which he, let alone the great majority of Marxists, had in mind. Yet, the intended audience, the industrial proletariat, had rarely been receptive.... Within the framework of this complex movement, only segments of its student and intellectual currents revived the young L.'s ideas. Yet the underlying source of this revival was not that his ideas provided a long-lost clue to the puzzle of how the proletariat becomes revolutionary. On the contrary, the young L.'s heirs in the 1960s reinterpreted his work as a critique of their own experience in capitalist (and socialist) society—as a contribution to their own radicalization. For at its root, the rebellion of students and intellectuals was directed against the reification of everyday life, the process by which human life is transformed under modern conditions of production into things, marketable goods, numbers. A critique of reification lay at the heart of the young L.'s work, pre-Marxist and post-Marxist. In that work, sections of the New Left grasped a vital theoretical anticipation of their own activity.

Andrew Arato and Paul Breines, *The Young L. and the Origins of Western Marxism* (1979), pp. 224

Adorno pointed out that the supreme criterion of L.'s aesthetics, "the postulate of a reality which must be depicted as an unbroken continuum joining subject and object," assumes that a reconciliation has already taken place, "that all is well with society, that the individual has come into his own and feels at home in the world." Besides, L. could not reconcile the Marxist cause with the fact that the novel of Realism he praised was a bourgeois invention. Like Marx, he hoped not to reject bourgeois achievements but to appropriate them: still, it was obviously insulting to offer Brecht and other Marxist writers the edifying examples of Scott and Balzac. But he remains an important figure for anyone who regards the relation between fiction, politics, and ideology as a crucial matter.

Dennis Donoghue, "The Real McCoy: *Essays on Realism* by G. L.," *NYRB*, 19 Nov. 1981, 45

LUNDKVIST, Artur

Swedish poet, novelist, and essayist, b. 3 March 1906, Hagstad

L. was born into relatively modest circumstances, and his formal education was not extensive. He has read widely, however, in his native Swedish as well as in nearly a dozen other languages, and his travels have taken him throughout most of the world. L. has assiduously guarded his personal and aesthetic independence by never associating too closely with any movement or any particular line of thought. He has surprised some by his lack of loyalty to social realism or organized labor movements and by his advocacy, during the 1950s and 1960s, of a political position beholden to neither the U.S. nor the Soviet Union. In 1968 he was elected a member of the Swedish Academy.

L.'s first volume of poetry, *Glöd* (1928; embers), and others of the early 1930s celebrate life, energy, and power portrayed as absolute values in lusty imagery and surging free verse. By 1932 L. had come under the influence of surrealism (q.v.), from which he learned much about liberating mankind from its fears, apprehensions, and anxieties. The impact of L.'s surrealistic meditations can be most clearly observed in *Nattens broar* (1936; the bridges of night) and *Sirensång* (1937; siren song).

During World War II and the subsequent years of political unrest, L.'s compassion for the powerless and his sympathy for human misery became more apparent in his poetry. One of his most accomplished works is the long poem *Agadir* (1961; *Agadir,* 1979), which describes the earthquake that struck that Moroccan city in 1960. In its evocation of heroic humility in the face of dreadful fact the poem transcends the specific event that is its subject to become universal in theme. Since 1960 L. has made effective use of the prose poem in such a way that the antithetical relationships inherent in the genre emerge in bold relief.

The growing prominence of prose in L.'s writing, suggested by the prose poems, is amplified by a series of longer, more integrated narratives that approach the novel in scope. These works, written for the most part since 1970, were by no means L.'s first narrative efforts, but they have a particular power deriving from their common concern with characters who break out of established social molds—Genghis Khan, Goya, Alexander the Great, and Viking heroes—to go on journeys that extend their horizons of personal understanding.

Two other prose forms have also been especially important: the travel narrative and the critical essay. L., an inveterate traveler, has used his accounts of sojourns abroad to describe the vast range of human possibilities as well as his impressions of exotic places and people. His most significant critical essays have also had a similar purpose: the introduction of important contemporary foreign writers to the Swedish reading public. His advocacy of writers as diverse as William Faulkner, Pablo Neruda, and Czesław Miłosz (qq.v.) has made him one of the most insistent and articulate spokesmen for 20th-c. modernism in Sweden.

L.'s most significant contributions to Swedish and world literature are not to be seen in terms of intellectual profundity or formal innovations but rather in the arresting articulation of his extremely broad interests and his genuine concern about the human condition. Both his poetry and poetics are grounded in the world of experience heightened by power of imagination. He has argued that literature should not exist for its own sake but for man's sake; it should thus defend and promote man's fundamental humanity and suggest ways in which he can become ever more humane.

FURTHER WORKS: *Naket liv* (1929); *Jordisk prosa* (1930); *Svart stad* (1930); *Atlantvind* (1932); *Vit man* (1932); *Negerkust* (1933); *Floderna flyter mot havet* (1934); *Himmelsfärd* (1935); *Drakblod* (1936); *Eldtema* (1939); *Ikarus flykt* (1939); *Vandrarens träd* (1941); *Diktare och avslöjare i Amerikas nya litteratur* (1942); *Korsväg* (1942); *Dikter mellan djur och Gud* (1944); *Skinn över sten* (1947); *Fotspår i vattnet* (1949); *Negerland* (1949); *Indiabrand* (1950); *Malinga* (1952); *Vallmor från Taschkent* (1952); *Spegel för dag och natt* (1953); *Darunga* (1954); *Liv som gräs* (1954); *Den förvandlade draken* (1955); *Vindrosor, moteld* (1955); *Vindingevals* (1956); *Berget och svalorna* (1957); *Vulkanisk kontinent* (1957); *Ur en befolkad ensamhet* (1958); *Komedi i Hägerskog* (1959); *Utsikter över utländsk prosa* (1959); *Det talande trädet* (1960); *Orians upplevelser* (1960); *Berättelser för vilsekomna* (1961); *Ögonblick och vågor* (1962); *Sida vid sida* (1962); *Drömmar i ovädrens tid* (1963); *Från utsiktstornet* (1963); *Hägringar i handen* (1964); *Texter i snön* (1964); *Sällskap för natten* (1965); *Så lever Kuba* (1965); *Självporträtt av en drömmare med öppna ögon* (1966), *Mörkskogen* (1967); *Brottställen* (1968); *Snapphanens liv och död* (1968); *Historier mellan åsarna* (1969); *Utflykter med utländska författare* (1969); *Besvärjelser till tröst* (1969); *Långt borta, mycket nära* (1970); *Himlens vilja* (1970); *Antipodien* (1971); *Tvivla, korsfarare!* (1972); *Läsefrukter* (1973); *Lustgårdens demoni* (1973); *Livsälskare, svartmålare* (1974); *Fantasins slott och vardagens stenar* (1974); *Världens härlighet* (1975); *Krigarens dikt* (1976); *Flykten och överlevandet* (1977); *Slavar för Särkland* (1978); *Sett i det strömmande vattnet* (1978); *Utvandring till paradiset* (1979); *Skrivet mot kvällen* (1980); *Babylon, gudarnas sköka* (1981); *Sinnebilder* (1982). FURTHER VOLUME IN ENGLISH: *The Talking Tree, and Other Poems* (1982)

BIBLIOGRAPHY: Vowles, R. B., "From Pan to Panic: The Poetry of A. L.," *NMQ*, 22 (1952), 288–303; Sjöberg, L., "An Interview with A. L.," *BA*, 50 (1976), 329–36; Miłosz, C., "Reflections on A. L.'s *Agadir*," *WLT*, 54 (1980), 367–68; Sondrup, S. P., "A. L. and Knowledge for Man's Sake," *WLT*, 55 (1981), 233–38

STEVEN P. SONDRUP

LUO LITERATURE

See Kenyan Literature and Ugandan Literature

LUSATIAN LITERATURE

The Lusatians (also known as Sorbs and Wends) are descendants of Slavic tribes who at the beginning of the first millennium occupied the territory between the Oder River on the east and the Elbe and Saale rivers on the west. Today, they constitute a separate national minority in East Germany, inhabiting the area southeast of Berlin, traditionally divided into Upper and Lower Lusatia.

From its beginnings in the days of the Reformation to the present, the literature of the Lusatians has reflected the struggle of this smallest Slavic group to preserve its cultural identity. Following a 19th-c. revival of national consciousness brought about by the romantic movement, a period of decline set in at the turn of the century. During that critical time, the continuity of Lusatian culture was preserved largely through the efforts of Catholic men of letters, such as the priests Jurij Winger (1872–1918), author of the popular historical tale *Hronow* (1893; Hronow); Mikławš Andricki (1871–1908), who edited the leading Lusatian periodical, *Łužica,* between 1896 and 1904; and Jurij Deleńk (1882–1918), editor of the Catholic paper *Katolski posoł.*

World War I and its aftermath brought about a new wave of patriotism and a renewed belief in the viability of Lusatian culture. Among the leading figures of that period were the writers of fiction Jakub Lorenc-Zalěski (1874–1939) and Romuald Domaška (1869–1945); the poets Jan Skala (1889–1945) and Józef Nowak (b. 1895); and the historian, poet, and critic Ota Wićaz (1874–1952).

After World War II Lusatian literature experienced another revival. Writers whose literary activities were restricted or altogether suppressed during the Third Reich, such as Michał Nawka (1885–1968), Mina Witkojc (b. 1893), Marja Kubašec (b. 1890), Měrćin Nowak (b. 1900), and Wylem Bjero (b. 1902), began to publish again with new vigor. These and younger writers have added new dimensions to Lusatian literature. Traditional subjects—the glorious past and village life—dealt with chiefly in poetry and short stories, have now been augmented by full-fledged novels about both life under the Nazis and contemporary social and political problems.

The most successful Lusatian novelist is Jurij Brězan (b. 1916), who also writes in German. The trilogy *Feliks Hanuš: Generacija horkich nazhonjenjow* (1958–66; Feliks Hanuš: generation of bitter experiences)—published first in German under the titles *Der Gymnasiast* (1958; the high-school student), *Semester der verlorenen Zeit* (1960; semester of lost time), and *Mannesjahre* (1966; years of maturity)—is an autobiographical and social novel dealing with the dilemma of being a Lusatian in the modern world. *Krabat; oder, Die Verwandlung der Welt* (1975; Krabat; or, the transformation of the world), a philosophical work published first in German, is a semimythical history of the Lusatian people and their strivings for an existence without fear, told from a contemporary perspective. Other novels and plays of Brězan have appeared in both Lusatian and German. Younger writers who deal with contemporary themes are Marja Młynkowa (b. 1934), author of the collection of stories *Kostrjanc a čerwjeny mak* (1965; the cornflower and the red poppy), and the poet and translator Jurij Koch (b. 1936), whose novel *Mjez sydom mostami* (1968; between seven bridges) was adapted for the stage in 1970.

Poetry, however, remains the principal genre in Lusatian literature. Leading contemporary exponents are the literary scholar and translator Jurij Młyńk (b. 1927), whose poems are filled with love and pride for Lusatia and its culture; and Kito Lorenc (b. 1938), who writes philosophical and social poetry.

Members of the younger generation, organized in the Circle of Young Sorbian Authors, at times voice controversial and (from the official Communist viewpoint) even heretical views on various ideological issues. Most official literary and cultural activities in Lusatia revolve around the national organization Domowina ("homeland")—banned in 1937 during the Nazi period—which has been the center of Lusatian cultural life since 1912.

Although favored by a contemporary literary boom and government subsidies, Lusatian culture is threatened by apparently benevolent but insidiously exploitive official policies and Germanization.

BIBLIOGRAPHY: Stone, G., *The Smallest Slavonic Nation* (1972); Jokostra, P., "Ein Ar-

chipel von Sprachinseln: Bericht über die Literatur der sorbischen Minderheit in der DDR," *DSt,* 15 (1977), 277–84

GREGORY LUZNYCKY
LEO D. RUDNYTZKY

LUSTIG, Arnošt

Czechoslovak short-story writer, novelist, and screenwriter (writing in Czech), b. 21 Dec. 1926, Prague

At an early age L. was exposed to the drastic experience of several Nazi concentration camps; toward the end of World War II he escaped from a transport train headed for Dachau. After the war he studied journalism in Prague and in 1948–49 covered the Arab-Israeli war as a radio correspondent. He continued to work for Czechoslovak Radio until 1958, then became an editor of a youth magazine, and from 1960 was a screenwriter with Czechoslovak State Film. In 1968 L. left Czechoslovakia and, following stays in Israel and Yugoslavia, settled in 1970 in the U.S.

L. was one of the younger writers who came to the fore during the slight political relaxation in the late 1950s and whose work signaled a break with the propagandist literature of the first half of the decade. In quick succession he published two volumes of short stories, *Noc a naděje* (1958; *Night and Hope,* 1962) and *Démanty noci* (1958; *Diamonds in the Night,* 1962; later tr., *Diamonds of the Night,* 1978), in which he examined the behavior of people under extreme pressure. L.'s approach was considerably influenced by modern American fiction, particularly that of William Faulkner (q.v.). His stories, which take place in Nazi concentration camps, on death transports, and during the turbulent last days of World War II, contain little action and only the rudiments of a plot. The characters, most of them children or old people, are sketchily drawn, since the author is less concerned with their psychological development than with their momentous reaction when faced with a moral dilemma. The crucial act of making an ethical decision under conditions of ultimate inhumanity is presented as proof that man can be destroyed but not vanquished.

The static nature of the stories, which seek to evoke an atmosphere and to explore the very essence of humanity, obliged L. to pay great attention to composition and style. The degree of sophistication that he achieved in this respect, however, sometimes unfavorably contrasted with the paucity of dramatic action. This imbalance marks some of his work in which he ventured onto other ground than that of the camp experience. Lack of action was also considered to be the main shortcoming of his next collection of short stories, *Ulice ztracených bratří* (1959; the street of lost brothers).

In the novella *Dita Saxová* (1962; *Dita Sax,* 1966) L. deals with the psychological wounds of those who survived the camps. Dita is "too young to be left to herself and too old to allow anyone to take care of her." Unable to adjust to postwar times, suffering from mistrust and loneliness, she commits suicide. Another novella, *Modlitba pro Kateřinu Horovitzovou* (1964; *A Prayer for Katerina Horovitzova,* 1973), describes both defiance and passivity in the face of death. Kateřina, a beautiful Jewish girl, is saved from the gas chamber on her arrival in the camp and allowed to join a group of rich European Jews caught by the Nazis when they had prematurely returned to Italy from their refuge in America. By deception and psychological manipulation they are gradually deprived of their wealth and reduced to sheeplike docility, with which they go to their slaughter, while Kateřina, even in the last hopeless moment, saves her dignity and humanity by the act of attacking the torturers. The novel is one of several of L.'s works that have been made into remarkable films.

New aspects of L.'s talent were revealed in *Hořká vůně mandlí* (1968; the bitter smell of almonds), which is composed of a novella and three short stories. While in the stories L. returned to subjects familiar from his earlier books, in the novella, *Dům vrácené ozvěny* (the house of the returned echo), he portrayed with great insight an unsuccessful and helpless Jewish businessman and his family as they inexorably follow the road that leads them to destruction. Set in Prague just before the war and during the early years of the Nazi occupation and war, the pitiful heroes and their small world are viewed by L. with a slightly ironic compassion.

L.'s last book published in Czechoslovakia, a novel, *Miláček* (1969; darling), is a rather tenuous love story set against the background of the first Arab-Israeli war. The matter-of-fact heroism that is supposed to lurk behind the façade of self-denigrating Jewish humor, as well as the tenderness covered up by rough

talk, are in fact only too often obliterated by these devices.

L.'s first book written in exile, *Z deníku sedmnáctileté Perly Sch.* (1979; from the diary of seventeen-year-old Perla Sch.), shows L.'s mastery of style and structure. But there may be some doubt whether the subject (a Jewish prostitute in Terezín concentration camp commits a ghoulish act of revenge on a Nazi officer) is not too melodramatic to justify such refined treatment.

L. is one of the few writers who succeeded in exorcising the tragic experience of the death camps by transforming it into art. In his search for the qualities that make man indomitable, he has endowed the fate of the Jews with a universal human dimension.

FURTHER WORKS: *Můj známý Vili Feld* (1961); *Nikoho neponížíš* (1963); *Bílé břízy na podzim* (1966); *Tma nemá stín* (unpub. expanded version of short story; *Darkness Casts No Shadow,* 1977)

BIBLIOGRAPHY: Hájek, I., comp., "A. L.," in Mihailovich, V. D., et al., eds., *Modern Slavic Literatures* (1976), Vol. II, pp. 142–45; Sherwin, B. L., "The Holocaust Universe of A. L.," *Midstream,* Aug.–Sept. 1979, 44–48

IGOR HÁJEK

LUXEMBOURG LITERATURE

From the early Middle Ages Luxembourg was divided into French- and German-speaking provinces. In 1659 the country lost part of its French-speaking territory to France; in 1839 the remaining French region became part of the newly established kingdom of Belgium. The people in what remained of Luxembourg speak a Moselle-Franconian dialect of German, the Luxembourg patois. Children are taught both German and French in elementary school. Thus, citizens of the Grand Duchy of Luxembourg can express themselves in three languages, and Luxembourg has three literatures.

In the Luxembourg Dialect

In the 19th c., after political autonomy had been reestablished, a nationalist spirit gave rise to a written literature in the Luxembourg dialect. Dialect writers created lyrical, epic, and satirical poetry as well as plays, mostly comedies. Michel Rodange (1827–1876) wrote the greatest book in Luxembourg dialect, the long poem *De Rénert* (1872; Reynard the fox), which has become a national epic. The playwright Andréï Duchscher (1840–1911) gave Luxembourg its first social drama, *Franz Pinell* (1899; Franz Pinell), about the conflict between a foundry owner and his workers. Batty Weber (1860–1940) wrote the first tragedy in dialect, *De Sche'fer vun Aasselburn* (1898; the shepherd of Asselborn); the hero is a historical figure who participated in the uprising of the Luxembourg peasants against the French Directoire in 1798.

Dialect literature developed along the lines of 19th-c. models during the first decades of the century and had an upsurge during the German occupation of Luxembourg in World War II, in reaction to the Nazi terror. Since World War II dialect writers have also turned to the essay, the short story, and the novel. Dialect drama was revitalized in the late 1950s by Norbert Weber (b. 1925), who introduced the techniques of the international avant-garde. The hero of his historical drama *Jean Chalop* (1963; Jean Chalop) is an alderman who was killed by the Burgundians when they penetrated the fortress of Luxembourg in 1443. Dialect theater, which had been dominated by light comedy, including musical comedy, today convincingly treats serious subjects.

In German

All the literary genres are employed by authors writing in German, but it is mainly the novelists who stress particularly Luxembourg problems. The Catholic influence has for a long time been dominant in the country, but it has also provoked criticism. In Batty Weber's novel *Fenn Kass* (1913; Fenn Kass), for example, a Catholic priest falls prey to doubt and eventually leaves the Church. Jean-Pierre Erpelding (1884–1977), in *Bärnd Bichel* (1917; Bärnd Bichel), analyzes avarice and moral degeneration. His trilogy *Adelheid François* (1936–38; Adelheid François) is concerned with the Luxembourg intellect torn between French and German cultures. His *Peter Brendel* (1959; Peter Brendel) deals with a Luxembourg peasant who nearly endorses the Nazi "blood and earth" theory; only hardship and tragedy make Brendel understand that mankind is more worthy of love than the soil.

Nicolas Hein (1889–1969), in some of the stories in the collection *Unterwegs* (1939; on the road), focuses on the sufferings of the Luxembourg intellectual in the provincial and narrow-minded atmosphere of his small country. Other of his stories relate the difficult life of Moselle wine growers. In a short novel, *Der Verräter* (1948; the traitor), Hein describes the awakening of national identity between 1830 and 1839. Historical subject matter is also treated in the posthumously published *Job, der Baumeister* (1961; Job the architect) by Paul Noesen (1891–1960), about the Swiss architect Ulrich Job, who directed the building of the Luxembourg cathedral (finished in 1621); the novel explores the religious faith of the Luxembourgers of the time. In the short novel *Kleines Schicksal* (1934: humble destiny) Joseph Funck (1902–1978) poignantly portrayed a miserly member of Luxembourg's subproletariat.

Mimy Tidick-Ulveling (b. 1892) is concerned with moral and intellectual progress toward individual freedom and responsibility, from the late Middle Ages until today. In the novel *Im Zeichen der Flamme* (1961; under the sign of the flame) she uses the trial and execution of a young woman accused of being a witch to develop these ideas. Fernand Hoffmann's (b. 1929) novel *Die Grenze* (1972; the borderline) tackles the problem of political and moral responsibility in a story about resistance to Nazi oppression. Roger Manderscheid (b. 1933), in his critical and satirical novel *Die Dromedare: Stilleben für Johann den Blinden* (1973; the dromedaries: still life for John the Blind), attacks the mediocrity of the national Spirit and human insufficiency in general. *Schumann* (1976; Schumann) by Cornel Meder (b. 1938) is the fictitious diary of a young woman teacher who lucidly analyzes her own situation, world problems, and the social and political life of Luxembourg.

The poet Paul Henkes (b. 1898) is more interested in universal than in specifically national subjects. In such works as *Ölbaum und Schlehdorn* (1968; olive tree and blackthorn), *Das Bernsteinhorn* (1973; the amber horn), and *Gitter und Harfe* (1977; grille and harp) he expresses with subtle means a profound concern for the dilemmas of Western man.

In French

Some Luxembourgers writing in French see in their choice of language a signal of their desire to assert Luxembourg's liberty and independence. The most striking of these is Marcel Noppeney (1877–1966), a poet, essayist, and polemicist, author of *Le prince Avril* (1907; Prince April) a volume of poetry in the Parnassian vein. Nicolas Ries's (1876–1941) two novels, *Le diable aux champs* (1936; the devil in the country) and *Sens unique* (1940; one way only), depict rural life in Luxembourg. Nicolas Konert's (b. 1891), novel *Folle jeunesse* (1938; crazy youth) portrays an upstart's life in the wine-growing Moselle region in eastern Luxembourg. Joseph Leydenbach's (b. 1903) most interesting novel is *Les désirs de Jean Bachelin* (1948; the longings of Jean Bachelin); Leydenbach's protagonists are from his own upper-class background and are torn between wordly dissipation and spiritual aspiration. Albert Borschette's (1920–1976) one novel, *Continuez à mourir* (1959; go on dying), is about Nazi-occupied western Europe and the hardships suffered by Luxembourg's young men, who were forced to serve in the German army.

Paul Palgen (1883–1966), who wrote *Oratorio pour la mort d'un poète* (1957; oratorio for the death of a poet), was a sensuous, perhaps decadent poet. Edmond Dune (b. 1914), poet, playwright, and essayist, on the other hand, is a grim critic of material and intellectual pollution. In spite of the restraints he puts on his feelings, he reveals himself, in *Poèmes en prose* (1973; prose poems), for instance, as a fervent lover of life, nature, and art.

BIBLIOGRAPHY: Hoffmann, F., *Geschichte der luxemburger Mundartdichtung* (2 vols., 1964–67); Gérard, M., *Le roman français de chez nous* (1968); Hoffmann, F., *Standort Luxemburg* (1974); Kieffer, R., "Luxembourg Literature Today," *BA*, 48 (1974), 515–19; Christophory, J., *The Luxembourgers in Their Own Words* (1978); Kieffer, R., ed., *Littérature luxembourgeoise de langue française* (1980)

ROSEMARIE KIEFFER

LUZI, Mario

Italian poet and essayist, b. 20 Oct. 1914, Florence

L. obtained a degree in literature with a dissertation on François Mauriac (q.v.) and taught in various high schools in Italy. He was among the first contributors to the Italian literary journals *Frontespizio, Letteratura,* and *Campo di Marte*. He now teaches French literature at the University of Florence.

With the collections *La barca* (1935; the boat) and *Avvento notturno* (1940; nocturnal advent) L. showed himself to be one of the most interesting and original poets of the movement known as hermeticism (q.v.). This early stage of his production is characterized by a refined, sometimes precious linguistic experimentation, which tends toward fragmentation and strong condensation of language and reveals literary influences ranging from Mallarmé to French surrealism (q.v.).

His postwar poetry—in *Un brindisi* (1946; a toast), *Quaderno gotico* (1947; gothic notebook), *Primizie del deserto* (1952; first fruits of the desert), *Onore del vero* (1957; truth's honor)—all collected in the volume *Il giusto della vita* (1960; what is right in life), moves away from his early symbolism and opens itself to a more discursive style. This need to embrace a more narrative mode emerges more clearly in the collections *Nel magma* (1963; in the magma), *Dal fondo delle campagne* (1965; from the bottom of the fields), *Su fondamenti invisibili* (1971; on invisible foundations), and *Al fuoco della controversia* (1978; in the fire of the controversy)—now all included in the volume *Nell'opera del mondo* (1979; in the world's work).

The abandonment of his early Parnassian style, with its refinements, reflects a stronger urge to explore human relationships and existential conflicts and to debate moral truths. L. examines the Christian message, conveying it in images of the suffering of a harsh, wintry, snowy landscape, in a rural, precapitalistic world. But these images do not define a closed, dogmatic religion or an easy escape into metaphysics. L.'s religion presents itself as a witness of a suffering common to all people that is too often overlooked by the official philosophies and ideologies. Far from being a resigned act of isolation, his Christianity constitutes the difficult choice to live with other men, to divide a common burden, to share a violent desire to hope, even knowing that perhaps salvation may not occur in the course of human history. In this lucid acceptance of pain L. places himself, along with Eugenio Montale (q.v.), in that line of Italian cultural tradition embracing the lesson of Giacomo Leopardi's (1798–1837) poem "La ginestra" ("The Broom"). This

159

poetry is characterized by its uncompromising denunciation of every ideological attempt to simplify the harsh history of man, by its will to penetrate the contradictions and limitations of human reality without escaping into easy consolations, and by its courage to maintain a generous pessimism, open to the tragic beauty of man.

In addition to poetry, L. has written essays and other prose works, and has done several translations—of Shakespeare, Coleridge, and Racine. His critical writings give intelligent, sensitive, and elegant analyses of Italian and European literatures and disclose strong and precise cultural preferences as well as his particular concept of the function of the poet. Through them the reader can gain a greater understanding of the development and maturation of his poetic methods and philosophy.

FURTHER WORKS: *L'opium chrétien* (1938); *Un'illusione platonica* (1941); *Biografia a Ebe* (1942); *Vita e letteratura* (1943); *L'inferno e il limbo* (1949); *Studio su Mallarmé* (1952); *Aspetti della generazione napoleonica, e altri saggi* (1956); *L'idea simbolista* (1959); *Lo stile di Constant* (1962); *Trame* (1963); *Tutto in questione* (1965); *Poesia e romanzo* (1973, with Carlo Cassola); *Libro di Ipazia* (1978)

BIBLIOGRAPHY: Sampoli, M. S., "An Italian Contemporary Poet: M. L.," *IQ,* 6, 23–24 (1962), 3–20; Merry, B., "The Anti-Oracle in M. L.'s Recent Poetry," *MLR,* 68 (1973), 333–43; Craft, W., "M. L.," *BA,* 49 (1975), 33–40

GOFFREDO PALLUCCHINI

SINCLAIR LEWIS

VÄINÖ LINNA

ROBERT LOWELL

GYÖRGY LUKÁCS

MAURICE MAETERLINCK

NORMAN MAILER

MACAULAY, Rose
English novelist, essayist, and poet, b. 1 Aug. 1881, Rugby; d. 30 Oct. 1958, London

The families from whom M. was descended on both sides belonged to an interrelated intellectual complex. Between her father's teaching appointments at Rugby and Cambridge, the family spent seven years on the Mediterranean shore near Genoa, where the children lived an unceremonious free outdoor life; a "gauche tomboy" of thirteen when they returned to England, she found the life there painfully restricting. But in the intellectual atmosphere of Somerville College, Oxford, she became lively and outgoing. She studied history, specializing in the 17th c.— her lifelong favorite. Going with her family to a small university town in Wales, she found these three years an exile; her first novel, *Abbots Verney* (1906), presents what was to be her main theme: the conflict between the alert and adventurous mentality and the dull and ungenerous. From 1913 on, London and its literary life became her ambience. During World War I, after much self-questioning, she entered upon an attachment with a married man that lasted until his death in 1942. For much of her adult life she found spiritual support in the Anglican Church.

The last of M.'s twenty-two novels, *The Towers of Trebizond* (1956)—some find it her best—was published fifty years after her first. She also produced two books of verse; three books of literary criticism, including *The Writings of E. M. Forster* (1938), a friend and fellow-Cantabridgian; several books of light, satirical essays; a weekly column in *Spectator* during part of the interwar period, and other journalism; and three remarkable books combining travel and history. *They Went to Portugal* (1946) presents the experiences of a great variety of English visitors to that country during seven centuries; in *Fabled Shore* (1949) all the past of Spain is with her on a trip in 1947 around the Iberian coasts in a battered car; in *Pleasure of Ruins* (1953) she considers the fear and fascination that the world's many ruins have inspired.

Abbots Verney and her fourth novel, *The Valley Captives* (1911) illustrated the cruelty that can result from ignorance. Her second, however, *The Furnace* (1907), introduced a theme that arose from her childhood in Italy and reappeared importantly in several later novels, including *The Lee Shore* (1912): the possibility of leading a simple, generous, delighted life outside the superfluities and limiting thought of mundane society. Her wit became more sophisticated in *The Making of a Bigot* (1914), with the relentless logic of its charmingly absurd plot. The horror of the war, its numbing of sympathies, and the need to work for a negotiated armistice were the themes of the courageous *Non-Combatants and Others* (1916).

International fame came with *Potterism* (1920), which satirizes, with a carefully controlled style, the senselessness of the popular press and of gushing lady novelists. By this time M. was considered one of the leading wits of London. *Dangerous Ages* (1921), which sensitively treats the lives of several women, won the Fémina-Vie Heureuse prize, a French award given to British writers in the 1920s and 1930s. The brilliant *Told by an Idiot* (1923) presents the history of upper-middle-class England through three generations. *Orphan Island* (1924) is a comic South Seas tour de force. M.'s interest in the 17th c. produced the strong historical novel *They Were Defeated* (1932); here again, extremists at both ends defeat moderates. A similar conflict, but conceived as light comedy, is found in *Going Abroad* (1934), laid in the Spanish Basque country. *And No Man's Wit* (1940) gives a rueful retrospective of the Spanish Civil War as World War II menaces; *The World My Wilderness* (1950) shows the moral destitution at the end of World War II.

The Towers of Trebizond brings together the themes, the erudition, the depth, and the comedy of all of M.'s work. Laurie's journey takes place on two levels: on a realistic one and on one of witty fantasy, of charade. As she travels along the Turkish coast, mulling over her extramarital love affair, which has alienated her from the Church of England, a poem emerges that envisions the old Byzantine city projected as the Church transcendent, ever there but ever beyond.

FURTHER WORKS: *The Secret River* (1909); *Views and Vagabonds* (1912); *The Two Blind Countries* (1914); *What Not: A Prophetic Comedy* (1918); *Three Days* (1919); *Mystery at Geneva* (1922); *A Casual Commentary* (1925); *Catchwords and Claptrap* (1926); *Crewe Train* (1926); *Keeping Up Appearances* (1928; Am., *Daisy and Daphne*); *Staying with Relations* (1930); *Some Religious Elements in English Literature* (1931); *They Were Defeated* (1932; Am., *The Shadow Flies*); *Milton* (1934); *Personal Pleasures* (1935); *I Would Be Private* (1937); *Life among the English* (1942); *Letters to a Friend* (1961); *Last Letters to a Friend* (1962); *Letters to a Sister* (1964)

BIBLIOGRAPHY: "Miss M.'s Novels," *TLS,* 12 May 1950, 292; Annan, N., "The Intellectual Aristocracy," in Plumb, J. H., ed., *Studies in Social History* (1955), pp. 241–87; Nicolson, H., et al., "The Pleasures of Knowing R. M.," *Encounter,* March 1950, 23–31; Lockwood, W. J., "R. M.," in Hoyt, C. A., ed., *Minor British Novelists* (1967), pp. 135–56; Swinnerton, F., "R. M.," *KR,* 29 (1967), 591–608; Bensen, A. R., *R. M.* (1969); Smith, C. B., *R. M.: A Biography* (1972)

ALICE R. BENSEN

MACCAIG, Norman
Scottish poet, b. 14 Nov. 1910, Edinburgh

M., brought up in his native city, received an honors M.A. in classics from Edinburgh University. After many years of schoolteaching and having made his mark as a poet in the 1960s, he was made Fellow in Creative Writing and Lecturer in English Studies at Edinburgh University. Later he became Reader in Poetry at the University of Stirling.

Although M. is city-born and city-bred, his roots are largely elsewhere; although not a Gaelic speaker, he thinks of himself as "threequarter Gael." His poetry, he feels, was shaped by a combination of classical training and what he calls the "extreme formality" of Celtic art. In form, theme, and tone his poems are marked by restraint, and with few exceptions they do not exceed a page in length. He abstains almost entirely from the kind of Scots vocabulary cultivated by the "Lallans" poets.

His poetic world is not the public one of social commitment or indignation, nor one of strong emotions. In several poems he speaks about his own art with gentle irony, but sometimes also in self-defense or self-assertion, wanting to make it clear that he looks upon himself, not as a Blake or a Hieronymus Bosch but rather as a Breughel who takes note of "unemphatic marvels": every kind of object penetrates his vision and is made welcome.

Geographically M.'s world is restricted: the setting of his poems is either Edinburgh or (rather more frequently) the West Highlands (the exceptions are a handful of poems set in Tuscany and New York). His landscapes are either small-scaled and intimately observed, or majestic depictions of wide spaces, distant horizons, monumental hills and mountains. Few of his poems are, however, purely descriptive: a recurring pattern is for a landscape to turn into a mindscape, into an observation on the speaker's own situation. In this regard, the critic is tempted to see the influence of Robert Frost (q.v.). Often the center of interest is the poet himself; but in a number of poems it is instead other people: admired Highland characters, eccentrics, or occasionally individuals who are seen ironically or even attacked, usually because they represent pomposity or abused power. Whoever or whatever M. studies, his poems usually give impressions of the here and now; he seldom pries into roots and beginnings or explores history on a wide scale.

M.'s descriptions of animal life are sensitive yet unsentimental; they often deal with ordinary creatures: a goat, a crow, a house sparrow. Here as elsewhere, M. demonstrates his facility at metaphor making, at times rather too obtrusively. While his images are often memorable, occasionally they become a little too ingenious and the thought they convey rather too precious, particularly in the love poems, which often relate feelings of frustration, of insuperable separation, sometimes expressed in terms of physical distance.

Anthropomorphizing metaphors are numerous in M.'s verse. Objects of nature, animals, sometimes even abstractions are often portrayed as individualized human types. At times the comparison is focused on a particular physical characteristic or mental state.

Some of M.'s creative processes and devices are present in his first two volumes of verse, although he chooses to disregard them, considering them exercises in a pretentiously abstruse modernist manner. But after that—with the exception of some relapsing in his fourth collection, *The Sinai Sort* (1957)—he has stuck tenaciously to his own ideals of style and theme. He cannot be said to have developed in any striking manner. He speaks engagingly of his verse as "fairly low-falutin'." He distrusts big words, the flaunting of extreme feelings, "the fake, the inflated, the imprecise, and the dishonest." On guard against such phenomena, he can speak ironically both about himself and others; but his poems, for the most part, are celebrations of the natural dignity of people and places and expressions of an unorthodox, unsolemn credo of joy in the manifoldness of the created world.

FURTHER WORKS: *Far Cry* (1943); *The Inward Eye* (1946); *Riding Lights* (1955); *A Common Grace* (1960); *A Round of Applause* (1962); *Measures* (1965); *Surroundings* (1966); *Rings on a Tree* (1968); *A Man in My Position* (1969); *Selected Poems* (1971); *The White Bird* (1973); *The World's Room* (1974); *Tree of Strings* (1977); *Old Maps and New: Selected Poems* (1978); *The Equal Skies* (1980)

BIBLIOGRAPHY: Press, J., *Rule and Energy* (1963), pp. 172–81; special M. section, *Akros*, 3, 7 (1968), 21–47; Fulton, R., "Ishmael among the Phenomena: The Poetry of N. M.," *ScotIR*, 5, 8 (1972), 22–27 (repr. in Fulton, R., *Contemporary Scottish Poetry: Individuals and Contexts* [1974], pp. 69–87); Scott, M. J. W., "Neoclassical M.," *SSL*, 10, 3 (1973), 135–44; Porter, W. S., "The Poetry of N. M.," *Akros*, 11, 32 (1976), 37–53; Frykman, E., *"Unemphatic Marvels": A Study of N. M.'s Poetry* (1977); Keir, W., "The Poetry of N. M.," *ScotR*, No. 21 (1981), 27–32

ERIK FRYKMAN

MACDIARMID, Hugh

(pseud. of Christopher Murray Grieve) Scottish poet and essayist, b. 11 Aug. 1892, Langholm; d. 9 Sept., 1978, Edinburgh

The son of a rural postman, M. grew up in the Border region of Scotland. Although his formal education was brief, he received encouragement early from excellent teachers who recognized his talent and continued to correspond with him. After leaving school at fourteen, he supported himself as a journalist while concentrating his real interest on poetry. As an editor and publisher of his own journal (*The Scottish Chapbook,* 1922–23) and three collections of modern Scottish verse (*Northern Numbers,* 1920–22) he was a key figure in the literary and cultural movement called the Scottish Renaissance; his journalistic prose defined and supported it, and his early poetry was its greatest achievement. Both a nationalist and a communist, M. joined political activism with his interest in cultural change, serving as a town councillor and justice of the peace, helping to found the National Party of Scotland, and running for various offices. During the 1930s he lived an isolated life on Whalsey, a small island in the Shetlands. In his later years he returned to the Borders. He remained active in cultural and political affairs and traveled extensively, including trips to Russia and China.

M.'s poetry shows great technical variety, developing from brief, intense lyrics in dense Scots through long poetic sequences to increasingly long and difficult philosophical poems in English. Major themes are the dialectic nature of reality; the relationships among Scotland, self, and poetry; human aspiration toward higher consciousness; and the nature of the creative act. The personal and political concerns running through his work reflect his sense of the artist's struggle to penetrate and reveal the unknown and the social need to free all people from economic constraints. His technical experimentation focused largely on vocabulary and imagery; both show his interest in using the widest resources of sound and meaning in both Scots and English. His dominant images—the Scottish thistle, the Celtic snake, water, and stones—represent changing ways to symbolize a complex modern vision of reality.

M.'s early Scots lyrics were an experiment aimed at reviving the language. He wrote a "synthetic" Scots: by using Scots vocabulary from any time or region, he sought to assimilate into literature the full range of Scottish life. Reacting against a limited and sentimental tradition, he called for an intellectual poetry showing a mastery of style and thought. His first two volumes of poetry, *Sangschaw* (1925) and *Penny Wheep* (1926) consist primarily of brief lyrics that gain their musical and thematic effects from the sounds and significance of Scots. M. believed that the Scottish vernacular was unique in its capacity to effect swift and subtle shifts in tone and to render uncanny spiritual and pathological perceptions. In his early poems unusual images, often extremely compressed and densely packed, are joined with words chosen for their multiple significance or for their precise expression of unusual moods in order to create such effects. Characteristically assuming a stance outside ordinary experience, these poems often convey wry humor, pathos, or a startling unease through subverting conventional assumptions. Frequently moving between the cosmic and the minute, they extend the Scottish experience to the universe, while recurrent images of seas, darkness, the moon, and the night sustain the sense of being outside conventional vision. Many of these lyrics depend on rare words or complex images to effect a sudden insight or alternative mode of seeing.

M.'s interest in expressing the whole of Scottish experience led to a series of increasingly longer poems. His first and greatest long poem, *A Drunk Man Looks at the Thistle* (1926), retains early techniques. Combining intense lyrics with descriptive and philosophic passages, it carries the use of dense Scots and swift shifts of mood into an extended poetic sequence with a large and inclusive vision of life. Composed of many loosely related sections forming thematic and tonal sequences and climaxes, *A Drunk Man Looks at the Thistle* embodies M.'s commitment to join unity and diversity. Its unity derives from a single image capable of endless transformations and containing paradox and contradiction. The thistle, Scotland's national emblem, symbolizes for M. what he considers the fundamental Scottish character: a yoking of contraries and freedom in passing from one mood to another, which has been called the "Caledonian antisyzygy." The poem's key themes focus on a union of various poles of experience: life and death, evolution and decline, self and world, bestiality and beauty. Other key ideas are the struggle of

the human soul for higher vision, the poet's special burden as center of creative energy, and Scotland's need to rise above sentiment and commercial values. These themes unite in a distinctly modern statement of the nature of reality as complex, contradictory, and endlessly transformational.

In *To Circumjack Cencrastus* (1930) M. attempted to use his early techniques for a new purpose: rather than contraries and struggle he wished to express the unity underlying all change. Cencrastus, the curly snake, is the Celtic image of eternity. M. was less able, in *To Circumjack Cencrastus,* to sustain a sense of unity through a single image, but the poem indicates important changes in style and theme. His last long poem in a lyric mode, it shows M.'s increasing interest in Gaelic culture, in direct expression of ideas, and in the use of English.

In the 1930s M. moved from a consistent line of lyric development to wide-ranging experiments in style and theme. After *To Circumjack Cencrastus* several volumes of shorter pieces appeared: *First Hymn to Lenin* (1931), *Scots Unbound* (1932), *Stony Limits* (1934), and *Second Hymn to Lenin* (1935). Along with Scots lyrics in the early style, these volumes include a series of poems on his own origins in Langholm, in Dumfriesshire, explicitly political poems, and long philosophical poems in English. Many return to speculation on the nature of reality, the creative act, and the role of Scotland in history. M.'s interest in Gaelic values appears in several philosophical poems as well as translations from the Gaelic. In *Stony Limits* M. also experimented with using obscure and technical English vocabulary to express modern complexity. His most fundamental change was a shift in emphasis from sound to content. This shift parallels an increasing detachment from personal experience and emotion and a commitment to poetry of thought. After 1935 M. wrote almost no lyrics and almost nothing in Scots. His major late works include the long poem *The Kind of Poetry I Want* (1961)—sections of it had been previously published in his autobiography, *Lucky Poet* (1943)—and *In Memoriam James Joyce* (1955), which were apparently intended to be parts of a single gigantic work, *Mature Art,* never published. These pieces, which he calls "poetry of fact," contain lengthy quotations, lists of names and facts, and obscure words and references. Extended images are embedded in long discursive commentaries. They explore the nature of poetry, art, and world languages, aspiring to an encyclopedic inclusiveness of detail. Like Ezra Pound's (q.v.) *Cantos* they aim at what M. calls "opening out" and taking in more and more of reality. He continued as well to write individual pieces, such as *Dìreadh I, II, III* (1974), a group of three poems, using nature images and developing sustained ideas. Nearly all of M.'s late work, which continued to appear into the 1970s, was written in the 1930s.

In addition to original poems, M. did verse translations, edited books and journals, and wrote short stories, biographies, autobiography, and an enormous body of polemical prose. In *Lucky Poet*, an autobiography of his intellectual life, he attempted a synthesis of his vast and varied interests, chiefly Scottish nationalism, communism, language, and the nature and function of poetry. His own early poetry is influenced by traditional Scottish folk songs and ballads and John Jamieson's (1759–1838) *Etymological Dictionary of the Scottish Language* (1808). His late work is more allied with the looser rhythms and massed detail of Whitman and Pound. Other important influences, formal and intellectual, include Dostoevsky, Lev Shestov (1866–1938), Vladimir Solovyov (1853–1900), John MacLean (1879–1923), the Scots communist-nationalist, Paul Valéry, James Joyce (qq.v.), Francis George Scott (1880–1958), the Scottish composer, and Charles Doughty (1843–1926). In turn he influenced a generation of Scots poets who joined in the aims of the Scottish Renaissance, which called for a return to the pre-Robert Burns Scottish tradition of William Dunbar (1460?–1520?) and Robert Henryson (1430?–1506?), characterized by intellect, sophistication, distinctive nationality, and links with international literary trends. His influence remains in current Scottish poetry in the vernacular, and his commitment to long poems on native tradition has influenced such contemporary Irish poets as John Montague (b. 1929) and Seamus Heaney (q.v.). M.'s work compares with that of T. S. Eliot, W. B. Yeats (qq.v), and Pound as a major statement of the modern condition.

FURTHER WORKS: *Annals of the Five Senses* (1923); *Contemporary Scottish Studies* (1926; enlarged ed., 1976); *Albyn, or Scotland and the Future* (1927); *At the Sign of the Thistle* (1934); *Scottish Scene* (with L. G. Gibbon, 1934); *Scottish Eccentrics* (1936); *The Is-*

lands of Scotland (1939); A Kist of Whistles (1947); *Cunningham Graham* (1952); *Francis George Scott* (1955); *Three Hymns to Lenin* (1957); *The Battle Continues* (1957); *Burns Today and Tomorrow* (1959); *Collected Poems* (1962; rev. ed., 1967); *The Company I've Kept* (1966); *A Lap of Honour* (1967); *The Uncanny Scot* (1968); *Early Lyrics* (1968); *A Clyack-Sheaf* (1969); *Selected Essays* (1969); *More Collected Poems* (1970); *Selected Poems* (1970); *The H. M. Anthology* (1972); *A Political Speech* (1972); *Metaphysics and Poetry* (1975); *Complete Poems* (1978)

BIBLIOGRAPHY: Leavis, F. R., "H. M.," *Scrutiny,* 4 (1935), 305; Daiches, D., "M. and Scottish Poetry," *Poetry,* 72 (1948), 202–18; Scott, T., "Some Poets of the Scottish Renaissance," *Poetry,* 88 (1956), 43–47; Wittig, K., *The Scottish Tradition in Literature* (1958), pp. 281–88; Duval, K., and Smith, S. G., eds., *H. M.: A Festschrift* (1962); Buthlay, K., *H. M.* (1964); Glen, D., *H. M. and the Scottish Renaissance* (1964); National Library of Scotland, *H. M., Catalogue No. 7* (1967); special M. and Scottish poetry double issue, *Agenda,* 5, 4/6, 1 (1967–68); Glen, D., ed., *H. M.: A Critical Survey* (1972); special issue, *Akros,* 12, 34–35 (1977); Wright, G., *M.: An Illustrated Biography* (1977); special M. issue, *Chapman 22,* 5, 4 (1978); Gish, N., "An Interview with H. M.," *ConL,* 20, 2 (1979), 135–54; Boutelle, A., *Thistle and Rose: A Study of H. M.'s Poetry* (1980); Scott, P. H., and Davis, A. C., eds., *The Age of M.* (1980)

NANCY K. GISH

Such a socially effective idiom is what M. has always been looking for. He is thus related analogically, rather than linealogically, to earlier Scots poetry. The Border Ballads set out to inspire a bundle of cattle thieves to the hazards of a life of murder, robbery, and rape. The complex sonorities of Dunbar, on the other hand, were addressed to the king and his contingent noblemen. Hence the difference between these two types of verse. M.'s public is of another kind altogether. His purpose lies with "the wisest and learnedest of mankind, who have this one great gift of reason, to answer solidly or to be convinced." The people he wishes to influence are the scientists, administrators, and scholars of his time. In their hands lies the fate of the world and it is their present insensitivity to those diabolical and illogical influences, explicit only in art, that today endangers humanity. He is therefore anxious to persuade them of the finally objective importance of the aesthetic exploration. [1957]

Burns Singer, "Scarlet Eminence," in Duncan Glen, ed., *H. M.: A Critical Survey* (1972), p. 41

What M. seems to be adumbrating in *The Kind of Poetry I Want*—it is nowhere made sharp and definite—is a poetry which is highly organised in parts, but not prescriptively with regard to the whole. It is not so much an organism as a colony, a living and in one sense formless association of organisms which share a common experience. Shape and architectonics are not so important as the quick movements of the thought—the feelers in the water, moved partly by the surrounding currents and partly by their own volition and partly in response to the movement of neighbor tentacles—while a succession of images, illustrations, and analogies is presented to it. As zoologists may argue whether a colony is an organism, critics may hesitate to say that the kind of *poetry* M. wants is a kind of *poem*. A movement towards a more "open" conception of the poem than has prevailed in the modern period is however gaining ground, and I see no reason why we should deny ourselves, for love of architectonics, the ingredient and emergent pleasures of a poetry in evolution. [1962]

Edwin Morgan, "Poetry and Knowledge in M.'s Later Work," in Duncan Glen, ed., *H. M.: A Critical Survey* (1972), pp. 201–2

It is not only M.'s happy use of his native tongue and his folk song rhythms that suggest Hopkins. There is his overt expression of the "red opinions" that the Jesuit confided to a private letter. Thus, the Scotsman writes a lyric to "The Dead Liebknecht," the Spartacist victimized by the Germans, and celebrates the idol of the Russian communists in more than one hymn to Lenin. There is also M.'s evident delight in nature's wilder inscapes—trees and waters, earth and sky, the uncertain or headlong movement of a mountain stream, the moon like a weird pale crow above the spinning earth, the tough willows that never come down from their stormy moods; there is his hurrahing in the Hebridean harvest as he watches the herring fishers, when the catch swims in as if of its own accord. And there is the counterpart of Hopkins' darker humours, when sand churns in his ears, the grave of all mankind opens before him, and he groans that no man can know his own heart until life's tide uncovers it.

Babette Deutsch, *Poetry in Our Time* (1963), pp. 343–44

M. had never recognised this kind of absentee landlordism of the spirit: one of the aspects of his achievement worth stressing is the way he has got most of himself onto the page even preoccupations one may dislike. The contemplative centre we value so much in Eliot and Edwin Muir is there, but also the coarser activity, the sparks from the rim of the wheel. Pride, humour, contrariness; patriotism, hatred, nostalgia; love, lust, longing: there is no contemporary poem more varied in mood than [*A*] *Drunk Man Looks at the Thistle*. And since there is no achievement without an accompanying technique, the poem is a showpiece of M.'s early virtuosity, like [Pound's] *Hugh Selwyn Mauberley,* another poem in which a poet examines the civilisation he is involved with.

John Montague, "The Seamless Garment and the Muse," *Agenda,* 5, 4/6, 1 (1967–68), 27

When M. came back to Scotland after military service in the eastern Mediterranean and started to write (just at the point when Eliot, Pound, Joyce, and the mature Yeats were bringing out their crucial work), he set himself, deliberately, to remake a style for poetry in his country. He took words and phrases from folksong, dictionaries, and his native speech, and he also took symbols and forms from Continental writers (Dostoevsky, Rilke). Many of his earlier lyrics are exercises, he was trying out a whole gamut of styles, in the way of so many modern artists (Eliot, Picasso, Stravinsky). But his own vision starts to emerge—a very modern sense of the world as an arena of conflict, a site of organic evolution, where vital instability is a permanent condition of life and human nature, human feelings, are always mixed and ambiguous.

David Craig, "A Great Radical: H. M., 1892–1978," *Marxism Today,* 23, 2 (1979), 57

Again and again in the lyrics in *Sangschaw* (1925) and *Penny Wheep* (1926), M. suggests a multidimensional view of reality by contrasting our usual viewpoint with a God's-eye-view of the universe; this cosmic outlook simultaneously shrinks the world to socially manageable proportions and suggests the imaginative majesty of man who is capable of possessing the cosmos through creativity alone. M. used God as an instantly accessible image of a meaningful universe and avoided the theological stereotype. For example, the God of "Crowdieknowe" is no awesome patriarch but an odious observer who has to contend with the truculent force of humanity in the shape of the Langholm locals who are unwillingly resurrected. . . . The faith that the mature M. put in scientific insights was already present in the early lyrics. In "The Eemis Stane" he saw a poignancy in the spectacle of the planet earth trembling in space.... That visionary approach could be extended to almost mystical levels, but for M. even the most puzzling elements of existence still deserved a human solution.

Alan Bold, "Dr. Grieve and Mr. M.," P. H. Scott and A. C. Davis, eds., *The Age of M.* (1980), p. 46

In M.'s case it isn't simply a question of his changing his mind from time to time, though of course he has done that like everybody else, nor—in spite of some important similarities with Whitman . . . —is it a question of Whitmanesque largeness. Self-contradiction is for him a mode of poetic awareness. This fact is easily obscured if we look at his work chronologically and chart carefully the different phases in his career. If we do that we will talk of his earliest quasi-mystical poetry in English, his perfectly wrought little lyrics in Scots, and his later massively discursive poems in what might be called a lexicographical English. We will distinguish between these, and say which we prefer and why. But if we take a comprehensive, synchronistic view of M.'s work we begin to see certain kinds of unity amid all this diversity. And two things will emerge. The first is that the counterpointing of unity and diversity is central to his poetic character. And the second is that such a counterpointing is bound up with M.'s view of the nature of the Scottish literary character.

David Daiches, "H. M. and the Scottish Literary Tradition," in P. H. Scott and A. C. Davis, eds., *The Age of M.* (1980), p. 60

MACEDONIAN LITERATURE
See Yugoslav Literature

MACHADO, Antonio
Spanish poet, b. 26 July 1875, Seville; d. 22 Feb. 1939, Collioure, France

Educated at the Institution of Free Learning of Madrid, Spain's most innovative, progressive, and liberal school, where the influence of the German philosopher Karl Christian Friedrich Krause (1781–1832) was strong, M., one of Spain's greatest poets, wrote the most representative poetry of the Generation of '98. His brother Manuel (1874–1947) was also a poet. In 1909 M. married a sixteen-year-old girl, Leonor, who died three years later. In the 1920s he again sought personal

happiness and a poetic muse through Guiomar, the other great love of his life. A teacher as well as a writer, he was an ardent antifascist and supporter of the Republic. He wrote poetry about war and peace, including a moving elegy on the death of García Lorca (q.v.). He died, a victim of the civil war, in a foreign land.

Not unaware of the modernist (q.v.) innovations, M. himself utilized them only briefly, early in his career, although on deeper levels much of his poetry continued to be symbolist (q.v.) and modernist. His early poetry is often autobiographical, and he used typically Andalusian symbols like the lemon tree. In *Soledades, galerías, y otros poemas* (1907; solitudes, galleries, and other poems), an expanded edition of *Soledades* (1903; solitudes), he showed that poetry, for him, was a profoundly spiritual enterprise. Solitude, in this collection, is conveyed through a fusing of the poet's soul and the landscape, of inner and outer realities. His themes include a lack of illusion and of love, nostalgia for childhood as memory becomes the mirror of time, the stirrings of an existential anguish, and a paradoxical hope. Dream and fantasy spur on his quest for love and his lifelong search for God through time, symbolized as a fountain or flowing water, the flow of life into death.

In *Campos de Castilla* (1912; fields of Castile), which one critic called the "poetic breviary of the Generation of '98," M. is an outstanding interpreter of the Spanish soul. Based on five years he spent in the province of Soria, which represented the essential Castilian spirit for him, this volume combines images of earth and countryside with patriotic fervor. M. attempts to rouse his countrymen from their complacency as he shows a once great nation fallen on evil days. Still, the austere and melancholy Castilian landscape is symbolized by the sturdy oak; and whatever the bitterness and injustices suffered by its inhabitants, there remains a special kind of beauty. M. fuses a personal emotion with objective description, searching for love, for a metaphysical God, and for values that may no longer exist. Exploring the tragic sense of life, M. also meditates on the philosophy of Henri Bergson (q.v.).

Included in *Campos de Castilla* is "La tierra de Alvargonzález" ("The House of Alvargonzález," 1961), M.'s one great effort at the Spanish ballad form. Set in a rugged mountain area of Soria, it depicts greed, patricide and vengeance. Two older brothers, scheming and evil, resent the virtuous and loving younger brother. Eventually the assassins, unable to stay away from the scene of their father's murder, fall to their deaths. Infused with the ideas and imagery of the passing of time, dream, mystery, the supernatural, and brooding terror, the poem stresses tragic fate.

In *Nuevas canciones* (1924; new songs) M. develops the theme of love, combining the sensual and the colorful, against background images of gray olive trees, blue mountains, brown oaks, and white lightning. Expanding a series of proverbs and songs he first published in a new version of *Campos de Castilla* included in *Poesías completas* (1917; complete poetry), M. experiments with a kind of Japanese haikai form. Life is a path without guidance, and M. becomes a "perpetual sailor of the eternal earth." Love, life and death, dream and reality, and dual personality are themes of these epigrammatic and at times satirical and skeptical poems.

In addition to plays written in collaboration with his brother Manuel, M. also wrote penetrating prose memoirs: *Juan de Mairena: Sentencias, donaires, apuntes y recuerdos de un profesor apócrifo* (1936; *Juan de Mairena: Epigrams, Maxims, Memoranda, and Memoirs of an Apocryphal Professor*, 1963). The invented, "apochryphal" professor Mairena, critic and moralist, whom M. labels his "philosophical alter ego" and who died young, offers philosophy, irony, humor, poetic anguish, and an explanation of M.'s existential outlook. Mairena rejects the power of pure reason and science and examines the problem of existence and death. Skeptical but not dogmatic, Mairena and M. explore literature, truth, liberty, politics, language, and philosophic works, although they also lampoon philosophers as of little use in an "apocryphal" world. Lacking God and Christ, M. in his solitude turns to man and nature.

Portions of *Los complementarios* (1972; the complementaries), written from 1912 on, were published over a period of years, in spite of M.'s prohibition. In part a diary, which enhances his reputation as a moral and ethical man, it also contains poetry and prose of various kinds, anecdotes, political and philosophical writings, and perceptive literary criticism.

M. combined the traditional and the modern. A dreamer, he wove his poems from landscape and memory, as he explored the hidden secrets in man's soul. Called "luminous and profound" by Rubén Darío (q.v.), M. rejected verbal pyrotechnics for a spiritual search for eternity, but his poetry is delicate as well as profound. The poet yearned for immortality, but his poetry, which he defined as the "essential word in time," could not provide him with a faith in God. A good and modest man, stoical in the face of lost love and life's blows, he asserted, in spite of his resigned pessimism, the spirit and dignity of man. In sincere, simple, and evocative words, M. proclaimed: "The essence of all noble fighters is never the certainty of victory but the fervent desire to deserve it."

FURTHER WORKS: *Canciones del alto Duero* (1922); *Juan de Mañara* (1927, with Manuel M.); *Las adelfas: La Lola se va a los puertos* (1930, with Manuel M.); *La guerra* (1937); *El hombre que murió en la guerra* (1947); *Obras completas de Manuel y A. M.* (4 vols., 1947); *Cartas de A. M. a Miguel de Unamuno* (1957); *Cartas de A. M. a Juan Ramón Jiménez* (1959); *Prosas y poesías olvidadas* (1964); *Poesías completas* (1973). FURTHER VOLUMES IN ENGLISH: *Zero* (1947, bilingual); *Eighty Poems of A. M.* (1959, bilingual); selected poems in McVan, A. J., *A. M.* (1959); *Castilian Ilexes* (1963); *Still Waters of the Air* (1970); *I Go Dreaming Roads* (1973); *Sunlight and Scarlet* (1973); *Del Camino* (1974); *Selected Poems of A. M.* (1978); *The Dream below the Sun: Selected Poems of A. M.* (1981, bilingual); *Selected Poems* (1982, bilingual)

BIBLIOGRAPHY: Trend, J. B., *A. M.* (1953); Serrano Poncela, S., *A. M.: Su mundo y su obra* (1954); Zubiría, R. de, *La poesía de A. M.* (1955); McVan, A. J., *A. M.* (1959); Cobos, P. de, *Humor y pensamiento de A. M. en la metafísica poética* (1963); Tuñón de Lara, M., *A. M.: Poeta del pueblo* (1967); Sánchez Barbudo, A., *Los poemas de A. M.* (1969); Gullón, R., *Una poética para A. M.* (1970); Cobb, C. W., *A. M.* (1971); Aguirre, J. M., *A. M.: Poeta simbolista* (1973); Valverde, J. M., *A. M.* (1975); Luis, L., *A. M.: Ejemplo y lección* (1975); Schulman, I. A., "A. M. and Enrique González Martínez: A Study in Internal and External Dynamics," *JSSTC,* 4 (1976), 29–46

KESSEL SCHWARTZ

MACHAR, Josef Svatopluk

Czechoslovak poet and essayist (writing in Czech), b. 29 Feb. 1864, Kolín; d. 17 March 1942, Prague

Son of a miller's foreman, M. grew up in Prague. After abandoning the study of law, he took a clerical job at a financial institution in Vienna. While living there, he wrote for a number of Czech literary reviews and associated with progressive writers who opposed the Hapsburg regime. In 1916 he was imprisoned in Vienna—he wrote of this experience in *Kriminál* (1918; *The Jail,* 1921). Returned to Prague before the end of World War I, in 1918 he became inspector general in and cultural adviser to the newly created Czechoslovak army. An idealist and man of strong views, he gave up his post after five years, as well as some valuable friendships, including that with President T. G. Masaryk, because of numerous disagreements over both public and personal matters.

M.'s strongly argumentative personality is reflected in all his works. He represented realism in Czech poetry, and his verse is sober, terse, and factual—very different from the emotionalism and ornate verbosity of the school of Svatopluk Čech (1846–1908) and Jaroslav Vrchlický (pseud. of Emil Frída, 1853–1912). His three volumes of subjective lyrical poems, *Confiteor* (1887–92; Latin: I confess), express M.'s disillusionment after an unhappy love affair, a disillusionment that in part led to his attacks on the morals of contemporary society. Gloom also marks a number of poems in *Čtyři knihy sonetů* (1903; four books of sonnets). The political lyrics of *Tristium Vindobona* (1893; Latin: Vienna elegy) convey a nostalgia similar to that of the exiled Ovid; aware of a writer's responsibility to his nation, M. deplored flaws in the national character and inveighed against the evils in Czech public life.

Two of M.'s best volumes of poetry can be described as feminist: *Zde by měly kvést růže* (1894; roses should bloom here) contains lyrical portraits of suffering women humiliated by an insensitive, narrow-minded society; *Magdaléna* (1894; *Magdalen,* 1916), a novel in verse, subtly presents a young reformed prostitute's vain effort to rehabilitate herself in a world of provincial pharisees, political careerists, and snobbish egoists.

Golgata (1901; Golgotha), in which M. sets patriotism and religion in the context of the historical development of mankind, anticipates his magnificent cycle *Svědomím věků* (9 vols., 1906–26; the conscience of the ages). Unable to find a true ideal in the present, M. here tries to formulate the lessons man can learn from the past. Strongly influenced by Nietzsche, M. is pessimistic as he finds the aristocratic paganism of the ancient world superior to democratic, austere, and sense-suppressing Christianity. In the ancient world M. discovers his ideal of a strong personality, a fully integrated individual. One of his last important books of poetry, *Tristium Praga* (1926; Prague elegy), however, sounds a more optimistic note.

M. was also a well-known journalist, and his prose is characterized by the same sobriety, eloquence, and pugnacity as his poetry. Among his numerous prose works, *Konfese literáta* (2 vols., 1902; the confessions of a writer) is outstanding. Other important essayistic works are *Řím* (1907; Rome), a collection of polemical essays on classical antiquity, Christianity, Roman Catholicism, among other subjects; *Katolické povídky* (1901; Catholic stories), a collection of short fiction that gives vent to his strong anti-Catholic feelings; *Antika a křest'anství* (1919; the ancient world and Christianity); *Pod sluncem italským* (1918; under the Italian sun), a travel book; *Čtyřicet let s Aloisem Jiráskem* (1931; forty years with Alois Jirásek), a collection of correspondence.

A prolific writer, M. was a leading member of the important Czech literary generation of the 1890s. With his rather pessimistic, frequently satirical and polemical poetry and prose, he brought social evils to the attention of a wide public.

FURTHER WORKS: *Bez názvu* (1889); *Letní sonety* (1891); *Zimní sonety* (1892); *Jarní sonety* (1893); *Podzimní sonety* (1893); *Třetí kniha lyriky* (1892); *Pêle-mêle* (1892); *1893–96* (1897); *Boží bojovníci* (1897); *Výlet na Krym* (1900); *Knihy fejetonů I* (1901; repr. as *Za rána*, 1920); *Knihy fejetonů II* (1902; repr. as *Trofeje*, 1903, 1920); *Stará próza* (1902); *Satiricon* (1903); *Próza z let 1901–1903* (1904); *Hrst beletrie* (1905); *Vteřiny* (1905); *V záři helenského slunce* (1906); *Jed z Judey* (1906); *Próza z let 1904–1905* (1906); *Próza z r. 1906* (1907); *Veršem i prózou* (1908); *Klerikalismus mrtev!* (1910); *Krajiny, lidé a netopýři* (1910); *Barbaři* (1911); *Pohanské plameny* (1911); *Apoštolové*

(1911); *Českým životem* (1912); *Nemocnice* (1913); *Význam Volné myšlenky v českém národě* (1914); *Krůpěje* (1915); *Životem zrazeni* (1915); *Franz Josef* (1918); *O Habsburcích* (1918); *Vídeň* (1919); *Třicet roků* (1919); *Vídeňské profily* (1919); *Časové kapitoly* (1920); *Vzpomíná se . . .* (1920); *V poledne* (1921); *Oni* (1921); *On* (1921); *Krůčky dějin* (1926); *Kam to spěje?* (1926); *Na křižovatkách* (1927); *Pět roků v kasárnách* (1927); *Oni i já* (1927); *Zapomínaní i zapomenutí* (1929); *Při sklence vína* (1929); *Dvacet pohlednic z Kysiblu* (1931); *Dva výlety do historie* (1932); *Peníze* (1932); *Filmy* (1934); *Na okraj dnů* (1935); *Rozmary* (1937); *První dějství* (1939)

BIBLIOGRAPHY: Harkins, W. E., *Anthology of Czech Literature* (1953), pp. 142–44; French, A., *Czech Poetry* (1973), p. 315; Novák, A., *Czech Literature,* (1976), pp. 233–36

B. R. BRADBROOK

MACLEISH, Archibald

American poet, dramatist, and essayist, b. 7 May 1892, Glencoe, Ill.; d. 20 April 1982, Boston, Mass.

After taking degrees at Yale and at Harvard Law School, M. studied independently and wrote poetry in France (1923–28); there, Ernest Hemingway, James Joyce, and Saint-John Perse (qq.v.) became his personal friends. During the 1930s M. wrote lucid essays for *Fortune* magazine. Under Roosevelt he became Librarian of Congress (1939–44) and Assistant Secretary of State (1944–45). Following an affiliation with UNESCO (1946–49), M. taught poetry at Harvard (1949–62) and Amherst (1963–67).

Under the spell of the symbolists (q.v.), M.'s early works, such as *Streets in the Moon* (1926), are introspective and filled with archetypal patterns. Often his poems are responses to cultural giants like Shakespeare or Freud (q.v.); sometimes, to modern masters like Charles Baudelaire. Not only significant cultural achievements but also verse forms and dramatic structures find their analogues in these as well as later works; *Conquistador* (1932), winner of a Pulitzer Prize, repeats Dante's terza rima in an assonant pattern so that the *Inferno* is felt as the force behind Cortez's monumental journey through Mexico; in *The Hamlet of A. M.* (1928), in part a

reply to *The Waste Land* of T. S. Eliot (q.v.), marginal annotations to Shakespeare's play make M.'s anxieties seem recapitulations of Hamlet's.

Responding to social and political issues during the Depression and World War II, M. wrote verse any concerned adult can grasp—like "Speech to Those Who Say Comrade" (1936). He wrote radio scripts and documentary films, and in *Land of the Free—U.S.A.* (1938) photographs of disgruntled Americans are counterpointed against a poem asking if the American Dream has failed. *Freedom Is the Right to Choose* (1951) is a selection of essays answering that the "American experiment" is the very belief in the worth of mankind. The "original documents" of democracy, however, must be deciphered, restored from beneath the palimpsest of their prostitutions, argues *Frescoes for Mr. Rockefeller's City* (1933). Finally, in *Actfive, and Other Poems* (1948), the false gods are exposed: science as miracle worker, the state as a savior, crowd consciousness as a center of existence. Instead, there persists the "responsible man" of "flesh and bone."

Archetypal images and the paradigms of masterpieces also give substance to M.'s plays. Typical of his radio plays is *The Fall of the City* (1937), in which citizens are paralyzed before a huge enemy in hollow armor. *J. B.* (1958) depicts modern man as a Job who can resist all loss and yet retain his love of life. Memorable in this Pulitzer Prize-winning play is the framework: a mock quarrel between a clown and a peanut vendor, wearing God and Satan masks. *Herakles* (1967) dramatizes the plight of a scientist struggling to remain a humanist; earlier, in *Nobodaddy* (1926), M. had represented Cain as the prototype of a man wrestling against superstition, and in the long poem *Einstein* (1929) M., skillfully blending puzzlement and awe, had suggested the ultimate limitations of natural science. During the 1970s M. reiterated his central motifs: *Scratch* (1971) is a political *J. B.* and *The Great American Fourth of July Parade* (1975) is an affirmation of democracy written on the occasion of the bicentennial celebration.

Throughout his career M. regarded himself as an aesthetician. In the famous "Ars Poetica" (1926) he wrote, "A poem should not mean/But be." By 1955 (in the essay "The Proper Pose for Poetry") this symbolist stance was converted into the view that "the poem is an action, not an urn," and by 1964 (in the essay "The Gift Outright") into the concept that poetry is "a speaking voice," the embodiment of each poet's unique synthesis of body, mind, and feeling. For M., a poem therefore has a definite tone and tempo—the adagio of "Immortal Autumn" (1930), for instance, or the scherzo of "The End of the World" (1926). Whatever M.'s music, though, his central purpose is clear: to mend the breach between the ancients and the moderns, between "private worlds" and "the public world," between mankind and the "unanswering universe."

FURTHER WORKS: *Songs for a Summer's Day* (1915); *Tower of Ivory* (1917); *The Happy Marriage, and Other Poems* (1924); *The Pot of Earth* (1925); *New Found Land* (1930); *Poems, 1924–1933* (1933); *Panic* (1935); *Public Speech* (1936); *Air Raid* (1938); *America was Promises* (1939); *Union Pacific* (1939); *The Irresponsibles* (1940); *The Next Harvard* (1941); *The American Cause* (1941); *A Time to Speak* (1941); *American Opinion and the War* (1942); *A Time to Act* (1943); *Colloquy for the States* (1943); *The American Story* (1944); *Poetry and Opinion* (1950); *The Trojan Horse* (1952); *Collected Poems, 1917–1952* (1952); *This Music Crept by Me upon the Waters* (1953); *Songs for Eve* (1954); *Poetry and Journalism* (1958); *The Secret of Freedom* (1959); *Three Short Plays* (1961); *Poetry and Experience* (1961); *The Collected Poems of A. M.* (1962); *The Dialogues of A. M. and Mark Van Doren* (1964); *The Eleanor Roosevelt Story* (1965); *An Evening's Journey to Conway, Massachusetts* (1967); *The Wild Old Wicked Man, and Other Poems* (1968); *A Continuing Journey* (1968); *Champion of a Cause* (1971); *The Human Season* (1972); *New and Collected Poems, 1917–1976* (1976); *Riders on the Earth* (1978); *Six Plays* (1980)

BIBLIOGRAPHY: Waggoner, H. H., "A. M. and the Aspect of Eternity," *CE,* 4 (1943), 402–12; Sickels, E., "A. M. and American Democracy," *AL,* 15 (1943), 223–37; Beach, J. W., *Obsessive Images: Symbolism in Poetry of the 1930's and 1940's* (1960), passim; Falk, S. L., *A. M.* (1965); Goodwin, K. L., *The Influence of Ezra Pound* (1967), pp. 175–83 and passim; Gianakaris, C. J., "M.'s *Herakles:* Myth for the Modern World," *CentR,* 15 (1971), 445–63; Smith, G., *A. M.* (1971)

BEN MCKULIK

MACLENNAN, Hugh

Canadian novelist and essayist, b. 20 March 1907, Cape Breton Island, N.S.

After a Scots-Presbyterian upbringing, M. studied at Dalhousie University, where he excelled in classics. He received graduate degrees at Oxford University and at Princeton University. Since he joined the McGill University faculty in 1951, teaching and writing have been the chief activities of an outwardly uneventful life. Widely read abroad, M. is not without recognition in Canada, where he has won several awards for his contributions to Canadian literature.

Set in Halifax during World War I, M.'s first novel, *Barometer Rising* (1941), deals with the disastrous explosion in the harbor of a munitions ship bound for the European theater of war. Revelations in the lives of M.'s symbolic characters coincide with this watershed event in the emergence of Canadian nationhood. It dramatizes the need for a national identity that includes an independent, mediating role in international affairs. Several elements of the novel were to become characteristic of M.'s art: the well-realized sense of place, the echoes of Greek myth that reverberate behind the narrative, and the somewhat contrived plot.

Two Solitudes (1945) deals with the uneasy coexistence of French and English Canada, the two solitudes of the title. Up to the death of wise old Athanase Tallard, the seigneur who typifies the French Canadian, the epic story is masterfully told, recalling Hardy (q.v.) and Balzac at their best. The second part, however, suffers from characters that are more symbolic than real and from the intrusion of M.'s views on war, social change, and the impact of other cultures on Canada. Perhaps the most remarkable quality of the book lies in its overarching historical and geographical imagination.

The setting of *Each Man's Son* (1951) is a coal-mining town on Cape Breton Island, M.'s birthplace. Departing from the sweeping concerns of previous novels, M. minutely examines the relationship between a doctor and the young boy whose life he wishes to shape. Beyond the question of willful manipulation of one personality by another, the book has much to say about the lingering effects of puritanism on Canada. In craftsmanship *Each Man's Son* marks a considerable advance. The technique of telling the story as filtered through the consciousness of several characters no longer impairs overall unity, while character and situation are handled with a new deftness and assurance.

The Return of the Sphinx (1967) continues the story of *Each Man's Son.* In the polarized 1960s, though, the solution to the French-English dilemma envisioned in *Two Solitudes,* an ethnic pluralism based on mutual respect and protection of differences, seems an impossibility. After several ultimately optimistic books on Canada's problems, M. suggested here that Canada is under a curse that renders its future enigmatic. A novel of its time, *The Return of the Sphinx* skillfully weaves cogitation on the forces of history with fictional episodes illustrating the manifestations of such forces. Such are the gulfs separating parents from children and those separating the generation of the Great Depression from the post-World War II generation.

In his four volumes of collected essays, M. frequently elaborates on such matters as the Canadian identity problem, the prospects for revitalizing society through Christianity, the relationship between Canada and the U.S., and the transcending question of purpose in life. Undistracted by the need to invent fictional vehicles for thought, M. is often more cogently persuasive in his essays.

Despite their conservative and occasionally uncertain technique, M.'s novels as a whole constitute an impressive achievement. He has pointed a new direction for Canadian fiction through his original treatment of Canadian themes and his attempt to define the moral and ideological dimensions of the Canadian mind.

FURTHER WORKS: *Oxyrhynchus: An Economic and Social Study* (1935); *The Precipice* (1948); *Cross Country* (1949); *Thirty and Three* (1955); *The Watch That Ends the Night* (1959); *Scotchman's Return, and Other Essays* (1961); *Seven Rivers of Canada* (1961; expanded ed., *Rivers of Canada,* 1974); *The Colour of Canada* (1967); *The Other Side of H. M.: Selected Essays Old and New* (1978); *Voices in Time* (1980)

BIBLIOGRAPHY: McPherson, H., "The Novels of H. M.," *QQ,* 60 (1953–54), 186–98; Wilson, E., *O Canada* (1965), pp. 59–80; Buitenhuis, P., *H. M.* (1969); Morley, P., *The Immoral Moralists: H. M. and Leonard Cohen* (1972); Mathews, R., "H. M.: The Nationalist Dilemma in Canada," *SCL,* 1 (1976), 49–63; Staines, D., "Mapping the Terrain," *Mosaic,* 11 (1978), 137–51; Cameron, E., *H. M.: A Writer's Life* (1981)

JOHN H. FERRES

MACNEICE, Louis

Anglo-Irish poet, radio dramatist, critic, and novelist, b. 12 Sept. 1907, Belfast, Northern Ireland; d. 3 Sept. 1963, London

Son of a bishop of the Anglican Church, M. early established his special affinity for pivotal groups of friends. At Sherbourne Preparatory School in Dorset and Marlborough College in Wiltshire, his first small group of intimates included the future poets Bernard Spencer (1909–1963) and John Betjeman (b. 1906). At Merton College, Oxford, where he excelled in classics and philosophy, he added Stephen Spender and W. H. Auden (qq.v.) to his circle.

The chronology of M.'s poetry reflects the international currents of his era; the budding, then disillusioned liberalism of his personal experience tends to mirror the rather repentant liberalism of the 1940s. His association with other poets caused him to be labeled a member of the group, yet he fulfilled his early promise and became a distinctively original writer.

M. was coeditor with Stephen Spender of *Oxford Poetry: 1929.* His first volume, *Blind Fireworks,* appeared in the same year; it displayed the philosophic bent of his mind and the wit of his expression. More surprisingly, the poems "Neurotics" and "Middle Age" describe a moribund culture at the moment of its death throes with a witty bathos rather than with pathos.

Poems (1935) appeared after he had become a "junior member of the Auden-Isherwood-Spender literary axis" and before he had visited Iceland with Auden—see *Letters from Iceland* (1937). With C. Day Lewis (q.v.) in place of Christopher Isherwood (q.v.), these four young British poets, grouped by the critics as the "Proletarian Poets," predicted the doom of contemporary culture, in a breezy manner set to jazz tunes. But hardly had he become a member of the left-of-center proletarian poets (all themselves upper-class) than Barcelona was bombed (December 7, 1937), and he confessed in *Autumn Journal* (1939) that vague, diffuse good will would be ineffectual against the screaming radio voices of Mussolini and

Hitler. At the outbreak of World War II he volunteered for the Royal Navy but was rejected because of poor eyesight, and instead served as a London fire watcher. In 1941 he began writing radio dramas for the BBC, continuing his services as a scriptwriter and producer for fourteen years.

The Dark Tower, and Other Radio Scripts (1947) and *Persons from Porlock, and Other Plays for Radio* (1969) contain the best of his verse plays—which were often produced with stunning casts, including Laurence Olivier, and with music by Benjamin Britten or William Walton. M. defended radio verse drama by the claim that, since poetry began with Homeric bards and Icelandic skalds shouting over banqueting guests, squalling babies, fighting dogs, and snoring oldsters, it could triumph over the interruptions of radio transmission.

M.'s sense of the failure of liberalism led inevitably to *The Last Ditch* (1940). Thus, when, in *Plant and Phantom* (1941) he attacks monism, the intellectual argument has the emotional overtone of despair of any attempt at establishing an orderly world. In *Springboard* (1945) he frankly describes the prewar liberal as a kind of ethical "Bottleneck," so high-minded he will fight only for pure motives. *Holes in the Sky: Poems 1944–1947* (1948) shows the poet caught in the straitjacket of an improvisational style suitable for stating the old social criticisms with tongue in cheek but inadequate for new themes.

Ten Burnt Offerings (1952) contains the best writing of the mature, reflective M. Longer, structurally more complex, more substantial in theme than his earlier work, and often religious in topic and tone, these poems are also richer and more deeply moving than the old flippant ditties. This and the last two volumes published in his lifetime are often marked by mystical vision. The final seven poems of *Visitations* (1958) practice the "immediate experience of mystery." *Solstices* (1961), taking its title from the semiannual points at which the sun is farthest from the celestial equator, represents the cyclical motion of M.'s career: classical scholar, teacher of Greek, very modern poet of social and political satire, prolific writer of radio plays, and then, at the end, once again back to the classics.

The Burning Perch, published posthumously in 1963, is the most eschatological of M.'s poetry. The bird flutters on a burning perch. Is it only supreme egotism that shrilly demands the world's attention to its midget dilemma? Clearly the budgerigar represents a world on fire with no place to escape. But in the final poem, "Memoranda to Horace," M. reveals his sense of literary kinship to the classical poet's polished style of sophisticated satire, moving like Horace in "court circles" and yet maintaining his independence of thought.

FURTHER WORKS: *Roundabout Way* (1932, under pseud. Louis Malone); *The "Agamemnon" of Aeschylus* (1936; tr. from Greek); *Out of the Picture: A Play in Two Acts* (1938); *Zoo* (1938); *The Earth Compels: Poems* (1938); *I Crossed the Minch* (1938); *Modern Poetry: A Personal Essay* (1938); *Selected Poems* (1940); *The Poetry of W. B. Yeats* (1941); *Christopher Columbus: A Radio Play* (1944); *Springboard: Poems 1941–1944* (1944); *Collected Poems: 1925–1948* (1949); *Goethe's Faust* (1951; tr. with Ernst Stahl); *Autumn Sequel* (1954); *Traitors in Our Way* (1957); *Eighty-five Poems* (1959); *Astrology* (1964); *The Mad Islands and The Administrator* (1964); *Varieties of Parable* (1965); *The Strings Are False: An Unfinished Autobiography* (1965); *Collected Poems* (1966); *One for the Grave: A Modern Morality Play* (1968)

BIBLIOGRAPHY: Spender, S., "Songs of an Unsung Classicist," *SatR,* 7 Sept. 1963, 25–33; Auden, W. H., "L. M.: 1907–1963," *Listener,* 24 Oct. 1963, 646; Smith, E. E., *L. M.* (1970); McKinnon, W. T., *Apollo's Blended Dream: A Study of the Poetry of L. M.* (1971); Moore, D. B., *The Poetry of L. M.* (1972); Brown, T., *L. M.: Sceptical Vision* (1975); Coulton, B., *L. M. in the BBC* (1980)

ELTON E. SMITH

MADAGASCAR LITERATURE
See Malagasy Literature

MAETERLINCK, Maurice
Belgian dramatist, poet, and essayist (writing in French), b. 29 Aug. 1862, Ghent; d. 6 May 1949, Nice, France

After earning a law degree in 1885, M. went to Paris, where he became familiar with the poetry of Verlaine, Rimbaud, Villiers de l'Isle Adam, and Mallarmé. M.'s long liaison with the actress-singer Georgette Leblanc was followed by his marriage to Renée Dahon (1919). He won the Nobel Prize for literature in 1911.

M.'s collection of poems *Serres chaudes* (1889; hothouses) showed his affinity to symbolism (q.v.): repetition of words, images, and sonorities; protracted silences; imperceptible tonal nuances ushering in soul-scapes tinged with discord; variety of color ranges; and a dreamy ambience broken by the intrusion of aggressive feelings.

M.'s early plays brought symbolism into the theater and can be considered precursors of modern avant-garde drama. Language, setting, lighting, and gesture flow into one central image. Their impact has a cumulative effect on the audience: the nuances and emotions become painful, until the weight of the experience becomes almost unbearable. The exteriorization of the protagonists' moods and feelings is effected by their physical demeanor and by the incantatory quality of their speech. M.'s dialogue relies heavily on repetition of sounds and phrases that frequently take on the power of a litany; the original function of language—its supernatural and religious characteristics—is thus revived. Gone are the platitudes and banalities of everyday speech. Words are no longer used in their habitual sense but usher in a world of magic, arousing a multitude of associations and sensations that act and react viscerally upon the onlooker—not by brash or obvious means, but rather by imposed restraints, nuances, and subtleties.

La princesse Maleine (1889; *Princess Maleine*, 1894), which Octave Mirbeau (1850–1917) called a masterpiece, is a symbolic drama incarnating the worlds of nightmare and joy. Its themes are the inexorable march of fate and man's feeble attempt to circumvent destined misfortunes; it is also a dramatic fairy tale, and as such it permitted M. to inject a sense of timelessness into the characters.

L'intruse (1890; *The Intruder*, 1894), a play about death, is constructed almost exclusively on inner states. The actors remain virtually immobile throughout the performance; their gestures, pared down to the barest suggestions of movement, underscore by their restraint the mounting terror of the situation. The dialogue is sparse, taking on at times the solemnity of a religious chant. Divested of personal elements, the characters

take on mythical qualities. They flay each other on stage in the subtlest of ways, compelled to do so by some invisible network of fatal forces.

Les aveugles (1890; *The Blind*, 1894) is metaphysical in dimension and dramatizes what psychologists call the "dying complex." A sense of isolation, loneliness, and fear pervades the atmosphere. With no real plot, its strength and beauty lie in its concise language, economy of gesture, and emotional restraint. Suspense consists in waiting; in this sense it may be likened in theme to Beckett's (q.v.) *Waiting for Godot*.

For M., as for Emerson, whose influence upon him was great, the poet is a superior being, a "representative" man: intuitive, inspired, and imaginative. Through his art, the poet gives form to the realities experienced in his unconscious and to the spiritual forces discovered within his depths. Influenced also by Plato, Swedenborg, and the medieval Flemish mystic Jan van Ruysbroeck (1293–1381), whose *The Adornment of the Spiritual Marriage* M. translated (1891), M. suggested that the world was to be perceived not through the intellect but through the senses. It was man's obligation to ascend the spiritual ladder, from sightlessness to illumination and from constriction of the soul to its liberation.

Pelléas et Mélisande (1892; *Pelléas and Mélisande*, 1894), M.'s greatest theatrical success, was first staged by Lugné-Poë in an innovative production that emphasized the play's dreaminess and mystery. Its central theme is the birth and burgeoning of love and the destruction of the protagonists by passion. The fairy-tale structure, with its obstacles, its inexplicable appearances and disappearances, its unaccountable dangers, and its concern with fate and death, was the perfect vehicle for this symbolic drama.

M. wrote three plays for marionettes, having been drawn to this form by the ambiguity and mystery of these wooden creatures—their simultaneous helplessness and power, their archetypal and collective nature: *Alladine et Palomides* (1894; *Alladine and Palomides*, 1896), *Intérieur* (1894; *Interior*, 1899), and *La mort de Tintagiles* (1894; *The Death of Tintagiles*, 1896).

M.'s plays henceforth became more conventional and realistic: *Aglavaine et Sélysette* (1896; *Aglavaine and Selysette*, 1897), in which love becomes an instrument of destruction; *Ariane et Barbe-Bleu* (1901; *Ariad-*

ne and Barbe-Bleu, 1901), a feminist play; *Monna Vanna* (1902; *Monna Vanna,* 1903), a play set in the 15th c. about self-sacrifice as a regenerative force; and *Marie Magdaleine* (1909; *Mary Magdalene,* 1910), a liturgical drama.

L'oiseau bleu (1909; *The Blue Bird,* 1909), first performed in Moscow (1907) and then in Paris (1911), was an enormous success. The play dramatizes a creation myth—the spiritual awakening of children—and reveals M.'s preoccupation with theosophy and the unconscious.

A philosopher and mystic, M. wrote essays that reflect his profound understanding of the mysteries of matter and the need of modern man for unfathomable domains in his overly scientific, mechanized, and industrial society. *Le trésor des humbles* (1896; *The Treasure of the Humble,* 1897) is a metaphysical inquiry into themes such as the value of silence and secrecy as being essential to the well-being of the soul. *La vie des abeilles* (1901; *The Life of the Bee,* 1901) draws parallels between the bee and man; each bee carries out his precise function in terms of the evolution of the group. *La vie des termites* (1926; *The Life of the White Ant,* 1927) is a very pessimistic work: M. compares man's future existence with that of the termite, who inhabits a world of darkness, feeds on its own dejecta and dead, and lives in a collective and utilitarian society.

To the extent that M.'s plays are based on symbols, gestures, and ritual they may be considered precursors of the Theater of the Absurd (q.v.). Like Antonin Artaud (q.v.), M. looked upon theater as a sacred ceremony. His dialogue, like Samuel Beckett's (q.v.), is stripped to its essentials, pared of its conventional meanings. In his mystical writings too he anticipated a trend of the later 20th c.: the need for the mysterious and religious in a technological world.

FURTHER WORKS: *Les sept princesses* (1891; *The Seven Princesses,* 1894); *Douze chansons* (1896); *La sagesse et la destinée* (1898; *Wisdom and Destiny,* 1898); *Sœur Béatrice* (1901; *Sister Beatrice,* 1901); *Le temple enseveli* (1902; *The Buried Temple,* 1902); *Joyzelle* (1903; *Joyzelle,* 1906); *Le double jardin* (1904; *The Double Garden,* 1904); *L'intelligence des fleurs* (1907; *The Intelligence of the Flowers,* 1907); *La mort* (1913; *Death,* 1911); *L'hôte inconnu* (pub. 1917; *The Unknown Guest,* 1914); *Deux contes* (1918); *Le*

bourgmestre de Stilmonde (1918; *The Burgomaster of Stilemonde,* 1918); *Les fiançailles* (pub. 1922; *The Betrothal,* 1918); *Le miracle de Saint-Antoine* (pub. 1919; *A Miracle of St. Anthony,* 1917); *Le grand secret* (1921; *The Great Secret,* 1922); *Le malheur passe* (pub. 1925; *The Cloud That Lifted,* 1923); *La puissance des morts* (pub. 1926; *The Power of the Dead,* 1923); *Marie Victoire* (1927); *La vie de l'espace* (1927; *The Life of Space,* 1928); *Juda de Kérioth* (1929); *La grande féerie* (1929); *La vie des fourmis* (1930; *The Life of the Ant,* 1930); *Avant le grand silence* (1934; *Before the Great Silence,* 1935); *Devant Dieu* (1934); *Princesse Isabelle* (1935); *La grande porte* (1939); *L'autre monde* (1942; *The Great Beyond,* 1947); *Bulles bleues, souvenirs heureux* (1948); *Jeanne d'Arc* (1948); *Théâtre inédit I* (1959). FURTHER VOLUMES IN ENGLISH: *Old Fashioned Flowers, and Other Open-Air Essays* (1905); *Chrysanthemums, and Other Essays* (1907); *Life and Flowers* (1907); *The Measures of the Hours* (1907); *The Inner Beauty* (1910); *On Emerson, and Other Essays* (1912); *Hours of Gladness* (1912); *News of Spring, and Other Nature Studies* (1913); *Our Eternity* (1913); *Poems* (1915); *The Wrack of the Storm* (1916); *The Light Beyond* (1917); *Mountain Paths* (1919); *Ancient Egypt* (1925); *The Magic of the Stars* (1930); *The Supreme Law* (1934); *Pigeons and Spiders; The Water Spider; The Life of the Pigeon* (1935); *The Hour Glass* (1936)

BIBLIOGRAPHY: Harry, G., *M. M.* (1910); Bithell, J., *Life and Writings of M. M.* (1913); Taylor, U., *M. M.* (1914); Halls, W. D., *M. M.: A Study of His Life and Thought* (1960); Donneux, G., *M. M.* (1961); Postic, M., *M. M. et le symbolisme* (1970); Knapp, B. L., *M. M.* (1975); Valency, M., *The End of the World: An Introduction to Contemporary Drama* (1980), pp. 62–83

BETTINA L. KNAPP

MAGDALENO, Mauricio

Mexican novelist, short-story writer, dramatist, essayist, and critic, b. 13 May 1906, Villa del Refugio

M. developed emotionally and matured intellectually during the violence-ridden period of the Mexican revolution, an epochal upheaval that was to influence much of his literary production. The years he spent in Spain in

175

the early 1930s sharpened his critical acumen and tempered his nationalism with cosmopolitan cultural assimilations, evident in collections of essays such as *Vida y poesía* (1936; life and poetry) and *Tierra y viento* (1948; land and wind). Back from Spain in 1934, M. cofounded the important theatrical group Today's Theater, which presented social dramas. Since that time he has concentrated primarily on fiction and the essay.

M.'s masterpiece, and the best Mexican novel of the 1930s, is *El resplandor* (1937; *Sunburst,* 1944), the action of which, although set in the 1920s, reflects the revolutionary fervor of the Cárdenas regime (1934–40). The collective protagonist is an impoverished Otomí Indian community exploited by corrupt politicians and generations of wealthy landowners. Departing from the usual straightforward style and linear structure of his Mexican contemporaries, M. presents flashbacks into the remote past, which serve to explain the present-day situation, and uses innovative techniques such as stream of consciousness (q.v.) and dream sequences, which broaden both the aesthetic and psychological dimensions of the novel. The cyclical recurrence of hope, betrayal, and violence in the lives of the Indians not only underscores the social protest theme but also suggests a pessimistic view of the historical process. Although *El resplandor* is occasionally marred by verbose descriptions and tendentious rhetoric, it effectively dramatizes the failure of the revolution to integrate the oppressed Indian into the mainstream of Mexican society.

Cabello de Elote (1949; Blondie) depicts a Mexican town on the eve of and during World War II. The protagonist of this popular novel is a blonde mestiza whose Indian heritage frustrates her attempts to attain the social prestige she so ardently desires. M. adroitly utilizes contrasting montage structures and surrealistic probes of the subconscious in order to highlight racial dichotomies and capture the confusion of a rapidly evolving society. Aesthetic cohesion and dramatic impact suffer, however, because the proliferation of characters and events, although not without interest, obscures the psychological development of the central figure.

M. stands out as an innovative regionalist whose works reflect a profound understanding of modern Mexico and an intuitive insight into the universal human experience.

FURTHER WORKS: *Mapimí 37* (1927); *Teatro revolucionario mexicano: Pánuco 137, Emiliano Zapata, Trópico* (1933); *Campo Celis* (1935); *Concha Bretón* (1936); *Rango* (1941); *Sonata* (1941); *La tierra grande* (1949); *El ardiente verano* (1954); *Ritual del año* (1955); *Las palabras perdidas* (1956); *El compromiso de las letras* (1958); *La voz y el eco* (1964); *Retórica de la Revolución* (1978); *Escritores extranjeros en la Revolución* (1979)

BIBLIOGRAPHY: Stanton, R., "The Realism of M. M.," *Hispania* 24 (1939), 345–53; Morton, F. R., *Los novelistas de la Revolución mexicana* (1949), pp. 207–13; Brushwood, J. S., *Mexico in Its Novel* (1966), pp. 19–21, 217–18; Carter, B. G., "*El resplandor* de M.: Su estructura clásica," *Revista mexicana de cultura,* 25 Feb. 1968, 1–2; Sommers, J., *After the Storm: Landmarks of the Modern Mexican Novel* (1968), pp. 23–33; Parle, D. J., "Las funciones del tiempo en la estructura de *El resplandor* de M.," *Hispania,* 63 (1980), 58–68

BOYD G. CARTER

MAGIC REALISM

"Magic realism" does not refer to a specific literary movement or period of modern Western literature. Long before Spanish American critics began labeling the prose works of certain authors as magic realist, there was a coalescence of diverse cultural perspectives and conceptions in Latin America which foreshadowed the invention and use of this literary expression. The modern perception of the reality found in Latin America was the result of a unique fusion of the beliefs and superstitions of different cultural groups that included the Hispanic conqueror, his *criollo* (creole) descendants, the native peoples, and the African slaves. The shared experiences of each one of these groups colored the accounts of America's discovery and colonization by both native and European chroniclers. In addition to his erroneous preconceptions and utopian images of the New World, the European chronicler often patterned his narrative on the *Libros de caballerías* (books of chivalry), which related fantastic and incredible feats realized by fictional heroes. Little distinction was made between fact and fiction within the traditions of European Renaissance historiography and rhetoric. By relying on the oral storytelling traditions of their ancestors' fables and myths as the primary source for their history, the native chroniclers also combined truth and fantasy. Today, many critics often note that magic realism, like myth, also provides an essentially synthetic or totalizing way of depicting reality.

Franz Roh (1890–1965), a German art critic, first mentioned magic realism in his book *Nach Expressionismus: Magischer Realismus: Probleme der neusten europäischen Malerei* (1925; after expressionism: magic realism: problems of the newest European painting), which was partially translated into Spanish in 1927 and appeared in Ortega y Gasset's (q.v.) journal, *Revista de Occidente.* Although Massimo Bontempelli (q.v.) and others around the Italian journal *'900* also advocated a "magic realism," the term never found general favor among European critics and was soon discarded. In Roh's original conception, magic realism was considered to be synonymous with postexpressionist painting (1920–25), which was thought to be magical because it revealed the mysterious elements hidden in everyday reality. Even when applied to literature, magic realism never signified for Roh the mixture of fantasy and reality. It was firmly grounded in daily reality and expressed man's astonishment before the wonders of the real world.

The Venezuelan writer Arturo Uslar Pietri (q.v.) was the first Latin American to speak of magic realism, but he did not mention Roh in his book, *Hombres y letras de Venezuela* (1948; men and letters of Venezuela). His use of the term essentially agreed with Roh's formulation and was applied to a few Venezuelan short stories that contained strange characters and themes based on real life situations and were written in a poetic prose style. Soon afterward, the Cuban writer Alejo Carpentier (q.v.) talked about "marvelous American reality" in the prologue to his novel *El reino de este mundo* (1949; *The Kingdom of This World,* 1957). Carpentier emphasized the importance of the American cultural experience and history in his notion of "marvelous American reality." Later, in *Tientos y diferencias* (1964; touches and differences), Carpentier had to concede that the marvelous aspects of reality were not limited to America. Carpentier criticized surrealism

(q.v.) as an artificial invention of a reality that already contained many intrinsic marvels of its own. He conceived "marvelous American reality" as a moment of awareness akin to poetic epiphany and based on a faith in the miraculous that allowed the writer to convey to his readers through the characters a vision of the fantastic features of reality. The conceptions of magic realism posited by Carpentier and Uslar Pietri corresponded to a transitory phase of their own fiction and critical theories of the narrative art.

The critic Ángel Flores (b. 1900) popularized the term among critics in a famous essay "Magical Realism in Spanish American Fiction" (1955). He widened the scope of its original meaning and applied it to a very diverse group of writers, which included Jorge Luis Borges and Miguel Ángel Asturias (qq.v.). Magic realism was simplified to mean an amalgam of the real and the fantastic. The Mexican critic Luis Leal (b. 1907) posed some objections to Flores's definition of magic realism and returned to Roh's original conception by stressing that the phrase meant an attitude toward reality in which the poetic or mysterious facets of daily life stood out and all fantastic elements were excluded. Many critics now consider Uslar Pietri, Carpentier, and Asturias as the initial theoreticians and exponents of magic realism because of their common insistence on its mimetic and regionalist aspects.

Although the concept of magic realism has been extended to some younger writers such as the Colombian Gabriel García Márquez and the Mexican Juan Rulfo (qq.v.), lately, its ambivalence and inexactness have been attacked by a score of critics who favor replacing it with a more precise exegetical term. Some view magic realism as a technique for creating or inventing a fantasy that is made to appear verisimilar. This view in turn implies a relativist concept of the real that can be distorted or manipulated through shifts in the narrative point of view. Here, the tradional emphasis on mimesis in magic realism is replaced by genesis or the artistic re-creation of reality. Virtually all critics now agree that magic realism constitutes a narrative tendency that is distinct and separate from fantastic literature. Many would also agree that magic realism is a thematic rather than a structural term because its usefulness for literary analysis is so imprecise. For some critics magic realism has been construed as a cultural or ontological view of reality that Latin Americans readily accepted while they sought autonomy from European prose models in the first half of the 20th c.

BIBLIOGRAPHY: Ben-Ur, L. E., "El realismo mágico en la crítica hispanoamericana," *JSSTC,* 4 (1976), 149–63; Flores, Á., "Magical Realism in Spanish American Fiction," *Hispania,* 38 (1955), 187–92; Leal, L., "El realismo mágico en la literatura hispanoamericana," *CA,* 153 (1967), 230–35; Merrell, F., "The Ideal World in Search of Its Reference: An Inquiry into the Underlying Nature of Magical Realism," *Chasqui,* 4 (1975), 5–17; Yates, D. A., ed., *Fantasía y realismo mágico en Iberoamérica* (1975)

JAMES J. ALSTRUM

MAHFŪZ, Najīb

Egyptian novelist and short-story writer, b. 11 Dec. 1911, Cairo

M. is the Arab world's most famous novelist, and he has also made contributions to the short story and drama. Born in Cairo, he has spent his entire life in Egypt, much of it as a civil servant within the cultural sector. At the University of Cairo M. studied philosophy, and it was while he was contemplating entering a graduate degree program that he began to write the series of short stories that appeared in his first collection, *Hams al-junūn* (1939; whisper of madness).

The stories in this earliest collection show clearly what has remained one of M.'s principal concerns: the individual and the question of the nature of the absurd. Following this volume however, M. pursued an earlier interest in the history of ancient Egypt by writing three novels set in that period and even made plans for a whole series of such works. It is the immense gain of the modern Arabic novel that he changed his mind and turned his attention to the circumstances of his own contemporaries within the older quarters of Cairo itself. The series of novels that appeared during the late 1940s and early 1950s demonstrated the maturity of the realistic novel in Arabic literature. This was a period of tremendous political unrest in Egypt, with terrorism and assassination being clear signs of the social turmoil preceding the revolution of 1952. M.'s novels succeed in capturing the

atmosphere of these times, and no more brilliantly than in *Zuqāq al-Midaqq* (1947; *Midaq Alley,* 1966), *Al-Qāhira al-jadīda* (1946; modern Cairo), and *Bidāya wa nihāya* (1951?; beginning and end). This series of novels was to culminate in a huge project that took M. five years to complete, the monumental *Al-Thulāthiyya* (1956–57; the trilogy), consisting of three novels, *Bayn al-Qasrayn* (1956), *Qasr al-Shawq* (1956), and *Al-Sukkariyya* (1957), each named after a different quarter of Cairo. This huge work of over fifteen hundred pages presents three generations of the family of 'Abd al-Jawwād, seen during the period 1917–44. As the narrative moves from one part of Cairo to another, we witness through the infinite care and subtlety that M. applies to his task the way in which this family is a microcosm of the forces of change within Egyptian society as a whole.

M. has said that this work was completed just before the 1952 revolution, in which King Farouk was overthrown, and that he was uncertain about publishing it until the nature of the revolution itself was clearer. The publication of *Al-Thulāthiyya* brought him instant fame and the State Prize for Literature. In 1959 the newspaper *Al-Ahrām* serialized his most controversial work, *Awlād hāratinā* (*Children of Gebelawi,* 1981), which caused a sufficient outcry among the conservative religious establishment to prevent its publication in book form in Egypt (it was published in Lebanon in 1967). An allegory concerning the development of the great religions and man's attitude to them, it surveys the careers of Adam, Moses, Jesus, and Muhammad before posing in the fifth section the question of the relationship between science and religion, strongly implying that the former has destroyed the latter. While this work was satisfyingly controversial, it was not a success from a literary point of view: the level of allegory was too inconsistent and the major purpose of the entire work—to suggest that science might be the cause of the destruction of religion—was too obvious.

During the 1960s M. wrote another series of novels in which he is more concerned with the individual in society than he was in his earlier work. Descriptions are more economical than previously, the symbolism is more pronounced, and there is much use of interior monologue and stream of consciousness (q.v.). Outstanding among these works are

Al-Liss wa al-kilāb (1961; the thief and the dogs), with its scarcely veiled criticism of the fair-weather socialists and opportunists within society; and *Tharthara fawq al-Nīl* (1966; chatter on the Nile), in which a houseboat symbolizing Egypt itself is the setting for the meetings of a group of intellectuals and artists who have retreated from society because they feel that they have no role to play. The final novel in this series, *Mīrāmār* (1966; *Miramar,* 1978), is a yet franker exposé of corruption in the public sector of Egypt, but the kind of exploitation that M. describes seems insignificant in the wake of the circumstances surrounding the defeat by Israel in the 1967 Six-Day War.

Following this disaster, M. addressed himself to the issue of civic responsibility and the maintenance of values in a series of lengthy short stories, often cyclical in form, which were published in collections between 1967 and 1971. The publication of his novels had been interpersed previously with a few short-story collections, of which *Dunyā Allāh* (1963; God's world) and *Khamārat al-Qitt al-Aswad* (1968; Black Cat Tavern), contain some of the best examples of M.'s contributions to this genre.

In 1971 M. surveyed the course of his career and the intellectual life of Egypt in the first half of this century in a work entitled *Al-Marāyā* (1972; *Mirrors,* 1977), purportedly a series of fifty-five vignettes but actually a commentary on education, morals, religion, international relations, and a whole host of other topics. Since then, M. has written a number of other novels, of which the most famous, *Al-Karnak* (1974; Karnak Café), paints a gruesome picture of the methods of the secret police against various opposition groups during the 1960s.

M.'s style has changed relatively little during the course of his career, and his vocabulary is quite small in comparison with some other writers of fiction in the Arab world today. His mastery of the use of language to create scene and mood, more expansive in his realistic period, more economical and symbolic during the 1960s, is complete, and has allowed him to create some memorable pages of Arabic fiction. His total oeuvre is vast, and not all his works are of equal quality, particularly his more recent novels. When the history of 20th-c. Arabic fiction comes to be written, however, he will undoubtedly be regarded as the first Arab novelist to bring

full mastery to the genre and to produce works of world stature.

FURTHER WORKS: *'Abath al-aqdār* (1939); *Radūbīs* (1943); *Kifāh Tībā* (1944); *Khān al-Khalīlī* (1946); *Al-Sarāb* (1948); *Al-Summān wa al-kharīf* (1962); *Al-Tarīq* (1964); *Bayt say' al-sum'a* (1965); *Al-Shahhādh* (1965); *Taht al-mazalla* (1969); *Hikāya bilā bidāya wa lā nihāya* (1969); *Shahr al-'asal* (1971); *Al-Hubb tahta al-matar* (1973); *Al-Jarīma* (1973); *Hikāyāt hāratinā* (1975); *Qalb al-layl* (1975); *Hadrat al-muhtaram* (1975); *Malhamat al-harāfīsh* (1977); *Al-Hubb fawqa hadbat al-haram* (1979); *Al-Shaytān ya'iz* (1979); *Afrāh al-qubba* (1980); *'Asr al-hubb* (1980); *Layālī alf layla* (1982); *Ra'aytu fīmā yarā al-nā'im* (1982). FURTHER VOLUME IN ENGLISH: *God's World* (1973)

BIBLIOGRAPHY: Le Gassick, T., "The *Trilogy* of N. M.," *MEF,* 39, 2 (1963), 31–34; Milson, M., "N. M. and the Quest for Meaning," *Arabica,* 17 (1970), 177–86; Allen, R., "Mirrors by N. M.," *MW,* 62, 2 (1972), 115–25, and 63, 1 (1973), 15–27; Somekh, S., *The Changing Rhythm: A Study of N. M.'s Novels* (1973); Sakkut, H., "N. M.'s Short Stories," and Le Gassick, T., "An Analysis of *Al-Hubb tahta al-matar,*" in Ostle, R. C., ed., *Studies in Modern Arabic Literature* (1975), pp. 114–25, 140–51; Milson, M., "Reality, Allegory and Myth in the Work of N. M.," *AAS,* 11 (1976), 157–79; Allen, R., "Some Recent Works of N. M.," *JARCE,* 14 (1977), 101–10; Allen, R. M. A., *The Arabic Novel: An Historical and Critical Introduction* (1982), pp. 55–62, 101–7

ROGER M. A. ALLEN

MAILER, Norman

American novelist, essayist, journalist, and screenwriter, b. 31 Jan. 1923, Long Branch, N.J.

M. had a conventional upbringing by a supportive family in a middle-class section of Brooklyn, N.Y. While at Harvard M. became so infused with literature and with the idea of creating great literary works which would attract acclaim that he began to write fiction. Upon graduation in 1943 M. entered the army and served in the Pacific.

M.'s writing has increasingly focused upon

his life, lived broadly in a variety of realms: a prominent public personality, M. cofounded *The Village Voice* newspaper (1955); campaigned to be mayor of New York City (1969); actively participated in political protest and cultural dissent; launched several conspicuous literary feuds; acted in a few films; was arrested several times, most notoriously for stabbing his wife (1960); and has flamboyantly been married six times.

The Naked and the Dead (1948), M.'s first novel, was a great critical success and launched M.'s career. It depicted the past and present lives of an ethnically diverse group of soldiers involved in a South Pacific campaign during World War II. The novel displays the influence of several American social realists: James T. Farrell (q.v.) in the overall style; John Dos Passos (q.v.) in the flashback technique, called in the novel the "Time Machine," and in the authorial perspective and structure; John Steinbeck (q.v.) in the propensity for elaborate imagery and metaphorical allusions.

Barbary Shore (1951), a more ambitious novel, was a critical failure: whereas his first novel grew out of America's general wartime experience, his second grounded itself in the particular political and philosophical concerns of the American left, reflecting such contemporary events as the Alger Hiss trial. The influence of F. Scott Fitzgerald (q.v.) is apparent in the stylized grafting of an Arthurian allegory (of the search for the Grail) upon the Stalinist-Trotskyite affinities of the residents of a Brooklyn rooming house.

In *The Deer Park* (1955), a novel about the Hollywood community (building upon M.'s observations as an unsuccessful screenwriter in 1949), M. began to demonstrate his notion that the sexual qualities of fictional characters might be connected to their moral nature; the novel was influenced by M.'s belief in the prototypical masculinity that he saw as existing in the fiction of Ernest Hemingway and Henry Miller (qq.v.). Because of the personal aspect of the novel's themes, M. held the work in high esteem; when it was rejected by six publishers before ultimately appearing in print to ambiguous reviews, M. experienced a sense of depression, an artistic turbulence in keeping with the indecisive and derivative nature of his early work.

M.'s resurgence occurred with *Advertisements for Myself* (1959), a bold and idiosyncratic work in which he not only assembled a retrospective of his literary career, but interpreted his work through a vitalized critical commentary. He announced his desire to stimulate "a revolution in the consciousness of our time"; accordingly, he affirmed his confidence that "it is my present and future work which will have the deepest influence of any work being done by an American novelist in these years." Evident in this work transcending generic classification is M.'s sense of himself as being exemplary of his age—a figure of dramatic individuality and dynamic creative vigor who would embody through literature the great themes of the era. Also characteristic are his increasing interest in existentialism (q.v.), his reliance upon evocative contemporary material, and his utilization of paradoxical metaphors to accommodate his philosophical formulations: thus, in the essay "The White Negro" (originally published in 1957), M. presents the "psychopathic hipster," whom he sees as being inherently creative and in tune with life, in opposition to the conventional citizen, whom he views as being repressed and alienated.

An American Dream (1965) expresses many of M.'s themes in mature fictional form: the war between God and the Devil for possession of the earth; sex as an encompassing metaphor for time and theology; the literary form of history; the viability of paranoia; the underlying morality and creativity behind deviant behavior. The protagonist, Rojack (a war hero who is a former politician and television talk-show host), does not achieve genuine heroic stature until he murders his wife and frees himself from the oppressive influence of the economic and political institutions with which he has previously been involved. Newly receptive to the poetic guidance of the moon, he attains individual fulfillment and expression of his personal being by gradually sloughing off the skins of conventional American existence. Central to this novel is M.'s prevailing conviction that any person in the United States is "a member of a minority group if he contains two opposed notions of himself at the same time."

A novel reminiscent stylistically of William Burroughs (q.v.) and thematically of William Faulkner (q.v.), *Why Are We in Vietnam?* (1967) offers a frenetic Alaskan bear hunt as a metaphor for the American involvement in southeast Asia. M.'s desire to exert an "influence" upon his time and to shape his history through literary vision resulted in *The Armies of the Night* (1968), which won a Pulitzer Prize and a National Book Award. This is a novelistic description of his participation in (and arrest during) the actual 1967 march on the Pentagon. M.'s use of the third person to relate a narrative in which he himself emerges as the protagonist excited the imagination of a decade eager to achieve immediacy and straightforwardness; it exerted a considerable influence upon the style of popular writing called the "New Journalism."

Fueled by his success, M. continued to explore the state of society from his own tempestuous vantage point. He twice interpreted Presidential contests—in *Miami and the Siege of Chicago* (1968) and *St. George and the Godfather* (1972). *The Prisoner of Sex* (1971), M.'s response to the feminist movement, proposed that gender might determine the way a person perceives and orders reality. *The Fight* (1975) analyzed the bout between Muhammad Ali and George Foreman as a metaphorical joust between cosmic animism and death.

M.'s account of the life and execution of the convict Gary Gilmore, the Pulitzer Prize-winning *The Executioner's Song* (1979), is an impressive and dramatic work that is both fiction and journalism. Drawing on actual interviews and records, M., for the first time, submerges himself in another's tale, with the result that M.'s own world vision is convincingly established.

Although M. has frequently announced his intention to create the ultimate novel of our age, it may well be that his body of work, when considered together, reflects most keenly the volatile state of the American nation. Often infuriating—reveling in a stylish nonconformity and a self-indulgence that often conceal a fundamental conservatism of values and a desire for popular adulation—flawed, poetic, crass, brilliant, M. has succeeded in making our contemporary era the "time of his time."

FURTHER WORKS: *Deaths for the Ladies (and Other Disasters)* (1962); *The Presidential Papers* (1963); *Cannibals and Christians* (1966); *The Bullfight* (1967); *The Deer Park: A Play* (1967); *The Short Fiction of N. M.* (1967); *The Idol and the Octopus* (1968); *Of a Fire on the Moon* (1971); *On the Fight of the Century: King of the Hill* (1971); *Maidstone: A Mystery* (1971); *Existential Errands* (1972); *Marilyn: A Biography* (1973); *The Faith of Graffiti* (1974); *Genius and Lust: A Journey through the Major Writings of Henry Miller* (1976); *Some Honorable Men* (1976); *Of Women and Their Elegance* (1980); *Pieces and Pontifications* (1982)

BIBLIOGRAPHY: Schulz, M., *Radical Sophistication* (1969), pp. 69–110; Tanner, T., *City of Words* (1971), pp. 344–71; Braudy, L., ed., *N. M.: A Collection of Critical Essays* (1972); Poirier, R., *N. M.* (1972); Kazin, A., *Bright Book of Life* (1973), passim; Adams, L., *A Bibliography of N. M.* (1974); Solotaroff, R., *Down M.'s Way* (1974); Zavarzadeh, M., *The Mythopoeic Reality: The Postwar American Nonfiction Novel* (1976), pp. 153–76; McConnell, F. D., *Four Postwar American Novelists* (1977), pp. 58–107; Bufithis, P., *N. M.* (1978)

GEOFFREY GREEN

MAJEROVÁ, Marie

Czechoslovak novelist and short-story writer (writing in Czech), b. 1 Feb. 1882, Úvaly; d. 16 Jan. 1967, Prague

M.'s writing, with its ideological bent toward socialism, was shaped by the experiences of her working-class childhood and adolescence. Her first years were spent in Prague. In 1894 the family moved to Kladno, a major center of heavy industry based on coal and iron ore. There the intellectually precocious girl discovered the joys of reading and assimilated the defiant spirit of nascent Czech proletarian consciousness. In the cosmopolitan atmosphere of Vienna, where she moved with her husband, M. turned to writing and also participated in the general strike of 1905. Under the influence of the Czech poet Stanislav Kostka Neumann (1875–1947), she was first drawn to social anarchism. A stay in Paris—the writers, including Romain Rolland (q.v.) she met there; the lectures she heard—led to a decisive break with the politics of anarchism, later recorded in her second novel, *Náměstí Republiky* (1914; Place de la République). In 1908 she officially joined the Czech Social Democratic Party and in 1921 was a founding member of the Communist Party of Czechoslovakia. In 1947 the Czechoslovak government awarded her the title of National Artist.

M.'s first novel, *Panenství* (1907; virginity), deals with the fashionable fin-de-siècle issue of woman's virginity in the grim social context of the proletarian condition. In spite of its melodramatic dénouement, the novel shows originality in its characterization and use of atmosphere. The central crisis of the plot places the heroine, a spirited servant girl, between two equally strong imperatives. Her devotion to an impoverished young journalist prompts her secretly to offer her virginity to a senile rake in exchange for enough money to obtain medical care for her consumptive beloved. When the sacrificial instant is upon her, the body's instinct for health prevails, and she runs away with her honor intact.

M.'s interest in the woman question never waned. In a collection of short stories, *Mučenky* (1921; the women martyrs), she casts an ironic but compassionate eye on the fate of middle-class women trapped by the hypocrisies of the double standard of sexual morality and by their own romantic delusions.

M.'s masterpiece is the novel *Siréna* (1935; *The Siren,* 1953). It is a chronicle of three generations of the Hudec family, iron and coal workers of Kladno. The theme of generations interacts with the historical and social background. The action, which begins in the 1850s and ends around 1918, illustrates the region's progression toward industrialization, with the accompanying emergence of class consciousness among the workers, who take their time shedding the more individualistic guild attachments. The dominant personality of a woman spans the life of the three generations: Hudcovka's village roots prove a solid foundation for her role as daughter-in-law, wife, and mother of workers and rebels. The linguistic texture of this novel is rich and varied, with M. drawing on the resources of the regional idiom. Her description of the 1905 strike, which briefly closed all the coal mines of the Austrian Empire, has the raw, convincing quality of an eyewitness account.

M. was a prolific writer of novels, short stories, and feuilletons whose lifelong commitment to socialism earned her the reputation of being the leading Czech Socialist Realist (q.v.). Her writings are widely translated in all socialist countries. Her major novel *Siréna,* however, stands on its own as a fine example of pure realism.

FURTHER WORKS: *Povídky z pekla a jiné* (1907); *Plané milování* (1908); *Nepřítel v domě* (1909); *Dcery země* (1910); *Červené kvítí* (1911); *Rézinka* (1912); *Čarovný svět* (1913); *Zlatý pramen* (1918); *Z luhů a hor* (1919); *Ze Slovenska* (1920); *Dojmy z Ame-*

riky (1920); *Nejkrásnější svět* (1923); *Zázračná hodinka* (1923); *Den po revoluci* (1925); *Pohled do dílny* (1929); *Bruno* (1930); *Přehrada* (1932); *Parta na křižovatce* (1933); *Africké vteřiny* (1933); *Kde je Charlie?* (1934); *Květná neděle* (1936); *Výlet do Československa* (1937); *Havířská balada* (1938; *Ballad of a Miner,* 1960); *Robinsonka* (1940); *Město ve znamení ohně* (1940); *Nespokojený králíček* (1946); *Deset tisíc kilometrů nad Sovětským svazem* (1948); *Cesta blesku* (1949); *Pravda veliké doby* (1950); *Sebrané spisy* (19 vols., 1952–61)

BIBLIOGRAPHY: Mihailovich, V. D., et al., eds., *Modern Slavic Literatures* (1976), Vol. II, pp. 148–51; Novák, A., *Czech Literature* (1976), pp. 285–88

MARIA NĚMCOVÁ BANERJEE

MAKSIMOVIĆ, Desanka

Yugoslav poet, translator, short-story writer, novelist, travel writer, and children's-book writer (writing in Serbian), b. 16 May 1898, Rabrovica (near Valjevo)

M. grew up in Brankovina and Valjevo, in an area where the people were strongly aware of the Serbian national heritage and heroic traditions. She studied comparative literature, world history, and history of art at the University of Belgrade (1919–23) and in Paris (1924–25). Upon graduation she was appointed a high-school teacher in Belgrade and remained in that position until her retirement in 1953. Recipient of innumerable literary awards and honors, she has been a member of Serbian Academy of Sciences and Arts since 1959.

In her very first collection, *Pesme* (1924; poems), M. emerged as a sensitive lyric poet, fascinated with nature, of which she has felt an integral part and in which she has confided and searched for joy, beauty, and comfort ever since. M.'s prewar poetic work includes mainly love and descriptive poems in which the poet confesses her own youthful anxieties and curiosity in front of the great mysteries of life and love. As she matured M. widened the scope and depth of her preoccupations, and her poetry came to have a more universal character. The suffering of her nation in World War II inspired a series of beautiful, humane patriotic poems, of which *Krvava bajka* (1951; *A Legend of Blood,* 1962), occasioned by the German massacre of schoolboys in Kragujevac in 1943, is the best known and most widely translated.

M. reached her peak in the 1960s and 1970s. The collection *Tražim pomilovanje* (1964; I plead for mercy), subtitled "Lyrical Discussions with Tsar Dushan's Medieval Code of Laws," glorifies forgiveness and compassion as the most noble of human virtues. Among those for whom the poet pleads are both the oppressed and the oppressors, the humble and the vain, the naïve and the sly, the poor and the rich, women, monks, soldiers, sinners, and dreamers—all her fellow human beings. In the collection *Nemam više vremena* (1973; my time is running short) the aging poet meditates on death and dying and reminisces about the passing of her loved ones. With calm resignation, M. accepts death as a component of life and prepares herself for the last journey, which for her means returning to nature and merging with eternity.

Like many great literary figures, M. does not belong to any specific 20th-c. literary movement or fad. Anything that might have influenced her is filtered through the prism of her own talent and her strong poetic individuality and is fully and harmoniously integrated in an entirely original poetic whole. With its accent on love, beauty, and universal ethical principles, her poetry, written in a superb style, represents M.'s most valuable contribution to Serbian literature. In addition, she has presented to Yugoslav readers many outstanding Slavic and French writers in excellent translations, and has been a prolific and popular author of literature for children and young adults. Besides poetry, she wrote several novels and many short stories for young people, all of which abound with lyricism and with beautiful descriptions of nature. They are aimed not only at entertaining young readers but at developing in them ethical values and love and respect for their fellow human beings.

M.'s travel books, *Praznici putovanja* (1972; the festive days of traveling) and *Snimci iz Švajcarske* (1978; snapshots from Switzerland), provide a valuable insight into the poet's personality. In both of them M. focuses her attention on her favorite subjects: the people whom she met during her many travels, and the natural beauties of the places she visited.

One of the few best-selling poets of our nonpoetic era, M. is today the dean of the Serbian literary scene, and her opus has become an integral part of Serbian national culture.

FURTHER WORKS: *Zeleni vitez* (1930); *Ludilo srca* (1931); *Gozba na livadi* (1932); *Kako oni žive* (1935); *Nove pesme* (1936); *Oslobodjenje Cvete Andrić* (1945); *Pesnik i zavičaj* (1946); *Otadžbina u prvomajskoj povorci* (1949); *Izabrane pesme* (1950); *Otadžbino, tu sam* (1951); *Otvoren prozor* (1954); *Strašna igra* (1954); *Miris zemlje* (1955); *Izabrane pjesme* (1958); *Buntovan razred* (1960); *Zarobljenik snova* (1960); *Govori tiho* (1961); *Pesme* (1963); *Pesme* (1964); *Pesme* (1965); *Pesme* (1966); *Pesme* (1966); *Deset mojih pesama* (1967); *Pesme* (1967); *Stihovi* (1967); *Vratnice* (1968); *Ne zaboraviti* (1969); *Sabrana dela* (7 vols., 1969); *Verujem* (1969); *Pradevojčica* (1970); *Izabrane pesme* (1972); *Izbor iz dela* (1974); *Letopis Perunovih potomaka* (1976); *Pesme iz Norveške* (1976); *Pjesme* (1977); *Ničija zemlja* (1979); *lzbrana dela: Poezija* (5 vols., 1980). FURTHER VOLUME IN ENGLISH: *Greetings from the Old Country* (1976, bilingual)

BIBLIOGRAPHY: Klančar, A. J., on *Nove pesme, BA,* 11 (1937), 512; Petrov, A., on *Tražim pomilovanje, IBSB,* 15 (1964), 267–68; Mihailovich, V. D., on *Tražim pomilovanje, BA,* 40 (1966), 355; Matejić, M., on *Neman više vremena, BA,* 48 (1974), 395–96; Surdučki, M., Preface to D. M., *Greetings from the Old Country* (1976), pp. ix–xiv; Šljivić-Šimšić, B., on *Letopis Perunovih potomaka, WLT,* 51 (1977), 305–6; Eekman, T., *Thirty Years of Yugoslav Literature (1945–1975)* (1978), pp. 25–26

BILJANA ŠLJIVIĆ-ŠIMŠIĆ

MALAGASY LITERATURE

In Malagasy

Before European missionaries introduced the printing press in the 19th c., Madagascar possessed highly developed forms of oral art: the most widely practiced genres were the proverbs (*ohabolana*), public oratory (*kabary*), the folktale (*angano*), and the fashionable poetic competitions known as *hain-teny;* also popular were dramatic rituals and festivities in which dancing and music by professional performers called *mpilalao* were as important as plot and the spoken word.

In 1818 King Radama I allowed the London Missionary Society to settle on the island. The first printing press was built in 1827, and in 1835 the Bible was the first book to be printed; the first vernacular newspaper, *Teny soa,* came out in 1866. Since then journalistic life in Madagascar has always been uncommonly lively: no other area of the French empire could boast as large a number of vernacular newspapers and little magazines, which fostered the promotion of literature; indeed, most Malagasy novels were first printed in serial form.

Imaginative writing in Malagasy can be said to begin in 1889 with *Fanoharana* (fables), a free adaptation of La Fontaine's *Fables* by a French-educated Jesuit priest, Basilide Rahidy (1839–1883), and with the tales and *hain-teny* of an L.M.S.-educated Protestant minister, Ingahibe Rainitovo (1852–?).

Apart from the edifying sentimental novels of Rev. Andriamatoa Rabary (1864–1947), the next generation was remarkable principally for its theatrical achievements. Its best representatives were exceptionally versatile, being journalists, novelists, poets, and musical composers as well as playwrights. But the chief contribution of Alexis Rakotobe (dates n.a.), Justin Rainizanabololona (1861–1938), and Tselatra Rajaonah (1863–1931) at the turn of the century was the creation of Malagasy musical comedy, which fused the native tradition of the *mpilalao* and the influence of the French operetta; their favorite theme is love, but the plays usually end on a moralizing note. Further, they gave instruction and encouragement to such younger dramatists as Dondavitra (pseud. of Charles-Aubert Razafimahefa, 1880–1936), whose best-known play, *Peratra Mahavariana* (the magic ring) was performed in 1906; Wast Ravelomoria (1886–1951), who wrote comedies of manners; Romain Andrianjafy (1888–1917), who directed his own company, Tananarive-Theatre; Jasmina Ratsimiseta (1890–1946), who imitated the French boulevard theater; and Naka Rabemanantsoa (1892–1943) and Justin Rajoro (1893–1949), the founders of the first Malagasy acting company, Telonorefy. Most of the early 20th-c. plays never reached print.

Madagascar became a French protectorate in 1895 and a French colony in 1905. All teaching was henceforth done in French; no native could be appointed to an official position if he did not know French. Although a number of writers were imprisoned in 1915 during the ruthless suppression of a plot engineered by the cultural association Vy Vato Sakelika, the colonial regime did not put an immediate end to the ebullient literary activity of the Malagasy people. Together with Justin Rainizanabololona, Edouard Andrianjafintrimo (1881–1972) experimented with rhyme and new metrical schemes based on French and Latin prosody. Rev. Maurice Rasamuel (1886–1954), chiefly known for his historical and oratorical works, wrote his novel *Tao Manjakadoria* (1942; formerly in Manjakadoria). Madagascar's first woman novelist, Charlotte Razafiniaina (b. 1894), who wrote plays, poems, and *hain-teny* as well, produced several social novels dealing with the problems of acculturation. This was also the generation of the greatest lyric poet in the Malagasy language, Ramanantoanina (1891–1940); his nostalgic work was studied by the first notable Malagasy critic, Charles Rajoelisolo (1896–1966), who was also a historian and a gifted short-story writer. Another prominent representative of this generation was Rodlish (pseud. of Arthur Razakarivony, 1897–1967), the author of serious dramas such as *Ranomody* (1926; the whirlpool) and *Sangy mahery* (1936; violent games), which deal with the theme of frustrated love and offer a critique of the native caste system; he also published in collaboration with Jean Narivony (b. 1898), two anthologies of Malagasy poetry, *Amboara voafantina* (1926; selected poems) and *Kolokalo tatsinana* (1929; songs from the east).

Among the writers born after Madagascar came under French authority, there was a noticeable estrangement from the use of the vernacular language for literary purposes. On the other hand, there arose a gifted school of French-writing poets. Although many popular novelettes were printed in the capital, Tananarive, there was a steady decline in the number of legitimate writers in the vernacular. Apart from the short stories of Elie Raharolahy (b.1901), the bulk of later Malagasy creative writing consists of the lyric poetry of Fredy Rajaofera (1902–1968) and especially the plays of J. V. S. Razakandrainy (b. 1913), better known under the pseudonym of Dox. Madagascar shares with the Cape Verde Islands and northern Nigeria the peculiarity of having bilingual poets, such as Fidelis-Justin Rabestimanandranto (b. 1907) and Régis Rajemisa-Raolison (b. 1913), who handle their mother tongue and French with equal ease.

After Madagascar became the independent Malagasy Republic in 1960, official encouragement given to the national language resulted in the rapid growth of the novel, examples of which are Alphonse Ravoajanahary's (dates n.a.) *Tao anatin'ny sarotra* (1967; in big trouble), Jean-Louis Rasamizafy's (dates n.a.) *Mandrakizay ho doria* (1967; forever), Michel Paul Abraham-Razafimaharo's (b. 1926) *Valin-keloka* (1968; the punishment of sin), and E. D. Andriamalala's (dates n.a.) *Fofombadiko* (1971; betrothal).

BIBLIOGRAPHY: Aly, J. M., "Où en est la littérature malgache depuis 1960?" and Andriantsilaniarivo, E., "Où en sont les lettres malgaches?" in *Réflexions sur la première décennie des indépendances en Afrique noire/ Reflections on the First Decade of Negro-African Independence*, special issue of *PA* (1971), pp. 272–82, 343–56; Gérard, A. S., *African Language Literature: An Introduction to the Literary History of Sub-Saharan Africa* (1981), pp. 75–91

ALBERT S. GÉRARD

In French

Malagasy literature in French began in the 1920s, with the publication of Édouard Bezoro's (dates n.a.) novel *La sœur inconnue* (1923; the unknown sister); it celebrates the success of the French military conquest of Madagascar in the late 19th c., which resulted in the abolition of slavery, practiced until then by the Hova rulers of the island.

Bezoro's attitude was not, however, to become typical, and subsequent writing in French was to be almost wholly dominated by the cultural and political tensions created by colonialism. This became evident very early on in the work of the country's most outstanding poet, Jean-Joseph Rabearivelo (1901–1937), whose poetry reflects his deep distress at the undermining of traditional Malagasy literature and his equally sensitive appreciation of contemporary French poetry. Rabearivelo suffered greatly from the isolation of the black writer in colonial society of the interwar years, an isolation that seemed to be intensified by Madagascar's geographical distance from France and the poet's frustration at being cut off from the intellectual life of the French capital. *La coupe de cendres* (1924; cup of ashes), *Sylves* (1927; woods), and *Volumes* (1928; volumes) follow conventional French verse forms, but the mature poetry of *Presque-songes* (1934; near-dreams) and *Traduit de la nuit* (1935; translated from the night) combines a mastery of modern French free verse and the traditional *hain-teny* (a prose poem in the form of a dialogue) to achieve a thoroughly personal style that fully reflects the poet's sense of his inner tensions. The poems in his *Vieilles chansons des pays d'Imerina* (1939; old songs of Imerina) are entirely based on the *hain-teny*.

The two best-known writers of the post-World War II period are Jacques Rabemananjara (b. 1913) and Flavien Ranaivo (b. 1914). Rabemananjara's most forceful poetry, in volumes such as *Antsa* (1956; Malagasy: eulogy), *Lamba* (1956; Malagasy: strip of cloth used as traditional article of clothing), and *Antidote* (1961; antidote), was inspired by the anticolonial violence that erupted in Madagascar in 1947 and expresses his bitter disillusionment with French policies, largely prompted by his experience of prison at the time. Plays like *Les boutriers de l'aurore* (1957; vessels of the dawn) and *Agapes des dieux* (1962; love feasts of the gods) are an attempt to evaluate the Malagasy past in keeping with the Negritude (q.v.) ideals of the day. Flavien Ranaivo's *L'ombre et le vent* (1947; the shade and the wind), *Mes chansons de toujours* (1955; my everlasting songs) and *Le retour au bercail* (1962; return to the fold) are modeled almost entirely on the traditional *hain-teny* and show how effectively the subtleties of Malagasy poetry can be conveyed in French.

A number of minor writers, chiefly poets, have helped to sustain the vitality of Malagasy writing in French since the 1920s. The best-known among these are Michel-François Robinary (1892–1971), whose *Fleurs défuntes* (1927; dead flowers) has survived remarkably well in spite of its heavy reliance on French romantic models, and Régis Rajemisa-Raolison (b. 1913), who continued the very fruitful exploitation of the *hain-teny* in his collection *Les fleurs de l'île rouge* (1948; the flowers of the red island).

As in the case of the vernacular literature, the constant regeneration of ephemeral literary journals was of considerable importance in the stimulation of creative writing in French and in keeping alive critical reflection on the problems confronting writers caught between two cultures. Another factor has been the existence of small local printing firms and an enterprising official printing house (which also publishes the only long-standing journal, the influential *Revue de Madagascar*). Apart from Rabemananjara, whose work has been published in France by the Présence Africaine publishing house, the majority of Malagasy writers, including Rabearivelo, have been dependent on these local publishers.

Madagascar obtained its independence from France in 1960, becoming the Malagasy Republic. Unlike most of the black states on the African continent, independence did not bring with it a continuing expansion of creative writing in French, and, since the military coup of 1972, the two most prominent living Malagasy writers, Jacques Rabemananjara and Flavien Ranaivo, have lived in political exile in France.

BIBLIOGRAPHY: Wake, C. H., and Reed, J. O., "Modern Malagasy Literature in French," *BA,* 38 (1964), 14–19; Cornevin, R., *Le théâtre en Afrique noir et à Madagascar* (1970), pp. 263–87

CLIVE WAKE

MALAMUD, Bernard

American novelist and short-story writer, b. 26 April 1914, Brooklyn, N.Y.

Born to Russian-Jewish immigrant parents, M. spent his childhood and much of his adult life in New York. He attended City College, where he received his B.A. in 1936. After working for several years as a clerk for the Bureau of the Census in Washington, D.C., M. returned to New York, teaching evening high school and earning his M.A. in English from Columbia University in 1942. In 1949 he accepted a position in the English Department at Oregon State University, where he remained for the next twelve years. In 1961 he joined the faculty of Bennington College, Vermont. He has served as a visiting lecturer at Harvard University and has traveled extensively in Europe. He now divides his time between Bennington and his home in New York.

M.'s fiction, although difficult to classify, often has its roots in the Jewish experience—both ancient and modern. His prose style alternates between surrealistic fantasy (his stories have been compared to the paintings of Marc Chagall) and detailed realism. The

themes of suffering, redemption, and moral responsibility recur throughout his work, from his early short stories to his latest novels.

M.'s first novel, *The Natural* (1952), stands apart as his only work without Jewish characters or background. Nevertheless, the theme of suffering and the myth of salvation, which dominate much of M.'s later fiction, are central to the novel. Here, however, M. presents a vision of man defeated rather than renewed. Roy Hobbs, the novel's mythical baseball hero, does not possess the sense of moral responsibility that redeems many of M.'s later Jewish characters. Roy fails to learn from his experiences, and the novel ends on a note of loss and despair.

In relation to M.'s subsequent fiction, *The Natural* appears uneven and overly reliant on its mythological allusions and structure. *The Assistant* (1957), by contrast, is one of M.'s most satisfying achievements. The novel is pessimistic in tone and starkly realistic in its presentation of the bleak, urban world of New York City. Imprisoned within his failing grocery store, Morris Bober, like many of M.'s Jewish immigrants, struggles against the overpowering forces of his environment. But the book's focus is on Frank Alpine, the grocer's assistant, who undergoes a transformation from victimizer to helper and from Christian to Jew. More than anything else in the novel, Frank's conversion represents M.'s belief in man's capacity for renewal and for self-creation.

A New Life (1961), as the title indicates, continues M.'s exploration of the theme of redemption. S. Levin, the novel's protagonist, journeys from his native New York to the Northwest in search of a new beginning as a college English instructor. Levin, the archetypal Jewish schlemiel, is more bungler than moral hero, and his exploits at Cascadia College are more comic than serious. But like Frank Alpine, Levin grows and changes and ultimately learns to accept the weight of moral entanglement.

Similarly, Yakov Bok, the hero of *The Fixer* (1966)—the novel for which M. received both the National Book Award and the Pulitzer Prize—comes to understand that the path to true redefinition of self is difficult and intricate. The novel represents the culmination of M.'s earlier themes and motifs and is considered by many to be his most successful effort. Here the metaphor of man imprisoned is translated into physical reality, and the story of Bok (based on the famous Mendel Beiliss case in tsarist Russia) becomes the perfect vehicle for M.'s themes of redemptive suffering, moral growth, and the acceptance of one's fate.

M.'s two novels of the 1970s, *The Tenants* (1971) and *Dubin's Lives* (1979), take greater risks and make greater demands on the reader than his previous works. Although they both demonstrate M.'s willingness to strike out in new directions, neither contains the rich and complex view of human existence presented in his earlier novels and stories. *The Tenants* ironically and pessimistically depicts the bitter and fatal struggle between two writers: one Jewish, the other black. The issue is once again man's moral involvement with his fellow man, but M. concludes *The Tenants* with an image of apocalyptic destruction. With *Dubin's Lives,* M. departed from all but the slightest connection with the Jewish experience, as well as with former themes. The motif of death and resurrection is present, but only in relation to the artistic and sexual endeavors of William Dubin, the novel's central figure. Intricate in its exposition of the character of Dubin, the novel contains some of M.'s finest prose but remains somewhat confined within its limited thematic concerns.

Perhaps M.'s greatest achievement lies in his short stories, especially those collected in his first volume, *The Magic Barrel* (1958), for which M. received his first National Book Award. The most successful of these—"The Magic Barrel" and "The Last Mohican," for example—possess a haunting magical quality that brings the reader to an understanding of the mystery of human existence. M. writes of misery and suffering, yet there remains throughout these stories the suggestion of fragile optimism.

At the center of M.'s fiction is the possibility of human growth, of man's ability to transcend old, unsatisfactory roles and to create new, more positive ones. In his finest works, of which *The Assistant, The Fixer,* and several of the early short stories are the best examples, there is a carefully balanced view of existence: an understanding of man's defeats and an appreciation of his triumphs. M. remains one of the few contemporary authors who has made us feel the richness of his moral imagination and the force of his affirmative vision.

FURTHER WORKS: *Idiots First* (1963); *A M. Reader* (1967); *Pictures of Fidelman: An Exhibition* (1969); *Rembrandt's Hat* (1973); *God's Grace* (1982)

BIBLIOGRAPHY: Richman, S., *B. M.* (1966); Meeter, G., *B. M. and Philip Roth: A Critical Essay* (1968); Field, L., and Field, J., eds., *B. M. and the Critics* (1970); Pinsker, S., *The Schlemiel as Metaphor: Studies in the Yiddish and American Jewish Novel* (1971), pp. 87–124; Ducharme, R., *Art and Idea in the Novels of B. M.: Toward "The Fixer"* (1974); Cohen, S., *B. M. and the Trial by Love* (1974); Field, L., and Field, J., eds., *B. M.: A Collection of Critical Essays* (1975); Astro, R., and Benson, J., eds., *The Fiction of B. M.* (1977); special M. issue, *SAJL,* 4, 1 (1978); Avery, E., *Rebels and Victims: The Fiction of Richard Wright and B. M.* (1979); Alter, I., *The Good Man's Dilemma: Social Criticism in the Fiction of B. M.* (1981)

STEVEN J. RUBIN

MALAWIAN LITERATURE

Malawi, formerly Nyasaland, became independent in 1964 after the Federation of Rhodesia and Nyasaland (1953–63) fell apart. There has been some publication in indigenous languages. Samuel Ntara (b. 1905) has published several novels in Nyanja, most importantly *Mnyamboza* (1949; *Headman's Enterprise,* 1949), a fictionalized biography of a chieftain of the Cewa tribe. Several of English Chafulumira's (b. 1930) short narratives in *Nyanja* were published in London. There has also been creative writing in the Tumbuka language.

The limitations of publishing opportunities at home and the likelihood that literacy will be achieved in English reduce the options for writers in every formerly British African country who might prefer to write in an indigenous language. When English is elected, there is usually a transitional type of writing, which draws heavily upon the admired formal accomplishments of the language taught at school. The poet Katoki Mwalilino (b. 1942?) exemplifies this unselective borrowing; he takes the style and diction of British poetry and tries to apply its unsuitable qualities to topics of African content—even the subject of African nationalism. The nature of Mwalilino's verse can be surmised from the Poet Laureate-like title of one of his more famous poems, "The Awakening Malawi on July 6th 1964" (1966).

There are only three contemporary Malawian writers of serious consequence. Legson Kayira (b. 1940) first achieved recognition for an extraordinary account of his "walk": he hiked some 2,500 miles from Malawi north to the Sudan, where he was befriended by the U.S. consul, who arranged for him to come to America for education. His autobiography, *I Will Try* (1965), if lacking much literary merit, is an impressive account of determination and commitment. Subsequently, Kayira settled in England, from where he has written three novels with themes also applicable to other parts of Africa. *The Looming Shadow* (1967) deals with the complexities of traditional life and belief, while *Jingala* (1969) confronts the generational conflict in its story of a young man who wishes to become a Catholic priest. These works are readable enough, without suggesting that the writer has the ability to give Malawian writing an individual stamp.

More competent technically is Aubrey Kachingwe (b. 1926), whose single novel, *No Easy Task* (1966), makes very clear that his training is as a journalist. It touches upon the inevitable problems that arise when a nation confronts the barriers to independence. It is less an imaginative creation than a documentation drawn from experiences both in Malawi and elsewhere in Africa. It is not clear whether Kachingwe will be able to move beyond reportage to true novel writing.

Superior to both these writers is the poet, novelist, and critic David Rubadiri (b. 1930). He is the most original Malawian literary figure, although he has spent much of his adult life outside the country. His single novel, *No Bride Price* (1967), deals, as do so many African novels, with the problems of coping with the incompetence and corruption of many African governments. More generally, it deals with the issue of establishing appropriate moral values to be retained in a violently transitional society. In Rubadiri's novel there is a coup, and the protagonist is imprisoned. The personal disaster of losing his child compounds his political distress, but he learns to comprehend the advantages and virtues of the traditional beliefs. He discerns belatedly that it is the false expecta-

tions raised by independence that are responsible for many of the problems afflicting modern Africa. Rubadiri is also a significant poet. He has not yet had his poetry collected in book form, but his verse is regularly anthologized, not only for its inherent quality but also because it treats of some of the more crucial issues confronting contemporary Africans. "The Tide That from the West Washes Africa to the Bone" (1970) is a powerful denunciation of the despoiling of the continent.

More recently, in the areas of drama and poetry Malawi has shown a far livelier development than is apparent from international lists of publications. There is an ambitious traveling theater, sustained by the university, for which several authors, including James Mgombe (dates n.a.), Innocent Banda (dates n.a.), and Chris Kamlongera (dates n.a.) have written plays published in the local Malawian Writers Series. The most ambitious dramatist is Steve Chimombo (dates n.a.), whose play *The Rainmaker* (1975) deals with the early rituals of the M'bona cult.

Similarly, the impetus for poetry derives from an active university poetry workshop. Felix Mnthali (dates n.a.) and Steve Chimombo, both significant poets, are on the faculty. Among this highly eclectic group, Jack Mapanje (dates n.a.) and Lupenga Mphande (dates n.a.) are promising poets who write sensitively on local themes. Frank Chipasula (dates n.a.) is the only one yet to have published a volume of verse, *Visions and Reflections* (1973). This vigorous array of local talent suggests a potential for a broadly based, specifically Malawian literature, which is being furthered by a literary quarterly, *Odi*.

BIBLIOGRAPHY: Kerr, D., "New Writing from Malawi," *Afriscope*, 3, 12 (1973), 54–59; Roscoe, A. A., *Uhuru's Fire: African Literature East to South* (1977), pp. 134–49, 215–25, 267–73; Gibbs, J., "Theatre in Malawi," *Afriscope*, 7, 11–12 (1977), 69–71; Mapanje, J., "New Verse in Malawi," *Odi*, 2, 1 (1977), 24–28; Namponya, C. R., "History and Development of Printing and Publishing in Malawi," *Libri*, 28 (1978), 167–81; Calder, A., "Under Zomba Plateau: The New Malawian Poetry," *Kunapipi*, 1, 2 (1979), 59–67; Gérard, A. S., *African Language Literatures* (1981), pp. 204–7, 226–33

JOHN POVEY

MALAY LITERATURE

See Malaysian Literature and Singapore Literature

MALAYALAM LITERATURE

See Indian Literature

MALAYSIAN LITERATURE

In Malay

Fiction

Modern writing in the Malay language began in the 19th c. with the works of Abdullah bin Abdul Kadir Munshi (1796–1854), but it was not until the 1920s that truly modern literature took shape. Short stories and novels appeared that were no longer the classical *hikayat* fairy tales of princes and princesses but works depicting true-to-life characters facing the problems of contemporary society. *Hikayat Faridah Hanum* (1925; the story of Faridah Hanum) by Syed Sheikh al-Hady (1867–1934) was the prototype of early Malay novels. An adaptation of an Egyptian novel, the characters and setting were therefore not Malayan. Still, it focused on the chief preoccupation of the Malayan elite at the time: to resolve the sociocultural conflicts arising from the confrontation between traditional culture and modern Western civilization. The main message was that the ethics of Islam, especially pertaining to relationships between the sexes, could not be compromised.

Many Malay novels until the outbreak of war in the Pacific in 1942 carried a similar message: the best defense against the problems of modern life is strict observance of the Islamic moral code. While there continued to be novels with foreign settings, Malay fiction had shifted to local scenes and situations. A love story is set against the background of urban life, often portrayed as full of evil. Surprisingly, criticism of old customs and outdated beliefs did not find fertile ground among Malay novelists, as it did among Indonesian novelists writing in Malay (Indonesian) at the same time.

During the 1930s publication of novels in Malay became widespread. About half were short penny-novels telling romantic stories. Many were more serious, concerned with moral questions and national aspirations. *Putera Gunung Tahan* (1936; the prince of Mount Tahan) by Ishak Haji Muhammad (b. 1910) and *Mari kita berjuang* (1940; let us struggle) by Abdullah Sidik (1913–1973) are representative. *Putera Gunung Tahan* satirizes the attitudes of the British colonial rulers toward their subjects. *Mari kita berjuang* is a straightforward narrative aimed at inspiring young Malayans to be self-reliant economically and politically.

The rise of the short story in the 1920s and 1930s coincided with the proliferation of magazines and newspapers in Malay. Many were simple romantic tales interlaced with moral teachings. The leading short-story writer of the period was Abdul Rahim Kajai (1894–1943).

During the Japanese occupation (1942–45) literary production almost ceased. The end of the war ushered in a period of nationalist struggle, first for cultural identity and later for political independence. New importance was placed on Malay language and literature. At first, however, novels continued prewar traditions. The moralistic novels of Ahmad Lutfi (1911–1966), like *Bilik 69* (1949; room 69) and *Joget moden* (1949; modern dance) were reminiscent of *Hikayat Faridah Hanum,* although they presented contemporary situations and spicy bedroom scenes. Ahmad Bachtiar (1902–1961) continued the prewar trend of the historical novel with nationalist overtones, while Salleh Ghani (dates n.a.) in *Seruan merdeka* (1949; the call of freedom) and Hamdan (dates n.a.) in *Barisan Zubaidah* (1950; the Zubaidah movement), treated nationalism in a more contemporary way.

A truly fresh approach to the novel did not appear until the late 1950s, and during the 1960s writing became more sophisticated. Abdul Samad Said (b. 1935), for instance, wanted to make Malay writing more realistic. His graphic portrayal of Singapore slum life in *Salina* (1961; Salina) brought a new dimension to fiction: the purpose of the novel is not to moralize but to capture contemporary society. While *Hikayat Faridah Hanum* and the novels of Ahmad Lutfi reflected fears that Malay traditions were losing out to the modern way of life, the new novels lay bare contemporary social injustices. *Tak ada jalan keluar* (1962; there is no way out) by

Suratman Markasan (b. 1930) presents a typical moral compromise: a divorcée resorts to prostitution so that her children can have a better future. *Desa pingitan* (1964; nurturing village) by Ibrahim Omar (b. 1936) and *Angin hitam dari kota* (1968; dark wind from the city) by A. Wahab Ali (b. 1941) are two prize-winning novels that deal with the conflicts between urban and rural values.

A prolific writer in the 1960s, who by the 1970s had become the leading fiction writer, is Shahnon Ahmad (q.v.). His novels mostly deal with controversial issues of the day. *Rentong* (1965; burned to ashes) and *Ranjau sepanjang jalan* (1966; *No Harvest but a Thorn,* 1972) are about the hard life of rural rice farmers, while *Protes* (1967; protest) raises touchy religious issues.

Women writers brought a new perspective to Malay fiction. Salmi Manja's (b. 1936) youthful novel *Hari mana bulan mana* (1960; which day, which month) depicts a woman's everyday experiences in a changing society. Adibah Amin's (b. 1934) *Seroja masih di kolam* (1968; the lily is still in the pond) focuses on the difficulties women face in trying to eschew traditions. Khadijah Hashim's (b. 1945) novel *Merpati putih terbang lagi* (1971; the white dove flies again) rearticulates the age-old Malayan ideal of honesty and goodness surmounting all obstacles.

While novelists have grappled with language and narrative techniques, they have not been able to deal successfully with new social experiences: the multiethnicity of the Malaysian population, political processes, and economic problems are hardly touched on.

The short story has played a more important role than the novel. Moralizing tales yielded to new trends during the 1950s, spurred on by a radical group known as Asas '50 (generation of the 1950s). Writers like Keris Mas (b. 1922), Awam-il-Sarkam (b. 1918), Wijaya Mala (b. 1923), Hamzah Hussein (b. 1927), and Asmal (pseud. of Abdul Samad bin Ismail, b. 1924), began to deal realistically with social problems. Anticolonial sentiments also appeared, but the main concern was the injustices suffered by the urban poor, rural peasants, and fishermen. The members of Asas '50 were political activists, but they were also concerned with the improvement of literary techniques and a more penetrating approach to themes.

The influence of Asas '50 continued into the mid-1960s. Asmal's "Ingin jadi pujangga" (1959; aspiring poet) is a self-caricature of the young writers who, in trying to live up to the ideals of serious writing, fall prey to their own artificialities. Asmal's "Ah Kau masuk syurga" (1959; Ah Kau goes to heaven) exposes the tendency of Malayans to accept symbols rather than substance. Keris Mas's collection *Patah tumbuh* (1962; continuity) shows not only the progress in Malay short-story writing after the war but also the writer's view of events that led to independence.

By the mid-1960s, the leading short-story writers were Abdul Samad Said and Shahnon Ahmad. Themes were still mainly social, but now set against the problems of a newly independent nation. Short-story writers portrayed emergent types: corrupt politicians, status-conscious civil servants, university-educated social climbers. Younger writers like Mohd. Affandi Hassan (b. 1940), S. Othman Kelantan (b. 1938), Ali Majod (b. 1940), Azizi Abdullah (b. 1942), and the women writers Khadijah Hashim and Fatimah Busu (b. 1943) have broadened the horizons of the short story and evinced a more polished technique. Since the late 1960s social themes have been balanced by a more introspective and penetrating look at human life.

Poetry

The first attempts to break away from traditional *syair* and *pantun* verse forms were made in the early 1930s. The new poetic expression, collectively called *sajak,* was influenced by the rise of modern poetry in Indonesia in the 1920s and 1930s. Although it took hold slowly, *sajak* bloomed after World War II. The early *sajak* poems often expressed Malayan nationalism in romantic terms.

Asas '50 viewed the *pantun* and the *syair* as too rigid for the philosophy the group advocated: they favored the free-verse expression of the *sajak.* The *sajaks* of Usman Awang (q.v.) and Mahsuri Salikon (b. 1927) became models for younger writers. Usman Awang's collection *Gelombang* (1961; waves) is representative of modern poetry of the time. The early *pantun* forms, the later free verse, his preoccupation with freeing himself from the shackles of tradition, his opposition to colonialism, and his concern for social justice are clearly arrayed chronologically in this volume. His second collection, *Duri dan api* (1969; thorns and fire), shows his ease with the free-verse forms and at the same time his widening vision, moving beyond his homeland.

There was a time when some poets thought that free verse was a license to experiment without constraint; this concept brought about the phenomenon of *sajak kabur* (obscure poems) in the 1950s and early 1960s. *Sajaks* proliferated: there was hardly a magazine or newspaper that did not print them.

Poets debuting since the late 1960s and the 1970s have had the advantage of greater education, including some knowledge of foreign literatures. Muhammed Haji Salleh (b. 1942), Firdaus Abdullah (b. 1944), Kassim Ahmad (b. 1933), Latif Mohidin (b. 1941), Zurinah Hassan (b. 1949), and Baharuddin Zainal (b. 1939) are among those who have written serious works of poetry. Poetry has moved away from social and political problems, concentrating instead on personal, philosophical, and aesthetic themes. A woman poet, Zanariah Wan Abdul Rahman (b. 1940), using traditional imagery, has written about the dilemmas of a young girl in love. Even in religious poems, thunderous exhortations and evangelistic fervor have given way to a more philosophical expression.

Drama

Malay drama in the 20th c. has had varied sources: it springs from folk-ritualistic drama, from the traditional shadow play, from the popular theater called the *bangsawan* (plays on romantic or historical themes interspersed with songs and comic sketches), and from the Western plays that were introduced through the schools. Before World War II the *bangsawan* was the main form of urban theater and the main expression of the rising urban culture. Traditional folk performances continued to thrive in the villages.

Modern Malay theater started with school performances, during the colonial period of Shakespeare and other European dramatists. During the Japanese occupation *sandiwara* plays, similar to *bangsawan* but with contemporary themes, to some extent replaced the *bangsawan;* this form of theater was inspired by Indonesian drama. Not until the 1950s was there a deliberate effort to create truly Malayan (later Malaysian) plays. The result was not only plays with modern social themes, but also, following the *bangsawan,* themes drawn from the historical and legendary past. The latter is usually referred to as *purbawara.* Shahrum Hussein (b. 1919) has written plays about past heroes, such as *Si bongkok Tanjung Puteri* (1961; the hunchbacked warrior of Tanjung Puteri) and *Tun Fatimah* (1964; Tun Fatimah [the woman warrior of old Malacca]). Mustapha Kamal Yassin (b. 1925) has dealt with contemporary subjects. His *Atap genting atap rembia* (1963; tiled and thatched roofs) attacks those who put status and wealth above love in marriage. Ali Aziz (b. 1935), in *Hang Jebat menderhaka* (1957; Hang Jebat rebels), tried to apply techniques of Shakespearean tragedy to the duel between two blood brothers: Hang Tuah, who upholds the cardinal Malayan traditional value of unquestioning loyalty to the sultan; and Hang Jebat, who rebels for the sake of justice. Usman Awang's *Muzika Uda dan Dara* (1976; the musical play of Uda and Dara), a simple tale of unrequited love between two young villagers, has been presented as a musical play as well as a dance drama.

Since the late 1960s, dramatists like Syed Alwi (b. 1930) and Nordin Hassan (b. 1929) have experimented with techniques from the traditional drama: images reflected on a screen, as in the shadow play, have been used for special effects or to convey a character's past experiences. And drama in the round often uses the techniques of traditional dance theater like the *randai.*

In Chinese

Before the Pacific War writings in Chinese echoed those of China proper. Early Chinese writers in Malaya had migrated from China, and sentiments expressed were mainly directed at the homeland. In the 1930s, after the Japanese invaded China, nationalism dominated the writing of overseas Chinese. Chinese writing had to go underground during the Japanese occupation of Malaya (1942–45). From prison Siew Yang (dates n.a.) and Chin Chung (dates n.a.) wrote clandestine anti-Japanese works.

The early postwar years saw a revival of literary activity, but writing in Chinese again suffered a setback after the communist insurrection of 1948. Between 1948 and 1957 hardly any literary activity took place, partly because of the local situation and partly because of the break in communication with China.

The desire to produce a truly *Ma-hoa,* or Malaysian Chinese, literature was nurtured

191

in the years following independence in 1957. Young writers who had grown up in Malaysia realized that *Ma-hoa* literature should have its own identity, but the legacy and influence of classical Chinese literature remained formidable.

The preferred genre of Chinese literature in Malaysia has been the short story. Between 1945 and 1965, works were mostly anticolonial and antifeudal. They reflected the life of the middle and lower classes. Since 1965 Malaysian settings and problems specifically related to the country have characterized Chinese writing in Malaysia.

In Tamil

Tamil writing in Malaysia began with religious poetry toward the end of the 19th c. The first Tamil novel was Venkitarattinam's (dates n.a.) *Karunacakaran; allathu, Kathalinmatchi* (1917; Karunacakaran; or, the glory of love). Short stories appeared during the 1930s, coinciding with the proliferation of Tamil newspapers. Many of the stories were moralizing. During this period those writing for local publications were in constant contact with developments in the homeland in south India. The influence of the Indian Tamil journal *Manikkodi* brought new themes into Malaysian Tamil short stories: political, economic, and social questions were raised.

Poetry has dominated Tamil literature in Malaysia. And the majority of poems until the 1940s were religious in content. Since the 1950s Tamil poetry had a variety of themes, ranging from social reform and patriotism to romantic love, nature, and the mother tongue.

Short stories became more numerous in the 1950s. The periodical *Tamil necan* regularly published stories by Suba Narayanan (b. 1938) and Bairoji Narayanan (b. 1931). Contact with the Tamil homeland still provided the literary guide for local writers. S. Vadivelu's (b. 1929) stories show an unusual ability to create a vivid setting; his stories that take place during the Japanese occupation are especially notable. Short stories now have a variety of themes: politics, education, economics, citizenship problems, family organization, human relationships, alcoholism, and national unity.

Only in 1958, a year after Malaysian independence, did the Association of Tamil Writers in Malaya come into being. By the 1960s there was a marked shift in Tamil literature toward Malaysian themes and problems. S. Vadivelu, who has continued to be a leading figure, published the collection of stories *Irunda ulagam* (1970; dark world) dealing with the problems of the Indian community in Malaysia.

In English

Literature in English can be called Malaysian after Malaysian writers began to write a distinctive literature in English. Before that there was only writing in English with a Malayan setting, written both by foreigners living in the country and by locals. Of the former, the most notable is Anthony Burgess (q.v.), who served as an education officer toward the end of British rule and wrote *The Malayan Trilogy* (1956–59). Gregory de Silva (dates n.a.) with *Sulaiman Goes to London* (1938), Chin Kee Onn (b. 1908) with *Malaya Upside Down* (1946), Ooi Cheng Teck (dates n.a.) with *Red Sun over Malaya: John Man's Ordeal* (1948), and Gurchan Singh (dates n.a.) with *Singa: The Lion of Malaya* (1959) represent the latter.

The seeds of Malaysian literature in English were sown by natives who used English because it was the language of their education, and hence the only language they were proficient in. Although some of them were conscious of their dilemma—inheriting a colonial culture while the country was readying itself for independence—they still could not shake off the influence of English. The best they could do was to adopt certain Malayan elements in their writings.

Wang Gungwu (b. 1930) was one of the early writers who attempted to forge a Malayan identity while using English; the poems in his collection *Pulse* (1950) have a definite Malayan quality. There were others like Wang Gungwu, but they could not sustain their creativity, and after a year or two they would stop publishing. Of the few who continued writing consistently, the leading poets have been Ee Tiang Hong (b. 1933), Wong Phui Nam (b. 1936), and Muhammed Haji Salleh. Ee Tiang Hong is fond of writing about different places in Malaysia. In "Heeren Street, Malacca" (1968), for example, he sees the old Baba Chinese culture, a relic of a past age, coming face to face with modern times. His early poems are collected in *I of the Many Faces* (1960). His tone became more critical of society as years went by. Wong Phui Nam excels in beautiful descriptions. Muhammed Haji Salleh, who studied in England and first wrote in English, now writes in Malay.

In prose, there are almost no novels, but short stories appear regularly in both popular magazines and more serious journals, like *Tenggara* and *Lidra*. Of the novels, *Scorpion Orchid* (1976) by Lloyd Fernando (b. 1926) is the best. Innovative in form, it deals with that period when the struggle for independence was not a clear-cut issue for the English-educated elite.

BIBLIOGRAPHY: Mohd. Taib bin Osman, *An Introduction to the Development of Modern Malay Language and Literature* (1961); Kirkup, J., Introduction to Majid, A., and Rice, O., eds., *Modern Malay Verse* (1963), pp. vii–xiv; Subramaniam, M., "Growth of Modern Tamil Literature in Malaysia," *Proceedings of the First International Conference-Seminar of Tamil Studies* (1969), Vol. II, pp. 304–8; Dhandayudham, R., "The Development of the Tamil Short Story in Malaysia," *JTamS*, No. 3 (1973), 7–16; Mohd. Taib bin Osman, "Classical and Modern Malay Literature," *Handbuch der Orientalistik*, 3, 3, 1 (1976), pp. 116–86; Zainal, B., "A Guide to Malay Literature (1970–76)," *Tenggara*, 8 (1976), 70–79; Wahab Ali, A., "The Role of Literature in Transmitting National Values: Malaysia," in Bresnahan, R. J., ed., *Literature and Society: Cross-Cultural Perspectives* (1977), pp. 32–42; Bennett, B., "The Subdued Ego: Poetry from Malaysia and Singapore," *Meanjin*, 37 (1978), 240–46; Ismail, Y., "The National Language and Literature of Malaysia," in Perez, A. Q., et al., eds., *Papers from the Conference on the Standardisation of Asian Languages, Manila, Philippines, December 16–21, 1974* (1978), pp. 93–103; Hong, E. T., "Malaysian Poetry in English: Influence and Independence," *PQM*, 4 (1979), 69–73; Simms, N., "The Future of English as a Poetic Language in Singapore and Malaysia," *CNLR*, 2, 2 (1979), 9–13; 3, 1 (1980), 10–14; and 3, 2 (1980), 8–12; Wong, S., "The Influence of China's Literary Movement on Malaysia's Vernacular Chinese Literature in the 1930's," *TkR*, 10 (1980), 517–34

MOHD. TAIB BIN OSMAN

See also Singapore Literature

MALGONKAR, Manohar

Indian novelist, short-story writer, and journalist (writing in English), b. 12 July 1913, Bombay

Educated at Karnatak College, Dharwar, M. then attended Bombay University, receiving a B. A. (honours) degree in English and Sanskrit in 1936. From 1935 to 1937, he arranged tiger shoots for maharajahs and worked as a professional big-game hunter. He held the post of cantonment executive officer, Government of India, 1937 to 1942. As a career military man, he served in the Maratha Light Infantry, worked on the British Army's general staff during World War II, and rose to the rank of lieutenant colonel. From 1953 to 1959 M. owned the Jagalbet Manganese Mining Syndicate, and since 1959 he has farmed a remote estate in Jagalbet, Belgaum District, Maharashtra. He has twice run, unsuccessfully, for the Indian Parliament.

In 1948 M. began writing stories for All-India Radio and *The Illustrated Weekly of India*. One need only look at his background to understand that M.'s writing is based largely on the values of the aristocracy—both Indian and British. His novels and stories have been severely criticized for dealing with the elite and ignoring the reality of India's dirt and poverty. His first two novels, *Distant Drum* (1960) and *Combat of Shadows* (1962), largely romantic tales of action and intrigue, fail most obviously in character development. His longer narratives tend to be strong in idea, but somewhat weak in execution.

This defect is particularly apparent in *A Bend in the Ganges* (1964), which deals with the violence of the 1947 partition and faults Gandhi for setting unrealistic expectations as a political expedient. M.'s best novel, *The Princes* (1963) deals with the absorption of the princely states into modern India at the time of independence, but is also a successful *Bildungsroman*. *The Devil's Wind* (1972), an engrossing historical novel, presents the Sepoy Mutiny of 1857 through the eyes of Nana Sahib, leader of the revolt.

M. has also written three works of Indian history, more than fifty short stories, at least a hundred articles, and several film scripts, one of which, *Spy in Amber* (1971), was fashioned into a novel by his daughter. Although M.'s writing deals with an era now past, his work has value as historical fiction, written from a distinctly feudal point of view no longer celebrated by Indian writers attuned to India's contemporary problems.

FURTHER WORKS: *Kanhoji Angray, Maratha Admiral* (1959); *Puars of Dewas Senior* (1963); *The Chhatrapatis of Kolhapur* (1971); *Toast in Warm Wine* (1974); *In Uniform* (1975); *Line of Mars* (1979)

BIBLIOGRAPHY: Gemmill, J. P., "Three by M. M.," *Mahfil,* 3 (1966), 76–84; Amur, G. S., *M. M.* (1973); Dayananda, Y. J., "The Novelist as Historian," *JSoAL,* 10 (1974), 55–67; Asnani, S. M., "A Study of the Novels of M. M.," *LHY,* 16 (1975), 71–98; Dayananda, J. Y., *M. M.,* (1975); Jayashri, I., "Women versus Tradition in the Novels of M. M.," *Triveni,* 45, 2 (1976), 73–80; Amur, G. S., "M. M. and the Problems of the Indian Novelist in English," in Mohan, R., ed., *Indian Writing in English* (1978), pp. 37–46

JANET POWERS GEMMILL

MALI LITERATURE

Vast, sparsely populated, predominantly agricultural, Mali has an illustrious history going back to medieval times. Under French rule the territory was called French Sudan. An independent nation since 1960, Mali has launched various campaigns to fight illiteracy, educating the masses in both French and Bambara, a Mandé language spoken by the largest ethnic group in the country. As literacy increases, interest in the arts grows as well. The rich oral tradition has given rise to theater groups. Since the early 1970s the government-owned publishing company, Éditions Populaires, has published historical, anthropological, and literary works. It limits publication to noncontroversial subject matter, however, emphasizing the glorification of the past rather than the examination of the present with a critical eye.

Among the most renowned African historians is Amadou Hampaté Bâ (b. 1920), who has published important works in the field of African religion and Islamic theology. Having developed an Arabic script for the Fulani language, Bâ published *Kaidara* (1965; Kaidara), a traditional allegorical poem in a bilingual Fulani/French edition.

Emphasis upon history and Mali's rich oral tradition is also apparent in the work of Bâ's contemporary, Djibril Tamsir Niane (b. 1920), who was born either in Mali or northern Guinea and whose ancestors were Malinké *griots* (oral historians). Niane's version of the Malinké epic *Soundjata; ou, L'épopée mandingue* (1960; *Sundiata: An Epic of Old Mali,* 1965) retells the legend of the crippled boy who grew up to become an outstanding military and political leader and rule the Mali Empire (1230–55). In the introduction to the epic, Niane emphasizes the importance of the *griot;* "We are vessels of speech, we are the repositories that harbor secrets many centuries old."

A younger generation has taken up the same tradition of glorifying the past. Massa Maken Diabaté (b. 1936) has rewritten the Sundiata legend as *Kala Jata* (1965; Kala Jata). Combining his talents as a poet and an anthropologist, Diabaté uses words and expressions in the Malinké language interspersed within the French text in an attempt to capture the rhythms of Malinké poetry.

Seydou Kouyaté Badian (b. 1928) is known as a poet, playwright, and novelist. His novel *Sous l'orage* (1963; under the storm) examines the conflict between generations in a changing society. When two lovers challenge their parents by deciding to marry, they involve the entire village in the conflict. Badian has also turned to African history for inspiration. His play *La mort de Chaka* (1962; the death of Chaka) treats the theme of the Zulu king first presented in literature by the Lesotho writer Thomas Mofolo (q.v.), in his novel *Chaka* (1925; *Chaka the Zulu,* 1931), written in the Bantu language South Sotho.

Drawing upon ancient Mali history to challenge modern perceptions of Africa's past, Yambo Ouologuem (b. 1940) published an important and controversial novel, *Le devoir de violence* (1968; *Bound to Violence,* 1971), in which he created the fictional African kingdom of Makem, ruled by the violent despots of the Saif dynasty. He advances the thesis that violence and slavery existed long before the colonial powers' scramble for the continent. The first African novel to receive the Renaudot Prize in France, *Le devoir de violence* has been attacked by critics for its brutality, eroticism, and alleged plagiarism. Ouologuem uses violence to shock the reader. In addition, he blends legend with realism, African and Arabic expressions with French. He forces the reader to react to his prose, to come to grips with his expression of the eternal problem of man's inhumanity to man.

Mali is committed to affirming a rich cultural tradition. Its writers today reveal a genuine commitment to studying the present and the past and to synthesizing the old and the new.

BIBLIOGRAPHY: Larson, C., *The Emergence of African Fiction* (1972), passim; Rubin, J. S., "Mali: New Writing from an Ancient Civilization," *SBL,* 4, 3 (1973), 15–18; Olney, J., "Of Griots and Heroes," *SBL,* 6, 1 (1975), 14–17; Diawara, G., "Literature and the New Generations," *LAAW,* 31 (1977), 114–17; Singare, T., "Où en sont les lettres maliennes?" *Études maliennes,* 22 (1977), 1–23; Palmer, E., *The Growth of the African Novel* (1979), pp. 199–220; Decraene, P., "Le Mali: Tradition, arts et littérature," *FE,* 294 (1980), 34–37

MILDRED MORTIMER

MALINKÉ LITERATURE
See Mali Literature

MALINOVSKI, Ivan
Danish poet, b. 18 Feb. 1926, Copenhagen

M. lived in Sweden during the German occupation of Denmark and afterward studied Slavic languages at the University of Århus, 1947–52. He has written for numerous newspapers and magazines and has translated such writers as Brecht, Enzensberger, García Lorca, Neruda, Pasternak, and Chekhov (qq.v.). In 1970 M. received the Prize of the Danish Academy.

M. made what he considers his debut as a poet at a relatively mature age with *Galgenfrist* (1958; respite from the gallows), having disavowed his first two collections of poems from the 1940s. His closest literary affinities are to the Swedish modernists (q.v.) of the 1940s—Karl Vennberg (b. 1910), Erik Lindegren, and Gunnar Ekelöf (qq.v.)—rather than to contemporary Danish poets. M. shares with the Swedish poets their rigor of expression, formal density, deep pessimism, and criticism of capitalist society.

Galgenfrist occupies a central position in M.'s oeuvre. The basis of these modernist poems is a total nihilism that leaves no room for any metaphysics, in contrast to most postwar Danish modernist writing. M. shows a complete distrust of any belief, theory, or ideology. This very attitude, according to M., may serve as a starting point for truthful artistic creativity.

One might expect this extreme nihilism to be at odds with M.'s Marxist-oriented criticism of society. To M., however, the two attitudes are not mutually exclusive; rather, they are a necessary outcome of our painful reality and as such constitute the fruitful tension that gives impetus to M.'s poetic creativity. He distinguishes between an objective inhumanity and a subjective human experience; when the suffering caused by the inhuman forces becomes unbearable, the human being will revolt.

Åbne digte (1963; open-ended poems) and *Romerske bassiner* (1963; Roman pools), with their portrayal of a repressive society and their treatment of contemporary events, are explicitly political. M.'s Marxist orientation, however, is only part of an existentialist (q.v.) attitude. It is the fundamental dichotomies of the human condition that M. has put into literary form. In *Romerske bassiner* a collage technique is used to describe society through its own distorted language. The cliché-ridden language of radio, magazines, advertisements, and speeches is captured in all its fraudulence and meaninglessness.

M.'s most prevalent technique has been described as a "strategy of opposition," whereby the compressed antithetical form reflects the antinomy between subjective and objective forces. *Poetomatic* (1965; poetomatic) is an accomplished structure of abrupt, irreconcilable opposites. The closed, aphoristic form is not easily accessible, but it aptly underscores the sense of discontinuity and nothingness. M.'s fast-growing reputation testifies to his success in finding an appropriate form for the complex experiences of modern man.

FURTHER WORKS: *Ting* (1945); *De tabte slag* (1947); *Vejen* (1954); *Glemmebogen: Femten digtere i dansk gendigtning* (1962); *Med solen i ryggen* (1963); *De tomme sokler* (1963); *Leve som var der en fremtid og et håb* (1968); *Misnøje til skade for mandstugten: Et digtudvalg* (1969); *Samlede digte* (1970); *Kritik af tavsheden* (1974); *Vinterens hjerte* (1980)

BIBLIOGRAPHY: King, C., *An Introduction to I. M.* (1975)

CHARLOTTE SCHIANDER GRAY

MALLEA, Eduardo

Argentine novelist, short-story writer, and essayist, b. 14 Aug. 1903, Bahía Blanca

M.'s father, a physician, instilled in his son a love of humanity and a respect for the downtrodden. M. first studied law in Buenos Aires, before finding his true vocation in literature. Central in his life and in his fiction is his impassioned, anguished search for what he calls the real Argentina, the Argentina that lies beneath the surface of the ostentation, materialism, and false values he sees enshrined in his country. M. has been a lifelong contributor to the newspaper *La nación* and directed its literary supplement for many years. He has also written frequently for the prestigious journal *Sur*.

At the beginning of his career M. was influenced by the European avant-garde writers of the 1920s. His first work, *Cuentos para una inglesa desesperada* (1926; stories for a desperate Englishwoman), revealed aesthetic sensitivity and refinement. More than stories, the narrations in this volume are poetic expressions in prose of moods and feelings, couched in delicate and at times affected language. Before M. wrote his first novel, he published *Historia de una pasión argentina* (1937; history of an Argentine passion), a seminal essay that stands as his intellectual and philosophical credo. It contains many themes that were to appear in M.'s fiction, the most important being his concept of the two Argentinas—the visible Argentina and the invisible one. The visible is the pretentious, artificial, and hypocritical veneer that the country lives with from day to day; the invisible is the heart, the genuine soul of the country, its true but hidden values.

M. is an intellectual and psychological novelist who sees man's anguish resulting more from a struggle of forces within his own psyche than from external, environmental ones. In this sense, novels such as *Fiesta en noviembre* (1938; *Fiesta in November,* 1966) and *La bahía de silencio* (1940; *The Bay of Silence* 1944) represent the counterpoise to the *criollista* novel, or novel of the land that held sway in Spanish America from about 1920 to 1940, in which hostile nature was the protagonist and man its helpless victim. M. is an existential writer who penetrates to the inner core of man's feelings and states of mind to reveal his basic loneliness, lack of communication, and alienation. In *Fiesta en no-*

viembre, inspired by the murder of Federico García Lorca (q.v.) during the Spanish Civil War, M. juxtaposes two distinct and ironically incompatible narratives: the frivolous party given by Señora Rague, and the Kafkaesque kidnapping and execution of a young poet. The autobiographical *La bahía de silencio,* which established M. as one of the most important writers in Argentina, represents his struggle to affirm his social ideals in the face of an impersonal and uncaring public. The torment and disillusion of Martín Tregua as he views his misguided Argentina forms the central theme of the novel.

In *Todo verdor perecerá* (1941; *All Green Shall Perish,* 1966) the cold, arid, and reticent nature of Agata and Nicanor Cruz leads to their ultimate destruction. Emotional withdrawal appears as a leitmotif in many of M.'s novels and stories and as the central theme in *Chaves* (1953; *Chaves,* 1966), a brief, intense novel about a sawmill worker whose inexorable taciturnity is symptomatic of profound grief and frustration.

M. is as fine a short-story writer as he is a novelist. *La sala de espera* (1953; the waiting room) consists of seven independent stories unified spatially by their setting at a train station, where each of the protagonists awaits the train back to Buenos Aires, back to a life of pain and despair.

There is little external action in most of M.'s fiction; it is almost static, the conflicts arising from the inner turmoil of the characters. Instead of movement in the form of a linear narrative, the reader senses a tension, a stress, an internal struggle between reason and emotion, or between will and feeling. M.'s characters are unhappy, unfulfilled, and isolated souls; his women are cold and distant, indifferent, ungiving, haughty, "alone in their aloneness." The people in his fiction are seeking to find themselves, to find their own set of values, whether it be in crass Buenos Aires, as in the case of Jacobo Uber in the story "La causa de Jacobo Uber, perdida" (1936; "The Lost Cause of Jacob Uber," 1966), or in the inner provinces, as with the wealthy Román Ricarte in *Las águilas* (1943; the eagles).

M.'s style is original, distinctive, and highly suitable for the penetrating analysis of character on which his fiction depends. His language, expansive rather than succinct or precise, can be heavy, dense, and inclined toward the abstract, but it can also be lyrical and poetic. At his best, M. uses ingenious linguistic play to capture the intensity and subtlety of his intellectual and emotional world.

M.'s place in Spanish American literature is secure. Although he is perhaps too cerebral ever to be a popular novelist, he has examined human emotions with great understanding and sensitivity.

FURTHER WORKS: *Conocimiento y expresión de la Argentina* (1935); *Nocturno europeo* (1935); *La ciudad junto al río inmóvil* (1936); *Meditación en la costa* (1939); *El sayal y la púrpura* (1941); *Rodeada está de sueño* (1944); *El retorno* (1946); *El vínculo* (1946); *Los enemigos del alma* (1950); *La torre* (1951); *Notas de un novelista* (1954); *El gajo de enebro* (1957); *Simbad* (1957); *Posesión* (1958); *La raza humana* (1959); *La vida blanca* (1959); *Las travesías* (2 vols., 1961–62); *La representación de los aficionados: Un juego* (1962); *La guerra interior* (1963); *El resentimiento* (1966); *La barca de hielo* (1967); *La red* (1968); *La penúltima puerta* (1969); *Gabriel Andaral* (1971); *Triste piel del universo* (1971); *En la creciente oscuridad* (1972); *Los papeles privados* (1974). FURTHER VOLUME IN ENGLISH: *All Green Shall Perish* (1966; contains three novellas and four short stories)

BIBLIOGRAPHY: Dudgeon, P., *E. M.: A Personal Study of His Work* (1949); Chapman, A., "Terms of Spiritual Isolation in E. M.," *MLF,* 37, 1–2 (1952), 21–27; Polt, J. H. R., *The Writings of E. M.* (1959); Peterson, F., "Notes on M.'s Definition of Argentina," *Hispania,* 45 (1962), 621–24; Lichtblau, M., *El arte estilístico de E. M.* (1967); Rivelli, C., *E. M.: La continuidad temática de su obra* (1969); Lewald, E. H., *E. M.* (1977)

MYRON I. LICHTBLAU

MALLET-JORIS, Françoise

(pseud. of Françoise Lilar) Belgian novelist, poet, short-story writer, and memoirist (writing in French), b. 6 July 1930, Antwerp

Daughter of a Belgian statesman and of the writer Suzanne Lilar (b. 1901), M.-J. now resides in France with her third husband; she has four children. Her conversion to Catholicism had a great impact on her life. An edi-

tor for the Grasset publishing house, M.-J. also serves on the juries of the Fémina Prize and the Goncourt Academy.

Since the publication, when she was seventeen, of a book of verse, M.-J.'s production has been steady and varied. Besides the novels and memoirs that have won her wide public recognition, M.-J. has translated English books and has written children's stories, song lyrics, prefaces for classics, and historical novels. Relatively unconcerned by problems of form, M.-J. admits that style is not of primary importance in her work, and she is resolutely opposed to the imitation of contemporary fads and New Novel (q.v.) innovations.

Le rempart des béguines (1951; *The Illusionist,* 1952) had a *succès de scandale* because of its lesbian theme, while the detached directness of the young author's approach suggested echoes of *Les liaisons dangereuses* by Choderlos de Laclos (1741–1803). *La chambre rouge* (1955; *The Red Room,* 1956), a sequel, continues focusing on the evolution of an adolescent facing a disillusioning adult world.

The title of *Les mensonges* (1956; *House of Lies,* 1957) emphasizes a theme that is becoming predominant in M.-J.'s work: the conflict between the characters' inner nature, hidden from others and even from themselves, and their social roles. This preoccupation slowly unfolds in *L'Empire Céleste* (1958; *Café Céleste,* 1959) until the main character, forced to act in accordance with the image others have of him, is faced with nothing but a mask. Winner of the Fémina Prize, this novel reveals an increased technical mastery in its handling of a great many characters of extreme diversity.

In *Le jeu du souterrain* (1973; *The Underground Game,* 1975) M.-J. deemphasizes precisely drawn descriptions, adopts a more fragmented technique, and conveys a much lighter atmosphere tinged with irony: a writer's relative failure in productive creativity has a humorous counterpart in the modest archaeological find that crowns another man's endless years of solitary underground labor. *Allegra* (1976; Allegra) portrays with deft and convincing touches the type of heroine often found in M.-J.'s world. Completely herself, Allegra is unaware that her innocence looks suspicious in a society used to compromises and role playing. Counterpointed with Allegra's instinctive nonconformism, the theme of women's guilt whenever they deviate from what is normally expected of them becomes more explicit than in earlier works.

M.-J. has been compared to Flemish painters for the precision and realism of her settings, and to Balzac for her adroit handling of a wide social spectrum. Already evident in her first novel, M.-J.'s talent over the years has consistently matured; the scope of her social observation has widened as well as deepened. There has been no sudden transformation in her narrative technique, which has remained fairly traditional, although it does not rely on introspection and leaves a margin of ambiguity behind everyone's actions. Rather pessimistic in outlook, most of M.-J.'s characters retain, nevertheless, a dynamic resilience and an intuitive belief in the value of living. The pursuit of authenticity and the search for identity may be the unifying trend in M.-J.'s world, while her lucid observation of human frailties makes M.-J. essentially a moralist. Her interest in people, men as well as women, of varying backgrounds and personalities may have ensured her success as a novelist.

FURTHER WORKS: *Poèmes du dimanche* (1942); *Cordélia* (1956; *Cordelia, and Other Stories,* 1965); *Les personnages* (1961; *The Favourite,* 1962); *Lettre à moi-même* (1963; *A Letter to Myself,* 1964); *Marie Mancini, le premier amour de Louis XIV* (1964; *The Uncompromising Heart: A Life of Marie Mancini, Louis XIV's First Love,* 1966); *Les signes et les prodiges* (1966; *Signs and Wonders,* 1967); *Trois âges de la nuit* (1968; *The Witches,* 1969); *La maison de papier* (1970); *The Paper House,* 1971); *J'aurais voulu jouer de l'accordéon* (1976); *Jeanne Guyon* (1978); *Dickie-Roi (1979); Un chagrin d'amour et d'ailleurs* (1981)

BIBLIOGRAPHY: Reck, R. D., "M.-J. and the Anatomy of the Will," *YFS,* 24 (1959), 74–79; Delattre, G., "Mirrors and Masks in the World of M.-J.," *YFS,* 27 (1961), 121–26; Crosland, M., *Women of Iron and Velvet: French Women Writers after George Sand* (1976), pp. 180–91; Detry, M., *M.-J.: Dossier critique et inédits* (1976); Rumeau-Smith, M., "Rôles, images et authenticité dans *Allegra* de F. M.-J.," *SPFA* (1980–81), 91–102

YVONNE GUERS-VILLATE

MALRAUX, André

French novelist and essayist, b. 3 Nov. 1901, Paris; d. 23 Nov. 1976, Paris

The son of separated parents, M. early established his independence by leaving school to frequent Parisian literary and artistic circles of the post-World War I period. In a spirit of adventure, he abruptly went to Cambodia in 1923 and was arrested for the theft of art treasures from a temple; he stayed on in Indochina to edit an anticolonial newspaper in Saigon. In 1936 he commanded an international air squadron on the Loyalist side during the Spanish Civil War. When World War II erupted, M. disappeared into the French underground and later joined General de Gaulle's 1945–46 government as Minister of Cultural Affairs. Recognized since 1928 as a major novelist, M. devoted the last several decades of his life to writing voluminously on art and also to publishing his personal reminiscences. In both literature and politics, M. proved to be one of the most prominent and controversial figures of the 20th c.

M. wrote quickly and was not given to rewriting for polished effect. His style is alternately reportorial and poetic; his characters speak in the vernacular of fighting men, yet sometimes sound like philosophers. In their structure, M.'s novels rely heavily on cinematic technique, with sudden "fade-outs" and abrupt transitions of scene, time, and place.

Two major influences on the young M. were Dostoevsky, whose psychological complexities he sought to capture in his own characters, and Nietzsche, who had portrayed the human will as an almost tangible force. M. was also fascinated by T. E. Lawrence, the British soldier-adventurer-writer known as "Lawrence of Arabia."

At the heart of M.'s work one senses not only a personal dynamism but the underlying tensions that motivated him to write. We are witness to a fierce struggle between the egocentric, rugged individualist—a romantic 19th-c. "conquering hero" type—and the modern hero who becomes increasingly aware of his isolation unless he recognizes his identity as a social and political being with an obligation to pursue collective action and international brotherhood.

M.'s first published novel, *Les conquérants* (1928; *The Conquerors,* 1929), deals with the revolutionary upsrisings in Canton, Hong

Kong, and Shanghai in 1925. Although he had only briefly visited China at that time, *Les conquérants* was generally, if erroneously, considered to be a documentary novel of events in which he had personally participated. Its hard-hitting journalistic style and vivid descriptions of revolutionary activity do create a "documentary" flavor, and the novel abounds in action and violence, but M. was actually seeking to create a gallery of human portraits to probe why and how men will fight for a given cause.

In particular, he contrasts the pure anarchist with the methodical and calculating revolutionary "organizer," and juxtaposes the sincere, dedicated revolutionary with his cynical, ruthless, and opportunistic counterpart. The central figure, Garine, is something of a cross between these two extremes. Sympathetic to the downtrodden, he believes that men must be manipulated and molded by a leader if they are to attain their collective goals. He has commitment but lacks idealistic fervor, and is, one senses, potentially a dangerous totalitarian tyrant. Despite his devotion to the revolutionary cause, Garine remains a self-centered individualist who never attains a true feeling of communal brotherhood.

The same characteristics are exhibited by the hero of *La voie royale* (1930; *The Royal Way*, 1935), another foreign adventurer in the Far East who wants to "leave a scar on the map." Perken becomes involved in a scheme to unearth Cambodian art treasures in order to sell them and obtain money for supplying a native tribe with modern weapons to fight off the colonial French, who would bring "civilization" to the jungle. He dies realizing that there are no true "causes," no authentic heroism, only solitary individuals who in the end die solitary deaths. *La voie royale* is based in part on M.'s own experience but also seems to derive from Joseph Conrad's (q.v.) *Heart of Darkness*, transcending the framework of the adventure tale to deal with the very meaning of life and death.

In *La condition humaine* (1933; *Man's Fate*, 1934) M. returns to the Chinese revolution of the 1920s, exploring in still greater depth the reasons men fight and die for what they believe in. It is in this novel that a strongly positive new element enters his philosophical thinking. Kyo, the Eurasian hero, discovers that death can be "con-

quered" in a sense if a man gives his life for the good of a communal cause, and, in so doing, acquires a deep personal experience of brotherhood and fraternity. While the "human condition" described by the 17th-c. philosopher Pascal (from whom M. took his title) is bleak, tragic, and meaningless without the grace of God, M. sees man's fate as lofty and meaningful when we consciously choose a course of action that transcends destiny and earns for us our individual human dignity. This expression of a new, agnostic, and altogether contemporary tragic humanism, along with M.'s positing of the "absurd," make him a precursor of Sartre, Camus, and existentialism (qq.v.).

On a grander scale than in his previous novels, *L'espoir* (1937; *Man's Hope*, 1938) once more embodies the basic stylistic characteristics and philosophical dialectic that marked both *La condition humaine* and *Les conquérants*. *L'espoir* records the early months of the Spanish Civil War, which eventually led to the victory of Generalissimo Francisco Franco. M.'s novel, however, ends on a note of hope that the fraternal spirit of the antifascist forces in Spain may yet triumph. Although he may have written *L'espoir* at least partly for its propaganda effect, and while it is a rather sprawling novel, it is also a powerful and epic work of fiction, adding to M.'s stature as a novelist of international importance.

When M. published *Les voix du silence* (1951; *The Voices of Silence*, 1953), followed by an impressive series of other volumes on painting and sculpture, he was attacked by art critics and historians for his unorthodox views and his cryptic, often paradoxical, commentary. In essence, M. was writing less about art per se than about the rise and fall of civilization and the destiny of mankind. Continuing the dialogue of his novels, M. advances the theory that the artist is a hero who triumphs over chaos by imposing form, meaning, and truth, and that art is our key to earthly immortality. It is art, M. believes, that defines man's continuity from civilization to civilization.

Great anticipation preceded the publication of what had been rumored to be M.'s "memoirs"; but he perversely called the first volume of his personal recollections *Antimémoires* (1967; *Anti-Memoirs*, 1968). Devoid of the customary anecdotes and gossip, and bypassing the author's childhood and youth completely, *Antimémoires* defies the conventions of autobiography. As a challenge to accepted notions of "reality," M. also juggles fact and fiction by interspersing excerpts from his novels. In lieu of following normal chronology, he dates certain chapters with several different years (for example, "1934 Saba/1965 Aden"), in order to alert the reader that his thoughts on certain civilizations are not just past impressions or just present impressions but rather a literary distillation of both. The result is an astonishing tour de force, highly demanding on the reader, but creating a unique, extratemporal "surreality" of almost mythic proportions.

Just as M.'s life had become a legend in his own time, he sought to re-create that life in legendary fashion by circumventing the devices of traditional literary memoirs. Subsequent volumes of his personal recollections include memorable portraits of such diverse personalities as Léopold Sédar Senghor (q.v.), Pablo Picasso, and M.'s political idol, de Gaulle.

"What then is the relationship between a man and the myth that he embodies?" M. teasingly asks in one of these last volumes. Throughout his colorful and stormy career, M. remained a resolutely private person, letting his public image grow to fantastic proportions with neither comment nor denial. Widely admired as an adventurer, soldier, novelist, essayist, and statesman, he was nonetheless frequently attacked as a hypocrite, opportunist, even charlatan. Because he had fought side by side with communists, and wrote sympathetically about them, M. was believed to have been himself a communist. Yet despite his prorevolutionary stance, M. was fundamentally simply antifascist. He early saw the Soviet Union as a police state, and long before his postwar diatribes against official Russian communism, such anti-Stalinist attitudes are apparent in his novels.

M. remains the prototype of his own fictional hero: the man who repeatedly defies death as a means of asserting and confirming his indomitable faith in life. *Les voix du silence* and *Antimémoires* are recognized as two of the most original and provocative works of nonfiction of our time; *La condition humaine,* which won the Goncourt Prize in 1933, continues to be acknowledged as one of the indisputedly great novels of this century.

FURTHER WORKS: *Lunes en papier* (1921); *La tentation de l'Occident* (1926; *The Temp-*

tation of the West, 1961); *Le temps du mépris* (1935; *Days of Wrath,* 1936); *Les noyers de l'Altenburg* (1943; *The Walnut Trees of Altenburg,* 1952); *Esquisse d'une psychologie du cinéma* (1946); *La psychologie de l'art* (3 vols., 1947–50): *Le musée imaginaire, La création artistique, La monnaie de l'absolu (The Psychology of Art,* 3 vols., 1949–50: *Museum without Walls, The Creative Act, The Twilight of the Absolute); Saturne* (1950; *Saturn: An Essay on Goya,* 1957); *Le musée imaginaire de la sculpture mondiale* (3 vols., 1952–54); *La métamorphose des dieux* (1957; *The Metamorphosis of the Gods,* 1960); *Le triangle noir* (1970); *Les chênes qu'on abat* (1971; *Felled Oaks: Conservation with de Gaulle,* 1972); *Oraisons funèbres* (1971); *Paroles et écrits politiques 1947–1972* (1973); *La tête d'obsidienne* (1974; *Picasso's Mask,* 1976); *Lazare* (1974; *Lazarus,* 1977); *L'irréel* (1974); *Hôtes de passage* (1975); *L'intemporel* (1976); *La corde et les souris* (1976); *Le miroir des limbes* (1976); *L'homme précaire et la littérature* (1977); *Le surnaturel* (1977)

BIBLIOGRAPHY: Frohock, W. M., *A. M. and the Tragic Imagination* (1952); Blend, C. D., *A. M.: Tragic Humanist* (1963); Lewis, R. W. B., ed., *M.: A Collection of Critical Essays* (1964); Righter, W., *The Rhetorical Hero: An Essay on the Aesthetics of A. M.* (1964); Langlois, W. G., *A. M.: The Indochina Adventure* (1966); Wilkinson, D., *M.: An Essay in Political Criticism* (1967); Horvath, V., *A. M.: The Human Adventure* (1969); Kline, T. J., *A. M. and the Metamorphosis of Death* (1973); Greenlee, J. W., *M.'s Heroes and History* (1975); Lacouture, J., *A. M.* (1975); de Courcel, M., ed., *M.: Life and Work* (1976); Hewitt, J. R., *A. M.* (1978); special M. issue, *TCL,* 24, 3 (1978); "A. M.: Metamorphosis and Imagination," special M. issue, *NYLF,* No. 3 (1979)

JAMES ROBERT HEWITT

One may well agree with Marcel Savane's judgment that *Man's Hope* will endure into the twenty-first century as one of the best revelations to later readers of what it meant to live in the twentieth. But if so, it will survive more by its value as a document than as a piece of literature, and by its appeal to the comprehending intellect rather than to the emotions. Its confusions, its loose ends, its diffuseness, may even increase its documentary interest. In its consciousness of what the fighting was about, *Man's Hope* towers above the book that is inevitably compared with it, *For Whom the Bell Tolls.* But Hemingway's book has the tight unity, the coherence, the constant emotional tension, and the finish, that M.'s does not. The difference is that Hemingway intended a novel while M. intended a novel and something more. The books are thus not entirely commensurable. If M.'s book outlasts Hemingway's, all that will be proved is that novels are not necessarily the most durable of books.

Wilbur M. Frohock, *A. M. and the Tragic Imagination* (1952), p. 125

La condition humaine is not a novel of ideas, although it forces one to think. It is even less a novel of propaganda. The Chinese revolution in Shanghai provides it with its general theme, but it is in no way dependent upon a historical framework for its major interest. Balzac would have described the city of Shanghai, its geography and appearance, its motley crowd of natives and foreign traders, its smells, and some of its shops and houses. Tolstoy might have written at length of the great and small causes that had brought about the revolt and of the way in which events had been determined. M.'s method, like that of most moderns, makes greater demands on the reader's brain. Nowhere is the confused skein of factions and assassinations and plots unraveled for his benefit. The traditional disorder of history is scrupulously respected. M. relates the struggle as an actor in those events and not as an omniscient and reflective spectator. The contemporary public, which has lived through one or more wars, is learning daily, through the press and the radio, how disconnected and futile are most of the events in which they are forced to take an interest, do not balk at the efforts they are asked to make. They know too well that men are not heroes curbing fate at will and that betrayals, contradictions, and dissonances are the common occurrence of any war, civil or foreign.

Henri Peyre, *The Contemporary French Novel* (1955), p. 197

His early novels (*Les conquérants, La voie royale*) are perhaps even a little excessive in their lyrical praise of the adventurer. No wonder Gaëtan Picon calls him and his generation romantic. But even in his later and more mature works, he consciously shuns the analytical novel, both introspective and retrospective. His is a literature of the present, a literature of "extreme situations," as Sartre calls it; a literature of war and death, in which evil, as represented by the sadistic will to degrade, remains pure and consequently redeemable. In the revealing preface to *Le temps du mépris*, M. fervently takes issue with the cerebral (and pathologically impartial) kind of novelist who, obsessed by the notion of individualism and individual antago-

nisms, forever explores the "inner world" of his characters, but neglects to find solidarity in common action.

Victor Brombert, *The Intellectual Hero: Studies in the French Novel 1880–1955* (1961), p. 166

The word "lucid," which M. sometimes applies to the heroes of his early novels, has frequently been applied to M. himself. Nonetheless, when we come to examine the meaning of his text, we find that he is very far from lucid as this word is generally understood in France. All the words that M. loves so well, that he uses over and over and over again—fraternity, destiny, fate, eternity, centuries-old, millennary—are just the resonant type of word that sets us dreaming. Whatever precise contents these words may originally have had is soon dissipated by incessant reiteration. Yet there is something in these vague and shapeless words, and in the emotions that are clustered around them, that is essential to M.'s meaning. M. truly believes—and he has become increasingly explicit on this point in his later writings—that the really important, fundamental aspects of human experience are mysteries that cannot be elucidated but only revealed. Death is a mystery; human fraternity, a mystery; art, a mystery; and behind them all, the great impenetrable mystery of man himself. "The word 'to know' as applied to human beings has always stupefied me. I believe that we know no one." But we do have, according to M., an immediate intuition of this mystery in certain moments that transcend our normal experience of life. And the vague abstractions, progressively depleted of rational content during the unfolding of a M. novel, are suddenly brought to life at the end, by the impact of approaching death. Death gives the dimension of the absolute to that which was relative, the depth of eternity to that which was transient. And the emotional illumination is reinforced by the strange nocturnal lighting effects that are characteristic of so many of M.'s climactic scenes.

Germaine Brée and Margaret Guiton, *The French Novel from Gide to Camus* (1962), p. 189

Essentially, it is the idea of the chaos of appearance or the chaos of the world as given by creation that makes it possible for M. to find unity in all artistic creation, whether it be religious or secular in nature. "All art," he declares, "seems to begin with a struggle against chaos." If art is also the expression of the artist's feeling about the universe, it follows that in M.'s philosophy the artist begins by feeling that the universe is chaotic, at least as it appears on the surface. This is no less true for the artist whose inspiration is religious in nature than for one for whom there is only man. For the former, the chaotic nature of appearance hides a truth "beyond," which he seeks to attain and, in one way or another, to manifest. The religious artist, then, takes the apparent chaos and orders it in terms of the truth that is the dominant value in his life. For the nonreligious artist, there may well be no order behind the chaos except what he can impose in terms of artistic truth as he sees it; this will be a human order, one determined by man's desires. Malraux dramatized this by his now famous remark on the Greek acanthus. The acanthus, he said, is a stylized artichoke; it is what an artichoke would have been if man had been God. This is nothing other than a restatement of Baudelaire's *dictum*, "The primary business of an artist is to substitute man for nature."

Charles D. Blend, *A. M.: Tragic Humanist* (1963), p. 149

M.'s career begins in mystery with the expedition to Indo-China, the obscure affair of the missing statues, a short term of imprisonment, and a plunge into Eastern politics. The details of these matters are still unknown to us, but it is their resonance that counts. With all their shadow and uncertainty they nevertheless suggest a purity of adventure. M. entered the European consciousness not as a writer but as an event, as a symbolic figure somehow combining the magical qualities of youth and heroism with a sense of unlimited promise. Here was no longer an air of defeat or fatigue, the melancholy self-deprecating "Hamlet" figure, but an insatiable cultural pirate, ransacking the four corners of the earth for some mysterious yet significant end, a last incarnation of "Faustian man." . . .

Such a symbolic existence, at a high level of self-consciousness, has complex responsibilities, above all the painful one of remaining true to itself. And no paradox of M.'s career has more puzzled and inflamed both critics and admirers than the particular metamorphosis that has transformed the novelist of violence into a critic and curator, or the ardent revolutionary into a fixture of the established order.

William Righter, *The Rhetorical Hero: An Essay on the Aesthetics of A. M.* (1964), pp. 2–3

It is important to bear in mind that it is an *individual* that M. would reintegrate into the society of men—a being who is fully aware of his stature as a man and who, by conscious choice, is willing to dedicate himself to elevating all men to a level of human dignity. This explains why all of M.'s heroes are intellectuals who have broken with a society in which they themselves suffered humiliation or in which dignity was denied their fellow men; they are lucid heroes, conscious of their world, and activated by a desire to either escape from the imperfect world into which they were born or to refashion it.

M.'s individual is born of a break with what he considers a world in need of rectification—a world conceived as a prison from which he must escape in order to forge his own destiny. M. himself is perhaps the chief protagonist of his own works. Whether the individual be a man of action or an artist, his origin is the same: he is born of a rupture with the world he has inherited. This world might be the political structure of society in the case of the former, or the world of pictures in the case of the latter.

Violet Horvath, *A. M.: The Human Adventure* (1969), p. 107

MALTESE LITERATURE

Malta (including Gozo), Christian in religion and European in culture, with a population of over 300,000 (there are additional Maltese overseas, in Australia and North America), was under foreign domination until 1964, when it achieved independence from Britain. Malta's earliest official written language was Old Sicilian, often interlarded with Vulgar Latin and Old Italian. This was the linguistic heritage of the Normans, who in 1090 captured Malta from the Arabs, and of their European successors. Italian continued to enjoy cultural and official preeminence during British rule from 1813 onward, at first alone and later together with English. It lost its official status when the Italian Fascists' propaganda machine began to describe Malta as *terra irredenta* (that is, Italian-speaking territory under foreign rule).

The first Chair of Maltese and Oriental languages at the Old University, held by the author of this article for nearly forty years, was established in 1937. The study of Maltese literature and language was thus given academic status. The by-product of this situation was the creation of a trilingual Maltese literature.

The Maltese language, basically Semitic but with a large superstructure of Romance and English loan words, for many centuries played second fiddle to Italian. There has been a smaller literary output in English, which continued to be a co-official with Maltese after independence.

In Italian

Historical circumstances explain why Maltese literature in the early 20th c. was mainly in Italian. Poets writing in Italian had as a common theme Maltese patriotism, often identified with love for Italy and its culture; but they also sounded personal notes and used local themes. Among the fourteen or so regularly anthologized poets are Carmelo Psaila (q.v.), better known as Dun Karm, who later established himself as the national poet in the Maltese language; Alberto Cesareo (1877–1943), at his best in the personal poems in *Risveglio* (1931; awakening); Carmelo Mifsud-Bonnici (1897–1948), who in *Canti della patria* (1924; songs of the homeland) created powerful patriotic verse; Vincenzo Frendo-Azzopardi (1895–1955), author of *Canti patriottici* (1924; patriotic cantos); and Giovanni Curmi (1900–1973), poet and novelist of a sad, sentimental bent, whose work is reminiscent of that of the Italian writer Edmondo De Amicis (1846–1908). The only living poet still writing in Italian is Vincenzo Maria Pellegrini (b. 1911), although he also writes in Maltese. The echoes of his Italian models, however, are too audible.

In English

Maltese authors using English (some of them also writing in Maltese) include a few young men still finding their voices, experimenting in a modern style inspired by contemporary English poets. There are also several significant older writers.

George Zammit's (b. 1908) colorful poetry is rooted in Maltese tradition and history. Most of it is collected in two volumes, *Lyrical Moments* (1939) and *Adrift* (1946). Another prominent English-language poet is John Cremona (b. 1918), former Chief Justice of Malta and International Judge at the European Court of Human Rights in Strasbourg. In *Songbook of the South* (1940) the main impulse is love of the Maltese landscape. His poetry abounds in striking topographic images. Edward Ellul (b. 1894), although now long silent as a poet, was in his time a prolific master of parody and humorous verse, in such volumes as *Merry Go Round* (1937), *The Primrose Path* (1939), and *Arctic Conditions: Sonnets* (1942).

Francis Ebejer (b. 1925) has written several plays and five novels in English: *A Wreath for the Innocents* (1958), *Evil of the King Cockroach* (1960), *In the Eye of the Sun* (1969), *Come Again in Spring* (1973), and *Requiem for a Malta Fascist* (1980). His nov-

els deal with British colonialism in Malta and with political issues during the 1950s and after.

In Maltese

Writers in Maltese have been laying the foundations of a literary national identity. Among the best Maltese-language poets are Carmelo Psaila, the most significant poet in Maltese literature; Anton Buttigieg (b. 1912), president of Malta, 1976–81, a poet of nature; Ġużè Chetcuti (b. 1914), a poet who extols family life; Ružar Briffa (1906–1963), a prosodically experimental lyricist; Ġorġ Pisani (b. 1909), a poet of landscape and history; George Zammit, the bilingual poet who apotheosizes Maltese legend and faith; Karmenu Vassallo (b. 1913), a poet of powerful anger; Wallace Gulia (b. 1926), master of intellectual verse; and Mario Azzopardi (b. 1944), whose prosodically antitraditional poetry is remarkable for its imagery and innovative themes.

Juan Mamo's (dates n.a.) novel *Ulied in-Nanna Venut fl'Amerca* (1930; the children of Grandma Venut in America) is a bitter but very humorous satire of Maltese society. Ġużè Muscat-Azzopardi's (1853–1927) *Nazju Ellul* (1909; Nazju Ellul) tells the story of a Maltese hero. Sir Themistocles Zammit (1864–1935) wrote humorous sketches. Ġużè (Joseph) Aquilina's (b. 1911) *Tant tliet salt-niet* (1938; under three flags) is a socioreligious novel. Frans Sammut's (b. 1945) *Il-Gaġġa* (1971; the cage) and *Samuraj* (1975; samurai) are two socially oriented novels.

The two best Maltese playwrights are Francis Ebejer, (who writes in Maltese as well as English), who focuses on social conflicts, and Ġużè Diacono (b. 1912), who, using remarkable dialogue, explores personal psychological conflicts.

These writers and many others, especially in the postwar generation, are creating true images of their country, interpreting the people in light of history as Mediterranean Europeans concerned with social progress.

BIBLIOGRAPHY: Aquilina, J., "The Maltese and Their Poetry," *Poetry Review,* 30, 1 (1939), 21–28; Arberry, A. J., comp., Introduction to *A Maltese Anthology* (1960), pp. xi–xxxvii; Aquilina, J., "Malta's Current

Contribution to Commonwealth Literature," in Goodwin, K. L., ed., *National Identity, Papers Delivered at the Commonwealth Literature Conference, University of Queensland, Brisbane, Australia* (1968), pp. 104–14; Ebejer, F., Introduction to Azzopardi, M., ed., *Malta: The New Poetry* (1971), pp. 4–13; Inglott, P. S., Introduction to Massa, D., ed., *Limestone 84: Poems from Malta* (1978), pp. 1–9; Massa, D., "Contemporary Maltese Literature," *ComQ*, 2, 7 (1978), 11–26; Friggieri, J., "Disillusionment after Independence in Maltese Literature," in Massa, D., ed., *Individual and Community in Commonwealth Literature* (1979), pp. 217–23

JOSEPH AQUILINA

MAMEDKULIZADE, Djalil

Azerbaijani journalist, short-story writer, and dramatist, b. 22 Feb. 1866, Nakhichevan; d. 4 Jan. 1932, Baku

M. taught school and studied law before finding his true vocation as a journalist and social critic. In 1906 in Baku he founded the weekly *Molla Nasreddin,* in which he perfected the satirical-realist style that became the hallmark of his finest stories and plays of the pre-Soviet period. After the Russian Revolution he lived for a time in Tabriz, in northern Iran. Returning home in 1922, he revived *Molla Nasreddin* and continued writing, but he could not adjust completely to the new political and cultural order. Although the Soviet state has acknowledged his remarkable gifts, it has found his cosmopolitan views and independent stance often incompatible with its ideal of the proletarian writer.

M.'s reputation rests primarily upon his editorship of *Molla Nasreddin.* Named after the half-legendary sage who made the rich and powerful the butt of his wit, it achieved an influence unrivaled by any similar publication in the Muslim world before World War I. Nonconformist and radical, M. attacked all forms of conservatism, but reserved special venom for the Shiite Muslim clergy, whose ignorance and depravity he held responsible for the backwardness of Azerbaijani society.

From his first collection of stories, *Danabash kendinin ehvalatlary* (1894; events in the village of Danabash), to the pieces written after 1922 M. carried on the realist tradition of 19th-c. Azerbaijani prose. His

instrument was the spoken language; his subject matter, the peasantry. To portray the daily sufferings and aspirations of ordinary people, he used the simple narrative form of the popular tale, which he honed in editorials and sketches written for *Molla Nasreddin.* The natural, outwardly impassive flow of the narrative and the tightly controlled selection of details, quite new to Azerbaijani prose, are reminiscent of Chekhov (q.v.) and de Maupassant. Despite the obvious aim of social criticism, these stories are never didactic. M.'s subtle art did not allow direct commentary; an ironic intonation here and a satirical wink there were enough to convey his intent.

Although he called them "comedies," M.'s plays were in reality serious meditations on the meaning of life. The two most important—*Ölüler* (1909; the victims) and *Deli yighinjagy* (1922; the assembly of the mad)—have an atmosphere of religious fanaticism and moral degradation that warps the human personality and undermines the general good. The "victims" and the "madmen" are the pious who in the name of religion ignore the most elemental rules of civilized behavior toward their fellow men, while the "normal" are those who flout the mores of Muslim society in the service of fundamental human values. As in his stories, M. used clarity, humor, and understatement to achieve his ends.

M. made two lasting contributions to Azerbaijani prose and drama: a realistic style that combined simplicity and satire; and complex characterization, such as that of the heroes of his plays, who, although keen observers of society, are of natures too flawed to change it.

FURTHER WORKS: *Sechilmish eserleri* (2 vols., 1951–54)

BIBLIOGRAPHY: Bennigsen, A., "*Molla Nasreddin* et la presse satirique musulmane de Russie avant 1917," *CMRS,* 3 (1962), 505–20; Caferoglu, A., "Die aserbeidschanische Literatur," *Philologiae turcicae fundamenta,* 2 (1964), 679, 684–85

KEITH HITCHINS

MAMET, David

American dramatist and screenwriter, b. 30 Nov. 1947, Chicago, Ill.

The title of one of M.'s plays, *A Life in the Theater* (perf. 1977, pub. 1978), epitomizes his career. He attended the Neighborhood Playhouse School of the Theater and was graduated in 1969 from Goddard College, where he was later artist in residence. At Yale and the University of Chicago he has taught drama and playwriting. He has served as artistic director for both the St. Nicholas Theater Company and the Goodman Theater in Chicago. Among his awards are an "Obie" in 1976 for the best new American plays produced off-Broadway, *American Buffalo* (perf. 1975, pub. 1977) and *Sexual Perversity in Chicago* (perf. 1974, pub. 1978) and the New York Drama Critics Circle Award in 1977 for *American Buffalo* as the best American play of the year. Lately he has turned to writing for radio, television, and films.

M. first gained recognition with *The Duck Variations* (perf. 1972, pub. 1978). Critics immediately made comparisons to Beckett and Pinter (qq.v.) because of the play's lurking air of menace, its aphasic dialogue, and its limited palette of characters and props. But his early plays are less derivative than they are assertive: they announce M.'s talent for quickly and deftly etching a character's desperate pain and tenuous sense of self. Whether dealing with the panic people feel at mutual commitment (*Sexual Perversity in Chicago*) or with the ironic awareness that "business" is "people taking *care* of themselves" (*American Buffalo*), M. proves that the way characters talk causes them both to perform self-destructive actions and to fix themselves in frustration.

Because M., like Voltaire, believes that language conceals feelings, he strives in three recent plays to lay bare his characters' hearts, but in a language that modulates from merciless profanity through querulousness to abstract poetry. Originally a radio play, *The Water Engine* (perf. 1977, pub. 1978) also satirizes the commercial ethic, but it demonstrates that the system corrupts the hearts of heroes and villains alike. M. raises the ante in *A Life in the Theater*. Confronting two actors, professionally adept at disguise, he discovers that only attitudes constitute their core. And *The Woods* (perf. 1977, pub. 1979) abstractly suggests the flight from intimacy felt by two lovers ignorant about their hearts.

M.'s admirers credit him with the subtlest ear for language among living American dramatists. Any event in his characters' lives results directly from that person's particular habits of using language. Because friendship and loyalty form the nexus of our social

lives, M. focuses on these themes, which he conveys through fragmented structures. But none of these characteristics accounts for the empathy, understanding, and affection that M. has for his characters and that the audience feels for both them and him.

FURTHER WORKS: *Lakeboat* (perf. 1970, pub. 1981); *Reunion* (perf. 1976, pub. 1979); *Dark Pony* (perf. 1977, pub. 1979); *The Revenge of the Space Pandas; or, Binky Rudich and the Two-Speed Clocks* (perf. 1977, pub. 1978); *Mr. Happiness* (1978)

BIBLIOGRAPHY: Eder, R., "D. M.'s New Realism," *NYTMag*, 12 March 1978, 40–47; Storey, R., "The Making of D. M.," *HC*, 16, 4 (1979), 1–11; Ditsky, J., " 'He Lets You See the Thought There': The Theater of D. M.," *KanQ*, 12, 4 (1980), 25–34

JAMES B. ATKINSON

MAMMERI, Mouloud

Algerian novelist, essayist, dramatist, and translator (writing in French), b. 28 Dec. 1917, Traourt-Mimoun

After attending the local primary school of his Berber village, where he learned French, M. pursued his studies in Rabat, Morocco, in Algiers, and in Paris. During World War II he fought in Algeria and later in Europe after the liberation of North Africa. After the war M. worked as a teacher. In 1957 he went to Morocco, returning after Algeria achieved independence in 1962 to Algiers, where he has been professor of ethnology at the University of Algiers and director of a research center at the Bardo Museum.

M. belongs to the first wave of major Algerian Francophone authors, called by some the "generation of '52"—for the year in which M. and Mohammed Dib (q.v.) published their first novels. M.'s novel, *La colline oubliée* (the forgotten hill), is set in a remote Kabyle village in the late 1930s and early 1940s. The book is presented in the form of a diary kept by Mokrane Chaalal. Near the end of the book, the diary breaks off and the narrator intervenes to tell what happens thereafter. The novel provides interesting sociological insights into such local customs as fertility rites and vendettas based on the male-honor code.

The action of M.'s second novel, *Le sommeil du juste* (1955; *The Sleep of the Just*,

1958), takes place during World War II; in it we see the notions of independence and an Algerian entity beginning to stir in the minds of the young Kabyles. M. shows greater technical mastery in this novel than in his first, which had numerous subplots; here he limits the number of major characters and increases the density of action. Much of *Le sommeil du juste* consists of a long letter the main character, Arezki, writes to his old French schoolteacher. The letter, like the novel in general, is an indictment of the inequality imposed by the colonial system.

M.'s third novel, *L'opium et le bâton* (1965; opium and the stick), although in some ways less unified in creative vision than M.'s earlier works, is nevertheless his most successful. It is an ambitious fresco of the liberation struggle in Algeria, presenting particular moments of the revolution.

In *La traversée* (1982; the crossing)—an impressionistic novel that makes frequent use of dreams, letters, and diary entries—the notion of "crossing" is explored on four levels: the title and theme of a controversial political fable by the journalist Mourad, which causes his resignation; an actual Sahara crossing; the trajectory of a human life; and the inexorability of historical movements. Mourad, cynical and alienated, tries to recover his Berber roots, but dies of a fever on arriving in his native village.

The evolution of M.'s protagonists—within each book, as well as from book to book—has been from rural security toward a vaster but more fragmented cosmopolitan humanism. Even as his protagonists have become more disenfranchised, M. has become increasingly aware of the implications of their loss and increasingly involved in a quest to preserve the cultural roots some of his younger characters have forsaken.

M.'s later works have addressed the possible decline of Berber civilization, owing to a worldwide trend toward uniformity of culture. In 1969 M. brought out *Les isefra: Poèmes de Si Mohand-ou-Mhand* (the *isefra:* poems of Si Mohand-ou-Mhand), a large bilingual collection of the traditional nine-line *isefra* by the great Kabyle wandering bard (1845–1906), who sang of, among other things, Kabylia's degeneration after French colonization. In 1980 M. published an anthology, *Poèmes kabyles anciens* (old Kabyle poems). A play, *Le banquet* (1973; the banquet), preceded by an essay entitled "La mort absurde des Aztèques" (the absurd

death of the Aztecs), deals ostensibly with Cortés's destruction of Montezuma and his people, but it also explores ethnocide in general and the dual threat that European colonialism and Arab-Muslim nationalism pose to the traditional values of Kabyle society.

BIBLIOGRAPHY: Dembri, M. S., "L'itinéraire du héros dans l'œuvre romanesque de M. M.," *CALC*, No. 3 (1968), 79–99; Ortzen, L., ed., *North African Writing* (1970), pp. 1–3, 90–99; Mortimer, M., "M. M. Bridges Cultural Worlds," *AfricaR*, 16, 6 (1971), 26–28; Yetiv, I., *Le thème de l'aliénation dans le roman maghrébin d'expression française, 1952–1956* (1972), pp. 114–33; Déjeux, J., *Littérature maghrébine de langue française* (1973), pp. 180–208; Adam, J., "Le jeune intellectuel dans les romans de M. M.," *RUO*, No. 46 (1976), 278–87; Déjeux, J., "*La colline oubliée* (1952) de M. M., un prix littéraire, une polémique politique," *O&C*, 4, 2 (1979), 69–80

ERIC SELLIN

MANDELSHTAM, Osip Emilevich

(often spelled Mandelstam in English) Russian poet and prose writer, b. 15 Jan. 1891, Warsaw, Poland; d. 27 Dec. 1938, near Vladivostok

From an assimilated middle-class Jewish family, M. grew up in St. Petersburg, where his family had moved when he was very young and where he received a classical education at the Tenishev School. He spent the greater part of the years 1907–10 in western Europe, discovering the French symbolists (q.v.) in Paris, visiting Italy and Switzerland, and studying Old French literature at Heidelberg University. In 1911, while at St. Petersburg University, he joined Nikolay Gumilyov and Anna Akhmatova (qq.v.) in launching Acmeism. During World War I and the Russian Revolution, in which he took no active role, M. continued to write, publish, and travel within Russia. During the civil-war years, he worked briefly for Anatoly Lunacharsky's (1875–1933) Education Ministry in Moscow and traveled to Kiev, Georgia, and the Crimea.

Although he was able to publish until 1928, M. supported himself during the 1920s largely by translating and by writing children's books. His arrest in May 1934 was connected with his poem denouncing Stalin as a "peasant slayer." At the end of his three-year term of exile in Voronezh, he was at first allowed to return to Moscow, then banished to its outskirts. The months before his second arrest in May 1938 were spent in search of work and money from sympathetic friends. Sentenced to five years at hard labor for counterrevolutionary activities, he was sent to a transit camp near Vladivostok, where, according to an official notice, he died two months later, of heart failure.

In the spare, traditionally structured verses of his first book, *Kamen* (1913; *Stone,* 1973), he is the poet of a confrontation between the universal emptiness, palpably evoked, and the fragile, yet indestructible pattern of individual, artistic consciousness. In their preoccupation with poetry itself, M.'s first poems evoke a primordial silence, from which both music and the word are born. The poet's terror before the abyss of eternity and his feeling of impotence over not possessing sufficient language are counterbalanced by the serene assertion of his own significance and the word he has to speak. He embraces the "poverty" of the tangible world as the raw material from which enduring art is made. His poems about famous buildings are celebrations of man's ability to overcome both the "cruel weight" of matter and the emptiness of space.

In the longer, more richly imagistic poems of his second collection, *Tristia* (1922; Latin: sad things [from Ovid]), M. continued to be the poet of civilization. St. Petersburg, Rome, Florence, Moscow, Venice, Troy, Siena, Theodosia in the Crimea—all appear as emanations of an integral and timeless "world culture" (centered in the Mediterranean, as the birthplace of Christianity), the longing for which he would later give as his definition of Acmeism. His tragic sense of the meaning of Russia's cataclysmic years is reflected in his poetry on the death of his beloved St. Petersburg. Yet, even as he re-creates the Ovidian theme of a poet's exile from his native city, he affirms the inevitable homecoming inherent in the survival of the "blessed, meaningless word" of poetry, an absolute aesthetic value, eternally new, eternally repeated. In the image of poetry as a plow churning up the layers of time, M. expressed his faith in the survival of the positive values created by each age.

But in *Stikhotvorenia 1921–25* (1928; *Poems 1921–25,* 1973), containing some of M.'s most profound philosophical meditations on

time and the age, the concept of creative time is opposed and overshadowed by the image of inimical time: the "Age-Ruler." The painful ambivalence of the poet, who wishes to belong to his own age yet cannot escape his internal estrangement from it, gives rise to repeated images of personal diminution and of the encroaching poetic muteness that would, in fact, envelop him from 1926–1930.

M.'s later poetry, contained in the two "Moskovskie tetradi" (1930–34; Moscow notebooks) and the three "Voronezhskie tetradi" (1935–37; Voronezh notebooks), was not published in his lifetime and survived only through the efforts of his widow, Nadezhda Yakovlevna Mandelshtam (née Khazin, 1899–1980). The stature of this large (over two thirds of his poetic output) and varied body of work has attained only belated recognition. Closely linked with M.'s personal fate, it centers upon the struggle of the poet, who is "not a wolf by blood," against the relentless "age-wolfhound." The possibility of survival is strongly linked with place. St. Petersburg-Leningrad has become a coffin. Armenia, which M. visited in 1930, becomes in his poetry an "outpost of Christendom"; yet the purity and vitality of this "land of the Sabbath" sustains him only temporarily, before his return to "Buddhist Moscow," the inert, menacing landscape of the Soviet era, where defiant assertions of his continued existence alternate feverishly with the resigned certainty of his impending exile and death. If his deserted, "quiet as paper" Moscow apartment represents the city's silencing of his voice, it is not a final defeat. In exile, he insists upon his "moving lips" as the symbol of his poetic immortality. Locked in the plains of his Voronezh exile, he preserved a vision of the waters and mountains of his ideal Hellenic landscape, "man's place in the universe."

The substantial body of M.'s prose writings, which include his autobiographical evocation of prerevolutionary Russia, "Shum vremeni" (1925; "The Noise of Time," 1965), the surrealistic Petersburg tale "Egipetskaya marka" (1928; "The Egyptian Stamp," 1965), and a number of critical-philosophical essays, displays the brilliance and originality of his poetry. Linked by countless conceptual and imagistic threads to his poetry, to which they provide a vital gloss, they demonstrate the essential unity of M.'s creative oeuvre.

M. stands alongside Boris Pasternak, Marina Tsvetaeva (qq.v.), and Anna Akhmatova as one of the great voices of 20th-c. Russian poetry. His many-layered verse, built upon a complex system of verbal and euphonic echoes and a broad network of literary and historical allusion, yields its fullness only to that ideal, culturally literate "reader in posterity," whom M. envisioned in an early essay. The survival of his work is ensured by the sheer beauty and power of the language in which he conducted his lifelong defense of culture against barbarism and fixed the image of history's fragile "victim," the indestructible poet.

FURTHER WORKS: *Sobranie sochineny* (3 vols., 1964–71); *Stikhotvorenia* (1974). FURTHER VOLUMES IN ENGLISH: *The Prose of O. M.* (1965); *The Complete Poetry of O. E. M.* (1973); *Selected Poems* (1973); *Selected Poems* (1975); *Selected Essays* (1977); *Selected Works* (1977); *O. M.* (1977); *Journey to Armenia* (1977); *The Complete Critical Prose and Letters* (1979)

BIBLIOGRAPHY: Terras, V., "Classical Motives in the Poetry of O. M.," *SEEJ*, 3 (1966), 25–67; Mandelstam, N., *Hope against Hope* (1970); Brown, C., *M.* (1973); Mandelstam, N., *Hope Abandoned* (1974); Nilsson, N. A., *O. M.: Five Poems* (1974); Broyde, S., *O. M. and His Age* (1975); Rayfield, D., "M.'s Voronezh Poetry," *RLT,* 11 (1975), 323–62; Baines, J., *M.: The Later Poetry* (1976); Taranovsky, K., *Essays on M.* (1976); Harris, J. G., Introduction to *The Complete Critical Prose and Letters* (1979), pp. 3–49; Leiter, S., "M.'s Moscow: Eclipse of the Holy City," *RusL,* 7, 2 (1980), 167–97

SHARON L. LEITER

MANGER, Itsik

Yiddish poet, b. 28 May 1901, Czernowitz, Austro-Hungarian Empire (now Chernovtsy, Ukrainian S.S.R.); d. 20 Feb. 1969, Tel Aviv, Israel

M. was born in the Bukovina region. His father, a tailor and "a storyteller, a compulsive rhymster who often drowned his sorrow in the wine cellar," hardly ever earned enough to support his family. His mother "filled the house with folk songs and songs of the Yiddish theater." M. attended the Czernowitz high school for two years, but was expelled because he could not "endure the discipline."

He then served several years in the Austrian army.

M. wrote his first poems in German, but from 1921 on he wrote exclusively in Yiddish. In 1928 he went to Warsaw, and his first collection of poems, *Shtern oyfn dakh* (1929; stars on the roof), appeared the following year. His whimsy and tender lyricism, and the touch of the grotesque in his work won him immediate acceptance and popularity. Many of his poems were set to music.

M. was in Paris at the time it fell to the Nazis. He escaped to Marseille and tried, in vain, for many months to get to Palestine. He finally reached London, and in 1951 came to New York. He was officially received by the American Poetry Society in 1961.

His years in the U.S. were difficult. M. was alone, desperate, and embittered. The title of his last collection of poetry, published in New York, was, significantly enough, *Shtern in shtoyb* (1967; stars in the dust). He became ill in New York and was invited by the Israeli government to settle in Israel as a guest of the state. He suffered a stroke and died in 1969.

M. occupies a place apart in modern Yiddish poetry. Despite modernist, impressionist, expressionist (q.v.), and futurist (q.v.) trends in Yiddish poetry of the day (in Poland, the Soviet Union, and the U.S.), he remained "old-fashioned" and classical in his versification. Yet his imagery was dramatically explosive, nightmarishly surrealistic, expressing not only the dilemma but the "sweat of the soul-anguish" (M.'s evaluation of Franz Kafka [q.v.]) of modern man. He is at once lucidly simple yet maturely sophisticated; naïve yet wondrously wise; soberly observant yet obsessed by the most phantasmagoric visions; alert to the tragic social misery of the present yet steeped in the past. He carries the weight of countless generations who nurtured him.

In a certain way he can be likened to the master humorist of Yiddish literature, Sholom Aleichem: both obliterated the boundary between a smile and a tear. Each sums up the sadness, wisdom, skepticism, and hope of his epoch. Both describe the bizarre nightmare of an era in the life of their people with compassion and forgiveness, and both possess the uncanny wisdom of approaching the edge of despair and drawing back on a narrow path of faith in man and affirmation of life.

M. saw his poetry as a mission entrusted to him, whose purpose, as he rides the "winged colt," Pegasus, fusing "vision with music," is to reach that elusive goal where "beauty wipes away the tears of all pain and anguish." He saw himself as the distilled continuum of centuries of Yiddish folk singers and writers—especially the "Broder Singers" at the end of the 19th c. and Abraham Goldfaden (1840–1908), the "father" of the Yiddish theater. He often uses their idiom and style—a creative and wise ruse of simplicity—to convey the most sophisticated and complex images and ideas. The effect of this synthesis is often startling: he is at once familiar and frighteningly strange, seemingly transparent and obscure, obliterating the thin line between wakefulness and dream.

M. goes back to the very headwaters of the Jewish mythos, creating a new biblical epos—in *Khumesh-lider* (1935; songs of the Pentateuch), the eight poems of the "Rut" (1935; Ruth) cycle, and *Megile-lider* (1936; songs of the Book of Esther). His biblical personages, however, even the Patriarchs, look, act, and speak as if they emerged out of an eastern European shtetl. Even the landscape is more Slavic than Asian. He makes the biblical characters and their relationships contemporary. With the removal of the patina of history and the hyperbole of the biblical text, they become not only more intimate and homey, they become us—modern people grappling with everlasting problems and interrelationships, and painfully trying to understand the sense—if any—of life.

M. achieved a complete conquest and/or denial of time (very like, in a sense, Marc Chagall's biblical figures portrayed as shtetl Jews). M. realized the same purpose in his whimsical novel *Dos bukh fun gan-eydn* (1939; *The Book of Paradise*, 1965), a tongue-in-cheek sad and dreamy depiction of heaven. The sardonic quality is heightened because Everyman's hometown, with its foibles and evils and drollness, is so easily recognizable in this mock-paradise.

M. carried within him the creativity of a people—past, present, and future. He was in eternal combat with the dark shadows of his moods and fears, and he sought not only to give them substance, but also to dissipate them through "vision and music," the two ever-reverberating strings of his poetic instrument, a fantastic hybrid of an old lyre and a dreamlike flute of tomorrow.

FURTHER WORKS: *Lamtern in vint* (1933); *Felker zingen* (1936); *Demerung in shpigl:*

Lid un balade (1937); *Velvl Zbarzher shraybt briv tsu Malkhele der sheyner* (1937); *Noente geshtaltn* (1938); *Volkens ibern dakh: Lid un balade* (1942); *Hotsmakh-shpil* (1947); *Der shnayder-gezeln Note Manger zingt* (1948); *Gezamelte shrifin* (1950); *Medresh Itsik* (1951); *Lid un balade* (1952); *Noente geshtaltn, un andere shrifin* (1961)

BIBLIOGRAPHY: Leftwich, J., "M.: Wandering Poet," *Menorah Journal,* Spring 1952, 55–80; Rais, E., and Jassine, D., "Poésie yiddish: I. M.," *Évidences,* No. 32 (1953), 34–38; Madison, C., *Yiddish Literature* (1968), pp. 317–18; Biletzky, I. C., *Essays on Yiddish Poetry and Prose Writers of the Twentieth Century* (1969), pp. 195–206; Liptzin, S., *The Maturing of Yiddish Literature* (1970), pp. 232–38

ITCHE GOLDBERG

MANIU, Adrian

Romanian poet, dramatist, and essayist, b. 6 Feb. 1891, Bucharest; d. 20 April 1968, Bucharest

Son of a lawyer, M. studied law at the University of Bucharest, but soon after graduation he dedicated himself exclusively to an artistic career. For a short period he frequented the symbolist (q.v.) circle of Alexandru Macedonski (1854–1920), and together with such leading figures as Tristan Tzara and Ion Pillat (qq.v.), founded and edited several journals, among which the most influential was *Gîndirea*. Between 1928 and 1946 he was an art inspector for the State Cultural Commission and regularly contributed to the art columns of several leading magazines. After 1948 his work was banned and he disappeared, for political reasons, from Romanian public life. Shortly before his death he was "rehabilitated" and allowed to publish a volume of poetry, significantly entitled *Cîntece tăcute* (1965; silent songs).

M.'s early poetry was characterized by an avant-garde, iconoclastic spirit, especially in *Salomeea* (1915; Salome). The caustic tone of his poems is reminiscent of such modernists as Jules Laforgue (1860–1887) and the young T. S. Eliot (q.v.), and remained a constant trait throughout M.'s literary career. *Lîngă pămînt* (1924; near the earth) bore the traditionalist mark of *Gîndirea* but was not free of parodic and self-parodic undertones. With

Drumul spre stele (1930; road to the stars)
and *Cîntece de dragoste și moarte* (1935;
songs of love and death), M. achieved a harmonious synthesis between his traditionalism
and modernism. He made such skillful use of
his interest in painting, and especially in iconography, that he was generally regarded as
the leading Romanian imagist (q.v.) poet.
Many of his poems capture states of anxiety
and forebodings of decomposition, in the
guise of threatening landscapes.

Between 1922 and 1929 M. wrote several
plays, such as *Meșterul* (1922; the master-
builder), based on Romanian legends and
fairy tales and informed by a populist ideology. It was his poetry, however, especially his
prose-poems, such as *Jupînul care făcea aur*
(1930; the man who would make gold), in
which he combined startling pictorial imagery with sarcastic antilyricism, that established him as one of the most complex
artistic personalities in contemporary Romanian literature.

FURTHER WORKS: *Figurile de ceară* (1912);
Din paharul cu otravă (1919); *Dinu Păturică*
(1925, with Ion Pillat); *Tinerețe fără bătrî-
nețe* (1926, with Ion Pillat); *Lupii de aramă*
(1929); *Cartea țării* (1934); *Focurile primă-
verii și flăcări de toamnă* (1935); *Versuri*
(1938); *Scrieri* (2 vols., 1968)

BIBLIOGRAPHY: Munteanu, B., *Panorama
de la littérature roumaine contemporaine*
(1938), pp. 293–97

                                        MIHAI SPARIOSU

MANN, Heinrich

German novelist, dramatist, and essayist, b.
27 March, 1871, Lübeck; d. 12 March, 1950,
Santa Monica, Cal., U.S.A.

Generally overshadowed by his brother
Thomas Mann (q.v.), M. has been one of the
least familiar of important 20th-c. German
writers to English-speaking readers. He was
the eldest son of a prominent Lübeck grain
merchant and his Brazilian-born wife. After
early forays into bookselling, publishing, and
painting, he visited France, and lived for five
years (1893–98) in Italy, the setting for much

of his writing. As a self-supporting writer he
lived in Munich and, after 1928, in Berlin. In
1931 he was named president of the Prussian
Academy of the Arts, Division of Literature,
a post he was forced to leave in 1933, when
the Nazis assumed power. The exiled author,
an active antifascist, resided in France until
it was occupied in 1940; he then emigrated to
southern California. In 1949 he received the
first National Prize of the German Democratic Republic. Shortly before his sudden
death, he was offered the presidency of the
East German Academy of the Arts.

M.'s debt to 19th-c. French literature and
culture is immediately evident in his first
important work, *Im Schlaraffenland* (1900;
In the Land of Cockaigne, 1925). The novel
is modeled along the lines of Maupassant's
Bel Ami: its protagonist, Andreas Zumsee,
also resembles the ambitious heroes of Stendhal and Balzac. The naïve young man from
the provinces penetrates the superficial and
modish elite society of Berlin, which M. satirically exposes as morally decadent and aesthetically vulgar.

M.'s other early novels, influenced by
Flaubert and Nietzsche, deal with the perverted vitalism and hectic eroticism of both
the bohemian and bourgeois elements of capitalist society. *Professor Unrat* (1905; *Small
Town Tyrant,* 1944) follows the career of a
pompous, repressed schoolmaster in Wilhel-
minian Germany, who, having fallen in love
with a low-life *chanteuse,* manages to corrupt
his Baltic home town. In 1930 this satire of a
petty tyrant was filmed, with significant
changes, as *The Blue Angel* (directed by Josef von Sternberg, with Emil Jannings and
Marlene Dietrich); in this form it is the internationally best-known of M.'s works.

M.'s masterpiece is his satirical novel *Der
Untertan* (1918; *The Patrioteer,* 1921). It is
the first book of a trilogy—also including *Die
Armen* (1917; *The Poor,* 1917) and *Der Kopf*
(1925; *The Chief,* 1925)—about Prussian
militarism and imperialism. Full of grotesque
caricature, it follows the rise of the opportunist Diedrich Hessling, unmasking along
the way the corruption of the Social Democrats, the impotence of the liberals, and the
moral bankruptcy of the bourgeoisie. After
many early failures, M. finally achieved great
literary fame with this novel.

During his years of exile in France, M.
wrote what some consider to represent the
pinnacle of his work: *Die Jugend des Königs*

Henri Quatre (1935; *Young Henry of Navarre,* 1937) and *Die Vollendung des Königs Henri Quatre* (1937; *Henry, King of Navarre,* 1939). The two novels offer a historically accurate and psychologically detailed portrait of the 16th-c. French king (M. also endowed him with many of his own traits). In this humanist of another time, M. found a model defender of tolerance and social equity. The novels are an optimistic demonstration of how political ideals can find pragmatic realization. Rather than attacking contemporary society with the sharp satire typical of his early work, M. here uses the high-minded realism of his historical pageant to address the abstract issues of power.

M. is an uneven, sometimes impatient writer. While his short narratives—above all the celebrated novella *Pippo Spano* (1905; Pippo Spano), a tragic farce about the isolation of the artist in bourgeois society—are often powerful, his translations—for example his 1905 translation of *Les liaisons dangereuses* by Choderlos de Laclos (1741–1803)—and his plays are less successful. His essays are brilliant: written at the height of Franco-German hostility, his controversial essay "Zola" (1915; Zola), on the crusading French writer, pleads for a socially committed art. Numerous essays written during World War II argue the cause of democracy. In 1945 he published his autobiographical meditations, *Ein Zeitalter wird besichtigt* (1945; reviewing an epoch).

Throughout his life M. and his younger brother Thomas influenced each other, sometimes criticizing, sometimes championing the other's work. Thomas's early literary success and Heinrich's early difficulties exacerbated their jealous competitiveness. During World War I, M. had been almost alone in denouncing the German intellectuals' support of the war. At that time Thomas referred to his brother as a *Zivilisationsliterat* ("cultural man of letters"), a derogatory term that demeans the cosmopolitan, overtly political orientation of his brother's world view and his art. But Thomas later acknowledged M.'s greater political sagacity.

A lifelong critic of authoritarianism, militarism, and bourgeois complacency, a supporter of the 1918 revolution in Germany, a friend of socialism (although never a communist), M. is more and more recognized as one of the most acute political critics of his day. His early writing, with its feverish tempo, anticipates expressionism (q.v.), and all his work is aimed at his fellow Germans; his art, however, unlike his brother's, is not rooted in the German romantic tradition, but rather in the spirit of the French tradition of reason.

FURTHER WORKS: *In einer Familie* (1894); *Das Wunderbare* (1897); *Ein Verbrechen, und andere Geschichten* (1898); *Die Göttinnen* (1903; *Diana,* 1929); *Die Jagd nach Liebe* (1903); *Flöten und Dolche* (1905); *Eine Freundschaft* (1905); *Mnais und Ginevra* (1906); *Schauspielerin* (1906); *Stürmische Morgen* (1906); *Zwischen den Rassen* (1907); *Die Bösen* (1908); *Das Herz* (1910); *Die kleine Stadt* (1909; *The Little Town,* 1930); *Die Rückkehr vom Hades* (1911); *Schauspielerin* (1911); *Die große Liebe* (1912); *Madame Legros* (1913); *Auferstehung* (1913); *Brabach* (1917); *Bunte Gesellschaft* (1917); *Drei Akte* (1918); *Macht und Mensch* (1919); *Der Weg zur Macht* (1919); *Der Sohn* (1919); *Die Ehrgeizige* (1920); *Die Tote, und andere Novellen* (1921); *Diktatur der Vernunft* (1923); *Das gastliche Haus* (1924); *Der Jüngling* (1924); *Abrechnungen* (1925); *Kobes* (1925); *Liliane und Paul* (1926); *Mutter Marie* (1927); *Eugenie; oder, Die Bürgerzeit* (1928; *The Royal Woman,* 1931); *Sie sind jung* (1929); *Sieben Jahre* (1929); *Die große Sache* (1930); *Geist und Tat* (1931); *Ein ernstes Leben* (1932; *The Hill of Lies,* 1934); *Das öffentliche Leben* (1932); *Die Welt der Herzen* (1932); *Der Haß* (1933); *Es kommt der Tag* (1936); *Lidice* (1943); *Mut* (1943); *Der Atem* (1949); *Empfang bei der Welt* (1956); *Eine Liebesgeschichte* (1953); *Unser natürlicher Freund* (1957); *Traurige Geschichte von Friedrich dem Großen* (1960); *Friedrich der Große* (1961); *Briefe an Karl Lemke und Klaus Pinkus* (1964); *Thomas Mann–H. M. Briefwechsel* (1965); *Gesammelte Werke* (18 vols., 1965–78); *Verteidigung der Kultur* (1971)

BIBLIOGRAPHY: Weisstein, U., *H. M.: Eine historisch-kritische Einführung in sein dichterisches Werk* (1962); Schröter, K., *H. M.* (1967); Linn, R. N., *H. M.* (1967); Banuls, A., *H. M.* (1970); Winter, L., *H. M. and His Public* (1970); Roberts, D., *Artistic Consciousness and Political Conscience: The Novels of H. M. 1900–1938* (1971); Hamilton, N., *The Brothers M.* (1978)

MARION FABER

MANN, Thomas

German novelist, short-story writer, and essayist, b. 6 June 1875, Lübeck; d. 12 Aug. 1955, Zurich, Switzerland

M. was the son of the patrician-burgher, Consul and later Senator of the Free City of Lübeck, Johann Heinrich Mann and his wife Julia, née da Silva Bruhns, of German and Portuguese stock, a southern element in his inheritance to which he often ascribed the burgher-artist conflict in himself. It also is a recurring theme in his works. A much younger brother Viktor wrote the story of the family *Wir waren Fünf* (1949; we were five). After the death of M.'s father in 1891 and the liquidation of his old and once prosperous firm of grain merchants, his widow, with the three youngest children, moved to Munich. Upon finishing—with difficulties—his Lübeck school, Thomas followed them. In Munich he worked for a short time in an insurance company and registered as an external student at the Technical University with the intention of becoming a journalist. After some of his early writings had been published, he traveled, spending some considerable time in the company of his older brother Heinrich (q.v.) in Italy, particularly in Rome and Palestrina. There, in 1897, he wrote a substantial part of his first novel, *Buddenbrooks* (1901; *Buddenbrooks,* 1924), which was to establish him as a major writer (it was completed in Munich in 1900). Before that he had written several novellas and, for a short time, belonged to the editorial staff of the satirical magazine *Simplizissimus.*

In 1905 he married Katia Pringsheim, who came from a wealthy family of bankers and scholars of Jewish extraction. He undoubtedly expected the marriage to settle his marked sexual ambivalence. Still, homoerotic love retained a place in his life and played a role in many of his works. Katia bore him six children, three boys and three girls, all of them gifted, particularly the eldest son, Klaus (1906–1949), who became a writer.

With the exception of *Buddenbrooks,* all M.'s major works were written during the years of his married life, which, after Hitler had come to power in Germany, turned into years of exile. Its stations were Switzerland, the south of France, and from 1938 on, the U.S. He spent some months as visiting professor at Princeton and then lived for ten years as an American citizen in his own house in Pacific Palisades, California. After

the war he visited Europe on several occasions, particularly Germany. He finally chose Switzerland as his domicile living in Kilchberg near Zurich. Among the many literary honors he received, the most distinguished was the Nobel Prize in 1929.

The history of the German novel culminates in M.'s work. He restored to German prose literature the international status that it had not enjoyed since the time of Jean Paul (1763–1825) and the romantics. His name is bound to appear, together with those of Proust and Joyce (qq.v.), in any discussion of the modern novel in Europe. The intellectual and spiritual features of his epoch are clearly recognizable in his writing, which represents that moment in the development of literary realism when its fundamental humanistic assumptions were called into question. Yet whereas his illustrious contemporaries such as Proust or Joyce expressed this predicament through the very form of their writing, M. preserved the outward conventions of realistic fiction but charged them with a new irony. From the outset his work is pervaded by the sense that art has become suspect if not impossible. Even his seemingly most conservative creation, his first novel, *Buddenbrooks,* fascinated its most sophisticated readers by the internal contrast between the meaning of the story—the decline, indeed the collapse, of the burgher tradition—and the telling of it in a manner that, by virtue of the faithful obedience to the inherited form, seems to intimate the unruffled integrity of that civilization. When an avant-garde woman artist from Munich had finished reading *Buddenbrooks,* she said to M.: "I was not bored by your novel, and with every page I read I was astonished that I was not bored." She was both not bored and astonished at not being bored because of the tension produced by that ironical juxtaposition.

The autobiographical character of *Buddenbrooks* is unmistakable, so much so that the Lübeck house of the family Mann became a kind of national monument. Destroyed by bombs during World War II, the "Buddenbrooks House" was rebuilt after the war in its original form and persists in being a tourist attraction, testimony to the enduring fame of the novel. It is safe to say that no other German work of fiction, on this level of artistic refinement, with the exception of Goethe's *Werther,* took with such spectacular success the very hurdle which in this case is its theme: the incompatibility of aesthetic sensibility and robust health, indeed, the separation of art from those for whom, after all, it is meant: the general public. For the historically inevitable decline of all Buddenbrook-like businesses, dignified by the name of a respected family and conducted by the successive heirs, does in this novel not appear to be solely determined by economic and social causes; with the Buddenbrooks, at least, it is accompanied, internally even caused, by the emergence of a consciousness that is more complex and troublesome than is good for the simple and tough practices of commerce. Would Hamlet ever have made an effective king? Thomas, the last owner of the firm of Buddenbrooks, is a kind of merchant Hamlet. He is certainly the most interesting of the three generations we come to know before his only child, Hanno, a precocious musical talent, dies—and dies as much of the inability to live as of typhoid fever.

If *Buddenbrooks* is the story of the fall of a family, it is, at the same time, M.'s first allegory of the Fall of Man. The Buddenbrooks are doomed because, in the person of Thomas, they have come to know; and it is no whim of literary ornamentation that invokes the memory of Hamlet in the novella that followed upon *Buddenbrooks: Tonio Kröger* (1903; *Tonio Kröger,* 1914). "There is something I call being sick of knowledge . . . ," says Tonio, "when it is enough for a man to see through a thing in order to be sick to death of it—the case of Hamlet . . ." This is also, attuned to his burgher existence, the case of Thomas Buddenbrook, just as it is the case of the burgher-artist Tonio Kröger. Only love, as Tonio comes to see in the end, could save him from the curse of his intellectual-aesthetic detachment and overcome his inability to "live." But when love comes to Gustav von Aschenbach, the artist hero of M.'s next novella, *Der Tod in Venedig* (1913; *Death in Venice,* 1925), and invades the insulated sphere of his exquisite artistry, the hopeless love for the boy Tadzio destroys the lover. This is the consummation of the-tragic sense that until then dominated M.'s experience of his "vocation" as an artist.

It was exactly this tragic sense of life that, during the years of World War I, M. passionately defended against any form of "Western" rationalism, enlightenment, or political "progress." He went so far as to interpret the war as Germany's defense against the intellectual conspiracy of the West to impose its shallow philosophy of life upon Germany—a country resolved to protect the spirit of music, irony, and the tragic profundities from the threatening encroachments of the rhetorical politics of reason. The enemy within Germany was the liberal-radical intellectual for whom M. coined the name "Zivilisationsliterat," the literary propagandist of those elegantly aggressive "political virtues." The living embodiment of the "Zivilisationsliterat" was his own brother Heinrich, his rival for literary honors and intimate friend of many years. Thus, for M., the most formidable and catastrophic event of the first decades of the 20th c. turned partially into a fraternal battle. Its fascinating record is the book of more than six hundred pages, *Betrachtungen eines Unpolitischen* (1918; *Reflections of a Nonpolitical Man,* 1983). The title is not quite as ironical as it seems. It is the burden of the book that politics is held to be the domain of "the West," indeed of M.'s Westernized brother, while he himself, like the "true" Germany, is unpolitical, imbued with musical intimations of the futility of political change. At the same time, the book ends on a note of irony. M. himself, simply as a man of literature, will have contributed, he confesses, to what is historically inevitable in any case: the transformation of Germany into a political and democratic country.

The writing of *Betrachtungen eines Unpolitischen* took up all M.'s literary energies during the years of the war. He himself called the strenuous effort it demanded his "military service." The problems clamoring for a solution, or rather the oppressions of the soul crying out for an articulate liberation, made it impossible for him to become engaged in a work of the imagination. This book is, in M.'s own words, the "work of an artist whose existence was shaken to its foundations, whose self-respect was brought into question, and whose troubled condition was such that he was completely unable to produce anything else." It is the work that fills the great literary vacuum of his career between 1912 and 1924, between *Der Tod in Venedig* and *Der Zauberberg* (1924; *The Magic Mountain,* 1927).

Der Zauberberg is clearly the work of the same intelligence that was responsible for *Betrachtungen eines Unpolitischen,* but also of an imagination that has reconquered its freedom from the stifling intellectual and spiritual disquiet. At times it has the serenity of a late summer day in the mountains that are its setting: a Swiss sanatorium in the Alps. As soon as one realizes—perhaps by recognizing in their utterances verbatim quotations from *Betrachtungen*—that two of the main figures of *Der Zauberberg,* the antagonists Settembrini and Naphta, closely resemble, at least with regard to their casts of mind, respectively, the "Zivilisationsliterat" of *Betrachtungen* and its author, one also fathoms with pleasurable surprise the depth of self-irony that M. has gained: Settembrini is a most amiable version of the once hated stranger to the musical and tragic depths, while Naphta, his bitter, resentful, and altogether unpleasant opponent, is, in his convictions, quite close to the M. of those wartime reflections. Naphta's suicide stands for the end of a long phase in M.'s life. Nothing now prevented a reconciliation of the two brothers.

Der Zauberberg is also the ironical consummation of the dominant genre of the 19th-c. German novel, the *Bildungsroman,* always the story of a young man's intellectual and sentimental education. While, for instance, Goethe's Wilhelm Meister or Gottfried Keller's Grüner Heinrich set out on their life-journey with highly problematical natures and move toward increasing firmness of character and acceptance of their places in human society, the unheroic hero of *Der Zauberberg,* Hans Castorp, enters the story as an unproblematical, perfectly "adjusted" young engineer and receives his unnerving initiation at the hands of a sick community, representative of the moral and intellectual chaos of the modern world. He, too, in an exalted moment of his story, has a vision of the good life, but the vision remains a dream dreamt at the threshold of death in a mountain-desert of snow and ice, a dream without hope of ever coming true either amid the eccentricities of this alpine "pedagogical province" (to use a term from *Wilhelm Meister*) or down in the "flatland" of bourgeois triviality. Hans Castorp, too, like the hero of every *Bildungsroman,* finally enters life again, but life is death on a battlefield of Flanders. Thus, *Der Zauberberg* is the most radical reversal of the educational optimism that is at the core of every *Bildungsroman.*

Mario und der Zauberer (1930; *Mario and the Magician,* 1930) is written in a manner that was to be developed on the grandest scale in *Doktor Faustus* (1947; *Doctor Faustus,* 1948). Although it is a novella in its own right, it is also a political allegory, the highly particularized and even grotesque portrayal of a social cataclysm: the subjugation of individual wills within an amorphous society "on vacation" from its disciplined commitments, which is finally forced into uniformity. The tyrant, in this case, is the theatrically displayed vulgar will of a hypnotist—read *duce.* The rebellion of violated human dignity comes too late and, therefore, issues in catastrophe.

In *Doktor Faustus,* M.'s persistently warring opposites, life and spirit, society and art, have come together at last—not in the harmony of a good life, but in the unison of hell. Both are doomed. In this extraordinary work—a work of old age, but, ironically, distinguished among M.'s productions by a youthful luxuriance of invention and composition that would usually suggest the storm-and-stress period of a writer—a musical Tonio Kröger, demonically enhanced in stature and destiny, is no longer confronted, as the young writer Tonio Kröger was, by "Life" in its lovable innocence, but by a life that, tired of its own blue-eyed banality, has "spiritualized" itself and entered, like the artist himself, into an alliance with the forces of "the deep that lieth under." For this is what, under Hitler, has become of the Germany that, thirty years before, had been the unjustly besieged and immoderately loved hero of *Betrachtungen eines Unpolitischen.*

M.'s most despairing book was, however, preceded by his most serene achievements: the Joseph tetralogy, *Joseph und seine Brüder* (1933–42; *Joseph and his Brothers,* 1934–45), of which the first two volumes, *Die Geschichten Jaakobs* (1933; *The Tales of Jacob,* 1934) and *Der junge Joseph* (1934; *The Young Joseph,* 1935) appeared in Germany, while the third and fourth volumes, *Joseph in Ägypten* (1936; *Joseph in Egypt,* 1938) and *Joseph der Ernährer* (1943; *Joseph the Provider,* 1945) had to be published abroad, after M. had written his classic rejection of Nazism in his 1937 letter to the University of Bonn upon having been deprived of his honorary doctorate. In between those volumes he wrote the Goethe novel *Lotte in Weimar* (1939; *The Beloved Returns,* 1940). Both works are distinguished by an amazing combination of encyclopedic knowledge, enduring inspiration, and eminent literary skill. Although biographically *Joseph und seine Brüder* looks like the imaginative outcome of the writer's émigré existence reflected in his mind's flight back to the wellsprings of the myth, it is at the same time the poetically realized hope of which *Doktor Faustus* despairs: the hope of a life that is friend to the spirit, and of a spirit that is no deserter from life. The biblical story of the dreamer, who also is the interpreter of dreams, and who, estranged from his crudely wakeful brothers, is reunited with them in their hour of need as the provider of bread, has been retold and vastly enlarged by M. with an artistic intelligence and graceful irony that, rainbowlike, spans the gulf between ancient myth and modern psychology, divine and human comedy. With this work M. definitely settled in the rank of those writers whom Stendhal praised as the most excellent for "kindling that delicious smile that is a sign of the highest intellectual pleasure."

In the end the smile turned to laughter—in the enlarged version of a fragment that he abandoned in 1911 in order to write *Der Tod in Venedig* (because, he said, he could at that time not sustain the consistently parodistic tone of voice), namely, *Die Bekenntnisse des Hochstaplers Felix Krull* (1922; enlarged ed., 1936; finished version of Vol. I, 1954; *Confessions of Felix Krull, Confidence Man,* 1955). In this unfinished book art takes its revenge upon "life" for all that it had had to suffer, but this time with unrestrained gaiety and scandalous insolence at the expense of a world that genius may at least deceive, even if it can teach it nothing. After this masterly extravagance M. devoted his last words to the memory of Friedrich Schiller in *Versuch über Schiller* (1955; *On Schiller,* 1958), the poet to whom literature meant little except as an expression of concern for the spiritual fate of mankind.

FURTHER WORKS: *Der kleine Herr Friedemann, und andere Novellen* (1898); *Tristan* (1903; *Tristan,* 1925); *Fiorenza* (1906); *Königliche Hoheit* (1909; *Royal Highness,* 1916); *Herr und Hund* (1918; *Bashan and I,* 1923); *Gesang vom Kindchen* (1919); *Wälsungenblut* (1921); *Erzählungen* (2 vols., 1922); *Gesammelte Werke* (15 vols., 1922–35); *Rede und Antwort* (1922); *Bemühungen* (1925); *Pariser Rechenschaft* (1926); *Unordnung und frühes Leid* (1926; *Disorder and Early Sorrow,* 1929); *Die Forderung des Tages* (1930; *Order of the Day,* 1942); *Lebensabriß* (1930; *A Sketch of My Life,* 1960); *Leiden und Größe der Meister* (1935); *Ein Briefwechsel* (1937; *An Exchange of Letters,* 1937); *Dieser Friede* (1938; *This Peace,* 1938); *Achtung, Europa!* (1938); *Die vertauschten Köpfe: Eine indische Legende*

(1940; *The Transposed Heads: A Legend of India,* 1941); *Das Gesetz* (1944; *The Tables of the Law,* 1945); *Ausgewählte Erzählungen* (1945); *Adel des Geistes: Sechzehn Versuche zum Problem der Humanität* (1945; *Essays of Three Decades,* 1947); *Leiden an Deutschland* (1946); *Neue Studien* (1948); *Die Enstehung des "Doktor Faustus": Roman eines Romans* (1949; *The Story of a Novel: The Genesis of "Doctor Faustus,"* 1961); *Michelangelo in seinen Dichtungen* (1950); *Der Erwählte* (1951; *The Holy Sinner,* 1952); *Altes und Neues* (1953); *Die Betrogene* (1953; *The Black Swan,* 1954); *Nachlese, Prosa 1951–1955* (1956); *Briefe an Paul Amann, 1915–1952* (1959); *T. M. an Ernst Bertram, 1910–1955* (1960); *T. M.–Karl Kerenyi, Gespräch in Briefen* (1960); *Gesammelte Werke* (12 vols., 1960); *Briefe, 1889–1955* (3 vols., 1961–65); *T. M.–Robert Faesi: Briefwechsel* (1962); *Reden und Aufsätze* (2 vols., 1965); *T. M.–Heinrich Mann: Briefwechsel, 1900–1949* (1968); *Hermann Hesse–T. M. Briefwechsel* (1968; *The Hesse/M. Letters, 1910–1955,* 1975); *T. M. und Hans Friedrich Blunck: Briefwechsel und Aufzeichnungen* (1969); *T. M.: Briefwechsel mit seinem Verleger Bermann-Fischer, 1932–1955* (1973); *Notizen* (1973); *Gesammelte Werke* (13 vols., 1974); *Essays* (3 vols., 1977); *T. M.–Alfred Neumann Briefwechsel* (1977); *Tagebücher* (4 vols., 1977–80; abridged tr., *Diaries: 1918–21/1933–39,* 1982); *Werkausgabe* (20 vols., 1980 ff.). FURTHER VOLUMES IN ENGLISH: *Children and Fools* (1928); *Three Essays* (1929); *Past Masters, and Other Papers* (1933); *Stories of Three Decades* (1936); *Freud, Goethe, Wagner* (1937); *Order of the Day: Political Essays and Speeches of Two Decades* (1942); *Listen, Germany!* (1943); *Last Essays* (1959); *Stories of a Lifetime* (1961); *Letters of T. M., 1889–1955* (1970); *An Exceptional Friendship: The Correspondence of T. M. and Erich Kahler* (1975)

BIBLIOGRAPHY: Weigand, H. J., *T. M.'s Novel "Der Zauberberg"* (1933); Brennan, J. G., *T. M.'s World* (1942); Neider, C., ed., *The Stature of T. M.* (1947); Hatfield, H., *T. M.* (1951; rev. ed., 1962); Lindsay, J. M., *T. M.* (1954); Jonas, K. W., *Fifty Years of T. M. Studies: A Bibliography* (1955); Faesi, R., *T. M.* (1955); Stresau, H., *T. M. und sein Werk* (1955); Nicholls, R. A. *Nietzsche in the Early Work of T. M.* (1955); Lion, F., *T. M.* (1955); Thomas, E. H., *T. M.: The Mediation of Art* (1956); Mayer, H., *Leiden und Größe*

T. M.s (1956); Kantorowicz, A., *Heinrich und T. M.* (1956); Kaufmann, F., *T. M.: The World as Will and Representation* (1957); Mann, E., *The Last Year of T. M.* (1958); Heller, E., *The Ironic German: A Study of T. M.* (1958); Altenberg, P., *Die Romane T. M.s* (1961); Hatfield, H., ed., *T. M.: A Collection of Critical Essays* (1964); Lukács, G., *Essays on T. M.* (1965); Feuerlicht, I., *T. M.* (1968); Bürgin, H., and Mayer, H.-O., *T. M.: A Chronicle of His Life* (1969); Kahler, E., *The Orbit of T. M.* (1969); Gronicka, A. von, *T. M.: Profile and Perspective* (1970); Bauer, A., *T. M.* (1971); Hollingdale, R. J., *T. M.: A Critical Study* (1971); Reed, T. J., *T. M.: The Uses of Tradition* (1974); Apter, T. E., *T. M.: The Devil's Advocate* (1979); Hatfield, H., *From "The Magic Mountain": M.'s Later Masterpieces* (1979); Winston, R., *T. M.: The Making of an Artist, 1875–1911* (1981)

ERICH HELLER

T. M.'s *Dr. Faustus* and the cycle of *Joseph* novels are a remarkable achievement to represent the mature work of a single writer. They form a monumental recapitulation and systematization of the subject-matter of his earlier period. What were previously études, capriccios and sonatas have become whole symphonies. This formal development, however, is not just a formal matter; it never is in the work of really significant artists. The symphonic complications and syntheses issue from a widening, deepening and generalizing of the content of M.'s original subject-matter. The growing formal complexity is dictated by the inner logic of his early themes. The characters, their relationships and experiences tended towards universality. If one looks at his early writing, one can see how little his development may be understood in formal terms. True, he starts off with a large novel which is pronouncedly universal in character, *Buddenbrooks*. In a certain sense it strikes all the notes of his later critique of capitalist society. And yet, compared even with later short stories, the first novel is much sparser, much less polyphonic.

It is along these lines that one should view M.'s development. The *Joseph* cycle and *Dr. Faustus* mark the culmination. They form a mature *œuvre* of a very special type. They were specifically conditioned by the epoch in which they were conceived, that is by the culture of the imperialist period and its particular German variant. [1948]

Georg Lukács, *Essays on T. M.* (1965), p. 47

. . . M. never conceived of progress in terms of a simple break with the past. His interest in the forward movement of history always embraced equally the notion of return. Particularly in *The Magic

Mountain* and *Joseph* special significance attaches therefore to the conception of the circular motion of time, implying the double process of return to a point of departure and advance from it. Its attraction for M. lay also in its inverse suggestion of the proximity of progress and reaction—a theme of *Doktor Faustus*. The preoccupation with the idea of return, linked to the search for a basis of advance, corresponds to this belief in an earlier tradition of middle-class culture, which is "classical" in his definition of the term as a "basic type" in the sense rather of Goethe's "Urphänomen"—"a primal type moulded by the patriarchs of the race, in which later life will recognize itself, in the footsteps of which it will walk, a myth, that is to say, for the type is mythical, and the essence of the mythical is return, timelessness, the eternally present" [*Adel des Geistes*]. "That which has once been lived is weak, it must be lived anew, strengthened in the sphere of the spirit"—the quotation from *Lotte in Weimar* implies the dual aspect involved in M.'s relationship to the middle-class culture of an earlier period, the process at once of leave-taking and renewal.

R. Hinton Thomas, *T. M.: The Mediation of Art* (1956), pp. 16–17

T. M.'s responsible and zealous love for the full growth, the pure form and representation of mankind came into conflict with the glowing love for his own people for which he had labored in the *Reflections* [*of an Unpolitical Man*]. But this love for man that made him choose the martyrdom of the exile is not foreign to the love which is at the roots of vicarious suffering—this religious aspect of artistic representation, the experience of the writer who spends his life in the Inferno of the human soul. . . .

This search for the soul, a religion of self-concern, is the animating power in the concern with and for the soul of man as the center of T. M.'s work. It gives the artist's approach to human life legitimacy, vigor, and warmth because the self finds itself and is consummated only as it finds its way into the life of others. Thus is begotten a spirit of infinite sympathy in which the respect for the dignity of man and the compassion for him in his "eminent" exposure are one. In communicating to us this sense for man's great predicament as it is experienced in the elations and agonies of the soul, the artist may contribute his mite to a new ethos in a new covenant.

Fritz Kaufman, *T. M.: The World as Will and Representation* (1957), pp. 237–38

Regarded as a whole, M.'s career is a striking example of the "repeated puberty" which Goethe thought characteristic of the genius. In technique as well as in thought, he experimented far more daringly than is generally realized. In *Budden-

BERNARD MALAMUD

ANDRÉ MALRAUX

OSIP MANDELSHTAM

THOMAS MANN

brooks he wrote one of the last of the great "old-fashioned" novels, a patient, thorough tracing of the fortunes of a family. The novel, far from naturalistic in spirit, demonstrates his mastery of the techniques of naturalism and impressionism: elaborate accounts of the dinners, the bank balances, and the ailments of the Buddenbrooks alternate with swift evocations of mood. Primarily—and hence no doubt its enormous popularity—the novel tells a story in a solid, conventional, unilinear way. From *The Magic Mountain* on, the secure ground of the nineteenth-century novel has been left for good. Daring experiments with the same sense, lack of interest, for long periods, in narration as such, and mythical associations are characteristic. In the climactic chapter of *The Beloved Returns* M. uses the technique of the stream of consciousness, which he ventures to apply to the mind of Goethe. Still more audacious is the attempt, in *Doctor Faustus,* to render in words the spirit and the impact of both actual and imaginary works of music. All of the later novels are in some sense experimental. M. says somewhere that the great novel transcends the limits of the genre; this, like so many of his general statements, probably refers primarily to his own work.

Henry Hatfield, *T. M.,* rev. ed. (1962), pp. 2–3

T. M.'s development as a novelist comprises the whole development of modern narrative prose. He began his career with a book that, though marked by the destiny of modern art, still resembled the traditional realistic novel. Indeed, he has gone on using the comfortably circumstantial, digressive manner of the nineteenth-century novel right up into the latest, "structuralist" stages of his work—even in this last summing-up, his *Faust.* Yet what a long way from *Buddenbrooks* to *Doctor Faustus!* All that has happened to us, to the world, to art, during the last half-century, can be read in the course of this journey.

M.'s whole *œuvre,* we have said, must be regarded as a single, consistent creation because, throughout, there may be felt in it an unconscious or semi-conscious tendency toward a structural unity of the whole. It is a dynamic macrocosm, a more and more dense and comprehensive complex of developing motifs, exhibiting as a whole a fugal character such as is otherwise found only in single novels or works of art. Just as each work gains increasing symbolic richness by the use and intensification of a leitmotif and the fusing of several leitmotifs, so on a larger scale the work as a whole exhibits the progressive exfoliation and metamorphosis of one single all-pervasive theme. . . .

The lifelong central theme of M.'s books has been an inquiry into the function of art and the artist, of culture and the intellectual in modern society.

Erich Kahler, *The Orbit of T. M.* (1969), pp. 22–23

This, then, is T. M.'s solution: The arcane magic of a dialectical process enabled the author without recourse to black art or a devil's pact to carry forward his immense life's work to ever more startling achievements. He reached a high point in the novel that holds the key to the triumph of the modern artist over seemingly insurmountable difficulties. In writing this "book of the end" [*Doctor Faustus*], M. has, in fact, made a new beginning for the novel. He proved that this form of art is indeed still possible, perhaps not in its traditional aspect, but as a work that combines self-conscious artistry with intensity of feeling and Romantic irony with objective epic narration. M. demonstrated that the modern novel, on its multiple interrelated levels, can offer the reader the sophisticated pleasure of an oratorio, magically recreated in words, together with as unsophisticated and popular a thrill as an eyewitness account of betrayed love avenged by murder in a streetcar.

André von Gronicka, *T. M.: Profile and Perspectives* (1970), pp. 15–16

Perhaps it is precisely culture, M.'s use of traditional means, which sticks in the throat. For the critic harrowed by harsh realities, T. M.'s cultural language may seem too coherent, too readily disponible, his technique too sovereign. Altogether he has something too much like mastery. And mastery is unpalatable in a world the critic believes is unmastered.

Yet the mastery was not easy. It was an achievement, demanding all the creative effort that word implies. M.'s culture was not complacent—only the legend of the solemn polymath makes it seem that—nor was it exhaustive or static. It was purposefully acquired, personally turned, and subtly used. Over a long lifetime it also acquired, inevitably, its own coherence of theme and substance; but this personal synthesis was incidental to M.'s work as an artist, using materials like any other artist. If the result is open to objection in principle, then it is doubtful whether any culture can subsist. The order established by art seldom rests on an ideally ordered world. It nevertheless has a value in proportion as the artist has taken issue with the disorder of the real world—we have seen how conscientiously T. M. did that—and contributed, by whatever means, to understanding it. For understanding is the first small step towards control.

T. J. Reed, *T. M.: The Uses of Tradition* (1974), p. 414

T. M. tried to state every claim in the devil's favour. He hoped, with a would-be humanism, that an investigation of evil's force and fascination would result in refreshing disgust with evil, that evil, once exposed, would shrivel in sunlight and crumble in the hands of the clear-eyed. This hope, however, is the point against which his novels, stories and essays move. As he boldly underlines the sometimes grotesque, sometimes elegant course the daemonic and decadent take, the dark river of corruption fails to reveal an unqualified ugliness; unflaggingly it glows with an hypnotic iridescence and flows with a silky vitality that promises rich and good things.

M. had to face the crisis of morality, the transformation of values he found in the works of Schopenhauer, Nietzsche and Freud. A person could no longer be seen as governed primarily by consciousness, nor could human impulses be supposed to be educable and enlightened. The will to live was not simply a prudent desire to survive; it was a will to power, constantly in conflict with other wills which in turn seek power.... Genius and creativeness, even in their brightest, most liberating forms, were not simple children of light, but were born of energies that are themselves amoral and which, in their unusually excessive strength, are akin to the daemonic.

This is the basic world picture M. inherited from Schopenhauer and Nietzsche, and his own moral development can be seen as a result of the tension between these philosophers' opposing recommendations of which value-systems should function within this world.

T. E. Apter, *T. M.: The Devil's Advocate* (1979), pp. 1–2

MANNER, Eeva-Liisa

Finnish poet, dramatist, novelist, short-story writer, and translator, b. 5 Dec. 1921, Helsinki

M.'s formal education stopped after junior high school. She worked for an insurance company from 1940 to 1944 and for a publisher from 1944 to 1946. Since then she has been a full-time writer and translator of numerous works—by, among others, Hesse, Kafka (qq.v.), Büchner, and Shakespeare. Shy and retiring, partly because of illness, unmarried, she lives in Tampere, the second city of Finland, but has traveled widely in southern Europe, especially Andalusia, Spain, a region that is evoked in several of her works.

Although M. published two collections of poems and one of short stories between 1944 and 1951, it was not until the verse collection *Tämä matka* (1956; rev. ed., 1963; this journey) that she received wide recognition. It was one of the most successful among the works of the 1950s that reacted against traditionalism in Finnish poetry. With the poets of the 1950s M. shares an elaborately struc-

tured, freely associative imagism (q.v.) and a rejection of strict form.

For M., the ideal poet possesses a wisdom transcending knowledge, like the ancient Greek philosophers. She shares with her generation an interest in Chinese mysticism, adding to it astrology, troubadour poetry, and other esoteric studies, but she uses these subjects allusively to express her own views. Music is important to her; she develops synesthetic visions suggested by composers like Bach, Haydn, Mozart, or Webern and models her poems on musical forms, discovering polyphonic structures in the universe.

According to M., sterile intellectualism has all but annihilated the Western world; the poem "Strontium" (strontium), in *Orfiset laulut* (1960; orphic songs) states: "strange smokes are rising/invisible ashes are raining/bartering death./ For they, the Skilled Ones,/ are almost destroying the whole world/ although it is half dream." The poems "Descartes" (Descartes) and "Spinoza" (Spinoza) in *Tämä matka* criticize these philosophers, but M. is not an antiintellectual poet. She says in the essay "Moderni runo" (1957; modern poetry): "The new form, as I understand it, requires that the reader's ... reason participate in the movement of the poem."

To M., established religions are cold and hostile systems, a part of the "logical disorder" that destroys the "magical order" of the world; this view is expressed in her novel *Tyttö taivaan laiturilla* (1951; the girl on the pier of heaven) and the poem "Lapsuuden hämärästä" (from the twilight of childhood) in *Tämä matka*. She understands the poor and the humble, who appear in her poems on Andalusia, and she has a quiet, slightly whimsical sense of humor, prevalent especially in her most recent book of poems, *Kamala kissa* (1976; that horrible cat).

M. has also written several plays, of which the dreamy and lyrical *Eros ja Psykhe* (1959; Eros and Psyche), although never a great success, has been repeatedly performed.

Although the general trend of Finnish poetry has changed more than once since M. published her principal works, the span of her interests, the depth and intensity of her intellect and feeling, and her mastery of language make her one of the foremost Finnish poets of our time.

FURTHER WORKS: *Mustaa ja punaista* (1944); *Kuin tuuli ja pilvi* (1949); *Kävelymusiikkia pienille virtahevoille* (1957); *Oliko murhaaja enkeli* (1963, under pseud. Anna September); *Niin vaihtuivat vuoden ajat* (1964); *Uuden vuoden yö* (1965); *Toukokuun lumi* (1966); *Kirjoitettu kivi* (1966); *Poltettu oranssi* (1968); *Fahrenheit 121* (1968); *Varjoon jäänyt unien lähde* (1969); *Paetkaa purjet kevein purjein* (1971); *Varokaa voittajat* (1972); *Kuolleet vedet* (1977); *Viimeinen kesä* (1977); *Runoja 1956–1977* (1980)

BIBLIOGRAPHY: Dauenhauer, R., "The Literature of Finland," *LitR,* 14, 1 (1970), 9–10; Ahokas, J. A., "E.-L. M.: Dropping from Reality into Life," *BA,* 47 (1973), 60–65; Sala, K., "E.-L. M.: A Literary Portrait," in Dauenhauer, R., and Binham, P., eds., *Snow in May: An Anthology of Finnish Writing 1945–1972* (1978), pp. 58–59

JAAKKO A. AHOKAS

MANNING, Olivia

English novelist and short-story writer, b. 1915, Portsmouth; d. 23 July 1980, Isle of Wight

Daughter of a commander in the Royal Navy, M. grew up in Portsmouth. In 1939 she married Reginald Donald Smith, whose work as a producer for the BBC took the couple to many countries. Eventually settling in London, M. avoided publicity but wrote prolifically on a wide variety of subjects, including history—*The Remarkable Expedition* (1947; Am., *The Reluctant Rescue*), an account of Stanley's rescue of Emin Pasha; travel—*The Dreaming Shore* (1950), about a visit to Ireland; and pets—*Extraordinary Cats* (1967). She also wrote articles for many periodicals. In 1976 she was appointed Commander of the Order of the British Empire.

M.'s first novel, *The Wind Changes* (1937), is set in Dublin just before the English-Irish truce of 1920. Its principal characters—an artist, a writer, and a revolutionary—carry on an emotional war that serves as counterpoint to the larger struggle. The book received mixed reviews, but in retrospect, it displays M.'s major characteristics: emphasis on sensuous detail, and an antiromantic point of view that portrays individuals as mirrors of common venality and confusion.

M.'s literary reputation was firmly established with her Balkan Trilogy, whose major characters, Harriet Pringle, a sensitive young wife, and Guy Pringle, a thoughtless young professor working for an official British cultural program in a foreign country, are fictional portraits of the author herself and her husband. The young couple's problems of learning to understand each other are compounded by the economic and political uncertainties of the first years of World War II. *The Great Fortune* (1960) introduces Harriet to Bucharest, a city exotic, gay, and still friendly to the British, and ends with the barely mentioned fall of Paris. *The Spoilt City* (1962) traces the day-to-day rumors and the terrifying disintegration that lead to the German occupation. *Friends and Heroes* (1965) takes place in Athens, to which the Pringles and their compatriots have fled, revealing the gradual involvement and suffering of the Greeks and ending with the fall of Crete and yet another escape, this time to Alexandria.

A convincing portrayal of civilian life in wartime, the trilogy produces a cumulative impression of a nonstructured world, a literary slice of life, without definite beginning, climax, or resolution of conflicts—only flow. Harriet concludes at the end of the first book that "the great fortune is life," and at the end of the third book that the couple's remaining together is the only certainty they can expect. In the late 1970s M. extended the Pringles' adventures to a Levant Trilogy: *The Danger Tree* (1977), *The Battle Lost and Won* (1978), and *The Sum of Things,* published posthumously in 1981; the six volumes are called collectively *The Fortunes of War.*

While M.'s precise observations capture the sights, sounds, smells, and moods of many exotic settings, the objective tone she uses with autobiographical material—hometown, childhood, marital experiences, international acquaintances—barely masks a strong antiromantic point of view. None of her "friends and heroes" is either a true friend or heroic. *A Different Face* (1953) makes postwar Coldmouth (Portsmouth) the chief cause of an expatriate's depression. In *The Play Room* (1969; Am., *The Camperlea Girls*) M.'s schoolgirl-spokesman suffers the nagging claims of a self-pitying mother (only slightly improved from the mother in the short stories in *A Romantic Hero,* 1966); with her brother (named for the author's brother) is exposed to an elderly transvestite and a macabre "play room" (based on an actual vacation incident); and understands too late the strangeness of the rich and beautiful classmate who dies in a rape-murder.

The total effect of M.'s artistry is realism that is ironically sympathetic, uncomfortably persuasive.

FURTHER WORKS: *Growing Up* (1948); *Artist Among the Missing* (1949); *School for Love* (1951); *The Doves of Venus* (1955); *My Husband Cartwright* (1956); *The Rain Forest* (1974)

BIBLIOGRAPHY: Rees, G., on *The Wind Changes, Spectator,* 30 April 1937, 832–34; Jones, H. M., on *The Wind Changes, SatR,* 9 April 1938, 12; Alpert, H., on *The Doves of Venus, SatR,* 18 Nov. 1956, 18–19; Bostwick, J., on *The Great Fortune, SatR,* 22 July 1961, 24; Morris, R. K., *Continuance and Change: The Contemporary British Novel Sequence* (1972), pp. 24–49; Trickett, R., on *The Battle Lost and Won, TLS,* 24 Nov. 1978, 1358; Milton, E., on *The Battle Lost and Won, Christian Science Monitor,* 9 April 1979, B7

ESTHER M. G. SMITH

MANSFIELD, Katherine

(pseud. of Kathleen Beauchamp) English short-story writer, b. 14 Oct. 1888, Wellington, New Zealand; d. 9 Jan. 1923, Fontainebleau, France

Much of M.'s early life was a rebellion against her origins: her birth in provincial and unsophisticated Wellington, her philistine upbringing by a banker father and a genteel mother, with all the concomitant restrictions placed upon her as a daughter in a pretentious colonial household. The result was enthusiastic withdrawal to a school for girls in London, a determination to be a woman writer in a man's world, and a loosening of moral and societal restrictions to permit experimentation with premarital affairs, with lesbianism, with abortion—in short, with a way of life antithetical to her upbringing.

Paradoxically, the last portion of her short career was devoted to exploring her roots proudly by re-creating in fiction the New Zealand of her brother "Chummie"—killed at the front in World War I—her beloved grandmother, her parents, and particularly the little girl and young woman who resembles so powerfully the developing M. Perhaps

this psychological need for identification with place owes much to the tormented, gypsylike existence of M.'s mature years when a combination of eventually fatal illnesses forced her from the uncongenial climate of England to medical exile on the French Riviera, in Switzerland, in Italy, and elsewhere, seeking the healing sun, but without the company of friends, family, or even of her husband, John Middleton Murry (1889–1957). For many of these latter years, she relived in her memories and her fiction the childhood period of belonging to a land, a family, and a distinct culture.

Although M. wrote about one hundred stories, her fame rests on fewer than twenty wrought with precise and calculated craftsmanship. James Joyce (q.v.) had earlier made the "epiphany" his trademark. M. independently used the technique repeatedly and effectively in her best stories. Her heroes and heroines are presented to the reader at a climactic, or at least psychologically traumatic, moment in their lives, when they see incisively into the mystery of their being. Bertha Young in "Bliss" (1918) approaches the abyss of her husband's infidelity; Mr. Salesby in "The Man without a Temperament" (1920) becomes painfully aware that his relationship to his wife has deteriorated to "rot"; and, in "The Stranger" (1920) Mr. Hammond, like Gabriel Conroy in Joyce's "The Dead," must forever after feel more a "stranger" to his own wife than does the dying male acquaintance on the ship as he expires in Mrs. Hammond's arms. Her most memorable fiction is thus devoted to subtle but momentous alterations in marital and family relationships—changes long in the coming but necessitated and focused by the revelatory instant.

Like Anton Chekhov (q.v.), whose work M. revered, she is most at home with the short sketch, the quiet vignette, in which little occurs on the surface. Insects drone, nature dozes, a character daydreams of past or future. But both character and reader are, often unwittingly, involved through the magic of image, symbol, word rhythm, repetitive patterns of gesture, color, sound, in a transformation that brings one or both to a new level of awareness of reality.

Because M.'s reality was abnormally bleak—her creative years full of physical pain and weakness, loneliness, exile, jealousy, frustration, alienation—her protagonists ordinarily reflect the bitter world of their creator. There are few happy characters in M.'s stories. Death and consciousness of class impinge on young Laura's rapture in "The Garden Party" (1921); time and age wear down the two sisters in "The Daughters of the Late Colonel" (1920); and in "Marriage à la Mode" (1921) the whole brittle underpinning of England's smart set is shown to be crumbling.

M. misses greatness as a writer of fiction, although in a few stories she comes very close. Her importance lies in her willingness to discard the stuffy post-Victorian drawing room of fiction for the modernist approach in which she excelled. She used the tools of psychology, not mechanically but creatively, to examine characters from within as well as without, concentrating on spirit rather than material circumstance. In her best work she surely attains her aim of tunneling beneath life's ostensible ugliness to reveal the beauty beneath.

FURTHER WORKS: *In a German Pension* (1911); *Prelude* (1918); *Je Ne Parle Pas Français* (1920); *Bliss, and Other Stories* (1921); *The Garden Party, and Other Stories* (1922); *The Dove's Nest, and Other Stories* (1923); *Poems* (1924); *Something Childish, and Other Stories* (1924); *The Journal of K. M.* (1927); *The Letters of K. M.* (1928); *The Aloe* (1930); *Novels and Novelists* (1930); *Stories by K. M.* (1930); *The Scrapbook of K. M.* (1937); *Collected Stories* (1945); *K. M.'s Letters to John Middleton Murry, 1913–1922* (1951); *Journal of K. M., Definitive Edition* (1954)

BIBLIOGRAPHY: Murry, J. M., *The Autobiography of John Middleton Murry: Between Two Worlds* (1936); Berkman, S., *K. M.: A Critical Study* (1951); Daly, S., *K. M.* (1965); Magalaner, M., *The Fiction of K. M.* (1971); Alpers, A., *The Life of K. M.* (1980); Hanson, C., and Gurr, A., *K. M.* (1981)

MARVIN MAGALANER

MAŃSI LITERATURE
See Finno-Ugric Literatures of the Soviet Union

MAO TUN
(pseud. of Shen Yen-ping) Chinese novelist and short-story writer, b. 25 June 1896, Tung-hsiang, Chekiang Province; d. 27 March 1981, Peking

M. T. came from a small-town, middle-class family and was educated in the big cities. After graduation from the junior division of the National Peking University, he worked in the editorial office of the Commercial Press, one of the large publishing houses in Shanghai. In 1921 he became editor of the company's *Hsiao-shuo yüeh-pao,* a monthly that published fiction. He was also one of the founding members, in 1920, of the Literary Research Association. With the support of the Association members, *Hsiao-shuo yüeh pao* soon became a leading literary periodical of the time (1921–32); many important works of modern Chinese fiction, including those of M.T. himself, were published in it.

M. T.'s most popular novels are the trilogy *Shih* (1930; eclipse)—consisting of *Huan-mieh* (disillusion), *Tung-yao* (vacillation), and *Chui-ch'iu* (pursuit)—which depicts in successive stages the tensions and struggles of young Chinese intellectuals prior to Nationalist victory in China; *Hung* (1930; rainbow), detailing the adventures of an innocent and intelligent girl thrust into the maelstrom of life in a complex society; and *Tzu-yeh* (1933; *Midnight,* 1957), his best-known novel, about the filth and corruption of the business and industrial communities in metropolitan Shanghai. He also published several story collections, which include "Ch'un ts'an" (1932; "Spring Silkworms," 1956) and "Lin-chia p'u-tzu" (1932; "The Shop of the Lin Family," 1956). Both stories narrate with sympathy and pathos the sufferings respectively of peasants and small-townsfolk.

During the Sino-Japanese War (1937–45) M. T. joined the exodus of Chinese intellectuals to the southwest interior. His important works of this period are the novels *Fu-shih* (1941; corrosion) and *Shuang-yeh hung szu erh-yüeh hua* (1943; frosted leaves as red as flowers in February), and the play *Ch'ing-ming ch'ien hou* (1945; before and after the spring festival).

M. T. shared the modern Chinese writers' interest in politics, which was often inseparable from literature. Although he was not a member of the Communist Party early in his career, he had pronounced leftist tendencies

221

and associated with authors who were ardent in their denunciation of the Nationalist government. After the founding of the People's Republic in 1949, he rose high in the literary hierarchy of the new regime and was elected chairman of the All-China Federation of Literary Workers (later called the Chinese Writers' Union). For sixteen years (1949–65) he was Minister of Culture in the Communist government. Beginning in 1951, he also served as editor of *Chinese Literature,* an official literary organ of Communist China, published in several languages for foreign readers. But he did little creative writing beyond revising and reissuing his earlier works in the ten-volume *M. T. wen-chi* (1958–61; M. T.'s collected works). He survived the purges of the intellectuals during the Cultural Revolution, but the most productive period of his life as a writer was long past.

A faithful chronicler of his time, M. T. recorded in a realistic manner the men and events of modern Chinese society, focusing on its ugliness and evils and on class distinctions that separate the rich from the poor. He analyzed with meticulous care the disruptive social and political forces that plunged the country into chaos in the most critical years prior to the socialist revolution that ushered in the Communist regime. After the establishment of the People's Republic, his political activities and administrative duties all but superseded his role as the most accomplished and versatile author of modern China.

FURTHER WORKS: *Yeh ch'iang-wei* (1929); *San-jen hsing* (1931); *Lu* (1932); *Hua hsia-tzu* (1934); *M. T. tuan-p'ien hsiao-shuo chi* (1934); *Su-hsieh yü sui-pi* (1935); *Yin-hsiang kan-hsiang hui-i* (1936); *To-chiao kuan hsi* (1936); *Ti-i chiai-tuan ti ku-shih* (1945); *Wei-ch'ü* (1945); *Su-lien chien-wen lu* (1947). FURTHER VOLUME IN ENGLISH: *Spring Silkworms, and Other Stories* (1956)

BIBLIOGRAPHY: Liu Wu-chi, "The Modern Period, 1900–1950," supplement to Giles, H. A., *A History of Chinese Literature,* enlarged ed. (1967), pp. 490–92; Hsia, C. T., *A History of Modern Chinese Fiction* (1971), pp. 140–64, 350–59; Berninghausen, J., "The Central Contradiction in Mao Dun's Earliest Fiction," and Chen, Y., "Mao Dun and the Use of Political Allegory in Fiction: A Case Study of His 'Autumn in Kuling,'" in Goldman, M., ed., *Modern Chinese Literature in the May Fourth Era* (1977), pp. 233–59, 261–80; Gálik, M., *The Genesis of Modern Chinese Literary Criticism* (1980), pp. 191–213; Průšek, J., "M. T. and Yü Ta-fu," in Lee, O., ed., *The Lyric and the Epic: Studies of Modern Chinese Literature* (1980), pp. 121–77

LIU WU-CHI

MAORI LITERATURE
See New Zealand Literature and Pacific Islands Literatures

MARAN, René
Martinican poet, novelist, and biographer, b. 15 Nov. 1887, Fort-de-France; d. 8 May 1960, Paris, France

M. started writing poetry while he was still in high school in Bordeaux, France, where he had been sent by his parents when he was about six years old. By the age of sixteen he was already publishing poems, and before leaving for Equatorial Africa in 1909 to serve as a colonial officer, his first volume *La maison du bonheur* (1909; home of happiness), had appeared to be followed by *La vie intérieure* (1912; the inner life). These collections and *Le livre du souvenir* (1958; the book of remembrance) constitute M.'s major poetic works. His main themes include love, the loneliness of a sensitive mind, and the inevitability of sorrow and its acceptance with fortitude. His quest for the right word and for the perfect rhythm and rhyme was almost fanatical, yet he did not sacrifice sense to sound.

Between 1912 and 1958 M. wrote mainly fiction, essays, and biographies. He returned to France in 1923, making his home in Paris. He was, in the 1920s, in contact with the New Negro movement in the U.S. Thus, in 1924 he was invited to be a judge in a literary contest organized by *The Crisis* (the house organ of the NAACP) and in 1926 to participate in the Albert and Charles Boni Novel Competition. Through articles and radio talks he promoted, in France and many other European countries, the writings of the New Negro authors. M.'s Friday evening receptions at his Paris home in the 1930s not only helped to bring black intellectuals into contact with men and women of letters from other parts of the world, but also provided a forum for discussion that fostered the emergence of Negritude (q.v.).

M.'s first novel, *Batouala, véritable roman nègre* (1921; *Batouala*, 1922), won the enviable Goncourt Prize in 1921. *Batouala* was the first attempt by a black writer to present an objective picture of the African in literature. Whether the attempt succeeded or failed is still an open question. What is certain is that, when it was published, *Batouala* with its preface, which attacked the French *method* (as distinct from *principle*) of colonization in Africa, was as controversial as M.'s own ambivalent attitude toward his African ancestral roots. Some critics commended his exposure of the dehumanizing effects of the French method of colonization in Africa—with its excessive taxation, forced labor, and attempts to make Africans renounce their customs and traditions—but condemned his portrayal of the African chief Batouala and his people as unmitigatedly primitive. Some agents and admirers of the French colonial administration saw the preface of *Batouala* not only as a misrepresentation of French activities in Africa but also as anti-French ammunition in the hands of Germany and other enemies of France. Others saw the portrayal of the African life style—characterized by idleness, cannibalism, and excessive sexual appetite—as justification for the colonization of Africa.

M. continued his attack on the French method of colonization in his later works. *Le Tchad de sable et d'or* (1931; Chad of sand and gold) demonstrated Africans' need for the protection of Europe. *Livingstone et l'exploration de l'Afrique* (1938; Livingstone and the exploration of Africa) celebrated David Livingstone's exploits.

M.'s perception of Africa and its reality was colored by his French upbringing. A great stylist, he saw himself first and foremost as a French writer. His writing, especially his poetry, is dominated by the stoic philosophy of Marcus Aurelius.

FURTHER WORKS: *Le visage calme* (1922); *Le petit roi de Chiméerie* (1924); *Djouma, chien de brousse* (1927); *Le cœur serré* (1931); *Le livre de la brousse* (1934); *Les belles images* (1935); *Savorgnan de Brazza* (1941); *Bêtes de la brousse* (1942); *Les pionniers de l'empire* (3 vols., 1943–55); *Mbala l'éléphant* (1944); *Peines de cœur* (1944); *Un homme pareil aux autres* (1947); *Bacouya le cynocéphale* (1953); *Félix Eboué, grand homme et loyal

serviteur (1957); *Bertrand du Guesclin* (1961)

BIBLIOGRAPHY: Vandérem, F., "Le Prix Goncourt," *La revue de France*, 1 (1922), 386–91; Cook, M., *Five French Negro Authors* (1943), pp. 123–48; *Hommage à R. M.* (1965); Kesteloot, L., *Black Writers in French: A Literary History of Negritude* (1974), pp. 75–79 and passim; Hausser, M., *Les deux Batouala de R. M.* (1975); Ikonné, C., "R. M. and the New Negro," *CLQ*, 15, 4 (1979), 224–39; Ade, F. O., "R. M. devant la critique," *O&C*, 3, 2–4, 1 (1979), 143–55

                                    CHIDI IKONNÉ

MARATHI LITERATURE

See Indian Literature

MARCEL, Gabriel

French philosopher, dramatist, and critic, b. 7 Dec. 1889, Paris; d. 8 Oct. 1973, Paris

After extensive travels with his diplomat father, M. took a degree in philosophy at the Sorbonne (1910) and afterward taught in secondary schools for a number of years. Later he worked for two Paris publishing houses, and was drama and music critic for various periodicals. His early publications included plays, essays, and critical articles, and in 1927 his *Journal métaphysique* (*Metaphysical Journal*, 1952) won him attention as a serious philosopher. Already acquainted with the works of Kirkegaard and the German philosopher Karl Jaspers (1883–1969), he crystallized his own religious thinking and, in 1929, embraced Catholicism. Recipient, over the years, of a goodly number of awards and prizes in France and abroad, M. was elected to the Academy of Moral and Political Sciences in 1952, named to other prestigious organizations, and invited to lecture all over the world. Some of his personal reminiscences can be found in *En chemin vers quel éveil?* (1971; en route toward what awakening?).

M. is usually identified as a "Christian existentialist" despite his repudiation of the term (he preferred Christian-Socratic). He insisted that his philosophical writings were not intended to constitute a closed "system" nor to be considered treatises in the usual sense. Often in the form of journals, collected essays, or public lectures, they are concerned with human existence and the search for authentic being and personal transcendence. In them M. offers critiques of several contemporary philosophical systems and points to the irreligion of our age. He distinguishes between modern man's obsession with "having"—both in the Christian sense of the "flesh" and its wants, and in the sense of the desire for possession in our technocratic world—and striving for "being," necessary elements of which include love for and direct and open communication with others, the more fully to find one's authentic self. Being is a "mystery," experienced and felt through involvement even in a "broken world." This mystery of being cannot be analyzed, just as faith in God is felt through concrete experience, not through abstract "proofs." M. considered his *Positions et approches concrètes du mystère ontologique* (1933; *Philosophy of Existence,* 1948; repr. as *The Philosophy of Existentialism,* 1961) the most succinct expression of his contribution to contemporary thought.

M. insisted, however, that in order fully to understand his philosophy one must know his plays, for he viewed them as the concrete revelation of his metaphysical thought. Although he refused to call them thesis plays—in the sense that he had no wish to impose any ready-made truth on his public—it is nonetheless true that he intended them to free the individual spectator from whatever opinions or prejudices might keep him from having access to his self or communication with others. The plays therefore aim at a spiritual and intellectual renewal for the audience and as a result are heavily intellectual. They do not always escape the wordiness of even indirectly didactic theater of a metaphysical thrust. They too frequently lack a true dramatic dynamic and rely on the last act or scene's making all the rest clear. They deal with arresting personalities, however—souls in exile, as M. called them. Especially absorbing in this respect are *Un homme de Dieu* (1925; *A Man of God,* 1958), *La chapelle ardente* (1925; *The Funeral Pyre,* 1958; later retitled *The Votive Candle,* 1965), and *Le chemin de Crête* (1936; *Ariadne,* 1958).

While M.'s perception of the difficulties of the human condition in the modern world is in some ways akin to that of Jean-Paul Sartre (q.v.) and other atheistic existentialists (q.v.),

his faith militates against his searching for "being" without a sense of hope.

FURTHER WORKS: *La grâce* (1911); *Le palais du sable* (1913); *Le seuil invisible* (1914); *Le cœur des autres* (1921); *L'iconoclaste* (1923); *Le quatuor en fa dièse* (1925); *Trois pièces: Le regard neuf, Le mort de demain, La chapelle ardente* (1931); *Le monde cassé* (1933); *Être et avoir* (1935; *Being and having,* 1949); *Le fanal* (1936); *Le dard* (1938); *La soif (Les cœurs avides)* (1938); *Du refus à l'invocation* (1940; *Creative Fidelity,* 1964); *Homo viator* (1944; *Homo Viator: Introduction to a Metaphysic of Hope,* 1951); *L'horizon* (1945); *La métaphysique de Royce* (1945; *Royce's Metaphysics,* 1956); *Théâtre comique* (1947); *Vers un autre royaume: L'émissaire et Le signe de la croix* (1949); *La fin des temps* (1950); *Le mystère de l'être* (2 vols., 1951; *The Mystery of Being,* 2 vols., 1950–51); *Les hommes contre l'humain* (1951; *Man against Mass Society,* 1952); *Rome n'est plus dans Rome* (1951); *La dimension Florestan* (1952); *Le déclin de la sagesse* (1954; *The Decline of Wisdom,* 1954); *Mon temps n'est pas le vôtre* (1955); *Croissez et multipliez* (1955); *L'homme problématique* (1955; *Problematic Man,* 1967); *Théâtre et religion* (1958); *Présence et immortalité* (1959; *Presence and Immortality,* 1967); *L'heure théâtrale de Giraudoux à Jean-Paul Sartre* (1959); *Fragments philosophiques, 1909–1914* (1962; *Philosophical Fragments and The Philosopher and Peace,* 1965); *La dignité humaine et ses assises existentielles* (1964; *The Existential Background of Human Dignity,* 1963); *Auf der Suche nach Wahrheit und Gerechtigkeit* (1964; *Searchings,* 1967); *Regards sur le théâtre de Claudel* (1964); *Paix sur la terre: Deux discours, une tragédie* (1965); *Le secret est dans les îles: Le dard, L'émissaire, La fin des temps* (1967); *Pour une sagesse tragique et son au-delà* (1968; *Tragic Wisdom and Beyond,* 1973); *Entretiens Paul Ricœur, G. M.* (1968; in *Tragic Wisdom and Beyond,* 1973); *Percées vers un ailleurs: L'iconoclaste, L'horizon, suivi de L'audace en métaphysique* (1973)

BIBLIOGRAPHY: Ricœur, P., *G. M. et Karl Jaspers: Philosophie du mystère et philosophie du paradoxe* (1947); Chénu, J., *Le théâtre de G. M. et sa signification métaphysique* (1948); Gallagher, K. T., *The Philosophy of G. M.* (1962); Cain, S., *G. M.* (1963);

Miceli, V., *Ascent to Being: G. M.'s Philosophy of Communion* (1965); Troisfontaines, R., *De l'existence à l'être: La philosophie de G. M.*, new ed. (1968); Widner, C., *G. M. et le théisme existentiel* (1971)

RUTH B. YORK

MARECHAL, Leopoldo

Argentine novelist, poet, and dramatist, b. 11 June 1900, Buenos Aires; d. 26 June 1970, Buenos Aires

M., like his celebrated contemporary Jorge Luis Borges (q.v.), began his career as an avant-garde, ultraist (q.v.) poet in the Buenos Aires of the 1920s and only much later achieved lonely distinction (and some notoriety) as a writer of fiction. His father was a worker who died in the influenza epidemic of 1918, and his maternal grandfather had been an exiled Paris Communard; M. regarded himself as a revolutionary, first as a socialist and later an an ardent supporter of Juan Perón. He made his living for many years as a schoolteacher and journalist and between 1944 and 1955 held various public posts, including the Cultural Directorship of the Argentine Ministry of Education.

M.'s identification with Peronism was to isolate him from most of the dominant writers of his generation and led to a decade of almost complete seclusion following Perón's fall in 1955 and to general critical neglect of his work, including the monumental city novel *Adán Buenosayres* (1948; Adam Buenosayres). The appearance of a second, slighter, novel, *El banquete de Severo Arcángelo* (1965; the banquet of Severo Arcángelo) an immediate popular and critical success, has stimulated a reassessment of M.'s position among Argentine writers of the 20th c.

Unlike his fiction, M.'s poetry received early and continuing recognition. His development was from the self-consciously modernist (q.v.) free verse of *Días como flechas* (1926; days like arrows), characterized by a perhaps too great reliance on startling metaphor, to a more ordered and formal poetry, metaphysical in theme, and in manner often closely related to the tradition of the Spanish past. *Odas para el hombre y la mujer* (1929; odes for man and woman) was awarded first prize in a competition sponsored by the municipality of Buenos Aires. M.'s religious conversion in the early 1930s is reflected in

the austerity of the collections *Cinco poemas australes* (1937; five southern poems) and *El centauro* (1940; the centaur), which together with *Sonetas a Sophia, y otros poemas* (1940; sonnets to Sophia, and other poems) won for M. in 1941 the coveted National Prize in poetry.

The classicism and restraint of the later poetry hardly prepared M.'s readers for the immense novel *Adán Buenosayres,* begun in Paris in 1930 and written and rewritten during the following eighteen years. Julio Cortázar (q.v.), who greeted its publication as "an extraordinary event in Argentine letters," also conceded, "Seldom has a book appeared that is less coherent." Autobiographical and fantastic by turns, Rabelaisian in parts and tender in others, scatological and eschatological often at the same time, it is a mélange of dreams, jokes, metaphysics, farce, and history. One early reviewer complained that *Adán Buenosayres* employed more bad words than *Ulysses,* and indeed it is with the comic epic of James Joyce (q.v.) that its closest affinities are found. As in *Ulysses,* a story of the present, or near present, is overlaid upon Greek myth, a device that M. used again in his play *Antígona Vélez* (1965; Antigone Vélez).

By comparison, the less ambitious later novels *El banquete de Severo Arcángelo* (which won the Forti Glori prize in 1966) and *Megafón; o, La guerra* (1970); Megafón; or, war) are more coherent, although still strange, blends of farce, melodrama, and religious allegory. In Argentina they have been well received.

M. is perhaps less well known by English-speaking readers than any other Latin American writer of comparable stature. Aside from the poems "Cortejo" (1937; "Cortège," 1942) and "El centauro" (1939; "The Centaur," 1944), almost nothing by, and very little about, M. is presently available in English. The curious reader who wishes to encounter one of the most surprising and often rewarding writers of this hemisphere has no recourse but to turn to the original.

FURTHER WORKS: *Los aguilochos* (1922); *Laberinto de amor* (1936); *Historia de la calle Corrientes* (1937); *Vida de Santa Rosa de Lima* (1943); *La rosa en la balanza* (1944); *El viaje de la primavera* (1945); *La alegropeya* (1962); *Cuaderno de navegación* (1966); *Las tres caras de Venus* (1966); *El poema de*

Robot (1966); *La batalla de José Luna* (1970); *Don Juan* (1978)

BIBLIOGRAPHY: Marechal, L., *Las claves de "Adán Buenosayres" y tres artículos de Julio Cortázar, Adolfo Prieto, Graciela de Sola* (1966); Andrés, A., *Palabras con L. M.* (1968); Coulson, G., *M.: La pasión metafísica* (1974); Kuehne, A., "M.'s Antígona: More Greek than French," *LATR*, 9, 1 (1975), 19–27; Gordon, A., "Dublin and Buenos Aires, Joyce and M.," *CLS*, 19 (1982), 208–19

AMBROSE GORDON

MARI LITERATURE

See Finno-Ugric Literatures of the Soviet Union

MARINETTI, Filippo Tommaso

Italian critic, journalist, novelist, poet, and dramatist (also writing in French), b. 22 Dec. 1876, Alexandria, Egypt; d. 2 Dec. 1944, Bellagio

The son of a prominent Italian lawyer residing in Egypt, M. moved to Paris in his early youth, while his family returned to Italy, and spent his formative years studying at the Sorbonne, where he received a degree. Later he attended the University of Pavia and graduated from the law school of the University of Genoa.

He began to write in French, and his first literary production includes, among other things, an epic poem, *La conquête des étoiles* (1902; the conquest of the stars). In 1905 M. moved to Milan and founded *Poesia*, an international journal of poetry that was partly committed to the propagation of French symbolism (q.v.) and Decadence but also accepted the work of Italian writers of the younger as well as the older generation. In connection with that review M. also organized a group of "poètes incendiaires," which can be regarded as one of the first rallies of futurism (q.v.). All the innovative ferment of M.'s work was to break out a few years later with the publication of the first manifesto of futurism, which appeared almost simultaneously in French in *Le Figaro* (February 20, 1909) as "Manifeste du futurisme" ("The Founding and Manifesto of Fu-

turism," 1972), and in Italian in *Poesia* (February–March 1909). It was followed by other "technical" proclamations of the futurist theory, as applied to literature and the arts—for example, "Manifesto tecnico della letteratura futurista" (1912; "Technical Manifesto of Futurist Literature," 1972).

M. advocated, among other things, daring and temerity, action and aggressiveness, militarism and patriotism, and open rebellion against all traditional forms of culture. He called for the liquidation of all values and institutions of the past and exalted modern dynamism and industry, the myth of the machine, and the unrestrained cult of the individual.

In the fields of poetry and other creative writing M. urged the dismantling of syntax, the abolition of punctuation, and the adoption of unorthodox typographical devices and techniques that would assure the reader's attention and participation—the style he called *parole in libertà* (words freed). These ideas, some of which were inherent in the development of modern irrationalism, M. attempted to exemplify in subsequent writings and particularly in the novel *Mafarka le futuriste: Roman africain* (1909; Mafarka the futurist: African novel), first published in French, a work whose overt iconoclasm and avowal of heroic vitalism has at times suggested definition in terms of "political" propaganda.

Both in his manifestos on the theater and in his "syntheses" (short dramatic pieces) M., rejecting the analytical pedantry of psychological drama and the static and diluted style of the stage of his time, aimed at revolutionizing the values and conventions of the traditional theater with ideas and methods whose seminal originality and vitality opened the way to a new age of experimentation in the performing arts.

M. also attempted to apply the principles of futurism, intended as a living doctrine and a global theory, to all aspects of social, cultural, and political life, even to the extent of actively supporting the policies of Mussolini and his Fascist regime.

Beyond his colorful and controversial activity as propagandist and committed writer, however, M.'s prominence remains confined mainly to his original function as ideologue and spokesman of one of the first avant-garde movements in 20th-c. art and literature. In this sense it can be said that his futurist manifestos represent his main literary contribution and can justifiably be valued for their special role in establishing a new "genre" that effectively blends the rhetoric of slogans and theoretical pronouncements with timely insights and highly innovative ideas for the development of all art forms.

SELECTED FURTHER WORKS: *D'Annunzio intime* (1903); *Destruction: Poèmes lyriques* (1904); *La momie sanglante* (1904); *Le roi Bombance: Tragédie satirique en 4 actes* (1905); *La ville charnelle* (1908; It., *Lussuria-velocità*, 1920); *Les dieux s'en vont, D'Annunzio reste* (1908); *Poupées électriques* (1909); *Uccidiamo il chiaro di luna!* (1911); *Le futurisme: Théories et mouvement* (1911); *Le monoplan du pape* (1912); *La battaglia di Tripoli* (1912); *Manifeste technique de la littérature futuriste* (1912); *I manifesti del futurismo* (1914); *Guerra sola igiene del mondo* (1915); *Come si seducono le donne* (1917); *Scelta di poesie e parole in libertà* (1918); *I manifesti del futurismo* (4 vols., 1919); *8 anime in una bomba: Romanzo esplosivo* (1919); *Democrazia futurista: Dinamismo politico* (1919); *Elettricità sessuale* (1919); *Al di là del comunismo* (1920); *L'alcova d'acciaio* (1921); *Il tamburo di fuoco* (1922); *Gli amori futuristi* (1922); *Gli indomabili* (1922); *Futurismo e Fascismo* (1924); *Scatole d'amore in conserva* (1927); *Prigionieri e vulcani* (1927); *L'oceano del cuore* (1928); *Primo dizionario aereo italiano* (1929); *Il suggeritore nudo* (1930); *Novelle colle labbra tinte* (1930); *Futurismo e novecentismo* (1931); *Il paesaggio e l'estetica futurista della macchina* (1931); *Ali d'Italia* (1931); *Il fascino dell'Egitto* (1933); *Poemi simultanei futuristi* (1933); *L'aeropoema del Golfo della Spezia* (1935); *L'originalità napoletana del poeta Salvatore di Giacomo* (1936); *Il poema africano della divisione "XXVIII ottobre"* (1937); *Patriottismo insetticida* (1939); *Il poema non umano dei tecnicismi* (1940); *Carlinga di aeropoeti futuristi di guerra, collaudata da F. T. M.* (1941); *Canto eroi e macchine della guerra mussoliniana* (1942); *Quarto d'ora di poesia della X Mas* (1945); *Teatro* (3 vols., 1960); *Il teatro della sorpresa* (1968); *Teoria e invenzione futurista* (1968); *La grande Milano tradizionale e futurista; Una sensibilità italiana nata in Egitto* (1969); *Lettere ruggenti* (1970); *Poesie a Beny* (1971); *Collaudi futuristi* (1977); *M. futurista: Pagine disperse, documenti e antologia critica* (1977). FURTHER VOLUMES IN ENGLISH: *Selected Writings* (1972); *Short Plays* (1973)

BIBLIOGRAPHY: Clough Trillo, R., *Futurism* (1961); Martin, M. W., *Futurist Art and Theory* (1968); Apollonio, U., ed., *Futurist Manifestos* (1973); Darío, R., "M. and Futurism" [tr. of 1909 article], *DQ*, 12 (1977), 147–52; Bronner, S. E., "F. T. M.: The Theory and Practice of Futurism," *BUJ*, 25 (1977), 48–56; Festa-McCormick, D., "M.'s Murder of the Moonlight and the Kinetics of Time," *Centerpoint*, 2 (1977), 50–54; Tindall, C., and Bozzolla, A., *Futurism* (1980)

A. ILLIANO

MARKANDAYA, Kamala

(pseud. of Kamala Purnaiya Taylor) Indian novelist (writing in English), b. 1924, Chimakurti

Born into a Madhwa Brahmin family of south India, M. was educated at various schools there and attended Madras University. She later worked as a journalist and moved to England, where she married. M. has been writing steadily since the publication of her widely acclaimed first novel, *Nectar in a Sieve* (1954), which has been translated into seventeen languages.

Nearly all of M.'s writing deals with the conflict between East and West or its more subtle form: tension between tradition and modernity in Indian life styles. In her novels British and urban elements are portrayed as agents of dynamic change, whereas native-born and village folk manifest cohesive but static social structures. *Nectar in a Sieve* conveys a romantic view of the Indian villager struggling against unending poverty. Yet at core, M. lacks familiarity with village life and writes more successfully, in *A Handful of Rice* (1966), of the overcrowded conditions and the angry young men that are the results of migration to the cities.

Two Virgins (1973) is an absorbing *Bildungsroman*, which explores the minds of two sisters as they encounter a rapidly changing external world as well as the puzzling internal world of emotions and growing sexuality. M. departs from her usual themes in *The Nowhere Man* (1972), which depicts the plight of an aged Indian merchant living in London and caught in the backlash of anti-Asian feeling fueled by Pakistani and Indian immigration. *The Golden Honeycomb* (1979) is a historical novel set in a princely state around 1900.

M. has shown an admirable willingness to

tackle a number of contemporary issues, to the extent that her writing may be considered socioliterature. Indeed, her conscious use of sociological imagery has increased as her writing has matured; wherever possible, she concentrates on demolishing stereotypes in favor of presenting truth. Role-assignment according to sex is a major concern in her work. M.'s novels intelligently illustrate the major social issues confronting India and its citizens, beginning with the struggle for independence. Most are fine stories as well.

FURTHER WORKS: *Some Inner Fury* (1955); *A Silence of Desire* (1960); *Possession* (1963); *The Coffer Dams* (1969)

BIBLIOGRAPHY: Shiv, K. "Tradition and Change in the Novels of K. M.," *BA,* 43 (1969), 508–13; Rao, K. S. N., "K. M.: The Novelist as Craftsman," *IWT,* 8 (1969), 32–40; Harrex, S. C., "A Sense of Identity: The Novels of K. M.," *JCL,* 6 (1971), 68–78; Adkins, J. F., "K. M.: Indo-Anglican Conflict as Unity," *JSoAL,* 10 (1974), 89–102; Shimer, D. B., "Sociological Imagery in the Novels of K. M.," *WLWE,* 14 (1975), 357–70; Rao, K. S. N., "Religious Elements in K. M.'s Novels," *ArielE,* 8, 1 (1977), 35–50; Prasad, H. M., "The Quintessence of K. M.'s Art," *ComQ,* 3, 9 (1978), 173–85

JANET POWERS GEMMILL

MARKISH, Peretz

Yiddish poet, novelist, and dramatist, b. 7 Dec. 1895, Polone, Russia; d. 12 Aug. 1952, Moscow, U.S.S.R.

M. was born and raised in a town in Volhynia. War and revolution were the crucible of M.'s life and work. He served in the tsar's army in World War I, was wounded at the front, and was thought for a time to have perished in the Ukrainian pogroms of 1918–19. In 1921 M. left the Soviet Union for Warsaw, where he launched the Yiddish expressionist (q.v.) group Di khalyastre (The Gang) with Melech Ravitch (1893–1976) and Uri Zvi Greenberg (q.v.). Wanderlust took him to Berlin, Paris, London, and Palestine, but Poland remained the center of his intense literary activity until he returned to the Soviet Union in 1926. Soon thereafter he came under vicious attack for maintaining ties with the "bourgeois reactionary circles in the West" and for "misrepresenting Soviet reali-

ty." Although M. bravely challenged his critics, he eventually submitted to Party control and subjected his own works to self-censorship and ideological revision. In 1939 he was awarded the Order of Lenin. M.'s response in his writings to the Nazi conquest of Poland was immediate and profound, but these intensely Jewish works could not be published until his country entered the war. Arrested on January 27, 1949, during the purge of the Jewish cultural figures, he was shot in the Lubyanka Prison on August 12, 1952.

For M., the revolution meant freedom from the neoromantic, melancholy, and stylized verse that had dominated Yiddish poetry of the previous decade; it meant the physical freedom to travel and work wherever he chose, striking roots nowhere. The titles of his earliest collections of poetry best illustrate this mood: *Shveln* (1919; thresholds), *Pust un pas* (1919; idle), *Shtiferish* (1919; mischievous), and *Stam* (1921; just like that). By the time he left for Poland, he had become the poetic voice of the revolution in Yiddish literature.

Influenced by two very different strands of Russian modernism—futurism (q.v.) and Acmeism—M. introduced a new Yiddish poetics: inverted syntax, the use of regional and unusual words, wild metonymies instead of metaphors, assonance, and wrenched rhyme. His most dazzling lyric poems applied classical forms (notably the sonnet) to such modernist themes as the city, chaos, and technology. Throughout his career, M. favored a dramatic, exclamatory style, which he managed to combine with long descriptive passages. This tension between classical form and modernist theory, between egocentric pathos and the need to chronicle the historical present, between the lyric and the epic, is at the heart of M.'s achievement.

The balance shifted from one period to another. M.'s early poetry was an exalted, personal celebration of the present, with its boundless possibilities. When he tried to capture the shtetl of his childhood in the narrative poem *Volin* (written 1918, pub. 1921; Volhynia), the people were portrayed dispassionately and as lacking all sense of the present moment. In his expressionist period (1921–26), external reality existed only to the extent that it was reflected within the poet's own ego—and reality could be anything from Ukrainian pogroms to the Eiffel Tower. In *Di kupe* (1921; the corpse heap), for instance, his major expressionist work, the poet is overwhelmed by the physicality of the po-grom, by the revolting smell of decomposing bodies. The egocentric vision allowed for no temporal development. Each poem captured a single moment, and even the poetic "I" had no biographical past: he was society at large or every "I" reading the poem.

M.'s narrative poem *Brider* (1929; broth-ers) marked a turning point and synthesis. M. returned to the shtetl setting to show it transformed by human experience. In the tale of two Jewish brothers who gave their lives to the revolution, a sense of history was achieved through highly figurative language, haunting repetitions, a fusion of lyric and narrative, high and low diction. Most innova-tive was M.'s elliptic throwing together of detail instead of a full narrative development. The social, political, and generational aspects of this theme received a more sustained, if more conventional treatment in M.'s first novel, *Dor oys dor ayn* (1929; generations come and go).

The 1930s were essentially a period of con-solidation and revision. M. adapted his more popular works for the Soviet Yiddish theater, then in its heyday, and saw an impressive number of his works appear in Russian trans-lation.

In his last, most tragic period, M. became the supreme elegist of Polish Jewry. In his finest poem, *Tsu a yidisher tentserin* (written 1940, pub. 1959; to a Jewish dancer), he treated the unfathomable tragedy through the fate of a single victim, the artistic em-bodiment of her people. Less successful were his all-encompassing epic poem *Milkhome* (1948; war) and his novel about the Warsaw Ghetto uprising, *Trot fun doyres* (written 1947–48; pub. [in censored version] 1966; the tread of generations). In 1948 M. wrote a de-fiant elegy for his close friend Solomon Mik-hoels, the preeminent actor and director of the Yiddish theater whom the Soviet secret police had just murdered. With its total poet-ic control and classical locutions, this poem is a fitting requiem for all of Soviet Yiddish culture.

FURTHER WORKS: *In mitn veg* (1919); *Nokhn telerl fun himl* (1919); *Farbaygeyendik (eseyen)* (1921); *Radio* (1922); *Der galaganer hon* (1922); *Nakhtroyb* (1922); *Farklepte tsi-ferblatn* (1929); *Nit gedayget* (1931); *Vokhn-teg* (1931); *Gezamlte verk* (3 vols., 1933–37); *Eyns af eyns* (1934); *Dem balegufs toyt* (1935; also pub. as *Anshl der zalyaznik*); *Oyf-*

gang afn Dnyeper (1937); *Lider vegn Shpanye* (1938); *Foterlekhe erd* (1938); *Der-tseylungen* (1939); *Di naye mishpokhe* (1939); *Mikhoels* (1939); *Poemen vegn Stalinen* (1940); *Roytarmeyishe balades* (1940); *Dor oys dor ayn*, Vol. II (1941); *A toyt di kani-baln!* (1941); *Farn folk un heymland* (1943); *Yerushe* (1959); *Der fertsikyoriker man* (1978)

BIBLIOGRAPHY: Shmeruk, C., "Yiddish Lit-erature in the U.S.S.R.," in Kochan, L., ed., *The Jews in Soviet Russia since 1917* (1970), pp. 232–68; Markish, E., *The Long Return* (1978); Roskies, D. G., "The Pogrom Poem and the Literature of Destruction," *NDEJ*, 11 (1979), 89–113

DAVID G. ROSKIES

MARQUAND, J(ohn) P(hillips)
American novelist, b. 10 Nov. 1893, Wil-mington, Del.; d. 16 July 1960, Newbury-port, Mass.

Born into New England literary society, M. majored in chemistry at Harvard. After grad-uation he took up magazine editing for *The Boston Transcript* and later worked in adver-tising and journalism following his military service as an artillery lieutenant during World War I. Married three times, M. had two sons and a daughter.

M. began his career by writing popular, melodramatic tales like the Mr. Moto stories, and costume romances like *The Black Cargo* (1925) and *Haven's End* (1937). *The Late George Apley* (1937), a satiric rendering of upper-class Bostonian traditions, made him known as a serious novelist, set the tone of subsequent works, and won him a Pulitzer Prize in 1938. *Wickford Point* (1939) em-ploys the same setting to explore the career of a slick, popular writer from a decaying New England family through M.'s favorite narrative techniques of ironic point of view and flashback. Similarly, *H. M. Pulham, Esq.* (1941) is the portrait of a Boston busi-nessman, the symbol of a vanishing order, who ineffectually rebels against social class and customs.

Turning to other cities and professions for subjects, M. continued to build on the theme of American social manners in his novels. *So Little Time* (1943) suggests the unrelenting passage of time in the life of a middle-aged playwright. Following an inferior war novel,

Repent in Haste (1945), *B. F.'s Daughter* (1946) reveals the effects of the wartime mood on big business and the Washington bureaucracy. In the postwar *Point of No Return* (1949) M. revived his earlier brilliance in satire and sociological study: a successful banker realizes too late in his career that the competitive ethics of American business have left him spiritually bankrupt. The past in inaccessible; he can only complete a dead life.

In *Melville Goodwin, U.S.A.* (1951) M. pictures the military world through the eyes of a journalist and achieves a double-edged irony that reflects both the shallowness of the reporter's medium and deceit among the Army's higher echelons. More purely in the tradition of Sinclair Lewis (q.v.), *Sincerely, Willis Wayde* (1955) brutally relates the lack of morality and character in the life of an American entrepreneur. M.'s last important and most autobiographically interesting novel, *Women and Thomas Harrow* (1958), is the story of a successful playwright and his three marriages. M. again uncovers spiritual mediocrity in American society.

M. was one of the most consistently popular and best-selling social novelists of his age. His thorough and detailed canvases of America, the grace of his parody and irony, and the power of his themes about the conflict between the individual and conformity speak of an artistic vision and sensibility fundamental to American literature.

FURTHER WORKS: *Prince and Boatswain* (1915); *The Unspeakable Gentleman* (1922); *Four of a Kind* (1923); *Lord Timothy Dexter* (1925); *Do Tell Me, Doctor Johnson* (1928); *Warning Hill* (1930); *Ming Yellow* (1935); *No Hero* (1935); *Thank You, Mr. Moto* (1936); *Think Fast, Mr. Moto* (1937); *Mr. Moto Is So Sorry* (1938); *Mr. Moto Takes a Hand* (1940); *Don't Ask Questions* (1941); *Last Laugh, Mr. Moto* (1942); *It's Loaded, Mr. Bauer* (1949); *Stopover, Tokyo* (1957); *Life at Happy Knoll* (1957); *Timothy Dexter Revisted* (1960)

BIBLIOGRAPHY: Hicks, G., "M. of Newburyport," *Harper's,* April 1950, 105–8; Brady, C. A., "J. P. M.," in Gardner, H. C., ed., *Fifty Years of the American Novel, 1900–1950* (1952), pp. 107–34; Kazin, A., "J. P. M. and the American Failure," *Atlantic,* Nov. 1958, 152–54; Gross, J J., *J. P. M.* (1963); Holman, C. H., *J. P. M.* (1965); Bell, M., *M.: An American Life* (1979); Green, G., "J. M.: The Reluctant Prophet," *NER,* 2 (1980), 614–24

LYNN DEVORE

MARQUÉS, René

Puerto Rican dramatist, short-story writer, novelist, essayist, and poet, b. 4 Oct. 1919, Arecibo; d. 22 March 1979, San Juan

After earning an agronomy degree in 1942, M. attended the University of Madrid, where he took courses in literature. In 1949 he received a Rockefeller grant to study theater arts at Columbia University, and upon returning to Puerto Rico he began a literary career that would make him the island's best-known contemporary man of letters.

M.'s basic preoccupation as a writer was Puerto Rico's political future. An outspoken advocate of independence, he abhorred the domination of his homeland by the U.S., which has led to the industrialization of the island's agricultural economy and to the contamination of its Hispanic culture. M. also condemned his fellow countrymen who barter their national identity for economic gain.

Most critics agree that M. will be remembered primarily as a dramatist whose works revitalized the modern Puerto Rican theater. His most popular play is *La carreta* (1951; *The Oxcart,* 1960), which depicts the plight of peasants who leave their farm in search of a better life, first in San Juan and then in New York. After suffering the dehumanizing misfortunes of slum life, they return to the land they never should have abandoned.

M.'s most highly acclaimed critical successes were *Un niño azul para esa sombra* (1958; a blue child for that shadow) and *Los soles truncos* (1958; *The House of the Setting Suns,* 1965). *Un niño azul para esa sombra* is a poetic tragedy of an alienated child whose suicide results from the rift between his Americanized mother and his revolutionary father. The color blue symbolizes idealism; the shadow, Puerto Rico's submission to American influence. In *Los soles truncos* two guilt-ridden old maids relive the past on the day of their sister's death. A series of flashbacks explains their mental torment, a metaphor of the collective guilt weighing on the Puerto Rican psyche. The theme of purification is suggested when the sisters set fire to their decaying mansion to prevent American entrepreneurs from converting it into a hotel.

Innovations in M.'s theater include striking visual and auditory effects as well as abrupt temporal and spatial dislocations. M. also injected elements of pantomime, farce, and Theater of the Absurd (q.v.) into his dramas in order to poeticize his political ideas. His last plays treat biblical themes that draw parallels between past and present-day situations and thus deny temporal progression.

M.'s short stories are considered second only to his theater, a fine example of this genre being the prize-winning "Tres hombres junto al río" (1960; "Three Men near the River," 1978), in which three Indians drown a white man to test the validity of, and ultimately destroy, the resurrection myth.

Although M. has been labeled a pessimist because of the adversity most of his protagonists experience, he was, in reality, an optimist who considered man capable of change once he is made aware of his foibles. His incessant search for new artistic horizons lent universal dimensions to his work, elevating it above most social-protest literature written in Spanish.

FURTHER WORKS: *Peregrinacíon* (1944); *El hombre y sus sueños* (1946); *El sol y los Mac-Donald* (1947); *Juan Bobo y la Dama de Occidente* (1955); *Otro día nuestro* (1955); *La muerte no entrará en palacio* (1956); *La víspera del hombre* (1957); *Carnaval afuera, carnaval adentro* (1960); *La casa sin reloj* (1960); *En una ciudad llamada San Juan* (1960); *El apartamiento* (1964); *Mariana; o, El alba* (1965); *Sacrificio en el Monte Moriah* (1969); *David y Jonathan* (1970); *Tito y Berenice* (1970); *Vía crucis del hombre puertorriqueño* (1970); *Ensayos (1953–1971)* (1971); *Inmersos en el silencio* (1976); *La mirada* (1976)

BIBLIOGRAPHY: Dauster, F., "The Theater of R. M.," *Symposium,* 18, 1 (1964), 35–45; Shaw, D. L., "R. M.'s *La muerte no entrará en palacio:* An Analysis," *LATR,* 2, 1 (1968), 31–38; Siemens, W. L., "Assault on the Schizoid Wasteland: R. M.'s *El apartamiento,*" *LATR,* 7, 2 (1974), 17–23; Holzaphel, T., "The Theater of R. M.: In Search of Identity and Form," in Lyday, L. F., and Woodyard, G. W., eds., *Dramatists in Revolt: The New Latin American Theater* (1976), pp. 146–66; Rodríguez-Seda, A.,

"Puerto Rican Narrative: Aspects of Frustration," *PCL*, 2, 2 (1976), 53–62; Pilditch, C., *R. M.: A Study of His Fiction* (1977); Martin, E. J., *R. M.* (1979)

GEORGE R. MCMURRAY

MARSMAN, Hendrik

Dutch poet and critic, b. 30 Sept. 1899, Zeist; d. 21 June 1940, English Channel

Only M.'s death sets his biography apart from those of many other middle-class, university-trained professional literati. He served brief and relatively unsuccessful stints as editor of a literary journal and newspaper critic, which failed to further his ambition to play a leadership role in the world of letters. Such influence as he did exert, especially over minor talents, was based more on his often forceful reviews, in which he developed his programmatic opinions. In 1921 and 1922 M. made an extensive journey through Germany, and later he lived for more than a decade on the Mediterranean: in Italy, Spain, and France. The political developments in Germany in the 1930s aroused his opposition to fascism, and when Hitler's troops invaded the Netherlands in May 1940, he decided to seek sanctuary in England. The ship on which he was making the crossing from the French port of Bordeaux was sunk by a German submarine, and M. drowned.

A selection of M.'s earliest poems, which had appeared in various journals since 1919, was published in the volume *Verzen* (1923; verse), followed some years later by a more extensive collection, *Paradise regained* (1927; title in English). These texts were dominated by a pseudoexpressionistic style, which reflected M.'s perception of such German poets as Herwarth Walden (1878–1941) and Hermann Kasack (1896–1966). In essence, M.'s lyric stance was impressionistic and individualistic in this so-called "vitalistic" phase, whose end he proclaimed in 1933.

Actually, he had abandoned this style in his poetry several years earlier. Even in the 1927 volume, occasional works had foreshadowed the new direction of his poetry in a basically romantic preoccupation with loneliness and death. The earlier tendency toward exaggerated diction gave way to a simpler and more colloquial mode of expression. The principal yield of this second phase was collected in *Porta Nigra* (1934; Latin: Black

Gate)—the title derives from the monumental "black gate" built by the Romans in the city that is now Trier, West Germany—which won a prestigious official literary award. Thematically related to these poems was one of M.'s few attempts at fiction, the novel *De dood van Angèle Degroux* (1933; the death of Angèle Degroux).

After a period of reduced literary productivity, from about 1936 on M. reasserted his prominent position in the Dutch world of letters with his poetry and criticism, and with another novelistic venture, written in collaboration with Simon Vestdijk (q.v.), *Heden ik, morgen gij* (1937; today I, tomorrow thou). But the most important work by far of these years, and of M.'s entire creative career, was the collection of verse *Tempel en kruis* (1940; temple and cross). In a variety of poetic forms, M. addressed himself to the dual roots of Western civilization in Greek antiquity and Christian religion. While acknowledging early Christianity as a positive force, he subscribed to the Nietzschean idea of its progressive decline into sterile dogmatism. On the other hand, the spirit of antiquity appeared to M. as a vital and enduring civilizing influence.

Tempel en kruis, the last work to be completed by M., was one of the very few successful lyric statements concerning the advent of fascism, because it avoided the pitfall of explicit politicizing. Instead, M. sublimated his misgivings about the political trends of his day in a grandiose vision of the civilization whose continued existence was threatened by the totalitarian and collectivistic movements that were sweeping Europe. M.'s death as a victim of World War II not only added a note of personal tragedy to his literary concern over the fate of Western culture but also deprived Netherlandic literature of a major lyric talent.

FURTHER WORKS: *Penthesilea* (1925); *De anatomische les* (1926); *De vliegende Hollander* (1927); *De lamp van Diogenes* (1928); *De vijf vingers* (1929); *Witte vrouwen* (1930); *Voorpost* (1931); *Kort geding* (1931); *Herman Gorter* (1937); *Menno ter Braak* (1939); *Verzameld werk* (3 vols., 1938); *Brieven over literatuur* (1945, with Simon Vestdijk); *Verzameld werk IV* (1947); *H. M. voor de spiegel* (1966); *De briefwisseling tussen P. N. van Eyck en H. M.* (1968); *Ik zoek bezielden* (1978)

BIBLIOGRAPHY: Meijer, R. P., *Literature of the Low Countries* (1978), pp. 316–21
EGBERT KRISPYN

MARTIN DU GARD, Roger
French novelist and dramatist, b. 23 March 1881, Neuilly-sur-Seine; d. 23 Aug. 1958, Bellême

M.'s father was a lawyer in Paris, and the long legal tradition in M.'s family is reflected in the careful preparation and documentation that went into M.'s novels. M. devoted himself almost exclusively to his writing, choosing to work in isolated country retreats, where he kept huge files of documentation on his characters and on historical events. An extremely ambitious writer who modeled himself after Tolstoy and sought to write epic novels like *War and Peace,* M. set such high standards for himself that he destroyed several completed manuscripts and could not complete his last novel, *Le journal du Colonel de Maumort* (Colonel de Maumort's diary), to his satisfaction. M. was awarded the Nobel Prize for literature in 1937.

M. made his literary debut with *Devenir!* (1909; to become!), a novel about a selfish, ambitious young writer who fails to measure up to his own expectations. Both the protagonist, André Mazarelles, and the plot of *Devenir!* are remarkably similar to those of *The Immoralist* (1902) by André Gide (q.v.). M. and Gide had a long, close friendship, which is revealed in their letters published in *Correspondance* (2 vols., 1968; correspondence) and in M.'s *Notes sur André Gide* (1951; *Recollections of André Gide,* 1953). M. shared with Gide, twelve years his senior, many literary and social concerns, although their approaches to writing were totally different. While Gide wrote directly and passionately, revealing much of himself in his fictional works, M. sought to remain impersonal and objective and strove for a transparent style in the manner of Flaubert.

M.'s first major novel was *Jean Barois* (1913; *Jean Barois,* 1949), the story of a young man's attempt to free himself from religion and spread the doctrine of rationalism and scientific truth. *Jean Barois,* which quickly became a best seller, provides one of the most accurate and moving accounts of the Dreyfus Affair, a series of events that shattered French political and social life. In writing *Jean Barois*, M. sought to innovate by eliminating the third person omniscient narrator and relating events directly through dialogue (as in the theater) and through documentation (excerpts from speeches and newspaper articles dealing with the Dreyfus Affair). With the novel, M. succeeded in the very goal that the unsuccessful protagonist of his first novel had set for himself: the creation of a new kind of novel that combines historical and psychological truth. The circumstances of Barois's death, which takes place in the same house and the same bed where his father had died at the beginning of the novel, give the work its cyclical unity. M. himself never had a feeling for religion, but in *Jean Barois* and in the sixth volume of *Les Thibault* (8 vols., 1922–40; Vols. 1–6, *The Thibaults,* 1939; Vols. 7–8, *Summer 1914,* 1941), M. powerfully depicts the comfort and solace that Christianity offers to those who are about to die.

Les Thibault, an eight-volume novel that traces the lives of two very different brothers from adolescence to adulthood, is undoubtedly M.'s masterpiece. It consists of *Le cahier gris* (1922; the gray notebook), *Le pénitencier* (1922; the penitentiary), *La belle saison* (1923; the springtime of life), *La consultation* (1928; the consultation), *La sorellina* (1928; the sorellina), *La mort du père* (1929; the father's death), *L'été 1914* (1936; summer 1914), and *Épilogue* (1940; epilogue). In depicting the two brothers—Jacques, the maladjusted adolescent who seeks purity and eventually joins the socialist revolutionary movement, and Antoine, the older, more conformist, hard-working doctor who seeks change through evolution—M. actually depicted two conflicting aspects of his own personality: his sense of rebellion and his need for order. The conflict between the two brothers and their ultraconservative, egotistical bourgeois father provides the focus for the first two volumes of the series. Although both brothers are extremely critical of their father's harsh authoritarian ways, they begin to recognize his reflection in themselves as they grow older. Many disgruntled adolescents of the 1920s identified with Jacques and wrote letters to M. empathizing with his young protagonist. Yet M. himself judged Jacques harshly and ironically, stating that Jacques "lived and died like an idiot." M. identified most closely with the older brother Antoine, and it is Antoine who, in his diary

in the last volume, *Épilogue,* delivers the final message of humanism and hope for the betterment of humanity in a new (socialist) society.

An automobile accident in 1931 in which he and his wife were injured led M. to reexamine his plans for the rest of *Les Thibault.* He decided to reduce the scope of his epic novel and change its very nature from a primarily psychological study to a historical study of the events that led to the outbreak of World War I during the summer of 1914. In the penultimate volume of the series, *L'été 1914,* Jacques, the young writer who has become an adamant pacifist, tries desperately and feverishly to avert a war. Using a technique similar to his documentation in *Jean Barois,* M. lengthily explores the negotiations and diplomatic missions that immediately preceded World War I. He sought to prove that World War I could easily have been avoided if only the socialist-pacifists had published certain revealing documents. The war, with its unnecessary bloodshed and the subsequent destruction of the entire European way of life, is shown to have been the result of blind nationalism and selfish propaganda on the part of political leaders on both sides.

M.'s one serious drama, *Un taciturne* (1932; a silent man), which explores the tragic consequences of the hero's discovery of his own latent homosexuality, was not as well received as M.'s novels, although its powerful confrontation scenes are dramatically effective.

M. did not write about extraordinary individuals; his goal was to reflect life itself, with its tedium and complexities, to present life in the rough as it appears to ordinary people. His frank explorations of the moral issue of euthanasia and the question of suicide in *Jean Barois* and in *Les Thibault* make his works relevant to the moral debates of the 1980s.

By stressing the emptiness of life led in isolation and insisting on the need for the individual to become involved with the collectivity, M. anticipated the writings of André Malraux, Jean-Paul Sartre (qq.v.), and M.'s friend and admirer Albert Camus (q.v.). Like the existentialists (q.v.) who followed, M. dealt with man's need to define himself, to discover his own identity through action in a world without God. The recent publication of M.'s personal correspondence,

Correspondance générale (2 vols., 1980; general correspondence), which reveals a passionate yet puritanical man who concealed his personality under a self-imposed literary straitjacket, will certainly lead to a better appreciation of M., the moralist and the man.

FURTHER WORKS: *L'abbaye de Jumièges: Étude archéologique des ruines* (1909); *L'une de nous* (1910); *Le testament du père Leleu* (1920; *Papa Leleu's Will,* 1921); *La gonfle, farce paysanne* (1928); *La confidence africaine* (1930); *Vieille France* (1933; *The Postman,* 1954); *Souvenirs autobiographiques et littéraires* (1955); *Œuvres complètes* (2 vols., 1955)

BIBLIOGRAPHY: Lalou, R., *R. M.* (1937); Brodin, P., *Les écrivains français d l'entre-deux-guerres* (1942), pp. 183–201; Magny, C.-E., *Histoire du roman français depuis 1918* (1950), pp. 305–50; Camus, A., "R. M." (1955), *Lyrical and Critical Essays* (1968), pp. 254–87; Brombert, V., *The Intellectual Hero: Studies in the French Novel 1880–1955* (1961), pp. 94–118; Boak, D., *R. M.* (1963); Schalk, D., *R. M.: The Novelist and History* (1967); Savage, C., *R. M.* (1968); Howe, I., "M.: The Novelty of Goodness" (1968), *The Decline of the New* (1970), pp. 43–53; Taylor, M., *M.: "Jean Barois"* (1974); Fernandez, D., "M. sans corset," *L'express,* 12 April 1980, 86–88

DEBRA POPKIN

MARTÍNEZ ESTRADA, Ezequiel

Argentine essayist, poet, critic, short-story writer, and dramatist, b. 14 Sept. 1895, San José de la Esquina; d. 4 Nov. 1964, Bahía Blanca

For some thirty years (1915–46) M. E. held various positions in the Argentine postal system. His literary work was probably influenced by such factors as economic pressures that trapped him in the bureaucratic routine of this job, a childless marriage, the frequently unenthusiastic critical reception of his work, extended travels (1961–62) in Castro's Cuba, and perhaps most of all, the experience of witnessing Argentina's steady drift toward reaction, dictatorship, and loss of national purpose.

Like many Latin Americans, M. E. began his literary career as a poet, although it was as an essayist that he was to achieve wide acclaim. The six volumes of verse published between 1918 and 1929 gained him only a modicum of recognition, but he won the National Prize for Literature for the collection *Humoresca y títeres de pies ligeros* (1929; humoresque and light-footed puppets).

M. E.'s position as one of Latin America's leading writers rests chiefly on a series of brilliant essays, in which he relentlessly probed Argentine history, character, and values. The first and most celebrated of these works, *Radiografía de la pampa* (1933; *X-Ray of the Pampa,* 1971), appeared at a time of economic depression and political instability. But in analyzing Argentina's plight M. E. chose to examine certain deep-lying historical, geographic, and social factors, suggesting that there exists a basic dysfunction in Argentine culture, born of a decadent medieval Spanish tradition that prolonged itself in the New World. In his assessment of geographic factors he found—as the Spanish thinker Ortega y Gasset (q.v.) had found earlier—that the vast, featureless pampa impeded normal social relationships and infused in the people intense feelings of solitude. The illusion of glory that motivated the conquistador, the belief in progress and plenty, typical of the 19th-c. positivist, and the dream of the immigrant that the New World was indeed a promised land, have, in M. E.'s iconoclastic view, served chiefly to obscure the real characteristics of Argentine life—solitude, resentment, frustration, aloofness, and subterfuge. Not surprisingly, when *Radiografía de la pampa* first appeared, many critics attacked it mercilessly; in recent decades, however, it has come to be considered M. E.'s masterpiece and his special contribution to Argentine letters.

Several other essays of M. E. are worthy of note, although it has been pointed out that virtually all of his later works are, in a sense, footnotes to *Radiografía de la pampa.* In the *Cabeza de Goliat* (1940; Goliath's head) he dissects the metropolis of Buenos Aires, which he describes as a "Goliath's head" on the body of a dwarf. This essay is especially rich in striking images: at one point the city and its inhabitants are likened to prisoners in a jail whose jailer has disappeared, and on another page the railroad system is compared to an octopus whose head is in the city but whose tentacles suck the sustenance out of the rich hinterland.

In *Muerte y transfiguración de Martín*

Fierro (2 vols., 1948; death and transfiguration of Martín Fierro) M. E. continued his analysis of Argentine rural life by focusing on the genesis, development, and mythification of the gaucho hero. In two short, highly charged essays, *Qué es esto?* (1956; what's this?) and *Exhortaciones* (1957; exhortations), he decries the fact that the post-Perón governments were guided more by a desire to return to normality than by the conviction that the nation needed basic, if not radical, changes in its political, economic, and social order.

M. E. also published a number of literary studies, several plays, and a series of well-regarded novellas and short stories.

M. E. occupied a very special position among Argentine writers of his generation in that he became a genuine mentor for younger writers. Moreover, his radical critique of society transcends national boundaries and has thus established him as one of Latin America's most provocative and stimulating essayists.

FURTHER WORKS: *Oro y piedra* (1918); *Nefelibal* (1922); *Motivos del cielo* (1924); *Argentina* (1927); *Sarmiento* (1946); *Panorama de las literaturas* (1946); *Los invariantes históricos en el Facundo* (1947); *El mundo maravilloso de Guillermo Enrique Hudson* (1951); *Sábado de gloria* (1956); *Cuadrante del pampero* (1956); *Marta Riquelme* (1956); *Tres cuentos sin amor* (1956); *Tres dramas* (1957); *El hermano Quiroga* (1957); *Las 40* (1957); *La tos y otros entretenimientos* (1957); *Heraldos de la verdad* (1958); *Coplas de ciego* (1959); *Mensaje a los escritores* (1959); *Análisis funcional de la cultura* (1960); *Diferencias y semejanzas entre los países de la América Latina* (1962); *El verdadero cuento del tío Sam* (1963); *Realidad y fantasía en Balzac* (1964); *Antología* (1964); *Mi experiencia cubana* (1965); *La poesía afrocubana de Nicolás Guillén* (1966); *Martí, revolucionario* (1967); *Para una revisión de las letras argentinas* (1967); *En torno a Kafka, y otros ensayos* (1967); *Meditaciones sarmientinas* (1968); *Leopoldo Lugones: Retrato sin retocar* (1968); *Leer y escribir* (1969)

BIBLIOGRAPHY: Murena, H. A., *El pecado original de América* (1954), pp. 43–65, 105–29; Ghiano, J. C., "M. E. narrador," *Ficción*, No. 4 (1956), 139–48; Sebreli, J. J., *M. E.: Una rebelión inutil* (1960); Stabb, M. S., "E. M. E.: The Formative Writings," *Hispania*, 49, 1 (1966), 54–60; Adam, C., *Bibliografía y documentos de E. M. E.* (1968); Earle, P., *Prophet in the Wilderness: The Works of E. M. E.* (1971); Maharg, J., *A Call to Authenticity: The Essays of E. M. E.* (1977)

MARTIN S. STABB

MARTÍNEZ SIERRA, Gregorio and María

Spanish dramatists, novelists, essayists, poets, Gregorio b. 6 May 1881, Madrid; d. 1 Oct. 1947, Madrid; María b. 28 Dec. 1874, San Millán de la Cogolla; d. 28 June, 1974, Buenos Aires, Argentina

María M. S., in all probability the principal writer in this unusual literary partnership, wanted all works, whether written by her alone or in collaboration with her husband, to be published under Gregorio's name. Gregorio, an important theatrical director and producer as well as a writer, founded and managed Spain's most avant-garde and prestigious theatrical company of the period, the Compañía Lírico-Dramática Gregorio Martínez Sierra. With leading lady Catalina Bárcena, the actress for whom Gregorio eventually left María, the company toured Europe and the Americas for five years during the 1920s with an international repertory that included works by Shakespeare, Dumas, and Shaw, as well as M. S. In the 1930s Gregorio spent several years in Hollywood supervising film versions of his plays and writing scripts for movie companies. When the Spanish Civil War (1936–39) began, Gregorio and Catalina moved to Buenos Aires, Argentina, where they lived until returning to Madrid only weeks before Gregorio's death in 1947. In the pre-civil war period, María remained in Spain to write. She also took an active role in Spanish politics and in the nascent feminist movement. During the Republic (1931–36) she was elected Socialist deputy to the Cortes (parliament). After the civil war she lived in Switzerland and France before settling in 1952 in Buenos Aires, her home until her death at exactly ninety nine and a half years of age.

Although M. S. also wrote novels, short stories, essays, and poetry, it is as a dramatist that he is best remembered. M. S.'s most successful play, *Canción de cuna* (1911; *The Cradle Song*, 1917), remains a standard inclusion in the modern international repertory. This delicate play features cloistered

235

nuns who adopt a foundling, and illustrate poignantly the author's reverence for motherhood. Yet despite the admiration for nuns depicted in this and in several other plays, such as *El reino de Diós* (1916; *The Kingdom of God,* 1923) and *Lirio entre espinas* (1911; *A Lily Among Thorns,* 1930), M. S. did not favor the cloistered life. In all of his plays women are happiest when actively expressing their social impulses. In works that focus principally on women M. S. favored a balance of physical, emotional, and spiritual participation in life and effectively blended idealism with realism. Unaware, perhaps, of María's major contribution to the M. S. signature, some critics have chided Gregorio for a lack of masculine vigor and worldly sophistication; others strongly defend the optimism and healthy enthusiasm for life so strongly associated with his works.

Despite an insistence that women are essentially mothers and that maternity is the loftiest expression of femininity, M. S. was a staunch apologist for women's rights. His feminism, individual and personal, relates almost exclusively to the social situation of the Spanish woman of the early 20th c. The feminist heroines of the plays (never members of an organization for women's rights) are diplomatically aggressive as they charmingly push for equality of responsibilities as well as of rights. In *Cada uno y su vida* (1924; to each his own) and *Seamos felices* (1929; let's be happy), for example, they contend that women have as much duty as men to support the family materially. It is interesting to note, moreover, that rather than claim as theirs the moral standard associated with the men of the period, these feminists insist that both sexes adhere to the more stringent code of behavior expected of women. M. S. repeatedly advocated careers for women, particularly in education, medicine, and the social services. The ideal career, M. S. suggests, is the professional collaboration of husband and wife, as illustrated in *Amanecer* (1915; dawn) and *Sueño de una noche de agosto* (1918; *The Romantic Young Lady,* 1923). This ideal of professional collaboration was one that Gregorio and María lived for many years and partially accounts for the frequency with which it appears in their works.

FURTHER WORKS: *Tú eres la paz* (1906; *Ana María,* 1921); *Primavera en otoño* (1911); *Mamá* (1913); *El amor brujo* (1915; music by Manuel de Falla); *El sombrero de tres picos*

(1916; music by Manuel de Falla); *Obras completas* (14 vols., 1920–30); *Mujer* (1925); *Triángulo* (1930; *Take Two from One: A Farce in Three Acts,* 1931). FURTHER VOLUMES IN ENGLISH: *The Plays of G. M. S.* (2 vols., 1923)

BIBLIOGRAPHY: Gardner, M., Introduction to *Sueño de una noche de agosto* (1921), pp. vii–xxv; Douglas, F., "G. M. S.," *Hispania,* 5, 5 (1922), 257–68, and 6, 1 (1923), 1–13; Martínez Sierra, M., *Gregorio y yo* (1953); O'Connor, P. W., *Women in the Theater of G. M. S.* (1967); O'Connor, P. W., *G. and M. M. S.* (1977)

PATRICIA W. O'CONNOR

MARTINICAN LITERATURE
See French-Caribbean Literature

MARTÍN-SANTOS, Luis
Spanish novelist and short-story writer, b. 11 Nov. 1924, Larache, Morocco; d. 21 Jan. 1964, San Sebastián

M.-S. was educated at the Marian Brothers School in San Sebastián. He studied medicine at the University of Salamanca and was a medical researcher as well as a surgeon. His interest turned to psychiatry, which he studied both in Spain and Germany, and he became the director of the Psychiatric Asylum of San Sebastián. At the time of his death, as a result of an automobile accident, he was considered a significant figure in contemporary psychiatry.

M.-S. was also an avid fiction reader, particularly of Joyce, Proust, Mann, and Sartre (qq.v.). While a student, he was active in a literary group whose members came into their own as writers in the 1960s.

M.-S.'s *Tiempo de silencio* (1962; *Time of Silence,* 1964), a major novel whose structure has been compared to that of Joyce's *Ulysses,* appeared at a time when Spanish fiction was still mired in repetitive social-realist themes. Set in Madrid in 1949, the novel has a protagonist who becomes involved in a series of misadventures as he attempts to carry out his medical research. The desperate conditions of social and professional life in the post-civil-war era are revealed through multiple narrative points of view.

The protagonist's "travels" bring him to the dead end of both personal and national silence. The work attained instant critical praise, with prime attention given to its intellectual and poetic depths blended with an ironic and satiric perspective.

Apólogos, y otras prosas inéditas (1970; apologues, and other unpublished prose works), a collection of some of M.-S.'s short fiction and sketches of other planned works, was published posthumously. It includes a tale about bullfighting (a recurrent image in M.-S.'s works), in which the narrator attempts to decipher the crucial importance to Spanish life of this diversion. Another story offers an insight into Basque mentality. Fragments of a novel that was to be called *Tiempo de destrucción* (1975; time of destruction) were also published.

M.-S.'s brief career was of considerable consequence. His one novel represented a significant breakthrough in modern Spanish fiction. Following the stylistic paths opened by the early works of Camilo José Cela and Rafael Sánchez Ferlosio (qq.v.), he surpassed them to achieve a fiction of intellectual rage, which has since been widely imitated.

FURTHER WORKS: *Dilthey, Jaspers y la comprensión del enfermo mental* (1955); *Libertad, temporalidad y transferencia en el psicoanálisis existencial* (1964)

BIBLIOGRAPHY: Díaz, J. W., "L. M.-S. and the Contemporary Spanish Novel," *Hispania,* 51 (1968), 232–38; Seale, M. L., "Hangman and Victim: An Analysis of M.-S.'s *Tiempo de silencio,*" *Hispano,* 44 (1972), 45–52; Rey, A., *Construcción y sentido de "Tiempo de silencio"* (1977); Caviglia, J., "A Simple Question of Symmetry: Psyche as Structure in *Tiempo de silencio,*" *Hispania,* 60 (1977), 452–60; Anderson, R. K., "Self-Estrangement in *Tiempo de silencio,*" *REH,* 13 (1979), 299–317

IRWIN STERN

MARTINSON, Harry
Swedish poet, novelist, and essayist, b. 6 May 1904, Jämshög, d. 11 Feb. 1978, Gnesta

M. lost his father early, and in 1910 his mother emigrated to America, leaving the boy and his sisters to become wards of the home parish. His childhood was marked by hard work, unfeeling guardians, and several attempts to run away. At the age of sixteen M. went to sea and worked for seven years as a stoker, with periods of vagabondage in South America and India. After contracting tuberculosis, he settled in Sweden, married Helga Swartz (who began a writing career in 1933 as Moa Martinson [1890–1964]), and established himself as a writer with the "vitalist-primitivist" literary group Fem Unga. In 1934 he attended the writers' conference in the Soviet Union from which he returned politically disillusioned. During the 1939–40 Winter War between Finland and the U.S.S.R. he volunteered on the Finnish side. M. never completely regained his health, and after his divorce and remarriage he spent most of his life in Gnesta. He was the recipient of a number of major literary prizes. In 1949 he became the first self-educated writer of working-class background to be elected to the Swedish Academy; in 1954 he received an honorary doctorate at the University of Göteborg; and in 1974 he shared the Nobel Prize in literature with Eyvind Johnson (q.v.).

M.'s poetry is characterized by a masterful use of language, bold innovations, and a brilliant employment of metaphors and similes in playful juxtapositions that are always based on an astonishing precision of observation. As a nature poet, he has few if any equals. In his early collection *Nomad* (1930; nomad) he formulates his particular philosophy of acceptance of the gentle forces in life and nature. In *Passad* (1945; trade winds) he hails the trade winds as a symbol of openness, undogmatic mobility, and the fresh renewing forces of humanity, as opposed to the mechanized "tyranny of the engineers." His "nomadic" philosophy is here deepened to include the conquest of inner distances in meditative quietism of a Taoist brand.

M.'s strong interest in the natural sciences enabled him to join in a single vision the small detail and the universal whole. His criticism of man's heedless use of modern technology, which made him an early spokesman for ecological concerns, is given powerful expression in the chilling verse epic *Aniara* (1956; *Aniara: A Review of Man in Time and Space,* 1963). This cycle of 103 cantos is a science-fiction epos of technological triumph and catastrophe, a tragic and horrifying vision of a future: earth has become uninhabitable through man's hubris about conquering nature, and the off-course spaceship becomes a symbol of modern man's alienation. Of central importance in *Aniara* is the Mima, a highly advanced computer/robot with a soul that is a source of distraction and consolation for the spaceship passengers.

M.'s prose works display the same virtuosity as his poetry in the use of the Swedish language. *Resor utan mål* (1932; travels without destination) and *Kap Farväl* (1933; *Cape Farewell*, 1934) present kaleidoscopic impressions of his years at sea and sojourns on different continents. In the novel *Nässlorna blomma* (1935; *Flowering Nettle*, 1936) and its sequel, *Vägen ut* (1936; the way out), M. gives a moving and unsentimental account of his difficult childhood and adolescence, making a lasting contribution to the autobiographical "proletarian" literature of the period. Two collections of lyrical philosophical essays, *Midsommardalen* (1938; the midsummer valley) and *Det enkla och det svåra* (1930; the simple and the difficult) excel in nature descriptions, and in *Verklighet till döds* (1940; reality to death) M. settles his personal account with Soviet ideology. Many of M.'s concerns—his advocacy of tolerance, pacifism, and humaneness, his admiration of Oriental philosophy, and his love of the Swedish countryside—find a mature synthesis in the novel *Vägen till Klockrike* (1948; *The Road*, 1955). This book about tramps and vagrants is a mixture of philosophical dialogue, satire, rhapsodic lyricism, social criticism, autobiography, and allegory; it marks a high point in M.'s writing.

M. was recognized from the very beginning as a truly original literary genius. Over the years he consolidated his position as one of Sweden's best-loved and most widely read authors. His linguistic innovations, often presenting insurmountable difficulties to his translators, may be an obstacle to a full appreciation of M. abroad, but the message of his works is of universal concern.

FURTHER WORKS: *Spökskepp* (1929); *Svärmare och harkrank* (1937); *Den förlorade jaguaren* (1941); *Cikada* (1953); *Gräsen i Thule* (1958); *Vagnen* (1960); *Utsikt från en grästuva* (1963); *Tre knivar från Wei* (1964); *Dikter om ljus och mörker* (1971); *Tuvor* (1973); *Längs ekots stigar* (1978); *Doriderna* (1980). FURTHER VOLUME IN ENGLISH: *Friends, You Drank Some Darkness: Three Swedish Poets* (1975)

BIBLIOGRAPHY: Johannesson, E. O., "*Aniara*: Poetry and the Poet in the Modern World," *SS*, 32 (1961), 185–202; Steene, B., "The Role of the Mima: A Note on M.'s *Aniara*," in Bayerschmidt, C. F., and Friis, E. J., eds., *Scandinavian Studies: Essays Presented to Henry Goddard Leach* (1965), pp. 311–19; Bergmann, S. A., "H. M. and Science," *Proceedings of the Fifth International Study Conference on Scandinavian Literature* (1966), pp. 99–120; Sjöberg, L., "H. M.: Writer in Quest of Harmony," *ASR*, 60 (1972), 360–71; "H. M.: From Vagabond to Space Explorer," *BA*, 48 (1974), 476–85; Sjöberg, L., "The 1974 Nobel Prize in Literature: Eyvind Johnson and H. M.," *BA*, 49 (1975), 407–21; Brennecke, D., "Beardsley und der Mimarob," *Skandinavistik*, 6 (1976), 37–50

LARS G. WARME

MASAOKA Shiki

(pseud. of Masaoka Tsunenori) Japanese poet, diarist, critic, essayist, and journalist, b. 14 Oct. 1867, Matsuyama; d. 19 Sept. 1902, Tokyo.

After studying philosophy and Japanese literature for two years at the University of Tokyo, M. left to become the haiku (traditional seventeen-syllable verse form) editor of the newspaper *Nippon*, from whose pages he launched his reform of the haiku in 1892. In 1895 he went to China as a war correspondent for *Nippon* but became so ill (with tuberculosis) on the return trip that he nearly died. For the rest of his life M. was an invalid.

Nevertheless, he managed to lead a very active literary life from his sickbed. In 1897, he and his disciples founded the literary journal *Hototogisu*. The next year he launched a reform of the tanka (traditional thirty-one-syllable verse form) similar in aim to his earlier reform of the haiku, and also turned his attention to autobiographical essays.

When M. began his career, the haiku and the tanka had come to be regarded as frivolous pastimes incapable of expressing the complexities of modern life. The necessary premise of M.'s haiku reform, as well as his most important contribution as a critic, was his insistence on the potential of the haiku and the tanka as serious literature. The second pillar of M.'s haiku reform was his commitment to realism as the aim of literature. His reevaluation of the 18th-c. poet Yosa Buson (1716–1783) in the light of the ideal of realism was responsible for Buson's reputation today as one of the greatest haiku poets. His most important writings on haiku are *Dassai sho-oku haiwa* (1892; talks on haiku from the otter's den), *Haikai taiyō* (1895; the essence of haikai), and *Haijin Buson* (1897; the haiku poet Buson).

At first M.'s poems (both his haiku and tanka) were derivative. Later they became efforts to depict real scenes from nature or daily life, and finally, in the last few years of his life, he created a literary persona, a semifictional "I," who became the central character of his most affecting works while he still retained the realism of his earlier works. The recurring theme of his later work, especially of the two diaries that he published in his last two years, *Bokujū itteki* (1901; partial tr., "A Drop of Ink," 1975) and *Byōshō rokushaku* (1902; a six-foot sickbed), is the juxtaposition of M.'s own suffering mortality with the ongoing life of nature and the human world. The prose style he used in these works had been developed through his experiments with the short essay beginning in 1898 and later influenced a significant number of Japanese novelists, including Natsume Sōseki and Shiga Naoya (qq.v.). Thus, as well as having brought haiku into the modern age and having established the dominant tone of the modern tanka, M. was instrumental in the evolution of modern Japanese prose style.

There is no room to doubt M.'s crucial importance as a critic and charismatic literary figure who inspired an entire generation of haiku poets. On the other hand, there has been a wrong-headed tendency for critics and scholars (now beginning to change) to question his merits as a poet and virtually ignore the diaries and essays. M.'s excellence as a writer lies in neither his poetry nor his prose but in writing that is on the border between the two. The two diaries mentioned above best exemplify this style, in that they combine qualities of the classical Japanese poetic diary with the self-revelation of modern autobiography.

FURTHER WORKS: *Shiki zenshū* (25 vols., 1975–78). FURTHER VOLUME IN ENGLISH: *Peonies Kana: Haiku by the Upsasak Shiki* (1972)

BIBLIOGRAPHY: Brower, R. H., "M. S. and Tanka Reform," in Shively, D. H., ed., *Tradition and Modernization in Japanese Culture* (1971), pp. 379–418; Keene, D., "S. and

Takuboku," *Landscapes and Portraits: Appreciations of Japanese Culture* (1971), pp. 157–70; Beichman-Yamamoto, J., "M. S.'s *A Drop of Ink*," *MN*, 30 (1975), 291–302; Ueda, M., "M. S.," *Modern Japanese Haiku: An Anthology*, pp. 3–8, 25; Beichman, J., *M. S.* (1982)

JANINE BEICHMAN

MASEFIELD, John

English poet, novelist, and dramatist, b. 1 June 1878, Ledbury; d. 12 May 1967, Abingdon

Born in Herefordshire, in the rural English west, M. was orphaned at thirteen and became a cadet on the training ship *Conway;* after rounding Cape Horn on a sailing vessel, he left his ship and the sea at New York City in 1895. Attracted to writing by his reading of Chaucer, Keats, Shelley, and Shakespeare, M. returned to England in 1897, worked for the Manchester *Guardian,* and produced a succession of little-noticed books, beginning with *Salt-Water Ballads* (1902). In 1911 *The Everlasting Mercy,* an astonishing rhymed narrative about a tavern brawler converted to the Christian life, brought M. sudden fame; *Dauber* (1913) and two other long narrative poems appeared before World War I. From his war experience came the much-praised prose history *Gallipoli* (1916) and the poem "August 1914" (1914), followed by reflective sonnets and five other long narratives, including *Reynard the Fox* (1919) and *King Cole* (1921). M. lived out his long life quietly with his family near Oxford. In 1930 he was named Poet Laureate and became an eloquent advocate for the speaking of verse.

Critical and popular opinion tend to agree that M.'s twenty-two novels and fifteen plays are less likely to survive than his poetry. Most successful of his novels are probably the children's story *The Midnight Folk* (1927) and the sea tale *The Bird of Dawning* (1933), while the three-act folk melodrama *The Tragedy of Nan* (1909), influenced by J. M. Synge (q.v.), has been his best-liked play.

Reynard the Fox reveals M.'s skill in storytelling and in painting the countryside and a gallery of country portraits. Part I of the poem introduces a cross section of society in the participants and onlookers at a traditional fox hunt. Part II takes the reader on the exciting hunt itself, at the end of which the fox has become the hero and escapes, while the killing of another fox, a stranger to the reader, sends the hunters home happy. This vivid pageant, even more than the tragic Cape Horn epic *Dauber* or the quietly magical *King Cole,* is often believed to have won M. the Laureateship.

In most of his work M. celebrates his country and countrymen—the English heritage and landscape; English people, arts, and games; the English soldier, ship, and sailor. His chief dedication is to the English spirit rather than to the sea and the common man of his early writing. For him Saint George, not John Bull, is the symbol of the nation he strives to interpret, and the spirit of Saint George shines brightest in the brief lyrics and these longer narratives that are most likely to live: *The Everlasting Mercy, Dauber,* "August 1914," *Gallipoli,* and *Reynard the Fox.* M.'s work is uneven, partly because of its sheer volume, but it is hard to see, as the critic Newman Ivey White has pointed out, how one can avoid assigning him a lasting place in early-20th-c. English literature without rejecting the whole tradition of English poetry.

FURTHER WORKS: *Ballads* (1903); *A Mainsail Haul* (1905); *Sea Life in Nelson's Time* (1905); *On the Spanish Main* (1905); *A Tarpaulin Muster* (1907); *Captain Margaret* (1908); *Multitude and Solitude* (1909); *The Tragedy of Pompey the Great* (1910); *Ballads and Poems* (1910); *Martin Hyde* (1910); *A Book of Discoveries* (1910); *Lost Endeavour* (1910); *The Street of Today* (1911); *William Shakespeare* (1911); *Jim Davis* (1911); *The Story of a Round-House* (1912); *The Widow in the Bye Street* (1912); *The Daffodil Fields* (1913); *Philip the King* (1914); *The Faithful* (1915); *John M. Synge* (1915); *The Locked Chest; The Sweeps of Ninety-Eight* (1916); *Good Friday* (1916); *Sonnets and Poems* (1916); *The Old Front Line* (1917); *Lollingdon Downs* (1917); *Rosas* (1918); *Collected Poems and Plays* (1919); *Right Royal* (1920); *Enslaved* (1920); *Esther and Berenice* (1922); *Melloney Holtspur* (1922); *The Dream* (1922); *Selected Poems* (1922); *A King's Daughter* (1923); *The Taking of Helen* (1923); *Collected Poems* (1923; rev. eds., 1932, 1946); *Recent Prose* (1924; rev. ed., 1932); *Shakespeare and Spiritual Life* (1924); *Sard Harker* (1924); *With the Living Voice* (1925); *The Trial of Jesus* (1925); *Collected Works* (4 vols., 1925); *ODTAA* (1926); *Tristan and Isolt* (1927); *The Coming of*

Christ (1928); *Midsummer Night* (1928); *Poems* (1929); *Easter* (1929); *The Hawbucks* (1929); *The Wanderer of Liverpool* (1930); *Chaucer* (1931); *Minnie Maylow's Story* (1931); *Poetry* (1931); *A Tale of Troy* (1932); *The Conway* (1933); *End and Beginning* (1933); *The Taking of the Gry* (1934); *The Box of Delights* (1935); *Victorious Troy* (1935); *Poems: Complete Edition* (1935; rev. ed., 1953); *Eggs and Baker* (1936); *A Letter from Pontus* (1936); *The Square Peg* (1937); *The Country Scene* (1937); *Dead Ned* (1938); *Tribute to Ballet* (1938); *Live and Kicking Ned* (1939); *Some Verses to Some Germans* (1939); *Some Memories of W. B. Yeats* (1940); *Basilissa* (1940); *In the Mill* (1941); *The Nine Days Wonder* (1941); *Gautama the Enlightened* (1941); *Conquer* (1941); *A Generation Risen* (1942); *Land Workers* (1942); *Wonderings* (1943); *New Chum* (1944); *A Macbeth Production* (1945); *Thanks before Going* (1946); *A Book of Both Sorts* (1947); *Badon Parchments* (1947); *A Play of St. George* (1948); *On the Hill* (1949); *In Praise of Nurses* (1950); *Selected Poems* (1950); *St. Katherine of Ledbury, and Other Ledbury Papers* (1951); *So Long to Learn* (1952); *The Bluebells* (1961); *Old Raiger* (1964); *Grace before Ploughing* (1966); *In Glad Thanksgiving* (1967); *Letters of J. M. to Florence Lamont* (1979)

BIBLIOGRAPHY: Simmons, C., *Bibliography of J. M.* (1930); Spark, M., *J. M.* (1953); Drew, F., *Contributions to Bibliography of J. M.* (1959); Handley-Taylor, G., *J. M., O.M.: A Bibliography* (1960); Lamont, C., *Remembering J. M.* (1971); Drew, F., *J. M.'s England* (1973); Sternlicht, S., *J. M.* (1977); Babington Smith, C., *J. M.: A Life* (1978)

FRASER DREW

MASING, Uku

Estonian poet and essayist, b. 11 Aug. 1909, Raikküla

After studying theology and Semitic languages, M. taught in the department of theology at the University of Tartu from 1933 to 1940. During this early period he was associated with the famous Arbujad (Soothsayers) group of poets. Since the Soviet takeover of Estonia in 1940 M. has remained silent as a poet, but three books by him have been published in the West.

M.'s first book of poetry, *Neemed vihmade*

lahte (1935; promontories into the gulf of rains), remains his most esteemed and best-known work. In his three subsequent books, M. has continued to explore visionary mystical themes in alternately lyrical and prophetic veins. Exactingly and intimately, M., a neosymbolist, celebrates details of nature, particularly flowers, trees, birds, clouds, winds, and stars. Yet he is most original in his steady reaching upward through interstellar space for the hand of God. One of the most cosmopolitan and complex of Estonian poets, M. uses musical free verse as well as traditional forms for his often symbolic and occasionally surreal poetic style. He is noted for coining words and for employing manneristic and archaic expressions.

Neemed vihmade lahte consists of fifty-one poems, whose titles are given only in the table of contents, allowing the text to be read as one extended work. M. centers the book in the mystical search for a full, steady, and unbroken consciousness of God's presence. Along the way M. experiences both joyous intimacy and complete faith in God, as well as anger at and despair over God's distantness from man. He portrays God at one point as a listless and decadent ruler shut behind gates of tourmaline in a drug-induced dream. Yet he realizes and admits, "We may long for angel's wings, but the stubborn urge of Thy slaves, O God, is powerless to hold Thy vision."

M.'s hallucinatory tableaux, spiritual themes, and allusive style often remind critics of William Blake, Gerard Manley Hopkins, Rabindranath Tagore (q.v.), whom he translated, and T. S. Eliot (q.v.). Like them, M. envisions life from the vantage point of eternity, as in *Piiridele pyydes* (1974; straining toward limits), where he feels "I am damned like an elevator which gets stuck between two floors for all eternity." Yet he goes on to advise devotion to the severest asceticism of Jesus, Buddha, and Lao Tzu. With this universal mysticism and poetic vision M. ranks among the finest modern religious poets.

FURTHER WORKS: *Džunglilaulud* (1965); *Udu Toonela jõelt* (1974)

BIBLIOGRAPHY: Oras, A., *Acht estnische Dichter* (1964), pp. 9–19; Ivask, I., "The Main Tradition of Estonian Poetry," in Kõressaar, V., and Rannit, A., eds., *Estonian Poetry and Language* (1965), pp. 292–96; Mägi, A., *Estonian Literature: An Outline* (1968), pp. 48–54; Leitch, V. B., "Religious Vision in Modern Poetry: U. M. Compared with Hopkins and Eliot," *JBalS*, 5 (1974), 281–94; Ivask, I., "U. M.: A Poet between East and West," *JBalS*, 8 (1977), 16–21

VINCENT B. LEITCH

MASTERS, Edgar Lee

American poet, novelist, biographer, dramatist, historian, and essayist, b. 23 Aug. 1868, Garnett, Kan.; d. 5 March 1950, Melrose Park, Pa.

M. spent most of his early life in small Illinois towns; his careers in law and literature combined the interests of his father, an attorney and sometime politician, and his mother, interested in music, literature, and religion. Largely self-taught, M. spent a year at Knox College. He began writing verse pseudonymously for several newspapers in Chicago, moving there in 1890, and he was admitted to the bar in 1891; eight of the following twenty-five years as a successful attorney were spent as a partner of Clarence Darrow. The first of M.'s more than fifty books, a compilation of verse published under a pen name, appeared in 1898; he published several other volumes of verse and seven unproduced plays by 1915, when the English critic John Cowper Powys (q.v.) cited him as one of three significant new American poets. For several years he had also been contributing verse to William Marion Reedy's St. Louis *Mirror;* Reedy's introducing M. to J. W. Mackail's (1859–1949) translations in *Select Epigrams from the Greek Anthology* influenced him to write first-person epitaphs of ordinary small-town people, subsequently published as *Spoon River Anthology* (1915). As his fame grew, M. gave up law and moved to New York. A fellowship M. received in 1946, the first awarded by the Academy of American Poets, helped make up for his by then diminished reputation and income, but poor health forced him to spend his last years in convalescent homes.

Spoon River Anthology went through seventy editions by the time of M.'s death; it has served as source material for plays, an opera, and dramatic readings, and it has been translated into many languages. The book—244 dramatic monologues, mostly in free verse—was both a critical and popular success. The book faithfully depicts characters representative of various small-town social levels and occupations, all sharing a sense of frustration at their dreary, unfulfilled, confined lives. Although it seemed to some, in the dying days of the "genteel tradition," unnecessarily defeatist and even obscene, M. stated elsewhere that his aim had been "to awaken the American vision [and] love of liberty." As with Whitman, M. succeeded not only in dramatizing this vision but also in shocking through the honesty of his portrayals. M. was less successful with *The New Spoon River* (1922); its 321 portraits were repetitious and too polemical and violent.

M.'s many other volumes of verse include *Towards the Gulf* (1918), worth noting because of a long tribute to Reedy. *Domesday Book* (1920) dramatized reactions to a young woman's death; *The Fate of the Jury* (1929), subtitled "An Epilogue to *Domesday Book*," continued the narrative, focusing on members of a coroner's jury. None of these other volumes (mostly dramatic narratives or collections of shorter lyrical work) received much praise; nor did his novels, although *Mitch Miller* (1920) was compared to *Tom Sawyer*.

But his nonfictional prose did attract attention, partly because of his sometimes iconoclastic handling of familiar subjects. Of his six biographies—including *Vachel Lindsay* (1935), *Whitman* (1937), and *Mark Twain* (1938)—*Lincoln the Man* (1931) was the most controversial because of his attempt to destroy the "Lincoln myth"; he accused Lincoln of chicanery, laziness, and other vices, and as a Democratic partisan he emphasized Stephen A. Douglas's posthumous stature. M.'s book on Lindsay (q.v.), by contrast, was praised for its scholarship and sympathy.

Aside from *The Sangamon* (1942), in the "Rivers of America" series, his most important prose work was his autobiography, *Across Spoon River* (1936). A candid and eccentric work—he indexes fifteen love affairs but never mentions Clarence Darrow at all— it is a revealing, tormented love-hate account of his small-town heritage, family, wives and lovers, careers, and changing fortunes. It is thus a valuable, unrestrained account of a particularly lively period in American history and culture.

The sheer amount and variety of M.'s writing—much verse has never been collected, he tried every poetic form and technique, and he treated a vast array of topics—necessarily re-

sulted in unevenness, repetitiveness, and superficiality. At his worst he produced mere magazine verse. Yet his best work supersedes changes in literary fashion and even his own frequent lapses in taste, style, and technique. His prolific versatility and occasional successes give him a permanent place among 20th-c. writers.

FURTHER WORKS: *Maximilian: A Play* (1902); *The New Star Chamber, and Other Essays* (1904); *The Blood of the Prophets* (1905); *Althea: A Play* (1907); *The Trifler: A Play* (1908); *The Leaves of the Tree: A Play* (1909); *Songs and Sonnets* (1910); *Eileen: A Play* (1910); *The Locket: A Play* (1910); *The Bread of Idleness: A Play* (1911); *Songs and Sonnets, Second Series* (1912); *Songs and Satires* (1916); *The Great Valley* (1916); *Toward the Gulf* (1918); *Starved Rock* (1919); *The Open Sea* (1921); *Children of the Market Place* (1922); *Skeeters Kirby* (1923); *The Nuptial Flight* (1923); *Mirage* (1924); *Selected Poems* (1925); *Lee: A Dramatic Poem* (1926); *Kit O'Brien* (1927); *Levy Mayer and the New Industrial Era* (1927); *Jack Kelso: A Dramatic Poem* (1928); *Lichee Nuts* (1930); *Gettysburg, Manila, Acoma* (1930); *Godbey: A Dramatic Poem* (1931); *The Serpent in the Wilderness* (1933); *The Tale of Chicago* (1933); *Dramatic Duologues: Four Short Plays in Verse* (1934); *Richmond: A Dramatic Poem* (1934); *Invisible Landscapes* (1935); *Poems of People* (1936); *The Golden Fleece of California* (1936); *The Tide of Time* (1937); *The New World* (1937); *More People* (1939); *Illinois Poems* (1941); *Along the Illinois* (1942); *The Harmony of Deeper Music: Posthumous Poems* (1976)

BIBLIOGRAPHY: Flanagan, J., "The Spoon River Poet," *SWR*, 38 (1953), 226–37; Hartley, L., *Spoon River Revisited* (1963); Earnest, E., "Spoon River Revisited," *WHR*, 21 (1968), 59–65; Flanagan, J., *E. L. M.: The Spoon River Poet and His Critics* (1974); Burgess, C. E., "E. L. M.: The Lawyer as Writer," and Russell, H., "After *Spoon River*: M.'s Poetic Development 1916–1919," in Hallwas, J. E., and Reader, D. J., eds., *The Vision of This Land: Studies of Vachel Lindsay, E. L. M., and Carl Sandburg* (1976), pp. 55–73, 74–81; Masters, H., *E. L. M.: A Biographical Sketchbook about a Famous American Author* (1978); Primeau, R., *Beyond Spoon River: The Legacy of E. L. M.* (1980)

PAUL SCHLUETER

MASTRONARDI, Lucio
Italian novelist, b. 28 June 1930, Vigevano;
d. 29 April 1979, Vigevano

M. was the son of schoolteachers; his father
was from the Abruzzi region, and his mother
from Vigevano, near Milan. Professionally,
he followed in his parents' footsteps, but in
time he became disenchanted with teaching
and looked to writing as the chief object of
his lonely and troubled life. M. suffered from
a serious neurotic condition that eventually
led to his suicide.

The town of Vigevano, with its thriving
shoe industry and enterprising inhabitants,
forms the nucleus of M.'s work. It is a nucleus rich in sociological interest, which takes
on added value as a microcosm of provincial
life in the industrialized north. *Il calzolaio di
Vigevano* (1962; the shoemaker of Vigevano),
the first part of what might be called a trilogy about life in Vigevano, was originally published in 1959 in Elio Vittorini's (q.v.)
avant-garde review *Il menabò*. The work explores the obsession with material success
through the depiction of the experiences of a
shoe-factory worker who rises to become a
small entrepreneur. A novella with a heavy
infusion of Milanese dialect, *Il calzolaio di
Vigevano* reflects the type of linguistic experimentation through which Carlo Emilio
Gadda and Pier Paolo Pasolini (qq.v.) sought
to recapture the immediacy and pristine flavor of the spoken language.

In *Il maestro di Vigevano* (1962; the
schoolteacher of Vigevano) M.'s own experiences as a teacher, enriched by a mordant
satire often laced with humor, are used to
expose the stifling environment, the bureaucracy, and the formalistic pedagogy of elementary education. The dreary atmosphere
of a small town, with its monotonous life and
puppetlike parade of familiar faces, contributes to the portrayal of the protagonist's sterile existence, which he tries to escape by
daydreaming and with absurd erotic fixations. *Il meridionale di Vigevano* (1964; a
southerner in Vigevano) offers another, and
equally deft, exercise in formal experimentation. The main character is a southern bureaucrat whose quest for social acceptance
meets with deep-seated prejudices against
southern Italians. The discordant mixture of
Milanese and Neapolitan dialects points to
the postwar immigration of southern Italians
to the north, bringing to light the problems

of social adjustment in an unreceptive environment.

M.'s last work, *A casa tua ridono* (1971;
your own family is laughing at you), with its
fragmented narrative, is more attuned to the
trends of structuralist (q.v.) narrative. Superseding the story of a misfit in the industrial
setting of a large city is the steady, albeit
oblique, effort to delve into the consciousness
of the main character and to highlight those
incidents that define his distorted psyche.

M.'s critical recognition in Italy stems
from his experimentation with language and
his incisive, satirical treatment of life in a social environment dominated by material
gains and technological advancement.

FURTHER WORK: *L'assicuratore* (1975)
AUGUSTUS PALLOTTA

MATEVOSSIAN, Hrant
Armenian novelist, short-story writer, and
screenwriter, b. 13 March 1935, Ahnitsor

Often compared to Vahan Totovents (1894–
1938), the American-educated Soviet Armenian writer who wrote about rural life in a
previous generation, M. is the most widely
praised contemporary Armenian prose writer. After receiving a degree from the Apovian
Institute, he graduated from the Moscow
School of Scenarists in 1967, and now works
for the Hayfilm studio in Armenia.

Sociopolitical phenomena have occupied a
large place in Armenian literature since the
turn of the century, when the population (not
yet massacred and dispersed) was under
Turkish rule. The "noble peasant" was used
by such writers as Siamanto (pseud. of Adom
Yarjanian, 1878–1915) and Eroukhan (pseud.
of Ervand Srmakeshkhanlian, 1870–1915)
not only to personify the victim of oppression
but to symbolize energy and hope. The peasants in M.'s fiction, although no longer in
danger of losing life and property, are in peril of seduction by the evil metropolis. Erevan
has replaced Constantinople as the lure.
While Eroukhan's themes were tragic, like
his time, M.'s concerns are agrarian and his
style has lyrical and light touches.

M.'s career began with assignments from
the literary periodicals *Sovetagan kraganootioon* and *Kragan tert* to write feature stories
and essays on agricultural students reclaiming land. His fresh style and his treatment of

the underlying social problems drew immediate praise, and he continued his pastoral themes in fiction. But whereas Totovents's stories of rural life were bathed in sweet nostalgia, M.'s work is both more contemporary and more mythic. In his short novel *Menk enk mer sareruh* (1965; we are our mountains) a seemingly commonplace quarrel among shepherds over stolen sheep becomes an allegory of truth versus hypocrisy in a tale told without any moralizing. In the story "Komesh" (1978; the buffalo) a female water buffalo in heat, roaming the countryside in search of a male, symbolizes the Armenian nation's will to survive and to do creative work. Use of pagan images is typical of M.'s work. His themes, his portrayals of rites of passage and crisis, and his characters fall within the naturalistic tradition but always have mythic overtones.

In his most famous work, the short-story collection *Narinch zampiguh* (1964; *The Orange Herd,* 1976), the wild red mountain horses are reminiscent of the red horses used by Eghishe Charents (q.v.) to symbolize the spirit of the revolution, and of the Pegasus poems of Daniel Varoujan (q.v.), in which the winged horse is symbolic of freedom. M.'s horses, however, are not political; their mystery is more Freudian and surreal.

In the Armenian short story plot is usually secondary to characterization. M. has followed this practice but has given greater psychological depth to his characters than earlier writers. M.'s villages, although microcosms of the universe, are firmly linked to real villages of the past in the same way that M. is linked to older Armenian literary traditions.

FURTHER WORKS: *Okostos* (1967); *Dsareruh* (1978); *Mer vazkuh* (1978)

DIANA DER HOVANESSIAN
MARZBED MARGOSSIAN

MATUTE, Ana María
Spanish novelist and short-story writer, b. 26 July 1925, Barcelona

Born into a middle-class family, M. attended a religious school until the outbreak of the Spanish Civil War. The war left an indelible mark on her life: she suddenly discovered that "the world was hunger, the world was hate. It was also the desire for justice; and it

was egotism, fear, horror, cruelty, and death." M. published her first story in 1942—during what she called the horrors of peace—working in an atmosphere of indifference, censorship, and fear. To protest "against all that represents oppression, hypocrisy, and injustice" was the objective that underlay her decision to devote herself to writing.

The civil war is a recurring theme in M.'s novels. Sometimes it serves only as the background to the action—as in *Pequeño teatro* (1954; little theater)—but often it is at the center of the work—as in *En esta tierra* (1955; in this land), a revised version of the censored *Las luciérnagas* (the fireflies), and *Los hijos muertos* (1958; *The Lost Children,* 1965).

The Cain and Abel theme, present in M.'s first novel, *Los Abel* (1948; the Abel family), and in *La torre vigía* (1971; the watchtower), among others, receives its strongest and most artistic treatment in *Fiesta al Noroeste* (1959; celebration in the Northwest), one of her best novels. The frame of the plot is the accidental death of a child caused by the arrival of a puppeteer; this device serves to introduce the protagonist, whose life is told in retrospect in two stages: his own evocation of childhood and family, and his confession to a priest of his sins of pride, wrath, envy, and avarice. This technique, as well as the themes in the novel—social injustice, solitude, the impossibility of communication, alienation—is characteristic of the style of M., a style rich in rhetorical figures, colorful descriptions, striking and contrasting images, and lyric exaltation.

M.'s most ambitious work is the trilogy *Los mercaderes* (the merchants), comprising *Primera memoria* (1960; *School of the Sun,* 1963), *Los soldados lloran de noche* (1964; soldiers cry at night), and *La trampa* (1969; the trap). Together these novels present a vast panorama of Spain from 1936 to the late 1960s. Her subjects are the basic philosophical and existential dilemmas and conflicts of man. *Primera memoria,* set against the background of the civil war and a country divided by hatred, is told from the perspective of a fourteen-year-old girl who feels only fear and abhorrence for the world of adults. Many of the characters also appear in *Los soldados lloran de noche,* which deals with the continuing bloody war. In *La trampa* the war has ended, and an authoritarian government has seized power. Hatred still divides Spain, and corruption and degeneration pervade every area of life.

M. has published several books of short stories, similar to her novels in their themes and settings. Children and adolescents are often the main characters, as in the collections *Los niños tontos* (1956; the stupid children) and *Algunos muchachos* (1968; a few kids); they are seen as lonely and alienated victims of the cruelty and incomprehension of adults. M. has also written excellent short stories for children.

Although her style has been faulted for rhetorical excesses, most critics place M. among the leading contemporary Spanish novelists. She has been awarded many literary prizes and her books have been translated into twenty-two languages.

FURTHER WORKS: *El tiempo* (1957); *Paulina, el mundo y las estrellas* (1960); *El arrepentido* (1961); *Historias de la Artámila* (1961); *El país de la pizarra* (1961); *Tres y un sueño* (1961); *Libro de juegos para los niños de los otros* (1961); *A la mitad del camino* (1961); *Caballito loco* (1962); *El río* (1963); *El polizón del Ulises* (1964)

BIBLIOGRAPHY: Alborg, J. L., *Hora actual de la novela española* (1958), Vol. I, pp. 181–90; Couffon, C., "Una joven novelista, A. M. M.," *CHA*, 44, (1961), 52–55; Jones, M., *The Literary World of A. M. M.* (1970); Nora, E. de, *La novela española contemporánea* (1970), Vol. III, pp. 264–73; Sobejano, G., *Novela española de nuestro tiempo* (1970), pp. 366–80; Weitzner, M., *The World of A. M. M.* (1970); Díaz, J. W., *A. M. M.* (1971)

MARÍA-LUISA OSORIO

MAUGHAM, W(illiam) Somerset

English novelist, dramatist, and short-story writer, b. 25 Jan. 1874, Paris, France; d. 15 Dec. 1965, Cap Ferrat, France

M.'s father was the solicitor for the British embassy in Paris. His mother died when he was eight, and after his father died, when M. was ten, the boy was sent to England to live with relatives. He took a medical degree but never practiced. With the publication of the novel *Liza of Lambeth* (1897) he began a sixty-five-year writing career. Although he never achieved true greatness in any genre, he nevertheless earned a place in the history of the English novel, drama, and short fiction.

Written under the influence of the English and French realists, especially Guy de Maupassant, *Liza of Lambeth* was based on M.'s experiences as a medical student in the slums of London. Although he followed this good first novel with seven more, it was not until *Of Human Bondage* (1915) that he produced another significant fictional work. Highly autobiographical, this *Bildungsroman* has come to be considered M.'s most important work. In tracing the life of a young man from childhood to maturity, M. demonstrates the importance of truth, beauty, and goodness, and, under the influence of Spinoza, reveals how reason can be subjugated by emotion. In this novel M. expressed more strongly than in any of his other works the central concern of his writing: the importance of the physical, intellectual, and spiritual freedom of the individual.

In *The Moon and Sixpence* (1919) M. presented a portrait of the artist as a man possessed by an inescapable impulse to paint and for whom freedom can come only when he expresses his inner vision through the act of creation. *Cakes and Ale* (1930), M.'s most skillfully written work, is both a masterful satire on the world of art and society and a study of those who find freedom amid social restrictions. M.'s last important novel, *The Razor's Edge* (1944), anticipates the interest in Indian mysticism of the 1960s through its hero's search for spiritual liberation in Vedanta.

M. wrote thirty-two plays; from 1908, when he suddenly had four plays running simultaneously in London, to 1933, he was a dominant dramatist in Europe and America. Although his plays generally lack the thematic substance of his fiction, some are excellently crafted examples of comedies of manners and will continue to be performed. *Our Betters* (1917) is a penetrating satiric treatment of the London upper-class milieu and the enterprising American women who marry into it. *The Circle* (1921), M.'s best play, is a shrewd examination of social façades and restrictions in English life, and here, as in many of his plays, he uses marriage as a metaphor for the individual's contract with society as a whole. *The Constant Wife* (1926) is an Ibsenesque treatment of the state of marriage as it exists among the British upper classes, and as it is especially restricting for women. In his penultimate play, *For Services Rendered* (1932), M. abandoned the comic mode to present a blistering attack on war profiteers and jingoists and to present a strong argument for pacifism.

M.'s more than one hundred short stories are among the best in English. Many follow the pattern of Maupassant's tales, with the reader given a shock in the final lines, but M. uses the form to explore a great variety of themes and situations. "Rain" (1921) is an effective study of sexuality, repression, and hypocrisy, and "The Letter" (1924) skillfully delineates the mores and ethos of British colonialism at its height. M. is best known for these stories set in the Far East, but others— for example, "The Alien Corn" (1931), "Virtue" (1931), "Sanatorium" (1938), and "The Kite" (1947)—perceptively explore psychological, sociological, moral, and philosophical themes.

Although M.'s lack of innovation in form has led critics and scholars generally to ignore him, his craftsmanship and skill as a storyteller has made him one of the world's most widely read authors. His stature as a serious writer should increase as his work is examined more thoroughly.

FURTHER WORKS: *The Making of a Saint* (1898); *Orientations* (1899); *The Hero* (1901); *Mrs. Craddock* (1902); *A Man of Honour* (1903); *The Merry-Go-Round* (1904); *The Land of the Blessed Virgin* (1905); *The Bishop's Apron* (1906); *The Explorer* (1907); *The Magician* (1908); *Lady Frederick* (1911); *Jack Straw* (1911); *Mrs. Dot* (1912); *Penelope* (1912); *The Tenth Man* (1913); *Landed Gentry* (1913); *Smith* (1913); *The Land of Promise* (1913); *The Unknown* (1920); *The Trembling of a Leaf* (1921); *Caesar's Wife* (1922); *East of Suez* (1922); *On a Chinese Screen* (1922); *Home and Beauty* (1923); *The Unattainable* (1923); *Loaves and Fishes* (1924); *The Painted Veil* (1925); *The Casuarina Tree* (1926); *Ashenden* (1928); *The Sacred Flame* (1928); *The Gentleman in the Parlour* (1930); *The Bread-Winner* (1931); *Six Stories Written in the First Person Singular* (1931); *The Book Bag* (1932); *The Narrow Corner* (1932); *Ah King* (1933); *Sheppey* (1933); *Altogether* (1934; Am., *East and West*); *Don Fernando* (1935); *Cosmopolitans* (1936); *Six Comedies* (1937); *Theatre* (1937); *The Favourite Short Stories* (1937); *The Summing Up* (1938); *The Round Dozen* (1938); *Christmas Holiday* (1939);

Princess September and the Nightingale (1939); *France at War* (1940); *Books and You* (1940); *The Mixture as Before* (1940); *Up at the Villa* (1941); *Strictly Personal* (1941); *The Hour before the Dawn* (1942); *The S. M. Sampler* (1943); *The Unconquered* (1944); *Then and Now* (1946); *Creatures of Circumstance* (1947); *Catalina* (1948); *Great Novelists and Their Novels* (1948; rev. enlarged ed., *Ten Novels and Their Authors*, 1954; Am., *The Art of Fiction*); *Quartet* (1948); *Here and There* (1948); *East of Suez* (1948); *A Writer's Notebook* (1949); *Trio* (1950); *The M. Reader* (1950); *The Complete Short Stories* (1951); *The Vagrant Mood* (1952); *Encore* (1952); *The Collected Plays* (1952); *The World Over* (1952); *The Selected Novels* (1953); *The Partial View* (1954); *Mr. M. Himself* (1954); *The Travel Books* (1955); *The Best Short Stories* (1957); *Points of View* (1958); *Purely for My Pleasure* (1962); *Husbands and Wives* (1963); *The Kite, and Other Stories* (1963); *Selected Prefaces and Introductions* (1963); *The Sinners* (1964); *Essays on Literature* (1967); *M.'s Malaysian Stories* (1969); *Seventeen Lost Stories* (1969); *A Baker's Dozen* (1969); *A Second Baker's Dozen* (1970); *Plays* (3 vols., 1970)

BIBLIOGRAPHY: Mander, R., and Mitchenson, J., *Theatrical Companion to M.* (1955); Cordell, R., *S. M.: A Biographical and Critical Study* (1961); Brander, L., *S. M.: A Guide* (1963); Naik, M. K., *W. S. M.* (1966); Barnes, R. E., *The Dramatic Comedy of W. S. M.* (1968); Calder, R. L., *W. S. M. and the Quest for Freedom* (1972); Curtis, A., *The Pattern of M.* (1974); Dobrinsky, J., *La jeunesse de S. M.* (1975); Raphael, F., *S. M. and His World* (1976)

ROBERT L. CALDER

MAURIAC, Claude

French novelist and essayist, b. 25 April 1914, Paris

M., son of Nobel laureate François Mauriac (q.v.), grew up in close contact with many of France's most prestigious writers. His own activities, especially his six years as private secretary to Charles de Gaulle and his reviewing assignments for *Le Figaro* and *Le monde*, vastly expanded his circle of celebrated acquaintances. The value for M. of his relations with the great political and literary figures of his era is among the principal messages of his major recent publication, nine volumes of extracts from the journals he began to keep as an adolescent.

M.'s importance derives from his contributions to developing the New Novel (q.v.) in France. His principal fictional work is a series of four novels that feature Bertrand Carnéjoux as their protagonist: *Toutes les femmes sont fatales* (1957; *All Women Are Fatal,* 1964), *Le dîner en ville* (1959; *The Dinner Party,* 1960), *La marquise sortit à cinq heures* (1961; *The Marquise Went Out at Five,* 1962), and *L'agrandissement* (1963; the enlargement). Striking technical experiments characterize the form of all four works, while preoccupation with human experience of time creates their thematic unity. The tetralogy's first novel presents Bertrand and his thoughts on four different days across a span of sixteen years; its last unfolds during the few seconds necessary for a stoplight to pass through two cycles of red, yellow, and green. To this temporal compression corresponds an expansion of devices for depicting the almost unimaginable variety of external and internal events that constitute any given moment of human existence.

By common consent, M.'s most successful novels are the tetralogy's second and third volumes. *Le dîner en ville* consists of the thoughts and words of eight characters around a dinner table at Bertrand's expensive Paris apartment. All eight characters are fully individualized, although no authorial intervention ever names or otherwise identifies them. The novel is rich in the kinds of unspoken conversation whose name M. retroactively made the overall title for all four Bertrand Carnéjoux novels: *Le dialogue intérieur* (interior dialogue). *La marquise sortit à cinq heures,* responding to the challenge of Paul Valéry's (q.v.) celebrated statement that he (Valéry) could never write a sentence as banal as "La marquise sortit à cinq heures," both illustrates how the New Novel has transformed our concept of narrative statements and exemplifies M.'s personal vision of time as an endless present. The novel's characters observe a Paris intersection during a single evening hour, but the text makes the intersection's eight centuries of history as significant as the sixty minutes actually depicted. This vision of the past's living participation in the present is also crucial to the form M. has chosen for publishing his diaries. Grouped by subject instead of by date, the three thousand pages of printed journals

juxtapose chronologically disconnected entries in continuous reiteration of the message communicated by the journal's collective title, *Le temps immobile* (stationary time).

M.'s concern with time places him in the great tradition of French literature epitomized by Marcel Proust (q.v.), yet his innovative representations of characters' simultaneous perceptions and thought processes link him with the central names in recent experimental fiction. His critical works, especially *L'alittérature contemporaine* (1958; *The New Literature,* 1959), are invaluable to study of how and why the New Novel came into being.

FURTHER WORKS: *Introduction à une mystique de l'enfer* (1938); *La corporation dans l'état* (1941); *Aimer Balzac* (1945); *Jean Cocteau* (1945); *La trahison d'un clerc* (1945); *Malraux* (1946); *André Breton* (1949); *Conversations avec André Gide* (1951; *Conversations with André Gide,* 1965); *Proust,* (1953); *Hommes et idées d'aujourd'hui* (1953); *L'amour du cinéma* (1954); *Petite littérature du cinéma* (1957); *La conversation* (1964); *L'oubli* (1966); *Théâtre* (1968); *De la littérature à l'alittérature* (1969); *Une amitié contrariée* (1970); *Un autre de Gaulle* (1971; *The Other de Gaulle,* 1973); *Le temps immobile* (1974); *Les espaces imaginaires* (1975); *Et comme l'espérance est violente* (1976); *La terrasse de Malagar* (1977); *Une certaine rage* (1977); *Aimer de Gaulle* (1978); *Le Bouddha s'est mis à trembler* (1979); *L'éternité parfois* (1978); *Un cœur tout neuf* (1980); *Laurent Terzieff* (1980); *Le rire des pères dans les yeux des enfants* (1981)

BIBLIOGRAPHY: Johnston, S. L., "Structure in the Novels of C. M.," *FR*, 38 (1965) 451–58; Mercier, V., *The New Novel from Queneau to Pinget* (1971), pp. 315–62; Roudiez, L. S., *French Fiction Today* (1972), pp. 132–51; Boschett, S. M., "Silence as an Element of Dialogue in C. M.," *IFR*, 7, 1 (1980), 35–38

SANDY PETREY

MAURIAC, François

French novelist, poet, essayist, critic, and dramatist, b. 11 Oct. 1885, Bordeaux; d. 1 Sept. 1970, Paris

M., who is best known as a Catholic writer, came from a home divided in religious background. His father, a freethinker, died when M. was not yet two years old. His mother, a devout Catholic influenced by Jansenist thought, gave M. a distinctly pious education. His attendance from the age of five at the Catholic College of Grand-Lebrun, taught by the Marist Fathers, turned him toward introspective self-analysis and scrupulosity. The mature writer never ceased to acknowledge his grateful recognition of this early tutelage and the preservation from evil it afforded him.

M. likewise was ambivalent in his attitude toward his childhood surroundings. He always loved Malagar, the family estate bought by his great-grandfather, whose formula was "order, work, economy." M.'s novels are filled with the atmosphere of the Landes, the region of marsh and pine near Bordeaux. This fact has led some critics to call M. a regionalist writer. Yet one of M.'s chief themes was his rebellion against the bourgeois farmers—his bitter criticism of the tenaciousness with which they clung to material goods and of their avaricious spirit. In politics he was likewise severe toward middle-class conservatism.

M.'s early literary influences are many. Often they reflect his personal relationship and debt to the writers rather than a detached objective judgment on his part. *Mes grands hommes* (1950; *Men I Hold Great,* 1952) has as chapter headings the names of Pascal, Molière, Voltaire, Rousseau, Chateaubriand, Maurice de Guérin (1810–1839) and his sister Eugénie de Guérin (1805–1848), Balzac, Flaubert, Maurice Barrès (1862–1923), André Gide (q.v.), Graham Greene (q.v.), and others. M. also wrote studies on Racine and Marcel Proust (q.v.), and the poet and novelist André Lafon (1883–1915). The French names predominating in such a list are indicative of his nationalistic orientation. The variety and number of the types represented suggest the rich complexity of M.'s mind.

Of all these writers, Pascal seems foremost in his influence on M. A sensitive Christian intellectual, deeply conscious primarily of his direct relationship with a personal God, Pascal is a type attractive to M., whose spiritual ordeal resembles that of the great 17th-c. writer. The constant, absorbing consciousness of God's presence and the concomitant anxiety about the conscious conflict between nature and grace are Pascal's legacy to M.

To this must be added M.'s admiration for Proust and for the subtle psychological explorations that mark Proust's work. When critics called M. the greatest French novelist since Proust, they were no doubt allying the two because of their poetic style, their reliance on remembrance of things past, and their use of interior monologue. Yet Proust's interior world never revolves about a personal God.

Although M.'s first publication was a book of poetry, *Les mains jointes* (1909; clasped hands), it was with his novels that M. was to achieve fame. His first novel, *L'enfant chargé de chaînes* (1913; *Young Man in Chains,* 1963), was followed by, among others, *La robe prétexte* (1914; *The Stuff of Youth,* 1960), *La chair et le sang* (1920; *Flesh and Blood,* 1955), and *Le fleuve de feu* (1923; *The River of Fire,* 1954). The first novel shares with its immediate successor a considerable sentimentality and reflects M.'s enthusiasm at the time for religious and romantic literature. But gradually M. developed control over his material. Using adolescent boys as central figures in his early novels, and depicting their maturation, he satirizes bourgeois society and focuses on the struggle of spirit and flesh, with profound reflections on the conflict between piety and the world—themes he never completely abandoned in his mature work.

Le baiser au lépreux (1922; *A Kiss for the Leper,* 1950) is the first of M.'s better-known novels. Here the theme that became closely identified with M.—the distrust of human love—first made a notable appearance. For M., each person is marked by isolation; the novelist seems deeply convinced of the futility of human love in people's attempts at communion with another. Ultimately, as many of M.'s novels demonstrate, the human heart finds its solace in confrontation with the "Other," with God alone.

"Those who love us form us," M. reflects in *Le jeune homme* (1926; the young man). The restraints that love puts upon us sometimes result in rebellion. The same theme in a different context, family love, is seen at its epitome in *Génitrix* (1923; *Genetrix,* 1950).

M. once wrote: "'The Desert of Love' might serve as the title for my entire work." With the work bearing this title began the publication of M.'s three greatest novels: *Le désert de l'amour* (1925; *The Desert of Love,* 1929); *Thérèse Desqueyroux* (1927; *Thérèse,*

1928), and *Le nœud de vipères* (1932; *Viper's Tangle,* 1933; also tr. as *The Knot of Vipers,* 1951).

In *Le désert de l'amour* Maria Cross, a self-centered young widow, deliberately provokes the passions of both her physician, Dr. Courrèges, and his adolescent son, Raymond. Viewed again after an interval of seventeen years, the trio has found love a place of solitude rather than union, a place of utter desolation, a temporary oasis inevitably to become a mirage.

In *Thérèse Desqueyroux* the futility of passion is pictured through the complex character of a strong young woman who finds her marriage to a complacent, coarse landowner intolerable. She becomes his would-be murderess, but her innermost feelings are surrounded by an atmosphere of mystery, and her conversion is both an artistic and a moral problem for M. He is confronted with the paradox of Thérèse, who is desperately seeking freedom at the cost of murder, yet who is unable to acknowledge her guilt in terms of repentance.

Before M. wrote the third novel of this distinguished trio, he seemed to have resolved the tragic struggle between passion and conscience that had marked his earlier writing, where nature itself seems allied with pagan sensuality against God. No reconciliation had appeared possible for M. when he wrote the essay "Souffrances du pécheur" (1928; sufferings of the sinner)—later published together with "Bonheur du chrétien" (1929; joy of the Christian) under the title *Souffrances et bonheur du chrétien* (1931; *Anguish and Joy of the Christian Life,* 1964). In "Souffrances du pécheur" he expresses the Jansenist paradox in his opening sentence: "Christianity makes no provision for the flesh. It suppresses it." However, the retraction of this extreme statement, "Bonheur du chrétien," was hailed by Charles du Bos (1882–1939) as the record of a conversion, a peace treaty achieved within M. himself. In "Bonheur du chrétien" M. acknowledges "Souffrances du pécheur" as the rebellious outpourings of a man who "accuses the Author of life of failing to make provision for the flesh, and the Author of life takes vengeance by overwhelming this soul and this body in his love to the point that he confesses the law of the spirit to be, indeed, the law of the flesh."

It may be that M.'s newly achieved seren-ity of spirit provided the creative stimulus for *Le nœud de vipères,* which is probably his greatest work. It is written almost entirely in the first person from the point of view of Louis, an embittered old man, whose determination to keep his money from his wife and children is motivated not by miserliness but by a sense of abandonment. His children and his illegitimate son are engaged in a counterplot against him. He finally realizes he has pursued an illusion and dies just as he discovers that the few loves he has known are revelations of the one true Love. *Thérèse Desqueyroux* is artistically admirable because of M.'s restraint in introducing the intervention of the supernatural. *Le nœud de vipères* also serves as a synthesis of characteristic M. themes: the bourgeois family as an institution, the mediocrity of innumerable Christians, the disillusionment seemingly inevitable in human love, the isolation of the individual.

Several later novels—*Galigaï* (1952; *The Loved and the Unloved,* 1952), *Les anges noirs* (1936; *The Mask of Innocence,* 1953), and *L'agneau* (1954; *The Lamb,* 1955)—are marked by the theme of isolation, but only once in the remainder of his writing did M. show comparable achievement. This was in his *La Pharisienne* (1941; *Woman of the Pharisees,* 1946), where his theme is the subtlety of a complacent Christian's hypocritical self-delusion, which results in the spiritual destruction of the "woman," Brigitte Pian. The novel is powerful, although perhaps less moving than *Le nœud de vipères.*

The fictional world M. created is acknowledged to be sharply limited; it exists only in the particular atmosphere he creates. His style is highly poetic—rhythmic, economical, full of suggestion. Of the poetry of the novel M. said: "There is little danger in the novel's invading the rest of literature. I believe that only poetry counts and that only through the poetical elements enclosed in a work of art of any genre whatever does that work deserve to last. A great novelist is first of all a great poet. Both Proust and Tolstoy were because their power of suggestion was boundless."

M.'s work as a dramatist, beginning with *Asmodée* (1937; *Asmodée; or, The Intruder,* 1939), never achieved the success of his novels. Indeed, his plays tend now to seem dated in comparison with the drama of metaphysical freedom that was being written at the same time by other playwrights. His characters often seem starkly outlined, without the nuances of background that enrich the novels; the "atmosphere" is lost. This is particularly true of *Asmodée,* in which the conflict of characters seems at times implausible. His best play is *Les mal aimés* (1945; the badly loved), a drama of frustrated love, which has a classically sharp construction.

M.'s religious writings are searching, at times anguished, always highly relevant to the troubled times in which he lived. Best among them is probably *Le fils de l'homme* (1958; *The Son of Man,* 1960), a meditation on the life of Christ. It is less controversial than his *Vie de Jésus* (1936; *Life of Jesus,* 1937), which emphasizes the human qualities of Christ.

As a journalist he made his mark in the columns of *Le Figaro* and in *La table ronde.* His collected articles, *Journal* (5 vols., 1934–51; journal), include some of the best of M.'s prose.

The highest tribute to M.'s art came with his winning of the Nobel Prize for literature in 1952. He is held by many to be the greatest French novelist of his time.

FURTHER WORKS: *L'adieu à l'adolescence* (1911); *De quelques cœurs inquiets: Petits essais de psychologie religieuse* (1920); *Préséances* (1921; *Questions of Precedence,* 1958); *Le mal* (1924; *The Enemy,* 1952); *La vie et la mort d'un poète* (1924); *Orages* (1925); *Bordeaux* (1926); *Proust* (1926); *Fabien* (1926); *La province* (1926); *La rencontre avec Pascal* (1926); *Le tourment de Jacques Rivière* (1926); *Destins* (1928; *Destinies,* 1929; also tr. as *Lines of Life,* 1957); *Le roman* (1928); *La vie de Racine* (1928); *Trois recits* (1929); *Dieu et Mammon* (1929; *God and Mammon,* 1936); *Voltaire contre Pascal* (1930); *Trois grands hommes devant Dieu* (1930); *Ce qui était perdu* (1930; *That Which Was Lost,* 1951); *Commencement d'une vie, suivi de Bordeaux; ou, L'adolescence* (1931); *Jeudi saint* (1931; *The Eucharist: The Mystery of Holy Thursday,* 1944); *L'affaire Favre-Bulle* (1931); *Blaise Pascal et sa sœur Jacqueline* (1931); *René Bazin* (1931); *Pèlerins de Lourdes* (1933); *Le mystère Frontenac* (1933; *The Frontenacs,* 1961); *Le romancier et ses personnages* (1933); *Le drôle* (1933; *The Holy Terror,* 1964); *La fin de la nuit* (1935; *The End of the Night,* in *Therese: A Portrait in Four Parts,* 1947); *Plongées* (1938); *Les maisons fugitives* (1939); *Les chemins de la mer* (1939; *The Unknown Sea,*

1948); *Le sang d'Atys* (1941); *Ne pas se renier* (1944); *La rencontre avec Barrès* (1945); *Sainte Marguerite de Cortone* (1945; *Saint Margaret of Cortona,* 1948); *Le bâillon dénoué* (1945); *Du côté de chez Proust* (1947; *Proust's Way,* 1947); *Passage du malin* (1948); *Journal d'un homme de trente ans* (1948); *Terres franciscaines: Actualités de St-François d'Assise* (1950); *Le sagouin* (1951; *The Weakling,* 1952); *La pierre d'achoppement* (1951; *The Stumbling Block,* 1952); *Le feu sur la terre* (1951); *Lettres ouvertes* (1952; *Letters on Art and Literature,* 1953); *Écrits intimes* (1953); *Paroles catholiques* (1954; *Words of Faith,* 1955); *Le pain vivant* (1955); *Bloc-notes, 1952–1957* (1958); *Mémoires intérieurs* (1959; *Mémoires Intérieurs,* 1960); *Nouveaux bloc-notes, 1958–1960* (1961); *La vie de Racine* (1962); *Ce que je crois* (1962; *What I Believe,* 1963); *De Gaulle* (1964; *De Gaulle,* 1966); *Nouveaux mémoires intérieurs* (1965); *Nouveaux bloc-notes, 1961–1964* (1965); *D'autres et moi* (1966); *Mémoires politiques* (1967); *Un adolescent d'autrefois* (1969; *Malteverne,* 1970); *Derniers bloc-notes, 1968–1970* (1971); *Correspondance André Gide–F. M., 1912–1950* (1971); *Correspondance F. M.–Jacques-Émile Blanche, 1916–1942* (1976); *Œuvres romanesques et théâtrales complètes* (1978 ff.). FURTHER VOLUMES IN ENGLISH: *Therese: A Portrait in Four Parts* (1947); *Second Thoughts: Reflections on Literature and Life* (1961); *Cain, Where Is Your Brother?* (1962)

BIBLIOGRAPHY: Heppenstall, R., *The Double Image* (1947), pp. 45–63; O'Donnell, D. [Conor Cruise O'Brien], *Maria Cross: Imaginative Patterns in a Group of Modern Catholic Writers* (1952), pp. 3–37; Simon, P. H., ed., *M. par lui-même* (1953); Robichon, J., *F. M.* (1953); Jarrett-Kerr, M., *F. M.* (1954); Peyre, H., *The Contemporary French Novel* (1955; new ed., *French Novelists of Today,* 1967), pp. 101–22; Moloney, M. F., *F. M.: A Critical Study* (1958); Turnell, M., *The Art of French Fiction* (1959), pp. 287–360; Alyn, M., *F. M.* (1960); Jenkins, C., *M.* (1965); Flower, J. E., *Intention and Achievement: An Essay on the Novels of F. M.* (1969); Smith, M. A., *F. M.* (1970); Kushner, E., *M.* (1972); Lacouture, J., *F. M.* (1980); Scott, M., *M.: The Politics of a Novelist* (1980)

ANITA MARIE CASPARY, I.H.M.

M.'s originality as a novelist lies in his Catholic vision of the world, in his analysis of love and es-

ROGER MARTIN DU GARD

FRANÇOIS MAURIAC

VLADIMIR MAYAKOVSKY

H. L. MENCKEN

HENRI MICHAUX

pecially of middle-aged women and adolescents led by a love affair to explore the bitter depths of love. It lies, too, in his craftsmanship, which, conscious and subtle as it is, contrives to leave in the novel the element by which it is most likely to challenge time—poetry.

Love hallowed by the sacrament of marriage and embellished by the devotion of the Christian couple to the service of God is hardly a theme for Catholic novelists. Happiness does not interest a creator. The radiating joy of lovers who might find an absolute in physical love is the foe M. pursues relentlessly. . . . To him, desire is always hideous. "It transforms the person who draws near us into a monster that is no longer like him. Nothing then stands any longer between us and our accomplice." His married women have, of course, ceased to expect any pleasure or joy. No mutual esteem, no admiration ever precedes or prolongs physical love. Love is nothing but a delusion that makes us feel our loneliness more acutely, or a fleeting sadistic impulse to humiliate our partner. More often still, with M., love is the inordinate power to torment us with which we have suddenly invested another creature.

Henri Peyre, *The Contemporary French Novel* (1955), pp. 118–19

The lucidity of the literary tradition in which he writes barred M. from the linguistic and structural exploration of a Joyce or the syntactical freedoms of a Faulkner, but he is no less concerned than they with the dark and lawless forces which well up from man's inmost being. Equally with them he testifies to modern man's recognition of the mystery of his nature. Unlike most contemporary novelists of the unconscious, however, M. has not been content merely to chart the ebb and flow of psychic currents. His identifying procedural trait has been his projection of himself *qua* artist into the full stream of the action which he narrates. The reader of a M. novel never escapes the presence of the novelist who is at the same time a poet of extreme lyric sensibility. [Ramon] Fernandez's declaration that a novel is, above all, the bringing to light of the interior world of the novelist is highly relevant to his manner of creation. No more than that of Dostoievski, or of his contemporary, Bernanos, is M.'s a reportorial art. His characters do not have their literal counterparts in the world of everyday experience. Here he breaks with the naturalistic tradition with which in so many ways he is closely identified. He is primarily the chronicler not of human actions separate and distinct from himself but of his own real and imagined life.

Michael F. Moloney, *F. M.* (1958), pp. 121–22

The truth is that in M. religion is translated not simply into concrete, but into physical terms. I think that we can go on to conclude that "pas-

sion" and "belief" are made of the same stuff, that though "belief" clearly implies a religious nuance which is not present in "passion," "belief" is nevertheless a form of "passion" as "passion is a form of "belief." While it is true that "passion" may provide "belief" with its driving power and "belief" may colour "passion," there is generally a conflict between the two, a conflict which is never resolved because the novelist does not wish to resolve it. His religion is not the source of harmony or unity; it is the disruptive element that creates the drama which is at the heart of all his work.

We can appreciate now the force of his statement that "this religion was *imposed* on me at birth," and the felicity of the image of the tide ebbing and flowing round the "central rock" and recoiling to form "whirlpools." The "whirlpools" are the conflicts which threaten the individual: the conflicts between love of God and love of the creature; between the Church and the world; between the individual and his environment; the individual and the family; the individual and the community.

Martin Turnell, *The Art of French Fiction* (1959), p. 288

It is certain . . . that with a certain feverish yet precisely evocative quality of style, immediately involving the physical in the metaphysical, M. has enriched the contemporary novel with a rare and distinctive tone. And it might seem that in such works as *Le désert de l'amour* and *Thérèse Desqueyroux*—perhaps also *Genitrix*, *Le nœud de vipères* and, of the plays, *Les mal aimés*—he has produced imaginative writing of lasting importance. That the Catholic novelist should achieve permanence through the more rebellious or troubled of his writings may well appear paradoxical, but this is hardly new in Catholic writing and M. himself has come to believe that, ultimately, the paradox is only an apparent one. Insofar as the value of the testimony is a function of the quality of the art, he is probably right. In the longer perspective, his contribution to his faith is not only to have maintained it in its public application against opposition from whatever quarter, but to have produced writings which—through the reality of their tensions—bear witness to the continuance of the Christian sense of life as an element in the culture of his time.

Cecil Jenkins, *M.* (1965), p. 114

M.'s aims and intentions as a novelist during some forty years of writing have been to exemplify to others his own firm conviction that mankind is assured of God's love . . . . Yet against this stands his description of a particular segment of bourgeois society with its families decaying and doomed to extinction. This is the problem stated in its simplest terms and one of which M. becomes increasingly aware in the course of his career. Implied values are not sufficient, particularly for the demanding Catholic critic, yet as a novelist M. is very aware of the danger of didactic literature. His attempts to incorporate his personal faith in the public statements that are his novels are various: the semi-autobiographical account of his relationship with Social Catholicism as a young man, the harsh castigation of the attitude of mind which raises material values over spiritual ones, the idealized portrait of a family in *Le mystère Frontenac,* or the allegory of Christ's passion in *L'agneau.* Too frequently, however, such attempts are doomed to fail and M. is open to the accusation of having implanted a particular view and in consequence of having falsified his picture of society. In order to avoid the charge of didacticism or of manipulation, therefore, the Catholic element of the novel must be included in such a way that it is an essential part of the structure of the book which without it would crumble.

J. E. Flower, *Intention and Achievement: An Essay on the Novels of F. M.* (1969), pp. 6–7

Throughout M\'s work we have observed three predominant themes, all of them present in the personality of this most subjective of writers. First, there is the essential element of tension and conflict: sometimes between Cybele and God, passionate and pagan love of nature versus religious faith; sometimes between God and Mammon, worldliness and sensual passion combating the desire for purity and saintliness. Second, we have the desperate loneliness and solitude of the individual, unable to communicate with others, even those most beloved. We recall in this regard M.'s own admission that "desert of love" might well serve as title of his entire work. Third, there is the flagellation of bourgeois smugness, social conformity, and lack of true Christian compassion a theme first appearing in the early *Préséances* but cropping up in most of the later works, particularly in that savage *Nœud de vipères.*

Maxwell A. Smith, *F. M.* (1970), p. 158

MAURITIAN LITERATURE

For a long time, Mauritius, in the Indian Ocean—or Île de France, as it was called until it was ceded by France to Britain in 1814—remained culturally a distant province of France. During the first part of the 19th c. the group of the Oval Table, led by Thomi Pitot de la Beaujardière (1779–1857), reflected the style of the popular French poet and song writer Pierre-Jean de Béranger (1780–1857). The first poet to depart from exclusively French themes and style was François

Chrestien (1767–1846), whose *Le bobre african* (1822; the African guitar) even included poems in Creole.

The "father of Mauritian poetry," Léoville L'Homme (1857–1928), and the more important poet Robert Edward Hart (1891–1954) gradually moved from romanticism to symbolism (q.v.). Over the course of thirty-three volumes, Loys Masson (1915–1969) achieved the transition to surrealism (q.v.) in poetry, while his *Le notaire des Noirs* (1961; the notary of Les Noirs) was a high point in the Mauritian novel. In poetry, Malcolm de Chazal (1904–1981) followed André Breton's (q.v.) surrealism, notably in *Sens plastique* (1947; plastic sense), while André Masson (b. 1927) veered toward esoteric themes, and Édouard J. Maunick (b. 1934) emphasized the African element in the inspired lyrics of *Ensoleillé vif* (1977; sunstruck alive). In fiction, Marcel Cabon (1912–1972) depicted indigenous life with realism and authenticity, even using local phrases occasionally in the novel *Namasté* (1965; Namasté).

Beginning with *Folklore de l'Île Maurice* (1888; folklore of Mauritius)—a collection of works, some in Creole, gathered by Charles Baissac (1831–1892), a white ethnographer—tales and *sega* (a local musical form) songs in Creole have been an important component of Mauritian literature. It took René Noyau (b. 1912), however, to "decolonize" such tales—that is, to use Creole as a challenge to French cultural ascendancy—and to assert the claims of the folk tradition in *Tention caïma* (1971; beware, crocodile), reworkings of folktales in Creole. Today, Dev Virshsawmy (b. 1940) is the major champion of Creole literature as a means of achieving cultural unity and as an alternative to the belleslettres of the French-speaking elite. His best-known work, *Li* (1976; him), a play whose production was banned by the government then in power, blends cultural and political satire. Another Creole writer, Renée Asgarally (b. 1942), also denounced social barriers in *Quand montagne prend difé . . .* (1977; when the mountain catches fire . . .).

Writing in English has always been on a limited scale, although English is the official administrative and school language, even since independence in 1968. Two worthy writers have emerged: Azize Asgarally (b. 1933), whose plays, mostly political and metaphysical, earned him an international reputation before he turned to writing in

Creole with *Ratsitatane* (1980; Ratsitatane), a play about the Malagasy leader of a 19th-c. revolt of native workers; and Deepchand Beeharry (b. 1927), whose novel *That Others Might Live* (1976) graphically evokes the plight of Indian indentured workers at the turn of the century.

Mauritian literature in English seems to have little future. There remains a strong French tradition—more than eighty percent of literary publications are still in French—but Creole writing is assuming an increasingly important position.

BIBLIOGRAPHY: Prosper, J.-G., ed., *Mauritius Anthology of Literature in the African Context* (1977); Hazareesingh, K., ed., *Anthologie des lettres mauriciennes* (1978); Prosper, J.-G., *Histoire de la littérature mauricienne de langue française* (1978); Furlong, R., ed., "La production littéraire à l'Île Maurice," special issue, *Journal of the Mauritius Institute of Education,* No. 3 (1979); Fabre, M., "Mauritian Voices: A Panorama of Contemporary Creative Writing in English," *WLWE,* 19 (1980), 121–37; Fabre, M., and Quet, D., "A Checklist of Mauritian Creative Writing in English (1920–1980)," *WLWE,* 19 (1980), 138–43

MICHEL FABRE

MAUROIS, André

(pseud. of Émile Herzog) French biographer, novelist, and historian, b. 26 July 1885, Elbeuf; d. 9 Oct. 1967, Neuilly

M. was born into a family of Jewish industrialists who had fled Alsace after the Franco-Prussian War (1870) and taken refuge in Normandy, where they owned a woolen mill at Elbeuf. He was a brilliant student at secondary school in Rouen, where he came under the influence of a famous teacher who wrote under the name Alain (q.v.). Young M.'s fluency in English led to his appointment during World War I as liaison officer with the British. The result was a series of sketches entitled *Les silences du colonel Bramble* (1918; *The Silence of Colonel Bramble,* 1920), which was an instant success in both France and England.

Peacetime found M. back at the family mill. But the success of *Les silences du Colonel Bramble* whetted his appetite for writing and attracted him to England. His next suc-

cess was *Ariel; ou, La vie de Shelley* (1923; *Ariel: The Life of Shelley,* 1924), a light-hearted biography. Readers were delighted, but not so the critics. M.'s accuracy was attacked. Since *Ariel* was not intended as a work of scholarship, these attacks were manifestly unfair, but thereafter his biographies adhered to academic standards.

M.'s next important biography was *La vie de Disraëli* (1927; *Disraeli: A Picture of the Victorian Age,* 1928). Asked if he saw himself in the prime minister of Jewish background, he replied "sometimes," but M. remained outside formal religion. For his biography of Byron, *Don Juan; ou, La vie de Byron* (1930; *Byron,* 1930), he studied his subject's poetry carefully.

M.'s first biography of a French figure was *Lyautey* (1931; *Lyautey,* 1931), about the empire builder and Marshal of France. Many others followed: *Chateaubriand* (1938; *Chateaubriand: Poet, Statesman, Lover,* 1938); *À la recherche de Marcel Proust* (1949; *Proust: The Portrait of a Genius,* 1950), a meticulous study; *Lélia; ou, La vie de George Sand* (1952; *Lelia: The Life of George Sand,* 1953); *Olympio; ou, La vie de Victor Hugo* (1954; *Olympio: The Life of Victor Hugo,* 1956); and *Les trois Dumas* (1957; *The Titans: A Three-Generation Biography of the Dumas,* 1957). He returned to an English subject with *La vie de Sir Alexander Fleming* (1959; *The Life of Sir Alexander Fleming, Discoverer of Penicillin,* 1959). Next came *Adrienne; ou, La vie de Mme de La Fayette* (1961; *Adrienne: The Life of the Marquise de La Fayette,* 1961), and finally *Prométhée; ou, La vie de Balzac* (1964; *Prometheus: The Life of Balzac,* 1965). All these biographies are distinguished by their delightful style; meticulously researched, they present vivid and realistic portraits of their subjects.

M. channeled his craft into history in *Histoire d'Angleterre* (1937; *The Miracle of England,* 1937), *Histoire des États-Unis* (2 vols., 1943; *The Miracle of America,* 1944), and *Histoire de la France* (1947; *The Miracle of France,* 1948). These works had all the charm lacking in the usual histories, and they won an enthusiastic readership.

Meanwhile M. was writing novels. *Ni ange, ni bête* (1919; neither angel nor beast), written during World War I, was inferior to *Les silences du colonel Bramble.* Fortunately, three major novels followed. All dealt with marital problems: *Bernard Quesnay*

(1926; *Bernard Quesnay,* 1927), is a story of love among industrialists; *Climats* (1928; *Atmosphere of Love,* 1929) relates the story of a man's two successive marriages; *L'instinct du bonheur* (1934; *A Time for Silence,* 1942) is his one truly happy novel. A later novel, *Les roses de septembre* (1956; *September Roses,* 1958), is the story of an old man's loves.

These activities as novelist, biographer, and historian would have satisfied most men, but M. was a man of extraordinary energy. He also wrote short stories, short biographies, children's books, literary criticism, and science fiction. He was an indefatigable lecturer on the writer and his problems.

In 1929 he received an invitation from Princeton to teach there for a semester. Subsequently his interest in America never flagged. When France fell, he and his wife escaped to the U.S., where he lectured at University of Kansas City and Mills College. He joined the Book-of-the-Month Club jury, and his varied contacts resulted in books about America and in defense of France. He saw his role as a sort of bridge between France and the Anglo-Saxon cultures.

When M. returned to France after World War II, he helped in the reconstruction with tongue and pen. He was already a member of the French Academy (1939), but new honors came to him.

M.'s place in the pantheon of letters is not yet sure. As a novelist he competed with distinguished compeers. His histories, too, have an uncertain position. But as a biographer he is unsurpassed. His studies will long be consulted by specialists. He tried to do everything well. As he once said: "I am never satisfied to do a hasty or improvised job when asked to write or speak."

FURTHER WORKS: *Le général Bramble* (1918; *General Bramble,* 1922); *Les bourgeois de Witzheim* (1920); *Les discours du docteur O'Grady* (1922); *Dialogues sur le commandement* (1924; *Captains and Kings: Three Dialogues on Leadership,* 1925); *Arabesques* (1925); *Les Anglais* (1926); *Meipe* (1926; *Mape: The World of Illusion,* 1926); *Conseils à un jeune Français partant pour l'Angleterre* (1927); *La conversation* (1927; *Conversation,* 1930); *Petite histoire de l'espèce humaine* (1927); *Un essai sur Dickens* (1927; *Dickens,* 1935); *Études anglaises* (1927); *Le chapitre suivant* (1927; *The Next Chapter: The War*

against the Moon, 1927); *Rouen* (1927); *Deux fragments d'une histoire universelle* (1928); *Aspects de la biographie* (1928; *Aspects of Biography,* 1929); *Voyage au pays des Articoles* (1928; *A Voyage to the Island of the Articoles,* 1929); *Contact* (1928); *Le pays des trente-six mille volontés* (1928; *The Country of Thirty-six Thousand Wishes,* 1930); *Fragments d'un journal de vacances* (1928); *Le côté de Chelsea* (1929; *The Chelsea Way; or, Marcel in England: A Proustian Parody,* 1930); *Relativisme* (1930); *Patapoufs et Filifers* (1930; *Fatapoufs and Thinifers,* 1940); *Sur le vif—L'exposition coloniale de Paris* (1931); *Tourgueniev* (1931); *Le peseur d'âmes* (1931; *The Weigher of Souls,* 1931); *L'Amérique inattendue* (1931); *Proust et Ruskin* (1932); *Le cercle de famille* (1932; *The Family Circle,* 1932); *L'Anglaise et d'autres femmes* (1932; *Ricochets: Miniature Tales of Human Life,* 1935); *Mes songes que voici* (1933); *Introduction à la méthode de Paul Valéry* (1933); *Chantiers américains* (1933); *Édouard VII et son temps* (1933; *The Edwardian Era,* 1933); *Sentiments et coutumes* (1934); *Voltaire* (1935; *Voltaire,* 1932); *Magiciens et logiciens* (1935; *Prophets and Poets,* 1935; enlarged ed. pub. as *Points of View,* 1968); *Premiers contes* (1935); *La machine à lire les pensées* (1937; *The Thought-Reading Machine,* 1938); *Un art de vivre* (1939; *The Art of Living,* 1940); *Discours de réception à l'Académie Française* (1939); *États-Unis 39* (1939); *Journal d'un voyage en Amérique* (1939); *Les origines de la guerre de 1939* (1939); *Tragédie en France* (1940; *Tragedy in France,* 1940); *Études littéraires* (2 vols., 1941–44); *Frédéric Chopin* (1942; *Frederic Chopin,* 1942); *Mémoires* (1942; *I Remember, I Remember,* 1942); *Cinq visages de l'amour* (1942; rev. ed., *Sept visages de l'amour,* 1946; *Seven Faces of Love,* 1944); *Toujours l'inattendu arrive* (1943); *Espoirs et souvenirs* (1943); *Eisenhower* (1945; *Eisenhower, the Liberator,* 1945); *Franklin: La vie d'un optimiste* (1945; *Franklin: The Life of an Optimist,* 1945); *Terre promise* (1945; *Women without Love,* 1945); *Études américaines* (1945); *Washington* (1946; *Washington: The Life of a Patriot,* 1946); *États-Unis 46* (1946; *From My Journal,* 1948); *Journal d'un tour en Suisse* (1946); *Conseils à un jeune Français partant pour les États-Unis* (1947); *Retour en France* (1947); *Les mondes impossibles* (1947); *Quand la France s'enrichissait* (1947); *Rouen dévasté* (1947); *Jour-*

nal d'un tour en Amérique Latine (1948; *My Latin-American Diary,* 1953); *Alain* (1950); *Les nouveaux discours du docteur O'Grady* (1950; *The Return of Doctor O'Grady,* 1951); *Le dîner sous les marroniers* (1951); *Cours de bonheur conjugal* (1951; *The Art of Being Happily Married,* 1953); *Ce que je crois* (1951); *Destins exemplaires* (1952); *La vie de Cecil Rhodes* (1953; *Cecil Rhodes,* 1953); *Lettres à l'inconnue* (1953; *To an Unknown Lady,* 1957); *Portrait de la France et des Français* (1955); *Aux innocents les mains pleines* (1955); *Hollande* (1955); *Périgord* (1955); *Discours prononcé à l'Académie Française pour la réception de Jean Cocteau* (1955); *Robert et Elizabeth Browning* (1955); *Louis XIV à Versailles* (1955); *La France change de visage* (1956); *Lecture mon doux plaisir* (1957; *The Art of Writing,* 1960); *Dialogue des vivants* (1957); *Portrait d'un ami qui s'appelait moi* (1959); *Pour piano seul: Toutes les nouvelles d'A. M.* (1960); *Histoire parallèle: Histoire des États-Unis de 1917 à 1961* (4 vols., 1962, with Louis Aragon; also pub. as *Les deux géants: Histoire des États-Unis et de l'URSS de 1917 à nos jours,* 1962–64; *From the New Freedom to the New Frontier: A History of the United States from 1917 to the Present,* 1963); *De Proust à Camus* (1963; *From Proust to Camus: Profiles of French Writers,* 1966); *Choses nues* (1963); *Napoléon* (1963; *Napoleon: A Pictorial Biography,* 1964); *De La Bruyère à Proust* (1964); *Histoire d'Allemagne* (1965; *An Illustrated History of Germany,* 1966); *De Gide à Sartre* (1965); *Lettre ouverte à un jeune homme sur la conduite de la vie* (1965); *Au commencement était l'action* (1966); *Soixante ans de ma vie littéraire* (1966); *D'Aragon à Montherlant* (1967); *La conquête de l'Angleterre par les Normands* (1967); *Les illusions* (1968). FURTHER VOLUMES IN ENGLISH: *A Private Universe* (1932); *Women of Paris* (1955); *A M. Reader* (1949); *Collected Stories of A. M.* (1967)

BIBLIOGRAPHY: Droit, M., *A. M.* (1953); Suffel, J., *A. M.* (1963); Keating, L. C., *A. M.* (1965); Kolbert, J., "The Worlds of A. M.," *SUS,* 7 (1965), 215–30; Kolbert, J., "A. M.'s Esthetics of Biography," *BRMMLA,* 20 (1967), 45–51; Lemaitre, G., *M.: The Writer and His Work* (1968); *Exposition organisée à l'occasion du dixième anniversaire de la mort d'A. M.* (1977)

L. CLARK KEATING

MAYAKOVSKY, Vladimir Vladimirovich

Russian poet and dramatist, b. 19 July 1893, Bagdadi (now Mayakovsky), Georgia; d. 14 April 1930, Moscow

M., Soviet poet laureate and major revolutionary artist, was born the son of a forest ranger in Georgia. After the sudden death of his father in 1906, the family moved to Moscow, where M. became involved in the Bolshevik movement. By the age of sixteen the youth had been arrested three times for anti-tsarist activities. While serving five months of a prison term in solitary confinement, he began to write verses and decided to suspend Party work to pursue an education. With his talent for drawing, M. won entrance in 1910 to the Moscow School of Painting, Sculpture, and Architecture. Here he met the radical painter-poet David Burlyuk (1882–1967). With the support of Burlyuk, who first recognized M.'s poetic genius, M. plunged into a literary career in the ranks of the cubo-futurists (see Futurism). This group of highly inventive writers, with their avid interest in avant-garde painting, sought to free the arts from academic traditions. Their flamboyant public performances created scandals across Russia, and M.'s association with this artistic modernism led to his expulsion from the Moscow School. A leading member of the artistic avant-garde, M. lived the life of a café bohemian. When the Bolsheviks took power in Russia in 1917, he enthusiastically welcomed the event. The poet-rebel now sought to become a poet of revolution.

M.'s literary debut took place in the notorious futurist collection *Poshchechina po obshchestvennomu vkusu* (1912; a slap in the face of public taste), which contained the famous manifesto of the same title. Despite the massive quantity and diversity of the art that followed, M.'s work as a whole consistently describes a persona closely identifiable with the poet himself. His first separate publication took the emphatic title *Ya!* (1913; "I," 1933); in essence it is a four-part portrait in verse. Like all of M.'s poetry, *Ya!* is striking in its manipulation of imagery. Cosmic and religious motifs take an irreverent tumble as the pain of the persona parallels his vividly distorted vision of urban life. The year 1913 also marked the premiere of his first play, the "monodrama" *Vladimir Mayakovsky, Tragedia* (*Vladimir Mayakovsky, a Tragedy,* 1963), in which he performed the title role. The play, a summation of many motifs and ideas in M.'s early lyrics, highlights the recurrent theme of the poet-martyr.

Among the finest vehicles of M.'s persona are his long poems (*poemy*). The first was *Oblako v shtanakh* (1915; "The Cloud in Trousers," 1933)—one of several dedicated to Lily Brik (1891–1978), wife of the critic Osip Brik (1888–1945)—which offers a vivid exposé of the torment of unrequited love. The work is also significant for its juxtaposition of sharply intense personal emotions with revolutionary challenges to do away with the old love, art, society, and religion. The hyperbolic sensitivity characteristic of M.'s persona acquired a well-known form in the early long poem *Fleyta-pozvonochnik* (1915; "The Backbone Flute," 1960), and the theme of love merged with that of the stages of life in the long work *Lyublyu* (1922; "I Love," 1960). In *Voyna i mir* (1916; war and universe), a text interspersed with bars of music, the poet confronts the horrors of war with a glimpse of utopia. Conflict also arises in *Chelovek* (1916; "A Man," 1975), when the persona's persistent pull toward the future is countered by the forces of philistinism. The clichéd existence of everyday life (*byt*) is a constant enemy in M.'s world view and plays a major role in his superb long poem dedicated to love, *Pro eto* (1923; "About This," 1965).

M.'s art has a strong utilitarian dimension. During World War I he wrote a series of satirical "hymns" for the journal *Novy satirikon* and designed posters. After the 1917 revolution he sketched and captioned propaganda posters for ROSTA, the Russian telegraph agency. He wrote political verses, poem-marches, children's poetry, and commercial jingles for state enterprises. His *Misteria-buff* (1918; 2nd version, 1921; *Mystery-Bouffe,* 1933), considered the first Soviet play on a current topic, is a modern morality play that, in its parody of Noah's Ark, reveals the superiority of the "unclean" (the proletariat) over the "clean" (the bourgeoisie). Two later plays, the satires *Klop* (1928; *The Bedbug,* 1960) and *Banya* (1929; *The Bathhouse,* 1963) were banned temporarily because they dealt critically with bureaucratic corruption and hypocrisy in early Soviet Russia. The plays also bring on stage representatives of the communist future. M. wrote many topical poems for Soviet papers, and

traveled to western Europe, the U.S., and Mexico as a Soviet representative. These trips resulted in a series of articles and poems.

A master of realized metaphor and unusual literary images, M. was also fascinated by the art of film. He wrote several film scenarios, and sequences in many of his poems recall film techniques. Along with imaginative use and choice of imagery, the originality of M.'s work lies in its wealth of verbal play, neologisms, innovative rhymes and rhythms. Linked in part to the declamatory "velvet bass" of his recitation methods, M.'s style reflects an effort to bring art closer to the content and cadences of normal speech. Peppering his texts with crude phrases, slogans, and advertisements of the day, he mixes rhythm patterns, regularly employs accentual verse, and heightens prosodic features with typesetting styles like the "short column" and "staircase" arrangements of verse lines on the page. His emphasis upon concrete images and rich sound textures lends a special tactile quality to his writing. While motifs of movement enhance the dynamism of his work, those of fire, water, and stars share the poetic field with heavy metals, weapons, and machines.

A sense of the monumental pervades M.'s poetry. It fills the emotions of his hulking persona and underlies his glorification of common Soviet citizens as well as his testimonial *Vladimir Ilyich Lenin* (1924; "Vladimir Ilyich Lenin [A Poem]," 1939). A pride equal to the epic event of the October Revolution evinced in *Khorosho!* (1927; "Good!," 1939) remains undiminished in a later poem dedicated to a Soviet passport, *Stikhi o sovetskom pasporte* (1930; "Soviet Passport," 1938). As part of the new symbolics, M. frequently engaged his lyric "I" with the concept of "we." For the long poem *150 000 000* (1921; partial tr., "150,000,000," 1949), the population figure of the Soviet state in 1919, an entire nation is claimed as the author of a poem. Yet the voice in the verse remains unmistakably M.'s. Audacious political agitator, irreverent destroyer of old myths, or delicate cloud in trousers, his poetic "I" stands ultimately alone in its own hyperbole. Like the title of his last, unfinished work, the poem *Vo ves golos* (1930; "At the Top of My Voice," 1940), the song of the poet approaches the tension of a cry.

M.'s career was surrounded by sharp controversy. As editor of the futurist journals

Lef (1923–25) and *Novy lef* (1927–28) he was embroiled in debates over matters of formalism. In 1930 he abruptly joined the dominant proletarian writers organization RAPP. A few months later M., who had earlier condemned in verse, in "Sereyu Yeseninu" (1926; "To Sergei Yessenin," 1965), the suicide of the poet Sergey Yesenin (q.v.), took his own life.

M. is a major writer of this century, and since 1935, when Stalin proclaimed indifference to M.'s works a crime, his place in Soviet literary history has been assured. Aspects of his work have been admired by other great Russian writers, such as Boris Pasternak, Anna Akhmatova, and Maxim Gorky (qq.v.). He has had a strong influence on later generations of Soviet poets, as well as on such foreign writers as Louis Aragon and Pablo Neruda (qq.v.).

FURTHER WORKS: *Kak delat stikhi?* (1926; *How Are Verses Made?*, 1970); *Moe otkrytie Ameriki* (1926); *Ispania; Okean; Gavana; Meksika; Amerika* (1926); *Kon-ogon* (1928; *Timothy's Horse*, 1970); *Polnoe sobranie sochineny* (12 vols., 1934–38); *Polnoe sobranie sochineny* (12 vols., 1939–49); *Polnoe sobranie sochineny* (13 vols., 1955–61); *Novoe o M.* (1958); *M.—khudozhnik* (1963); *Izbrannye proizvedenia* (2 vols., 1963); *Sobranie sochineny* (8 vols., 1968); *Semya M. v pismakh* (1978); *Sochinenia* (3 vols., 1978); *Izbrannye sochinenia* (2 vols., 1982). FURTHER VOLUMES IN ENGLISH: *M. and His Poetry* (1945); *The Bedbug, and Selected Poetry* (1960); *M.* (1965); *The Complete Plays of V. M.* (1968); *Electric Iron* (1971); *V. M.: Poems* (1972); *Essays on Paris* (1975)

BIBLIOGRAPHY: Jakobson, R., "On a Generation That Squandered Its Poets" (1931), in Brown, E. J., ed., *Major Soviet Writers* (1973), pp. 7–32; Bowra, C. M., "The Futurism of V. M.," *The Creative Experiment* (1949), pp. 94–127; Muchnic, H., *From Gorky to Pasternak* (1961), pp. 185–275; Humesky, A., *M. and His Neologisms* (1964); Stahlberger, L., *The Symbolic System of M.* (1964); Woroszylski, W., *The Life of M.* (1970); Shklovsky, V., *M. and His Circle* (1972); Brown, E. J., *M.: A Poet in the Revolution* (1973); Jangfeldt, B., *M. and Futurism, 1917–1921* (1976); Miller, A., tr., *V. M.: Innovator* [collection of essays] (1976); Barooshian, V., *Brik and M.* (1978)

JULIETTE R. STAPANIAN

MCCARTHY, Mary

American novelist, short-story writer, and critic, b. 21 June 1912, Seattle, Wash.

Orphaned by the 1918 influenza epidemic, M. was raised successively by two sets of rich but austere grandparents, one Catholic and one Protestant. She attended Catholic, public, and Episcopal schools and graduated Phi Beta Kappa from Vassar College in 1933. She then worked as an editor and theater critic (for *Partisan Review*) and briefly taught English at two American women's colleges. She has been married four times, the second to literary critic Edmund Wilson (q.v.), by whom she had her only child.

M.'s fiction, often described as witty, sophisticated, and savagely satiric, is distinguished by a relentlessly frank analysis of sexuality, political commitment, social pretense (especially in artists and intellectuals), and the effects of the modern world on people with middle-class values. Her first book, *The Company She Keeps* (1942), is a collection of loosely linked stories, some admittedly autobiographical, about a woman who decides to get a "fashionable" divorce, join a literary-political coterie, and go through analysis. *The Oasis* (1949) is a short novel about a well-meaning but incompetent utopian society of artists and intellectuals.

The Groves of Academe (1952) tells of an incompetent liberal professor who spreads the rumor that a Joseph McCarthy-style of witch hunt is behind moves to dismiss him; other liberals support him (on political rather than academic grounds), and he remains while the college president is forced to resign—a satiric inversion of justice and freedom that questions the authenticity of the liberals' integrity and intellectualism. *A Charmed Life* (1955) is set in an artists' colony; the central character returns with a new husband, is seduced by her former husband, and dies en route to an abortionist; with little plot, this book contains long digressions on art and literature and ruthless dissections of character. *The Group* (1963), M.'s most famous work, concerns eight Vassar graduates of M.'s own class who find their lives in turmoil regarding sex, politics, and art.

Birds of America (1971) is M.'s only comic—albeit sharply satiric—novel; it is told by a youth whose mother refuses to accept modern conveniences, although she changes husbands and life styles with impunity. Gradually the boy's naïve beliefs—beliefs in people's innate goodness, in nature's benevolence, in truth itself—are shattered, and only after these abstractions are eliminated can he really understand his mother's lack of sympathy with "progress," for this kind of "progress," M. would have us believe, leads man to the same danger of extinction identified with the birds of the novel's title. *Cannibals and Missionaries* (1979), a topical work unlike any of M.'s earlier fiction, concerns a hijacked airliner and two groups of hostages, liberal human-rights activists and wealthy art collectors. Although tied in to current events, this novel is not convincing as realistic political fiction because of M.'s confused handling of character relationships and responses to terrorism.

M.'s critical writing, by contrast, is consistently evocative of particular settings and concepts, whether this be in an autobiographical work, such as her fine *Memories of a Catholic Girlhood* (1957), her books on Venice and Florence, or her various theater essays. In more recent years she has turned to political reportage, with short but brilliant analyses of Vietnam and Watergate.

M.'s strengths as a novelist are a cold, calculating eye for hypocrisy, a piercing, honest examination into motivation, a pervasive sense of wit and intelligence, and a fine style; her weaknesses include forced polemics, philosophical digressions, stereotyped, repetitive characters, and a poor sense of structure (especially in regard to the endings of her novels). These strengths and weaknesses combine to make her nonfiction especially effective as topical commentary and her fiction often appear more like extended polemical, satiric, and philosophical exercises than like works concerned with plot, structure, and character.

FURTHER WORKS: *Sights and Spectacles: 1937–1956* (1956; repub. and expanded as *Sights and Spectacles: Theatre Chronicles 1937–1958* [1959] and *Theatre Chronicles 1937–1962* [1963]); *Venice Observed* (1956); *The Stones of Florence* (1959); *On the Contrary: Articles of Belief 1946–1961* (1961); *The Humanist in the Bathtub* (1964); *Vietnam* (1967); *Hanoi* (1968); *The Writing on the Wall, and Other Literary Essays* (1970); *Medina* (1972); *The Mask of State: Watergate Portraits* (1974); *The Seventeenth Degree* (1974); *Can There Be a Gothic*

Literature? (1975); *Ideas and the Novel* (1980)

BIBLIOGRAPHY: Niebuhr, E., "The Art of Fiction XXVII: M. M.," *Paris Review,* 27 (1962), 58–94; Schlueter, P., "The Dissections of M. M.," in Moore, H. T., ed., *Contemporary American Novelists* (1964), pp. 54–64; Auchincloss, L., *Pioneers and Caretakers: A Study of Nine American Women Novelists* (1965), pp. 170–86; Aldridge, J., *Time to Murder and Create: The Contemporary Novel in Crisis* (1966), pp. 95–132; McKenzie, B., *M. M.* (1966); Grumbach, D., *The Company She Kept: A Revealing Portrait of M. M.* (1967); Stock, I., *M. M.* (1968); Widmer, E., "Finally a Lady: M. M.," in French, W., ed., *The Fifties* (1970), pp. 93–102

PAUL SCHLUETER

MCCULLERS, Carson

American novelist, short-story writer, and dramatist, b. 19 Feb. 1917, Columbus, Ga.; d. 29 Sept. 1967, Nyack, N.Y.

M. was herself as peculiar and egocentric a person as any of her characters. An overindulgent mother encouraged her from her earliest years to behave exactly as she chose, and at the age of thirteen she was accustomed to hearing the catcall "freak!" from her schoolmates. In later years her determination to succeed as a writer and her bisexual proclivity so undermined her husband's self-esteem that he was driven to suicide, and M. refused not only to mourn her husband but even to pay the cost of having his ashes sent from France for interment in the U.S. In short, M. was an eccentric, self-centered woman, preoccupied with money, with literary success, and with the satisfaction of her own emotional needs. No one else was quite real to her.

But the failings of M.'s life were the material of her art, and all of her characters share her egocentricity and suffer the pangs of its attendant loneliness. Indeed, egocentricity and loneliness are facts of the human condition for them, not personal failings, and M.'s fiction has in consequence an air of stark, existential angst. Her view of the human condition is especially clear in her first novel, *The Heart Is a Lonely Hunter* (1940). The main character is a deaf-mute who receives uncomprehendingly the confidences of four characters who mistakenly think him sympathetic, and the deaf-mute in turn confides his heartaches to a man who is feeble-minded as well as mute, extending the line of meaningless communication. The novel is successful because its plain, grave style suits its rigid architecture, and because its characters touch the heart. M.'s second novel, *Reflections in a Golden Eye* (1941), is less successful. Its characters are Krafft-Ebing grotesques, clearly beyond M.'s ken, and its style tends toward the portentously abstract—a failing toward which M.'s work always tends, but more egregiously so in this novel than elsewhere.

The long story "The Ballad of the Sad Café" (1943) is M.'s most startling work. Its grotesqueries include a brooding, two-fisted Amazon, a hunchbacked confidence man, and a climactic wrestling match between the Amazon and her former husband. But the effect of the story is more archetypal than grotesque, for an anonymous narrator recounts the story in a folk idiom, and an *envoi* recasts the events of the story into vast, analogical terms. Many critics think it is M.'s finest work.

Yet *The Member of the Wedding* (1946) vies with "The Ballad of the Sad Café" for literary distinction. Its central character, Frankie Addams, is a motherless tomboy who decides to become a member of her brother's wedding in an attempt to be someone more than herself. Reality eventually compels her accommodation to selfhood, but not before a world of adolescent loneliness is laid out for the reader with bittersweet realism and marvelous delicacy. M. adapted this story for the stage at the suggestion of her friend Tennessee Williams (q.v.), and the Broadway production of *The Member of the Wedding* had a successful run in 1950–51. It is considered today one of the outstanding adaptations from a novel in the history of the American theater. M. was not able to repeat the theatrical success of *Member* with her subsequent play, *The Square Root of Wonderful* (1956), however, and declining health made it impossible for her to maintain the quality of her earlier fiction in her final novel, *Clock without Hands* (1961).

M.'s work is often compared to that of Eudora Welty, Flannery O'Connor, and Katherine Anne Porter (qq.v.), somewhat to its disadvantage. M.'s artistry is less sophisticated than that of these other writers, to be sure, and her understanding of the dark corners of the mind is certainly less astute than theirs. But M.'s writing is distinguished from her fellow Southerners' work by an empathy for the disaffiliate so profound that she is his preeminent spokesman in modern American literature. No one has written more feelingly than she about the plight of the eccentric, and no one has written more understandingly than she about adolescent loneliness and desperation.

FURTHER WORKS: *The Ballad of the Sad Café: The Novels and Stories of C. M.* (1951); *Sweet as a Pickle and Clean as a Pig* (1964); *The Mortgaged Heart* (1972)

BIBLIOGRAPHY: Hassan, I., "C. M.: The Alchemy of Love and the Aesthetics of Pain," *MFS*, 5 (1959), 311–26; Evans, O., *The Ballad of C. M.* (1966); Edmonds, D., *C. M.* (1969); Graver, L., *C. M.* (1969); Carr, V. S., *The Lonely Hunter: A Biography of C. M.* (1975); Cook, R. M., *C. M.* (1975); Kiernan, R. F., *Katherine Anne Porter and C. M.: A Reference Guide* (1976)

ROBERT F. KIERNAN

MCKAY, Claude

Jamaican-American poet, novelist, short-story writer, and journalist, b. 15 Sept. 1889, Sunny Ville, Jamaica; d. 22 May 1948, Chicago, Ill.

M. came from a petit-bourgeois agricultural family; his father claimed Ashanti origins, his mother, Madagascan. Both were Baptists, but M. was more strongly influenced by the rationalism of his brother, who was his teacher and guardian for some years, and of Walter Jekyll, a British expatriate writer who was his literary mentor and patron.

Undecided on a career, M. joined the Jamaica Constabulary in 1911 but gained release after a year upon the publication of poems first in the *Daily Gleaner* (Kingston) and then in two small volumes, *Songs of Jamaica* (1912) and *Constab Ballads* (1912), through the efforts of Jekyll. M. was hailed as the "Robert Burns of Jamaica," an undeserved sobriquet, since his work lacked the philosophical content of the Scot and M. himself deprecated dialect—which he henceforth rejected except for disparagement of characters.

In 1912 he left Jamaica forever, although it remained for him the main source of inspiration and a constant and Edenic frame of reference. Its many shortcomings he rigorously overlooked: as in the poem "North and South" (1920), Jamaica (and the other West Indian islands) represented the antithesis of the degeneration, impersonality, and racial antagonism of North American cities. Although he entered Tuskegee Institute and then Kansas State College, he soon left both; he worked as railroad waiter between New York and Pittsburgh, and did odd jobs in Harlem before joining the leftist literary circles in New York. He was associate editor of *The Liberator,* but a contretemps over the paper's position on the race-versus-class issue precipitated his resignation. Meanwhile, his "If We Must Die" (1919), occasioned by the 1919 race riots in several American cities, had made M. the leading poet of the "black belt." His *Spring in New Hampshire* (1920) and *Harlem Shadows* (1922)—again suggesting the antithesis of country and city—established his position as a leader of the Harlem Renaissance.

In 1922 M. visited Russia and addressed the Third International. While there he produced two works both written in English, then translated into and published in Russian, and later retranslated into English: *Sudom lyncha* (1922; *Trial by Lynching,* 1977) and *Negry v Amerike* (1923; *The Negroes in America,* 1979). The first was M.'s initial volume of short fiction and developed themes that are to be found also in the poetry but more clearly in the subsequent prose: the horrendous treatment of black people in America, the uncertain role of the mulatto, and the "use" made of blacks.

The Negroes in America, a work of popular sociology that is really a superior form of journalism, indicated what the neo-Marxist M. thought his Russian hosts and readers would appreciate. It nonetheless contains many astute observations: M. suggested that the 1920s was the age of Negro art and race consciousness (some years before Alain Locke's [1886–1954] similar declaration); that race liberation and women's liberation are inextricable; that black and white workers must appreciate their common interests; that the black middle class can not be trusted with the black masses' welfare; that whites' fears of blacks' sexuality is psychologically revealing.

After his "magic pilgrimage" to Russia, M. drifted around Europe and North Africa. His *Home to Harlem* (1928), the first of a

genre of realistic novels of urban black life written by a black, was a great success, although it was censured by W. E. B. DuBois (1868–1963) for catering to the "prurient interests" of whites. M. responded that he was giving a realistic picture of black life.

In 1934 M. returned to the U.S., but his long absence and his recantation of his Communist beliefs distanced him from his former associates. *Banana Bottom* (1933), a nostalgic idyll of Jamaica, and *Gingertown* (1932), a collection of short stories, represented a retreat from proletarian, or "protest," literature and suggested that M. was writing for yet another audience. His conversion to Catholicism in 1945 further isolated him from his political and social origins.

In his last years he became a Catholic apologist, wrote *My Green Hills of Jamaica* (pub. 1980), and completed a large cycle of poems (all in the sonnet form that he most readily worked in), which remain unpublished, as do two unfinished and unsatisfactory novels.

The reputation of M. rests principally on *Selected Poems* (1953), which reprints the best work of his earlier volumes, excluding the dialect verse. Although he is associated now with the Harlem Renaissance, ironically he was abroad during the whole of that movement's vital decade.

FURTHER WORKS: *Banjo* (1929); *Harlem: Negro Metropolis* (1940)

BIBLIOGRAPHY: Gayle, A., Jr., *C. M.: The Black Poet at War* (1972); Cooper, W., ed., *The Passion of C. M.* (1972); Wagner, J., *Black Poets of the United States* (1972), pp. 211–81; Giles, J. R., *C. M.* (1976); McLeod, A. L., "Memory and the Edenic Myth: C. M.'s *Green Hills of Jamaica,*" *WLWE,* 18 (1979), 245–54; McLeod, A. L., "C. M.'s Adaptation to Audience," *Kunapipi,* 2, 1 (1980), 123–34

A. L. MCLEOD

MEHREN, Stein

Norwegian poet, essayist, dramatist, and novelist, b. 16 May 1935, Oslo

M. is one of Norway's strongest lyrical talents of recent times. His university studies in philosophy and biology, combined with his position as secretary to an art collector, have contributed to the high intellectual awareness and logical consistency of his work, while his experience as a ski instructor and guide have strengthened his love of nature and his feeling for the concrete image.

M.'s many poems have a resonance, beauty, and poetic magic that carry the reader along even when interpretation becomes difficult. A lover of words and ideas, he has attempted to go his own way to find his view of life and the human being. Longing for the inexpressible, for childhood, and for direct experience is joined in his poetry with philosophical reflections on the situation of modern man.

In *Gjennom stillheten en natt* (1960; through the silence one night) M. created bold comparisons and nature images while revealing feelings of unrest, alienation, and unreality. He has also always been preoccupied with problems of language. In *Hildring i speil* (1961; reflected illusion), he shows how language not only distorts experience but also creates expectations that life cannot fulfill.

In his subsequent poetic works, M.'s field expands to include all of European tradition. With daring linguistic inventiveness, he attacks all forms of prejudice and false assumptions in modern society, everything that makes the human being alien to himself and the world.

M.'s essays, which deal with modern isolation, neurosis, and fear, but which also emphasize the positive virtues of nature and love, parallel his lyrics. In *Aurora, det niende mørke* (1971; Aurora, the ninth darkness) and *Kongespillet* (1971; the royal game) M. mixes poems, essays, and aphorisms to show a romantic preference for a mythical explanation of the world and a mythical path to wisdom and at the same time to oppose the modern tendency toward the demythologizing of society.

M.'s novels deal with people's struggles to find their way through modern ideological difficulties. Both *De utydelige* (1972; the vague ones) and *Titanene* (1974; the titans) deal with the same three intellectuals from Oslo and their attempts to avoid the pitfalls of fixed ways of thinking. For M., ideologies are modern illusions that lead people away from themselves and their fellow men. One must seek freedom and self-awareness by going one's own way.

M.'s drama *Narren og hans hertug* (1968; the fool and his duke) deals with an actual historical revolt of the 1400s but seeks time-less psychological and political insights into the phenomenon of revolt in general. Idealism, immaturity, and ineffectiveness are reflected in the fool, Fastelan, who leads the revolt, and in the people, while the leaders, who hold fast to power in spite of momentary urges to allow justice to hold sway, symbolize the sophistication of power.

All of M.'s works are meant to give strength and freedom—to the reader, to his characters, and to himself—to break the grip of the times on us, and to save our deepest thoughts from destruction by the modern world.

FURTHER WORKS: *Alene med en himmel* (1962); *Mot en verden av lys* (1963); *Gobelin Europa* (1965); *Tids alder* (1966); *Vind runer* (1967); *Maskinen og menneskekroppen: En pastorale* (1970); *Veier til et bilde* (1971); *Den store frigjøring* (1973); *Dikt for enhver som våger* (1973); *Kunstens vilkår og den nye puritanismen* (1974); *En rytter til fots* (1975); *Menneske bære ditt bilde frem* (1975); *Den store søndagsfrokosten* (1976); *Det opprinnelige landskapet* (1976); *Det trettende stjernebilde* (1977); *Myten og den irrasjonelle fornuft* (2 vols., 1977–80); *Vintersolhverv* (1979); *50 60 70 80* (1980)

BIBLIOGRAPHY: Naess, H. "S. M.: Dialectic Poet of Light and Dreams," *BA*, 47 (1973), 66–69

                                    WALTER D. MORRIS

MEHRING, Walter

German poet, satirist, novelist, essayist, and dramatist, b. 29 April 1896, Berlin; d. 3 Oct. 1981, Zurich, Switzerland

After being expelled from secondary school for "unpatriotic conduct," M. studied art history and in 1916 published his first poems in the expressionist (q.v.) journal *Der Sturm*. He was one of the founders of the Berlin Dada (q.v.) movement, and in the early days of the Weimar Republic his songs and skits were performed in a number of Berlin cabarets. During most of the 1920s M. lived in Paris, working as a correspondent for German publications, including *Die Weltbühne*, the leading periodical of the intellectual left. Immediately after the Reichstag fire M. fled Berlin; ten of his books were burned by the Nazis. Until the annexation of Austria in 1938 M. was a correspondent in Paris and

Vienna for an exiles' newspaper. He was interned several times in Vichy, France, but escaped and eventually reached the U.S. In the 1950s M. returned to Europe, choosing to live in Switzerland. In spite of his reputation as a leading literary figure in prewar Germany, M. was largely ignored by postwar writers and critics. He continued to publish— reminiscences, a book of essays on "painters, connoisseurs, and collectors," new collections of earlier work—but in 1976 the disappearance of an eight-hundred-page manuscript, a semifictional autobiography, proved to be the "greatest catastrophe" of a life marked by loss and calamity.

In the 1920s M. published several volumes of poetry. Inspired by François Villon, Heinrich Heine, traditional German folk songs and ballads, Baroque poetry, and American jazz, his poems captured the rhythms of life in bustling modern cities and attacked prejudice, injustice, and hypocrisy in pre-Hitler Germany. He was one of the chief creators of the modern German chanson and pioneered in developing the montage poem and what he called "verbal ragtime." The songs in the plays of Bertolt Brecht (q.v.) reveal a substantial (unacknowledged) debt to M.

In 1929 M.'s play *Der Kaufmann von Berlin* (the merchant of Berlin) was a theatrical and political scandal. The play savagely exposed the shameless profiteering that had occurred during the inflation of 1923 and pointed up the pervasiveness of anti-Semitism in German society.

In exile M. wrote the satirical novel *Müller: Chronik einer deutschen Sippe von Tacitus bis Hitler* (1935; chronicle of a German tribe from Tacitus to Hitler), in which he mocked the Nazis' ideal of racial purity by tracing a "Germanic" family tree back to Roman times and showing how peoples of different racial stocks had met and mingled on German territory. In the poetic cycle "Briefe aus der Mitternacht" (1944; separate book pub., 1971; "Odyssey out of Midnight," 1944) M. depicts the stages of his exile in a world that has fallen into the grip of evil. The counterpoint to this apocalyptic vision is his love for the woman who accompanied him during much of his odyssey, either in person or in his thoughts. In *Die verlorene Bibliothek* (1952; *The Lost Library*, 1951), first published in English translation, M. summons up memories of his father's library, left behind when he fled Vienna, in order to reconstruct a highly subjective intellectual history of the Western world.

Throughout his career M. opposed bourgeois complacency and greed, and political extremism of all kinds. As a believer in the power of the word, he pointed out the falsehoods in propaganda and stereotyped thought and speech. Neither his poetry nor his prose writings have received the critical attention they deserve, either as documents of their time or as literature of enduring value. M.'s poetry appears readily accessible, but it is actually highly intricate in form and sophisticated in content. Most of M.'s prose works lack a clear narrative thread; with their webs of images, allusions, and associations they seem at first to be Dadaistic or impressionistic jottings. Careful analysis, however, reveals an elaborate inner structure.

FURTHER WORKS: *Die Frühe der Städte* (1918); *Das politische Cabaret* (1919); *Das Ketzerbrevier* (1921); *Wedding-Montmartre* (1923); *Europäische Nächte* (1924); *In Menschenhaut, aus Menschenhaut, um Menschenhaut herum* (1924); *Westnordwestviertelwest* (1925); *Neubestelltes abenteuerliches Tierhaus* (1925); *Algier; oder, Die 13 Oasenwunder* (1927); *Paris in Brand* (1927); *Gedichte, Lieder und Chansons* (1929); *Sahara* (1929); *Arche Noah SOS* (1930); *Die höllische Komödie* (1932); *. . . und euch zum Trotz* (1934); *Die Nacht des Tyrannen* (1938); *Timoshenko, Marshal of the Red Army* (1942); *George Grosz* (1946); *Edgar Degas* (1946); *Verrufene Malerei* (1958); *Der Zeitpuls fliegt* (1958); *Berlin-Dada* (1959); *Morgenlied eines Gepäckträgers* (1959); *Neues Ketzerbrevier* (1962); *Kleines Lumpenbrevier* (1965); *Großes Ketzerbrevier* (1974); *Werke* (1978 ff.); *Wir müssen weiter: Fragmente aus dem Exil* (1979). FURTHER VOLUME IN ENGLISH: *No Road Back* (1944, bilingual)

BIBLIOGRAPHY: Schwab-Felisch, H., "W. M.: Dichter am Rand der Zeit," *Der Monat,* July 1953, 403–6; Pesel, P., " 'Und sie werden mich also nicht hören': Versuch über W. M.," *Deutsche Rundschau,* 85 (1959), 1090–95; Geuner, R., "W. M.: Provokation durch Satire," *Gegenspieler* (1969); Denker, K. P., "Staatenlos im Nirgendwo: W. M.," *Akzente,* 22 (1975), 258–73; Serke, "W. M.: Schüsse mitten ins deutsche Gemüt," *Die verbrannten Dichter* (1979), pp. 98–113; Hansen, T.,

"W. M.s antifaschistische Romane: Ein Beitrag zur politischen Prosa im Exil," in Elfe, W., et al., eds., *Deutsche Exilliteratur: Literatur im 3. Reich* (1979), pp. 132–40

KRISHNA WINSTON

MEIRELES, Cecília

Brazilian poet, b. 7 Nov. 1901, Rio de Janeiro; d. 9 Nov. 1964, Rio de Janeiro

Orphaned at the age of three, M. was raised by her maternal grandmother in Rio de Janeiro. By the time she graduated from normal school in 1917 M. had already demonstrated a strong enthusiasm for music and foreign languages. In later years, she became a noted orientalist as well. In 1934 M. delivered a series of lectures on Brazilian literature at the universities of Lisbon and Coimbra, and in 1935 she taught at the newly formed University of the Federal District. In 1940 she lectured on Brazilian literature and culture at the University of Texas. As a teacher, which she was for most of her adult life, M. did much to promote educational reforms and to foster the construction of children's libraries in Brazil.

M. began composing simple rhymes and songs even in grade school. Her first book of poems, *Espectros* (1919; specters), was published when she was eighteen. During the 1930s, M. matured as an artist. One of her most respected works, *Viagem* (1938; voyage), won the coveted poetry prize of the Brazilian Academy of Letters. Often mystical in tone and consistently universal in scope, *Viagem* ranks among the most significant of all Brazil's modernist (q.v.) poetic achievements. *Vaga música* (1942; vague music) reflects a rather disillusioned, skeptical, and world-weary author, as do *Mar absoluto* (1945; absolute sea) and, to a lesser degree, *Retrato natural* (1949; natural portrait), a work in which the commonplaces of everyday life come to the fore.

The high point of M.'s career as a poet is *Romanceiro da inconfidência* (1953; songbook of the revolution), a long and inspired narrative poem that, by presenting in closely interlocking patterns several different perspectives on the same subject matter, blends the style of the medieval Portuguese troubadour with a chronicler's sense of people and event. Widely held to be M.'s most original and imaginative work, this challenging poem

is a paean to liberty and, in its entirety, amounts to a virtual apotheosis of "Tiradentes" (the dentist who was the leader of the aborted revolt) and his confederates, the men involved in the ill-fated independence movement of 1789.

Often counted among the Brazilian modernists, M.'s best work really places her more squarely in the symbolist (q.v.) tradition. Unlike the more radical modernists, such as Mário de Andrade and Oswald de Andrade (qq.v.), M. did not advocate a total break with the Portuguese language's rich poetic traditions. Rather, she synthesized what were essentially established forms and metrical patterns with new images and the modernist's world view. The result, eclectic in nature, was a corpus of poetic works outstanding in their musicality, their fluidity, and their evocative power.

Much of M.'s poetry is intensely personal and reflects a quest for self-discovery in which certain motifs recur, especially those involving the sea, space, and solitude. M.'s lyric poetry is characteristically visual in essence. M. tended to praise the simple beauties of the natural world while rebuking mankind for its selfishness, egoism, and vanity. A pure poet, M.'s poems, which resist strict classification, cut back and forth across the arbitrary divisions of time and fashion.

FURTHER WORKS: *Nunca mais . . . e Poema dos poemas* (1923); *Baladas para El-Rei* (1925); *Criança: Meu amor* (1933); *Poetas novos de Portugal* (1944); *Rui: Pequena história de uma grande vida* (1949); *Problemas de literatura infantil* (1950); *Amor em Lenoreta* (1952); *Doze noturnos da Holanda, e O aeronauta* (1952); *Pequeno oratório de Santa Cecília* (1955); *Pistóia, cemitério militar brasileiro* (1955); *Panorama folclórico dos Açores* (1955); *Canções* (1956); *Giroflé, giroflá* (1956); *Romance de Santa Cecília* (1957); *A rosa* (1957); *Obra poética* (1958); *Metal rosicler* (1960); *Poemas escritos na Índia* (1961); *Antologia poética de C. M.* (1963); *Solombra* (1963); *Escolha o seu sonho* (1964); *Crônica trovada da cidade de Sam Sebastiam* (1965); *Inéditas* (1967); *Poesia* (1967). FURTHER VOLUME IN ENGLISH: *C. M.: Poems in Translation* (1977, bilingual)

BIBLIOGRAPHY: Nist, J., *The Modernist Movement in Brazil* (1967), pp. 190–204; Coutinho, A., *An Introduction to Literature in Brazil* (1969), pp. 187, 224, 244; Martins, W., *The Modernist Idea* (1970), pp. 13, 108–9; Keith, H., and Sayers, R., Introduction to *C. M.: Poems in Translation* (1977); García, R., "Symbolism in the Early Works of C. M.," *RomN,* 21 (1980), 16–22; Sadlier, D. J., "Metaphor and Metamorphosis: A Study of the Sea Imagery in C. M.'s *Mar absoluto,*" *KRQ,* 27 (1980), 361–70

EARL E. FITZ

MENCKEN, H(enry) L(ouis)

American essayist, political and social commentator, and literary critic, b. 12 Sept 1880, Baltimore, Md., d. 29 Jan. 1956, Baltimore, Md.

M. grew up in the pace of small-city life, enjoying the "great protein factory of the Chesapeake," and later rejecting the allure of literary New York for quiet amenities and old friends. At age eleven he forsook, in his words, "Christian Endeavor" and became "contumacious of Holy Men and resigned to Hell." After graduating from Baltimore Polytechnic Institute, he continued to study literature with a private tutor. In 1899 his father died, and M. went to work immediately as a newspaperman with the *Baltimore Herald.* Here his study of "life" rather than the liberal arts allowed him to "lay in all the worldly wisdom of a police lieutenant, a bartender, a shyster lawyer, and a midwife." He rose to the position of editor in chief, but switched to the *Baltimore Sunpapers* in 1906 and retained his connection with them for a lifetime. In 1908 he began doing book reviews for *Smart Set,* and by 1914 he was editing the magazine with George Jean Nathan (1882–1958) as well as writing monthly articles of five thousand words. This prodigious schedule lasted until 1923, when he launched the *American Mercury;* his work now became increasingly political, and his reputation as the scourge of public men grew to national proportions. His characteristic skepticism caused him to be somewhat eclipsed during the intensely committed period of the Great Depression, but he continued to comment unfavorably on the political scene while also pursuing his lifelong interests in the American language. He reported vigorously until suffering a stroke in 1948.

M.'s mind is an amalgam of Nietzschean exaltation and deadly comic skepticism about human progress. Great artists can create ecstatic experience for the few, but most men are trapped by their own smallness. M. spent his career anatomizing the "booboisie," the benighted joiners who fear and despise excellence in the arts and life. On a more abstract level, he rejected the pursuit of truth and attacked all forms of idealism. His critical work was accomplished in a razzle-dazzle style: one part Carlyle's outrageous diction, a second part Swift's abuse, and a final measure of nativist American plain talk reminiscent of Mark Twain.

M.'s range and relish for ideas and events are seemingly boundless: philosophy and literature, politics and popular culture, language and religion are explored with enthusiasm and relentless wit. *George Bernard Shaw: His Plays* (1905) and *The Philosophy of Friedrich Nietzsche* (1908) established his learning, but his manner of employing knowledge in the essay form is his distinctive attribute. As a literary critic he is neither original nor in any way systematic, yet his finest essays are keenly sensitive to the writer's special gifts and place in culture. In *A Book of Prefaces* (1917) he captures Theodore Dreiser's (q.v.) talent for "depicting the spirit in disintegration" and humorously analyzes his clumsy prose. Of the latter M. says "there are no charms of style to mitigate the rigours of these vast steppes and pampas of narration." When M. turns to the fate of American literature in "The National Letters," published in *Prejudices: Second Series* (1920), he employs a cultural argument—or more properly a tirade. American literature is "thin and watery" because of the national fear of ideas; this quality in turn is traced to democratic conformity and plutocratic domination. Such a diatribe is typical of M. and tends to draw us away from the texture of literature and into a criticism of life: one genteel critic's "lack of humor is almost that of a Fifth Avenue divine"; another moralistic type "tries to save Shakespeare for the right thinking by proving that he was an Iowa Methodist."

M.'s rough-and-tumble debunking is most effective when used on politicians, Elks Club members, and high-minded reformers. In *A Carnival of Buncombe* (1956), a collection of essays on the American presidency, as well as in numerous other political pieces, M. exposes the self-importance and inconsequence of men in the arena. In a 1921 essay called

"The Archangel Woodrow," Woodrow Wilson is described as a "pedagogue gone mashugga." In *A Carnival of Buncombe* Harding's windy, confused writing and thinking are labeled "Gamalielese." Calvin Coolidge's intelligence is compared to that of a "cast-iron lawn dog." The New Deal is dismissed as a "milch cow with 125,000,000 teats." This tradition of abuse is also found in "On Being an American," published in *Prejudices: Third Series* (1922). Here the idea of American civilization as the greatest clown show on earth is by no means as arresting as the style. M. the social critic becomes a Tocqueville lost in the funhouse of insulting language. Our selfishness is a matter of keeping a "place at the trough." America is a "glorious commonwealth of morons," a "paradise of back-slappers, of democrats, of mixers, of go-getters." Elsewhere in his six volumes of *Prejudices* (1919–27) M. swings at chiropractors, Southern culture, professors, farmers, fundamentalists, and reformers of all shades. These last he calls "wowsers"—people with a "divine commission to regulate or improve the rest of us."

M.'s more reflective longer works are no less controversial; in *Treatise on the Gods* (1930) religion is a con game; in *The American Language* (1919; rev. and enlarged ed., 1936) scholarship coexists with lively excursions into national bigotry, prudery, and stupidity.

While sometimes provincial and noisy, M. is a continuing resource for social critics, despisers of cant, and all lovers of extravagant language. He assaulted public issues with a penetrating style unrivaled in the American essay form.

FURTHER WORKS: *Ventures into Verses* (1903); *The Gist of Nietzsche* (1910); *What You Ought to Know about Your Baby* (1910, with Leonard Keen Hirshberg); *Men versus Man* (1910, with Robert Rives La Monte); *The Artists* (1912); *Europe after 8:15* (1914, with George Jean Nathan); *A Book of Burlesques* (1916); *A Little Book in C Major* (1916); *Pistols for Two* (1917, with George Jean Nathan); *Damn! A Book of Calumny* (1918); *In Defense of Women* (1919); *The American Credo* (1920); *The Literary Capital of the United States* (1920); *Heliogabalus* (1920, with George Jean Nathan); *Americana 1925* (1925); *Notes on Democracy* (1926); *Americana 1926* (1926); *James Branch Ca-* *bell* (1927); *Menckeneana: A Schimpflexikon* (1928); *Making a President* (1932); *Treatise on Right and Wrong* (1933); *The Sunpapers of Baltimore* (1937, with others); *Happy Days, 1880–1892* (1940); *Newspaper Days, 1899–1906* (1941); *A Dictionary of Quotations* (1942); *Heathen Days, 1890–1936* (1943); *The American Language, Supplement I* (1945); *Christmas Story* (1946); *The Days of H. L. M.* (1947); *The American Language, Supplement II* (1948); *A M. Chrestomathy* (1949); *The Vintage M.* (1955); *Minority Report: H. L. M.'s Notebooks* (1956); *The Bathtub Hoax, and Other Blasts and Bravos from the Chicago Tribune* (1958); *H. L. M. on Music* (1961); *Letters* (1961); *H. L. M.'s Smart Set Criticism* (1968); *A Choice of Days* (1981)

BIBLIOGRAPHY: Manchester, W., *Disturber of the Peace: The Life of H. L. M.* (1950); Wilson, E., "M.'s Democratic Man," *The Shores of Light* (1952), pp. 293–98; Cooke, A., Preface to *The Vintage M.* (1955), pp. v–xii; Angoff, C., *H. L. M.: A Portrait from Memory* (1956); Adler, B., *H. L. M.: The M. Bibliography* (1961); Nolte, W. H., *H. L. M.: Literary Critic* (1966); Wagner, P. M., *H. L. M.* (1966); Stenerson, D., *H. L. M.: Iconoclast from Baltimore* (1971); Cooke, A., "H. L. M.: The Public and the Private Face," *Six Men* (1977), pp. 93–133; Fecher, C. A., *M.: A Study of His Thought* (1978); Dorsey, J., ed., *On M.* (1980)

DAVID CASTRONOVO

MENON, Vallathol Narayana

Indian poet and translator (writing in Malayalam), b. 16 Oct. 1878, Chennara; d. 13 March 1958, Cochin

Born in the state of Kerala, M., usually known in India as Vallathol, studied Malayalam and Sanskrit, and Ayurvedic medicine. In 1902 he married and worked for a time as editor of the literary journal *Atmaposhini*. Around 1910 he became deaf. In 1927 M. started the Kerala Kalamandalam, a school for the training of performers of the traditional dance-drama known as Kathakali. He participated in the World Peace Conference at Warsaw in 1950 and later visited England, Russia, China, Singapore, and Malaya.

Along with N. Kumaran Asan (1873–1924) and Ulloor Parameswara Iyer (1877–

1949) M. was responsible for ushering in a romantic renascence in Malayalam literature. They began as imitators of the neoclassical tradition of the 19th c., but in the first quarter of the 20th they changed the trends chiefly through their *khanda kavyas* (short narratives) and *bhava kavyas* (lyrics).

M. was a prolific writer. In addition to verses on medicine and critical reviews, he has to his credit a substantial body of translations from Sanskrit into Malayalam. His reputation, however, rests largely on his poetry, which falls into two main groups: the narrative poems, such as *Chitrayogam* (1912; the strange union), *Bandhanastanaya Aniruddhan* (1914; Aniruddha in captivity), and *Magdalana Mariam* (1921; "Mary Magdalene," 1980); and the lyrics, mostly collected in *Sahitya manjari* (11 vols., 1916–70; cluster of literary flowers). These lyrics are written in a simple diction using mostly Dravidian meters, and cover a wide variety of themes such as political freedom, social equality, religious tolerance, domestic happiness, and the appreciation of the beauty of nature. His best poems are melodious and full of sensuous imagery. His later poems are marked by an increasing awareness of the plight of the poor.

A patriot, a humanist, a rebel with an insatiable zest for life, never an ascetic, always an optimist, M. embodies in his writings the tropical splendors of the land of his birth as well as the irrepressible adaptability of his people and the vibrant melody of their language.

FURTHER WORKS: *Badhiravilapam* (1910); *Ganapati* (1913); *Sishyanum makanum* (1918); *Kochu Sita* (1926); *Grantha viharam* (1927); *Acchanum makalum* (1941); *Vallathol Russiayil* (1951); *Abhivadyam* (1957). FURTHER VOLUMES IN ENGLISH: *Selected Poems* (1978); *The Song of the Peasants* (1978)

BIBLIOGRAPHY: George, K. M., *A Survey of Malayalam Literature* (1968), pp. 151–57; Chaitanya, K., *A History of Malayalam Literature* (1971), pp. 235–48; George, K. M., *Western Influence on Malayalam Language and Literature* (1972), pp. 120–30; Hrdayakumari, B., *Vallathol* (1974); Paniker, K. A., *A Short History of Malayalam Literature* (1977), pp. 50–53; Sarma, S., et al., eds., *Vallathol: A Centenary Perspective* (1978)

K. AYYAPPA PANIKER

MEREZHKOVSKY, Dmitry Sergeevich

Russian novelist, poet, dramatist, critic, and religious and social thinker, b. 14 Aug. 1865, St. Petersburg (now Leningrad); d. 7 Dec. 1941, Paris, France

After taking a degree in philosophy at St. Petersburg University, M. married the poet Zinaida Hippius (q.v.). Active in literary and religious circles, M. assisted in the establishment of the Religious Philosophical Meetings and founded the journal *Novy put* in 1903. In 1920 he and his wife fled the U.S.S.R. and settled in Paris.

M. began as a poet in the tradition of Russian populism but abandoned civic idealism to initiate the symbolist (q.v.) movement with his collection of verse *Simvoly* (1892; symbols) and the manifesto *O prichinakh upadka i o novykh techeniakh sovremennoy russkoy literatury* (1893; on the reasons for the decline and on new trends in contemporary Russian literature), in which he advocated mystic content, symbols, and artistic impressionism as the primary elements of the new art. In his verse he expressed his aristocratic outlook, his love of beauty, and his attraction to the attributes of Greek and Roman antiquity. Yet poetry was too constraining to permit full expression of M.'s ideas, and aestheticism could not long suppress his innate religiosity.

In his many essays and his excellent study *L. Tolstoy i Dostoevsky* (2 vols., 1901–2; *Tolstoy as Man and Artist, with an Essay on Dostoievski,* 1902) M. attempted to resolve the contradiction between the human virtues of Hellenic paganism and Christ's spirituality. Renouncing "historic" Christianity, he formulated his apocalyptic Christianity of the Third Testament, in which a synthesis would occur when history had come to an end. M. supported the revolutionary movement of 1905, and in his essays of the period, especially those in *Le tsar et la révolution* (1907; the tsar and the revolution), written with his wife and Dmitry Filosofov (1872–1940), which was published only in French, *Gryadushchy Kham* (1906; the coming Ham), and *Ne mir, no mech* (1908; not peace, but a sword), he called for a religious revolution to overthrow all forms of church and state and to establish a religious social order and the Kingdom of God on earth.

M.'s first trilogy of historical novels, *Smert bogov: Yulian Otstupnik* (1896; *The Death of the Gods,* 1901; later tr., *Julian the*

Apostate, 1929), *Voskresshie bogi: Leonardo da Vinci* (1901; *The Romance of Leonardo da Vinci, the Forerunner,* 1902; later tr., 1928) and *Antikhrist: Pyotr i Alexey* (1905; *Peter and Alexis,* 1906; later tr., 1931), which mark the apogee of his career and for which he is renowned in the West, not only surpasses his other belles-lettres in artistic merit, but also occupies a central position among his religiophilosophical works. He gives brilliant re-creations, lavishly embellished with archaeological details and enlivened by the introduction of numerous historical characters and incidents, of three dynamic eras: the reign of the 3rd-c. Roman emperor Julian the Apostate, the Renaissance, and the reign of Peter the Great. At the same time he invests the genre of the historical novel with philosophical argumentation. The primary aim of these novels is to show the conflict between Christianity and paganism in the past, to reveal why attempts at reconciliation failed, and to allow M. to present his panacea for the problem. Similarly, in his later historical novels, *Alexandr I* (1913; Alexander I) and *Chetyrnadtsatoe dekabrya* (1918; combined and abridged as *December the Fourteenth,* 1923), *Rozhdenie bogov: Tutankamon na Krite* (1925; *The Birth of the Gods,* 1926), and *Messia* (1928; *Akhnaton, King of Egypt,* 1927), as well as in his dramas, M. disseminated his latest socioreligious views in the guise of fiction.

As an émigré M. remained an outspoken opponent of Soviet Communism. Turning from belles-lettres after 1925, he continued to elaborate his religious thought in collections of aphorisms and in a series of biographies, primarily those of Christian saints and religious thinkers. Although he complained of being misunderstood both in Russia and Western Europe, M.'s recognition of modern man's spiritual dilemma and his efforts to find a solution to it add universal significance to his work.

FURTHER WORKS: *Stikhotvorenia, 1883–1887* (1888); *Novye stikhotvorenia, 1891–1895* (1896); *Vechnye sputniki* (1897); *"Ottsy i deti" russkogo liberalizma* (1901); *Stikhotvorenia, 1888–1902* (1902); *Lyubov silnee smerti* (1902); *Sobranie stikhov, 1883–1903* (1904); *Pushkin* (1906); *Gogol i chort* (1906); *Prorok russkoy revolyutsii* (1906); *Teper ili nikogda* (1906); *Pavel I* (1908); *Makov tsvet* (1908, with Zinaida Hippius and Dmitry Filosofov); *V tikhom omute* (1908); *M. Y.*

Lermontov: Poet sverkhchelovechestva (1909); *Sobranie stikhov, 1883–1910* (1910); *Bolnaya Rossia* (1910); *Lermontov; Gogol* (1911); *Polnoe sobranie sochineny* (17 vols., 1911–13); *Polnoe sobranie sochineny* (24 vols., 1914); *Bylo i budet: Dnevnik 1910–1914* (1915); *Dve tayny russkoy poezii: Nekrasov i Tyutchev* (1915); *Zavet Belinskogo* (1915); *Budet radost* (1916); *Zachem voskres* (1916); *Nevoenny dnevnik, 1914–1916* (1917); *Ot voyny k revolyutsii* (1917); *Perventsy svobody* (1917); *Romantiki* (1917); *Tsarevich Alexey* (1920); *Tsarstvo Antikhrista* (1921, with Z. Hippius, D. Filosofov, and Vladimir Zlobin); *Tayna tryokh: Egipet i Vavilon* (1925); *Napoleon* (1929; *Napoleon: A Study,* 1929); *Tayna zapada: Atlantida-Evropa* (1930; *The Secret of the West,* 1933); *Iisus neizvestny* (2 vols., 1931; *Jesus the Unknown,* 1933; *Jesus Manifest,* 1935); *Pavel, Avgustin* (1936); *Frantsisk Assissky* (1938); *Zhanna d Ark* (1938); *Dante* (1939); *Luther* (1941); *Pascal* (1941); *Calvin* (1942). FURTHER VOLUMES IN ENGLISH: *Daphnis and Chloe* (1905); *The Life Work of Calderon* (n.d.); *The Life Work of Henrik Ibsen* (n.d.); *The Life Work of Montaigne* (n.d.); *The Life Work of Pliny the Younger* (n.d.); *The Life Work of Flaubert* (n.d.); *The Life Work of Marcus Aurelius* (n.d.); *The Life Work of Dostoievski* (n.d.); *The Acropolis* (n.d.); *Joseph Pilsudski* (1921); *The Menace of the Mob* (1921); *Michael Angelo, and Other Sketches* (1930)

BIBLIOGRAPHY: Chuzeville, J., *D. M.* (1922); Matlaw, R. E., "The Manifesto of Russian Symbolism," *SEEJ,* 3 (1957), 177–91; Schmourlo, A. de, *Le pensée de M.* (1957); Bedford, C. H., *The Seeker: D. S. M.* (1975); Rosenthal, B. G., *M. and the Silver Age* (1975)

C. HAROLD BEDFORD

MERI, Veijo

Finnish novelist, short-story writer, dramatist, poet, and essayist, b. 31 Dec. 1928, Viipuri (now Vyborg, U.S.S.R.)

Son of a noncommissioned officer in the Finnish army who was promoted to commissioned rank for conspicuous gallantry during the war of 1941–44, M. grew up in garrison towns and graduated from secondary school in 1948, but did not pursue his studies further. Since the publication of his first collection of short stories, *Ettei maa viheriöisi*

267

(1954; so that the earth might not grow green), he has devoted himself entirely to literature. He was awarded the Finnish government's Sillanpää Prize for Literature in 1963, the government's Pro Finlandia Medal for artistic merit in 1967, the Nordic (Scandinavian) Council Literary Prize in 1973, and the honorary title of Artist Professor in 1975.

M. has stated that he was deeply marked by the wartime atmosphere in which he grew up; in the preface to the novel *Manillaköysi* (1957; *The Manila Rope,* 1964), for instance, he writes, in an ironic vein satirizing patriotic bombast: "Our generation had also been morally trained to be soldiers. . . . Life is a short and simple thing and requires of every individual that he live and die fearlessly for his country on land, on the sea, and in the air." M. indicates in this statement, by slight twists on patriotic rhetoric, that he does not take war and life in general quite so seriously as most people do. The adjective "absurd" has often been applied to his works; they are, however, not like Beckett's or Ionesco's (qq.v.). His characters are often energetic and articulate. But misunderstandings and lack of proper communication frustrate their efforts and lead to confused situations or sudden eruptions of violence. Such events may be taken humorously; M. himself says about humor in his essay "Huumorista ja humoristeista" (1968; on humor and humorists): "It is a bad mistake to think that humor is tragedy that falls flat. One-hundred-percent-effective tragedy is humor. When a person is shy and weak and cannot run very well, and, in spite of that, he is roughed up and chased, that is humor (Chaplin)."

War and military life, which are frequent subjects in M.'s earlier works, give him ample opportunity to describe meaningless violence which is rendered even more absurd by an insistence on rigid regulations—a nuisance that can be skillfully bypassed in peacetime, as in the novel *Yhden yön tarinat* (1967; the tales of one night), but is positively dangerous in war, as in another novel, *Sujut* (1961; quits), in which the main character is sentenced and nearly shot by his own officers because he fights efficiently, but not according to regulations.

Relations between the sexes play a larger part in M.'s works on civilian life than in those on war, as in, for example, the short-story collection *Sata metriä korkeat kirjaimet* (1969; letters one hundred meters high),

the title story of which was adapted for the stage as *Sano Oili vaan* (1974; just say Oili), and the novel *Jääkiekkoilijan kesä* (1980; the summer of an ice-hockey player). These relations are somewhat less frustrating than others described by M., for the partners often achieve an enjoyable sexual union; nevertheless, they find it difficult, if not impossible, to have a life together, not so much because of emotional incompatibility as because of difficulties arising from their surroundings. In some of M.'s works, the realistic depiction of characters and actions is at times interrupted by sudden visions of dreamlike landscapes, conceived not as symbols or metaphors but rather as projections of the character's psychic processes.

In recent years M. has published three collections of poems: *Mielen lähtölasku* (1976; the countdown of the mind), *Toinen sydän* (1978; another heart), and *Ylimpänä pieni höyhen* (1980; uppermost a small feather). His verse is a natural offshoot of his prose style: nonrealistic, although not fantastic images are combined with views of everyday life into a personal vision of the world.

M.'s nonfictional work covers a variety of subjects: his travels, people he has met, and famous figures of the past. His well-documented biography of the great 19th-c. Finnish writer who published under the pseudonym Aleksis Kivi (1834–1872), *Aleksis Stenvallin elämä* (1973; enlarged ed., 1975; the life of Aleksis Stenvall), was adapted for the stage as *Aleksis Kivi* (1974; Aleksis Kivi). Because of the conjectural elements in it, this work elicited adverse criticism from some literary scholars.

M. belongs to the generation of writers of the 1950s, who brought about considerable changes in Finnish literature, although they did not have a common program or literary theory. While no mere entertainer, M. is probably the most popular among them, as well as the most prolific through the present day. With his rough humor and his penetrating view of the absurdities of everyday life, he has contributed to demolishing a number of myths and taboos—especially about war and sex.

FURTHER WORKS: *Irralliset* (1959); *Vuoden 1918 tapahtumat* (1960); *Tilanteita* (1962); *Peiliin piirretty nainen* (1963); *Suomen paras näyttelija* (1963); *Tukikohta* (1964); *Sotamies Jokisen vihkiloma* (1965); *Everstin autonkuljettaja* (1966); *Kaksitoista artikkelia*

(1968); *Suku* (1968); *Neljä näytelmää* (1970); *Kersantin poika* (1971); *Morsiamen sisar ja muita novelleja* (1972); *Leiri* (1972); *Kuviteltu kuolema* (1974); *Kaksi komediaa* (1978); *Goethen tammi* (1978); *Tuusulan rantatie* (1981)

BIBLIOGRAPHY: Bolgár, M., and Sylvian, C., Afterword to V. M.'s *Une histoire de corde* [French tr. of *Manillaköysi*] (1962), pp. 139–45; Laitinen, K., "Väinö Linna and V. M.: Two Aspects of War," *BA,* 36 (1962), 365–67; Starkmann, A., "Ein großer finnischer Erzähler: Drei Werke V. M.s wurden ins Deutsche übersetzt," *Die Welt der Literatur,* 14 Sept. 1967, 1–2; Stormbom, N.-B., "V. M. and the New Finnish Novel," *ASR,* 55 (1967), 264–69; Dauenhauer, R., "The Literature of Finland," *LitR,* 14, 1 (1970), 18–22; Ahokas, J. A., "The Short Story in Finnish Literature," in Dauenhauer, R., and Binham, P., eds., *Snow in May: An Anthology of Finnish Writing 1945–1972* (1978), pp. 35–37

JAAKKO A. AHOKAS

MERRILL, James

American poet, novelist, dramatist, and essayist, b. 3 March 1926, New York, N.Y.

M.'s father, Charles E. Merrill, was a wealthy financier and founder of America's premier investment firm. This accident of fate was decisive in two ways: it allowed M. the luxury of cultivating a considerable poetic talent without any other career or any financial restraints, and the connection to fabulous wealth helped to develop in him a sense of the extraordinary—the mythical. Educated in both America and Europe, beginning with undergraduate years at Amherst College (B.A., 1947), M. worked hard at the traditional stanzaic patterns, meter, and rhyme of English poetry. He studied music and classical and modern languages and read extensively in literature and the arts.

While he has worked with success at both drama—*The Immortal Husband* (1956); *The Bait* (1960)—and the novel—*The Seraglio* (1957), *The (Diblos) Notebook* (1965)—M. has most distinguished himself as a lyric poet in the pure sense of poetry as rooted in musical expression. Although his sheer mastery of prosody was evident from the earliest volumes—*The Black Swan* (1946), *First Poems* (1951), *The Country of a Thousand Years of Peace* (1959)—their highly formal and, to

some extent, hermetic poems revealed the strain of imposing the traditional forms of prosody on contemporary English. M. persisted in his poetic craftmanship, and several volumes later—by the time of *The Fire Screen* (1969) and *Braving the Elements* (1972)—critics and award committees agreed that he had become a master of lyric expression. Many critics feel he is the finest lyric voice in America today, and some have claimed him to be the finest lyric poet since Yeats (q.v.).

Until recently M.'s themes have been the familiar ones of lyric poetry: autobiography, nature, the particularities of time and place (especially his several homes), the adventures of travel, the stages of love and death, the ecstasies and agonies of encounter and departure, and his memory of literature and the other arts. His approach to these themes is essentially a combination of 17th-c. English metaphysical poetry, the great romantic odes, and French symbolism (q.v.): nature and the arts are both symbolic of the spirit, words carefully chosen and used are pregnant with presences; meditated on long enough through symbols and words, nature reveals transcendent messages, and a series of lovers or landscapes coalesce into a platonic essence. Several of the poems in *Braving the Elements*—"Willoware Cup," "Up and Down"—and *Divine Comedies* (1976)— "*Lost in Translation*"—are masterpieces in the genre. These lyrics are so multifaceted and highly polished that they reflect almost any light the reader brings to them.

In addition to this lyric voice, M. has long cultivated a narrative voice in verse: long, discursive narrative poems like "From the Cupola" (1963), "Days of 1935" (1972), and "Days of 1971" (1972). These poems, which like his plays and novels compound myth and biography—sometimes indistinguishably— have found their fulfillment recently in a three-volume visionary epic: *The Book of Ephraim* (printed in *Divine Comedies*), *Mirabell: Books of Number* (1978), and *Scripts for the Pageant* (1980). In this extraordinary but flawed work, M., through the medium of a Ouija board, communicates with the dead and with the spirits and forces of the universe, including God Biology. In an endlessly unfurling mock-heroic pageant, M. has all his questions about the nature of the universe and the evolution of life answered. The epic, whose three parts are published together under the title *Changing Lights at Sandover*

(1982), delineates dazzling contemporary analogies to Dante's vision while gathering into itself practically every form of the pop-spiritualism of modern times, including ESP, reincarnation, mediums, astrology, and numerology.

In its autobiographical dimensions, the epic serves as M.'s poetics—revisiting at length the scenes and personae of his life—as well as the first epic with a specifically homosexual content. On another level, it is one of the few apocalyptic epics since the Bible to respond to the evolving modes—from animism through monotheism to the mysteries of contemporary science—of man's spiritual awareness. Ironically, to achieve this vision, M. has surrendered his miraculous poetic craft by accepting the mechanistic dictates of the Ouija board. But lyric poems contained within the epic as well as several published subsequently indicate that M.'s lyric voice is still masterfully mature: it is somewhat looser and therefore broader in its scope; somewhat less hermetic and therefore closer to the luminous wisdom of the greatest lyricism.

FURTHER WORKS: *Short Stories* (1954); *Selected Poems* (1961); *Water Street* (1962); *Nights and Days* (1966); *The Yellow Pages* (1974); *From the First Nine: Poems 1946–1978* (1982)

BIBLIOGRAPHY: Yenser, S., on *Braving the Elements, Poetry,* 122 (1973), 163–68; Sáez, R., "J. M.'s Oedipal Fire," *Parnassus,* 3, 1 (1974), 159–84; Kalstone, D., "J. M.," *Five Temperaments* (1977), pp. 77–128; Yenser, S., on *Mirabell, YR,* 68 (1979), 556–66; Vendler, H., "V Work," *New Yorker,* 3 Sept. 1979, 95–105; Howard, R., *Alone with America,* enl. ed. (1980), pp. 386–441; Lehman, D., and Berger, C., *J. M.: Essays in Criticism* (1982)

RICHARD SÁEZ

MERWIN, W(illiam) S(tanley)

American poet and translator, b. 30 Sept. 1927, New York, N.Y.

Son of a Presbyterian minister, M. grew up in Scranton, Pennsylvania, and attended Princeton (A.B., 1947), where R. P. Blackmur (q.v.) was his mentor. M. moved to Europe in 1949 to work as a tutor; in 1950 he tutored Robert Graves's (q.v.) son. In Lon-

don (1951–54), he did translations of Spanish and French classics for the BBC Third Programme. Returning to America in 1956, M. wrote plays for The Poets' Theatre in Cambridge, Massachusetts, and served as poetry editor of *The Nation* (1961–63) before going again to France. Since 1968 he has lived in the U.S.

M.'s poetry reveals a Wallace Stevens-like quest for harmony, for a satisfactory statement of the relationship of man's order to natural order. His work, therefore, is process-oriented, as the motifs of the aborted journey and of the inadequately defined experience suggest. In his early work, for example, *A Mask for Janus* (1952), M.'s search is inhibited by his virtuosity in traditional, inherited techniques and forms. His skepticism about the possibility of a reconciliation between man and nature produce the bleakness of vision and the humorlessness in his poetry.

M. wrote in the essay "On Open Form" (1967) that poetry requires "an unduplicative resonance, something that would be like an echo except that it is repeating no sound. Something that always belonged to it; its sense and its conformation before it entered words. . . . poetry seems to have to keep reverting to its naked condition, where it touches on all that is unrealized."

In *The Drunk in the Furnace* (1960), M. broke away from traditional poetic structures and conventions and began to compose poetry better suited to his personal vision. The new style, marked by colloquialism and syntactical structures that permitted greater ambiguity, strikingly resembles that of Robert Frost (q.v.). *The Moving Target* (1963), which won the National Book Award, confirmed the new direction M. had taken. In his indictment of "a society whose triumphs one after the other emerge as new symbols of death, and that feeds itself by poisoning the earth," M. bears comparison to Robinson Jeffers (q.v.).

Miner's Pale Children (1970) and *Houses and Travelers* (1977) include numerous stories and sketches that contain mythic, fabulous, and legendary elements in a prose style that is essentially poetic. M. has also been a prolific translator of works both classic and esoteric.

Although M. has published widely in various journals and continues to appear in *The New Yorker,* he has not received much attention from the general public, who may find his sobriety and sophistication to be more vexatious than solacing. Most other poets and the critics, however, have praised M.'s craft and intellect. Useful comparisons and contrasts between M.'s work and that of others remain to be made before M.'s final position in American letters will be defined.

FURTHER WORKS: *The Dancing Bears* (1954); *Green with Beasts* (1956); *Darkling Child* (1956, with Dido Milroy); *Favor Island* (1957); Lope Felix de Vega Carpio, *Punishment without Vengeance* (1958, trans.); *The Poem of the Cid* (1959, trans.); *Spanish Ballads* (1960, trans.); *The Satires of Persius* (1960, trans.); *The Gilded West* (1961); *The Life of Lazarillo de Tormes* (1962, trans.); *The Song of Roland* (1963, trans.); *The Lice* (1967); *Three Poems* (1968); *Selected Translations: 1948–1968* (1968); *Animae* (1969); *Transparence of the World: Poems of Jean Follain* (1969, trans.); *Voices: Selected Writings of Antonio Porchia* (1969, trans.); Pablo Neruda, *Twenty Love Poems* (1969, trans.); *The Carrier of Ladders* (1970); *Writings to an Unfinished Accompaniment* (1973); *Asian Figures* (1973, trans.); Osip Mandelstam, *Selected Poems* (1974, trans. with Clarence Brown); *The Compass Flower* (1977); *Sanskrit Love Poems* (1977, trans. with J. Moussaieff Masson); Euripides, *Iphigenia at Aulis* (1978, trans. with George E. Dimock, Jr.); *Selected Translations: 1968–1978* (1979); *Unframed Originals: Recollections* (1982)

BIBLIOGRAPHY: Benston, A. N., "Myth in the Poetry of W. S. M.," in Hungerford, E., ed., *Poets in Progress* (1962), pp. 179–204; Howard, R., *Alone with America: Essays on the Art of Poetry in the United States since 1950* (1969), pp. 349–81; Atlas, J., "Diminishing Returns: The Writings of W. S. M.," in Shaw, R. B., ed., *American Poetry since 1960: Some Critical Perspectives* (1973), pp. 69–81; Davis, C. C., "Time and Timelessness in the Poetry of W. S. M.," *MPS,* 6 (1975), 224–36; Watkins, E., "W. S. M.: A Critical Accompaniment," *Boundary 2,* 4 (1976), 187–200; Christhilf, M., "W. S. M.: The Poet as Creative Conservator," *ModA,* 23 (1979), 167–77; Contoski, V., "W. S. M.: Rational and Irrational Poetry," *LitR,* 22 (1979), 309–320

ARTHUR B. COFFIN

MEXICAN LITERATURE

Mexican literature in the 19th c. was dominated by romanticism, a movement well suited to the national character as well as to the historical situation of the time. Toward 1880 realist and modernist (q.v.) writers reacted against the excesses of the romanticists, occupying the literary stage for approximately the next thirty years. Although both of these schools would leave their mark on future generations, it was the aesthetically oriented elite-minded modernist poets such as Manuel Gutiérrez Nájera (1859–1895), Salvador Díaz Mirón (1853–1928), Amado Nervo (q.v.), and José Juan Tablada (1871–1945) who produced works of the most lasting literary value. Influenced by the French Parnassians and symbolists (q.v.), these writers emphasized perfection of form while experimenting with new metrical rhythms in order to enhance the flexibility and musicality of the Spanish language. They also sought to revitalize Spanish American literature by injecting exotic or fantastic elements, thus rendering its content more cosmopolitan and universal.

The political regime of Porfirio Díaz, which was overthrown by the revolution of 1910, coincided with the domination of Mexican education by positivism, a scientifically oriented philosophy imported from France. In 1908 Justo Sierra (1848–1912), Mexico's leading intellectual of the time, rejected positivism for the more subjective philosophy of Henri Bergson (q.v.), and the following year there appeared a group of writers known as the Atheneum of Youth, who sought not only to strengthen Mexican ties with classical European thought but also to create a culture more in tune with the realities of Mexican life. The literature of the thirty years between 1915 and 1945 is characterized by two basic trends: in fiction, the realistic dramatization of social issues; and in poetry, the search for innovative forms.

Fiction

The Mexican Revolution and its aftermath provided the warp and woof of many novels, the best of which was *Los de abajo* (1916; *The Underdogs,* 1929) by Mariano Azuela (q.v.). This naturalistic epic captures the immediacy of the revolution in a montage of fast-moving scenes depicting the initial enthusiasm, the brutality, and the eventual disillusionment of its exhausted peasant participants. Although often referred to as an epic, it also conveys the author's disenchantment with the revolution, which he suspects will be betrayed by a new class of oppressors. Another fine account of the revolution is *El águila y la serpiente* (1928; *The Eagle and the Serpent,* 1930) by Martín Luis Guzmán (q.v.), whose role as Pancho Villa's secretary enabled him to observe the manipulation of power by leading figures of the movement.

The most outstanding political novel of this period is Guzmán's *La sombra del caudillo* (1929; in the leader's shadow), a roman à clef based on a power struggle during the regime (1924–28) of President Plutarco Elías Calles. *Indigenista* fiction, which describes the lives of oppressed Indians, is best represented by *El resplandor* (1937; *Sunburst,* 1944) by Mauricio Magdaleno (q.v.), and *El indio* (1935; *El Indio,* 1937) by Gregorio López y Fuentes (q.v.). José Rubén Romero's (q.v.) excellent picaresque novel *La vida inútil de Pito Pérez* (1938; *The Futile Life of Pito Pérez,* 1967) satirizes the society that emerged after the Revolution.

Mexican fiction of the 1940s and 1950s was characterized by universal themes and structural innovations reflecting the intellectual and social impact of World War II. Most representative of this period are four gifted writers: José Revueltas (1914–1976), who focused on human suffering and injustice in works such as *El luto humano* (1943; *The Stone Knife,* 1947); Agustín Yáñez (q.v.), whose *Al filo del agua* (1947; *The Edge of the Storm,* 1963) is considered a landmark novel because of its Freudian analysis of repressed villagers just before the revolution of 1910; Juan Rulfo (q.v.), whose complex masterpiece *Pedro Páramo* (1955; *Pedro Páramo,* 1959) evokes the past of a ghost town and its corrupt political boss; and Juan José Arreola (q.v.), a cosmopolitan humorist known above all for his impeccably stylized philosophical tales collected in *Confabulario* (1952; *Confabulario, and Other Inventions,* 1964).

During the past twenty years an unprecedented explosion of talent in fiction has tended to overshadow other genres in Mexico. Carlos Fuentes (q.v.) has emerged not only as the nation's leading novelist but also as a major figure of international stature. His experiments with a wide variety of techniques and his broad knowledge of philosophy and other literatures have enhanced his ability to capture the Mexican experience in universal terms. Two of Fuentes's finest novels are *La muerte de Artemio Cruz* (1962; *The Death of Artemio Cruz,* 1964), in which a dying Mexican tycoon relives the existential decisions of his life that ultimately determine his essence; and *Terra Nostra* (1975; *Terra nostra,* 1976), a quest for the origins of absolute authority in Hispanic America through an insightful examination of European culture.

After Rulfo, Arreola, and Fuentes, Mexico's most important living writers of fiction are Vicente Leñero, Salvador Elizondo, Gustavo Sainz, and José Agustín (qq.v.). Leñero shares Fuentes's preoccupation with literary technique, as evidenced by *Los albañiles* (1964; the bricklayers), a fascinating murder mystery with profound social and philosophical overtones. Like Fuentes, Elizondo is a cosmopolitan man of letters whose most intriguing novel, *Farabeuf* (1965; Farabeuf), demonstrates his ability to assimilate foreign philosophies and techniques such as those of the New Novel (q.v.). Sainz and Agustín typify the Onda (Wave), a movement of young, irreverent writers of the 1960s whose works mock the time-honored values of the establishment. Typical examples of the Wave are Sainz's *Gazapo* (1965; *Gazapo,* 1968) and Agustín's *De perfil* (1966; from the side). Now more mature, these two authors are continuing to impress their reading public with avant-garde portraits of disoriented youths caught up in the chaotic life of the burgeoning Mexican capital.

Many other novelists have contributed to the enrichment of contemporary Mexican fiction. In works such as *Las muertas* (1977; the dead ones) and *Dos crímenes* (1979; two crimes) Jorge Ibargüengoitia (b. 1928) demonstrates his mastery of irony by portraying characters trapped in a labyrinthine world beyond their comprehension. Unlike Ibargüengoitia, who fabricates clear, well-constructed plots, Sergio Fernández (b. 1926) relies on stylistic devices likely to appeal to the more sophisticated reader. His novels, a fine example of which is *Los peces* (1968; the fish), express the disillusionment and alienation so characteristic of life in a modern metropolis. In his complex, prize-winning *Palinuro de México* (1977; Palinuro of Mexico) Fernando del Paso (b. 1935) utilizes classical myth as a point of departure for his treatment of the massacre by army troops of demonstrating students in Tlatelolco Square in 1968. Mexico's best-known living female novelist, Elena Poniatowska (b. 1933), has sensitively captured the atmosphere of the Mexican Revolution in her fine novel *Hasta no verte Jesús mío* (1969; farewell, my Jesus), which dramatizes an uneducated woman's experiences during the uprising. And, although hardly known for his literary artistry, Luis Spota (b. 1925) is Mexico's most popular writer, having published more than twenty best sellers on subjects ranging from bullfighting and wetbacks to the Tlatelolco tragedy and urban guerrilla warfare. One of Spota's most successful novels is *Casi el paraíso* (1956; *Almost Paradise,* 1964), an ingeniously structured satire of Mexico's shallow, hypocritical nouveaux riches.

Poetry

The works of Enrique González Martínez (q.v.) and Ramón López Velarde (1888–1921) best exemplify the poetry of the postmodernist period (1915–22). González Martínez's famous poem "Tuércele el cuello al cisne" (1911; "Wring the Neck of the Swan," 1958) expresses his desire to replace the superficial artistry of modernism with a movement of deeper philosophical content symbolized by the meditative owl; and "La suave patria" (1919; "Gentle Fatherland," 1943) by López Velarde represents a richly symbolic, impressionistic mural that not only captures the soul of Mexican life but also marks a complete break with the preceding generation.

The most significant avant-garde schools of poetry are the Estridentistas (the Strident Ones), who flourished 1922–27 and whose tenets reflect Italian futurism and Spanish ultraism (q.v.), and the Contemporáneos (Contemporaries), who flourished 1928–31, a group of talented poets consisting of Jaime Torres Bodet (1902–1974), Xavier Villaurrutia (q.v.), Salvador Novo (1904–1974), Carlos Pellicer (1899–1977), and José Gorostiza (1901–1973). Inspired by Tablada, González Martínez, and López Velarde, as well as by numerous European writers, the Contemporáneos ignored social problems and concentrated on aesthetic questions, such as the manipulation of free verse and the creation of fresh imagery. The most memorable of the works produced by this school is Gorostiza's long poem *Muerte sin fin* (1939; *Death without End,* 1969), which conveys an existentialist (q.v.) awareness of, and fascination with, nothingness. In a somewhat similar vein, Vi-

llaurrutia's *Nostalgia de la muerte* (1938; nostalgia of death) views death as a previous form of life, a kind of limbo or womb to which man longs to return.

The undisputed leader of postvanguardist poetry, a movement dating back to the late 1930s, is Octavio Paz (q.v.), Mexico's most esteemed living author. The underlying theme in Paz's work is the quest for a better world, a vaster and more magnificent world in which time is obliterated and man no longer experiences existential anguish. This quest is perhaps best expressed in the poem *Piedra de sol* (1957; *Sunstone* 1963), which records life's endless cycles of ecstatic moments and their inevitable collapse in the face of everyday banality. Also characteristic of Paz's verse is his use of surrealistic imagery to capture a dialectical reality generated by opposites, such as life and death, the real and the masked self, progressive and static time.

Outstanding contemporaries of Paz are Efraín Huerta (1914–1982) and Alí Chamucero (b. 1918), the former for his masterful use of popular language to depict the modern metropolis, the latter for his remarkable perfection of form and evocative leitmotifs. During the 1950s four exceptionally gifted poets began their careers: Rubén Bonifaz Nuño (b. 1923), Jaime García Terrés (b. 1924), Jaime Sabines (b. 1925), and Rosario Castellanos (q.v.). Despite their many differences, these writers share a number of traits, including the description of everyday life, the rejection of rhetorical language, a belief in the supremacy of the metaphor, and a preoccupation with solitude and time. The poets of the 1960s present themes similar to those of their immediate predecessors, but their imagery suggests the influence of surrealism (q.v.), and their styles tend to be more literary and subjective. Prominent representatives of this generation are Marco Antonio Montes de Oca (b. 1932), José Emilio Pacheco (b. 1939), and Homero Aridjis (b. 1940).

The Essay

The essay has been a source of cultural enrichment in Mexico throughout the 20th c. The group known as the Atheneum of Youth included such masters as the eminent professor and philosopher Antonio Caso (1883–1946), who inspired the younger generation to abandon positivistic materialism for spiritual values; the political activist and mystical thinker José Vasconcelos (1882–1959), whose famous treatise *La raza cósmica* (1925; the cosmic race) views Latin America as a kind of melting pot for the emergence of a new race; and Alfonso Reyes (q.v.), the brilliant stylist and cosmopolitan humanist.

The first in a long series of essays on the Mexican character is *El perfil del hombre y la cultura en México* (1934; *Profile of Man and Culture in Mexico,* 1962) by Samuel Ramos (1897–1959). According to Ramos, Mexicans should strive for a more universal culture but, at the same time, for a culture that expresses the national soul and will. He inspired a group of thinkers known as the Hyperion, which, under the leadership of the well-known philosopher Leopoldo Zea (b. 1912), continued his investigations of what it means to be Mexican. The most significant examination of this subject is Octavio Paz's *El laberinto de la soledad* (1950; *The Labyrinth of Solitude,* 1961), a penetrating psychological study of the effects of the past on his fellow countrymen's search for identity in the 20th c. Paz is also a perceptive analyst of Mexican politics, his most original and interesting pieces having appeared in *Posdata* (1970; *The Other Mexico,* 1972). And his contributions to literary criticism are evidenced by his recent founding of two journals of exceptionally high quality: *Plural* (1971) and *Vuelta* (1976).

Drama

Mexican playwrights produced little of significance prior to 1928, when the experimental Ulises Theater was formed by Xavier Villaurrutia, Salvador Novo, and Celestino Gorostiza (1904–1967). These talented writers, together with their famous colleague Rodolfo Usigli (q.v.), eventually emerged as the creators of the modern Mexican theater. Perhaps the most noteworthy drama of this period is Usigli's *El gesticulador* (1943; the impostor), a gripping portrayal of the Mexican identity crisis that would be explored in greater depth by Octavio Paz. *El gesticulador* also illustrates the role of myth in Mexican history, that is, the emergence of a charismatic figure who embodies the Mexican Revolution and thus attains mythical stature.

During the past three decades the Mexican theater has developed a repertoire of works focusing on both national and universal issues. The nation's leading contemporary playwright is Emilio Carballido (b. 1925),

whose works range from the realistic comedy of manners to a more poetic drama characterized by the irrational and the fantastic. His masterpiece, *Yo también hablo de la rosa* (1966; *I Too Speak of the Rose,* 1971) is representative of much of his production. *Los frutos caídos* (1956; the fallen fruit) by Luisa Josefina Hernández (b. 1928) is typical of her representations of the emptiness and futility of middle-class life, and Elena Garro (b. 1920) combines a magical, poetic reality with elements of social protest in her best plays, *La mudanza* (1959; the move) and *Los perros* (1965; the dogs).

The works of three additional playwrights have continued to broaden the aesthetic scope of the Mexican stage. Vicente Leñero has achieved considerable success as the initiator of documentary theater, a genre that seeks to edu- cate the public by constructing dramatic plots on materials taken from the news media and court records. A notable example is *El juicio* (1972; the trial), a taut representation of the 1928 trial and conviction of President-Elect Alvaro Obregón's assassins. In contrast to this objective art form, Carlos Fuentes's *Todos los gatos son pardos* (1970; all the cats are dark) has imaginatively probed Mexico's mythical past in order to explain present-day phenomena. And absurdist works such as *Nada como el piso 16* (1977; nothing like the sixteenth floor) by Maruxa Vilalta (b. 1932) satirize the effects of alienation in a complex, urbanized society.

Mexican literature in the 20th c. reveals a remarkable sensitivity to national realities, reflecting above all the upheaval wrought by the revolution of 1910 and the changes brought about by the urban growth of the post-World War II years. This sensitivity is further illustrated by the great quantity of essays, poetry, and fiction protesting the massacre of students in 1968. The emergence of numerous gifted writers in a society fraught with political, social, and intellectual tensions would seem to portend a bright future for Mexican letters.

BIBLIOGRAPHY: Martínez, J. L., ed., Introduction to *The Modern Mexican Essay* (1965), pp. 3–19; Brushwood, J. S., *Mexico in Its Novel* (1966); Millán, M. del C., *Diccionario de escritores mexicanos* (1967); Nomland, J. B., *Teatro mexicano contemporáneo (1900–1950)* (1967); González Peña, C., *History of Mexican Literature,* 3rd ed.

(1968); Leal, L., *Panorama de la literatura mexicana actual* (1968); Sommers, J., *After the Storm: Landmarks of the Modern Mexican Novel* (1968); Langford, W. M., *The Mexican Novel Comes of Age* (1971); Usigli, R., *Mexico in Its Theater* (1976); Debicki, A. P., ed., Introduction to *Antología de la poesía mexicana moderna* (1977), pp. 11–30; Larson, R., *Fantasy and Imagination in the Mexican Narrative* (1977); Agustín, J., "Contemporary Mexican Fiction," *University of Denver Occasional Papers,* No. 1 (1978), 15–29

GEORGE R. MCMURRAY

MEYRINK, Gustav

(born Gustav Meyer) Austrian novelist and short-story writer, b. 19 Jan. 1868, Vienna; d. 4 Dec. 1932, Starnberg, Germany

M. was the illegitimate son of a Bavarian actress and a Swabian baron. After secondary schooling in Munich and business college in Prague, he joined a Prague banking firm. A growing interest in the occult and the esoteric led him to the study of the cabala, yoga, and Rosicrucianism. In 1902 M. went bankrupt; he subsequently left Prague for Vienna, and after a year moved on to Munich, making a not always easy living from his literary endeavors. From 1911 until his death M. made his home in Starnberg, near Munich.

M., best known for his novel *Der Golem* (1915; *The Golem,* 1928), began his literary career as a contributor to the satirical weekly *Simplicissimus,* in which his first published story appeared in 1901. The collection *Des deutschen Spießers Wunderhorn* (3 vols., 1913; the German philistine's magic horn) shows M. a mordant critic of society. Through caricature and parody that abound in grotesque and fantastic elements, he unmasks the spiritual hollowness and philistine mediocrity of bourgeois civilization, with its narrowminded prejudices; the military and jingoism are favorite targets of his caustic wit. This satirical verve is, however, only one aspect of M.'s cultural criticism, which springs from his grave concern over the despiritualization of life in the name of positivism and materialism. His turning toward the realities of man's inner life, his interest in the mysteries of esoteric teachings and the occult, must be seen as its complementary aspect.

Der Golem, the novel that made M. fam-

ous, can be read on two levels. It can be taken as a mystery, in which M., with an unerring flair for effect, fuses sensational, fantastic, grotesque, and nightmarish elements to create the uncanny atmosphere of a horror story, whereby the old Prague ghetto acquires a mysterious life of its own. But it can also be read as a novel of initiation, as the dream story of Athanasius Pernath's awakening to a higher life according to the mysteries of the cabala.

The theme of spiritual awakening is central to M.'s other novels as well. They can be characterized as esoteric novels of education, depicting rites of passage to a higher, cosmic awareness, inspired by a variety of arcane teachings: yoga in *Das grüne Gesicht* (1916; the green face), Taoism in *Der weiße Dominikaner* (1921; the white Dominican), alchemy and tantrism in *Der Engel vom westlichen Fenster* (1927; the angel of the west window). In his quest for spiritual self-knowledge, the elect often becomes conscious of the greater possibilities within himself through the experience of living past lives, identifying himself with different manifestations of unique spiritual states of being.

Beginning with *Das grüne Gesicht* M. adopted an ever more pronounced attitude of initiate and prophet, to the detriment of the literary qualities of the later novels, which often show a certain lack of balance between didactic intention and artistic realization. His earlier works, however, notably his short stories, show M. at his best, as a master of fantasy.

FURTHER WORKS: *Der heiße Soldat* (1903); *Orchideen* (1904); *Das Wachsfigurenkabinett* (1907); *Jörn Uhl und Hilligenlei* (1908); *Der Sanitätsrat* (1912, with Roda Roda); *Bubi* (1912, with Roda Roda); *Die Sklavin aus Rhodos* (1912, with Roda Roda); *Die Uhr* (1914, with Roda Roda); *Der Kardinal Napellus* (1915); *Fledermäuse* (1916); *Der Löwe Alois, und andere Geschichten* (1917); *Walpurgisnacht* (1917); *Gesammelte Werke* (6 vols., 1917); *Der violette Tod, und andere Novellen* (1922); *An der Schwelle des Jenseits* (1925); *Die heimtückischen Champignons, und andere Geschichten* (1925); *Meister Leonhard* (1925); *Das Haus zur letzten Laterne* (1973)

BIBLIOGRAPHY: Sperber, H., *Motiv und Wort bei M.* (1918); Frank E., *G. M.: Werk und Wirkung* (1957); Bithell, J., *Modern German Literature 1880–1950* (1959), pp. 72–74;

Schwarz, T., "Die Bedeutung des Phantastisch-Mystischen bei G. M.," *WB*, 12 (1966), 716–19; Schödel, S., "Über G. M. und die phantastische Literatur," in Burger, H. O., ed., *Studien zur Trivialliteratur* (1968), pp. 209–24; Abret, H., *G. M., conteur* (1976); Aster, E., *Personalbibliographie von G. M.* (1980)

FRIEDHELM RICKERT

MICHAUX, Henri

Belgian poet and essayist (writing in French), b. 24 May 1899, Namur

M. grew up in Brussels. An introspective child out of step with reality, by his own account estranged from his parents, he discovered early his imaginative gifts, read extensively, and for a while felt a deep affinity with several mystical writers. But he was also drawn to scientific literature, and prepared to study medicine; then, at the age of twenty-one, signed up as a sailor. A reading of Lautréamont's (1846–1870) *Maldoror* rekindled M.'s desire to write and inspired his first essays, published by the Brussels review *Le disque vert.* In 1924, having settled in Paris, M. began painting. To support himself he worked as teacher and secretary and in 1938–39, as coeditor of the mystical review *Hermès.* Despite extended travels, he kept abreast of the Parisian artistic movements and for a while frequented the surrealists (q.v.). Since the death of his wife in 1948 M. has lived in profound solitude in Paris, writing and painting.

M.'s work stems from psychological, not aesthetic concerns. It seeks access to man's inner realm and focuses on the experience of existing in a flawed universe. *Qui je fus* (1927; who I was), M.'s first full-length work, a mixture of poetry, prose, and prose poems, opposes the inchoate flux within the self to the outer space of fixed forms, codes, and orderly processes and opts for the former as the ground of poetry. *Écuador* (1929; *Ecuador: A Travel Journal by H. M.,* 1970), a journal of travel in South America, is a work of severed contacts. It traces M.'s personal trajectory away from the experiences of the journey, which he found disappointing. *Un barbare en Asie* (1933; *A Barbarian in Asia,* 1949), M.'s second book of reportage, recounts a more successful trip to the Far East. It retains the picturesqueness of a travelogue, and through a series of essays on ideas and

attitudes creates a narrative of visual and moral perception where facts are used as a point of departure for self-analysis. The work signaled M.'s break with Western culture, hastened by his discovery of Hindu spirituality.

Mes propriétés (1929; my properties) opened an era of exploration of mental and psychic phenomena that extends through five collections, ending with *L'espace du dedans* (1944; *Selected Writings: The Space Within,* 1951), a selection of tales, verse, and prose poems from the 1927–40 period. Originating in the will to extend consciousness, these highly charged, fluid texts explore unconscious drives, wishes, impulses, and emotional turbulences and define the self as a momentary point of balance amid divergent forces, threatened by both inner formlessness, that is, nonbeing, and external restraints. To the latter M. opposes the gesture of refusal. He structures his poems so as to negate the world and creates imaginary zones—places of change, of births and deaths of various objects, of shifting relationships, of rising tensions, which are reworked into concrete manifestations of inner states, into dream images, myths, monsters, allegorical figures, animal species.

In M.'s work internal projections also assume human shapes, bearing the name of Plume, among others. Plume, the bewildered protagonist and victim of tragicomic adventures, represents man's alienation and serves as an artistic mask ensuring painless exchanges between the poet and the outside world. While the Plume stories relieve tensions through humor, other texts of this period maintain a turbulent, aggressive tone. Rhythms surge, strike, hammer; images explode under pressure; sentences are pushed beyond the limits of conventional syntax, giving rise to moments of extreme tension between thought and language. M. puts to the test the very possibility of verbal articulation.

The imaginary voyages of *Ailleurs* (1948; elsewhere) impose order upon mental chaos through the creation of a narrative. Here M. portrays half-real, half-imaginary lands, inhabited by semicorporeal creatures whose life and gestures reenact man's inner conflicts. In the earlier *Au pays de la magie* (1941; in the land of magic), the workings of the poetic mind are explored. Opening up to humanitarian concerns, *Ici Poddema* (1948; Poddema calling) captures the horrors of contemporary society. Taken together, these imaginary voyages hold a mirror up to human strengths and aberrations; while maintaining a spirit of play, they propose a serious reevaluation of human nature.

M.'s poetry written between 1940 and 1948 brings together two notions: creativity and power. In 1940 he fled to southern France to escape the German occupation and there pursued a course of internal resistance that surfaced in the commitment to human values of his wartime poems. *Épreuves-exorcismes* (1945; trials-exorcisms) pits poetic language against the war, unfolding a passionate litany of human suffering and directing anathemas against man's demonic skills. It transforms the desire to oppose into the very act of opposition, giving birth to a poetry of concentrated will, of action. Poets, M. believed, can reach a threshold of intensity beyond which thoughts and feelings assume power. Their poems become actions undertaken against evil, explosive charges introduced into the very center of suffering, acts of magical retaliation. To M., they are also a healing response to life's hurts, a means to achieve liberation.

Beginning in 1948 Promethean attitudes gave way to a more willing acceptance of the world, and ultimately to serenity. Written in response to his wife's death, *Nous deux encore* (1948; two of us still) expresses the pain of loss in plaintive, lyric notes. *Face aux verrous* (1954; facing the bolts) and especially the later *Vents et poussières* (1962; winds and dusts) temper anguish into aphorisms where only occasional sharp tones betray the underlying pressures. *Meidosems* (1948; Meidosems [a fictitious nationality invented by M.]), which is about spiritual aspiration, conveys a sense of man's limits. Despite the new tone of his work in this period, the thrust to extend boundaries persists, reflected in M.'s evocations of the world beyond or in his visionary poems, which present human experience as a continuum. Essays on poetry, graphic arts, and dreams complement M.'s imaginative production of the postwar period, demonstrating his range and his understanding of the creative processes.

M.'s discovery of the drug mescaline in the mid-1950s ushered in a decade of experimentation with hallucinogenic substances and opened the door in M.'s work to a variety of transcendent states: ecstasy, limitless expansion, soaring, the experience of infinity or of total involvement with the universe. Undertaken in a spirit of scientific inquiry, these experiments produced five major works, among them *Misérable miracle* (1956; *Miserable Miracle,* 1963) and *L'infini turbulent* (1957; turbulent infinity), in both of which objective analysis and lyrical evocation fuse to close the gap between science and poetry. Lucid even while under the influence of drugs, M. demystifies experience. But he also struggles to remain a visionary and thus takes consciousness to its furthest limits. *Paix dans les brisements* (1959; peace among the windbreaks) is the most interesting mescaline text. It creates a sense of plenitude by bringing into a perfect symbiotic relationship prose commentary, poems, and drawings.

M.'s work embraces a hundred variations ranging from free verse to clinical studies of drug-induced states to painting. It developed independently and achieved an extraordinary degree of freedom from existing literary forms. Restless, spasmodic, in constant pursuit of experiences, it accelerated the pace of poetic language and, by insisting that flights of the imagination are a proper instrument of inquiry, extended the boundaries of both knowledge and poetry.

SELECTED FURTHER WORKS: *La nuit remue* (1935); *Voyage en Grande Garabagne* (1936); *La ralentie* (1937); *Plume, précédé de Lointain intérieur* (1938); *Peintures* (1939); *Arbres des tropiques* (1942); *Je vous écris d'un pays lointain* (1942); *Exorcismes* (1943); *Labyrinthes* (1944); *Le lobe des monstres* (1944); *Apparitions* (1946); *Peintures et dessins* (1946); *La vie dans les plis* (1949); *Poésie pour pouvoir* (1949); *Passages* (1950); *Tranches de savoir, suivi de Secret de la situation politique* (1950); *Mouvements* (1951); *Connaissance par les gouffres* (1961; *Light through Darkness,* 1963); *Les grandes épreuves de l'esprit et les innombrables petites* (1966; *The Major Ordeals of the Mind and the Countless Minor Ones,* 1974); *Parcours* (1966); *Vers la complétude: Saisie et dessaisies* (1966); *Façons d'endormi, façons d'éveillé* (1969); *Poteaux d'angle* (1971); *Émergences-resurgences* (1972); *En rêvant à partir des peintures énigmatiques* (1972); *Bras cassé* (1973); *Moments: Traversées du champ* (1973); *Moriturus* (1974); *Par la voie des rhythmes* (1974); *Face à ce qui se dérobe* (1976); *Saisir* (1979). FURTHER VOLUME IN ENGLISH: *H. M.* (1967)

BIBLIOGRAPHY: Belaval, Y., *H. M.: Une magie rationelle* (1951); Bertelé, R., *H. M.*

(1957); Bréchon, R., *M.* (1959); Leonhart, K., *H. M.* (1967); Bowie, M., *H. M.: A Study of His Literary Works* (1973); La Charité, V., *H. M.* (1977); Velinsky, L. A., *From the Gloom of Today to New Greatness of Man: Itinerary by H. M., Builder of New Poetry* (1977)

VIKTORIA SKRUPSKELIS

MIHARDJA, Achdiat Karta
See Achdiat Karta Mihardja

MILLAY, Edna St. Vincent
American poet, b. 22 Feb. 1892, Rockland, Maine; d. 19 Oct. 1950, Steepletop (near Austerlitz), N.Y.

M. wrote poetry long before she went to college and won several prizes from *St. Nicholas Magazine.* She received a solid education at Barnard and Vassar colleges. "Renascence" (1912), her first major poem, was written when she was only nineteen years old, in the year widely regarded as the one that marked the dawning of a poetic renascence in both England and the U.S.—the same year that the magazine *Poetry* was launched by Harriet Monroe (1860–1936). Simple diction masked her wonderment and love of "The How and Why of all things, past, and present, and forevermore": the poem, published in the anthology *The Lyric Year,* made her famous. Subsequent volumes of poetry preached hedonism, anger that death should be so powerful, and love of the arts ("On Hearing a Symphony by Beethoven," 1928). Her tone was that of a young girl new to a big city (New York) who was shocked by its evil but had decided to master its tempo. Despite their bravura, her lyrics communicated a girlish innocence that won her large audiences.

M. admired classical poets like Catullus, but observed nature closely. Her work with the Provincetown Players and her experiments with verse drama (notably *Aria Da Capo,* 1920) made her a Greenwich Village celebrity. Her libretto for *The King's Henchman* (music by Deems Taylor, produced in 1927) was a serious contribution to American opera. She won the Pulitzer Prize in 1922 for *The Harp-Weaver, and Other Poems;* married Eugen Jan Boissevain the following year;

and moved in 1925 to a farm in the Berkshires.

During the 1920s M. was tremendously excited by the Sacco-Vanzetti case, wrote several poems on the subject, and pleaded with the government of Massachusetts to commute the death sentence.. What began as a concern with social injustice broadened, with the appearance of *Conversation at Midnight* (1937), into a consideration of international problems. Much of her later poetry was censured by critics as didactic and journalistic, and she agreed that she had not learned how to convert the ideals of a beleaguered democratic world into poetry of the first order. Her final years were spent fighting illness, personal disappointment, and a declining reputation.

A brief revival followed the posthumous publication of *Collected Poems* (1956). Over a longer period she has attracted new generations of readers. Many of her books remain in print, and her recordings of poems are widely available. In general, however, critics during the last three decades have chosen either to belittle M.'s self-dramatizations as immature and period-dated, or to ignore her entirely. But the record shows that she was the most exciting American woman poet since Emily Dickinson, and a distinguished contributor to both the lyric and the sonnet traditions.

FURTHER WORKS: *Renascence* (1917); *A Few Figs from Thistles* (1920); *The Lamp and the Bell* (1921); *Second April* (1921); *Two Slatterns and a King* (1921); *Poems* (1923); *Distressing Dialogues* (1924); *The Buck in the Snow, and Other Poems* (1928); *Poems Selected for Young People* (1929); *Fatal Interview* (1931); *The Princess Marries the Page* (1932); *Wine from These Grapes* (1934, with George Dillon); *Flowers of Evil* (tr. of Baudelaire, 1936); *Huntsman, What Quarry?* (1939); *Make Bright the Arrows* (1940); *Collected Sonnets* (1941); *The Murder of Lidice* (1942); *Letters of E. St. V. M.* (1952); *Mine the Harvest* (1954)

BIBLIOGRAPHY: Atkins, A., *E. St. V. M. and Her Times* (1936); Sheean, V., *The Indigo Bunting: A Memoir of E. St. V. M.* (1951); Gurko, M., *Restless Spirit: The Life of E. St. V. M.* (1962); Brittin, N. A., *E. St. V. M.* (1967); Gould, J., *The Poet and Her Book: A Biography of E. St. V. M.* (1969); Cheney, A., *M. in Greenwich Village* (1975); Nier-

ARTHUR MILLER

HENRY MILLER

CZESŁAW MIŁOSZ

GABRIELA MISTRAL

MISHIMA YUKIO

man, J., *E. St. V. M.: A Reference Guide* (1977)

HAROLD OREL

MILLER, Arthur

American dramatist, essayist, and novelist, b. 17 Oct. 1915, New York, N.Y.

Son of a well-to-do New York Jewish couple, the young M. was an indifferent student who devoted his attention chiefly to sports. It was not until entering the University of Michigan that he developed an interest in writing. He received his B.A. degree from Michigan in 1938 and spent the next five years as a script writer for NBC, CBS, and the Federal Theatre Project. M. won the Theatre Guild National Award for his play *The Man Who Had All the Luck* in 1944 and soon earned a reputation as a major new American playwright with his successful drama *All My Sons* (1947) which won the New York Drama Critics' Circle Award. In 1956 M. was called before the House Committee on Un-American Activities and was asked to identify colleagues who were suspected of communist activities. He refused and was found in contempt of Congress in 1957, although his conviction was reversed by the U.S. Court of Appeals in the following year. It was also in 1956 that M. married the film actress Marilyn Monroe, a marriage that he dramatized in *After the Fall* (1964). They were divorced in 1961. In 1958 M. was elected to the National Institute of Arts and Letters, winning its Gold Medal for Drama in 1959. He was elected to a four-year term as president of PEN, the international literary association, in 1965. A prolific essayist, M. has articulated his views on literature both in writing and in scores of interviews.

M.'s minor early works—more than thirty plays written for production in colleges, on radio, and in amateur theaters—advanced the ethical concepts and social themes that were later to dominate his major plays. They exhibited as well M.'s penchant for dramatizing the father-son relationships that are central to most of his mature works. Among these early works is M.'s only novel, *Focus* (1945), a narrative that explores the nature of prejudice and anti-Semitism.

The ideas somewhat imperfectly expressed in M.'s early works reached fruition in *All My Sons,* a powerful drama of betrayal and disloyalty within a father-son relationship. The major advance here over M.'s previous playwriting is the achievement of a style of dialogue that allows its characters to convey and explore ideas with a minimum of explicit moralizing or declaiming of principles. In this play, M. proved himself a master in capturing the rhythms of middle-American speech, including its slang and clichés, and in imbuing such realistic, pedestrian dialogue with considerable dramatic power. The play's chief flaw is its weak ending, a denouement that calls attention to the essentially melodramatic devices of the plot. The father's suicide, for example, seems weakly motivated.

M.'s next play remains perhaps his finest. *Death of a Salesman* (1949), often called the most outstanding modern tragedy, received numerous awards, including the Pulitzer Prize for drama and the New York Drama Critics' Circle Award. It substantiates M.'s thesis—advanced repeatedly in essays and interviews—that the common man is an apt subject for contemporary tragedy. In *Death of a Salesman,* M. achieved the remarkable feat of heightening realistic, everyday speech to a level of eloquence bordering on the poetic. The play's dialogue powerfully expresses the thoughts and feelings of characters who are essentially inarticulate, relying upon repetition, rhythm, and other poetic techniques in place of extensive vocabulary.

Of all M.'s plays, *The Crucible* (1953) is the one most clearly focused upon social commentary. A drama of the 1692 Salem witch trials in colonial Massachusetts, it is often said to be M.'s allegorical commentary on the McCarthy-era persecution of suspected communists, a witch hunt of which M. himself was to become a victim three years later. Thus, *The Crucible* confirmed M.'s reputation as a topical playwright and crusader against social injustice. The play is, however, a viable drama in its own right, apart from its applicability to the red-baiting of the early 1950s. Its topic is the phenomenon of mass hysteria and its effect upon a heroic figure who chooses death rather than submit to the injustice spawned by that hysteria.

Most of M.'s work is to some extent autobiographical; his plays frequently portray characters and situations derived from his own past. The most purely autobiographical is *After the Fall*, a quasi-expressionistic (q.v.) exercise in guilt and self-discovery that most critics have seen as M.'s apologia for his own life. The parallels between the play's hero-narrator, Quentin, and M. himself are inescapable—especially in their reference to the HUAC hearings and to M.'s marriage to Marilyn Monroe (Maggie in the play). The latter subject especially brought critical scorn upon M. for the frank exposure of his relationship with the actress, who had died only two years earlier. Despite the critical attention given to *After the Fall,* it is one of M.'s weaker plays. It is marred by the excessive narration of its hero; its supporting characters are but vaguely sketched; and Quentin's pseudopoetic monologues frequently seem convoluted and pretentious, serving only to obscure the narrative line rather than elucidate it.

By his own admission, M. has been strongly influenced by the plays of Henrik Ibsen. He greatly admires the Norwegian dramatist's ability to objectify human situations and relationships in terms of actions and deeds, rather than in mere declamation and philosophical pronouncements. Nevertheless, M. is a decidedly American playwright—one whose settings and characters are redolent of modern American life. This is attributable principally to M.'s facility with dialogue and his keen ear for ethnic and regional speech. More than any other American dramatist, M. has captured the rhythms and syntax of a wide range of the American people and has rendered their speech both expressive and dramatic.

M.'s heroes—whether from the Midwest, from colonial Salem, or from the Brooklyn waterfront—appear before us as husbands and fathers caught in familial crises. They are portrayed as common folk, struggling to define their existence within the limitations imposed upon them by hostile—or at least indifferent—social and domestic forces. Although they are little people—salesmen, longshoremen, policemen—their creator has often endowed them with tragic stature. They are as fixed and uncompromising in their exertion of self-will as were the Greek heroes in their exercise of hubris. M. has brought the common man within the reach of tragedy.

FURTHER WORKS: *Situation Normal* (1944); *A Memory of Two Mondays* (1955); *A View From the Bridge* (1955); *Collected Plays* (1957); *The Misfits* (1961); *Incident at Vichy*

(1965); *I Don't Need You Any More* (1967); *The Price* (1968); *The Creation of the World and Other Business* (1973); *The Portable A. M.* (1977); *The Theater Essays of A. M.* (1978); *Chinese Encounters* (1979, with Inge Morath); *The American Clock* (1980); *Collected Plays, Vol. II* (1981)

BIBLIOGRAPHY: Welland, D., *A. M.* (1961); McAnany, E. G., "The Tragic Commitment: Some Notes on A. M.," *MD,* 5 (1962), 11–20; Prudhoe, J., "A. M. and the Tradition of Tragedy," *ES,* 43 (1962), 430–39; Weales, G., "A. M.: A Man and His Image," *TDR,* 7, 1 (1962), 165–80; Huftel, S., *A. M.: The Burning Glass* (1965); Murray, E., *A. M., Dramatist* (1967); Corrigan, R. W., ed., *A. M.: A Collection of Critical Essays* (1969); Hayman, R., *A. M.* (1970); Nelson, B., *A. M.* (1970); Moss, L., *A. M.*, rev. ed. (1980)

JACK A. VAUGHN

MILLER, Henry

American novelist, essayist, travel writer, and dramatist, b. 26 Dec. 1891, New York, N.Y.; d. 7 June 1980, Pacific Palisades, Cal.

Born of middle-class German-Americans, M. spent his early years, as he puts it, getting an education on the streets of Brooklyn. He worked at innumerable jobs: for the Atlas Portland Cement Company, in his father's tailor shop, for the U.S. Bureau of Economic Research, for Western Union, and for the Queens County Park Department, among many others. He sold prose-poems ("mezzo-tints") door to door, ran a speakeasy, and wrote three still-unpublished novels. He lived in Europe (mostly Paris) in the 1930s under impoverished circumstances, doing odd jobs, and writing prolifically work that, for years, was published almost exclusively by the Obelisk Press, Paris. After an extended stay in Greece, M. returned to America following the outbreak of war. Until his death he lived in California (mostly Big Sur)—writing, painting water colors, and revisiting Europe numerous times. In 1957 he was elected to the National Institute of Arts and Letters.

M.'s major literary achievement is a pair of "autobiographical" trilogies: *Tropic of Cancer* (1934), *Black Spring* (1936), and *Tropic of Capricorn* (1939); and *The Rosy Crucifixion: Sexus* (1949), *Plexus* (1953), and *Nexus* (1960). These books, plus *Quiet Days in Cli-*

chy (1956), fictionalize M.'s life in a kind of free-form *Bildungsroman,* a loosely connected, anecdotal narrative. They depict an aging expatriate American writer who bears M.'s name and experience, divides his thoughts and energies between intoxicating Paris and frenzied New York, and discovers that the world is generally uncongenial to his sensitivities and needs. A "lost generation" writer of what might be called the second phase, Paris of the Depression, M. uses themes—cadging for food, shelter, and sex; attacks on such bourgeois values as work and marriage; denunciations of traditional art and literature—and imagery—wild, exuberant, often shockingly frank—that together represent a savage, nihilistic (and at times enormously funny) revulsion against a world of stupidity and ugliness.

The contradiction on which these books depend is that the picaro, gaining knowledge of the world's endless frustrations, squalor, and disasters, attains a disproportionate sense of triumph for each small victory in daily survival. Another meal, a free bed, a beautiful sky, a warm and willing female body—from these emerge a free-spirited exuberance for life, a sense of initiation and self-liberation, despite the world and his own instincts. The mask of alienation slips often, revealing a would-be eternal outsider whose exile is self-imposed, a buffoon-lecher who spouts wisdom in the guise of foolishness, while seducing, indiscriminately, virgins and whores.

M. called his fiction "auto-novels," and maintained that, like his protagonist, the work is natural, spontaneous, uncontaminated by reason or recollection. Yet M. was as much craftsman as free-spirited artist, and his "spontaneous" effects are calculated: the first-draft manuscript of *Tropic of Cancer* was three times the length of the published version, and M. rewrote the book three times. And despite his scorning of critics (whom he called "bastards" and for whom, to throw them "off the track," he planted lies in his autobiographical chronology, published in *The H. M. Reader* [1959], edited by his friend Lawrence Durrell [q.v.]), he expended enormous energy on criticism: *Hamlet* (2 vols., 1939, 1941, with Michael Fraenkel); *The Plight of the Creative Artist in the United States of America* (1944); *Patchen: Man of Anger and Light* (1947); *The Books in My Life* (1952); *The Time of the*

Assassins: A Study of Rimbaud (1956); plus a huge, never-completed study of D. H. Lawrence (q.v.), *The World of Lawrence: A Passionate Appreciation* (1980).

Since the 1960s, when all of M.'s controversial writings were finally published in America, his reputation has declined. No longer underground, M.'s fiction lost first its influence and then its popularity. The world of sexual freedom, anarchism, and Oriental philosophy he helped to create no longer finds him shocking—or even particularly relevant. Now, or soon, we will be able to take his measure as artist, rather than as cause. A likely point of emphasis should be his peculiarly American posture—iconoclastic, self-educated, naturalistic, strongly antipathetic toward modern industrial society. M.'s powerful imagistic language, the lyrical intensity with which he endows our daily activities, and his brilliant re-creation of the bum's rejection of society are among those features of his work that will insure him a continuing readership.

FURTHER WORKS: *Aller Retour New York* (1935); *Money and How It Gets That Way* (1938); *Max and the White Phagocytes* (1938); *The Cosmological Eye* (1939); *The World of Sex* (1940; rev. ed., 1957); *The Wisdom of the Heart* (1940); *The Colossus of Maroussi* (1941); *Sunday after the War* (1944); *The Air-Conditioned Nightmare* (1945); *Obscenity and the Law of Reflection* (1945); *Maurizius Forever* (1946); *Of, by, and about H. M.* (1947); *Remember to Remember* (1947); *The Smile at the Foot of the Ladder* (1948); *Nights of Love and Laughter* (1955); *A Devil in Paradise* (1956); *Big Sur and the Oranges of Hieronymus Bosch* (1957); *The Red Notebook* (1958); *The Intimate H. M.* (1959); *Stand Still Like the Hummingbird* (1962); *Lawrence Durrell and H. M.: A Private Correspondence* (1963); *H. M. on Writing* (1964); *Letters to Anaïs Nin* (1965); *Selected Prose* (1965); *Writer and Critic: A Correspondence with H. M.* (1968, with William A. Gordon); *My Life and Times* (1971); *H. M. in Conversation with Georges Belmont* (1972); *Insomnia; or, The Devil at Large* (1974); *Letters of H. M. and Wallace Fowlie* (1975); *The Nightmare Notebook* (1975); *H. M.'s Book of Friends: A Tribute to Friends of Long Ago* (1976); *Sextet* (1977); *Correspondance privée 1935–1978* (1980, with Joseph Delteil)

BIBLIOGRAPHY: Porter, B., ed., *Happy Rock: A Book about H. M.* (1945); Durrell, L., and Perlès, A., *Art and Outrage: A Correspondence about H. M.* (1959); Baxter, A. K., *H. M., Expatriate* (1961); Wickes, G., ed., *H. M. and the Critics* (1963); Widmer, K., *H. M.* (1963); Wickes, G., *H. M.* (1966); Dick, K. C., *H. M.: Colossus of One* (1967); Gordon, W. A., *The Mind and Art of H. M.* (1967); Hassan, I., *The Literature of Silence: H. M. and Samuel Beckett* (1968); Nelson, J. A., *Form and Image in the Fiction of H. M.* (1970); Mitchell, E. B., ed., *H. M.: Three Decades of Criticism* (1971); Mathieu, B., *Orpheus in Brooklyn: Orphism, Rimbaud, and H. M.* (1976)

ALAN WARREN FRIEDMAN

MILLIN, Sarah Gertrude

South African novelist, biographer, and diarist (writing in English), b. 3 March 1888, Zagar, Lithuania; d. 16 July 1968, Johannesburg

M.'s Jewish parents emigrated to South Africa when she was five months old. The family settled on alluvial diamond diggings on the Vaal River near Kimberley. M. spent her early years keenly observing the diggers whose lives were to form the major inspiration for her fiction. Her disapproval of the racial mixing she saw on the river developed into a lifelong obsession with miscegenation. In later life she turned her back on the liberal tradition established by her fellow writers in South Africa and became instead a supporter of apartheid and of white supremacy in southern Africa. An interest in the work of her husband, Philip Millin, a barrister and judge, led to her familiarity with the law courts of Johannesburg. She attended trials and based some of her plots on them.

At the end of a long life, M. claimed that she had provided South African literature with "bulk." Apart from fifteen novels and a volume of short stories, *Two Bucks without Hair* (1957), interest in politics and history resulted in a two-volume biography of the famous Boer soldier and statesman Jan Smuts, *General Smuts* (1936), another biography, *Cecil Rhodes* (1933), and an autobiography, *The Night is Long* (1941), which she saw as a prelude to her ambitious 1,600-page *War Diary* (6 vols., 1944–48).

M. chose a dynastic structure for several novels *God's Stepchildren* (1924), *King of the*

Bastards (1949), and *The Burning Man* (1952). *God's Stepchildren,* her most popular work, covers four generations of South African life, and the theme of biological destiny is prominent. In the somber, tragic world of her novels miscegenation is the physical manifestation of original sin. Sometimes M.'s characters are disgraced by poor and demanding relations, whose connections with darker people are economic rather than sexual, as in *The Jordans* (1923). The belief in superior or inferior genes, however, is germane to M.'s world view.

M.'s numerous female characters are striking for their emotional strength and their ruthlessness. They will often stop at nothing to indulge an obsession. In *Mary Glenn* (1925) M. describes feminine ambition in a small provincial town. Typically, Mary marries for social advantage and not for love. Many of M.'s women are haunted by the fear of spinsterhood; the dread of remaining sexually unfulfilled poisons their lives.

M. sees money as the driving force in modern society. Her characters come from the deprived classes of South Africa. They are landless, uneducated, temperamentally unstable—social outcasts, poor whites, half-breeds, or simply "bastards" (that is, people of mixed race). In M.'s fiction, crimes are committed and lives blighted over trifling sums of money. Even if the economic problem is solved, M.'s protagonists are frequently unable to arrive at self-determination. Guilt, fear, or an innate self-destructiveness prevent them from rising above an inferior background.

Despite her color prejudice, incorporated in a deterministic world view, M.'s fiction is of a distinguished caliber. She writes in a tragic mode, achieving real poignancy in a style that is at once plain and forceful. She is a master of dialogue and situation, and her portraits of the poor and degenerate families who eked out a living in a provincial and rural South Africa during the first decades of the 20th c. are both emotionally compelling and authentic.

FURTHER WORKS: *The Dark River* (1919); *Middle-Class* (1921); *Adam's Rest* (1922); *The South Africans* (1926); *An Artist in the Family* (1928); *The Coming of the Lord* (1928); *The Fiddler* (1929); *Men on a Voyage* (1930); *The Sons of Mrs. Aab* (1931); *What Hath a Man?* (1938); *South Africa* (1941); *The Herr Witchdoctor* (1941; Am., *The Dark*

Gods); *The People of South Africa* (1951); *The Measure of My Days* (1955); *The Wizard Bird* (1962); *Goodbye, Dear England* (1965); *White Africans Are Also People* (1966)

BIBLIOGRAPHY: Snyman, P. P. L., *The Works of S. G. M.* (1955); Rubin, M., *S. G. M.: A South African Life* (1977); Rabkin, D., "Race and Fiction: *God's Stepchildren* and [William Plomer's] *Turbott Wolfe*," in Parker, K., ed., *The South African Novel in English: Essays in Criticism and Society* (1978), pp. 77–94; Sarvan, C., and Sarvan, L., "*God's Stepchildren* and *Lady Chatterley's Lover:* Failure and Triumph," *JCL*, 14, 1 (1979), 53–57; Coetzee, J. M., "Blood, Flaw, Taint, Degeneration: The Case of S. G. M.," *ESA*, 23 (1980), 41–58

JEAN MARQUARD

MIŁOSZ, Czesław

Polish poet, novelist, essayist, and critic (also writing in English), b. 30 June 1911, Seteiniai (Szetejnie), Lithuania

M. is Polish although his native country is Lithuania. From the 14th to the 18th cs., Poland and Lithuania were part of the same commonwealth ruled by the Polish king, who was also the Lithuanian grand prince. Owing to intermarriage and cultural assimilation, many Lithuanian families eventually became ethnically Polish; M.'s family was one of them.

M. began to publish poetry when he was a law student at the University of Wilno (Vilnius). From 1946 to 1951 he served as a Polish diplomat in Washington and Paris, but in 1951 he broke with the Communist government of Poland, and after spending nine years in France came to the U.S. Since that time he has been a professor of Slavic languages and literatures at the University of California at Berkeley. In 1978 he received the Neustadt Prize, and in 1980 the Nobel Prize for literature. In connection with the Nobel Prize he was asked about his plans for the future, to which he replied: "I intend to continue my private occupation of translating the Bible from Hebrew and Greek into Polish."

M. has written poetry, novels, short stories, philosophical and literary essays, and political pamphlets. Most of his works are in Polish, but some were written in English. His autobiography *Rodzinna Europa* (1959; *Na-tive Realm: A Search for Self-Definition*, 1968) speaks about the formation of an intellectual amid the social and political upheavals that took place in eastern Europe during the first part of the 20th c. It succeeds in demonstrating the psychological differences between the intellectuals of eastern and western Europe.

Notwithstanding the variety of his occupations and activities, M. has remained primarily a poet. His poetry is crisp, laconic, and cerebral, and it often verges on rhythmical prose, especially in the middle and later periods. The essentials of M.'s poetic style have not changed much over the years. His determination as a poet to use the smallest possible number of words to express an idea or an emotion has contributed to making him one of the great stylists of Polish literature. Some of his poems indicate that he has been influenced by the Manichean vision of the world. Throughout his life, M. has had a profound interest in nature; this interest was reflected in his early poetry in the portrayals of the Lithuanian countryside, and in later poetry in the landscapes of California.

M.'s poetic themes have been nature, philosophy, Poland and Lithuania, and himself. In contrast to many of his contemporaries in Poland and abroad, he has been more interested in thoughts than in words, and he has sought to provide definitions of things, events, and people rather than the impressions of them. In this he is a born classicist, differing sharply from the futurists (q.v.), the impressionists, and other modernist poets of his time.

Traktat poetycki (1957; the poetic treatise) is M.'s most significant poetic work. The dry title hides a dynamic content. It is a spirited defense of poetry in an age in which most significant writing has been done in prose. In verse, M. argues that poetry is essential for every human community wanting to survive as a community. It alone is capable of condensing the community's experience in a form that is understandable to all. Following his thesis, M. surveys Polish history from 1918 to the 1950s. He deals with poets, thinkers, and sacrifices, rather than with governments and political declarations. In this work, M. tries to express the experience of his lifetime, that is to say, the experience of a Pole who lived in independent Poland between the two world wars, survived the war and lived on afterward, and who eventually came to view his native country from a geographical and emotional distance. *Król Popiel, i inne wiersze* (1962; King Popiel, and other poems) contains the famous "Ballada" (ballad) commemorating the inhabitants of Warsaw who had been decimated by the uprising of 1944. "Gdzie wschodzi słońce i kędy zapada" (1974; partial tr., "From the Rising of the Sun," 1978) is a poem in rhythmical prose in which M. comes to terms with his own personal victories and defeats.

Of M.'s prose works, *Zniewolony umysł* (1953; *The Captive Mind,* 1953) has enjoyed the greatest popularity. It tells the story of four eastern European intellectuals who adapted themselves to the Communist system while at the same time preserving their belief in their own personal integrity. This book resembles the French writer Julien Benda's (1867–1956) *The Treason of the Intellectuals* (1927) in decrying the betrayal of reason by 20th-c. intellectuals.

The novel *Dolina Issy* (1955; *The Issa Valley,* 1981) deals with M.'s childhood in Lithuania. Old Lithuania, which M. describes in this work, was a rural country in which Poles, Lithuanians, and Jews lived and died in obscurity, their conflicts ignored or misunderstood by conquerors from the East and observers from the West. In the novel, a boy lives with his grandparents on a small country estate. He absorbs the adults' conversations about wars and uprisings, and he watches the dark passions and evil obsessions they try to conceal from him. As often happens in books about rural life, the peaceful milieu of the boy's childhood conceals an undercurrent of unresolved psychological conflicts. While shedding a tear over a world that is no more, M. provides a glimpse into the dark side of human nature. Another novel, *Zdobycie władzy* (1955; *The Seizure of Power,* 1955), deals with quite different subject matter: the Communist takeover of Poland.

In recent years, M. has published two books of essays, *Emperor of the Earth: Modes of Eccentric Vision* (1977) and *Ogród nauk* (1979; the garden of learning), that contain his critique of contemporary Western culture. M. feels that the spiritual ingredient of this culture, conceived in ancient Israel, Greece, and Rome, has all but disappeared in the Western world. It has been preserved on the frontiers of Western culture, however, in countries such as Poland and some of the other eastern European nations. M.'s *The History of Polish Literature* (1969), a critical

and historical work of taste and style, has become an indispensable reference tool to English-speaking students of Polish literature.

FURTHER WORKS: *Poemat o czasie zastygłym* (1933); *Trzy zimy* (1936); *Ocalenie* (1945); *Światło dzienne* (1953); *Gucio zaczarowany* (1965); *Wiersze* (1967); *Widzenie nad zatoką San Francisco* (1969; *Visions from San Francisco Bay,* 1982); *Miasto bez imienia* (1969); *Prywatne obowiązki* (1972); *Człowiek wśród skorpionów: Studium o Stanisławie Brzozowskim* (1972); *Gdzie wschodzi słońce i kędy zapada* (1974); *Ziemia Ulro* (1977); *Utwory poetyckie: Poems* (1976); *Księga Psalmów* (1979); *Nobel Lecture* (1981). FURTHER VOLUMES IN ENGLISH: *Selected Poems* (1973; rev. ed., 1981); *Bells in Winter* (1978)

BIBLIOGRAPHY: Folejewski, Z., "C. M.: A Poet's Road to Ithaca between Worlds, Wars and Poetics," *BA,* 43 (1969), 17–24; Contoski, V., "C. M. and the Quest for the Critical Perspective," *BA,* 47 (1973), 35–41; Schenker, A. M., Introduction to C. M., *Utwory poetyckie: Poems* (1976), pp. xv–xxvii; Bayley, J., "Return of the Native," *NYRB,* 25 June 1981, 29–33; Stone, J., "C. M., Child and Man," *NYTBR,* 28 June 1981, 7, 16–19; Zweig, P., on *The Issa Valley, NYTBR,* 28 June 1981, 7, 29

EWA THOMPSON

MINANGKABAU LITERATURE
See Indonesian Literature

MIRÓ, Gabriel
Spanish novelist, short-story writer, and essayist, b. 28 July 1879, Alicante, d. 27 May 1930, Madrid

M. took a degree in law after studies at the universities of Valencia and Granada, but his education as a writer came from elsewhere: the Spiritual Exercises at the Jesuit-run school he attended in Orihuela, which trained his sensual imagination; his uncle's academy for painters (in Alicante), where he was taught that the eye should be a veritable camera obscura; Pérez Galdós's (q.v.) noninstitutional Christianity; the critic and novelist Juan Valera's (1824–1905) aestheticism; years of reading and seeing for a blind friend. Because M. requires closer attention than many readers are willing to give, he never achieved the popular success that would enable him to live from his writing, and he had to support himself by taking various positions in Alicante, Barcelona, and Madrid.

M.'s densely populated "city" novel about the clergy and people of Oleza (Orihuela rearranged) was published as two books, *Nuestro Padre San Daniel: Novela de capellanes y devotos* (1921; *Our Father San Daniel: Scenes of Clerical Life,* 1930) and *El obispo leproso* (1926; the leper bishop). Dozens of characters painted as in enamel; many episodes; lengthy flashbacks and side flashes; morbid Catholic orthodoxy and traditionalism against life-serving Christianity and progressivism—all are presented through a technique of such intense linguistic concentration, heavy with nouns and metaphors, poor in verbs, that at the end one feels enveloped by a vast series of shimmering mosaics, with time held poignantly at bay.

"There is only one heroism, to see the world as it is and to love it," a remark of Romain Rolland's (q.v.), was appropriated by M. as his own ethical and aesthetic principle. The absence of love and the presence of human suffering and cruelty, most often physical and depicted by M. with chilling candor, are therefore his most obsessive subjects, beginning with his first mature work, *Del vivir* (1904; about being alive), an account of the visit by Sigüenza, M.'s alter ego, to a leper colony. M.'s general characteristics here did not change in later works: an almost intolerable pathos attenuated by gentler modes of irony and wit, as well as outright comedy and the expression of astonishment (*pasmo*) that what is there is there (antisubjectivism). These qualities are notable in the numerous short pieces—anecdotes devolving into meditations—brought together in *Libro de Sigüenza* (1917; Sigüenza's book) and in the neo-Parnassian heroism of M.'s last book, *Años y leguas* (1928; years and leagues), where Sigüenza takes spiritual possession, through the word, of the days and places of his youth: the towns and trails, mountains and valleys, and peasant characters of the region around Alicante.

Although not a practicing Catholic, the adult M. retained a lifelong loving obsession with the Church's liturgies, lore, and teachings, especially the doctrines of the incarnate word and transubstantiation, seen in *El humo dormido* (1919; the sleeping smoke) as elaborate human inventions satisfying the need for the illusion of transcendence and obscuring the truth of radical alienation. M.'s works abound with cases of orphanhood, estrangement, separation, and unprovoked cruelty. In *Figuras de la Pasión del Señor* (2 vols., 1916–17; *Figures of the Passion of Our Lord,* 1924) M. shows the Disciples in their anxiety as they face the loss of Christ their transcending mediator, and Christ himself as He is abandoned by God to utterly human agony on the cross.

M. did not share with his contemporaries, the so-called Generation of '98, their abiding preoccupation with the "problem of Spain." Rather, exploiting the most idiosyncratic resources of the Spanish language, he set forth the problem of man, and in so doing achieved a power of expression unique and unsurpassed in Spanish prose.

FURTHER WORKS: *Nómada* (1908); *La novela de mi amigo* (1908); *La palma rota* (1909); *El hijo santo* (1909); *Las cerezas del cementerio* (1910); *Del huerto provinciano* (1912); *Los amigos, los amantes y la muerte* (1915); *El abuelo del rey* (1915); *Dentro del cercado* (1916); *El ángel, El molino, El caracol del faro* (1921); *Niño y grande* (1922); *Obras completas* (1 vol., 1943)

BIBLIOGRAPHY: Guillén, J., "Adequate Language: G. M.," *Language and Poetry: Some Poets of Spain* (1961), pp. 157–97; Casalduero, J., "G. M. y el cubismo," *Estudios de literatura* (1962), pp. 219–66; Vidal, R., *G. M.: Le style, les moyens d'expression* (1964); King, E. L., Introduction to G. M., *El humo dormido* (1967), pp. 15–53; Macdonald, I., *G. M.: His Private Library and His Literary Background* (1975); Landeira, R., *An Annotated Bibliography of G. M. (1900–1978)* (1978); Ramos, V., *G. M.* (1979)

EDMUND L. KING

MISHIMA Yukio

(pseud. of Hiraoka Kimitake) Japanese novelist, short-story writer, dramatist, and essayist, b. 14 Jan. 1925, Tokyo; d. 25 Nov. 1970, Tokyo

M., the son of a government official, was raised mainly by his paternal grandmother, who hardly permitted the boy out of her sight. This fact has frequently been cited to explain both his fragility and oversensitivity as an adolescent.

In 1944, the year in which he entered Tokyo University, his first book, *Hanazakari no mori* (the forest in full bloom), was published. In 1945 he took his physical examination for military service, but was rejected.

In 1946 M. met Kawabata Yasunari (q.v.). The older novelist took an interest in his work and not only introduced him to the literary world but recommended his stories to important magazines. M. continued his law studies at Tokyo University, but found after graduation in 1947 that he could not combine a career as a civil servant with that of a writer; he resigned his post in the finance ministry in 1948 to devote himself entirely to his writings. M. was not an avant-garde writer and showed relatively little interest in the work of foreign contemporary writers; he drew greater inspiration from premodern literature, both Japanese and Western. His absorption with classical Japanese literature sets him off from other writers of his generation.

Kamen no kokuhaku (1948; *Confessions of a Mask,* 1968) was the novel that established M.'s literary reputation. In the opinion of some critics, this is his best work. It describes in thinly disguised form M.'s childhood memories, his life as a student, and his wartime experiences It is a record of the significant steps in the development of the narrator's awareness that he would have to wear a mask before the world because of his abnormal sexual preferences.

The central character of M.'s next major novel, *Ai no kawaki* (1950; *Thirst for Love,* 1969), is Etsuko, a woman who has become the mistress of her late husband's father. M. admitted that he had written this novel under the influence of François Mauriac (q.v.), and it is not difficult to detect similarities between Etsuko and various Mauriac protagonists. But the climactic moments when Etsuko gashes the back of the young man she loves as he cavorts at a festival, or when in the final scene she kills him, continue the mood of *Kamen no kokuhaku*. Etsuko's victim is the strong, sunburned youth untroubled by intellectual concerns who seemed to embody for M. the most attractive aspect of traditional Japan.

Perhaps M.'s finest novel is *Kinkakuji* (1956; *The Temple of the Golden Pavilion,* 1959). The central incident, the burning of the celebrated temple by a deranged monk, was inspired by an actual event of 1950. M.'s concern here was not with uncovering the

facts but with establishing circumstances that would make the act seem logical and even inevitable.

Many of M.'s later novels were intended as experiments. In the unsuccessful *Kyōko no ie* (1959; Kyoko's house) he apportioned different aspects of his life among the four main characters in the detached manner of a "study in nihilism," to use his description. He followed this with the less ambitious but nearly flawless *Utage no ato* (1960; *After the Banquet,* 1963), a story so closely based on the personal life of a well-known politician that M. lost the ensuing suit for invasion of privacy.

Even as he was writing these novels, M. wrote many short stories and novellas. His best novella, *Yūkoku* (1960; *Patriotism,* 1966), describes the suicides of a young army officer and his wife. This was the first manifestation of M.'s absorption with the February 26, 1936, army coup, when young officers attempted to wrest power from the politicians in the name of the emperor. M. contrasted the purity of their motives with the greed of the old politicians and businessmen. His fascination with their ideals led him to emulate them.

His plays, especially those included in *Kindai nōgaku shū* (1956; *Five Modern Nō Plays,* 1957), were the finest written in Japan in the postwar years. M.'s plays were cast in many idioms, and their contents ranged from contemporary events to themes inspired by the Nōo dramas and the tragedies of Euripides and Racine. His best full-length play was *Sado kōshaku fujin* (1965; *Madame de Sade,* 1967), of which he wrote: "I felt obliged to dispense entirely with the usual, trivial stage effects, and to control the action exclusively by dialogue; collisions of ideas had to create the shape of the drama, and sentiments had to be paraded throughout in the garb of reason." The play was clearly in the tradition of Racine, M.'s favorite among Western dramatists. Each of the six women of the play stands for a particular kind of feminine personality as it reacts to the offstage presence of the Marquis de Sade.

M.'s last work of fiction, the tetralogy *Hōjō no umi* (1969–71; the sea of fertility), is loosely based on an 11th-c. Japanese tale of dreams and reincarnation. In his own opinion, this was the grand summation of his work as a novelist. The first volume, *Haru no yuki* (1969; *Spring Snow,* 1972), evoked the world of the aristocracy in 1912. This story, told with exceptional beauty of style and detail, was an expression of the feminine ideals of Japan. The second volume, *Homba* (1969; *Runaway Horses,* 1972), by contrast, describes the masculine ideals of the way of the Japanese warrior. It takes place in the 1930s, and its protagonist, the stern young Isao, is the reincarnation of the rather effeminate protagonist of *Haru no yuki*. In *Homba* M. gave his most powerful expression of the themes of loyalty and devotion to Japanese ideals that had occupied him since *Yūkoku*.

The third volume, *Akatsuki no tera* (1970; *The Temple of Dawn,* 1973), is divided into two parts: the first is set in southeast Asia, where we first see the Thai princess who is the reincarnation of Isao; the second takes place in Japan after World War II, when the old values of society have been corrupted. The last volume, *Tennin gosui* (1971; *The Decay of the Angel,* 1974), carries the story into the future, and describes the conflict between the reincarnation of the Thai princess and the one man who has observed the four transformations of the being whose decay presages his end. The novel concludes with a superbly written scene that casts doubt on the reality of the events described in the four volumes. In the end we discover that the "sea of fertility" may be as arid as the region of that name on the moon, although it seems to suggest infinite richness.

On the day that M. delivered the final instalment of *Tennin gosui* to his publisher he and members of his private "army" broke into the headquarters of the Japanese Self-Defense Force. He unsuccessfully harangued a crowd of soldiers, and soon afterward committed *seppuku* in the traditional manner, apparently in the hopes of inducing the Japanese to reflect on what they had lost of their cultural heritage. The incident created an immense sensation, but M.'s reputation was to be determined not by this act but by the brilliant works in many genres he wrote during his short life. Long before his suicide he had established himself as the first Japanese writer whose fame was worldwide.

FURTHER WORKS: *Kinjiki* (1951–53; *Forbidden Colors,* 1968); *Manatsu no shi* (1953; *Death in Midsummer,* 1966); *Yoru no himawari* (1953; *Twilight Sunflower,* 1958); *Shiosai* (1954; *The Sound of Waves,* 1956); *Shizumeru Taki* (1955); *Shiroari no su* (1956); *Shi wo kaku shōnen* (1956; *The Boy Who Wrote Poetry,* 1977); *Bitoku no yoro-*meki (1957); *Rokumeikan* (1957); *Bara to kaizoku* (1958); *Ratai to ishō* (1959); *Yoroboshi* (1960; *Yoroboshi: The Blind Young Man,* 1979); *Kemono no tawamure* (1961); *Utsukushii hoshi* (1962); *Gogo no eikō* (1963; *The Sailor Who Fell from Grace with the Sea,* 1965); *Watakushi no henreki jidai* (1964); *Kinu to meisatsu* (1964); *Mikumano mōde* (1965); *Eirei no koe* (1966); *Suzaku-ke no metsubō* (1967); *Hagakure nyūmon* (1967; *The Way of the Samurai,* 1977); *Wa ga tomo Hittorā* (1968; *My Friend Hitler,* 1977); *Taiyō to tetsu* (1968; *Sun and Steel,* 1970); *Bunka bōei ron* (1969)

BIBLIOGRAPHY: Keene, D., *Landscapes and Portraits: Appreciations of Japanese Culture* (1971), pp. 204–25; Kimball, A. G., *Crisis in Identity and Contemporary Japanese Novels* (1973), pp. 75–93; Keene, D., "The Death of M.," in Dillon, W. S., ed., *The Cultural Drama: Modern Identities and Social Ferment* (1974), pp. 271–87; Nathan, J., *M.: A Biography* (1974); Miyoshi, M., *Accomplices of Silence: The Modern Japanese Novel* (1974), pp. 141–80; Scott-Stokes, H., *The Life and Death of Y. M.* (1974); McCarthy, P., "M. Y.'s *Confessions of a Mask,"* in Tsuruta, K., and Swann, T. E., eds., *Approaches to the Modern Japanese Novel* (1976), pp. 112–28; Ueda, M., *Modern Japanese Writers and the Nature of Literature* (1976), pp. 219–59; Yamanouchi, H., *The Search for Authenticity in Modern Japanese Literature* (1978), pp. 137–52

DONALD KEENE

MISTRAL, Gabriela

(pseud. of Lucila Godoy Alcayaga) Chilean poet, b. 7 April 1889, Vicuña; d. 10 Jan. 1957, Hempstead, N.Y., U.S.A.

As a young woman M. worked as a rural schoolteacher in various parts of Chile; she went to Mexico in 1922 as an educational consultant. In 1925 she joined the Chilean diplomatic service, representing Chile in Spain, Portugal, France, Brazil, and the U.S. M.'s first literary triumph came in 1914, when a group of sonnets, "Sonetos de la muerte" (sonnets of death), won a prize in Santiago. In 1945 she received the Nobel Prize for literature.

The major themes throughout M.'s work are the humanistic ones of love and respect for all people, especially children, women, and country folk. Another important motif is admiration for the natural world, which she often presents in specifically American or Chilean contexts and which she describes with great detail and clarity. Many of her poems reflect a preoccupation with death and with the passing of time, expressed at first, in *Desolación* (1922; desolation), as a blunt cry of personal anguish and in later works as a theme of universal application.

In *Desolación* M. describes herself as the "rural schoolteacher," a strong, compassionate woman dedicated to her work. In a brief section on nature she presents both such universal subjects as mountains, clouds, rain, stars, pine trees, and autumn, and specific places—Patagonia, and Iztaccíhuatl in Mexico. In the first section of *Desolación*, "Vida" (life), Christian faith is the main theme, and biblical imagery is abundant. The most important parts of the book deal with death as a dark, quiet, and impenetrable barrier separating people into two parallel worlds. The section "Dolor" (pain) includes the three autobiographical "Sonetos de la muerte," which reflect M.'s own feelings of loneliness and despair as she confronts the loss, by suicide, of the man she loved. These sonnets take the form of a spiritual monologue directed at the beloved. They promise that, after the death of the poet, the dark and cold image of death will become, for all eternity, a "sunny land" in which roses and lilies, symbols of hope beyond death, grow from decay and spread pollen over the earth. In the final sonnet M. alludes to her own selfish prayers, asking for the death of the beloved should he share his love with another woman. She expresses faith in a forgiving God who understands the exclusive nature of her love.

Many of the poems in *Ternura* (1924; tenderness) deal with children and the world as seen by them. This collection demonstrates M.'s ability to write simple yet elegant verse. She describes the precariousness of a young child's life, in which death is as near as sleep. A major section in *Ternura,* "Canciones de cuna" (cradle songs), has a pronounced melodic verse form, with a refrain. These lullabies focus on maternal love and care, and contain frequent references by M. to "my child," reflecting her deep longing for children of her own. The group "Cuentamundo" (tales of the world) contains descriptions of simple things basic to a complex world: air, light, water, animals, fruit.

M. continued her inventory of these basics in *Tala* (1938; devastation). In the "Materias" (matter) section she writes of bread, salt, water, rainfall, and air in the same manner as in *Ternura*. The opening of *Tala* is a group of somber personal poems focusing on the death of the poet's mother, in which M. expresses, through Christian imagery, belief in spiritual life after death. In other poems in *Tala* there are views of the Chilean landscape, the Caribbean Sea, tropical sun, and corn growing.

M.'s interest in nature continued in the collection *Lagar* (1954; wine press), in which her descriptions of nature are extended to areas as distant as Uruguay, Cuba, and California.

Intertwined throughout both *Tala* and *Lagar* are two contrasting worlds—the timeless and the evanescent. M. suggests that freedom from the confines of time, change, and rational cause-and-effect relationships is both desirable and inevitable. Escape from changes due to the passing of time can be found in constant elements in nature: the eternal air and sea, the centuries-old plants native to America. Another form of escape from the rational effects of the passing of time may be found in an irrational approach to life. In the section called "Locas mujeres" (mad women) in *Lagar* M. sketches women who find entrance to a timeless existence through obliteration of memory and logic by means of insanity—a state similar to death.

In the metaphysical poems of *Tala* and *Lagar* M. suggests that life is a mysterious pilgrimage leading to death, which she portrays as a final and complete liberation from the confines of both time and the rational world. Time, measured by each person as a succession of permanent memories, can bring people to a negation of the present, if they desire only to relive and eternalize moments remembered from the past. M. implies that she herself was caught in this paradox, for she describes herself poetically as wanting things she has never had or no longer has. It is the continuous presence of the past that makes the women of the poems "La abandonada" (the abandoned woman), "La humillada" (the humiliated woman), and others in *Lagar* seek refuge in irrationality or in death. M. traces a mystical progression, from harmony with the permanence of nature, from irrationality, or from death, to liberation from the earthly limits of time and to a sense of becoming part of a greater, mysterious, yet compelling universe.

In her work M. reveals a great understanding of and concern for humanity. The problems of individuals are presented specifically, although these same problems may be extended to a universal interpretation. Her love of nature is basic to her metaphysical poetry, in which the earth is found to be an unchanging source of hope and security. Death, seen in her early work as an enemy, is, in *Tala* and *Lagar,* a source of mystical beauty.

FURTHER WORKS: *Lecturas para mujeres* (1923); *Rondas para niños* (1930); *Nubes blancas* (1930); *La Oración de la maestra* (1930); *Antología* (1941); *Poemas de las madres* (1950); *Poesías completas* (1958); *Motivas de San Francisco* (1965); *Antología de G. M.* (1967). FURTHER VOLUME IN ENGLISH: *Selected Poems of G. M.* (1957)

BIBLIOGRAPHY: Pinilla, N., *Biografía de M.* (1946); Saavedra Molina, J., *G. M.: Su vida y su obra* (1946); Iglesias, A., *G. M. y el modernismo en Chile* (1950); Figueira, G., *G. M.: Fuerza y ternura de América* (1952); Ladrón de Guevara, M., *G. M.: Magnificent Rebel* (1962); Torres-Rioseco, A., *G. M. (una profunda amistad, una dulce recuerdo)* (1962); Arce de Vásquez, M., *G. M.: The Poet and Her Work* (1964); Preston, M. C. A., *A Study of Significant Variants in the Poetry of G. M.* (1964); Taylor, M. C., *G. M.'s Religious Sensibility* (1968)

CATHERINE VERA

MITTELHOLZER, Edgar

Guyanese novelist, b. 16 Dec. 1909, New Amsterdam; d. 6 May 1965, Farnham, England

M. was born in what was then British Guiana to mixed-blood, middle-class parents who, he claims, were bitterly disappointed in his swarthy complexion. Educated at the local secondary school, he seemed destined for a career in the civil service. He determined early on to become a writer, however, and worked at various times as a customs officer, meteorological observer, cinema inspector, journalist, and hotel receptionist to support himself while he wrote. He left for England in 1948 to become a professional novelist.

Although M.'s first novel, *Corentyne Thunder* (1941), is of considerable historical significance in the West Indies, since it was the first work of fiction to deal in depth with the Guyanese peasantry, it went largely unnoticed because of World War II. His second, *A Morning at the Office* (1950; Am., *Morning in Trinidad*), however, attracted much attention not only to M. himself but more generally to English-Caribbean writing, which was beginning to appear in London and New York. The analysis of race and class in these early works and the massive interpretation of Guyanese history in his Kaywana trilogy—*Children of Kaywana* (1952; repub. as two volumes, *Children of Kaywana* and *Kaywana Heritage,* 1976), *The Harrowing of Hubertus* (1954; Am., *Hubertus;* repub. as *Kaywana Stock,* 1959), and *Kaywana Blood* (1958; Am., *The Old Blood*)—no doubt helped to establish race and history as basic themes in West Indian writing. A more general assessment of his twenty-five books indicates, however, that West Indian society is less intrinsic to his works than such concerns as the situations of the strong and the weak in society, and such problems as those caused by "racial, cultural and psychic disorientation," referred to by the critic Michael Gilkes as "the Divided Consciousness."

These themes are explored on a very personal level in M.'s autobiography *A Swarthy Boy* (1963), on a social and historical level in the works mentioned above and in such others set in the West Indies as *A Tale of Three Places* (1957) and *Latticed Echoes* (1960), and on a very didactic level in such novels set in England as *The Weather in Middenshot* (1952) and *The Aloneness of Mrs. Chatham* (1965). As his career as a novelist progressed, M. became less interested in depicting people and more interested in expounding his ideas. The world of his West Indian novels, created with some understanding and sympathy, accommodates more organically his themes of strength, weakness, and disorientation than does the English world of his later novels, which is merely a framework into which these themes are obsessively forced.

In the majority of his novels, from the first to the last, M.'s characters resort to suicide as the only satisfactory way to cope with the anguish caused by disorientation and alienation. The reader of M.'s work who has come to recognize so many of M.'s own interests and obsessions in his characters is hardly surprised to learn that M. burned himself to death in a manner similar to that used by a character in his last novel, *The Jilkington Drama* (1965).

While M.'s work at its worst descends to obsessively haranguing the reader to accept an extreme and warped vision of the world, at its best it does lay bare the anguish of an intense and passionate personality.

FURTHER WORKS: *Shadows Move among Them* (1951); *The Life and Death of Sylvia* (1953; repub. as *Sylvia,* 1963); *The Adding Machine* (1954); *My Bones and My Flute* (1955); *Of Trees and the Sea* (1956); *The Weather Family* (1958); *With a Carib Eye* (1958); *A Tinkling in the Twilight* (1959); *The Mad MacMullochs* (1959, under pseud. H. Austin Woodsley); *Eltonsbrody* (1960); *Thunder Returning* (1961); *The Piling of Clouds* (1961); *The Wounded and the Worried* (1962); *Uncle Paul* (1963)

BIBLIOGRAPHY: Cartey, W., "The Rhythm of Society and Landscape (M., Carew, Williams, Dathorne)," *New World,* Guyana Independence Issue (1966), 97–104; Birbalsingh, F. M., "E. M.: Moralist or Pornographer?" *JCL,* No. 7 (1961), 88–103; Howard, W. J., "E. M.'s Tragic Vision," *CarQ,* 16, 4 (1970), 19–28; James, L., Introduction to *Corentyne Thunder* (1970), pp. 1–6; Gilkes, M., *Racial Identity and Individual Consciousness in the Caribbean Novel* (1975), pp. 5–35; Gilkes, M., "E. M.," in King, B., ed., *West Indian Literature* (1979), pp. 95–110; Gilkes, M., *The West Indian Novel* (1981), pp. 41–85

ANTHONY BOXILL

MIYAZAWA Kenji

Japanese poet and writer of children's stories, b. 27 Aug. 1896, Hanamaki; d. 21 Sept. 1933, Hanamaki

M. went to an agricultural college and taught at an agricultural school. Both institutions had been established to meet the special need of his region, Iwate, which suffered from chronic crop failures because of the harsh climate and backward agricultural methods. A devout Buddhist of an activist sect, M. resigned from his school in 1926 and turned to

farming to put his teachings into practice. During the next few years he forced himself to subsist on a poorer diet than even the local farmers were used to, and ruined his health.

M.'s scientific training, Buddhist vision, and concern for the plight of the local farmers, combined with his hallucinatory imagination, sense of drama, and humor, resulted in a highly distinctive body of work. His poems are laced with precise technical terms and vivid descriptions, but they seldom become trivial or simply curious, supported as they are by a larger view of life, a combination of Buddhist pantheism and the belief that science can solve all problems. At the center of his poetic world is the poet himself, presented as an *asura* (a Sanskrit word), in Buddhist belief a contentious, arrogant, malevolent giant somewhere between a human and a beast. As described in the title poem of his first book, *Haru to shura* (1924; spring and asura), M.'s *asura* is unenlightened and restless. Still, M.'s poetic self is far from being egotistic. Even when he describes himself, he externalizes the description. More often, he is concerned with people and phenomena: his dead sister, a bull enjoying himself in the night mist, a horse that died from overwork, a tired farm boy, the movement of clouds, a rainstorm, a country doctor. It is the depth and range of M.'s mind apparent in such poems that make him outstanding.

The stories M. wrote for children share similar qualities, here often extended in a fantastic way. M. describes a great variety of animals and objects, such as a slug, a cat, a fox, a nighthawk, a lark, an ant, a frog, a birch tree, a constellation, and an electric pole, as if he let them project their qualities onto himself, rather than projecting his emotions onto them. The stories are often stark, sometimes brutal. Even where compassion is the theme, the resolution of the conflict of the story is usually realistic and credible.

M. wrote prolifically, and although he revised many of his poems and stories, a good number of them give the impression of being roughhewn and unfinished. Not widely known while alive, he is now considered one of the three or four greatest poets, and surely the most imaginative writer of children's stories, of 20th-c. Japan.

FURTHER WORKS: *M. K. zenshū* (15 vols., 1973–77); *M. K. zenshū* (16 vols., 1979–80). FURTHER VOLUMES IN ENGLISH: *Winds from*

Afar (1972); *Spring and Asura: Poems of K. M.* (1973)

HIROAKI SATO

MŇAČKO, Ladislav

Czechoslovak novelist, journalist, dramatist, and poet (writing in Slovak), b. 29 Jan. 1919, Valašské Klobouky

M. is of working-class origin and had no formal higher education. When the Nazi occupation of Czechoslovakia began, he joined the partisans operating in the mountains that lie between Moravia and Slovakia. After the war he embarked on a varied and tumultuous literary career. In 1967 M. traveled to Israel despite being expressly forbidden by his government to do so. As a result he was deprived of citizenship. Nevertheless, he returned to Czechoslovakia in 1968, but left again when the U.S.S.R. forcibly stamped out the reforms instituted by the Dubček regime. The novel *Die siebente Nacht* (pub. in German, 1968; *The Seventh Night,* 1969) is his account of the 1968 invasion of Czechoslovakia. Since 1968 M. has been living in western Europe.

In the early 1950s M. started to write that particular blend of reportage and fiction for which he has become known. His reportage uses techniques of fiction, and his fiction has substantial factual content.

As a roving reporter M. explored neglected regions of Czechoslovakia and brought back vivid, and sometimes deeply disturbing, reports of the problems people had to cope with in the building of socialism in remote and impoverished parts of the country.

M. achieved his greatest success as a novelist with the publication of *Smrt' sa volá Engelchen* (1959; *Death Is Called Engelchen,* 1961). In this clearly autobiographical book (which was made into a successful film) he returned to his experience as a partisan during the Nazi occupation. He did not present the war in the simplistic terms common to most Czech and Slovak fiction of the period. Instead, he dealt with the demoralization and brutalization brought about by war and affecting both the Nazis and the partisan fighters.

A special problem facing the partisans was that of not jeopardizing the lives of the civilian population, who were subject to dreadful punishment for aiding them. The proceeds from *Smrt' sa volá Engelchen* were donated to the surviving inhabitants of Ploština, which was destroyed by the Nazis in reprisal for just such aid to the partisan group of which M. had been a member.

Although a convinced Communist, M. grew more and more disllusioned with Communist Czechoslovakia. In *Oneskorené reportáže* (1962; belated reportages) M. shows the perversion of the revolutionary spirit in the 1950s. The book presents a stark description of the great suffering inflicted on innocent people by the government and by local Party chiefs under the flimsiest pretexts. M. did not exempt himself from guilt, as he too had contributed to bringing about the debasement of more humane goals. *Oneskorené reportáže* was meant as a warning against the repetition of similar outrages and was written to reestablish trust among men. It was one of the most widely read books of the postwar era.

Ako chutí moc (1968; *The Taste of Power,* 1967) widened the rift between M. and the Novotný group, which had developed with the publication of *Oneskorené reportáže.* President Novotný felt he was being caricatured in this new novel about the gradual corruption of a revolutionary leader. The story is one of a man who started out as an idealistic revolutionist and ended as a venal politician. The novel is also a condemnation of a system that has failed, one that has devoured many of its children.

In his lively journalistic style, M. exposed evils that at that time few other writers dared to tackle.

FURTHER WORKS: *Partyzáni* (1945); *Piesne ingotov* (1950); *Mosty na východ* (1952); *Bubny a činely* (1954); *Živá voda* (1954); *Vody Orava* (1955); *Marxova ulica* (1957); *D'aleko je do Whampoa* (1958); *Aj taký človek* (1960); *Kde končia prašné cesty* (1963); *Dlouhá bílá přerušovaná čára* (1965; tr. into Czech from the manuscript); *Nočný rozhovor* (1966); *Der Vorgang* (1970; tr. into German from the manuscript); *Súdruh Münchhausen* (1972)

BIBLIOGRAPHY: Součková, M., *A Literary Satellite* (1970), pp. 150–53; Hájek, I., comp., "L. M.," in Mihailovich, V. D., et al., eds., *Modern Slavic Literatures* (1976), Vol. II, pp. 154–57

IGOR HÁJEK

MOBERG, Vilhelm

Swedish novelist and dramatist, b. 20 Aug. 1898, Algutsboda; d. 8 Aug. 1973, Väddö

M.'s forebears were soldiers and small farmers in the province of Småland, in southern Sweden. Largely self-educated, M. worked in the glassblowing industry and as a farm laborer before turning to journalism in his early twenties. The critical and popular success of *Raskens* (1927; the Rask family), a carefully documented novel based on family tradition about the daily life of a soldier and his family in late-19th-c. rural Småaland, enabled M. to concentrate on literary endeavors.

In the partly autobiographical trilogy comprising *Sänkt sedebetyg* (1935; *Memory of Youth*, 1937), *Sömnlös* (1937; *Sleepless Nights*, 1940), and *Giv oss jorden!* (1939; *The Earth Is Ours*, 1940)—one-volume translation of complete trilogy, *The Earth Is Ours*, 1940—the protagonist Knut Toring's inability to find happiness either in the rural Småland of his youth, where he lacks intellectual stimulation, or in Stockholm, where he feels cut off from his roots, becomes a metaphor for existential homelessness. The final volume culminates in an impassioned plea for the defense of humanitarian principles against encroaching fascism, a theme M. expands on in the historical novel *Rid i natt!* (1941; *Ride This Night!*, 1943), which M. made into a play in 1942.

Soldat med brutet gevär (1944; partial tr., *When I Was a Child*, 1956) also incorporates considerable autobiographical material, but the focus is on social history rather than psychological conflict. By tracing the influences of various social and political movements on his fictional alter ego, Valter Sträng, M. portrays the confrontation between the innate conservatism of rural culture and the political radicalism that accompanied rapid industrialization in the early 1900s.

M.'s best-known work is the four-volume epic about mid-19th-c. emigration to America: *Utvandrarna* (1949; *The Emigrants*, 1951), *Invandrarna* (1952; *Unto a Good Land*, 1954), *Nybyggarna* (1956; *The Settlers*, 1978), and *Sista brevet till Sverige* (1959; *Last Letter Home*, 1978). In *Utvandrarna* M.'s representative characters, a group of Småland peasants, collectively illustrate the historical causes of emigration: poverty, religious persecution, and the desire for personal freedom and social betterment.

While never abandoning documentary realism, M. places increasing emphasis in the later volumes on the psychological cost of the uprooting. The work connects thematically both with the Knut Toring trilogy and with *Din stund på jorden* (1961, dramatized 1967; *A Time on Earth*, 1965), in which the protagonist is a Swedish-American of M.'s own generation.

M. wrote more than thirty plays, primarily folk comedies set in rural Småland, such as *Marknadsafton* (1929; market day eve) and *Än keman Jarl* (1940; Jarl the widower); or serious contemporary dramas about moral or social issues, like *Vår ofödde son* (1945; our unborn son) and *Domaren* (1957; the judge). In Scandinavia M. was also known for speaking out in defense of individual freedoms and for his attacks on corruption in government. Before his death he had completed two volumes of *Min svenska historia* (1970, 1972; *A History of the Swedish People*, 1972).

M.'s strengths are his straightforward narrative style and epic breadth combined, in his best works, with penetrating psychological insight and a lyricism rooted in the natural rhythms of the language. Like other working-class writers of his generation, he deliberately set out to tell about the people from whom he came, and his works are important documents of social history. Still the most widely read serious novelist in Sweden today, he is also among the few Swedish writers to have achieved international renown.

FURTHER WORKS: *I vapenrock och linnebyxor* (1921); *Kassabrist* (1925); *Hustrun* (1928); *Bröllopssalut* (1929); *Långt från landsvägen* (1929); *De knutna händerna* (1930); *A. P. Rosell, bankdirektör* (1932); *Mans kvinna* (1933); *Våld* (1933); *Kyskhet* (1936); *Jungfrukammare* (1938); *En löskekarl* (1940); *Hundra gånger gifta* (1941); *Sanningen kryper fram* (1943); *Segerstedtstriden* (1945); *Brudarnas källa* (1946); *Gudens hustru* (1946); *Fallet Krukmakaregatan* (1951); *Det gamla riket* (1953); *Att övervaka överheten* (1953); *Lea och Rakel* (1954); *Därför är jag republikan* (1955); *Komplotterna* (1956); *Dramatik* (3 vols., 1957); *Nattkyparen* (1961); *Sagoprinsen* (1962); *Förrädarland* (1968); *Berättelser ur min levnad* (1968)

BIBLIOGRAPHY: Winther, S. K., "M. and a New Genre for the Emigrant Novel," *SS*, 34 (1962), 170–82; Moberg, V., "Why I Wrote the Novel about Swedish Emigrants," *SPHQ*, 17 (1966), 63–77; Alexis, G. T., "Sweden to Minnesota: V. M.'s Fictional Reconstruction," *AQ*, 18 (1966), 81–94; Holmes, P. A., "Symbol, Theme and Structure in *Utvandrarromanen*," in Lagerroth, E. and U.-B., eds., *Perspektiv på Utvandrarromanen* (1971), pp. 239–48; Orton, G., and Holmes, P., "Memoirs of an Idealist: V. M.'s *Soldat med brutet gevär*," *SS*, 48 (1976), 29–51; McKnight, R., *M.'s Emigrant Novels and the Journals of Andrew Peterson: A Study of Influences and Parallels* (1979); Holmes, P., *V. M.* (1980)

ROCHELLE WRIGHT

MODERNISM

In its general sense as applied to literature and art, "modernism" connotes change and innovation, a break with the past, a rejection of the traditional and conventional, and a search for new means of expression. In the 20th c. the word has been loosely used to describe art and literature which broke from the dominant 19th-c. modes of romanticism and realism and which, in the case of literature, experimented with language and form, found new subject matter, was antimimetic, and frequently self-consciously delved into the inner states of the writer.

"Modernism," however, is more narrowly applied to specific literary movements in Latin America and Europe, the most prominent being the *modernismo* of Spanish America. It has been customary to date Spanish American modernism from the publication in Chile of a collection of stories and poems entitled *Azul* (1888; blue) by the Nicaraguan writer Rubén Darío (q.v.). In fact, although *Azul* was a landmark of the movement and although Darío was the first to use the term, the modernist writings of the Cuban José Martí (1853–1895) and the Mexican Manuel Gutiérrez Nájera (1859–1895), as well as works by the Cuban poet Julián del Casal (1863–1893) and the Colombian poet José Asunción Silva (1865–1896) predate *Azul*. Nevertheless, Darío is the central figure of the movement.

Spanish American modernism originated in a dissatisfaction with the provincial Hispanic tradition of poetry and perhaps also from a loss of religious faith. The modernists desired to free Spanish American poetry

from didactic purposes and to make it more cosmopolitan. They first turned for inspiration to the French Parnassians—Leconte de Lisle (1818–1894), José María de Hérédia (1842–1905), Catulle Mendès (1843–1909)—with their emphasis on concision, color, form, metrical perfection, and emotional detachment, and their "art for art's sake" theory derived from Théophile Gautier. French symbolism (q.v.)—Verlaine, Rimbaud, Mallarmé—also exerted a strong influence, adding musical flow, verbal hermeticism, conceptual complexity, synesthetic imagery, and a mystical undercurrent to the modernist esthetic. The examples of Victor Hugo, Charles Baudelaire, and Edgar Allan Poe also had an influence on Spanish American modernism.

In Darío's work the modernist tendency is epitomized. He wrote in highly literary language, experimented with unusual meters, added color and innovative imagery to Spanish-language verse, and enriched his texts with classical and mythological allusions and philosophical undertones.

The leading Argentine modernist poet was Leopoldo Lugones (q.v.), whose verse was influenced by Hugo and Jules Laforgue (1860–1887). Lugones and other major modernist poets—the Mexican Amado Nervo (q.v.), the Uruguayan Julio Herrera y Reissig (q.v.), the Bolivian Ricardo Jaimes Freyre (1868–1933), the last of whom used Nordic themes, and the Peruvian José Santos Chocano (q.v.)—reflect awareness not only of symbolism and other vanguardist tendencies but also sensitive and intelligent identification with New World problems and cultures; although they looked to Europe (but not Spain), they also tried to be essentially American.

The Mexican poet Enrique González Martínez (q.v.) is considered by many the transitional figure between modernism and postmodernism in Spanish American poetry. While his verse is marked by Parnassian and symbolist elements, his sonnet "Tuércele el cuello al cisne" (1911; "Wring the Neck of the Swan," 1958), in which he replaces the swan, the symbol of elaborate modernist rhetoric, with the wise owl, is seen by many critics as signaling the end of the modernist period. Among postmodernists who broke away from the ornate language of Darío and his contemporaries were the Mexican Ramón López Velarde (1888–1921), who wrote with linguistic brilliance about the corruption of the city and about erotic subjects, and the Chilean poet Gabriela Mistral (q.v.), a Nobel Prize winner.

Spanish American prose writers also participated in the modernist movement. The Uruguayan José Enrique Rodó (q.v.) was the foremost essayist of the group; in *Ariel* (1900; *Ariel,* 1922) and other works he pleads for spiritual values in a materialistic world. The Venezuelan novelist Manuel Díaz Rodríguez (1871–1927), in *Ídolos rotos* (1901; broken idols) and *Sangre patricia* (1902; patrician blood), wrote in highly chiseled prose on symbolic themes. The Guatemalan literary journalist Enrique Gómez Carillo (1873–1927) kept the New World's Hispanic public abreast of modernist and vanguardist developments in Europe.

The Spanish American War and the arrival of Darío in Europe in 1898 hastened the impact of modernism in Spain. The war caused intellectuals to reassess Spanish culture, and Darío's innovations had an influence on such writers as Juan Ramón Jiménez (q.v.); the poet and dramatist Francisco Villaespesa (1877–1936), who popularized the movement in Spain; and Manuel Machado (1874–1947), a poet who combined Andalusian folklore with the musicality of modernism. The impact of Spanish American modernism, with its roots in symbolism, was also felt in Portugal, where its most eminent representative was the poet Eugénio de Castro (1869–1944).

The term "modernism" has also been used to describe specific avant-garde literary manifestations in countries outside of Spanish America—in particular, Russia, the Ukraine, the Swedish-speaking part of Finland, and Brazil.

In Russia the term is identified with the "decadent" foreign influences (primarily French) of the turn of the century and is used more or less interchangeably with symbolism. Pioneered by Dmitry Merezhkovsky (q.v.), with the mystical philosophy of Vladimir Solovyov (1853–1900) as a precursor, Russian modernism was dominated in its early phase by the poets Konstantin Balmont, Valery Bryusov, and Fyodor Sologub (qq.v.) and later by Alexandr Blok, Andrey Bely, and Vyacheslav Ivanov (qq.v.). The movement was notable for its aesthetic individualism tinged with anarchism and for its rejection of moralizing realism in literature. In the Ukraine the relaxation of censorship after the revolution of 1905 led to a period of

modernism influenced by symbolism and the concept of art for art's sake. While continuing to deal with Ukrainian subject matter, particularly village life and the role of the intelligentsia in the Ukraine, modernist prose writers and poets searched for new forms. In the 1920s the Soviet government put a stop to the development of modernist writing in the Ukraine, imposing the strictures of socialist ideology.

Finland-Swedish modernism came about around the time of Finland's independence from Russia (1917), the victory of the Whites in the 1918 civil war, and the establishment of the Republic of Finland (1919), when an atmosphere of optimism was pervasive. Poetry was freed from traditional rhyme and meter and came under the influence of such avant-garde movements as Dadaism and surrealism (qq.v.). Edith Södergran (q.v.) introduced modernism into Finland-Swedish poetry and had an enormous influence on later Finland-Swedish and Swedish poets. Along with her, Elmer Diktonius, Gunnar Björling, and Rabbe Enckell (qq.v.) were the leading modernist poets, while Hagar Olsson (1893–1978), in her criticism, fiction, and drama, epitomizes Finland-Swedish modernist prose writing.

Modernism in Brazil (see also Brazilian Literature) had almost no links with the Spanish American modernism of the turn of the century. Coming somewhat later than Darío's brand of modernism, it had its sources in futurism, expressionism, and cubism (qq.v.); gathering momentum during the first decades of the century, Brazilian modernism was proclaimed and celebrated at a series of sessions on the arts called the Modern Art Week, held in 1922 in São Paulo. Its tenets were that art (all art, not just literature) was to utilize native and folkloric sources, that the Brazilian vernacular rather than "classical" Portuguese was to be used, and avant-garde movements of Europe and North America were to be adapted to Brazilian themes. (A later development was the idea that Brazilian literature was to be free from foreign influences.) Modernism dominated all the arts in Brazil until after World War II, and its influence is still felt.

Monteiro Lobato's (q.v.) early stories and critical writings are of great importance to the beginnings of Brazilian modernism. Its outstanding exponent, however, was Mário de Andrade (q.v.), who in his poetry, fiction—in particular, *Macunaíma* (1928; Macunaíma)—and essays embodied the iconoclastic spirit of the movement. The essayist José da Graça Aranha (q.v.) was the strongest defender of the modernists. Oswald de Andrade (q.v.), one of the organizers of the Modern Art Week, in his poetry and prose exemplifies the modernist idiom—informal, irreverent, exalting the primitive. One faction of modernism was highly nationalistic and somewhat fascistic; Ricardo Cassiano (q.v.), a member of this group, wrote *Martim Cererê* (1928; Martim Cererê), the epic poem of the modernist movement.

To mention outstanding writers of Brazilian modernism is to list all the outstanding writers of the first half of the century. Major poets include Manuel Bandeira (q.v.), who became the leader of the Rio de Janeiro modernists; Cecília Meireles (q.v.), considered by many to be the most important woman poet writing in Portuguese; Carlos Drummond de Andrade (q.v.), one of the greatest of Latin American poets; Jorge de Lima (1895–1951), from the Northeast, who wrote excellent Negro poetry and religious verse; and the younger João Cabral de Melo Neto (b. 1920), who carried on the regionalist orientation of the movement.

The Northeast developed its own form of modernism, particularly in the regional novel. The seminal influence was the anthropologist and novelist Gilberto Freyre (q.v.), who dealt with the distinctive culture of the region. Jorge Amado, Graciliano Ramos, and José Lins do Rêgo (qq.v.) were the outstanding modernist novelists of the Brazilian Northeast, while João Guimarães Rosa (q.v.), innovative in style and technique, wrote of the region of Minas Gerais. There is hardly a Brazilian writer today who has not in some way been touched by the modernism of the 1920s, 1930s, and 1940s.

BIBLIOGRAPHY: Goldberg, I., *Studies in Spanish American Literature* (1920); Craig, G. D., *The Modernist Trend in Spanish American Poetry* (1934); Spender, S., *The Struggle of the Modern* (1963); Davison, N. J., *The Concept of Modernism in Hispanic Criticism* (1966); Nist, J., *The Modernist Movement in Brazil* (1967); Howe, I., ed., *The Idea of the Modern in Literature and the Arts* (1968); Anderson, R. R., *Spanish American Modernism: A Selected Bibliography* (1970); Chiari, J., *The Aesthetics of Modernism* (1970); Martins, W., *The Modernist Idea* (1970); Bradbury, M., and McFarlane, J., *Modernism 1890–1930* (1974); Forster, M. H., ed., *Tradition and Renewal: Essays on Twentieth-Century Latin American Literature and Culture* (1975); Ackroyd, P., *Notes for a New Culture: An Essay on Modernism* (1976); Bender, T. K., et al., *Modernism in Literature* (1977); Faulkner, P., *Modernism* (1977)

BOYD G. CARTER

MOFOLO, Thomas

Lesotho novelist (writing in South Sotho), b. 2 Aug. 1875, Khojane, Basutoland (now Lesotho); d. 8 Sept. 1948, Teyateyaneng

When M. was five, his Christian parents moved to the Qomoqomong Valley, Quthing District. There M. met the black Christian missionary teacher whose devotion to education M. was to idealize in the figure of Reverend Katse in the novel *Pitseng* (1910; Pitseng). M. became a houseboy to Alfred Casalis, who was the head of the Bible school, the printing press, and the book depot in Morija. Recognizing M.'s potential, Casalis sent him to the Bible School and then to the teachers' college, from which M. received certification. Casalis also encouraged him to write.

M.'s first novel, *Moeti oa bochabela* (1907; *The Traveller of the East,* 1934), had first been serialized in *Leselinyana,* a Sotho journal. It is probably the first novel by a black to be published in southern Africa. Set in Basutoland, the action of the morality tale centers around the quest of the young protagonist, Fekisi, for the causes of the presence of evil in the world. Although he does not find the answer, his journey ends in his ascent to a Christian heaven where all is honesty and virtue.

In this novel Christian morality is idealized, while that of the African is shown to be in decline. M. tried to integrate African values with Christian values in a harmonious synthesis; Christianity for him was a way of restoring the purity of ancient African civilization.

The plot of *Pitseng,* M.'s second novel, concerns the marriage between two young Christianized Africans. In showing the moderation, discipline, and patience of both Alfred and Aria, qualities that make their marriage bond secure, M. alluded to marriage as the symbol of the relationship between the Church and Christ. Much emphasis is given to the character portrayal of the simple people who live in the secluded valley of Pitseng. In contrast to the virtue and piety of Alfred and Aria, M. pictures the hypocrisies of many other Christian Africans, black and white. M. here focuses on the discrepancy between the teachings of Christianity and the behavior of many Christians.

M.'s masterpiece, *Chaka* (1925; *Chaka the Zulu,* 1931; new tr., 1981), the last of his three novels, was written in 1910, but it was considered unsuitable for publication by M.'s only recourse, the missionary press, which did not alter this position for fifteen years. Disillusioned, M. gave up writing at thirty-five and devoted the next years to building a successful business. In 1937 he retired to his farm. But he was not to be allowed to enjoy it. M.'s farm was expropriated in 1940 when the government proceeded to enforce a prohibition of the Land Act of 1914—that a black could not own land that abuts the property of a white. Thus victimized by the whites and having lost the financial security obtained by years of work, he became a broken man. His last years were redeemed from grim poverty only by a small pension.

Chaka, a dramatic departure from M.'s earlier books, is the tragic study of a man who, once accustomed to the gratifications of power, can no longer live according to common morality. The novel is based on the history of an African conqueror, the "black Napoleon," who in the early 19th c. amassed an army of close to a million Zulu warriors and ruled over half of Africa, from the Congo to South Africa. In M.'s version, Chaka becomes evil when he succeeds to the chiefdom at his father's death; from that point on Chaka develops from a moral man into a monster. He sinks into the dark world of sorcery and paganism, bartering his soul for power. There is no turning back for Chaka, and he goes on to extraordinary success on the battlefields. But the code of power and violence by which he lives in the end devours him as well, when he is assassinated by his two half-brothers.

The appeal of Chaka is mythic; about him is the light of the fallen prince; he is Satan, Tamburlaine, and Faust. Although he destroys himself, his is a magnificent adventure. There is poetry in his evilness, fascination in his decline. Chaka chose the way of power, violence, cruelty. M. was attracted to another way—that of love and

trust in humanity—but he understood the frustration and rage at the root of Chaka's evilness, and as an African he could even glory in Chaka's magnificent conquests.

Soon after its publication *Chaka* was a best seller in Africa, both in South Sotho and in other African and European-language editions, and M., who by then had long stopped writing, enjoyed its success.

M., both in the virtues he exhibited during his lifetime and in the themes he conveyed through his novels, belongs to a transitional African period, one in which conflict between traditional and modern values resulted in a painful distortion of both value systems. His work illustrates the tragic irony that angels as well as monsters are swallowed up when violence overtakes the African terrain.

BIBLIOGRAPHY: Kunene, D. P., *The Works of T. M.: Summaries and Critiques* (1967); Gérard, A. S., *Four African Literatures: Xhosa, Sotho, Zulu, Amharic* (1974), pp. 125–30; Mphahlele, E., *The African Image,* rev. ed. (1974), pp. 206–10, 223; Ikonné, C., "Purpose versus Plot: The Double Vision of T. M.'s Narrator," in Heywood, C., ed., *Aspects of South African Literature* (1976), pp. 54–65; Burness, D., ed., *Shaka, King of Zulus* (1976), passim; Swanepoel, C. F., "Reflections on the Art of T. M.," *Limi,* 7 (1979), 63–76

MARTIN TUCKER

MOHANTY, Gopinath

Indian novelist and short-story writer (writing in Oriya), b. 1 April 1914, Cuttack

M. was born into an aristocratic landowning family, the ninth and youngest child of his parents. He earned an M.A. in English literature at Ravenshaw College in Cuttack and then entered government service as a subdeputy collector under the British administration. While holding a variety of jobs in his home state of Orissa, he came into contact with a cross section of different groups, particularly the Adibasis, a tribal people. He mastered the Adibasi language, and has often used Adibasi words and phrases in his novels. He was further inspired, if not influenced, by the literary achievement of his elder brother, Khanu Charan Mohanty (b. 1906), a novelist of high repute. M. is a polyglot, a man of culture, and also a keen observer of human nature. He received the

Sahitya Akademi Award in 1955 and the highest Indian literary prize, the Jnanpith Award, in 1974.

M.'s major novels are *Paraja* (1945; subjects), *Amritara santan* (1949; son of the nectar), *Danapani* (1955; bread and butter), and *Mati matal* (1964; *matal* soil). The central theme of *Paraja* is the exploitation of the poor by landlords. *Amnitara santan* deals with the Kondha, an Adibasi tribe, and focuses on the life of a village woman. In *Danapani* M. lays bare the hypocrisy of a "town man," showing how he exploits people, including his wife, in his ambition to rise to high position. *Mati matal* is an in-depth study of the nature of an individual and his efforts to come to terms with the environment and with changing society.

M. has also written numerous short stories; two of the best known are "Ghasara phula" (1957; flower of grass) and "Na mane nahin" (1968; name not remembered).

M. brought glory to the Oriya language and raised its status among other Indian languages. He has great insight into human nature. His special contribution is his depiction of the Adibasis' way of life, which no writer had done before. His awareness of changing times and values is evident in his work. Above all, he is an outstanding craftsman.

FURTHER WORKS: *Managahirara chhasa* (1940); *Dadi Buddha* (1944); *Harijana* (1948); *Sarata babunka gali* (1950); *Rahura chhaya* (1952); *Dwipatra* (1954); *Sapana mati* (1954); *Naba badhu* (1956); *Chhai alua* (1956); *Sarala Mahabharata* (1956); *Siba bhai* (1958); *Poda kapala* (1958); *Mahapurusa* (1958); *Mukti Pathe* (1958); *Apahancha* (1961); *Tantrikar* (1963); *Ranadhandola* (1963); *Dipang jyoti* (1965); *Utkala mani* (1967); *Gupta ganga* (1967); *Pahanta* (1970); *Udanta khai* (1971); *Akash sundari* (1972); *Analanala* (1973). FURTHER VOLUME IN ENGLISH: *Ants, and Other Stories* (1979)

BIBLIOGRAPHY: Mansinha, M., *History of Oriya Literature* (1962), pp. 268–70; Mohanty, J. M., *There Where Trees Flower* (1980), pp. 62–79

BIJAY KUMAR DAS

MOLDAVIAN (S.S.R.) LITERATURE

The literature of the Moldavian Soviet Socialist Republic must be treated as distinct from that of Romania. Created in 1940 by a merger of the former Romanian province of Bessarabia (1918–40) and the small Moldavian Autonomous Soviet Socialist Republic, which had been organized in 1924 east of the interwar Soviet–Romanian border, the Moldavian S.S.R., except during World War II, has been completely incorporated into the Soviet political and social system. In literature the symbol of the incorporation was the adoption of a modified Cyrillic alphabet (a version of this alphabet had been in use since 1924 in the Moldavian A.S.S.R., but this tiny region—created as a symbol of the Soviet intention to reacquire Bessarabia—did not produce any literature of consequence). Although Moldavian differs only slightly from standard Romanian, and Moldavian writers could not but draw inspiration from Romanian as well as Soviet sources, since 1945 Moldavian writers have been fully integrated into Soviet cultural life, and their themes and methods have reflected Soviet rather than Romanian realities.

The major themes of poetry immediately after World War II were patriotism and the building of socialism; the epic, well suited to civic poetry, was the favorite genre. The work of Emilian Bukov (b. 1909) and Andrei Lupan (b. 1912) was typical, for in it ideological and social considerations prevailed over aesthetic requirements. Since the 1950s subject matter and means of expression have diversified, as the poetry of Emil Lotianu (b. 1936) reveals. His work runs the gamut from civic to love poetry, conveying sentiment and conviction through striking images.

Fiction has generally followed the same evolution as poetry. At first, the peasant and his adjustment to collectivized society was the dominant theme, but in the 1950s other heroes and new techniques came to the fore. The first Moldavian novel, Bukov's *Kresk etazhele* (1952; the floors grow), dealt with the urban working class, and Adriadna Shalar's (b. 1923) novel *Neastymper* (1961; restlessness) described the spiritual formation of the new generation. One of the major innovators in prose has been Ion Drutse (b. 1928), whose novels, among them *Balade din kympie* (1963; ballads of the steppes), pursue the fortunes of the peasantry between the world wars. Telling his stories in the laconic, figurative language reminiscent of popular fables, he displays a keen appreciation of the material and psychological foundations of village life.

297

Moldavian drama reached maturity more slowly than poetry and prose. The first important Moldavian play, *Lumina* (1948; light), by Lupan, was typical of the early preoccupation of dramatists with broad social problems and their relative lack of interest in individual psychology and experimentation with form. Drutse's *Kasa mare* (1962; the festive room) was a promising new departure. The story of a young wife whose soldier-husband has been killed at the front, it probes with sympathy and insight her inner struggles with loneliness and suggests some universal truths about the purity of the human conscience.

KEITH HITCHINS

MOLNÁR, Ferenc

Hungarian dramatist, novelist, short-story writer, and journalist (also writing in English), b. 12 Jan. 1878, Budapest; d. 1 April 1952, New York, N.Y., U.S.A.

Son of a physician, M. studied law in Budapest and Geneva but soon began writing feuilletons and novels. In 1896 he joined the editorial staff of *Budapesti napló* and later that of several other newspapers. His early writings gained wide recognition, and he soon became a prominent dramatist and novelist. During World War I M. was a war correspondent. In the 1920s his plays achieved worldwide fame. He spent many years abroad, and in 1939 left Hungary permanently because of the menace of fascism. He settled in New York City and continued writing—sometimes in English—until his death.

As a journalist, M. valued keen observation, precise description, suave mischievousness, and wit. His urbane, vibrant short stories, mainly featuring lovelorn men and cunning women engaged in the battle of sexes, are meticulously constructed. His novels are characterized by clever plots and stylistic brilliance, although their range is rather narrow. Only the early *A Pál-utcai fiúk* (1907; *The Paul Street Boys*, 1927) is a masterpiece. It is a moving, realistic tale about youngsters playing adults. M. depicts their nobility, innocence, camaraderie, and love of freedom, but also their innate cruelty. Their gang life is an allegory of a problem-ridden age. M.'s insights into young people's psyches, his sympathies with their boundless hopes and dreams, are communicated to the reader in a succinct, poetic style.

M.'s chief contribution to world literature was as a dramatist. He was a natural playwright with a mesmerizing, unerring dramatic instinct, originality, and dazzling technique and craftsmanship. His whimsical, sophisticated drawing-room comedies show the influence of Oscar Wilde, of the French boulevard playwrights, and of Shaw, Schnitzler, and Pirandello (qq.v.). M. achieved a felicitous synthesis of realism and romanticism, cynicism and sentimentality, the profane and the sublime. His elegant, satiric plays about manners, frailties, and illusions are built on precisely timed, sparkling dialogue.

M.'s first great success was *Az ördög* (1907; *The Devil*, 1908), a comedy in which the devil forces two people together who might have remained virtuous without him. From powdered dandies and scheming ladies, M. turned to thugs and simple servants in his next play, *Liliom* (1909; *Liliom*, 1921), his most famous work. Staged worldwide and filmed, both the play and its Americanized musical version, *Carousel* (1946), are classics. Combining naturalism and fantasy, this touching allegory examines the problem of redemption while portraying human suffering in Budapest's underworld. Liliom, a tough barker at an amusement park, marries Juli, a naïve servant. Failing in his efforts to steal and kill for money, he commits suicide. At a celestial court, he learns that after purging himself for sixteen years, he could gain salvation by one good deed. After his probation he returns to earth, but when his daughter refuses his gift, a stolen star, Liliom strikes her in exasperation, although the girl says the slap felt like a caress. Thus, the incorrigible sinner is escorted back to hell as irredeemable. Liliom is M.'s paradoxical Everyman, Juli the eternal female ideal.

M. developed one of his favorite themes, the contrast of relative and absolute truth, of illusion and reality, by using actors as characters in two of his most famous plays. *A testőr* (1910; *The Guardsman*, 1924), a sparkling comedy, presents the predicament of an actor who feels he is not loved for what he is and needs to masquerade as what he believes his wife wants. Using his histrionic powers to impersonate the guardsman (his new "rival"), he sets out to seduce his own wife. In *Játék a kastélyban* (1926; *The Play's* the Thing, 1927), the distinctions between theater and life are again blurred. The play is a dazzling, mercilessly cynical farce proving that our lives are mere role-playing.

Equally entertaining are his facile farces portraying romance among the aristocracy. *A hattyú* (1921; *The Swan,* 1929) is a witty satire about a princess who is compelled to forsake genuine love because of family obligations. Elaborating on a similar theme in *Olympia* (1928; *Olympia,* 1928), M. assails the cruelty of aristocracy toward the common man.

M. achieved international fame by amusing audiences everywhere for five decades. Instead of conveying social messages, this prolific, imaginative, witty writer aimed merely to entertain by transforming his colorful, stormy personal experience into effective works of art. M. excelled as an observer, a storyteller, and a humorist. A master of stagecraft, he provided escape and gaiety in an illusory world in which conflicts were amenable to solution.

FURTHER WORKS: *Magdolna és egyéb elbeszélések* (1898); *A csókok éjszakája és elbeszélések* (1899); *Az éhes város* (1901); *Egy gazdátlan csónak története* (1901; *The Derelict Boat,* 1924); *A doktor úr* (1902; *The Lawyer,* 1927); *Éva* (1903; *Eva,* 1924); *Józsi* (1904); *Gyerekek* (1905); *Egy pesti lány története* (1905); *Rabok* (1908; *Prisoners,* 1924); *Muzsika* (1908); *Ketten beszélnek* (1909; *Stories for Two,* 1950); *Pesti erkölcsök* (1909); *Hétágú síp* (1911); *A farkas* (1912; *The Wolf,* 1925); *Ma, tegnap, tegnapelőtt* (1912); *Báró Márczius és egyéb elbeszélések* (1913); *Kis hármaskönyv* (1914); *Az aruvimi erdő titka és egyéb szatirák* (1916); *A fehér felhő* (1916; *The White Cloud,* 1927); *Egy haditudósito emlékei* (1916); *Farsang* (1917; *Carnival,* 1924); *Ismerősök* (1917); *Úri divat* (1917; *Fashions for Men,* 1922); *Andor* (1918); *Széntolvajok* (1918); *Szinház* (1921); *Égi és földi szerelem* (1922; *Launzi—Heavenly and Earthly Love,* 1923); *A vörös malom* (1923; *The Red Mill,* 1928); *Az üvegcipő* (1924, *The Glass Slipper,* 1925); *A gőzoszlop* (1926; *The Captain of St. Margaret's,* 1945); *Riviera* (1926; *Riviera,* 1927); *Összes munkái* (20 vols., 1928); *Egy kettő, három* (1929; *The President,* 1930); *A jó tündér* (1930; *The Good Fairy,* 1932); *Harmonia* (1932); *Valaki* (1932; *Arthur or Somebody,* 1952); *Csoda a hegyek közt* (1933; *Miracle in the Mountain,*

1947); *A zenélő angyal* (1933; *Angel Making Music,* 1935); *Az ismeretlen lány* (1934); *A cukrászné* (1935; *Delicate Story,* 1941); *Nagy szerelem* (1935); *A királynő szolgálólánya* (1936; *The King's Maid,* 1941); *Delila* (1937; *Blue Danube,* 1952); *A zöld huszár* (1937); *Őszi utazás* (1939); *Panoptikum* (1942; *Waxworks,* 1952); *A császár* (1942; *The Emperor,* 1942); *The Blue-Eyed Lady* (1942); *Farewell My Heart* (1945); *Szivdobogás* (1947; *Game of Hearts,* 1952); *Companion in Exile: Notes for an Autobiography* (1950). FURTHER VOLUMES IN ENGLISH: *Husbands and Lovers* (1924); *Plays of M.* (1927); *The Plays of F. M.* (1929; repr. as *All the Plays of M.,* 1937); *Romantic Comedies: Eight Plays* (1952)

BIBLIOGRAPHY: Chandler, F. W., "Hungarian and Czech Innovators: M. and the Capeks," *Modern Continental Playwrights* (1931), pp. 438–53; Gassner, J., "M. and the Hungarians," *Masters of the Drama* (1945), pp. 478–81; Behrman, S. N., "Playwright: F. M." (1946), *The Suspended Drawing Room* (1965), pp. 191–253; Gergely, E. J., *Hungarian Drama in New York: American Adaptations 1908–1940* (1947), pp. 9–60, 181–90; Middleton, G., "F. M.," *These Things Are Mine* (1947), pp. 363–69; Reményi, J., *Hungarian Writers and Literature* (1964), pp. 348–62; Györgyey, C., *F. M.* (1980)

CLARA GYÖRGYEY

MONGOLIAN LITERATURE

Mongolian literature begins with Chinggis Khan (Genghis Khan) in the early 1200s and the famous *Secret History of the Mongols,* an imperial chronicle of family genealogy and conflict. The later centuries of internal warfare were not conducive to writing or preserving literature. Not until the introduction of Lamaist Buddhism in the late 1500s did an upsurge occur. The next centuries saw a prodigious output of translations from Tibetan sacred scriptures, but only rarely histories or epics.

There was a widespread and popular oral literature, which encompassed: central Asian story cycles, some from Indian sources; didactic literature; stories, poems, legends; and particularly heroic epics, lengthy verse compositions about mighty heroes, their steeds, beautiful heavenly daughters, marvelous palaces, and the many-headed mangus, the monster of Mongolian folklore. In the last decades of the 19th c. collectors of folklore and epics began to transcribe many of these long works, saving them from extinction as old cultural ways yielded to incursions of the West.

At the fall of the Manchu (Ch'ing) dynasty under revolutionary pressures around 1910, the new government of the Chinese Republic was no longer able to exert effective control over its more distant provinces; Inner Mongolia, beyond the Great Wall, heavily settled with Chinese agriculturalists, remained part of the Republic, but Outer Mongolia cast off its ties to the Manchus and declared itself autonomous.

Outer Mongolian Literature

The proclaiming in 1924 of the Mongolian People's Republic, the first political satellite of the U.S.S.R., with its attendant socialization and collectivization of the economy, led to the creation of a new literature of Socialist Realism (q.v.), in line with similar developments in the U.S.S.R. itself. The creation of an educational system, where none had existed before (except for training for the religious hierarchy), presented young Mongols with the possibility of becoming writers, artists, and intellectuals.

Dashdorjiin Natsagdorj (1906–1937), called the founder of modern Mongolian literature, is known for fiction, drama, poetry, and translations. His poem "Minii nutag" (1933; "My Native Land," 1967) is almost an anthem for Mongolia and is known to everyone. He wrote a libretto for an opera on native Mongolian themes, *Uchirtai gurvan tolgoi* (the three hills of sorrow), which was first produced in 1934 and is still performed regularly in Ulan Bator. Another important achievement is his short story "Tsagaan sar ba khar nulims" (1932; New Year's and bitter tears), which compares the life of a rich landlord's daughter with that of a poor servant girl.

Tsendiin Damdinsüren (b. 1908) is a noteworthy poet, translator, literary critic, and scholar. His first success was *Gologdson khüükhen* (1929; the rejected girl), the first Mongolian novel, a story of class struggle in the feudal countryside and the changes in a poor hired girl's life brought about by the revolution. It was considerably influenced by traditional folklore. His most famous poem is probably "Buural iiji minii" (1934; my gray-

haired mother), a letter-dialogue whose theme is the tender affection between mother and son. He contributed to scholarship by editing an immensely important anthology, *Monggol uran jokiyal-un degeji jagun bilig* (1959; the hundred best selections of Mongolian literature), revealing hitherto unsuspected depth and richness in the literature of his country. He also published a study of the Geser epic, which appeared in Russian under the title *Istoricheskie korni Geseriady* (1957; historical bases of the Geser cycle).

Chadraavolyn Lodoidamba's (1917–1970) famous adventure novel *Altaid* (1949–51; in the Altai range) which, typically for Mongolian fiction, focuses more on exciting events than on character development, was followed by *Tungalag Tamir* (1962; the transparent Tamir River), the latter made into a successful motion picture. The dean of academics, Byamba Rinchen (1905–1977), wrote a three-volume historical novel, *Üüriin tuya* (1951–55; the ray of dawn), a detailed and historically accurate reconstruction of prerevolutionary times, treating battles, trials, social structure, shamanism, love and politics.

A number of other versatile authors have all written poetry, short stories, novels, and plays: Bökhiin Baast (b. 1921), Shanjmyatavyn Gaadamba (b. 1924), Püreviin Khorloo (b. 1917), Erdenebatyn Oyuun (b. 1913), Dashzevegiin Sengee (1916–1959). Sengiin Erdene (b. 1929) became a spokesman for his generation with his lyrical novels, whose heroes have some psychological depth.

Inner Mongolian Literature

Although in the mid- and late-19th c. there were noted writers of Inner Mongolian origin and residence, their works formed part of a general Mongolian culture. Nonetheless, such writers as Khesigbatu (1849–1916), Güleranja (1820–1851), Gelegbalsan (1846–1923), Injannashi (1837–1892), and Ishidanzanwangjil (1854–1907) were important forerunners of a 20th-c. Inner Mongolian literature.

During the period when the young Mongolian People's Republic was launching Communism, the Inner Mongolian region of China was struggling with factions of Chinese nationalism (later to result in the split between Nationalists and Communists), a struggle followed by hegemony by Japan until the end of World War II. Among young Mongolian nationalists sent to Japan for education was the essayist and poet Saichungga (later known as Na. Sainchogtu, b. 1914).

After the Chinese Communist victory in 1949, writers in Inner Mongolia, still heavily Chinese in settlement (ten to one in some areas), were permitted as a minority to publish in their native script. One figure who kept old traditions alive was the bard Pajai (1902–?), an original poet as well as a singer of epic poems.

During the Cultural Revolution in the 1960s it was difficult to secure information about literary figures and publications, a situation that holds true even today. The continued use of traditional script in Inner Mongolia now acts as a barrier to literary exchange with the Mongolian People's Republic, where a modified Cyrillic alphabet is used. And the decades-long Sino-Soviet tensions have played their roles, too. Inner Mongolian literature today is largely a vehicle for socialist thought, dominated by the Chinese (Han) educational and administrative system.

BIBLIOGRAPHY: Poppe, N., *Mongolische Volksdichtung* (1955); Gerasimovich, L. K., *History of Modern Mongolian Literature (1921–1964)* (1970); Heissig, W., *Geschichte der mongolischen Literatur*, Vol. II (1972)

JOHN R. KRUEGER

MONTALE, Eugenio

Italian poet, b. 12 Oct. 1896, Genoa; d. 12 Sept. 1981, Milan

M. spent his childhood and early adult years in Genoa and the Cinque Terre, a rugged marine area on the Ligurian coast that figures prominently in his first collection of poetry, *Ossi di seppia* (1925; cuttlefish bones). In 1915 he began the serious study of singing. Although he had already dabbled a bit in verse by then, he did not commit himself entirely to the writing of poetry until he abandoned his operatic career in 1916. He was drafted during World War I, returning to his family home in 1919, where he remained for the next ten years. In 1929 he took on the directorship of the Vieusseux Research Library in Florence and held this post until 1938, when he was dismissed because of his refusal to join the Fascist Party. M. spent the years of World War II in Florence, during which time he made a living by translating French, English, American, and Spanish works, and

by contributing to various literary journals. In 1948 the poet was hired by the Milanese newspaper *Corriere della sera* and remained active in journalism until 1967. His collected essays, short stories, and travel pieces are all the fruit of his years as a journalist. M. was given the honorary position of Senator for Life in 1967 and won the Nobel Prize for literature in 1975.

M.'s first published poetry, "Accordi" (1922; chords), was a series of seven poems that sought to imitate the sounds of musical instruments. This impressionistic phase was soon replaced, however, by the "countereloquence" of *Ossi di seppia*. Although this volume contains many poems that speak of the rocky landscape and ever-present Mediterranean of Liguria, it is clear that M.'s real interest is not in the representation of the physical world but rather in the search for some metaphysical and cognitive certainties in the midst of what he feels is an obdurately uncertain reality. This search is carried out in a pared-down, harsh poetic style that avoids the inherent lyricism of the Italian language. The title points, therefore, not only to its thematic center—the sea and the marine atmosphere surrounding it—but also to M.'s stylistic ideal of a honed, essential poetry.

M.'s second volume, *Le occasioni* (1939; occasions), also contains in its title an indication of its origins and goals, "occasions" being those rare, private moments of illumination that are best re-created in brief "flashes" of lyric. The central series of the collection—"Mottetti" (motets)—is made up of twenty very short love poems written to and about a beloved woman who is now absent from the poet's life, but who provides him with continued hope for success in his search for meaning. In this volume M. suppresses any discursive, descriptive elements in favor of an elliptic, allusive style, somewhat analogous to T. S. Eliot's (q.v.) "objective correlative."

The third collection, *La bufera, e altro* (1956; *The Storm, and Other Poems*, 1978), develops fully the figure of the beloved, who is now called Clizia, and who is the bearer of transcendental salvation to the poet as well as to the war-torn world. This is a much less "hermetic" volume than the second, for M. here is deeply involved in the "storm" of the directly experienced historical events of the 1940s, even though he is still pursuing his own personal dream of fulfillment through

301

love. The poet experiments with traditional poetic forms, most notably the sonnet, in a continuing dedication to the creation of a powerful style.

M.'s three late collections—*Satura* (1971; Latin: satire), *Diario del '71 e del '72* (1973; diary of '71 and '72), and *Quaderno di quattro anni* (1977; *It Depends: A Poet's Notebook,* 1980)—represent a new direction, for they are written in a prosaic, satiric style, providing an ironic commentary on the first three volumes. They find much of their inspiration in the poet's daily life, in current events, and in retrospective self-evaluation. The "Xenia" series of *Satura,* poems written to his wife, who was called Mosca, are exquisite examples of the way in which language can be used to express great emotion in an understated, even humorous manner while losing none of its power to move and enthrall.

M.'s poetry, although superficially related to hermeticism (q.v.), representative poets of which are Giuseppe Ungaretti and Salvatore Quasimodo (qq.v.), does not belong to any school. It is rather the product of a lifelong dedication to poetry understood as the solitary pursuit of knowledge and perfected form. M. is a master in pointing to the uncertainties, ambiguities, and moral complexities of our century. His difficult poetry does not offer any sure solutions to the existential and spiritual problems with which it deals, but rather finds its abiding power in its unforgettable formal beauty, its incisive, profoundly intelligent first-person voice, and its commitment to the importance of the individual, to what M. has called "daily decency," and to the essential seriousness of artistic creation.

FURTHER WORKS: *La casa dei doganieri, e altri versi* (1932); *Finisterre* (1943); *Quaderno di traduzioni* (1948); *Farfalla di Dinard* (1956; *Butterfly of Dinard,* 1971); *Auto da fé* (1966); *Fuori di casa* (1969); *La poesia non esiste* (1971); *Nel nostro tempo* (1973; *Poet in Our Time,* 1976); *Trentadue variazioni* (1973); *Sulla poesia* (1976); *Tutte le poesie* (1977). FURTHER VOLUMES IN ENGLISH: *Poems* (1959); *Poesie di M.* (1960, bilingual); *Poesie/Poems* (1964, bilingual); *Selected Poems* (1965, bilingual); *Provisional Conclusions* (1970); *New Poems* (1976); *The Second Life of Art: Selected Essays* (1982)

BIBLIOGRAPHY: Cambon, G., "E. M.'s 'Motets': The Occasions of Epiphany," *PMLA,*

82 (1967), 471–84; Pipa, A., *M. and Dante* (1968); Cary, J., *Three Modern Italian Poets: Saba, Ungaretti, M.* (1969); Singh, G., *E. M.: A Critical Study of His Poetry, Prose and Criticism* (1973); Almansi, G., and Merry, B., *E. M.: The Private Language of Poetry* (1977); Huffman, C., "Structuralist Criticism and the Interpretation of M.," *MLR,* 72 (1977), 322–34; West, R. J., *E. M.: Poet on the Edge* (1981)

REBECCA J. WEST

MONTEIRO LOBATO
See Lobato, Monteiro

MONTHERLANT, Henry de
French novelist, dramatist, essayist and poet, b. 20 April 1895, Paris; d. 21 Sept. 1972, Paris

M. lied about the date of his birth by one year (1896 instead of 1895) to make himself younger and by one day (April 21 instead of April 20) to have his birthday coincide with the legendary date of the founding of Rome. He also chose the date of his death by committing suicide on the day of the autumnal equinox. These choices are typical of his deliberate efforts to shape his biography and give a heroic dimension to an otherwise rather uneventful and protected life devoted mainly to reading and writing. They also indicate to what extent Rome and a particular idea about Roman stoicism took hold of his imagination. It had started very early, since at nine he wrote a "Roman" novel inspired by Henryk Sienkiewicz's (q.v.) *Quo Vadis?* In conformity to his wish, his ashes were scattered over the ruins of the Forum in Rome.

Since M.'s writings are often autobiographical and always marked by his egotistical personality, the books he wrote are inseparable from the various events and experiences of his life. Conversely, some of his books had a decisive influence on the course of his life. An only child, M. was born into a conservative, aristocratic family and educated in private Catholic schools. This experience, marked by a passionate friendship for a boy who was schoolmate, which caused his dismissal at seventeen from the École Saint-Croix, was to be the source of many fictional transmutations. It inspired his first book, *La relève du matin* (1920; the morning relief), a collection of lyrical essays published at his own expense but immediately greeted as a work of great promise. The same incident provided the subject matter of what many consider M.'s best play, *La ville dont le prince est un enfant* (1951; the city whose prince is a child). It finally inspired a long novel, *Les garçons* (1969; the boys), published three years before M.'s death.

M. had been declared unfit for military service, and he kept away from the front during three years, completing his education by vast reading. In the last months of World War I he managed, through family connections, to be attached to an infantry regiment. He was wounded by a bursting shell on June 6, 1918. This very limited experience allowed him to use war as the background of his first novel, *Le songe* (1922; *The Dream*, 1963). The hero, Alban de Bricoule, a fictional double of the author, is the prototype of later M. heroes: he enjoys only the sensual love of his undemanding mistress, Douce; through his indifference he tortures Dominique Soubrier, a bright, beautiful, and athletic girl whom he finally rejects because she does love him in a sentimental way and has followed him to the front as a nurse. Alban's friendship for Stanislas Prinet, which has brought him to the front, means much more to him than his love for women. But he displays the same kind of sadism toward his comrade, whom he reprimands for being a weak, clumsy, sentimental bourgeois. When Prinet is killed, Alban regrets his cruelty and sinks into a depression. This apparently tough character, who takes pride in his strength and independence, is in fact totally dependent on other human beings yet afraid of making lasting commitments. At the end of the book, he is utterly alone and cut off from society.

This brilliant novel is also one of the first in the post-World War I period to present an existentialist (q.v.) hero, who, thrown into exceptional circumstances, rejects the conventional values of his education, discovers himself in the face of impending death during a bombardment, and makes decisive choices. M., who had played soccer and enjoyed cross-country running, celebrated athletes and praised the moral values bred by the practice of sport in *Les Olympiques* (1924; enlarged ed., 1938; the Olympic Games). *Les bestiaires* (1926; *The Bullfighters*, 1927; later tr., *The Matador*, 1957) is a novel based on M.'s early experience when he visited Spain before the war. Once again Alban de Bricoule

is the protagonist, an adolescent who "merits" the love of a Spanish girl, Soledad, by overcoming his fear and killing a particularly mean bull; but he rejects her love after his victory. M., however, transcends this rather thin plot by giving the bullfight a dimension of mythical timelessness by associating it with the ancient Mithraic cult.

In 1925, after the death of his grandmother, with whom he had lived since his parents' death ten years earlier, M. sold all his belongings and left France. He traveled in Spain, Italy, and North Africa for the next ten years. In *Les voyageurs traqués* (1927; the hunted travelers) he described the "metaphysical crisis" he underwent. It consisted mainly of an encounter with the absurd leading to nihilism and despair. Alternating his moods, M. at times abandoned himself to a strong impulse toward asceticism, renunciation, detachment, and indifference and then practiced absolute self-indulgence, acting as an apologist of sensual pleasure.

The lesson he drew from this crisis and its resolution is summed up in an important volume of essays, *Service inutile* (1935; useless service), which made a strong impression on the young Albert Camus (q.v.). While emphasizing the folly of all human ambitions and the vanity of all human undertakings in tones reminiscent of the Book of Ecclesiastes, M. preaches a philosophy of action.

He had managed to surmount his emotional crisis by writing two long novels. *La rose de sable* (1968; the desert rose)—part of which had earlier been published as *L'histoire d'amour de la rose de sable* (1952; *Desert Love*, 1957)—is a condemnation of French colonialism as M. had observed it in North Africa. He had finished it by 1932 but postponed its publication for fear of further hurting his country's tottering prestige. It was published in its entirety five years after the end of the Algerian war. The book is disappointing for the lack of inventiveness in its form and the timidity of its content. *Les célibataires* (1934; *Perish in Their Pride*, 1936; later tr., *The Bachelors*, 1960), on the other hand, in which M. created two unforgettable characters—pitiful aristocrats modeled on his own uncle and great-uncle—is a masterpiece of craftsmanship full of incisive humor, subtlety, and verve.

In 1934 M. met a twenty-three-year-old girl from a respectable middle-class family. During the next two years they were engaged, had a liaison, broke off, were several times on the point of getting married before they finally separated in 1936. This young woman was to be the model of the main female character, Solange Dandillot, and the central thread of a four-volume novel under the general title of *Les jeunes filles: Les jeunes filles* (1936; *The Young Girls,* 1938), *Pitié pour les femmes* (1936; *Pity for Women,* 1938)—these first two English translations published together in one volume—*Le démon du bien* (1937), and *Les lépreuses* (1939)—these last two published together in English as *Costals and the Hippogriff* (1940); the tetralogy was later translated as *The Girls* (1968). Costals, the hero of the novel, a libertine, shares many of M.'s traits and opinions. He is a creative writer, believes that sensuality should be kept separate from love, and does not think that the dignity and honesty of frank voluptuousness is compatible with the traditional marriage relationship, at least for men and women of outstanding gifts. The novel exalts the joy of artistic creation and attacks "shop-girl morality," sentimentality, the cult of suffering, and romantic love. It is often irritating and even deliberately infuriating, but it illustrates a point that has often been made since by feminist writers: women have created themselves in the image that men have of them. It is the virtuoso performance of a consummate craftsman who exploits all forms of narrative technique with great verve. The novel was an immediate best seller; its *succès de scandale* gave M. a widespread notoriety.

By 1939 M. had become a legendary figure, and his shrewdly provocative statements contributed to his image as an anticonformist and a maverick in French literature not unlike Rousseau in his time. He was contributing articles to both the communist and the conservative press, and he was praised by both the left and the right.

The publication of *Le solstice de juin* (1941; the June solstice) tarnished M.'s image and irretrievably damaged his reputation. The title refers to 24 June 1940, the date on which the French signed the armistice after being defeated by Nazi Germany. The essays entitled "Épuration" (purification) and "Les chenilles" (caterpillars) represent what is most objectionable in the book. In them M. gives vent to his contempt for Christianity and expresses satisfaction at the victory of the solar wheel (swastika) over the cross.

After the war M. was blacklisted by the National Committee of Writers (C.N.E.) and as a result did not play any role in the moral and ideological debates of postwar France. But he did pursue a glorious career as a playwright, a career that had started during the war with the immensely successful premiere of *La reine morte* (1942; *Queen after Death,* 1951) in December 1942 at the Comédie Française.

Whether his plays are set in the contemporary period—*Fils de personne* (1943; *No Man's Son,* 1951), *Demain il fera jour* (1949; *Tomorrow the Dawn,* 1951)—or classified as "costume" tragedies and set in 14th-c. Portugal—*La reine morte;* 15th-c. Italy—*Malatesta* (1946; *Malatesta,* 1951); or 15th-c. Spain—*Le maître de Santiago* (1947; *The Master of Santiago,* 1951)—M. always gives expression to his own many contradictory selves. He was never more personal than in his plays, and yet he preserved the appearance of objectivity, since he could not be totally identified with any single character.

The pessimism and nihilism earlier present in his essays and novels are exacerbated in the aging heroes of his plays. In *Fils de personne* and *Demain il fera jour* the theme of the conflict between a haughty and rigid father and his mediocre illegitimate son is apparently borrowed from the author's personal situation (he had an illegitimate son himself). M.'s plays are psychological and devoted to the exploration of proud, cruel, ruthless, lonely, self-deceiving, and world-weary protagonists. They are characterized by a great economy of means, tightly woven plots, and a sumptuous language verging sometimes on bombast. They have been criticized for being too static, too stylized, too remote from modern tastes. Many critics consider them in the tradition of the classic French theater of Racine and Corneille. Others emphasize the modernity of their themes and more particularly their preoccupation with the absurdity of life.

In spite of unpleasant personality traits, frankly repellent aspects of his ideology, and some obvious shortcomings in his works, M. holds an important place in contemporary French literature as a consummate craftsman both in fiction and drama. He is one of the great French prose writers, in the tradition of Rousseau, Chateaubriand, and Maurice Barrès (1862–1923).

FURTHER WORKS: *Chant funèbre pour les morts de Verdun* (1924); *Aux fontaines du désir* (1927); *La petite Infante de Castille*

304

(1929); *L'exil* (1929); *Hispano-mauresque* (1929); *Pour une vierge noire* (1932); *Mors et vita* (1932); *Encore un instant de bonheur* (1934); *Pasiphaë* (1936); *L'équinoxe de septembre* (1938); *Fils des autres, un incompris* (1944); *Notes sur mon théâtre* (1950); *Celles qu'on prend dans ses bras* (1950); *Coups de soleil* (1950); *Le fichier parisien* (1952); *Textes sous une occupation* (1953); *Port-Royal* (1954); *Un voyageur solitaire est un diable* (1955); *Brocéliande* (1956); *Carnets années 1930 à 1944* (4 vols., 1947–56); *Don Juan* (1958); *Romans et œuvres de fiction non théâtrale* (1959); *Le cardinal d'Espagne* (1960); *Le chaos et la nuit* (1963; *Chaos and Night,* 1964); *Discours de réception à l'Académie Française* (1963); *Essais* (1963); *La guerre civile* (1965; *Civil War,* 1967); *Va jouer avec cette poussière* (1966); *Un assassin est mon maître* (1971); *Théâtre* (1972); *La marée du soir 1968–71* (1972). FURTHER VOLUME IN ENGLISH: *Selected Essays* (1961)

BIBLIOGRAPHY: Faure-Biguet, J. N., *Les enfances de M.* (1941); Sipriot, P., *M. par lui-même* (1953); Chiari, J., *The Contemporary French Theatre* (1958), pp. 205–22; Perruchot, H., *M.* (1959); Norrish, P. J., "M.'s Conception of the Tragic Hero," *FS,* 14 (1960), 18–37; Beer, J. de, *M.; ou, L'homme encombré de Dieu* (1963); Cruickshank, J., *M.* (1964); Guicharnaud, J., *Modern French Theater from Giraudoux to Genet* (1967), pp. 98–116, Batchelor, J., *Existence and Imagination: The Theatre of H. de M.* (1967); Johnson, R. B., *H. de M.* (1968); Grover, F. J., "The Inheritors of Maurice Barrès," *MLR,* 64 (1969), 529–45; Mason, H. T., "M.," in Fletcher, J., ed., *Forces in Modern French Drama,* (1972), pp. 68–85; Robichez, J., *Le théâtre de M.* (1973); Sipriot, P., *Album M.* (1979)

FREDERIC J. GROVER

It is noteworthy that *no one* of M.'s works paints for us a man-to-man conflict; coexistence is the great living drama, but it eludes him. His hero always stands alone before animals, children, women, landscapes; he is the prey of his own desires (like the queen in *Pasiphaë*) or of his own demands (like the master of Santiago in *The Master of Santiago*), but there is never anyone at his side. Alban in *The Dream* has a comrade: he disdains Prinet alive, and becomes excited about him only over his corpse. M.'s works, like his life, admit of only one consciousness. . . .

M.'s lofty indifference to all causes and his preference for the pseudo-sublime are illustrated in *The Dead Queen* and *The Master of Santiago.* In these dramas, both significant in their pretentiousness, we see two imperial males who sacrifice to their empty pride women guilty of nothing more than being human: for punishment one loses her life, the other her soul. Once again, if we ask in the name of what, the author haughtily answers: in the name of nothing. He did not want the King to have too clear motives of state for killing Inès, for then this murder would be only a commonplace political crime. [1949]

Simone de Beauvoir, *The Second Sex* (1953), pp. 210, 213

If one day, we rediscover the commonplace truth that there is such a thing as a literary art, just as there is a pictorial or a musical art, and if writers—they alone are guilty in this—finally stop treating "literature" with contempt (it sometimes returns the favor), then M.'s works will provide proof that the rare fusion of irony and majestic writing was also part of the art of our age.

André Malraux, in a letter dated October 19, 1952, to French Radio and Television (R.T.F.) for a radio program on M.: "Fifteen Evenings with M."

M. is for me the very model of a certain clan of French writers (Chateaubriand, Barrès), and I flatter myself that I am one of them. A common trait unites the members of this group, which includes such fraternal enemies as Aragon and Malraux. Since I consider myself a part of the family, I hope I may be forgiven for saying that this element of kinship is based on a kind of imposture. The word is not intended here in its sinister sense, as in the title of Molière's *Tartuffe* (*Tartuffe; or, The Impostor*). Don Juan too is an impostor and that is the kind of deceit I have in mind, the deceit of style. Writers of that breed all strive for effect and cocky posturing, for music and the advantageous pose.

François Mauriac, "Bloc-notes," *Figaro,* 8 March 1960, 16

M. emphasizes the fact that "the tragedies of the Ancients were tragedies not only among members of the same family but between the different selves making up any single individual." This latter form of tragic characterisation plays a dominant part in most of M.'s plays. Ferrante, in *The Dead Queen,* is tempted to do good yet finally does evil. He does so partly in order to "cut the fearful knot of contradictions" within himself so that he can learn at last who he really is. La Soeur Angélique, in *Port-Royal,* suffers from self-division in an acute form as she battles with the fear of losing her faith. . . . *Le Cardinal d'Espagne* follows the same pattern. Cardinal Cisneros, the principal character, has a nature split into two warring parts. One element in him withdraws into his religion in reaction to the vanity of human life; another enjoys power, particularly the power of life and death over his fellow-men.

John Cruickshank, *M.* (1964), p. 112

Style is a quality that seldom ranks very high in the contemporary critic's scale of values: but it would be impossible to discuss M. the novelist without considering his achievement as a modern master of the French language. His prose style is uncommonly rich and various—tart, idiomatic, incisive, when he attacks some typical or controversial issue; measured, euphonious, poetic, when he deals with wider and less transitory themes.... Like every genuine style, that of M. is no mere adventitious decoration, but arises from his subject as he enlarges and develops it. M.'s efforts as a controversialist should never blind us to the fact that he is primarily an accomplished artist. *The Girls* may be read as a deliberately controversial book—an attack on "the cult of woman," on the place that Woman has come to occupy in the modern European world; and as such it may have helped to break down many masculine taboos and phobias. But it is also an imaginative work of art, which, having absorbed and digested its subject matter, presents us with something far more valuable and lasting.... So long as literature continues to play a part in our lives, M.'s story of *Les jeunes filles* is a book that will retain its youthful freshness.

Peter Quennell, Introduction to *The Girls* (1968), p. 15

"I am a poet," says M., "and only a poet." Why do critics with unusual stubbornness—whether it is to praise or damn him—continue to see in M. first of all a thinker? ... They talk too much about ethics concerning him and never enough about aesthetics, which in fact informs everything in his work. His work is essentially dramatic, based on conflict and contrast. The contrast is everywhere: in words, images and themes.... It is this law of contrast that brings M. to unite voluptuousness and chastity, life and death, desire and renunciation. The famous *alternance* [i.e., alternation] is a principle of art before it became a principle of life. This aesthetic principle of conflict explains why M. came quite naturally to the theater. Actually, he had started his writing career at eighteen with a play, *L'exil*. The same aesthetic law governs a novel like *Les jeunes filles*, in which the male and female principles are set in conflict by means of a comic method that is but another form of dramatic art.... This writer, in whom everyone tries to find the man and the thinker, needs more than any other to be exposed to "formalist" types of criticism. He has nothing to lose from

this critical approach, which on the contrary will establish his greatness and endurance.

Jacqueline Piatier, "M. et la contradiction," *Le monde,* 19 April 1969, 17

The despair occasioned by the recognition of the absurdity of human existence has led writers like Camus and Sartre to propound a new humanism to palliate the anguish of modern man. M.'s response, however, is a purely personal code of ethics. Recognizing that there is no reward for man either on this earth or in another life, M. has set up as a *raison d'être* the superior qualities which characterize his hero. His search for an answer to the problem facing the twentieth century of how to live, and for what reasons to live, when all traditional philosophical systems have proved inadequate, has led M. to his concept of the hero. This lucid individual, having rejected all hope of immortal life or of recompense in this life, having realized the vanity of all human things, must still go forward, must accomplish, despite the absurdity of man's destiny. Thus, he attempts to make his experiences as intense and as varied as possible.... Responsible only to himself, he goes forward to meet his destiny, heedless of others. Whatever wrongs he may commit are justified if they serve him in his quest for self-realization. Recognizing that human existence is essentially tragic, the hero cannot content himself with his despair, but must act in order to find deliverance.

Lucille Becker, *H. de M.: A Critical Biography* (1970), pp. 114–15

We may discern dramatically important links between parent and child in all but four of M.'s plays and in all the important ones.... If Georges [in *Fils de personne*], Ferrante [in *La reine morte*], and Alvaro [in *Le maître de Santiago*] express in varying degree the anguished fear of betrayal by their progeny, it is more than the simple disappointment of a father. These children strike at something fundamental in the parent himself.... Inès [in *La reine morte*] represents for Ferrante a weakness to which he is in danger of consenting, and Georges abandons Gillou in *Fils de personne* because the latter does not give back to him a satisfactory image of himself. Just as Ferrante seeks to discover his own identity and in so doing strikes at his children, so are Georges and Alvaro seeking their true self-image in those they have brought into the world. Alvaro's love of God, says M., is "love for the idea he has of himself"; so is his love of Mariana.... In acting thus, these fathers are acting against themselves.... Thereby they relate to another great theme in M.—the theme of suicide.

H. T. Mason, "M.," in John Fletcher, ed., *Forces in Modern French Drama* (1972), pp. 82–84

MOORE, Brian

Irish-Canadian novelist, b. 25 Aug. 1921, Belfast, Northern Ireland

Raised as a Catholic in Belfast, M. emigrated to Canada in 1948. Although now a Canadian citizen, he has lived in the U.S. since 1959. Thus, he has had access to three cultures, and his novels accordingly explore Irish, Canadian, and American life. M.'s reputation was established with his first novel, *The Lonely Passion of Judith Hearne* (1955), a remorselessly realistic study of the disintegration of a Belfast spinster. In the novels that have followed it, M. has by and large continued his commitment to the techniques of realism.

M.'s first two novels—the second was *The Feast of Lupercal* (1957; repub. as *A Moment of Love,* 1960)—presented the entrapment of his characters within the religious and familial structures of Belfast Catholic life. Later novels reveal a complex reaction to this concern with entrapment. Much of M.'s work deals with the guilt feelings of the person who liberates himself from religious values and stable cultural traditions. These guilt-ridden characters may be Irish-born writers living in the U.S., as in *An Answer from Limbo* (1962) and *Fergus* (1970); or they may be unfaithful wives who have renounced their Catholicism, as in *I Am Mary Dunne* (1968) and *The Doctor's Wife* (1976). These novels present central characters free from belief and from the demands of a life conducted according to traditional values, but isolated in a despair that is sometimes suicidal. In the short novel *Catholics* (1972) M. created a brilliant variation on this theme by presenting the orderly and beautiful life of Irish monks in a remote island monastery presided over by an abbot who has lost his faith and who lives daily in despair at its loss. A longing for the discarded Latin liturgy of Catholicism suffuses the book, and the abbot, who does not rebel against anything, is in his suffering a kind of saint.

M.'s work, in its diversity of setting and its preoccupation with substantial themes, is a serious contribution to the literature of the latter half of the 20th c. Considered both an Irish and a Canadian novelist, he has created a fictional world that expresses the painful condition of the culturally displaced and the religiously alienated. His novels, no matter the setting, are always realized with the greatest particularity. Yet beyond the satisfying realistic surfaces of his novels lie expressions of the powerful and insoluble conflicts between freedom and security, personal fulfillment and love, religious belief and suicidal despair.

FURTHER WORKS: *The Luck of Ginger Coffey* (1960); *The Emperor of Ice-Cream* (1965); *The Revolution Script* (1971); *The Great Victorian Collection* (1975); *The Mangan Inheritance* (1979); *The Temptation of Eileen Hughes* (1981)

BIBLIOGRAPHY: Dahlie, H., *B. M.* (1969); Flood, J., *B. M.* (1974); McSweeney, K., "B. M.: Past and Present," *CritQ,* 18 (1976), 53–66; Scanlan, J., "The Artist-in-Exile: B. M.'s North American Novels," *Éire,* 12 (1977), 14–33; Shepherd, A., "Place and Meaning in B. M.'s *Catholics,*" *Éire,* 15 (1980), 134–40

JEANNE A. FLOOD

MOORE, George

Anglo-Irish poet, novelist, dramatist, and essayist, b. 24 Feb. 1852, Moore Hall, County Mayo, Ireland; d. 20 Jan. 1933, London

After a haphazard education, with considerable freedom to do as he pleased, and equipped with a lively imagination and a sound knowledge of the racing stables, M. at eighteen was left with an adequate income and no professional training. In 1873, after spending a few years in London, he went to Paris to study painting, soon finding himself on the periphery of the group of French impressionists. Most of his fiction reflects his interest in and knowledge of painting.

The practical result of these studies and friendships was *Modern Painting* (1893), mainly essays he had contributed to *The Speaker.* Without talent for painting and having been introduced between 1877 and 1880 to some of the French writers associated with the naturalist movement in fiction and the symbolist (q.v.) movement in poetry, M. turned to writing. *Flowers of Passion* (1878) and *Pagan Poems* (1881), in the main poor imitations of Baudelaire, showed M. he had no great talent in this genre. He wrote *A Modern Lover* (1883; rev. as *Lewis Seymour and Some Women,* 1917) in imitation of Zola, and there followed such volumes as *A Mummer's Wife* (1885), *A Drama in Muslin*

(1886), and *Spring Days* (1888), each in various ways a modification of Zola's manner.

Even in these early years of his career M. was dissatisfied with what he considered the surface psychological portraiture in the French novel and in the work of, among other English writers, Fielding. He was already searching for a way of expressing states of mind and emotions more subtly and penetratingly. In *Esther Waters* (1894), his greatest success, his use of the impressionistic painter's techniques and his counterpointing of tones showed a marked shift away from the naturalistic manner. Some of his early short stories, as in *Celibates* (1895), are in a sense exercises in subtle psychological portraiture.

M.'s lifelong interest in the short story is demonstrated in *"Minor Keys": G. M.'s Uncollected Short Stories* (1982). This volume and the five volumes of short stories published in his lifetime make a convincing case for him as a major writer in this genre.

In midcareer, with *Evelyn Innes* (1898) and *Sister Teresa* (1901), M. carried the search for a new technique still further by adapting to fiction Wagner's innovations in music. His subject often became the private inner life in conflict with the public life. His techniques increasingly borrowed from painting and music. The effects of these experiments on his fiction are next seen in the short-story collection *The Untilled Field* (1903) and the novel *The Lake* (1905), written during the ten-year period of his return to Ireland. This period is recorded in his novelistic autobiography, *Hail and Farewell* (3 vols., 1911–14). As this work reveals, M. clashed with other leaders of the Irish literary renaissance, and he soon realized that this movement could no longer serve his interests and talents.

From about 1915 to 1933 M. published most of his work in expensive limited editions. His later work, that of the "melodic line," is thus little known. The complex, supple style is perhaps best illustrated by his brilliant novel *The Brook Kerith* (1916) and his prose epic *Héloïse and Abélard* (1921).

Although M.'s career after about 1915 has received little attention, it was, despite his illness and exhaustion, very active and fruitful. By refusing to deal significantly with the problem of modern times, as he had done during the earlier phases of his career, he lost many readers. Much of the later work was misjudged as being insufficiently original but relying too heavily on translations of classical and biblical stories, biographies, and histories. But M.'s "re-creations" did have claim to originality in the same sense as the classical dramatists' individual treatments of well-known myths. Thus, *The Brook Kerith* is a re-creation of biblical history, *Héloïse and Abélard* of biography, *The Pastoral Loves of Daphnis and Chloe* (1924) of myth, *Ulick and Soracha* (1926) of Irish history, and *Aphrodite in Aulis* (1930) of the Greece of the 5th c. B.C.

M. also played an important role in the development of the modern drama. Early in his career he became very knowledgeable in practical aspects of the theater. He contributed significantly to the Independent Theatre, which performed Ibsen, and later was instrumental in helping to launch the Irish Literary Theatre; and he wrote a number of very competent plays.

M. will probably be longest remembered for his novels, his essays, his imaginative autobiographical writings, and, above all, for being one of the most influential molders of taste of the last two decades of the 19th c. and forerunner of many modern techniques in the novel and short story.

FURTHER WORKS: *Martin Luther* (1879, with Bernard Lopez); *Literature at Nurse; or, Circulating Morals* (1885); *Confessions of a Young Man* (1886); *A Mere Accident* (1887); *Parnell and His Island* (1887); *Mike Fletcher* (1889); *Impressions and Opinions* (1891); *Vain Fortune* (1892); *The Strike at Arlingford* (1893); *The Bending of the Bough* (1900); *Diarmuid and Grania* (1901, with W. B. Yeats); *Memoirs of My Dead Life* (1906); *The Apostle* (1911; final version, *The Passing of the Essenes,* 1930); *Esther Waters* (play, 1913); *A Story-Teller's Holiday* (1918); *Avowals* (1919); *The Coming of Gabrielle* (1920); *In Single Strictness* (1922; rev. as *Celibate Lives,* 1927); *Conversations in Ebury Street* (1924); *Peronnick the Fool* (1924); *The Making of an Immortal* (1927); *Letters to Edouard Dujardin, 1886–1922* (1929); *A Communication to My Friends* (1933); *Letters to John Eglinton* (1942); *Letters to Lady Cunard* (1957); *G. M. in Transition: Letters to T. Fisher Unwin and Lena Milman, 1894–1910* (1968); *G. M. on Parnassus: Letters (1900–1933) to Secretaries, Publishers, Printers, Agents, Literati, Friends and Acquaintances* (1982)

BIBLIOGRAPHY: Morgan, C., *Epitaph for G. M.* (1935); Hone, J. M., *The Life of G. M.* (1936); Nejdefors-Frisk, S., *G. M.'s Naturalistic Prose* (1952); Brown, M., *G. M.: A Reconsideration* (1955); Cunard, N., *G. M.* (1956); Collet, G.-P., *G. M. et la France* (1957); Gilcher, E., *A Bibliography of G. M.* (1970); Dunleavy, J. E., *G. M.: The Artist's Vision, the Storyteller's Art* (1973); Gerber, H. E., "G. M.," in Finneran, R. J., ed., *Anglo-Irish Literature: A Review of Research* (1976), pp. 138–66; Farrow, A., *G. M.* (1978)

HELMUT E. GERBER

MOORE, Marianne

American poet, translator, and essayist, b. 15 Nov. 1887, Kirkwood, Mo.; d. 5 Feb. 1972, New York, N.Y.

After graduating from Bryn Mawr in 1909, and from the Carlisle (Pennsylvania) Commercial College in 1910, M. taught commercial subjects at the United States Indian School in Carlisle. She began publishing poems in periodicals in 1915. She moved to New Jersey in 1916, to Manhattan in 1918, to Brooklyn in 1929, and back to Manhattan in 1966. She worked in a private school and in the New York Public Library until 1925, when she was appointed acting editor of *The Dial,* becoming editor the following year, a position she held until 1929. Thereafter she lived as a free-lance poet, translator, reviewer, and critic, receiving many recognitions of excellence, culminating in her selection in 1955 for membership in the American Academy of Arts and Letters.

M.'s first volume, entitled simply *Poems* (1921), was published by friends, without M.'s prior knowledge. Although she chose to omit almost half of the 1921 poems from her *Complete Poems* (1967), her most characteristic qualities were visible from the start—astringently judgmental wit, fastidious intellectual detachment, cryptic or eccentric associational logic, and a prosody that was syllabic rather than metrical, rhyming lightly when it rhymed at all, and rigorously regular in its stanzaic designs, although a persistent habit of revising earlier poems, sometimes radically, subsequently obscured that regularity. While not prosaic, the voice was that of elegantly lucid prose, given to quoting passages from other sources, not for purposes of allusion but because M. found the phrasing

attractive or appropriate for her own purposes.

Early reviewers were not sure what to make of M., although Ezra Pound, T. S. Eliot, and William Carlos Williams (qq.v.) were sympathetic. But *Observations* (1924) received the Dial Award, and *Selected Poems* (1935), by appearing in London and New York editions, indicated that she was receiving international recognition, a fact confirmed by the appearance of French, Spanish, German, and Italian translations of her poems. And *Collected Poems* (1951) received a National Book Award, a Pulitzer Prize, and the Bollingen Prize.

By the time of the 1951 *Collected Poems,* three things of importance for M. had happened—the outbreak of war in 1939, an eight-year commitment to translating *The Fables of La Fontaine* (1954), and her mother's death in 1947, when M. herself was sixty. Mary Warner Moore appears to have been M.'s closest friend (M. never married); M. kept a notebook of her mother's sayings, and regarded her as almost a collaborator. Her involvement with La Fontaine may have been a means of keeping herself alive as a writer through a time of deep personal loss; she apparently wrote no poems of her own during these years, and her later poems satisfied her less than her earlier ones.

World War II seems to have forced, or at least hastened, M. to a personal reassessment which was fundamentally religious in nature (she was a lifelong member of the Presbyterian Church) and which becomes especially visible in her books of the 1940s—*What Are Years?* (1941) and *Nevertheless* (1944)—although some of the poems registering that reassessment were written before the war's actual outbreak. In "Virginia Britannia" (1935) and "The Pangolin" (1936), which later appeared in *What Are Years?*, the frequently caustic and intolerant brilliance of her treatment of the human in her earlier work has yielded almost entirely to a deeper, more complex affirmation of understanding, acceptance, and affection. "Virginia Britannia" is a poem about colonization in all its ruthlessness and arrogance, and also in its courage and creativeness, inextricably interlocked in the burden of history. "The Pangolin" juxtaposes anteaters—graceful, humble, self-effacing, admirably adapted to survive without aggressiveness—against men, their absurd, aggressive, creative, humorous, vulnerable, engaging, and imperfectly admirable cousins—juxtaposes, and accepts the less graceful of the two. "Virginia Britannia" is elegiac, "The Pangolin" ruefully comic, but both are deeply human in a way that had not been much evident in M.'s earlier work.

"What Are Years?" (1940), which opens its volume, and "In Distrust of Merits" (1943), which closes *Nevertheless,* are clearly wartime poems, and in them affirmation deepens to an impassioned and tragic identification with the world of pain and responsibility. "What Are Years?" has to do with the reality and the mystery of human courage, affirming that freedom of the spirit exists only in the context of a confining necessity. But "In Distrust of Merits" finds even such moral formulations inadequate in the face of a devastating sense of personal involvement in and sin-ridden responsibility for the intolerable facts of war. In a 1961 *Paris Review* interview with Donald Hall, M. said it was hardly a poem at all, and in a way she was right; the intolerable remains intolerable, not reduced or reducible to aesthetic form. But in that respect, "In Distrust of Merits" is comparable with Eliot's "The Waste Land," Picasso's "Guernica," and the monument at Treblinka. It seems safe to suppose, on the strength of these poems of the 1930s and 1940s, that M.'s permanence is assured among the poets of this century, and perhaps of any century.

FURTHER WORKS: *Marriage* (1923); *The Pangolin, and Other Verse* (1936); *Rock Crystal* (1945); *Predilections* (1955); *Selected Fables of La Fontaine* (1955); *Like a Bulwark* (1956); *O to Be a Dragon* (1959); *A M. M. Reader* (1961); *The Absentee* (1962); *Puss in Boots, The Sleeping Beauty & Cinderella* (1963); *The Arctic Ox* (1964); *Tell Me, Tell Me: Granite, Steel and Other Topics* (1966); *Selected Poems* (1969); *The Complete Poems,* rev. ed. (1981)

BIBLIOGRAPHY: Engel, B. F., *M. M.* (1964); Tambimuttu, M. J., ed., *Festschrift for M. M.'s Seventy-seventh Birthday* (1964); Nitchie, G. W., *M. M.: An Introduction to the Poetry* (1969); Abbott, C. S., *M. M.: A Reference Guide* (1978); Stapleton, L., *M. M.: The Poet's Advance* (1978); Borroff, M., *Language and the Poet: Verbal Artistry in Frost, Stevens, and M.* (1979), pp. 80–135; Costello, B., *M. M.: Imaginary Possessions* (1981)

GEORGE W. NITCHIE

310

MORAND, Paul

French novelist, short-story writer, poet, and essayist, b. 13 March 1888, Paris; d. 24 July 1976, Paris

M. was born into a bourgeois family with artistic, political, and literary connections and with whom he early on had the opportunity to begin the extensive travels that were to dominate his life and his works. His studies at the Faculty of Law of the University of Paris and the School of Political Sciences, interrupted by a year at Oxford, his travels, and his military service, were completed just before World War I, and he became a diplomat. Named to posts around the world, he continued in this profession until the end of World War II, when the provisional government removed him because of his connection with the Vichy government; he did not return to diplomacy until 1953. He retired in 1955. While one can say that his autobiography is in much of what he wrote in the way of travel notes, chronicles, and essays, one can consult in particular *Mes débuts* (1934; my beginnings), in which he describes his family background and early years; *Papiers d'identité* (1931; identity papers), a miscellany of reflections and impressions; *Le visiteur du soir* (1949; evening visitor), reminiscences of Marcel Proust (q.v.), in which the sentimental side of M. is revealed; and *Venises* (1971; Venices), which contains memories of his whole life.

M. began his literary career with two volumes of poetry, *Lampes à arc* (1920; arc lamps) and *Feuilles de température* (1920; temperature charts), both striking in their modernism. These were followed by three books of short stories, *Tendres stocks* (1921; *Green Shoots,* 1923), *Ouvert la nuit* (1922; *Open All Night,* 1923), and *Fermé la nuit* (1923; *Closed All Night,* 1924), which solidified his reputation as an extremely fastidious portrayer of telling details and a stylist with some of the preciosity one associates with his friend Jean Giraudoux (q.v.).

M.'s style is more subdued in his first novel, *Lewis et Irène* (1924; *Lewis and Irene,* 1925), which has a feminist theme; in *L'Europe galante* (1926; *Europe at Love,* 1927), satirical sketches of eroticism in postwar Europe; in *Rien que la terre* (1926; *Nothing but the Earth,* 1927); and in *Champions du monde* (1930; *World Champions,* 1931)—all of which show his fine skills of observation. The cosmopolitan aspect of his work is reflected in *Magie noire* (1928; *Black Magic,* 1929), a description of blacks in Africa and America; his highly successful place-sketches like *New York* (1930; *New York,* 1930) and *Londres* (1933; *A Frenchman's London,* 1934); or his numerous essays on travel, full of picturesque images, rapid descriptions, and silhouettelike characters.

One critic sees his *Bouddha vivant* (1927; *The Living Buddha,* 1928), a novel contrasting Europe and Asia, as a pivotal work, and it is true that its themes are more serious than in his earlier work, as are the subjects and techniques of his later novels and novellas, such as *Hécate et ses chiens* (1954; Hecate and her dogs) and *La folle amoureuse* (1956; the mad woman in love), where one finds more thoughtful, more psychologically probing portrayals. These, his historical studies, and his *Venises* are considered by many to be his best.

Although dismissed by certain detractors as a superficial cosmopolitan, too rapid, too aloof, or too ironic to be taken very seriously, M. was nevertheless a moralist in the French sense of the word—a close observer of and commentator on his times. And there is no denying the fact that both his observations and his manner have had an influence on a younger generation of French writers.

FURTHER WORKS: *Poèmes, 1914–1924* (1924); *La fleur double* (1924); *Rain, Steam, Speed* (1926); *Le voyage* (1927); *L'innocente à Paris; ou, La jolie fille de Perth* (1927); *U.S.A.* (1927); *Paris-Tombouctou* (1928); *Hiver caraïbe* (1929); *À la Frégate* (1930); *Conseils pour voyager sans argent* (1930); *1900* (1931; *1900 A.D.,* 1931); *Air indien* (1932; *Indian Air: Impressions of Travel in South America,* 1933); *Flèche d'Orient* (1932; *Orient Air Express,* 1932); *L'art de mourir, suivi de Le suicide en littérature* (1932); *Paris de nuit* (1933; *Paris to the Life: A Sketchbook,* 1933); *Rococo* (1933); *Paysages méditerranéens* (1933); *France la doulce* (1934; *The Epic-Makers,* 1935); *La femme agenouillée* (1934); *Rond-point des Champs-Elysées* (1934); *Bucarest* (1935); *La route des Indes* (1936; *The Road to India,* 1937); *Les extravagants* (1936); *Apprendre à se reposer* (1937); *Le réveille-matin* (1937); *Méditerranée, mer des surprises* (1938); *L'heure qu'il est* (1938); *Isabeau de Bavière, femme de Charles VI* (1938); *Réflexes et réflexions* (1939); *Chroniques de l'homme maigre, suivi de Propos d'hier* (1941); *L'homme pressé* (1941); *Feu monsieur le duc, avec Bug O'Shea* (1942); *Vie de Guy de Maupassant* (1942); *Petit théâtre* (1942); *Propos de 52 semaines* (1942); *Excursions immobiles* (1944); *Adieu à Giraudoux* (1944); *Montociel, rajah aux Grandes Indes* (1947; *Montociel, Rajah of Greater India,* 1962); *Journal d'un attaché d'ambassade, 1916–17* (1948); *Giraudoux, souvenirs de notre jeunesse* (1948); *L'Europe russe annoncée par Dostoïevsky* (1948); *Le flagellant de Séville* (1951; *The Flagellant of Seville,* 1953); *L'eau sous les ponts* (1954); *Fin de siècle* (1957); *Le prisonnier de Cintra* (1958); *Le lion écarlate, précédé de La fin de Byzance* (1959); *Bains de mer, bains de rêve* (1960); *Fouquet; ou, Le soleil offusqué* (1961); *Le nouveau Londres* (1962); *Majorque* (1963); *La dame blanche des Habsbourg* (1963); *Tais-toi* (1965); *Mon plaisir en littérature* (1967); *Ci-gît Sophie Dorothée de Celle* (1968); *Mon plaisir en histoire* (1969); *Les écarts amoureux* (1974); *L'allure de Chanel* (1976); *Lettres à des amis et à quelques autres* (1978). FURTHER VOLUME IN ENGLISH: *East India and Company* (1927)

BIBLIOGRAPHY: Lemaître, G., *Four French Novelists* (1938), pp. 301–92; Guitard-Auviste, G., *P. M.* (1956); Thiébaut, M., "P. M., l'amour et la vitesse," *Entre les lignes* (1962), pp. 107–29; Sarkany, S., *P. M. et le cosmopolitisme littéraire* (1968); Schneider, M., *M.* (1971)

RUTH B. YORK

MORANTE, Elsa

Italian novelist and poet, b. 18 Aug. 1918, Rome

Daughter of a Sicilian father and an Emilian mother, M. left home at the age of eighteen. In 1941 she married Alberto Moravia (q.v.)—they were later divorced. In 1943, during the German occupation, she lived the desperate life of a refugee in the countryside near Cassino, where she experienced that rural world of the south that plays an important part in her fiction. M. has lived most of her life in Rome, although she has traveled all over the world.

With her first two novels, *Menzogna e sortilegio* (1948; *House of Liars,* 1951) and *L'isola di Arturo* (1957; *Arturo's Island,* 1959), M. defined her literary universe: a world filtered through memory, a private, magical world whose jealously guarded dreams and obsessions cultivated in the secret silence of the heart are ever threatened by the encroachment of external reality. In *Menzogna e sortilegio* this conflict is depicted through the vicissitudes of three generations of a family—their obsessive dreams, brooding silences, narcissistic theatricality, and feudal stubbornness. *L'isola di Arturo* re-creates the painful maturation of a child caught between the attachment to his luminous fantasies, to the world of his private island, and an increasing awareness that this beauty is destined to dissolve. The narrator is Arturo himself, who, looking back at his life with a more adult consciousness, still oscillates between the tempting fantasies of his childhood and his new awareness.

To say that M. in these two novels develops a narrative style dominated by the magic, mythical dimension of the imagination does not do full justice to her literary strategies. She proceeds in her writing through a slow accumulation of details that balances the fantastic with a wide-ranging realism. M. herself rejects an interpretation of her work that stresses only the mythical, fantastic elements.

The theme of the conflict between a private, fantastic world and an external historical reality continues to dominate her later work. In *Il mondo salvato dai ragazzini* (1968; the world saved by the children), a collection of poems, popular songs, and a one-act play, it acquires more precise connotations than earlier: those who do not accept the logic of power and domination and whose innocent dreams can find no place within social norms, those whose innocence is the source of anarchic rebellion, inevitably come into conflict with the violent institutions and ideologies of society.

In *La storia* (1974; *History: A Novel,* 1977) the conflict between "outsiders" and institutions, society, and history is analyzed in a blend of the fantastic, the fairy tale, and the devices of the popular historical novel. Through the story of a timid schoolteacher, Ida Ramundo, her two sons, and many other defenseless characters, set during World War II and the immediate postwar period, M. condemns the arrogant falsifications of official history, which would like to present itself as a glorious process, but which in reality has been a long series of violent acts, persecutions, and injustices.

FURTHER WORKS: *Le bellissime avventure di Caterí dalla trecciolina* (1941); *Il gioco segreto* (1941); *Alibi* (1958); *Le straordinarie avventure di Caterina* (1959); *Lo scialle andaluso* (1963)

BIBLIOGRAPHY: Brennan, M., on *House of Liars, New Yorker,* 9 Feb. 1952, 106–9; Hicks, G., on *Arturo's Island, SatR,* 15 Aug. 1959, 16; Ferrucci, F., "E. M.: Limbo without Elysium," *IQ,* 7, 27–28 (1963), 28–52; McCormick, E. A., "Utopia and Point of View: Narrative Method in M.'s *L'isola di Arturo* and Keyserling's *Schwüle Tage,*" *Symposium,* 15 (1963), 114–30; Spender, S., on *History: A Novel, NYRB,* 28 April 1977, 31–34

GOFFREDO PALLUCCHINI

MORAVIA, Alberto

Italian novelist, short-story writer, dramatist, and essayist, b. 28 Nov. 1907, Rome

Born of well-to-do middle-class parents, M. was stricken with osteomyelitis at the age of nine and spent the next several years of his life bedridden and under treatment in sanatoriums. A precocious writer, he began working on his first major novel, *Gli indifferenti* (1929; *The Indifferent Ones,* 1932; new tr., *The Time of Indifference,* 1953), at the age of eighteen. In 1941 he married the novelist Elsa Morante (q.v.), from whom he was later divorced. Except for a period of exile in the Abruzzi region in 1943, M. has always lived in Rome, the city intimately associated with most of his fiction.

Always sharply critical of the middle class (the object of bitter irony in many of his stories), M. has stated that Marxism is one of the two main poles of his thought; Freudianism is the other. From his earliest works to his most recent, M.'s themes, characters, and ideas have remained remarkably constant.

M. has identified the main theme of all his writing as the "relationship between man and reality." The perspective from which he views this relationship is that of sexuality—indeed, for him, the relationship itself is sexual. The reality is the dehumanized, capitalist world that the bourgeoisie has created, a nightmare that causes lifelong anguish in every individual. His characters are shown to be creatures of their instincts, governed by the forces of a mysterious bond between sex and money, the root of their alienation and torment.

Gli indifferenti, with its portrayal of the despair of the individual who is trapped in what would later come to be known as "the absurd," may be considered the first European existentialist (q.v.) novel. It was an immediate success, despite its harsh description of the decadence and rot of the middle-class society of its day. M. has readily concurred with critics who claim that he has continued to rewrite this first book, for the seeds of virtually all his later works were sown here. In character types, there is the typical impotent intellectual hero who suffers from boredom and self-disgust and who is pitted against a virile, successful rival; there are the women who are presented as prey to their sexuality, either as unconsciously voluptuous seductresses or as pitiful but disgusting aging mistresses and courtesans.

Variations on the women of *Gli indifferenti* have figured prominently in M.'s fiction. Two of M.'s best-known novels, *La romana* (1947; *The Woman of Rome,* 1949) and *La ciociara* (1957; *Two Women,* 1958), trace the awakening consciousness of three women who slowly come to an understanding of their own nature and of the meaning of life. In *La romana* we watch the sixteen-year-old Adriana, a naïve, unconsciously sensual girl of the working class, become a prostitute because she discovers that she "likes love and money and the things that money can buy." At the core of the experiences she narrates is her existentialist crisis and her recurring feeling of despair, spawned by a sense of shame at her life. When we leave her at age twenty-one, she has learned to accept herself and all humanity with its entangled strands of evil, violence, and suffering; she can now look to the future with hope for happiness.

For the two women in *La ciociara* redemption comes through suffering. The war experiences of the middle-class businesswoman and her daughter in this novel are closely based on M.'s own experiences as a refugee in the Abruzzi during World War II. The two women finally break out of their "tomb of indifference and wickedness" and take up life again at a moment when they are able to feel grief and compassion. Through his description of the brutal, dehumanizing forces of war we see M.'s belief that man is man because he suffers most cogently illustrated. This novel is also probably the most poignant expression of M.'s view of the human condition.

Among the hundreds of short pieces of fiction M. has written, the 130 stories in the *Racconti romani* (1954; *Roman Tales,* 1957)

and *Nuovi racconti romani* (1959; *More Roman Tales,* 1964) are probably his best known. Originally published as a regular newspaper feature, they charmed readers all over Italy, but most especially the Romans, who saw themselves and their daily activities reflected in these brief, thumbnail sketches of working-class characters in everyday situations.

Most critics and readers of M. consider his earlier short works to be his finest, however. In three of these stories M. excels in portraying adolescents during a time of crisis in the painful period of growing up. "Inverno di malato" (1930; "A Sick Boy's Winter," 1954), is a delicately melancholy tale about a middle-class boy under treatment in a sanatorium, who tries to seduce a naïve but willing fourteen-year-old patient. His feelings of shame and guilt, combined with the tormenting despair at his unimproved condition, are rendered with masterful sensitivity. Both *Agostino* (1945; *Agostino*) and *La disubbedienza* (1948; *Luca*)—published together in English as *Two Adolescents* (1950)—relate the anguish of loss of purity and the intense suffering of a boy confronted with a harsh reality so different from his ideals. The intimate drama of fifteen-year-old Luca's initiation into the mysteries of sexual union in *La disubbedienza* provides a sequel to the story of thirteen-year-old Agostino's desperate but futile attempts to experience sex.

M. has not received the critical acclaim for his essays, plays, and travel books that he has for his stories and novels. Indeed, these do remain minor works. However, his collected essays provide clear summaries of his ideas, and are provocative and stimulating if at times highly questionable or even outrageous. M.'s plays are generally elaborations of a broad thesis and embodiments of themes that are not always as fully explored in his fiction. In his travel books M. has written some memorable passages of impressions of people and life styles in the various countries he has visited.

Throughout his career M. has been a figure of controversy. He has, however, remained faithful to his inner vision and in so doing has reflected the main preoccupations of 20th-c. thought. An expert storyteller, he is widely recognized as a master of plot and description.

FURTHER WORKS: *La bella vita* (1935); *Le ambizione sbagliate* (1935; *Wheel of Fortune,*

1937; repub. as *Mistaken Ambitions,* 1955); *L'imbroglio* (1937); *I sogni del pigro* (1940); *La mascherata* (1941; *The Fancy Dress Party,* 1952); *L'amante infelice* (1943); *L'epidemia: Racconti surrealistici e satirici* (1944); *La cetonia* (1944); *Due cortigiane, e Serata di Don Giovanni* (1945); *L'amore coniugale, e altri racconti* (1949; *Conjugal Love, 1951); Il conformista* (1951; *The Conformist,* 1951); *I racconti* (1952); *Il disprezzo* (1954; *A Ghost at Noon,* 1955); *Teatro* (1958; *Beatrice Cenci,* 1966, tr. of one play in the vol.); *Un mese in U.R.S.S.* (1958); *La noia* (1960; *The Empty Canvas,* 1961); *Saggi italiani* (1960, with Elémire Zolla); *Un'idea dell'India* (1962) *L'automa* (1963; *The Fetish, and Other Stories,* 1964); *L'uomo come fine e altri saggi* (1964; *Man as an End,* 1965); *L'attenzione* (1965; *The Lie,* 1966); *Il mondo è quello che è* (1966); *L'intervista* (1966); *Una cosa è una cosa* (1967; *Command and I Will Obey You,* 1968); *La rivoluzione culturale in Cina* (1967; *The Red Book and the Great Wall,* 1968); *Il dio Kurt* (1968); *La vita è gioco* (1969); *Il paradiso* (1970; *Bought and Sold,* 1973; repub. as *Paradise, and Other Stories*); *Io e lui* (1971; *Two: A Phallic Novel,* 1972); *A quale tribù appartieni?* (1972; *Which Tribe Do You Belong To?,* 1974); *Un altra vita* (1973; *Lady Godiva, and Other Stories,* 1975; also tr. as *Mother Love,* 1976); *Al cinema* (1975); *Boh* (1976; *The Voice of the Sea, and Other Stories,* 1978); *La vita interiore* (1978; *Time of Desecration,* 1980); *Un miliardo di anni fa* (1979); *Cosma e i briganti* (1980); *Impegno controvoglia: Saggi, articoli, interviste—trentacinque anni di scritti politici* (1980). FURTHER VOLUMES IN ENGLISH: *Bitter Honeymoon, and Other Stories* (1956); *The Wayward Wife, and Other Stories* (1960)

BIBLIOGRAPHY: Lewis, R. W. B., "A. M.: Eros and Existence," *The Picaresque Saint: Representative Figures in Contemporary Fiction* (1956), pp. 36–56; Pacifici, S., *A Guide to Contemporary Italian Literature* (1962), pp. 29–56; Dego, G., *M.* (1966); Rimanelli, G., "M. and the Philosophy of Personal Existence," *IQ,* 41 (1967), 39–68; Heiney, D., *Three Italian Novelists: M., Pavese, Vittorini* (1968), pp. 1–82; Ragusa, O., "A. M.: Voyeurism and Storytelling," *SoR,* 4 (1968), 127–41; Radcliff-Umstead, D., "M.'s Indifferent Puppets," *Symposium,* 24 (1970), 44–54; Ross, J., and Freed, D., *The Existentialism of A. M.* (1972); Kibler, L., "The Reality and Realism of A. M.," *IQ,* 65 (1973), 3–25; Cottrell, J., *A. M.* (1974)

JANE E. COTTRELL

MORDVIN LITERATURE
See Finno-Ugric Literatures of the Soviet Union

MORGENSTERN, Christian
German poet, critic, and translator, b. 6 May 1871, Munich; d. 31 March 1914, Merano, Italy

M. was born into a family of artists; because of family difficulties his education beyond secondary school was limited to one year at Breslau University. He moved to Berlin in 1894, working as a professional writer, contributing literary, drama, and art criticism to important journals in Germany and Austria. He soon joined the group of writers and artists known as the Friedrichshagen circle, so named after the Berlin suburb where its founders, the Hart brothers, lived, and where meetings were held. Through the Harts— Heinrich (1855–1906) and Julius (1859–1930)—M. met many of Berlin's intellectual elite. His interest in theater led him to found a theatrical journal, *Das Theater* (1903–5), during the time he worked for the publisher Bruno Cassirer. Between 1897 and 1903 M. was also active as a translator, being particularly commended for his renditions of Ibsen.

M. considered poetry a sacred mission and regarded himself as a serious poet, but he also believed that humor and seriousness grew from common roots. While his first collection, *In Phantas Schloß* (1895; in fancy's castle), combined humor and fantasy, subsequent early works struck a more serious, romantic, and melancholy note. However, in *Galgenlieder* (1905; *The Gallows Songs,* 1964), his most enduring volume, M. reverted to a satiric voice to express his rejection of literary naturalism. Written during a period of skepticism, the poems play with language and present objects in a grotesque and surreal manner as a protest against man's manipulation of nature.

Most of the poetry he published between 1910 and 1914 had religious overtones and reflected his growing cosmic awareness, which extended even to the love lyrics for his wife in *Ich und Du* (1911; I and you). An exception to this preoccupation with religion and mysticism was *Palmström* (1910; Palmström), in which humor with a philosophical twist was directed at a complacent materialist society.

Although his serious writing was underrated in his lifetime, the depth of M.'s thought places him above most other German neoromantic poets. His tendency toward introspection and philosophy, including German and Oriental mysticism, was reinforced by long rest periods necessitated by tuberculosis. He acknowledged the influence of Nietzsche and Schopenhauer, of the controversial cultural philosopher Paul de Lagarde (1827–1891), and of the linguistic theorist Fritz Mauthner (1849–1923). Others have seen links in his humorous poetry with the satiric works of Clemens Brentano (1778–1842) and Wilhelm Busch (1832–1908), and with symbolism, Dadaism, and surrealism (qq.v.). M.'s last book, *Wir fanden einen Pfad* (1914; we found a path), was dedicated to Rudolf Steiner (1861–1925), founder of the anthroposophy movement, who was also his final mentor.

FURTHER WORKS: *Horatius travestitus* (1897); *Auf vielen Wegen* (1897); *Ich und die Welt* (1898); *Ein Sommer* (1900); *Und aber rundet sich ein Kranz* (1902); *Melancholie* (1906); *Einkehr* (1910); *Palma Kunkel* (1916); *Stufen* (1918); *Der Gingganz* (1919); *Der Melderbaum* (1920); *Epigramme und Sprüche* (1920); *Klein Irmchen* (1921); *Über die Galgenlieder* (1921); *. . . Daß auch sie einst Sonne werde* (1923); *Mensch Wanderer* (1927); *Die Schallmühle* (1928); *Meine Liebe ist groß wie die weite Welt* (1936); *Böhmischer Jahrmarkt* (1938); *Das aufgeklärte Mondschaf* (1938); *Wer vom Ziel nicht weiß, kann den Weg nicht haben* (1939); *Klaus Burrmann der Tierwelt Photograph* (1941); *Zeit und Ewigkeit* (1942); *Ausgewählte Gedichte* (1945); *Flugsand und Weidenflöten* (1945); *Stilles Reifen* (1945); *Mann muß aus einem Licht fort in das andre gehn* (1948); *Liebe Sonne, liebe Erde* (1949); *Egon und Emilie* (1950); *Quellen des Lebens hör ich in mir singen* (1951); *Sausebrand und Mausbarbier* (1951); *Ein Leben in Briefen* (1952); *Das Mondschaf* (1953; *The Moonsheep*, 1953); *Vom offenbaren Geheimnis* (1954); *Die drei Hasen* (1959); *Aphorismen und Sprüche* (1960); *Der Spielgast* (1960); *Alles um des Menschen Willen* (1962); *Eine*

Auswahl der schönsten Galgenlieder in deutscher und englischer Sprache (1964); *Der Sündfloh* (1965); *Gesammelte Werke* (1965); *Kindergedichte* (1965); *Heimlich träumen Mensch und Erde* (1967); *Versammlung der Nägel* (1969); *Gedenkausgabe 1871–1971* (1971); *Sämtliche Dichtungen* (16 vols., 1971–79); *Alle Galgenlieder* (1972); *Galgenlieder: Der Gingganz* (1973); *Gesammelte Werke* (1974); *Palmström: Palma Kunkel* (1974); *Das große C.-M.-Buch* (1976). FURTHER VOLUMES IN ENGLISH: *The Three Sparrows, and Other Nursery Poems* (1968); *The Great Lalula, and Other Nonsense Rhymes* (1969); *The Daynight Lamp, and Other Poems* (1973); *Selected Poems of C. M.* (1973)

BIBLIOGRAPHY: Bauer, M., *C. M.s Leben und Werk* (1933; 2nd ed., 1954); Hiebel, F., *C. M.: Wende und Aufbruch unseres Jahrhunderts* (1957); Beheim-Schwarzbach, M., *C. M. in Selbstzeugnissen und Bilddokumenten* (1964); Walter, J., *Sprache und Spiel in C. M.s Galgenliedern* (1966); Gumtau, H., *C. M.* (1971); Hofacker, E. P., *C. M.* (1978)

EVELINE L. KANES

MORI Ōgai

(pseud. of Mori Rintarō) Japanese novelist, short-story writer, and critic, b. 17 Feb. 1862, Tsuwano; d. 9 July 1922, Tokyo

M. followed his father by taking up a career in medicine, studying new Western scientific techniques, largely imported from Germany, which were taught in Tokyo in the 1870s. After joining the army, M. was sent to Germany to observe hygienic practices. He remained in Europe from 1884 to 1888, and on his return, fired by a new-found love for German literature and philosophy, began to pursue a double career as a writer and a bureaucrat that was to continue throughout his life. M. eventually obtained the rank of Surgeon General of the Japanese army, but his creative writing activities put him, along with his contemporary, Natsume Sōseki (q.v.), in the forefront of the writers of his generation.

Shortly after his return from Germany, M. wrote a trilogy of stories about his German experiences. The first of these, "Maihime" (1890; "The Girl Who Danced," 1964), chronicles the activities of a young Japanese in Europe who falls in love and then abandons his German mistress. The story, for all of its romantic trappings, concentrates on the conflict between self-fulfillment and social duty, a theme that finds repercussions in virtually every important M. work.

M.'s enthusiasms then turned to the preparation of a series of translations of works by Hans Christian Andersen, Goethe, Heine, and Kleist, among many others. He also did research in German aesthetic theory. M. wrote a number of stories and essays in the years that followed, but his first sustained period as a writer began in 1909, when, late in his forties, he began a series of novels and stories that allowed him to explore his own experience against the background of a rapidly modernizing society. The first of them, *Vita sexualis* (1909; *Vita Sexualis,* 1973), sketches with trenchant irony his development of feelings for the opposite sex. The second, *Seinen* (1910; youth), recounts the spiritual adventures of a young man struggling to become a novelist in modern Tokyo. In the third novel, *Gan* (1911; *Wild Geese,* 1959), M. creates as his heroine a woman caught between traditional and modern ways of behavior. She and the protagonist, a young student bound for study in Germany, are attracted to each other but never manage to meet in any meaningful way; her loneliness forces the woman to come alive to the forces of life that well up within her.

The protagonist of *Seinen* declares that art can only grow from a sense of the past, and by 1912 M. showed his commitment to this position in a series of historical stories and novels usually judged as his finest work. Among these, "Sanshō dayū" (1914; "Sanshō Dayū," 1952), a moving story, set in medieval times, of two children taken into slavery, shows M.'s ability to infuse traditional narrative with acute psychological and philosophical insight. Another notable story, "Kanzan Jittoku" (1915; "Han Shan and Shi Te," 1971) tells the legend of two Chinese Zen recluses with humor and wisdom. M.'s masterpiece is doubtless *Shibue Chūsai* (1916; Shibue Chūsai), the biography of a Confucian scholar and doctor who lived from 1805 to 1858, the period just prior to the modernization of Japan. M. reconstructs the details of the scholar's life, and, as he does so, shows his own affinities with this earlier figure, revealing both his and his subject's views on life in an intimate and compelling fashion.

M. continued to write and translate important works from European literature, including a number of Ibsen plays and Goethe's *Faust.* Although failing health caused him to curtail his activities, he continued to do research and writing until shortly before his death.

M.'s reputation is founded not only on his literary and critical works but also on a widespread admiration for the quality of the life that he led. His understanding of modern European culture, with its restless search for truth in an era when science was replacing metaphysics, helped him delineate the same changes in Japan. M.'s ironic detachment, which led him to an austere and poetic sense of philosophical resignation, reveals an atmosphere of moral courage that combines traditional Confucian virtue with modern sophistication.

FURTHER WORKS: *Omokage* (1889); *Utakata no ki* (1890; *Utakata No Ki,* 1974); *Kamen* (1909); "Hannichi" (1909; "Half a Day," 1974); "Hanako" (1910; "Hanako," 1918); *Ikutagawa* (1910); "Asobi" (1910); "Mōsō" (1911; "Delusion," 1970); *Hyaku monogatari* (1911); "Ka no yo ni" (1912; "As If," 1925); "Sakai jihen" (1914; "The Incident at Sakai," 1977); "Yasui Fujin" (1914; "The Wife of Yasui," 1977); *Oshio Heihachirō* (1915); "Takasebune" (1915; "Takase-bune," 1918); *Izawa Ranken* (1916); *Zenshū* (53 vols., 1951–56)

BIBLIOGRAPHY: Miyoshi, M., *Accomplices of Silence: The Modern Japanese Novel* (1974), pp. 38–54; Rimer, J. T., *M. Ō.* (1975); Johnson, E. W., "Ōgai's *The Wild Goose,*" in Tsuruta, K., and Swann, T., eds., *Approaches to the Modern Japanese Novel* (1976), pp. 129–47; Rimer, J. T., *Modern Japanese Fiction and Its Traditions* (1978), pp. 138–61; Bowring, R., *M. Ō. and the Modernization of Japanese Culture* (1979)

J. THOMAS RIMER

MÓRICZ, Zsigmond

Hungarian novelist, dramatist, and short-story writer, b. 30 June 1879, Tiszacsécse; d. 4 Sept. 1942, Budapest

Born in a small village in eastern Hungary, M. grew up among peasants, and although his mother, a descendant of impoverished Calvinist clergymen, instilled in him a respect for book learning, the adult M. identified more closely with his ambitious and hardworking peasant father. After attending some of the best church-run schools in provincial Hungary, M. enrolled in the Theological Seminary of Debrecen, but then switched to law, although he quit before receiving a degree. In 1900 he moved to Budapest and for a number of years made a meager living as a journalist and as a clerk in a government office. He also began to write essays and children's stories. In 1903, with a grant from a Hungarian learned society, he undertook a tour of the Hungarian countryside, collecting folktales and poetry in remote villages. This pioneering field trip, which may be compared with his compatriot Béla Bartók's researches into folk music, also begun around this time, signaled a turning point in his life as a writer. Not being interested in scholarship, M. did not publish his finds but the material he gathered—its spirit more than the narrative riches—fed his creative vein for many years to come.

With a poignant story in the manner of Chekhov (q.v.) about the dignity of the rural poor, "Hét krajcár" (1909; "Seven Pennies," 1962), M. established his name in Hungarian literature, and within a few years he came to be known as a modern master. He managed to incorporate the crises and conflicts of his personal life into his works, without making any of them transparently autobiographical. He was married twice, both times unhappily (his first wife committed suicide); in his novels male-female relationships are invariably tempestuous. Although M. was among the literary innovators who were associated with the modernist periodical *Nyugat*—between 1929 and 1933 he was one of the editors of the journal—at the time of his death in 1942 he was a father figure to Hungary's increasingly influential populist writers.

In M.'s mature fiction we encounter a new type of peasant: brooding, complex, violence-prone, a far cry from the docile and comically hapless figures familiar from earlier literature. His first important novel, *Sárarany* (1910; golden mud), shocked many people because in it the poverty and backwardness of the Hungarian village is described without palliative idealizations. The novel's peasant hero, a disturbingly robust, aggressive man with a huge appetite for life, was even more shocking. M.'s early conservative critics labeled him—disparagingly of course—a "naturalist"; the sexual excesses of

his characters, as well as the hints about biological determinism, were seen as evidence of a suspiciously radical, Zolaesque tilt. In truth, detached, slice-of-life naturalism was alien to M.'s temperament. He was attracted to the darker side of social and psychological reality, but an ingrained sense of morality also made him a passionate crusader for social justice. A quintessential realist, M. was nevertheless partial to strongly emotive language; he filled in background with bold colors and favored romantic hyperbole when depicting moments of high drama. Perhaps his most successfully realized novel, *A fáklya* (1918; *The Torch,* 1931), the story of a well-meaning though flawed Calvinist minister who tries to enlighten his narrow-minded parishioners, ends with a spectacular barn fire that claims the lives of hundreds of villagers, including the hero's.

M. was just as interested in the provincial middle class and the gentry as he was in the peasantry. The daydreaming, hopelessly frustrated heroine of *Az Isten háta mögött* (1911; behind God's country) has been called the Hungarian Madame Bovary; indeed, references to Flaubert's characters are made throughout the novel. Two more mature works, *Kivilágos kivirradtig* (1926; until daybreak) and *Úri muri* (1928; gentry roistering), also present a devastating picture of life in the Hungarian provinces. Descriptions of endless and almost desperate drinking and carousing, of arrogant posturing and nostalgic daydreaming, suggest not only the decadence of the gentry but the utter hollowness of its life style.

A far mellower and more serene novel, which has become a children's classic in Hungary, is *Légy jó mindhalálig* (1920; *Be Faithful unto Death,* 1962). Despite temptations, the earnest adolescent hero of this novel remains unaffected by the cruelties and corruptions of the adult world. M. himself, as he grew older, became more pessimistic about the possibility of reforming entrenched social institutions and alleviating social inequities. For example, his novel *Rokonok* (1932; the relatives), is a bitter exposé of machinations and cover-ups in high places.

M.'s most ambitious undertaking as a writer was the historical trilogy *Erdély* (1922–35; Transylvania), perhaps the most splendid historical novel in Hungarian literature. In it he pits two Transylvanian princes against each other—one a sober and effective compromiser, the other an anarchic and charismatic fighter. In addition to a host of fascinating characters, the trilogy also offers a rich tapestry of 17th-c. eastern European civilization.

M.'s most lasting achievements are his novels; as a playwright he was less successful (his works for the stage include adaptations of his popular novels). On the other hand, he was a master of the short story. Indeed his best stories—for example, "Barbárok" (1932; "Brutes," 1962) and "A világ végén már szép és jó" (1938; "Everythig Is Good at the End of the World," 1966)—have a balladlike terseness and intensity that his longer fiction lacks. Toward the end of his life M. befriended a young girl, a waif from the outskirts of Budapest who, when the author first met her, was about to commit suicide. M. wrote a number of stories about her harsh life, and through her learned a great deal about the urban poor. An avid note-taker and listener, M. was bent on discovering new worlds even in old age. He may have begun his career surveying peasant life only, but in time just about every stratum of Hungarian society fell under his careful, implacable scrutiny.

FURTHER WORKS: *Sári bíró* (1910), *Kerek Ferkó* (1913); *Mese a zöld füvön* (1915); *Nem élhetek muzsikaszó nélkül* (1916); *Szegény emberek* (1918); *Búzakalász* (1924); *Pillangó* (1925); *Forró mezők* (1929); *Esőleső társaság* (1931); *Az asszony közbeszól* (1934); *A boldog ember* (1935); *Rab oroszlán* (1936); *Életem regénye* (1939); *Árvácska* (1941); *Rózsa Sándor a lovát ugratja* (1941); *M. Z. összegyűjtött művei* (7 vols., 1953–59); *Színművei* (1956); *M. Z. hagyatékából* (1960); *Regényei és elbeszélései* (12 vols., 1961–65)

BIBLIOGRAPHY: Reményi, J., *Hungarian Writers and Literature* (1964), pp. 326–40; Klaniczay, T., Szauder, J., and Szabolcsi, M., *History of Hungarian Literature* (1964), pp. 199–205; Nagy, P., "How Modern Was Z. M.?" *NHQ*, No. 77 (1980), 29–42

IVAN SANDERS

MOROCCAN LITERATURE

In Arabic

The modern Arabic literary renascence known as "The Awakening," which began in the Levant in the second half of the 19th c., had for a long time only a minor effect in Morocco—on the western limit of the Arab world. There was not even a printing press in the country until 1865, when a lithograph press was opened in Fez, and no Arabic newspaper until 1889.

For the first two decades of the 20th c., literary endeavor in Morocco was confined primarily to the age-old forms of classical Arabic poetry and to traditional works of scholarship, such as treatises on law and liturgy, scriptural exegesis, local histories, and hagiologies. Few of these works enjoyed any sort of wide readership or lasting impact. A singular exception to the general obscurity is Muhammad al-Kattānī's (1858/9–c. 1927) *Salwat al-anfās wa-muhādathat al-akyās biman uqbira min al-'ulamā' wa al-sulahā' bi-Fās* (1899; solace for souls and discourses for the wise concerning the scholars and saints buried in Fez). The book is not only a biographical dictionary of the holy men of Fez, but a theoretical treatise on the doctrine of saint veneration and a defense of this typically Maghrebi (North African) form of Islam.

The earliest discernible influence of the Middle Eastern revival appeared in historical writing, the most important traditional Arabic literary genre after poetry. Muhammad al-Nāsirī's (1835–1897) *Kitāb al-istiqsā' li-akhbār duwal al-Maghrib al-Aqsā* (4 vols., 1894; 9 vols., 1954–56; a thorough investigation of the chronicles of the dynasties of Morocco), a monumental chronicle of Moroccan history from the Muslim conquest to the author's own time, had a profound impact upon the historical and national consciousness of the reading public and remains to this day the classic exposition of the national past. The *Kitāb al-istiqsā'* was followed by other works that tried to bridge the gap between traditional and modern Arabic historiography, such as 'Abd al-Rahmān ibn Zaydān's (dates n.a.) *Ithāf alām al-nās bi-jumāl akhbār hādirat Miknās* (5 vols., 1929–33; a presentation of the most learned men according to the finest accounts of the capital of Meknes), a history of the author's native city of Meknes and its elite. The first volume opens with a dedication to the young Sultan Sīdī Muhammad ibn Yūsuf (later Muhammad V), who had recently ascended the throne. Like the *Kitāb al-istiqsā'*, the *Ithāf* had the effect of further strengthening a national-historical awareness among Moroccans.

The first attempts at adopting truly modern literary forms came in drama after the highly successful tour of an Egyptian theatrical company in 1923. The early plays, such as *Al-Fadīla* (virtue) by 'Abd Allāh al-Jarārī (b. 1905), which was performed in Fez in the mid-1920s, and *Intisār al-haqq bi al-bātil* (the triumph of right over wrong) by 'Abd al-Khaliq al-Tarīs (dates n.a.), which was staged in Tetuan in 1933, were didactic and rather primitive works of no lasting importance. They were, however, the forerunners of the nationalist literature that became dominant in Morocco from the mid-1930s to the mid-1950s.

The new Arabic journals of the period, such as *Al-Maghrib, Al-Atlas, Al-Saʿāda,* and *Al-Salām,* became organs for essays on cultural themes by 'Abd Allāh Guennoun (dates n.a.) and Ahmad Bahnīnī (?–1971), for essays of literary criticism by Muhammad al-Qabbāj (pseud.: Ibn 'Abbād, dates n.a.) and Ahmad Ziyād (dates n.a.), and for patriotic poetry and stories in verse and prose by 'Allāl al-Fāsī (1910–1974), who became the leader of the nationalist movement, Mukhtār al-Sūsī (dates n.a.), who promoted Berber ethnic pride, and 'Abd al-Qādir Hasan (dates n.a.). During this period a new poetry, known as *al-shiʿr al-nidālī* (resistance poetry), developed. Written in the classical meters, it expressed the new themes of struggle, self-sacrifice, and the establishment of equity and justice, all of which were watchwords of the nationalists.

The most lasting body of literature to come out of the nationalist period consisted of short stories, again appearing mostly in journals. Sentimental vignettes of Moroccan life were in vogue. The bourgeoisie of Fez, which formed the backbone of the independence movement, was frequently depicted. Ahmad Bannānī's (dates n.a.) "Wafāʾ li-Fās wa-wafāʾ li al-hubb" (1940; fidelity to Fez and fidelity to love) was the first in a series of stories set in the author's native city. It is a work of pure, descriptive lyricism. The protagonist longs to return to his beloved Fez, "where everything talks of love," and to die there. Among the finest short stories of the period are those of 'Abd al-Majīd Ben-Jellūn (b. 1919). His collection of tales *Wādī al-dimāʾ* (1948; the valley of blood) depicts with great sensitivity the relations between Moroccans and Frenchmen at the time of the Protectorate. For example, in the pathetic story "Sāʾid al-asmāk" (the fisherman) Ben-Jellūn relates the tale of 'Abbās, a simple fisherman who cannot comprehend the changes wrought by the conquerors. Ben-Jellūn is one of the few Moroccan writers whose works have enjoyed some popularity in the Arab East.

In French

Alone among the writers of the nationalist period, Ahmed Sefrioui (b. 1915) employed French as his language of expression. Nevertheless, his stories exhibit the same romantic, patriotic sentiment found in the works of Moroccans writing in Arabic. Sefrioui's collection of tales *Le chapelet d'ambre* (1949; the amber necklace) has Fez as its principal setting. The stories have an almost fairy-tale quality. For Sefrioui, Morocco is an enchanted land whose daily life is "assuredly all poetry."

The only Moroccan writer to receive truly international attention stands totally outside the main current of nationalist literature as it developed from the 1930s through the 1950s. In 1954 Driss Chraïbi (b. 1926), a young Moroccan chemical engineer living in Paris, published his first novel, *Le passé simple* (the simple past), an angry, rebellious work, in part autobiographical, expressing the author's disgust for and rejection of traditional Moroccan Islamic society. *Le passé simple* was disconcerting both to the liberal French intellectual establishment and to the Moroccan public. It was denounced in the Moroccan nationalist press, and for a short while Chraïbi recanted and apologized to his countrymen for the book. He later admitted that the denial of his own work was made in a moment of weakness. The following year he published *Les boucs* (1955; billygoats). The hero of the book, Yalann Waldik (whose name means "may his father be cursed!") is an Algerian—not a Moroccan—living in France. The novel deals in part with the problem of North Africans in European society. Other novels in the same nervous, angry style followed, culminating in *Succession ouverte* (1962; unclaimed inheritance), a sequel to *Le passé simple,* in which the hero finally achieves a certain peace of mind after visiting Morocco to attend his father's funeral.

In the 1960s, a number of young Moroccans followed the trail blazed by Chraïbi, using similar subject matter and evincing the same spirit of rebelliousness against traditional Moroccan values. The most notable among these is the avant-garde poet and novelist Mohammed Khair-Eddine (b. 1941), whose novels *Agadir* (1967; Agadir) and

Corps négatif (1968; negative body) have been described by Moroccan critics as "savage literature." Khair-Eddine is a consummate rebel revolting against his family, his king, even his own blood. He calls for the complete destruction of the old in order to build anew.

Other young contemporary Moroccan authors writing in French, such as Abdelkébir Khatibi (b. 1938), Tahar Benjelloun (b. 1944), Zaghloul Morsy (b. 1933), and El Mostefa Nissaboury (b. 1943), who have chosen to remain in their native country, stand somewhere between the rebels Chraïbi and Khair-Eddine, on the one hand, and the senior establishment romanticists such as Sefrioui and Ben-Jellūn, on the other.

BIBLIOGRAPHY: Lévi-Provençal, E., *Les historiens des Chorfa* (1922); Germanus, A. K. J., "The Literature of Morocco," *IC,* 38 (1964), 213–41; Khatibi, A., *Le roman maghrébin* (1968); Ortzen, L., ed., *North African Writing* (1970); Yetiv, I., *Le thème de l'aliénation dans le roman maghrébin d'expression française* (1972); Déjeux, J., *Littérature mahgrébine de langue française* (1973); Lahbabi, M. A., "L'acculturation franco-marocaine en littérature," *Comptes rendus trimestriels des séances de l'Académie des Sciences d'Outre-Mer,* 37 (1977), 675–94; *La littérature maghrébine de langue française devant la critique,* special issue, *O&C,* 4, 2 (1979); special Moroccan issue, *Europe,* Nos. 602–3 (1979)

NORMAN A. STILLMAN

MORRIS, Wright

American novelist, essayist, critic, and short-story writer, b. 6 Jan. 1910, Central City, Nebr.

M. attended public schools in Chicago and studied at Pomona College in California, but left without graduating. After extensive travel in America and Europe—a long stay in Paris was artistically influential—he settled in California. He won Guggenheim awards in photography in 1942, 1946, and 1954. A member of the National Institute of Arts and Letters and of the American Academy of Arts and Sciences, M. received the National Book Award for the novel *The Field of Vision* (1956). He has honorary degrees from Westminster College (1968) and the University of Nebraska (1968). Since 1962 he has taught English at San Francisco State University.

My Uncle Dudley (1942), M.'s first novel, blends photographic realism and frontier nostalgia with overtones of myth. A jalopy full of social misfits heading eastward is observed through the eyes of a young man whose uncle, the group's leader, personifies the triumph of frontier independence over the contemporary wasteland. *The Man Who Was There* (1945) and *The World in the Attic* (1949) reveal M.'s eye for the minutiae of place, his ear for the mundane in dialogue. In sentences both stripped and evocative M. depicts characters who summon the past against the present in moods ranging from nostalgia to existential nausea. *The Works of Love* (1951), dedicated to Sherwood Anderson (q.v.), recounts the plight of another "grotesque," a small-town nonentity who defies puritan philistinism and bigotry. In *The Deep Sleep* (1953) M. works within the strict unities of place and time, crisscrossing them with kaleidoscopic flashbacks and multiple points of view. *The Huge Season* (1954) multiplies camera angles and truncates episodes to reveal the futility of the Jazz Age as seen in a handful of its aging children. Here M.'s earlier themes—mother domination, the ambivalence of love, the tyranny and richness of the past—are expanded and deepened. Landscape and inanimate objects increasingly take on a conscious life of their own, assuming both a dramatic and thematic role.

In midcareer M. focused on courage as the obverse of personal failure. *The Field of Vision* captures in a sequence of vividly realized monologues the reactions to a bullfight of five unfulfilled spectators whose memories of each other are stirred by its violence. *Ceremony in Lone Tree* (1960) is the account of a family gathering in a Nebraska ghost town on the occasion of its lone inhabitant's ninetieth birthday. Over M.'s flat landscape and the prosy exchanges of the trapped characters hangs a faint air of heroism. Perhaps the sole exception to this thematic pattern is his popular success *Love among the Cannibals* (1957), a sex comedy less evocative and mythical than brutally satirical.

What a Way to Go (1962), *Cause for Wonder* (1963), and *One Day* (1965) are expanded moments in what M. calls "durable experience," T. S. Eliot's (q.v.) "still point in a turning world." *In Orbit* (1967) re-creates a single day of mindless violence in the life of a sexual predator whose exploits arouse his neighbors' secret envy. Both picaresque and mythic, *Fire Sermon* (1971) dramatizes a boy's difficult choice between the values of an urban hippie couple and the aging plainsman he reveres. The struggle for release from the past continues in M.'s nineteenth novel, *The Fork River Space Project* (1977).

In 1981 M. won an American Book Award for *Plains Song: For Female Voices* (1980), a "chanted" lament for three generations of Midwestern women in their painful confrontation with a dying tradition. *Will's Boy: A Memoir* (1981) reconstructs the first thirty years of M.'s own life set against a bleak, even harsh, Midwestern heritage; it is rendered in a spare, emotionally powerful style.

M. has also produced a sizable body of essays on American society and culture, several distinguished photographic collections, and literary criticism highly revealing of his own artistic ends and means.

Despite the quantity and quality of M.'s work, his archetypal vision of the American Middle West, and his uniquely ironic "signature," the popular response to his more than twenty volumes continues to lag behind critical estimates, which place him alongside Saul Bellow, Bernard Malamud, and Ralph Ellison (qq.v.), leading novelists of America's "middle" generation. A chronicler of the American Dream in all its revealed absurdity and angst, M. salvages from the past a sense of the timeless, the heroic, and the real. These are the qualities he celebrates in the midst of the contemporary clichés and artifices his characters always reject before they discover the strength and freshness of ongoing life. Plainspoken Westerners, small communities on the plains, simple artifacts, and puzzled, groping, ordinary lives—M. sees in such ingredients a "functional and classic purity."

FURTHER WORKS: *The Inhabitants* (1946); *The Home Place* (1948); *Man and Boy* (1951); *A Bill of Rites, a Bill of Wrongs, a Bill of Goods* (1968); *God's Country and My People* (1968); *W. M.: A Reader* (1970); *Green Grass, Blue Sky, White House* (1970); *War Games* (1971); *Love Affair: A Venetian Journal* (1972); *Here is Einbaum* (1973); *A Life* (1973); *About Fiction* (1975); *Real Losses, Imaginary Gains* (1976); *Earthly Delights, Unearthly Adornments: American Writers as Image Makers* (1978)

BIBLIOGRAPHY: Trachtenberg, A., "The Craft of Vision," *Crit,* 4 (1961–62), 41–45;

Booth, W. C., "The Shaping of Prophecy: Craft and Idea in the Novels of W. M.," *ASch,* 31 (1962), 608–26; Klein, M., *After Alienation* (1964), pp. 196–246; Madden, D., *W. M.* (1964); Knoll, R. E., *Conversations with W. M.: Critical Views and Responses* (1977); Crump, G. B., *The Novels of W. M.: A Critical Interpretation* (1978)

JOHN G. HANNA

MORRISON, Toni

American novelist, b. 18 Feb. 1931, Lorain, Ohio

Unlike her Southern-born parents, M. grew up in the North relatively unscarred by racial prejudice. A good student and omnivorous reader, she received degrees in English from Howard and Cornell universities. Besides a novelist, M. has been a dancer and actress, a teacher, and an editor; she has also been a member of both the National Council on the Arts and the American Academy and Institute of Arts and Letters. M. has actively used her influence to defend the role of the artist and strongly encourage the publication of other black writers.

M.'s first novel, *The Bluest Eye* (1970), established the pattern of her later, more complex works of fiction: it is set in the black community of a small, Midwestern town, and its characters are all black. Here M. fulfills the need she felt existed for literature about the "nobody"—in this case, an ugly little girl whose imagination convinces her that her life would be happy if only she had blue eyes. Her second novel, *Sula* (1973), again has a female protagonist, whose flouting of society's mores earns her its condemnation. Both novels show a sensitivity that has become M.'s hallmark.

Song of Solomon (1977) won the National Book Critics' Circle Award for fiction and established M. as an important American writer. The book traces Milkman Dead's efforts to recover his "ancient properties," the family roots so important to M.; it also develops M.'s concern with signs of otherworldly portent, which can be seen in *Sula*. M.'s most recent novel, *Tar Baby* (1981), moves in a new direction: although it, too, is strongly reliant on myth, the setting has shifted to the Caribbean, and there are several important white characters. The protagonist is a new type: a highly educated young black woman whose white orientation prevents her from achieving a committed relationship with the black man she loves. Less emphasis is placed on narrative than in M.'s earlier novels, and the characters reveal themselves increasingly through their own words and actions.

M. is at the forefront of the group of intelligent, articulate black American woman novelists who began writing after the Black Power movement of the 1960s. M. universalizes the pain and beauty of the black experience, thus making it accessible to all readers. In so doing, in little over a decade M. has made herself a powerful voice in American literature.

BIBLIOGRAPHY: Bischoff, J., "The Novels of T. M.: Studies in Thwarted Sensitivity," SBL, 6 (1975), 21–23; Ogunyemi, C. O., "Order and Disorder in T. M.'s The Bluest Eye," Crit, 19 (1977), 112–20; Lounsberry, B., and Hovet, G. A., "Principles of Perception in T. M.'s Sula," BALF, 13 (1979), 126–29; Atlas, M. J., "A Woman Both Shiny and Brown: Feminine Strength in T. M.'s Song of Solomon," SSMLN, 9 (1979), 8–12; Blake, S. L., "Folklore and Community in Song of Solomon," MELUS, 7 (1979), 77–82; Christian, B., "Community and Nature: The Novels of T. M.," JEthS, 7 (1979), 65–78; Weever, J. de, "The Inverted World of T. M.'s The Bluest Eye and Sula," CLAJ, 22 (1979), 402–14

JOAN BISCHOFF

MOZAMBICAN LITERATURE

In the development of their respective indigenous, acculturated elites, Mozambique and Angola have much in common. But while Angolan intellectuals, starting in the late 19th c., had access, because of relatively open lines of communication with Portugal and Brazil, to many of the new, often progressive ideas generated in Europe and America, their counterparts in the east African colony of Mozambique were isolated from Europe and exposed to the conservative thinking of the ruling classes in South Africa and Rhodesia. The historical peculiarities of Portuguese settlement in Mozambique also contributed to greater separation of the races than in Angola, where the color line was more subtly drawn.

De facto racial segregation in colonial Mozambique resulted in the founding of three social clubs: the first, established in 1920, was made up almost entirely of mestizos; the second, founded in 1932, was composed of blacks; and the third, established in 1935, had a membership of native-born whites. The mestizo club, which eventually came to be known as the African Association, through O brado africano, its official news organ, promoted some of the first literary efforts by Africans in the form of poems and stories in Portuguese, with an occasional work in Ronga, one of the principal Bantu languages of southern Mozambique. The Association of Mozambique's Native Sons, made up exclusively of so-called second-class whites, Europeans born in the colony (beginning in the 1960s a few token blacks and mestizos were admitted as members), published A voz de Moçambique as its official newspaper. This newspaper and others, like Itinerário, became important outlets for the literary efforts of members of the three racial communities.

The Associative Center of the Colony's Negroes published no newspaper, but it did harbor a unique component known as the Secondary School Studies Nucleus. Eduardo Mondlane (1920–1969), the American-educated economist who headed the Mozambican Liberation Front (FRELIMO) until his assassination, founded the Nucleus in the early 1960s as an intellectual training ground for many of the militants, like Samora Machel, who would lead the rebellion against colonial rule. The Nucleus also served as a meeting place for writers.

Mozambique's acculturated literature, written in Portuguese, but from an African perspective, got under way with the posthumously published Sonetos (1949; sonnets) of Rui de Noronha (1909–1943) and the likewise posthumous Godido, e outros contos (1952; Godido, and other short stories) by João Dias (1926–1949). But in the absence of a coordinated sociocultural movement, as in Angola, and of a creole-African ethos, present in Angola's capital city of Luanda, the literary scene in Mozambique was fragmented and unsure.

Beginning in the 1950s the subject of Mozambican literature versus literature for its own sake reached the level of often heated debate, a debate that reached its peak in the late 1960s. Euro-Mozambicans, members of a white-dominated intellectual and literary clique in the city of Lourenço Marques (now Maputo), struggled with their own provincialism while denouncing black specificity and proclaiming a cultural universality that transcended ethnic, geographical, and political boundaries. But as the tide of national liberation swept across Portugal's colonial empire, advocates of a politically committed, authentically Mozambican literature came forward to contest art for art's sake. Ironically, from the ranks of Euro-Mozambican intellectuals emerged a few writers who did assure themselves a place in the history of Mozambican literature. Thus, Rui Knopfli (b. 1935), in his *Mangas verdes com sal* (1969; green mangoes with salt), produced "art" poems that express aspects of a black cultural reality through the codification of the tensions and ambivalences of the European born in Africa.

Some Euro-Mozambicans may have been appalled by what they saw as Noémia de Sousa's (b. 1927) stammering artlessness, but they could not help take note of her full-throated, frequently moving poetry of African revindication. But Sousa, one of sub-Saharan Africa's first female writers, never published a book of her poems, and her poetic voice became silent when, in the 1950s, she went into voluntary exile.

Meanwhile, José Craveirinha (b. 1922) was gaining attention with his vigorous poems, collected in *Chigubo* (1965; chigubo [a traditional Ronga dance]) and *Karingana ua karingana* (1974; a Ronga phrase roughly equivalent to "once upon a time"). Craveirinha's militancy, couched in the style of Negritude (q.v.), earned him an honored place among Mozambican nationalists, and his poetic phrasing and sensitivity brought him the respect and admiration of Euro-Mozambicans.

Craveirinha emerged as *the* poet of Mozambique; his counterpart in fiction was Luís Bernardo Honwana (b. 1942), whose short stories, such as those in *Nós matamos a cão tinhoso* (1964; *We Killed Mangy-Dog, and Other Mozambique Stories,* 1969), are artful elaborations of colonial social realities in the rural and semirural south. Some of Honwana's stories are clearly autobiographical; all play on the contradictions inherent in the relationship between the colonized and the colonizer. Both Craveirinha and Honwana were imprisoned in the 1960s for alleged subversive activities. Their status as political prisoners further enhanced their works in the eyes of many readers; but their literary pro-

duction was an isolated case in the generally depressed cultural climate of Mozambique in the decade or so before independence.

In 1963, with the outbreak of the war of independence, literary activity became even more fragmented as militant writers fled into exile, joined their guerrilla compatriots in the bush, were imprisoned as subversives, or simply became discreetly mute. Liberal, if not militant Euro-Mozambicans, who generally opposed the Portuguese dictatorship and its colonial policies, often collaborated with black and mestizo dissidents, at least on the level of civil rights. And this concern for individual freedoms and democratic institutions led some members of the European circle to take part in a kind of cultural resistance that incorporated elements of a more committed African perspective and that ultimately embraced the cause of Mozambican nationalism.

Meanwhile, a small corpus of patriotic and combative literature was being published in exile and distributed abroad and in the liberated zones of northern Mozambique. Chief among these combative writers was Marcelino dos Santos (b. 1929), who also wrote some of his pamphleteering but frequently powerful and widely anthologized poetry under the pseudonym Kalungano.

Unlike what occurred in Angola, independence in Mozambique did not bring about a flurry of literary activity. With the flight of most Euro-Mozambican intellectuals, the preindependence publishing base was all but obliterated, and the lines of literary continuity became tenuous. There were, however, isolated and often curious cases of literary activity. Orlando Mendes (b. 1916), for example, a white Mozambican and a prolific writer, published two volumes of patriotic poems, stories, and plays under the title of *País emerso* (1975, 1976; a country emerged). And in 1975, the year of Mozambican independence, a startling find was made in the form of a number of poems written by one Mutimati Bernabé João, presumably a guerrilla fighter who had died in battle. The poems, published under the title *Eu o povo* (1975; I, the people) were actually the product of António Quadros (b. 1933), a Portuguese who had come to Mozambique in 1964 and who had actively participated in the cosmopolitan cultural activities of the circle of Euro-Mozambican intellectuals. Despite what would seem to amount to a hoax, the poems stand as something of a monument to the idea that there can be such a thing as "good" political literature; and Quadros, who has never openly admitted to being the author and who, in fact, uses several different names, continues to live and work in Mozambique.

Even without a coordinated literary thrust, there was considerable literary activity in Mozambique. This activity was not limited to the major cities, and much of it took the form of grassroots organizing by the government and FRELIMO, the ruling party. Literary contests for students and workers resulted in the publication of prize-winning, albeit mainly technically weak poems and stories. Their amateurishness notwithstanding, these works contributed to the propagation of a taste for literature among a populace that was just beginning to learn to read, and they helped form a base upon which a more substantial literature could be built. And finally, in December 1980, the proclamation of the Association of Mozambican Writers set the stage for that more coordinated effort from which, Mozambicans hope, will emerge a national literature of universal appeal. If one new voice of recognizable merit has emerged since independence, it is that of Luís Patraquim (b. 1953), whose poems, collected in the small volume *Monção* (1980; monsoon), qualify him as Craveirinha's heir in terms of artistic quality.

BIBLIOGRAPHY: Moser, G. M., *Essays in Portuguese African Literature* (1969), passim; Honwana, L. B., "The Role of Poetry in the Mozambican Revolution," *LAAW*, No. 8 (1971), 148–66; Hamilton, R. G., *Voices from an Empire: A History of Afro-Portuguese Literature* (1975), pp. 163–229; Burness, D., *Fire: Six Writers from Angola, Mozambique, and Cape Verde* (1977); Hamilton, R. G., "Cultural Change and Literary Expression in Mozambique," *Issue,* 8, 1 (1978), 39–42

RUSSELL G. HAMILTON

MPHAHLELE, Ezekiel (Es'kia)

South African novelist, short-story writer, and essayist (writing in English), b. 17 Dec. 1919, Pretoria

Born in the slums of Pretoria, M. lived as a child on poor farms, then, as a teenager, re-turned to the urban life of Marabastad, the locale of his autobiography. He obtained a certificate in 1940 to teach English and Afrikaans in Johannesburg. In 1952 he was dismissed from his post because he protested apartheid. After working as a journalist, he left South Africa in 1957 to live in Nigeria. He moved to Nairobi, Kenya, in 1963 to teach English at University College; he also journeyed to England, the U.S., and France. The first draft of M.'s novel *The Wanderers* (1971) served as his dissertation for his degree from the University of Denver. He then moved to the University of Pennsylvania, where he taught English. He left that post in 1977 to return to his native land and changed his first name from Ezekiel to its corresponding African form, Es'kia. M. now teaches at the Center for African Studies of Witwatersrand University, on its Soweto campus.

M.'s views of human life have remained remarkably consistent. Always concerned about human rights, he has tried to avoid simplistic answers to the enormous racial problems of South Africa. His autobiography, *Down Second Avenue* (1959), exemplifies his wish to see people as human beings, not as "victims of political circumstance."

M.'s autobiographical novel *The Wanderers* is a lyric cry of pain for the many rootless black exiles who wander across the African continent searching for a new home. The protagonist, Timi Tabane, is a journalist forced to flee South Africa because he exposed the activities of a slave farm to which blacks were abducted and where they were beaten and murdered. Timi becomes an exile in more ways than just physically; he feels his alienation in free Nigeria and Kenya and in his job as a high-school teacher in eastern Africa; he even becomes alienated from his wife and children. Only in the tragic death of his son, who had joined an underground movement in South Africa, does a sense of catharsis and new resolution take hold in him.

In his second novel, *Chirundu* (1980), M. portrays an ambitious, self-made politician in a fictional country resembling Zambia. Chirundu, minister of transport and public works, is determined to gain power and wealth. He ends up in jail on a charge of bigamy brought by his first wife. Chirundu's "fall," however, is regarded by him as a boon to come later in the form of support by his tribal people, since bigamy is not recognized as a crime by his tribe. M. uses the bigamy trial to explore questions of modernism and tribalism, and of individualism and communal responsibility.

M. has also published three collections of short stories. *The Living and the Dead* (1961) and *In Corner B* (1967) portray life both in the urban slums and on the estates of wealthy English and Boer families. These stories are more charged with violence and with sexual imagery than M.'s other narrative work.

M.'s first critical study, *The African Image* (1962; rev. ed., 1974), is another attempt to gain perspective on himself and on his role as writer in a land torn by the struggle for political and human rights. In this book he attempts to reconstruct the image of the African as seen by white and black writers.

M.'s study *Voices in the Whirlwind* (1972) is a series of six essays on black culture. He expands his discussion of "African" to include black American and West Indian cultures. He remains conscious of the many differences among black men, just as he had earlier remained unconvinced by Negritude (q.v.). In the "whirlwind" created by the new awareness of black art and literature, M. sees education as the single most important force.

M. is also well known as an editor of many distinguished periodicals. His *African Writing Today* (1967), an anthology, is highly regarded, both for its comprehensiveness and for his illuminating introductions.

FURTHER WORK: *Man Must Live, and Other Stories* (1947)

BIBLIOGRAPHY: Cartey, W., *Whispers from a Continent* (1969), pp. 27–38, 110–22; Duerden, D., and Pieterse, C., eds., *African Writers Talking* (1972), pp. 95–115; Olney, J., *Tell Me, Africa* (1973), pp. 26–79; Barnett, U. A., *E. M.* (1976); Roscoe, A., *Uhuru's Fire: African Literature East to South* (1977), pp. 225–34; Moore, G., *Twelve African Writers* (1980), pp. 40–66; Tucker, M., on *Chirundu, Worldview,* June 1982, 25–26

MARTIN TUCKER

MROŻEK, Sławomir

Polish dramatist, b. 26 June 1930, Borzęcin

In 1950, when M. was an architecture student in Cracow, he began to publish cartoons in the daily press. The volume of ministories

Słoń (1957; *The Elephant*, 1962) won him the prestigious award of the literary review *Przegląd kulturalny* in 1957. The first collection of his plays, *Utwory sceniczne* (theatrical works) came out in 1963. These and other plays have often been performed in his native Poland and in many American and European cities. Since the early 1960s M. has lived mainly in France, and he is now a French citizen.

M. belongs to the tradition of the Theater of the Absurd (q.v.), which in Poland goes back to the plays of Stanisław Ignacy Witkiewicz and Witold Gombrowicz (qq.v.). Unlike these two, however, M. is an intensely moral writer. His basic technique consists of reducing political programs and social theories to the dimensions of one family or one man, and demonstrating what they entail for those individuals who have to pay the price for their implementation. His imagery partakes heavily of war, chase, and flight. His plays have few characters, often only two or three. The plays are brief. The language is simple, lively, and easy to translate, and the action proceeds swiftly to an absurdist end.

M.'s first play, *Policja* (1958; *The Police*, 1967), is a theatrical parable of a political system that manufactures fake political dissenters, whom it then proceeds to destroy for the sake of keeping the system functioning. In *Strip-tease* (1961; *Striptease*, 1972) an anonymous Hand deprives two citizens of their possessions, their clothes, and finally, their lives. In *Na pełnym morzu* (1960; *Out at Sea*, 1967) three shipwrecked individuals discuss the methods of survival at sea. At the end, the weakest of them agrees to be killed and devoured by the other two in order to assure their survival. In *Karol* (1963; *Charlie*, 1967) an old man and his grandson visit an optician to buy a pair of glasses, but instead they take away the optician's own glasses and nearly shoot him to death. In *Indyk* (1963; the turkey) and *Śmierć porucznika* (1963; death of a lieutenant) the meaning of the play emerges out of a web of ironic allusions to Polish romantic literature. *Emigranci* (1975; *Emigrés*, 1978) is a dialogue between the two refugees who room together even though they have little in common: one is a writer who has fled from his native country in search of intellectual freedom, and the other is a worker who has gone abroad with the hopes of making a fortune. In the course of their hostile verbal exchanges, they gradually discover the bondage created by interpersonal relationships. They have both fled from political oppression only to find out that there exist other limitations to man's freedom and that it is often impossible to escape them.

M.'s best-known play, *Tango* (1964; *Tango*, 1968), dramatizes the psychological situation in which bohemian and permissive parents produce in their son so strong a longing for fixed meanings that he decides to "reform" the world by force. Instead of turning to Marxist-inspired ideologies (a course of action common in the West), Artur turns to the ideologies of the national past (as has often been the case in Communist-dominated eastern Europe). He is finally defeated by the vulgar opportunist Edek, who emerges out of the turmoil as the new lawgiver to the society.

M.'s basic dramatic situation is that of the cornered man, or the man who has been manipulated by others to such a degree that he becomes their victim. Like Gogol in his attitude toward Akaky Akakievich in *The Overcoat*, M. both sympathizes with and laughs at the victims in his plays. Doubtless there is in his schlemiels a bit of the "Polish complex," the Poles often viewing themselves as victims of their stronger and more ruthless neighbors. M.'s plays can also be read as satires on totalitarian regimes, especially on their eastern European variety, or as commentaries on the theory of Alfred Adler that a desire for power is the motivating force behind all human behavior. Some plays lend themselves best to the political interpretation—*Policja, Męczeństwo Piotra Ohey'a* (1959; *The Martyrdom of Peter Ohey*, 1967), *Strip-tease*—others to the psychological one—*Emigranci, Na pełnym morzu, Karol, Tango.*

FURTHER WORKS: *Opowiadania z Trzmielowej Góry: Satyry* (1953); *Półpancerze praktyczne: Satyry* (1953); *Polska w obrazach: Satyry* (1957); *Maleńkie lato: Powieść* (1959); *Wesele w Atomicach: Opowiadania* (1959); *Postępowiec: Satyry* (1960); *Ucieczka na południe: Powieść satyryczna* (1962); *Kynolog w rozterce* (1962); *Racket baby* (1962); *Deszcz* (1962; *The Ugupu Bird*, 1968); *Zabawa* (1963; *The Party*, 1967); *Czarowna noc* (1963; *Enchanted Night*, 1967); *Opowiadania* (1964); *Dom na granicy* (1967); *Testarium* (1967; *The Prophets*, 1972); *Poczwórka* (retitled *Drugie danie;* unpub. in Polish, perf.

1968; *Repeat Performance*, 1972); *Przez okulary S. M.* (1968); *Vatzlav: Sztuka w 77 odsłonach* (written c. 1969, unpub. in Polish, perf. 1978; *Vatzlav: A Play in 77 Scenes*, 1970); *Dwa listy, i inne opowiadania* (1970); *Utwory sceniczne nowe* (1975)

BIBLIOGRAPHY: Kott, J., "M.'s Family," *Encounter*, Dec. 1965, 54–58; Czerwinski, E. J., "S. M.: Jester in Search of an Absolute," *CSS*, 3 (1969), 629–45; Krynski, M. J., "*Tango* and an American Campus," *PolR*, 15 (1970), 14–16; Stankiewicz, M. G., "S. M.: Two Forms of the Absurd," *ConL*, 12 (1971), 188–203; Galassi, F. S., "The Absurdist Vision of S. M.'s *Strip-tease*," *PolR*, 17 (1972), 74–79; Kejna-Sharratt, B., "S. M. and the Polish Tradition of the Absurd," *NZSJ*, 1 (1974), 75–86

EWA THOMPSON

MUIR, Edwin

Scottish poet, critic, essayist, translator, and novelist, b. 15 May 1887, Deerness, Orkney Islands; d. 3 Jan. 1959, Cambridge, England

At fourteen M. moved with his family from the Orkneys to Glasgow. His parents and two brothers soon died, and he supported himself by office work. In spite of ill health and emotional shock, he read widely, joined discussion groups, and in 1913 began writing for A. R. Orage's (1873–1934) *New Age*. After his marriage in 1919 to Willa Anderson (1890–1970), he moved to London, where he worked as assistant to Orage and wrote criticism and reviews. Not until he underwent psychoanalysis in 1920–21, after which he spent four years on the Continent, did he recover from his early trauma and begin to write poetry. At the same time, he and his wife began their long series of translations from Continental writers, which was to lead eventually, with the publication in 1930 of *The Castle*, to their introducing Franz Kafka (q.v.) to English-language readers. On their return home, M. also published an increasing amount of his own work, including several volumes of poems; collections of critical essays; a study in fiction theory, *The Structure of the Novel* (1928); three novels; and the first version of his autobiography, *The Story and the Fable* (1940). His return to the Continent, as director of the British Institute in

Prague from 1945 to 1948 and in Rome from 1948 to 1949, gave him material for poems included in his last two volumes, *The Labyrinth* (1949) and *One Foot in Eden* (1956), and for additions to *The Story and the Fable,* now published as *An Autobiography* (1954). His final, posthumously published work, *The Estate of Poetry* (1962), is a collection of the Charles Eliot Norton lectures he gave at Harvard in 1955–56, and his *Collected Poems* were published in 1965.

From the first, M.'s work as a poet was shaped more by his life experience and his own sensibility than by current literary trends. The verse in *First Poems* (1925), for example, was distinguished for its visionary power rather than for the wit and technical innovation so characteristic of the 1920s. Similarly, as each succeeding volume appeared, it was the increasing range and force of this vision that slowly won him recognition. For while the childhood memories and dream images of *First Poems,* with their intimations of some transcendent good, remained constants in his poetry, other, darker images entered as well. These images, derived from his Glasgow years, his stay on the Continent, and his immersion, as a translator, in European culture, all reflected, like Kafka's, the deep and growing anxieties of the time. Like Kafka's, too, they touched the imagination of readers beginning to sense the imminence of unimaginable horror.

Yet paradoxically, because M. was now reflecting on his past to write many of his poems and to prepare his autobiography, it was in this dark period that for the first time he was able to look back on his life and see it as a whole, where right and wrong each had a place. As a result, although the symbols of fear, frustration, and betrayal that had dominated his poems from the difficult *Variations on a Time Theme* (1934) until *The Narrow Place* (1943) continued to recur in his last three volumes of verse, *The Voyage* (1946), *The Labyrinth,* and *One Foot in Eden,* a growing number of poems in each of these later books showed a new openness. The strength he drew from his marriage, a restored faith in the natural harmony he had known as a child, the persistent intuitions of his dreams, and an increasingly deep, if unorthodox, religious sense all worked to counterbalance the forces of terror and inhumanity he saw gathering in the world about him. Even after the shock of witnessing the over-throw of the democratic government in Prague in 1948, he could still write the radiantly affirmative lines that appear in *One Foot in Eden.* Here the dark, the wrong, is not diminished, but it is included and thereby undone, in poems that establish M. beyond question as one of the major figures of modern English poetry.

At the same time, M. wrote several prose works of primary importance. His autobiography, an account of the inner as well as the outer events of his life, is a masterpiece of the genre. As the story of his first years in the Orkneys, where the ordinary and the fabulous blended together seamlessly, through the destruction of that harmony in Glasgow, to the recovery of a still deeper sense of wholeness, the autobiography documents a spiritual journey from faith through loss to new faith, justified at the end by a full recognition of evil. Further, it provides the single most valuable commentary on M.'s poetry. M.'s critical writings, too, provide insight into his poetry, but they are equally significant in their own right as balanced, perceptive, and humane discussions of a wide range of literature. As the title of his best-known collection, *Essays on Literature and Society* (1949; 2nd ed., 1965) suggests, it was his particular virtue as a critic to view literature in relation to the way human beings live and the values they hold.

Seen now against the background of his time, M.'s entire work becomes continually more impressive. In everything he wrote, there is an acute awareness of the dislocations of society in this century, of the assaults of the mechanized and the impersonal on the free human spirit, and of that spirit's miraculous capacity to endure. But above all, in his poetry M. created not only the haunting images necessary to show the times their face, but also glimpses of a reconciliation made credible by his awareness of the world's wrong and his unfailing humility before the mysteries of our being.

FURTHER WORKS: *We Moderns: Enigmas and Guesses* (1918); *Latitudes* (1924); *Chorus of the Newly Dead* (1926); *Transition* (1926); *The Marionette* (1927); *John Knox: Portrait of a Calvinist* (1929); *The Three Brothers* (1931); *Six Poems* (1932); *Poor Tom* (1932); *Scottish Journey* (1935); *Social Credit and the Labour Party* (1935); *Scott and Scotland: The Predicament of the Scottish Writer*

(1936); *Journeys and Places* (1937); *The Present Age* (1940); *The Scots and Their Country* (1946); *Prometheus* (1954); *Collected Poems 1921–1951* (1957); *Selected Poems* (1965); *Selected Letters* (1974); *Uncollected Scottish Criticism* (1981)

BIBLIOGRAPHY: Hall, J. C., *E. M.* (1956); Blackmur, R. P., "E. M.: 'Between the Tiger's Paws,' " *KR,* 21 (1959), 419–36; Hamburger, M., "E. M.," *Encounter,* Dec. 1960, 46–53; Butter, P. H., *E. M.* (1962); Mellown, E. W., *Bibliography of the Writings of E. M.* (1964; augmented ed., 1970, with Peter Hoy); Butter, P. H., *E. M.: Man and Poet* (1966); Muir, W., *Belonging: A Memoir* (1968); Huberman, E., *The Poetry of E. M.* (1971); Wiseman, C., *Beyond the Labyrinth: A Study of E. M.'s Poetry* (1978); Knight, R., *E. M.: An Introduction to His Work* (1980)

ELIZABETH HUBERMAN

MUJICA LÁINEZ, Manuel

Argentine novelist, short-story writer, biographer, poet, and essayist, b. 11 Sept. 1910, Buenos Aires

A member of his country's cosmopolitan elite and related to noted literary figures of Argentina's past, M. L. was educated in Buenos Aires and in France. Although he attended law school, he did not complete his studies and in 1932 began what was to become a lifelong association with the leading Latin American newspaper, *La nación,* on which he served as reporter, art critic, and travel chronicler.

M. L. began publishing short poems and tales in 1927. His first book, *Glosas castellanas* (1936); Castilian variations), was an evocation of old Spain, in the spirit of the Spaniard Azorín (q.v.). M. L.'s compatriot, the novelist Enrique Larreta (1875–1961), inspired his first full-length fictional work, the historical novel *Don Galaz de Buenos Aires* (1938; Don Galaz of Buenos Aires). M. L. considers both books, which reveal his ongoing concern with time, preparatory works. He did not establish a reputation as a writer of fiction until 1949. In the 1940s he became well known for his biographies of celebrated Argentines. He published *Canto a Buenos Aires* (1943; ode to Buenos Aires), which still sells as a gift volume; edited a number of works by 19th-c. Argentine writers; and pro-

duced the first of his "urban albums" (texts accompanied by etchings or photos).

The linked tales of *Aquí vivieron* (1949; here they lived) were followed by the collection of stories *Misteriosa Buenos Aires* (1950; mysterious Buenos Aires), both organized chronologically according to historical periods, from the 16th to 20th cs. Then four major works firmly established M. as the author of what has been called the "saga of Buenos Aires," which records, nostalgically and critically, the decadence of Argentina's wealthy and cultured elite. *Los ídolos* (1953; the idols) presents the poeticized memories of a bachelor in three related novelettes. In the novel *La casa* (1954; the mansion), M. L.'s best-known and perhaps best work, the house itself relates the downfall of one society family. Another novel, *Los viajeros* (1955; the travelers), deals with a family related to the one in *La casa;* these people perish while dreaming of a grand tour of Europe. *Invitados en El Paraíso* (1957; guests at Villa Paradise) follows the elite to its dissolution with the introduction of bohemian elements in the wake of World War II. M. L., who during this period had become a member of the Argentine Academy of Letters, developed a technique of his own, which includes having settings of sumptuous decay, making paintings "come to life," establishing links between his plots, and using repeated motifs and an elegant Spanish devoid of regional features.

His prestige in Argentine assured, M. L. turned to topics of universal interest. *Bomarzo* (1962; *Bomarzo,* 1969), the "autobiography" of an Italian Renaissance prince, who speaks from a 20th-c. perspective and who is "reincarnated" in the person of M. L. himself, shared the Kennedy Novel Prize of 1964 with Julio Cortázar's (q.v.) *Hopscotch.* *Bomarzo*'s international recognition was enhanced by the opera by Alberto Ginastera based on it. *El unicornio* (1965; the unicorn), narrated by a French fairy, evokes the time of the Crusades.

M. L. continued to depict splendor and decadence, but his ironic view of history became more and more humorous, especially in the linked novellas *Crónicas reales* (1967; royal chronicles), which relates the exploits of an imaginary European dynasty, and *De milagros y de melancolías* (1969; of miracles and melancholies), episodes in the evolution of a hypothetical Latin American city. The satire is less boisterous in the picaresque novel *El laberinto* (1974; the labyrinth), about life in Spain and colonial America under the Habsburgs, and *El viaje de los siete demonios* (1974; the tour of the seven devils), which depicts a hellish recruiting drive through time and space. M. L.'s essentially pessimistic view of humanity's sameness is attenuated by a smiling compassion and a stress on beauty. Tidbits of history and an "I was there" technique are common in these works, and well-known motifs of literature and art are consciously recycled.

After his formal retirement from *La nación* M. L. returned to Argentine settings in his creative writing. *Cecil* (1972; Cecil) is his dog's view of his master and the latter's creative process. The novels *Sergio* (1976; Sergio) and *Los cisnes* (1977; the swans) depict contemporary Argentine society with its frustrations, including sexual ones. Sexual problems also play a role in the novel *El gran teatro* (1979; the great theater), set in pre-Perón Buenos Aires. Here, real-life dramas are played out in the opera house simultaneously with the drama on the stage.

Although M. L. uses unusual topics and narrators, he is not an innovator, but rather a traditional writer. He has updated the techniques of the Spanish American modernists (q.v.) of the turn of the century with a considerable dose of social satire. Like Jorge Luis Borges (q.v.), M. L. represents an Argentina that considers itself European. Thus, his work is as appealing abroad as it is in Argentina itself.

FURTHER WORKS: *Miguel Cané (Padre)* (1942); *Vida de Aniceto el Gallo* (1943); *Vida de Anastasio el Pollo* (1948); *Cincuenta sonetos a Shakespeare* (1963); *Bomarzo* [bilingual libretto] (1967); *Obras completas* (3 vols., 1978–80); *El brazalete y otros cuentos* (1978); *Los porteños* (1979)

BIBLIOGRAPHY: Carsuzán, M., Introduction to *M. M. L.* (1962), pp. 7–56; Ghiano, J., Introduction to M. M. L., *Cuentos de Buenos Aires* (1972), pp. 5–62; Schanzer, G. O., "The Four Hundred Years of Myths and Melancholies of M. L.," *LALR*, 1, 2 (1973), 65–71; Font, E., *Realidad y fantasía en la narrativa de M. M. L.* (1976); Villena, L., *Antología general e introducción a la obra de M. M. L.* (1976), pp. 11–33; Cruz, J., *Genio y figura de M. M. L.* (1978)

GEORGE O. SCHANZER

MULISCH, Harry

Dutch novelist, short-story writer, dramatist, poet, essayist, librettist, and journalist, b. 29 July 1927, Haarlem

M. left school at the age of seventeen, at which time he started writing poems. From 1946 on, he also wrote many short stories. His first novel, *Archibald Strohalm* (1952; Archibald Strohalm), received an award, and since then he has enjoyed continued literary success. He is one of the few Dutch authors who have been full-time writers.

M.'s prolific output encompasses a wide variety of genres and modes. As a journalist he covered the Eichmann trial and wrote a book about it, *De zaak 40/61* (1962; case 40/61). During the 1960s he became a key figure of the new left in Amsterdam, expressing his political views in *Bericht aan de rattenkoning* (1966; report to the rat king). A trip to Cuba in 1967 resulted in the strongly partisan account *Het woord bij de daad* (1968; the word to the deed). In memory of Che Guevara he wrote the "total opera" *Reconstructie* (1969; *Reconstruction,* 1969) in collaboration with Hugo Claus (q.v.) and a group of composers; it was highly acclaimed at the Holland Festival.

M. became less outspoken politically during the 1970s, since he believes that a writer's political impact depends on a powerful movement sustaining his vision and that the 1970s lacked such a movement. An echo of the concerns of the 1960s—in its combination of radical politics and sexual liberation—was his very original analysis of the psychoanalyst Wilhelm Reich (1897–1957), *Het seksuele bolwerk* (1973; the sexual bulwark), which is also a fascinating self-analysis.

Important as M. has been in Holland as a political writer, his international reputation is based mainly on his fiction. Of his stories available in English translation, the best known is "Wat gebeurde er met sergeant Masuro?" (1957; "What Happened to Sergeant Masuro?," 1961), a dense and shocking tale brilliantly employing modernist techniques in its subtly shifting point of view and its playing with narrative sequence. It has been translated into eight languages.

M.'s most remarkable novel is *Het stenen bruidsbed* (1959; *The Stone Bridal Bed,* 1962). The germinal idea for the book had been the aftermath of World War II as seen in the fate of a Dutch war criminal, but gradually the focus shifted to the story of an American who participated in the bombing of Dresden and after a decade visits that city again. An affair with a German girl soon comes to an end because of his traumatic war memories. Interwoven with this story are flashbacks to his war experiences, related in mock-Homeric form, which creates an emotional distancing. But serious parallels between Troy and Dresden are also suggested. This mythic method reminds one of James Joyce's (q.v.) *Ulysses;* also Joycean is an interior monologue that resembles Molly Bloom's. The work as a whole, however, is not derivative and offers a highly distinctive vision as well as a crisp style.

After sophisticated experiments with fictional technique in *De verteller* (1970; the narrator) and after an exploration of "imaginary history" in *De toekomst van gisteren* (1972; the future of yesterday), an "alternate world" novel about what could have happened if Germany had won the war, M. returned to realistic narrative in *Twee vrouwen* (1975; *Two Women,* 1980), a tragic story of lesbianism, which was made into a film.

Unlike some writers, who keep reworking the same material (such as Simon Vestdijk [q.v.]), M. always seeks fresh subjects and stylistic experiments. His sense of irony and his capacity for felicitous expression, combined with striking psychological insight, make him one of the most gifted writers the Low Countries have produced.

FURTHER WORKS: *Chantage op het leven* (1953); *De diamant* (1954); *Het mirakel* (1955); *Het zwarte licht* (1956); *De versierde mens* (1957); *Tanchelijn* (1960); *De knop* (1960); *Voer voor psychologen* (1961); *Wenken voor de Jongste Dag* (1967); *Paralipomena Orphica* (1970); *De verteller verteld* (1971); *Over de affaire Padilla* (1971); *Soep lepelen met een vork* (1972); *Oidipous Oidipous* (1972); *Woorden, woorden, woorden* (1973); *De vogels: Drie balladen* (1974); *Bezoekuur* (1974); *Mijn getijdenboek* (1975); *Kind en kraai* (1975); *Tegenlicht* (1975); *Volk en vaderliefde* (1975); *De wijn is drinkbaar dank zij het glas* (1976); *De taal is een ei* (1976); *Axel* (1977); *Verzamelde verhalen 1947–1977* (1977); *Wat poëzie is* (1978); *Paniek der onschuld* (1979); *De compositie van de wereld* (1980); *De mythische formule* (1981)

BIBLIOGRAPHY: Meijer, R. P., *Literature of the Low Countries* (1978), pp. 356–59;

Byrne, J., on *Two Women, RCF,* 2 (1982), 180

JORIS DUYTSCHAEVER

MÜLLER, Heiner

East German dramatist, b. 9 Jan. 1929, Eppendorf

After World War II M. was employed briefly as a civil servant, and then worked as a journalist. In 1954 and 1955 he was a technical assistant in the East German Writers' Union. Thereafter he learned theater craft at the Maxim Gorki Theater in East Berlin. During the late 1950s, M. wrote three plays with his wife Inge Müller (1925–1966). They were awarded the Heinrich Mann Prize in 1959 for their joint efforts. Since 1959 M. has devoted himself to his writing. In 1979 he received the Drama Prize of the Mülheim Theater.

From the East German point of view, M. is a problematic figure. Although recognized by his critics as an important dramatist, he remains, nevertheless, an outsider. Much of his best work has been suppressed until recently. The theoretical direction of his plays has often been sharply discouraged by the East German regime. Presentations of his dramas have been more successful in the West than in East Germany.

Die Korrektur (1957; the revision), a play about the troublesome contradictions caused by the political demand for complete cooperation among the classes, and *Der Lohndrücker* (1958; the wage cutter) were among the first of the East German dialectic dramas. (The dialectic movement refused to whitewash negative aspects of early socialist reconstruction, but also declined to criticize them.)

M. was strongly influenced by Bertolt Brecht (q.v.). In form, M.'s plays are a continuation of Brecht's didactic drama and the agitprop theater of the 1920s. M., however, went further in presenting unpleasant realities of postwar East Germany than Brecht was willing to go. This fact is especially apparent in *Der Lohndrücker,* which treats material Brecht rejected as being too negative.

Der Lohndrücker examines East German reconstruction in a difficult era. The play portrays bad working conditions and a form of labor competition that generated sabotage, jealousy, and general worker unrest. The drama's "positive hero" adapts to this world but recognizes that it can be made better. He therefore works harder than the others and produces more. By thus increasing the demanded quota, he unintentionally pushes down the wages. Yet his nonideological striving is simply an attempt to better the standard of living through increased production.

Although *Der Lohndrücker* was initially praised, the dialectic theater soon lost headway because of its treatment of sensitive topics. M.'s other openly dialectic dramas were systematically suppressed. Even *Der Bau* (1965; the construction project), perhaps M.'s best play, based on the novel *Spur der Steine* (1964; trace of the stones) by Erik Neutsch (b. 1931), was published but never staged.

Attempting to salvage the dialectic theater in a disguised form, M. later turned to abstractions based on classical mythology. Despite the change in approach, however, his concerns remained the same. The best of the mythological dramas is *Philoktet* (1966; Philoctetes), in which M. changed the traditional Philoctetes (who was abandoned wounded by the Greeks, then coerced into fighting when it became apparent that he was needed) into a man who refused to return to the Trojan War because he has recognized the futility of militarism.

In more recent works, as for example *Hamletmaschine* (1977; the Hamlet machine), M. has used harsh and abrasive symbols to intensify the drama: Bits and pieces of rotting corpses, Hamlet's threat to choke the palace with royal excrement by stopping up the toilet with his mother's corpse, and Ophelia's macabre striptease after she emerges from a coffin are a few examples.

The originality with which M. has treated familiar materials has made M. a dramatist who can no longer be ignored, not even by his East German opponents and critics.

FURTHER WORKS: *Der Klettwitzer Bericht* (written 1959); *Herakles 5* (1966); *Das Laken* (1966); *Ödipus Tyrann* (1966); *Prometheus* (1968); *Horizonte* (1969); *Großer Wolf; Halbdeutsch* (1970); *Die Weiberkomödie* (1970); *Macbeth* (1971); *Der Horatier* (1972); *Geschichten aus der Produktion* (2 vols., 1974); *Zement* (1974; *Cement,* 1979); *Die Umsiedlerin; oder, Das Leben auf dem Lande* (1975); *Theater-Arbeit* (1975); *Traktor* (1975); *Stücke* (1975); *Mauser* (1976; *Mauser,* 1976); *Die Schlacht; Traktor; Leben Gündlings Friedrich von Preußen; Lessings*

Schlaf Traum Schrei (1977); *Germania Tod in Berlin* (1977); *Mauser* (collection, 1978); *Der Auftrag: Erinnerung an eine Revolution* (1980)

BIBLIOGRAPHY: Fehervary, H., "H. M.s Brigadenstücke," *Basis,* 2 (1971), 103–40; Schivelbusch, W., "Optimistic Tragedies: The Plays of H. M.," *NGC,* 2 (1974), 103–14; Bernhardt, R., "Antikrezeption im Werk H. M.s," *WB,* 22, 3 (1976), 83–122; Bathrick, D., and Huyssen, A., "Producing Revolution: H. M.'s *Mauser* as Learning Play," *NGC,* 8 (1976), 110–21; Schlechter, J., "H. M. and Other East German Dramaturgs," *Y/T,* 8, 2–3 (1977), 152–54; Milfull, J., " 'Gegenwart und Geschichte': H. M.s Weg von *Der Bau* zu *Zement,*" *AUMLA,* 48 (1977), 234–47; Schulz, G., *H. M.* (1980)

LOWELL A. BANGERTER

MUNK, Kaj

(born Petersen) Danish dramatist and essayist, b. 13 Jan. 1898, Maribo; d. 4 Jan. 1944, Silkeborg

M. was born on the island of Lolland. Having lost both parents at an early age, he was taken in by a small landowner, Peter Munk, and his wife and was formally adopted by them in 1916. The pietistic atmosphere of the home left a strong mark on M., influencing his decision to study theology at the University of Copenhagen, where he received a degree in 1924. He was ordained as a minister the same year and found a position as a pastor of the small community of Vedersø in western Jutland, where he remained until the time of his arrest and murder by Gestapo agents during the German occupation of Denmark.

Beginning shortly after World War I, M. wrote close to sixty plays, as well as numerous essays and sermons. To the Danish stage, then dominated by naturalism, he wanted to bring back elevated drama in the spirit of Shakespeare. Dominant features in his writing are a deep Christian faith and a fervent admiration for the strong-willed man of action. This worship of the man of power, coupled with the political chaos in the wake of the Treaty of Versailles, led to M.'s rejection of democracy as a political possibility and his advocacy of authoritarianism. But he was first and foremost a religious idealist who saw the tragedy of man symbolized in the conflict between God and man, between good and evil. With very few exceptions M.'s plays present an idealized hero who challenges the authority of God.

Although initially a failure when performed at the Royal Theater in Copenhagen, *En idealist* (1928; *Herod the King*, (1953) is one of the best of M.'s so-called dictatorship dramas. It tells of Herod, King of the Jews, who aspires to become independent of all authority. He is the greatest of M.'s heroic characters—strong, sly, and willing to play for the highest stakes, even the death of his wife Mariamne, who personifies nobility of mind, love, and compassion. After doing away with her, he has triumphed over all men. But he is unable to win over God, and the play culminates in a meeting between Herod and the Virgin Mary with the Christ child.

I brændingen (1929; in the breakers), dramatically weak but poetically alive, describes a seventy-year-old professor, modeled on the great Danish critic Georg Brandes (1842–1927), who is an idealist with negative tendencies. His contempt of his fellow human beings and his anti-Christian attitude bring about his fall. *Cant* (1931; *Cant*, 1953), a historical drama about Henry VIII of England and Anne Boleyn, was his first major success on stage. The title refers to a special type of hypocrisy: the embellishment of egotistical deeds with insincere excuses and pious phrases in order to gain a reputation for goodness. The king is presented as a ruthless despot who cleverly disguises his desires as divine commands and who becomes self-deluded in his belief in his own lies. The play, while well constructed, lacks psychological depth and shows M.'s limited understanding of the complexities of the mind.

Although Christianity and admiration for the exceptional human being are common denominators in M.'s dramas, one group of plays puts the religious issue in the foreground. *Ordet* (1932; *The Word*, 1953), a modern miracle play, is set among the peasants in West Jutland. It is probably the best known among M.'s works and possesses great dramatic force. Dealing with the problem of faith, it poses the question of whether God can still fill a person with such a strong belief that miracles are possible. A young woman, Inger, dies in childbirth but is brought back to life by a Christ figure, Johannes, with the help of an innocent girl. The biblical drama *De udvalgte* (1933; the chosen ones) de-

scribes the doubts, sins, and fall of King David, who is saved through his belief in God. M.'s last religious drama, *Egelykke* (1940; *Egelykke*, 1954), set in 1805–8, is about Danish romantic poet, minister, and theologian N. F. S. Grundtvig (1783–1872)—his crisis and the finding of his vocation.

During the 1930s the political unrest in the world began to undermine M.'s world view, and he reevaluated his concept of the hero. In *Sejren* (1936; the victory) and *Han sidder ved smeltediglen* (1938; *He Sits at the Melting Pot*, 1953), both political dramas, he tries to settle accounts with his position toward dictatorship. The second play is a violent protest against the Nazi persecution of the Jews; its central theme rests on the assumption that the Christian spirit can influence the lives of men. For the first time M. chooses a weak man as his hero: Professor Mensch at the beginning is willing to sacrifice everything for Germany, even the truth. At the end, he recognizes his horrendous mistake.

During the German occupation of Denmark M. showed great courage: the historical play *Niels Ebbesen* (1942; *Niels Ebbesen*, 1944) and the curtain raiser *Før Cannae* (1943; *Before Cannae*, 1953) are unequivocal attacks on the occupying power.

M. helped revitalize the Danish theater by his rejection of the shallow naturalistic drama and his attempts—very much in the romantic tradition—to replace it with a more spiritually significant drama.

FURTHER WORKS: *Rub og stub* (1922); *Vedersø-Jerusalem retur* (1934); *Os bærer den himmelske glæde* (1934); *10 Oxfordsnapshots* (1936); *Knaldperler* (1936); *Liv og glade dage* (1936); *Pilatus* (1937); *Himmel og jord* (1938); *Filmen om Christiern den anden* (1938); *Dette dødsens legeme* (1938); *Fugl fønix* (1939); *Tempelvers* (1939); *Navigare necesse* (1940); *Sværg det, drenge* (1941); *Ved Babylons floder* (1941; *By the Rivers of Babylon*, 1945); *Med ordets sværd* (1942); *Det unge Nord* (1942); *Foråret så sagte kommer* (1942); *Med sol og megen glade* (1942); *Småbyens sjæl* (1943); *Danmark* (1943); *Tre prædikener* (1943); *Den skæbne ej til os* (1943); *Jesus' historier* (1943); *Apostlenes gerninger* (1943); *Den blå anemone* (1943); *Sømandsvise* (1943); *Ewalds død* (1943; *The Death of Ewald*, 1949); *8 nye digte* (1944); *Et norsk digt om Norge* (1944); *Tre tusinde kroner* (1946): *I Guds bismer*

(1946); *Så fast en borg* (1946); *Sangen til vor ø* (1946); *Alverdens-Urostifterne* (1947); *Ansigter* (1947); *Landlige interiører i lollandsk bondemål* (1948); *Kardinalen og kongen* (1948); *Kærlighed* (1948); *Naturens egne drenge* (1948); *Diktatorinden* (1948); *Mindeudgave* (9 vols., 1948–49); *Puslespil* (1949); *Det onde liv og den gode Gud* (1951); *Vers on syndefaldet* (1951); *Julevers fra Landets Kirke på Lolland* (1956). FURTHER VOLUMES IN ENGLISH: *K. M.: Playwright, Priest, and Patriot* (1944); *Four Sermons* (1944)

BIBLIOGRAPHY: Schmidt, R., "K. M.: A New Danish Dramatist," *ASR,* 21 (1933), 227–32; Thompson, L., "The Actuality of K. M.'s Dramas," *BA,* 15 (1941), 267–72; Thompson, L., "A Voice Death Has Not Silenced," *BA,* 18 (1944), 126–27; Bang, C. K., "K. M.'s Autobiography," *ASR,* 33 (1945), 45–50; Keigwin, R. P., Introduction to *Five Plays by K. M.* (1953; 2nd ed., 1964), pp. 9–21; Arestad, S., "K. M. as a Dramatist (1898–1944)," *SS,* 26 (1954), 151–76; Harcourt, M., "K. M.," *Portraits of Destiny* (1969), pp. 1–47

MARIANNE FORSSBLAD

MURDOCH, Iris

English novelist and essayist, b. 15 July 1919, Dublin, Ireland

M. was born of Anglo-Irish parents but grew up in London. She earned first-class honors at Somerville College, Oxford, in 1942, served as an assistant principal in the British Treasury from 1942 to 1944, and was an administrative officer for UNRRA in Belgium and Austria from 1944 to 1946. She then returned to Oxford and in 1948 was appointed a fellow and tutor in philosophy at St. Anne's College. She is married to the novelist and critic John Oliver Bayley (b. 1925).

M.'s early publications were in philosophy. Her first work, *Sartre, Romantic Rationalist* (1953), gave evidence of literary concerns however, and it was here that she began developing her definitions of the novel. Later essays, especially "The Sublime and the Beautiful Revisited" (1960) and "Against Dryness" (1961), establish her argument that the prevalence of the current philosophies of existentialism (q.v.) and linguistic empiricism is the reason modern consciousness is dominated by either neurosis or convention. M. feels that the contemporary novel reflects these two states of mind and is usually a

"small, compact, crystalline, self-contained myth about the human condition" or a "loose journalistic epic, documentary or possibly even didactic in inspiration." Further, the "crystalline" novel is solipsistic, while the "journalistic" novel lacks vitality. Both sustain fantasy at the expense of imagination. The modern novel M. argues, must rediscover reality, must deal with solipsistic man, the nature of love and freedom, and man's behavior in times of contingency, that is, under conditions where chance and accident make unexpected demands on his moral judgments.

M.'s novels are not essentially philosophical, nor are they strict codifications of her literary criteria, but they do deal with solipsistic man, contingency, and the nature of freedom and love. Often M. uses gothic elements to create a twilight-of-the gods atmosphere in which a demonic figure is intent on imposing his system while other characters project their fantasies upon him in an attempt to give meaning and structure to their lives. *The Flight from the Enchanter* (1956) depicts such a demonic figure, Mischa Fox, and his influence on an assortment of alienated characters who not only are drawn to his enchanted world but also must escape it. *The Unicorn* (1963), M.'s most obviously gothic novel, describes the entry of characters from the world of convention into a medieval world of contingency, presided over by a recluse named Hannah. She is a scapegoat, a Christ-figure, a prisoner, and perhaps a murderess—her identity is a fiction created by the characters around her. Here existential concepts of freedom undergo a severe testing. *The Time of the Angels* (1966) focuses on a time of spiritual desolation in a world bereft of moral contexts and has as its main character an atheist priest who believes that the death of God has "set the angels free."

A number of M.'s novels can be broadly classified as domestic comedy. *A Severed Head* (1961) is this type of comedy contained in myth. A Medusa figure, Honor Klein, an anthropologist, involves a conventional male in a messy life of random pairings, passion, incest, and suicide. A complicated plot and overly self-conscious characters do not prevent this work from being a witty comment on moral responsibility. *The Bell* (1958) is set in a lay religious community that has attempted to create the sort of moral order society at large lacks. Here, the richly drawn characters, in contending with the dark side of human nature, discover something of love and the limits of human goodness. Some of M.'s domestic comedies have broader contexts and are more loosely structured. *The Nice and the Good* (1968) contains a large number of questing males, lovers, scholars, refugees, demons, and mystics, and deals with scandals, suicides, blackmail, violence, and the occult. Set in both London and the country, it is one of M.'s most successful treatments of love and the recognition of "otherness." *The Sacred and Profane Love Machine* (1974), another provocative if sometimes implausible work of this type, has at its center a love triangle. Through extensive use of dreams M. again comments on the problem of reality, the need for people to create fictions about one another, and the inability of most to handle emotional reality.

The Black Prince (1973), winner of the James Tait Black Memorial Prize for fiction, is one of M.'s finest works. It is experimental, containing prefaces and postscripts. The narrator is an excessively self-conscious and sterile writer who creates art only after a passionate love awakens his dark Eros. The art he creates brings destruction but also succeeds in helping him to retreat from his work until he finally becomes a true artist—"the lover who, nothing himself, lets other things be through him."

M.'s occasionally predictable patternings and elaborate plots sometimes undercut her stated intention to free characters to be themselves. Yet her wit, imagination, and comic inventiveness, her talent for brilliant scene-making and rich characterization, combined with a compelling moral vision, make her a major figure in 20th-c. fiction.

FURTHER WORKS: *Under the Net* (1954); *The Sandcastle* (1957); *An Unofficial Rose* (1962); *The Italian Girl* (1964); *A Severed Head* (play, 1964, with J. B. Priestley); *The Red and the Green* (1965); *Bruno's Dream* (1969); *A Fairly Honourable Defeat* (1970); *The Sovereignty of Good* (1970); *An Accidental Man* (1971); *The Three Arrows, and The Servants and the Snow* (1973); *A Word Child* (1975); *Henry and Cato* (1976); *The Sea, the Sea* (1978); *Nuns and Soldiers* (1980)

BIBLIOGRAPHY: O'Connor, W. V., *The New University Wits and the End of Modernism* (1963), pp. 54–74; Byatt, A. S., *Degrees of Freedom: The Novels of I. M.* (1966); Wolfe, P., *The Disciplined Heart: I. M. and Her Novels* (1966); Rabinovitz, R., *I. M.* (1968); Gerstenberger, D., *I. M.* (1975); Scholes, R., *Fabulation and Metafiction* (1979), pp. 56–74; Dipple, E., *I. M.: Work for the Spirit* (1982)

LINDSEY TUCKER

MURPHY, Richard
Irish poet, 6 Aug. 1927, Galway

Born into an Anglo-Irish Protestant (Ascendancy) family, M. traveled widely in his youth and early adulthood. Fascinated with the boat life in the west of Ireland, he has lived most of his life since 1959 in Cleggan and the nearby islands, including High Island, purchased by M. in 1969. During the 1970s he was a visiting poet at Colgate, Princeton, Bard College, and the University of Iowa.

M. has been called the poet of two traditions. In some of his early poems in *The Archaeology of Love* (1955) and especially in *The Woman of the House* (1959), he expresses a fondness and deep respect for the "Big House" (that is, the Ascendancy class), while accepting the decline of its traditions. *The Battle of Aughrim* (1968), a long narrative poem, represents M.'s most complex study of his Anglo-Irish Protestant background. On the other hand, M., in the poem "Sailing to an Island" (1955), describes his difficult and painful initiation into the primitive, Catholic life of the islands in the west of Ireland. That initiation became complete with the writing of "The Last Galway Hooker" (1961) and "The Cleggan Disaster" (1963), narrative poems that record M.'s acceptance for himself of the harsh experiences of fishermen and of peasants and his desire to preserve their simple traditions.

M.'s poetry has been characterized by its detached observation, its physical energy, and its classical simplicity. In *High Island* (1974), however, the poems—while capturing in content and imagery the violence of the island life, the itinerant life of Irish tinkers, and the poet's own youth in Ceylon—are more self-exploratory than his earlier work. They examine the poet's relationship to the harsh realities he has chosen as subject matter, as well as his difficulties with language and craft in expressing his conflicts and discoveries.

M. is the most important Irish poet since Yeats (q.v.) to write about the fading Anglo-Irish culture and the primitive life of the

Irish peasant. M.'s encounter with the two traditions is less visionary than Yeats's, but his poetry creates a vivid impression of the Ascendancy pleasure ground of his youth and the primitive, harsh landscape of his maturity.

FURTHER WORKS: *Sailing to an Island* (1963); *The Battle of Aughrim, and The God Who Eats Corn* (1968); *High Island: New and Selected Poems* (1974); *Selected Poems* (1979)

BIBLIOGRAPHY: Longley, E., "Searching the Darkness: R. M., Thomas Kinsella, John Montague, and James Simmons," in Dunn, D., ed., *Two Decades of Irish Writing* (1975), pp. 118–53; Kersnowski, F., *The Outsiders: Poets of Contemporary Ireland* (1975), pp. 93–98; Harmon, M., ed., *R. M.: Poet of Two Traditions* (1978); Kilroy, M., "R. M.'s Connemara Locale," *Éire*, 15, 3 (1980), 127–34

RICHARD F. PETERSON

MUSIL, Robert

Austrian novelist, dramatist, and essayist, b. 6 Nov. 1880, Klagenfurt; d. 15 April 1942, Geneva, Switzerland

The son of a professor of engineering and a high-strung, sensuous mother, M. was early given to experiences of isolation and withdrawal. Sent to military school at the age of eleven, he graduated as a second lieutenant but quickly rejected the army for the study of engineering at the Technical University in Brno, where his father taught. Only then did he become acquainted with the German literature of his day, with the French symbolists (q.v.), with Nietzsche, and with Emerson. M. graduated as an engineer in 1901 and, after spending a year as an assistant at the Technical University in Stuttgart, turned to the study of philosophy and experimental psychology at the University of Berlin, at the same time pursuing his interest in literature, especially in the German romantics.

M.'s personal life remained difficult. He was financially dependent on his parents, who objected to M.'s liaison with a working-class girl. Only his marriage in 1911 to a Jewish painter brought him a measure of happiness.

M. completed his studies with his dissertation on the physicist and philosopher Ernst Mach (1838–1916), *Beitrag zur Beurteilung*

der Lehren Machs (1908; rpt. with additions, 1980; a contribution toward a critical judgment of Mach's philosophy). Unwilling to become a university lecturer (he turned down an assistantship at the University of Graz) and unable to make a living by his pen, M. accepted a position as a librarian at the Technical University in Vienna (1911–14). From February to August 1914 he was an editor of *Die neue Rundschau* in Berlin. He was called up at the outbreak of World War I and served as an officer on the Italian front. Discharged because of illness, M. served as an editor of a military newspaper. He returned to civilian life and to Vienna at the end of the war and was for some years a civil servant in the ministries of foreign affairs and defense, while at the same time writing.

For a short while M. experienced a modest degree of prosperity. After 1924 he turned entirely to writing, becoming dependent on advances from his publisher and later on occasional help from a circle of friends. In 1938 he emigrated to Switzerland. During his last years he lived in poverty and died virtually forgotten.

M.'s work represents a lifelong preoccupation with the ethical human being in whose character rigidity, disproportion, and polarities have been overcome for the sake of genuine wholeness and integration. His first novel, *Die Verwirrungen des Zöglings Törleß* (1906; *Young Törless*, 1955), has as its setting a military school, like the one M. himself attended. While the foreground is filled with the brutalities and humiliations endemic to the milieu, the real theme of the novel is the development of a teenager who for the first time encounters his unconscious and his creative energies. At first he fails to understand his intense emotions, but in his painful process of self-discovery he comes to terms with the conflict between reason and logic on the one hand and his emotional and imaginative faculties on the other, gaining insight into a possible fusion of these two aspects of his psyche. The immediate success of this first novel was due not only to M.'s bold treatment of the subject but even more so to his insight into human motivation, his rich symbolism, and his succinct style.

The search for new, integrated identities is also the theme of the slim volume *Vereinigungen* (1911; unions)—comprising the two stories "Die Vollendung der Liebe" ("The Perfecting of a Love," 1966) and "Die Versuchung der stillen Veronika" ("The Temptation of Quiet Veronica," 1966)—some seventy pages on which M. had worked to the point of exhaustion for two and a half years. Being totally concerned with the portrayal of the feelings and thoughts of his heroines, M., in a radical experiment, did away with plot and perspective, rendering their inner lives through a succession of metaphors arranged with the greatest of precision. He thus paired ambiguity and icy rationality into a new whole. Even though M. considered *Vereinigungen* one of his best works, because of its hermetic quality it did not meet with popular success.

The failure of *Vereinigungen* caused M. to turn to a more objective genre. In a series of essays that appeared in liberal periodicals he dealt with problems in art, aesthetics, politics, and ethics posed by the complexities of modern civilization. Apart from the interruptions of the war, M. continued to write on questions of the day well into the mid-1920s.

With his return to civilian life and to creative writing at the end of the war, M. singled out the theater as the most rigid cultural institution. Hence his plays were to ventilate the stage and make it more receptive to new ideas. Both *Die Schwärmer* (1921; the enthusiasts) and *Vinzenz und die Freundin bedeutender Männer* (1923; Vinzenz and the girl friend of important men), the first a serious drama, the second a comedy, contrast the inauthenticity of bourgeois life, as it is evidenced in the institution of marriage and in the professions, with a new kind of man, an isolated individual, indifferent to all conventions, dependent only on his inner motivation, and because of his freedom able to love others, even if only for a short period. While the strident tone and the intensity especially of *Die Schwärmer* again made the public reject the plays, they are an important milestone in M.'s work. For the first time he introduced irony and satire into his portrayal of the bourgeoisie.

As if trying to show that he could also write in a more traditional manner, M. produced a collection of stories published under the title *Drei Frauen* (1925; three women), consisting of "Grigia" ("Grigia," 1966), "Die Portugiesin" ("The Lady from Portugal," 1966), and "Tonka" ("Tonka," 1966), in which he reverts to a more conservative form. Drawing on his own experiences during the war, among them a constant awareness of death and an intense longing for a

distant love, M. created three male protagonists who are all isolated and inactive outside their familiar environment. Each of these heroes achieves a heightened state of understanding through the mediation of a woman.

The first volume of the novel *Der Mann ohne Eigenschaften* (1930–43; partial tr., *The Man without Qualities,* 1953) was immediately hailed as a great and unusual work. The publication of a second volume coincided with the coming of the Third Reich (1933). M.'s widow published the finished chapters of the third part, found among M.'s papers, in 1943. Against the pattern of the modern world, the regularity of statistics, of science, and of technology, the hero of the novel, Ulrich, experiences his ego only as a point of intersections of impersonal functions. Having lost all ambition, he cannot take his qualities, of which he has many and very good ones, seriously; they belong more to each other than they belong to him. Like his creator M., Ulrich has been in turn a soldier, an engineer, and a mathematician. His skeptical attitude, the result of his scientific training, make him critical of all culture. His citizenship in "Kakanien" (M.'s name for the old Austro-Hungarian monarchy), whose contradicting cultures and multiple nationalities mirror the disintegration of the 20th c., is another aspect of his floating kind of life.

Ulrich's search for a more authentic and meaningful life is the theme of the novel. His conversations with a group of Austrian politicians and intellectuals gathered together for the so-called *Parallelaktion,* a patriotic undertaking ostensibly planned to celebrate the sixtieth anniversary of the ascension to the throne of the aging emperor Franz Josef, to occur in 1918, are an attempt to give new meaning to the crumbling culture of the 19th and by implication also of the 20th c. Although the discussants are divided between those who rule and want to maintain the status quo and those who rebel and want to destroy it, both parties suffer from a lack of ideas aggravated by the emptiness of their personal lives and by their susceptibility to "great" and aggressive solutions.

A corollary to Ulrich's weak and fragmented sense of identity, however, is expressed in his sense of "possibility"—that is, his notion that imagination is as significant as reality, his conscious utopianism—which arises precisely from his intellectual freedom and mobility. It causes him to contemplate life as a laboratory, to consider fusing polarities for the sake of a life that is fulfilling both intellectually and emotionally. He is more open than his partners in the patriotic action to memories of a state of love and of union with the world and with others. Thus, his suggestion at the end of Volume I for an inventory of the historical evidence for such a state (a task that would be undertaken with the precision of science)—to be done by the "general secretariat of precision and soul"—would represent an attempted reordering of society.

The rejection of Ulrich's suggestion by his friends suggests that the chances for such a reform do not exist. Ulrich's fulfillment thus depends on his meeting his sister Agathe, whose existence M. has kept secret in Volume I. It is the encounter with the human being that is most like him and yet not like him, the near-twin of the opposite sex, that causes Ulrich to reconcile his fragmented ego. In his closeness to Agathe, Ulrich's dominant intellect and his suppressed feeling unite, and from his tendencies toward activity and amorality he turns toward inactivity and rest. The second part of the novel is made up of Ulrich's and Agathe's conversations regarding a new morality. Together they search for a state in which the individual is enhanced, in which his ego rises and does not fall until they both experience the "other state," in which the borders and limits between human beings slowly diminish. The question of how Ulrich's and Agathe's relationship would end has never been adequately resolved, since M. never finished the novel.

The style of *Der Mann ohne Eigenschaften* represents the highest achievement of M. as a writer. It is forever open, rejecting all firm norms, all systems. In an infinite range of possibilities it forever balances opposites, hovering between subjectivity and truth, between imagination and reality, between logic and the affective emotion, between unequivocality and the metaphor. What M. calls irony is the stylistic rendering of the profound relationship that exists between opposites. It is expressed in every chapter, page, and line, indeed in every figure of speech and in every metaphor.

M.'s work, in the intensity of his fusion of imagination and precision, is a profound attempt in modern literature to create a new man, to move mankind toward new life

forms, to regain a lost potential for the sake of a richer and more rewarding life.

FURTHER WORKS: *Rede zur Rilke-Feier* (1927); *Nachlaß zu Lebzeiten* (1927); *Über die Dummheit* (1937); *Briefe nach Prag* (1971); *Tagebücher* (1976); *Gesammelte Werke* (1978); *Briefe 1901–1942* (1981). FURTHER VOLUME IN ENGLISH: *Five Women* (1966)

BIBLIOGRAPHY: Dinklage, K., ed., *R. M.: Leben, Werk, Wirkung* (1960); Arntzen, H., *Satirischer Stil: Zur Satire R. M.s im "Mann ohne Eigenschaften,"* (1960); Pike, B., *R. M.: An Introduction to His Work* (1961); Kaiser, E., and Wilkins, E., *R. M.: Eine Einführung in das Werk* (1962); Dinklage, K., ed., *R. M.: Studien zu seinem Werk* (1970); Roth, M.-L., *R. M.: Ethik und Aesthetik: Zum Theoretischen Werk des Dichters* (1972); Reniers-Servranckx, A., *R. M.: Konstanz und Entwicklung von Themen, Motiven und Strukturen in den Dichtungen* (1972); Appignanesi, L., *Femininity and the Creative Imagination: A Study of Henry James, R. M., and Marcel Proust* (1973); Williams, C. E., *The Broken Eagle: The Politics of Austrian Literature from Empire to Anschluss* (1974), pp. 148–86; Peters, F. G., *R. M.: Master of the Hovering Life* (1978); Luft, D. S., *R. M. and the Crisis of European Culture 1880–1942* (1980); Arntzen, H., *Kommentar sämtlicher zu Lebzeiten erschienener Schriften ausser dem Roman "Der Mann ohne Eigenschaften"* (1980)

WILHELM BRAUN

When an author promises to furnish a positive construction with his work, he exposes himself to an examination not only of his poetic but also of his intellectual capacity. M. once suggested that the following words be added to the graduation certificate with which he wanted to leave German literature: "Behavior unusual, talent tender, even though inclining to excesses." But the critics noticed one day that his novel [*The Man without Qualities*] was the greatest experiment in the philosophy of history and the most relentless criticism of *Weltanschauung* since Voltaire's *Candide*. Thus some justice has been done to M.; because he wanted much more than to write a novel, more than to tell the story of the decline of Kakanien and more than to offer criticism regarding the obsolete ideas of his time.

But he did not want—and that is what he is reproached for sometimes—to go beyond his competence. He was always conscious of the fact that the poet cannot and should not penetrate into a philosophical system.

He did not go for the "whole," but gave models and prototypes, partial solutions, not *the* solution. He did not want to communicate only about reality, but also include possibility. Or as his hero Ulrich once expressed himself, "to take in the open horizon, from where life is fitted to the spirit."

Ingeborg Bachmann, "Ins tausendjährige Reich," *Akzente,* No. 1 (1954), 50–51

In a world in which facts are so preponderant, in the aridity of feelings that follows from that, the appeal to the emotions is a very understandable resistance-reflex. When everything overflows with energy, when economics is more important than the human being, the workbench more important than the worker who stands at it, then one longs for a soul that like moist winds blows from the sea into the dryness. If one, however, wants to speak of a task, it can only consist of carrying benevolent feelings into the world, into the world as it is, with its facts that overpower men, with its troubles and sorrows, its hundredfold difficulties that harden the heart, but not of retreating out of this state into the "other," and of making a poem out of one's own life, torn out of any inconvenient reality. But precisely this, the world-denying sinking into the other state, into private life, not shrinking like that of the petit bourgeois, but blossoming like a fairy tale, of an overflowing feeling of love, tenderness and happiness—that is what M. lets his hero Ulrich try. He chooses the motif of the brother-sister love as a most favorable condition because the exclusion of any social aspect is given through the prohibition of the relationship as necessary. That is the secret that removes it from the world. But in the nature of the twin sister, mystically similar, so deeply related to his own nature, Ulrich continuously experiences himself, his own ego in the mirror of the other character.

Ernst Fischer, "Das Werk R. M.s," *SuF,* 9, 5 (1957), 894–95

Whatever R. M., the great Austrian writer, touched, was or became difficult. Simplicity was not for him: in style, thought, or life. But the M. touch, which turns everything into subtlety, complexity, ambiguity, is not, like the Midas touch, a curse. It is an honest awareness that life is difficult—or, as we read in Rilke, whom M. revered, "There are no classes for beginners in life"—and that a mere simplistic acceptance of that fact will lessen the difficulty.

But the fascination of what is difficult does not, as Yeats would have it in an early poem, dry the sap out of the veins, whatever it may do to spontaneous joy. Besides, difficulty in M. is always both there and not there. He is not like the phony weight lifter who grunts and snarles as he lifts a weight which may be heavy, but not all that heavy; he is rather like a master juggler who would make us forget how hard his cavalierly performed feats are if we did not notice with anxiety the fearful swelling of his jugular vein.

John Simon, Afterword to *Young Törless* (1964), p. 175

[In *Vereinigungen*] each situation unites contradictions and in each moment numerous ego possibilities meet each other—a few emerge into the light, most of them stay in the shadow; repression is found next to enticement, revolt next to apathy; there are no irrevocable divisions between yesterday and today, between good and evil; rather everything has only a functional value, dependent upon circumstances and connections as well as upon the use that is made of it. Reality is accidental, and often it remains imponderable why this or that constellation becomes firm in order to fit itself to some set of circumstances. Whatever characteristics exist next to each other seem to be born to oppose each other; the challenge through contrast, however, results in a union originating out of this tension. At the same time, effect and counter-effect are so closely connected, so braided into unity "that it would be in vain . . . to want to determine . . . phases of development." This mutual development does not form a succession but a togetherness. The one exists only through the other; events outside and within man create a complimentary relationship. Thus "infidelity may be union in a deeper interior zone."

Gerhart Baumann, *R. M.: Zur Erkenntnis der Dichtung* (1965), p. 133

M.'s is notoriously a world in political collapse, the end of a great empire; but more central to his poetic writing (at times he makes one think of a prose Rilke) is the sense of a world in metaphysical collapse, a universe of hideously heaped contingency, in which there are nonetheless transcendent human powers. These he represents always by the same complex and various image of eroticism, which reaches its fullest expression in the big novel. *The Man without Qualities* has among its themes nymphomania, incest, and sex murder, not at all for their prurient interest but as indices of the reaches of consciousness. Moosbrugger, the murderer, thinks, when he is not killing, that he is by his personal effort holding together the world; the story of the love between Ulrich, the book's hero, and his sister was, according to M., to take us to the "farthest limits of the possible and unnatural, even of the repulsive"; and yet if one theme can be called central in *The Man without Qualities* it is this one, and nobody could think M. anything but overwhelmingly serious in his treatment of it. Erotic ecstasy is beyond good

HENRY DE MONTHERLANT

ALBERTO MORAVIA

ZSIGMOND MÓRICZ

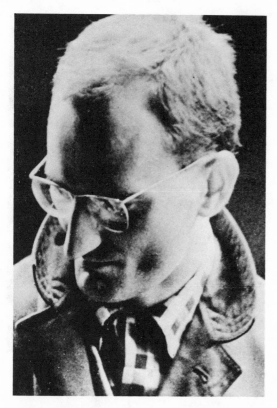

SŁAWOMIR MROZEK

IRIS MURDOCH

ROBERT MUSIL

and evil ("all moral propositions refer to a sort of a dream condition that's long ago taken wing") and exemplifies the power of our consciousness to cross the borderline formerly protected by what are now the obsolete fortresses of traditional ethics and metaphysics.

Frank Kermode, Preface to R. M., *Five Women* (1966), p. 9

M. intended not to be one of those old-fashioned novelists who refuse to take the decisive step into the twentieth century. Since he was unable to perceive a divinely ordained narrative order in existence, M. believed that he could not allow himself to create a traditional novel with a plot. M. consciously decided that his novel, *The Man without Qualities,* should not follow "the law of this life, for which one yearns," that is to say, it should not present a series of actions in a unidimensional order. In fact, his novel had to be written precisely against the psychological grain of the old-fashioned reader who yearns for a plot. *The Man without Qualities,* lacking a plot, is not a novel of action but rather the supreme example in Western literature of the novel of ideas. So, too, is Ulrich a protagonist who exists not at all through his actions but mainly through his ideas, which seem to be constantly "spreading out as an infinitely interwoven surface."

Frederick G. Peters, *R. M.: Master of the Hovering Life* (1978), pp. 189–190

The poetry of *Bilder* (images) (in *Nachlaß zu Lebzeiten*) pertains not only to the practice in words but to the experience in living. It is a question of how words seize existence, of their ambiguous and complex richness, of how to integrate subjectivity and emotion into the world from which they are excluded. The question is less to know and to distinguish than to experience reality and its mechanisms in all its profundity, both visible and hidden, and to show its numerous facets and variations. One sees throughout *Bilder* a man, avidly anxious to meet the phenomena, to penetrate life, to restore authenticity to things. The exterior facts are seized with meticulous precision, which is again found everywhere in the description of persons, of women in particular, of nature, of scenes with animals. M. evokes the houses of a market square, with their identical structures, the details of doors and portals, the architecture of administrative buildings in Vienna, the monuments, the behavior of men and animals. He narrates life with its eroticism, its needs, its complications, its battles, and its failures.

Marie-Louise Roth, *R. M.: Biographie et écriture* (1980), pp. 101–2

Strangely enough, certain interpreters have seen in the portrayal of the afterglow of the old monarchy at the Danube in this novel [*The Man without Qualities*] either a bitter satire or a hymn to this state completely free of any criticism. A more serious investigation of the chapters in question makes this seeming contradiction understandable and eliminates it. It appears that M. softens the irony of his description so much with love, or, conversely, has intermingled the approving portrayal with so much fine irony that they both merge into one another. The unconditional supporters of the old state see only one side of the presentation, and the unconditional opponents only the other side.

Even further, if one investigates the novel more precisely, one finds that the problem of Kakanien is treated exactly like all other problems. Both the pro and anti-Kakanien attitudes are represented by positive and negative ideas and bearers of ideas. The "World-Austrian" impulses of Diotima are, for example, the fantastic hopeless chimeras of a slightly overwrought unsuspecting lady, while the not less pro-Kakanien ideas of her husband, Sektionschef Tuzzi, have not only common sense but also the strength of a decisive and conclusive conviction. The importance that such a consequent thinker and great intellect as M. puts upon precision and truth excludes from the beginning any kind of oversimplification and any kind of black and white representation that would tend to incline towards untruth.

Joseph P. Strelka, "Der Nachglanz der alten Monarchie bei R. M.," *M. Forum,* 6, 1 (1980), 69–70

MYERS, L(eopold) H(amilton)
English novelist, b. 6 Sept 1881, Cambridge; d. 8 April 1944, London

Son of F. W. H. Myers, a noted Cambridge intellectual, M. was educated at Cambridge but left without taking a degree. M. passed much of his life disengaging himself from various social and ideological circles with which he was successively associated, ranging from upper-class English snobs through Bloomsbury and Chelsea aesthetes to pro-Soviet communists. Sometimes called a misanthrope, M. reserved his chief distaste usually for the materialism of his own privileged class after his youthful submersion in its pleasures and pursuits. Of considerable importance to his fiction was a mystical experience M. had as a young man in a Chicago hotel room, for the theme of a spiritual quest persists throughout his canon. Despite a generally happy marriage to an extremely wealthy woman and the comfort of two daughters, M. suffered periodic bouts of deep depression in his later years and finally committed suicide. It is regrettable that, shortly before his death, M. destroyed all copies of an autobiography in progress and urged his friends, who were often compliant, to destroy their letters from him. These materials might have shed additional light on a distinguished, provocative, but ultimately mysterious man of letters.

M.'s first novel, *The Orissers* (1922), which required nearly twelve years to reach its final form, presents in overly schematic fashion the difficulties of the sensitive and isolated moral individual caught in an unsatisfactory materialist society. As epigraph to the novel M. included Sir Francis Bacon's description of the Illusions of the Tribe, Den, Market, and Schools and then examined the role of such illusions in the lives of the novel's characters. This early work, rather reminiscent of E. M. Forster's (q.v.) *Howard's End,* stresses the inherent value of ideas and the inner life, which can encourage and deepen a sense of vocation—a theme M. continued to find congenial.

M.'s next novel, *The Clio* (1925), somewhat resembling lightweight Aldous Huxley (q.v.), takes place on "probably the most expensive steam yacht in the world," which sails up the Amazon, where the wealthy passengers confront the jungle, South American revolutions, and the shallowness of their own supposed civilization. Absurdity on this ship of fools is redeemed only by the wit and intelligence revealed in the dialogue.

Although shorter than his other novels, *Strange Glory* (1936) contributes to the unfolding quasi-mystical vision in M.'s fiction. It is set in the bayous of Louisiana—M. habitually eschewing the home grounds of England and traditional British society as source material. M.'s characters negotiate between two curious species of mysticism in this novel: one a sort of nature worship and the other a rarefied form of idealistic communism. Perhaps as much as mysticism, M. informs his novel with myth, defined in the Jungian sense as a turning point in consciousness, with the end being to submit to destiny—finding a place in the world rather than finding oneself, or perhaps finding one through the other.

M.'s masterpiece is the tetralogy, published finally in a collected volume under the title of the first book, *The Near and the Far* (1943). The immediate model for the work is doubtless Arthur Waley's translation of Lady Murasaki's 11th-c. Japanese masterpiece *The Tale of Genji,* with its study of love and intrigue conducted in a highly polished and civilized manner. The tetralogy comprises *The Near and the Far* (1929), *Prince Jali* (1931), *Rajah Amar* (1935)—these three novels were collected as a trilogy under the title *The Root and the Flower* (1935)—and *The Pool of Vishnu* (1940). Taken together these novels demonstrate M.'s ability to transcend the "low, dishonest decade," as W. H. Auden (q.v.) termed the 1930s. Set in an imaginary 16th-c. India during the reign of Akbar, as his two sons, Daniyal and Salim, struggle for succession, *The Near and the Far* represents a profound philosophical novel about the convergence in one country of Christianity, Buddhism, Islam, and Hinduism, as well as depiction of the clash of other more secular sanctions and persuasions, including sexuality, militarism, aestheticism, and humanism. M. attempts to take measure of the spiritual dimensions of human nature and to gauge the possibilities of the self's and civilization's honorable survival. Many readers perceived the contemporary relevance of M.'s tetralogy. With his interest in the issues of history and man's place in the world, M. keeps returning to the question of what is worthwhile and how it can be achieved. Beneath all of India's divisions and diversities M. shows the unity possible through modes of feeling and standards of value more fundamental than any of the things over which the country is divided.

The first three books of the tetralogy were widely read and critically acclaimed; the fourth was generally considered inferior to its predecessors and overly abstract. Years ago M. attracted much attention from the critics associated with *Scrutiny* for his satire on the Bloomsbury group shown not so obliquely in *Rajah Amar* as Prince Daniyal's Pleasance of the Arts, and this vein has not yet been exhausted. With the current veneration of Bloomsbury's loving friends, other aspects of the tetralogy seem due for renewed attention after an extended period of neglect. If a return to an awareness of sacred order in life is imminent, then M. the moralist should speak once more to readers. M. remains stimulating and complex in his political ideas, aphoristically memorable, stylistically graceful, and often numinous in his spiritual insights, a combination of excellence rarely found in British novelists of this or any other century.

FURTHER WORKS: *Arvat: A Dramatic Poem* (1908)

BIBLIOGRAPHY: Simon, I., *L. H. M.* (1948); Bantock, G. H., *L. H. M.: A Critical Study* (1956); Hartley, L. P., Introduction to *The Near and the Far* (1956), pp. 1–6; Gupta, B. S., "L. H. M.'s Treatment of Buddhism in *The Near and the Far,*" *RLV,* 37 (1970), 64–74; Grant, R. A. D., "Art versus Ideology: The Case of L. H. M.," *CQ,* 6 (1974), 214–40; Cockshut, A. O. J., *Man and Woman: A Study of Love and the Novel, 1740–1940* (1978), pp. 181–85; Rao, V. A., "*The Near and the Far:* A Note on the Structure," *RLV,* 44 (1978), 275–84

EDWARD T. JONES

MYKOLAITIS, Vincas

(pseud.: Putinas) Lithuanian poet and novelist, b. 6 Jan. 1893, Pilotiškės; d. 7 June 1967, Kačerginė

M. studied for the Roman Catholic priesthood in Seinai and took his vows in 1915, while a refugee in Russia, where he and many other Lithuanians retreated from the German advance during World War I. During his stay in Petrograd, M. was influenced by the Russian symbolists (q.v.), particularly the philosopher-poet Vladimir Solovyov (1853–1900), whose aesthetics M. later studied in Switzerland (1918–22). After additional study of art in Munich, he was appointed to a teaching position at the University of Kaunas, Lithuania, in 1923.

While still in the seminary, M. had begun to have doubts about his religious calling. During his study abroad, his uncertainty developed into a conflict between the vocation of a priest and that of a poet. Another element was added to this inner struggle when M. fell in love with one of his students. These conflicts are reflected in his novel *Altorių šešėly* (1933; in the shadow of the altars). In 1935 the couple were secretly married, and in 1936 M. was excommunicated, although in his later years he became reconciled with the Catholic Church.

It was during his years at the University of Kaunas that M. first established a reputation as a poet. His main collections of verse of that period are *Tarp dviejų aušrų* (1927; between two dawns) and *Keliai ir kryžkeliai* (1936; roads and crossroads).

The key emotional elements in M.'s poetry are repression, rebellion, and intense yearning to reconcile his priestly vows with the poet's need for a fuller life. His success as a poet derived from his ability to sublimate these contradictory impulses in poetic structures of balanced tension, expressing his turbulent feelings in pithy, disciplined poetic language. The early influences of the Russian symbolists nourished in M. a vague existential longing and—as, for example, in the famous poem "Stella Maris" (Latin: star of the sea) in *Raudoni žiedai; Kunigaikštis Žvainys* (1917; red blossoms; Prince Žvainys)—turned his eyes toward evening horizons, the sea, and the stars as radiant points of unreachable perfection. These spacious, abstract settings in themselves became the symbols of a philosophical quest after the meaning of God. The visage of God in M.'s poetry underwent cyclical changes: from that of a cold and distant ruler, removed from human suffering by the vast, dark cosmic distances, to one of a sorrowful Christ, carved by peasant hands, contemplating man's fate on an empty roadside under the starry skies. In the service of this elusive unknown God, M. alternated between grand gestures of revolt and worshipful tenderness. Images of nature complement these transitory states of mind as vibrant spring gives way to gloomy autumn, mountain heights, to shadowy depths. Affection for the warm and sinful earth is counterpointed by moments of cosmic solitude. Love seeks its difficult path between similar antitheses, often appearing in the form of struggle between the ardent and the pious heart. In his last years, M. was caught in still another painful dichotomy: between gropings toward a "socialist consciousness" and the insistent returns of the God who will not be ignored. Stylistically, M. enriched Lithuanian poetry by his use of fresh and original rhythms and by his extraordinary musicality of language.

M.'s novel *Altorių šešėly* established the psychological genre in Lithuanian fiction. Liudas Vasaris, the semiautobiographical protagonist of this work, for many years huddles unhappily as a novice priest in the "shadow of the altars," trying at the same time to squelch the fires of erotic temptation and to warm the cooling embers of his love for God. As a budding poet he finds his passionate, suffering soul can see beauty only as it is reflected in troubled, imperfect Creation, not as it exists in the perfection of God. He yearns for a woman's love and for the chal-

341

lenge of the affairs of the world. With the encouragement of a devoted woman, Liudas leaves the priesthood, rebelling not against God but against the earthly law of the Church. *Altorių šešėly* provoked bitterness and shock in conservative and Catholic Lithuanian circles; only now has it become accepted on the strength of M.'s stature as a literary figure.

After World War II M. had to adjust some of his past views to the demands of the Communist regime. His second important novel, *Sukilėliai* (1957; the rebels), shows clear signs of his efforts to stay within the ideological framework of Socialist Realism (q.v.). It is the story of another young priest who makes a conscious decision to leave the contemplative life, joining the tumult of the Lithuanian uprising against the Russians in 1863. Despite M.'s efforts to give credit to the "progressive influences of Russian democratic thought" that inspired the rebellion, the novel was frowned upon by Soviet authorities. The theme was too reminiscent of Lithuania's present situation to give the Communist censors much peace of mind.

FURTHER WORKS: *Raštai* (2 vols., 1921); *Valdovas* (1930); *Naujoji lietuvių literatūra,* Vol. I (1936); *Krizė* (1937); *Literatūros etiudai* (1937); *Lietuviškoji tematika Adomo Mickevičiaus kūryboje* (1949); *Sveikinu žeme* (1950); *Rūsčios dienos* (1952); *Vakarėj žaroj* (1959); *Raštai* (8 vols., 1959–62); *Būties valanda* (1963); *Langas* (1966); *Poezija* (2 vols., 1973)

BIBLIOGRAPHY: Jungfer, V., "V. M.-P. und Krėvė," *Litauen: Antlitz eines Volkes* (1948), pp. 296–314; Grinius, J., *V. M.-P. als Dichter* (1964); Sietynas, A., "The Condition of Free Prisoner: Poetry and Prose of V. M.-P.," *Lituanus,* 11, 1 (1965), 48–63

RIMVYDAS ŠILBAJORIS

MYRIVILIS, Stratis

(pseud. of Stratis Stamatopoulos) Greek novelist and short-story writer, b. 30 June 1892, Sykamia, Lesbos; d. 9 Sept. 1969, Athens

M. was old enough to fight in the Balkan wars of 1912–13 and also to observe at close range the critical events that preceded and followed the 1922 Greek catastrophe in Asia Minor. All three of his novels and several of his short stories draw their inspiration from those experiences of war and political and social conflict. He was very active as a publisher and journalist, first on his native island of Lesbos (also called Mytilene), later in Athens. Between 1936 and 1951 M. was the general program director of the Greek National Radio and wrote for newspapers. In the 1950s he visited America and described his impressions in a series of newspaper articles. He was a member of the Academy of Athens.

M.'s first collection of short stories, *To kokkino vivlio* (1915; rev. ed., 1952; the red book), and the first and best-known of his novels, *I zoi en tafo* (1924; rev. ed., 1930; *Life in the Tomb,* 1977), show him to be a great craftsman in the tradition of Greek demoticism (that is, the literary movement that worked for the promotion of the vernacular over the purist language in literature and education). The novel is a Greek equivalent, broadly speaking, of the antiwar novels of Erich Maria Remarque and Ernest Hemingway (qq.v.). The main character of the story, Sergeant Kostoulas, gradually loses faith in the purpose of the Balkan wars, in which he had initially volunteered to fight, and is quite disillusioned when he dies. A diary he leaves behind describes his life in the trenches. This is supposedly found and published by a friend (the first-person narrator). The book combines stark realism with lyrical descriptions of nature and human feeling.

In M.'s second novel, *I dhaskala me ta hrissa matia* (1933; *The Schoolmistress with the Golden Eyes,* 1951), which may be seen as the center link in a loose trilogy of novels, the chief character, Leonis Drivas, returns to his native Mytilene from the war his country has lost in Anatolia, unharmed in body but badly affected in spirit. His mental convalescence is long, hampered by the shallow, naïve, or cynical attitudes of the island society, people whom the war seems to have taught nothing. Drivas is, moreover, divided between loyalty to a friend killed in the war and passion for that man's widow, Sappho, the schoolmistress of the title.

Here, and also in his third novel, *I panaghia i ghorghona* (1949; *The Mermaid Madonna,* 1959), M. mixes realistic narration and description with a lyrical, almost sensuous feeling for nature, and with detailed psychological analysis of some of the more significant characters. This work deals with the settlement on Mytilene of a group of Greek refugees from Anatolia. In time, they acquire roots in the new soil, although some among them will not relinquish easily the dream of going back to their old homes. Against this background M. weaves the story of Smaragdhi (the name means "emerald girl"), a foundling, believed by the people to be of supernatural origin. She is an ideal as well as a source of torment for the men of her village, and chooses, at the end, to become a devotee of the Virgin, the Mermaid Madonna, whose icon (depicting her as half human and half fish) oversees and protects the village. The use of myth to deepen the understanding of history as well as to relieve the characters of some of the burden of the past, a technique that characterizes M.'s mature period, is also found in his novella *O Vassilis o Arvanitis* (1943; Vassilis the Albanian), a portrait of a Zorba-like character who, pushed by an irresistible lust for life, commits the inevitable hubris that leads to ruin.

To some critics, M. was particularly successful as a short-story writer. Important collections, like *To prassino vivlio* (1935; the green book), *To ghalazio vivlio* (1939; the blue book), the revised version of *To kokkino vivlio,* and *To vissini vivlio* (1959; the purple book), in fact, contain some of the best-crafted specimens of the genre in modern Greek literature. In one of his most memorable stories, "To sakki" (the sack), in *To prassino vivlio,* a middle-aged soldier of World War I carries, on his return journey, a sack with his brother's bones, which others mistake for hardtack, a luxury in those days when even bread had become scarce. The macabre as well as humorous discovery of the sack's real contents elicits, in both narrator and reader, feelings of sympathy and admiration for the poor soldier's faithfulness in carrying out a promise to his mother: to find and bring home for proper burial the remains of his younger brother, killed in battle in an earlier year of the war.

It is not for dealing with great spiritual questions (in the manner, let us say, of Nikos Kazantzakis [q.v.] or for thematic and stylistic variety that M. is to be remembered, but instead for his rich and varied elaboration of the Greek vernacular, his talent for vivid characterization, and the interplay in his works of realism and myth. Ideologically, he remained inward-looking, from his early "angry" days to his later embrace of a wider Hellenic tradition. His overall significance lies in the role he played in realizing better than most of his predecessors the ideals of demoticism: to cultivate the popular language as a literary instrument and to provide a realistic picture of modern Greek society.

FURTHER WORKS: *O arghonaftis* (1936); *Traghoudi tis yis* (1937); *Mikres foties* (1942); *Ta paghana* (1944); *O Pan* (1946); *Ap'tin Elladha* (1956); *Pteroenta* (1964)

BIBLIOGRAPHY: Mirambel, A., "S. M., romancier de la Grèce des légendes et de la réalité," *Mercure de France,* No. 1165 (1960), 90–112; Dimaras, C. T., *A History of Modern Greek Literature* (1972), passim; Politis, L., *A History of Modern Greek Literature* (1973), passim; Doulis, T., *Disaster and Fiction: Modern Greek Fiction and the Asia Minor Disaster of 1922* (1977), passim; Rexine, J. E., on *Life in the Tomb, WLT,* 51 (1977), 661

GEORGE THANIEL

NABOKOV, Vladimir

(pseud. until 1940: V. Sirin) Russian-American novelist, short-story writer, memoirist, essayist, critic, translator, and poet, b. 23 April 1899, St. Petersburg (now Leningrad); d. 2 July 1977, Montreux, Switzerland

N. was born into an ancient aristocratic family; his father was a prominent liberal politician and scholar. The Nabokovs were forced to leave Russia after the Bolsheviks took power in 1917, but young N.'s first books of poetry appeared before he emigrated to England. N. graduated from Cambridge in 1922 and moved to Berlin (1922–37), where his verse, stories, plays, and novels established his Russian reputation. His misleadingly simple prose style was noted by every critic. N.'s alienated and obsessive heroes, His harsh treatment of his characters, and his avoidance of popular social and political topics led most Russian critics to brand him "un-Russian" and an outsider.

Leaving Nazi Germany, N. moved to Paris, where he and his wife lived from 1937 to 1940. In May 1940 N. fled to the U.S. where he became a teacher of Russian language and literature, notably at Cornell University from 1948 to 1958. His lectures, published as *Lectures on Literature* (1980) and *Lectures on Russian Literature* (1981), became very popular among students. N. continued to pursue his avocations of chess, tennis, and lepidopterology, all of which figure prominently in his works. Although he spoke English almost as early as he had Russian and French, he switched to English for his writing only in the 1940s. He published stories in the *New Yorker,* and his novel *The Real Life of Se-*

bastian Knight (1941) marked the final turning point. *Bend Sinister* (1947) followed, but it was the sensational publication of *Lolita* (1955) that made N.'s name and fortune in popular terms.

N. retired from teaching and in 1960 moved to Montreux, Switzerland (retaining his American citizenship), where he lived until his death. During the years in Switzerland he translated, or oversaw translations, of nearly all of his Russian works into English. He also translated two English works back into Russian: *Speak, Memory* (1966; orig. pub. as *Conclusive Evidence,* 1951; *Drugie berega,* 1954) and *Lolita* (*Lolita,* 1967). Moreover, all of his Russian works were reissued in the original, making his two separate but interrelated bodies of writing known all over the world—except in the U.S.S.R., where none of his works has ever been permitted to appear.

N. is one of the few writers who are major figures in two languages; moreover, both his Russian and his English styles have been lauded by fellow writers and critics. Although his poetry is not considered his highest achievement, it is clear that from his first book, *Stikhi* (1916; verse) to his last collection, *Stikhi* (1979; verse), including his poems in English (*Poems and Problems,* 1970), his poetry served as a stylistic laboratory. The richly metaphorical language of his poems is vital to the structure of his prose. His lines are alive with metaphor, and key image clusters play important roles not only in foreshadowing but in developing themes and characterization.

N.'s short stories are often elegantly poetic and as neatly structured as sonnets. The three Russian collections, *Vozvrashchenie Chorba* (1930; the return of Chorb), *Soglyadatay* (1938; the eye), and *Vesna v Fialte* (1956; spring in Fialta), were among the last things N. put into English—in collections not corresponding exactly to the originals in content, notably *Tyrants Destroyed* (1975), *A Russian Beauty, and Other Stories* (1975) and *Details of a Sunset, and Other Stories* (1976). Some are seemingly conventional character studies, with Russian émigré heroes. Others are set in fantastic worlds of the sort that later developed into *Pale Fire* (1962). In his stories as in his other fiction N. liberally uses puzzles, anagrams, allusions, and fatidic dates, challenging readers to penetrate beyond the apparent meaning of the work and discover more subtle designs.

N. forces one to be more than a passive receiver of information. The reader must use all his faculties of perception, memory, and imagination if he wants to participate in the discoveries N.'s fictional world offers.

The theme of memory is the key to his first novel, *Mashenka* (1926; *Mary,* 1970) and many of N.'s other novels. The hero, Ganin, learns that his first love is soon to arrive in Berlin, and decides to renew their relationship, even though she is now married. But after spending days remembering his childhood in Russia, reliving the development of his love, and doing this all with a wealth of very specific sensory detail (typical of N.), he realizes that he has recaptured that lost time the only way humans can, and therefore does not confront Mary when she arrives. Man is unique because in his consciousness, with his retrospective faculty, he can conquer time and space.

The burlesque *Korol, dama, valet* (1928; *King, Queen, Knave,* 1968) is a rather mechanical series of variations on themes from *Madame Bovary.* Among N.'s books it was the only one he changed substantially when translating it. The bumbling hero of *Zashchita Luzhina* (1930; *The Defense,* 1964) is a monomaniac chess master; images of the board gradually take over his entire life. His ultimate defense against the moves of these images is suicide. The subject matter of this novel is well suited for N.'s use of repeated and anticipatory images. In his English foreword N. mocks the "careful reader" by saying he will notice specific passages containing what N. calls a significant system of chessboard images. However, for seventeen years no reviewer, critic, or scholar noticed that the images that N. specifies do not in fact occur in the novel. N. the illusionist, like a magician or chess player, loved such misdirections.

Kamera obskura (1932; *Laughter in the Dark,* 1938) deals with literal blindness and moral blindness, and foreshadows in some ways *Lolita. Podvig* (1932; *Glory,* 1971) tells the story of a Russian émigré who decides to return secretly to his homeland; the faculty of memory and what it re-creates is again vital. In *Otchayanie* (1934; *Despair,* 1937; rev. ed., 1966) N.'s obsessed first-person narrator believes he has discovered his physical double and plots to commit the perfect murder. Hermann's madness becomes clear to the reader in spite of his efforts to deny it. N.'s world is filled with moral degenerates dis-

guised as intelligent and witty characters; his seemingly objective treatment of these figures led some critics to the erroneous conclusion that N. could create only cold and inhuman characters, and that he had no feelings about them himself.

The late 1930s was the creative climax of N.'s Russian career. *Priglashenie na kazn* (1938; *Invitation to a Beheading,* 1959), first published serially in the leading Paris émigré journal, *Sovremennye zapiski,* describes the sentencing, incarceration, and apparent execution of a man named Cincinnatus. It has usually been interpreted as a purely political novel, a Kafkaesque spoof of 20th-c. totalitarian regimes. In fact, it was N.'s first achievement of what he called "fairytale freedom." The setting of the novel seems very concrete, but on close examination it is another planned mirage; no specific place or time is ever mentioned. With difficulty one can deduce that it takes place in an imaginary future so distant that matter itself has almost worn out and all invention has ceased. The prison described is a prison in imagination only, and the book is about the creative process of writing a book. The liberating power of fantasy and imagination becomes one of N.'s main themes. The longest of N.'s Russian novels, *Dar* (1937–38; *The Gift,* 1963), also first published in *Sovremennye zapiski,* is about a poet; in it N. strives to show what creative imagination, wedded to memory, can accomplish. It is also a kind of encyclopedia of Russian literature, teeming with allusions and parodies, and written in N.'s most dazzling style.

The Real Life of Sebastian Knight marks N.'s shift to English. The central problem of the novel is how one determines the true identity of another person, and how one puts that into words. In *Bend Sinister* N. returns to a fantasy land and political themes, with the process of novel-writing itself a key concern. As in *Invitation to a Beheading,* the ancient symbols of the soul, lepidoptera, are used to suggest life beyond what humans regard as the real world. The setting is a vaguely Slavic world of mediocre absolutism, but in general, references to the totalitarianism of the Communist U.S.S.R. are quite rare in N.'s works. No other Russian writer could have written memoirs, as N. did in *Speak, Memory,* that dismiss the revolution in passing, treating it as a minor interruption in butterfly hunting.

Lolita eclipsed N.'s earlier American novels. While it was first rejected by many publishers, and later attacked by critics from many pulpits, it has come to be recognized not as a pornographic book but as a poetically written love story, whose hero suffers from an obsession: the desire to possess "nymphets," as he terms a rare type of barely adolescent girl. Humbert Humbert, the condemned hero-narrator, is a mixture of comic and tragic features, as is the whole novel. In his urbanity, wit, and erudition he is attractive; but as usual in N., one must go beyond what the narrator tells one to what he lets slip. N. allows Humbert to apologize for his actions profusely, but he also makes him a madman and a murderer, who in moments of lucidity realizes exactly how he destroyed Lolita's childhood. N.'s foreign-eye view of American life is alternately comic and lyric, poetic and satirical.

Because its incompetent hero, an émigré professor of Russian, is so lovable, *Pnin* (1957) is often seen as the warmest and most affectionate of N.'s books. *Pale Fire* (1962) is perhaps his most experimental. Its core is an epic poem, and this is surrounded by Introduction, Commentaries, and Index, written by a mad and footnote-drugged narrator named Charles Kinbote. The structure of the narrative is so complex that critics cannot agree about the true identity of the narrator, or which characters have a "real" existence in the book. It is N.'s paradox that the madman's world, Zembla, an imaginary world, is the most realistic and vivid world in the book. N. calls into question the very nature of reality and our ability to perceive it. *Pale Fire* cannot be read in the usual linear manner, nor does it make complete sense except on subsequent readings.

This is also true of N.'s longest and most complex work, *Ada; or, Ardor: A Family Chronicle* (1969). N.'s two worlds, Russia and America, are joined in a fantasy antiworld where normal Earth geography, chronology, and history are mixed in delightful and informative ways. The hero and heroine turn out to be, on close reading, brother and sister, and their lifelong sexual passion for each other provides the sensational element in an otherwise learned and poetic novel containing dissertations on such subjects as the nature of time and space. In *Transparent Things* (1972) N. goes beyond normal time to use characters who have already died, but who in another dimension watch over the living. *Look at the Harlequins!* (1974) was

N.'s attempt to recapitulate both his Russian and American careers in fictional form, using a variety of styles, each imitating his own style at various stages of his sixty-year-long career.

N.'s literary translations and criticism form a significant part of his work. He wrote an insightful critical study called *Nikolai Gogol* (1944). He practiced his carefully worked-out theory of literal translation in *The Song of Igor's Campaign: An Epic of the Twelfth Century* (1960) and Lermontov's *A Hero of Our Time* (1958). His four-volume edition of Pushkin's *Eugene Onegin* (1964; rev. ed., 1975), with translation, copious commentaries, and interpolated essays, is a unique gift from one culture to another. Many of his essays and his iconoclastic, scrupulously *written* interviews were collected in *Strong Opinions* (1973).

A brilliant style is partly a function of imagination, and it is probably the concept of imagination that is the key to most of N. He celebrates it, as he celebrates liberty, language, love, and beauty. He asserts the sanctity of individual human life. He prizes wit, and his own wit is always directed against those who by normal moral standards deserve it: people who do not love, destroyers of freedom, preachers of mediocrity, anyone who maims or kills to force his ideas on other human beings, people who are ignorant of themselves or the physical and intellectual world around them. N. has no sermons. He loathed propaganda fiction. But these values are constants in his world.

FURTHER WORKS: *Dva puti* (1918); *Gorny put* (1923); *Izobretenie valsa* (1938; *The Waltz Invention,* 1966); *Three Russian Poets: Selections from Pushkin, Lermontov, and Tyutchev* (1944); *Nine Stories* (1947); *Stikhotvorenia 1929–51* (1952); *N's Dozen: A Collection of Thirteen Stories* (1958); *Poems* (1959); *The Eye* (1965); *N.'s Quartet* (1966); *Lolita: A Screenplay* (1974); *The N.–Wilson letters 1940–1971* (1979)

BIBLIOGRAPHY: Dembo, L. S., ed. *N.: The Man and His Work* (1967); Field, A., *N.: His Life in Art* (1967); Proffer, C. R., *Keys to "Lolita"* (1968); Appel, A., Jr., ed., *The Annotated "Lolita"* (1970); Appel, A., Jr., and Newman, C., eds., *N.: Criticism, Reminiscences, Translations, and Tributes* (1970); Rowe, W. W., *N.'s Deceptive World* (1971); Field, A., comp., *N.: A Bibliography* (1973);

Fowler, D., *Reading N.* (1974); Mason, B. A., *N.'s Garden: A Guide to "Ada"* (1974); Proffer, C. R., ed., *A Book of Things about V. N.* (1974); Updike, J., *Picked-Up Pieces* (1975), pp. 191–222; Lee, L. L., *V. N.* (1976); Bodenstein, J., *The Excitement of Verbal Adventure: A Study of V. N.'s English Prose* (1977); Grayson, J., *N. Translated* (1977); Quennell, P., ed., *V. N.: A Tribute* (1979); Schuman, S., *V. N.: A Reference Guide* (1979); Pifer, E., *N. and the Novel* (1980); Rowe, W. W., *N.'s Spectral Dimension* (1981); Rivers, J. E., and Nicol, C., eds., *N.'s Fifth Arc: N. and Others on His Life's Work* (1982)

CARL R. PROFFER

Under thorough scrutiny Sirin proves for the most part to be an artist of form, of the writer's device, and not only in that well-known and universally recognized sense in which the formal aspect of his writing is distinguished by exceptional diversity, complexity, brillance and novelty. All this is recognized and known precisely because it catches everyone's eye. But it catches the eye because Sirin not only does not mask, does not hide his devices, as is most frequently done by others (and in which, for example, Dostoevsky attained startling perfection) but, on the contrary, because Sirin himself places them in full view like a magician who, having amazed his audience, reveals on the very spot the laboratory of his miracles. This, it seems to me, is the key to all of Sirin. His works are populated not only with the characters, but with an infinite number of devices which, like elves or gnomes, scurry back and forth among the characters and perform an enormous amount of work. They saw and carve and nail and paint, in front of the audience, setting up and clearing away those stage sets amid which the play is performed. They construct the world of the book and they function as indispensably important characters. Sirin does not hide them because one of his major tasks is just that—to show how the devices live and work. [1937]

Vladislav Khodasevich, "On Sirin," in Alfred Appel, Jr., and Charles Newman, eds., *N.: Criticism, Reminiscences, Translations, and Tributes* (1970), p. 97

As a literal image and overriding metaphor, the mirror is central to the form and content of N. novels. If one perceives *Pale Fire* spatially, with John Shade's poem on the "left" and Charles Kinbote's Commentary on the "right," the poem is seen as an object to be perceived, and the Commentary becomes the world seen through the distorting prism of a mind, a monstrous concave mirror held up to an objective "reality." The narrator of *Despair* (1934) loathes mirrors, avoids

them, and comments on those "monsters of mirrors," the "crooked ones," in which a man is stripped, squashed, or "pulled out like dough and then torn in two." N. has placed these crooked reflectors everywhere in his fiction: Doubles, parodies and self-parodies (literature trapped in a prison of amusement park mirrors), works within works, mirror-games of chess, translations ("a crazy-mirror of terror and art"), and language games. He manipulates the basic linguistic devices—auditory, morphological, and alphabetical, most conspicuously the latter. In *Pale Fire*, Zemblan is "the tongue of the mirror," and the fragmentation or total annihilation of the self reverberates in the verbal distortions in *Bend Sinister's* police state, "where everybody is merely an anagram of everybody else," and in the alphabetical and psychic inversions and reversals in *Pale Fire*.

Alfred Appel, Jr., "*Lolita:* The Springboard of Parody," in L. S. Dembo, ed., *N.: The Man and His Work* (1967), pp. 107–8

One of the commonest words in the Nabokovian lexicon is fate. It is fate who wills the unity of all things, who prompts the little unity of alliteration and the other poetic devices of sound repetition so common in the prose of N., who seeks out for words of one language unsuspected cousins in another language, who provides that abundance of Pasternakian and Lermontovian coincidence which informs the novels. In his translation of Lermontov's novel *A Hero of Our Time* Nabokov refers to all these lucky encounters and overheard conversations as "the barely noticeable routine of fate." N.'s account of his own life in *Speak, Memory* is a kind of diary of the workings of fate. Fate is really one of the guises of the muse of N.

If we turn to one of the larger elements of N.'s art, the structure of the character relationships, we find fate busily at work, inevitably with the same result, since fate has only one passion—the passion for unity. In these character relationships we begin, typically, with an apparent duality, which is then reduced to unity—two men who in the course of the novel strangely coalesce. "The only real number is one, the rest are mere repetition." The central position in the novel is usually occupied by the charismatic figure of some poet or novelist of genius. The other figure is the person in the foreground, usually the narrator, whose entire function consists in surrounding the genius at the middle. He researches this genius, seeks him out, comments upon him and in fact draws his existence from him. We know the character at the center only through the efforts of our narrator and guide, who is himself a sympathetic but a less interesting, less gifted, and somehow flawed, incomplete figure.

Clarence Brown, "N.'s Pushkin," in L. S. Dembo, ed., *N.: The Man and His Work* (1967), pp. 201–2

His passion for exactitude is necessarily coupled with a love of synonymy. Without a large bag of words, the wordman is incapable of providing the right word for the right occasion. When there are semantic equals, rhythm and sound determine choice. If *whin* won't fit, *gorse* or *furze* might do. If it is a time for Elizabethan flyting and digladiation, one may grow wrathful with an unctuous mome and let fly *cudden* and *dawkin* and *mooncalf*. If it is a matter, say, of Kinbote's catamites and urning-yearnings, it helps to have *ingle* and *gunsil, bardash* and *pathic,* in verbal reserve. Most of N.'s resources, of course, are not at all rare or recherché. He is a master of the familiar word. But when he does embrace a neglected one, "it lives again, sobs again, stumbles all over the cemetery in doublet and trunk hose, and will keep annoying stodgy gravediggers" as long as literature itself endures.

Peter Lubin, "Kickshaws & Motley," in Alfred Appel and Charles Newman, eds., *N.: Criticism, Reminiscences, Translations, and Tributes* (1970), pp. 190

I have expressed in print my opinion that he is now an American writer and the best living; I have also expressed my doubt that his aesthetic models—chess puzzles and protective colorations in lepidoptera—can be very helpful ideals for the rest of us. His importance for me as a writer has been his holding high, in an age when the phrase "artistic integrity" has a somewhat paradoxical if not reactionary ring, the stony image of his self-sufficiency: perverse he can be, but not abject; prankish but not hasty; sterile but not impotent. Even the least warming aspects of his image—the implacable hatreds, the reflexive contempt—testify, like fortress walls, to the reality of the siege this strange century lays against our privacy and pride.

As a reader, I want to register my impression that N. does not (as Philip Toynbee, and other critics, have claimed) lack heart. *Speak, Memory* and *Lolita* fairly bulge with heart, and even the less ingratiating works, such as *King, Queen, Knave,* show, in the interstices of their rigorous designs, a plenitude of human understanding. The ability to animate into memorability minor, disagreeable characters bespeaks a kind of love. The little prostitute that Humbert Humbert recalls undressing herself so quickly, the fatally homely daughter of John Shade, the intolerably pretentious and sloppy-minded woman whom Pnin undyingly loves, the German street figures in *The Gift,* the extras momentarily on-screen in the American novels—all make a nick in the mind. Even characters N. himself was plainly prejudiced against, like the toadlike heroine of *King, Queen, Knave,* linger vividly, with the outlines of the case they must plead on Judgment Day etched in the air; how fully we feel, for example, her descent

into fever at the end. And only an artist full of emotion could make us hate the way we hate Axel Rex in *Laughter in the Dark.* If we feel that Nabokov is keeping, for all his expenditure of verbal small coin, some treasure in reserve, it is because of the riches he has revealed. Far from cold, he has access to European vaults of sentiment sealed to Americans; if he feasts the mind like a prodigal son, it is because the heart's patrimony is assured.[1970]

John Updike, "A Tribute," *Picked-Up Pieces* (1975), pp. 221–22

N.'s haunting magic rests precisely in the telling— in his particular combination of sounds works, ideas.... The mechanisms ... are both subtle and complex. For N.'s world breathes with a teasing and unseen deception. Describing himself as a Russian writer, he has aptly emphasized "the mirror-like angles of his clear but weirdly misleading sentences."

A faintly Russian coloration further contributes to the "live iridescence" of N.'s English prose. His writings evince a unique perspective on especially these two languages and cultures.

But N.'s uniquely controlled "reality" is surely his most mysterious product. Elusive inter-echoes, from line to line, from book to book, subtly expand. Systematic networks of ironic foreshadowings produce a background unsettling in its depth. Hidden levels of meaning effect a striking range of dimension.

Nabokovian "reality" also illustrates his belief that imagination is a form of memory. His narrators ... view and present their stories throught the lenses of their own imaginations. Memory and imagination systematically overlap. And the clear, vivid results of their purposely blurred interaction consistently make up for a negation of time.

William Woodin Rowe, *N.'s Deceptive World* (1971), pp. 151–62

In his fiction N. is always concerned with both a world and a world apart, with an objective reality on which we can more or less agree ("There is no Zembla") and a consciousness which creates a subjective world of its own ("There is not only a Zembla, but I am its king"). The conflict between these two worlds may be that between art and life, as in *Bend Sinister,* or that between the present and the past, as in *Pnin.* The extremely complex relationship of these two sets of realities is the mark of N.'s most advanced fiction; earlier European fiction like *King, Queen, Knave* does not employ it, or employs it, as in *Despair,* in a comparatively simple fashion. The idea reaches its apotheosis in *Ada,* where the world is wholly reimagined, and it is our Terra that is the dream— or the nightmare.

The real complexities of N.'s art lie in the grazing, mirroring, adjacent planes of objective and subjective "realities," and in the complicated statements about consciousness, art, and imagination. With these interactions we must be very careful. But there are few major artists whose emotional appeals are so direct and unambiguous, and whose favorites are so obviously meant to awe us with their heroics of deed and perception.

Douglas Fowler, *Reading N.* (1974), p. 202

N. has often been celebrated for his brilliance as a stylist; but it is important to recognize that this brilliance, perhaps most centrally in *Ada,* is not ornamental, as in some of his American imitators, but the necessary instrument of a serious ontological enterprise: to rescue reality from the bland nonentity of stereotypicality and from the terrifying rush of mortality by reshaping objects, relations, existential states, through the power of metaphor and wit, so that they become endowed with an arresting life of their own. An incidental samovar, observed in passing, "expressed fragments of its surroundings in demented fantasies of a primitive genre." Lucette drowning sees her existence dissolve in a receding series of selves and perceives that "what death amounted to was only a more complete assortment of the infinite fractions of solitude." Van Veen, driving through the Alps to his first rendezvous with Ada after a separation of fifteen years, sees from his flesh (to borrow an apposite idiom from Job) the palpable reality of time as his recent telephone conversation with Ada and his view of the landscape around him are transformed in the alembic of consciousness into a summarizing metaphor.

Robert Alter, "*Ada,* or the Perils of Paradise," in Peter Quennell, ed., *V. N.: A Tribute* (1979), pp. 105–6

NAGAI Kafū

(pseud. of Nagai Sōkichi) Japanese novelist, short-story writer, essayist, and critic, b. 3 Dec. 1879, Tokyo; d. 10 April 1959, Tokyo

As a young man, N. was sent by his father to the U.S. and to France to learn the banking trade, but his love of the traditional Kabuki theater and of Japanese and French literature caused him upon his return to Japan in 1908 to take up a career as novelist, professor of French literature, literary editor, and translator, most notably of French symbolist (q.v.) poetry.

In an early masterpiece, the novel *Sumidagawa* (1909; *The River Sumida,* 1965), N. already shows certain of the hallmarks of his mature style, which include an ability to create an ironic view of the present reflected

through an appreciation of the beauties of traditional urban Japanese culture, an elegant and elegiac prose style, and an interest in the nuances of the erotic lives of his characters, many of them from the demimonde. N. came to write about such supposedly degraded persons because he felt they represented the truth about society; for him, middle-class respectability represented an essential falsehood.

From the beginning of his career, N. showed great skill in capturing nuances in characterization and setting. In *Sumidagawa,* N. achieved a consonance of setting, mood, and character that set him apart and ahead of all other writers of his generation. In that novel, the sections on the Kabuki theater are particularly vivid. N. continued to adapt certain elements from this theatrical form to his fiction, including the use of surprising happenings and of characters with unusual and colorful personalities.

In 1916 N., increasingly disillusioned with the reactionary policies of the Japanese government, abandoned public life after the death of his father, never again assuming any kind of public position. He continued to write about the byways of contemporary Japanese culture, finding lyric impetus in the erotic world of the geishas and mistresses who functioned in perhaps the only area of life that remained resistant to change in a rapidly modernizing Japan. In an oblique fashion, N. served as a sort of cultural critic through his evocation, half lyrical, half ironic, of a vanishing lifestyle that represented for him a time when Japanese culture had been of a piece. In this one regard, his attitude of irony and detachment resembles that of his mentor, the novelist Mori Ōgai (q.v.).

Of N.'s many pre-World War II works, *Bokutō kidan* (1937; *A Strange Tale from East of the River,* 1965) is perhaps the finest, a remarkable evocation of the atmosphere of a poor section of Tokyo, written as a story within a story, in which the protagonist, a novelist, has an affair with a prostitute while composing his own story about an affair with a prostitute. A brilliant command of detail combined with a sense of evanescence allows N. to produce a striking evocation of psychology, time, and place. N.'s treatment of the liaison mixes introspection, literary reference, and acute observation with an expression of his own intense disdain for the forces of order in society.

During the war years N. refused to cooperate with the government authorities; because of his fiercely independent attitude he became something of a culture hero after 1945. In his short stories written during the postwar period, N. continued to examine changes in Japan with an aristocratic and acerbic eye.

N. continues to be appreciated for his brilliant, evocative style as well as for the special atmosphere and psychological insight of all his works. In spite of the charges of decadence that have often been brought against him, he is, in his own way, a moralist.

FURTHER WORKS: *Amerika monogatari* (1908); *Furansu monogatari* (1909); *Kazagokochi* (1912); *Udekurabe* (1917; *Geisha in Rivalry,* 1963); *Okamezasa* (1918); *Ame shōshō* (1921); *Enoki monogatari* (1931); *Odoriko* (1944); *Towazugatari* (1945); *Zenshū* (24 vols., 1948–53). FURTHER VOLUME IN ENGLISH: *Kafū the Scribbler: The Life and Writings of N. K., 1879–1959* (1965)

BIBLIOGRAPHY: Seidensticker, E., *Kafū the Scribbler: The Life and Writings of N. K., 1879–1959* (1965); Ueda, M., *Modern Japanese Writers and the Nature of Literature* (1976), pp. 26–53; Rimer, J. T., *Modern Japanese Fiction and Its Traditions* (1978), pp. 138–61

J. THOMAS RIMER

NAGY, Lajos

Hungarian short-story writer, novelist, and essayist, b. 5 Feb. 1883, Apostag; d. 28 Oct. 1954, Budapest

The illegitimate son of a housemaid, N. lived with his farm-laborer grandparents until the age of six. The "shame" of his origin and the first experiences of his awakening consciousness left their marks both on his life and his art. Eager to break away from the kind of life he was born into, he untiringly worked to get an education. He studied law, worked as a tutor with an aristocratic family, and, for a short period, as a civil servant. From 1912 on he made his living as a writer, often under severely strained financial circumstances.

In 1919, at the time of Béla Kun's short-lived communist regime, N. favored Kun's administration. The Hungarian Commune, however, which established a classification of writers, relegated him to second-class status. Yet N. was one of those few writers who, after the collapse of Béla Kun's government,

were unwilling to listen to the siren song of the Christian Nationalists. On the contrary, he responded to Horthy's counterrevolutionary regime with remarkable personal courage. In *Képtelen természetrajz* (1921; an improbable bestiary) he attacked human selfishness, violence, and stupidity with the unmistakable images of animal allegory; *Találkozásaim az antiszemitizmussal* (1922; my encounters with anti-Semitism) is a spirited defense of the Jews being persecuted by the Horthy government.

N. always went his way alone. Although a socialist, he did not join the Social Democratic Party. Although as a writer he was aware of his intellectual affinity to the period's most important literary circle, the group around the magazine *Nyugat,* he did not associate himself with these writers, who viewed him with a mixture of respect and aversion.

N. published several novels and a monthly magazine, *N. külövéleménye* (N.'s dissent), written entirely by himself, but he was at his best in the short story. In his first stories, "Özvegy asszonyok" (1908; windows) and "Egy délután a Grün irodában" (1910; an afternoon in the Grün office), the problems that were to become the central concerns of his later work are already present: the recognition that women are commonly treated as objects; the power of the sex drive; and the conflict between the rich and the poor, in which N.'s stand is unequivocally anticapitalist without romanticizing the poor.

In the 1920s, the naturalistic realism of N.'s work was modified by expressionism (q.v.). Some of his most significant stories— for instance, "Napirend" (1927; agenda), "Razzia" (1929; raid), "Január" (1929; January), "A lecke" (1930; the lesson), "Bérház" (1931; tenement), and "Anya" (1931; mother)—show the influence of the cult of the proletarian, the "new factualism" of German literature, the writings of Upton Sinclair and John Dos Passos (qq.v.), and the new cinematic montage technique.

In *Kiskúnhalom* (1934; Kiskúnhalom), which is about one day in his native village, N. turned away from expressionism. This synthesis of literature and sociology, reportage and Freudian analysis, can, in contemporary terms, be called an "antinovel." That airless dustbowl of a Hungarian village, according to N., can be described only by portraying the pettiness, hatred, hopeless poverty, and rigid oppression of its inhabitants. N.'s precise, cold descriptions resemble the articles in a technical journal; but the impact of the novel is achieved by exactly this method. *Kiskúnhalom* is the archetype of the sociological novel, the "village-exploring" fiction, that was to become an important genre in Hungary.

In the summer of 1934 N. was one of the two Hungarian writers invited to Moscow to attend the First Congress of Soviet Writers. For him, the journey was a disappointment. This disappointment became the main theme in his series of reports, *Tizezer kilóméter Oroszország földjén* (1934; ten thousand kilometers in Russia).

In 1945 N. joined the Communist Party and became the feuilletonist for *Szabad Nép,* the central organ of the Party in Hungary. In 1948 he was awarded the highest literary honor of the country. Yet he recognized the impossibility of writing honestly about current problems. He escaped into the past—into his own past—and began working on his autobiography; the first volume *A lázadó ember* (the rebel) was published in 1949.

At the first Congress of the Hungarian Writers' Association, in 1950, a leading Party functionary characterized N. as a "coffeehouse writer," one who "can view and portray the world only through the window of a coffeehouse." This official attack spelled the end of N.'s writing career; the second volume of his autobiography, *A menekülő ember* (the fugitive), was rejected by the state publishing house and was not published until after his death in 1954, during the short-lived, comparatively liberal government of Imre Nagy.

N. is the most important Hungarian short-story writer of the first half of the 20th c. Although he urged social change, his work is basically and deeply pessimistic. It is characterized by an exceptional talent for observation, by scathing irony, and by a deep-rooted respect for truth.

FURTHER WORKS: *Az asszony, a szeretöje és a férje* (1911); *A szobalány* (1913); *Egy leány, több férfi* (1915); *Egy berlini leány* (1917); *Az Andrássy-út* (1918); *A jó fiú* (1919); *Fiatal emberek* (1920); *Vadember* (1926); *Egyszerüség* (n.d.); *Három magyar város* (1933); *Utcai baleset* (1935); *Budapest Nagykávéház* (1936); *A falu álarca* (1937); *Három boltoskisasszony* (1938); *Egy lány a századfordulón* (1940); *A fiatalúr megnösül* (1941); *Pincenapló* (1945); *A tanitvány* (1945); *A falu*

(1946); *A három éhenkórász* (1946); *Emberek, állatok* (1947); *Január* (1948); *Farkas és bárány* (1948); *Új vendég érkezett* (1954); *Válogatott elbeszélések* (3 vols., 1956); *Válogatott karcolatok* (1957); *Iró, könyv, olvasó, Tanulmányok és cikkek* (2 vols., 1959); *N. válogatott müvei* (1962)

BIBLIOGRAPHY: Aczel, T., and Méray, T., *The Revolt of the Mind* (1959), pp. 21–33; Klaniczay, T., Szauder, J., and Szabolcsi, M., *History of Hungarian Literature* (1964), pp. 298–301; Erdei, F., *Information Hungary* (1968), pp. 796–97

TIBOR MÉRAY
UPDATED BY TAMAS ACZEL

NAIDU, Sarojini

Indian poet (writing in English), b. 13 Feb. 1879, Hyderabad; d. 2 March 1949, Lucknow

The precocious eldest child of an eminent, highly Westernized family, N. began to write English poetry as a child. In 1895 she went to study at King's College, London, where she became friends with the critic Edmund Gosse (1849–1928) and later at Girton College, Cambridge, where she was introduced to members of the famous Rhymer's Club by the critic Arthur Symons (1865–1945). She returned to India in 1898, and because of her family's position in the vanguard of India's intellectual and literary renascence, she came into close contact with many of the country's most prominent writers, political figures, and reformers. She continued to write poetry until the period of World War I, then abruptly stopped. The remainder of her life was spent as an active political worker for the Indian National Congress Party. A close friend and confidante of Mahatma Gandhi, N. also campaigned vigorously for women's rights in India.

Gosse had advised N. to eschew Anglo-Saxon themes in her poetry and to concentrate on subjects from her native India. That she heeded this advice is evident in her first volume of poems, *The Golden Threshold* (1905), published in England and boasting an introduction by Symons. It is replete with descriptive pieces on snake charmers, dancers, weavers, and palanquin-bearers, as well as Indian flora and monuments. The book was well received, and N. was immediately given the epithet "nightingale of India."

Her second collection, *The Bird of Time*

351

(1912), included an enthusiastic foreword by Gosse, who noted that the poems in this volume express a "graver music" than her earlier ones, for they treat such themes as melancholy, death, and bereavement. Others take the form of Indian folk songs and present ardent religious sentiment mixed with patriotic fervor.

The third collection, *The Broken Wing* (1917), contains a number of poems dedicated to Indian patriots, including N.'s father, G. K. Gokhale, and Mahatma Gandhi. Others are the usual sorts of descriptions of Indian cities, festivals, and monuments that were already considered standard fare in N.'s verse. The last section of this volume, however, is given over to a sequence of twenty-four poems entitled "The Temple: A Pilgrimage of Love," which is considered by many as N.'s foremost literary achievement. Here the beloved expresses a wide spectrum of emotions in relationship to her lover: the ecstasy of union, the sadness of separation, anguish over supposed infidelity, and finally silence and acceptance. The poems are replete with images of withered leaves, crushed fruit, and trampled, broken stones and clay lamps. The final section of the cycle identifies the lover with the Almighty and depicts in vivid, violent imagery the inevitability of death.

In 1961 N.'s daughter published a small collection of poems written between July and August 1927 under the title *The Feather of the Dawn*. Many of these are patriotic expressions written to Indian leaders; others are passionate love songs addressed to the god Krishna; and still others portray scenes from Indian life, festivals, and flora. In terms of style, technique, and sentiment, these poems are not notably distinguishable from those found in the earlier collections.

The heir to a tradition of English poetry started by another Indian woman, Toru Dutt (1856–1877), N. initially attracted a great deal of attention in Britain because of her remarkably idiomatic and technically accomplished verse. She offered Edwardians an unprecedented view of Indian exotica which they could readily understand and with which they could easily identify. As her later poetry became suffused with patriotic themes and a seeming preoccupation with death, she began to fall out of favor with the British literary establishment. The reason for her sudden absence from print after 1917 has been the subject of a great deal of speculation. Some suggest that she had developed a certain morbidity in outlook, whose roots were to be found in her personal life, which as a result prevented her from writing. Others submit that she was stunned into silence by the overwhelming popularity of her countryman, Rabindranath Tagore (q.v.), winner of the 1913 Nobel Prize for Literature. Still others point out that her thoroughgoing commitment to the Indian nationalist movement did not allow her the necessary time and solitude required to write poetry. Evidence suggests that all three reasons, and possibly others, contributed to her withdrawal from the literary scene.

Today N.'s poetry is generally ignored in the West. In India N.'s poetry has recently become the subject of reevaluation by critics of Indian writing in English, some of whom suggest that many of N.'s poems are among the most distinguished written in India during the 20th c.

FURTHER WORKS: *The Gift of India* (1914); *The Sceptered Flute* (1943)

BIBLIOGRAPHY: Dastoor, P. *S. N.* (1961); Iyengar, K., *Indian Writing in English* (1962), pp. 173–87; Sengupta, P., *S. N.: A Biography* (1966); Mokashi-Punekar, S., "A Note on S. N.," *Critical Essays on Indian Writing in English* (1972), pp. 72–82; Blackwell, F., "Krishna Motifs in the Poetry of S. N. and Kamala Das," *JSoAL*, 13, 1–4 (1977–78), 9–14; Ramamurti, K., "The Indianness of S. N.'s Poetry," *IndSch*, 1, 2 (1979), 101–9; special N. issue, *OJES*, 16, 1 (1980)

CARLO COPPOLA

NAIPAUL, V(idiadhar) S(urajprasad)

Trinidadian novelist and essayist, b. 17 Aug. 1932, Chaguanas

N., whose grandfather had come from India to the Caribbean as an indentured laborer, completed his early education in Port of Spain, Trinidad, and, after emigrating to England, was graduated from Oxford in 1954. These facts are of considerable importance for understanding N.'s progressive alienation from the three cultures that shaped him, his disaffection from any particular literary community or tradition, and his concern with political and moral freedom, exile, and the quest for order. These are the themes that, in one way or another, find their way into his writing.

Such themes are but thinly articulated in the first three novels. In *Miguel Street* (written 1954, pub. 1959) they are parceled out among several dozen inhabitants of a slum street in Port of Spain. Their activity on the street is perceived through the intelligence of the young narrator—a street "rab" of rare sensitivity and humanity who is able to transmit something poignant and comic, but at the same time profound, about lives governed by poverty, frustration, aborted ambition, and superstitious fatalism.

N.'s next two novels focus on a single protagonist. They, too, generate their satire and irony from the culturally and racially disordered world of Trinidad. In *The Mystic Masseur* (1957) the naïve Ganesh Ramsumair, through a concatenation of chance, island superstition (*obeah*), autodidacticism, and corruption, rises to become first a popular masseur, then a mystic, writer, pundit, politico, and finally a representative to the legislature. Inevitably, Ganesh loses his stature as cult figure and hero of the people, and, capping his progress, anglicizes his name to G. Ramsay Muir.

In *The Suffrage of Elvira* (1958) Surujupat Harban's shaky course to the legislature careers through the comic intrigue, boondoggling, and logrolling that accompanies democracy's rise in Trinidad and its first general election. "Pat" sells out totally to win the seat, and, winning, disowns all those factions that helped him—Hindu, Muslim, black. For the fascination of power that transports him from Trinidad's backward counties to the capital, he surrenders honesty, innocence, and wonder.

N., in these rather slight novels, seems clinically accurate about the logical progression from self-abasement to self-advertisement to selfishness; he is scrupulous in rendering the motives of the little man who must flog his egotism in order to succeed in a care-little, do-nothing, failure-prone society.

A House for Mr. Biswas (1961) was N.'s first major novel, and perhaps the best novel yet to emerge from the English-speaking Caribbean. This feat was achieved by linking one of the most notable characters in contemporary fiction with the extraordinary multiethnicity of Trinidad. Epic in conception and panoramic in execution, the novel spans three generations of West Indian Hindus and centers on Mohun Biswas, a poor, diligent Brahman, and his quest for a house of his own. *A House for Mr. Biswas* is nothing less than a small odyssey. From his inauspicious, unlucky birth, through childhood misfortunes, a too-hasty marriage, years of domination by in-laws (the power-hungry, status-seeking Tulsis), to his success as a journalist, the purchase of the house, and his death by cardiac arrest, Mr. Biswas moves through life confronting and overcoming exhaustion and loss. In the course of his forty-three years he is flogged, duped, thwarted, maligned, robbed, humiliated, frustrated, defeated, sickened, and frightened; yet he remains throughout stoic and hopeful. The house, when it at last becomes his, has come not only to symbolize his yearning for freedom and identity but his triumph over the lovelessness, waste, and chaos of his society.

Six years later—after traveling in the Americas and India and writing books about the experience—N. published his most profound book to date, *The Mimic Men* (1967). It is a novel of colonial disintegration on a par with George Orwell's (q.v.) *Burmese Days* and E. M. Forster's (q.v.) *A Passage to India;* but its focus is on the disintegration of the natives rather than that of the colonialists.

The "mimic men" of the title refer to men of older cultures who have been educated to be mimics of contemporary cultures. Consequently, such a man is deprived of the authenticity of living in terms of one's own culture. The novel explores the rise to and fall from power of Ralph Singh, a West Indian Hindu. At forty, having exhausted his roles as friend, countryman, lover, son, husband, student, businessman, politician, and diplomat, he now writes his autobiography. Living in a London hotel, he strives to obtain from the "inaction" imposed upon him the "final emptiness."

Born on the island of "Isabella" and educated in England, Singh, the imperfectly Westernized Hindu, drives toward wealth and power, always under the illusion that he is free to choose, although in reality he can never overcome his past or his heritage. The novel is a monumental study of the evils and perversions of double-faced colonial exploitation, but it is also a profound study of a single life, drained by the flux of history, defeated by personal, social, political, and cultural forces, and fated for shipwreck.

An inveterate traveler and confirmed expatriate, N., always in search of new settings for his themes, offers a most searching evaluation of several important themes in *In a*

Free State (1971). The volume's three stories—ranging in tone from farce to tragedy, and in locale from Washington, D.C., to a fictional African state—are linked by the themes of freedom and exile. They are framed by two excerpts from N.'s journals, which also brood on these themes, seeing them as basic to his existence. The longest (and title) story of the volume, tells of the growing fears and ultimate neurotic collapse of two British colonials (a man and a woman) as they travel by car across a small African nation in the throes of revolution. Seeking order, safety, and freedom, Bobby and Linda experience only disillusion and the claustrophobic confinement of an English compound in the heart of Black Africa.

Guerrillas (1975) continues the theme of *In a Free State,* but the virulence of colonialism—its self- and universal destructiveness—has been translated to a nameless, if prototypical Caribbean island just on the verge of realizing its infection. To the island—divided racially, politically, and economically—comes Peter Roche, a white South African liberal who is hired as a kind of public relations liaison between the Establishment and Jimmy Ahmed, the half-caste leader of the revolutionary group. Within the ideological struggles of these two men—one who "cannot see the future," and the other who seems to hold it in the palm of his hand—N. constructs variations on the evils and disasters that liberalism, colonialism, and militancy have wrought. Every man is a guerrilla, he suggests, fighting his own war.

The nihilism of N.'s recent novels is not solely the result of the author's private pessimism; it grows out of history, out of the colonial dilemma and paradox. Colonialism leads to decay, decay to revolution, revolution to chaos and rootlessness, then back again to revolution. It is of course the individual, caught up in this dialectic, who suffers. Such is the major theme of *A Bend in the River* (1979), N.'s tenth novel. Isolated at "a bend in the river," Salim, an East African of East Indian origin, an expatriate trying to build his life out of the rubble left by postindependence revolution, finds that such "freedom" plunges him further into spiritual, cultural, and inevitably political imprisonment. His false hopes of constructing anything—a new life or new self—are scrapped for the matter of merely surviving in, and then escaping from a country that is suspiciously like Zaire with a crude, energetic, insane president that uncomfortably resembles Mobutu.

N.'s five most recent novels paint a bleak, but compelling and realistic picture of the colonial experience: of the betrayers and of the betrayed who in turn become the betrayers. One, he seems to say, may accept the order of things, the other may create the chaos, but neither, alas, is able to create order. N.'s treatment of so complex a theme, and his fluid, challenging ideas on other problems fundamental to our times, have made him one of the most original and thoughtful writers of the postwar period.

FURTHER WORKS: *The Middle Passage* (1962); *Mr. Stone and the Knights Companion* (1964); *An Area of Darkness: An Experience of India* (1964); *A Flag on the Island* (1967); *The Loss of El Dorado: A History* (1969); *The Overcrowded Barracoon: Selected Articles 1958–1972* (1972); *India: A Wounded Civilization* (1977); *The Return of Eva Perón, with The Killings in Trinidad* (1980); *Among the Believers: An Islamic Journey* (1981)

BIBLIOGRAPHY: Walsh, W., *A Manifold Voice: Studies in Commonwealth Literature* (1970), pp. 62–85; Ramchand, K., *The West Indian Novel* (1970), pp. 189–204; Theroux, P., *V. S. N.: An Introduction to His Work* (1972); Hamner, R. D., *V. S. N.* (1973); Walsh, W., *V. S. N.* (1973); Morris, R. K., *Paradoxes of Order: Some Perspectives on the Fiction of V. S. N.* (1975); White, L., *V. S. N.: A Critical Introduction* (1975); Boxill, A., "The Paradox of Freedom: V. S. N.'s *In a Free State,*" *Crit,* 18 (1976), 81–91; Hamner, R. D., ed., *Critical Perspectives on V. S. N.* (1977); Morris, R. K., "Shadow into Substance: V. S. N.'s *The Mimic Men,*" in Morris, R. K., ed., *Old Lines, New Forces* (1977), pp. 131–50

ROBERT K. MORRIS

NAŁKOWSKA, Zofia

Polish novelist, short-story writer, and dramatist, b. 10 Nov. 1884, Warsaw; d. 17 Dec. 1954, Warsaw

Daughter of a renowned scholar, N. grew up in an intellectual, progressive, and sophisticated milieu. She was introduced early to philosophical ideas and modern literary trends that influenced her creative work from the start and left their mark on her *Weltan-schauung* as well as on her political stances at different times of her life. A prolific writer, N. started her career with the publication of modernistic verse, but abandoned the genre for prose—mainly the novel and the short story, later the drama.

The novel *Kobiety* (1906; *Women,* 1920) is typical of N.'s approach to the theme of women's emancipation, seen as the right to love and to experience the dark mysteries of sex—which, however, her cerebral heroines invariably fail to understand. The theme, treated by N. philosophically, realistically, or as a psychological experiment, never ceased to fascinate her throughout her writing career; but historical events—World War I, Poland's regaining of independence, World War II and the German occupation of Poland, and the postwar political situation there—developed in turn other themes, relegating feminism to a secondary interest.

Rumblings of the approaching worldwide upheaval are reflected in N.'s earlier works in the revolutionary activities of her male protagonists, but these works chiefly explore the "battle of sexes." They are written in the fin-de-siècle spirit and the ornamental style of "Young Poland," the Polish counterpart of the symbolist (q.v.), and especially the Decadent movements of the period. Some critics accused her of psychologism—applying psychological conceptions to the interpretation of historical events—and of exaggerated philosophical thinking, which often deprive N.'s characters of warmth and realistically motivated behavior.

N.'s most significant work dates from the 1920s and 1930s. Her style by then had acquired simplicity and lucidity, and her characters had become less self-centered and more psychologically realistic. She has a penchant for *romans à these:* her plots tend to serve as illustrations of her favorite maxims, which are also clearly spelled out in characters' remarks or the narrator's asides, such as "one dies at just any random moment of life," or "we really are what we appear to be in the eyes of other people." Some maxims reappear in different novels. Yet, an element of social awareness and a desire to probe deeper into the complexities of life and human relationships lend authenticity even to N.'s far-fetched aphorisms.

While N.'s two plays, *Dom kobiet* (1930; the house of women) and *Dzień jego powrotu* (1930; *The Day of His Return,* 1931), still focus primarily on the vicissitudes of the human condition, her best novel, *Granica* (1935; the boundary) is different. The boundary of the title is the farthest limit of the compromise an individual can make with his conscience without jeopardizing his identity. However, since everyone is a pawn in the social "scheme" to which he belongs by birth, occupation, or financial situation, the line is certain to be gradually approached and eventually crossed. This being N.'s fatalistic premise, the plot ends in total catastrophe. *Granica* can be, and was, viewed as an indictment of the social order, symbolically dividing the protagonists into inhabitants of the upper floors and those of the cellars in an apartment house; or as an affirmation of the Bible's pronouncement that the wages of sin (in this case the seduction of a servant girl) is death.

N. met with success and recognition at practically all stages of her artistic career, especially in the final stage of her life and work following the global catastrophe of World War II, when she became a deputy to the Polish Diet and member of the Commission for the Investigation of Nazi Crimes. The latter position resulted in the publication of her documentary, *Medaliony* (1946; medallions), awesome in its stark realism. N.'s work was shaped as much by her sensitivity to social ills and her intellectual curiosity as by her talent. It also faithfully reflects the stormy historical events and the variegated literary trends of her entire lifetime.

FURTHER WORKS: *Książę* (1907); *Koteczka albo białe tulipany* (1909); *Rówieśnice* (1909); *Narcyza* (1910); *Węże i róże* (1915); *Tajemnice krwi* (1917); *Hrabia Emil* (1920); *Charaktery* (1922); *Romans Teresy Hennert* (1924); *Dom nad łąkami* (1925); *Małżeństwo* (1925); *Choucas* (1927); *Niedobra miłość* (1928); *Między zwierzętami* (1934); *Niecierpliwi* (1939); *Węzły życia* (1948; enlarged ed., 2 vols., 1950–54); *Pisma wybrane* (1954; enlarged ed., 2 vols., 1956); *Widzenie bliskie i dalekie* (1957); *Dzienniki czasu wojny* (1970); *Dzienniki* (3 vols., 1975–76)

BIBLIOGRAPHY: Kridl, M., *A Survey of Polish Literature and Culture* (1956), pp. 495–97, 503; Miłosz, C., *The History of Polish Literature* (1969), pp. 431–32; Krzyżanowski, J., *A History of Polish Literature* (1978), pp. 624–27

XENIA GASIOROWSKA

NAMORA, Fernando Gonçalves

Portuguese novelist, short-story writer, and poet, b. 15 April 1919, Condeixa

N. was raised in rural central Portugal. While studying medicine at the University of Coimbra, he was the director of several small literary reviews, in which he published his first poems. N.'s works reflect his professional experiences as a rural and urban physician, as well as his interest in the role of the intellectual in a politically repressed society.

N.'s first volume of poetry, *Relevos* (1938; reliefs), displayed the confessional tone of the Presença literary group. His *Terra* (1941; soil) was the initial volume in the major series of Portuguese neorealist poetry collectively titled *Novo Cancioneiro* (new songbook). In 1959 he published his collected poems, *As frias madrugadas* (the cold dawns), to be followed by another volume of poetry, *Marketing* (1969; title in English). But N. himself has recognized his lack of a true poetic bent and has more successfully cultivated fiction.

As sete partidas do mundo (1939; the world's seven parts) and *Fogo na noite escura* (1943; fire in the dark night) are autobiographical novels, treating respectively his adolescent years at a Coimbra high school and the members of his circle at the university at the time of their graduation during World War II. The technique of both works reflects N.'s interest in psychological detail and in the then-growing importance of the neorealist movement. *A casa da malta* (1945; the transient's house) is a complex yet well-developed narrative in which the author presents the lives of poor, wandering rural types.

In his novels of the 1950s N. turned to more existential preoccupations, through his presentation of the exploitation of tungsten miners during World War II and also that of farmers and rural workers. While *O trigo e o joio* (1954; *Fields of Fate,* 1970) is a whimsical tale of rural life, his most provocative work of this period was the novel *O homem disfarçado* (1957; the masked man), a penetrating portrait of the medical profession in Portugal.

N.'s two very notable companion volumes of short fiction, *Retalhos da vida de um médico* (1949, 1963; sketches of a doctor's life; Vol. I tr. as *Mountain Doctor,* 1956), poignantly portray characters who not only are physically ill but also, owing to their chronic misery, have been emotionally and

mentally dehumanized. Among N.'s more recent novels, *Os clandestinos* (1972; the clandestine ones), is a striking view of the struggles of his own generation of Portuguese intellectuals under harsh dictatorial repression. He has also written popular biographies of figures of Portuguese medical history, a short history of the neorealist movement in Portugal, and commentaries on contemporary topics.

N.'s works have followed the prevalent trends of modern Portuguese literature, but his doctor's point of view has given his fiction a distinctive narrative voice.

FURTHER WORKS: *Mar de sargaços* (1940); *Minas de S. Francisco* (1946); *A noite e a madrugada* (1950); *Deuses e demónios da medicina* (1952); *Cidade solitária* (1959); *Domingo à tarde* (1961); *Esboço histórico do neo-realismo* (1961); *Aquilino Ribeiro* (1963); *Diálogo em Setembro* (1966); *Um sino na montanha* (1968); *Os adoradores do sol* (1971); *Estamos no vento* (1974); *A nave de pedra* (1975); *Cavalgada cinzenta* (1977); *Encontros* (1979); *Resposta a Matilde* (1980); *O rio triste* (1982)

BIBLIOGRAPHY: Gil, I. M., "La obra novelística de F. N.," *CHA,* 105 (1958), 325–32; Rogers, W. G., on *Fields of Fate, NYTBR,* 22 March 1970, 38; Ares Montes, J., on *Os adoradores do sol, Ínsula,* 270 (1972), 14

IRWIN STERN

NARAYAN, R(asipuram) K(rishnaswamy)

Indian novelist, short-story writer, and essayist (writing in English), b. 10 Oct. 1906, Madras

Of all Indian novelists writing in English, N. is the best known to Westerners. Born of an old Brahmin family that moved to Mysore when he was young, N. learned in school the language that was to become the medium of his own reading and writing (his first languages were Tamil and Kannada). His higher education was acquired at Maharajah's College (now part of the University of Mysore), from which he graduated in 1930. N. burst on the literary scene with the publication of the novel *Swami and Friends* (1935) and since then has produced a continuous stream of novels, short stories, and essays. Early in his career, N. received encouragement from Graham Greene (q.v.).

Over the years N. has contributed several hundred short stories and sketches to the Madras newspaper *Hindu*. In 1960 he received the Sahitya Akademi Award for *The Guide* (1958). Recent work has involved shortened modern prose versions in English of India's great epics, the *Mahabharata* (1978) and the 13th-c. Tamil poet Kamban's version of the *Ramayana* (1972). *Gods, Demons, and Others* (1964) contains similar prose versions of shorter sacred tales. N. has also written two travel books on Karnataka state, *Mysore* (1939) and *The Emerald Route* (1977).

N.'s novels appear at first to be gently humorous stories of Indian family life set in an imaginary town called Malgudi, where nothing of consequences happens and life goes on as usual. Despite their deceptively simple prose style, however, N.'s novels are in fact complex artistic statements adhering closely to the canons of classical Indian literature. His heroes, generally middle-class types—a printer, a teacher, a student, a sweet-vendor—usually struggle against sudden movements of fate and ensuing ethical dilemmas. Through self-discipline and self-conquest, each hero eventually attains a spiritual insight that enables him to ignore his material circumstances; spiritual knowledge thus renders further action unnecessary. The story usually ends on a note of resolution or harmony in which the equilibrium of life in Malgudi is preserved.

The Man-Eater of Malgudi (1961) involves a taxidermist, an anomaly in Hindu society, who is literally a demon erupted into a hitherto peaceful world. His role as an elemental force of disorder requires that he be eliminated by an equally potent force—divine fate. Appropriately, the demon-taxidermist oversteps his own limits and unintentionally kills himself. Margayya, in *The Financial Expert* (1952), is unable to comprehend the complexities of land banks and credit unions, and instead builds his own financial empire out of a little black box and later out of elegant offices on Market Road. When all his depositors demand their capital at once, the hero is ruined and returns to his humble seat under the banyan tree, wiser for having experienced a foolish attachment to wealth.

Most of N.'s novels also deal with deep conflicts between the traditional way of life and forces emanating from contact with the West. Malgudi changes in the course of N.'s career; the intensity of such conflicts deepens along with India's own predicaments in the real world. *Mr. Sampath* (1949; Am., *The Printer of Malgudi*, 1957), deals with the financial killing to be made in the newly developing film industry. In *The Guide* a tourist guide builds a career for a Bharata Natyam dancer. After the would-be impresario is jailed for forging the dancer's Rosie's signature, he eventually makes his way to a village where he is mistaken for a holy man. Gradually he accepts this role; he is forced into fasting to placate the gods after the monsoon rains fail to come, and he dies as a result.

Although in N.'s fiction the gap between action and consequence is great, this disparity serves to point up the Hindu world view and man's incapacity to influence events. The Western view, insistent on cause-and-effect logic, never prevails, yet N.'s reconciliation of opposites is always surprising, often humorous, and spiritually ennobling. His characters, moreover, meet frustration with unfailing optimism, so that N.'s novels seem to mirror India in every aspect.

FURTHER WORKS: *The Bachelor of Arts* (1937); *The Dark Room* (1938); *Malgudi Days* (1941); *Dodu, and Other Stories* (194?); *Cyclone, and Other Stories* (1944); *The English Teacher* (1945; Am., *Grateful to Life and Death*, 1953); *An Astrologer's Day, and Other Stories* (1947); *Waiting for the Mahatma* (1955); *Lawley Road, and Other Stories* (1956); *My Dateless Diary* (1960); *Next Sunday: Sketches and Essays* (1960); *The Sweet-Vendor* (1967; Am., *The Vendor of Sweets*, 1971); *A Horse and Two Goats, and Other Stories* (1970); *My Days* (1974); *Reluctant Guru* (1975); *A Painter of Signs* (1976); *Malgudi Days* (1982)

BIBLIOGRAPHY: Gerow, E., "The Quintessential N.," *LE&W*, 10 (1966), 1–18; Narasimhaiah, C. D., "R. K. N.: The Comic as a Mode of Study in Maturity," *The Swan and the Eagle* (1969), pp. 135–58; Holmstrom, L., *The Novels of R. K. N.* (1973); Kaul, A. N., "R. K. N. and the East-West Theme," in Mukherjee, M., ed., *Considerations* (1977), pp. 43–65; Vanden Driesen, C., "The Achievement of R. K. N.," *LE&W*, 21 (1977), 51–64; Harrex, S. C., "R. K. N.: Some Miscellaneous Writings," *JCL*, 13, 1 (1978), 64–76; Walsh, W., *R. K. N.: A Critical Appreciation* (1982)

JANET POWERS GEMMILL

NATSUME Sōseki

(pseud. of Natsume Kin'nosuke) Japanese novelist, b. 5 Jan. 1867, Tokyo; d. 9 Dec. 1916, Tokyo

N. (usually called Sōseki) was born to a family that had fallen on hard times as a result of the Meiji Restoration. His parents were embarrassed at having a child late in life and tried unsuccessfully to have him adopted, and he was left permanently with a feeling of being unwanted. After a brilliant career as a student of English at Tokyo Imperial University, he abandoned his native city and accepted a series of rural teaching positions. In 1900 the government sent him to England for further study of English. He returned to Japan in early 1903, after having suffered a nervous breakdown. Nerves and ulcers were to plague him for the rest of his life. Although he decided, while in England, to become a creative writer rather than a literary scholar, he took a position as professor of English literature at Tokyo University, succeeding the American writer Lafcadio Hearn (1850–1904). In 1907 N. resigned his professorship to become literary editor of the newspaper *Asahi shimbun*. The ensuing decade was a period of intense literary activity until the very moment of his death from ulcers in 1916.

N.'s work can be divided into several groups representing stages in his developing philosophy. He began with experimental works, trying several fictional techniques. His first major work was *Wagahai wa neko de aru* (1905; *I Am a Cat*, 1961), a satire depicting modern Japanese society as seen from the point of view of a cat. The idea for this story was apparently derived from E. T. A. Hoffmann's (1776–1822) *Kater Murr*. At the time he wrote this book N. was still developing his narrative style, and it is not so much a unified novel as a loosely related series of amusing episodes poking fun at many aspects of Japan's modernization.

Another work from this experimental phase is *Kusamakura* (1906; *Unhuman Tour*, 1927; new tr., *Three-Cornered World*, 1965). N. said this was intended as a novel in the manner of a haiku. In one sense he uses the work to contrast Western and Eastern aesthetic values, arguing that the West emphasizes the individual while the East denies individuality. N. also said that his broader intention with *Kusamakura* was simply to

leave an impression of beauty in the reader's mind.

Shortly after joining the newspaper staff and devoting himself to writing full time, there appeared his first trilogy, composed of *Sanshirō* (1908; *Sanshiro*, 1977), *Sorekara* (1909; *And Then*, 1978), and *Mon* (1909; *Mon*, 1972). In these works he introduced themes he consistently used throughout his career. One is initiation, usually taking the form of a youth who comes to Tokyo and learns to deal with adult life in the modern world. As these young men struggle to come to terms with life, they end up making decisions or taking actions, and then have to live with their consequences for the rest of their lives. Usually the consequence is feeling guilty of having been greedy or selfish. Where, asks N., can man find solace to assuage this feeling of guilt? In this trilogy he suggests love and religion to relieve the burden of guilt.

N.'s second trilogy consists of *Higan sugi made* (1910; until after the spring equinox), *Kōjin* (1912–13: *The Wayfarer*, 1967), and *Kokoro* (1914; *Kokoro*, 1941; new tr., 1957). In these works the mood is darker, as N. probes more deeply the themes of loneliness, alienation, and guilt. The avenues of relief he offers here are much less hopeful than the ones presented in earlier works. In *Kōjin*, Ichirō, the central figure, declares that the only solutions to modern man's dilemma are suicide, insanity, and religion. In exploring insanity, N. more clearly defines his philosophy: man must learn to surrender his own self to something larger.

Kokoro is probably the best and certainly the most widely read of all of N.'s novels. Here again he shows that mistrust and self-ishness lead to betrayal, guilt, and alienation, which are the normal condition of modern man. N. also reflects on the merits of suicide as a means of atonement, and the theme of initiation is prominent, as in earlier works. N.'s narrative technique here is still fragmentary, but it is also highly imaginative. The first part tells of the youthful narrator going to college in the city and being exposed to modern life. The second part shows the youth at home in the country caring for his dying father, and traditional Japanese life is contrasted to the modern. The third part is in the form of a long letter and suicide note from Sensei, the youth's mentor and also a surrogate father figure. With stark simplicity

N. presents the unendurable loneliness of the modern intellectual, which cannot be breached either by the ties of love and family or by intellectual companionship.

At the time of his death N. had completed several hundred pages of the novel *Meian* (1916; *Light and Darkness,* 1971). Since the work is incomplete, we have no way of knowing for certain how he would have ended it. Critical opinion is sharply divided. Some feel that the characters are headed for the same sort of gloomy dilemma we see in N.'s earlier works. Others say that he had come to terms with life by developing his philosophy of "sokuten kyoshi," which means to seek heaven by abandoning the self. Certainly, egoism or the burden of self-consciousness is at the heart of all the problems N.'s characters struggle with.

It is no exaggeration to say that N. has been the single most popular writer in Japan in the 20th c. Not only do his works give expression to the social and moral problems faced by Japan as it became Westernized and modernized; he also introduced a philosophical approach to literature. This represents a remarkable development, since traditionally fiction had been considered only frivolous and entertaining. N. raised it to the level of a serious medium for artistic expression and philosophical thought.

FURTHER WORKS: *Botchan* (1906; *Botchan,* 1970); *Yokyoshu* (1906); *Gubijinso* (1908); *Kusa awase* (1908); *Shihen* (1910); *Garasudo no naka* (1915); *Michikusa* (1915; *Grass on the Wayside,* 1969)

BIBLIOGRAPHY: McClellan, E., "An Introduction to Sōseki," *HJAS,* 20 (1959), 150–208; Viglielmo, V. H., "An Introduction to the Later Novels of N. S.," *MN,* 19 (1964), 1–36; Eto, J., "N. S.: A Japanese Meiji Intellectual," *ASch,* 34 (1965), 603–19; McClellan, E., *Two Japanese Novelists: Sōseki and Tōson* (1969), pp. 3–69; Yu, B., *N. S.* (1969); Miyoshi, M., *Accomplices of Silence: The Modern Japanese Novel* (1974), pp. 55–92; Doi, T., *The Psychological World of N. S.* (1976); Jones, S., "N. S.'s *Botchan:* The Outer World through Edo Eyes," in Tsuruta, K., and Swann, T., eds., *Approaches to the Modern Japanese Novel* (1976), pp. 148–65; Viglielmo, V. H., "Sōseki's *Kokoro:* A Descent into the Heart of Man," in Tsuruta, K., and Swann, T., eds., *Approaches to the Modern Japanese Novel* (1976), pp. 166–79; McClain, Y., "Sōseki: A Tragic Father," *MN,* 33 (1978), 461–69

STEPHEN W. KOHL

NAZRUL ISLAM

Indian poet, short-story writer, novelist, and dramatist (writing in Bengali), b. 14 May 1899, Churulia; d. 29 Aug. 1976, Dacca, Bangladesh

N. enlisted in the Indian Army in 1917 and served in Karachi and later Iraq during World War I. During this time he came into contact with a *maulvi,* or Muslim religious teacher, in the same regiment, with whom he read the works of the Persian poet Hafiz (1327–1390). This poetry had a profound effect on N. It was at about this time that he assumed the honorific title of Kazi (a type of Muslim judge), which remained with him throughout his life. He returned to India in 1918 and in 1922 published his first major poem, "Vidrohi" ("The Rebel," 1963). Its appearance was considered a major literary event, and the poem made its author an instant celebrity. That same year N. established *Dhumketu,* a radical weekly newspaper in which he published anti-British editorials and essays. The newspaper was closed down, and eventually N. was jailed for a year by the British for sedition. During the 1920s and 1930s he continued to write and to participate actively in numerous leftist political organizations. In 1942, however, he suffered a complete mental breakdown as a result of syphylis contracted while he was in the army. Never recovering his mental facilities, he lived in seclusion in Calcutta until 1974, at which time he moved to Dacca, where he died.

N. published a number of volumes of fiction, plays, and essays, which exhibit his commitment to leftist ideology. He was first and foremost a poet, however. The publication of "Vidrohi" has been described by critics as a monumental event in Bengali literature. In this poem he displays a keen sense of self-assurance, even arrogance, in proclaiming himself a rebel-hero, a destroyer of oppression (that is, by the British) and of outmoded, conservative ideals. As a result of this work N. became known as the "rebel poet" of Bengal. In that the Bengali poetry of this period was dominated by the ethereal, other-worldly verse of Rabindranath Tagore (q.v.), N.'s compositions, replete with political activism and Marxist ideology, came as a surprise to Bengali intellectuals. It is also significant that N. was a peasant, and, to an extent, used rustic diction in his poetry. He was, in addition, a Muslim, and many of his poems are replete with allusions to Islamic history, heroes, and culture, facts that did not go unnoticed by the predominantly Hindu literary circles of Calcutta.

Most of N.'s early poems, especially those in his first collection, *Agni vina* (1922; lute of fire), are hyperbolical, enthusiastic expressions of patriotic sentiment. Numerous volumes followed in rapid succession, notably *Bhangar gan* (1924; songs of destruction), *Biser banshi* (1924; flute of poison), and *Pralay shikha* (1924; flames of destruction), which were proscribed by the British authorities. These are filled with volatile nationalist sentiments in which the poet exhorts patriots to drive the British from the motherland and demands that the downtrodden masses take up arms against their capitalist exploiters.

In addition to patriotic works, N. also wrote numerous love songs, called *ghazals,* a genre popular in Persian and Urdu literature, which he is credited with having introduced into Bengali. A proficient singer and guitarist, he set many of these compositions, which number about 3,300, to music. Many of these poems deal with the requited love. Such love poems can also be read metaphorically as the human soul's expressions of love toward God.

N. continues to be one of the most popular poets of Bengal. He is sometimes criticized for the rather narrow scope of his poetic themes and his facile use of prosody, but while some of his poems may seem dated, his songs exhibit a timeless appeal that assures his position as one of the greatest lyric poets in 20th-c. Indian literature.

FURTHER WORKS: *Vyathar dan* (1921); *Chayanat* (1923); *Dolan campa* (1923); *Jhine phul* (1923); *Rajbandir jabanbandi* (1923); *Rikter vedan* (1924); *Citta nama* (1925); *Puver haoay* (1925); *Samyavadi* (1925); *Sancita* (1925); *Durdiner yatri* (1926); *Sarvahara* (1926); *Namaskar* (c. 1926); *Bandhan hara* (1927); *Phani manasa* (1927); *Shat bhay campa* (1927); *Sindhu hindol* (1927); *Bulbul, Part I* (1928); *Zinzir* (1928); *Nirjhar* (c. 1928); *Cakravak* (1929); *Cokher catak* (1929); *Sandhya* (1929); *Candrabindu*

(1930); *Jhili-mili* (1930); *Mrtyu-khuda* (1930); *N. gitika* (1930); *Pralayankar* (c. 1930); *Kuhelika* 1931); *Nazrul swarlipi* (1931); *Putuler biye* (1931); *Shiuli mala* (1931); *Aleya* (1932); *Ban giti* (1932); *Siraj* (1932); *Sur saqi* (1932); *Zulfikar* (1932); *Gul bagica* (1933); *Sonali swapan* (1933); *Ganer mala* (1934); *Giti shatadal* (1934); *Sur mukur* (1934); *Suro lipi* (1934); *Rudramangal* (c. 1935); *Maktab sahitya* (1936); *Jivaner jay yatra* (1939); *Nutan cand* (1945); *Maru bhaskar* (1950); *Bulbul, Part II* (1952); *Sancayan* (1957); *Shesh sougat* (1958); *Dhumketu* (1962); *Yugbani* (1970). FURTHER VOLUMES IN ENGLISH: *Selected Poems of Kazi N. I.* (1963); *The Rebel, and Other Poems of Kazi N. I.* (1974); *The Fiery Lyre of N. I.* (1974)

BIBLIOGRAPHY: Rahman, M., *N. I.* (1955); Chaudhury, S., *Introducing N. I.* (1965); Chakravarty, B., *Kazi N. I.* (1968); Haldar, G., *Kazi N. I.* (1974)

CARLO COPPOLA

NDEBELE LITERATURE
See Zimbabwean Literature

NEGOIŢESCU, Ion
Romanian critic and poet, b. 10 Aug. 1921, Cluj

After graduating from secondary school in Cluj, N. majored in literature and philosophy at the University of Cluj, after studying under Lucian Blaga (q.v.) at Sibiu, where with Stefan Augustin Doinaş (q.v.) and others he organized a literary and ideological group that in a flamboyant manifesto (1943) opposed the cultural policies of fascism. After 1947 N.'s work was virtually banned from publication, and he was imprisoned for political reasons between 1961 and 1964. After 1965 he was allowed to publish again and served briefly on the editorial staffs of several literary journals, but he continued his activities of cultural and political dissidence and was subject to harassment and press attacks. Since 1980 he has lived in Cologne, West Germany.

N. was influenced by German romanticism and French surrealism (q.v.). From the beginning, as it later became clear, his purpose was to rewrite Romanian literary history from the point of view of a modern lyrical sensitivity such as had been formed between the two world wars. Most of his critical volumes, from *Scriitori moderni* (1966; modern writers) to *Analize și sinteze* (1976; analyses and syntheses), are collections of fragments of a large historical work, the plan of which he published in an article in 1968. N.'s critical method mixes archetypal elements with empathetic and impressionist procedures; it aims primarily at discovering lyrical and irrational nuclei around which the work is organized. The approach worked best in the study of Mihai Eminescu (1850–1889), Romania's great romantic poet, where it led to the rejection of the sentimental and nostalgic strata of Eminescu's work, which were familiar to the public and had been officially emphasized for decades, in favor of a visionary and eruptive substructure apparent in the posthumously published work of the poet. In discussing contemporary literature, N. has vigorously defended aesthetic values against social and political criteria. He considers his work a continuation of that of Eugen Lovinescu (q.v.) and thus a defense of competence and objective truth against topical interests.

N. also published several volumes of hermetic and erotic poetry, as well as an early surrealist story. His work synthesizes the aesthetic consciousness of Romanian culture in its attempt to offer an alternative to the politicization of human relations.

FURTHER WORKS: *Povestea tristă a lui Ramon Ocg* (1941); *Sabasios* (1968); *Poezia lui Eminescu* (1968); *Eugen Lovinescu* (1970); *Poemele lui Balduin de Tyaormin* (1970); *Însemnări critice* (1970); *Lampa lui Aladin* (1971); *Moartea unui contabil* (1972); *Engrame* (1975); *Un roman epistolar* (1975, with Radu Stanca); *Alte însemnări critice* (1980)

BIBLIOGRAPHY: Nemoianu, V., on *Engrame*, *BA*, 50 (1976), 388–89; Nemoianu, V., "Romanian Revolutions," *TLS*, 8 July 1977, 824; Nemoianu, V., on *Un roman epistolar*, *SEEJ*, 23 (1979), 315–16

VIRGIL NEMOIANU

NEGRITUDE

Negritude emerged in Paris around 1934, among a group of Caribbean and African students including Aimé Césaire (q.v.) from

Martinique and Léopold Sédar Senghor (q.v.) from Senegal. The word itself first appeared in print in Césaire's poem *Cahier d'un retour au pays natal* (1939; *Memorandum on My Martinique,* 1947; later tr., *Return to My Native Land,* 1969). It was only after World War II, in the late 1940s and 1950s, however, that the term and the concept acquired extensive currency. In the minds of its founders, Negritude was a reaction against the French colonial policy of assimilation and especially against the readiness of the older generation to accept assimilation as a goal. Negritude writers asserted instead the existence of an independent African culture and sought to define its distinctive values. They argued that all cultures have distinctive characteristics owing to biological differences between the races.

Although the term has been applied, often very loosely, to a wide variety of French-speaking black writers, there has never been a Negritude school. The concept itself has very little substance, in fact, outside its use by its main founders, Senghor and Césaire, and a few of their contemporaries, such as Léon Gontran Damas and Birago Diop (qq.v.). It is Senghor alone who has, since the end of World War II, consistently developed and expounded Negritude as an ideology in his poetry, speeches, and essays. He has listed and defined the fundamental, permanent values of African culture—emotion, rhythm, religious spirit, community—contrasting them with the European values of reason, skepticism, and individualism.

At first, Senghor viewed these characteristics as conflicting opposites, with the virtue of creativity on the African side. Jean-Paul Sartre (q.v.), in his important essay on Negritude, "Orphée noir" (1948; *Black Orpheus,* 1963), therefore described it as an "antiracist racism." Senghor was, however, more inclined by temperament to reconciliation, and increasingly stressed the complementarity and interdependence of cultures and their evolution toward the "civilization of the universal."

While Césaire, too, stresses some of the African values invoked by Senghor (especially the African's essential quality of emotion as opposed to the European's reason), he has concentrated more on attacking the European stereotype of the black man as a cultural and racial inferior and the black man's readiness to acknowledge this stereotype. In his poetry Césaire presents the black man as much closer to the natural, real world than the white man, and therefore as much more vital and creative. Unlike Senghor, Césaire has not sought to develop Negritude as an ideology and has even tended to avoid the use of the term itself.

Since the 1960s, Negritude has been increasingly criticized by black writers. This criticism has been partly directed against the Negritude definition of African culture, which is seen as being too simplistic and too close to Western racist ideologies, but also against the conservative and neocolonialist politics considered to derive from Senghor's concept of Negritude. It is now being acknowledged, however, that during the 1950s Negritude was very influential in changing black, as well as white, attitudes toward the black peoples of Africa and the Caribbean; Sartre was therefore right to see it, in his 1948 essay, as a crucial but passing historical phenomenon.

BIBLIOGRAPHY: Jahn, J., *Muntu: An Outline of Neo-African Culture* (1961); Jahn, J., *Neo-African Literature: A History of Black Writing* (1969); Moore, G., "The Politics of Negritude," in Pieterse, C., and Munro, D., eds., *Protest and Conflict in African Literature* (1969), pp. 26–42; Adotevi, S., *Négritude et négrologues* (1972); Kesteloot, L., *Black Writers in French: A Literary History of Negritude* (1974); Steins, M., "La Négritude: Un second souffle?" *Cultures et Développement,* 12 (1980), 3–43; Irele, A., *The African Experience in Literature and Ideology* (1981)

CLIVE WAKE

NELLIGAN, Émile

Canadian poet (writing in French), b. 24 Dec. 1879, Montreal, Que.; d. 18 Nov. 1941, Montreal, Que.

Born of an Irish father and French-Canadian mother, N. received a typical 19th-c. classical education. But he dropped out of a Jesuit college at the age of seventeen to devote himself to poetry.

Quebec's first *poète maudit,* N.'s meteoric career was compressed into three years, beginning with the publication of his first poem, "Rêve fantasque" (1896; fantastic dream), which showed his predilection for dream landscapes. In August 1899, schizo-

phrenic, N. entered the mental hospital where he remained until his death.

The apogee of N.'s career was his recitation of "Rêve d'artiste" ("A Poet's Dream," 1960) and "La romance du vin" ("The Poet's Wine," 1960) in May 1899 at a public meeting of the École Littéraire of Montreal, from which he was borne triumphantly on the shoulders of his fellow poets. A first collection of poems, *É. N. et son œuvre* (1904; É. N. and his work) appeared thanks to the efforts of a writer friend, Louis Dantin (pseud. of Eugène Seers, 1865–1945).

Little development marks the 175 poems constituting N.'s corpus, all of which were published in *Poésies complètes, 1896–1899* (1952; complete poems, 1896–1899). The teenager quickly mastered prosody, experimenting with unusual feminine rhymes in his favorite forms, the sonnet and the rondel. The melancholy "Soir d'hiver" ("Winter Evening," 1960) haunts the reader with its verbal melodies. Music, in fact, is a constant theme in N.'s poetry, as is evident in "Tombeau de Chopin" (Chopin's tomb) and "Pour Ignace Paderewski" (for Ignace Paderewski). In "Vieux piano" (old piano) it is associated with memories of childhood and his mother's playing. Above all, N.'s poetry aspires to the state of music, exhibiting the symbolist (q.v.) penchant for synaesthesia in works like "Rythmes du soir" (rhythms of evening).

Despite some Parnassian exoticism and objectivity in the cycle "Pastels et porcelaines" (pastels and porcelains), N.'s poetry is essentially private, the external landscapes composed of artifacts reflexively mirroring his emotions. His objective correlatives correspond, like Baudelaire's, to a black spirit.

N. makes a personal myth of his despair, charting a journey between the heights and the abyss. In his most famous sonnet, "Le vaisseau d'or" ("The Golden Ship," 1960), the ship, his "heart," which he calls "that work of art," falls into the abyss of dream, locus of death and poetry. The paradoxes of Baudelairean romanticism abound: cradle and grave are confounded in "Devant mon berceau" (in front of my cradle), a lament for lost childhood. The interrelationship of creation and destruction, life and death, is located in his repeated symbols: piano, ship of life, chapel, garden of childhood, black virgin, crows.

N.'s obsession with death and madness has assumed the proportions of a national myth in French Canada in light of its development by younger poets, fascinated with the state of life-in-death. Within the poetic movements of the turn of the century N. developed his own imagery and form and determined the direction of modern poetry in Quebec. He was its first great poet.

FURTHER WORK: *Poèmes choisis* (1966). FURTHER VOLUME IN ENGLISH: *Selected Poems* (1960)

BIBLIOGRAPHY: Dantin, L., *Gloses critiques* (1931), pp. 179–99; Lacourcière, L., Introduction to *Poésies complètes* (1952), pp. 7–38; Bessette, G., *Les images en poésie canadienne-française* (1960), pp. 215–75, Wyczynski, P., *É. N.* (1967); Mezei, K., "Lampman and N.: Dream Landscapes," *CRCL,* 6 (1979), 151–65; Mezei, K., "É. N.: A Dreamer Passing By," *CanL,* 87 (1980), 81–99

BARBARA GODARD

NEMEROV, Howard

American poet, critic, and novelist, b. 1 March 1920, New York, N.Y.

N. was graduated from Harvard University in 1941, served briefly as a flyer in World War II, and since that time has taught at a number of colleges and universities, including Bennington, Brandeis, and Washington University in St. Louis. In 1963–64 N. was consultant in poetry to the Library of Congress. He has received many literary awards, and in 1977 was inducted into the American Academy and Institute of Arts and Letters.

Although he is competent and prolific in many genres, N. is best known as a poet. His fictions are, for the most part, entertaining and forgettable: typical is the novel *The Homecoming Game* (1957), which was adapted for the screen as *Tall Story.*

N.'s early poetry draws heavily on biblical themes and is obsessed with the presence of death. At the same time, however, it displays wit, iconoclasm, and an almost haughty technical virtuosity. N.'s attention to formal alignments of verse (sonnets, quatrains, couplets, villanelles, and sestinas) in *Guide to the Ruins* (1950) becomes a kind of obsession. Virtually every poem follows a program to its appointed end. Because of N.'s formalism, many critics treated him harshly in the

decades of the beat poets Allen Ginsberg (q.v.) and Lawrence Ferlinghetti (b. 1919) and of formlessness. The critic M. L. Rosenthal mutes his criticism by calling him an "independent," working apart from the trends and movements of his time, but recognizing N.'s distinct modernity.

N. has composed a number of superb dramatic monologues, in which he tries to capture the temper of the present by using a voice from the mythic past. One of his best-known works in this genre is "Lot Later," in *The Next Room of the Dream* (1962). In this lengthy, rambling, chatty disquisition the biblical character Lot ruminates about the destruction of Sodom and Gomorrah ("the whole/Outfit went up in smoke"), and about his own predicament ("neither permitted the pleasure of his sins/Nor punished for them"). Several of N.'s publications in the 1960s are conceived as poetic dramas, exploring philosophical and aesthetic themes without using any of the poetic forms that had been his mainstay.

In *The Western Approaches* (1975) N. returned to the formalism of his earlier years. Here, however, it is a conscious eccentricity, adapted to precise effect. N. asserts that technology, the preoccupation of the Western mind, represents a profound abstraction, an approach for rediscovering a sense of wonder at the infinite mysteries of the universe.

The musical technology of J. S. Bach is N.'s subject in "Playing the Inventions" in *The Western Approaches.* The "perfect courtesy of music" provides a parallel to poetic thought: it cannot exist without form, it cannot be paraphrased, it cannot know "except by modeling what it would know." This poem combines sensual and intellectual delight, describing shadow-dappled pages of music where the accidents of wind and sun expand upon the incidents of the composer's imagination to create a beatific dream world. There the centuries that separate the poet from the composer "are for a while as thought/Dissolved in the clear streams of your songs."

Science and technology, for N., are not necessarily opposed to human values. The need to catalogue the natural world, to build knowledge by increments, to test, challenge, and probe, to assay proof and root out doubt—these activities arise out of the same spirit that fears the dark, that embraces ritual or superstition, that seeks faith. The two faculties, reason and faith, are not necessarily at war; N. suggests that we do our culture and our intellect a disservice when we worship one at the expense of the other.

Western humanity, at its best, begins by tinkering with the mechanics of an entity (a poem, a miracle, a fugue, a rocket), and ends with the nervous, uncertain belief that there is more to know. As a consummate technician of poetry, N. illuminates the mind's progress from ignorance to knowledge to recognition of a wider ignorance. This progress has always been his subject.

FURTHER WORKS: *The Image & the Law* (1947); *The Melodramatists* (1949); *Federigo; or, The Power of Love* (1954); *The Salt Garden* (1955); *Mirrors and Windows* (1958); *A Commodity of Dreams* (1959); *New and Selected Poems* (1960); *Ender* (1962); *Poetry and Fiction* (1963); *Journal of the Fictive Life* (1965); *The Blue Swallows* (1967); *The Winter Lightning: Selected Poems* (1968); *Stories, Fables, and Other Divisions* (1971); *Reflexions on Poetry & Poetics* (1972); *Gnomes and Occasions* (1973); *The Collected Poems of H. N.* (1977); *Figures of Thought* (1978); *Sentences* (1980)

BIBLIOGRAPHY: Rosenthal, M. L., *The Modern Poets* (1960), pp. 255–62; Hungerford, E. B., ed., *Poets in Progress* (1962), pp. 116–33; Meinke, P., *H. N.* (1968); Duncan, B., ed., *The Critical Reception of H. N.* (1971); Donoghue, D., *Seven American Poets from MacLeish to N.* (1975), pp. 250–88; Labrie, R., *H. N.* (1980)

LARRY TEN HARMSEL

NÉMETH, László

Hungarian novelist, dramatist, essayist, and translator, b. 18 April 1901, Nagybánya (now Baia-Mare, Romania); d. 3 March 1975, Budapest

A physician by training, N. burst on the literary scene in 1925 with a prize-winning short story about the death of a peasant woman, "Horváthné meghal" (Mrs. Horváth dies). Although he grew up in Budapest, N. came from a peasant background, and his knowledge of village life stood him in good stead: his best novels have a rural setting and delve into peasant psyches. Indeed, during the 1930s, after he had made a name for himself as a polemicist as well as a novelist and

playwright, the Hungarian populists looked to N. as the potential ideologist of their movement. But direct involvement in politics was alien to N.'s temperament. Never lacking for disciples and partisans, N. clashed often with his fellow writers and the literary establishment. For a time in the 1930s he edited a periodical, *Tanu,* which was one of those curious ventures not entirely unprecedented in Hungarian literature: a journal written by one man. On the eve of World War II N. formulated his most controversial ideas on race and ethnic viability, for which he was attacked both from the left and the right. After the war he virtually disappeared from the literary scene and for several years earned his living by teaching and translating. Toward the end of his life, however, he was acclaimed both at home and abroad as one of the leading figures in modern Hungarian literature.

N. was a man of bold vision. Basing his ideological conviction on an odd mixture of Nietzschean elitism and Christian and socialist egalitarianism, he became an advocate of a "revolution of quality," that is, a moral revolution. The basic tenet of his writing is that life's deep-seated ills can be remedied only by moral example. Before and during World War II N. rejected both capitalism and communism, believing that the real revolution must take place within the individual's consciousness. This ethical impulse informs virtually all of his novels and plays, which deal invariably with the noble and tragic struggle of individual genius against mass stupidity and intolerance. The names alone of the historical personages around whom he built some of his dramas—Galileo, Jan Hus, Mahatma Gandhi—indicate the nature of his theme.

In subtler, more provocative ways, his novels exemplify the same outlook. The nonconformist hero of *Emberi színjáték* (1929; the human comedy) becomes a Nietzschean moral hero; and the heroines of *Égető Eszter* (2 vols., 1956; Eszter Égető) and *Irgalom* (1965; compassion), although realistically conceived, are symbols of human goodness and endurance. The father of four daughters, N. had a predilection for strong female characters. The novel *Gyász* (1935; mourning), for example, is the finely wrought story of a proud peasant widow whose grief over her husband's death turns into an awe-inspiring obsession. And N.'s best novel, *Iszony* (1947; *Revulsion,* 1965), is about a cold, virginal, but highly sensitive woman's tragic marriage to a jovial, sensuous man. *Bűn* (1936; *Guilt*, 1966) is N.'s most "Russian" novel. The title refers to the guilt felt by thoughtful members of the upper class—here represented by a wealthy intellectual—in the face of social inequality.

Marxist critics have dismissed N.'s ethical-ideological conviction as illusionary utopianism. In his later years N. came to accept Hungarian-style communism. But even in his final works the redeeming power of solitary moral exemplars remains strong.

FURTHER WORKS: *Ember és szerep* (1934); *Kocsik szeptemberben* (1937); *Alsóvárosi búcsú* (1939); *A minőség forradalma* (4 vols., 1940–43); *Lányaim* (1942); *Kisebbségben* (2 vols., 1942); *Magam helyett* (1943); *A Medve utcai polgári* (1943); *Társadalmi drámák* (2 vols., 1958); *Történelmi drámák* (2 vols., 1963); *A kísérletező ember* (1964); *Kiadatlan tanulmányok* (2 vols., 1968); *N. L. munkái* (1969 ff.)

BIBLIOGRAPHY: Kerényi, K., "On L. N.," *HungQ*, 3 (1962), 33–38; Reményi, J., *Hungarian Writers and Literature* (1964), pp. 394–401; Stillwell, R., on *Revulsion, SatR*, 12 March 1966, 36; Ozsvath, Z., "L. N.'s *Revulsion:* Violence and Freedom," *CARHS*, 6 (1979), 67–77; Sanders, I., "Post-Trianon Searching: The Early Career of L. N.," in Király, B. K., Pastor, P., and Sanders, I., eds., *Total War and Peacemaking: A Case Study on Trianon* (1982)

IVAN SANDERS

NENETS LITERATURE
See Finno-Ugric Literatures of the Soviet Union

NEOREALISM

The term "neorealism," first coined by the critic Arnaldo Bocelli (1900–1976) in 1930, describes a movement in modern Italian literature, cinema, and figurative arts. The term has subsequently—and less precisely—been applied by critics writing on other European literatures to identify similar tendencies.

Never organized into a school with specific aesthetic norms or recognized leaders, neorealism was a movement of hybrid compo-

nents, internal ambiguities, and indistinct contours. Therefore, setting chronological limits and identifying chief representatives are quite difficult. In general terms, neorealism can be defined as a trend most important during the period 1930–55 and characterized by a pervasive preoccupation with social issues.

After the opening decades of the century there was a marked return in the Western world to forms of realism: in Russia, coinciding with the Bolshevik revolution, from the cinematic work of Sergey Eisenstein (1898–1948) and Vsevolod Pudovkin (1893–1953) to the establishment of Socialist Realism (q.v.); in Germany, with the literary suggestions of the "new factualism" of the 1920s; in England, with the documentaries of John Grierson (1898–1972) and Basil Wright (b. 1907) depicting the world of the workers. These movements led to seemingly endless polemics in Europe on the function of art as a mode of social commitment, from Jean-Paul Sartre (q.v.) to the present. Within this shared framework, however, neorealism shows unique characteristics ascribable to factors peculiar to the Italian situation: opposition to the Fascist regime and to the bourgeois complicity in it, together with rebellion against the aristocratic view of art as self-sufficient and detached from the conflicts of the real world.

The aim of neorealism was to describe authentically the human condition, the social and political milieu, and the role of the intellectual in it. What results is a tragic sense of human existence, marked by solitude and the absence of communication. The solitude is perceived not elegiacally but historically, with war seen as a deformation, a vision of what man has made of man. From this effort at objectivity, there follows the discovery of a social perspective—a perspective typically focused on the lower classes, with their immediate problems and disarticulated language. Fascism, World War II, and the Resistance all molded the neorealist stance. This era gave rise to a belief in the possibility of creating at least the illusion of a radical revolt against the past and a significant metamorphosis of consciousness—in order to create a new society from zero, to create a new culture.

In literature, the neorealists advocated that the writer be politically involved, at least in terms of healing the traditional rupture between literature and the masses, between the written word and the spoken word. Reality should be approached through a narrative mode following the models of Ernest Hemingway (q.v.), Russian realists like Isaak Babel and Alexandr Fadeev (qq.v), and the Italian writers Cesare Pavese and Elio Vittorini (qq.v.), who were also responsible for introducing the American novel into Italian culture. The result should be a documentary literature, in which facts are viewed as protagonists, a literature that would reject lyrical expression and would instead use an immediate, antirhetorical, spoken, dialectal language. Writers who in varying degree exemplify such a literature are Vasco Pratolini, Francesco Jovine, Italo Calvino, Beppe Fenoglio, Ignazio Silone, Carlo Levi, Giuseppe Berto, Domenico Rea (qq.v.), Silvio Micheli (b. 1911), Renata Viganò (1900–1976), and Oreste Del Buono (b. 1923).

Perhaps it was in the cinema that neorealism attained its most eloquent form. Films like *Roma, città aperta* (1945; *Rome, Open City*) and *Paisà* (1946) by Roberto Rossellini (1906–1977), *Ladri di biciclette* (1948; *Bicycle Thieves*) by Vittorio De Sica (1902–1974), *La terra trema* (1948) by Luchino Visconti (1906–1976), and *Sciuscià* (1946; *Shoeshine*) by De Sica and Cesare Zavattini (b. 1902), among others, have become exemplary of and synonymous with that movement. They were instrumental not only in the expansion of cinematic art but also in the projection of a particular image of Italy to the world.

BIBLIOGRAPHY: Pacifici, S., *A Guide to Contemporary Italian Literature: From Futurism to Neorealism* (1962), pp. 114–49, 226–50; Armes, R., *Patterns of Realism: A Study of Italian Neo-Realist Cinema* (1971)

ANTONINO MUSUMECI

NEPALESE LITERATURE

Poetry

Traditional Sanskrit diction and themes characterized poetry in Nepali in the early 20th c. The *gajal* (ghazal) style, introduced during the 19th c. and used to express witty amorous emotions, lost its appeal as Nepali poets increasingly felt the need to handle the complexities of the modern age. Additionally, the spread of Western education influ-

366

enced the thought and technique of Nepali writers.

According to some critics, modern Nepalese literature began with Lekha Nath Paudyal's (1885–1966) poetic works *Ritu bicar* (1916; thoughts on seasons) and *Satya kali sambad* (1919; conversations of the golden age and iron age), both departures from earlier devotional poetry. Although Paudyal remained in the classical Sanskrit tradition in his meter, precision of expression, and imagery, his poetry is also full of images drawn from modern science, as he expresses a sense of gloom at the growth of technology. Still, even in his much later long reflective poem *Tarun tapasi* (1953; the young ascetic) ancient Vedic philosophy is predominant. He seeks a panacea for inequality, injustice, and the disharmony of the industrial age in religious retreat.

The real break with tradition in Nepalese literature was the poetic play *Mutuko byatha* (1929; heart's agony) by Bal Krishna Sama (b. 1903). Using a genre outside the Sanskrit tradition—tragedy—Sama deals with love, jealousy, compassion, hatred, and avarice.

Nationalism is a recurrent theme in modern Nepalese literature. Paudyal's simple love of country becomes more complex in the poetry of Sama, Laxmi Prasad Devkota (1909–1959), Gopal Prasad Rimal (1916–1973), Bhupi Sherchan (b. 1936), and Kali Prasad Rijal (b. 1940). Sama's patriotism is argumentative and extremely cerebral. Devkota, regarded as the leading modern poet of Nepal, on the other hand, expresses his love with warm and unbridled emotion. Sama's intellectual acrobatics in the long narrative poem *Ciso culho* (1958; cold hearth) is less convincing in its appeal for equality of the castes than is Devkota's *Muna Madan* (1939; Muna and Madan), a narrative poem on a folk theme depicting the pathetic life of a young and beautiful lovelorn wife.

In their early works Sama and Devkota followed Sanskrit metrics. But both turned to prose poems, since they found that the intricacies of modern life could not be expressed in restrictive Sanskrit meters. Sama, in the long poem *Ago ra pani* (1954; fire and water), attacks incompetence, stagnation, and ignorance. The perennial struggle between good and evil is presented with logical precision. Like Sama, Devkota explored the lofty ideals of humanism. In "Pagal" (1953; "Crazy," 1980) he satirizes social maladies and expresses the desire for individual dignity. In the prose poem *Amako sapana* (1942; mother's dream) Rimal decries the appalling tyranny of the Rana oligarchy, and his "Jangi nisan hamro" (1946; our battle ensign) was the first Nepalese song of revolution.

Even after the overthrow of the oligarchy in 1951, Sama, Devkota, Rimal, Sherchan, and Rijal, as well as Vijaya Malla (b. 1925) and Mohan Koirala (b. 1926), wrote poetry attacking continuing conditions of misery and ignorance. Sherchan in "Hami" (1965; we) and Rijal in *Abakas prapta lahureko atamakatha* (1968; autobiography of a retired soldier) use bitter irony to expose economic exploitation and lack of education and freedom. The struggle for emancipation from social malaise is amply present in contemporary Nepalese poetry.

The more traditional Sanskrit style of Paudyal was notably continued by Madhav Prasad Ghimire (b. 1919), especially in the collection *Gauri* (1947; Gauri). But even their works and those of Dharani Dhar Sharma (1893–1980) address contemporary problems of tyranny and injustice. Because of Sharma's Western education his poems focus more on the spread of education and modernization.

Drama

Nepalese drama has been equally successful in depicting contemporary social problems. Influences from Chekhov, Shaw (qq.v.), and Ibsen were adapted to Nepalese themes and settings. In Rimal's plays, for example, women consciously rebel against the age-old cultural and economic bondage. In *Masan* (1946; graveyard) the heroine bolts from her husband's house, since his house for her is nothing but a graveyard where both femininity and rationality are dead.

Sama, in *Boksi* (1942; witch), uses psychoanalysis in his portrayal of the main character and dismisses the traditional belief in witches, and in *Bhater* (1952; feast) he attacks the caste system. Sama's comedies *Mukunda Indira* (1937; Mukunda and Indira) and *Ma* (1945; I) are as brilliant as his many tragedies. The central themes of his plays are humanism and patriotism. *Prempinda* (1952; lump of love) is a vivid and scathing portrait of a Rana despot. His historical plays express national pride in their depiction of heroic historical figures and of revered poets of the past.

Vijaya Malla and Govinda Bahadur Gothale (b. 1922) also experimented with the psychoanalytical approach to character delineation. Gothale's *Cyatieko parda* (1960s; torn blinds) and *Bhusko ago* (1960s; fire of husk) advocate equality for women. The cry for freedom and an end to social abuses reached its height in Malla's *Pattharko katha* (1971; the story of a stone).

The Essay

Social protest in modern Nepalese literature is best represented by the personal essay. Devkota's essays in *Laxmi nibandha sangraha* (1930s; collection of Laxmi's essays) were the first examples of humor and satire in the genre. Later essayistic works of merit are the collections *Khai khai* (1960; please let me have it) by Keshav Raj Pindale (b. 1915) and *Jaya bhudi* (1965; long live the stomach) by Bhairav Arayal (1937–1976). While Devkota's essays are full of poetic imagination, Pindale and Arayal are pure humorists and at times bitter satirists. Scathing criticism of contemporary ills can be found in essays by Shyam Prasad (b. 1929), Bal Krishna Pokharel (b. 1933), and Tara Nath Sharma (b. 1934).

Fiction

Fiction in Nepali is a recent development and is characterized, by and large, by social awareness and agitation for reform. Guru Prasad Mainali's (1900–1971) short stories, which first appeared in the 1930s, are about poverty, inequality, and superstition. These stories paved the way for modern Nepali fiction.

"Biha" (1938; marriage) and "Shatru" (1938; foe), short stories by Bishweshwar Prasad Koirala (b. 1915), are effective attacks on social injustices. Pushkar Shumshere Rana (1902–1961), in "Paribanda" (1938; circumstantial evidence) and other stories, describes rampant evils in Nepalese society. Sama, in the stories "Parai ghar" (1935; stranger's home) and "Sharan" (1938; shelter), also explored deep-rooted social problems, and this approach was pursued by Ramesh Bikal (b. 1932) in the collection *Naya sadakko git* (1960; song of New Road).

The psychological short story was introduced by B. P. Koirala with "Candrabadan" (1935; Candrabadan). His "Karnelko ghoda"

(1949; the colonel's horse) is a supreme example of psychoanalytical technique. In the novels *Tin ghumti* (1969; three turnings) and *Narendra dai* (1970; brother Narendra) Koirala gives a sweeping picture of the mental states of modern Nepalese, dealing with conflicts that arise from the disintegration of traditional values.

Bhavani Bhikshu (1914–1981) wrote many stories exploring the psychology of women; representative is the novelette *Paip nambar dui* (1977; pipe number two). In Bhikshu's fiction female characters display a rare quality among Nepalese—intellectual curiosity—but they are almost always victims of their own frailties. Vijaya Malla's novel *Anuradha* (1961; Anuradha) probes the mind of an educated woman victimized by her husband.

Sama's story "Taltal" (1936; persistent desire) and Tarini Prasad Koirala's (1922–1974) novel *Sarpa damsa* (1969; snakebite) delve deeply into child psychology. In both works the pure and innocent world of children is contrasted with the ugly and selfish world of adults.

The Rana regime is presented in two novels, *Basanti* (1949; Basanti) and *Seto bagh* (1974; white tiger), by Diamond Shumshere Rana (b. 1919). In *Eka deshki maharani* (1960s; princess of a certain country), by Keshav Raj Pindali, the secret tortures perpetrated on servants and innocent poor people inside the Rana mansions are vividly exposed. (The horrors of the Rana age, however, are best described in *Jelma bis barsa* [1975; twenty years in jail], the autobiography of Khadga Man Singh [b. 1908].)

History is not only an account of rulers. The novels *Basai* (1960s; moving out) by Lil Bahadur Kshatri (b. 1932) and *Ek paluwa anekau yam* (1968; a young shoot in many seasons) by Daulat Bikram Bista (b. 1926) depict the misery of the masses under the Rana aristocrats.

A kaleidoscopic picture of a noble family whose old values are collapsing under the impact of political and social upheaval is beautifully presented in *Agat* (1975; oncoming), a novel by Bhikshu. It is a story of changing Nepal, a country trying to take its place in the comity of developing nations.

BIBLIOGRAPHY: Subedi, A., *Nepali Literature: Background and History* (1978)

MANINDRA K. VERMA
TARA NATH SHARMA

NERUDA, Pablo

(pseud. of Neftalí Reyes Basualto) Chilean poet, b. 12 July 1904, Parral; d. 23 Sept. 1973, Santiago

Although N. did not receive the Nobel Prize for literature until 1971, he was already considered to be the most important Spanish American poet of the 20th c. because of his innovative techniques and contributions to most major trends and formal developments of the genre.

After his mother's death when he was just a month old, N.'s family moved to Temuco. N. attended schools there and came to Santiago to study French at the University of Chile. By his twentieth birthday N. had already published several books of poetry, including the international best seller, *Veinte poemas de amor y una canción desesperada* (1924; *Twenty Love Poems and a Song of Despair,* 1969), which established his reputation.

N. soon obtained an appointment in the Chilean diplomatic service and was sent to Burma as Chilean consul in Rangoon. While in the Far East (1927–31) N. completed the first volume of *Residencia en la tierra* (1933; *Residence on Earth,* 1946; later tr., 1973). After returning to Chile in 1933, N. was reassigned to Buenos Aires, where he befriended the Spanish poet Federico García Lorca (q.v.). When N. was named Chilean consul in Barcelona in 1934, García Lorca and other Spanish poets of the Generation of 1927 hailed him as a major voice of Hispanic poetry. N. published his second *Residencia en la tierra* (1935; *Residence on Earth,* 1946; later tr., 1973) volume in Spain.

After the outbreak of the Spanish Civil War, N. changed the course of his life and poetry. Beginning with his book *España en el corazón* (1937; *Spain in the Heart,* in *Residence on Earth, and Other Poems,* 1946), N.'s poetry became less personal and depicted the sociopolitical concerns of man from a socialist ideological perspective. N. partipated actively in leftist political causes until he announced his membership in the Chilean Communist Party in 1945. As early as 1938, N. had organized support for the Spanish Republic and found asylum for Spanish refugees in Chile. While still a diplomat assigned to Mexico City, N. provoked the ire of pro-Nazi groups because of his public support of the Soviet Union. N. was assaulted by Nazis in

Cuernavaca in 1941, and his poem praising the defenders of Stalingrad produced such controversy that he was forced to relinquish his diplomatic post.

N. visited the Incan ruins of Macchu Picchu in 1943 and was inspired to write his acclaimed poem, *Alturas de Macchu Picchu* (1943; *The Heights of Macchu Picchu,* 1967), which was later incorporated into *Canto general* (1950; general song). His last volume of *Residencia en la tierra* (1947; *Residence on Earth,* 1973) contained poems written between 1935 and 1945. N. was elected to the Chilean senate in 1946, and when he denounced the government's anticommunist witch hunt, he was indicted and forced to flee his country in 1949 as a political exile. During this period he traveled extensively, finished *Canto general,* and met Matilde Urrutia, who later became his wife and inspired most of his mature love poetry. While in exile, N. was awarded the Stalin Prize for literature and the Lenin Peace Prize. He returned to Chile in 1952.

N.'s work cannot be easily classified within a single movement or style because it constantly changed and evolved as the personal and historical circumstances of his life and world were altered. Most critics arrange N.'s poetry according to different cyles or periods of development. Nevertheless, there are thematic and stylistic constants present throughout his work. His themes include an obsession with the sensual and material objects of the natural world and human society; an interest in both the frustration and enjoyment of material and erotic pleasures, especially in relation to telluric forces and the organic cycle of nature; a heroic view of the poet as a spokesman for the voiceless; recurring mythical archetypes; and the illogical association of images as found in dreams and the subconscious. N. assumed varying poetic personae or masks, eventually voicing not only his personal concerns but also the universal aspirations of the common man of the Third World for social justice, dignity, and respect. In style, N. made use of a wide range of techniques: the expansive employment of hermetic metaphors and polysemic imagery; chaotic enumerations of concrete objects; reiteration, alliteration, and interior rhyme; an alternating application of free unpunctuated verse and more conventional metric forms and syntax; and shifts in point of view and tone expressed by multiple voices.

Veinte poemas de amor y una canción desesperada is now considered to be a classic of Hispanic erotic poetry. It represented the highest achievement of N.'s early poetry because it marked his first successful attempt to write a book with a central theme and cohesive vision. Although the book still retained some trappings of the modernist (q.v.) style, it initially shocked some critics because of its prosaic language and explicit celebration of amorous ecstasy, lovemaking, and heartbreak. This book led to a series of subsequent volumes dedicated to erotic themes, in which woman is represented as both an alluring seductress and man's vital link with mother-earth and the cycles of nature. N. broadened and enriched his vision of love in *Cien sonetos de amor* (1959; one hundred love sonnets) and *Los versos del capitán* (1952; *The Captain's Verses,* 1972).

Tentativa del hombre infinito (1926; attempt for the infinite man) is now regarded as one of N.'s major works, although it was misunderstood and overlooked for many years by the critics. It represented an important transitional phase between the lucid, more conventional lyricism of *Veinte poemas de amor y una canción desesperada* and the dense hermetic language of *Residencia en la tierra.* As the book's title implied, it signified a bold new experiment and a departure from N.'s earlier poetry. Here, N. attempted to create a new poetic system, which better reflected the poet's inner torment, together with an anguished vision of a disordered and disintegrating cosmos. This book marked the first use of interior monologue in N.'s poetry, as he broke with conventional punctuation, syntax, rhyme, and stanzaic organization.

The first volume of *Residencia en la tierra* initiated a period in N.'s poetry that critics have called his *Residencia* cycle. Most poems of Volume I were written in the Far East at a time of loneliness and personal crisis. Although critics have often viewed the three volumes of the cycle as a unit because of their apparent continuity, one can discern differences in emphases and style as well as a progressive shift in tone in each book, as the poet moved from existential pessimism to resignation and, ultimately, to an optimistic faith in a political solution for the world's problems. "Galope muerto" ("Dead Gallop," 1946), the introductory poem of Volume I, set the pessimistic tone of frustration for the entire book as well as providing its central theme, a vision of life in perpetual disintegration driven on a whirlwind dash toward death and oblivion.

Volume II of the *Residencia* cycle signaled a shift in poetic diction and posture. Interior monologue was replaced by a dialogue with the reader, as the poet came to realize the necessity of communicating with an audience and assumed a more public voice and declamatory style. The introspective soul-searching and dense language of the first volume was supplanted by a lighter, more digressive style and a more extroverted outlook. The poet spoke more directly to his reader and became more resigned to life's vicissitudes and less guilty about his inability to find an explanation for life's paradoxes. The images became more realistic and less "purely poetic." This movement away from a private, lyrical stance in Volume II toward a public voice and narrative style would become more pronounced as N.'s work evolved.

The publication of the third *Residencia* volume consummated the cyclical evolution of N.'s poetry: he turned away from egocentric angst toward an open espousal of social concern and ideological commitment. The poem "Las furias y las penas" ("The Furies and the Sorrows," 1973) was a poetic confession that the author's verse had changed as both his personal circumstances and the world itself had become transformed during two turbulent decades in which humanity had witnessed economic depression, the Spanish Civil War, the outbreak of World War II, and the triumph over fascism. Because of its marked political character, the last volume of the *Residencia* cycle was the most controversial: N. sought to persuade the reader that his new-found ideological commitment offered the only solution for a world in turmoil.

N.'s next major work, *Canto general,* was even more explicitly political and autobiographical, but many critics consider it to be N.'s masterpiece because of the artistry with which he effectively communicated his theme of the historic quest and epic struggle of the Latin American for social justice from time immemorial to the moment of the poet's own persecution and exile for his political ideas. The book's obvious Marxist content was presented in the lucid narrative style of the epic, whereby each canto could be read like a chapter from a novel and contained its own theme but was linked sequentially and the-

matically to the entire poem. Cinematic effects and the documentary character of a newsreel are achieved by shifting multiple narrators who dramatize events or disclose factual information at opportune moments through their narrative commentaries. N. re-created and mythified Latin American history in accordance with Marxist philosophy, attempting to raise the reader's social consciousness and enlist his support for the Communist cause. These shifts in point of view created a distancing effect that enabled N. to make his arguments more convincing.

The publication of *Odas elementales* (1954; *Elementary Odes,* 1961) inaugurated a new cycle in N.'s poetry. It also marked another break with his previous poetics, as he turned from the grandiose and heroic tone of the epic poem to a humorous and occasionally sardonic exaltation of the most banal objects and aspects of daily life. His language became more plainspoken and apparently artless and free of any ideological purpose. Through his odes, N. finally was able to write for the people. The odes departed from the classic tradition of employing only well-defined metric forms. They were written in free verse with a thematic orientation both lyrical and public in character. By writing about ordinary objects like fruits and vegetables, he made these subjects worthy of the solemn and serious tradition of the ode. N. wrote in a jocular and benign tone, implicitly mocking the tradition of the conventional ode. N. wrote three more books of odes, his writing becoming for the first time an act of sheer pleasure and entertainment free of soul-searching or explicit ideological commitment.

One of his major works, *Estravagario* (1958; *Extravagaria,* 1972) began the last stage of N.'s poetry, in which he returned to egocentric concerns, self-indulgence, and frivolous individuality. Like Whitman, N. wrote a song about himself, but in an irreverent tone of self-parody and criticism of his own life and works. The book was unashamedly personal in the poet's return to some of the earliest themes of his poetic repertory. He used humor to mock his own previously held conception of the poetic artist as a hero endowed with special gifts. In N.'s new anti-poetry the poem was viewed as an entertaining word game. Rhetoric and graphic effects complemented one another. The poet's personal experience was made ironic and his work desanctified. Through *Estravagario* N. was able to extricate himself from his own literary tradition of personal and social concerns, while pointing toward the varied directions the books of his final decade would take. Among the more salient tendencies of N.'s last decade of poetry are his politically committed verse with touches of didacticism and satire; the simple, humorous poetry of everyday living; the antipoetic and parodic strophes devoted to the theme of the absurd; and the more solemn and prophetic lyricism present in his work since "Alturas de Macchu Picchu." Often these diverse tendencies would converge and overlap in different books as N. furiously sought to bring his poetic outpouring full circle before succumbing to cancer in 1973.

FURTHER WORKS: *Crepusculario* (1923); *El habitante y su esperanza* (1926); *Anillos* (1926); *El hondero entusiasta* (1933); *Las uvas y el viento* (1954); *Viajes* (1955); *Nuevas odas elementales* (1956); *Tercer libro de odas* (1957); *Navegaciones y regresos* (1959); *Canción de gesta* (1960; *Song of Protest,* 1976); *Las piedras de Chile* (1961); *Cantos ceremoniales* (1961); *Plenos poderes* (1962; *Fully Empowered,* 1976); *Memorial de Isla Negra* (5 vols.: *Donde nace la lluvia; La luna en el laberinto; El fuego cruel; El cazador de raíces; Sonata crítica;* 1964; *Isla Negra: A Notebook,* 1981); *Arte de pájaros* (1966); *Una casa en la arena* (1966); *Fulgor y muerte de Joaquín Murieta* (1967; *The Splendor and Death of Joaquín Murieta,* 1972); *La Barcarola* (1968); *Las manos del día* (1968); *Fin del mundo* (1969); *Aún* (1969); *Comiendo en Hungría* (1969); *La espada encendida* (1970); *Las piedras del cielo* (1970); *Geografía infructuosa* (1972); *La rosa separada* (1972); *Incitación al Nixoncidio y alabanza de la revolución chilena* (1973; *A Call for the Destruction of Nixon and Praise for the Chilean Revolution,* 1980); *El mar y las campanas* (1973); *Jardín de invierno* (1974); *El corazón amarillo* (1974); *Libro de las preguntas* (1974); *Elegía* (1974); *Defectos escogidos* (1974); *2,000* (1974); *Confieso que he vivido: Memorias* (1974; *Memoirs,* 1977); *Elrío invisible: Poesía y prosa de juventud* (1980) FURTHER VOLUMES IN ENGLISH: *Three Spanish American Poets: Pellicer, N., Andrade* (1942); *Three Material Songs* (1948); *Selected Poems* (1961); *Twenty Poems* (1967); *We Are Many* (1967); *A New De-cade: Poems 1958–1967* (1969); *P. N.: The Early Poems* (1969); *New Poems: 1968–1970* (1972); *Selected Poems of P. N.* (1972); *Five Decades: Poems 1925–1970* (1974)

BIBLIOGRAPHY: Alonso, A., *Poesía y estilo de P. N.* (1940); Alazraki, J., *Poética y poesía de P. N.* (1965); Loyola, H., *Ser y morir en P. N.* (1967); Ellis, K., "Poema XX, a Structural Approach," *RomN,* 11 (1970), 507–17; Riess, F. J., *The Word and the Stone: Language and Imagery in N.'s "Canto general,"* (1972); "Focus on P. N.'s *Residence on Earth,*" special section, *Review,* No. 11 (1974), 6–37; Kauffmann, L., "N.'s Last Residence: Translations and Notes on Four Poems," *NewS,* 5 (1975), 119–41; Rodríguez Monegal, E., *N.: El viajero inmóvil* (1977); Camacho Guizado, E., *P. N.: Naturaleza, história y poética* (1978); Rosales, L., *La poesía de N.* (1978); Costa, R. de, *The Poetry of P. N.* (1979); Alegría, F., "The State and the Poet: An Art of Resistance," *PCP,* 15 (1980), 1–9; Felstiner, J., *Translating N.: The Way to Macchu Picchu* (1980); Durán, M., and Safir, M., *Earth Tones: The Poetry of P. N.* (1981); Santi, E. M., *P. N.: The Poetics of Prophecy* (1982)

JAMES J. ALSTRUM

By becoming a political poet, N. faced a serious dilemma: how to meet his obligation as a militant, which demanded from him simplicity and social realism in literature, and at the same time maintain the hermetic beauty of his surrealist art. He would have to either purify his poetry of all decadent elements or give up revolutionary militancy. He could not, of course, follow either of these paths. In *Canto general* he openly condemned the poetry of his youth—everything written before *España en el corazón*—and proclaimed his faith in the social function of art. He would be a popular poet, to be sure, optimistic, dynamic in his expression of the world of the future. Nevertheless, in the purest and deepest zone of his poetry, N. continued to be a surrealist and, as a consequence, remained incomprehensible for the masses. It would be a serious error to doubt his sincerity, as it would be to believe that his political message fell on deaf ears because of the complex literary form in which it is expressed. . . .

Fernando Alegría, *Las fronteras del realismo: Literatura chilena del siglo XX* (1962), pp. 184–85

The N. we have come to expect is a poet in which one of the essentials of great poetry, continual surprise and revelation *in the language itself,* is always present. The typical *form* which that revelation assumes in his work is that of the unexpected coupling of qualities, or of the discovery of unexpected analogies and "irrational" relationships—"a swan of felt," "rawhide tranquility," an "explosion of feathers," "a proletariat of petals and bullets," "destitute bread." In many ways N. seems to be the poet of the adjective. Generally, adjectives simply add or subtract. N.'s multiply—or, better yet: transform; and they do this by discovering new qualities in *objects*.... Perhaps the best way to put it is to say that N. is the poet of the transformation of nouns.

Thomas McGrath, "The Poetry of P. N.," *Mainstream,* 15, 6 (1962), 44

There are so many N.s, so many manners—his early apprenticeship to Modernism, the wild and sometimes incoherent extravagance of his three *Residencias,* the prophetic and incantatory tone of his *Canto general,* the political travelogues in *Las uvas y el viento,* the intimacy and humour of the three books of Odes, and then the lucidity and serenity of all he has written since *Estravagario* in 1958. He has always been not so much looking for a new style as discarding his previous one, like a worn lizard skin. For this reason, everyone has his own N.; and for this reason, his work has provoked the whole gamut of criticism, from hatred to idolatry, to all of which he is indifferent. He has to be taken whole, or not at all. But there is such a lot to take! What N. has done is to keep bursting at the seams, breaking the sound barrier, swallowing the world whole and regurgitating it in an endless stream of poems that he seems to leave behind him like footprints—one might as well mix the metaphor, for N. certainly would not hesitate to do so. He has not bothered to write much *about* poetry; he has too much poetry on the boil all the time....

Alastair Reid, "A Visit to N.," *Encounter,* Sept. 1965, 67

Each important book, each distinct period of N.'s poetic career produced not only *poetry* but also a *persona*.... In the course of his long career, N. has projected several distinct personae in his poetry: the lost boy amidst the west winds of the hostile city in his first book, *Crepusculario;* the enthusiastic soldier who is enraptured by the contemplation of infinite space ... the new American Bécquer who reveals the melancholy and desperate art of adolescent love to several generations; the unrestrained and disconnected poet of *Tentativa del hombre infinito* ... the somnambulistic, terrified spectator of a world undergoing a permanent process of disintegration, which *Residencia en la tierra* documents; the witness who has seen the blood in the streets and creates a deliberately impure poetry to transmit the stupor and hope of

España en el corazón; the narrator who rises from the nourishing sand and the ocean to sing the glory and the misery of Latin America in *Canto general;* the satisfied and amorous traveler of the world who orders his poetic duties in *Las uvas y el viento;* the popular poet who plays the guitar of the poor man in order to sing ... [in] *Odas elementales ...;* the contemplative poet who turns his gaze more and more toward his own life and lets loose the powerful forces of memory in the autobiographical book that is the culmination of his poetry [*Los versos del capitán*].

Emir Rodríguez Monegal, *El viajero inmóvil: Introducción a P. N.* (1966), p. 20

The tendency to self-imitation makes the *Canto general* a watershed in the development of his poetry; it synthesizes much of the previous work and clarifies abiding associations between major images which N. had not fully worked out in his earlier poetry. Finally, the *Canto general* provides him with a set of themes that he never abandons, especially the social, historical and political phenomena set down in the poem.... The reason why he refuses to forgo these themes is that N. has always sought to discover in his poetry the nature of man: to do this, he has to find his way back to an understanding of how man is related to nature.

Frank Riess, *The Word and the Stone: Language and Imagery in N.'s "Canto general"* (1972), p. 164

N. was a poet of many styles and many voices, one whose multitudinous work is central to almost every important development in twentieth-century Spanish and Spanish American poetry. He was once referred to as the Picasso of poetry, alluding to his protean ability to be always in the vanguard of change. And he himself has often alluded to his personal struggle with his own tradition, to his constant need to search for a new system of expression in each book. N. was, until very recently in his later years, a poet perpetually in revolution against himself, against his own tradition.

René de Costa, *The Poetry of P. N.* (1979), p. 1

NERVO, Amado
Mexican poet, b. 27 Aug. 1870, Tepic; d. 24 May 1919, Montevideo, Uruguay

A student of theology and jurisprudence, N. practiced briefly as a lawyer in provincial Mazatlán before moving to Mexico City, where he worked as a journalist from 1894 to 1898. The publication of his naturalistic novel *El bachiller* (1895; the bachelor of arts) quickly established his name in Mexican literary circles. N. contributed to the famed modernist (q.v.) *Revista azul,* a magazine that reflected the influence of the French symbolists (q.v.). In 1900, as a member of the Mexican press, he traveled to Paris, where he met the famous modernist poet Rubén Darío (q.v.). In 1905 N. entered the diplomatic corps, serving as secretary of the Mexican legation in Madrid (1905–18) and minister to Argentina and Uruguay (1919).

Although he wrote short stories in the fantastic vein, such as *Cuentos misteriosos* (1921; mysterious tales), and literary criticism, including a long study on the Mexican poet Sor Juana Inés de la Cruz (1651–1695), N. is recognized primarily as a poet. His evolution as a writer can be seen in three periods. His verse written prior to 1900—*Perlas negras* (1898; black pearls) and *Poemas* (1900; poems)—reflects the strong influence of the Mexican writer Manuel Gutiérrez Nájera (1859–1895) and the preoccupation of the early modernists with Parnassian poetic themes and forms. Even at this early stage, however, in poems such as "A Kempis" (1898; A Kempis) N. exhibited an abiding interest with spiritual concerns.

N.'s second and most prolific period coincides with his stay in Europe and his association with Darío. In collections such as *Los jardines interiores* (1905; the inner gardens), *En voz baja* (1909; in a low voice), and *Serenidad* (1914; serenity), N. became increasingly introspective; modernist pomp yielded to metaphysical anguish. The death of Ana Cecilia Luisa Dalliez, the woman he loved, inspired his best-known book, *La amada inmóvil* (1920; the motionless lover), a collection of poems that reflects the intense personal anguish caused by the loss of his beloved and marks the last period in his evolution. N's preoccupation with death, his growing pantheism, and his progression toward simplicity are clearly evidenced in *El estanque de los lotos* (1919; the lotus pond), his last collection of poetry.

Together with Gutiérrez Nájera, N. is considered Mexico's most important writer of the modernist period. Prolific and varied, N. exerted considerable influence on Mexican literature.

FURTHER WORKS: *Místicas* (1898); *El donador de almas* (1899); *La hermana agua* (1901); *El éxodo y las flores del camino* (1902); *Lira heroica* (1902); *Almas que pasan* (1906); *El glosario de la vida vulgar* (1916);

El diablo desinteresado (1916); *El diamante de la inquietud* (1917); *Una mentira* (1917); *Un sueño* (1917); *Elevación* (1917); *Plentitud* (1918; *Plenitude,* 1928); *El sexto sentido* (1918); *Amnesia* (1918); *Parábolas, y otros poemas* (1918); *El arquero divino* (1922); *Obras completas* (2 vols., 1967). FURTHER VOLUME IN ENGLISH: *Confessions of a Modern Poet* (1935)

BIBLIOGRAPHY: Meléndez, C., *A. N.* (1926); Wellman, E. T., *A. N.: Mexico's Religious Poet* (1936); Montellano, B. O. de, *Figura, amor y muerte de A. N.* (1943); Leal, L., "La poesía de A. N.," *Hispania,* 43 (1960), 43–47; García Prado, C., "A. N.," *Américas,* 22, 10 (1970), 9–14

EDWARD MULLEN

NESİN, Aziz

(pseud. of Mehmet Nusret Nesin) Turkish satirist, short-story writer, novelist, and dramatist, b. 1915, Istanbul

Born into a lower-middle-class family, N. first received traditional Muslim education and then was admitted to the Orphans' School on account of his family's poverty. He later enrolled in military colleges. N. began his professional writing career as a journalist in 1944, when he resigned his military commission. Two years later, in collaboration with the short-story writer Sabahattin Ali (1907–1948), he began publishing a highly popular satirical magazine of leftist leanings, *Marko Paşa,* which was closed several times by the authorities, only to reappear under a different name. Struggling to earn a living in these early years, N. also worked as a grocer, photographer, bookseller, and accountant. On account of his socialism, he was prosecuted several times, and was sentenced to prison terms in 1947 and 1950.

A period of silence until 1954 was followed by a second beginning of N.'s prolific career. The next two years saw the publication of a novel, *Kadın olan erkek* (1955; the man who became a woman) and four volumes of short stories. The title story of *Fil Hamdi* (1956; Fil Hamdi) earned the Italian Golden Palm Award (1956). "Fil Hamdi," along with the title story of *Kazan töreni* (1957; ceremony for a boiler)—a story for which he won the Golden Palm Award for the second year running—are satirical masterpieces dwelling on the absurdities of officialdom. The helplessness of the individual against the ridiculous but powerful bureaucracy is a major theme of N.'s stories: "İnsanlar uyanıyor" (1969; people are waking up), tells, with pathos and humor, of how a paroled political convict comes to terms with life after prison. N.'s stories about the absurdities of everyday life and habits are more overtly comic.

Most of N.'s novels are conceived as lengthier versions of his short stories and reflect his interest in satire over plot. He excels in presenting types rather than developing characters. *Zübük* (1961; Zübük) tells the story of a charlatan from the viewpoint of several characters cheated by him. In some works of fiction N. also successfully employs the narrative techniques of the tale in creating a version of humorous parable.

N. has written numerous plays, ranging from farces to existentialist dramas. The exuberance that marks his satires is noticeably absent from his best-known plays, which examine the loneliness and meaninglessness of life. *Çiçu* (1969; Çiçu) reveals the near total alienation of a man who is capable of living only with his plants, pets, and inflatable doll.

N.'s childhood experiences served to heighten his awareness of the pathetic and ludicrous aspects of human life at the mercy of social forces. In his memoirs, *Böyle gelmiş böyle gitmez* (2 vols., 1966, 1972; *Istanbul Boy*, 2 vols., 1977, 1979), he focuses on the contrasts between the lifestyles of the rich and the poor; between the enormous piety of his parents and the profligate degeneracy in the side streets of a metropolis in transition; and between the traditionalism of the lower middle class and the rapid modernization undertaken by the newly established republic. His later confrontations with officialdom reinforced his idealism. N.'s piercing satire derives from the tension between his profound social commitment and the extravagant way in which he portrays absurd situations.

N.'s work appeals to a broad range of readership. Along with Yaşar Kemal (q.v.), he is one of the two best-selling authors in Turkey. N.'s work has been translated into twenty-five languages and has won various foreign prizes. Because of the particular cultural context and N.'s special sense of humor, however, his work does not lend itself easily to translation into English.

FURTHER WORKS: *Azizname* (1948); *Geriye kalan* (1948); *It kuyruğu* (1955); *Yedek parça* (1955); *Düğülü mendil* (1955); *Damda

deli var (1956); *On dakika* (1957); *Koltuk* (1957); *Gol kralı* (1957); *Toros canavarı* (1957); *Deliler boşandı* (1957); *Hangi parti kazanacak* (1957); *Ölmüş eşek* (1957); *Bir sürgünün hatıraları* (1957); *Erkek Sabahat* (1957); *Mahallenin kısmeti* (1957); *Havadan sudan* (1958); *Bay düdük* (1958); *Nazik âlet* (1958); *Memleketin birinde* (1958); *Biraz gelir misiniz* (1958); *Gıdıgıdı* (1958); *Nutuk makinesi* (1958); *Kördöğüşü* (1959); *Aferin* (1959); *Az gittik uz gittik* (1959); *Mahmut ile Nigar* (1959); *Saçkıran* (1959); *Bir şey yap Met* (1959); *Ah biz eşekler* (1960); *Gözüne gözlük* (1960); *Hoptirinam* (1960); *Bir koltuk nasıl devrilir* (1961); *Yüz liraya bir deli* (1961); *Biz adam olmayız* (1962); *Namus gazı* (1964); *Sosyalizm geliyor savulun* (1965); *Canavar* (1965); *Rıfat bey neden kaşınıyor* (1965); *İhtilâli nasıl yaptık* (1965); *Şimdiki çocuklar harika* (1967); *Poliste* (1967); *Vatan sağolsun* (1968); *Düdükçülerle fırçacıların savaşı* (1968); *Üç karagöz oyunu* (1969); *Tut elimden Rovni* (1970); *Hadi öldürsene* (1970); *Merhaba* (1971); *Leylâ ile Mecnun* (1972); *Hayvan deyip de geçme* (1973); *Tatlı Betüş* (1974); *Bu yurdu bize verenler* (1975); *Borçlu olduklarımız* (1976); *Surname* (1976); *Seyyahatname* (1976); *Pırtlatan bal* (1976); *Duyduk duymadık demeyin* (1976); *Yaşar ne yaşar ne yaşamaz* (1977); *Dünya kazan ben kepçe* (1977); *Büyük grev* (1978); *Tek yol* (1978); *Beş kısa oyun* (1979)

BIBLIOGRAPHY: Halman, T. S., "Turkish Literature in the 1960's," *LitR*, 15 (1972), 387–402

AHMET Ö. EVIN

NETHERLANDS LITERATURE

Dutch Literature

At the beginning of the 20th c. the literature of the Netherlands was still dominated by the artistic ideals and methods of the Beweging van Tachtig (Movement of the Eighties)—the literary and spiritual upheaval that in the 1880s had raised Dutch culture from the slough of mediocrity in which it had been sunk for close to two centuries. The program of this movement, although enunciated with all the polemic violence of which brash youth is capable, had been strangely indecisive, being indebted both to Zola's naturalism and to the impressionism of French painting. It was also strongly influenced by English romantic poetry. The poems of Jacques Perk (1859–1881), dead at the age of twenty-two, borrowed from Shelley, and Herman Gorter's (1864–1927) *Mei* (1889; May), one of the principal monuments of the movement, was modeled on Keats's *Endymion*. The aesthetics of the Movement of the Eighties, particularly in poetry, constituted a highly unstable compound, and it was bound to dissolve.

As the 20th c. got under way, Willem Kloos (1859–1938) proved to be the only one of the Eighties group who clung stubbornly to the radical individualism that had originally characterized the movement. Albert Verwey (q.v.) came to stress more and more the opposed values of the communal—the claims of society and brotherhood as opposed to those of the individual. Frederick van Eeden (q.v.) sought spiritual direction first in Thoreau, later in Roman Catholicism; and Gorter turned to communism, as did Henriette Roland Holst van den Schalk (q.v.). The individual and the community—the tension between these concepts is, to be sure, found at all times and in all places, at least in the West, but it has always had a particular thematic prominence in Dutch culture. The intransigent individualism cultivated by the Beweging van Tachtig was bound to be followed by a reaction.

In style as well as in theme, lyric poetry in the first quarter of the century developed away from the belated romanticism of Tachtig. Verwey, partly under the influence of his German friend Stefan George (q.v.), moved in the direction of symbolism, as did such younger poets as J. H. Leopold (q.v.), Pieter Cornelis Boutens (q.v.), and Adriaan Roland Holst (q.v.). A chastened classicism of expression also manifested itself in Leopold and Boutens (both of whom were classical scholars), and the influence of W. B. Yeats (q.v.) was as important for Roland Holst as that of George was for Verwey. Classicism is also a feature of the poetic work of Jacobus Cornelis Bloem (1887–1966), who was associated with Verwey and Verwey's journal *De beweging;* Bloem explored the themes of nostalgia and regret.

Poetry has historically been the dominant form in the literature of the Netherlands, in contrast to the Flemish part of Belgium, where fiction has been more eminent. There are exceptions, of course: Multatuli (pseud.

of Eduard Douwes Dekker, 1820–1887), author of the novel *Max Havelaar* (1860; *Max Havelaar,* 1868), the only giant figure in Dutch literature between the 17th c. and the 1880s; or Simon Vestdijk (q.v.) in our own time. Still, in the 20th c. the old pattern has been basically repeated. The poetic dramas of van Eeden proved essentially for the study alone; the only significant dramatist of the early 20th c. was Herman Heijermans (q.v.), whose *Op hoop van zegen* (1901; *The Good Hope,* 1928) enjoyed great popularity in the early years of the century. Heijermans was a naturalist, but, like his coeval Gerhart Hauptmann (q.v.), he made occasional excursions into the fantastic, as, for example, in *Uitkomst* (1907; deliverance).

The greatest Dutch novelist of the early part of the century was Louis Couperus (q.v.). Although he had many affinities with the Movement of the Eighties, he remained, as both artist and man, somewhat aloof from the group. His early novel *Eline Vere* (1889; *Eline Vere,* 1892) was markedly naturalistic; later works such as *Van oude mensen, de dingen die voorbijgaan* (1906; *Old People and the Things That Pass,* 1918) and *De boeken der kleine zielen* (4 vols., 1901–3; *The Books of the Small Souls,* 1914) revealed more subtle gifts of psychological perception. Couperus was a notable stylist, occasionally "precious" in a fin-de-siècle manner, but clearly a master of verbal art. His oeuvre also includes a series of historical novels set in antiquity at the time of its decadence.

The curious alliance of naturalism and aestheticism that Couperus was able to effect in so masterful a way is also to be noted in *Een liefde* (1888; a love) by Lodewijk van Deyssel (q.v.) and in the fiction of Marcellus Emants (1848–1923). Van Deyssel, the ideologue and polemicist of the Movement of the Eighties, was also the dominant—and representative—critic of Dutch letters in the late 19th and early 20th cs. His judgments, which were violent, abusive, and often unjust, nevertheless did much to clear away the sentimentality and obtuseness of the 19th-c. heritage; his methods, which were impressionistic and subjective, left much to be corrected by his critical successors.

Among other prose writers, Arthur van Schendel (q.v.) is eminently deserving of mention. In *Het fregatschip Johanna Maria* (1930; *The Johanna Maria,* 1935), *De waterman* (1933; *The Waterman,* 1963), and many other novels he proved a distinguished stylist and a painstaking craftsman, with considerable psychological profundity.

The period between the two world wars was, in Holland as elsewhere in the West, the age of triumphant high modernism. Kloos and Verwey continued as significant poets, but the dominant figures in poetry were Roland Holst, Martinus Nijhoff, Hendrik Marsman, and Gerrit Achterberg (qq.v.). Nijhoff had connections with the artistic movement known as De Stijl. Marsman was the leader of an important school of expressionism (q.v.); his death on a ship torpedoed by the Germans in 1940 robbed 20th-c. Dutch poetry of one of its most vital presences. Achterberg, who emerged in the 1930s, was perhaps an even greater poet; had he written in a more widely known language, he would probably enjoy an international reputation as a major figure. His achievement rests on a delicate tension among a number of opposed elements: verbal experimentation versus a traditional sense of form, thematic limitation (his virtually sole theme is communication with the dead beloved) versus imagistic variety, colloquial versus technical vocabulary. In many ways he is a modern metaphysical poet.

Other important poets of the interwar period include Jan Slauerhoff (q.v.), Victor van Vriesland (1892–1974), Anton van Duinkerken (pseud. of Willem Anton Asselberg, 1903–1968), Jan Greshoff (1888–1971), and Anthonie Donker (psued. of Nicolaas Anthonie Donkersloot, 1902–1965). Another prolific and significant poet was Simon Vestdijk, but he, unquestionably the greatest writer of 20th-c. Holland, is better known for his work as a novelist. Vestdijk was extremely prolific, producing a huge number of novels and collections of short stories and poetry, as well as numerous essays on philosophy, music, and other subjects and in literary criticism. The variety of his novelistic production is also impressive, ranging from the autobiographical *Anton Wachter* cycle (1934–50), with its clear relation to Proust (q.v.), to a number of historical novels with diverse settings, to contemporary realistic works such as *De koperen tuin* (1950; *The Garden Where the Brass Band Played,* 1965), to metaphysical fantasies such as *De kellner en de levenden* (1949; the waiter and the living ones). The metaphysical and the psychological are perhaps the constants of his oeuvre: his first historical novel, *Het vijfde zegel* (1937; the fifth seal), aims at accuracy

as a re-creation of the life and times of El Greco; later work in this genre, such as *Rumeiland* (1940; *Rum Island,* 1963) uses history as an agency for creating myth. Vestdijk's late Victor Slingeland trilogy—*Het glinsterend pantser* (1956; the shining armor), *Open boek* (1957; open book), and *De arme Heinrich* (1958; poor Heinrich)—explores in depth the preoccupation with music that is one of the recurrent themes of his work, the work of an author who, as one critic remarked, wrote "faster than God can read."

Were his work internationally known, Vestdijk might rank with Mann, Joyce, and Kafka (qq.v.), and Proust. Within the Dutch framework he was for some time before World War II associated with the group around the periodical *Forum,* headed by the essayist Menno ter Braak (q.v.) and the novelist and essayist Edgar du Perron (q.v.). The *Forum* group, manifesting again the familiar Dutch dialectic, emphasized the claims of the social, communal, and ethical as opposed to those of the intransigently individual. Vestdijk's position was less simplified and clear-cut than that of his friends. Neither ter Braak nor du Perron survived the first year of World War II: the former committed suicide on learning of the Nazi invasion of the Netherlands; the latter died of a heart attack during an air raid. Like Marsman's, their deaths constituted a severe loss for Dutch letters.

Other important novelists of the period between the wars include the poet Slauerhoff, Frans Coenen (1866–1936), Ferdinand Bordewijk (q.v.), Top Naeff (1878–1953), and Jeanne van Schaik-Willing (b. 1895), the last of whom also wrote plays. Bordewijk's *Karakter* (1938; *Character,* 1966) is one of the most impressive novels of the period between the wars. In nonfiction prose, in addition to the *Forum* group, there was the philosopher and historian Johan Huizinga (1872–1945), a towering figure in 20th-c. Dutch culture.

Note should be taken of Anne Frank's (1929–1945) *Het achterhuis* (1947; *The Diary of a Young Girl,* 1952), which retains its considerable personal and historical, although largely extra-literary, interest as an account of a gifted and sensitive adolescent's experiences during the Nazi occupation.

Achterberg remained the most influential poet during the decades following World War II, but other poets also established themselves: the "moderate surrealist" Eduard Hoornik (1910–1970), who also wrote plays and an epic entitled *Matthaeus* (1937; Matthaeus), and the Catholic Bertus Aafjes (b. 1912). (It is worth noting that, even in contemporary Dutch poetry, a specifically Christian orientation, either Catholic or Calvinist, continues to be a significant factor.) The 1950s witnessed a poetic revolution of sorts, with the advent of the group called Vijftigers ("Writers of the Fifties"): the analogy with the Movement of the Eighties is clear. These young poets—chief among them Gerrit Kouwenaar (b. 1923), Remco Campert (b. 1929), Jan Elburg (b. 1919), Lucebert (q.v.), and Bert Schierbeek (b. 1918)—distanced themselves from contemporary society and literary tradition alike, seeking to achieve above all immediacy, sincerity, and totality of expression. They proved hospitable to foreign influences, among them those of such American poets as William Carlos Williams and Marianne Moore (qq.v.). To their number should be added the name of the somewhat older Leo Vroman (b. 1915), who now lives and works in the U.S.

Lucebert has proven perhaps the most talented of the group, Campert perhaps the wittiest. Another gifted experimental poet of similar orientation is Simon Vinkenoog (b. 1928). Mention should also be made of the short-lived Hans Lodeizen (1924–1950), whose radically associational poems clearly anticipated those of the experimental poets of the 1950s. More traditional poets include Vasalis (pseud. of Margaretha Drooglever Fortuyn-Leenmans, b. 1909) and Ellen Warmond (pseud. of Pieternella Cornelia van Yperen, b. 1930).

The Vijftigers did not constitute a school or even, really, a movement. As one of their spokesmen, Kouwenaar, has noted, it was really more a case of a number of young literary artists moving independently in the same general direction—a direction defined by a break with traditional conceptions of form, by a strong concern with the unconscious, by a distinct antiintellectualism, and by a high degree of individualism. Their poetry has some links with Dadaism, surrealism (qq.v.), and expressionism, particularly in its distrust of bourgeois society, but it differs in its absence of program, in its radical lack of belief in anything at all.

Nevertheless, Vijftiger poetry retains from earlier generations the concept of the poem as an autonomous verbal artifact rather than an unmediated expression of the author's personality. As in other Western literatures, the 1960s and 1970s saw a progressive erosion of this sense of the autonomy and integrity of the work of art. Some of the more recent Dutch poets who epitomize this tendency are J. Bernlef (pseud. of Hendrik Jan Marsman, b. 1937; not to be confused with the older poet Hendrik Marsman), Herman Hendrik ter Balkt (b. 1938), Hans van Waarsenburg (b. 1943), Frank Koenegracht (b. 1945), and Sjoerd Kuyper (b. 1952).

Contemporary Dutch drama has not achieved real distinction. Hoornik fails to reach it, both in his earlier poetic drama and in such later, realistic work as *Het water* (1957; the water). Absurdism, as exemplified by Schierbeek's *Een groot dood dier* (1963; *A Big Dead Beast,* 1963), does not rise above the fashionable. Perhaps the best Dutch dramatist of the age is the popular Jan de Hartog (b. 1914), whose *Schipper naast God* (1942; *Skipper Next to God,* 1949) and *Het hemelbed* (1943; *The Fourposter,* 1947) achieved notable commercial success even outside the boundaries of the Netherlands.

The giant figure of the late Simon Vestdijk continues to dominate Dutch fiction, but other currents began to manifest themselves from the late 1940s on—in the work of Maria Dermoût (1888–1962), whose belated literary career began with the publication of *Nog pas gisteren* (1951; *Only Yesterday,* 1959) and who evoked life in the Indies with lyrical nostalgia, and in that of Anna Blaman (q.v.), whose existentialist (q.v.) novels include *Eenzaam avontuur* (1948; lonely adventure) and her masterpiece, *Op leven en dood* (1954; *A Matter of Life and Death,* 1974). Blaman's frank treatment of such themes as homosexuality caused controversy at the time.

Blaman seems, however, downright decorous in the light of the themes and treatments favored by the younger novelists who made their debuts in the 1950s, chief among them Willem Frederik Hermans (b. 1921) and Gerard Cornelis van het Reve (b. 1923). They share a vision of unrelieved bleakness and negativism, and motifs of violence, betrayal, and degradation permeate their work. The dream of a better society, so strong an impulse in Dutch civilization from the 17th c. down to the writers of the *Forum* group of the 1930s, is in their novels vehemently exposed as no more than a dream. Hermans's best work is probably *De donker kamer van Damocles* (1958; *The Dark Room of Damo-*

377

cles, 1962). Like his earlier novel, *De tranen der acacia's* (1949; the tears of the acacias), it is set in Holland at the time of the Nazi occupation and is preoccupied with murder, violence, and intense sexuality. Society is seen as wholly a sham. Van het Reve, who now prefers to call himself Gerard Reve, made his debut with *De ondergang van de familie Boslowits* (1946; the fall of the Boslowits family); in this work and in *De avonden* (1947; the evenings) he expressed a comparable negativism. Another writer much concerned with dark and tragic themes is Harry Mulisch (q.v.), whose most important work to date is *Het stenen bruidsbed* (1959; *The Stone Bridal Bed,* 1962), dealing with the fire-bombing of Dresden near the end of World War II. In other works, such as *Het zwarte licht* (1956; the black light), Mulisch differs from Hermans and van het Reve in a free use of fantasy.

Impulses of rejection and rebellion, conspicuously present in the poetry of the Vijftigers, are the dominant element in the novels written by the generation born in the 1920s, the generation that came to maturity during the war and the Nazi occupation. The obsessively sexual and frequently scatological fictions of Jan Wolkers (b. 1925) carry these impulses to a kind of extreme. Even in his best works, *Een roos van vlees* (1963; *A Rose of Flesh,* 1967) and *Turks fruit* (1969; *Turkish Delight,* 1974), a self-indulgent desire to shock weakens the general effect. (The rebellion syndrome is particularly strong in Wolkers as a result of a strict Calvinist upbringing.) Self-indulgence, a flaw in Wolkers, becomes a principle of being in Jan Cremer (b. 1940), whose *Ik, Jan Cremer* (1964; *I, Jan Cremer,* 1966) was hailed by some critics as a bold document of self-revelation and censured by others as an exercise in adolescent narcissism.

The stance of revolt has to some extent hardened into a literary convention, and negativism has become almost a conditioned reflex. There were some signs of change, however, in the fiction of Heere Heeresma (b. 1932), as in that of the somewhat older Adriaan van der Veen (b. 1916) and Hella Haasse (Hélène Serafia Haasse, b. 1918). The vision of life in Heeresma's novel *Een dagje op het strand* (1962; *A Day at the Beach,* 1967) is undeniably bleak, but the work possesses an awareness of human relationships that frees it from the solipsism that marks much contemporary Dutch fiction. The same

observation can be made with regard to van der Veen's work, particularly *Het wilde feest* (1952; *The Intruder,* 1958) and *Doen alsof* (1960; *Make Believe,* 1963), and to Haasse's—*De scharlaken stad* (1952; *The Scarlet City,* 1954), a historical novel, and *De ingewijden* (1957; the initiated). Margo Minco (b. 1920), who is married to the poet Bert Voeten (b. 1918), dealt movingly with the persecution of the Jews in German-occupied Holland in her short novel *Het bittere kruid* (1957; *Bitter Herbs,* 1960).

The current situation in Dutch letters is rather static. There is much activity and a high degree of cosmopolitanism, but the revolutionary drives of the 1950s and 1960s have spent their force, and no countermovement has yet asserted itself. No new Multatuli has appeared on the scene, no new Couperus or Vestdijk. Lucebert is giving more time to his painting and Wolkers to his sculpture.

As previously observed, Dutch literature presents a kind of dialectic between the claims of the individual and the claims of the community. It is, in the 20th c. as in the 17th, the natural expression of a culture in which the polarity is felt with particular force. The Dutch have old and strong traditions of respect for personal freedom and of tolerance of diverse viewpoints, but they are also used to living under circumstances of population density that enforce an awareness of the claims of community. Add to that the sense of mutual dependency aroused by the centuries-long and continuing battle with the sea. Add to that the fact that Holland has always been, preeminently, a bourgeois country, with the pressures toward conformity that the adjective implies. Add, finally, that the two main religious traditions, Calvinist and Catholic, can both be rigid, dogmatic, and authoritarian. There are good historical reasons for the Dutch to be especially aware of the conflicts between the individual and the community. The defense of the individual occasioned the rebellious outburst of van Deyssel and the other Tachtigers as well as the antisocial gestures of so many later Dutch writers. A sense of communal responsibility was as central to the thought of the *Forum* group in the 1930s as it was to Pieter Corneliszoon Hooft (1582–1647) or Hugo Grotius (Huig de Groot, 1583–1645) in the 17th c.

The greatest Dutch writers hold the claims of individual and community in delicate balance. In the play *Lucifer* (1654; *Lucifer,* 1898), the 17th-c. masterpiece of Joost van den Vondel (1587–1679), greatest of Dutch poets, the hero-villain is Lucifer—arch-rebel but also Prince of Darkness. His individualistic rebellion is titanic, but the evil to which it is dedicated leads the reader to question the validity of uncontrolled individualism. Multatuli's titanic satirical rage is triggered equally by communal irresponsibility and by the desecration of individual rights. In our own century the greatest novelists, Couperus and Vestdijk, have probed the relationship with profundity, sympathy, and insight. It is likely to remain the great theme of Dutch literature.

BIBLIOGRAPHY: Verschool, A. R., *Silt and Sky: Men and Movements in Modern Dutch Literature* (1950); Weevers, T., *Poetry of the Netherlands in Its European Context* (1960); Flaxman, S. L., "The Modern Novel in the Low Countries," in Peyre, H., ed., *Fiction in Several Languages* (1968), pp. 141–61; Snapper, J. P., *Post-War Dutch Literature: A Harp Full of Nails* (1971); Krispyn, E., ed., Introduction to *Modern Stories from Holland and Flanders* (1973), pp. ix–xii; Bulhoff, F., ed., *Nijhoff, van Ostaijen, "De Stijl": Modernism in the Netherlands and Belgium in the First Quarter of the 20th Century* (1976); special Holland issue, *RNL,* 8 (1977); Meijer, R. P., *Literature of the Low Countries,* new ed. (1978)

FRANK J. WARNKE

Frisian Literature

Frisian, the West Germanic language that is most closely related to English, has three branches: West Frisian (Netherlands), and East and North Frisian (Germany). West Frisian, in spite of past suppression, now has official rights in the Netherlands. Its literature, dating back to the 11th c., reached its first peak in the 17th c., but declined in the 18th and 19th cs., when, with some notable exceptions, it was shallow, unaesthetic, and provincial.

At the beginning of the 20th c., however, a new wind began to blow across Friesland. Its freshness and vigor was perhaps most obvious in the graceful poems and lyrical fiction of Simke Kloosterman (1876–1938). *De Hoara's fan Hastings* (1921; the Hoaras of Hastings), her best novel, poignantly depicts the relations between the rich Frisian land-

owners and the poor, dependent farm workers who, at the turn of the century, were beginning to assert their rights.

The new wind was also evident in the spontaneous poetry of Hendrika Akke van Dorssen (pseud.: Rixt, 1887–1978), whose collected poetry was published in *De gouden rider* (1952; the golden rider). A broader talent was discernible in the short stories and novels of Reinder Brolsma (1882–1953), who focused on the lives of little people and in his best novels painted a broad and colorful canvas of Frisian life in the early decades of the century.

The Young Frisian Movement, launched in 1915 by the determined nationalist Douwe Kalma (1896–1953), produced a national awakening and a vigorous literary renaissance. Kalma, who began his literary career as a critic who roundly denounced the mediocrity and provincialism of 19th-c. literature, was a poet, dramatist, translator, and literary historian. Owing to his efforts, Frisian literature has gained intellectual breadth. Kalma's poetic art is perhaps most impressive in *Keningen fan Fryslân* (2 vols., 1949–51; kings of Friesland), a series of epic dramas in blank verse that began with *Kening Aldgillis* (King Aldgillis), published separately in 1920. His lyric poetry, largely in the classical tradition, has grandeur and shows great technical skill but suffers somewhat from a dreamy vagueness and an overuse of both archaisms and neologisms.

Another significant figure in the Young Frisian Movement was Rintsje Piter Sybesma (1894–1975), who in *Ta de moarn* (1927, toward morning) showed himself to be a first-rate sonneteer. Douwe Hermans Kiestra (1899–1970) was a vigorous poet of the soil, and Jelle Hindriks Brouwer (1900–1981) wrote verse that is sonorous and well crafted. Obe Postma (1868–1963), although not of the Young Frisian school, won high praise from Kalma. His quiet and unpretentious poetry is rich in suggestiveness and imagery. Fedde Schurer (1898–1968), who in his early work was influenced by the aestheticism of the Young Frisian school, became the most popular and widely read poet of his time. Much of his verse centers around national, social, and religious themes.

Around 1935 a few of the younger poets began to break away from the Young Frisian tradition both in themes and in poetic idiom. Johannes Doedes de Jong (b. 1912) wrote the innovative and refreshing volume *Lunchroom*

(1936; lunchroom). Douwe Annes Tamminga (b. 1909), in *Balladen en lieten* (1942; ballads and songs) and other volumes, cast aside the lofty, ornate language of the Young Frisians in favor of the more virile language of the people, which he carefully refined into durable art.

Some talented novelists appeared during the interwar period. Ulbe van Houten (1904–1974) is known especially for *De sûnde fan Haitze Holwerda* (1939; the sin of Haitze Holwerda), a novel that probes moral conflicts. Nyckle J. Haisma (1907–1943), who like Van Houten wrote a good many short stories, is remembered for his moving novel *Peke Donia, de koloniaal* (2 vols., 1937–40; Peke Donia, the colonial), about the alienation of a Frisian returned from the Dutch East Indies.

After World War II significant innovative poets were Germant Nico Visser (b. 1910) and Sjoerd Spanninga (pseud. of Jan Dykstra, b. 1906). Visser's work reflects postwar disillusionment and pessimism; Spanninga's, on the other hand, introduced an exotic flavor into Frisian verse.

After the demise in 1968 of the important but conservative literary journal *De tsjerne* (founded in 1946 by Fedde Schurer), Frisian letters increasingly showed the impact of a twofold emancipation already underway: from traditional moral codes, especially in sexual matters; and from the influence of the national movement. Emphasis shifted from the romantic to the psychological, from the realistic to the abstract, from the conventional to the experimental, from the rural to the cosmopolitan.

Perhaps no figure contributed so greatly to these changes as Anne Sybe Wadman (b. 1919), who is not only an incisive literary critic but also an able essayist, novelist, and short-story writer, whose works often attack social evils. In the novel *De smearlappen* (1963; the scoundrels) he did much to open the way for a frank treatment of sex.

Ypk fan der Fear (pseud. of Lipkje Beuckens Post, b. 1908) in her boldly conceived fiction often features women who are physically handicapped, mentally disturbed, or mystically religious. Ype Poortinga (b. 1910) has published poetry, short stories, novels, and seven volumes of Frisian folk tales. His best work is probably *Elbrich* (2 vols., 1947–49), a historical novel set in the 16th c., centering on the quest of a nobleman for the ideal woman. Rink van der Velde (b. 1932) is a

prolific and popular novelist. Several of his works of fiction are set outside Friesland, in such countries as France, Greece, Czechoslovakia, and Israel. His best novel to date is *De fûke* (1966; the trap), in which he vividly portrays the tenacious resistance of a lone Frisian fisherman to Nazi terror.

Perhaps the most talented of the younger writers is Trinus Riemersma (b. 1938), whose work displays both high intelligence and honesty. His first novel, *Fabryk* (1964; factory), which caused a considerable stir because of its sexual explicitness, deals with a factory worker who feels himself estranged, lonely, and helpless amid modern cultural and technological forces. Riemersma's works, often experimental in form, usually center around problems of religion or sex. Durk van der Ploeg (b. 1930) is a novelist preoccupied largely with human weakness and failure, with physical and mental decay, and with death itself.

In contemporary poetry, which in language and form continues to show the influence of the experimentalists of the 1950s, there is much of the same pessimism found in fiction. It is well represented by the work of Jan Wybenga (b. 1917), whose doleful subjects are deserted villages and deteriorating cities, autumn and winter, dissolution and death. The verse of Daniël Daen (pseud. of Gerben Willem Abma, b. 1942) has a philosophic bent. Much of it, although it has universal overtones, concentrates upon himself and constitutes an attack on the strictures imposed upon him as a youth in a conservative family. Much more positive and optimistic is Tiny Mulder (b. 1918), whose buoyant and playful poems are often a joyous paean to life.

Contemporary Frisian literature reflects artistic and intellectual movements from elsewhere in the world.

BIBLIOGRAPHY: Fridsma, B. J., "Frisian Literature," in Shipley, J. T., ed. *Encyclopedia of Literature* (1946), pp. 317–24; Poortinga, Y., "Die westfriesische 'schöne' Literatur nach dem Kriege," *Friesisches Jahrbuch,* 30 (1955), 180–93; Harris, E. H., *The Literature of Friesland* (1956); Fridsma, B. J., "Frisian Poetry," in Preminger, A., et al., eds., *Encyclopedia of Poetry and Poetics* (1965), pp. 301–2; Brouwer, J. H., "A Committed Lot: Frisian Writers," *Delta,* 8, 4 (1965–66), 39–45

BERNARD J. FRIDSMA, SR.

VLADIMIR NABOKOV

V. S. NAIPAUL

PABLO NERUDA

SEAN O'CASEY

NETHERLANDS ANTILLES LITERATURE
See Dutch-Caribbean Literature

NEW NOVEL

During the years immediately following World War II French literature was dominated by Albert Camus, André Malraux, and Jean-Paul Sartre (qq.v.). Camus's *La peste* (1947; *The Plague,* 1948) is an expression of faith in human solidarity; Malraux's work on the philosophy of art, *Les voix du silence* (1951; *The Voices of Silence,* 1953), extols universal brotherhood; and Sartre's *Les chemins de la liberté* (3 vols., 1945–49; *The Roads to Freedom,* 3 vols., 1947–51) points out that freedom is meaningful only when accompanied by social commitment. For these writers, literature was a tool to make people aware of their human condition and of the problems of the contemporary world.

Concurrently, another group of writers began questioning the purpose of literature as interpreted by Camus, Malraux, and Sartre. What is really the essence of writing fiction? they asked. Is the writer above all a philosopher, social critic, visionary? Or is the writer's genuine function simply to write, to combine words into patterns on the blank piece of paper? Gradually the focus shifted from content to form, and the process of writing itself became the chief subject of exploration. The first New Novels were Samuel Beckett's (q.v.) *Molloy* (1951; *Molloy,* 1955) and Alain Robbe-Grillet's (q.v.) *Les gommes* (1953; *The Erasers,* 1964).

In addition to Beckett and Robbe-Grillet, the novelists most frequently associated with this new trend in fiction are Michel Butor, Marguerite Duras, Claude Mauriac, Claude Ollier, Nathalie Sarraute, Claude Simon, and Philippe Sollers (qq.v.), the last also a critic and one of the founders, in 1960, of the influential journal *Tel Quel,* which in its early years was closely associated with the New Novel writers. While these are highly individualistic writers, they nevertheless have enough in common to justify categorization as New Novelists. Still, no theory applies equally well to all of them. Moreover, each writer's work has evolved considerably. For instance, there is little in common between Simon's first novel, *Le tricheur* (1945; the trickster) and his most recent one, *Les Géorgiques* (1981; the Georgics).

Nevertheless, all the New Novelists would probably agree that the true writer has no particular message or insight to convey to the world. In *Pour un nouveau roman* (1963; *For a New Novel,* 1965) Robbe-Grillet states that for him the term "New Novel" is associated with all those who are exploring new forms. The New Novelists believe that writing is a perpetual quest. The work of the novelist is equivalent to that of the laboratory scientist. Without specifically attempting to do so, each may stumble upon a key that will open a door to a better world. This, however, would always be a secondary achievement, since the central one has to be the research itself.

The New Novelists are ambivalent toward literary tradition, comprehending their role within it at the same time they desire the freedom to look at the world in a direct, unobstructed way. The New Novel is frequently referred to as the *école du regard,* since vision is customarily perceived as the most objective of the senses, permitting the writer to define as far as humanly possible what is his situation in the world. The New Novelists all share the desire to see reality without the intermediary of learned responses. Moreover, they all agree that the natural world simply *is* and that the only way we can learn to understand it better is through detailed description. A willow does not weep, but its leaves have an infinite variety of colors and shapes that the writer can observe, describe, and relate to images that compose his own mental universe. Description, then, is a key word in the New Novel; however, the distance is great indeed between the geometric surfaces of Robbe-Grillet and the metaphorical, expanding descriptions in the novels of Beckett, Butor, and Simon.

As description becomes gradually more important, characters and plot cease to dominate the novel. Above all, the hero is dethroned, and in his place we find antiheroes who frequently parody the narrator's quest. This is true, for instance, in Beckett's *Molloy,* Butor's *La modification* (1957; *A Change of Heart,* 1959), and Simon's *La route des Flandres* (1960; *The Flanders Road,* 1961).

While the New Novelists reject the traditional plot, with incidents following upon one another and building to a climax, their books nevertheless are filled with stories and anecdotes. These stories, however, are not intended to reproduce the real world, recapture the past, and mirror society. An anecdote may be repeated several times, often in contradictory fashion, leaving the reader without a firm grasp as to what is happening. Moreover, since chronology has been dispensed with, the reader is unable to fix events in time, or even decide whether a given event is supposed to have taken place or is merely a figment of the imagination of the narrator or protagonist.

The New Novel has been closely associated with theory, and several of its proponents, including Robbe-Grillet, Butor, and to a lesser extent Sarraute, have written commentary on their own fiction. One of the leading theoreticians is Jean Ricardou (q.v.), author of *Problèmes du nouveau roman* (1967; problems of the new novel), *Pour une théorie du nouveau roman* (1971; for a theory of the new novel), and *Le nouveau roman* (1973; the new novel). While the theory is a reflection on the fiction for these writers, it is by no means an attempt to set up absolute rules. On the contrary, while fiction stimulates theory, theory will in turn inspire new experiments in fiction, in a dialectical pattern.

Although essentially a French phenomenon, the New Novel has made its appearance in other countries. In England, Rayner Heppenstall (q.v.), who wrote two studies of Raymond Roussel (q.v.)—one of the forerunners of the New Novelists—used its techniques in his novels *The Woodshed* (1962) and *The Connecting Door* (1962). The English writer Christine Brooke-Rose (q.v.), a resident of France, has employed a variation of New Novel methods in much of her fiction. In the 1960s Spanish American writers such as the Argentines Julio Cortázar and Ernesto Sábato (qq.v.) and the Mexican Carlos Fuentes (q.v.), among others, produced what could be considered New Novels in the formal sense, but with the metaphysical overtones and linguistic and structural innovations that distinguish contemporary Latin American fiction.

The New Novel demands from its readers a high degree of participation. Without the support of a dependable narrator, a central plot, and characters with comprehensible histories, the reader frequently feels lost. All one has is a skeletal structure inviting the reader to explore but not to create an artificial coherence. Instead, the reader is asked to accept the book as it is, delve into its internal structure, and work through the intricate analogies formed in the narrator's mind. In

proportion to the work he is willing to put in, his own creativity is set in motion, until in the end the distinction between writer and reader is blurred, and the reader becomes creator of his own novel.

BIBLIOGRAPHY: Janvier, L., *Une parole exigeante: Le Nouveau Roman* (1964); Robbe-Grillet, A., *For a New Novel* (1965); Astier, P., *La crise du roman français et le nouveau réalisme* (1968); Sturrock, J., *The French New Novel: Claude Simon, Michel Butor, Alain Robbe-Grillet* (1969); Mercier, V., *A Reader's Guide to the New Novel* (1971); Heath, S., *The Nouveau Roman: A Study in the Practice of Writing* (1972); Roudiez, L., *French Fiction Today: A New Direction* (1972)

RANDI BIRN

NEW ZEALAND LITERATURE

New Zealand literature is the issue of an uneasy union between a transplanted British tradition and a new environment. The task of New Zealand writers has been to harness individual vision to the creative tensions arising from the vicissitudes of this union. Literally at the far ends of the earth from Mother England, the literature both values the protective isolation geography affords and laments a concomitant sense of remoteness and cultural stagnation. This ambivalence makes for a fruitful balance of idealism and reality in the work of the best New Zealand writers, although it has also made expatriates of many of them.

Fiction

New Zealand fiction of the 19th c. is mainly of historical interest. Deference to English literary tradition, colonial attitudes on race, and a dearth of New Zealand-born writers early insured an unsympathetic, alien view of the antipodean environment. In the 20th c., however, at least five writers have successfully explored the mutations of consciousness and climate inherent in the New Zealand experience. The best known of these, Katherine Mansfield (q.v.) holds a secure place in the front rank of English-language writers in this century. As an expatriate in England Mansfield excelled at sensitive, subtle stories of her New Zealand childhood and brilliantly spontaneous letters. Innocence, isolation, war, idealism, independence, conflicting loyalties, the nature of love—these are both Mansfield's and New Zealand literature's characteristic themes.

Influenced by America's literary realists and naturalists, Frank Sargeson (q.v.) is credited with reviving the moribund short story in New Zealand. From the social realism of his early stories about the impact of the 1930s depression on New Zealand, collected in *A Man and His Wife* (1940), the prolific Sargeson has matured into the skillful, original writer of fiction in *That Summer, and Other Stories* (1946), *I Saw in My Dream* (1949), *Memoirs of a Peon* (1965), *Joy of the Worm* (1969), and *Man of England Now* (1972). Sylvia Ashton-Warner's (b. 1908) first novel, *Spinster* (1958), a pedagogically challenging account of teaching in a Maori school as well as a meditation on the accommodation that a sophisticated intelligence must make with a limited environment, is perhaps her best, although *Greenstone* (1966) aspires higher artistically, with its complex allegory of New Zealand's dual racial heritage deepening the meaning of a story of relationships among several generations of a New Zealand family.

The most arrestingly different of New Zealand writers is Janet Frame (q.v.). In her novels published between 1957 and 1970 virtually all the protagonists are isolated in the terrain of the self by their paranoid visions of a society that worships technical efficiency and little else. The structure and coherence of Frame's fiction, however, sometimes threatens to disintegrate under the pressure of an apocalyptic language that seeks to penetrate these private, tormented consciousnesses. In *The New Zealanders* (1959) Maurice Shadbolt (b. 1932) deftly handles the short-story form and the theme of adolescence, while his darkening vision of humanity and the future is apparent in a novel, *This Summer's Dolphin* (1969), and later books dealing with the forces he sees as destroying and polluting the world.

Poetry

Not surprisingly, the development of New Zealand poetry corresponds to that of English poetry over the last hundred years. Few of the antipodean Victorians, Edwardians, or Georgians, however, were vital poetic voices. After World War I, three poets stand out from an impressive crop by dint of originality

and craftsmanship. Allen Curnow's (b. 1911) meditative poetry, especially *Sailing or Drowning* (1943), *At Dead Low Water* (1949), and *Poems, 1949–1957* (1957), typically deals with New Zealand myths of origin and identity such as the islands' discovery by Europeans, and the alienation of European colonizers from the native Maori culture. Protean in mood and form, James Baxter's (q.v.) poetry is also concerned with the theme of exile—more broadly, man's exile from heaven. In *Blow, Wind of Fruitfulness* (1948), *The Fallen House* (1953), *In Fires of No Return* (1958), and *The Rock Woman* (1969) Baxter combines a Catholic cosmic view with a counterculture compassion for society's rejects, whose refusal to embrace the success ethic safeguards them against a greater Fall. Less accessible but equally impressive, Kendrick Smithyman (b. 1922) transforms the accents of common speech into an intricate, resourceful poetic music capable of treating such universal themes as youth, age, love, death, and war. His often difficult *The Blind Mountain* (1950) presents at once a challenge to the reader and proof positive of the hard-won maturity of New Zealand poetry.

On the whole, New Zealand literature has successfully freed itself from its colonial origins, although its achievements remain modest by world standards. The present literary situation is one of diversity, scope, sophistication, and self-confidence. A growing number of readers, too, find value in a literature that is at last interpreting the New Zealand experience independently of literary stereotypes or inherited conflicts from abroad. Two particularly encouraging trends are the emergence in recent decades of several noteworthy playwrights using indigenous subjects, and a nascent Maori literature written in English led by the poet Hone Tuwhare (b. 1922) and the novelist Witi Ihimaera (b. 1944), which, through integration of the Maori and European traditions, also seeks new definitions of culture and self.

BIBLIOGRAPHY: McCormick, E. H., *New Zealand Literature: A Survey* (1959); Stevens, J., *The New Zealand Novel: 1860–1960* (1962); Rhodes, W. H., *New Zealand Fiction since 1945* (1968); Wilkes, G. A., and Reid, J. C., *Australian and New Zealand Literature* (1970); Curnow, W., ed., *Essays on New Zealand Literature* (1973); Pearson, B., *Fret-*

ful Sleepers, and Other Essays (1974); Mc-Naughton, H., *New Zealand Drama* (1981)

JOHN H. FERRES

NEXØ, Martin Andersen

(original family name Andersen) Danish novelist and short-story writer, b. 26 June 1869, Copenhagen; d. 1 June 1954, Dresden, East Germany

N. was one of the first Danish writers of proletarian background. He lived in poverty in Copenhagen for the first eight years of his life; his family then moved to the town of Nexø on the island of Bornholm, whose name he later (1894) adopted as his own. There he worked as a farmhand and later as a cobbler. He received some further education and briefly worked as a teacher.

N.'s early novels reflect fin-de-siècle taste, but *Dryss* (1902; waste) is also a protest against the age's introversion and decadence. During 1894–96 he traveled in Italy and Spain, and his encounter with the proletariat there renewed his solidarity with the lower classes. In his short stories of this period that solidarity is expressed in some sharply edged portrayals of extreme poverty and social injustice. In the 1930s N. recalled the formative years of his life in an admirable memoir, *Erindringer* (4 vols., 1932–39; tr. of Vols. 1–2, *Under the Open Sky*, 1938).

His first major work was *Pelle erobreren* (4 vols., 1906–10; *Pelle the Conqueror*, 4 vols., 1913–16). Pelle is a poor boy whose childhood years on Bornholm bear a resemblance to N.'s. As a young man Pelle experiences the misery of the exploited workers in Copenhagen; he becomes a trade unionist and strike leader, and eventually he leads his proletarian followers to a momentous victory. The first part of the book seems very authentic, but its utopian ending lacks verisimilitude.

Critics have maintained that N. is best when he omits his political convictions, but that view warrants revision: some of N.'s best short stories are permeated by social indignation and read as convincing arguments against capitalistic society. The truth is rather that N. is a fairly limited writer who reached excellence only when he depicted those fates or milieus that he knew from experience. It is correct—and common—to call him a first-rate social realist, but it should not be overlooked that his works also contain symbolic structures and numerous references to the lore of the rural proletariat. Pelle, for example, besides being a very real person who engages in a struggle for social equality, is also the folktale hero who conquers all obstacles and fulfills a dream of happiness.

N.'s next major work, *Ditte menneskebarn* (5 vols., 1917–21; *Ditte: Girl Alive,* 1920; *Ditte: Daughter of Man,* 1922; *Ditte: Towards the Stars,* 1922), once more records the life of a child of the rural proletariat; like Pelle, she moves to Copenhagen, where she quite literally works herself to death at an early age. The book offers a starker picture of the ghastliness of poverty than does *Pelle erobreren,* but it is a mistake to assume that N. had lost his optimistic vision of the proletariat's march toward the light. Ditte's suffering is not meaningless, but rather a sacrifice for the sake of future generations. As with *Pelle erobreren,* this novel has mythical overtones.

The remainder of N.'s fiction is uneven in quality. Some of his short stories are excellent. More ambitious is the novel *Morten hin røde* (3 vols., 1945, 1948, 1957; Morten the red), which reveals its author's growing radicalism. In 1922, after a trip to the Soviet Union, N. had joined the Communist Party. *Morten hin røde* shows how social democrats like Pelle have adopted bourgeois values. Morten, a childhood friend of Pelle's, is, on the other hand, a man who remains true to the revolutionary ideals of his class. This novel, which never was finished, lacks the vividness of the earlier works.

The older N. was primarily a political activist. His numerous articles reflect his engagement in the political and humanitarian issues of his day. His views did not make him popular in Denmark, and he spent the years after World War II in the German Democratic Republic. Although theory-oriented Marxists may find flaws in N.'s works, he remains an immensely popular author in communist countries.

FURTHER WORKS: *Skygger* (1899); *Det bødes der for* (1899); *En moder* (1900); *Muldskud* (3 vols., 1900, 1924, 1926); *Familien Frank* (1901); *Soldage* (1903; *Days in the Sun,* 1929); *Af dybets lovsang* (1908); *Barndommens kyst* (1911); *Lykken* (1913); *Bornholmer noveller* (1913); *Under himlen den blå* (1915); *Folkene på Dangården* (1915); *Dybvandsfisk* (1918); *Lotterisvensken* (1919); *De tomme pladsers passagerer* (1921); *Mod dagningen* (1923); *Digte* (1926; rev. enl. ed., 1951); *Midt i en jærntid* (2 vols., 1929; *In God's Land,* 1933); *To verdener* (1934); *Mod lyset* (1938); *Et skriftemål* (1946); *Hænderne væk!* (1953); *Taler og artikler* (3 vols., 1954–55); *Breve fra M. A. N.* (3 vols., 1969–72)

BIBLIOGRAPHY: Slochower, H., *Three Ways of Modern Man* (1937), pp. 105–44; Berendsohn, W. A., *M. A. N.s Weg in die Weltliteratur* (1949); *M. A. N. als Dichter und Mensch* (1966); Koefoed, H. A., "M. A. N.: Some Viewpoints," *Scan,* 4 (1965), 27–37; "M. A. N.: A Symposium," special section, *Scan,* 8 (1969), 121–35; Le Bras-Barret, J., *M. A. N.: Écrivain du prolétariat* (1969)

NIELS INGWERSEN

NEZVAL, Vítězslav

Czechoslovak poet (writing in Czech), b. 26 May 1900, Biskoupky; d. 6 April 1958, Prague

N.'s childhood and adolescence were spent in the Moravian village of Šemkovice, where his father was a schoolteacher. He developed an early interest in musical composition and wrote poetry seriously by the time he was sixteen. His first publication was a confessional prose piece, "Jak se mnou příroda zahovořila" (1919; how nature began talking to me), in the student journal of his secondary school in Třebíč.

He arrived in Prague in 1920 and immediately plunged into its vibrant literary life. In 1922 he joined the newly formed avant-garde group Devětsil (Nine Powers), soon becoming one of its most passionate spokesmen. Named in honor of all the nine Muses, this association of poets, artists, and critics sought a radical transformation of society by way of a revolution in the arts. When the internal debate between the young proletarian poet Jiří Wolker (q.v.) and the leader of Devětsil, the brilliant art theoretician Karel Teige (1900–1951) broke into the open, N. joined in with a spirited defense of fantasy and formal experimentation. His first volume of poetry, *Most* (1922; the bridge), was a display of verbal pyrotechnics, evincing an imagination untrammeled by logic or convention. In his second collection, *Podivuhodný kouzelník* (1922; marvelous magician), he records the poet's descent from the daylight of the modern city, with its violent social struggles, into the nurturing darkness of a subjective underworld. This book, recognized by Devětsil as a fulfillment of its theories, gave an additional impetus to the nascent movement of poetism, whose main theses Teige and the poet Jaroslav Seifert (q.v.) were then in the process of formulating. N.'s magician showed the way to a complete liberation of the human spirit, including liberation from the psychological oppression of fear and guilt. It heralded this revolution by the unleashing of the carnival mood of spontaneous playfulness. Czech poetism, like its precursors Italian and Russian futurism (q.v.), delighted in film, sport, the music hall, and all other manifestations of speed and technological virtuosity, which were the hallmarks of the still young and cocky 20th c. In the same year as Teige coined the name for the new movement, N. contributed to it his own manifesto, *Papoušek na motocyklu* (1924; parrot on a motorcycle). Throughout the 1920s, N. participated in all the activities of poetism, while publishing thirteen volumes of original poetry.

N.'s two poetic masterpieces belong to the end of this period. The long poem *Edison* (1928; Edison) is probably the most explosive example of free verse in the Czech language. Like *Podivuhodný kouzelník, Edison* is a work about a quest. Its protagonist is the American inventor, seen as the symbol of the eternal anxiety that propels mankind to seek to change and manipulate nature. The poem pits Edison's restlessness against the illusion of an ever-expanding American landscape, as if seen from a speeding train. Breaking loose from the constraints of traditional metrics and the tyranny of the habitual end rhyme, N. achieves rhythmic intensity by charging his lines with the dynamo of anaphoric repetition and the hypnotic frequency of verbal parallelism. *Básně noci* (1930; poems of the night), a collection of lyric rhapsodies united by the leitmotif of the contrast between light and darkness, rivals *Edison* in the power and originality of its imagination. Here, the magic of the speaker's intonation yields a rich harvest of startling visual effects.

In the 1930s, under the influence of his readings and translations from French poets, as well as eye-opening visits to Paris, N. discovered surrealism (q.v.). As revolutionary as Czech poetism, surrealism had the advantage of being a truly international movement. Moreover, it had incorporated Freud's (q.v.) discoveries about dreams into its comprehensive and quasi-scientific doctrines about the layers of consciousness. In 1934 N. founded the Czech branch of surrealism with the poet Konstantín Biebl (1898–1951) and the painter Toyen (pseud. of Marie Čermínová, 1902–1980). He published his own manifesto, *Surrealismus v Č.S.R.* (1934; surrealism in the Czechoslovak Republic) and invited the French leaders of the movement, André Breton and Paul Éluard (qq.v.), to bring their "theses of hope" to Prague. At the 1934 Congress of Writers in Moscow, N. defended the surrealist position as a synthesis of discipline and freedom.

The finest example of N.'s surrealist poetry is the cycle *Praha s prsty deště* (1936; Prague with Fingers of Rain," 1971), published a year after his first volume of surrealist verse, *Žena v množném čísle* (1935; woman in plural), which was inspired by and dedicated to Paul Éluard. The Prague cycle creates a polythematic image of the city whose "mysterious order" the poet-lover discovers after awakening her dormant beauty by the fiat of his magic invocation.

In 1938, after the Munich agreement, N. disbanded the Czech surrealist group, in a public show of solidarity with the Communists, whose political, if not literary, ranks he had joined as early as 1924. He now considered them as the undisputed leaders of the struggle against fascism. N. spent the war years in Nazi-occupied Prague, having declined the option of exile. While his writing was banned, he turned to painting. After the liberation of Czechoslovakia, he assumed a leading position among those writers who welcomed the Communist regime. His poetic cycle *Zpěv míru* (1950; *Song of Peace,* 1951), which asserted the justice of the Soviet position in the Korean conflict, was acclaimed in his country and the U.S.S.R. A year earlier N. had published *Stalin* (1949; Stalin), a poetic biography that marks his literary nadir. The only poems that rise above the level of propaganda in this last period of his life are those collected in the book *Chrpy a města* (1955; cornflowers and towns). Many of them were inspired by a return to France and echo the playfulness of his prewar writing.

N. was the most prolific, versatile, and elemental poet of the 20th-c. Czech avant-garde. He has been criticized for his lack of intellectual discipline and for his refusal to give up his posture of perpetual boyhood. But even his critics admit that he is one of the supreme magicians of the Czech word, who wielded the power of the original metaphor with an intensity unmatched since Karel Hynek Mácha (1810–1836).

FURTHER WORKS: *Pantomima* (1924); *Falešný mariáš* (1925); *Wolker* (1925); *Abeceda* (1926); *Básně na pohlednice* (1926); *Diabolo* (1926); *Karneval* (1926); *Menší růžová zahrada* (1926); *Nápisy na hroby* (1927); *Akrobat* (1927); *Blíženci* (1927); *Dobrodružství noci a vějíře* (1927); *Manifesty poetismu* (1928); *Židovský hřbitov* (1928); *Hra v kostky* (1928); *Kronika z konce tisíciletí* (1929); *Smuteční hrana za Otokara Březinu* (1929); *Silvestrovská noc* (1930); *Chtěla okrást Lorda Blamingtona* (1930); *Jan ve smutku* (1930); *Posedlost* (1930); *Slepec a labuť* (1930); *Snídaně v trávě* (1930); *Strach* (1930); *Dolce far niente* (1931); *Schovávaná na schodech* (1931); *Signál času* (1931); *Tyranie nebo láska* (1931); *Milenci v kiosku* (1932); *Pan Marat* (1932); *Pět prstů* (1932); *Skleněný havelok* (1932); *Jak vejce vejci* (1933); *Zpáteční lístek* (1932); *Monaco* (1934); *Sbohem a šáteček* (1933); *Neviditelná Moskva* (1935); *Věštírna delfská* (1935); *Anička skřítek a slaměný Hubert* (1936); *Frivolní báseň pro slečnu Marion* (1936); *Řetěz štěstí* (1936); *Ulice Gît-le-Cœur* (1936); *52 hořkých balad věčného studenta Roberta Davida* (1936); *Absolutní hrobař* (1937); *Josef Čapek* (1937); *Moderní básnické směry* (1937); *V říši loutek* (1937); *100 sonetů zachránkyni věčného studenta Roberta Davida* (1937); *Matka naděje* (1938); *Pražský chodec* (1938); *70 básní z podsvětí na rozloučenou se stínem věčného studenta Roberta Davida* (1938); *Historický obraz* (1939); *Manon Lescaut* (1940); *Óda na smrt Karla Hynka Máchy* (1940); *Pět minut za městem* (1940); *Loretka* (1941); *Balady Manoně* (1945); *Historický obraz: Část I–III* (1945); *Rudé armádě!* (1945); *Švábi* (1945); *Valerie a týden divů* (1945); *Veselohra s dvojníkem* (1946); *Veliký orloj* (1949); *Dílo* (38 vols., 1950–70); *Z domoviny* (1951); *Křídla* (1952); *Věci, květiny, zvířátka a lidé pro děti* (1953); *Dnes ještě zapadá slunce nad Atlantidou* (1956); *O některých problémech současné poesie* (1956); *Sloky o Praze* (1956); *Čtvero pozdravení* (1957); *Nebylo marné žít a umírat* (1957); *Veselá Praha* (1957); *Zlatý věk* (1957); *Moderní poesie* (1958); *Šípková růže* (1958); *Z mého života* (1959); *Jiřímu Wolkrovi* (1959); *Nedokončena* (1960)

BIBLIOGRAPHY: French, A., *The Poets of Prague* (1969) pp. 29–119; Martin, G., Introduction to *Three Czech Poets: V. N., Antonín Bartušek, Josef Hanzlík* (1971), pp. 11–14; Novák, A., *Czech Literature* (1976), pp. 319–31; Banerjee, M. N., "N.'s *Prague with Fingers of Rain:* A Surrealistic Image," *SEEJ*, 23 (1979), 505–14; Hansen-Löve, C., "Die Wurzeln des tschechischen Surrealismus: V. N.," *WSIA*, 4 (1979), 313–77

MARIA NĚMCOVÁ BANERJEE

NGUGI wa Thiong'o

(formerly James Ngugi) Kenyan novelist, dramatist, and essayist (writing in English and Kikuyu), b. 5 Jan. 1938, Limuru

After receiving a B.A. in English at Makerere University College (Uganda) in 1964, N. worked briefly as a journalist in Nairobi before leaving for England to pursue graduate studies at the University of Leeds. Upon returning to Kenya in 1967, he taught at the University of Nairobi, eventually becoming head of the literature department, a position he held until 1978, when he was put in detention for nearly a year by the Kenyan government. After being released, he was not reinstated in his university post; in recent years he has supported himself entirely by writing.

N. is known best for his novels, which have focused on colonial and postcolonial problems in Kenya. *Weep Not, Child* (1964), the first novel in English to be published by an East African, tells the story of a young man who loses his opportunity for further education when his family is torn apart by the violence of the Mau Mau rebellion. *The River Between* (1965), written during N.'s undergraduate years, deals with an unhappy love affair in a rural community divided between Christian converts and non-Christians; the hero is a young schoolteacher who is trying to unite his people through Western education. Both books end tragically, emphasizing the difficulty of reconciling the old with the new in a society undergoing the trauma of cultural and political transition.

N.'s later novels, written after Kenya attained independence, concentrate on the legacy of colonialism in a new nation-state. In *A Grain of Wheat* (1967) the people who sacrificed most during the liberation struggle discover that their future has been blighted by their past and that the fruits of independence are being consumed by predatory political leaders. *Petals of Blood* (1977) carries this

theme further by indicting wealthy landowners as well as politicians who capitalize on the miseries of others, thereby perpetuating economic inequality and social injustice. N. always sides with the poor, weak, and oppressed, exposing the cruelties they suffer in an exploitative neocolonial world. His most recent narrative, *Caitaani mūtharaba-Inī* (1980; *Devil on the Cross,* 1982), an allegorical novel written in Kikuyu, is an effort to make peasants and workers aware of the powerful political forces that shape their lives.

N.'s plays display the same gradual shift from colonial cultural concerns to contemporary social preoccupations. The early plays deal mainly with conflicts between parent and child and between the old and the new, but N. later teamed up with Micere Githae-Mugo (b. 1942) to write *The Trial of Dedan Kimathi* (1977), a dramatization of an episode in the career of Kenya's most prominent Mau Mau leader, and in 1977 he coauthored with Ngugi wa Mirii (b. 1951) *Ngaahika ndeenda* (1980; *I Will Marry When I Want,* 1982), a play in Kikuyu that depicts social, economic, and religious exploitation in the Kikuyu highlands. It was the staging of the latter play in Limuru, his hometown, that led to N.'s incarceration for nearly twelve months. Although no formal charges were ever filed against him, he apparently had offended members of the ruling elite in Kenya.

N.'s essays express very clearly and concisely the ideas that have animated his fiction and drama. *Homecoming: Essays on African and Caribbean Literature, Culture and Politics* (1972) places emphasis on coming to terms with the past and resisting colonial domination. *Writers in Politics* (1981) speaks of the postcolonial struggle for a patriotic national culture and outlines the writer's role in combating political repression. *Detained: A Writer's Prison Diary* (1981) provides a detailed account of his own involvement in efforts to increase the political awareness of his people.

N. remains East Africa's most articulate social commentator, someone whose works accurately reflect the tone and temper of his time and place.

FURTHER WORKS: *The Black Hermit* (1968); *This Time Tomorrow* (c. 1970); *Secret Lives* (1976)

BIBLIOGRAPHY: Roscoe, A., *Uhuru's Fire: African Literature East to South* (1977), pp.

170–90; Githae-Mugo, M., *Visions of Africa: The Fiction of Chinua Achebe, Margaret Laurence, Elspeth Huxley and N.* (1978), passim; Moore, G., *Twelve African Writers* (1980), pp. 262–88; Robson, C. B., *N.* (1980); Killam, G. D., *An Introduction to the Writings of N.* (1980); Gurr, A., *Writers in Exile: The Creative Use of Home in Modern Literature* (1981), pp. 92–121; Killman, G. D., ed., *Critical Perspectives on N.* (1982)

BERNTH LINDFORS

NGUYỄN Công Hoan

Vietnamese novelist and short-story writer, b. 6 March 1903, Bắc-ninh; d. 6 June 1977, Hanoi

Scenes N. witnessed in French Indochina—first as a boy aware of the plight of peasants pitilessly exploited by village bullies and greedy, corrupt mandarins; later as a teacher assigned to different areas of the country—he incorporated into some twenty novels and over three hundred short stories. N., who began writing in the 1920s, became one of the most accomplished representatives of social realism in modern Vietnamese literature.

N.'s finest works, which offer insight into Vietnam's outmoded customs and the life of the peasantry and the urban middle class, appeared before the 1945 revolution. His most important novel, *Bước đường cùng* (1938; *Impasse,* 1963), portrays the miserable existence of a poor, debt-ridden peasant whose life is constantly threatened by natural disasters. The protagonist dares to rise up against his enemies: the landlords, the usurers, the petty local officials. This book was banned by the colonial administration.

N. is at his best when, using clear and witty language, he lashes out against injustices and corruption condoned by the French administration and against injustice and oppression in his feudal and colonial society. He treats bribery, for example, in about ten stories.

In N.'s novels plot is secondary to theme and style. For example, family conflicts, occasioned by the influence of Confucian ethics, are analyzed through skillfully constructed dialogue, as in *Cô giáo Minh* (1936; teacher Minh). Whether he portrays an audience unwittingly forcing an actor to prolong his jokes at the very time when his father is about to die, or a rickshaw boy getting stuck on New Year's Eve with a penniless prostitute as his passenger, or a mother leaving her child home to go out with her lover, N. exposes the meanness, wickedness, and deceit of people around him.

After 1954, when the French were defeated and a Communist government was established in North Vietnam, N.'s central themes became nationalism and socialist construction. In 1957 he was elected president of the Vietnam Writers' Association in Hanoi.

FURTHER WORKS: *Kiếp hồng nhan* (1923); *Những cảnh khốn nạn* (1932); *Ông chủ* (1934); *Bà chủ* (1935); *Kép Tư Bền* (1935); *Tấm lòng vàng* (1937); *Tờ vường* (1938); *Lá ngọc cành vàng* (1938); *Tay trắng, trắng tay* (1940); *Chiếc nhẫn vàng* (1940); *Nợ nần* (1940); *Lê Dung* (1944); *Đồng-chí Tư* (1946); *Xổng cũi* (1947); *Tranh tối tranh sáng* (1956); *Hỗn canh hỗn cư* (1961); *Đống rác cũ* (1963)

BIBLIOGRAPHY: Durand, M. M., and Nguyễn-Trần Huân, *Introduction à la littérature vietnamienne* (1969), p. 197; Hoàng Ngọc-Thành, *The Social and Political Development of Vietnam as Seen through the Modern Novel* (1969), pp. 222–30; Bùi Xuân-Bào, *Le roman vietnamien contemporain* (1972), pp. 218–28; Trương Đình Hùng, "N. C. H. (1903–1977): A Realist Writer," *Viet Nam Courier,* Oct. 1977, 26–29

DINH-HOA NGUYEN

NHẤT-LINH

(pseud. of Nguyễn Tường-Tam) Vietnamese novelist and short-story writer, b. 25 July 1906, Hai-duong; d. 7 July 1963, Saigon

N.-L. was one of the founders, in 1933, of the "Self-Reliant" group, which rejected traditional Vietnamese literature. He was also a social reformer and a political leader. He served as foreign minister in the Vietminh-dominated government of the Democratic Republic of Vietnam, took part in the negotiations with the French, and at the time of partition chose to live in South Vietnam. He committed suicide while a political prisoner of the Ngo Dinh Diem regime.

N.-L. began writing early: the short stories "Nho phong" (1926; the scholars' tradition) and "Người quay tơ" (1927; the spinner) appeared before his three-year stay in Paris (1927–30) as a student. These romantic and traditional stories contrast with his later works, which are realistic, patriotic, and revolutionary.

N.-L.'s most famous novel, *Đoạn tuyệt* (1934; break-off), is a sophisticated and resolute work championing individual freedom and the pursuit of happiness. The heroine, Loan, is ill-treated by a superstitious, cruel, and greedy mother-in-law; Loan, who kills her husband by accident, is acquitted because she is seen as a victim of the conflict between traditions and the new concept of women's rights. The title of the book pinpoints the movement away from the oppressive paternalistic kinship system.

The novels N.-L. wrote between 1935 and 1942 all depict the weaknesses of Vietnamese family and social structures. His characters, struggling for changes in their own lives and in society, rebel against age-old traditions. *Lạnh lùng* (1937; loneliness) tells the story of a young widow in love with her son's tutor. The happiness she feels in the tutor's arms cannot last, since she is afraid of social ostracism. In *Đôi bạn* (1938; two friends), a sequel to *Đoạn tuyệt*, N.-L.'s revolutionary ideals are evident. Patriotic zeal and anticolonialism are equated with dreams of individual freedom and a youthful thirst for heroic action.

In collaboration with Khái-Hưng (pseud. of Trần Khánh-Giư, 1896–1947), N.-L. wrote two excellent novels: *Gánh hàng hoa* (1934; the florist's load), about the innocent love of a young florist, and *Đời mưa gió* (1936; a stormy life), which depicts the life of a girl who, emancipated from the shackles of tradtional clan life, has to become a prostitute to earn her rights as an individual.

N.-L.'s style is alternately poetic and precise. In a work like *Lạnh lùng* it is a model of clarity, precision, and balance.

FURTHER WORKS: *Anh phải sống* (1933, with Khái-Hưng); *Tối tăm* (1936); *Hai buổi chiều vàng* (1937); *Bướm trắng* (1941); *Nắng thu* (1948); *Xóm Cầu mới* (1958); *Dòng sông Thanh-thuỷ* (1961); *Mối tình "Chân"* (1961); *Thương chồng* (1961); *Viết vàđọc tiểu-thuyết* (1961)

BIBLIOGRAPHY: O'Harrow, S., "Some Background Notes on N.-L. (Nguyễn Tường Tam, 1906–1963)," *France-Asie,* 22 (1968), 205–20; Durand, M. M., and Nguyễn-Trần Huân, *Introduction à la littérature vietnamienne* (1969), passim; Hoàng Ngọc-Thành, *The Social and Political Development of Vietnam as*

Seen through the Modern Novel (1969), pp. 182–204; Bùi Xuân-Bào, *Le roman vietnamien contemporain* (1972), pp. 164–83, 364–72

DINH-HOA NGUYEN

NICARAGUAN LITERATURE
See Central American Literature

NIGERIAN LITERATURE

In addition to oral art, which has been produced in the course of the centuries in the more than two hundred languages and dialects spoken by a population of nearly eighty million, Nigeria has been a prolific producer of written poetry, which began in the Muslim north, in the Arabic language, in the 15th c. The late 18th c. saw the emergence of *ajami*-type literature—that is, literature written in Arabic script used for the transliteration of such non-Arabic languages as Fula and Hausa.

In Hausa

Hausa, which is the main language of northern Nigeria, became all the more important as Western missionaries adapted the Roman alphabet to it for printing. In the 1930s the Literature Bureau at Zaria encouraged young literati to create prose fiction in Hausa: one of these early writers, who signed himself Abubakar Bauchi, was to become the first prime minister of independent Nigeria as Sir Abubakar Tafawa Balewa (1912–1966). Nevertheless, poetry has remained the most widely practiced and respected genre, with such talented authors as Sa'adu Zungur (1915–1958), Mudi Sipikim (b. 1930), and Mu'azu Hadejia (1920–1955). Formal drama, which had been initiated in the 1930s by Abubakar Imam (b. 1911), does not seem to be very popular, although it is practiced by a few members of the younger generation, such as Shu'aibu Makarfi (dates n.a.) and Umaru A. Dembo (b. 1945). Significantly, the Hausa have produced hardly any imaginative writing in English.

In Yoruba

Literacy was brought to the Yoruba of western Nigeria in the mid-19th c. by one of their own, Samuel Crowther (1809–1891), a freed slave who had been educated in Sierra Leone; he put the language in writing in order to translate the Bible. Although Yoruba was used for writing purposes from the late 19th c. on, especially in local newspapers, it did not reach its literary maturity until Daniel O. Fagunwa (1910–1963) had his first, highly original works of prose fiction printed in the 1950s; often described as "romances," these are traditional oral tales woven onto a central narrative thread, and slightly modernized to bring them in harmony with the moral tenets of Christianity. One of them was translated into English by Wole Soyinka (q.v.) as *The Forest of a Thousand Daemons* (1968). Novels closer to Western models were produced almost simultaneously by Chief Isaac O. Delano (b. 1904). Two distinct trends were thus initiated: one, originating in the rich store of local lore, was pursued by Gabriel E. Ojo (1925–1962), Olaya Fagbamigbe (b. 1930), Ogunsina Ogundele (b. 1925), and D. J. Fantanmi (b. 1938). The other, which seeks to reflect the problems of contemporary life, has on the whole been less successful: its main representative is Femi Jeboda (b. 1933). But while most of those writers were trained as schoolteachers, after independence Yoruba literature was enriched by the emergence of a number of university-educated authors who gave it greater complexity: Adeboye Babalola (b. 1926), a playwright and a well-known student of oral art, Adebayo Faleti (b. 1935), a versatile writer who has been active in narrative poetry and prose as well as in drama, and Afolabi Olabimtan (b. 1932). Yet another strikingly original Nigerian contribution to African literature is the dramatic genre known as the "Yoruba opera" because of the strong admixture of music and dance. Rooted in the biblical plays that were performed in mission schools in the 1930s, it made its real beginning in the early 1940s when Hubert Ogunde (b. 1916) founded his Concert Company; he produced a satirical play with definitely political overtones that became well known throughout West Africa, and his example was soon followed by E. Kola Ogunmola (1925–1973) and his traveling theater, whose outlook was conspicuously Christian and moralizing. The most widely known representative was Duro Ladipo (1931–1978), who was chiefly inspired by Yoruba myths and historical legends: his company was famed even in Europe, and several of his works

were translated into English (*Three Yoruba Plays,* 1964).

In English

While the Yoruba had started creating a written art in their own language by the middle of the century, they, unlike the Hausa, also contributed significantly to the emergence and growth of Nigerian literature in English. Until the late 1950s, this had been represented only by the mediocre versifying of Denis Osadebay (b. 1911). The first Nigerian writer to reach international fame was Amos Tutuola (q.v.), whose first piece of prose fiction, *The Palm-Wine Drinkard and his Dead Palm-Wine Tapster in the Dead's Town* (1952) was enormously successful throughout Western countries, not only because of the author's highly idiosyncratic style but also because of the striking originality of the tale itself, which was derived, in fact, from the oral tradition and from Daniel O. Fagunwa's own recordings of it. Timothy M. Aluko (b. 1918) with *One Man, One Wife* (1959) inaugurated a series of satirical novels of a more conventional type, which constitute an imaginative chronicle of the evolution of Nigerian society and mores. And on the occasion of independence in 1960, Wole Soyinka produced *A Dance of the Forests,* a powerful drama in which elements drawn from the Yoruba tradition are combined to convey a message of national unity.

Besides Yoruba folklore and satirical wit, modern Nigerian literature is also rooted in a different, urban form of popular art: the so-called "Onitsha chapbooks" of the Igbo people. Written in substandard but often picturesque English, printed mostly in the Igbo market town of Onitsha, these became exceedingly popular among the Igbo lower middle class during the 1950s. It was as a purveyor of such subliterary pamphlets that Cyprian Ekwensi (q.v.) made his beginnings with a mawkish novelette, *When Love Whispers* (1948); but his *People of the City* (1954) made him known throughout the English-speaking world as the novelist of Nigerian city life. Although there are nearly ten million Igbo people in southeastern Nigeria, hardly any creative writing has been produced in the vernacular in spite of the efforts of Peter Nwana (dates n.a.) with *Omenuko* (1933; Omenuko) and, three decades later, of Leopold Bell-Gam (dates n.a.) with *Ije Odumodu jere* (1963; Odumodu's travels).

There is no doubt that the element that was chiefly responsible for giving Nigerian writing the decisive impetus that was to win for Nigeria undisputed leadership in black African literature in English was the cluster of initiatives that were taken around 1960 in the university town of Ibadan. The university college had been created in 1947. Ten years later its English department had become a hatching place for young writers, who could find an outlet for their youthful efforts in the student magazine *The Horn;* contributors from 1957 to 1960 included John Pepper Clark, Christopher Okigbo (qq.v), Wole Soyinka, and several other Ibadan students and graduates. While these were trying their hand in *The Horn,* two Germans, Janheinz Jahn (1918–1973) and Ulli Beier (b. 1922), launched (also in 1957 at Ibadan) a literary periodical named *Black Orpheus* after the title of Jean-Paul Sartre's (q.v.) famous preface to Leopold Sédar Senghor's (q.v.) *Anthologie de la nouvelle poésie nègre et malgache de langue française* (1948; anthology of the new black poetry in the French language). The journal's first task was to make available, to African readers of English, the already abundant amount of creative writing that had been produced in French during the 1950s in Africa and in the West Indies. After a few issues, however, original African contributions in English became more and more numerous, coming not only from Nigeria but also from elsewhere in West Africa and other parts of the continent. These two modest streams coalesced more or less formally when Ulli Beier founded (still at Ibadan) the Mbari Club, the name of which (meaning a certain kind of shrine) was suggested by the novelist Chinua Achebe (q.v.); while spreading to other parts of Nigeria (Duro Ladipo founded a Mbari Club in his hometown of Oshogbo), Mbari generated its own publishing firm and issued, between 1961 and 1964, several plays, novels, and collections of poetry by writers who now appear as the founding fathers of modern English-language literature in Africa.

By the time the civil war broke out in 1966, Nigeria could boast impressive achievements in creative writing. Poetry was dominated by Christopher Okigbo, who was killed during the Biafra war; his two slender collections, *Heavensgate* (1962) and *Limits* (1964), contain poems of exceptional excellence, some of which had previously appeared in *The Horn* and in *Black Orpheus;* they focus on familiar areas of experience, such as nostalgia for the African past, the sociopolitical problems of the present, and the eternal theme of the nature of love; but in spite of their social and historical relevance, they are first and foremost works of art, whose incantatory quality owes much to the music of Igbo oral art, even though Okigbo's techniques in the use of imagery may have been partly derived from English poetry of the generation of Yeats and Eliot (qq.v.). Another promising poet was Michael Echeruo (b. 1937), who seems to have given up poetry in favor of scholarship and criticism after his only collection, *Morality* (1968).

During the early years of independence, drama was entirely dominated by Wole Soyinka, who easily outclassed James Ene Henshaw (b. 1924), a popular author of "well-made" comedies such as *This Is Our Chance* (1956), and even his contemporary John Pepper Clark, whose *Song of a Goat* (1961) was more successful perhaps as poetry than as tragedy; Clark soon turned to the study of his native Ijaw folk tradition, editing its oral epic and giving it dramatic shape in *Ozidi* (1966). But it was Soyinka who chronicled—not only in dramatic terms, but also in his novel *The Interpreters* (1965)—Africa's dizzy descent toward the murky depths of despotism or anarchy. Whereas his 1960 play *A Dance of the Forests* had been a celebration calling on traditional myth and performance practice, *Kongi's Harvest* (1967) and *Madmen and Specialists* (1971), "enriched" by direct experience of civil war, were, as Soyinka himself put it, "an ironic expression of horror at the universal triumph of expediency and power lust."

Meanwhile, the vitality and attractiveness of Yoruba culture were illustrated in a very odd way in *The Imprisonment of Obatala, and Other Plays* (1966), whose author, who called himself "Obotunde Ijimere," was none other than Ulli Beier, translating into modern drama in English episodes from Nigerian folklore. Until the late 1970s Yoruba playwrights maintained a privileged (although by no means monopolistic) position in Nigerian drama, with such younger authors as Ola Rotimi (b. 1938) and Wale Ogunyemi (b. 1939).

In the making of the Nigerian novel, however, Igbo writers, led by Chinua Achebe, provided the main impetus. Achebe's early novels either explored the weakness that had caused the traditional society to collapse so easily under the impact of Europe—*Things Fall Apart* (1958), *Arrow of God* (1964)—or else analyzed the inner culture clash tormenting the Westernized African—*No Longer at Ease* (1960). In some way, the conflict between native tradition and imported novelty was basic to the Nigerian novel of the early 1960s; some writers—like Onuora Nzekwu (b. 1928), Ntieyong U. Akpan (b. 1924), and Obi Egbuna (b. 1938), who is also a playwright—chose to lament, sometimes in a humorous way, the disappearance of age-old customs and beliefs, while others—such as Timothy M. Aluko and Vincent C. Ike (b. 1931)—chose to welcome the winds of change.

In the mid-1960s, while a number of other young Igbo novelists—Nkem Nwankwo (b. 1936), Flora Nwapa (b. 1931), and especially Elechi Amadi (b. 1934) with his second novel, *The Great Ponds* (1969)—turned to the tribal past for literary inspiration, setting their stories in rural communities that had little or no contact with the outside world, the moral, social, and above all political deliquescence of the country was increasingly preoccupying the more sensitive observers. Frank criticism of the corruption of the leading classes, which had played a peripheral role in some of Ekwensi's novels—*Jagua Nana* (1961), *Beautiful Feathers* (1963)—and in *The Voice* (1964), the strange allegorical and experimental novel of Ijaw writer Gabriel Okara (q.v.), became the main theme of more ambitious works with ironic titles such as Achebe's *A Man of the People* (1966) or Aluko's *Chief the Honourable Minister* (1970).

The Biafra war thus broke out in an atmosphere of disillusionment. Its traumatic impact made itself felt throughout Nigeria's literature with unprecedented intensity. The death of Okigbo was felt as a symbol of Africa destroying the best of her own substance in old-fashioned tribal quarrels. Some of the major writers turned to new modes of expression: while Clark voiced his despair in poetry—*Casualties: Poems 1966–1968* (1970)—Achebe gave up the novel in favor of poetry—*Beware, Soul Brother, and Other Poems* (1971)—and the short story—*Girls at War, and Other Stories* (1972); besides *Madmen and Specialists,* Wole Soyinka expressed his own concern and experience in an autobiography, *The Man Died: Prison Notes* (1972) (as did Elechi Amadi with *Sunset in Biafra: A Civil War Diary* [1973]), in poetry in *A Shuttle in the Crypt* (1972), and in his second novel, *Season of Anomy* (1973).

With John Munonye's (b. 1929) novel *A Wreath for the Maidens* (1973) and Flora Nwapa's novel *Never Again* (1974), it became clear that the civil war was on its way to becoming a mere literary cliché. It had nevertheless provided genuine inspiration for a younger generation of writers, who had been in their twenties when it broke out. These included Sebastian O. Mezu (b. 1941), with *Behind the Rising Sun* (1971), and Kole Omotoso (b. 1943), with *The Combat* (1972). But the restoration of peace in 1970, the comparative orderliness maintained by moderate military regimes, and the economic prosperity resulting from the discovery of oil also had their literary aftermath throughout the 1970s. For the new generation of writers, born in the 1940s, who had little knowledge of the colonial regime and of the struggle for independence, who were thoroughly urbanized and found traditional mores and ideas totally irrelevant to life in a modern society, who had attended one or several of Nigeria's eighteen universities and/or foreign institutions of higher learning as a matter of course, and for whom the rapid growth of the educational system had prepared a sizable public of literate readers, the Biafra war belonged to an outdated tribal past, the obsolete tensions of which were profitably manipulated by foreign capitalistic interests. What they regarded as the elitist posture of their elders, who had been trying to graft their own work onto a venerable but alien tradition ranging from Shakespeare through Jane Austen to Yeats and Eliot, was as anachronistically irrelevant as their alleged veneration for the so-called "African" values, the legends, the memories, the myths, and the superstitious creeds of a society that Nigeria, they felt, had outgrown.

Although a playwright of such exceptional ability as Ola Rotimi successfully managed, in *The Gods Are Not to Blame* (1968) and in ensuing plays, to put modern scenic techniques and the manipulation of dramatic space to the service of a type of inspiration that remained recognizably Yoruba, the novel outpaced both drama and poetry in the 1970s. Given the rebellious outlook of the post-civil-war generation, it is not surprising that they should have chosen for their masters, guides, and models, two writers whom academic criticism had hitherto regarded as comparatively minor: Cyprian Ekwensi, the founder of the urban novel, and John Munonye, whose many novels, from *The Only Son* (1966) to *Bridge to a Wedding* (1978), had mostly been devoted to recording the condition of the common man. This revulsion from profundity led to a literature that was at the same time popular and populist, and whose diffusion was greatly helped by the multiplication of private publishing houses, aiming, perhaps, to fill the void created by the destruction of Onitsha during the civil war. Since 1956 Ogali A. Ogali (b. 1935) had been one of the most prolific purveyors of popular reading, and during the 1970s there were many who shared with him the rewards of this profitable branch of the entertainment business. Some of the novelists who had already emerged before the civil war, such as Nkem Nwankwo, Obi Egbuna, and Vincent C. Ike, turned their satirical glance toward the ebullient urban society of the new Nigeria, and so did (although with angrier overtones) the younger writer Femi Osofisan (b. 1946) in his novel *Kolera Kolej* (1975) and especially in his various plays, such as *The Chattering and the Song* (1975), which "offers a model of the new society as well as a condemnation of the old" (Gerald Moore). But others, like Isidore Okpewho (b. 1941) in *The Victims* (1970), I. N. C. Aniebo (b. 1939) in *The Journey Within* (1978), and many of their generation—for instance, Charles Njoku (dates n.a.) in *The New Breed* (1978) or Festus Iyayi (dates n.a.) in *Violence* (1979)—chose to offer a realistic depiction of the common town dweller's experiences and ordeals, as did Nigeria's first woman playwright, Zulu Sofola (b. 1935). The theme of the culture clash and the motif of the "been-to" (returnee), both of which had been prominent in pre-civil-war writing, received new dimensions with *The Edifice* (1971) by Kole Omotoso, who has since become one of the dynamic leaders of the new Nigerian literature, and with *Second Class Citizen* (1976) by Buchi Emecheta (b. 1944), whose later novels gave ever more compelling voice to the new militancy of African womanhood.

As the 1980s dawned, it was clear that Nigerian literature, having outgrown its pioneering period, still remained the herald and the model it had been (although with Kenya close on its heels): it provided articulate evidence that this enormous, populous, and resourceful new republic had at last joined the modern society of nations, the modern world of industrialization and urbanization, with its standardized universal conflicts and tensions taking the place of the futile idealizations, the pointless nostalgia, the small-scale, parochial-tribal confrontations that had provided earlier writers with their usual subject matter.

BIBLIOGRAPHY: Laurence, M., *Long Drums and Cannons: Nigerian Dramatists and Novelists 1952–1966* (1968); Klíma, V., *Modern Nigerian Novels* (1969); King, B., ed., *Introduction to Nigerian Literature* (1971); Roscoe, A. A., *Mother Is Gold: A Study in West African Literature* (1971); Obiechina, E., *An African Popular Literature: A Study of Onitsha Market Pamphlets* (1973); Udeyop, N. J., *Three Nigerian Poets* (1973); Lindfors, B., ed., *Critical Perspectives on Nigerian Literature* (1976); Momodu, A. G. S., and Schild, U., eds., *Nigerian Writing: Nigeria as Seen by Her Own Writers as Well as by German Authors* (1976); Emenyonou, E., *The Rise of the Igbo Novel* (1978); Baldwin, C., comp., *Nigerian Literature: A Bibliography of Criticism, 1952–1976* (1980); Booth, J., *Writers and Politics in Nigeria* (1981)

ALBERT S. GÉRARD

NIJHOFF, Martinus

Dutch poet and dramatist, b. 20 April 1894, The Hague; d. 26 Jan. 1953, The Hague

N. studied law in Amsterdam and later Dutch literature in Utrecht, and served as editor of *De gids* from 1926 to 1933. His poetry began to appear at the time of World War I, and he established himself as one of the most eminent Dutch literary figures of his time.

His poetry, notable for its lucidity, is carefully crafted: N. sometimes reworked already published poems. In his earlier work he makes effective use of the sonnet. Later in his career he often used looser forms, and in the verse dramas that absorbed much of his literary energy later in his life he developed a flowing verse line closer to the conversational.

A central theme in his work is the confusion of individual lives in contrast to a higher or deeper order, perhaps that established by God. This sharply etched poetry, never vague or indefinite, is full of unexpected images: the moon as a muffled sun, a satyr offering currants to the infant Christ, Saint Sebastian removing his arrows and finding himself in a modern Dutch landscape. It is poetry informed by a sense of disquiet, at times of anguish, and a recurring thematic action is breaking, both in the sense of giving way and of breaking through.

N.'s early inspiration was often religious, although the nature and degree of his belief has been a much discussed subject. Related to this impulse is the frequent return to the theme of the dead mother, a subject handled in a sensitive yet unsentimental way. N.'s later lyrics become more sensual although without losing the delicacy of tone and feeling of the earlier poems. They are more musical, and music enters as a theme. The tone of his best poems is that of a dark romanticism, where life and death exist as attractive counterweights.

Of his longer poems, *Awater* (1934; "Awater," 1954) and *Het uur U* (1942; H-hour) are the most noteworthy. Both are concerned with the unexpected effect the passage of a stranger has on the emotional lives of others, a heightening of emotions not without surrealistic overtones. Each poem leaves the reader with a sense that some breach in the order of things has been accomplished. The failure of the narrator and of others to make any but the most fleeting contact with the passing stranger is related to the theme of leaving others and of being left, a theme that recurs in the shorter poems as well.

N. was also a popular and effective writer of verse drama. His most important work of this kind is the series of three plays for Christmas, Easter, and Pentecost respectively written during World War II and later collected under the title *Het heilige hout* (1950; the sacred wood): *De ster van Bethlehem* (1942; the star of Bethlehem), *De Dag des Heren* (1949; the Lord's Day), and *Des Heilands tuin* (1950; the Savior's garden). He has also been much admired for his translations, notably of Euripides' *Iphigenia in Tauris* and T. S. Eliot's (q.v.) *The Cocktail Party*.

FURTHER WORKS: *De wandelaar* (1916); *Pierrot aan de lantaarn* (1919); *Vormen* (1924); *De pen op papier* (1926); *De vliegende Hollander* (1930); *Gedachten op dinsdag* (1931); *Halewijn* (1933); *Nieuwe gedichten* (1934); *Een idylle* (1940); *Verzameld werk* (3 vols., 1954–61)

BIBLIOGRAPHY: Sötemann, A. L., " 'Non-spectacular' Modernism: M. N.'s Poetry in Its European Context," in Bulhof, F., ed., *N., Van Ostaijen, De Stijl* (1976), pp. 95–116; Fokkema, D. W., "N.'s Modernist Poetics in European Perspective," in Fokkema, D. W., et al., eds., *Comparative Poetics* (1976), pp. 63–87

FRED J. NICHOLS

NIN, Anaïs

American diarist, novelist, and critic, b. 21 Feb. 1903, Paris, France; d. 14 Jan. 1977, Los Angeles, Cal.

After a cosmopolitan childhood in Europe, N. came to the U.S. with her Danish mother and two brothers in 1914, following the desertion of the father, the Cuban-born composer-pianist Joaquin Nin. Largely self-educated, she spent her youth reading and keeping a journal, which she initially wrote in French and did not begin to write in English until she was seventeen. In 1923 she married Hugh Guiler, who later became known as an engraver and filmmaker under the name of Ian Hugo; N. reproduced a number of his engravings in her fiction and appeared in his early films. During the 1930s N. lived in Paris, where she became the confidante and promoter of such writers as Henry Miller, Lawrence Durrell, Antonin Artaud (qq.v.) and of the psychologist Otto Rank, with whom she worked as a lay analyst. Returning to the U.S. at the outbreak of World War II, she set up her own printing press when publishers refused her work, and in the 1940s and 1950s she became allied with such younger writers as Robert Duncan, Gore Vidal (qq.v.), and James Leo Herlihy (b. 1927). Following the success of the publication of the first volume of *The Diary* (7 vols., 1966–80), N. became a much sought-after public speaker. In 1973 she was the subject of a documentary film, *Anaïs Observed*.

Although a highly poetic style and emphasis upon psychological reality are the distinguishing features of all of N.'s writing, if viewed chronologically her fiction also presents a movement from the inner to the outer, from the subjective to the objective, which dramatizes her general conviction that self-realization must precede social commitment. *House of Incest* (1936), her first fictional work, is a surrealistic prose poem wherein a self-obsessed narrator encounters fragments of herself in a desperate quest to find the core of her identity; *Collages* (1964), N.'s last work of fiction, is a loosely connected series of portraits of a wide variety of characters, and the prevailing tone is a combination of social criticism and good humor.

Published collectively under the title of *Cities of the Interior* (1959; enlarged version, 1974), five novels constitute the central core of N.'s fiction: *Ladders to Fire* (1946), *Children of the Albatross* (1947), *The Four-Chambered Heart* (1950), *A Spy in the House of Love* (1954), and *Solar Barque* (1958; enlarged and pub. as *Seduction of the Minotaur,* 1961). Designed to explore the nature and causes of discontent in four basic female types, the series illustrates N.'s grounding in contemporary psychological theory as well as the extent to which such theory was grounded in the four-humors psychology of the past. The problem of each female type is to reconcile her basic nature with the image she has projected and to admit to her own responsibility for the conflict between the two. At the same time, N.'s concern is to demonstrate the limitations of type-casting and the need to recognize that each type represents merely the ascendancy of one aspect of woman, who is in actuality a composite.

In keeping with general trends in early-20th-c. fiction, N.'s novels utilize limited point of view, stream of consciousness (q.v.), and association rather than sequence as a structural principle, but she employs these devices to an extreme that makes her work very different from that of Virginia Woolf, James Joyce, or Ernest Hemingway (qq.v.). Characterized by the elimination of all sociological details or sense of historical time, N.'s method of composition has more in common with modern trends in music and the pictorial arts, analogues that she herself emphasizes in her literary manifesto, *The Novel of the Future* (1968).

It is, however, *The Diary of A. N.* that is her masterpiece and her most significant contribution. Covering the years from 1931 to 1977, based on the original private journal N. kept during this period, and including correspondence and photographs, *The Diary* provides fascinating insights into her development as a woman and artist, although because it is a highly edited version of the original, *The Diary* should not be read as a biographical document but rather as a work of art. Each volume has a controlling theme and is structured as an aesthetic whole, while the series itself reflects the movement from inner to outer which characterizes her fiction. Internally, the art of *The Diary* lies in the quality of N.'s prose, which is rich and

rhythmic to the point of incantation; its literary merits also derive from N.'s sense of the dramatic: individuals and scenes are vividly and concretely realized; conversations are presented in dialogue form; episodes are narrated in the present tense; lengthy observations are juxtaposed with cryptic comments; related themes are introduced after the fashion of subplots; and finally, the N. persona herself is a multifaceted protagonist whose various selves are continually in conflict with each other. Aside from the contemporaneity of the issues N. addresses, it is this dramatic flair which makes *The Diary* seem so immediate, and which in turn distinguishes it from other memoirs and journals.

Also characterized by its presentness is *A Woman Speaks: The Lectures, Seminars, and Interviews of A. N.* (1975), wherein are represented N.'s attitudes toward current trends in general and toward the women's liberation movement in particular. Dissociating herself from the political activism of feminists, N. advocates journal keeping as a preliminary requirement for a liberated self, to be followed by cooperation with men in the interests of mutual growth—ideas she also explores in *In Favor of the Sensitive Man* (1976).

Influenced by D. H. Lawrence (q.v.), about whom she wrote her first critical work, *D. H. Lawrence: An Unprofessional Study* (1932), all of N.'s writing has an erotic quality. In the early 1940s, however, she wrote a series of specifically sexual pieces, which were edited and published posthumously as *Delta of Venus* (1977) and *Little Birds* (1979). Although the quality is uneven, these pieces do as a whole illustrate in a subtle way N.'s contention that women's writing about sex differs from men's and that the difference between pornography and erotica lies in the poetic quality of the latter.

Largely ignored until the 1960s, N. is today rightly regarded as one of the leading women writers of the 20th c., and the one who has done most to pioneer and perfect a distinctly feminine mode of perception and articulation. She has also become a source of inspiration for those who would respond creatively to the self-destructive features of our time and who would see obstacles as challenges and life as an adventure.

FURTHER WORKS: *Winter of Artifice* (1939); *Under a Glass Bell* (1944); *Realism and Reality* (1946); *On Writing* (1947); *Waste of*

Timelessness, and Other Early Stories (1977); *Linotte: The Early Diary of A. N. 1914–1920* (1978); *The Early Diary of A. N.: Volume Two, 1920–1923* (1982)

BIBLIOGRAPHY: Evans, O., *A. N.* (1968); Hinz, E., *The Mirror and the Garden: Realism and Reality in the Writings of A. N.*, rev. ed. (1973); Zaller, R., ed., *A Casebook on A. N.* (1974); Spencer, S., *Collage of Dreams: The Writings of A. N.* (1977); Knapp, B., *A. N.* (1978); special N. issue, *Mosaic*, 11, 2 (1978); Cutting, R., *A. N.: A Reference Guide* (1978); Franklin, B., and Schneider, D., *A. N.: An Introduction* (1979)

EVELYN J. HINZ

DER NISTER

(pseud. [Yiddish, "the concealed one"] of Pinkhes Kahanovitsh) Yiddish novelist and short-story writer, b. 1 Nov. 1884, Berdichev, Ukraine; d. 4 June 1950, a labor-camp hospital, U.S.S.R.

N. received a traditional Jewish education but also read widely in Russian. His spiritual and literary development was greatly influenced by his older brother, a Bratzlaver Hasid, who is reflected in the character of Luzi in N.'s magnum opus the novel *Di mishpokhe Mashber* (2 vols., 1939, 1948; the Mashber family). His first book, *Gedanken un motivn* (1907; thoughts and motifs), a collection of short poetic prose pieces, contains the universal themes that recur in his later works: man's divine-satanic duality, the eternal contradiction between aspiration and reality, and the ebb and flow of human emotion. *Hekher fun der erd* (1910; higher than the earth) represents an attempt to write modern Kabbalistic tales.

N. left Soviet Russia in 1921 for Berlin, where he published *Gedakht* (2 vols., 1922–23; imagined), the first collection of his visionary and fantastic tales. He revived the Hasidic symbolic tale created by Rabbi Nachman of Bratzlav (1772–1811) and developed a very distinctive style in Yiddish literature, one synthesizing the Jewish mystical tradition with world mythology. Influenced by Russian symbolism (q.v.), N. integrated its characteristic symbols, verb inversions, and lyrical effects into his Yiddish writing. The hypnotic rhythms of his long sentences and their special musicality, his archaic diction and the repeated use of "and" demand and hold the reader's attention and usher him into a surrealistic atmosphere.

N. returned to the Soviet Union in 1926 and contributed to those publications still open to "fellow-traveling" writers. He also produced works for children and translations into Yiddish, literary activities he had begun during his residence in Kiev (1918–20). With the triumph of the "proletarian" critics in 1929, his work was violently condemned. He ceased publishing for a time. His last symbolist story, the complex "Unter a ployt" (1929; "Under a Fence," 1977), is both a concealed protest against regimentation of the arts and a tortured self-accusation for abandoning his symbolist art.

N. subsequently conceived a literary stratagem to rescue his artistic conscience as well as his existence as a Soviet writer. His family saga, *Di mishpokhe Mashber,* appeared on the surface to comply with the tenets of realism but it still served the author's intimate aesthetic, philosophical, and Jewish national purposes. It absorbed much from his symbolist period. This novel, perhaps the greatest work of Soviet-Yiddish prose, was conceived as the portrait of a traditional society in dissolution: N. intended to depict eastern European Jewry from the 1870s to the Russian Revolution. The two published volumes (the third may exist in manuscript), however, cover less than a year of the 1870s in the most Jewish town of the Ukraine, Berdichev. The depiction of Jewish life, particularly of the Bratzlaver Hasidim, is deeply sympathetic rather than critical. The novel's chief protagonists are the same anguished seekers found in the earlier tales.

N. perished in the liquidation of Yiddish writers following the suppression of Jewish cultural life in the Soviet Union in 1948.

FURTHER WORKS: *Gezang un gebet* (1912); *Mayselekh in ferzn* (1918); *A bove-mayse; oder, Di mayse mit di melokhim* (1921); *Motivn* (1922); *Fun mayne giter* (1929); *Dray hoyptshtet* (1934); *Karbones* (1943); *Der zeyde mitn eynikl* (1943); *Heshl Ansheles* (1943); *Inem okupirtn Polyn* (1945); *Dersteylungen un eseyen* (1957)

BIBLIOGRAPHY: Shmeruk, K., "D. N.'s 'Under a Fence': Tribulations of a Soviet Yiddish Symbolist," in Weinreich, U., ed., *The Field of Yiddish: Studies in Language, Folklore and Literature, Second Collection* (1965), pp. 263–87; Madison, C. A., *Yiddish Literature:*

Its Scope and Major Writers (1968), pp. 415–23; Liptzin, S., *A History of Yiddish Literature* (1972), pp. 199–203; Shmeruk, C., "Yiddish Literature in the U.S.S.R.," in Kochan, L., ed., *The Jews in Soviet Russia since 1917* (1978), pp. 242–80

EUGENE ORENSTEIN

NIZAN, Paul

French novelist and essayist, b. 7 Feb. 1905, Tours; d. 23 May 1940, Saint-Omer

The son of a middle-class mother and of a father who had worked his way up from the proletariat, N., according to his friend Jean-Paul Sartre (q.v.), may have lived out this class conflict all of his short life. The two were classmates at secondary school and at the École Normale Supérieure in Paris, where N. excelled in philosophy. He flirted briefly with fascism and religion, but soon gravitated to the Communist Party, where he remained until he resigned in the wake of the Hitler-Stalin Pact in 1939. N. was killed by a stray bullet early in World War II.

A voyage to Aden in 1926 resulted in his first book, *Aden-Arabie* (1931; *Aden-Arabie,* 1968), an account of his youthful flight to the East that turns into a bitter attack on European capitalism. This was followed by *Les chiens de garde* (1932; *The Watchdogs,* 1971), a polemic in which he argued that philosophy as such does not exist, only philosophies as expressions of a class or an age.

Antoine Bloyé (1933; *Antoine Bloyé,* 1973), the story of a laborer who rises to the middle class only to discover the emptiness of his life, is a rare example of a successful proletarian novel. Although written from a Marxist perspective, it does not view existence as determined solely by economic considerations; the unconscious and its dreams, religion, and the libido play their roles as well. *Le cheval de Troie* (1935; *The Trojan Horse,* 1975) is a political novel, the account of an attempt to organize the workers of a provincial town. Although it rises above the stereotypical strategies of Socialist Realism (q.v.), the novel was not well received.

La conspiration (1938; the conspiracy) better illustrates N.'s strengths. It is an ironic but sobering look at the follies of intellectual youth who act out their inarticulate rebellion against family and society in irresponsible ways. Thanks in part to the ambiguity of its point of view, it becomes as much a novel about the rites of passage into modern capitalist society as it is a plot of passwords and betrayal and an indictment of the void at the heart of bourgeois life.

N.'s brief career disproves the notion held by some critics that commitment to an ideology makes it impossible to write well. His books are being republished and read again today, after a period of oblivion.

FURTHER WORKS: *Les matérialistes de l'antiquité* (1936); *Chronique de septembre* (1939); *P. N., intellectuel communiste* (1967); *Pour une nouvelle culture* (1971)

BIBLIOGRAPHY: Sartre, J.-P., *Situations* (1965), pp. 115–73; Ginsbourg, A., *P. N.* (1966); Leiner, J., *Le destin littéraire de P. N. et ses étapes successives* (1970); Redfern, W. D., *P. N.: Committed Literature in a Conspiratorial World* (1972); Nizan, H., and Cohen-Solal, A., *P. N., communiste impossible* (1980); Ory, P., *N.: Destin d'un révolté* (1980); Suleiman, S. R., "The Structure of Confrontation: N., Barrès, Malraux," *MLN,* 95 (1980), 938–67

RANDOLPH RUNYON

NORTH CAUCASIAN LITERATURES

The languages of the Caucasus (exclusive of isolated Indo-European and Turkic areas) are usually classified by linguists in three groups: Southern (or Kartvelian, of which Georgian [q.v.] is the only written member), Northwestern (or Abkhaz-Adyghe, including also Abaza and Kabardian), and Northeastern (or Nakh-Daghestan; this large group comprises twenty-nine spoken languages, of which only Chechen, Ingush, Avar, Dargin, Lak, Lezgin, and Tabasaran have been accorded the status of literary languages).

Until the 20th c. the literary heritage of the North Caucasian peoples was composed almost exclusively of oral epics (the "Nart" cycles in particular among the Abkhaz, Adyghes, and Kabardians) and folklore of a highly imaginative type. Attempts at writing in several languages were made in an adapted Arabic alphabet, but these were minimal except in Daghestan, where literary works were composed as early as the 18th c. The late 19th c. and the early 20th witnessed a sudden development in written literature throughout most regions of the North Caucasus. In Daghestan the Dargin poet Sukur Kurban

(1842–1922), the Lak poet Mallei (186?–190?) and the Avar poet Mahmud (1870–1919) may be considered the founders of their native belles-lettres. The Abkhaz national poet Dimitri Gulia (1874–1960) published his first work in 1912, effectively establishing the literary form of his language, which was given further impetus by the newspaper he began in 1919, *Apsny,* in which young Abkhaz writers obtained their first exposure. Bekmurza Pachev (1854–1936) published his work in Kabardian at the beginning of the 20th c., utilizing an alphabet of his own invention. One of the first dramas to be written in any North Caucasian language was *Makhadjiry* (1920; Makhadjiry), by the Abkhaz author Samson Chanba (1886–1937).

With the reconquest of the North Caucasus by the Russians in 1921, after a brief period of independence begun in 1918, the emerging generation of writers was, for the most part, constrained to utilize its talents to further the ends of communist propaganda. Despite the extraordinary difficulties of these first years of Soviet rule, a number of writers did manage to contribute works to their native literatures that avoided political saturation. Works by the Chechen writer Saidbek Baduev (1904–1943), for example, included a collection of stories, *Maccalla* (1925; hunger), a play, *Daj nizamoš* (1929; the law of the fathers), and a novel—the first in Chechen—*Petimat* (1930; Petimat), about the life of his mountain people. In Daghestan, a group of poets made their first appearance in print during the 1920s, among them the Avar Zagid Gadjiev (b. 1898), the Dargin Sagid Abdullaev (1903–1952), the Lak Mugutin Charinov (1893–1937), and the Lezgin Alibek Fatakhov (1910–1935). In Kabardian, an interesting play on folk themes from the heroic epics, *Korigot* (193?; Korigot), was written by P. Shekikhachev (1879–1937). During the 1930s many of the most talented and promising young writers were purged by Stalin and either executed or sent to labor camps, where the majority died. Among these were the gifted Adyghe poet Akhmet Khatkov (1901–1937), as well as Chanba, Fatakhov, Charinov, and Shekikhachev.

Little original work of literary value was produced during World War II, although Gulia's novel *Kamachich* (1940; Kamachich) achieved great success in Abkhazia. The Chechen and Ingush peoples were deported to Central Asia immediately after the war,

suffering extremely high mortality; they were not permitted to return to the Caucasus until after Stalin's death. Since that time more creative literature has begun to appear throughout the North Caucasus, although ideological restrictions continue to be applied forcibly. In Chechen, Nadjmuddin Muzaev's (b. 1913) novels *Orgona tolloskox̌* (1965; in the valley of the Orgun) and *Dogdoxara x̌üpara* (1971; the power of wishes) are worthy of note. Although he has demonstrated unswerving subservience to the Party line in both his public statements and in his writing, the nonpolitical poems, sketches, and reminiscences of the Avar author Rasul Gamzatov (b. 1923) rank among the best literary productions of the North Caucasus and have achieved wide popularity throughout the Soviet Union.

BIBLIOGRAPHY: "The Literature and the Arts of Soviet Daghestan" (special issue), *SovL,* No. 10 (1980)

LEONARD FOX

NORTHERN SOTHO LITERATURE
See South African Literature: In Pedi

NORWEGIAN LITERATURE

Norway began the 20th c. with a newly obtained independence and with literary bravura. The struggle for national identity, beginning with independence from Denmark in 1814, and culminating in the dissolution of the union with Sweden in 1905, had left the country free from foreign domination for the first time since the Middle Ages. The poets Henrik Wergeland (1808–1845) and Johann S. Welhaven (1807–1873) had extolled national ideals and goals; the novelists Jonas Lie (1833–1908) and Alexander Kielland (1849–1906) had critically examined Norwegian social structure; and the dramatists Bjørnstjerne Bjørnson (1832–1910) and Henrik Ibsen (1828–1906) had won international fame. By the 1890s Norway's literary output matched that of any other nation in quality.

As was true with their predecessors, modern Norwegian writers have been greatly influenced by their country's rugged landscape; the ancient granite mountains, fertile valleys, fjords, and sea coasts. Nature may sometimes symbolize romantic escape or danger, but it may also represent mystical and religious feelings, the possibilities of human development, and national identity.

Modern Norwegian literature often reflects a fierce desire for personal and political independence, which may range from defiant self-reliance to sensitive, considerate social consciousness. There is a long tradition of writing by women that describes the struggle of women for liberation and for equality with men. A sense of history is also pervasive; the Viking times, the Middle Ages, the domination by the Hanseatic League and by Denmark, and the struggle for independence are common themes, as are disillusionment with modern industrialization and despair at war and at the growing alienation of modern man.

Norway has two languages: the dominant *bokmål* ("book language," formerly called, and still commonly referred to among its users as *riksmål,* "state language"), of Dano-Norwegian origin, which is somewhat more urban; and *nynorsk* ("new Norwegian," formerly known as *landsmål,* "rural language"), fashioned in the 19th c. by Ivar Aasen (1813–1896) and Aasmund Vinje (1818–1870) from various Norwegian dialects, which is centered more in the rural, "country interest." Compromises and spelling reforms have brought the languages closer together, until today both are truly Norwegian and representative.

Fiction

Outstanding among the new writers of fiction in the 1890s were Knut Hamsun (q.v.) and Hans Kinck (1865–1926). Both eschewed the older generation, sought rural "truths," rejected themes from classical antiquity, neglected the church and other traditional cultural mores, worshiped life in a Nietzschean sense, and opposed enveloping materialism. As part of general European neoromanticism, they embraced art for art's sake as opposed to social criticism, and sought to describe inner, psychological life. Kinck was the more intellectual, with a tendency to preach and to solve conflicts, while Hamsun was a consummate story teller and ironic stylist. Hamsun never forsook his aristocratic, antidemocratic ideas that led him to criticize America and the West and to remain spiritually close to Germany, even to the extent of supporting Nazism. In the novels *Pan* (1894; *Pan,* 1920), and *Markens grøde* (1917; *Growth of the Soil,* 1920) he produced powerful, almost

mythical characters who made their own worlds outside society.

Other novelists who emerged in the 1890s whose productive careers lasted well into the 20th c. were Peter Egge (1869–1959), Johan Bojer (q.v.), and Gabriel Scott (1874–1958). Egge wrote stories about his native region of Trøndelag, his best work being *Hansine Solstad* (1925; *Hansine Solstad,* 1929), a novel portraying a working woman struggling to survive while resisting corruption. Bojer described the Trøndelag crofter fishermen in *Den siste Viking* (1921; *The Last of the Vikings,* 1923), one of the finest Norwegian novels of the sea. Scott, more poetic and spiritual, is best known for *Jernbyrden* (1915; *The Ordeal,* 1935), which has been compared to Hamsun's *Markens grøde.*

By the turn of the century, the symbolic and neoromantic movements were giving way before the new realism. In the vanguard were four female authors whose themes were the struggles of women for emancipation and emotional, intellectual, and spiritual independence: Ragnhild Hølsen (1875–1908), Nini Roll Anker (1873–1942), Barbra Ring (1870–1955), and Regine Normann (1867–1939). Anker's *Det svake kjøn* (1915; the weak sex), is typical. The early works of Sigrid Undset (q.v.) dealt with similar themes, but gradually her interest in detail and historical accuracy led her to studies of the sagas, folklore, and the Norwegian Middle Ages. The result was *Kristin Lavransdatter* (3 vols., 1920–22; *Kristin Lavransdatter,* 3 vols., 1923–27), regarded by many as the greatest novel in Norwegian. Set in the 13th c. and containing finely drawn characters, the novel follows the relationship of Kristin to her father and her husband until her martyrdom during the Black Death epidemic; psychologically compelling are the heroine's struggles between the urge to obedience and the desire for happiness, between the earthly and the spiritual.

Contemporary with Undset were Olav Duun (q.v.), Kristofer Uppdal (1878–1961), and Johan Falkberget (q.v.), all of humble Trøndelag origin, a background pervasive in their works. Uppdal's *Dansen gjennom skuggeheiman* (10 vols., 1911–24; the dance through the realm of the shadows) treats the transformation of farmers into factory workers and the rise of the labor unions. Falkberget's novels deal mostly with the exploited miners of his native Røros. Many think of Duun as the giant of 20th-c. Norwegian literature. His *Juvikfolke* (6 vols., 1918–23; *The*

People of Juvik, 6 vols., 1930–35) covers four hundred years but concentrates on the period from 1814 to the start of the industrial era in Norway in the early 20th c. It portrays the moral development of a family from blind, ruthless individualism to ethical and social responsibility.

Although World War I did not have a strong psychological effect on Norway, there was still some weakened faith in the future, increasing social criticism, and growing fear of industrialization and urbanization. During the 1920s the socialist journal *Mot dag,* edited by Sigurd Hoel (q.v.) and Erling Falk (1887–1940), attracted many excellent writers attuned to social and psychological themes, as did the more conservative *Vor verden* under Ronald Fangen (q.v.). A great stimulus to Norwegian writing and understanding was *Den gule serie,* edited by Hoel, whose appearance in 1929 first brought to Norway translations of Franz Kafka, François Mauriac, Graham Greene, William Faulkner, Ernest Hemingway (qq.v.), and other major foreign writers.

In the 1930s, Hoel's works and those of Tarjei Vesaas (q.v.) began to enjoy wide acceptance. At the same time, several new novelists came into their own, among them Cora Sandel (1880–1974), Inge Krokann (1893–1962), and Aksel Sandemose (q.v.). In addition to his essays, criticism, and editing, Hoel wrote sensitive, thoughtful novels influenced by Freud (q.v.) and Kafka, and reflecting disenchantment with the world. Typical are his novel of childhood, *Veien til verdens ende* (1933; the road to the end of the world), and of psychoanalysis, *Fjorten dager før frostnettene* (1935; fourteen days before the frosty nights). Sandel's ironic novels about the talented and ambitious Alberte follow the heroine from a cruel and insensitive home milieu to Paris, where she flowers as an artist. Sandemose is an impressive story teller, at best in his psychological analysis of a criminal's childhood in *En flyktning krysser sitt spor* (1933; *A Fugitive Crosses His Tracks,* 1936) and of an amoral manipulator of people in *Det svundne er en drøm* (1946; the past is a dream). Krokann's historical novels set in Oppdal reflect the efforts of native leaders to unify their people against foreign oppression. Vesaas is a lyrical, symbolic writer who celebrates the human need for compassionate communication. A fine example is *Is-slottet* (1963; *The Ice Palace,* 1966), a tender story of friendship between two young girls.

With the exception of Hamsun and a handful of others, the Norwegian literary world joined in the fight against Nazism. After the war, bookstalls were flooded with versions of what had happened. From concentration camps came two books of high literary quality, Odd Nansen's (1901–1973) secret diary of Grini and Sachsenhausen, *Fra dag til dag* (1946; *From Day to Day,* 1949), and Petter Moèn's (1901–1944) posthumously published *Dagbok* (1949; *Diary,* 1951), written for the most part in solitary confinement. Sigurd Evensmo's (b. 1912) war novels, which deal with the struggle for integrity and loyalty in the face of torture, can be read as social history, while Kåre Holt's (q.v.) highly successful *Det store veiskillet* (1949; at the crossroads) analyzes the possible courses open to young Norwegians during the war, emphasizing decision and responsibility.

The 1950s were years of experimentation, exemplified by the masterful short stories of Vesaas, Nils Johan Rud (b. 1908), and particularly Johan Borgen (q.v.). Finn Carling (q.v.) and Solveig Christov (q.v.) investigated the moral and psychological implications of dreams, while Finn Bjørnseth (b. 1924) wrote of the ethical and mythical components of physical love. Agnar Mykle's (b. 1915) novel *Sangen om den røde rubin* (1956; song of the red ruby) contained such explicit sexuality that he was tried on charges of pornography, although he was acquitted. Jens Bjørneboe (q.v.) investigated the misuse of power in education, medicine, law, and government.

In 1964 Norwegian literature received a new stimulus from a ruling by the Norwegian Cultural Council that insured a minimum sale for all new Norwegian belles lettres. A new generation without memories of the Depression and of World War II began to write on the issues of the day: imperialism, underdeveloped countries, starvation, environmental pollution, women's liberation, and Vietnam. Among those who are of a revolutionary bent are Dag Solstad (b. 1941), Tor Obrestad (b. 1938), and Espen Haavardsholm (b. 1945). Solstad's novels examine late-capitalistic man, confused and caught by social forces, struggling toward socialism. Obrestad's *Sauda! Streik!* (1972; Sauda! strike!), a fictional-documentary account of the smelting plant strike in Sauda in 1970, draws lessons from the writings of Lenin. Haavardsholm's stories and essays involve the alienated individual who is exploited by the power structure.

Many contemporary writers, such as Mona Lyngar (b. 1944), Gunnar Lunde (b. 1944), and Øystein Lønn (b. 1936), regard modern alienation as something absurd, but they offer no political solutions. Alfred Hauge (b. 1915) seeks Christian existentialist (q.v.) answers for people in crisis who must choose the right path to salvation. In literature written about women by women, Bjørg Vik (b. 1935), Karin Bang (b. 1928), and Bergljot Hobæk Haff (b. 1925) stand out in their descriptions of love, marriage, exploitation, and victimization.

Despite the new trends, many excellent writers stay closer to traditional writing. Both Finn Alnæs (b. 1932) and Knud Faldbakken (b. 1941), for instance, describe modern people who are guided by more conventional goals in ambition and love.

Drama

At the beginning of the 20th c., permanent, successful theaters were established in Oslo, Bergen, Trondheim, and Stavanger, providing opportunity for native dramatists. Several writers from other fields tried their hands at drama with varying success. Knut Hamsun's plays have a lyrical tone; *Munken Vendt* (1902; Monk Vendt) owes much to Ibsen's *Peer Gynt* in its excellent treatment of the wanderer motif. Technical difficulties often hindered the production of Hans Kinck's excellent dramas. Peter Egge, Nils Collett Vogt (1864–1937), and Nils Kjær (1870–1924), produced good psychological plays.

Of paramount importance before World War I was Gunnar Heiberg (1857–1929), who continued the psychological, moral, and political problem drama set in a middle-class milieu that Ibsen had begun. Heiberg's thirteen plays almost all shock either by their eroticism or their social criticism. In *Kjærlighetens tragedie* (1904; *The Tragedy of Love*, 1921), the heroine kills herself in despair of attaining unremitting carnal satisfaction, while the hero of *Jeg vil verge mit land* (1912; I will defend my country) ends his life in dissappointment over the concessions made by Norway to Sweden in 1905.

Between the wars, Helge Krog (1889–1962) followed the Ibsen-Heiberg tradition with logical, dialectical attacks on society reminiscent of Bernard Shaw. His plays often involve erotic conflicts. In *Underveis* (1931; *On the Way*, 1939) and *Opbrudd* (1936; *Break-Up*, 1939) women play progressive,

positive roles in an outmoded, corrupt male society. Krog's contemporary, Nordahl Grieg (q.v.), wrote powerful revolutionary dramas: *Vår ære og vår makt* (1935; *Our Power and Our Glory*, 1971) attacks the exploitation of seamen during World War I, while *Nederlaget* (1937; *Defeat*, 1944), about the Paris Commune of 1871, analyzes the correct use of power.

German expressionism (q.v.) influenced the dramas of Ronald Fagen. His *Den Forjættede dag* (1926; the promised day), *Syndefald* (1920; the fall), and *Fienden* (1922; the enemy) show how the coldness, emptiness and spiritual homelessness of modern life can result in criminal behavior. Johan Borgen, Arnulf Øverland (q.v.) and Sigurd Christiansen (1891–1947) produced excellent dramas dealing with the problem of self-fulfillment. Øverland's *Gi meg ditt hjerte* (1930; give me your heart), contrasts intellect and sensuality, while Borgen's *Høit var du elsket* (1937; greatly were you loved) shows how hypocrisy can keep people from being themselves. Christiansen's *Offerdøden* (1919; the sacrificial death) is a highly ethical drama, Ibsen-like in its demand for heroic honesty.

Among the more traditional postwar dramatists in the Ibsen-Heiberg-Krog tradition are Victor Borg (b. 1916), Arne Skouen (b. 1913), Hans Heiberg (b. 1904), Finn Havrevold (b. 1905), Helge Hagerup (b. 1933), and Alex Kielland (1907–1963). They deal with moral decisions, capitalistic exploitation, postwar superficiality, and the conflict of generations. Kielland's plays, such as *Han som sa nei* (1959; he who said no), about a soldier's duty to obey, have aroused international attention.

There has also been much experimentation in the theater. The disintegration of middle-class society and of the traditional image of reality, together with the influence of foreign dramatists such as Strindberg, Lagerkvist, Eliot, Brecht, Ionesco, and Beckett (qq.v.) have contributed to the new theater. In this avant-garde drama there is usually stylization of milieu and character, action and dialogue, with the search for symbols representing general truths; the plays often contain verses, music, song, dance, and pantomime.

The first Norwegian dramatist after the war to experiment with new form was Odd Eidem (q.v.) in *Spillet om Bly-Petter* (1946; the play about Bly-Petter), a strongly stylized drama, not bound to time or place, with the main character representing the oppressed proletariat. Tormod Skagestad's (b. 1920) poetic dramas, *Under treet ligg øksa* (1955; the axe lay under the tree), and *I byen ved havet* (1962; in the city by the sea), as well as his radio plays, are general, timeless, and symbolic, involving the use of chorus and allegory. Jens Bjørneboe's satirical musical, *Til lykke med dagen* (1965; many happy returns), clearly inspired by Brecht, sharply and satirically attacks the prison system. Finn Carling's *Gitrene* (1966; bars), *Slangen* (1969; the snake), and *Skudd* (1971; shot) treat biblical themes in highly unusual ways. Stein Mehren's (q.v.) complicated, difficult *Narren og hans hertug* (1968; the fool and his duke), a historical drama that is meant to have contemporary significance, has dramatic appeal in spite of its heavy intellectual content.

Poetry

In the 1890s the lyric poetry of Nils Collett Vogt, Sigbjørn Obstfelder (1866–1900) and Vilhelm Krag (1871–1933), liberated fancy and imagination, and portrayed moods, reveries, and "soul-life." This melancholy and alienation gave way about 1905 to a full-blooded flowering of new poetry, realistic in attitude, subjects, and language. The highly popular Herman Wildenvey (1886–1959) was a word artist full of humor and warmth, a happy troubador, summer's poet of beauty, but also mature and sometimes melancholy. The verse of Olaf Bull (q.v.) one of the greatest Norwegian poets of the 20th c., is more profound and symbolic than Wildenvey's. His themes are the passing of time, the relationship of life and art, and often erotic passion.

The poetry of the 1905 generation also had a strong local character. Alf Larsen (1885–1967), Tore Ørjasæter (1886–1968), Olav Aukrust (1883–1929), and Olav Nygard (1884–1924) sang of the sea, the coastal lands, and the mountains, combining a love of nature with deep religious feeling, earthly passion, and mystical ecstasy.

Arnulf Øverland was a contemporary of the 1905 generation, but more influenced by World War I and by social problems. Well-educated, sophisticated, a socialist, and atheist, Øverland became a leader of his people. His simple but meaningful poems are objec-

tive and warm, with subdued passion and sometimes a touch of grandeur.

In the 1920s, regional tradition continued in the verse of Jakob Sande (1906–1967) and Louis Kvalstad (1905–1952), who wrote romantically about nature, particularly the sea. Gunnar Reiss-Andersen (1896–1964), like Bull and Wildenvey, was elegant, witty and sophisticated, while Halldis Moren Vesaas (b. 1907) and Einar Skæraasen (1900–1966) show a love of home and happiness in close, trusting relationships. In contrast, Aslaug Vaa's (1889–1965) poetry about Telemark is abstract and tense, reflecting her moods and conflicts.

The 1930s brought greater depth to the continued trend toward concrete, everyday language. Rolf Jacobsen (b. 1907) first praised and later criticized the new technology, factories, and metropolitan life. Like Jacobsen, Claes Gill (1910–1973) was a stylistic innovator: images pile up in an illogical, associational sequence; his treatment of love, art, and death is very effective. Emil Boyson (b. 1897) favors timeless and universal themes, as evidenced especially in his fine translations from many periods and languages.

During World War II a great deal of poetry was written; much of it was circulated illegally and dealt with anti-Nazi themes, political and social ideals, and postwar goals, but also with problems created by the war, such as human debasement and fear. Nordahl Grieg's war poems, in particular, are well remembered.

Since 1945 there has been a great variation in motifs and styles. Around 1950 symbolic modernism came to Norway. At the forefront were Tarjei Vesaas, Peter R. Holm (b. 1931) and Stein Mehren. They use free rhythms, suggestive sounds, new, unexpected connections and sentence combinations, and sometimes language freed from conventional syntax. Mehren is perhaps the most restless, seeking, questioning one, concerned with poetry as a means of learning and perception. The movement declined in the early 1960s, to be replaced by concretists such as Jan Erik Vold (b. 1939), who have experimented with deliberately simple and naïve language and unusual typographical arrangement.

The changeover from symbolism to realism can also be seen in some of the social and political poets of the 1960s. Whereas many of them remained somewhat esoteric in their use of irony, satire, and metaphor, others, such as Tor Obrestad, eschewed subtle effects in order to speak directly and clearly to the masses.

Among those holding to traditional verse forms and themes have been Inger Hagerup (b. 1905) with her biblical motifs and folksongs; Tor Jonsson (1916–1951), full of strong contrasts and longing, expressing hope for a better future; Alf Prøysen (1914–1970), great song writer, social realist, and smiling satirist; and André Bjerke (q.v.), whose sensitive artistry in poems about children, love, adventure, art, and nature have marked him as one of the great contemporary poets.

The 1970s saw ever-increasing amounts of poetry published. There was also a great variety in theme and subject matter. It has been suggested that much of this output is not of high quality, and that an effort on the part of Norwegian publishers and critics is necessary to bring some order out of the chaos. Part of the difficulty can be traced to the government's support of belles lettres.

One of the themes that has often appeared in recent poetry is the combination of a love of tradition with a fear of modern change. Poets react with humor, fantasy, and sometimes terror to the threat of decay, destruction, and loss. Sigmund Skard (b. 1903) has given excellent voice to these thoughts in his glimpses of the world that contrast sharply with his love of simple Norwegian tradition. Einar Økland (b. 1940) is strongly critical of politics and politicians while at the same time presenting attractive descriptions of life in western Norway. Two others who see the world on the brink are Annie Riis (b. 1955) and Liv Lundbert (b. 1944).

Three notable poets of the 1970s are Paal-Helge Haugen (b. 1945), who, in clear, precise language, attempts to understand "the world" and to come to terms with it; Frank Stubb Micaelsen (b. 1947), whose poems show a connection between people and things throughout history, suggesting a mystical unity of all matter; and Ove Røsbak (b. 1960), whose strong, robust poems with their eagerness for life and love show excellent talent and promise.

BIBLIOGRAPHY: Bach, G., *The History of Scandinavian Literatures* (1938), pp. 11–87; Koht, H., and Skard, S., *Voice of Norway* (1944); Christiansen, H., *Norwegische Literaturgeschichte* (1953); Beyer, H., *A History of Norwegian Literature* (1956); Downs, B. W., *Modern Norwegian Literature, 1860–1918* (1966); Jorgensen, T., *History of Norwegian Literature* (1970); Rossel, S. H., *A History of Scandinavian Literature, 1870–1980* (1982)

WALTER D. MORRIS

NOSSACK, Hans Erich

West German novelist, essayist, poet, and dramatist, b. 30 Jan. 1901, Hamburg; d. 2 Nov. 1977, Hamburg

Son of a merchant, N. studied philosophy and law, then held jobs as a factory worker, traveling salesman, and journalist before reluctantly joining his father's business.

An important and distinguished writer to whom recognition was denied until relatively late in his career, N. did not see his first work published until 1947. Proscribed from publishing by the Nazis because of former left-wing affiliations, N. continued to write clandestinely, but lost all his manuscripts during the Allied bombing raids on Hamburg in 1943. The ensuing physical and emotional devastation marked the turning point in N.'s life, for by associating Hamburg's fate with his own, he effectively freed himself from the coils of the past. The situation was graphically and soberly recorded in "Der Untergang" (the destruction), a piece from *Interview mit dem Tode* (1948; interview with death)—republished as *Dorothea* (1950; Dorothea)—in which N. recognized and welcomed the chance to make a complete break with a bankrupt society.

It is this theme of the total rejection of the past, of release from societies inimical to the real development of man—and the implications of this idea for the whole question of personal identity—that forms the nucleus of his work.

In his early—and only—volume of verse, *Gedichte* (1947; poems), N. explores the inner man and his motivations, and clearly enunciates his belief in moral and intellectual integrity. N. believed in pushing out to the very limits of experience, into the unknown and uncertain, into "extraterritoriality," as he called it. In *Spätestens im November* (1955; *Wait for November*, 1982) protest against the conventional and the norm is seen as the first step toward self-fulfillment, even though the outcome ends in disaster. The very fact that a stale and meaningless pattern of existence has been recognized as such and questioned was sufficient for N. The important thing was to have the courage to be oneself, to be an individual.

This concern also dominates N.'s three plays—*Die Rotte Kain* (1949; the band of Cain), *Die Hauptprobe* (1956; the main test), and *Ein Sonderfall* (1963; a special case)—which, however, despite the strength and clarity of their language and, in the case of the last two, the tragicomic effects, never enjoyed popular or critical success.

The brilliant novel *Unmögliche Beweisaufnahme* (1959; *The Impossible Proof,* 1968) deals with the problem of trying to live by two different realities: what man really is, and the image society has of man. The "account" takes the form of a trial in which communication between a judge and a defendant is reduced to a minimum, in a witty and often ironic dialogue, as the two realities are explored. This failure of understanding that occurs between these two men is seen by N. as a consequence of the increasing bureaucratization and institutionalization of society against which N. believed it was his duty to warn—and he did so repeatedly.

The distinction between what is real and unreal became increasingly blurred in N.'s work, his characters moving in mysterious and strange settings that were at one and the same time tangible and recognizable yet also vaguely unfamiliar. This precarious focus was cleverly broadened in *Der jüngere Bruder* (1958; the younger brother) to examine not only the protagonist's own nebulous identity and relationship to others but also to juxtapose a physically recognizable Europe with disturbingly out-of-focus elements.

The ever-present tendency to fuse the real and the unreal in surrealistic or mythical forms reached a climax in *Nach dem letzten Aufstand* (1961; after the last revolt), which comprises an often bewilderingly rich mixture of complex time and space elements welded together to create an alliance between this world and the other more mysterious one, in which there is a highly stylized reflection of postwar Germany's dilemmas. Protest against frozen attitudes, the quest for self-realization, and the attempt to create a new mythology out of our reality also characterize the important *Der Fall d'Arthez* (1968; *The D'Arthez Case,* 1971), while N.'s sense of comic satire was ably demonstrated in *Dem unbekannten Sieger* (1969; *To the Unknown Hero,* 1974), which attacks the sterile

systematizing of politicohistorical reality, a process N. believed denied the essential spontaneity and multidimensionality of man's experiences.

In the few years before his death, N. returned to his main themes with increasing urgency and subtlety. *Die gestohlene Melodie* (1972; the stolen melody) took the question of outsiderness a stage further, dealing with "remigrants," that is, those who had actually returned from the "other side" of being, but whose newly acquired awareness now excluded them from the familiar. In *Bereitschaftsdienst* (1973; emergency service) the feasibility of the act of suicide was seen as an apparent way out, although confusingly it was not so much extinction that was sought, but escape from the sterility of conventional norms and atrophied social forms. N.'s last novel, *Ein glücklicher Mensch* (1975; a happy man), assembled most of N.'s driving concerns to form a quintessential statement of his intellectual position.

In cool, lucid, and restrained prose, this "dispassionate visionary" portrayed with striking forcefulness man's precarious and threatened condition, his inner loneliness and basic unrelatedness. His works are inner explorations, attempts to reach the emotional centers that lie within us and to examine the manifold possibilities of human existence that lie in the pursuit of individual freedom.

An understanding of N.'s artistic purpose and *Weltanschauung* can be obtained by reading his essays, the most important of which are contained in *Die schwache Position der Literatur* (1966; the weak position of literature), in which N.'s special moralistic stance, somewhat akin to Albert Camus's (q.v.), is well defined, and in *Pseudoautobiographische Glossen* (1971; pseudoautobiographical glosses).

N. was a percipient and relentless critic of his society who, through reasoned and always quiet argument, never wavered from his firm conviction that the solution to man's problems lies within man himself, and that all he, as a writer, could do was "to render an account."

FURTHER WORKS: *Nekyia: Bericht eines Überlebenden* (1947); *Publikum und Dichter* (1950); *Der Neugierige* (1955); *Die Begnadigung* (1955); *Spirale: Roman einer schlaflosen Nacht* (1956); *Über den Einsatz* (1956); *Begegnung im Vorraum* (1958); *Freizeitliteratur: Eine Fastenpredigt* (1959); *Das kennt man* (1964); *Sechs Etüden* (1964); *Das Testament des Lucius Eurinus* (1964); *Das Mal, und andere Erzählungen* (1965); *Der König geht ins Kino* (1974); *Um es kurz zu machen* (1975); *Dieser Andere: Ein Lesebuch mit Briefen, Gedichten, Prosa* (1976)

BIBLIOGRAPHY: Kasack, H., "Rede auf den Preisträger," *Jahrbuch der deutschen Akademie für Sprache und Dichtung* (1961), pp. 79–89; Boehlich, W., Afterword to *Der Untergang* (1963), pp. 55–60; Keith-Smith, B., "H. E. N.," in Keith-Smith, B., ed., *Essays on Contemporary German Literature* (1966), pp. 63–85; Prochnik, P., "Controlling Thoughts in the Work of H. E. N.," *GL&L*, 19 (1965), 68–75; Prochnik, P., "First Words: The Poetry of H. E. N.," *MLR*, 64 (1969), 100–110; Schmid, C., ed., *Über H. E. N.* (1970)

PETER PROCHNIK

NOUVEAU ROMAN
See New Novel

NOVOMESKÝ, Laco (Ladislav)
Czechoslovak poet and journalist (writing in Slovak), b. 27 Dec. 1904, Budapest, Hungary; d. 4 Sept. 1976, Bratislava

The evolution of N.'s poetic talent and the recognition his work currently enjoys are both intertwined with the vagaries of his lifelong career as a leading activist of the Slovak Communist Party. N. received his early education in Hungary. His family left for Slovakia in 1919. In 1923 N. graduated from the Teacher's College in Modra, Slovakia. He had published his first poem in 1921, and by the time he entered Bratislava University, in 1923, he was a regular contributor to the radical journal *Mladé Slovensko*.

N. joined the Communist Party of Slovakia in 1925. Two years later he published his first volume of poems, *Nedeľa* (1927; Sunday). It was followed, in the next decade, by three more books of poems. During these years, N. served the Party as a journalist and cultural propagandist, working in close collaboration with the Communist leader Klement Gottwald (1896–1953) on the editorial board of the Party organ *Rudé právo*. In the divisive debate at the Fifth Party Congress in 1929, N., together with his fellow Slovak

Vladimír Clementis (1902–1952), threw their support behind Gottwald's position of militant opposition to the Versailles-created Czechoslovak Republic. In 1934 he attended the First Congress of Soviet Writers in Moscow.

In 1939, after the breakup of the Czechoslovak Republic, N. left Prague for Slovakia, there to participate in the underground life of the Slovak Communist Party. The Politburo sent him to London in 1943, with the mission of explaining the aims of the incipient Slovak uprising to the president-in-exile, Eduard Beneš. From London N. flew to Moscow, where he remained until his return to Slovakia in January 1945, after it was liberated from the Nazis.

Between 1945 and 1950 N. was a prominent participant in the cultural politics of the Party and his country. But in 1950 he was accused of "bourgeois nationalism," an official term for the separatist, anti-Czech tendencies that the Party in Slovakia had previously encouraged. In 1951 N. was imprisoned. He was released at the end of 1955 and allowed to live and even publish quietly in Prague. His official rehabilitation came in 1963, followed by national honors.

N. played an important role in the traumatic year 1968. After giving a cautious endorsement to the reforms put into effect, he broke ranks with the vast majority of Czechoslovak writers and called for an end of the Prague experiment with democracy, even before the Soviet military intervention. Until his withdrawal from public life in 1970 for reasons of health, N. remained a vocal supporter of the policies of "normalization" of the Husák regime. He was a Lenin Prize winner and a Hero of the U.S.S.R.

N.'s poetic legacy is contained in the two volumes of his collected poems, *Básnické dielo* (1971; poetic works), which include all the prewar and postwar cycles of verse. In his earliest poems, N. had been primarily the poet of the proletarian suburbs, celebrating, in an aggressively prosaic idiom, man-made things and mankind's irrepressible quest for happiness. The 1930s brought more linguistic sophistication to his poetry and, here and there, the occasionally daring stab of a surrealistic (q.v.) image. In the last cycle published before the war, the native Slovak rural strain asserts itself in poems of uncomplicated sensuality.

Villa Teréza (1963; Villa Teréza), the most important cycle of poems, was written by N.

405

after the Communists came to power in his country. It is an ironic meditation about the individual in history, dedicated to the memory of Vladimir Antonov-Ovseenko, the hero of Red Petrograd, who later became a Soviet nonperson. N. had known him in the 1920s as the Soviet envoy to Czechoslovakia during the presidency of T. G. Masaryk. In this cycle of poems, N.'s historical subject has a very personal subtext.

N.'s literary achievement is that of a minor but authentic poet. He will also be remembered for the crucial role he has played in his country's recent history. His life exemplifies the evolution of an official Communist writer from the youthful time when poetry and revolution seemed to be one, to the sobering realities and the historical compromises of entrenched political power.

FURTHER WORKS: *Pred nedeľou* (written 1924–26, pub. 1971); *Znejúce ozveny* (written 1924–32, pub. 1969); *Romboid* (1932); *Marx a slovenský národ* (1933); *Manifesty a protesty* (written 1924–37, pub. 1970); *Čestná povinnost* (written 1933–44, pub. 1968); *Otvorené okna* (1936); *Slávnost istoty* (written 1938–44, pub. 1970); *Svätý za dedinou* (1939); *Zväzky a záväzky* (written 1945–50, pub. 1972); *Komunizmus v slovenskej národnej idei* (1946); *Pašovanou ceruzkou* (1948); *Hviezdoslav* (1949); *Výchova socialistického pokolenia* (1949); *T. G. Masaryk* (1950); *Do mesta 30 min.* (1963); *Samodtiaľ a iné* (1964); *Nezbadaný svet* (1964); *Dobrý deň, vám* (1964); *Dom, kde žijem* (1966); *Otvorená kronika: Scenár o živote a diele Vladimíra Clementisa* (1969); *Z piesní o jednote* (1971); *O literatúre* (1971); *Z úrodných podstát človečích* (1976)

BIBLIOGRAPHY: Banerjee, M. N., on *Básnické dielo, BA,* 47 (1973), 185; Mihailovich, V. D., et al., eds., *Modern Slavic Literatures* (1976), Vol. II, pp. 172–75

MARIA NĚMCOVÁ BANERJEE

NUŠIĆ, Branislav

Yugoslav dramatist, short-story writer, novelist, and essayist (writing in Serbian), b. 8 Oct. 1864, Belgrade; d. 19 Jan. 1938, Belgrade

N. grew up in Belgrade and studied law there. Subsequently he held a number of government and diplomatic posts in the Serbian ministries of foreign affairs and education and later served as director of several state subsidized theaters in Belgrade, Novi Sad, Skopje, and Sarajevo.

N. was both a prolific and versatile author. Aside from his sizable fictional oeuvre, his twenty-five volumes of collected works include practically every kind of dramatic composition, from farce to tragedy. His early historical patriotic plays *Knez Ivo od Semberije* (1902; Duke Ivo of Semberia) and *Hadži Loja* (1908; Hadži Loja), several lachrymose romantic pieces, and the tragedy *Nahod* (1923; the foundling) initially enjoyed some popularity, but ultimately failed to survive the test of time. Only when N. turned to comedy did his dramatic talent attain its fullest potential. A satirist of the first rank, he revealed a true panorama of the late-blossoming Serbian bourgeois society plagued by abuses of political, bureaucratic, and police power, the peddling of influence, greed for money, and the craving for advancement and honors. Such memorable plays as *Narodni poslanik* (1883; the member of parliament), *Sumnjivo lice* (1887; the suspicious individual), *Protekcija* (1889; favoritism), *Običan čovek* (1900; an ordinary man), *Svet* (1906; the world), and *Put oko sveta* (1910; a trip around the world), all written in pre-World War I Serbia, display his satirical powers. His satirical bite increased in the interwar period, when he completed *Gospodja ministarka* (1931; the cabinet member's wife), *Ožalošćena porodica* (1934; the bereaved family), *UJEŽ* (1935; acronym for Association of Yugoslav Emancipated Women), and *Pokojnik* (1937; the late departed), in which the picture of the well-known social ills of the new south Slav state, Yugoslavia, was amply augmented by a devastating satirical comment upon more universal human foibles.

Among N.'s nondramatic prose writings, of particular note are his three volumes of short stories—*Pripovetke jednoga kaplara* (1886; tales of a corporal), *Listići* (1889; leaflets), and *Ramazanske večeri* (1898; Ramazan evenings)—and the novel *Opštinsko dete* (1902; the municipal child), characterized by a wealth of humorous detail, lively characters, and the authenticity of its Serbian provincial petit-bourgeois milieu. Although in both his dramatic and fictional works N. occasionally succumbed to his audience's thirst for easy comic effects and laughter for its own sake, his work still remains a striking exposé of that upstart segment of the Serbian bourgeois society that sacrificed everything to its frenzied pursuit of wealth, privilege, political influence, and fashion.

FURTHER WORKS: *Pučina* (1901); *Autobiografija* (1924); *Analfabeta* (1935); *Sabrana dela* (25 vols., 1966)

BIBLIOGRAPHY: Barac, A., *A History of Yugoslav Literature* (1955), pp. 206–8; Kadić, A., *Contemporary Serbian Literature* (1964), pp. 37–40; Nikolić, M., "Die Entstehung des serbischen Nationaltheaters im 19. Jahrhundert," *MuK,* 12 (1966), 203–9

NICHOLAS MORAVČEVICH

NYANJA LITERATURE
See Malawian Literature

NYORO-TORO LITERATURE
See Ugandan Literature

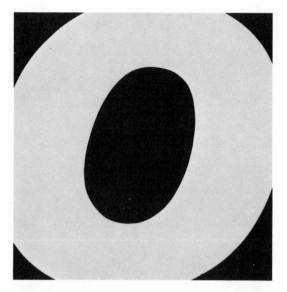

OATES, Joyce Carol

American novelist, short-story writer, critic, poet, and dramatist, b. 16 June 1938, Millersport, N.Y.

O. grew up in a rural area near Lockport, New York. Her family background is blue-collar Catholic. She graduated with a B.A. in English from Syracuse University, and received her M.A., also in English, at the University of Wisconsin. She is a recipient of the O. Henry Special Award for Continuing Achievement (1967) among other awards. After teaching English at the University of Windsor in Ontario, Canada, for a number of years, she accepted a post at Princeton University.

O. is an extraordinarily versatile and prolific writer. Among her best works are her short stories. Since her first collection, *By the North Gate* (1963), she has published many short stories, both traditional and experimental in form. *The Wheel of Love* (1970) is her best-known collection. Typically, her characters find that love brings anguish and bitterness rather than fulfillment. "Accomplished Desires" (1968) depicts a student who marries the professor of her dreams, only to learn she is still unhappy. "How I Contemplated the World from the Detroit House of Correction and Began My Life Over Again" (1969) concerns a teenager alienated from her suburban parents, who runs away from home and turns to shoplifting, drugs, and prostitution. "In the Region of Ice" (1965) shows an isolated student demanding that his nun-professor be a Christian. "Where Are You Going, Where Have You Been?" (1966) is an allegory that applies existential initiation rites to the biblical se-

duction myth. O.'s stories are replete with realistic details and plausible characters. Frequently, they have violent resolutions.

Her novels, too, more often than not, are resolved by violent death. O. believes her fiction reflects a contemporary American society in which an ordinary day can suddenly be filled with horror. Each novel of her early trilogy—*A Garden of Earthly Delights* (1967), *Expensive People* (1968), and *them* (1969), the last of which won a National Book Award—ends in murder or suicide. Whether rich or poor, the male protagonists act out their frustrations savagely.

Not all of O.'s works are violent. When she satirizes the university world in *Unholy Loves* (1979) she delineates with psychological realism college administrators and professors vying to identify with a famous visiting poet. *Do with Me What You Will* (1973) contains a rare heroine for O.: Elena achieves self-actualization through love, and feels that she has a chance for happiness.

A recurrent O. theme is the loss of the American Eden. Like Thoreau, whom she admires, she decries the destruction of the natural world and the related decay of moral fiber. In her poem "Dreaming America" (1973) she shows the loss of game animals and then a time when teenagers do not realize what is missing. Her ambitious gothic saga, the novel *Bellefleur* (1980), depicts six generations of a mythic American family. The Bellefleurs wantonly slaughter deer, exploit people and the land, and at times metamorphose into animals or disappear entirely. *Angel of Light* (1981), dedicated to the "Lost Generations," is a complex political novel set in the late 1970s, which dramatizes the alienation of the American people from those in positions of power.

O. is emerging as a great writer who illuminates contemporary American life with dazzling versatility. Her best short stories are masterpieces in the tradition of Nathaniel Hawthorne and Flannery O'Connor (q.v.). Her fiction reveals an America peopled with inarticulate, violent men and unliberated, passive women. Her countrysides are replete with decimation; her polluted cities reflect racial and class tensions, as papers and dust blow through desolate streets. The world she portrays shows little social cohesion; this fragmented society is a result of a loss of spirituality and sense of community. Her vision is chilling, yet as a chronicler of narcissism and of consequent chaos, O. acts as an instrument of cultural synthesis in her assessment of modern life.

FURTHER WORKS: *With Shuddering Fall* (1964); *Upon the Sweeping Flood* (1966); *Women in Love, and Other Poems* (1969); *Anonymous Sins, and Other Poems* (1969); *Wonderland* (1971); *The Edge of Impossibility: Tragic Forms in Literature* (1972); *Marriages and Infidelities* (1972); *Angel Fire* (1973); *The Hostile Sun: The Poetry of D. H. Lawrence* (1973); *Love and Its Derangements, and Other Poems* (1974); *Miracle Play* (1974); *New Heaven, New Earth: The Visionary Experience in Literature* (1974); *The Hungry Ghosts: Seven Allusive Comedies* (1974); *Where Are You Going, Where Have You Been?: Stories of Young America* (1974); *The Goddess and Other Women* (1974); *The Seduction, and Other Stories* (1975); *The Assassins: A Book of Hours* (1975); *The Poisoned Kiss, and Other Stories from the Portuguese* (1975); *The Fabulous Beasts* (1975); *Childwold* (1976); *The Triumph of the Spider Monkey* (1976); *Crossing the Border: Fifteen Tales* (1976); *Night-Side: Eighteen Tales* (1977); *Season of Peril* (1977); *Son of the Morning* (1978); *All the Good People I've Left Behind* (1979); *Women Whose Lives Are Food, Men Whose Lives Are Money* (1978); *Cybele* (1979); *Three Plays* (1980); *A Sentimental Education: Stories* (1981); *Contraries: Essays* (1981); *Invisible Woman: New and Selected Poems 1970–1982* (1982); *A Bloodsmoor Romance* (1982)

BIBLIOGRAPHY: Burwell, R., "J. C. O. and an Old Master," *Crit*, 15 (1973), 48–57; Grant, M., *The Tragic Vision of J. C. O.* (1978); Urbanski, M., "Existential Allegory: J. C. O.'s 'Where Are You Going, Where Have You Been?'" *SSF*, 15 (1978), 200–203; Phillips, R., "J. C. O.: The Art of Fiction LXXII," *Paris Review*, 74 (1978), 198–226; Creighton, J., *J. C. O.* (1979); Wagner, L. W., *Critical Essays on J. C. O.* (1979); Franks, L., "The Emergence of J. C. O.," *NYTMag*, 27 July 1980, 22 ff.

MARIE OLESEN URBANSKI

O'BRIEN, Edna

Irish novelist, short-story writer, dramatist, and screenwriter, b. 15 Dec. 1930, Tuamgraney

After growing up in the rural west of Ireland, O. attended the Pharmaceutical College in Dublin from 1946 to 1950. Married in 1951, she moved with her husband and two sons to London in 1959. Since her divorce in 1964, O. has remained in England. The author of several novels and short-story collections, she has also written for theater and films and in 1976 published *Mother Ireland,* a study of Irish culture and society.

The major characteristic of O.'s fiction is its frank portrayal of emotional and sexual relationships (her works usually have been censored in her native country). Her first three novels, *The Country Girls* (1960), *The Lonely Girl* (1962)—filmed (1964) with screenplay by O. under the title *The Girl with Green Eyes,* and later republished under that title—and *Girls in Their Married Bliss* (1964), form a trilogy about Caithleen Brady's painful journey from an awkward teenager growing up in the repressive atmosphere of rural Catholic Ireland to a young woman wounded by a bad marriage and forced to face her self-doubts and loneliness.

Her subsequent novels, with the exception of *A Pagan Place* (1970)—made into a play in 1973—which returns to the difficulties of childhood in the west of Ireland, explore the loneliness, suffering, and bitterness endured by women who have experienced emotional failure and betrayal in their relationships with men. *August Is a Wicked Month* (1965), perhaps O.'s best-written novel, with its wasteland imagery and atmosphere, and *Casualties of Peace* (1966), with its main character murdered in a case of mistaken identity, are particularly bleak studies of female isolation. *Night* (1972), whose heroine, Mary Holligan, recalls her history of emotions, desires, and loves, manages to reconcile life's pain with its promise, but *Johnny I Hardly Knew You* (1977) marks a return to a harsher world and vision, as its female victim turned avenger murders her younger lover for the past betrayals of her other loves.

O.'s collections of short stories, *The Love Object* (1960), *A Scandalous Woman* (1974), and *Mrs. Reinhardt* (1978), also develop a pattern of childhood disappointment and adult betrayals. Taken together, her novels and short stories, usually told from a personal viewpoint that has become more experimental in the later fiction, reveals a deepening probe into the desires, commitments, and betrayals of women who search for love and find a terrible sense of loss and loneliness at the end of their quest.

FURTHER WORKS: *A Nice Bunch of Flowers* (1963); *Zee and Co.* (screenplay, 1971); *Seven Novels, and Other Short Stories* (1978); *Virginia: A Play* (1981)

BIBILIOGRAPHY: McMahon, S., "A Sex by Themselves: An Interim Report on the Novels of E. O.," *Éire*, 2, 1 (1967), 79–87; Kiely, B., "The Whores on the Half-Doors," in Edwards, O. D., ed., *Conor Cruise O'Brien Introduces Ireland* (1969), pp. 148–61; Eckley, G., *E. O.* (1974); Snow, L., " 'That Trenchant Childhood Route?' Quest in E. O.'s Novels," *Éire*, 14, 1 (1979), 74–83

RICHARD F. PETERSON

O'BRIEN, Flann

(pseud. of Brian O'Nolan) Irish novelist, dramatist, and journalist, (writing in English and Irish), b. 5 Oct. 1911, Strabane; d. 1 April 1966, Dublin

Both of O.'s parents came from County Tyrone; because of the father's position as a customs and excise officer, the family moved frequently to various parts of Ireland. O. was the third child in a family of twelve that eventually settled in Dublin and environs. He was educated at Blackrock College and University College, Dublin.

As Brian O'Nolan (or, in its Irish form, Briain Ó Nualláin) O. spent much of his adult life as a civil servant in Dublin, chafing at the restrictions of his position and eventually losing it. As Myles na gCopaleen (or Gopaleen)—the name means "Myles of the little horse (or pony)"—he had an even longer career writing "Cruiskeen Lawn," a column for the *Irish Times,* mostly in English, sometimes in Irish, and even in French. His plurality of names, like his adroit shifts in languages, mirrored a multifaceted talent and a variety of literary modes, all of which came to a premature end when he died of cancer in his fifty-fifth year.

At Swim-Two-Birds (1939) established O.'s reputation and brought praise from James Joyce (q.v.), who called him a "real writer, with the true comic spirit." It remains one of the few examples of experimental modernism in Irish prose literature. Failure to have his second novel published during the war years embittered O., and he retreated from the audacities of his first novel, thereafter continuing to write comic works, but with neither the structural complexities nor the stylistic

intricacies of *At Swim-Two-Birds.* He reacted against Joyce as well, publishing "A Bash in the Tunnel" (1951), an unusual critical essay on Joyce, and resurrecting Joyce as a character in the novel *The Dalkey Archive* (1964)— as a bartender and writer of religious tracts.

The amount of time that elapsed between the publication of *At Swim-Two-Birds* and the three other novels in English published under the Flann O'Brien pseudonym—*The Hard Life* (1961), *The Dalkey Archive,* and the posthumously published *The Third Policeman* (1967)—attest to the difficulty of his literary career. The last novel duplicates material from its immediate predecessor and appears to be the lost manuscript rejected in 1940, from which O. had already cannibalized. A fifth novel, *Slattery's Sago Saga,* existed for years only as a rumor, but seven chapters were unearthed and published in 1973.

The missing decades between *At Swim-Two-Birds* and *The Hard Life* were years in which the Myles-of-the-little-horse persona dominated, not only in the scurrilous and hilarious columns but also on the stage—and in the Irish language. As Myles he wrote *An béal bocht* (1941; *The Poor Mouth,* 1973), which because of its complex Irish puns was long considered untranslatable, and his first drama, *Faustus Kelly* (1943), which was produced at the Abbey Theatre. Regardless of the artistic medium or the operative language, everything written by Brian-Flann-Myles reveals an irreverent comic touch veering from frivolity to satiric bitterness.

Although some critics, primarily in Ireland, relegate *At-Swim-Two-Birds* to the status of an oddity and prefer the later works, his international reputation rests essentially on that novel-within-a-novel-within-another-novel. The multiple frame, the diabolism, the conspiracy of the fictional characters against their creator, the fiendish speculations on human folly, the unexpected transcendence of folly and fate—these features characterize this unusual work. His later novels abandon complex plot structure for linear narrative but retain the wildly comic tone, the agony of despair, the pretended indifference that underlines an acceptance of futility, the lugubriousness that nonetheless hints at religious miracle, and the skillful blend into near-plausible fantasy that characterize the first novel.

Satiric and cynical, outrageous and outlandish, O.'s world is remembered for the small-town Irish politics with the devil stuffing the ballot boxes, the smoke-filled rural kitchens with obese pigs jammed in the door-frame, the cracks in the ceiling that are maps of hell, the bicycles that take on the human characteristics of their owners, the Irish uncles who attempt to convince the Pope to provide public conveniences for women who, having consumed "gravid water," fall to their death through the floorboards, and James Joyce writing for the Catholic Truth Society. These diverse elements locate O. within the Irish comic tradition, and he persisted as a jaundiced commentator on the Irish nation that emerged in the 20th c.

FURTHER WORKS: *The Best of Myles* (1968); *Stories and Plays* (1973); *The Various Lives of Keats and Chapman, and The Brother* (1976); *A F. O. Reader* (1978)

BIBLIOGRAPHY: Wain, J., "To Write for My Own Race," *Encounter,* July 1967, 71–85; O'Keeffe, T., ed., *Myles: Portraits of Brian O'Nolan* (1968); Benstock, B., "The Three Faces of Brian Nolan," *Éire,* 3, 3 (1968), 51–65; Janik, D. I., "F. O.: The Novelist as Critic," *Éire,* 4, 4 (1969), 64–72; Lee, L. L., "The Dublin Cowboys of F. O.," *WAL,* 4 (1969), 219–25; Clissmann, A., *F. O.: A Critical Introduction to His Writings* (1975); Power, M., "F. O. and Classical Satire: An Exegesis of *The Hard Life,*" *Éire,* 13, 1 (1978), 87–102

BERNARD BENSTOCK

O'CASEY, Sean

(born John Casey; name Gaelicized, first as Sean Ó Cathasaigh) Irish dramatist, autobiographer, and essayist, b. 30 March 1880, Dublin; d. 18 Sept. 1964, St. Marychurch, England

Much of O.'s life was fraught with controversy, including the facts of his biography. He began his autobiography with "In Dublin, sometime in the early eighties, on the last day of the month of March" (even the date is erroneous), a purposely vague beginning to the story of "Johnny/Sean Casside" in a novelized version. O. had previously set his birth year ahead in order to pass as a young new playwright to qualify for the Hawthornden Prize when he was forty-six. His first play had been staged by the Abbey Theatre in Dublin three years earlier, when its author

was still earning his meager living with a pick and shovel.

O. was actually born into reasonably comfortable circumstances, the last of thirteen children; the previous two had also been christened John, and both had died in infancy. His parents were lower-middle-class Protestants, but with the death of the father when O. was only six, the family became progressively poorer but never less proud. Eventually, he lived alone with his aged mother, her sole means of support during years in which he remained mostly unemployed. Impaired eyesight during childhood kept him away from school; at times tutored by his school-teacher sister, he was essentially self-taught from books he bought or stole. During his thirties he wrote poems, songs, and journalistic political pieces, learned Irish and joined the Gaelic League, and served as secretary for various organizations, primarily the Irish Citizen Army, the militant arm of the trade-union movement. He broke with the Nationalist cause because he insisted on a socialist base for its political activities, and despite his bourgeois origins he strongly identified with the working class, remaining a lifelong communist. From 1918 on he persisted in submitting plays to the Abbey Theatre, all of them rejected until *The Shadow of a Gunman* (1923) was produced; it brought instant success to him and the theater, probably saving the Abbey from bankruptcy and eventually rescuing O. from manual labor.

The next two plays, *Juno and the Paycock* (1924) and *The Plough and the Stars* (1926), confirmed O.'s reputation and are still considered his greatest, although the latter caused a recurrence of Abbey riots (there had previously been disturbances over plays by Yeats and Synge [qq.v.]). While the voice of a Nationalist leader can be heard outside a pub extolling patriotic bloodletting, a happy-go-luckless prostitute is present within peddling her wares. When Nationalists in the audience erupted in anger at the idea of the flag of the Citizens Army being brought into a pub and at the portrayal of an Irish woman as a prostitute, William Butler Yeats announced from the stage the apotheosis of a new Irish genius. In 1926 O. went to London for the opening of *Juno and the Paycock* and the Hawthornden Prize, and married a young Irish actress. The rejection of *The Silver Tassie* (1928) by the Abbey (and Yeats in particular) in 1928 changed the residence in England into permanent self-exile, and in

411

1938 he moved his wife and two sons to Devon, where his daughter was born the next year. From his Tor Bay-area vantage point O. surveyed events in Ireland with interest, wrote plays, essays, and autobiographies, and received visitors from all over the world; his vintage years were tragically marred by the premature death of his son Niall. His turbulent love affair with Ireland and the Abbey Theatre and his numerous quarrels with both persisted throughout, and two of his comic self-personifications—guises of a Socratic gadfly and a raucous voice insisting on joy in life, good drama, and working-class ideals—provided titles for books of fugitive essays, *The Flying Wasp* (1937) and *The Green Crow* (1956).

The twenty-two plays (plus a recently published early rejected play) constitute the primary corpus of O.'s creativity. Directly or obliquely most of the plays mirrored the historical events in Ireland (and the world at large) during O.'s lifetime: the first four major Dublin-set tragicomedies deal with the era of the "Troubles" (*The Shadow of a Gunman*), the civil war (*Juno and the Paycock*), the Easter Rising (*The Plough and the Stars*), and World War I (*The Silver Tassie).*

Two later plays have an English setting: *Within the Gates* (1934), a morality play about the economic depression set in Hyde Park, and *Oak Leaves and Lavender* (1946), a drama of the Battle of Britain set in rural England, with two Irishmen as its protagonists. The latter is among O.'s most outspoken propaganda pieces, along with *The Star Turns Red* (1940), which hypothesized for Ireland an ultimate confrontation between communist and fascist forces based on the circumstances of the Spanish Civil War. His most personal drama, *Red Roses for Me* (1943), is also his most successful political statement in favor of militant trade unionism; it is based on his own experiences during the 1911 railway strike, which had previously served as plot material for the rejected play, *The Harvest Festival* (written 1918–19, pub. 1980).

The Abbey triumphs of the 1920s established O. as a presumed master of naturalistic drama, a designation he was never comfortable with, and it was not until the expressionist (q.v.) second act of *The Silver Tassie* that he demonstrated his bent for experimentation. His ear for working-class Dublin speech, the settings in the slums, the depiction of tenement life during periods of

upheaval and hardship had fixed critical assumptions of "photographic realism," but these plays were also distinguished for the ironic juxtapositions of the tragic and the comic. Having learned his craft from reading such diverse authors as Shakespeare and Dion Boucicault (1820?–1890), O. did not hesitate to mix genres and styles, and to deploy strong elements of the melodramatic. During the 1940s and 1950s he wrote several joyous and bitter comedies, beginning with *Purple Dust* (1940), in which two English businessmen make magnificent fools of themselves in attempting to restore a Tudor mansion in Ireland, losing their mistresses to militant and romantic Irish workmen, and their manor and lives to an apocalyptic flood. *Cock-a-Doodle Dandy* (1949) and *The Drums of Father Ned* (1958) are also set in rural Ireland—priest-ridden, puritanical, and bourgeois—where only an occasional free spirit, several strong-minded women, and some amorous young people can break free and possibly upset the apple cart. The most libertine and licentious comedy, however, is *Figuro in the Night* (1961), written when O. was already an octogenarian, a parable extolling the Mannequin Pis running amock in theocratic Dublin. In *The Bishop's Bonfire* (1955) O. dissected what he viewed as constricted Irish society in a drama that retains some of his zesty comic elements, but is essentially his most somber play.

Rivaling his dramatic output is his alternate career as a dynamic and caustic writer of autobiographies that transcend the genre to include aspects of the novel, imaginative fictions, and the expository essay. *I Knock at the Door* (1939), *Pictures in the Hallway* (1942), and *Drums under the Windows* (1945) are poignant, exciting, and often poetic, many of the incidents paralleling those of the plays. *Inishfallen, Fare Thee Well* (1949) marks a transition as the playwright leaves Ireland, and it points toward the later volumes of commentary and criticism in which O. indulged in acerbic observations and opinions, as well as verbal high jinks. *Rose and Crown* (1952) and *Sunset and Evening Star* (1954) are filled with warmth, compassion, good humor, and a healthy dollop of sentimentality. (The six volumes were republished as *Mirror in My House,* 2 vols., 1956).

O.'s reputation as Ireland's premier dramatist and a major figure in 20th-c. literature has consolidated since his death in 1964, although productions of any but his major plays are not as frequent as his fixed position deserves. The vagaries of fantasy, the controversial political and anticlerical elements, the subtle balances of comic and tragic, the broad nature of slapstick comedy and melodrama, and the difficulty of reproducing the mellifluous and mordant Irish speech remain inhibiting factors, yet the technological advances in stage machinery reduce some of the technical problems of production: several productions have been innovative in enacting the vast deluge that covers the stage at the end of *Purple Dust,* for instance. *Mirror in My House* has recently become an increasingly important component of O.'s body of work, and an alternate reputation has been developing for him as a fanciful chronicler of his time and a writer of creative autobiography. Despite the negative attitudes of various detractors, there are few who would deny that O. has achieved a permanent position in literary history as the creator of such immortal characters as Captain Boyle, "Joxer" Daly, and Fluther Good to share the world stage with Falstaff and Tartuffe.

FURTHER WORKS: *Windfalls* (1934); *Collected Plays* (4 vols., 1949–51); *Behind the Green Curtains* (1961); *Feathers from the Green Crow* (1962); *Under a Colored Cap* (1964); *Blasts and Benedictions* (1967); *The S. O. Reader* (1968); *The Letters of S. O.* (2 vols., 1975, 1980); *The Harvest Festival* (written 1919, pub. 1979)

BIBLIOGRAPHY: Krause, D., *S. O.: The Man and His Work* (1960); Hogan, R., *The Experiments of S. O.* (1960); McCann, S., ed., *The World of S. O.* (1966); Ayling, R., ed., *S. O.* (1969); O'Casey, E., *Sean* (1971); Mikhail, E. H., ed., *S. O.: A Bibliography of Criticism* (1972); Mikhail, E. H., and O'Riordan, J., eds., *The Sting and the Twinkle: Conversations with S. O.* (1974); *S. O. Review* (1974 ff.); Kilroy, T., ed., *S. O.: A Collection of Critical Essays* (1975); Benstock, B., *Paycocks and Others: S. O.'s World* (1976); Smith, B. L., *O.'s Satiric Vision* (1978); Ayling, R., and Durkin, M., eds., *S. O.: A Bibliography* (1978); Murray, C., ed., special O. issue, *IUR,* 10, 1 (1980)

BERNARD BENSTOCK

O. is a master of knockabout in this very serious and honourable sense—that he discerns the principle of disintegration in even the most complacent solidities, and activates it to their explosion. This is the energy of his theatre, the triumph of the principle of knockabout in situation, in all its elements and on all its planes, from the furniture to the higher centres. If *Juno and the Paycock,* as seems likely, is his best work so far, it is because it communicates most fully this dramatic dishiscence, mind and world come asunder in irreparable dissociation—"chassis" (the credit of having readapted Aguecheek and Belch in Joxer and the Captain being incidental to the larger credit of having dramatised the slump in the human solid).

Samuel Beckett, *The Bookman,* 86 (1934), 111

The manifest fact is that O. is a baroque dramatic poet in a largely trivial and constricted theatre given over to neat construction and small-beer feeling. He is as baroque, as lavish and prodigal, as were Marlowe, Shakespeare, Jonson, and John Webster. He belongs to the spacious days of the theatre. And since he will not make himself smaller for anything as inconsequential to him as material success, the theatre will simply have to be made larger if O. is to have his rightful place. . . .

He was formed as a writer neither by educational institutions nor by the theatre but by a turbulent life equally remote from the academy and the stage. It has never been possible to subjugate him to either institution. Nor could he accept the rule of any established dramatic form. Realistic group drama suited his needs in *The Shadow of a Gunman,* family drama in *Juno and the Paycock,* mass drama in *The Plough and the Stars.* His passion forced him to adopt expressionism in *The Silver Tassie* and choral drama in *Within the Gates.* Rather simplified drama was his natural mode in *The Star Turns Red* when he polarized the world into revolutionary and counterrevolutionary factions. A lyrical realism was proper to his elegaic mood when he commemorated the great Transport Strike of 1913 in *Red Roses for Me.* A turbulent fantasy was the inevitable choice for his desire to assert the claims of nature against cowardice in *Cock-a-Doodle Dandy.* . . .

Neither in tragedy nor comedy can he be circumspect, cautious, or calculating. His artistry remains pure self-expression and spins everything out of his emotion and immediate observation.

John Gassner, *The Theatre in Our Time* (1954), pp. 244–45

S. O.—whose own youth was bitter—believed that life was a joyful inspiration that should never be tarnished by anything that even remotely resembled a sense of sin. He believed in the dignity of freedom and the liberty of joy; nothing, one imagines, would have given him more pleasure than an opportunity of joining God in declaring that Nietzsche was dead. He was a man of powerful vision and enormous energy, the most irrational yet likeable voice in twentieth-century theatre. An early and most vocal member of the Disestablishment, he was unable to resist sitting targets but he knocked them with brilliance and built alternatives with fierce integrity and considerable compassion. He added several new dimensions to the theatre, influenced many of the best contemporary dramatists of whom one can think, and wrote the most brilliant dialogue of our time.

Don't be misled by those who say that he was out of touch with Ireland. He wasn't. His plays have real relevance for they go back, in modern dress, to investigate the archaic, hypocritical and furtively puritanical thinking of the Irish past which still so strongly influences the mildly sophisticated thinking of the Irish present. Some day our society will change, broaden, solidify, and the old crawthumpers will be safely stored away and something approaching honesty will take the place of compromise in our politics, our religion and our thought. Then we will realise the extent of his genius. Or will we?

Kevin Casey, "The Excitements and the Disappointments," in Sean McCann, ed., *The World of S. O.* (1966), p. 233

But it was faith in life, love for his family and friends, and belief in a cheerful destiny that kept him going through a life of indigence and several personal catastrophes. He was affectionate, generous, and loyal towards those he loved and respected. His hatreds were confined to people and institutions that, in his opinion, impeded or impaired the normal joyousness of human existence. Among the advertising cards inside a Second Avenue bus in New York I was once surprised and delighted to find a quotation from O.: "I have found life an enjoyable, enchanting, active and sometimes terrifying experience, and I've enjoyed it completely. A lament in one ear, maybe, but always a song in the other." This turned out to be a quotation from one of the hundreds of personal letters he wrote to hundreds of anonymous admirers, particularly in the United States, of which he was especially fond. O. was a believer; it is a temptation to misuse a religious term and call him an Old Believer. That was his strength as a writer. The fire was in his hatred. The strength was in his love.

He was a frail man, afflicted all his life with ulcerated eyes that resulted in almost total blindness in his last years. He suffered from lumbago that made movement painful; he had bronchial and respiratory troubles that consigned him to nursing homes repeatedly. But he left a prodigious body of exuberant work. Beginning at the age of thirty-eight, when his first writings were published ("Songs of the Wren" and "The Story of Thomas Ashe") he wrote twelve full-length plays, fifteen one-act plays, six volumes of autobiography and four volumes of poems, short stories, reviews, articles and jeremiads. Although the literary forms

changed, the basic point of view remained consistent.

Brooks Atkinson, Introduction to *The S. O. Reader* (1968), pp. xi–xii

In his beginning and in his ending, words were the weapons of his idealism and discontent. Words for him were a delight and a defense, a way of playing with dramatic images and developing his working-class values, a way of compensating for his lack of formal education; but ultimately and of necessity words were a way of defending himself in an Ireland torn by economic and political revolt, religious conflict and literary backbiting. If he was poor in material things, he could be rich, even profligate with words. In some of his earliest extant letters he is in his most characteristic moods when as a St. Lawrence O'Toole piper in 1910 he defends the glory of the ancient Irish war pipes, in English and later in Gaelic; and when as an unemployed railway laborer in 1913 he defends Irish freedom and socialism in a letter to the *Irish Worker* that is subtitled, "A Challenge to Verbal Combat." He was to spend the rest of his life piping the tragicomic music of Irish life and seeking verbal combat whenever honor was at stake. He was incapable of turning away from a fight; he courted conflict, even when it was apparent that he would probably win the argument but lose the battle. As he once wrote about himself in later years in the persona of "The Green Crow": "Some Latin writer once said, 'If a crow could feed in quiet, it would have more meat.' A thing this Green Crow could never do: it had always, and has still, to speak and speak while it seeks and finds its food, and so has had less meat than it might have had if only it had kept its big beak shut." Suffering in silence would have been an unbearable sign of humiliation and defeat—to him the ultimate despair, and a sin against the Holy Ghost which he never committed.

David Krause, Introduction to *The Letters of S. O., Volume I, 1910–1941* (1975), p. ix

O. was a "realist": his plays and his prose works present a picture of life as he saw it, with the exploited working class engaged in constant struggle not only against their capitalist and imperialist masters but also against their own human weaknesses and petty meannesses. But he was not a "naturalist." His realistic picture is constantly modified by the introduction of allegorical or mythological characters and incidents. Because the culture he writes about is Christian and largely Catholic, many of these "imaginary" elements take the form of, or are presented in language derived from, the Christian religious iconography. Because he was an Irishman (who had in his youth been a keen member of the Gaelic Revival movement) he also reflects the prevailing divine machinery of the pre-Christian Gaelic legends.

John Arden, "Ecce Hobo Sapiens: O.'s Theatre," in T. Kilroy, ed., *S. O.: A Collection of Critical Essays* (1975), p. 65

O.'s achievement, for all the unevenness and occasional failures, can be fully comprehended only by approaching his work as the product of a sensitive and well-read man, to be evaluated within the broad context of the English literary tradition that he knew so well and of modern developments in world theatre, and not merely the context of Dublin or even Anglo-Irish culture. He was a conscious literary artist, aware of what he was doing and what was going on in the world at large. His profound identification with the consciousness of Dublin, and of the Dublin proletariat in particular, is a characteristic that cannot be ignored, of course; but, at best—and this is more often than is usually recognised—his plays and prose works project a deeply realised experience of Irish life on a universal plane. If it is wrong to view James Joyce merely in parochial or regional terms, then it is equally absurd to approach O. as a provincial writer in any narrow sense, or, because of the proletarian background to his writings, to label him, even appreciatively, as a wild, untutored primitive. He was, from first to last, a deliberate and pioneering dramatic artist and his style and technique, constantly adapted and modified to display basic recurrent themes in new and theatrically exciting ways, invites analysis by virtue of its variety and originality. Criticism of O. as a playwright, therefore, should bear in mind that his command of stagecraft was no happy accident but the result of a lifetime's sustained exploration of diverse modes of dramatic expression.

Ronald Ayling, *Continuity and Innovation in S. O.'s Drama* (1976), pp. vi–vii

OCCITAN LITERATURE
See under French Literature

O'CONNOR, Flannery
American novelist and short-story writer, b. 25 March 1925, Savannah, Ga., d. 3 Aug. 1964, Milledgeville, Ga.

O.'s life was in many ways tightly circumscribed. With the exception of two years spent at the University of Iowa acquiring a Master of Fine Arts degree, she spent her entire life in her native Georgia, the first thirteen years in Savannah, and the remainder in Milledgeville, where she lived on a farm with her mother. In part, the circumscription of O.'s life was due to illness, for she was a victim after 1950 of disseminated lupus, a debilitating blood disease. Yet O. knew nothing of self-pity: her attitude toward her illness was distinctly cavalier, and she liked to affect a broad, down-home manner in an apparent parody of her provincial existence. Nor was O. a recluse. She regularly issued invitations to friends and correspondents to visit her in Milledgeville, and she numbered Caroline Gordon, John Hawkes, Robert Lowell, Katherine Anne Porter (qq.v.), Andrew Lytle (b. 1902), and Robert Fitzgerald (b. 1910) among her friends and callers. Nor was O. a dropout from the cultural mainstream. She read carefully such contemporary thinkers as Pierre Teilhard de Chardin (1881–1955), Hannah Arendt (1906–1975), and Jacques Maritain (1882–1973), and she read with discernment such formidable novelists as Vladimir Nabokov, Muriel Spark, and Henry James (qq.v.).

But O. knew that her strength was in her roots, and all but two of her stories are set among the cities, towns, and farms of the Piedmont region, where "Jesus Saves" signs punctuate a landscape too often squalid and mean. Drawing on that intermixture of squalor and backwoods Protestantism, O. wrote stories in which ill-favored characters are engaged in an unsettling relationship with God, who tends to erupt into their lives violently and unexpectedly. Humor attends her macabre stories of God and man, for many of O.'s characters exult in their malfeasance and delight us with their unregenerate willfulness. Nonetheless, O. was herself a deeply religious Roman Catholic (a "hillbilly Thomist," she once called herself), and her characters ultimately risk condemnation for their disbelief.

O.'s two novels, *Wise Blood* (1952) and *The Violent Bear It Away* (1960), are both studies in disbelief and the saving ways of grace. Hazel Motes of *Wise Blood* goes so far as to preach the "Church without Christ," believing himself liberated from his childhood obsession with sin and Jesus, and determined to free others from the tyranny of Christian faith. Motes cannot sustain his defiance of Christ, however, and he finally embraces a life of penance as grotesque as his defiance of God had been. Marion Tarwater, the protagonist of *The Violent Bear It Away,* is a mirror-opposite of Motes, for Tarwater

415

accepts an early call to prophetic ministry without genuine faith in his calling. Like Motes in *Wise Blood,* Tarwater comes finally to faith, but through an acceptance of his prophetic burden rather than through a rejection of it. Ironically, it is in committing murder that both Motes and Tarwater suddenly know their identities and their conversions to Christ: in O.'s fictive world, the ways of grace are eccentric as well as salvific.

O.'s short stories are not so explicitly theological in framework or in reference as her novels, and the protagonists of the short stories tend to suffer abrupt revelations about themselves rather than revelations of God. But in stories such as "The Geranium" (1946), "The Artificial Nigger" (1955), and "Everything That Rises Must Converge" (1961), the protagonists experience dark nights of the soul as profound as those of Motes and Tarwater; in stories such as "Good Country People" (1955), "The Life You Save May Be Your Own" (1953), and "A Good Man Is Hard to Find" (1953), violence erupts as shatteringly as the violence of God erupts in the novels, and it is never clear that the violence in such stories is *not* of God, for O.'s stories are always open to theological interpretation.

In many ways, O.'s short stories are more successful than her novels. *Wise Blood* and *The Violent Bear It Away* are thinly textured at best, whereas the short stories are typically thick with incident; moreover, the frigidly unsentimental tone of O.'s fiction tends to cloy in the novels, while it remains startling and effective in the more brief compass of the stories. The bite of O.'s humor is more successful in the stories than in the novels, too, for in the span of the novels the humor cumulates with an oddly saddening effect, while in the stories it remains crisp and morally authoritative, entirely an agent of the mixed effect that is O.'s aesthetic signature. Indeed, the incongruity between style and subject in O.'s fiction—a kind of poker-face she turns to the extraordinary—is what distinguishes O.'s vision from that of such kindred writers as Carson McCullers and Tennessee Williams (qq.v.).

If O. was not the ignorant provincial that she sometimes pretended to be, she was still less the backwoods natural she is sometimes thought to have been. As her collected letters, published as *The Habit of Being* (1979), make clear, she was a conscious craftsman,

not unsophisticated in technique, and she had a masterful sense of the nuances of manners and social class, a fine sense of timing, and an exact ear for speech. Her prose may seem artless to the casual glance, but its rhythms are precisely modulated, its vocabulary is concretely evocative, and its tone is marvelously calculated to embrace dark humor and religious exultation alike. Her body of work is small, consisting of only thirty-one stories, two novels, and some speeches and letters, but her achievement is major, transcending both the religious beliefs and the regionalism that so deeply inform her work.

FURTHER WORKS: *A Good Man Is Hard to Find, and Other Stories* (1955); *Everything That Rises Must Converge* (1965); *Mystery and Manners: Occasional Prose* (1969); *The Complete Stories of F. O.* (1971)

BIBLIOGRAPHY: Friedman, M. J., and Lawson, L. A., eds., *The Added Dimension: The Art and Mind of F. O.* (1966); Driskell, L. V., and Brittain, J. T., *The Eternal Crossroads: The Art of F. O.* (1971); Feeley, K., *F. O.: Voice of the Peacock* (1972); Muller, G. H., *Nightmares and Visions: F. O. and the Catholic Grotesque* (1972); Orvell, M., *Invisible Parade: The Fiction of F. O.* (1972); May, J. R., *The Pruning Word: The Parables of F. O.* (1976); McFarland, D. T., *F. O.* (1976); Shloss, C., *F. O.'s Dark Comedies: The Limits of Inference* (1980)

ROBERT F. KIERNAN

O'CONNOR, Frank

(pseud. of Michael O'Donovan) Irish short-story writer, novelist, dramatist, literary critic, biographer, and translator, b. 17 Sept. 1903, Cork; d. 10 March 1966, Dublin

O.'s early years, the subject of his *An Only Child* (1961), the first of two autobiographies, were spent in terrible poverty. Although he had to leave school in his early teens, he continued his studies, especially of the Irish language and culture, and became active in politics. But after fighting on the losing Republican side in the Irish civil war and spending a year in an internment camp, he turned away from politics. In his second autobiography, *My Father's Son* (1969), O. describes his frustrations as a librarian in Cork and the controversies during his early literary career in Dublin. He became a director of the Abbey Theatre in 1935 but re-signed after W. B. Yeats's (q.v.) death in 1939 and devoted his energies to writing. After a decade of struggling against Irish provincialism, O. went to America, where he taught at several universities during the 1950s. In his later years O. received long-overdue acclaim in Ireland and abroad as one of the world's finest short-story writers.

Although he also published translations from the Irish, as well as a biography, two novels, and several books of literary criticism, O. has been recognized and honored mainly for his short stories. Most of the stories in *Guests of the Nation* (1931), his first volume, are reflections of his war experiences. In *Bones of Contention* (1936) the focus is on peasant characters at odds with authority. In *Crab-Apple Jelly* (1944), one of his best collections, and *The Common Chord* (1948) O. concentrates on lonely, isolated characters, their frustrations and failures, and their occasional triumphs of the spirit. In later collections, *Traveller's Samples* (1951) and *Domestic Relations* (1957), the stories are dominated by first-person narratives, often told humorously by Larry Delaney, a spokesman for O., about the problems of growing up in Ireland.

In *The Lonely Voice* (1962), an influential study of the modern short story, O. points out that the proper subject matter for the short story, because it is a solitary art intended for the solitary reader, is the lonely, even outlawed individual who appears so frequently in Irish, American, and Russian fiction. Although he believes that the short story developed from the oral tradition, he sees the modern story as dominated by a detached, objective point of view that often makes narrative approach the mode of dramatic art.

A member of a generation that also produced Liam O'Flaherty (b. 1897) and Sean O'Faoláin (b. 1900), O. is generally regarded as Ireland's most important writer of short fiction. At their best, his stories illuminate the loneliness endured by those isolated from society by their own sensitivity, desire, or sense of failure. While several of his masterpieces are written in a detached manner, most of his stories are first-person narratives that capture the human voice speaking. O.'s popularity is largely dependent upon the charm and humor of his narrators, but his reputation as a master of the short-story form is based on his ability to write with ob-jectivity and with insight into the lonely characters who populate his fictional world.

FURTHER WORKS: *The Saint and Mary Kate* (1932); *Three Old Brothers* (1936); *The Big Fellow: A Life of Michael Collins* (1937); *Dutch Interior* (1940); *Towards an Appreciation of Literature* (1945); *Irish Miles* (1947); *The Art of the Theatre* (1947); *The Road to Stratford* (1948; rev. ed., *Shakespeare's Progress,* 1960); *Leinster, Munster, and Connaught* (1950); *The Stories of F. O.* (1952); *More Stories* (1954; rev. ed., *Collection Two,* 1964); *The Mirror in the Roadway* (1956); *Stories by F. O.* (1956); *The Backward Look: A Survey of Irish Literature* (1967); *Collection Three* (1969); *A Set of Variations* (1969); *Collected Stories* (1981); *The Cornet-Player Who Betrayed Ireland* (1981)

BIBLIOGRAPHY: Sheehy, M., ed., *Michael/Frank: Studies on F. O.* (1969); Matthews, J., *F. O.* (1976); Wohlgelernter, M., *F. O.: An Introduction* (1977); Tomory, W., *F. O.* (1980); Chatalic, R., "F. O. and the Desolation of Reality," in Rafroidi, P., and Brown, T., eds., *The Irish Short Story* (1980), pp. 189–204; Averill, D., *The Irish Short Story from George Moore to F. O.* (1981), pp. 227–305; Peterson, R. F., "F. O. and the Modern Irish Short Story," *MFS,* 28 (1982), 53–67

RICHARD F. PETERSON

ODETS, Clifford

American dramatist and screenwriter, b. 18 July 1906, Philadelphia, Pa.; d. 14 Aug. 1963, Los Angeles, Cal.

O.'s parents were originally of the working class, but his father became the owner of a printing plant after the family moved to the Bronx in 1912, and O. grew up in a comfortable, middle-class milieu. He dropped out of high school in 1923 to become an actor but his essentially unsuccessful experiences with the Theatre Guild (1923–27), Harry Kemp's Poets' Theatre (1925–27), Mae Desmond and Her Players (1927–31), and the Group Theatre (1930–35) caused him to give up the stage. His subsequent career as a dramatist reflects major trends in American playwriting of the next three decades: O. wrote proletarian, social-problem plays in the 1930s, plays dealing with loneliness and personal disorientation in the late 1930s and early

1940s, and psychological dramas for the Broadway stage in the late 1940s and early 1950s. In 1961 O. received the Drama Award of the American Academy of Arts and Letters.

O.'s best plays were produced between 1935 and 1937. *Waiting for Lefty* (1935), a one-act play in the agitprop tradition, is concerned with the situation of striking taxicab drivers. It took first prize from a field of 220 entries in the New Theatre–New Masses Theatre Contest as well as winning the George Pierce Baker Drama Prize at Yale. The play, while depicting a specific strike, offers a vigorous and searching commentary on the overall labor and social unrest of the times.

I've Got the Blues (1935), later retitled *Awake and Sing!* (1935), displays at its best O.'s talent for psychological characterization and for well-balanced tragicomedy. The play portrays the tensions of three generations of a working-class Jewish family living together in a Bronx apartment. *Awake and Sing!* and *Paradise Lost* (1935) both deal with the lives of families whose very existence is threatened by the economic problems of the Great Depression. *Awake and Sing!* is the stronger play in that its characters are more convincingly developed and tend to be less stereotypical than those in *Paradise Lost*. Both plays demonstrate clearly O.'s fine ear for Jewish-American idiom and his ability to record it credibly. *Till the Day I Die* (1935), an agitprop play about the problems of communists in Nazi Germany, was hastily (and carelessly) written and produced hurriedly so that it might be part of a double bill. It was paired first with *Waiting for Lefty* and later with *Awake and Sing!* Some crudely presented elements in this play (for example, the smashing of Ernst Tausig's hand by a sadistic SS trooper) were refined and used productively in subsequent plays such as *Golden Boy* (1937), which, like the latter plays *The Big Knife* (1948) and *The Country Girl* (1950), is concerned with the unconscionable exploitation of talent. *Golden Boy*, the story of a sensitive violinist who is forced by economic necessity to go into professional boxing, thereby destroying his hands, retains many of the proletarian overtones of O.'s earliest work.

Of O.'s middle group of plays, *Night Music* (1940) is the most sensitive and the one with the greatest artistic integrity. It deals with homelessness and loneliness, presenting these themes with delicacy, although at times too

romantically. *Rocket to the Moon* (1938) and *Clash by Night* (1941) are dependent for their development upon the hackneyed and formulaic love triangle. Only intermittently do they rise above banality.

The Big Knife is the most vitriolic of O.'s late plays. It demonstrates O.'s anger and disenchantment with Hollywood and the film industry—he had written the scripts for *The General Died at Dawn* (1937), *None But the Lonely Heart* (1944), which he also directed, *Deadline at Dawn* (1946), and *Humoresque* (1946), and would later write the screenplays for *The Sweet Smell of Success* (1957), *The Story on Page One* (1960), which he directed, and *Wild in the Country* (1961). *The Country Girl* is psychologically more profound than most of his earlier plays, save *Awake and Sing!* It focuses on the battle of an aging actor with alcoholism and on the struggle of his younger wife to help him overcome his problem and to remain loyal to him despite her romantic attraction to his director.

O.'s final stage play, *The Flowering Peach* (1954), a warm and witty allegory based on the biblical story of Noah and the flood, is one of his stronger works. In it he returns to the theme of preserving the family during times of great strain.

O.'s early contributions to proletarian drama in the U.S. belong to the best of that genre. His later work, while highly competent, was not charged with the energy, vitality, or verisimilitude of his purely proletarian plays. O.'s anger in *The Big Knife* is relatively trivial compared to his anger in a play like *Waiting for Lefty*, while *The Flowering Peach* is a comfortable, mellow play, one of resignation rather than of rebellion.

FURTHER WORKS: *Rifle Rule in Cuba* (1935, with Carleton Beales); *I Can't Sleep* (1936); *The Silent Partner* (1936); *Six Plays by C. O.* (1939)

BIBLIOGRAPHY: Shuman, R. B., *C. O.* (1962); Murray, E., *C. O.: The Thirties and After* (1968); Mendelsohn, M. J., *C. O.: Humane Dramatist* (1969); Weales, G., *C. O.: Playwright* (1971); Shuman, R. B., "C. O.: A Playwright and His Jewish Background," *SAQ*, 71 (1972), 225–33; Cantor, H., *C. O.: Playwright-Poet* (1978); Brenman-Gibson, M., *C. O., American Playwright: The Years from 1906 to 1940* (1981)

R. BAIRD SHUMAN

ŌE Kenzaburō

Japanese novelist, short-story writer, and essayist, b. 31 Jan. 1935, Ōsemura (now Uchiko-cho)

Ō. was born and raised in an isolated rural region of the small island of Shikoku. He made his literary appearance in 1957 while still a student at Tokyo University. His early works, published between 1957 and 1963, express his sense of the degradation, humiliation, and disorientation caused by Japan's surrender at the end of World War II. Since 1964 his writing has focused on themes of madness and idiocy, themes that give expression to his personal experience as the father of a brain-damaged child and that are metaphors for the human condition. Ō. has a strong sense of social involvement, which began with the anti-American Security Treaty protests in 1960, and which encompasses his role as an antinuclear spokesman, involvements in radical causes, and numerous essays on political and social topics. Given Ō.'s commitment to social action as a way of authenticating his existence, it is not surprising that his literary mentors include Jean-Paul Sartre, Albert Camus, and Norman Mailer (qq.v.).

One of the finest of Ō.'s early stories is "Shiiku" (1958; "Prize Stock," 1977), in which the hero is propelled from the innocent world of childhood into adulthood by various acts of madness ranging from the madness of war to the temporary insanity of his father, who murders a prisoner of war with an ax. Other early stories, such as "Kimyō na shigoto" (1957; an odd job) and "Shisha no ogori" (1957; "Lavish Are the Dead," 1965), also have protagonists who are alienated and disoriented in a world where gratuitous degradation and abuse are commonplace. Ō.'s heroes fight back with hostility and rebellion, or escape into fantasies and perverse sex.

In 1964 Ō. simultaneously published *Kojinteki na taiken* (1964; *A Personal Matter,* 1968) and *Hiroshima nooto* (1964; Hiroshima notes), both dealing with madness-producing events. The latter is an essay about the public madness of nuclear warfare. The former is more personal, a fictional account of coming to terms with the birth of a brain-damaged son. This novel was followed by several stories outlining other possible relationships between the corpulent father and the idiot son.

Although many would argue that Ō. is the finest writer in Japan today, he has been criticized by those who feel his rage against complacency is out of line in view of Japan's prosperity. Others criticize his style for being so rough it sometimes sounds as though his novels have been ineptly translated into Japanese from some other language. These complaints aside, Ō. has achieved and maintained an impressive level of literary excellence.

FURTHER WORKS: *Megumushiri kouchi* (1958); *Warera no jidai* (1959); *Seinen no omei* (1959); *Sakebigoe* (1962); *Nichijō seikatsu no bōken* (1963); *Man'en gannen no futtobōru* (1967; *Silent Cry,* 1974); *Warera no kyōki o iki nobiru michi o oshieyo* (1969; *Teach Us to Outgrow Our Madness,* 1972); *Kōzui wa waga tamashii ni oyobi* (1973); *Pinchiranna chōsho* (1976)

BIBLIOGRAPHY: Rabson, S., "A Personal Matter," in Tsuruta, K., and Swann, T., eds., *Approaches to the Modern Japanese Novel* (1976), pp. 180–98; Iwamoto, Y., "The 'Mad' World of Ō. K.," *JATJ,* 14 (1979), 66–83; Wilson, M. N., "Ō.'s Obsessive Metaphor, Mori the Idiot Son: Toward the Imagination of Satire, Regeneration, and Grotesque Realism," *JJS,* 7 (1981), 23–52

STEPHEN W. KOHL

O'HARA, Frank

American poet and art critic, b. 27 June 1926, Baltimore, Md.; d. 25 July 1966, Mastic Beach, N.Y.

O. received his B.A. in 1950 from Harvard, where he met the poet John Ashbery (b. 1927) and helped found the Cambridge Poets' Theater. In 1951 he received an M.A. in English from the University of Michigan as well as a Major Hopwood Award for poetry. Having moved to New York, he worked briefly at the Museum of Modern Art, wrote for *Art News* and other publications, and became part of several artistic and literary circles that included the poet Kenneth Koch (b. 1925), the painters Larry Rivers, Franz Kline, Willem de Kooning, Jackson Pollock, Robert Motherwell, and Helen Frankenthaler, and the composer Ned Rorem. In 1955 O. rejoined the museum, eventually becoming associate curator of painting; he organized several major exhibitions and wrote the catalogues for them. O. was relatively unknown as a poet during his lifetime (he died young from injuries sustained after being struck by a car), and his present reputation owes much to efforts of poet friends and students.

O. worked in several genres: poetry, poem-painting collaborations, plays, and film. His poetry, however, is the most substantial in volume, range, and achievement. He began with relatively straightforward and formally traditional short lyrics—a period of "muscle-flexing," as Ashbery called it. Nevertheless, even these early works differ from the production of other poets at the time. Instead of learning from the dominant school of T. S. Eliot and Wallace Stevens (qq.v.), O. modeled his procedures and tone on an individual mox of "underground" sources: Gertrude Stein, William Carlos Williams, W. H. Auden, Pierre Reverdy, Guillaume Apollinaire, Vladimir Mayakovsky, Federico García Lorca, Boris Pasternak (qq.v.), and Arthur Rimbaud. O. strove to unify surrealistic (q.v.) technique with American colloquial poetic diction. The early work, not surprisingly, consists largely of worshipful imitations and arguments and agreements with O.'s models. Nevertheless, O. transcended his apprenticeship to make a poetry that did not hide its debts, yet remained his own.

O. treated an astonishingly large number of subjects—art, trashy films, cityscapes (mainly New York), the demimonde, as well as more usual lyrical themes. Love and friendship figure in much of his work. Many of the poems are addressed to friends; friends are very often characters in the poems. He is happy and vivacious in a new affair, resigned or hurt or foolishly hopeful at a break-up. Yet, contrary to the charges often made against him, O. does more than merely record; his selection of detail comments indirectly.

Despite his many subjects, one theme, generally unstated, has great significance for O.'s technique: the value of intensely experiencing the moment and unwillingness to contemplate, to impose order by distancing, as preventing full participation in the moment. O.'s poems give the illusion of automatic writing, when in fact their speed and spontaneity result from craft. From the Dadaists (q.v.) and surrealists, O. learned how to include objects bound not by verisimilitude or logic but by psychic association with the event. In Gertrude Stein he had a model for re-creating the mind's language as it receives perceptions and before it begins to shape them into grammatical form, and he extend-

ed many of her innovations: coordination rather than subordination, to emphasize the simultaneity of multiple perceptions; syntactic but logically irrelevant conjunctions; suppressed pronoun references, radically condensed syntax, and "floating" modifiers that create at least two readings of the same semantic unit. Yet O.'s surface is much more dense than Stein's: complex images follow one another more quickly, and there is little repetition. If one compares Stein's surface to the open spaces and two-dimensional emphasis of cubist art, O.'s analogue is to the restless, intricate surfaces of "action" painters like Pollock, for whom O. proselytized in his art criticism.

O.'s commitment to capturing sensation almost for its own sake has its successes and dangers. At their best, the poems are fast, intimate, and reveal a persona of great wit and complexity. When they fail, they seem orphically incomprehensible, mere exercises in constructing complex images, or simply too personal, so "in" they have confused even O.'s friends. It is no coincidence that O.'s best-known works are also his more comprehensible: "Chez Jane" (1952), "On Rachmaninoff's Birthday (Quick! a last poem before I go)" (1953), the James Dean elegies (1955–56), "To the Film Industry in Crisis" (1955), "Rhapsody" (1959), "The Day Lady Died" (1959), and many of the lyrics titled "Poem." Long works like "Second Avenue" (1953) and "Biotherm" (1961–62) tend to collapse from their length and extreme density. Such generalizations are dangerous, however; critics and sophisticated readers are discovering meaningful threads in O.'s difficult poems.

FURTHER WORKS: *A City Winter, and Other Poems* (1952); *Oranges* (1953); *Meditations in an Emergency* (1957); *Stones* (1958, with Larry Rivers); *Jackson Pollock* (1959); *Odes* (1960); *Second Avenue* (1960); *The New Spanish Painting and Sculpture* (1960); *Awake in Spain* (1960); *Try! Try!* (1960); *Lunch Poems* (1964); *The General Returns from One Place to Another* (1964); *Franz Kline: A Retrospective Exhibition* (1964); *Love Poems (Tentative Title)* (1965); *Robert Motherwell* (1965); *David Smith* (1966); *Nakian* (1966); *In Memory of My Feelings* (1967); *The Collected Poems of F. O.* (1971); *The Selected Poems of F. O.* (1973); *Hymns to St. Bridget* (1974, with Bill Berkson); *Art Chronicles, 1954–1966* (1975); *Early Writing, 1946–1951* (1975); *Standing Still and*

Walking in New York (1975); *Poems Retrieved* (1977); *Selected Plays* (1978)

BIBLIOGRAPHY: Berkson, B., "F. O. and His Poems," *Art and Literature,* No. 12 (1967), 53–63; Koch, K., "All the Imagination Can Hold," *New Republic,* 1–8 Jan. 1972, 23–25; Vendler, H., "The Virtues of the Alterable," *Parnassus,* 1, 1 (1972), 9–20; Perloff, M., *F. O.: Poet among Painters* (1977); Meyer, T., "Glistening Torsos, Sandwiches, and Coca-Cola," *Parnassus,* 6, 1 (1979), 241–57; Smith, A., Jr., *F. O.: A Comprehensive Bibliography* (1979)

STEVEN SCHWARTZ

O'HARA, John

American novelist and short-story writer, b. 31 Jan. 1905, Pottsville, Pa.; d. 11 April 1970, Princeton, N.J.

The eldest of eight children of a prosperous doctor, O. had a privileged youth. But at the time he was admitted to Yale University, his father died, and O. lost financial security. O. had to leave school; he worked as a reporter and clerk in Pennsylvania and New York and began publishing stories in *The New Yorker* in 1928. A successful writer by 1934, O. took up film-script writing in Hollywood and by the mid-1950s had received numerous honors, including the National Book Award.

O.'s first and perhaps best novel, *Appointment in Samarra* (1934), chronicles the destructive effects of money, sex, and social status in the life of a wealthy Cadillac dealer and introduces the fictional world of Gibbsville, the center of O.'s Pennsylvania settings for dramatizing the themes of love, failure, and death in almost half of his stories. The ironic tales of *The Doctor's Son, and Other Stories* (1935) intricately detail a wide range of Gibbsville characters and relationships. The central focus of *A Rage to Live* (1949), while it also documents social history among the rich of the state capital from 1900 to 1920, is a woman's inability to control her passion and the tragic end of her marriage. In *Ten North Frederick* (1955) O. studies the subtleties of existence that bring a leading, well-adjusted citizen to ruin and suicide.

Life in the worlds of Broadway and Hollywood is a major O. concern. The roman à clef *Butterfield 8* (1935) re-creates the events behind the suicide of the beautiful celebrity, Starr Faithfull, through the eyes of the protagonist-narrator and O.'s alter ego, Jimmy Malloy. This persona figures as well in the minor *Hope of Heaven* (1938) and later in the three novellas of *Sermons and Soda Water* (1960), which feature the subject of loneliness. O.'s stories of a second-rate nightclub singer collected as *Pal Joey* (1940) represent a triumph of American vernacular; the book was made into a successful Broadway musical shortly after its publication. Numerous short stories in *Files on Parade* (1939), *Pipe Night* (1945), and *Hellbox* (1947) effectively satirize various stage and screen personalities and situations. Although weak in structure and characterization, the Hollywood novel *The Big Laugh* (1962) offers authentic American idiom and bawdy humor.

O.'s later works include a minor academic novel, *Elizabeth Appleton* (1963), and the expansive *The Lockwood Concern* (1965), which covers a family dynasty over four generations. The book's center, George Lockwood, compulsively drives his son to crime and thus disintegrates the heritage. *The Instrument* (1967) revolves about a parasitic playwright and his relationship to a star actress, and *Lovely Childs: A Philadelphian's Story* (1969) deals with a 1920s celebrity heiress and her playboy husband. By the time of his death, O. had completed *The Ewings* (1972), the tale of a young lawyer making his fortune during World War I, and was working on a sequel, also posthumously published, entitled *The Second Ewings* (1977).

As a social commentator O. wrote in the tradition of Theodore Dreiser and F. Scott Fitzgerald (qq.v.), laying life in the United States bare through a deft ear for American dialogue, accurate details, and penetrating glimpses into the human heart. While now unfashionable in the opinion of some readers, O. will remain a professional and poignant chronicler of the American scene from 1900 to 1970.

FURTHER WORKS: *Here's O.* (1946); *All the Girls He Wanted* (1949); *The Farmers Hotel* (1951); *Sweet and Sour* (1954); *A Family Party* (1956); *The Great Short Stories of O.* (1956); *Selected Short Stories* (1956); *Three Views of the Novel* (1957, with Irving Stone and MacKinlay Kantor); *From the Terrace* (1958); *Ourselves to Know* (1960); *Assembly* (1961); *Five Plays* (1961); *The Cape Cod Lighter* (1962); *49 Stories* (1963); *The Hat on the Bed* (1963); *The Horse Knows the Way* (1964); *Waiting for Winter* (1966); *And Oth-*

er Stories (1968); *The O. Generation* (1969); *The Time Element, and Other Stories* (1972); *Good Samaritan, and Other Stories* (1974); *"An Artist Is His Own Fault": J. O. on Writers and Writing* (1977); *Selected Letters of J. O.* (1978)

BIBLIOGRAPHY: Trilling, L., "J. O. Observes Our Mores," *NYTBR,* 18 March 1945, 1, 9; Carson, E. R., *The Fiction of J. O.* (1961); Grebstein, S., *J. O.* (1966); Walcutt, C. C., *J. O.* (1969); Farr, F., *O.* (1973); *J. O. Journal* (1977 ff.); MacShane, F., *The Life of J. O.* (1981)

LYNN DEVORE

OKARA, Gabriel

Nigerian poet and novelist (writing in English), b. 24 April 1921, Bumodi

O. attended school in Umuahia and then worked as a printer and bookbinder in Lagos and Enugu. In 1956 he studied journalism in the U.S. at Northwestern University and has been involved in information-media work ever since, most recently as editor of the newspaper *Nigerian Tide.*

O.'s first poems were published in the maiden issue of *Black Orpheus* (1957), an influential Nigerian literary magazine that later carried some of his fiction, translations of Ijaw myths, and experimental verse. His poetry and fiction have also appeared in numerous anthologies and literary publications outside of Nigeria and have won him an international reputation as one of Nigeria's most innovative stylists.

O.'s poetry tends to be simple, lyrical, and polyrhythmic. He writes free verse disciplined by subtly controlled metrics and amplified by sharply defined images and richly ambiguous symbols. In his early poetry he frequently combined native and nonnative imagery (oil palm and snowflake, drum and piano) as a metaphoric way of communicating the confused psychological state of the Westernized African. He was one of the first African writers to introduce into English verse uncompromisingly literal translations of metaphors, idioms, and philosophical concepts from an African vernacular language. His most recent poetry is his most explicitly political, reflecting his intense personal reaction to the horrors of the Nigerian-Biafran conflict (1967–70). The first collection of his poetry, *The Fisherman's Invocation* (1978),

was awarded the Commonwealth Poetry Prize.

Although O. originally made his mark as a poet, he is perhaps better known as the author of *The Voice* (1964), an imaginative novel written in an unorthodox prose style simulating idiomatic expression in Ijaw. *The Voice* is a moral allegory about man's quest for faith, truth, and the meaning of life in a corrupted world. An idealistic hero discomfits leaders in his village by initiating a search for coherent moral values. Soon he is expelled from the village and sent into exile, but he defies the ban, returns home, and confronts those in power who had sought to obstruct his quest. He is put to death, but his words and deeds have made an impact on his people. A moral revolution has begun.

Some critics have been harsh on the radical verbal and syntactical innovations O. introduced in *The Voice,* but others think the strangeness of the style superbly suited to the strangeness of the tale. The unnatural inversions and neologisms tend to enhance the hallucinatory, dreamlike quality of the protagonist's quest, giving it an appropriate parabolic flavor. It is a poet's concern for form, awareness of symbol, and sensitivity to language that make O.'s novel a brilliant literary achievement.

O.'s experimental style and poetic vision place him in the forefront of the movement to indigenize African literature by investing it with local sonority as well as pan-African significance.

BIBLIOGRAPHY: Anozie, S. O., "The Theme of Alienation and Commitment in O.'s *The Voice,*" *BAALE,* 3 (1965), 54–67; Shiarella, J., "G. O.'s *The Voice:* A Study in the Poetic Novel," *BO,* 2, 5–6 (1970), 45–49; Palmer, E., "G. O.: *The Voice,*" *An Introduction to the African Novel* (1972), pp. 155–67; Webb, H., "Allegory: O.'s *The Voice,*" *EinA,* 5, 2 (1978), 66–73; Egudu, R. N., "A Study of Five of G. O.'s Poems," *Okike,* 13 (1979), 93–110

BERNTH LINDFORS

OKIGBO, Christopher

Nigerian poet (writing in English), b. 16 Aug. 1932, Ojoto; d. Aug. 1967, near Nsukka

O. studied in Umuahia and then went on to study classics at Ibadan University. Between

1956 and 1962 he worked in business and in government and as a teacher and a librarian. In the Nigerian-Biafran conflict (1967–70), he joined the Biafran army as a major in July 1967 and was killed in action the following month.

O. began to attract attention in 1962, when three publications of his appeared: a sequence of poems in Nigeria's influential literary magazine *Black Orpheus;* a pamphlet, entitled *Heavensgate,* in a poetry series published in Ibadan; and a long poem, *Limits,* in the Ugandan cultural magazine *Transition.* (*Limits* appeared independently in 1964.) During the next few years O. continued to contribute poetry to *Black Orpheus* and *Transition.*

In his earliest verse—"Moonglow" and "Four Canzones," written between 1957 and 1961—one finds echoes of T. S. Eliot, Ezra Pound (qq.v.), Gerard Manley Hopkins, and other modern poets, echoes that O. deliberately evoked in order to give greater sonority to the verbal music he was intent on creating. As he matured and discovered his own distinctive poetic idiom, the greatest influence on him may have been Peter Thomas (b. 1928), an English poet who taught at the University of Nigeria at Nsukka for several years and encouraged O. through discussion and enthusiastic readings of successive drafts of his poems. O. was also remarkably responsive to instrumental music, both African and Western, and he incorporated in his verse motifs inspired by symphonies, songs, and traditional percussive rhythms. Many critics have noted that O.'s work may appeal to the ear more than to the eye, for subtle nuances of sound meant more to him than mere certainties of sense.

In *Heavensgate* O. began to speak in a poetic voice informed by a judicious blend of African and Western poetic elements. This mature verse tends to be difficult, cryptically allusive, and sinuously musical, yet it achieves remarkably vivid pictorial effects by juxtaposing fresh images and compressing ideas into spare, metaphorical statements that have the lucidity of proverbs. *Heavensgate,* which O. said was originally conceived as an Easter sequence, traces the spiritual journey of a celebrant through several levels of ritual.

In *Limits* the same poet-protagonist sets out on a mystical quest for something unattainable and loses himself to his obsession. *Distances* (1964), described by O. as "a poem

of homecoming," deals with the psychic and spiritual fulfillment that the writer must achieve before he can create. *Silences* (1965), inspired by tragic events in Nigeria and the Congo, is a poetic investigation of the music of mourning, with drums symbolizing the spirits of the ancestors. The poems in *Path of Thunder* (in *Black Orpheus,* 1968) reflect O.'s pessimistic response to the tensions in Nigeria in the mid-1960s, a crisis that he felt presaged war and possibly his own death. His last poems, by far his most political utterances, indicate that he was moving toward a less oblique mode of expression that could articulate moral and patriotic concerns in images accessible to the ordinary reader.

O. believed that his poems, although written and published separately, were organically related and could be read as one poetic statement. After his death, final versions of his poems, which he had himself edited, were published in the collection *Labyrinths with Path of Thunder* (1971). It has been reported that he had been working on a novel before his death, but the manuscript of this venture into prose apparently was lost during the Nigerian-Biafran war.

O.'s work defies easy explication and rational analysis. He was often more concerned with the resonance of sound and symbol than he was with communicating an intelligible meaning. His imagination played upon the rich suggestiveness of rhythm, image, and allusion, creating a subtle fusion of curiously disparate associations. He found trenchancy in obscurity, precision in ambiguity, form in formlessness. These qualities make him the most modern of African poets.

BIBLIOGRAPHY: Whitelaw, M., "Interview with C. O.," *JCL,* 9 (1970), 28–37; Anozie, S. O., *C. O.* (1972); Izevbaye, D. S., "O.'s Portrait of the Artist as a Sunbird: A Reading of *Heavensgate,*" *ALT,* 6 (1973), 1–13; Udoeyop, N. J., *Three Nigerian Poets: A Critical Study of the Poetry of Soyinka, Clark and O.* (1973), pp. 101–57; Anafulu, J. C., "C. O., 1932–1967: A Bio-bibliography," *RAL,* 9 (1978), 65–78; Achebe, C., Preface to Achebe, C., and Okafor, D., eds., *Don't Let Him Die: An Anthology of Memorial Poems for C. O. (1932–1967)* (1978), pp. v–ix; Nwoga, D. I., *Critical Perspectives on C. O.* (1982)

BERNTH LINDFORS

OKUDZHAVA, Bulat Shalvovich

Russian poet, balladeer, novelist, and screen-writer, b. 9 May 1924, Moscow

During World War II, at the age of eighteen, O. volunteered for service in the Soviet army and was later wounded. In 1950 he completed his education at Tbilisi State University and became a village schoolteacher. He began writing verse in 1953, and a few years later joined the editorial staff of *Literaturnaya gazeta,* the major Soviet cultural newspaper, in Moscow. By 1960 O. had already gained a reputation as a composer (and performer with guitar) of nonconformist ballads, a genre that subsequently brought him international fame as well as official condemnation at home. He has given concerts not only in the USSR but also in Poland and western Europe. He visited the U.S. for the first time in 1979. In the 1960s O. also began writing fiction, and in recent years he has concentrated on historical novels.

O.'s first collection of verse, *Lirika* (1956; lyrics), was later dismissed by the poet as immature. In the volumes *Ostrova* (1959; islands), *Vesyoly barabanshchik* (1964; the happy drummer), and *Mart velikodushny* (1967; generous March) the basic themes of O.'s poetry emerged: abhorrence of war, compassion and hope for ordinary human beings, tenderness toward youth and women, love of Moscow with its joys and sorrows. All these emotions are expressed in unpretentious, conversational language, in contrast to the stilted Soviet officialese. O. developed and reinforced these themes in dozens of short poems set to simple tunes, several of which have been published in the U.S.S.R., but which primarily exist on tape recordings that circulated privately inside the country and were clandestinely sent abroad, where many were published and reproduced on phonograph discs.

O. is considered to be the pioneer among contemporary national bards of *magnitizdat* ("publishing by tape recorder," a term derived from *samizdat:* uncensored, "self-published" typewritten pages). He ranks in popularity with Vladimir Vysotsky (1938–1980) and Alexander Galich (1919–1977), but he avoids their explicit and biting political satire, preferring gentle humor, subtle irony, and allegory in his statements about the quality of Soviet life. For example, in one of his most famous songs, "Pro chyornogo kota" (1964; "The Black Cat," 1966), he creates the image of a malevolent authority whom none dares oppose.

O.'s first work of fiction was the novella *Bud zdorov, shkolyar!* (1961; *Lots of Luck, Kid!,* 1963). Based on his frontline experiences as a young soldier, it is filled with antimilitarism. Like his many poems about the cruelty and senselessness of war, it provoked official criticism for "mawkish pacifism." Actually, the work belongs to the vanguard of post-Stalinist realism, which rejected the pompous patriotism and spurious pathos of canonical Socialist Realism (q.v.). In his later fiction O. has turned his attention to historical themes, skillfully juxtaposing authentic figures from early 19th-c. Russia with memorable imaginary heroes, such as the comic bungler in *Bedny Avrosimov* (1969; poor Avrosimov), which first appeared in a literary magazine and was later published under the title *Glotok svobody* (1971; gulp of freedom).

O. continues the humanitarian tradition in Russian literature. He reflects reality sincerely and articulates the genuine moods and aspirations of his fellow countrymen. In particular, his lyrical songs have ensured him the lasting respect and affection of people at home and abroad who value the age-old quest for truth and justice so characteristic of unfettered Russian writing.

FURTHER WORKS: *Po doroge k Tinatii* (1964); *Proza i stikhi* (1964); *Front prikhodit k nam* (1965); *Proza i poezia* (1968); *Mersi; ili, Pokhozhdenia Shipova* (1971); *Arbat, moy Arbat* (1976); *Puteshestvie diletantov* (1976; *Nocturne,* 1978). FURTHER VOLUME IN ENGLISH: *Sixty-five Songs/65 pesen* (1980, bilingual)

BIBLIOGRAPHY: Mihajlov, M., *Moscow Summer* (1965), pp. 104–14, 195–96; Langland, J., Aczel, T., and Tikos, L., eds., *Poetry from the Russian Underground* (1973), pp. 241–44; Sosin, G., "Magnitizdat: Uncensored Songs of Dissent," in Tökés, R. L., ed., *Dissent in the USSR* (1975), pp. 276–309; Smith, H., *The Russians* (1976), pp. 411–12; Brown, D., *Soviet Russian Literature since Stalin* (1978), pp. 98–105; Rishina, I., "I Am Not Abandoning History" (interview), *SSLit,* 15, 4 (1979), 74–81; Svirsky, G., *A History of Post-War Soviet Writing* (1981), pp. 351–67

GENE SOSIN

OLBRACHT, Ivan

(pseud. of Kamil Zeman) Czechoslovak novelist and short-story writer (writing in Czech), b. 6 Jan. 1882, Semily; d. 30 Dec. 1952, Prague

Son of the politically liberal writer Antal Stašek (pseud. of Antonín Zeman, 1843–1931), O. began his career as a journalist for the Social Democratic press. After attending a meeting of the Third International in Moscow, he became a Communist and edited the Czechoslovak Party newspaper *Rudé právo* during most of the 1920s. He always set aside time for creative writing, however, and during the 1930s, his richest period, he devoted himself entirely to literature. He spent the war with a partisan group and was active in postwar politics as a member of the National Assembly and the Central Committee of the Czechoslovak Communist Party.

The psychological novel *Podivné přátelství herce Jesenia* (1918; the peculiar friendship of the actor Jesenius) is typical of his early writings. It uses the Dostoevskian *Doppelgänger* theme to point up the opposing forces of individualism and anarchy. In *Anna proletářka* (1925, rev. eds., 1928, 1946; Anna the proletarian) this opposition metamorphoses into individualism versus the workers' movement. This novel about a rural servant girl who goes to the city and becomes involved in organizing the general strike of 1920 exists in three quite different versions, each exemplifying a distinct stage in O.'s development. In the first he highlights the heroine's inner struggles; in the second he expands on the historical events surrounding the strike; and in the final version he turns Anna into a socially aware, Socialist Realist (q.v.) heroine whose Social Democrat husband betrays the workers. All three versions show the pronounced influence of Gorky (q.v.).

O. came into his own with *Nikola Šuhaj loupežník* (1933; *Nikola Šuhaj, Robber,* 1954) and *Golet v údolí* (1937; *The Bitter and the Sweet,* 1965), both set in the Carpathians. In the former he begins with the true story of a local outlaw, but by skillfully combining the elemental with the monumental, he creates a kind of Robin Hood, a character of mythical dimensions, who fights for freedom and social justice against impossible odds. In the latter, three short stories of the Jewish Diaspora, he depicts ghetto life with great humor and sympathy, showing equal interest in realistic, even naturalistic, portrayals of its daily squalor and in mystical evocations of the Old Testament ethos that rules the lives of the inhabitants. These two volumes reveal an eye for local color and an ear for poetic diction completely lacking in his earlier work; they are ballads in prose and exhibit a consummate balance of documentary and fantasy.

Although the concerns in these two works do not differ essentially from those in, say, *Anna proletářka,* O. treats them less tendentiously. O.'s claim to recognition rests not so much on his social novels, which have faded with the events they portray, as on his studies of the social outcast, the archetypal outsider.

FURTHER WORKS: *O zlých samotářích* (1913); *Žalář nejtemější* (1916); *Pátý akt* (1919); *Obrazy ze soudobého Ruska* (2 vols., 1920–21); *Devět veselých povídek z Rakouska i republiky* (1927); *Zamřížované zrcadlo* (1930); *Dvě psaní a moták* (1931); *Země bez jména* (1932); *Hory a staletí* (1935); *Biblické příběhy* (1939); *Ze starých letopisů* (1940); *Dobyvatel* (1947); *O mudrci Bidpajovi a jeho zvířatkách* (1947); *Spisy* (15 vols., 1947–61)

BIBLIOGRAPHY: Opelík, J., "O.s reife Schaffensperiode," *ZS,* 12 (1967), 20–37; Kunstmann, H., *Tschechische Erzählkunst im 20. Jahrhundert* (1974), pp. 71–76; Novák, A., *Czech Literature* (1976), pp. 284–85

MICHAEL HEIM

OLESHA, Yury Karlovich

Russian novelist, short-story writer, and dramatist, b. 3 March 1899, Yelisavetgrad (now Kirovograd); d. 10 May 1960, Moscow

O. grew up in Odessa in a family of Polish origin. In 1922 he went to Moscow, where he made his literary debut with poems published in a railway workers' newspaper. His novel *Zavist* (1927; *Envy,* 1936) immediately established his reputation and made him one of the most controversial Soviet writers. It was followed by a fairy-tale account of the revolution, *Tri tolstyaka* (1928; *The Three Fat Men,* 1964), a number of short stories, and several plays.

O. found it more and more difficult to publish or even to write in the increasingly restrictive atmosphere of the 1930s. Announcing that the building of a new Soviet order was not his theme, he pleaded at the First Congress of Soviet Writers (1934) for a greater humanism in Soviet letters. But as the 1930s advanced, his published work became more and more fragmentary, and he busied himself writing film scenarios. After 1938 O. disappeared from the literary scene almost completely, and it was not until the "thaw" following Stalin's death that his works were again published. An interesting volume of reminiscences and reflections, *Ni dnya bez strochki* (1965; *No Day Without a Line,* 1979), was published posthumously.

O.'s masterpiece is *Zavist,* which deals in a symbolic and expressionistic (q.v.) style with the conflict between the old and new orders in Soviet life. Its hero, Kavalerov, longs for personal fame, success, and love, all of which he finds unattainable in Soviet society. Rejecting the new socialist order, which is personified by Andrey Babichev, a complacent and philistine food commissar who has perfected a new sausage and is trying to open a chain of cheap soup kitchens, Kavalerov sides with those who preach a "conspiracy of feelings" in the name of such emotions as love, ambition, and jealousy. After the conspiracy's failure, he attempts to salve his wounded ego in the suffocating embraces of a fat widow.

This comic novel has a rare freshness and originality of visual imagery. In a poet's prose rich in metaphors, similes, and conceits, O. rejects both the old and new orders—the one for its lack of progress and concern for social welfare, the other because it is too mechanical and unfeeling.

Influenced by the French philosopher Henri Bergson (q.v.), O. saw an irreparable dichotomy in life between the mechanical and the biological. Such is the theme of his stories "Lyubov" (1928; "Love," 1949) and "Vishnyovaya kostochka" (1930; "The Cherry Stone," 1934). In the latter the possibility of a synthesis is indicated when the architects of a new steel and concrete building remember to provide for a garden in their plans.

"Liompa" (1928; "Liompa," 1967) contrasts a dying man for whom the world has become a collection of meaningless names and a child for whom it is it is a bright chaos of nameless objects.

O. made a free adaptation of his *Zavist* as

a play, entitled *Zagovor chuvstv* (1930; *The Conspiracy of Feelings,* 1932). Although popular, the play lacks the freshness and incisiveness of the novel. Stronger is his original drama, *Spisok blagodeyany* (1931; *A List of Assets,* 1963), a fairly sensitive psychological portrayal of a Soviet actress who is destroyed by her attraction to the West.

The first critics of O.'s work took his writing as a negative comment on Soviet reality of the 1920s and early 1930s. Although this is undoubtedly true, it becomes increasingly clear that his expressionistic fiction fits into the context of Western literature of the period and that its universal theme is applicable to both Soviet and Western society.

Although O. never fulfilled the promise of his first brilliant novel, we can now see that he is one of the most vivid exponents of the European "vitalist" current of the 1920s. His profoundly philosophical work remains as readable and fresh as when it was written.

FURTHER WORKS: *Vishnyovaya kostochka* (1931); *Zapiski pisatelya* (1932); *Izbrannye sochinenia* (1956); *Povesti i rasskazy* (1965); *Pesy; Stati o teatre i dramaturgii* (1968). FURTHER VOLUMES IN ENGLISH: *The Wayward Comrade and the Commissar* (1960; repub. as *Envy, and Other Works,* 1967); *Love, and Other Stories* (1967); *The Complete Short Stories, and The Three Fat Men* (1979)

BIBLIOGRAPHY: Struve, G., *Soviet Russian Literature, 1917–1950* (1951), pp. 98–106, 219–30, 246–49; Brown, E. J., *Russian Literature since the Revolution* (1963), pp. 84–94; Alexandrova, V., *A History of Soviet Literature* (1964), pp. 188–202; Nilsson, N. A., "Through the Wrong End of Binoculars: An Introduction to Y. O.," *SSl,* 11 (1965), 40–68; Harkins, W. E., "The Theme of Sterility in O.'s *Envy,*" *SlavR,* 25 (1966), 443–57; Maguire, R. A., *Red Virgin Soil* (1968), pp. 338–44; Beaujour, E. K., *The Invisible Land: A Study of the Artistic Imagination of Y. O.* (1970)

                    WILLIAM E. HARKINS

OLLIER, Claude

French novelist, critic, radio dramatist, and poet, b. 17 Dec. 1922, Paris

O. first went to law school and worked in the business world before he devoted himself entirely to literature in 1955. He had started writing short stories as early as 1946. His first novel, *La mise en scène* (1958; the setting), a book of violence and mystery, which also began his first quartet of novels won the Médicis Prize. *Le maintien de l'ordre* (1961; *Law and Order,* 1976), *Été indien* (1963; Indian summer), and *L'échec de Nolan* (1967; Nolan's defeat) are the other volumes in the quartet.

According to O., all his novels are detective stories; for him, the primordial relationship of man and the world·is one of terror. He writes methodically, making use of scientific jargon. Proponents of the new French criticism have praised his concept of contemporary *écriture* (writing)—his use of elaborate and intricate poetic devices, metric relations, assonance, and rhythmic superimpositions.

In 1971 O. participated in a colloquium at Cerisy devoted to the New Novel (q.v.). He was at the time deeply involved in the writing of a second quartet of science-fiction-like New Novels, which he worked on for a decade. The first volume was *La vie sur Epsilon* (1972; life on Epsilon). In *Enigma* (1973; enigma) the vocabulary is Freudian. In *Our; ou, Vingt ans après* (1974; Ur; or, twenty years later), he uses literary texts as examples of cultural phenomena acquired automatically by the collective unconscious. He has voluminous notebooks describing his dreams and has said, "My most fertile inventions are those that arise out of periods of drowsiness or sudden awakening, at the end of dreams." This modern-day Jules Verne creates fables permeated by the writings of Joyce, Kafka (qq.v.), and the surrealists (q.v.). O. is also sensitive, perhaps more than anyone else, to the haunting, unreal world of Raymond Roussel (q.v.). In *Fuzzy sets* (1975; title in English) the forceful influx of the psychoanalytic theories of Jacques Lacan (1901–1981) are evident. In the fictional process, the author pinpoints criss-crossing influences determined by psychological conflicts originating in early childhood and contained in the unconscious, as well as those conflicts "born of belonging to a given social class or cultural sphere." The novels of the two quartets, to which O. gave the overall title *Le jeu d'enfant* (child's play), constitute a global, monumental work built on a "spiraloid structure."

In his North African colonial travelogue-novel, *Marrakch Medine* (1979; Marrakch Medine), which won the 1980 France-Culture Prize, he stresses dialectical materialism.

And in the introduction to his *Souvenirs écran* (1981; screen memories) he scrupulously, "clinically" traces the relationship of films to his own childhood. At the same time, he tightly links his own experience as a novelist with parallel practices evidenced in the films of the New Wave from 1958 to 1968. In the same vein, O. has written a number of radio plays and film scripts, which he considers to be "satellites" constituting an important part of his overall "network."

O. not only attempts to revolutionize fiction through the ever-changing manipulation of scientific techniques, erudite organization, and precise mathematical devices; he also strives to widen the "open" meaning of the linguistic, rhetorical, and narrative process in the "new New Novel": scorning the linear plot, he weaves his words on the page almost as if they had a physical weight. Language looms on paper and seems to change shape visually. His sonorities throb within our inner ear, thereby creating a new world of meaning through, he says, "expansion, deception, and riddle." Thus, for the serious reader, the impact of O.'s entire opus is that of an appealing, propelling, 21st-c. strangeness, stemming from the efforts of poets such as Mallarmé and Valéry (q.v.), thrusting past present materialism toward an abstract approach to visions of the future.

FURTHER WORKS: *La mort du personnage* (1964); *L'attentat en direct* (1965); *Régression* (1965); *Cinématographe* (1965, with Jean-André Fieschi); *Navettes* (1967); *La relève* (1968); *Luberon* (1969); *Réseau de blets rhizomes* (1969); *Le dit de ceux qui parlent* (1969); *Pèlerinage* (1969); *La fugue* (1969); *Les dires des années 30* (1970); *L'oreille au mur* (1971); *Une bosse dans la neige* (1971); *La recyclade* (1971); *Our-Musique* (1975); *Réseau Ollier Navettes* (1975); *Opérettes entre guillemets* (1977); *Loi d'écoute* (1979); *Computation* (1979); *Détour* (1980); *Bon entendeur* (1980, in *Agrafes,* with others); *Nébules* (1981); *Mon double à Malacca* (1982)

BIBLIOGRAPHY: Ricardou, J., *Pour une théorie du nouveau roman* (1971), pp. 159–99; Foucault, M., "Le langage de l'espace," Noguez, D.," 'Plus qu'un Borgès français,' " and Ricardou, J., "Textes 'mis en scène,' " in Ouellet, R., ed., *Les critiques de notre temps et le nouveau roman* (1972), pp. 118–27; Roudiez, L., *French Fiction Today* (1972), pp. 233–58; Houppermans, J., "Quelques rails (C. O., Roussel)," in Grivel, C., ed., *Écriture de la religion/Écriture du roman* (1979), pp. 195–210; Cali, A., *Pratiques de lecture et d'écriture: O., Robbe-Grillet, Simon* (1980); Steisel, M.-G., "O. ou l'Orient; Orient or O.," *CELFAN*, 2, 1 (1982), 20–23

MARIE-GEORGETTE STEISEL

OLSON, Charles

American poet and essayist, b. 27 Dec. 1910, Worcester, Mass., d. 10 Jan. 1970, New York, N.Y.

Best known as the author of the *Maximus Poems,* O. was the central figure of the Black Mountain school of poetry in the 1950s. His early poems and polemical essays attempt to define an American poetical tradition rooted in the innovations of Ezra Pound and William Carlos Williams (qq.v.). His essays, his letters, his teaching at Black Mountain College (1951–56), and the *Maximus Poems* themselves became the focal point for a number of post war poets, such as Robert Creeley, Robert Duncan (qq.v.), and Edward Dorn (b. 1929), who sought an alternative to the closed poetic forms that academic criticism had made fashionable.

After receiving B.A. and M.A. degrees from Wesleyan University, O. prepared for an academic career. He entered the Harvard American Studies program. Although he left without taking a degree, O.'s research on Herman Melville was later published as *Call Me Ishmael* (1947). O.'s study of Melville examined the Shakespearean sources of *Moby-Dick* and Melville's attempt to fashion a mythological system from the tragic figure of King Lear and the materials of American history.

Following a brief political career in the Roosevelt administration, O. began his poetic career. From 1946 to 1950, O. developed a political approach to poetry, and his use of poetry as a didactic instrument tended to divide his audience into disciples and detractors. From Pound, whom O. visited regularly at St. Elizabeths Hospital, O. derived a "spatial" sense of history, an understanding of the continuity of the past in the present. According to O., Pound's egotism allowed him to treat Western culture as contemporaneous with himself, but limited him to a nostalgic recovery of tradition. What was needed was a sense of place, a "polis," for which the poet could make himself useful and from which he could rediscover a sense of man more comprehensive than that offered by the Western traditions.

O. adopted the sense of the local from Williams's poetry, although he thought Williams's treatment of Paterson sentimental. Pound and Williams both had a profound influence on O.'s manifesto "Projective Verse" (1950), which argued for a "postmodern" poetics based on "open" verse forms. According to O., the poem is a "field of action," a process where energy is transferred from the poet by means of the poem to the reader. The poem is not an object that comments on nature but is continuous with nature and, like any other natural object or event, should have an immediate "kinetic" effect on the reader.

In the first volume of *The Maximus Poems* (1960), O. finds in Gloucester, Massachusetts, the "polis" he will address, teach, and learn from. Constructed as a series of letters, these poems attempt to define the stance of Maximus as he confronts his city and as O. confronts the voices of the American poetic tradition. In addressing his city, Maximus takes in his experience of it, criticizes its politics and rituals, argues for a new vision of politics, and turns to historical records in order to discern its origins and to recover the meaning immanent in its founding. Throughout, Maximus employs a variety of poetic forms as a commentary on the use of poetic languages and an attempt to dissolve himself in an almost Emersonian way into the experience of the city as a spatial or "horizontal" entity.

In *Maximus Poems IV, V, VI* (1968), Maximus explores the "vertical" dimension by turning inward. Literally, his attention shifts inland from the fishing village of Gloucester to the failed farming community of Dogtown. At the same time, his introduction of Jungian (q.v.) archetypes plunges him into an examination of his relations to mother figures, and this personal concern is reflected cosmologically in the turn to Algonquin and Hittite myths of genesis, nurturance, and rebirth. The narrower political, economic, and historical concerns of the first volume are displaced by intense sexual conflict and by wide-ranging speculation on geology, philosophy, and myth. The letter forms are replaced by several long meditations stitched together by fragments and notes, reflecting Maximus's attempt to stitch together the once unified but now disparate realms of self, world, and cosmos.

The Maximus Poems, Volume III (1975) is formally even more difficult than the second volume. Compiled posthumously, the work purports to be Maximus's "Republic." While critics disagree about the nature of this "Republic," all seem to agree that this volume is the weakest of the three. "Maximus" is discarded halfway through, and O. confronts his readers as his autobiographical self. His interest in mythology now appears obsessional as well as idiosyncratic, and the sexual and generational conflicts in those myths are exaggerated in the service of confession, as O. strains to unite himself with father and mother. The pervasive sense of loss and isolation in O.'s work, which gave urgency to his didacticism in volume I and his eccentric and passionate interest in arcane lore in volume II, begins to feed on itself in volume III as O. returns continually to autobiographical material in obsessive acts of reparation.

Since O.'s death his early poems have been reprinted in *Archaeologist of Morning* (1973) and his papers collected at the University of Connecticut continue to be published. Important and necessary tracing of O.'s sources has been done, and this research has helped make O.'s often obscure and difficult poetry more accessible. In addition to their intrinsic worth, O.'s poems and essays are themselves among the most useful commentaries on American modernism.

FURTHER WORKS: *Y & X* (1948); *Mayan Letters* (1953); *In Cold Hell, in Thicket* (1953); *The Distances* (1960); *Human Universe, and Other Essays* (1965); *Proprioception* (1965); *Selected Writings* (1967); *Pleistocene Man* (1968); *Causal Mythology* (1969); *Letters for Origin* (1970); *The Special View of History* (1970); *Poetry and Truth* (1971); *Additional Prose* (1974); *The Post Office* (1975); *C. O. and Ezra Pound: An Encounter at St. Elizabeths* (1975); *The Fiery Hunt, and Other Plays* (1977); *Muthologos* (1978)

BIBLIOGRAPHY: Altieri, C., "From Symbolist Thought to Immanence: The Ground of Postmodern American Poetics," *Boundary 2*, 1 (1973), 605–41; Perloff, M. G. "C. O. and the " 'Inferior Predecessors': 'Projective Verse' Revisited," *ELH*, 40 (1973), 285–305; Butterick, G. F., *A Guide to the Maximus Poems of C. O.* (1978); Paul, S., *O.'s Push* (1978); Hallberg, R. von, *C. O.: The Schol-

ar's Art* (1978); Christensen, P., *C. O.: Call Him Ishmael* (1979); Byrd, D., *C. O.'s Maximus* (1980)

JOHN FRANZOSA

O'NEILL, Eugene

American dramatist, b. 16 Oct. 1888, New York, N.Y., d. 27 Nov. 1953, Boston, Mass.

O.'s early life provided material for his dramas. The son of a famous actor, James O'Neill, he, along with the rest of his family, accompanied his father on tour. From ages seven to fourteen he was educated in Roman Catholic schools. After renouncing Catholicism, he attended a nonsectarian preparatory school and studied for a year at Princeton University. Events of special importance to his work included early voyages as a merchant seaman, interspersed with periods of beachcombing in Buenos Aires, and followed (1911–12) by a period of drinking and destitution on the New York waterfront. At this time O. suffered emotional depression and attempted suicide. He then stayed with his family in Connecticut, but was forced by the onset of tuberculosis to spend six months in a sanatorium. It was there that he determined to become a playwright. He had been reading widely, including some works of Nietzsche and plays by Strindberg (q.v.)—who would become his most important model—Ibsen, and Wedekind (q.v.). By 1914 he had become a working playwright, and in 1916 *Bound East for Cardiff* was produced by the Provincetown Players. After this success, O. lived for periods in the bohemian atmosphere of Greenwich Village in New York, which provided settings and characters for the plays. O.'s three stormy marriages were reflected in the relationship of the sexes in his dramas. O. was awarded the Nobel Prize for literature in 1936. A progressive disease of the nervous system forced him to stop writing in 1943.

O.'s plays fall into chronological groupings through which the changes and development of his art may be traced. According to their dates of composition, three groups emerge: those plays written from 1913 to 1925, 1926 to 1933, and 1939 to 1943. From his first to his final work, O.'s major characters—those with whom the author identified—are tormented misfits, searching for their lost selves or "souls." They are all, in some way, failed poets and dreamers who envision another world or life where they can, or once did, find fulfillment, innocence, relief from guilt and conflict. Throughout his first, highly prolific period O. looked upon this dream as an affirmation of human dignity—of the stubborn, often mystical, instinct for hope that keeps us alive, even when logic calls for despair. Death itself becomes a grand gesture, a ritual celebration of freedom, escape, or homecoming.

Of O.'s apprenticeship (1913–18) the most important plays are the one-act *Bound East for Cardiff* (written 1914, pub. 1916) and *Beyond the Horizon* (written 1918, pub. 1920). O. said that *Bound East for Cardiff* contained "the germ of the spirit, life-attitude of all [my] more important future work." The play broke with tradition in that it had no real plot; it depicted a badly injured seaman who, on his deathbed, reveals his simple values of courage and friendship, and his dream of some day owning a farm, a dream that made the drudgery of life at sea worthwhile.

Beyond the Horizon, O.'s first important full-length play, is the story of two brothers, the elder a practical realist and the younger a poetic idealist. His dreams about romantic love and the pastoral life keep the younger brother at home on the family farm, which he is incapable of managing. Poverty and tuberculosis kill him, but he dies joyfully affirming his idealism, his life-giving dream of some day voyaging beyond the horizon, and his final freedom in death. He leaves behind him, however, a bitter wife and an angry brother who must live on, coping with a bleak reality. Alternate indoor and outdoor settings represented, O. said, the rhythmic "alternation of longing and of loss"—a rhythm that was to flow through subsequent plays. *Beyond the Horizon* won the Pulitzer Prize (1920) and high praise from critics; it presaged a new era of serious art in the American theater.

Between 1918 and 1925 O. wrote fifteen plays. In 1920 and 1921 alone, he completed *Anna Christie* (pub. 1922) which won a Pulitzer Prize, *The Emperor Jones* (pub. 1921), and *The Hairy Ape* (pub. 1922).

Anna of *Anna Christie* is a prostitute who regains her lost innocence when her father, an ex-sailor, takes her to live with him aboard his coal barge. To Anna the sea and the fog come to represent freedom and cleanliness; to her father they represent fate, mystery, impending danger. The play ends with Anna's marriage to a sailor to whom, also, the sea represents freedom and hope. (But O.

pointed out that this was not intended to be a happy ending; the mystery and the danger would remain.)

The hero of *The Emperor Jones* begins life as a Pullman porter, who through luck and exploitation of the natives becomes ruler of an island in the West Indies. When his subjects rebel, he becomes a fugitive, pursued through the jungle to the beat of a drum in pulse rhythm. Scenes from his racial and personal history flash before him, stripping him down to the essentials of himself and of the past that shaped him. Jones dies in the end, and his death is a ritual expiation of guilt, but not all the guilt is his, and he dies on his own terms, in "the height of style."

Death as the grand gesture of ultimate escape and "belonging" is the finale, also, of *The Hairy Ape.* The protagonist, Yank, is a brawny stoker in the hold of an ocean liner, where he is proud of his occupation and his strength. His self-image is destroyed, however, when he hears a wealthy young woman call him, with revulsion, a "hairy ape." As a result he seeks vengeance on the society that he thinks has rejected his brute strength. His attempts fail, however, and in frustration and anger he goes to the zoo and harangues a real ape in a cage, with whom he identifies. In a fierce embrace, his "brother," the ape, kills him. The ape escapes and as Yank slips to the floor of the cage, O. comments that "perhaps the Hairy Ape at last belongs." Both *The Emperor Jones* and *The Hairy Ape* were highly effective dramaturgical experiments, using expressionist (q.v.) techniques to project the characters' feelings and the symbolic meaning of the action.

In most of the plays from the remaining years of this first period O.'s "dreamers" find the resolution of conflict and the peace they long for in mystical union or oneness with all life. To gain this unity with the whole they must sacrifice their individuality—not a very realistic solution for many of O.'s characters nor for the majority of his audiences. Most of these plays were failures, depending too heavily upon philosophical ideas derived from Nietzsche and Schopenhauer, Taoism, and psychoanalytic allusions to Jung and Freud (qq.v.). *All God's Chillun Got Wings* (written 1923, pub. 1924) created a sensation as the anguished love story of a black man and the white woman to whom he abases himself. *The Great God Brown* (written 1925, pub. 1926) is an intricate and confusing drama of masks in which the hero tries to find himself between conflicting self-images and conflicting forces of materialism and idealism, paganism and Christianity. *Marco Millions* (written 1923–25, pub. 1927) is a huge, spectacular pageant portraying Marco Polo as an American Babbitt who confronts the mysticism of the East with total incomprehension. *Lazarus Laughed* (written 1925–26, pub. 1927) was another enormous pageant, in which Lazarus has been reborn to bring the joyful tidings that there is really no death.

The only drama from this period that continues to be produced with popular success is *Desire under the Elms* (written 1924, pub. 1924). In this play O. moved away from mysticism and attempts at poetical diction to rustic New England dialect. It is a violent tale of a hard, realistic father in opposition to his dreamer-son. The characters are all rugged farm people, of Puritan stock, driven by the desire for sex, money, and vengeance but also by the need for warmth, love, and beauty. Even after the son has been intimate with his father's young wife, and she has murdered their child, the lovers feel that somehow their love transcends the reality of their crime and its imminent punishment. By suggesting that the characters of *Desire under the Elms* are victims of a wronged brooding maternal spirit that has demanded revenge and expiation, O. attempted to give them tragic stature. Although the two lovers go rapturously toward prison, the old father remains to work out his lonely destiny on the barren, rocky land.

He is a precursor of the protagonists of the plays written between 1926 and 1932. For them the long struggle for fulfillment and freedom ends in self-punishment or resignation. There is no ideal or transcendent world. Guilt is inescapable, and conflict ends only with the end of desire. The important plays of this period are *Strange Interlude* (written 1926–27, pub. 1928), which also won a Pulitzer Prize, and *Mourning Becomes Electra* (written 1929–31, pub. 1931).

Strange Interlude is a stream-of-consciousness (q.v.) novel in dramatic form. It consists of nine acts and takes five hours to perform, but it was the greatest popular success of O.'s career. The characters reveal their hidden motives in asides, exposing their Oedipal fixations or other drives and forces as described by Freud, Jung, and Schopenhauer. The central figure is Nina Leeds, a woman who must exploit the male characters in order to fulfill her needs for a father, lover, husband, and

son. The action of the play ceases only when Nina, all passion spent, gives up hope of fulfilling these needs and accepts old age. Her rebellion against sexual repression made the play seem shocking and revolutionary in its day. Now, however, it seems dated and often melodramatic.

Mourning Becomes Electra is O.'s version of the tragedy of the house of Atreus, set in 19th-c. New England. This trilogy (made up of *Homecoming, The Hunted,* and *The Haunted*) interprets, in psychoanalytic terms, the familiar story of the murder of Agamemnon and its consequences. The action centers around Lavinia (Electra), who avenges her father's murder by persuading her brother, Orin (Orestes) to kill her mother's (Christine-Clytemnestra) lover; the murder is followed by the suicide of the mother, and subsequently, of Orin when he discovers that he has an incestuous passion for his sister. Shouldering the family guilt, Lavinia locks herself in the family mansion to live with and be hounded by the ghosts of the past.

In a few weeks in 1932, O. wrote his only comedy, the highly successful *Ah, Wilderness!* (pub. 1933). Its nostalgic portrayal of middle-class American family life was based in part on O.'s family memories of his Connecticut days. Here the poetic dreamer is an adolescent boy in the throes of romantic love, whose introduction to sex and the adult world is treated with humor and sympathy.

O. was becoming increasingly preoccupied with his own past. In 1933 *Days without End* (pub. 1934) was completed only after many laborious drafts, each with a different ending. It is a drama of inner conflict, in which two actors play the two selves of the protagonist. One self is a gentle idealist who adores his wife; the other is a satanic mocker who hates her and life. The conflict is finally resolved in the love of Christ, as the hero returns to Catholicism. The conclusion was not very convincing, and the play was a theatrical failure. Although some critics saw in it O.'s return to his childhood faith, this was not the fact. Throughout his career, before and after *Days without End,* O. expressed his ambivalence toward Christianity in a longing to believe, on the one hand, and blasphemous contempt, on the other.

In 1935 O. began work on a cycle of eleven plays, to be called *A Tale of Possessors Dispossessed.* Its theme was the destructiveness of American greed and materialism, as seen in the two-hundred-year history of an Irish-American family. The cycle was never completed. Only two plays have survived: *A Touch of the Poet* (written 1935–43, pub. 1957) is the most finished; *More Stately Mansions* (written 1935–43, pub. 1964) was a lengthy rough draft, posthumously revised and shortened by its editors.

In his final productive period O. completed *The Iceman Cometh* (written 1939, pub. 1946), *Long Day's Journey into Night* (written 1940–41, pub. 1956), the one-act *Hughie* (written 1941–42, pub. 1959), and *A Moon for the Misbegotten* (written 1943, pub. 1952). In all these plays the characters long, still, for some kind of peace or fulfillment, but now any "dream" they have is a self-deceptive lie. Yet life is bearable to them only by virtue of these "pipe-dreams," and by the pity and sympathy they come to feel for one another. When death comes, it is no longer a grand gesture or a mystical experience, but simply a relief, a giving up.

The Iceman Cometh and *Long Day's Journey* reflect O.'s experiences in 1911–12, and his mood of depression at that time. *The Iceman Cometh* concerns a group of drunken derelicts (based on people O. knew on the waterfront and in Greenwich Village) who spend their time in the back room of Harry Hope's saloon on the lower west side of New York City. They live in an aura of alcohol and illusions about what they once were and hope to become again. These illusions are shattered when Hickey, a salesman whom they admire, appears as a messiah, offering them peace of mind if they will face reality and test their plans to rehabilitate themselves. They fail the test, and in despair are no longer able to forget their inadequacies in alcohol—until they discover that their quasi-redeemer is himself living a lie; is, indeed a madman and a murderer. Then they can again find solace and community in drinking with their cronies, in Hope's back room. For three characters, however, there can be no solace but death. Two of these, Hickey and a young ex-anarchist named Parritt, have destroyed women they loved—one a wife, the other a mother. They convince themselves for a while that their crimes were justified, but when the horror of what they have done comes through to them, death is the only expiation. The third of these, Larry, thinks of himself as a philosopher, a detached observer of the others. Events show him, however, that his supposed detachment is actually a

hopeless paralysis of will from which death can be the only release.

When read, the play seems to be repetitious as each character recites his own "pipe-dream" and subsequent disillusionment, and as the plots parallel each other. On the stage, however, and under good direction, the repetition becomes, as O. intended, an excitingly dramatic "theme and variations." The play typifies, also, another favorite device of O.'s: it begins as a comedy with the characters objectively portrayed as clowns; later, when their inner selves are revealed, they become pathetic and even tragic.

Long Day's Journey Into Night is O.'s agonized portrait of his own family, here called the Tyrones. The events take place in 1912. Edmund (the young O. himself) is staying with his family in Connecticut, before entering the tuberculosis sanatorium. O. reveals his mother's drug addiction and its effect upon the family relationships. Beginning on a note of affection and humor, the tone of the play changes to pain and bitterness as the father, the mother, and the two brothers reveal the secret springs of their own characters and the mixed love, hate, and guilt they feel toward the others. They shout recriminations at each other, then confess their own guilt and beg for forgiveness. Through it all the mother (called Mary) wanders in a morphine haze, in each scene regressing farther into the past where she thought she had once known peace, freedom, and innocence. *Long Day's Journey* is the most consistently powerful of all O.'s work.

The hauntingly effective one-act play, *Hughie,* continues the theme of *The Iceman Cometh; A Moon for the Misbegotten* continues the family history. In *Hughie* a small-time gambler cannot endure his life without someone to believe the lie that he was once in the "big time." In *A Moon for the Misbegotten,* James Tyrone, Jr., who represented O.'s older brother in *Long Day's Journey,* has been devastated by his mother's death and his guilt feelings toward her. He is a desperate alcoholic wreck. For a brief time he finds comfort in the arms of a large earthy woman who loves him, and who as a mother surrogate gives him a kind of absolution. In the end, however, the best she can hope for him is that he die in his sleep, and soon.

O. brought passion and art to the American stage. He believed that drama should attempt to project on the stage the deepest truths about human character and its relationship to the "mystery" of things. This subjective point of view led him to use a stylized rather than a literal approach to production. He employed such devices as the monologue and the aside; abstract, symbolic sets; symbolic masks, makeup and costumes; thematic repetition of spoken phrases, actions, and theatrical effects; and archetypal motifs drawn from mythology and religion. He was not above using old plot devices from melodrama or vaudeville if they served his purpose.

The depth of O.'s thought, and his knowledge of philosophy and psychology have been questioned, as has his use of language and the quality of his imagination. He is universally honored, however, for his skillful dramaturgy and especially for the emotional truth and intensity of some of his plays. Of these the ones most likely to survive as classic repertory are his one comedy, *Ah, Wilderness!;* his paean to the "pipe-dream," *The Iceman Cometh;* and his family confessional, *Long Day's Journey into Night.* Other plays are, and will continue to be revived experimentally now and then, but these three have already become a part of the American dramatic heritage.

FURTHER WORKS: *Thirst, and Other One-Act Plays* (1914); *Before Breakfast* (1916); *The Long Voyage Home* (1917); *The Moon of the Caribees* (1918); *In the Zone* (1919); *The Rope* (1919); *Where the Cross is Made* (1919); *The Dreamy Kid* (1920); *The Straw* (1921); *Gold* (1921); *Diff'rent* (1921); *The First Man* (1922); *Welded* (1924); *The Fountain* (1926); *Dynamo* (1929); *Lost Plays, 1913–15* (1950); *Plays of E. O.* (3 vols., 1955); *Ten "Lost" Plays* (1964); *Children of the Sea, and Three Other Unpublished Plays* (1972); *Poems 1912–1944* (1980); *E. O. at Work* (1981); *"The Theatre We Worked For": The Letters of E. O. to Kenneth Macgowan* (1982); *Chris Christophersen* (1982)

BIBLIOGRAPHY: Clark, B. H., *E. O.* (1926; rev. ed., 1947); Winther, S. K., *E. O.: A Critical Study* (1934; rev. ed., 1961); Engel, E. A., *The Haunted Heroes of E. O.* (1953); Falk, D. V., *E. O. and the Tragic Tension* (1958; rev. ed., 1982); Bowen, C., *Curse of the Misbegotten* (1959); Cargill, O., et al., eds., *O. and His Plays* (1961); Alexander, D., *The Tempering of E. O.* (1962); Gelb, A. and B., *O.* (1962); Leech, C., *E. O.* (1963);

Gassner, J., ed., *O.: A Collection of Critical Essays* (1964); Raleigh, J. H., *The Plays of E. O.* (1965); Sheaffer, L., *O., Son and Playwright* (1968); Tiusanen, T., *O.'s Scenic Images* (1968); Törnqvist, E., *A Drama of Souls: Studies in O.'s Super-Naturalistic Technique* (1969); Bogard, T., *Contour in Time: The Plays of E. O.* (1972); Sheaffer, L., *O., Son and Artist* (1973); Chabrowe, L., *Ritual and Pathos: The Theater of O.* (1976); Carpenter, F. I., *E. O.,* rev. ed. (1979); Chothia, J., *Forging a Language: A Study of the Plays of E. O.* (1979); Floyd, V., ed., *E. O.: A World View* (1979)

DORIS V. FALK

The dialogue of *The First Man* . . . proves in reading so tasteless and dreary that one does not see how one could sit through it.

But E. O. has another vein in which he is a literary artist of genius. When he is writing the more or less grammatical dialogue of the middle-class characters of his plays, his prose is heavy and indigestible even beyond the needs of naturalism. People say the same things to one another over and over again and never succeed in saying them any more effectively than the first time; long speeches shuffle dragging feet, marking time without progressing, for pages. But as soon as Mr. O. gets a character who can only talk some kind of vernacular, he begins to write like a poet. [1922]

Edmund Wilson, "E. O. and the Naturalists," *The Shores of Light* (1952), pp. 99–100

That he is the foremost dramatist in the American theatre is . . . generally granted. His eminence is predicated on the fact that no other has anywhere near his ability to delve into and appraise character, his depth of knowledge of his fellow man, his sweep and pulse and high resolve, his command of a theatre stage and all its manifold workings, and his mastery of the intricacies of dramaturgy. His plays at their best have in them a real universality. His characters are not specific, individual and isolated types but active symbols of mankind in general, with mankind's virtues and faults, gropings and findings, momentary triumphs and doomed defeats. He writes not for a single theatre but for all theatres of the world.

George Jean Nathan, "O.: A Critical Summation," *American Mercury,* Dec. 1946, 718

At one time he performed a historic function, that of helping the American theatre to grow up. In all his plays an earnest attempt is made to interpret life; this fact in itself places O. above his predecessors in American drama and beside his colleagues in the novel and poetry. He was a good playwright

433

insofar as he kept within the somewhat narrow range of his own sensibility. When he stays close to a fairly simple reality and when, by way of technique, he uses fairly simple forms of realism or fairly simple patterns of melodrama, he can render the bite and tang of reality or, alternatively, he can startle and stir us with his effects. . . . But the more he attempts, the less he succeeds. *Lazarus Laughed* and *The Great God Brown* and *Days without End* are inferior to *The Emperor Jones* and *Anna Christie* and *Ah, Wilderness!*

Eric Bentley, "Trying to Like O.," *KR,* 14 (1952), 488

O. was a faulty craftsman; he was not a sound thinker. . . . Yet to dwell on these shortcomings . . . is to confess one's own inadequate and bloodless response to the world we live in . . . . O. not only lived intensely but attempted with perilous honesty to contemplate, absorb and digest the meaning of his life and ours. He possessed an uncompromising devotion to the task he set himself: to present and interpret in stage terms what he had lived through and thought about—a devotion unique in our theatre. . . . O.'s work is more than realism. And if it is stammering—it is still the most eloquent and significant stammer of the American theatre. We have not yet developed a cultivated speech that is either superior to it or as good.

Harold Clurman, on *Long Day's Journey into Night, Nation,* 3 March 1956, 182–83

Compassion produced by a full understanding of man's circumstances and man's essential nature, a compassion which beggars analysis, is O.'s final achievement in theatre. The action of each of the four last plays rests in a tale to be told, a tale that is essentially a confession made in hope of absolution. Although the confessional tale is often plotless, often nothing more than a dream, it is a way of reaching out in the dark, of finding pity long denied to old sorrow.

The introspective qualities of the last plays account for their essential lyricism. When *The Iceman Cometh* was first produced in 1946, under the somewhat ponderously reverential conditions that O.'s "return" to the New York theatre necessarily occasioned, it brought with it, from producers and reviewers, charges that O. was indulging himself by refusing to cut the work. [Lawrence] Langner tells of a time during rehearsals when he timidly reminded O. that the same point had been made eighteen times. O. told him "in a particularly quiet voice, 'I *intended* it to be repeated eighteen times!' " Although it was obviously not a matter of calculated intention, O. did not indulge in such repetition without full awareness of its theatrical consequences. Like many of his earlier efforts, the repetition not only in *The Iceman*

Cometh but in *Long Day's Journey into Night* is essential to the lyric mode of the work, for in these plays O. became the poet he had earlier so often lamented he could not be.

Travis Bogard, *Contour in Time: The Plays of E. O.* (1972), pp. 408–9

As *Mourning Becomes Electra* was derived from the *Oresteia* in plot and structure, it had a considerable aesthetic distance from the audience. Its pathos was consequently muted, the tragic effect too removed. The fate equivalent could have its full impact only when cast in an intrinsically modern idiom. And not until *Long Day's Journey into Night,* written a decade later, did O. cast it in such an idiom. By then his philosophical outlook had turned despairing, a state of mind that worked against any spiritual triumph of the characters. But by purely aesthetic means he was able to bring about a greater release of tragic pathos than ever before. In the very defeat of man in the life struggle there was an exultation.

The fact is that O. achieved nothing less than a renaissance of an art form long thought dead. Since funeral orations have been delivered many times over the petrified body of tragedy, a renaissance is just what his work amounts to. The orations have usually been delivered by scholars and critics with a strictly Aristotelian or moral perspective, but O.'s perspective was more from the Nietzschean or aesthetic side. Through the magic of ritual and pathos he evoked the tragic emotions in the theater as of old. In varying degrees, depending on the play, he made the audience feel what life was in its essence, not think about how to deal with it in its detail. To instruct or shake the opinions of an audience—the aim of political theater—is no mean feat. Still it is less difficult and in the long run even less relevant than to move an audience to catharsis.

Leonard Chabrowe, *Ritual and Pathos—the Theater of O.* (1976), pp. xxii–xxiii

There is an element in his dialogue not captured by the traditional approaches of literary analysis. This element is movement. There is a constant pendulum movement between several polarities in O.'s dialogue: between such polarities as fear and laughter, love and hatred, tragedy and comedy, aversion and sympathy, search and finding, heroism and baseness, self-deception and honesty. The result of this movement is a grotesque, grand language of the stage, even in the apparently most traditional or realistic of his plays. This is the feature that makes O. modern even today, in this new age of drama after Samuel Beckett.

Timo Tiusanen, "O.'s Significance: A Scandinavian and European View," in Virginia Floyd, ed., *E. O.: A World View* (1979), p. 66

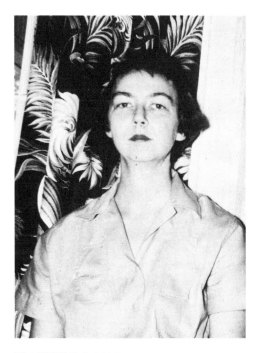

FLANNERY O'CONNOR

EUGENE O'NEILL

JOSÉ ORTEGA Y GASSET

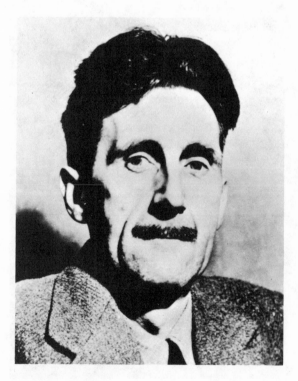

GEORGE ORWELL

O.'s drama found an audience in the late 1950s. At first sight, it seems remote from the dominant serious drama of this period, the post-realist drama that stemmed from Beckett's *Waiting for Godot.* A further wave of successful revivals of the late plays early in the 1970s suggests that O.'s appeal in 1956 was not, as might have been supposed, that of a voice from the past briefly resuscitated, but that of a voice speaking directly to audiences now. It is not a quaint voice but an urgent one that we hear, one that sounds both of and outside of its own time and presents us with pressing questions about our own being. O.'s writing differs from the ephemeral writing of those contemporaries of his who might seem to share his conventions because, in his drama, word and word, word and stage image, interact within a developing pattern of meaning, startling us, as members of the audience, with their echoic quality, informing us with their mutual suggestiveness, compelling us to see contrasts and new relationships.

Jean Chothia, *Forging a Language: A Study of the Plays of E. O.* (1979), p. 185

ONETTI, Juan Carlos

Uruguayan novelist and short-story writer, b. 1 July 1909, Montevideo

O. spent his first twenty years in his native Uruguay, but then moved to Buenos Aires, Argentina, where he worked quite successfully as a journalist. Despondent at the Argentine social and political situation, he returned in 1954 to Uruguay, where he spent some time as a librarian. Although not well known abroad then, he won the National Prize for Literature in Uruguay in 1962. The political changes in the 1970s in Uruguay resulted in his going into exile in Spain, where he has lived since 1975, winning the prestigious Critics' Prize in 1979 for his novel *Dejemos hablar al viento* (1979; let's speak with the wind) and Spain's highest literary award, the Miguel de Cervantes Prize, in 1980.

Many of O.'s existential novels and short stories are set in the fictional town of Santa María, a locale that is a microcosm of an absurd world. Most of his protagonists lead anguished, alienated, or frustrated lives in a sad and sordid world populated by unhappy people and corrupted by absurd values. His characters often live only through the remembrance of things past and—unfulfilled sexually, politically, socially, or morally—find death to be the only solution to a life of defeat.

O.'s first novel, *El pozo* (1939; the pit),

viewed by many critics as the first truly modern Spanish American novel because it gives expression to a peculiarly Spanish American mixture of dream and reality, explores the nightmarish world of its protagonist, Eladio Linacero. A solitary being who had dreamed of utopia, Linacero recalls his rape of an innocent girl, his moral degradation, and his nightly self-torture, although his confession gives him, briefly, self-awareness and an imagined potential for a different existence.

Tierra de nadie (1941; no-man's-land), stresses the sexual frustration and political disillusionment of an entire generation. Diego de Aránzuru, a typically ambiguous and ambivalent Onetti creation, abandons the legal profession to search in vain for meaning in life and love in an absurd universe indifferent to his needs.

Para esta noche (1943; for tonight) explores the world of dreams in a city under siege. Osorio, fleeing with the teenage daughter of the man he denounced to an enemy police agent, is himself killed. Again O. depicts a cynical, cruel, sterile world of moral indifference and lack of faith.

La vida breve (1950; *A Brief Life,* 1976), stylistically innovative, again portrays a world of hatred and frustration. The narrator, Brausen, unhappy with his married life, his routine, and his mediocrity, and seeking a "brief life" to transcend nothingness, invents a fantasy existence for himself as Díaz Grey, the protagonist of a screenplay he is writing, who is no more authentic than his inventor.

In a series of short novels set in Santa María, O. continued to dwell on earlier subjects: existentially isolated people who live in the past in *Los adioses* (1954; the good-byes); a man who is sexually obsessed with a prostitute in *Una tumba sin nombre* (1959; later title, *Para una tumba sin nombre;* [for] a nameless tomb); a guilt-ridden protagonist who accepts responsibility for the death of his brother and a young girl in *La cara de la desgracia* (1960; misfortune's face).

El astillero (1961; *The Shipyard,* 1968), an ironic allegory, presents in detail the frustrated and absurd life of Larsen, a middle-aged ex-owner of a whorehouse who, seeking escape from failure, works in Jeremías Petrus's rusting shipyard. Without a meaningful present or future—he fantasizes about managing the shipyard and having a relationship with Petrus's mad daughter—Larsen ends his wasted life in unheroic defeat, much as the shipyard, devoured by decay, will also disappear. *Juntacadáveres* (1964; the body collector) is about Larsen's earlier life as brothel owner, the psychologically troubled prostitutes and clients, and, despite Larsen's attempts to alter the situation, the closing of the brothel.

O.'s protagonists search in vain for an unattainable ideal love, which could give meaning to their absurd, alienated, and irrational lives. Betrayed and defeated, they often create imaginary doubles to obtain surcease from an unattractive world. This failure of escape through fantasy, reflecting the disintegration of modern urban life, often leads his characters to suicide.

A master in fusing fantasy and realism and in dealing with the mythopoetic faculties of creation, O., using a fluid style that some have compared to Faulkner's (q.v.), gives aesthetic expression to metaphysical preoccupations, as he ponders the human condition and the destiny of man.

FURTHER WORKS: *Un sueño realizado y otros cuentos* (1951); *El infierno tan temido* (1962); *Tan triste como ella* (1963); *Jacob y el otro, y otros cuentos* (1965); *Tres novelas* (1967); *Cuentos completos* (1967); *La novia robada, y otros cuentos* (1968); *Novelas cortas completas* (1968); *Obras completas* (1970); *La muerte y la niña* (1973); *Cuentos completos* (1974); *Tiempo de abrazar* (1974); *Réquiem por Faulkner* (1975)

BIBLIOGRAPHY: Jones, Y. P., *The Formal Expression of Meaning in J. C. O.'s Narrative Art* (1969); Gómez Mango, L., ed., *En torno a J. C. O.* (1970); Deredita, J., "The Shorter Works of J. C. O.," *SSF*, 8 (1971), 112–22; Ruffinelli, J., *O.* (1973); "Focus on J. C. O.'s *A Brief Life*," special section, *Review*, No. 16 (1975), 5–33; Giacoman, H. F., *Homenaje a J. C. O.* (1974); Kader, D., *J. C. O.* (1977)

KESSEL SCHWARTZ

ORIYA LITERATURE
See Indian Literature

ORTEGA Y GASSET, José
Spanish philosopher and essayist, b. 8 May 1883. Madrid; d. 18 Oct. 1955, Madrid

O. was the son of José Ortega Munilla (1856–1922), a noted journalist and novelist,

and the grandson of Eduardo Gasset, the founder of the newspaper *El imparcial.* He attended a Jesuit school in Málaga and the University of Madrid, where he received his doctorate in 1904. In 1906 he went to Leipzig and Berlin. Later he spent a year in Marburg, where he studied with Hermann Cohen (1842–1918), the Neo-Kantian philosopher. From 1910 to 1936 he was professor of metaphysics at the University of Madrid.

Eager to contribute to the creation in Spain of a climate suited to philosophical and systematic thought, O. sought to reach the public that did not attend universities by means of newspapers, journals, and public lectures. Two of his most significant social and political works, *España invertebrada* (1922; *Invertebrate Spain,* 1937) and *La rebelión de las masas* (1923; *The Revolt of the Masses,* 1932) were first published in installments in the periodical *El sol* (1920 and 1922). His lecture series on "What Is Philosophy?" in 1929 attracted a surprisingly large and varied audience. In 1916 he began the publication of a one-man review, *El espectador,* whose eight volumes appeared at irregular intervals from 1916 to 1934. In 1923 he founded the prestigious *Revista de Occidente,* which was decisive in the intellectual and artistic formation of many writers of his generation.

O.'s first trip to Buenos Aires in 1916 marked the beginning of his influence among Latin American writers. Throughout his life he made lecture tours to North and South America and to various European countries. O. lived outside Spain during the civil war and did not return until 1949.

O.'s works are extremely varied, for they reflect his constant interest in all the elements of his "circumstance." He wrote on philosophical, political, social, historical, and literary topics; he described the landscape of Castile, the phenomenology of love, the writings of Azorín, Pío Baroja, and Marcel Proust (qq.v.), the painting of Velázquez and Goya. In his preoccupation with the problem of Spain and the changes of values in modern technological society, he continued to develop some of the themes of the "Generation of 1898." Like Antonio Machado, Miguel de Unamuno (qq.v.), and Azorín, O. wanted to "save" the reality of Spain, to elevate even the humblest aspects of that world to their fullest meaning. But whereas the "Generation of 1898" effected the literary transformation of the Spanish landscape and of

Spanish psychology and history, O.'s confrontation of these circumstances led him to his central philosophical conceptions: perspectivism and historical or vital reason.

The formula "I am myself plus my circumstances"—stated in his first book, *Meditaciones del Quijote* (1914; *Meditations on Quixote,* 1961) and fully elaborated in *El tema de nuestro tiempo* (1923; *The Modern Theme,* 1933)—not only expresses the relation of the individual to his physical and cultural environment but forms the basis of the theory that the point of view is one of the components of reality. This theory must be distinguished from any purely psychological relativism; for O. perspective refers not only to the subject but to reality itself. As he wrote in the essay "Verdad y perspectiva" (1916; truth and perspective): "Truth, the real, the universe, life—whatever you want to call it—breaks into innumerable facets... each one of which faces a certain individual." Each point of view is unique and indispensable. Each person, nation, and historical period is an irreplaceable organ for the discovery of truth. The coincidence of two points of view can only mean that the object of focus is an abstraction and not reality; the real, the concrete, can only be grasped through infinite, diverse perspectives.

In *El tema de nuestro tiempo* O. argued in favor of a vital reason that, unlike the abstract reason of rationalism, would concern itself with the ever-changing phenomena of life. The modern theme is the need to place reason within the vital or biological sphere; thought is a biological function, and it is also the tool one must use in order to live. Reason is *not* a special gift to be employed at leisure; reason is something we must have recourse to in order to make our way in that "uncertain repertory of possibilities and difficulties" presented to us by the world, as he expressed it in *Ideas y creencias* (1940; ideas and beliefs).

In *¿Qué es filosofía?* (1929; *What Is Philosophy?,* 1960) and *Historia como sistema* (1941; *Toward a Philosophy of History,* 1941; repub. as *History as a System,* 1961), works that show the influence of existentialist (q.v.) ideas and vocabulary, O. defines human life as the radical reality because all other realities occur within it. And that reality is no specific thing: it cannot be fixed and defined; it is precisely the evasion of all definition. A person is neither a body nor a soul (which are both "things") but a series of choices and

actions—a drama. Life is not given to us already formed; on the contrary, it consists of continuously deciding what we are to do and be. This constant and constitutive instability is freedom. We are necessarily free. Since life has no stable, definable form, the only possible way of understanding anything human, whether personal or collective, is by telling a story, by relating its history.

Vital reason is the same as historical reason. "Man does not have a nature but a history." Historical reason adapts itself to the fluid course of life and situates the individual in relation to his specific environment; it is therefore more rigorous, more demanding, more "rational" than abstract reason.

Although O. views life as radically problematical and uncertain, he also portrays it as an immense festive or "sporting" phenomenon. He differentiates between a primary activity that is spontaneous, disinterested, and creative, and a secondary one that responds to demands imposed from without. The first, an effort we make for the sheer delight of making it, is sport; the second, necessary, dependent, utilitarian, and mechanized, is work. Since life itself serves no ulterior purpose, its highest products—scientific and artistic creations, political and moral heroism, religious sainthood—are the result of a playful, superfluous expenditure of energy (*El tema de nuestro tiempo*). It is in this sense that one should understand O.'s statements, in *La deshumanización del arte* (1925; *The Dehumanization of Art,* 1948), about the essentially ironical and playful nature of the new art, an art that claims to have no transcending consequences.

Whether considering it as insecurity or as play, O. defends life's flexibility and diverseness from all rigid schemes and rules. In the name of life values he attacks the superstitious deification of reason and culture. Art, science, philosophy, and ethics are interpretations or clarifications of life and should never be elevated to ends in themselves. In his political and social works—*España invertebrada, La rebelión de las masas, En torno a Galileo* (1933; *Man and Crisis,* 1958), *El hombre y la gente* (1957; *Man and People,* 1957)—O. sees society as a constant threat to individual authenticity. In the social realm, originally spontaneous acts become mere customary usages, empty gestures. O. often speaks of society as a fossilization of life, a mineralized excrescence of human existence. Against the danger of this degradation, O.

asserts, in *Ensimismamiento y alteración* (1939; self-absorption and otherness), the need continually to absorb one's circumstances, to retreat from the accumulated mass of cultural forms in order to make unique and personal responses.

O.'s simplistic and mechanical division of society into elites and masses makes his sociology unacceptable. His unwillingness to integrate the various aspects of his thought into a coherent system, as well as certain important contradictions and inconsistencies, has left some of his ideas—especially those on modern art—open to misinterpretation. Outside of Spain he is known for his least impressive works (*La rebelión de las masas,* for example). O.'s significant contributions to existentialism are to be found in the development of the concepts of perspectivism and historical or vital reason.

FURTHER WORKS: *Vieja y nueva política* (1914); *Personas, obras y cosas* (1916); *Ideas sobre la novela* (1925; *Notes on the Novel,* 1948); *La redención de las provincias y la decadencia nacional* (1931); *Rectificación de la república* (1931); *Pidiendo un Goethe desde dentro* (1932; "In Search of Goethe from Within," 1949); *Misión de la universidad* (1932; *Mission of the University,* 1966); *Estudios sobre el amor* (1939; *On Love: Aspects of a Single Theme,* 1957); *Teoría de Andalucía, y otros ensayos* (1942); *Del imperio romano* (1946; *Concord and Liberty,* 1963); *Obras completas* (11 vols., 1946–69); *Papeles sobre Velázquez y Goya* (1950; in *Velázquez, Goya, and The Dehumanization of Art,* 1972); *La idea de principio en Leibniz y la evolución de la teoría deductiva* (1958; *The Idea of Principle in Leibniz and the Evolution of Deductive Theory,* 1971); *Prólogo para alemanes* (1959); *Una interpretación de la historia universal* (1960; *An Interpretation of Universal History,* 1973); *Pasado y porvenir para el hombre actual* (1962); *Unas lecciones de metafísica* (1966; *Some Lessons in Metaphysics,* 1970); *Epistolario* (1974). FURTHER VOLUMES IN ENGLISH: *The Dehumanization of Art, and Other Writings on Art and Culture* (1956); *The Origin of Philosophy* (1967); *Meditations on Hunting* (1972; tr. of prologue to *Veinte años de caza mayor* by E. Figueroa and Alonso Martínez, Conde de Yebes, pub. 1943); *Phenomenology and Art* (1975)

BIBLIOGRAPHY: Livingstone, L., "O. y G.'s Philosophy of Art," *PMLA,* 67 (1952), 609–

54; Stern, A., "O. y G., Existentialist or Essentialist?" *La torre,* 4 (1956), 388–99; Ferrater Mora, J., *O. y G.: An Outline of His Philosophy* (1957); Gaete, A., *El sistema maduro de O.* (1962); Sebastian, E. G., "J. O. y G.," *Hispania,* 46 (1963), 490–95; Read, H., "High Noon and Darkest Night: Some Observations on O. y G.'s Philosophy of Art," *JAAC,* 23 (1964), 43–50; Weber, F., "An Approach to O.'s Idea of Culture," *HR,* 32 (1964), 142–56; Drijoune, L., *La concepción de la historia en la obra de O. y G.* (1968); Morón Arroyo, C., *El sistema de O. y G.* (1968); Marías, J., *J. O. y G.: Circumstance and Vocation* (1970); McClintock, R., *Man and His Circumstances: O. as Educator* (1971); Niedermayer, F., *J. O. y G.* (1973); Silver, P., *O. as Phenomenologist: The Genesis of "Meditations on Quixote"* (1978)

FRANCES WYERS

ORTESE, Anna Maria

Italian novelist, short-story writer, poet, and journalist, b. 1915, Rome

O. grew up, in squalid circumstances, in several towns in southern Italy and later in Tripoli, Libya; from 1928 until the start of World War II she resided with her family in Naples. During the war she lived in various cities and towns in central and northern Italy, and after the war continued to move from place to place. Poor health, poverty, and inferior formal education marred her childhood. She spent most of her time at home, reading mainly such foreign authors as Edgar Allan Poe, Robert Louis Stevenson, and Hans Christian Andersen, from whom she first learned of life as a kind of poetic vision.

O.'s first publication was a poem, "Manuele" (1933; Manuele), written at the death of her twenty-year-old brother, killed in a naval accident. It created such enthusiasm among young poets that Alfonso Gatto (q.v.) said: "[The] poem makes her a new Ungaretti [q.v.], the man of sorrows."

A few years later O. started writing short stories for the prestigious journal *L'Italia letteraria.* These stories—lyrical visions and private dreams—captured the attention of many writers, particularly of Massimo Bontempelli (q.v.), the father of "magic realism" (q.v.), who collected and published them under the title *Angelici dolori* (1937; angelic sorrows). In this book, which is the history of a life of "solitude," O. intertwines her life and her family's with the lives of such characters as American Indians or with fantastic adventures and dreams. These stories are a poetic amalgam of reality and fabulation. *Angelici dolori* is fundamental to the understanding of the rest of O.'s work.

Il mare non bagna Napoli (1953; *The Bay Is Not Naples,* 1955) received both national and international recognition. Translated into many languages, it contains touching stories of Neapolitan poverty. For example, "La città involontaria" ("Involuntary City") is a description, realistic yet compassionate, of a decrepit military barracks in which homeless people—like O. herself—live in subhuman conditions. She has been accused of "desecrating Naples," but it is truer to say that, as in the story "Il silenzio della ragione" ("Silence of Reason"), O.—together with a group of younger writers around the Neapolitan journal *Sud*—participates in the sorrows of her people and dreams of a better future for them.

In his remarks written for the jacket of *Il mare non bagna Napoli,* Elio Vittorini (q.v.) called O. "a gypsy absorbed in a dream." The "gypsy" (who had moved, and would move until 1975, from city to city in search of the financial stability she never had) always felt "poor and simple." It may be indicative of her lifelong "solitude" that in her fascinating fable-novel *L'iguana* (1965; the iguana) the "iguana"—Estrellita, the poor little faithful servant—works all her life for a rich family (who pay her not with money but with little stones) and lives otherwise isolated in the "absolute darkness" of a cellar.

Although O.'s works have been acclaimed by many critics and although several were translated into a number of languages, writing has not made her financially comfortable. Her major novel *Il porto di Toledo* (1975; the port of Toledo) cost her five years of strenuous effort. A profound reworking of nine stories in *Angelici dolori,* it is a lyrical work of mythopoeic power. Toledo is a metaphor for Naples, and O. incorporates her life and times from childhood to the end of World War II in a synthesis of reality and dreamlike transformation, hope and disappointment.

O. emphasizes these same ideas in her latest novel, *Il cappello piumato* (1979; the feathered hat), which is set in Milan in the aftermath of World War II. The narrator scrutinizes the interior lives of a "poor and simple" group of young intellectuals, whose efforts to preserve their belief in love and politics end in the complete failure of their dreams.

FURTHER WORKS: *Poesie* (1939); *L'infanta sepolta* (1950); *I giorni del cielo* (1958); *Silenzio a Milano* (1958); *Poveri e semplici* (1967); *La luna sul muro* (1968); *L'alone grigio* (1969)

BIBLIOGRAPHY: Nouat, R., "Le méridionalisme dans la littérature italienne d'aujourd'hui," *Critique,* No. 139 (1958), 1045–58; Ragusa, O., "Women Novelists in Postwar Italy," *BA,* 33 (1959), 5–9; Brandon-Albini, M., *Midi vivant* (1963), pp. 141–43; Pautasso, S., "Une approche de la littérature italienne," *Les lettres nouvelles,* 3–5 (1976), 7–31, 144–56

M. RICCIARDELLI

ORWELL, George

(pseud. of Eric Blair) English novelist, essayist, and social critic, b. 23 Jan. 1903, Motihari, India; d. 21 Jan 1950, London

O. was born in Bengal, the second child of Richard Walmesley Blair and Ida Mabel Limonzin. At the age of four he returned with his family to England, and four years later began his education by attending St. Cyprian's Preparatory School in Sussex until the age of thirteen. He then went by scholarship to Eton, where, after four and a half years, he completed his formal schooling. Following Eton, O. joined the Imperial Police in Burma in 1922; after serving for five years he resigned from the service. In 1928 O. decided definitely to become a writer and devoted the remainder of his life to that occupation. In 1933 he assumed the pseudonym by which he would sign all his publications.

O., who was primarily a novelist, nevertheless accomplished some of his best writing in autobiographical nonfiction and the polemical essay. These forms better served his strong sociopolitical concerns and the moral temper that led his contemporaries to call him the conscience of his age.

O.'s early work of the 1930s consists of social novels dealing largely with middle-class English life, and books of autobiographical reportage, drawn from his active involvement in the poverty and war that dominated the decade.

O.'s first book, *Down and Out in Paris and London* (1933), shows him to be a keen observer and penetrating social analyst, committed to recording accurately and imaginatively the plight of the poverty-stricken laborer and tramp on the Continent and in England. O.'s point of view in this book, that of the involved and sympathetic observer, reflects O.'s life style of subjecting himself to personal hardship in the interests of championing the underdog.

The Road to Wigan Pier (1937), in which the social protest is voiced even more articulately, was written for Victor Gollancz's Left Book Club as an exposé of the depressed living conditions of workers in the north of England. It contains a disturbingly sharp lengthy criticism of the weaknesses of contemporary socialism and socialists. Although O. belonged to the left, he remained to the end of his life an uncompromising individualist and political idealist, maintaining that the ends of socialism must be justice and freedom.

O.'s involvement in the Spanish Civil War as a common soldier attested to his need to act upon his political ideals. His experiences in Spain produced *Homage to Catalonia* (1938), still considered one of the best books in English on the Spanish war. The book records O.'s initiation into the international political turmoil of the late 1930s, and foreshadows his later political fiction. Many of O.'s attributes as a writer are evident in this personal account of life at the front and ideological conflict behind the lines. O. captures the image of war and its absurdities in the plain and vivid prose style that was to become so highly praised. Although the book is pervaded by O.'s disillusionment about the capability of party politics, its theme expresses O.'s abiding faith in the decency of the common man.

O.'s fiction of the same period is less distinguished. *Burmese Days* (1934) is O.'s sole novel related to his experiences in Burma. Like *A Clergyman's Daughter* (1935), *Keep the Aspidistra Flying* (1936), and *Coming Up for Air* (1939), *Burmese Days* depicts protagonists who are victims of their social environments and their own inner frustrations and doubts. In these novels O. deals with lonely, unhappy, sometimes oppressed people, with people who are nostalgic for the past because they live in the gray world of failure, religious doubt, poverty, or boredom.

Although linked thematically with much modern fiction, the early novels are technically unimpressive and fall far short of the achievements of writers like Aldous Huxley,

D. H. Lawrence, and James Joyce (qq.v.). O. had not yet found the literary medium that would express his most compelling vision of society.

In the 1940s O. set out "to make political writing an art," and in two estimable works of fiction he accomplished what he spoke of as the fusion of "political purpose and artistic purpose into one whole."

Animal Farm (1945), a political satire in the form of an animal fable, depicts the revolt of barnyard animals against their farmer oppressors and the establishment of an autonomous socialistic state. The original ideals of the animals rapidly degenerate at the hands of the pigs, who assume dictatorial power and turn the society into a police state. The animals—except for the pigs, of course—are returned to a bondage and misery more severe than they had initially suffered. Clearly an allegory of the Russian Revolution and particularly of the Stalinist regime, the novel avoids a narrow topicality by suggesting the disappointing aftermath of more than one revolution. O. directs his satire at a universal human condition, that is, that all political radicalisms inevitably become reactionary when based on power and power alone.

In 1949 O. published *1984*, his second political novel and last major work. This anti-utopian novel was influenced by O.'s reading in H. G. Wells, Yevgeny Zamyatin, Arthur Koestler (qq.v.), and Aldous Huxley. Precipitated by the international phenomenon of the rise of totalitarian states and the long, hard years of World War II, *1984* is a protest against the fearful direction in which O. believed the modern world was moving. Undoubtedly O. again wrote with the Stalinist regime in mind, but the machinery of his not so imaginary society is also drawn from the English scene of the war and postwar years.

The effectiveness of *1984* derives in part from an immediately recognizable reality, one whose atmosphere extends beyond any specific totalitarian state and includes even aspects of the so-called free societies. The book exposes the horror of totalitarianism whatever the form. O.'s pessimism is apparent throughout, and the final emotional and intellectual capitulation of the protagonist, another Orwellian victim, to Big Brother and the authority of the state is depressing rather than tragic. Yet O.'s purpose was to shock his readers into an awareness of the disastrous results of absolute power. Less a prophecy than a warning, the novel exists as a continual reminder to contemporary Western man that he is dangerously close to losing not only his freedom but the very attributes that make him human.

O.'s sense of social and political responsibility is as apparent in his early essay "A Hanging" (1931) and the many periodical contributions of almost twenty years as it is in *1984*. The first extensive collection of his major essays, *Critical Essays* (1946; Am., *Dickens, Dali and Others*), includes some of his most perceptive commentaries on important social and cultural issues of his time.

It has been said that in O.'s later work, and especially in his final novel, he registers a profound disillusionment about contemporary liberalism and that *1984* suffers aesthetically from an attitude of defeatism. Yet it has been equally observed that despite the pessimism of *1984*, O. never relinquished his commitment to Western liberal values, which include the freedom of mind and the sense of responsibility to acknowledge and to rectify social oppression whatever its nature, wherever it may appear, and to speak with an unadulterated truth of the ever-present threat of political totalitarianism in the 20th c.

Like Albert Camus (q.v.), O. was convinced that the contemporary writer must become involved, must take sides, with a sincerity that becomes the *sine qua non* of literary effectiveness. Few modern writers have been as assiduous as O. in devoting their lives and creative efforts to the cause of freedom and social amelioration. This commitment is the dominant force in all of his work.

FURTHER WORKS: *Inside the Whale, and Other Essays* (1940); *The Lion and the Unicorn: Socialism and the English Genius* (1941); *The English People* (1947); *Shooting an Elephant, and Other Essays* (1950); *England, Your England* (1953; Am., *Such, Such Were the Joys*); *The O. Reader: Fiction, Essays, and Reportage* (1956); *Selected Essays* (1957); *Collected Essays* (1961); *The Collected Essays, Journalism and Letters of G. O.* (4 vols., 1968)

BIBLIOGRAPHY: Brander, L., *G. O.* (1954); Hollis, C., *A Study of G. O.* (1956); Rees, R., *G. O.: Fugitive from the Camp of Victory* (1961); Voorhees, R., *The Paradox of G. O.* (1961); Woodcock, G., *The Crystal Spirit: A Study of G. O.* (1966); Oxley, B., *G. O.* (1967); Aldritt, K., *The Making of G. O.* (1969); Gross, M., ed., *The World of G. O.* (1971); Stansky, P., and Abrahams, W., *The Unknown O.* (1972); Steinhoff, W., *G. O. and the Origins of "1984"* (1975); Williams, R., *O.* (1975); Stansky, P., and Abrahams, W., *O.: The Transformation* (1980); Crick, B., *G. O.: A Life* (1981)

WAYNE WARNCKE

Mr. O. is a revolutionary who is in love with 1910. This ambivalence constitutes his strength and his weakness. Never before has a progressive political thinker been so handicapped by nostalgia for the Edwardian shabby-genteel or the under-dog. It is this political sentimentality which from the literary point of view is his most valid emotion. *Animal Farm* proves it, for it truly is a fairy story told by a great lover of liberty and a great lover of animals. The farm is real, the animals are moving. At the same time it is a devastating attack on Stalin and his "betrayal" of the Russian revolution, as seen by another revolutionary.

Cyril Connolly, on *Animal Farm, Horizon,* Sept. 1945, 215

The gist of O.'s criticism of the liberal intelligentsia was that they refused to understand the conditioned nature of life. He never quite puts it in this way but this is what he means. He himself knew what war and revolution were really like, what government and administration were really like. From first-hand experience he knew what Communism was. He could truly imagine what Nazism was. At a time when most intellectuals still thought of politics as a nightmare abstraction, pointing to the fearfulness of the nightmare as evidence of their sense of reality, O. was using the imagination of a man whose hands and eyes and whole body were part of his thinking apparatus.

Lionel Trilling, Introduction to *Homage to Catalonia* (1952), pp. xvi–xvii

I am at the moment engaged in trying to write a longer and better sketch of Eric [Blair, O.'s real name] than the one I wrote shortly after his death in which I try to show that his value consists in his having taken more seriously than most people the fundamental problem of religion. *Nineteen Eighty-Four*, for example, is more than a pessimistic prophesy. The crisis of the book is when the hero, under torture, says: "Do it to Julia, don't do it to me." Eric was appalled, like the saints, by the realization that human nature is fundamentally self-centered; and in *Nineteen Eighty-Four* the triumph of the totalitarian state is not complete until it has been demonstrated to the last resister that in the last resort he would sacrifice the person he loves best in order to save his own skin.

Richard Rees, Letter to Malcolm Muggeridge (March 8, 1955) in Miriam Gross, ed., *The World of G. O.* (1971), p. 167

O. was too solitary to be a symbol and too angry to be a saint. But he succeeded in becoming a writer who set down, in the purest English of his time, the thoughts and fantasies of an individual mind playing over the common problems of our age. What made him exceptional—and more than a little eccentric in the eyes of his contemporaries—was the fact that he also tried to work out his theories in action and then to give his actions shape in literature. The triad of thought, act and artifact runs through the whole of O.'s writing life.... Like Dr. Johnson, so many of whose attitudes he shared, he is likely to hold his place in English literature not only for what he wrote, but also for the man he was and for the fundamental honesties that he defended.

George Woodcock, *The Crystal Spirit: A Study of G. O.* (1966), p. 5

It is surely a permissible exaggeration to say that from first to last O., like George Eliot, was always writing the same novel. Not simply are his works marked by the same tone and style, but each one represents with variations the same troubled situation which he tries, without ever quite succeeding, to bring to an intellectually and emotionally satisfying outcome. Stated most generally, this central situation is a hidden or overt rebellion against a way of life accepted by most but intolerable to the protagonists. These, as O. sees them, are victims of forces they are never strong enough to oppose with any show of equality. Good is defeated by evil; the bully wins. Because of his constancy to this theme we can detect the seeds of *1984* in all O.'s published fiction, beginning with *Burmese Days,* his first novel.

William Steinhoff, *G. O. and the Origins of "1984"* (1975), p. 123

The key to O. as an individual is the problem of identity. Educated as he was to a particular consciousness, the key to his whole development is that he renounced it, or attempted to renounce it, and that he made a whole series of attempts to find a new social identity. Because of this process, we have a writer who was successively many things that would be unlikely in a normal trajectory: an imperial police officer, a resident of a casual ward, a revolutionary militiaman, a declassed intellectual, a middle-class English writer. And the strength of his work is that in the energy of his renunciation he was exceptionally open to each new experience as it came.... O. could connect as closely and with as many different kinds of people as he did, precisely because of his continual mobility, his successive and serious assumption of roles.

When he is in a situation, he is so dissolved into it that he is exceptionally convincing, and his kind of writing makes it easy for the reader to believe that this is also happening to himself. The absence of roots is also the absence of barriers.

Raymond Williams, *O.* (1975), pp. 87–88

OSBORNE, John
English dramatist, b. 12 Dec. 1929, London

Twenty-five years after *Look Back in Anger* (1956) opened at the Royal Court Theatre in London, making "angry young man" the standard label for the alienated and frustrated postwar generation and introducing a new language and a new hero into the genteel traditions of British drama, O. published his autobiography, *A Better Class of Person* (1981). Although the book ends with the opening night of *Look Back in Anger,* it nevertheless gives O. the opportunity to refute many of the biographical fallacies he claims critics have perpetrated upon his work. O., a socialist, an antinuclear activist, antiroyalty and antichurch, asserts in his book the strong influence of the view of Thomas de Quincy (1785–1859) on the necessity of always tearing away the "decent drapery" that hides the moral ulcers and scars from British sensitivity. O.'s new hero in *Look Back in Anger,* Jimmy Porter, is, like O., educated and married above his working-class origins and has little in the way of positive positions. In spite of the absence of good, brave causes, he feels the need to penetrate the indifference and apathy of the world surrounding him and to view its inherent wickedness as sufficient justification for his own vitriolic responses to it.

O. also refutes the common criticism that his works are essentially dramatic monologues delivered by the central characters who inhabit a world of dramatic nonentities. But it is precisely in the creation of these exceptional heroes, neurotic but self-aware, that O. has achieved his most notable successes.

In *The Entertainer* (1957), Archie Rice, the embodiment of the moribund traditions of both British music-hall comedians and, metaphorically, the British Empire, attacks his father, wife, and children in a series of domestic scenes, which are surrounded by vaudeville "turns." Although critics often point to this play and to *Luther* (1961), with its twelve scenes and a narrator, as examples of the influence of Bertolt Brecht's (q.v.) epic theater, O.'s plays differ from that mode in their appeal much more to feelings than to reason.

Inadmissible Evidence (1964), perhaps O.'s most accomplished play, has as its hero a loquacious and philandering lawyer, Bill Maitland, who exists for himself only to the extent that he remains an object in the existence of others. The dreamlike opening scene with Maitland on trial for commiting an obscenity, namely, his life, sets in motion a sequence of scenes that show the hero gradually abandoned by family, colleagues, and friends. In turn, these characters exist for the audience only as indicators of Maitland's progressive alienation. In the course of the play he increasingly relates to the outside world by means of the telephone.

The typical O. hero—Jimmy Porter, Archie Rice, Bill Maitland—talks in a language of bitter metaphors appropriate to his respective personal and social world. These protagonists are nostalgic for some golden age that was denied them, and envious of youth. They are incapable of living on a moment-to-moment basis with the people and situations surrounding them. The eponymous heroes of *Epitaph for George Dillon* (1958, with Anthony Creighton) and *Luther* share in comparable dilemmas. In *Luther* the hero and play are dominated by the central metaphor of purgation, which joins personal and theological themes. The hero, who is continually preoccupied with stomach disorders and the need to evacuate his bowels, likewise desires to purge the Church. He differs from other O. heroes in having a positive program. George Dillon, a writer who compromises his dubious standards, anticipates a subsequent writer-hero, Laurie of *The Hotel in Amsterdam* (1968). But Laurie is successful and surrounded by a balanced and mutually adjusted group of three couples. In this play, O. broke out of his prior mold; no longer is one character dominant and the others existing merely in terms of their interactions with his personal universe. And the hero, no longer looking back, now adjusts himself to the present. Yet even a play published in the same year, *Time Present* (1968), in ironic contrast with its title, has as its central character an actress, Pamela, whose values are dominated by those of her father, a famous actor who dies offstage during the course of the drama.

The earlier plays depend on central char-

acters with ambivalent values who await some outside force that will expose them: Archie Rice has his Tax Man, Bill Maitland, his Law Society Board; and Alfred Redl, the central character of *A Patriot for Me* (1965), fears the revelation of his homosexuality. A more dynamic interchange among several characters and a more secure treatment of exposition are developments in O.'s dramaturgy of the late 1960s and 1970s.

During the 1960s O. ventured into screenwriting, often working with the director Tony Richardson, his partner in Woodfall Productions; his screenplay for *Tom Jones* (1963) won an Academy Award. In the 1970s he began writing dramas for television with varying degrees of success.

O.'s place in the history of British drama is secure. His plays introduced a series of new attitudes and relevant themes into a theatrical tradition stagnating under the limitations of a 19th-c. view of the "well-made play." His muscular, aggressive dialogue, alive to the nuances of contemporary feelings and sensitive to the dramatic needs of the play, opened new experiences for audiences. Frequent successful revivals of O.'s major works testify to his success in both challenging and yet appealing to modern sensibilities.

FURTHER WORKS: *The World of Paul Slickey* (1959); *A Subject of Scandal and Concern* (1960); *Plays for England: The Blood of the Bambergs; Under Plain Cover* (1963); *A Bond Honoured* [from Lope de Vega] (1966); *The Right Prospectus* (1968); *Very Like a Whale* (1970); *West of Suez* (1971); *Hedda Gabler* [from Henrik Ibsen] (1972); *A Sense of Detachment* (1972); *The End of Me Old Cigar, and Jill and Jack* (1974); *The Gift of Friendship* (1974); *A Place Calling Itself Rome* [from Shakespeare's *Coriolanus*] (1975); *The Picture of Dorian Gray* [from Oscar Wilde] (1975); *Watch It Come Down* (1976); *You're Not Watching Me, Mummy, and Try a Little Tenderness: Two Plays for Television* (1978)

BIBLIOGRAPHY: Taylor, J. R., *Anger and After* (1964), pp. 37–58; Hayman, R., *J. O.* (1968); Brown, J. R., ed., *Modern British Dramatists* (1968), pp. 47–57, 117–21, and passim; Banham, M., *O.* (1969); Carter, A. V., *J. O.* (1969); Trussler, S., *The Plays of J. O.: An Assessment* (1969); Brown, J. R., *Theatre Language* (1972), pp. 118–57 and passim; Worth, K., *Revolutions in Modern*

English Drama (1972), pp. 67–85; Anderson, M., *Anger and Detachment* (1976), pp. 21–49 and passim

HOWARD B. WOLMAN

OSHAGAN, Hagop

(born Hagop Kiufejian) Armenian novelist, short-story writer, critic, and dramatist, b. 1883, Soelez, Turkey; d. 17 Feb. 1948, Aleppo, Syria

The first modern Armenian critic concerned with combining ethnological studies with literature and linguistics, O. first gained recognition as a writer with his frank, earthy fiction, then earned notoriety for his iconoclastic reviews, debunking contemporary literary idols. Championing a literature of Armenian imagery and content, he urged writers and critics to find spiritual and cultural regeneration through a national literature.

O. was educated at the seminary at Armash, Turkey, where he acquired fluency in French and German. He was fired from his first teaching job in his home village by a puritanical school board after the publication of his short story "Aracheen artsounk" (1902; the first tear). Familiar with the works of Freud (q.v.), O. believed that sexuality was the root of every human impulse. Such sexually explicit writing as his had not been seen before, and has seldom been matched since, in Armenian literature.

The material for the stories in O.'s first collection, *Khonarneruh* (1921; the humble ones), was gathered when he was forced to work as a wandering teacher. Village characters, much like those of Telkadintsi (pseud. of Hovaness Haroutiunian, 1860–1915) and Rouben Zartarian (1874–1915), animate his narratives.

In 1914 in Istanbul O. cofounded the literary magazine *Mehian* with the writers Daniel Varoujan (q.v.), Gosdam Zarian (1885–1969), and Aharon Dadourian (1887–1965). Their work soon became the standard for contemporary Armenian literature. The influence of Nietzsche and Schopenhauer was apparent in their manifesto, which stressed a literature of ideas instead of mere reportage and realistic description, and poetry above ideas: "Art should be concerned with beauty, truth, and the ideal, and the proper themes pursued by the Armenian writer should be national."

O.'s admiration for and the influence of the work of Dostoevsky, Balzac, and Proust (q.v.) is evident in his three-volume roman-fleuve *Menatsortatsuh* (1931–34; those who remained). The three books—*Arkantee jampov* (via the uterus), *Ariunee jampov* (via the blood), and *Tezhokhkee jampov* (via hell)—trace the development of an Armenian town up until the 1915 massacre through the lives of some of its inhabitants, who are either Armenian victims or Turkish murderers. Psychological motivation in character development and a baroque style are the two distinct characteristics of O.'s novels, such as *Dzag bedooguh* (1929; the pot with the hole), *Haji Murad* (1933; Haji Murad), and *Haji Abdullah* (1934; Haji Abdullah). His plays, the best known of which is *Stepanos Siunetsi* (1936; Stepanos of Siunik), were more literary than dramatic successes.

Most of O.'s writing was inaccessible to the general reader because of his convoluted style. Although his work reflects the national ethos, clarity and simplicity are secondary to his lush language and imagery. In his literary criticism, collected in *Hamabadker arevmedahay kraganootian* (10 vols., 1945–82; panorama of western Armenian literature), he claims that his ambition was the "discovery of my nation" and that "literature can free itself of morality but not of its bloodline." His own writing was true to those precepts.

FURTHER WORKS: *Khorhoortneroo mehianuh* (1922); *Erp badanee en* (1925); *Suleiman Effendi* (1936); *Meenchev oor* (1936); *Erkenkee jampov* (1936); *Hye kraganootioon* (1942); *Erp merneel keedenk* (1944); *Spiurkuh ev eerav panasdeghdsootioonuh* (1945); *Vegayootioon muh* (1945)

DIANA DER HOVANESSIAN
MARZBED MARGOSSIAN

OSSETIC LITERATURE

Written literature in Ossetic, an Iranian language spoken by some 430,000 people of the central Caucasus in the Soviet Union, came into being only at the beginning of the 19th c.; the earliest texts were translations of Christian liturgical books. But there is much evidence for the existence of a rich oral poetry in preliterary times, namely, the rich folklore of the present-day Ossets. Particularly important is the cycle of heroic legends about the Narts, superhuman beings who in mythical antiquity inhabited the plains north of the Caucasus. These legends are widespread over the whole of the north Caucasian area, but their Iranian origin is unquestionable.

The first Ossetic poet known by name is Mamsyraty Temyrbolat (1843–1898). His younger contemporary, Khetägkaty Kosta (1859–1906) is, however, usually regarded as the "father" of Ossetic literature and the creator of the literary language. Among writers of this period, Gädiaty Seka (1855–1915) created short stories that portray, with harsh realism, the unrelenting struggle for existence among the people of the Caucasian mountains. For the development of social realism and for Ossetic prose in general these stories have been of great significance. Gädiaty Seka also wrote lyric poetry.

The new cultural currents that came in the wake of tsarist conquests in the 19th c. brought about a profound change in the spiritual life of the Ossets. The break with the centuries-old traditions of tribal society became a frequent theme in the new literature. For the Ossets, as for the other peoples of the Caucasus, the 20th c. has been an era of national and cultural awakening, which is reflected especially in the growth of a varied literary production. Most genres of modern European literature—the novel, the short story, the drama, the essay—have taken root, and foreign literary works have been translated. Among those who began writing at the beginning of the century were Kotsoity Arsen (1872–1944), who as a journalist and short-story writer exerted considerable influence upon the formation of the new literature; and Britiaty Elbyzdyqo (1881–1923), the first dramatist of importance.

The Russian revolution and the policies of the Soviet regime led to great changes in Ossetic literature. The abolishment of illiteracy resulted in a large expansion of the reading public; literature took on an enormously important role in national life. In the biggest towns theaters were built, thereby encouraging original dramatic works. The founding of research institutes, and in recent years of a university, not only was of significance to the scholarly world but also became a major incentive to cultural activities and national consciousness.

In general, Ossetic literature has followed the pattern of that of other Soviet peoples. Themes have been sought in Caucasian situations at the time of the revolution and, later, of the collectivization. World War II made

its special thematic demands. At the same time, traditional oral poetry and episodes from national history have been a vitalizing force, and it is tempting to talk about a national-romantic vein, which has become more vigorous in the last decades. A prominent figure among the pre-World War II writers was Dzanaity Ivan (pseud.: Niger; 1896–1947), who tried his hand at most literary genres and, like most of his colleagues, was actively engaged in promoting education.

The postwar period has seen a steady increase in literary output. Thanks to improved material conditions, the demand for didactic literature has decreased. Lyric poetry is apparently much in vogue; the depiction of personal problems is more freely admitted. Literature has reached a higher degree of formal sophistication. Questions of national and cultural identity and the role of writers in a communist country are intensely debated. The strengthening of national feeling has led to enthusiasm for historical and mythological themes. A representative writer of the postwar period, Dzhusoity Nafi (b. 1925), is a dynamic humanist who, besides being a literary historian, has written both novels and lyric poetry and translated Pushkin and Greek drama into his mother tongue.

The Ossets are a small linguistic community; their language is not widely known, and their books are rarely translated. Literary works are written for a limited public with a somewhat uniform taste. As with other small groups, literature has to face the danger of parochialism and a restricted aesthetic scope. Yet, Ossetic literature has succeeded in meeting the cultural needs of the people and in invigorating their sense of historical continuity and national identity.

FRIDRIK THORDARSON

OSTAIJEN, Paul van

Belgian poet, short-story writer, and essayist (writing in Flemish), b. 22 Feb. 1896, Antwerp; d. 18 March 1928, Miavoye-Anthée

O. never finished his secondary education. While working as a clerk for the city of Antwerp, he began contributing to periodicals. Involvement with local politics forced him to flee abroad, and from 1918 to 1921 he lived in Berlin. On his return to Belgium he managed to eke out a living from his poetry and journalism, before dying of tuberculosis at the age of thirty-two.

O. made his literary debut with *Music-Hall* (1916; title in English), a volume of poems that were written when he was about eighteen. The book was immediately influential because its new vocabulary and rhythms were related to a new theme in Flemish poetry: the metropolis.

O.'s promise was fulfilled in his second volume of poems, *Het sienjaal* (1918; the signal). All the previous qualities, now openly joined by a strong humanist and apostolic credo, were developed into a verbal torrent typical of the heyday of German expressionism (q.v.). Striking individual lines and images blend into a paean to humanity and a newly blossoming earth. An important document in the development of expressionist poetry, the book set the tone for many of O.'s contemporaries.

O. seemed assured of a respectable and successful career, but during his years in Berlin, he essayed to redefine humanitarian expressionism and began writing the kind of poetry for which he is famous. Having experimented with cocaine and witnessed a revolution, he wrote in 1921 the tormented pages of *De feesten van angst en pijn (Feasts of Fear and Agony,* 1976). Not published until 1952, the volume is a haunting farewell to the past, testimony to the turmoil and pain of the present, and a dire prophecy of the future.

Having met and studied the work of kindred spirits of Dadaism (q.v.), O. published *Bezette stad* (1921; occupied city), a bitter and incisive indictment of war. A highly unusual poetic document, it describes the horror and desolation of war, as well as the cowardice of terrified citizens and the cynicism of the "State, Church, and Monarchy Corporation." Typographically, the texts explode from the page—poetic shrapnel of a generation that could no longer be deceived by slogans of any kind.

O.'s social criticism after 1921 was primarily continued in masterly tales he called "grotesques." Acerbic, absurdly reasoned, these satires have lost none of their force. Reminiscent of the writings of Swift and Kafka (q.v.), they present a world out of joint and and a society quite happily unaware of this condition. Some were printed during his lifetime, but most were published in posthumously issued collections that pleased few people.

O.'s poetic adventure continued in a series of texts that have become basic to modern Flemish poetry. He explained his objectives and techniques in a number of essays, and put his basic theory of thematic lyricism and association into practice in a series of masterful poems that were not printed in book form until the posthumously issued *Gedichten* (1928; poems). These profoundly simple and musical poems describe the mystery of the common and the commonplace of the metaphysical. Outstripping conventions and traditions, they reflect O.'s lifelong dilemma: the limitations of expression make it impossible to capture the primordial secret of existence and of nature. Truth lies in the attempt.

O. educated his countrymen to the significant innovations of modern culture in a series of essays that included both literary topics and discussions of the visual arts. He prepared one of the first translations of Kafka and wrote the only known Dadaistic film script, although it was never realized.

In his quest for the pure poem, in his cerebral and vitriolic satires, and in his important essays on the arts and literature, O. showed himself always ahead of the avantgarde. A major contribution to 20th-c. literature, his work reaches far beyond the confines of his native Flemish tongue to assure him a foremost and irrevocable place in the literary vanguard of this century. His poetry and prose are only now being accorded their proper prominence both in Belgium and in the wider context of European literature.

FURTHER WORKS: *De trust der vaderlandsliefde* (1925); *Het bordeel van Ika Loch* (1926); *Vogelvrij* (1928); *Intermezzo* (1929); *Het eerste boek van Schmoll* (1929); *Krities proza* (2 vols., 1929–31); *De bende van de Stronk* (1932); *Diergaarde voor kinderen van nu* (1932); *Self-Defense* (1933); *Verzameld werk* (4 vols., 1952–56). FURTHER VOLUMES IN ENGLISH: *Patriotism Inc., and Other Tales* (1970); *The First Book of Schmoll: Selected Poems 1920–1928* (1982)

BIBLIOGRAPHY: Beekman, E. M., *Homeopathy of the Absurd: The Grotesque in O.'s Creative Prose* (1970); Beekman, E. M., "Blue Skiff of the Soul: The Significance of the Color Blue in P. v. O.'s Poetry," *DutchS,* 1 (1974), 113–17; Hadermann, P., "P. v. O. and *Der Sturm,*" in Bulhof, F., ed., *Nijhoff, v. O., "De Stijl"* (1976), pp. 37–57; Beekman, E. M., "The Universal Hue: P. v. O.'s lyrisme à thème," *Dutch Crossing* (London), No. 13 (1981), 42–80; Beekman, E. M.,

"Dada in Holland," in Paulsen, W., and Hermann, H. G., eds., *Sinn aus Unsinn: Dada International* (1982), pp. 229–47

E. M. BEEKMAN

OSTROVSKY, Nikolay Alexeevich

Russian novelist, b. 16 Sept. 1904, Vilia, Ukraine; d. 22 Dec. 1936, Moscow

Son of a poor worker, before his fifteenth birthday O. was already a member of the Komsomol (Communist Youth League) and, by 1924, a member of the Communist Party. In 1919, during the civil war, without telling his family, he volunteered for the front. A year later he was seriously wounded and partially lost his vision. He continued to take an active part in the work of the Komsomol in his native Ukraine until he was found to be suffering from an incurable form of arthritis, which slowly debilitated him. Bedridden from 1927 until his death, he completely lost his sight in 1928. Thus began his career as a writer.

O.'s literary fame rests upon a single work, the novel *Kak zakalyalas stal* (1935; *The Making of a Hero,* 1937; also tr. as *How the Steel Was Tempered,* 1952), although, with the assistance of other writers and secretaries, he managed to complete the first part of a contemplated trilogy, *Rozhdennye burey* (1936; *Born of the Storm,* 1939). By the process of creating and writing, O. courageously kept up the struggle for life in the face of enormous physical handicaps.

By his own admission, when planning *Kak zakalyalas stal* O. attempted to "couch facts in literary form." His explicit wish was to provide young Soviet people with "memoirs in the form of a story." The main characters of the novel are all based on people the author knew; moreover, Pavel Korchagin, the protagonist, is an autobiographical portrait, "made from my brain and my blood," O. later said to an interviewer. The story unfolds during the decade preceding the October revolution, the civil war, the years of NEP (New Economic Policy), and the first Five-Year Plan, that is, during a stormy revolutionary period. In Pavel Korchagin, O. created a young revolutionary whose character, as the title clearly indicates, is tempered and directed as he begins to live and work for an idea—that of communism. The details of Korchagin's life and struggle closely parallel those of the author's; the novel even ends at the moment the manuscript of the novel Korchagin has written is accepted for publication.

In the Soviet Union, Pavel Korchagin was viewed as a sort of "hero of our time." The novel, which was deliberately promoted by Soviet critics in a literary propaganda campaign, attracted widespread attention. The personality of its author and the physical handicaps he valiantly sought to overcome contributed to making O. a legend in his own lifetime. Although the literary merits of the novel are far from outstanding, the book became a Soviet classic.

FURTHER WORKS: *Sobranie sochineny* (3 vols., 1967–68). FURTHER VOLUME IN ENGLISH: *Hail, Life! Articles, Speeches, Letters* (1955)

BIBLIOGRAPHY: Karavayeva, A., Introduction to *How the Steel Was Tempered* (1952), pp. 5–23; Van der Eng-Liedmeier, A., *Soviet Literary Characters* (1959), pp. 113–16; Alexandrova, V., *A History of Soviet Literature* (1963), pp. 43–44; Struve, G., *Russian Literature under Lenin and Stalin, 1917–1953* (1971), p. 287; Slonim, M., *Soviet Russian Literature: Writers and Problems, 1917–1967* (1973), pp. 181–83

NADJA JERNAKOFF

OTTIERI, Ottiero

Italian novelist, b. 29 March 1924, Rome

O. received a doctoral degree in languages and literature from the University of Rome in 1948, but his main interest was always in psychoanalysis. When he moved to Milan, he sought work that would allow him to put his interest in social psychology to use. After having worked for a few years for a publisher, O. accepted a position in the public and human relations department of the Olivetti company.

A highly autobiographical writer, O. has drawn most of his material from his own experiences. For his early novels he relied extensively on his work at Olivetti. *Tempi stretti* (1957; hard times) initiated the trend called "Literature and Industry," which received wide attention primarily because it was expected to bring linguistic innovations to literature, as well as a new view of alienation and other problems of an industrial society. *Tempi stretti* was acclaimed as an excellent inside view of workers in large factories around Milan. The novel focuses on their daily problems—mechanical, sociopolitical, and personal: on the production line, in commuting, at union meetings, in organizing strikes, and even in their most intimate moments at home.

From diaries he kept for nearly ten years O. drew the material for *Donnarumma all'assalto* (1959; *The Men at the Gate*, 1962), and *La linea gotica* (1963; the gothic line), both dealing with attempts at industrializing southern Italy and with the resulting clashes between the modern, technologically advanced north and the backward, poverty-stricken south. The psychologist's narration is based on O.'s frustrating experience as administrator of psychological and technical-skills tests to job applicants (mostly poor and illiterate) at a factory about to open in a small town near Naples. The author's pungent, ironic criticism is directed both at industry for its ridiculous hiring practices and at the government for not having prepared the south for industrialization. Using characters like Donnarumma, who aggressively demands a job while refusing to fill out an application, and portraying people who cannot cope with an eight-hour workday or with any form of organization, O. demonstrates that workers have to be educated and trained before they can function in modern industry.

With the rather technical *L'irrealtà quotidiana* (1966; everyday unreality) O. began a series of semiconfessional and documentary novels dealing with Jungian (q.v.) therapy, with clinics, and often with his own neuroses, his fears of impotence, and his excessive drinking and smoking. O. has stressed that writing can be a form of self-therapy—see especially *Il campo di concentrazione* (1972; the field of concentration [or concentration camp]).

Whether writing about industrialization or emotional disorder, O. always offers astute analyses of central problems of contemporary society.

FURTHER WORKS: *Memorie dell'incoscienza* (1954); *I venditori a Milano* (1960); *L'impagliatore de sedie* (1964); *I divini mondani* (1968); *Il pensiero perverso* (1971); *Contessa* (1976); *La corda rotta* (1978); *Di chi è la colpa* (1979)

BIBLIOGRAPHY: Rossi, J., on *Tempi stretti*, *BA*, 33 (1959), 334; De Bellis, A. C., on *I divini mondani*, *BA*, 43 (1969), 582; Fantazzi,

C., on *L'irrealtà quotidiana*, *BA*, 41 (1967), 338; Fantazzi, C., on *Contessa*, *WLT*, 51 (1977), 75–76

ROCCO CAPOZZI

ØVERLAND, Arnulf

Norwegian poet, essayist, short-story writer, and dramatist, b. 27 April 1889, Kristiansund; d. 25 March 1968, Oslo

Ø. came from a family of limited means, but he nevertheless finished secondary school, after which he studied literature and philosophy at the University of Oslo. He was particularly influenced by the Swedish writers August Strindberg and Hjalmar Söderberg (qq.v.). The events of World War I led him to become an active member of the Norwegian Communist Party, which he remained until he was disillusioned by the Moscow trials of the 1930s. He early warned of the danger represented by Hitler, and during the Nazi occupation of Norway in World War II, his poems of defiance were widely circulated. As a result, Ø. was arrested and in 1942 sent to the Sachsenhausen concentration camp. After the war Ø. was invited to live at Grotten, a government-supported residence for outstanding artists.

Ø.'s first published collection of Poetry was *Den ensomme fest* (1911; the lonely party). In it, as well as in all his subsequent collections, he deals with such universal themes as life, death, and love. Some of this poetry is extremely introspective; there is often irony directed at self, but also poignant expressions of the bitter loneliness of youth.

In *Brød og vin* (1919; bread and wine) Ø. moved away from his introspection and expressed a deep commitment to social justice. He makes extensive use of biblical motifs but employs them in such a manner that the message of the Norwegian Lutheran State Church appears as only one of several possible readings of the Bible. His aim is to awaken his audience not to the needs of the soul but to the material, emotional, and intellectual needs of human beings in a cruel and unjust world. In *Berget det blå* (1927; blue mountain) he used motifs from legend and folktale in order to achieve a similar effect.

Ø.'s masterwork as a poet is the collection *Hustavler* (1929; rules for living), which represents a synthesis of his early introspection and his later social commitment. The major theme is death, thoughts of which had long been familiar to the author because of his having suffered from pulmonary tuberculosis.

Ø.'s radical political stance, as well as his atheism, had made him unacceptable to large segments of the Norwegian population. World War II changed this public attitude, however, and the poet now became a symbol of patriotism. His war poetry was collected in *Vi overlever alt!* (1945; we will survive anything!) and *Tilbake til livet* (1946; back to life).

Ø. also presented his social and political views in essays and public lectures, and he is one of the foremost essayists in Norwegian literature. His lecture "Kristendommen—den tiende landeplage" (1933; Christianity—the tenth scourge) led to a trial for blasphemy in 1933. He was acquitted, but the so-called blasphemy paragraph in the criminal code was, as a result of the case, strengthened in order that it might cover similar situations in the future.

In the period after World War II Ø. battled with equal energy against a move to unify Norway's two official languages—the more urban *bokmål* and the more rural *nynorsk*—as well as against modernism in poetry. His lecture "Tungetale fra Parnasset" (1953; speaking in tongues heard from Parnassus) precipitated one of the liveliest debates in Norwegian cultural history.

Ø. is less important as a dramatist and short-story writer than as a poet and essayist. His two plays, *Venner* (1917; friends) and *Gi mig ditt hjerte* (1930; give me your heart), suffer from the author's lack of theatrical experience. The many short stories are thematically connected with the rest of his oeuvre and often satirize the same follies Ø. attacked in his essays.

Ø.'s best poetry is among the best in Norwegian literature. This holds true for both some of his poems of social commitment and many of those that deal with universal themes. Above all, Ø. was a man who refused to be silenced and whose words will continue to live.

FURTHER WORKS: *De hundrede violiner* (1912); *Advent* (1915); *Den hårde fred* (1916); *Deilig er jorden* (1923); *Gud planter en have* (1931); *Jeg besværger dig* (1934); *Samlede dikt* (2 vols., 1936); *Noveller i utvalg* (1939); *Er vårt sprog avskaffet?* (1940); *Ord i alvor til det norske folk* (1940); *Det har ringt for annen gang* (1946); *Samlede dikt* (3 vols., 1947); *Norden mellem øst og vest* (1947); *Nøitralitet eller vestblokk* (1948); *Hvor ofte skal vi skifte sprog?* (1948); *Nordiske randstater eller atlantisk fred* (1949); *Bokmålet—et avstumpet landsmål* (1949); *Fiskeren og hans sjel* (1950); *Har jorden plass til oss?* (1952); *I beundring og forargelse* (1954); *Riksmål, landsmål og slagsmål* (1956); *Sverdet bak døren* (1956); *Om Gud skulde bli lei av oss* (1958); *Verset—hvordan blir det til* (1959); *Den rykende tande* (1960); *Jeg gikk i rosengården: Kjærlighetsdikt i utvalg* (1960); *Samlede dikt IV* (1961); *På Nebo bjerg* (1962); *Hvor gammelt er Norge?* (1964); *Møllerupgåsens liv og himmelfart, og andre troverdige beretninger* (1964); *Livets minutter* (1965); *De hundrede fioliner: Dikt i utvalg* (1968)

BIBLIOGRAPHY: Beyer, H., *A History of Norwegian Literature* (1956), pp. 317–18; Boardman, P., "A. Ø.: Patriot, Religious Atheist, Poet Laureate," *Norseman,* No. 3 (1964), 71–74; Beyer, E., "Die norwegische Literatur nach 1900," *SchM,* 45 (1965), 473–83; Anon., "Er war immer unbequem: Zum Tode des norwegischen Dichters A. Ø.," *Ausblick,* 19 (1968), 17–20; Houm, P., "A. Ø.," *ASR,* 61 (1973), 268–72

JAN SJÅVIK

OWEN, Wilfred

English poet, b. 18 March 1893, Oswestry; d. 4 Nov. 1918, Landrécies, France

A true Shropshire lad, O. was born and raised on the Welsh border of rural England. He was a dreamy, sickly, somewhat bookish child, pampered and favored by his intensely devoted, rigidly Calvinist mother. Indeed, he never fully escaped the pull of either his mother's affection or her religion. Growing up to become an excellent amateur botanist, O. would later write that a visit to Broxton by the Hill at the age of ten first confirmed his poetic vocation. He wrote copiously, and his early poems are steeped in the romanticism of Keats and Shelley. After his education at the Birkenhead Institute, Liverpool, and the Technical College, Shrewsbury, he worked as an assistant at Dunsden vicarage (it was here he first suffered a crisis of faith) and spent two years teaching English in France (1913–15).

During World War I O. enlisted in the Artists' Rifles, was commissioned in the Manchester Regiment, and was assigned to the French battlefields. After several months at the front he finally suffered intolerable nervous stress, diagnosed as "neurasthenia," as a result of spending several days in a heavily shelled position staring at the scattered remnants of another officer's body. Sent to the Craiglockhart War Hospital to recover, he soon met the poet Siegfried Sassoon (q.v.), who encouraged him to write about the reality and outrage of war. This new subject matter—and the radical style that it required—liberated O.'s work, and almost all of his major poems were written during an intensely creative period from August 1917 to September 1918. In August 1918 he was sent back to France and, one week before the armistice, he was killed in action.

Before his death O. had begun to put together a small collection of poems, only four of which appeared in print during his lifetime. He also left the first draft of what has become one of the most celebrated literary prefaces in English poetry, published in *The Poems of W. O.* (1931). O.'s preface stated flatly that he was not concerned with "heroes," or with any other generalized abstractions like "glory" or "honor." Rather, as he said, "My subject is War, and the pity of War. The Poetry is in the pity." O. was shocked by the harshness of modern warfare and scandalized by the ironic discrepancy between what soldiers actually endured in the trenches and the English civilian's sentimental ideas about the war. His poems set out to dismantle once and for all any idealized or patriotic stereotypes of war by showing its terrible, brutal, dehumanizing reality. Two central principles predominate in O.'s most characteristic work: anger at the senseless destruction of war, and compassion or pity for the helpless, inarticulate victims that it drives to madness and death. The furious note of protest that prevails in such didactic poems as "Dulce et Decorum Est" (pub. 1920) and "Spring Offensive" (pub. 1920) is only balanced by the elegiac tone of such laments for the dead as "Anthem for Doomed Youth" (pub. 1920) and "Strange Meeting" (pub. 1919). Either directly or indirectly, all of O.'s work testifies to the terrible effects of war on ordinary soldiers.

O.'s characteristic poetic technique was to infuse new life into traditional forms by relying on highly sensuous imagery. His concentrated, almost homoerotic descriptions of exhausted, maimed, and slaughtered male bodies give a palpable immediacy to his poet-

ry. At the same time his consistent use of half rhyme (or pararhyme) creates a sense of discordance, delay, and frustration that is ideally suited to his subject matter. This matching of consonant assonance and vowel dissonance is especially powerful at echoing and conveying one of O.'s principle themes: that the war keeps young men from ever living out or fulfilling their lives. The slaughter and destruction of youth is always his first and final subject.

O.'s reputation has grown slowly but significantly since Edith Sitwell (q.v.) and Siegfried Sassoon first put together a volume of twenty-three poems from his surviving manuscripts, *Poems* (1920). This volume was supplanted by the textually more accurate and expanded 1931 volume, *The Poems of W. O.*, edited, with a "Memoir," by Edmund Blunden (1896–1974). It was this collection that significantly influenced the English political poets of the 1930s: W. H. Auden, Stephen Spender, and C. Day Lewis (qq.v.). O.'s audience was further enlarged when Benjamin Britten set some of the major poems to music in his *War Requiem,* which captures something of the intense anger and enormous sympathy for the suffering of young soldiers that flows through the poetry. O. is unquestionably the most important and central English poet associated with the Great War.

FURTHER WORKS: *The Collected Poems* (1963); *Collected Letters* (1967); *W. O.: War Poems and Others* (1973)

BIBLIOGRAPHY: Welland, D. S. R., *W. O.: A Critical Study* (1960); Owen, H., *Journey from Obscurity* (3 vols., 1963–65); Bergonzi, B., *Heroes' Twilight: A Study of the Literature of the Great War* (1965), pp. 121–35; White, W., *W. O.: A Bibliography* (1967); Silkin, J., *Out of Battle: The Poetry of the Great War* (1972), pp. 197–248; Stallworthy, J., *W. O.: A Biography* (1974); Hibberd, D., *W. O.* (1975)

EDWARD HIRSCH

OYONO, Ferdinand

Cameroonian novelist (writing in French), b. 14 Sept. 1929, N'Goulémakong, near Ebolowa

O.'s mother, a fervent Roman Catholic, left her husband because although professing to be a Catholic he continued to practice polygamy. O. was a choirboy and studied the classics with a priest; when he obtained his primary-school diploma, his father suddenly took pride in his son's education, sending him to the lycée of Ebolowa and urging him to study in France. Before going to France, O. worked for missionaries as a houseboy, a situation that served as the source of inspiration for his first novel, *Une vie de boy* (1956; *Boy!*, 1970). After receiving his diploma from the lycée of Provins near Paris, O. went on to study law and government administration. He has held several government positions.

O.'s three novels are rich in autobiographical material. *Une vie de boy* is the ironic tale of an innocent young African, Toundi, who works as a servant for a white missionary. After the missionary's death, Toundi is transferred to the service of the Commandant Decazy and his wife, a beautiful white woman whom Toundi idolizes, but who treats him with utter contempt. Like Voltaire's Candide, Toundi has an optimistic, easy-going nature and an unspoiled enthusiasm for life. His naïve frankness and sense of trust contrast sharply with the carefully calculated hypocrisy of the other Africans, who, while pretending to be subservient and obedient toward their masters, openly express their disgust and dissatisfaction when in their own private circles. Toundi's gradual awakening to the injustice of his colonial masters is pathetically demonstrated toward the end of the novel, but that awakening occurs too late for Toundi to save his own life.

His sad death is made known to the reader in an epilogue in which O., in his own voice, purports to be offering the reader Toundi's own diary. Since the narrative is presented as a translation into French from the unsophisticated houseboy's native Ewondo, its style is extremely simple and direct. *Une vie de boy* was one of the first novels to challenge openly the European's claim to being superior to the African.

In O.'s second novel, *Le vieux nègre et la médaille* (1956; *The Old Man and the Medal*, 1967), the satire is aimed not only at the whites but also at those blacks who fawn over and cringe before their masters. Meka, the old man of the title, is to be presented with a medal for his service to the administration. As naïve as Toundi, Meka is equally comical in his desire to impress his white superiors. His realization that he has been exploited also occurs late in the novel. Following the award ceremony, when Meka accidentally wanders into the white section of town, he finds himself suddenly imprisoned as a prowler and begins to rebel. He recognizes the meaninglessness of the sacrifices of his land to the Church mission and of his two sons, who died fighting in the French army. In the end Meka rejects European civilization and Christianity as he seeks to regain his original African identity.

O.'s third novel, *Chemin d'Europe* (1960; road to Europe) is his most ambitious. The subject is the many problems and frustrations a young native encounters when he seeks permission from the colonial authorities to study in Europe. *Chemin d'Europe* marks a departure from O.'s first two novels because it is sophisticated in tone and broader in scope. The protagonist, Aki Barnabas, is disillusioned and cynical from the start. He bitterly resents both Europeans who try to impose their culture upon Africans and those Africans who refuse to admit the need for change. Although skillfully written, this novel lacks the warmth, freshness, and humor of O.'s first two works.

O., committed to exposing the evils of colonialism, encouraged Africans to regain their native values. By blending humor with pathos, he awakens the reader to the oppression endured by blacks in the French African colonies just before those colonies gained their independence.

FURTHER WORK: *Le pandémonium* (c. 1971, unpublished)

BIBLIOGRAPHY: Diop, D., on *Une vie de boy* and *Le vieux nègre et la médaille*, PA, 11 (1956), 125–27; Moore, G., "F. O. and the Colonial Tragicomedy," *PA*, 18, 2 (1963), 61–73; Mercier, R., and Battestini, M. and S., *F. O.* (1964); Brench, A. C., *The Novelists' Inheritance in French Africa* (1967), pp. 47–63; Makward, E., Introduction to *Boy!* (1970), pp. v–xvi; Linneman, R., "The Anticolonialism of F. O.," YFS, 53 (1976), 64–77; Storzer, G. H., "Narrative Techniques and Social Realities in F. O.'s *Une vie de boy* and *Le vieux nègre et la médaille*," Crit, 19, 3 (1978), 89–101

DEBRA POPKIN

OZ, Amos

Israeli short-story writer, novelist, and essayist, b. 4 May 1939, Jerusalem

From a family of scholars and teachers, O. was educated at the Hebrew University, Jerusalem. At the age of fifteen he left home to settle at the Kibbutz Chulda, where to this day he divides his time between writing, farming, and teaching. After serving with a tank unit in the Six-Day War (1967) and the Yom Kippur War (1973), he published many articles and essays on the Arab-Israeli conflict, campaigning for a compromise based on mutual recognition and a Palestinian homeland in the West Bank and Gaza.

O.'s first collection of short stories, *Artsot hatan* (1965; *Where the Jackals Howl, and Other Stories,* 1981), was followed by a novel about loneliness on the kibbutz, *Makom acher* (1966; *Elsewhere Perhaps,* 1973), and his most widely known novel, *Michael sheli* (1968; *My Michael,* 1972), a tragic, loveless love story set in Jerusalem. His most demanding and controversial works—*Ad mavet* (1971; *Unto Death: Crusade and Late Love,* 1975), consisting of two novellas, and *Lagaat bamayim lagaat baruach* (1973; *Touch the Water, Touch the Wind,* 1974)—mark a turn from realistic style and subject matter toward surrealistic, archetypal studies of the deeper roots of Israeli loneliness, violence, and yearning for death. In the three novellas making up *Har haetsah haraah* (1976; *The Hill of Evil Counsel,* 1978) O. returns to a realistic mode but probes still more deeply into the Jewish soul, mentally in exile although physically at home. *Sumchi* (1978; Sumchi) is a child's tale of lonely adventure and love, and *Beor hatchelet haazah* (1979; under the blazing light) a collection of literary, ideological, and political essays. O.'s works have been translated into eighteen languages.

Unlike many Jewish writers—who portray the modern Jew as an uprooted stranger or prodigal son who, by repudiating his heritage, has turned into a self-centered materialist and his life into a wasteland devoid of dream, myth, and value—O. believes that the sabra's wanderlust, estrangement, and cynical ennui derive precisely from the mythic aura of Israel, the haunting presence of visionary forefathers, and the hovering shadow of their messianic dreams. The Earth Mother, under whose aegis Zionist fathers hoped to begin anew and heal the diseased spirituality of exilic Judaism, is portrayed as worshiped with the same sacrificial zeal as the forsaken Heavenly Father had been earlier. The ironic smile O.'s idealistic heroes wear is the scornful sneer of the apocalyptic redeemer poisoned by an exalted ideal he cannot re-

nounce, disillusioned with the sun-washed cities and cultivated fields of his homeland because of his yearning for a home somewhere over the rainbow. Tied to an age-old dream whose modest realization he disdains, O.'s sabra remains, like his forefathers in the Diaspora, divorced from earthly reality and relations.

In *Artsot hatan, Makom acher,* and *Michael sheli* O. dramatizes the ironic tragedy of real human estrangement—husbands from wives, parents from children, individuals from social bonds—arising from obsessive playing of archetypal roles, such as the Wandering Jew, dictated by a collective heritage from which Israelis believe themselves liberated. In *Ad mavet* and *Lagaat bamayim lagaat baruach* O. suggests, with none too subtle symbolic allusions, that his alienated protagonists are acting out in modern dress the role of crucifying and crucified saviors in a crusade against the world, the flesh, and the devil, a situation all the more ironic and tragic for being incarnate in men whose fathers yearned to touch the earth. In *Har haetsah haraah* O. suggests that to heal these "dream-crucified" children, Judaism must realize that there is no grace but the tender touch of a woman's hand, no redeemed life but the brief, finite, imperfect present, and no rest from lonely wandering save in the real embrace of real wives, parents, friends. Instead of the old dreams of redemption, O. calls for the little wonders achieved here and now by people committed to simple, everyday realities.

FURTHER WORK: *Mnuchah nchonah* (1982)

BIBLIOGRAPHY: Kazin, A., on *Touch the Water, Touch the Wind,* SatR/World, 2 Nov. 1974, 38; McElroy, J., on *Unto Death: Crusade and Late Love,* NYTBR, 26 Oct. 1975, 4; Porat, Z., "The Golem from Zion: Exile and Redemption in A. O.'s Legends of Israel," *Ariel* (Jerusalem), No. 47 (1978), 71–79; Bayley, J., on *The Hill of Evil Counsel,* NYRB, 20 July 1978, 35; Yudkin, L. I., "The Jackal and the Other Place: The Stories of A. O.," JSS, 23 (1978), 330–42; Vardi, D., "On A. O.: *Under the Blazing Light,*" MHL, 5, 4 (1979), 37–40; Mojtabi, A. G., on *Where the Jackals Howl, NYTBR,* 26 April 1981, 3

ZEPHYRA PORAT

JOHN OSBORNE

KOSTIS PALAMAS

PIER PAOLO PASOLINI

BORIS PASTERNAK

PA CHIN

(pseud. of Li Fei-kan) Chinese novelist, b. 25 Nov. 1904, Chengtu

One of the most popular writers of 20th-c. China, P. C. experienced the social turmoil that accompanied the birth of modern China and produced a generation of youth committed to revolution. Despite his upper-class family background he was a self-professed anarchist and found political inspiration in the writings of Pyotr Kropotkin (1842–1921) and of Emma Goldman (1869–1940), with whom he corresponded. His literary influences came from Russian fiction (he later translated works by Gorky [q.v.], Turgenev, and Tolstoy). After returning from France, where he lived from 1927 to 1929, he turned to social and political novels, which he produced prolifically during the 1930s and 1940s. After the Communist victory in 1949 he remained on the mainland; he was made a vice-chairman of the National Committee of the All China Federation of Literary and Art Circles and was given other assignments by the government. He was, however, persecuted during the Cultural Revolution in the late 1960s. Since his recent rehabilitation he has been twice nominated for the Nobel Prize in literature, and in 1981 was elected acting chairman of the Chinese Writers' Association. He was awarded the Dante International Prize by the Italian government in 1982.

P. C.'s first novel, *Mieh-wang* (1929; destruction), is noted more for its social message than for its literary excellence. The main character, Tu Ta-hsin ("Tu Big Heart"), hates the existing government so much that he plots its overthrow. Eventually he commits suicide after failing to assassinate a gar-

rison commander. *Hsin sheng* (1931; new life), another political novel about revolution, is distinguished by its portrayal of a Chinese "dangling man," Li Leng. A masochistic sufferer, despairing and alienated, Li finally finds himself in the anarchists' cause and dies for it.

P. C.'s most acclaimed work is the *Chi-liu* (turbulent stream) trilogy, comprising *Chia* (1931; *The Family,* 1958), *Ch'un* (1937; spring), and *Ch'iu* (1939; autumn). It traces the fortunes of the Kao family during the early 20th c., when old and new values clashed, and it treats comprehensively such related themes as frustrated young love, the low status of women, concubinage, enmity between parents and children, and harsh treatment of the young. Of the three novels in the trilogy, *Chia* is the most widely known and is considered one of his finest works. All three, however, were extremely popular with the readers of the 1930s and 1940s, who easily identified with the characters.

During the Sino-Japanese War (1937–45) P. C. at first supported the war effort by writing about the activities of patriots in the trilogy *Huo* (1938–43; fire). Despite the lack of exciting battles or moving love scenes, the trilogy is memorable for P. C.'s concentration on the emotions of patriotic men and women whose idealism and fiery zeal are symbolized by the title itself.

P. C.'s loss of enthusiasm for the war can be seen in *Hsiao-jen, hsiao-shih* (1947; little people, little events), a collection of short stories written during the war in which he stripped the war of its glamour and described the "little people" exactly as they were. His pessimism about China grew as the war dragged on and was further reflected in *Ti-ssu ping-shih* (1945; ward number four), a novelette about the inhumane conditions in a substandard hospital in the interior.

P. C.'s harshest attack on the war and the Nationalist government, however, was in *Han yeh* (1947; *Cold Nights,* 1978), regarded, along with *Chia,* as one of his two masterpieces. Set in Chungking at the end of World War II, *Han yeh* portrays the strained and deteriorating relationships among a mother, a son, and a daughter-in-law, against a background of the social weariness and ennui that pervaded China in the 1940s. In addition to the realistic presentation of the grim realities in wartime Chungking, *Han yeh* is notable in its exploration of human motives and behavior.

Because of the Communist Party's rigid control of literature, P. C. wrote little after 1949. His visits to Korea in the early 1950s, however, led to his writing about the Chinese who fought there in *Ying-hsiung ti ku-shih* (1954; *Living Among Heroes,* 1954). Adopting a cautious attitude toward the government, he revised many of his pre-1949 works, excising references to anarchism and changing some endings.

During the height of the Cultural Revolution in the late 1960s P. C. was silenced. When he resumed writing in the late 1970s he produced more than sixty essays on a variety of topics and translated two volumes of Alexandr Herzen's (1812–1870) memoirs. Most recently he has been working on a novel about an elderly intellectual couple during the Cultural Revolution.

In his heyday P. C. was regarded as a counselor to the young. He probed the dynamics of social institutions during a time of radical change, and through the medium of fiction he eloquently communicated his vision of China's character. With the passing of time, many of the issues he wrestled with will lose their immediacy, and his works will be judged more on purely aesthetic grounds—and found to be of high artistic quality.

FURTHER WORKS: *Ssu-ch'ü-ti t'ai-yang* (1930); *Ai-ch'ing-ti san-pu-ch'u* (3 vols., 1931–33); *Hai ti meng* (1932); *Li-na* (1934); *Ch'i yüan* (1945); *P. C. wen-chi* (14 vols., 1959–62)

BIBLIOGRAPHY: Chen, T., "P. C. the Novelist," *Chinese Literature,* No. 6 (1963), 84–92; Lang, O., *P. C. and His Writings* (1967); Hsia, C. T., *A History of Modern Chinese Fiction* (1971), pp. 237–56, 375–88; Mao, N. K., "P. C.'s Journey in Sentiment: From Hope to Despair," *JCLTA,* 11 (1976), 131–37; Mao, N. K., *P. C.* (1978)

NATHAN K. MAO
WINSTON YANG

PACIFIC ISLANDS LITERATURES

The Pacific Islands consist of about eighteen large islands and numberless smaller ones spread over an ocean area of about eight million square miles. They were colonized beginning in the mid-18th c. by waves of Dutch,

French, and English traders. Today the three large island-complexes—Fiji, Western Samoa, and Papua New Guinea—have political, economic, and cultural ties with England, the U.S., and Australia respectively.

Although the islands have an oral literature dating back a thousand years, they did not have a written literature until recently. In the last twenty years there has emerged a growing body of "South Pacific" literature from Fiji, Western Samoa, and Papua New Guinea that has been generated by an indigenous cultural renascence and supported by centers of learning such as the University of the South Pacific in Suva, Fiji, the Institute of Papua New Guinea Studies, and the South Pacific Creative Arts Society, which publishes *Mana,* the journal that introduced contemporary Pacific literature.

Fiji. Indo-Fijians were the first to produce written literature in the islands. Sixty thousand indentured laborers from India were brought to the sugar plantations of Fiji between 1879 and 1916. The second wave of immigrants were mainly educated middle-class people, and they drew upon India's heritage of thirty centuries of written literature to start a literature in Fiji. Totaram Sanadhya (dates n.a.), author of *Fiji dwip men mere ikkis varsh* (1919; my twenty-one years in the Fiji Islands), Pandit Amichand Sharma (dates n.a.), Kamla Prasad (dates n.a.), and Pandit Pratap Chandra Sharma (dates n.a.) wrote in Hindi and were published in India. Their writings describe and comment on their experiences; Sharma's *Pravas bhajanamjali* (1947; a foreign offering of verse) shows that an Indo-Fijian dialect had evolved; the volume is mainly a panegyric of India, however, and does not explore the meaning of the indenture or expatriate experience. Indeed, we have very few firsthand accounts of the *girmit* (distorted pronunciation of "agreement," i.e., the indenture contract) experience; *Turn North-East at the Tombstone* (1970) by Walter Gill (dates n.a.), an Australian who worked as an overseer, is one of the few books that reconstruct the indenture period.

Through the 1950s and 1960s, English became progressively more important as the literary medium of Fiji, and the 1970s saw the emergence of accomplished writers such as Satendra Nandan (b. 1939), Raymond C. Pillai (b. 1942), and Subramani (b. 1943) among Indo-Fijians, and Pio Manoa (b. 1940)

among Fijians. Vijay C. Mishra's (b. 1945) critical essays give a penetrating and cogent analysis of the ethos of Indo-Fijians.

Western Samoa. Whereas much of Indo-Fijian literature reflects the psychological interaction between the present and an idealized Indian past that Mishra calls a "sophisticated construct, false, but necessary," Western Samoan writers deal with the cultural interaction between the old and new dispensations, the ambivalence and triangular relationships between the white, native, and mixed components of the island's and islander's identity. Albert Wendt (b. 1939) put Western Samoa on the literary map in the 1960s with his short stories and poems. His first full-length publication was a novel, *Sons for the Return Home* (1973); this was followed by a short-story collection, *Flying Fox in a Freedom Tree* (1974); *Inside Us the Dead* (1976), a volume of poems; and the novels *Pouliuli* (1977) and *Leaves of the Banyan Tree* (1979); he has also edited an anthology of Pacific poetry, *Lali* (1980). *Sons for the Return Home* deals explicitly with the theme of the clash between old and new, but in having his nameless hero shake off all commitment to family and country at the end of the novel, Wendt is perhaps going beyond cultural and cross-cultural externals into a universal, personal dilemma. We see the same pattern in *Leaves of the Banyan Tree,* which has all the same tensions as *Sons for the Return Home,* but as the critic Chris Tiffin says, "overriding all these is the question of self-esteem," that is, the personal (and universal) problem of how to live with oneself.

Papua New Guinea. Although Papua New Guinea has its own growing core of fiction and poetry in English, its noteworthy feature lies in the creative use of native languages and in translations of folklore and chants. The German scholar Ulli Beier's (b. 1922) contribution in the latter field has been significant. In the last decade, Beier has edited several volumes of literary work, including *The Night Warrior, and Other Stories* (1972) and *Voices of Independence: New Black Writing from New Guinea* (1980).

The connections, and frictions, between the oral native traditions and the written Western tradition characterize both the form and content of contemporary Papua New Guinea literature. As in several other emerging nations, literature is often more preoccupied with political and sociological problems than with personal and psychological ones. Writers who were once expressing the hopes and ideologies of a nation fighting for independence are now expressing people's disillusionment with their politically independent but bureaucracy-enslaved country.

Several now-expatriate writers of Anglo-Saxon stock, including Edward Lindall (dates n.a.), Maslyn Williams (dates n.a.), and Margaret Reeson (dates n.a.), have written well about New Guinea. Among emerging native writers are the novelists Vincent Eri (b. 1936), author of *The Crocodile* (1970), and Albert Maori Kiki (b. 1931), who wrote *Ten Thousand Years in a Lifetime* (1968); and the poets Pokwari Kale (dates n.a.), John Kasaipwalova (b. 1949), who gained international recognition in 1972 with his long poem *Reluctant Flame,* and Kumalau Tawali (b. 1946). Russell Soaba (dates n.a.) is a versatile new writer who began as a poet with a Westernized voice and went on to become a short-story writer. Among his better-known stories are "A Portrait of the Odd Man Out" (1971), "A Glimpse of the Abyss" (1972), "The Victims" (1972), "The Villager's Request" (1974), and "Ijaya" (1977); in his play *Scattered by the Wind* (1972) he utilized the native oral tradition.

Some of the best contemporary works have appeared in the journals *Kovave* (1969–75), *New Guinea Writing* (1970–71), *Papua New Guinea Writing* (1970–78), and *Bikmans* (1980 ff.)

Two writers who belong to New Zealand literature but should be mentioned here because they bear a kinship to those of the other islands are the Maoris Witi Ihimaera (b. 1944) and Hone Tuwhare (b. 1922). Their work shows a degree of excellence that surpasses all others mentioned above.

BIBLIOGRAPHY: Arvidson, K. O., "The Emergence of Polynesian Literature," *WLWE,* 14 (1975), 91–115; Krauth, N., "Contemporary Literature from the South Pacific," *WLWE,* 17 (1978), 604–45; McDowell, R. E., and McDowell, J. H., eds., *Asian Pacific Literatures in English: Bibliographies* (1978); Tiffin, C., ed., *South Pacific Images* (1978); Mishra, V. C., ed., *Rama's Banishment: A Centenary Tribute to the Fiji Indians* (1979); Beier, U., ed., Introduction to *Voices of Independence: New Black Writ-*

ing from Papua New Guinea (1980), pp. i–xvi; Subramani, ed., *The Indo-Fijian Experience* (1980); Nandan, S., "Beginnings of a Literary Culture in Fiji: The Role of Language, Commonwealth Literature and the Writer," *Chimo* (Quebec), 2 (1980), 36–50

UMA PARAMESWARAN

PAGNOL, Marcel
French dramatist and filmmaker, b. 28 Feb. 1895, Aubagne; d. 18 April 1974, Paris

P. studied at the University of Aix-en-Provence, where in 1913 he helped found a student literary magazine, *Fantasio*. Later, as *Les cahiers du sud,* it was to become one of the most influential literary magazines of the century. From 1915 to 1927 P. taught English at various secondary schools; from then on he devoted himself wholly to writing plays, making films, and editing *Cahiers du cinéma*. In 1946 he became the first filmmaker to be elected to the French Academy.

Topaze (perf. 1928, pub. 1931; *Topaze,* 1958) was P.'s first great success. In this play he traces the metamorphosis of an obscure schoolteacher into a wily businessman. The principal themes are the lies of politicians, the venality of newspapers, the moral decline of an era in which money has become the key to success.

P.'s name is especially associated with a trilogy: the stage plays *Marius* (perf. 1929, pub. 1931; Marius) and *Fanny* (perf. 1931, pub. 1932; Fanny), also made into films; and the third, written directly for the screen, *César* (1936, pub. 1937; César). The setting of this cycle is the Vieux Port (old port) of Marseille; P. skillfully portrays its noisy, indolent life under the strong sunlight. He writes with affection about the people of Provence, their tenderness and their bravado, their dreams and their fears. The ebullient dialogue of *Marius* and *Fanny* in particular illustrates the temperament typical of the south of France—a sentimentality that easily becomes moralistic. (An American musical adaptation of the entire cycle was produced as *Fanny* in 1955.)

In his autobiography, *Souvenirs d'enfance* (4 vols., 1957–77; memories of childhood), P. describes with simplicity and charm his early years in Marseille and in the hills above the city. The first volume, *La gloire de mon père* (1957; *My Father's Glory*) is in praise of P.'s father, who was a schoolteacher. In the second volume, *Le château de ma mère* (1959; *My Mother's Castle*)—this and the first volume were published together in English as *The Days Were Too Short* (1960)—and in the third volume, *Le temps des secrets* (1960; *The Time of Secrets,* 1962), P. writes about his school years and summer vacations. The final volume, *Le temps des amours* (1977; the time of loves), incomplete and published posthumously, deals with P.'s adolescent loves.

P. will probably be better remembered as a filmmaker than as a playwright. His first two films, *Marius* (1931) and *Fanny* (1932), were actually directed by Alexander Korda and Marc Allégret respectively, but P. himself, as writer and producer, took such an active part in the coaching of the actors that subsequently he took over the full responsibility of directing *Topaze* (1932) and *César* (1936).

Besides the successful direction of movies based on his own plays, P.'s outstanding achievements are films based on texts by two other Provence writers. From Jean Giono's (q.v.) novels P. made three films: *Angèle* (1934; Angèle), after *Un de Baumugnes*; *Regain* (1937; harvest); and *La femme du boulanger* (1938; the baker's wife). From Alphonse Daudet's (1840–1897) *Lettres de mon moulin* (letters from my windmill), P. chose three episodes for a film (1954), the screenplay of which was published in *Trois lettres de mon moulin* (1954; three letters from my windmill).

The aesthetics of P.'s films is similar to that of his plays. In both genres he is primarily concerned with a poetic or picturesque interpretation of what is real, and not with dramatic or cinematic experimentation. In both media he uses the natural settings of the city, the harbor, and the countryside as a background for the garrulous southerner, successfully conveying this character's petulance, gaiety, and optimism.

FURTHER WORKS: *Catulle* (1922); *Tonton* (1924); *Les marchands de gloire* (1924); *Ulysse chez les Phéniciens* (1925); *Un direct au cœur* (1926); *Jazz* (1926); *Pirouettes* (1932); *Merlusse* (1935); *Cigalon* (1936); *Le Schpountz* (1938); *Le premier amour* (1946); *Notes sur le rire* (1947); *Critique des critiques* (1949); *Manon des sources* (1953); *Œuvres dramatiques* (2 vols., 1954); *Judas* (1955); *Fabien* (1956); *L'eau des collines* (2 vols., 1963); *Le masque de fer* (1964); *Œuvres complètes* (6 vols., 1964–73); *Le secret du masque de fer* (1973)

BIBLIOGRAPHY: Combaluzier, I., *Le jardin de P.* (1937); special P. issue, *Biblio,* 32, 3 (1964); Beylie, C., *M. P.* (1974); Berni, G., *M. P., enfant d'Aubagne et de la Treille* (1975); Caldicott, C. E. J., *M. P.* (1977); Castans, R., *Il était une fois M. P.* (1978)

CHARLES G. HILL

PAK Tu-jin

South Korean poet, essayist, and critic, b. 10 March 1916, Ansŏng

After graduating from a local high school, P. worked as a company employee. He made his literary debut in 1939 with a group of nature poems. Between 1941 and 1945, in response to Japanese repression and the prohibition of the use of the Korean language, he refused to write anything. In 1949 P. published his first poetry collection, *Hae* (the sun). In addition to eleven volumes of poetry, he has written essays and literary criticism, including interpretations of his own poems. P. is currently a professor of Korean literature at Yonsei University in Seoul. He is also an accomplished calligrapher. His many awards include the Free Literature Prize (1956), the Culture Prize of the City of Seoul (1962), the March First Literature Prize (1970), and the Korean Academy of Arts Prize (1976).

P. is credited with having imparted a new direction to modern Korean poetry through skillful use of such elemental images as mountains, rivers, stars, the sun, the sea, and the sky. He inspires hope for a new life, a prelapsarian cosmos of perfect harmony. During the Japanese occupation (1910–45), such a world symbolized not only moral perfection of men but also independence and freedom for Korea and the Koreans. But to P., nature has always been "the source of God's love, light, truth, goodness, and beauty," and his paeans to the beauty of the created world and his Blakean innocence became imbued with a moral vision as he came to view the world in terms of moral conflict. As political corruption and repression increased in South Korea, P.'s moral consciousness came to the fore, and his poems from the mid-1960s on are imbued with

a strong historical and cultural consciousness that bears testimony to contemporary reality.

P. is capable of a wide range of moods—angry accusation, fierce honesty, visionary serenity—and his language and style impart a distinctive tone to his Christian and nationalistic sentiments. Sonoric intricacies and incantatory rhythms, achieved by sporadic repetition of key words, are the hallmark of P.'s poetry. Of late, he has withdrawn into nature to perceive its creative power in water-washed stones, the topic of some two hundred of his poems. An authentic inheritor of the East Asian eremitic tradition, P. has consistently rejected the false allegiances demanded by a corrupt society.

FURTHER WORKS: *Ch'ŏngnok chip* (1946, with Pak Mogwŏl and Cho Chihun); *Odo* (1953); *P. T. sisŏn* (1956); *Ingan millim* (1963); *Kosan singmul* (1973); *Sado haengjŏn* (1973); *Susŏk yŏlchŏn* (1973); *Sok susŏk yŏlchŏn* (1976). FURTHER VOLUME IN ENGLISH: *Sea of Tomorrow: Forty Poems of P. T.* (1971)

BIBLIOGRAPHY: Lee, P. H., ed., *The Silence of Love: Twentieth Century Korean Poetry* (1980), p. xviii–xix, 136

PETER H. LEE

PAKISTANI LITERATURE

The demand of the Muslim League, led by Muhammad Ali Jinnah (1876–1948), for a homeland for South Asian Muslims, led to the partition of British India into India and the Islamic nation of Pakistan in 1947. Although the ideological basis for the existence of Pakistan as a state distinct from India was Islam, Islam alone did not prove sufficient to hold the two wings of Pakistan together, and East Pakistan seceded in 1971 to become the separate nation of Bangladesh. The area that now forms Pakistan has a wide variety of languages and literatures, including English, the classical languages of Arabic and Persian, the official language Urdu, the regional languages Sindhi, Punjabi, Balochi, and Pashto, and more localized languages like Brahui, Shina, Balti, and others. The most developed literature is that written in the national language, Urdu.

Although Urdu is not indigenous to the area that is now Pakistan, and is the mother tongue of only about eight percent of the population, most of them refugees from India at the time of partition and later, it is widely used as a second language and is the major language of literacy. Because each of the major languages of Pakistan is also found in neighboring countries, it is difficult to define what is specifically Pakistani about Pakistani culture and literature.

Since the creation of Pakistan in 1947, writers have been concerned with the question of Pakistani national identity and "Pakistani literature." Some, like the critic Vazir Agha (b. 1922), seek the identity of Pakistan and Pakistani literature in a synthesis of the material element of local cultures—including ancient pre-Islamic cultures—and the spiritual element of Islam. Other critics, like Jameel Jalebi (dates n.a.), go beyond the geographical limits of present-day Pakistan and see Pakistani culture as a continuation of the specifically Muslim culture that developed in the south-Asian subcontinent over the last thousand years. Some agree with Muhammad Hasan Askari (?–1974) that "Pakistani literature" should be "Islamic literature"; almost all agree that it should not be Westernized.

In English

English retains its prestige as a language of government, politics, science, and industry, but it is seldom used for creative writing. Among the very few authors now writing in English are the novelist Zulfikar Ghose (b. 1935), who lives in Texas, the poetess Maki Kureishy (dates n.a.), and the poets Kaleem Omar (dates n.a.) and Taufiq Rafat (dates n.a.). Rafat is noted for his use of themes derived from Pakistani culture, such as the Muslim rite of circumcision and the bride's departure from her parental home. The two novels of Ahmad Ali (b. 1910), *Twilight in Delhi* (1940) and *Ocean of Night* (1964), both set in British India before partition, have been widely acclaimed. *Twilight in Delhi* depicts the decline of the traditional Muslim culture of old Delhi and the growth of the nationalist movement; *Ocean of Night* describes the life of a courtesan in Lucknow. In comparison with his English works, Ahmad Ali's stories written in Urdu are more innovative in both subject and technique.

In Urdu

In the late 19th c. the poet Khwaja Altaf Husain Hali (1837–1914) protested against the cultivation of artificial diction, fixed and stereotyped themes, and borrowed imagery in classical Urdu. He felt that poetry should be natural, and should be used as a tool for reform. Among both Hindus and Muslims British influence had resulted first in an admiration for Western culture and a desire to emulate it in reforming their own cultures, and then in a reaction against the materialism of the West. Hali's revivalism coincided with the growing pan-Islamism of the Afghan Jamal al-din al-Afghani (1839–1897), who sought to unite all Islamic countries against their common enemy, the West.

Urdu prose developed during the 19th c. with the publication of a number of popular novels. Mirza Ruswa (1858–1931) is best known for his novel *Umrao Jan Ada* (1899; Umrao Jan Ada), the tale of a courtesan of Lucknow that is unusual for its considerable psychological realism.

Pan-Islamism continued in the works of Sir Muhammad Iqbal (q.v.), who, however, wrote most of his poetry in Persian rather than Urdu in order to reach the Muslim audience outside of south Asia. Influenced by Henri Bergson (q.v.) and Nietzsche, Iqbal preached action rather than inertia, and self-consciousness rather than the denial of self characteristic of Islamic mysticism.

The emphasis on reform became less religious and more social in nature in the Progressive Writers' Movement, which affected all the languages of south Asia and is still an important influence in the regional languages of Pakistan. The Progressives' ideals of social uplift and nationalism are found particularly in the novels and short stories of Premchand (q.v.). The first direct expression of Progressivism, however, was *Angare* (1932; live coals), a collection of ten stories by four writers, which was widely condemned for its criticism of Islam and its relatively open discussion of sex. It also experimented in form. Stream-of-consciousness (q.v.) technique was used in short stories by Ahmad Ali and Sajjad Zaheer (1905–1973). Its effect was not to reveal the psychology of their characters but to allow the characters to express their resentment of the oppression of women and of the evils resulting from an unequal distribution of wealth. The Progressives' goals were initially broadly defined and its membership included a wide variety of writers, but under the leadership of Sajjad Zaheer the movement gradually became more dogmatic. Authors were expected to write according to the dictates of Soviet Socialist Realism (q.v.), and those who did not conform were ostracized and their works censored. By the early 1950s the Progressive Movement had ceased to be an effective literary force.

The two most famous Progressive authors in Pakistan are Ahmad Nadim Qasmi (b. 1916), who writes both poetry and short stories, and the poet Faiz Ahmad Faiz (q.v.), winner of the Lenin Prize in 1962. Qasmi writes sociological stories based on village life in the Punjab. Faiz, the most popular poet in Pakistan, uses both free verse and the more traditional poetic forms. Like Iqbal, whom he admires, he reinterprets the imagery of classical Urdu poetry to express his message: the beloved of the *ghazal* becomes the longed-for new social order, the people, the country, or life itself.

In April 1939 a group of writers met at the home of Sayyid Nasir Ahmad Shah (dates n.a.) in Lahore to form the "Meeting of Story Writers." When poets also began to attend the weekly meetings, its name was changed to the "Assembly of the Men of Good Taste." Its purpose was to provide a forum for writers of every ideological bent. The poet Miraji (1913–1950) joined in 1940 and became its guiding spirit.

The first person to use free verse in Urdu was Tasaduq Hussain Khalid (b. 1900) who was inspired by Ezra Pound, D. H. Lawrence (qq.v.), and others while he was studying law in England. Free verse was developed and popularized first by Miraji, and later by N. M. Rashed (1910–1975). Miraji was one of the first to use his own symbolism rather than the traditional symbolism derived from Persian. N. M. Rashed's free-verse poems protest alien rule, religious dogmatism, and the breakdown of values.

Several important novels, including *Aisi bulandi, aisi pasti* (1948; *The Shore and the Wave,* 1971), about the upper classes of Hyderabad, were published in the 1940s by Aziz Ahmad (b. 1914), who is also a scholar and a leading authority on Islamic culture in Pakistan and India. In the 1950s the most notable fiction writers in Urdu were Qurrutulain Hyder (b. 1927) and Saadat Hasan Manto (1912–1955). Hyder's stories and novels are considered precursors of the modernist movement in their experiments with the stream-of-consciousness technique and in their subjective depiction of the loneliness and rootlessness of the individual cut off from his or her cultural moorings. Although

she has now returned to India and lives in Bombay, her novel *Ag ka darya* (1959; river of fire) was written while she was living in Karachi. Considered by many to be the best novel in Urdu, it is structurally unified by four main characters who all appear—seemingly reborn—in four historical periods encompassing 2,500 years of south Asian history. The characters identify themselves with the composite culture of India, including Hindu and Buddhist elements; thus the need for Pakistan's existence as a separate Islamic state is called into question.

Although Sadat Hasan Manto is best known for his depiction of tender-hearted prostitutes, he also wrote stories sympathetic to the oppressed members of society in general. The impassioned self-righteousness of his early political stories later gave way to a pessimistic and disillusioned view of political activity, which was described with bitter irony.

In the late 1950s and early 1960s both poets and fiction writers began to use highly metaphorical and symbolic language. This trend toward ambiguous and indirect statement may have been influenced by the declaration of martial law in 1958 and by the subsequent press censorship. In both prose and poetry, form was characterized by innovation, and subject by alienation, disillusionment, and a search for self-identity that was often combined with a questioning of national identity and purpose. The use of free verse popularized by Miraji continued, and the prose poem developed. The poet and theorist Iftikhar Jaleb (b. 1936) insisted on the indivisibility of form and content; tried to stretch the linguistic possibilities of individual words, using them in paradoxical and contradictory contexts; and juxtaposed apparently unrelated fragments of verse by free association. Zafar Iqbal (dates n.a.) has also experimented with coining new words and distorting the meanings of existing words. The poets Salimur Rahman (b. 1936) and Anis Nagi (b. 1939) are influenced by existentialism; Jilani Kamran (dates n.a.) tries to combine existentialism (q.v.) with Islamic mysticism.

The two most important modernist fiction writers are Intizar Husain (b. 1925?) and Anvar Sajjad (b. 1935). Husain's early works express nostalgic regret for the lost cultural traditions of prepartition India. Later stories show the sense of loss and the confused search for identity of the refugees who left India for Pakistan at partition. Sajjad's early concern with the symbolic and surrealistic expression of individual alienation shifted in the mid-1960s to the depiction of social and political oppression, both national and international. His stories of the 1970s often look to a new birth, brought about by previously oppressed characters.

A number of authors began writing modernist fiction in the mid-1960s, including Khalidah Asghar (dates n.a.), Masud Ashar (dates n.a.), Ahmad Hamesh (b. 1940), and Rashid Amjad (b. 1940). Asghar's early stories excel in creating an atmosphere of an unidentified impending doom. After her marriage (she now writes under the name of Khalidah Husain) her stories hint at what happens to a woman's identity in *purdah* (behind the veil). Ashar's early stories express an ambivalent search for self in which the desire to know the self is tempered by a fear of exposure of himself both to himself and to others. There is an outward turn in his stories of the 1970s, in which his search for self-knowledge is coupled with a moral concern for the actions of his countrymen, particularly in East Pakistan (now Bangladesh), and for the future direction of the country. Hamesh's stories are unusual in Urdu literature for their use of scatological references. His largely autobiographical fiction shows poverty in gruesome and bizarre detail.

In the 1970s writers began to combine the innovative literary techniques developed by the modernists in the 1960s with a concern for social problems, political repression, and the status of Third World nations, particularly in their relations with the superpowers.

In Sindhi

After the British conquest of Sind in 1843 Persian was no longer the court language. The British standardized the Sindhi script in 1852. As in Urdu, early Sindhi prose works were of two kinds: romances of adventure and magic, and didactic appeals for social reform. The prolific Mirza Qalich Beg (1853–1929) translated, compiled, or wrote over three hundred fifty works, including *Zeenat* (1890; Zeenat), the first novel in Sindhi, which advocated female education.

Sindhi poetry in the late 19th and early 20th cs. copied its forms and imagery from Persian verse and was frequently didactic. Kishin Chand Tirathdas Khatri (1885–1947), known as "Bewas," enlarged the subjects of poetry, writing about laborers and national-

ism during the 1930s. The ranks of Sindhi poets today include traditionalists who continue to use the Persian style, revivalists who are bringing back the classical Sindhi forms and subjects, and those influenced by the reformist trends of the Progressive Movement.

The leading Sindhi poet in Pakistan today is Sheikh Ayaz (b. 1923), who began writing in both Urdu and Sindhi at the age of fifteen. He later switched to Sindhi alone, in protest against Urdu, which he called a symbol of exploitation because it was spoken by the refugees who flooded Karachi after partition, and whose presence was resented by some Sindhis. Ayaz has long been associated with the Progressive Writers' Movement and feels that literature should be in a language easily understood by the common man, and about subjects close to the people. Ayaz, as well as Tanvir Abbasi (dates n.a.) and Niyaz Humayuni (dates n.a.) use imagery drawn from folk legends. In prose as in poetry, the Progressive Movement is still influential, most notably in the works of Jamal Abro (dates n.a.), whose short stories protest injustice and inhumanity toward the poor.

In Punjabi

Following the British conquest of the Punjab in 1849, the second half of the 19th c. saw the growth of a concern for social change, political awareness, and nationalism. The use of literature for social reform was intensified by the Progressive Movement. During this period, however, Punjabi had begun to be considered a sectarian language of the Sikhs, and the center for Progressive literature in Punjabi was Amritsar (now in India). The cultural language of Lahore was Urdu, and Muslim Punjabi speakers frequently wrote in Urdu rather than in Punjabi.

Since partition, Punjabi writers, most of whom write in Urdu as well, have been influenced by the Progressive Movement and by modernism. Ustad Daman (dates n.a.), Joshua Fazal-ud-din (dates n.a.), and Abdul Majid Bhatti (dates n.a.) were early users of social themes in their poetry. Recently the Writers' Guild Adamjee Prize was awarded to Pir Fazal (dates n.a.), who uses the *ghazal* of the classical Persian and Urdu traditions in Punjabi. The influence of modernism is evident in the works of Muhammad Azim Bhatti (dates n.a.), Anam Adib (dates n.a.), and Munir Niyazi (dates n.a.)—also famous for his Urdu poetry—who have produced

Punjabi poetry about alienation and fear in the city. The Urdu modernists' use of symbolism in fiction is also reflected in the symbolic Punjabi novels of Mustansar Husain Tarar (dates n.a.) and Ahsan Batalvi (dates n.a.).

In Balochi

Traditional Balochi literature includes epic war ballads and love lyrics, orally transmitted by hereditary minstrels and reflecting the tribal nomadic life of Balochi society, with its emphasis on hospitality and bravery.

During the period of English influence from 1854 to 1947, Balochi poets turned to Sufism and reformist literature, and adopted literary forms from Persian and the regional languages Sindhi and Siraiki. After 1947 several literary organizations were founded, and a radio program in Balochi was started. The leading Balochi poet today is Gul Khan Nasir (b. 1910). Azah Jamaldini (b. 1919), who edited the short-lived literary journal *Balochi,* is a poet who uses free verse as well as the classical forms. He has been influenced by the Progressive Movement and writes "message" poetry decrying the economic backwardness of the Balochis.

In Pashto

Pashto is spoken in the Northwest Frontier Province of Pakistan, as well as in the east, south, and southwest of Afghanistan, where it is one of the official languages. It is also spoken by smaller numbers in Balochistan and the Punjab. The Yusufzai dialect spoken near Peshawar is considered the standard Pashto literary dialect in Pakistan.

From the 18th c. until the modern era, Pashto authors wrote poetry using Persian forms and images, and some prose historical compositions. Recent Pashto literature in Pakistan has been influenced by the reformist impulse generated by the Progressive Movement. The short stories of Zaitun Banu (dates n.a.) show the conflict between the modernized younger generation and the more traditional older generation in Pathan society. Banu has said that she feels it is her mission to write against the oppression of women.

In Other Languages

A number of the regional languages of Pakistan remained unwritten until the introduction of government-sponsored radio programs in these languages during the last two decades necessitated their use of the Urdu script. Their oral literature consists of folk tales and folk songs. The recently developed written literature of the northern languages is influenced by the relatively more developed Pashto, and by Urdu and Persian. It includes poetry using the Persian *ghazal* form, religious poetry in praise of God and the Prophet, and patriotic songs. None of these languages has a well-developed prose literature.

The regional languages Balti, Shina, Brushuski, and Khowar in the north, and the Dravidian language Brahui in the south have primarily oral literatures. Balti, a language related to Tibetan, is known for its hymns in praise of the Prophet. Shina includes love poetry with a female persona, unlike love poetry in Persian and Arabic. The most famous poet of Shina, Khalifah Rahmat Malang (1879–19??) wrote poems describing his unsuccessful love for the lady Yurmas. Literature in Brahui has existed since the middle of the 18th c., but very little has been written in it until recently. Poetry in Hindko, the form of Punjabi spoken around Peshawar, dates from the 18th c. Most Hindko poets, like those writing in Brushuski and Khowar, write in Urdu, Pashto, and Persian as well, and their literature in their native languages is influenced by the traditions of the more established literatures.

BIBLIOGRAPHY: Sadiq, M., *A History of Urdu Literature* (1964); Ajwani, L. H., *History of Sindhi Literature* (1970); special Pakistani issue, *Mahfil,* 7, 1–2 (1971); Kalim, S., *Pakistan: A Cultural Spectrum* (1973); Jalal, H., et al., eds. *Pakistan: Past and Present* (1977), pp. 235–45

LINDA WENTINK

See also Bangladeshi Literature

PALAMAS, Kostis

Greek poet, b. 13 Jan. 1859, Patras; d. 27 Feb. 1943, Athens

At the age of seven P. lost both his parents; he was brought up by an uncle in Missolonghi, the town his family came from. In 1875 he went to Athens to study law at the university, but instead he devoted himself to literature. He first earned his living by contributing literary articles to newspapers

461

and periodicals, until he was appointed, in 1897, general secretary of the University of Athens, a post he held until his retirement in 1929. In Athens he lived a "life immovable," as he called it, and he died there while his country was under Nazi occupation.

P. was the central figure of the generation of the 1880s, the generation that brought Greece, which had been reborn from its ashes earlier in the 19th c., to its intellectual maturity. His wide familiarity with European literature and thought not only contributed greatly to his own originality and literary leadership; it also helped to modernize Greek literature in general and to broaden its horizons. As the leader of the group of poets known as the New Athenian School, he militantly embraced the cause of the demotic Greek language as a literary medium. He was influenced by the folk tradition; he also introduced Parnassianism to Greek poetry, and later symbolism (q.v.), and was the most gifted Greek practitioner of both. His continued popularity and influence was due not only to his talent but to the fact that his work reflected the Greek spirit during years frequently disturbed by political turmoil and tragedy.

P. was a very prolific poet. His three earliest collections—*Traghoudhia tis patridhos mou* (1886; songs of my country), *Imnos is tin Athinan* (1889; hymn to Athena), and *Ta matia tis psykhis mou* (1889; the eyes of my soul)—did not truly reveal his poetic personality, although the last two won prizes and in their quality surpassed any modern poetry in Greek up to that time. P. really came into his own as a poet with the Parnassian lucidity of the twelve sonnets entitled "Patridhes" (1895; homelands). *Iamvi ke anapesti* (1897; iambs and anapests) introduced the musical, oblique, evocative suggestiveness of symbolism to Greek literature. The poems in *O tafos* (1898; *The Grave*, 1930), in lamenting the death of his five-year-old son, range from the simplicity of the folk song to the sophistication of philosophic meditation. *I asalefti zoï* (1904; Part I, *Life Immovable*, 1919; Part II, *A Hundred Voices*, 1921), the product of a decade, contains most of his best lyrical poetry on a great variety of themes and in a number of different modes. The long poem "Finikia" ("Palm Tree," 1969) in this volume is the best and also the most difficult of his symbolist poems; "Askreos" (Askreos [P.'s name for Hesiod]), another long poem

in *I asalefti zoï*, is the first of what he called his "greater visions."

To these greater visions belong his next two synthesizing poems, both of epic length, *O dhodhekaloghos tou yiftou* (1907; *The Twelve Words of the Gypsy*, 1964; later tr., 1975) and *I floyiera tou vassilia* (1910; *The King's Flute*, 1967). *O dhodhekaloghos tou yiftou*, widely considered his masterpiece, is written in a variety of forms, moods, and rhythms. Its action takes place at the time preceding the fall of Constantinople to the Turks in 1453. The gypsy, who may represent the skeptical modern Greek or the poet himself reconsidering the Greek cultural experience, goes through all the stages of doubt and nihilistic negation until a violin befriends him and restores his spirits. The apparently simple symbolism of the violin becomes far more complex in its combined epic and lyrical associations. *I floyiera tou vassilia*, also epic in length and ambition, is not as successful as *O dhodhekaloghos tou yiftou*. In large part inspired by historians' recent discoveries about the cultural significance of Byzantium to modern Greece, the poem was composed and published ten years after the 1897 military débacle in which the Greek government had attempted to take possession of Crete, and shortly before the successful Balkan wars (1912–13). In this poem Emperor Basil II (958?–1025), who ruled at the time when the Byzantine Empire had reached its peak under the Macedonian dynasty, journeys through Greece to reach Athens, the ancient and modern cultural capital of Hellenism.

In his remaining books of poetry the aging P. wrote, with diminished power, lyrical verse. There are, however, exceptional moments in *O kyklos ton tetrastihon* (1919; cycle of quatrains) and elsewhere. Sadness prevails in his later verse, which reflects the impact on himself and his country of the two worlds wars. Of the few short stories he published from 1884 to 1901, "Thanatos pallikariou" (1901; "A Man's Death," 1934) is his best. He also wrote a poetic drama, *Trisevyeni* (1903; *Royal Blossom; or, Trisevyeni*, 1923), his only play. His voluminous critical writing had a considerable influence on his contemporaries and on younger writers.

P. was second only to Dionysios Solomos (1798–1857) in enriching Greek literature with a poetic language drawn from many eras, particularly the Byzantine. His poetry, in his ample drawing from Greek mythology, culture, literature, and history, encompasses the entire Greek world, both ancient and modern.

During his lifetime, his "greater visions" were deemed his major accomplishments. More recent criticism has shown a preference for the best of his shorter lyrical poetry. A duality inherent in his work—a wavering between enthusiasm and despair, affirmation and negation, action and contemplation, faith and faithlessness—has elicited many reservations from critics; what he posits beyond that wavering, however, is a faith in the capacity of art, of poetry, to transcend reality.

FURTHER WORKS: *To ergho tou Krystalli* (1894); *I heretizmi tis ilioyienitis* (1900); *Ghrammata* (2 vols., 1904, 1907); *I kaïmi tis limnothalassas ke ta satirika yimnasmata* (1912); *I politia ke i monaxia* (1912); *Ta prota kritika* (1913); *Aristoteles Valaoritis* (1914); *Vomi* (1915); *Ta parakera* (1919); *Ta dhekatetrastiha* (1919); *Dhiiyimata* (1920); *I pentasyllavi ke ta pathitika kryfomilimata* (1925); *Dhili ke skliri stikhi* (1928); *Pezi dhromi* (3 vols., 1928–34); *Perasmata ke heretizmi* (1931); *I nihtes tou Phimiou* (1931–32); *Dionysios Solomos* (1933); *Ta hronia mou ke ta hartia mou* (2 vols., 1933, 1940); *Vradhini fotia* (1944); *Apanta* (16 vols., 1962–69)

BIBLIOGRAPHY: Phoutrides, A., *A New World-Poet* (1919); Phoutrides, A., *A Living Poet of Greece: K. P.* (1921); Buck, C. D., Stevens, D. H., Skipis, S., Prior, M. E., and Argoe, K. T., Introductions (in English) to *K. P.: Dhili ke skliri stikhi* (1928), pp. 19–56; Palamas, L., *A Study on the "Palm Tree" of K. P.* (1931); Sherrard, P., *The Marble Threshing-Floor: Studies in Modern Greek Poetry* (1956), pp. 39–81; Maskaleris, T., *K. P.* (1972)

ANDONIS DECAVALLES

PALAZZESCHI, Aldo

(pseud. of Aldo Giurlani) Italian poet and novelist, b. 2 Feb. 1885, Florence; d. 18 Aug. 1974, Rome

P. was the only child of well-to-do parents. Although he studied accountancy, his real love since childhood had always been literature. In his youth P. spent a few years in Par-

is, where he was introduced to avant-garde circles.

P.'s earliest works include three volumes of poetry: *Cavalli bianchi* (1905; white horses), *Lanterna* (1907; lantern), and *Poemi* (1909; poems). *Poemi* in particular linked P. to futurism (q.v.). His short-lived association with that movement was based not on an acceptance of its theoretical assertions but rather on his own strong desire to "rejuvenate" Italian literature, which had come under the dominance of Gabriele D'Annunzio (q.v.).

Traces of futurism are present in the novel *Il codice di Perelà* (1911; *Perelà, the Man of Smoke*, 1936)—a revised edition was published as *Perelà, uomo di fumo* (1954). It is a fable about a man who has lived in a chimney for thirty-two years. When he emerges, he is at first welcomed by society and charged with the task of writing a "new code of freedom" for the state; later, rejected by the people, he is condemned to life in imprisonment but escapes and dissolves into smoke. *Il codice di Perelà* can be seen as a depiction of the crisis of values in the years preceding World War I. In this novel, as in all his other works, P. makes effective use of humor and irony.

Le sorelle Materassi (1934; *The Sisters Materassi*, 1953), one of P.'s best-known novels, recounts the story of two old-maid sisters who temporarily escape from their drab bourgeois life when their young, attractive nephew, Remo, comes to live with them. Sensing the sisters' infatuation for him, Remo exploits the situation. He eventually brings about their financial ruin, marries a wealthy American woman he has met in Venice, and leaves for a life in the U.S.

In later novels, *Il doge* (1967; the doge) and *Stefanino* (1969; Stefanino), P. returned to the fantastic mode evident in *Il codice di Perelà*. *Il doge* is a novel of Venice, which is seen in its legendary splendor; P. creates a surrealistic picture of the city through a language that combines the popular and the "cultured."

One of the most unusual figures in 20th-c. Italian literature, P. captured over fifty years of Italian life with a literary voice that was never content with conventional form. To reduce P. to a single attribute (such as the lyrical P.), as some critics have attempted to do, is to acknowledge only one aspect of his considerable and varied oeuvre. Even in his less successful works, such as *I fratelli Cuccoli* (1948; the Cuccoli brothers), whose characters are not fully developed, there are stylistic innovations, linguistic experiments, and an extraordinary imagination.

FURTHER WORKS: *Riflessi* (1908); *L'incendiario* (1910); *Il controdolore* (1914); *Due imperi mancati* (1920); *Il re bello* (1921); *Poesie* (1925; final version, 1930); *La piramide* (1926); *Stampe dell'Ottocento* (1932); *Il palio dei buffi* (1937); *Bestie del Novecento* (1951); *Roma* (1953; *Roma,* 1965); *Scherzi di gioventù* (1956); *Vita militare* (1959); *Il piacere della memoria* (1964); *Il buffo integrale* (1966); *Cuor mio* (1968); *Storia di un'amicizia* (1971); *Via della cento stelle* (1972)

BIBLIOGRAPHY: Riccio, P. M., *Italian Authors of Today* (1938), pp. 109–17; Singh, G., "A. P.: A Survey," in Pacifici, S., ed., *From Verismo to Experimentalism* (1969), pp. 81–101; Bever, P. van, "Révolution et restauration: De P. à Ungaretti," *Revue de l'Université de Bruxelles*, 2–3 (1971), 229–37; Bergin, T. G., "The Enjoyable Horrendous World of A. P.," *BA*, 46 (1972), 55–60; Pacifici, S., *The Modern Italian Novel* (1979), pp. 34–46

ANTHONY R. TERRIZZI

PALESTINIAN LITERATURE

Poetry

At the beginning of the 20th c. poetry in Palestine—as in other Arab provinces of the Ottoman Empire—was the main vehicle of literary expression. Its neoclassical style emphasized the importance of wording, and its subjects were for the most part traditional panegyric, elegiac, or religious topics. Under the influence of the wider concerns of a burgeoning society and the articulate prose of a growing Palestinian journalism beginning in 1908—when the Ottoman constitution was promulgated, granting greater freedoms—poets began increasingly to deal with social and political issues, among other things alerting people to the Zionist goals for Palestine and the threat posed by Zionism to the national aspirations of Palestinian Arabs. Poems like those of Is'āf al-Nashāshībī (1882–1948) used classical forms but had new themes and sociopolitical purposes.

Such an approach began to prevail in the works of poets like Wadī' al-Bustānī (1888–1954), Iskandar al-Khūrī al-Baytajālī (1890–1978), and Abū Salmā (1909–1980), especially after the Balfour Declaration of 1917 and the inception of the British mandate in 1922. The greatest poet of mandated Palestine was Ibrāhīm Tūqān (1905–1941), whose innovative technique equaled his fervent commitment to his people, whom he saw being gradually deprived of their land to accommodate Jewish immigrants. His poetry chides traitors and misguided leaders, celebrates Palestinian heroes and martyrs, challenges Zionist and British policies, and foretells the disaster of a homeless Palestinian nation. His disciple, 'Abd al-Rahīm Mahmūd (1913–1948), was killed in the war of 1948, along with many other Palestinians whose cause he, like Tūqān, commemorated in his poetry.

After the establishment of the State of Israel in 1948 at the end of the British mandate, Palestinians in exile or in refugee camps, as well as those under Israeli control, never ceased to denounce injustices. In the poetry of Mahmūd Darwīsh (b. 1942), who lived in Israel until 1971, and since then has resided in Lebanon, the love of Palestine is celebrated as an eternal attachment to the soil. His friends Samīh al-Qāsim (b. 1939), Tawfīq Zayyād (b. 1932), and Sālim Jubrān (b. 1941) continue to write similar poetry in Israel. Fadwā Tūqān (b. 1917), a leading woman poet of the West Bank (occupied by Israel since 1967), abandoned romantic topics in order to turn her attention to the more pressing issues of the Palestinian quest for justice and a homeland. Tawfīq Sāyigh (1923–1971) and Jabrā Ibrāhīm Jabrā (b. 1919), living in exile, reminisce in their verse about a happy youth in the homeland. Sāyigh deplores the immorality of a depraved modern world that remains silent at the injustice; Jabrā decries the inefficacy of Arab regimes in dealing with it. The poetry of Kamāl Nāsir (1925–1973), joyfully envisioning a victorious return to Palestine in the future, came to a halt in 1973, when he was gunned down by Israelis in Beirut. Meanwhile, a chorus of younger unrelenting poetic voices still goes on.

The Essay and Fiction

The importance of Palestinian prose increased with the growth of journalism and printing. The literary essay began as the main genre in prose, the two outstanding pioneers being Khalīl al-Sakākīnī (1878–1953), a bold, free spirit undaunted by tradition, and the poet Isʻāf al-Nashāshībī, an able writer despite an antiquarian style. Other essayists followed in the footsteps of al-Sakākīnī, opening wider vistas of thought. But they used prose increasingly for writing fiction, which began to vie with poetry as a vehicle of literary expression.

From the turn of the century on, the stories of Khalīl Baydas (1875–1949), as well as his translations, mainly from Russian, helped both to popularize the art of fiction and to give it respectability. By the end of World War II fiction writers and translators included Najātī Sidqī (b. 1905) and Mahmūd Sayf al-Dīn al-Īrānī (1914–1978), both noted for short stories that conveyed a social message sympathetic to the poor and the oppressed. Although Samīra ʻAzzām (1927–1967) offered similar stories, she also wrote several others that probed the anguish of individuals, especially women, in complicated situations and difficult relationships.

After midcentury the Palestinian novel advanced phenomenally. The poet Jabrā Ibrāhīm Jabrā, who also wrote short stories, published several novels. *Sayyādūn fī shāriʻ dayyiq* (1974; *Hunters in a Narrow Street,* 1960), originally published in English in London, deals with Iraqi society before the 1958 revolution. *Al-Safīna* (1970; the ship) exposes the degeneracy of bourgeoisie in Arab countries, in depicting passengers on a ship cruising the Mediterranean. Escaping failure at home as well as social and political pressures, they are as desperate by journey's end as they are at its beginning. The Palestinian, who alone among them is without a homeland, is ironically the only one with a strong attachment to his country's soil, despite his material success away from it. A similar character appears in Jabrā's novel *Al-Bahth ʻan Walīd Masʻūd* (1978; the search for Walīd Masʻūd), but here the well-to-do middle-aged Palestinian disappears mysteriously. The reader is left with the strong suggestion that he has gone to join the PLO commandos.

From the refugee camps in Damascus came the compelling fiction of Ghassān Kanafānī (1936–1972). His *Rijāl fī al-shams* (1963; *Men in the Sun,* 1978), the story of three Palestinian refugees who die in the empty water tank of a truck while waiting in the blazing sun to be smuggled into Kuwait to work there, portrays the docility of Palestinians at the stage when individual, not national, salvation was considered to be a way out. In Kanafānī's later novel, *ʻĀʼid ilā Haifā* (1968; return to Haifa), however, the protagonist comes to realize that armed struggle alone can bring about salvation, both individual and national.

Emile Habībī (b. 1921), an Israeli Arab who is a Communist and a former Knesset member, in *Sudāsiyyat al-ayyām al-sitta* (1969; sextet of the six days) expressed through fiction the mixed feelings of Palestinians meeting each other after the 1967 Six Day War following twenty years of separation; he blends memory with hope, reality with myth, to convey the unity of the Palestinians and the power of mutual support. His novel *Al-waqāʼiʻ al-gharība fī ikhtifā Saʻīd Abī al-Nahs al-mutashāʼil* (1974; *The Secret Life of Saeed, the Ill-fated Pessoptimist: A Palestinian Who Became a Citizen of Israel,* 1982), depicts the feelings of constant anguish and insecurity that Palestinians experience as Israeli citizens awaiting a solution. His dramatic narrative *Lukaʻ ibn Lukaʻ* (1980; Lukaʻ son of Lukaʻ) metaphorically suggests that Arabs ought finally to rise and demand that their governments face reality and stop their antics. Habībī remains the master of black humor and of symbolic language.

In *Najrān taht al-sifr* (1975; Narjrān below zero) Yahyā Yakhlif (b. 1945) deals with poverty and political coercion in Arab society by concentrating on life in the 1960s in Najrān and its vicinity, just across the northern border of the new Arab Republic of Yemen (North Yemen), where the Yemeni royalists and their mercenaries were finally defeated. The novel highlights the crushed individuality of the Arab and indicates that Arabs are in need of revolutionary change everywhere.

BIBLIOGRAPHY: Tibawi, A. L., "Visions of the Return: The Palestine Arab Refugees in Arabic Poetry and Art," *MEJ,* 17 (1963), 507–26; Kanafany, G., "Resistance Literature in Occupied Palestine," *AAW,* 1, 2–3 (1968), 65–79; Nakhleh, E., "Wells of Bitterness: A Survey of Israeli-Arab Political Poetry," *Arab World,* 16, 2 (1970), 30–36; Abu Ghazaleh, A., "Arab Cultural Nationalism in Palestine during the British Mandate," *JPalS,* 1, 3 (1972), 37–63; Germanus, J. A. K., "The New Palestinian Poetry from beneath the Crossfire," *IC*, 47 (1973), 127–58; Ashrawi, H. M., "The Contemporary Palestinian Poetry of Occupation," *JPalS*, 7, 3 (1978), 77–101; Ismael, J. S., "The Alienation of Palestine in Palestinian Poetry," *ASQ*, 3 (1981), 43–55; Elmessiri, A. M., "The Palestinian Wedding: Major Themes of Contemporary Palestinian Resistance Poetry," *JPalS*, 10, 3 (1981), 77–99

ISSA J. BOULLATA

PALUDAN, Jacob

Danish novelist and essayist, b. 7 Feb. 1896, Copenhagen; d. 26 Sept. 1975, Copenhagen

P. started his studies in pharmaceutical chemistry in 1912 and received his degree in 1918. From 1920 to 1921 he lived in Ecuador and the U.S.; after his return to Denmark he worked as a literary critic for various newspapers.

P.'s stay in America affected his whole conservative and romantic outlook on life. He saw materialism and superficiality as the threatening components of "Americanization," which would eventually destroy all traditional values. This critical point of view appears in P.'s very first work, the emigrant novel *De vestlige veje* (1922; the western roads), a satirical but somewhat rhetorical attack on American urban civilization. He also satirized urban life in the novel *Søgelys* (1923; searchlight), which is set in Copenhagen. *Søgelys* contains penetrating psychological studies that recur in *En vinter lang* (1924; all winter long), a lyrical novel of considerable artistic merit about loneliness and isolation that turn into defiance and frigidity.

More extroverted is P.'s next work, *Fugle omkring fyret* (1925; *Birds around the Light*, 1928), the semisymbolic, highly dramatic story of a harbor-building project in a small coastal town, illustrating the destructive forces of economic and technological progress. A more coherent character delineation is found in his most pessimistic novel, *Markerne modnes* (1927; the ripening fields). Here P. portrays two artistically gifted young men, a poet and a musician, who ultimately fail in their careers, the former because of too much popular success, which spoils him, the latter because of too much adversity in his environment, which is devoid of any true spiritual values.

P.'s most popular book—and a true masterpiece—is the two-volume novel *Jørgen Stein* (1932–33; *Jørgen Stein*, 1966). It is a social work depicting three generations: the first one is firmly rooted in the conservative pre-World War I period; the second is the "lost generation" whose values were destroyed through the war; the third is the young, disillusioned generation that takes life's emptiness for granted. At the same time, *Jørgen Stein* is a *Bildungsroman*. The individualistic but also weak and passive title character is emotionally split, at different times manifesting the attitudes of all three generations. He is unable to commit himself either to society or to a woman. The resultant catastrophe is the suicide of his girlfriend Nanna. Finally Jørgen overcomes his restlessness through resignation and by returning to nature and physical work. He gives up his illusory independence, chooses marriage, and accepts the duties of everyday life, finding at least a glimpse of hope in an otherwise meaningless world.

After *Jørgen Stein* P. turned to the essay, a genre indirectly anticipated in the numerous commentaries and reflective sections in his fictional writing. P.'s favorite targets are the American way of life and feminism, as in *Feodor Jansens jereminader* (1927; the jeremiads of Feodor Jansen). In *Året rundt* (1929; the year around), *Landluft* (1944; country air), and *Han gik ture* (1949; he took walks) contemplations on nature based on mystical experiences become predominant. Other essays pay particular attention to metapsychology, as in *Søgende ånder* (1943; searching spirits) and *Skribenter på yderposter* (1949; writers on outposts). P.'s most biting sarcasm appears in the two brilliant collections of aphorisms, *Tanker og bagtanker* (1937; thoughts and secret thoughts) and *Små apropos'er* (1943; aphorisms), which are aimed at the superficiality and vulgarization of the times and at current fashionable trends. From 1973 to 1975 P. published three volumes of anecdotal memoirs, *I høstens månefase* (1973; during the autumn moon), *Sløret sandhed* (1974; veiled truth), and *Vink fra en fjern virkelighed* (1975; waves from a distant reality). After his death another volume of memoirs, *Låsens klik* (1976; the click of the lock), was published.

P. was a sharp and critical commentator on his age. At the same time he had a deep affection for art and nature, where he discovered the harmony he could not find in the modern world. P.'s masterful style is characterized by a refined rhythm, and it maintains a subtle balance between a poetic and a purely intellectual approach. P. himself constantly strove to understand the interplay between the human mind and nature as well as man's situation in time and space.

FURTHER WORKS: *Urolige sange* (1923); *Landet forude* (1928); *Som om intet var hændt* (1938); *Mit kaktusvindue* (1944); *Bøger på min vej* (1946); *Prosa: Korte ting fra tyve år* (1946); *Facetter* (1947); *Retur til barndommen* (1951); *Fremad til nutiden* (1953); *Sagt i korthed* (1954); *Ålborg i min ungdoms vår* (1955); *Litterært selskab* (1956); *Skribent at være* (1957); *Røgringe* (1959); *En kunstsamlers meditationer* (1960); *Mørkeblåt og sort* (1965); *Siden De spørger* (1968); *Her omkring hjørnet blæser det mindre* (1969); *Dråbespil* (1971)

BIBLIOGRAPHY: Claudi, J., *Contemporary Danish Authors* (1952), pp. 57–61; Heltberg, N., "J. P.," *ASR,* 40 (1952), 142–45

SVEN H. ROSSEL

PANAMANIAN LITERATURE
See Central American Literature

PANAYOTOPOULOS, I(oannis) M(ichael)
Greek poet, novelist, short-story writer, critic, travel writer, and essayist, b. 23 Oct. 1901, Aitolikon

Educated at the University of Athens, P. combined writing with the teaching of Greek literature at private institutions. He also contributed to the cultural life of Greece by serving on the advisory board of the National Theater and as chairman of its committee on artistic affairs. In addition, he served on the editorial board of the "Basic Library," a series of books of history, literature, philosophy. Among P.'s many honors were the Palamas Prize, awarded in 1947 for four volumes he contributed to the series known as *Ta prosopa kai ta keimena* (individuals and their works); a First National Prize in 1957 for *Ta epta koimismena paidia* (1956; the seven sleepers) as the best novel of the year; and another National Prize awarded in 1964 for his travel book *E Afriki afipnizetai* (1963;

Africa awakens). Translations of his work have given P. an international reputation.

At the age of twenty P. published *To poeitiko ergo tou Kosti Palama* (1921; the poetic work of Kostis Palamas), testifying to his admiration for the great demotic poet. He followed this critical study with several poetry collections of his own, culminating in *To parathyro tou kosmou* (1962; window of the world). In 1970 he gathered and published his poetry in one large volume, *Ta poeimata* (the poems).

Like many authors of his generation, P. expresses in his poetry and fiction the moral dilemmas of man confronting an age of lost standards and eroded beliefs. His first novel, *Astrofengia* (1945; starlight), depicts the social and cultural chaos engendered by World War I. His second novel, *O aichmalatos* (1951; the captive), begins before the outbreak of World War II and describes defeated and occupied Greece. In the prize-winning *Ta epta koimismena paidia,* P. writes about 3rd-c. Rome, whose disintegration has parallels with our own time.

P. feels deeply the alienation that man suffers, a loneliness that he compares to that of God when He is abandoned by man. To be truly alive, P. believes, one must experience the agony of separation. These basic themes particularly permeate his three volumes of short stories: *To dachtilidi me ta paramythia* (1957; ring with the fairy tales), *Anthropini dipsa* (1959; human thirst), and *Flamingos* (1963; flamingos).

Like writers such as Nikos Kazantzakis, Elias Venezis, and Petros Haris (qq. v.), P. has also written about his travels. To this genre P. contributed several volumes that express his wanderlust and desire for fresh knowledge, ranging from *Ellenikoi orizondes* (1940; Greek horizons) to *Afrikaniki peripeteia* (1970; African travels). Committed to no particular politics or ideology, P. seeks in his journeys to learn what is vital for himself and for mankind.

In addition to poetry, fiction, and travel books, P. has published essays on literary and cultural subjects. His most ambitious effort consists of six volumes in the series *Ta prosopa kai ta keimena,* his last contribution being in 1956. In them he discusses both Greek and non-Greek authors. In a reminiscence touching upon his own past, *Hamozoe* (1945; "Humble Life," 1969), P. dramatizes various events in a poor section of Piraeus.

In a manner less fiery than that of Kazantzakis, P. also expresses the moral crises besetting modern man. *O synchronos anthropos* (1966; *The Contemporary Man,* 1970) is perhaps his best effort to study the "anatomy of modern reality."

FURTHER WORKS: *To biblio tis Mirandas* (1924); *Lyrika schedia* (1933); *Dromoi paralliloi* (1943); *Anisiha hronia* (1943); *Kostis Palamas* (1944); *Omilies tis yimnis psichis* (1946); *K. P. Kavafis* (1946); *O lyrikos logos* (1949); *Alcyone* (1950); *O kyklos tou zodion* (1950); *Scaravaios o ieros: E Egyptos* (1950); *Politeies tis Anatolis* (1954); *Stochasmos kai o logos* (1954); *Ta Ellenika kai ta xena* (1956); *E Kypros: Ena taxidi* (1961); *O kosmos tis Kinas* (1961)

BIBLIOGRAPHY: Gianos, M. P., ed., *Introduction to Modern Greek Literature* (1969), pp. 21, 32–33; Hogan, M. P., Preface to *The Contemporary Man* (1970), pp. v–xiv

ALEXANDER KARANIKAS

PANDURO, Leif

Danish novelist and dramatist, b. 18 April 1923, Copenhagen; d. 16 Jan. 1977, Asserbo

Having finished dental school in 1947, P. moved to Sweden in 1949, where he practiced dentistry until his return to Denmark in 1956. From 1961 to 1965 he divided his time between dentistry, television journalism, book reviewing, and creative writing. In 1965 he became a full-time writer.

P. made his literary debut with a radio play, *Historien om Ambrosius* (1956; the story of Ambrosius). His first novel, *Av, min guldtand* (1957; off, my good tooth), is partly autobiographical. Dominant in his early works is the theme of the adolescent's identity crisis and the question of how to achieve maturity for the individual, as well as for society as a whole.

P.'s first major work, *Rend mig i traditionerne* (1958; *Kick Me in the Traditions,* 1961), influenced by J. D. Salinger's (q.v.) *The Catcher in the Rye,* is a humorous description of a young boy's revolt against his surroundings and his confinement in a mental hospital as a result of his refusal to accept the adult world, with its conventions, deceits, and taboos. P.'s theme of rebellion is set against the German occupation of Denmark

during World War II in *De uanstændige* (1960; the immoral ones), a farcelike yet serious protrayal of the period, which focuses on the Danes' perception of one another and of morality. The protagonist has to eliminate part of his identity to fit into the so-called normal world.

Øgledage (1961; saurian days), P.'s most fantastic and modernist work, represents a determined effort to throw off the old literary bonds; it links him to the quest for linguistic liberation of the 1960s. Again, the main theme is that of the psychological problems of youth. According to P., the conventions of society force modern man to reject vitality and spontaneity, a situation that leads to schizophrenia. The author creates an inversion whereby the normal world is unbalanced and insanity is an intentional choice. The healing process for the sickness entails the assimilation into and the acceptance of bourgeois society, and these can be achieved only through the amputation of part of the self.

P.'s later novels deal with middle age. Martin Fern in *Fern fra Danmark* (1963; Fern from Denmark) rejects his limitations and the unpleasant sides of himself through loss of memory. The paranoid Marius Berg in *Fejltagelsen* (1964; the mistake) uses severe hypochondria as a shield against the demands of the outside world, and Edvard Morner in *Den gale mand* (1965; the crazy man) consciously chooses to live according to the strictest rules of society, rejecting all human emotions.

In P.'s novels of the 1970s his middle-class and middle-aged heroes are confronted with a younger generation of rebels. The main characters have isolated themselves in a self-created world of security, refusing all commitments and burdensome contacts. Yet reality intrudes upon them, bringing confusion and questions. *Daniels anden verden* (1970; Daniel's other world) depicts a society marked by chaos and dissolution. For Daniel, the title character, salvation lies in the meeting with the young, schizophrenic rebel Laila and his understanding of her world. *Amatørerne* (1972; the amateurs), as well as P.'s final two novels, *Den ubetænksomme elsker* (1973; the thoughtless lover) and *Høfeber* (1975; hay fever), also treat the problem of lack of commitment.

P.'s television dramas likewise center on the crisis of the middle class. The theme of insecurity and desperation in the supposedly well-organized modern welfare state is present in all of P.'s plays, beginning with *En af dagene* (1968; one of these days), which depicts the power struggle in an office where everybody watches everybody else because of the fear of losing the chance of advancement. *Farvel, Thomas* (1968; goodbye, Thomas) tells of a man who loses his own identity when he is abandoned by his wife. In *Hjemme hos William* (1971; at William's place) P. shows the private fiasco of a seemingly successful architect, while *Rundt om Selma* (1971; around Selma) depicts the failure of the whole middle-class life style. *Rundt om Selma* is P.'s most penetrating and also his most pessimistic analysis of bourgeois society. Every trace of humanity and love of fellow man has been displaced by callous tyranny. *I Adams verden* (1973; in Adam's world) and *Louises hus* (1974; Louise's house), among the best Scandinavian television dramas, continue P.'s attack on the "civilized" behavior of the bourgeoisie. P. became the most successful Danish dramatist of the 1970s. Paradoxically, he attacked exactly those values of the very audiences that held him in such high esteem.

As a novelist, P. occupies a central position in Danish literature; as a dramatist, his position is somewhat isolated, since, unlike most of the newer dramatists, his point of departure was not a political doctrine.

FURTHER WORKS: *Lollipop, og andre spil* (1966); *Vejen til Jylland* (1966; *One of Our Millionaires Is Missing,* 1967); *Farvel, Thomas, og andre TV-spil* (1968); *Bella, og Et godt liv: To TV-spil* (1971); *Vinduerne* (1971); *Selma, William, og Benny: Tre TV-spil* (1972); *Den store bandit* (1973); *Den bedste af alle verdener* (1974); *Bertram og Lisa, og Anne og Paul: To TV-spil* (1974); *Gris på gaflen* (1976); *Hvilken virkelighed?* (1977)

BIBLIOGRAPHY: Sokoll, G., "Mensch und Gesellschaft in L. P.s Dramatik," in Wrede, J., et al., eds., *20th Century Drama in Scandinavia: Proceedings of the International Association of Scandinavian Studies* (1978), pp. 197–204; Hugus, F., "The King's New Clothes: The Irreverent Portrayal of Royalty in the Works of L. P. and Finn Søeborg," *SS,* 51 (1979), 162–76

MARIANNE FORSSBLAD

PANOVA, Vera Fyodorovna

Russian novelist, dramatist, and short-story writer, b. 20 March 1905, Rostov-on-the-Don; d. 3 March 1973, Leningrad

P. began her career in her native city, where she worked as a journalist from 1922 to 1935. She returned to this profession for a period of three years while living in Perm, in the Urals, during World War II. Working for local newspapers and Komsomol (Communist Youth League) papers, she wrote sketches, feuilletons, and articles on a variety of subjects, while her stories for and about children were beginning to attract attention.

P. made her debut in the purely literary field with the publication of her first play, *Ilya Kosogor* (1939; Ilya Kosogor), which was followed by several more works for the theater. In her later years she returned to this genre and between 1956 and 1968 wrote and staged a number of plays.

It was not until shortly after the war, however, that P.'s first long story, "Semya Pirozhkovykh" (1945; the Pirozhkov family), was published, followed quickly by her first successful novel, *Sputniki* (1946; *The Train,* 1948), one of the finest Soviet books written about the war years. In this short, patriotic, and unpretentious tale of life on a hospital train P. resists presenting her characters as ideal positive heroes but strikes a genuinely human note.

Objectivity, understatement, and detachment in depicting existing Soviet reality are again present in her second novel, *Kruzhilikha* (1947; *The Factory,* 1949). These qualities earned P. the displeasure of Party critics. At a time of rampant "Zhdanovism"—after a partial liberalization of artistic and creative life immediately following the end of the war, Andrey Zhdanov, the Communist cultural "boss," had decreed a return and an undeviating adherence to Socialist Realism (q.v.)— P. was not spared the pressure. In her third short novel, *Yasny bereg* (1949; clear shore), set on a large state-owned stockbreeding farm, P. adhered to the dicta set forth by the Party, with all the concomitant mediocrity resulting therefrom.

P.'s first attempt at a full-length conventional novel was *Vremena goda* (1953; *Span of the Year,* 1957). Structurally, this work is less successful than her earlier books, for P.'s talent was that of a miniaturist. Nevertheless, *Vremena goda* and the novel that followed it,

Sentimentalny roman (1958; a sentimental novel), were major literary events inasmuch as they treated controversial subjects and were harbingers of things to come. Together with Ilya Ehrenburg's (q.v.) novel *The Thaw, Vremena goda* ushered in the post-Stalinist period in Soviet literature, marked by a bid for greater artistic freedom. In this novel, P. paints an unsavory, but truthful picture of large-scale corruption in everyday Soviet life and even dares to depict the criminal underworld.

Sentimentalny roman is a frankly autobiographical and sentimental novel in which P. uses Rostov-on-the-Don in the 1920s as background. The book is presented as the personal reminiscences of its hero, the journalist Sevastyanov, but it is based on P.'s own recollections, as was earlier the case with *Sputniki* and, partially, with *Vremena goda. Sentimentalny roman* is free of ideology, and the 1920s appear in it as a "golden age," seen from a distance of over thirty years. The lyricism of this almost entirely romantic work is the quality that sets it apart from other novels of the period.

P. had an extraordinary talent for writing about children, as evidenced by her novella *Seryozha* (1955; *Time Walked,* 1957) and the two complementary stories, "Valya" (1959; "Valya," 1976) and "Volodya" (1959; "Volodya," 1976). Clearly quite at home in the more limited genres of the novella and short story, P. produced in *Seryozha* a series of delightful scenes of life and events as seen from the point of view of a six-year-old boy. "Valya" and "Volodya" are set in wartime Leningrad and feature older children, with their own problems and tribulations in a time of crisis. In these stories, P. shows herself to be not only a sensitive, sympathetic, and keen-eyed observer but also a master at penetrating to the depths of youthful psychology.

In her later years, P.'s long-standing interest in history resulted in a collection of stories based on old Russian chronicles published under the title *Liki na zare* (1966; faces at dawn). She was also a prolific screenwriter: between 1960 and 1967 no fewer than eight films were made from her scenarios.

P.'s feminine sensitivity toward ordinary people is evident throughout her books, as is her lucid style and detached tone, reminiscent of Chekhov's (q.v.). While remaining within the confines of Soviet ideology, in most of her works P. was able to retain an objectivity of characterization that complemented her writer's talent but at times earned her severe criticism from the authorities.

FURTHER WORKS: *V staroy Moskve* (1940); *Devochki (1945); Metelitsa* (1956); *Evdokia* (1959); *Provody belykh nochey* (1961); *Kak pozhivaesh, paren?* (1962); *Skolko let, skolko zim!* (1962); *Tredyakovsky i Volynsky* (1968); *Sobranie sochineny* (5 vols., 1969–70); *O moey zhizni, knigakh i chitatelyakh* (1975)

BIBLIOGRAPHY: Alexandrova, V., *A History of Soviet Literature* (1963), pp. 272–83; Brown, E. J., *Russian Literature since the Revolution* (1963), pp. 243–45; Moody, C., Introduction to V. P., *"Serezha" and "Valya"* (1964), pp. xi–xxvi; Struve, G., *Russian Literature under Lenin and Stalin, 1917–1953* (1971), p. 383; Holthusen, J., *Twentieth-Century Russian Literature: A Critical Study* (1972), pp. 162–66; Slonim, M., *Soviet Russian Literature: Writers and Problems, 1917–1967* (1973), passim; Brown, D., *Soviet Russian Literature since Stalin* (1978), pp. 177–78, 264, 270, 287–89

NADJA JERNAKOFF

PAPADAT-BENGESCU, Hortensia

Romanian novelist and short-story writer, b. 8 Dec. 1876, Iveşti; d. 5 March 1955, Bucharest

An army officer's daughter, P.-B. married a provincial magistrate and had several children and a large household to take care of. This, in part, explains her belated literary debut: she started publishing short stories only in 1913. Although not exactly a feminist, P.-B. can be considered the most important representative to date of women's literature in Romania.

P.-B.'s literary career can be divided into two periods. The first, when she was associated with Garabet Ibrăileanu (1871–1936) and his journal *Viaţa românească,* was characterized by a lyrical, intimate prose that was a refreshing change from the objective, epic-oriented novelistic conventions of her contemporaries. Her most important work of this period is *Balaurul* (1923; the dragon), which drew upon P.-B.'s experience as a volunteer nurse during World War I. Written in diary form, the novel presents the atrocities of war through the eyes of a sheltered, sensitive woman, who initially volunteers for the medical corps not so much out of patriotism as out of a need to get over a painful romance. Confronted with the gruesome reality of her wounded patients, she comes to view her own sentimental drama as ludicrously insignificant.

The second period of P.-B.'s career, when she was associated with Eugen Lovinescu (q.v.) and his review *Sburătorul,* was marked by a shift, presumably under Lovinescu's influence, from subjectivism to a soul-probing objectivism that has led critics to compare her with Proust (q.v.). It was during this period that she wrote the "Halippa cycle," which brought her the highest Romanian literary awards and a seldom-contested reputation as a master of prose. This series of novels, of which the best-known is *Concert din muzică de Bach* (1927; a Bach concert), is a loose, unstructured narrative, mostly held together by Mini, the narrator—in many ways a female counterpart of Proust's narrator, Marcel—and by her friend Nory Baldovin, a sarcastic, upper-class feminist with whom she exchanges gossip. Like Marcel, Mini moves in upstart, pseudoaristocratic circles whose superficiality, venality, and snobbishness she exposes with devastating irony. Nevertheless, not unlike Marcel, she is at the same time curiously fascinated by and not unsympathetic to this world. She is also the exponent of the controversial theory, which appears in much of P.-B.'s work, of the "soul as bodily form." Attributing this theory to the author, some critics see it as trite or naïve, and others as hopelessly obscure. This "psychological" theory, however, should probably not be separated from its fictional context and from its inventor, Mini, who uses it as a convenient way of "understanding" and "categorizing" her friends.

Through her psychological narrative techniques and her shift from predominantly rural to urban settings and themes, P.-B. substantially contributed to the expansion of Romanian fiction beyond conventions of naturalism and external realism that prevailed in the late 19th and early 20th cs.

FURTHER WORKS: *Ape adînci* (1919); *Sfinxul* (1920); *Bătrînul* (1920); *Femeia in fața oglinzii* (1921); *Romanță provincială* (1925); *Fecioarele despletite* (1926); *Desenuri tragice*

(1927); *Drumul ascuns* (1933); *Logodnicul* (1935); *Rădăcini* (1938); *Sangvine* (1973); *Sărbătorile în familie* (1976)

BIBLIOGRAPHY: Munteanu, B., *Panorama de la littérature roumaine contemporaine* (1938), pp. 237–39; Reichman, E., "Les lettres roumaines: Un lent apprentissage à la liberté," *Preuves,* No. 175 (1965), 37–47; Philippide, A., "The Spirit and Tradition of Modern Romanian Literature," *RoR,* 21, 2 (1967), 5–10; Roceric, A., "La fonction du contexte dans l'œuvre de H. P.-B.," *Cahiers de linguistique théorique et appliqué,* 6 (1969), 183–91; Mihailescu, F., "Le centenaire d'H. P.-B.," *AUB-LLR,* 26 (1977), 73–82

MIHAI SPARIOSU

PAPADIAMANTIS, Alexandros

Greek short-story writer and novelist, b. 4 March 1851, Skiathos; d. 3 Jan. 1911, Skiathos

P., popularly called the "saint of Greek letters," was born into a pious island family; his father was a priest. P. spent most of his mature years in Athens with periodic and sometimes long extended visits to his native Skiathos. He studied literature at the University of Athens but never obtained a degree, and eventually settled down as a writer and translator for newspapers and literary journals. Humble and strongly religious, he often acted as a cantor at Greek Orthodox services in the chapels of Plaka, the district of Athens near the Acropolis, while at other times he sat and wrote his stories in modest restaurants and cafés of the same area, between glasses of wine and cups of coffee. His essential modesty shines both in the anecdote that tells of the time he felt embarrassed when he was offered a fee higher than he expected for his writings and in the fact that, in 1908, he stayed away from a public gathering in his honor at "Parnassos," a society of writers and artists.

P. began his career as a writer of historical novels at a time when the genre was going out of fashion. *I metanastis* (1879; the expatriate), *I embori ton ethnon* (1882; the merchants of nations), and *I yiftopoula* (1884; the gypsy girl) are written in purist rather than demotic Greek; they abound in romantic adventures and dramatic situations but have a loose construction and poor characterization. The novella *Christos Milionis* (1885; Christos Milionis), inspired by a folk song of the same name, suggests by its brevity and tight structure that P. was moving toward the short story.

In the following twenty-five years P. wrote about 170 short stories. Although some were set in Athens, most of them are centered around Skiathos. They are ethnographic and social stories, some very short and rapidly sketched, others longer and more elaborate, but all characterized by nostalgia, reverie, love of nature, and simple Christian piety. His characters, complex or simple, are always memorable: priests, fishermen, housewives, shepherds, sailors, described with sympathy, psychological knowledge, and an innocent kind of humor. Of the works written before 1900, the stories "I nostalghos" (1894; "She Who Was Homesick," 1920; also tr. as "The Dreamer," 1969), "O erotas sta hionia" (1896; love in the snow), and "Oloyira stin limni" (1892; all around the lake), as well as the novella *Vardhianos sta sporka* (1895; watchman of the infected ships), stand out. After 1900 P. became more lyrical and showed a greater command of language. Memorable stories from this, his last creative period, are "Oniro sto kima" (1900; dream on the waves), "Ta rhodhin' akroyalia (1908; rosy shores), and "To miroloyi tis fokias" (1908; the dirge of the seal).

P.'s greatest work for its dramatic quality and its social significance, is the novella *I fonissa* (1903; *The Murderess,* 1977). The old lady Frangoyiannou epitomizes the subservient role a woman must play in traditional Greek society and is described by P. at the point of revolt. Contemplating her past life, during which she graduated from slavery to her father to submission to her brothers and then to her husband, the old lady loses her mind and starts murdering baby girls with the purpose of sparing them future hardships. P. portrays Frangoyiannou as a tragic rather than as an evil character, who finally dies "halfway between divine and human justice." It is probable that Dostoevsky's *Crime and Punishment,* which P. had translated from a French version, influenced P. when he wrote *I fonissa.*

P.'s language is idiosyncratic. He wrote his stories at a time when the literary movement of the vernacular (demotic) Greek over the purist was making great advances; yet he consistently used the purist in description and lyrical digression, combining purist and demotic in the narrative parts and resorting to almost pure demotic (his island's idiom) in dialogue. He used the popular language also in most of the few poems he wrote.

P. has had great admirers, but he has also been the object of strong criticism for the loose construction and lack of artistic intention of his writings. Yet, as the modern Greek literary historian Linos Politis aptly stated, "the lack of construction is usually owing to the nature of his [P.'s] nostalgia and reverie; the ideas, not bound by any predetermined plan, follow the course of reverie—and the very lack of construction is a virtue and has charm." P.'s all-encompassing interest in his native island and its people was personal and inward-looking, but it could also be seen as a positive response to the folkloristic concerns among the educated Greeks of his time. Greek and non-Greek readers who have even a mild interest in the literature about the Aegean sea and its islands certainly cannot ignore P.

On the whole, it is purity of feeling and lack of artifice that have made P. a remarkable writer and motivated the 1979 Nobel Prize winner Odysseus Elytis (q.v.) to single out P., in his poem *The Axion Esti* (1959), as one of two Greek writers (the other is the poet Dionysios Solomos, 1798–1857) from whose work and example Greeks in distress can draw moral sustenance, and to write a lyrical commentary on P.

FURTHER WORKS: *Ta apanta* (5 vols., 1954–56)

BIBLIOGRAPHY: Dimaras, C. T., *A History of Modern Greek Literature* (1972), passim; Politis, L., *A History of Modern Greek Literature* (1973), passim; Xanthopoulides, G. X., Introduction to A. P., *The Murderess* (1977), pp. v–xv

GEORGE THANIEL

PAPIAMENTU LITERATURE
See Dutch-Caribbean Literature

PAPUA NEW GUINEA LITERATURE
See Pacific Islands Literatures

PARAGUAYAN LITERATURE

Before 1900 literary activity in Paraguay was a peripheral part of national life. There were poets and prose writers, but they never constituted an active group of intellectuals exercising a significant influence on the country's development. A truly Paraguayan literature began with the brilliant "Generation of 1900": Cecilio Báez (1862–1925), Juan E. O'Leary (1879–1969), Manuel Domínguez (1869–1935), Alejandro Guanes (1872–1925), Manuel Gondra (1871–1927), Fulgencio R. Moreno (1872–1935), and a few other writers of comparable merit.

Essayists and poets, the writers of the Generation of 1900 were also powerful polemical journalists. They had a cause: the reassertion of national values, including a reinterpretation of the War of the Triple Alliance (1864–70), which had left Paraguay desolate and almost extinct. The combined forces of Argentina, Brazil, and Uruguay had devastated the country in a genocidal campaign, which the allied invaders justified as a "crusade of liberation": Paraguay, according to them, was a barbaric country tyrannized by a monster, Marshal Francisco Solano López (1826–1870). The Generation of 1900 tried to show that Paraguay was far more civilized than its enemies when the conflict began and that López was a great patriot and the nation's supreme hero.

Cecilio Báez, the leader of this very prolific generation, wrote more than fifty books in addition to countless essays; Blas Garay (1873–1899), O'Leary, Domínguez, and Moreno all wrote historical works. Alejandro Guanes, the great poet of the group, achieved distinction with "Las leyendas" (1910; the legends) and "Recuerdos" (1910; memories). Fiction of literary merit, however, did not flourish at the beginning of the century.

Around 1915 a new generation of talented writers appeared. The four most important essayists of this group—Justo Pasto Benítez (1895–1962), Pablo Max Ynsfrán (1894–1972), Natalicio González (1897–1966), and Arturo Bray (1898–1977)—continued the historical work of their predecessors. Benítez and Max Ynsfrán wrote the best biographies and interpretations of recent events. By the 1930s (the period the Chaco War with Bolivia), Paraguayan historiography attained distinction, in the writings of Julio César Chaves (b. 1907) and Efraím Cardozo (1906–1975). The first and also the most important

woman prose writer of the first half of the century was Teresa Lamas de Rodríguez-Alcalá (1887–1976), while the most popular poet of this generation was Manuel Ortiz Guerrero (1897–1935), whose lyrics were set to music by a number of composers.

During the first forty years of the century the dominant literary genre was the historical essay. ("History," said one critic, "devoured literature.") During the 1940s, however, all genres began to flower with unprecedented fertility. Hérib Campos Cervera (1908–1953) won recognition throughout Spanish America for his surrealist (q.v.) poetry, which appeared in his only published volume, *Ceniza redimida* (1953; redeemed ashes). Josefina Plá (b. 1909), a dramatist, poet, and art historian, shared with Campos Cervera the leadership of the literary revival during this decisive decade. A surrealist during the 1940s, she later turned toward classical simplicity; *Rostros en el agua* (1963; faces on the water) is perhaps her greatest lyrical achievement. Among the next generation, Elvio Romero (b. 1926), a follower of Campos Cervera, became one of Latin America's outstanding contemporary poets. His *Antología poética* (1965; poetic anthology) reveals his virtuosity.

The Paraguayan novel finally achieved distinction in the 1950s and 1960s, although its two outstanding practitioners are expatriates. Gabriel Casaccia's (b. 1907) *La babosa* (1952; the driveler) caused a great stir when it was first published in Argentina. It is a searingly realistic study of a group of middle-class characters in Areguá, a resort town near Asunción, and depicts what the author sees as the corruption and vice of Paraguayan society. Augusto Roa Bastos (q.v.), also a poet, and the most distinguished writer of the Generation of 1940, is regarded as one of the leading novelists of Latin America. His novel *Hijo de hombre* (1960; *Son of Man,* 1965), one of the masterpieces of recent Latin American fiction, is a panorama of Paraguay's history, utilizing the techniques of magic realism (q.v.) in its interweaving of social and religious themes. His *Yo el Supremo* (1974; I the Supreme) constitutes an extraordinary literary experiment. It is a novel narrated in the first person from the complex and contradictory point of view of Dr. José Gaspar Rodríguez de Francia (1761?–1840), dictator of Paraguay from shortly after the time it gained its independence. Roa Bastos succeeds in brilliantly combining literary invention and the Paraguayan writer's traditional preoccupation with history.

BIBLIOGRAPHY: Centurión, C. R., *Historia de las letras paraguayas* (3 vols., 1947–57); Vallejos, R., *La literatura paraguaya como expresión de la realidad nacional* (1967); Rodríguez-Alcalá, H., *La literatura paraguaya* (1968); Pérez-Maricevich, F., *La poesía y la narrativa en el Paraguay* (1969); Rodríguez-Alcalá, H., *Historia de la literatura paraguaya* (1971)

HUGO RODRÍGUEZ-ALCALÁ

PÁRAL, Vladimír

Czechoslovak novelist (writing in Czech), b. 10 Aug. 1932, Prague

P. was trained as a chemical engineer and, before he devoted himself full-time to literature, worked for a dozen years in the research laboratory of a textile factory in northern Bohemia. Science and technology have exerted a strong influence on his fiction.

After a false start under a pseudonym, P. achieved overnight prominence with the novel *Veletrh splněných přání* (1964; the fair of dreams fulfilled). A new kind of character in Czech fiction made his appearance: in P.'s words, he was a "statistically significant sample" of an individual molded by and conforming to the socialist variant of consumer society. Looking for an easy way to comply with demands placed on him while at the same time obviating the need for risky initiative, the protagonist, a talented young chemist, systematically transforms his life into a repetitive sequence of automatic acts. As a consequence, he also has to eliminate from his life any irregularities, including genuine love.

P.'s next novel, *Soukromá vichřice* (1966; private hurricane), presents another laboratory report on mechanized characters. They are easily interchangeable, and indeed, the plot partly consists of the swapping of partners among the couples involved. P. adapted the form of his novel to its purpose, and its short chapters are identified by a combination of letters and numbers, as in a research report.

Sophisticated stylistic and compositional devices are also apparent in *Katapult* (1967; catapult). The hero, Jacek Jošt, a thirty-three-year-old chemist, attempts to escape from the banal routines of an unexciting marriage and boring work and begins several affairs simultaneously, only to find himself in a self-destructive vicious circle whose essential quality has not changed just because its diameter has increased.

P. has created in his novels a half-real world of his own, the center of which is the north Bohemian city of Ústí nad Labem, where many details of everyday life are faithfully recorded (including people on trains reading P.'s novels), but his work cannot be really described as realistic in the traditional sense. It is, in fact, a grotesquely exaggerated caricature, a schematic and analytic representation of a certain way of life.

P.'s irony is more apparent than in his earlier works in *Milenci a vrazi* (1969; lovers and murderers), in which he takes a skeptical view of the perpetual nature of the struggle between the haves and the have-nots. But the elusiveness of P.'s position, as well as his narrative virtuosity, is demonstrated in a "novel for everyone," *Profesionální žena* (1971; professional woman), a modern fairy tale that can be read as a sentimental and adventurous romance by the uninitiated and as an exhilarating spoof by more sophisticated readers. It appeared at a time when Communist Party controls over the ideological content of literature in Czechoslovakia were being tightened up, and P.'s last two novels were criticized for lack of a positive message of hope and aspiration.

The short novel *Mladý muž a bílá velryba* (1973; the young man and the white whale [Moby Dick]) seemed to be a response to such criticism. It is suffused with optimism even though its main character, a hero of labor, is killed in a work accident. The author's attitude has remained inscrutable and has made possible the interpretation voiced in the West that the novel is in fact a parody of Socialist Realism (q.v.). The same view may apply to *Radost až do rána* (1975; joy until the morning), which somewhat ambiguously suggests that happiness can be found in conformity.

With *Generální zázrak* (1977; universal miracle) P. returned to the theme of searching for a full life enriched by love. *Muka obraznosti* (1980; torment of imagination) has a strong autobiographical element combined with parallels to Stendhal's *The Red and the Black,* which is often quoted.

P. has been a major influence on Czech fiction of the 1960s and 1970s. He was the first to submit to scrutiny the lifestyle of the new socialist middle-class; he brought attention to the industrial region of northern Bohemia, which had never been so extensively described; he infused Czech literature, traditionally inclined to lyricism, with a strong epic element. Despite the demands that its sophisticated complexity makes on readers, P.'s work has enjoyed extraordinary popularity in Czechoslovakia. It has yet to achieve wider recognition abroad, particularly in the English-speaking world.

BIBLIOGRAPHY: Kunstmann, H., *Tschechische Erzählkunst im 20. Jahrhundert* (1974), pp. 370–73; Hájek, I., comp., "V. P.," in Mihailovich, V. D., et al., eds., *Modern Slavic Literatures* (1976), Vol. II, pp. 179–82; Harkins, W. E., "V. P.'s Novel *Catapult*," in Harkins, W. E., and Trensky, P. I., eds., *Czech Literature since 1956: A Symposium* (1980), pp. 62–73

IGOR HÁJEK

PARANDOWSKI, Jan

Polish novelist, essayist, and literary historian, b. 11 May 1895, Lvov; d. 26 Sept. 1978, Warsaw

While still attending secondary school in Lvov, at the time part of the Austro-Hungarian Empire, P. began to write. His first book was a literary study, *Rousseau* (1913; Rousseau). During World War I he was interned in central Russia. In 1918 P. returned to Lvov, where he resumed his university studies and received a degree in philosophy and archaeology. At that time he was also active as a journalist and theater critic.

From 1930 on P. lived in Warsaw. During World War II he was politically active in the anti-Nazi underground. After Poland was liberated by Soviet troops, he became a professor of comparative literature at Lublin Catholic University. He was president of the Polish PEN Club from 1933 to 1978, and vice-president of the International PEN Club from 1962 to 1978.

P. is perhaps best known as a devoted and erudite scholar of antiquity. *Mitologia* (1923; mythology) is a retelling of Greek myths for young readers, and the story collection *Eros na Olimpie* (1923; Eros on Olympus) is a ribald work depicting the amorous adventures of the Greek gods. *Dwie wiosny* (1927; two springs), a magnificent historical-literary travel book, was the result of his journeys to

Greece in 1925 and to Sicily in 1926. Through his translations (Caesar's *Civil Wars*, Longus' *Daphnis and Chloe*, Homer's *Odyssey*), P. made a substantial contribution to Polish cultural life. In 1930 P. published the penetrating and sensitive *Król życia* (king of life), a fictionalized biography of Oscar Wilde.

After another trip to Greece P. published *Dysk olimpijski* (1932; *The Olympic Discus*, 1939). Through this depiction of the Olympic Games in 476 B.C. P. reconstructs the life of ancient Greece. His unusual ability to render physical details and his meticulous research combine to make this one of the major representations of ancient Greece in modern fiction. For this novel P. was awarded a bronze medal at the Berlin Olympic Games in 1936, despite the protests of the Germans. It is this book, which was translated into several languages, that introduced P. to the Western European reader.

Niebo w płomieniach (1936; heaven in flames), undoubtedly one of P.'s best works, is a psychological novel that treats a subject previously unknown in Polish literature—a religious crisis in the soul of a young boy. It provoked keen criticism and controversy among Roman Catholics and writers of the right. The protagonist reappears as a grown man in *Powrót do życia* (1961; return to life), but the emphasis of this later novel is primarily on the Poland of World War II. *Wrześniowa noc* (1962; September night) is P.'s account of his personal experiences during the Nazi occupation of Poland.

Ideologically, P. occupies a detached, seemingly neutral position, and he considered himself a realist; he is often called a contemporary Polish humanist. His literary style reflects his equanimity, his optimism, and his unceasing search for harmony.

FURTHER WORKS: *Aspazja* (1925); *Odwiedziny i spotkania* (1933); *Trzy znaki zodiaku* (1939); *Godzina śródziemnomorska* (1949); *Alchemia słowa* (1950); *Zegar słoneczny* (1952); *Szkice* (1953); *Pisma wybrane* (1955); *Petrarka* (1956); *Z antycznego świata* (1958; rev. ed., 1971); *Podróże literackie* (1958); *Mój Rzym* (1959; enlarged ed., 1970); *Wspomnienia i sylwety* (1960); *Juvenilia* (1960); *Kiedy byłem recenzentem* (1963; enlarged ed., 1968); *Luźne kartki* (1965); *Szkice, seria druga* (1968); *Akacja* (1968); *Pod zamkniętymi drzwiami czasu* (1975)

BIBLIOGRAPHY: Harjan, G., "J. P.: A Contemporary Polish Humanist," *BA*, 34 (1960), 261–66; Harjan, G., Introduction to *The Olympic Discus* (1964), pp. 1–11; Backvis, C., "J. P.," *Flambeau*, 48 (1966), 281–89; Harjan, G., *J. P.* (1971); Natanson, W., "J. P.," *PolP*, 22, 2 (1979), 66–70

GEORGE HARJAN

PARNICKI, Teodor

Polish novelist and essayist, b. 5 March 1908, Berlin, Germany

P. was born into a strongly Germanized Polish family. Because of his father's travels as an engineer, P. spent his early years in Russia and China. He went to Poland in 1928 to study at the University of Lvov, where he quickly earned a reputation for his knowledge of Russian literature. His contributions to numerous magazines made him known as an essayist on the historical novel. During World War II he served as an attaché of the Polish government-in-exile at embassies in Moscow, Jerusalem, London, and Mexico City. In 1945 P. settled in Mexico, which he felt had an atmosphere favorable to his literary development. He has lived in Poland since 1967 and is the winner of several Polish literary prizes.

P. revitalized the Polish historical novel by bringing modern techniques and themes to the genre. His first novel, *Aecjusz, ostatni Rzymianin* (1937; Aetius, the last Roman), depicts the deeds of a Roman dictator during the 5th c., while *Srebrne orły* (1944; silver eagles) explores the origins of the medieval Polish state.

P.'s most important novels were written in Mexico. The uncompleted cycle known as *Światy mieszańców* (at the crossroads of civilizations), consisting of *Słowo i ciało* (2 vols., 1953, 1958; word and body) and *Koniec "zgody nardów"* (1955; the end of the "people's entente"), depicts the intrigues, customs, and ideas of ancient Mediterranean civilizations. *Twarz księżyca* (3 vols., 1961–67; the face of the moon) analyzes societies in the 3rd and 4th cs. A.D. And *Nowa baśń* (6 vols., 1962–70; the new fable) is a panorama of a medieval European culture that emerges from the confrontation between East and West. P.'s best novel is *Tylko Beatrycze* (1962; only for Beatrice), about a peasant insurrection in 12th-c. Poland. Since the publication of *Muza dalekich podróży* (1970; the

muse of distant journeys) his work has evolved toward fantasy historical novels.

The two main centers of interest in P.'s work are the development of the early Catholic Church and the birth of the medieval Polish state. Erudite, P. always chooses episodes of history that highlight intellectual, social, and religious ferment. He is fascinated by the interaction between cultures and by the transformations it produces. His heroes, living in a troubled world, are full of contradictions and conflicts. P's novels reflect his effort to organize the labyrinth of the past in order to build his own spiritual and mythical genealogy. His works have a chronological, thematic, and geographical cohesiveness comparable only to that of Proust's (q.v.) *Remembrance of Things Past*.

P.'s most original contribution to the historical novel is his conception of the historical fact. The past is seen through the eyes of an observer (the hero-narrator), through his beliefs and reactions; hence the work has a psychological foundation. The emphasis of the narration is on reflections about historical facts whose objectivity is questioned. Works such as *Staliśmy jak dwa sny* (1973; like two dreams) also analyze the art of writing a historical novel. This concern about theory is further demonstrated in a collection entitled *Szkice literackie* (1978; literary essays) and in a series of autobiographical lectures published as *Historia w literaturę przekuwana* (1980; making history into literature).

P.'s novels are not easy ones. Although detached from actuality, they address 20th-c. formal and moral questions, providing new insights into the problem of the extent to which the writing of history is an objective skill or imaginative, creative work. His philosophical attitude makes him akin to another specialist in the historical novel, Marguerite Yourcenar (q.v.).

FURTHER WORKS: *Trzy minuty po trzeciej* (1930); *Rozkaz nr. 94* (1930); *Opowiadania* (1958); *I u możnych dziwny* (1965); *Smierć Aecjusza* (1966); *Koła na piasku* (1966); *Zabij Kleopatrę* (1968); *Inne życie Kleopatry* (1969); *Tożsamość* (1970); *Przeobrażenie* (1973); *Sam wyjdę bezbronny* (1976); *Hrabia Julian i król Roderyk* (1976)

BIBLIOGRAPHY: Herman, M., *Histoire de la littérature polonaise des origines à 1961* (1963), pp. 593–761; Miłosz, C., *The History of Polish Literature* (1969), pp. 504–7 and passim

ALICE-CATHERINE CARLS

PARRA, Nicanor
Chilean poet, b. 5 Sept. 1914, Chillán

P. was the eldest son of a rural elementary-school teacher who had married a farmer's daughter. He began writing poetry as a student at the Pedagogical Institute of the University of Chile in Santiago, from which he graduated in 1938 with a degree in mathematics and physics. P.'s first book, *Cancionero sin nombre* (1937; songbook without a name), won the Municipal Poetry Prize of Santiago. P. taught in Chilean high schools until 1943, when he began graduate work at Brown University in advanced mechanics. While in the U.S., P. continued to write poetry and was influenced by Walt Whitman's *Leaves of Grass.* After his return to Chile in 1945, P. was appointed director of the School of Engineering at the University of Chile. From 1949 to 1951 he studied at Oxford University under a grant from the British Council. In 1952 he was named professor of theoretical physics at the University of Chile and has held this post ever since.

P.'s early poetry emulated the ballads found in García Lorca's (q.v.) *Gypsy Ballads* and was hailed by Chilean critics as marking a return to clarity and simpler poetic modes within the nation's rich lyric tradition. Today, however, P.'s first book has almost been forgotten because of the enormous success enjoyed by his *Poemas y antipoemas* (1954; *Poems and Antipoems,* 1967), which made a profound impact on Latin American poetry. Within Chile, this book represented a creative liberation and a new direction away from the overwhelming influence of Pablo Neruda's (q.v.) three volumes of *Residence on Earth,* which was written in a style typified by oneiric imagery, personal symbols, chaotic enumerations, and mythical archetypes. P.'s second book provided Latin American critics with the term "antipoem," which was an attractive name for a reaction to Nerudian surrealism and the traditionally elitist character of most lyric poetry. P. had created a tragicomic, prosaic poem characterized by biting irony, sardonic humor, and iconoclastic imagery.

Antipoetry represented more than just a dialectical reaction to the avant-garde verse in vogue up to the end of World War II. P. also attempted to refurbish lyric poetry and recapture its lost popular appeal through the incongruous juxtaposition of colloquial language and traditional poetic conceits, the employment of free verse and ironic humor, and the mordantly satirical depiction of the banal daily tribulations that afflict every 20th-c. man, including the poet himself. In short, P.'s radical departure from more conventional verse led to a thorough reexamination of the purposes and nature of the poetic art by poets and critics alike throughout Latin America.

In most of his later books P. has constantly mocked the social and literary conventions of the contemporary Western world. At the same time, P.'s own antipoetry has further evolved and replenished itself, until in *Artefactos* (1972; artifacts) he stripped poetry of all metaphorical adornments and reduced the antipoem to epigrammatic verses that still voice popular discontent with society. Almost all the characters found in P.'s poetic world are antiheroes who are obsessed with a fear of death, are prey to physical deterioration, have had disillusioning love affairs, and have a deep-felt sense of personal inadequacy and insignificance. They are trapped in the absurdly comic tragedy of daily living. Even the poet himself is presented as a pathetic figure no better off than any other man, hardly a "small god," as Vicente Huidobro (q.v.), another Chilean poet, once described him. Some critics view the language and form of the antipoetic texts as a reflection of the disarray of contemporary society. Religion is debunked and denigrated. Women, once the main source of poetic inspiration, are perceived as heartless, seductive adversaries of man or as his exploited sexual playmates.

P. has parodied most of the major themes and stylistic devices employed throughout the Western poetic tradition. P.'s antipoetry has now been translated into many languages. It ridicules modern man for his continued adherence to defunct myths promoted by the social establishment. It also radically subverts the established forms and language found in conventional lyric poetry. P.'s works have broadened the boundaries of poetic expression to include almost every individual and social dimension of the human experience and have made the genre more accessible to the common man.

FURTHER WORKS: *Discursos* (1962); *Versos de salón* (1962); *La cueca larga, y otros poemas* (1964); *Canciones rusas* (1967); *Obra gruesa* (1969); *Los profesores* (1971). FURTHER VOLUME IN ENGLISH: *Emergency Poems* (1972, bilingual)

BIBLIOGRAPHY: Hersh, B., "The Man in the Ironic Mask," *Horizon,* May 1962, 35–41; Lerzundi, P., "In Defense of Antipoetry: An Interview with N. P.," *Review,* Nos. 4–5 (1972), 65–72; Van Hooft, K., "The *Artefactos* of N. P.: The Explosion of the Antipoem," *RevB,* 1, 1 (1974), 67–80; Grossman, E., *The Antipoetry of N. P.* (1975); Gottlieb, M., *No se termina nunca de nacer: La poesía de N. P.* (1977)

JAMES J. ALSTRUM

PASCOAES, Teixeira de
See Teixeira de Pascoaes

PASCOLI, Giovanni
Italian poet, b. 31 Dec. 1855, San Mauro di Romagna; d. 18 Feb. 1912, Bologna

P.'s early life was darkened by a series of tragic events: at the age of eleven, by the unsolved murder of his father; later, by the deaths of his mother and three of his brothers and sisters. His university years in Bologna were marked by involvement in the socialist movement and active participation in the International. Upon graduation in 1882, he began teaching Latin and Greek in several schools and universities in southern and northern Italy, until, in 1905, he was appointed to succeed Giosuè Carducci (1835–1907), his former teacher and mentor, in the chair of Italian literature at the University of Bologna. With the proceeds of the sale of thirteen gold medals awarded him at the Hoeuft annual competition for Latin poetry in Amsterdam, he purchased a much longed-for country home at Castelvecchio di Barga, a locale that inspired much of his poetry.

P.'s first collection of poems, published under the title of *Myricae* (1891; Latin: tamarisks), consists mostly of scenic sketches and descriptions of rural life, created by juxtaposing short phrases that add up to vivid series of pictorial and musical impressions. The choice of themes is psychologically connected to remembrances of his serene early childhood in the country and to his persistent sense of happiness forever lost. As a consequence, many lyrics that at first appear to be only idyllic descriptive fragments take on a vague and obscure symbolic meaning. Other poems are directly inspired by P.'s domestic sorrows and are highly charged with personal emotion. In the last poems of the collection, his own grief expands to a deeply melancholic view of man's destiny, and the descriptions of nature become laden with pending danger or cosmic catastrophe. The technical means by which P. achieves these effects are deceptively simple. While the logical structure of his sentence is minimal but still intact, the order of descriptive elements is very effectively handled to suggest a sense of foreboding. The use of refrains, of popular songs, of insistent onomatopoeia, of synesthesia, create the suggestion of a different, impenetrable reality in which the fates of men and of other creatures in the universe are mysteriously connected.

The poems of *Canti di Castelvecchio* (1903; songs of Castelvecchio) successfully continue the themes and manner of *Myricae*. Many poems are descriptions of his childhood or evoke the painful events of his youthful years; nonetheless, realistic evocations of daily life at Barga are dominant in the collection and give it its pervasive tone.

Primi poemetti (1904; first minor poems) and *Nuovi poemetti* (1906; new minor poems) depict the serene life of a family of farmers, with descriptions of the various phases of home and field work, of country festivities, of seasonal changes, and of animals, plants, and trees. What gives a lyrical, almost religious quality to these humble subjects is both a sense of cosmic correspondence in the destinies of men and their fellow creatures and the poet's strong belief in the sacred value of human and animal labor.

Poemi conviviali (1904; *Convivial Poems,* 1979) re-create scenes and situations of the classical world, from Homeric times to the rise of Christianity. The subject is solemn and the language highly precious and erudite; but the poet's pervasive feeling is that all things must come to an end and die, and that the dissolution of ancient myths and of history is inevitable.

Odi e Inni (1906; odes and hymns) contains poems of a civic nature. They are noteworthy as examples of the repeated attempt on the part of the poet, who never renounced his ideal of humanitarian socialism, to rationalize and harmonize his stands on the many social and political problems of contemporary Italy; among these were the massive emigration, which he felt was a heartrendingly tragic solution to unemployment, and the foreign policies of the Italian and other European governments, which he interpreted in terms of a struggle between poor and powerful nations.

Compared with the robust strains of Giosuè Carducci's poetry and with the flamboyant verse of Gabriele D'Annunzio (q.v.), P.'s work was long considered to be that of a homely provincial poet, a sort of bucolic Vergil in minor key. During the past decades critics have come to recognize that his emphasis on personal sensations and emotions, his persistent sense of loss, his technical innovations—connotative and evocative use of words and sounds, coherence of mood in place of logical coherence, new verse rhythms—his theory and practice of poetry as a predominantly intuitive activity place him in the mainstream of the Decadent and symbolist (q.v.) movements in Europe. Moreover, he is now considered the most genuine voice in Italian poetry of his time and the primary influence on all subsequent avant-garde poets.

FURTHER WORKS: *Il fanciullino* (1897); *Minerva oscura* (1898); *Sotto il velame* (1900); *La mirabile visione* (1902); *Nell'anno mille* (1902); *Miei pensieri di varia umanità* (1903); *La messa d'oro* (1905); *Pensieri e discorsi* (1907); *Canzoni di Re Enzio* (1908–9); *Poemetti italici* (1911); *Poesie varie* (1912); *Traduzioni e riduzioni* (1913); *Poemi del Risorgimento* (1913); *Carmina* (2 vols., 1914, 1930); *Antico sempre nuovo* (1925); *Lettere agli amici lucchesi* (1960); *Lettere agli amici urbinati* (1963); *Lettere ad Alfredo Caselli* (1968); *Tutte le opere* (6 vols., 1970–71); *Lettere a Mario Novaro e ad altri amici* (1971); *Lettere alla gentile ignota* (1972). FURTHER VOLUMES IN ENGLISH: *Poems of G. P.* (1923); *Poems of G. P.* (1927); *Selected Poems of G. P.* (1938)

BIBLIOGRAPHY: Valentin, A., *G. P., poète lyrique: Les thèmes de son inspiration* (1925); Purkis, G. S., Introduction to *Selected Poems of G. P.* (1938), pp. 1–10; Wilkins, E. H., *A History of Italian Literature* (1966), pp. 461–64; Ukas, M., "Nature in the Poetry of G. P.," *KFLQ,* 13 (1966), 51–59

RINALDINA RUSSELL

PASHTO LITERATURE

See Afghan Literature and Pakistani Literature

PASOLINI, Pier Paolo

Italian poet, novelist, essayist, and film director (also writing in Friulian), b. 5 March 1922, Bologna; d. 2 Nov. 1975, Ostia

After passing a somewhat peripatetic existence in several northern Italian cities as a young boy, a style of life occasioned by his father's military career, P. returned to his native city in 1937 and enrolled at the University of Bologna. He studied literature and art history and began writing poems in Friulian, a Rhaeto-Romanic dialect, publishing his first collection of verse, *Poesie a Casarsa* (poems to Casarsa), at his own expense in 1942. The family had spent summers for many years in the town of Casarsa, P.'s mother's birthplace northeast of Venice, and it is to this place that the poems are dedicated. In 1943 the family moved there; during the stay of six years the young poet's philological and creative interests flourished as he became more deeply involved with the dialect of the region and wrote more poetry both in Friulian and in Italian. In 1949 P. and his mother went to Rome, where he lived and worked until his brutal murder in a suburb of Rome. In the last decade of his life P. attained international renown as a film director and became one of contemporary Italy's most outspoken and controversial figures, in political and personal as well as artistic debates.

The richness and variety of P.'s career are equaled in magnitude only by the complexities of his inner life, which drove him to attempt a merging of his politics, metaphysics, and homosexuality into a cohesive, meaningful artistic and existential unity of intent and result. When viewed retrospectively, each work represents a piece of the mosaic, no matter how disparate the individual elements might at first appear.

P.'s first collection of verse in Friulian reflects his intense love for his mother's place of origin, a love tied to its landscapes, its peasants, and, above all, its language. The concept of an intimate "maternal tongue," one more poetically valid than standard speech, had essential resonances for P. from very early on. This intuition soon merged with his political concerns for the uneducated, dialect-speaking, marginal classes of Italy. His move to Rome opened up yet another world of experience, which both intensified his interest in the oppressed and sharpened his critical and literary skills: the former by direct contact with the Roman proletariat; the latter by collaboration on literary journals and continued study of the linguistic and artistic heritage of Italy. As P. maintained his dedication to writing poetry, he also began, in the early 1950s, to turn to fiction. In the novel *Ragazzi di vita* (1955; *The Ragazzi,* 1968), written in P.'s version of Roman dialect, P.'s goal was to describe, in their own language, the Roman street hustlers' daily struggle for survival. The protagonists are Rome's uneducated youth, who live precariously and violently in a state of permanent personal and social alienation from the bourgeois mainstream.

During this same period P. also wrote several articles in which he attempted to clarify his ideological convictions—Marxist for the most part, but already personalized by the writer's insistence on the fundamental role of culture and language in the struggle for a new Italian society. P.'s relationship to the Communist Party was always troubled and questioning; his formal association with the Party had ended shortly before his move to Rome with his expulsion "for moral and political unworthiness" because of a homosexual incident with minors for which P. was prosecuted. As in all his work, therefore, both the personal and the ideological components of his stormy politics must be kept in mind if his beliefs are to be understood correctly.

One of the clearest expressions of P.'s beliefs is found in his collection of poetry *Le ceneri di Gramsci* (1957; the ashes of Gramsci), written in standard Italian. Here he shows his ambivalence toward the political and cultural philosophy of Antonio Gramsci (1891–1937). On the one hand, he accepts the rational arguments of the great early Communist; on the other, he cannot follow the implicit exhortation to become identified passionately and intimately with the working class and to see it as an autonomous, potentially self-sufficient force for the significant transformation of society. His sense of personal, intellectual, and spiritual distance from the poor, for whom he nonetheless cared intensely, would torment him throughout his life and eventually led him to deny the possibility of total integration he so desperately sought through his entire career.

In the late 1950s P. published many volumes that manifest his multiple interests: *L'usignolo della Chiesa Cattolica* (1958; the nightingale of the Catholic Church), a collection of the poetry written in Italian between 1943 and 1949, in which the influence of symbolist (q.v.) and Decadent poetry is evident; *Una vita violenta* (1959; *A Violent Life,* 1968), another novel written in Roman dialect, in which the central theme is the difficult struggle for dignity and betterment of the lower classes; *Passione e ideologia* (1960; passion and ideology), a collection of critical essays on dialect poetry, modern and contemporary Italian poets and novelists, and general literary, linguistic, and cultural topics.

P.'s debut as a film director was in 1961 with *Accattone*. As is the case of most of his films, P. wrote the script, which was also published in 1961. The film is a cinematic version of the preoccupations evident in the two dialect novels, and is distinguished by a highly effective mix of harsh realism and subtle poetic sensibility. Throughout the 1960s and up to the time of his death, P. was primarily involved in filmmaking; his best-known and most successful films are *Il vangelo secondo Matteo* (1964; the gospel according to Matthew), a moving reinterpretation of the story of Christ's life from a Marxist perspective; *Uccellacci e uccellini* (1964; hawks and sparrows), an allegorical tale also with political undertones; *Teorema* (1968; theorem), a highly symbolic story of a family seduced by a frighteningly erotic Christ-figure; *Medea* (1970; Medea, a version of the classic tragedy starring Maria Callas; and his last film, *Salò; o, le 120 giornate di Sodoma* (1975; Salò; or, the 120 days of Sodom), a violently pornographic meditation on Italian Fascism from an eroto-political perspective provided primarily by the works of the Marquis de Sade. The scripts for all of these films were written by Pasolini and published in the same years of the films' releases. In addition, there exists an English translation of the script for the film *Edipo Re* (1967; *Oedipus Rex,* 1971), and in 1975 the scripts for *Il Decamerone* (1971; the Decameron), *I racconti di Canterbury* (1972; the Canterbury Tales), and *Il fiore delle mille e una notte* (1974; the flower of the thousand and one nights) were published under the title *Trilogia della vita* (trilogy of life). These last three films, perhaps the most popularly successful of all P.'s cinema, are delightfully eccentric reworkings of literary classics.

P. did not, however, abandon other forms of creative expression during the last years of his life. He wrote several tragedies in verse and published another collection of poetry, *Trasumanar e organizzar* (1971; to transfigure, to organize); in 1972 his prolific critical writings were again collected and published under the title *Empirismo eretico* (heretical empiricism). P. contributed extensively to the Milanese newspaper *Corriere della sera* in the final few years of his career, writing on everything from language to current events to politics. Although filled more and more with a sense of despair, P. remained enormously productive right up to the moment of his death, intending to direct more films, complete a novel, write more poetry, and pursue his eternal goal of joining personal confession and clarification with political and cultural activism.

The controversy surrounding P.'s death—was he murdered by one young man in a violent homosexual encounter or was he deliberately killed by prior arrangement for political reasons?—remains active to this day, and adds to the mysterious, mythic dimensions of the man and his destiny. Whatever the answer to the why of his death, however, the more essential answer to the why of his life lies in his prolific and undeniably positive gifts through which he has enriched our century.

SELECTED FURTHER WORKS: *Poesie* (1945); *I pianti* (1946); *Tal cour di un frut* (1953); *La meglio gioventù* (1954); *Donne di Roma* (1960); *Roma 1950, diario* (1960); *La religione del mio tempo* (1961); *Mamma Roma* (1962); *Poesia in forma di rosa* (1964); *Orgia* (1969); *Calderón* (1973); *Il padre selvaggio* (1975); *Scritti corsari* (1975); *La divina mimesis* (1975); *Lettere agli amici* (1976); *Lettere luterane* (1977); *Affabulazione; Pilade* (1977); *Le belle bandiere* (1977). FURTHER VOLUME IN ENGLISH: *P. P. P.: Poems* (1982)

BIBLIOGRAPHY: Ragusa, O., "Gadda, P. and Experimentalism: Form or Ideology?," in Pacifici, S., ed., *From Verismo to Experimentalism* (1969), pp. 239–69; O'Neill, T., "P. P. P.'s Dialect Poetry," *FI*, 9 (1975), 343–67; Anderson, L. J., "Challenging the Norm: The Dialect Question in the Works of Gadda and P.," *SHEH*, 20 (1977), 1–63; Marcus, M., "P. P. P.'s Poetics of Film," *YItS*, 1 (1977), 184–94; Friedrich, P., *P. P. P.* (1982); Siciliano, E., *P.: A Biography* (1982);

White, E., on *P.: A Biography* and *P. P. P.: Poems, NYTBR,* 27 June 1982, 8–9, 14

REBECCA J. WEST

PASTERNAK, Boris

Russian poet and prose writer, b. 10 Feb. 1890, Moscow; d. 30 May 1960, Peredelkino

Born into a family of great talent—his father, Leonid Pasternak, was a well-known painter (a friend of Leo Tolstoy and illustrator of his works), and his mother, Rosalia Kaufmann, a concert pianist—P. was early exposed to the world of art. Under the influence of the music and personality of Alexander Scriabin (another P. family acquaintance), P. spent his adolescent years preparing for a career in music, but gave it up for philosophy, which he studied at the universities of Moscow and Marburg, Germany.

His first collection of verse, *Bliznets v tuchakh* (1914; a twin in the clouds), was followed by *Poverkh barerov* (1917; over the barriers). His following two books, *Sestra moya zhizn* (1922; *Sister My Life,* 1967) and *Temy i variatsii* (1923; themes and variations), brought him critical acclaim and wide recognition; they proved to be the most influential of his works. A trip to the Caucasus in 1931 established long-term friendships and collaborations with several Georgian poets. *Vtoroe rozhdenie* (1932; second birth) marks the beginning of P.'s consciously simpler style. After the mid-1930s P. led an increasingly secluded life at his country house outside Moscow. Two slim volumes of poems, *Na rannikh poezdakh* (1943; on early trains) and *Zemnoy prostor* (1945; earth's expanse), appeared during World War II. His novel, *Doktor Zhivago* (1957; *Doctor Zhivago,* 1958), was banned in the Soviet Union, but published abroad and translated into many languages; it brought P. worldwide recognition. In 1958 P. was awarded the Nobel prize for literature, which he was forced to refuse under pressure of an attack in the Soviet press. He died two years later.

During 1914–16, without sharing in the futurist (q.v.) poets' generally unconventional behavior or supporting their highly negative view of the art of the past, P. actively participated in Centrifuge, one of the modernist literary groups. More importantly, his handling of language and the deliberate use of nonaesthetic imagery in the poems of the period (most notably in *Poverkh barerov*) reveal P.'s more than casual relation to futurist poetics. While some critics (for example, Wladimir Weidlé) accept P.'s own retrospective view of this episode in his life as something transitory and unimportant for his development, others (such as Lazar Fleishman), although acknowledging his peripheral position, tend to view his futurist orientation as very significant until the 1930s.

Written in 1917 and 1918 respectively, but only published five years after their composition, *Sestra moya zhizn* and *Temy i variatsii* can be described as the "essential" P. The emotionally charged poems in these two books demonstrate well the fundamentals of P.'s poetry. Although the setting of the lyrics is often urban, it is through seasonal and natural changes that the emotional developments are conveyed. Transference of experiences between the subject and his surroundings—an effective device for depicting communion with nature and awareness of the surrounding physical world—testifies to a poetic point of view that embraces everything about the subject. The poet's never-failing surprise at returning spring or the joy brought by rain, for example, contribute toward the youthfulness and dynamism of this poetry. Many poems are about lovers' separations and disappointments, but the general tone is one of exaltation and exuberance. The complexity of imagery, the verbal richness, and the elliptic and unconventional syntax contribute to the appeal as well as the difficulty of this verse.

Publication of these two books established P. as a major poet of the period. The influence of his poetic manner of expression was soon seen in the work of his contemporaries and younger poets and even of some poets of the preceding generation.

One of the persistent criticisms directed at P. by establishment critics was his interest in the individual rather than in the collective. Ignoring the revolution was tantamount to rejecting it. But for P. himself, *Sestra moya zhizn* was a book about revolution, with the poet not chronicling events but conveying their essence.

During the 1920s P. published two longer narrative poems, "Devyatsot pyaty god" (1927; the year 1905) and "Leytenant Shmidt" (1927; Lieutenant Schmidt), in which he attempted to deal with the subject of the revolution. Just as in his shorter lyrics P. speaks not about himself but assigns his experiences to the surrounding world, here

he speaks not about the main event but about what led to it—about the 1905 rather than the 1917 revolution. Although reprinted many times, these poems were not as successful artistically as his short lyrics.

Along with his first poems, P. started experimenting in prose, although it was not until 1925 that a collection was published, under the title *Rasskazy* (*Zhenia's Childhood, and Other Stories,* 1982). The long prose piece "Detstvo Lyuvers" (written 1918; *The Adolescence of Zhenya Luvers,* 1961), showing the world through the perception of an adolescent girl, was singled out for particular praise by the critics. Other pieces in the volume deal mainly with the problems of art and the artist.

A major prose work, *Okhrannaya gramota* (1931; "A Safe-Conduct," 1949; later tr., 1977), is an autobiography that proposes to speak about the poet's own life only when prompted by the biographies of those who were important for his development as a human being and a poet. Complex and allusive, it is one of the high points of P.'s prose works. Beginning with a chance meeting in 1900 of P.'s family with Rainer Maria Rilke (q.v.), a significant influence acknowledged by P. himself, it ends in 1930, with the suicide of Vladimir Mayakovsky (q.v.), his contemporary, friend—and often antagonist.

P.'s simpler manner in the book of verse *Vtoroe rozhdenie* was to remain his goal until the end of his life. This programmatic desire for a less complex means of expression can be seen, at least in part, as a result of a genuine wish to become more accessible, aided, no doubt, by constant official criticism of his being incomprehensible to the mass reader. This new style, although strikingly different from his earlier work in some aspects, most notably in syntax, developed from P.'s original complexity and retained in a subdued form many of the stylistic features of his earlier poetry.

After Mayakovsky's death, P. was left the undisputed candidate for the role of the "first poet" of the Soviet state, and, indeed, his fortunes at that time stood very high. But the publication of *Okhrannaya gramota,* a highly complex and idiosyncratic work, was an indication that the poet remained his old self. Paradoxically, but consistent with P.'s temperament and position, it was at this time that he turned to translation, which became his primary occupation and main source of income until the end of his life.

P. translated Georgian poets and western European poets—Kleist, Keats, Shelley, Verlaine, Rilke. One of his last such enterprises was Goethe's *Faust*. Although prompted by the inability to publish his own works (between 1935 and 1943 no new book of his was published) and by the need to earn money to support his large family, translation, especially of Shakespeare's plays, gave P. the possibility of reaching large audiences and served as a tool for forging the simplicity of his mature work. In translating Shakespeare, P. consciously modernized the language in an attempt to make him easily comprehensible to contemporary audiences. Translations, however, were taking up most of his time and keeping him from his own work, and in his later years this complaint became one of the constant themes in his correspondence.

Doktor Zhivago, which P. considered his single greatest achievement, was conceived as a tribute to the memory of those of his friends and contemporaries who did not survive the years of Stalin's terror. From this concept stems the sense of urgency in P.'s letters of the period: in writing *Doktor Zhivago* he was paying his debt as one of the surviving witnesses of the epoch. The main conflict of the novel is between "living life" and dead ideology. The affirmation of life is couched in terms typical of P.: love and nature amid the day-to-day existence of the revolutionary and the civil-war years.

The social and economic changes brought about by the revolution initially are accepted by Zhivago without hesitation. It is the ideology that becomes an end in itself and thus turns against life that is rejected. Life is not "material" that can be shaped to fit an abstract scheme. In rejecting the regime that issued from the revolution, Zhivago defends the value of every individual and the value of life itself. In this he comes close to Christianity, the essence of which for him is precisely in its treatment of human personality as an absolute value.

The novel's protagonist, whose name means "life," is a physician and a poet. But he stops practicing his profession, is separated from his family, and is virtually unknown as a poet, and he dies in 1929 an apparent failure. But in the epilogue, his friends read Zhivago's poems and find a new significance in them: the poems speak of their time and its meaning. For P., a poet, apparently unconcerned with current events and out of step with the changing times, is in his art

able to touch upon the essence of history. This is the paradox of the timelessness of art and its inevitable connection with its time.

The epilogue, set in 1943 and later, is cautiously optimistic. This was the mood of P. during World War II, when he was writing the novel and hoped that the loyalty to the regime demonstrated by the Soviet people during the war would bring about a fundamental change in the system. This hope was revived again after Stalin's death.

The final section of the novel consists of the poems attributed to Zhivago. It is in his poetry that he fulfills himself and leaves a living legacy. Immortality for Zhivago is life in the memory of others, so it is through self-sacrifice that a meaningful life is achieved. The novel and especially the poems abound in New Testament symbols of death and resurrection.

The resounding success of the novel in the West was a source of joy for P., since it brought him in contact with fellow writers and readers around the world. The success, however, was also a source of constant anxiety for him, for by allowing it to be published in the West, he defied one of the basic tenets of Soviet society.

P. was one of the most original and influential Russian poets of the century. Whatever the official pronouncements, his poetry is well known and highly valued by poets and discerning readers. In publishing *Doktor Zhivago* he took his place at the head of what is now a long list of writers to publish despite official prohibition; in writing it, he was one of the first among Soviet Russian writers to express in a clear voice the truth about Soviet society.

FURTHER WORKS: *Spektorsky* (1931); *Vozdushnye puti* (1933); *Povest* (1934; *The Last Summer,* 1959); *Avtobiografichesky ocherk* (1961; also pub. as *Lyudi i polozhenia,* 1967; *I Remember: Sketch for an Autobiography,* 1959); *Kogda razgulyaetsya* (1959; *Poems 1955–1959,* 1960, bilingual ed.); *Sochinenia* (3 vols., 1961); *Stikhotvorenia i poemy* (1965); *Slepaya krasavitsa* (1969: *The Blind Beauty,* 1969); *Stikhotvorenia i poemy* (1976); *Perepiska s Olgoy Freydenberg* (1981; *The Correspondence of B. P. and Olga Freidenberg, 1910–1954,* 1982). FURTHER VOLUMES IN ENGLISH: *The Collected Prose Works* (1945); *Selected Poems* (1946); *Selected Writings* (1949); *Poems* (1959); *Safe Conduct: An Early Autobiography, and Other*

Works (1959); *The Poetry of B. P.: 1917–1959* (1959); *In the Interlude: Poems 1945–1960* (1962); *Poems* (1964); *Letters to Georgian Friends* (1967); *Collected Short Prose* (1977)

BIBLIOGRAPHY: Conquest, R., *The P. Affair: Courage of Genius* (1962); Davie, D., and Livingstone, A., eds., *P.: Modern Judgements* (1969); special P. section, *BA*, 44 (1970), 195–243; Hughes, O. R., *The Poetic World of B. P.* (1974); Pomorska, K., *Themes and Variations in P.'s Poetics* (1975); Nilsson, N. Å., ed., *B. P.: Essays* (1976); Gladkov, A., *Meetings with P.* (1977); Gifford, H., *P.: A Critical Study* (1977); France, A. K., *B. P.'s Translations of Shakespeare* (1978); Erlich, V., ed., *P.: Twentieth Century Views* (1978); Ivinskaya, O., *A Captive of Time* (1978); Mallac, G. de, *B. P.: His Life and Art* (1981)

OLGA RAEVSKY HUGHES

In the *Tales* there is neither the passionate intensity nor the verbal innovation [of P.'s poetry]. All attention is directed to a new manner of perception of reality and its interpretation. Liberation from the customary associations that give practical and facile explanations to the endless complexity of the world—this is the main goal of P. the prose writer.... "Childhood of Luvers" is a "psychological" history of a girl. But the "psychology" of this tale is not the least bit "psychological." It deals not with emotions or thoughts, but exclusively with perceptions ... and a gradual formation from them of a definitive picture of the world. It is interesting to compare the sober, dry, and tight "Childhood of Luvers" with the treatment of similar subjects by Andrey Bely and by Proust. Precision, aloofness, a kind of a scientific coolness, and the quiet attentiveness of P. are the complete opposite of Bely's manner. But just as striking is his dissimilarity from Proust: instead of the endless, almost lifelike unfolding of memory, [there are] specific, very precisely and concisely presented moments, like symbols on a relief map giving a complete picture of a locality.... And all this intellectuality is directed toward exploring the most inexpressible and irrational processes, which in strange ways and judgements, eventually completely forgotten, create an original world in the child's consciousness that is afterward "related" to the world of adults.

Dmitri Svyatopolk-Mirsky, on *Rasskazy, Sovremennye zapiski,* 25 (1925), 544

If his determination to maintain always a level of pure poetry sometimes makes him obscure or even awkward, it also means that he never writes below

a certain standard and never wastes his time on irrelevant matter. The close texture of his verse, which at times makes it difficult to grasp all his implications at a first reading, is an essential feature of his art. It helps him to convey his intense, concentrated experience and is a true mirror of his moods. He looks at objects not in isolation but as parts of a wider unity, marks their relations in a complex whole, and stresses the dominant character of a scene as much as the individual elements in it. His work is therefore extremely personal, but not so personal as to be beyond the understanding of other men. He assumes that others will recognise the truth of his vision and come to share it with him. For, in his view, what he gives them is not a scientific, photographic transcript of an impersonal, external reality but something intensely human, since reality and value are given to things by our appreciation of them and by our absorption of them into our consciousness. Man is the centre of the universe, and human consciousness is its uniting principle.

C. M. Bowra, "B. P., 1917–1923," *The Creative Experiment* (1949), pp. 133–34

The poet himself remarked somewhere that poetry or art is the natural object informed by, or seen under, the aspect of energy—the all pervasive *vis vivida* whose flow, at times broken and intermittent, is the world of things and persons, forces and states, acts and sensations. To attempt to give more precise significance to this kind of vision may be perilous and foolish, save by discrimination from what it is not: it is neither a pathetic fallacy whereby human experience is projected into inanimate objects, nor yet is it the inversion of this, to be found, for example, in the novels of Virginia Woolf, where the fixed structure of human beings and material objects is dissolved into the life and the properties of the shifting patterns of the data of the inner and outer senses.... There is, on the contrary, a sense of unity induced by the sense of the pervasiveness of cosmic categories ... which integrate all the orders of creation into a single, biologically and physiologically, emotionally and intellectually, interrelated universe.... Nor is this a consciously bold device or technical method of juxtaposing opposites to secure a spark or an explosion; it conveys a directly experienced vision of a single world-wide, world-long system of tensions and stresses, a perpetual ebb and flow of energy.

Isaiah Berlin, "The Energy of P.," *PR,* 7 (1950), 749–50

But, although in no vulgar sense subversive, the novel certainly contains a most devastating criticism of the very foundations of official Soviet enthusiasm. The real danger it presents to the régime is that it destroys the position of moral superiority of the political "activists" and restores the confidence of those who are seeking nothing more than their right to love nature and to follow in their actions the inclinations of their heart. The compelling power of P.'s argument is not based on any theoretical view, but on a direct poetical vision of Soviet society and of the mechanism by which its ideological foundations are maintained.... It is hardly probable that ... literary bureaucrats ... could understand and estimate all the dangers P.'s novel presents for the ideological foundations of the régime. But they must instinctively realise that once a work of art of such spontaneity has reached the public, they will not be able to look their readers in the eye when repeating the hackneyed, conventional phrases with which they fill their writings.

Max Hayward, "P.'s *Dr. Zhivago*," *Encounter*, May 1958, 48

In a way quite different from Mayakovsky's, without recourse to purely tonic verse, without doing violence to classical meters, P. approximates poetry to prose, gives his verse the intonations and cadences of ordinary colloquial speech, and yet achieves wonderful musical and rhythmical effects. He is nothing if not a musical poet. Some of his best poems ... may appear to defy normal semantic analysis, but as the reader is carried along on the waves of their sound magic, their hidden and profound meaning is revealed to him. Yet there is in P. nothing of the effeminate musicality of a Zhukovsky, a Fet, a Balmont, or a Verlaine. The texture of his verse is taut and muscular. His prosaisms, his bold enjambments, his paradoxical juxtaposition of poetic and unpoetic words and lavish use of metonymy, destroy the automatism of perception and enhance the effect of novelty and freshness. He has been compared with Donne, with Gerard Manley Hopkins (without his religion), and with Rilke (without his mysticism), but one might as well find in him parallels with T. S. Eliot and Dylan Thomas—and if poetry could develop untrammeled in the Soviet Union, his influence on the younger generation of poets would certainly be comparable to Eliot's in England and America.

Gleb Struve, *Russian Literature under Lenin and Stalin, 1917–1953* (1971), p. 182

Zhivago's vision of the wholly lived life transcends the claims of all factions and the savage meaningless wars they fight among themselves. He stands apart from this struggle, but later, as the revolution gains the upper hand, he cannot avoid total engagement in the deeper conflict between the new politics and life itself, a conflict which impinges on language, art, morality, religion, theories of history, and culture in the broadest sense: all the ceremonies, institutions, and explanations

men devise to ease their earthly situation. Zhivago defines and defends his view of these entities as he discovers that the revolution corrupts or destroys some aspects of each, ignores others, and proposes spurious substitutes for still others. Nothing of the revolution's total program except its initial grievances and its long-term aspirations—its ends—remains valid for him. The fanatical actions and doctrines that brought the revolution to power—its means—will apparently endure indefinitely, certainly beyond the span of his life. The interim men, who do not contemplate their own passing, will carry out their arrogant and misguided plans, as he sees it, at the expense of most of civilization's legacy. Alone, embattled and unknown, he must stand and fight.

Rufus W. Mathewson, Jr., "P.: 'An Inward Music,' " *The Positive Hero in Russian Literature* (1975), p. 261

P. builds his New Testament scenes by blending the miraculous and the humdrum, the exceptional and the workaday, the supernatural and the ordinary. The prosiness of some of the details and the everyday quality of the proceedings serve to authenticate the miracle of which the poem tells and lend the events of sacred history an emphatically contemporary and personal stamp. The author adheres strictly to the canonical story and reproduces it at times with textual precision, but in the language and the psychological and social detail he takes bold liberties which are taken, however, not in order to violate the canvas of the legend, but to make it more exact and tangible. He approaches this theme in roughly the same way as Breughel and Rembrandt did in their time.... As a result the Biblical text in P.'s version appears as the most contemporary, actual reality. His poems on evangelical themes leave us with the feeling that the sacred mystery has endured to this very day.

Andrey Sinyavsky, "P.'s Poetry," in Victor Erlich, ed., *P.: Twentieth Century Views* (1978), p. 101

It would be most unwise to see in the text of "Safe Conduct" a collection of veiled allusions to Lef [post-revolutionary futurism]. The work's complex philosophical meaning, which brings contradictory ideological intentions into a tragic opposition, would be overshadowed by merely clever and inventive theoretical discussions. And yet a register—as complete as possible—of [the book's] hidden polemical responses to contemporary developments and the elucidation of specific addressees, in our opinion, can explain both the meaning of a number of statements in "Safe Conduct" that have still not been explicated and their structural function in an autobiographical text.... [A] static and "dogmatic" expression of his own views is alien to P. in principle. Despite his distaste for public appearances, his conscious attempts to avoid organized forms of literary battles, and his avoidance of journalistic polemics, the very character of P.'s thinking (including aesthetic and theoretical problems) tended toward dynamic opposition, a kind of purgation that lays bare the internally contradictory essence of the conceptions at hand. This means that the omission of the hidden polemical (and autopolemical) intent of P.'s aesthetic declarations, the attempt to read them outside their temporal context diminishes their profoundly personal undercurrent and, instead of demonstrating the poet's ties with his time..., turns the protagonist of the autobiography into a rhetorical declaimer of abstract truths.

Lazar Fleishman, *B. P. v dvadtsatye gody* (1981), pp. 195–96

PATON, Alan

South African novelist, short-story writer, essayist, and poet (writing in English), b. 11 Jan. 1903, Pietermaritzburg

P.'s upbringing by deeply religious parents of English stock sensitized him to the moral and ethical principles underlying the racial conflicts in South Africa. He interprets the race struggle as a larger revolt of man against domination—against dominating and being dominated.

This view marked his innovations as principal of Diep Kloof Reformatory near Johannesburg, an experience that provided the material for several short stories and moved him to political action in the anti-apartheid Liberal Association, of which he was founder (1953) and president. The poles of his political views and literary themes are the same: the negative, a distrust of institutionalized power; the positive, a belief in the power of love expressed as human brotherhood.

The subject of an early, uncompleted novel—Christ's return to South Africa—anticipates the material of P.'s later fiction. His first published novel, *Cry, the Beloved Country* (1948), the story of Stephen Kumalo, a Zulu minister, and his search for his son in Johannesburg, is about racial tensions, but its primary theme is the brotherhood of man. His second, *Too Late the Phalarope* (1953), is about a white man destroyed because of an affair with a native girl. Again the primary object is to indict the inhumanity of racial separation as institutionalized in such legislation as the Immorality Act, which prohibits sexual relations between black and white.

Moving as these novels are, they are open to the charge that P. manipulates characters to conform to his thesis about the political and social situations they dramatize.

The death of P.'s wife in 1967 turned him to a self-searching analysis of domination in the complex structure of marriage in *Kontakion for You Departed* (1969). In this painful, sometimes moving account of the relationship with his wife, P. attempted to define marital communion as the sacramental point of transition from what is at best a flawed *agape* existing within society toward the perfection of the Creator's love.

Critics often overlook this thematic preoccupation when they object that humanitarian zeal sometimes reduces P.'s fiction to the level of propaganda. The charge is in any case more applicable to the volume of short stories *Debbie Go Home* (1961; Am., *Tales from a Troubled Land*) than to the novels.

The appeal of his fiction derives from the language—simple, seemingly unadorned, but modified by the rhythms of African languages and Afrikaans—and from an intricate symbolic interweaving of land, people, and theme.

In 1980 appeared *Towards the Mountain,* an account of P.'s life up to 1948. It deals largely with the public events of his life, as *Kontakion for You Departed* does with the private. The promised second part of the autobiography will likely also deal mainly with public involvements. But these have already been well documented in *The Long View* (1967), a selection of essays on political and social matters originally published in the South African journal *Contact* between 1955 and 1966, which exhibit the insistent reason of his arguments, and in *Knocking at the Door* (1976), a collection of short fiction, poems, and articles on various subjects, including politics and penal reform.

The nonfiction that P. produced in the 1960s and 1970s prepared the way for the novel *Ah, But Your Land Is Beautiful* (1981), a narrative marked by greater stylistic variety than his earlier fiction. He uses a sequence of poison-pen letters and speeches by public figures, which, although they newly dramatize his long-standing advocacy of individual freedom and racial equality, do little for characterization.

P.'s poetry is governed by the qualities so evident in his prose: feeling, reason, and clarity of expression. These qualities, however, work to disadvantage in the poetry, sometimes leaving the didactic element too apparent. The ideal medium for his characteristic intensity of feeling and simplicity of style is provided by *Instrument of Thy Peace* (1968), reflections on a prayer of Saint Francis of Assisi. In this meditative work P. confronts without equivocation the difficulties of the region in which personal and social relationships come into conflict. Wherever the uncertainties of this kind of conflict reach the danger stage, both P.'s personal commitment and his achievements in literature will be consulted as touchstones of courage and integrity.

FURTHER WORKS: *South Africa Today* (1953); *The Land and People of South Africa* (1955; rev. ed., 1972); *South Africa in Transition* (1956, with Dan Weiner); *Hope for South Africa* (1958); *Hofmeyr* (1964; Am., *South African Tragedy: The Life and Times of Jan Hofmeyr*); *Sponomo* (1965, with Krishna Shah); *Apartheid and the Archbishop: The Life and Times of Geoffrey Clayton, Archbishop of Cape Town* (1973)

BIBLIOGRAPHY: on *Cry, the Beloved Country, TLS,* 23 Oct. 1948, 593; on *Too Late the Phalarope, TLS,* 28 Aug. 1953, 545; Baker, S., "P.'s Beloved Country and the Morality of Geography," *CE,* 19, 2 (1957), 56–61; Callan, E., *A. P.* (1968); Breslin, J. B., "Inside South Africa," *America,* 17 April 1976, 344–46; Sharma, R. C., "A. P.'s *Cry, the Beloved Country:* The Parable of Compassion," *LHY,* 19, 2 (1978), 64–82; Cooke, J., " 'A Hunger of the Soul': *Too Late the Phalarope* Reconsidered," *ESA,* 22 (1979), 37–43

MANLY JOHNSON

PAULHAN, Jean

French literary critic, essayist, and novelist, b. 2 Dec. 1884, Nîmes; d. 9 Oct. 1968, Melun

After receiving his degree from the Sorbonne, P. spent several years prospecting for gold and teaching on the island of Madagascar. Upon his return to Paris, he became a professor of Malagasy at the School of Oriental Languages. From 1925 to 1940 he worked for *La nouvelle revue française,* succeeding Jacques Rivière (1886–1925) as its editor in 1925. During World War II he was instrumental in launching the clandestine *Les lettres françaises* and Éditions de Minuit, and he cooperated with the French resistance

movement. Later, however, he approved the return of those writers who had been collaborators.

P. was the recipient of the Grand Prize for Literature of the French Academy in 1945 and of the Grand Prize of the City of Paris in 1951. In 1953 he resumed his responsibilities as editor of *La nouvelle nouvelle revue française* and as a consultant to the Gallimard publishing house. In these capacities, he exercised a profound influence on new talents, whom he discovered and encouraged. He was elected to the French Academy in 1964. It was not until the last years of his life, when his *œuvres complètes* (1966 ff.; collected works) began to be published, that his writing won for him the widespread recognition that he so well deserved.

P. wrote the preface to the scandalous *L'histoire d'O.* (1954; *The Story of O.,* 1966), which was published under the pseudonym Pauline Réage, and he was for a long time presumed to be the author of the novel. The book was, however, apparently written by a woman long associated with him as friend and secretary.

P.'s interest in and exploration of the problem of language, his lifelong preoccupation, was stimulated by his sojourn as a young man in Madagascar. He brought back from there *Les hain-tenys* (1913; Malagasy: the hains-tenys), which contains the Malagasy songs and proverbs he had been collecting.

P. continued to be dominated by the idea of language when writing *Le guerrier appliqué* (1917; the diligent warrior), *Jacob Cow, le pirate* (1922; Jacob Cow, the pirate), *Le pont traversé* (1922; the crossed bridge), *La guérison sévère* (1925; the hard recovery), and *Aytré qui perd l'habitude* (1926; Aytré who loses the habit). The early *Le guerrier appliqué,* a curious war tale inspired by P.'s experiences during World War I, illustrates, through subtle reasonings, the interplay between the realities of a soldier's life and his dreams or reveries, the search for liberation through thought and language.

Complicated and mysterious, all these tales reveal, in the subtle analysis of the subconscious, how at best language merely approximates, or screens, the essence of thought and feeling. P. saw language as a trap, and in his demand for a means of expression that was more exact and authentic he rejected the eloquent, the commonplace, and the phrasing that reflects the thinking of acquired social habits.

Ultimately, to achieve his ideal, P. participated in what has been characterized as the "terror" of cubism and of surrealism (qq.v.), or, as one critic prefers to call it, "irrealism." Hostile toward the rhetorical, he favored the use of a hermetic and audacious vocabulary, one more consistent with the kind used by those who emulated Henry Miller (q.v.) or the Marquis de Sade.

Reveling in paradox and always ready to correct a previous metamorphosis, P. realized that extremes breed new extremes, that the "terror" he had helped to make happen had paralyzed or handicapped the writer's creativity. To remedy this, he later did an about-face in the hope of restoring liberty to the writer, and proceeded to demonstrate, in the voluminous essay *Les fleurs de Tarbes* (1941; the flowers of Tarbes), how rhetoric could be used effectively.

À demain la poésie (1947; good-bye until tomorrow, poetry), probably P.'s best and clearest work, is a denunciation of those who renounced completely the accepted means of expression and thought to embrace wholeheartedly the dream, automatic writing, and the irrational. While words are dangerous, demonstrably so in P.'s writing, they are undeniably at the root of thought.

Absorbed with problems of language and poetics, into whose meaning and scope he inquired, P. wrote with enigmatic precision, using in his essays and tales a style that is at once, in its associations and affectations, subtle and elegant. Like Mallarmé and Valéry (q.v.), he insisted on an absolute unity of word and meaning, of form and content. Like them, too, he fought relentlessly for the autonomy of literature. An iconoclast, he was an enemy of mediocrity, a friend to innovators, and a guardian of the avant-garde.

FURTHER WORKS: *Entretiens sur des faits divers* (1933); *Clef de la poésie* (1944); *Sept causes célèbres* (1946); *Petit guide d'un voyage en Suisse* (1947); *De la paille et du grain* (1948); *Lettre aux directeurs de la résistance* (1952)

BIBLIOGRAPHY: Toesca, M., *J. P.: L'écrivain appliqué* (1948); Carmody, F. M. "J. P.'s Imaginative Writings," *Occidental*, Nov.–Dec. 1949, 28–34; Lefèbvre, M. J., *J. P.: Une philosophie et une pratique de l'expression et de la réflexion* (1949); Judrin, R., *La vocation transparente de J. P.* (1961); Elsen, C., *J. P.: Histoire d'une amitié* (1968); Poulet, C., *J. P., l'écrivain* (1968); Hellens, F., *Adieu à J. P.* (1969)

SIDNEY D. BRAUN

PAUSTOVSKY, Konstantin Georgievich

Russian memoirist, short-story writer, and novelist, b. 31 May 1892, Moscow; d. 14 July 1968, Moscow

Son of a railroad statistician, P. grew up in Kiev. His father encouraged him to become a writer, and at an early age his imagination was excited by the tales of his grandfather, a proud descendent of the Zaporozhian Cossacks. In 1913, after two years of study at the University of Kiev, P. moved to Moscow. Soon after, his years of wandering began; they continued until 1929. During this time P. frequently changed jobs and absorbed countless experiences. He worked as a tram conductor and driver, a medical orderly for the imperial army during World War I, a factory worker, a fisherman, a teacher, and a journalist. He went to the front, returned to Moscow, made his way to Kiev, lived for a period in Odessa, and spent time in the Caucasus. In the late 1920s he returned to Moscow, where he spent the rest of his life, although he continued to travel extensively both in the Soviet Union and abroad (after World War II). During World War II he served as a war correspondent on the southern front.

P. published his first story in 1912 but did not turn to writing as a career until the early 1920s. At that time he worked with fellow writers Isaac Babel, Valentine Kataev, and Edvard Bagritsky (qq.v.) on the Odessa journal *Moryak*. His first collection of stories, *Morskie nabroski* (sea sketches), was published in 1925. This volume and two novels written in the same period, *Romantiki* (written 1916–23, pub. 1935; the romantics) and *Blistayushchie oblaka* (1929; shining clouds), are marked by a strong romantic coloring and by exoticism. P. writes about strange lands far across the seas and about dreamers, writers, and artists. It is not the biographies of his heroes that are important but their inner lives, their feelings.

Before long P. abandoned the exotic and began to write about everyday life. Even so, a romantic quality continued to permeate his writings. It was one of the most distinctive elements in his prose, as P. himself was later to acknowledge. P.'s short stories of the

1930s and 1940s are often marked by a wistful lyricism and by a suggestion of mysterious coincidence. Mood is heightened by evocative nature descriptions. In many stories the natural beauty of central Russia is celebrated: it is described in concise, harmonious language, conveying to the reader the simple splendor of the Russian landscape. Even in his longer historical works of the 1930s and 1940s—*Kara-Bugaz* (1932; *The Black Gulf,* 1946), *Chernoe more* (1936; the Black Sea), *Severnaya povest* (1939; a northern tale), and *Povest o lesakh* (1949; a tale of the forests)—P. plays on the reader's emotions rather than carefully reconstructing historical reality. He strives to evoke a feeling of kinship with the past and of awe before the courage and self-sacrifice of its heroes.

P.'s most important postwar work is his autobiography, *Povest o moey zhizni* (6 vols., 1946–63; *The Story of a Life,* 6 vols., 1964–74). The work consists of hundreds of short episodes unified by the personality of the author and by the underlying theme of Russian history on the march. P. does not simply recount his own life but evokes the turbulent times surrounding it. He captures vivid likenesses of famous contemporaries (Isaak Babel and Mikhail Bulgakov [q.v.], just to name two) as well as many ordinary people. The first volume, *Dalyokie gody* (1946; *Childhood and Schooldays,* 1964), focuses on P.'s childhood; the second, *Bespokoynaya yunost* (1955; *Slow Approach of Thunder,* 1965), deals with the period of World War I; the third, *Nachalo nevedomogo veka* (1957; *In That Dawn,* 1967), with the Russian Revolution and the civil war; the fourth, *Vremya bolshikh ozhidany* (1959; *Years of Hope,* 1968), with P.'s adventures in Odessa in 1921. The fifth, *Brosok na yug* (1960; *Southern Adventure,* 1969), and sixth, *Kniga skitany* (1963; *The Restless Years,* 1974), treat P.'s wanderings during the 1920s.

The translation of P.'s autobiography into several European languages in the 1960s won him wide acclaim abroad. He has always been extremely popular with Russian readers because of the romantic quality of his writings, the courage and idealism of his heroes, his poignant love stories, and his descriptions of Russian nature. P. was also greatly admired by younger writers for the sincerity and warmth of his writing and for his integrity. In the 1950s and 1960s he spoke out in defense of writers who came under attack by the regime. For over ten years he ran a seminar for young writers at Tarusa, an artists' colony south of Moscow. In the semiautobiographical *Zolotaya roza* (1956; *The Golden Rose,* 1957) P. talks about the creative process and discusses the origins of many of his own writings.

FURTHER WORKS: *Minetoza* (1927); *Vstrechnye korabli* (1929); *Sudba Charlya Lonsevilya* (1933); *Kolkhida* (1934); *Rasskazy* (1935); *Letnie dni* (1937); *Orest Kiprensky* (1937); *Isaak Levitan* (1937); *Povesti i rasskazy* (1939); *Taras Shevchenko* (1939); *Poruchik Lermontov* (1941); *Nash sovremennik: Pushkin* (1949); *Rozhdenie morya* (1952); *Perstenek* (1956); *Sobranie sochineny* (8 vols., 1967–70). FURTHER VOLUMES IN ENGLISH: *The Flight of Time: New Stories* (1955); *Selected Stories* (1967)

BIBLIOGRAPHY: Bondarev, Y., "A Master of Prose," *SovL,* No. 10 (1962), 166–69; Alexandrova, V., *A History of Soviet Literature* (1963), pp. 302–16; Lehrman, E. H., "K. G. P.," in Simmonds, G., ed., *Soviet Leaders* (1967), pp. 296–309; Urman, D., "K. P., Marcel Proust, and the Golden Rose of Memory," *CSS,* 2 (1968), 311–26; Kasack, W., *Der Stil K. G. P.s* (1971); Vatnikova-Prizel, Z., "P.'s *Povest o moey zhizni:* Autobiographical Techniques," *RLJ,* No. 105 (1976), 81–89; Slonim, M., *Soviet Russian Literature: Writers and Problems, 1917–1977,* 2nd rev. ed. (1977), pp. 118–27

SONA STEPHAN HOISINGTON

PAVESE, Cesare

Italian novelist, poet, short-story writer, and translator, b. 9 Sept. 1908, Santo Stefano Belbo; d. 27 Aug. 1950, Turin

P. was born in a village in the Piedmontese Langhe hills, where his family came on summer vacation and where P. returned all his life. He attended the University of Turin, specializing in American literature and graduating in 1930. His thesis on the poetry of Walt Whitman was first rejected for failing to follow the cultural directives of the Fascist regime and for being influenced by Benedetto Croce's (q.v.) aesthetic theories. P.'s love for English and especially American literature was lifelong. His first publications were translations of Sinclair Lewis's (q.v.) *Our Mr. Wrenn* and of Melville's *Moby-Dick.* He also translated works by Sherwood Anderson, John Dos Passos, William Faulkner, James Joyce, Gertrude Stein (qq.v.), Dickens, and Defoe. Various essays on American literature were collected posthumously in *La letteratura americana, e altri saggi* (1951; *American Literature: Essays and Opinions*, 1970).

In 1932 P. enrolled in the Fascist Party ("a thing against my conscience"), but in May 1935, after a mass arrest in Turin—the same one in which Carlo Levi (q.v.) was arrested—P. was exiled to Brancaleone Calabro, a southern village, for editing the anti-Fascist magazine *La cultura*, for working at the liberal publishing house Einaudi, and for the possession of some compromising letters. Sentenced to three years' confinement, he was pardoned the following year and returned to Turin, finding the woman he had loved married to another man.

In 1936 P. published his first collection of poetry, *Lavorare stanca* (*Hard Labor*, 1976) and reassumed his post as editor and translator for Einaudi. At the end of 1943 P. retreated to his sister's home in a small Piedmontese village, where he stayed until the war's end. In 1945 he became editorial director of Einaudi, joined the Italian Communist Party, and started writing for its newspaper, *L'unità*. Another romantic involvement inspired the poems of *La terra e la morte* (1947; earth and death); the collection *Verrà la morte e avrà i tuoi occhi* (1951; death will come and its eyes will be yours), written in 1950, was occasioned by another, final painful love affair. On the morning of August 27, 1950, P. was found dead, a suicide.

P. believed that "maturity is an isolation sufficient unto itself." He never reached this maturity; he wished to participate in the life around him, yet felt unable to communicate. P. thought of himself as an outsider. When he had the opportunity to fight for his ideas in the Resistance, he could not take arms. His love affairs were unsuccessful. He suffered from feelings of rejection, impotence (also in the clinical sense), and guilt.

In P.'s writings the failure to communicate takes the form of a tension between the active and contemplative life, work and idleness, country and city, nature and civilization, impulse and deliberate thought. Recurrent images—hill, tree, house, evening, bread, fruit, moon—come to signify deep-rooted symbols, leading to myths.

In the first poem of *Lavorare stanca*, "I mari del sud" ("Southern Seas," 1969), P. presents the return of a sailor to his native village. This theme recurs in his last novel, *La luna e i falò* (1950; *The Moon and the Bonfire*, 1952): escape and the impossibility of escape, return and the impossibility of return. In his first collection of poems P. forges a poetic expression completely different from the hermeticism (q.v.) of Italian poetry of the time. His poems are a kind of *poesia-racconto* (poem-story), almost epic in character, free of facile lyricism. His two other books of poetry, responses to unhappy love, are limited by the outpouring of sentiment and passion.

Three of P.'s novels, *Il compagno* (1947; *The Comrade*, 1959), and the two published together under the title *Prima che il gallo canti* (1949; before the cock crows)—*Il carcere* (*The Political Prisoner*, 1959) and *La casa in collina* (*The House on the Hill*, 1961)—deal with political themes. In *Il compagno*, P.'s only "positive" novel, the protagonist sheds his indifference and becomes politically involved. *Il carcere* recounts the confinement in southern Italy of a political prisoner who proves unable to find any ties with the people around him. *La casa in collina* depicts a protagonist in flight from the war.

P. also wrote a series of novels concerned largely with how an individual can remain authentic and whole through various crises: the failure to understand conjugal love in *La spiaggia* (1942; *The Beach*, 1963); the passage from innocent adolescence to corrupt adulthood in *La bella estate* (1949; *The Beautiful Summer*, 1959); the shock of leaving natural surroundings for the sophistication of the city in *Il diavolo sulle colline* (1949; *The Devil in the Hills*, 1959); the suicidal rejection of life owing to its lack of beauty and value in *Tra donne sole* (1949; *Among Women Only*, 1959). (The last three were first published together under the title *La bella estate*.)

P.'s most original works are about the soul. In *Paesi tuoi* (1941; *The Harvesters*, 1961) he examines the intensity of unreflective life and sexual violence, including incest. The novel is set in the hills of his childhood, and images of fire, blood, and the moon abound. His use of the Piedmontese dialect filtered through standard Italian adds to the impact of the novel, which is reminiscent of Verga (q.v.) in its intense realism.

In *Dialoghi con Leucò* (1947; *Dialogues*

with Leucò, 1965) P. tries to penetrate the collective unconscious in order to fathom the destiny of the human race. This work is a retelling of ancient myths, charged with a modern sensibility: Orpheus, for example, intentionally looks back at Eurydice. P. wishes to share his personal anxieties—or even exorcise them—by finding their archetypal force. *Dialoghi con Leucò* is written in a poetic prose, and the sound of words often communicates as much as their meaning.

It is not enough, however, for an artist to gaze upon the timeless unconscious; one must also accept time-bound consciousness. *La luna e i falò*, P.'s final novel, is an attempt to reconcile these two dimensions. There are, as in *Paesi tuoi*, images of violence, blood, hills, destructive fire, and the white, timeless, feminine moon representing the unconscious and myth; but now there are also the controlled bonfires, symbolizing the conscious forces of history. The protagonist, who goes to America, is even able to feel a continuity between the New World to which he has escaped and the ancient world of the Langhe hills to which he returns. He cannot remain on his native soil, however, for a permanent return has become impossible.

With both his poetry and his prose P. brought a new tone to Italian literature. His originality lies in his having found a spiritual chord for the prevailing neorealism (q.v.) of his time.

FURTHER WORKS: *Feria d'agosto* (1946; *Summer Storm, and Other Stories,* 1966); *Il mestiere di vivere: Diario 1935–1950* (1952; *The Burning Brand: Diaries 1935–1950,* 1961); *Notte di festa* (1953; *Festival Night, and Other Stories,* 1964); *Fuoco grande* (1959, with Bianca Garufi; *A Great Fire,* in *The Beach,* 1963); *Racconti* (1960); *Poesie edite ed inedite* (1962); *8 poesie e quattro lettere a un'amica* (1964); *Lettere 1924–1944* (1966); *Lettere 1945–1950* (1966); *Poesie del disamore* (1968). FURTHER VOLUMES IN ENGLISH: *Selected Works of C. P.* (1968); *A Mania for Solitude: Selected Poems 1930–1950* (1969); *Selected Letters 1924–1950* (1969); *Told in Confidence, and Other Stories* (1971)

BIBLIOGRAPHY: Milano, P., "P.'s Experiments in the Novel," *New Republic,* 4 May 1953, 18, 23; Freccero, J., "Mythos and Logos: *The Moon and the Bonfires,*" *IQ,* 4, 20 (1961), 3–16; Norton, P. M., "C. P. and the American Nightmare," *MLN,* 77 (1962), 24–36; Heiney, D., *America in Modern Italian Literature* (1964), pp. 171–86; Rimanelli, G., "The Conception of Time and Language in the Poetry of C. P.," *IQ,* 8, 30 (1964), 14–34; Hood, S., "A Protestant without God," *Encounter,* May 1966, 41–48; Sontag, S., *Against Interpretation* (1966), pp. 39–48; Biasin, G. P., *The Smile of the Gods: A Thematic Study of C. P.'s Works* (1968); Heiney, D., *Three Italian Novelists: Moravia, P., Vittorini* (1968), pp. 83–146; Renard, P., *P.: Prison de l'imaginaire, lieu de l'écriture* (1972); Rimanelli, G., "P.'s *Diario:* Why Suicide? Why Not?" in Rimanelli, G., and Atchity, K. J., eds., *Italian Literature: Roots and Branches* (1976), pp. 383–405; Thompson, D., *C. P.: A Study of the Major Novels and Poems* (1982)

EMANUELE LICASTRO

PAVLOVIĆ, Miodrag

Yugoslav poet and essayist (writing in Serbian), b. 28 Nov. 1928, Novi Sad

After graduating from the University of Belgrade Medical School, P. practiced medicine for a short time, but then decided to devote himself to a literary career. He lives in Belgrade and works as an editor for the Prosveta publishing company.

P. appeared on the Serbian literary scene in the early 1950s, while still a university student. His first collection, *87 pesama* (1952; 87 poems), full of dark moods and nightmarish visions of destruction and the horrors of war, stirred a great deal of controversy and brought the young poet almost instant prominence. In it, P. boldly rejected the traditional poetic forms and all the stifling norms and limitations prescribed by the regime-supported literary theories, thus assuming a major role in the struggle for freedom of poetic expression waged in Yugoslavia in the early 1950s. Together with Vasko Popa (q.v.), P. contributed a great deal to the successful outcome of that struggle and to the resulting integration of Serbian—and, more broadly, Yugoslav—poetry into the European and world literary mainstream.

At present, three major "chapters" can be distinguished in P.'s complex poetic corpus. In all of them, the poet is preoccupied with the fate of contemporary man, the means he possesses to resist ever-growing evil in the world, and the chances he has to preserve his humanity in the process. In the 1950s P. focused on the devastating effects of World War II on those who survived it and on the bleak prospects the future had in store for them. During the following decade (1963–71) the poet embarked on a long journey into the past in search of his nation's roots and his own, believing that the lost sense of identity must be restored before a new hope could be offered to man. Beginning with *Zavetine* (1976; country festivals), which, in P.'s own words, represents his "return to the modern world and the contemporary experience," P. once again addresses his contemporaries directly, although his preoccupations have not essentially changed. He ponders over the unity of time—past, present, and future,—and over the consistency with which human experiences repeat themselves, serving as links between generations.

P.'s verse is free and his poetic metaphor, although somewhat hermetic, is highly functional. In the collections aimed at direct communication, simple, short lines dominate. Long, solemn, and ornate verse is typical of the collections dealing with the past, which are peopled with gods and heroes.

P.'s anthologies of English, European romantic, and Serbian poetry, and his books of essays on Yugoslav poets and the art of poetry in general are a significant part of his literary output. The essays especially are a very important contribution to literary theory in Yugoslavia: they are models of erudite and objective essayistic prose that addresses itself to the rational mind of our era.

Because of its innovations, its concern with the universal problems of contemporary man, and its influence on younger Yugoslav poets, P.'s refined and humane intellectual poetry, founded on the experiences of the English poetic tradition, is one of the most impressive examples of the maturity and vitality of the contemporary Serbian—and Yugoslav—poetic art.

FURTHER WORKS: *Stub sećanja* (1953); *Most bez obala* (1956); *Oktave* (1957); *Rokovi poezije* (1959); *Igre bezimenih* (1963); *Mleko iskoni* (1963); *87 pesama: Izbor poezije* (1963); *Osam pesnika* (1964); *Velika Skitija* (1969); *Nova Skitija* (1970); *Hododarje* (1971); *Svetli i tamni praznici* (1971); *Velika Skitija, i druge pesme* (1972); *Dnevnik pene* (1972); *Poezija i kultura* (1974); *Karike* (1977); *Pevanja na viru* (1977); *Poetika modernog* (1978); *Bekstva po Srbiji* (1979); *Izabrane pesme* (1979); *Ništitelji i svadbari* (1979); *Vi-*

dovnica (1979); *Izabrana dela* (1981). FURTHER VOLUME IN ENGLISH: *The Conqueror in Constantinople: Poetry* (1976)

BIBLIOGRAPHY: Palavestra, P., on *Osam pesnika, LQ,* 1 (1965), 106; Simic, C., on *Velika Skitija, BA,* 44 (1970), 691; Popović, B. A., on *Hododarje, BA,* 46 (1972), 327; Mihailovich, V. D., on *Poezija i kultura, BA,* 49 (1975), 577; Eekman, T., *Thirty Years of Yugoslav Literature (1945–1975)* (1978), pp. 201–3; Mihailovich, V. D., "The Poetry of M. P.," *CSP,* 22 (1978), 358–68; Šljivić-Šimšic, B., on *Vidovnica, WLT,* 55 (1981), 140–41

BILJANA ŠLJIVIĆ-ŠIMSIĆ

PAYRÓ, Roberto Jorge

Argentine dramatist, short-story writer, and novelist, b. 19 April 1867, Mercedes; d. 5 April 1928, Buenos Aires

P. was brought up in Buenos Aires by his maternal grandmother. He disliked school and refused to study law, as his father wished, but he managed to educate himself and to pursue his interest in literature by his voracious reading. By the age of twenty-one he had published some stories and a novel. Even as a youth he had a passion for journalism. While visiting his father in Bahía Blanca in 1887, he contributed articles to the local newspaper and within two years had founded one of his own, *La tribuna*. Most importantly, however, he had an opportunity to observe provincial customs and manners, political mores, and character types, all of which bore fruit in his later fiction. In Buenos Aires, P. worked on the staff of *La nación;* his trips to Patagonia and Tierra del Fuego (1898) and the northern provinces (1899) resulted in two semidocumentary books, *La Australia argentina* (1898; the Argentine south) and *En las tierras de Inti* (1909; in the lands of Inti).

P. was also active in politics—he founded the Argentine Socialist Party with Leopoldo Lugones (q.v.)—and took part in literary gatherings. Although a friend of Rubén Darío's (q.v.), his own tastes in literature were in the direction of realism and naturalism rather than modernism (q.v.). He lectured on and translated some of the works of Émile Zola. From 1907 until 1919 P. lived in Spain and Belgium, primarily the latter, and continued to contribute to *La nación*.

Considering his dedication to newspaper columns, it is surprising that P. had time for creative writing. It is universally acknowledged, however, that even his best work suffers from a journalistic taint. P.'s first significant literary efforts were in the theater. *Sobre las ruinas* (1904; upon the ruins), his best-known play, was an important contribution to the developing Argentine National Theater. Although the play dramatizes the tragic failure of the old gaucho virtues as Don Pedro's ranch is destroyed by floods due to his stubborn refusal to accept modern engineering techniques, the hope is expressed in the end that a technologically based Argentine agricultural system will be built on the ruins of backward ways. The more melodramatic *Marco Severi* (1905; Marco Severi) is also a thesis play: should a former counterfeiter be extradited by his native Italy after he has lived his new life in Argentina as a model citizen? P.'s answer is "no," as he praises the opportunities for regeneration inherent in his native Argentina. Both plays are more valued today for their social documentation than for their intrinsic dramatic merit.

P.'s early plays are optimistic about his country; in the fiction that followed, however, there is a gradual descent into pessimism and even cynicism. To this second period belong *El casamiento de Laucha* (1906; Laucha's marriage), *Pago Chico* (1908; Pago Chico), and *Divertidas aventuras del nieto de Juan Moreira* (1910; amusing adventures of Juan Moreira's grandson). The first is a picaresque tale in the Spanish tradition but with a rural setting and colloquial language that are distinctly Argentine. Laucha, a clever but amoral gaucho trickster, obviously delights in the telling of his story, an extended joke centering around his fraudulent marriage to a hard-working Italian widow. Upon losing his money and his "wife's" business in a horse race, he simply abandons her and departs for greener pastures. In this brief work, atmosphere, character, and language combine to create a minor classic in which the satirical intent is clearly secondary to the humor. In *Pago Chico,* a volume of loosely interrelated sketches focusing on the men and women of influence in a turn-of-the-century Argentine provincial town, P. is more biting in his satire as he ridicules graft, pomposity, and moral laxity. The picaresque tone of Laucha's story is retained, as is the locale, but the narrative voice is a more ironic third

person. If the stories hold up today, it is because the characters are presented as genuinely human even in their foibles. For the most part, this is not true of the longer picaresque novel, *Divertidas aventuras del nieto de Juan Moreira*. Here the protagonist, Mauricio Gómez Herrera, a cynical opportunist who rises from small-town rogue to presidential sycophant as he betrays friends and lovers alike, is a contrived character with no redeeming qualities whatsoever. Despite its success as a satire, it suffers as a work of fiction from the manipulation of character and plot for the purpose of social criticism.

In his later years, P. returned to his earlier interest in the theater; his one-act humorous sketch (*sainete*), *Mientraiga* (1925; while they last), is considered to be an excellent example of the *costumbrista* genre, which satirizes popular customs and manners. P. also turned his attention to the historical novel. *El capitán Vergara* (1925; Captain Vergara) and *El mar dulce* (1927; freshwater sea) succeed in a modest way in dramatizing two significant moments in the discovery and conquest of Argentina.

P.'s universal appeal has diminished with the passing of time. Nevertheless, *El casamiento de Laucha* and *Pago Chico* can still be read for their humor, humanity, and vitality. They also immortalize a time and place in the Argentine scene that has for the most part passed away.

FURTHER WORKS: *Ensayos Poéticos* (1884); *Antígona* (1885); *Scripta* (1887); *Novelas y fantasías* (1888); *Los italianos en Argentina* (1895); *Canción trágica* (1900); *El falso Inca* (1905); *Violines y toneles* (1908); *Crónicas* (1909); *El triunfo de los otros* (1923); *Teatro: Vivir quiero conmigo, Fuego en el rastrojo, Mientraiga* (1925); *Nuevos cuentos de Pago Chico* (1929); *Chamijo* (1930); *Cuentos del otro barrio* (1931); *Siluetas* (1931); *Charlas de un optimista* (1931); *Los tesoros del rey blanco* (1935); *Alegría* (1936); *Teatro completo* (1956)

BIBLIOGRAPHY: special P. issue, *Nosotros,* May 1928; special P. issue, *Claridad,* April 1929; Larra, R., *P.: El hombre y la obra* (1938); Anderson-Imbert, E., *Tres novelas de P., con pícaros en tres meras* (1942); Jones, C., and Alonso, A., Introduction to *Sobre las ruinas* (1943), pp. vii–xx; García, G., *R. J. P.: Testimonio de una vida y realidad de una literatura* (1961); González Lanuza, E., *Genio y figura de R. J. P.* (1965)

ROBERT H. SCOTT

PAZ, Octavio

Mexican poet and essayist, b. 31 March 1914, Mexico City

P.'s long and productive autodidacticism began in the library of the decaying mansion of his grandfather, one of the first novelists to plead the cause of the Indians. His father, a lawyer who represented Zapata in the U.S. during the Mexican revolution, strengthened P.'s interest in social causes. Although P. attended the University of Mexico at an early age, he apparently outdistanced his professors before achieving formal degrees. His formative period was strongly shaped by his presence in Spain during the civil war. As one of the founders and most energetic editors of the literary journal *Taller* (1938–41), he had a direct influence on emerging writers. In 1943 he received a Guggenheim fellowship for travel and study in the U.S. A period of great literary activity coincided with the assumption of several high government posts (including service as Mexico's representative to UNESCO and ambassador to India), which he resigned to protest the Mexican government's handling of student demonstrations before the 1968 Olympic Games. Since then he has dedicated his time to writing and to teaching, particularly at Harvard, which awarded him an honorary degree in 1980. As the founder and chief editor first of *Plural* and then of *Vuelta,* he influences and challenges the intellectuals of Spanish America. His name is frequently cited among possible Latin American candidates for the Nobel Prize in literature. He won the prestigious Neustadt Prize in 1982.

P.'s impact as a poet preceded his accomplishments in the essay. Although he was recognized for his early poetic works, especially *A la orilla del mundo* (1942; on the world's shore), *Libertad bajo palabra* (1949; rev. eds., 1960, 1968; freedom and the word) represents the height of his talent. Employing a technique that is a mixture of symbolism and surrealism (qq.v.), the poet remains true to the necessities of his deeply personal creativity. His gift is to bridge the gap between the personal and the general, between man and society, and by defining his own alien-

ation and anxiety to provide some solace for these universal afflictions. Although many of his poems are developed within the discipline of regular meter and rhyme, the appeal of his work rests more on their reconstruction of reality than on brilliance of form.

If one were to ask readers and critics to select P.'s most successful long poem, the likely choice would be *Piedra de sol* (1957; *Sun Stone,* 1963). Written in 584 unpunctuated endecasyllabic lines, reflecting the synodic cycle of Venus, this carefully structured work is modeled after the famous Aztec calendar stone. In the same way that the calendar stone combines interlocking circular symmetries of time and religious symbolism to suggest a cosmology, the poem joins personal reminiscence and social commentary, illustrating the truth of Unamuno's (q.v.) observation that the universal is derived from the particular. Like its model, the poem too is circular, beginning in the middle of an experience and concluding with the six introductory verses, whose meaning has been broadened, if not transformed, by the development of the poem. Its two halves, separated by the recall of the poet's experience in wartime Madrid, compare and contrast the themes of love, of the nature of man, and of his place in the world, yet leave major questions to be answered only by the reader.

Like *Piedra de sol, Blanco* (1967; *Blanco,* 1971) is an experiment in form, whose complexity, however, demands more of the reader than does *Piedra del sol.* The poet suggests in an introduction to the poem that it can be read as a succession of signs on a single page (the original edition was printed on one long page that folded out); such a reading produces a text that is in constant flux. In addition, he indicates five other ways to comprehend the text, which is composed of three columns: (1) the center column alone, whose theme is the passage of speech from silence through four stages to an ultimate silence; (2) the left column alone, divided into four sections corresponding to the four traditional elements—earth, air, fire, and water; (3) the right column alone, the counterpoint of the left, whose divisions correspond to sensation, perception, imagination, and comprehension; (4) each one of the parts consisting of two columns read separately, comprising four independent poems (that is, the left and right columns read together); (5) each of the six center sections and each of the four left and four right sections as separate poems. The effect of these multiple readings is to instruct the reader in the technique of responding in various ways to the signs that have been presented.

In *Ladera este* (1969; east slope) the lack of punctuation of *Piedra de sol* and *Blanco* and the columnar structure of *Blanco* are utilized in many of the poems. The complexity in these cases, however, suggests not so much a programmed variety of opposing and/or complementary interpretations as an independent ambiguity whose solution is not only concealed by, but may even be unknown to, the poet. A phrase or noun, for example, may be read as a part of the preceding verse, or part of the following, or as part of the poet's thought independent of both. Perhaps as a compensation for increased difficulty of comprehension, the diction is simpler. As in much of P.'s other poetry, the theme involves the reconciliation of opposites, but here, as indicated by the title and textual references, Buddhist philosophy has a noticeable influence.

In *Pasado en claro* (1975; *A Draft of Shadows,* 1979) and *Vuelta* (1976; return) P. returned to a more conventional form. The reworking of his major themes—language, love, and metaphysics—shows a constant, and perhaps futile, striving for ultimate expression. At the same time, the demands on the reader not only in interpreting the poem but also in some measure creating it, are more apparent.

The publication of twenty-three volumes of essays to date is ample evidence of P.'s productivity as a thinker. Although these can be divided broadly into the large categories of social concerns on the one hand and arts and letters on the other, it is characteristic of his approach to take every opportunity to explore the relationship between the two. In *El laberinto de la soledad* (1950; *The Labyrinth of Solitude,* 1961) P. provided a complex and controversial analysis of the Mexican character. Taking as his point of departure the *pachuco,* the hybrid Mexican-American, P. identifies concealment, the use of a mask, as the most observable feature of the Mexican character. Much "illogical" social behavior is traceable to a profound individual insecurity, which is reflected in a collective identity crisis. The Mexican does not know who he is and is suspicious of others because he is suspicious of himself. In terms which are basi-

cally psychological but which P. extends to history, mythology, and social behavior, the Mexican is revealed as the defensive victim of the social rape in which he was engendered. The historical application of P.'s thesis reveals a Mexico (and, in fact, Spanish America) in quest of a national identity: America is not so much a tradition to be carried on as it is a future to be realized. In the book's final chapter on the dialectic of solitude, P. places the problems of individual integration and social communion in the center of modern existence. *Posdata* (1970; *The Other Mexico,* 1972) is an extension of his interpretation to the failure of Mexico's ruling party to maintain communication with the people and to continue the principles on which it was established. The massacre of students in 1968 is not only symbolic of that failure, but is a modern re-creation of ritual human sacrifice on which the Aztec state was based.

Just as the meaning of history underlies P.'s analyses of society, so does the significance of language connect his numerous essays on Hispanic and French poetry and art. Ranging from *El arco y la lira* (1956; *The Bow and the Lyre,* 1973)—a brilliant analysis of poetry as language, process, and social phenomenon—to his broad history of poetic evolution in the 1972 Charles Eliot Norton lectures at Harvard—*Los hijos del limo: Del romanticismo a la vanguardia* (1974; *Children of the Mire: Modern Poetry from Romanticism to the Avant-Garde,* 1974)—he views the distillation of language not as an adornment of mankind but as a key to its comprehension. His brief but seminal study of a French surrealist artist, *Marcel Duchamp; o, El castillo de la pureza* (1968; *Marcel Duchamp; or, The Castle of Purity,* 1970), provides insights into contemporary hermetic expression, including that of the poet's own work.

P.'s poetry and prose represent two aspects of a concern for the predicament of modern man, whom P. is not unique in viewing as fragmented and mutilated. In fact, all of his work is unified by a utopian wish for the fulfillment of man's wholeness in individual creativity and in the building of society, offering an ennobling vision of man to an uneasy world. This vision underlies his attempts to reconcile opposites, especially those of passion and reason, linear and circular time, society and the individual, and word and meaning. His ideal is perhaps expressed by a line from "Himno entre ruinas" (1948; "Hymn among the Ruins," 1963): "Words that are flowers that are fruit that are acts."

FURTHER WORKS: *La hija de Rappaccini* (1956); *Las peras del olmo* (1957); *La estación violenta* (1958); *Salamandra* (1962); *Cuadrivio* (1965); *Viento entero* (1965); *Puertas al campo* (1966); *Claude Lévi-Strauss; o, El nuevo festín de Esopo* (1967; *Claude Lévi-Strauss: An Introduction,* 1970); *Corriente alterna* (1967; *Alternating Current,* 1973); *Discos visuales* (1968); *Conjunciones y disyunciones* (1969; *Conjunctions and Disjunctions,* 1974); *Los signos en rotación, y otros ensayos* (1971); *Renga* (1971, with Edoardo Sanguineti, Charles Tomlinson, and Jacques Roubaud; *Renga: A Chain of Poems,* 1972); *Topoemas* (1971); *Traducción: Literatura y literalidad* (1971); *El signo y el garabato* (1973); *Sólo a dos voces* (1973, with Julian Rios); *El mono gramático* (1974; *The Monkey Grammarian,* 1981); *La búsqueda del comienzo* (1974); *Teatro de signos* (1974); *Versiones y diversiones* (1974); *In/Mediaciones* (1979); *Poemas (1935–1975)* (1979). FURTHER VOLUMES IN ENGLISH: *Configurations* (1971); *Early Poems* (1974); *The Siren and the Seashell, and Other Essays on Poets and Poetry* (1974); *A Draft of Shadows* (1979); *The Labyrinth of Solitude, and Other Essays,* rev. ed. (1982)

BIBLIOGRAPHY: Céa, C., *O. P.* (1965); Xirau, R., *O. P.: El sentido de la palabra* (1970); Phillips, R., *The Poetic Modes of O.P.* (1972); special P. section, *Review,* No. 6 (1972), 5–21; Gallagher, D. P., *Modern Latin American Literature* (1973), pp. 67–81; Ivask, I., ed., *The Perpetual Present: The Poetry and Prose of O. P.* (1973); Flores, A., ed., *Aproximaciones a O. P.* (1974); Rodman, S., *Tongues of Fallen Angels* (1974), pp. 135–61; Brotherston, G., *Latin American Poetry: Origins and Presence* (1975), pp. 138–68; Magis, C. H., *La poesía hermética de O. P.* (1978); Roggiano, A., ed., *O. P.* (1979); Wilson, J., *O. P.: A Study of His Poetics* (1979); Chantikian, K., ed., *O. P.: Homage to the Poet* (1981)

JOHN M. FEIN

There is no reason to require an essay to be systematic: it is enough that it be enlightening. But P. not only enlightens, he frequently arouses passion and sometimes irritates. It is interesting to follow the meanderings of his thinking with an ex-

pectant eye to the surprises his associative genius and the uniqueness of his knowledge can give us. To whom but him would it occur to note the lack of "a general history of the relations between body and soul, life and death, sex and the face"? . . .

The relationships of signs are by nature difficult. If, making use of relationships among them, one tries to establish a system of parallels and antitheses between different cultures, the exercise is hazardous and the positive results provisional. Even so, it is worth the trouble to attempt it for it is the only way to show precisely the affinities between those different cultures and the common roots shared by very different men. In sum, it is a way of showing that signs reveal a common identity among human beings, be they Protestant Europeans of the 16th century or Buddhists of the 6th century B.C.

Ricardo Gullón, "The Universalism of O. P.," *BA,* 46 (1972), 587

His demand that the world be different is the demand of a healthy man, untroubled by suffering. It is just that nothing can satisfy him that is not an all-embracing, time-destroying ecstasy. His poetry, whose central topics have remained more or less constant throughout his career, constitutes a search for a single moment of dizzy ecstasy, a splendid *instante* that will annul the world that is, and germinate instead an altogether new one, where a poplar, a stone, a mountain, or a river— or, above all, O. P.—will become transfigured from what they merely are to something immeasurably more vast and magnificent.

D. P. Gallagher, *Modern Latin American Literature* (1973), p. 67

In one of his essays P. says, "When we read or listen to a poem we do not smell, taste or touch the word. All of these sensations are mental images. In order to feel a poem one must understand it; in order to understand it, hear it, see it, contemplate it, change it into an echo, into shadow, into nothing. Comprehension is a spiritual exercise." Just as the experience of man in the world, the poem is incarnation and distance, plenitude and precariousness at the same time; like the world, the poem draws its life from the dialectic between affirmation and negation. In recent years, P. proposes a more and more radical *no:* "Take negation to its limit. There contemplation awaits us: the disincarnation of language, transparency."

Thus, transparency leads to silence: that which is true reality is inexpressible. In this way P. seems to come to the same conclusion as the Igitur of Mallarmé: "Nothingness having departed, there remains the castle of purity." But will not this purity be the ultimate form in which the word is revealed to us or becomes transparent, i.e., the ultimate form in which the world becomes incar-

CESARE PAVESE

OCTAVIO PAZ

CHARLES PÉGUY

RAMÓN PÉREZ DE AYALA

BENITO PÉREZ GALDÓS

nate and fully real, so real that it cannot be named? This, I believe, is P.'s utopian vision: the appearance of the world—of the world, it is understood, in its complete original state—implies the disappearance of language and of poetry. All that is left is to live poetry: to write the world.

Guillermo Sucre, "O. P.: Poetics of Vivacity," in Ivar Ivask, ed., *The Perpetual Present: The Poetry and Prose of O. P.* (1973), p. 19

In most respects P.'s biggest "Mexican" poem, "Sun Stone," in fact belongs more properly to the collection it appeared in: *La estación violenta*. . . . Complemented by P.'s first major work of criticism, *El arco y la lira* . . . these poems as a whole amount if anything to a certain scepticism about the idea of Mexico. At any event, he openly repudiates the indigenists and the social realists, and all forms of national concern with culture. Against these traditions he would set another, which had come to fascinate him more and more from the late 1940s onwards, that of the Surrealists. In a metaphor fundamental to all his writing, but especially to that of this period, he would break out of his labyrinth of solitude into new utterance. Out of empty constriction, in which man is fragmented socially and erotically, he would join the Surrealists in conjuring that marvellous instant when we truly "inhabit our names."

Gordon Brotherston, *Latin American Poetry: Origins and Presence* (1975), p. 146

Throughout P.'s writings there are many references to surrealism, especially in his *El arco y la lira* (1956). But all that he writes falls within the opposition between attitude and activity. What P. accepts and rejects follows a clear pattern of values based on that opposition. For P., surrealism as a historical movement degenerated into style and convention. All that is tainted with history, all that is subject to time's corrosion, is rejected by P.

P. has lifted surrealism out of time and social context, elevating it into an attitude of mind. This was possible because he arrived late at the surrealists' table. Sifting theory from practice also enabled P. to view surrealism as eternal, a universal constant impervious to time and change. Circumstantial involvement did not blur these clear distinctions.

First, P., like Villaurrutia and most of surrealism's detractors, rejected automatic writing, one of the theoretical and practical pillars of surrealism. . . .

In P.'s version of surrealism, all the techniques became commonplaces, or inevitable conventions because forming part of history. His attitude towards automatism became his attitude to hypnosis, dream *récits*, the mode of poem-objects, the collective games and so on.

Jason Wilson, *O. P.: A Study of His Poetics* (1979), pp. 23–24

P'BITEK, Okot

Ugandan poet, anthropologist, and social critic (writing in English and Luo), b. 1931, Gulu

Bursting onto the literary scene in the mid-1960s, p'B. drew to East Africa the attention and acclaim for literature in English that West Africa had long enjoyed. It was a fitting effect, for p'B. had all his life displayed an "unabashed commitment" to his native culture and to African standards and values.

Under the influence of his mother, a gifted singer and composer and a leader in her clan, p'B. early absorbed the rich songs, proverbs, and customs of the Luo people. He was also exposed to missionary training early, and after completing his secondary education in Gulu, attended King's College, Budo. He went abroad as a member of the Uganda national soccer team, and stayed in Britain to take a diploma in education in Bristol, a degree in law at Aberystwyth, and a further degree in social anthropology at Oxford. He returned home as lecturer at University College in Makerere, founded the Festival of African Arts in Gulu, and went on to serve as director of the National Cultural Center in Kampala. As a result of trenchant criticisms he uttered in Zambia, he made himself persona non grata to the Uganda government, and elected to move to Kenya. In 1971 he took up the post of senior research fellow at the Institute of African Studies in Nairobi.

As an administrator, p'B. has shown an intense practical involvement in the sociocultural life of East Africa, shifting the emphasis in song, dance, theater, and art from the dominant British to the basic African style. He has also emerged as an important champion of African values, in a somewhat polemical mode. He has corrected long-standing misapprehensions and created an enhanced view of African culture in such works as *African Religions and Western Scholarship* (1970), *Religion of the Central Luo* (1971), *Africa's Cultural Revolution* (1973), and the critical anthology of poetry and prose, *The Horn of My Love* (1974).

By his own testimony p'B. is less concerned with fixed "ontological definitions" than with "dynamic function," and he is at his most arresting and incisive in creative embodiments and complex dramatizations of the culture-conscious East African scene. His youthful novel in the Acholi dialect of Luo, *Lak tar miyo kinyero wi lobo* (1953; are your teeth white? then laugh), has perhaps been put into the shade by the rich suites of Songs: *Song of Lawino: A Lament* (1966), *Song of Ocol* (1970), *Song of (a) Prisoner* (1971), and *Two Songs: Song of Prisoner; Song of Malaya* (1971), which reprints the earlier title along with the new song. The first of these was composed in Acholi, and p'B. himself made the English translation that brought him international fame.

That fame has not been untouched by controversy. British observers have felt that the Songs convey animosity toward their ways and influence, while African observers have contended that African personalities and ways are exposed to satirical barbs. Access to the poems is simplified as soon as we realize they are dramatic monologues, that is, emotionally and intellectually partial utterances by characters who have silent interlocutors and who are in situations more complex than the characters directly apprehend. The reader must look through their eyes, but also into their minds—between the lines of overt statement—for the full values of the poems.

It helps further to recognize two facts: (1) that the acute social anthropologist in p'B. is not stifled in the poetry, for the main characters are really representative figures, distillations of major features of African experience in the aspiring and dislocating postindependence world; and (2) that the characters operate poetically in a kind of allegory of naïveté, where all impressions are curiously pursued by a mind too sensitive to withstand them and too fresh to organize them in a stable system.

The four Songs constitute veritable compass points of African experience. *Song of Lawino* is the plangent, minutely detailed utterance of resentment and grief by a traditional wife abandoned by her newfangled husband for a modernized woman and the new urban prosperity. *Song of Ocol* is the husband's overemphatic counterstatement, the last lines revealing his true character, one of selfish weakness and hidden anguish. *Song of a Prisoner* shows, in what appears to be a composite character, the ugly machinations and specious hopes of the new politics. And *Song of Malaya* sets forth the alternately harsh and tender world view of the new woman of pleasure in the new African town

(*malaya* means "prostitute").

Song of Lawino and *Song of a Prisoner* are poems of defense; *Song of Ocol* and *Song of Malaya* are poems of attack. All are poems of seething desperation, representing points of transition and crisis not only for the individuals speaking but also for their very culture. If we want to know what p'B. thinks, we may turn to his polemical anthropological writing. But if we want to know what he apprehends and what he aspires to, then we must turn to the poetry.

BIBLIOGRAPHY: Lo Lijong, T., *The Last Word* (1969), pp. 135–56; Blishen, E., Introduction to *Song of Prisoner* (1971), pp. 1–40; Cooke, M., on *Song of a Prisoner, Parnassus,* 1, 2 (1973), 115, 117–19; Heron, G., *The Poetry of O. p'B.* (1976); Asein, S. O., "O. p'B.: Literature and the Cultural Revolution in East Africa," *WLWE,* 16 (1977), 7–24; Heron, G., "O. p'B. and the Elite in African Writing," *LHY,* 19, 1 (1978), 66–93; Moore, G., *Twelve African Writers* (1980), pp. 170–90; Heywood, A., "Modes of Freedom: The Songs of O. p'B.," *JCL,* 15, 1 (1980), 65–83

MICHAEL G. COOKE

PEDI LITERATURE

See under South African Literature

PEDROLO, Manuel de

Spanish novelist, dramatist, short-story writer, poet, essayist, and translator (writing in Catalan), b. 1 April 1918, Aranyo

P., the child of middle-class landowners, earned his bachelor's degree in Barcelona in 1935. He served in the Spanish Republican Army until the end of the Spanish Civil War in 1939. After his release from a concentration camp in Valladolid he took up residence in Barcelona. In the 1950s and 1960s he ran a business and then worked in advertising and publishing; he also did translations, while continuing to pursue his literary career. Since around 1970 he has been a full-time writer. Because of the publishing difficulties for Catalan writers, many of P.'s works appeared long after their composition, and a large number remain unpublished. P. was awarded the Honor Prize of Catalan Letters of 1979.

The early novel *Cendra per Martina* (written 1952, pub. 1955; cinders for Martina) is a realistic love story; it constitutes the first great testimony in Catalan fiction of a generation morally destroyed by the Spanish Civil War.

Some of P.'s plays have been acclaimed as masterpieces of the Theater of the Absurd (q.v.). *Cruma* (written 1957, pub. 1958; *Cruma,* 1973)—the title is the name of an ancient unit of measurement—is a play about the existentialist (q.v.) problem of communication. Starting from the Heideggerian premise of the debatable "authenticity" of the human being, it portrays a search for scientific knowledge; the characters, however, must finally tacitly admit their inability to attain that knowledge. *Homes i no* (written 1957, pub. 1960; *Humans and No,* 1977), P.'s finest play, explores the meaning of personal freedom through the depiction of the struggle of some imprisoned people against their closed world. The play acknowledges the cosmological failure of man but concludes that man has at least succeeded in broadening his definition of freedom. Two other major plays, *Situació bis* (written 1958, pub. 1965; *Full Circle,* 1970) and *Tècnica de cambra* (written 1959, pub. 1964; *The Room,* 1972), both deal with rebellion—political and metaphysical—and the nature of freedom.

With *Un camí amb Eva* (written 1963, pub. 1968; a path with Eva) P. began a series of eleven novels called "Temps obert" (open time). In each one Daniel Bastida lives a different life—one he could have lived given new conditions and/or interests. This cycle constitutes the most ambitious mosaic of Catalan society after the civil war.

Totes les bèsties de càrrega (written 1965, pub. 1967; all the beasts of burden) is perhaps the masterpiece of contemporary Catalan fiction. It depicts, naturalistically and in a near-Kafkaesque fashion, the inhuman conditions imposed by an arbitrary state machinery and the heroism of a group of people who tenaciously fight for their human dignity.

Anònim I (written 1970, pub. 1978; anonym I) is the first of three novels that, although not a true trilogy, share the same political overtones and depict an absurd world ruled autocratically, in which an inversion of values, including especially sexual values, prevails.

In the novel, the genre that interests P. the most, he has tried all possible subgenres (including detective fiction and science fiction), frequently using a mixture of these, and employing all the modern literary techniques, including those of the New Novel (q.v.). P. is the most notable literary experimenter of Catalonia—and indeed of all Spain.

FURTHER WORKS: *Addenda* (wr. 1936–73); *Els tentacles* (wr. 1945); *Ésser en el món* (1949); *Ésser per a la mort* (wr. 1949); *Elena de segona mà* (wr. 1949, pub. 1967); *Documents* (wr. 1950); *Simplement sobre la terra* (wr. 1950); *Dimensions mentals* (wr. 1938–51); *Reixes a través* (wr. 1944–52); *Roba bruta* (wr. 1948–52); *Infant dels grans* (wr. 1952); *Es vessa una sang fàcil* (wr. 1952, pub. 1954); *He provat un gest amarg* (wr. 1952); *Mister Chase, podeu sortir* (wr. 1953, pub. 1955); *L'interior és al final* (wr. 1953, pub. 1974); *Domicili provisional* (wr. 1953, pub. 1956); *Balanç fins a la matinada* (wr. 1953, pub. 1963); *Avui es parla de mi* (wr. 1953, pub. 1966); *L'inspector arriba/fa tard* (wr. 1953, pub. 1960); *Visat de trànsit* (wr. 1952–54); *El temps a les venes* (wr. 1953–54, pub. 1974); *Els hereus de la cadira* (wr. 1954, pub. 1980); *Estrictament personal* (wr. 1954, pub. 1955); *Un món per a tothom* (wr. 1954, pub. 1956); *Cinc cordes* (wr. 1954, pub. 1974); *Sonda de temps* (wr. 1955); *Violació de límits* (wr. 1955, pub. 1957); *International Setting* (wr. 1955, pub. 1974); *Una selva com la teva* (wr. 1955, pub. 1960); *Nou pams de terra* (wr. 1955, pub. 1971); *Les finestres s'obren de nit* (wr. 1955, pub. 1957); *Esberla del silenci* (wr. 1956); *Crèdits humans* (wr. 1956, pub. 1957); *La nostra mort de cada dia* (wr. 1956, pub. 1958); *Introducció a l'ombra* (wr. 1956, pub. 1972); *Cops de bec a Pasadena* (wr. 1956, pub. 1972); *La mà contra l'horitzó* (wr. 1957, pub. 1961); *Pell vella al fons del pou* (wr. 1957, pub. 1975); *La terra prohibida, 1: Les portes del passat* (wr. 1957, pub. 1977); *LTP, 2: La paraula dels botxins* (wr. 1957, pub. 1977); *LTP, 3: Fronteres interiors* (wr. 1957, pub. 1978); *LTP, 4: La nit horitzontal* (wr. 1957, pub. 1979); *Entrada en blanc* (wr. 1958, pub. 1968); *Perquè ha mort una noia* (wr. 1958, pub. 1976); *Pas de ratlla* (wr. 1958, pub. 1972); *Algú a l'altre cap de peça* (wr. 1958, pub. 1975); *Darrera versió, per ara* (wr. 1958, pub. 1971); *Veus sense contacte* (wr. 1959); *Un amor fora ciutat* (wr. 1959, pub. 1970); *Tocats pel foc* (wr. 1959, pub. 1976); *Sóc el defecte* (wr. 1959, pub. 1975); *Contes fora recull* (wr. 1959–74, pub. 1975); *Solució de continuïtat* (wr. 1960, pub. 1968); *Si són roses, floriran* (wr. 1961, pub. 1971); *Acte de violència* (wr. 1961, pub. 1975); *Si em pregunten, responc* (wr. 1961–73, pub. 1974); *Viure a la intempèrie* (wr. 1962, pub. 1974); *M'enterro en els fonaments* (wr. 1962, pub. 1967); *Acompanyo qualsevol cos* (wr. 1962, pub. 1979); *Els elefants són contagiosos* (wr. 1962–72, pub. 1974); *Temps obert, 2: Se'n va un estrany* (wr. 1963, pub. 1968); *L'ús de la matèria* (wr. 1963, pub. 1977); *TO, 3: Falgueres informa* (wr. 1964, pub. 1968); *TO, 4: Situació analítica* (wr. 1964, pub. 1971); *TO, 5: Des d'uns ulls de dona* (wr. 1965, pub. 1972); *Joc brut* (wr. 1965, pub. 1965); *Arreu on valguin les paraules, els homes* (wr. 1966, pub. 1975); *La sentència* (wr. 1966); *TO, 6: Unes mans plenes de sol* (wr. 1966, pub. 1972); *TO, 7: L'ordenació dels maons* (wr. 1966, pub. 1974); *A cavall de dos cavalls* (wr. 1966, pub. 1967); *Mossegar-se la cua* (wr. 1967, pub. 1968); *TO, 8: S'alcen veus del soterrani* (wr. 1967, pub. 1976); *TO, 9: Pols nova de runes velles* (wr. 1967, pub. 1977); *TO, 10: Cartes a Jones Street* (wr. 1968, pub. 1978); *Milions d'ampolles buides* (wr. 1968, pub. 1976); *Hem posat les mans a la crònica* (wr. 1969, pub. 1977); *TO, 11: "Conjectures" de Daniel Bastida* (wr. 1969, pub. 1980); *Anònim II* (wr. 1970, pub. 1980); *Obres púbiques* (wr. 1971); *Anònim III* (wr. 1971, pub. 1981); *Algú que no hi havia de ser* (wr. 1972, pub. 1974); *Aquesta nit tanquem* (wr. 1973, pub. 1978); *Espais de fecunditat irregular/s* (1973); *Mecanoscrit del segon origen* (wr. 1973, pub. 1974); *Text/Càncer* (1974); *Contes i narracions* (3 vols., 1974–75); *Trajecte final* (wr. 1974, pub. 1975); *Dos quarts de set* (wr. 1974); *Xit* (wr. 1974); *Monòleg* (wr. 1974); *Sòlids en suspensió* (1975); *Detall d'una acció rutinària* (1975); *Procès de contradicció suficient* (wr. 1975, pub. 1976); *Lectura a banda i banda de paret* (wr. 1975, pub. 1977); *Bones noticies de Sister* (wr. 1975, pub. 1977); *D'esquerra a dreta, respectivament* (wr. 1976, pub. 1978); *Aquesta matinada i potser per sempre* (wr. 1976, pub. 1980); *Novel·les curtes* (4 vols., 1976–82); *A casa amb papers falsos* (wr. 1976–78, pub. 1981); *S'han deixat les claus sota l'estora* (1977); *D'ara a demà* (wr. 1977); *Baixeu a rècules i amb les mans alçades* (wr. 1977, pub. 1979); *Reserva d'inquisidors* (wr. 1978, pub. 1979); *Apòcrif u: Oriol* (wr. 1978); *Exemplar d'arxiu/únicament persones autoritzades* (wr. 1978); *Apòcrif dos: Tina* (wr. 1979); *Successimultani* (wr. 1979, pub. 1981); *Entrem més bigues mentre dormen*

(wr. 1980); *Ara (quan?) i aquí (però on?)* (wr. 1980); *Apòcrif tres: Verònica* (wr. 1981); *Crucifeminació* (wr. 1981)

BIBLIOGRAPHY: Esslin, M., *The Theatre of the Absurd* (1961), pp. 182–85; Wellwarth, G. E., *Spanish Underground Drama* (1972), pp. 139–47; Wellwarth, G. E., "M. de P. and Spanish Absurdism," *BA*, 46, (1972), 380–87; Wellwarth, G. E., Introduction to *3 Catalan Dramatists* (1976), pp. 1–7; Valdivieso, T., *España: Bibliografía de un teatro silenciado* (1979), pp. 67–72; Solanas, J. V., *Historia de la literatura catalana* (1980), pp. 278–81

ALBERT M. FORCADAS

PÉGUY, Charles

(pseuds.: Charles Pierre Baudouin, Pierre Deloire) French philosopher, poet, journalist, and essayist, b. 7 Jan. 1873, Orléans; d. 5 Sept. 1914, Villeroy

Born of a family of peasant craftsmen, P., an outstanding student at the lycée of Orléans, went on, after further study, to the prestigious École Normale Supérieure (1894); during 1897 he was enrolled at the Sorbonne. He took degrees in humanities and science but, having failed the *agrégation* (examination) in philosophy, abandoned academic life for journalism. His earliest works were written under pseudonyms.

His first articles expressed the utopian socialism he had adopted in place of a lost Catholic faith. By 1898 the Dreyfus affair had transformed P. into a militant for justice, and his bookshop near the Sorbonne was a rallying point for Dreyfus's socialist partisans. In 1900 he founded the *Cahiers de la quinzaine*, the journal which henceforth became the focus of his activities. Scrupulously committed to truth, it featured writers of every ideological stamp. Around 1908 P. rediscovered his faith but, for family reasons, never resumed formal practice. Intensely patriotic, he assiduously fulfilled his duties as a reserve officer, was among the first mobilized at the outbreak of World War I, and died in the Battle of the Marne.

As the major outlet for his work, the *Cahiers de la quinzaine* became the vehicle of *Péguysme*, a deeply personalist philosophy combining socialism, patriotism, and Catholicism. Less a systematic analysis than a stream of conscious meditation on the theme of the modern world, *Péguysme* constituted an organic body of thought that took shape in three distinct stages: (1) a formative period (1896–1904), culminating in a series of *Cahiers* attacking the anticlericalism and statism of modern secular society; (2) the critical middle years (1905–9), during which P. defined the situation of the modern world, while formulating in opposition to it a value system grounded in Henri Bergson's (q.v.) metaphysics, classical humanism, the traditions of old France, and a spirituality free of clericalism; (3) the major phase (1910–14), when he employed all his talent as essayist, dramatist, and poet to chart for a reinvigorated nation the mystical vocation he envisaged as hers.

A masterful pamphleteer who identified issues with personalities, P. wrote lengthy polemical essays denouncing whatever deviated from his ideal: the demagoguery of erstwhile Dreyfusist allies; the pacifism of his former mentor, the socialist politician Jean Jaurès, in *L'argent* (1913; money); a Catholicism as modernistic as its secular adversaries in *Un nouveau théologien, M. Fernand Laudet* (1911; Mr. Laudet, a new theologian); above all, the cult of science and sociology. In *Zangwill* (1904; Zangwill), the four essays, each titled *Situation* (1906–7; situation), *L'argent suite* (1913; money, continued) he focused on the party of intellectualism (Hippolyte Taine [1828–1893], Ernest Renan [1823–1892], the social and literary historians of the Sorbonne) to criticize a scientific method he deemed inadequate to describe a reality ever in process. Against them he invoked his "heroes"—the Greek poets, the historian Jules Michelet (1798–1874), and his true mentor, Bergson, whose vitalistic philosophy gave to *Péguysme* its intellectual armature. *Note sur M. Bergson et la philosophie bergsonienne* (1914; note on Monsieur Bergson and Bergsonian philosophy) and *Note conjointe sur M. Descartes et la philosophie cartésienne* (1914; added note on Monsieur Descartes and Cartesian philosophy) defended Bergson, after the Vatican had put some of his works on the Index, and reexamined, in Bergsonian terms, theological questions like freedom and grace.

Although fraught with flaws—inordinate length, endless digressions, repetitions that restate rather than developing ideas—the essays transcend their internal weaknesses to

express thought in the making. *Notre patrie* (1905; our fatherland) illustrates how P. formulated an idea, the need for a national awakening, while chronicling an event. He captures the ebb and flow of life in a Paris caught up in the state visit of King Alfonso XIII of Spain, only gradually revealing to an unthinking public that the crisis at Tangiers has made a European war something that is eventually inevitable.

Rooting an idea in the concrete is basic to *Péguysme,* whose dominant motif is the insertion of the eternal in the temporal. Just as in the Incarnation the divine became incorporated with the human, so the collective cultural past of a people perdures through memory, creating across time a sense of communion. This is the theme of the posthumously published two-part dialogue composed 1909–14 and generally referred to as *Clio I–II: Véronique: Dialogue de l'histoire et de l'âme charnelle* (pub. 1955; Veronica: dialogue of history and the carnal soul; Eng. adaptation, *Clio I,* in *Temporal and Eternal,* 1958) and *Clio: Dialogue de l'histoire et de l'âme païenne* (pub. 1917; Clio: dialogue of history and the pagan soul). This theme is also taken up in *Victor-Marie comte Hugo* (1911; Victor-Marie Count Hugo), where P. uses Corneille's theater to illustrate how sanctity represents the transfer of temporal heroism to the plane of the eternal. His contemporaries' infidelity to the heroic ideal saddened P., leading him to write *Notre jeunesse* (1910; *Memories of Youth,* in *Temporal and Eternal,* 1958), in which he recalled what the Dreyfus affair had meant to his generation and how, from being a mystique, it had degenerated into politics.

Out of this disillusionment emerged P. the lyricist, who turned to poetry not only to exorcise pain but to take a firmer hold on reality. P. wrote a genuinely popular poetry celebrating the organic life of old France. Its hypnotic rhythms resemble incantatory verse. But P. did not simply take over older forms; his prosody evolved naturally out of his prose style. The measured beat of the essays developed, through the free verse of the *Mystères* (mysteries), into the regular verse patterns of the quatrains of *La ballade du cœur qui a tant battu* (1911–12; new ed., 1973; the ballad of the heart that has beaten so much), of the two *tapisseries* (tapestries)—*La tapisserie de Sainte Geneviève et de Jeanne d'Arc* (1912; the tapestry of Saint Genevieve and Joan of Arc) and *La tapisserie de Notre Dame* (1913; the tapestry of Our Lady)—and of the eight thousand and more alexandrines of *Ève* (1913; Eve), the poem P. called his "Christian Iliad." At once elementary and sublime, abstract and colloquial, his poetry is written from the pseudonaïve viewpoint of the peasant, for whom the spiritual is firmly anchored in the carnal. P. innovated by renewing: he resurrected the medieval mystery play, infused incantatory rhythms into the classical alexandrine, and made poetry out of prayer.

All his essential motifs come together in the Joan of Arc theme. In the figure of the peasant-soldier-saint, P. fused the spiritual, humanitarian, and patriotic wellsprings of his thought. His oldest subject, it took shape initially in the three-part play in prose *Jeanne d'Arc* (1897) and was reworked, after P.'s conversion, into *Le mystère de la charité de Jeanne d'Arc* (1910; *The Mystery of the Charity of Joan of Arc,* 1950), a dialogue on heroism and sainthood, pitting Joan against prudential wisdom embodied in Madame Gervaise. It is the latter's voice we hear in *Le Porche du mystère de la deuxième vertu* (1911; *The Portico of the Mystery of the Second Virtue,* 1970) and *Le mystère des saints innocents* (1912; *The Mystery of the Holy Innocents,* 1956), celebrating the theological virtue of hope as the principle animating not only the believer but all mankind and nature as well.

Uneven in quality and almost impossible to stage, the *Mystères* can reach extraordinary lyricism, as in God's invocation to the night to envelope in its mantle the dead Christ, or in Joan's anguish lest all men not be saved. Eschatological themes preoccupy P., and, like Hugo, he tries to capture the sweep of history so as to situate man within a sacred context. This is the goal of *Ève*, a gigantic hymn to the mother of the human race, which contains P.'s prayer for those who have died in a just war.

Prayer, the essence of P.'s poetry, was increasingly expressed in more traditional forms (sonnets, quatrains), the climax of this development being the "Presentation" poems and accompanying prayers of *La tapisserie de Notre Dame.* In presenting the Beauce region of France to Our Lady of Chartres, P. recaptures his own pilgrimages there to petition God's grace, while rooting prayer in the blood and soil of the nation.

P. wrote as an antimodernist prophet, a fact that accounts for the discordant elements in his work—the alternance between popular mysticism and controlled intellectualism; the ease with which he moved from invective, to tender lyricism, to prayer; the coexistence of a profound sympathy for the oppressed (particularly the Jewish people) and an apology for war. A seminal figure in the Catholic Literary Revival, he influenced younger writers—Georges Bernanos, Julien Green (qq.v.)—but, overall, left a varied and somewhat contradictory legacy. In the aftermath of World War I, reactionary Catholics and nationalists sought to couple him with Charles Maurras (1868–1952) and Maurice Barrès (1862–1923), but his authentic successors have been the personalist thinkers, Emmanuel Mounier (1905–1950) and Albert Béguin (1901–1957), the Resistance poets (for example, Pierre Emmanuel [q.v.]), and reviews like *Esprit.* Ultimately unclassifiable, P. was a solitary, best remembered for resisting all forces seeking to make political capital out of moral issues.

FURTHER WORKS: *Œuvres complètes* (20 vols., 1916–55); *Avec C. P., de la Lorraine à la Marne* (1916); *Lettres et entretiens* (1927); *Ébauche d'une étude sur Alfred de Vigny, suivi de L'épreuve* (1931); *Œuvres poétiques complètes* (1941; new eds., 1966, 1975); *Du rôle de la volonté dans la croyance* (1943); *La république* (1946); *La route de Chartres* (1947); *P. et les "Cahiers": Notes de gérance 1900–1910* (1947); *Lettre à Franklin Bouillon* (1948); *Lettres à André Bourgeois* (1950); *Notes politiques et sociales* (1957); *Œuvres en prose 1909–1914* (1957); *Œuvres en prose 1898–1908* (1959); *Correspondance André Gide–C. P., 1905–1912* (1958); *C. P.–André Suarès correspondance* (1961); *Les œuvres posthumes de C. P.* (1968); *Marcel: Premier dialogue de la cité harmonieuse, accompagné d'une série d'articles publiés en 1897 et 1898 à la "Revue socialiste"* (1973); *Alain Fournier–C. P.: Correspondance 1910–14* (1973); *Pour l'honneur de l'esprit: Correspondance entre C. P. et Romain Rolland 1898–1914* (1973); *Claudel et P.: Correspondance* (1974); *Correspondance C. P.–Pierre Marcel, 1905–1914* (1980). FURTHER VOLUMES IN ENGLISH: *Basic Verities: Prose and Poetry* (1943); *Men and Saints: Prose and Poetry* (1944); *God Speaks: Religious Poetry* (1945)

BIBLIOGRAPHY: Servais, Y., *C. P.: The Pursuit of Salvation* (1953); Guyon, B., *P.* (1960); Nelson, R. J., *P.: Poète du sacré*

(1960); Duployé, P., *La religion de P.* (1965); Jussem-Wilson, N., *C. P.* (1965); Villiers, M., *C. P.: A Study in Integrity* (1965); Schmitt, H., *P.: The Decline of an Idealist* (1967); St. Aubyn, F. C., *C. P.* (1977); Centenary Colloquium 1973, *P. écrivain* (1977); Fraisse, S., *P.* (1979)

GEORGE E. GINGRAS

PERCY, Walker

American novelist and essayist, b. 28 May 1916, Birmingham, Ala.

After graduation from medical school and a brief career as a pathologist in New York City, P. was forced by illness to abandon the practice of medicine. He now lives in Covington, Louisiana.

A sizable selection of his philosophical essays on man and language, *The Message in the Bottle,* was published in 1975, but his reputation rests principally upon his five novels: *The Moviegoer* (1961), *The Last Gentleman* (1966), *Love in the Ruins* (1971), *Lancelot* (1977), and *The Second Coming* (1980). All are novels of spiritual quest, part romance and part satire. Only *Love in the Ruins*—subtitled *The Adventures of a Bad Catholic at a Time near the End of the World*—is futuristic. But in the other four as well, with their more or less realistic, contemporary settings, the atmosphere is distinctly that of life in the world's last days.

The amiable, diffidently alienated, bumblingly amorous heroes of the first three novels—Binx Bolling, the stockbroker and prospective medical student of *The Moviegoer;* Will Barrett, the sometime "humidification engineer" (janitor) who becomes a paid traveling companion to a dying youth, in *The Last Gentleman;* Dr. Thomas More, the alcoholic physician of *Love in the Ruins,* who has invented a machine that can diagnose, perhaps cure, all the ills of a dying world, but who finds that his patients, including at times himself, are not really interested in being healed—have so much in common that they seem to be studies of the same man in three different "phases." The novel most recently published, *The Second Coming,* is in fact a kind of "sequel" to *The Last Gentleman,* picking up the life of Will Barrett as a middle-aged widower, who falls in love with the daughter of the woman he had, in the earlier story, thought he would marry. And even the title character of *Lancelot,* the murderer and self-ordained mad prophet Lancelot Andrewes Lamar, has curious affinities with the other more genial heroes. Yet each of the books is endlessly surprising in its wealth of invention and observation; each creates its own world.

The central settings of P.'s fiction are Southern, and, clearly, P. is surest of himself in the Southern scene and idiom. Yet he is not primarily a regionalist. The other Southern writers to whom he is discernibly indebted—among them William Faulkner, Eudora Welty, and Flannery O'Connor (qq.v.)—are those who also, each in his or her own way, have used the South as the world's stage. And his writing has an urbanity that does not characterize his fellow Southerners of either his own or any previous generation. Both in its philosophical concerns and in its artistic form, P.'s work owes at least as much to Henry James and T. S. Eliot (qq.v.) and to English and European writers—for instance, Evelyn Waugh, Graham Greene, Albert Camus (qq.v.), and Dostoevsky—as it does to any of the Southerners.

Although the effects of P.'s medical training are readily apparent in his fiction, he is interested in the science of medicine, as it is representative of all modern science, more for what it cannot tell us about man than for what it can. But his existentialist (q.v.) Catholicism provides no very clear alternative to scientism or to all the other false faiths of our demented times, which the novels so brilliantly satirize. In the three first-person narratives, *The Moviegoer, Love in the Ruins,* and *Lancelot*—only a little more obviously in *Lancelot* than in the others—the narrator-heroes are not to be identified with P. himself. And even in the two Will Barrett novels, which are narrated in the third person, it is extremely difficult at any point to identify the authorial voice. Readers expecting any kind of clear-cut "affirmation" of conventional religious values, let alone suggestions for a program of militant action to right the wrongs of the everyday world, will be disappointed and bewildered by the deliberate ambiguities, and the frequently extravagant fantasy, the mere exuberant *fictitiousness,* of P.'s tales.

On the other hand, to those who look only for proof of the continuing vitality of the novelistic form, P.'s work is wonderfully rewarding. His talent is at once solidly traditional and unmistakably original. As both the considerable popular success of his

503

novels and the rapid development of a body of critical scholarship on all aspects of his art and thought attest, his place in American letters seems already assured, if not yet clearly defined.

BIBLIOGRAPHY: Luschei, M., *The Sovereign Wayfarer: W. P.'s Diagnosis of the Malaise* (1972); Broughton, P., ed., *The Art of W. P.: Stratagems for Being* (1979); Coles, R., *W. P.: An American Search* (1979); Tharpe, J., ed., *W. P.: Art and Ethics* (1980); Gilman, R., on *The Second Coming, New Republic,* 5–12 July 1980, 29–31; Towers, R., on *The Second Coming, NYRB,* 14 Aug. 1980, 39–41

JOHN EDWARD HARDY

PÉREZ DE AYALA, Ramón
Spanish novelist and poet, b. 9 Aug. 1880, Oviedo; d. 5 Aug. 1962, Madrid

Sent away to a Jesuit school at the age of eight, P. de A. received the beginnings of a solid classical education and acquired a fiercely negative attitude toward religion and authority. He set out early to explore Spanish life, but his contact with things English—he studied English early in life and served as Spanish ambassador to Great Britain in the 1930s—and his marriage to a young lady from Pennsylvania added a cosmopolitan dimension to his outlook. From the outset a writer of brilliant promise, he published his last major work in 1926; thereafter, he concentrated upon a diplomatic career, which itself was truncated by the civil war.

P. de A. began his literary career as a poet, a follower of Rubén Darío (q.v.) and perhaps Juan Ramón Jiménez (q.v.), although the latter was, in fact, younger than he. His first book, *La paz del sendero* (1905; the peace of the path), became a part of a proposed series on the grandiose theme of man's "path" through life. In this volume the poet goes back in both theme and time to the Asturias region of his childhood memories. In general following the French poet Francis Jammes (q.v.), he concentrates upon a return to a simpler pastoral world of yesteryear. In his second volume, *El sendero innumerable* (1916; the path of infinite variations), the poet broadens his outlook by choosing the sea as an essential symbol. A third "path," entitled *El sendero andante* (1921; the flow-

ing path), develops the symbol of the river and hence the theme of transitoriness. P. de A.'s early poetry showed great promise, but gradually his interest in fiction absorbed most of his energy.

As a novelist, P. de A. earned a certain amount of notoriety with *A. M. D. G.* (1910; A. M. D. G.), these initials being the Latin motto of the Jesuit Society: "Ad majorem Dei gloriam" (to the greater glory of God). This little novel is an emotional attack against the rigidity and cruelty of the Jesuit system of education. P. de A., who later repudiated this work, ultimately developed a much more balanced appreciation of the Christian tradition. In three other early novels—*Tinieblas en las cumbres* (1907; darkness on the heights), *La pata de la raposa* (1912; *The Fox's Paw,* 1924), and *Troteras y danzaderas* (1913; hustlers and dancers)—P. de A. developed a character, Alberto Díaz de Guzmán, who is a thinly disguised representation of the author himself. Alberto is a young man desperately seeking a philosophy of life (meaning, of course, that he had not received one). As he tests the old and explores the new, above all he intrudes in the area of the relations between the sexes (in Spain this whole area has been a problem complicated by reticence and hypocrisy). By hiding behind the device of a picaresque mode, which is frank and explicit, P. de A. is able to present sexual relations meaningfully. Although in these novels he revealed an impressive talent as a writer, he did not quite succeed in achieving a mastery of theme and form.

One of P. de A.'s enduring successes is a trilogy of short novels, each of which is subtitled *Novela poemática de la vida española* (poetic novel of Spanish life). These short novels are a showcase for P. de A.'s talents (and his weaknesses). In all three the theme is prefigured in poems placed before the prose chapters. In *Prometeo* (1916; *Prometheus,* 1920), before James Joyce (q.v.) and *Ulysses,* P. de A. discovers the technique of ironically pitting the heroic or the epic against everyday life; his hero revives the epic world and sets out to raise his Prometheus as a perfect son, only to crash against the insufficiencies of life itself. In *Luz de domingo* (1916; *Sunday Sunlight,* 1920), set in a provincial town, the hopes of a simple and innocent young engaged couple are blighted when the girl is brutally raped by a group of the town bullies. In *La caída de los Limones*

(1916; *The Fall of the House of Limón,* 1920)
P. de A. traces the rise and subsequent fall of
a *caudillo* (a local strongman) and his family.
Headed by the father, the family carves out a
high position in the town; later his psychotic
son commits a murder that destroys the family. All three of these short novels set out to
illustrate the tragic truth that life is insufficient to measure up to the dreams of man, especially in P. de A.'s Spain.

Although not very successful in his day, P.
de A.'s greatest novel is now considered to be
Belarmino y Apolonio (1921; *Belarmino and
Apolonio,* 1971). This is definitely an "intellectual" novel, like Joyce's *Ulysses,* above all
in the development of various levels of irony.
For example, it is very Spanish in its themes
and yet transcends the specifically Spanish; it
attacks religion and yet it exalts religion; it is
an intellectual tour de force and yet it glorifies simple love. The protagonists are both
shoemakers, but the passion of Belarmino is
philosophy and that of Apolonio the drama.
Belarmino has developed a zany philosophical system that has its own weird logic; Apolonio thinks in dramatic verse form. The
"love interest" is provided by Don Guillén
(the son of Apolonio), who is now a priest,
and Angustias (the daughter of Belarmino),
who is now a prostitute. The way P. de A.
weaves together several narrative strands and
handles many levels of irony is quite impressive, although admittedly one of the complexities is that perhaps some of them remain
unresolved. When the novel appeared, the
Spanish reading public was not ready for it;
later, critics both in Spain and in the Americas discovered its value.

P. de A.'s other truly major novel was published in two parts: *Tigre Juan* (1926; tiger
Juan) and *El curandero de su honra* (1926;
the healer of his honor), both parts translated into English as *Tiger Juan* (1933). This
work is another treatment of the Don Juan
theme, set in 20th-c. Spain. Tiger Juan is an
unusual character—a bloodletter, a public
scribe, and an herbal doctor in a provincial
town. This Tiger Juan has a tragic past: he
helped cause his wife's death in a mixup over
a matter of honor. When Tiger Juan sets out
to win Herminia, there is a potential for tragedy when she becomes attracted to a traveling salesman, a "superficial" Don Juan.
Although she runs off with this man, when
she returns Tiger Juan forgives her with understanding. Thus he becomes the "healer of

his honor" in loving forgiveness, not by having his wife killed as did the protagonist in
Calderón's fierce drama *The Surgeon of His
Honor.* This novel is P. de A.'s most solid attempt to write about relations between man
and woman based on sincere communication,
rather than hypocrisy and barbaric masculine
will.

P. de A. is an important novelist of the
generation that falls between that of Unamuno, Azorín, Valle-Inclán, and Baroja (qq.v.)
and that of Camilo José Cela (q.v.) following
the civil war. After showing initial promise
as a poet, he gradually saw his inspiration
wane, unlike that of his friend Jiménez. In
fiction, at least two of his works will surely
survive: *Novelas poemáticas de la vida
española* and *Belarmino y Apolonio.* In these
novels slices of Spanish life are presented
with unusual vividness; at the same time the
author's very modern and sophisticated use
of irony aptly demonstrates his talent as a
novelist.

FURTHER WORKS: *Las máscaras* (2 vols.,
1917, 1919); *Política y toros* (1918); *Luna de
miel, luna de hiel* (1923; this and following
title tr. as *Honeymoon, Bittermoon,* 1972);
Los trabajos de Urbano y Simona (1923); *El
ombligo del mundo* (1924); *Bajo el signo de
Artemisa* (1924); *Divagaciones literarias*
(1958); *Obras completas* (4 vols., 1964–69)

BIBLIOGRAPHY: Madariaga, S. de, *The Genius of Spain* (1923), pp. 71–86; Barja, C.,
Libros y autores contemporáneos (1935), pp.
439–66; Nora, E. de, *La novela española contemporánea* (1958), pp. 467–513; Reinink, K.
W., *Algunos aspectos literarios y lingüísticos
de la obra de Don R. P. de A.* (1959); Curtis,
E. R., *Ensayos críticos acerca de la literatura
española* (1959), Vol. II, pp. 109–21; Beck,
M. A., "La realidad artística en las tragedias
grotescas de P. de A.," *Hispania,* 46 (1963),
480–89; Weber, F. W., *The Literary Perspectivism of P. de A.* (1966); Rand, M. C., *P. de
A.* (1971); Feeny, T., "Maternal-Paternal Attitudes in the Fiction of R. P. de A.," *Hispano,* 62 (1978), 77–85; Macklin, J. J.,
"Myth and Mimesis: The Artistic Integrity
of P. de A.'s *Tigre Juan* and *El curandero de
su honra,*" *HR,* 48 (1980), 15–36; Newberry,
W., "R. P. de A.'s Concept of the *Doppelgänger* in *Belarmino y Apolonio,*" *Symposium,* 34 (1980), 56–67

CARL W. COBB

PÉREZ GALDÓS, Benito

Spanish novelist, dramatist, and journalist, b. 10 May 1843, Las Palmas, Canary Islands; d. 4 Jan. 1920, Madrid

Raised in the somewhat remote Canary Islands, where he attended an English high school, P. G. moved to Madrid in 1862 to attend the University of Madrid. He enrolled as a student of law, a course of study he never completed—nor did he ever intend to. His time was occupied with his observations of the city, his work as a journalist for the prestigious newspaper *La nación,* and his own writing. In 1867 P. G. went to Paris, where he became familiar with the works of Balzac.

P. G. was an outspoken liberal and republican. In 1886 he was elected to Parliament; in 1907 he was again elected, as a representative for Madrid, and once more in 1914 for the Canary Islands. Although he was a member of the Royal Spanish Academy and a novelist and dramatist of great success, he died poor and broken, totally blind—and never succeeded in being nominated by the Spanish Academy for the Nobel Prize.

That P. G. is Spain's greatest novelist after Cervantes there is no debate. With *La fontana de oro* (1870; the fountain of gold), which portrays the political struggles of the minority Liberal faction against the reactionary reign of Ferdinand VII in 1822–23, P. G. began to revitalize the Spanish novel. He also created a model for Spanish fiction that was to be highly influential throughout the 20th c. It is difficult to imagine how the work of Blasco Ibáñez, Unamuno, Baroja, Pérez de Ayala, Sender (qq.v.), and many others would have come into being without the legacy of P. G. Although reacted to with hostility by some of these later writers, P. G. was a strong force in their development as well as in the careers of some of the objectivist writers of the 1950s and in some of the dialectical realists of the 1960s.

When P. G. began to write, the novel in Spain was almost completely stagnant. Vacuous, mindless romantic fiction abounded. P. G. had a strong conviction that novels should be written with a keen regard for accurate observation and natural dialogue. Fiction should reflect all the good and evil in society, since it must be a moral response to reality. As a reformer and moralist who was convinced that love was the principal salvation, P. G. was fond of the dialectical process. He often proceeded along Hegelian lines, believing that only through opposition and struggle could there be growth and transcendence.

P. G.'s lifelong undertaking was the historical portrait of 19th-c. Spain, embodied in the *Episodios nacionales* (national episodes), five series comprising forty-six novels in all, beginning with *Trafalgar* (1873; *Trafalgar,* 1884), a quasi-journalistic account of that sea battle against the British, and ending with *Cánovas* (1912; Cánovas), a highly fictionalized account of the regime of Prime Minister Antonio Cánovas in 1906. In this mammoth undertaking P. G. sought the proper balance among fact, fiction, description, and commentary; he always tried to avoid any one ideology, lest his panorama turn into propaganda. In doing so, he created a paradigm for the historical novel that many 20th-c. writers would later utilize.

In the category P. G. called "Novels of the First Period," *Doña Perfecta* (1876; *Doña Perfecta,* 1880; new tr., 1960) is the most popular work. Dickensian in its characterizations, it portrays Doña Perfecta, the venerable widow of Orbajosa, a backward town located somewhere in the "heart of Spain," known solely for its prodigious production of garlic. *Doña Perfecta,* a somewhat melodramatic although cogent tract against religious fanaticism, which is personified by Doña Perfecta and her cohorts, is a strong plea for scientific progress, symbolized by Pepe Rey, her nephew, who wishes to marry her daughter Rosario. The rather *imperfect* protagonist, Doña Perfecta, finds this situation totally intolerable and has Pepe murdered. Although clearly a thesis novel, *Doña Perfecta* achieves the necessary balance between abstract ideas and concrete human concerns and character development. The reader is deeply moved by the death of Pepe Rey and scornfully outraged at Doña Perfecta, one of Spanish literature's most heinous characters.

P. G.'s masterpiece is the panoramic and meticulously detailed four-volume work, *Fortunata y Jacinta* (1886–87; *Fortunata and Jacinta: Two Stories of Married Women,* 1973). The novel concerns a love triangle, in which two women are desperately in love with the same man, Juanito Santa Cruz, an idle son of a very wealthy family. He loves each woman in a different way. Jacinta, his barren wife, represents the social forces or civilization, and Fortunata, who is beautiful beyond words, the natural forces or barbarism. At the end of this many-tiered and highly symbolic novel P. G.'s Hegelian bent can be fully comprehended. When Fortunata is slowly dying after having given birth to her second child by Juanito (their first one had died young), she decides to give it to the childless Jacinta, who will become its mother. Only through dialectical opposition and struggle can there be the fusion and synthesis to insure growth and genuine progress.

Also important is the Torquemada series, comprising four novels: *Torquemada en la hoguera* (1889; *Torquemada in the Flames,* 1956), *Torquemada en la cruz* (1893; Torquemada on the cross), *Torquemada en al Purgatorio* (1894; Torquemada in purgatory), and *Torquemada y San Pedro* (1895; Torquemada and Saint Peter). This series is an exhaustive psychological portrait of a small-time usurer who tries to become a respected businessman. P. G. shows his opprobrium for materialistic values and their incompatibility with spiritual growth.

Spiritual growth, Christian charity, and the unselfish belief in others are the qualities that Benina, a self-effacing servant, possesses in P. G.'s most humanistic novel, *Misericordia* (1897; *Compassion,* 1962), in which he reached the height of his disenchantment with positivism, as he moved away from realism toward a kind of spiritual naturalism.

Although P. G. admitted that he was attracted to the drama more than to any other genre, his first play was not performed until 1892. He never became as fine a dramatist as he was a novelist, but his concerns were the same: honesty, social justice and truth, individual liberty and freedom from stultifying Spanish traditionalism and clericalism.

Electra (1901; *Electra,* 1919), one of P. G.'s most successful plays, caused a near riot at the time of its premiere, in spite of its simple, if not simplistic plot about Electra, the illegitimate daughter of a woman of "bad blood." At the end of the play Electra emerges victorious, overcoming those ill-intentioned traditionalists who desired to thwart her marriage to a man of progress. Reason, truth, and liberal ideals win out; heredity—"bad genes"—and the forces of repression lose.

P. G.'s oeuvre has a very special place in Spanish letters. His patience, tolerance, and constant striving to reform the individual are awesome. It is this legacy—the need to reform on a microcosmic, that is, an individual, scale—that the members of the Generation of 1898 received from P. G. as their mission.

FURTHER WORKS: *La sombra* (1870; *The Shadow,* 1980); *El audaz* (1871); *Bailén* (1873); *La corte de Carlos IV* (1873; *The Court of Charles IV: A Romance of the Escorial,* 1888); *El 19 de marzo y el 2 de mayo* (1873); *Cádiz* (1874); *Gerona* (1874); *Juan Martín el Empecinado* (1874); *Napoleón en Chamartín* (1874); *La batalla de los Arapiles* (1875; *The Battle of Salamanca: A Tale of the Napoleonic War,* 1895); *El equipaje del Rey José* (1875); *Memorias de un cortesano* (1875); *El Grande Oriente* (1876); *La segunda casaca* (1876); *El 7 de julio* (1876); *Gloria* (2 vols., 1876–77; *Gloria,* 1879); *El terror de 1824* (1877); *Los cien mil hijos de San Luis* (1877); *Marianela* (1878; *Marianela,* 1883); *Un voluntario realista* (1878); *La familia de León Roch* (3 vols., 1878–79; *Leon Roch: A Romance,* 1888); *Los apostólicos* (1879); *El amigo Manso* (1881); *La desheredada* (1881; *The Disinherited Lady,* 1957); *El doctor Centeno* (2 vols., 1883); *La de Bringas* (1884; *The Spendthrifts,* 1951); *Tormento* (1884; *Torment,* 1952); *Lo prohibido* (2 vols., 1884–85); *Miau* (1888; *Miau,* 1963); *La incógnita* (1888–89); *Realidad* (1889); *Crónicas de Portugal* (1890); *De vuelta de Italia* (1890); *Angel Guerra* (3 vols., 1890–91); *La loca de la casa* (1892); *Realidad* (play, 1892); *Tristana* (1892; *Tristana,* 1961); *Gerona* (play, 1893); *La loca de la casa* (play, 1893); *La de San Quintín* (1894; *The Duchess of San Quintin,* 1917); *Los condenados* (1894); *Zaragoza* (1894; *Saragossa: A Story of Spanish Valor,* 1899); *Halma* (1895); *Nazarín* (1895); *Voluntad* (1895); *Doña Perfecta* (play, 1896); *La fiera* (1896); *El abuelo* (1897); *De Oñate a la Granja* (1898); *Zumalacárregui* (1898); *La campaña del Maestrazgo* (1899); *La estafeta romántica* (1899); *Ludana* (1899); *Vergara* (1899); *Bodas reales* (1900); *Los ayacuchas* (1900); *Montes de Oca* (1900); *Alma y vida* (1902); *Las tormentas del 48* (1902); *Narváez* (1902); *Los duendes de la camarilla* (1903); *Mariucha* (1903); *La revolución de julio* (1904); *El abuelo* (play, 1904; *The Grandfather,* 1910); *O'Donnell* (1904); *Aita Tettauen* (1905); *Amor y ciencia* (1905); *Bárbara* (1905); *Carlos VI en la Rápita (1905); Casandra* (1905); *La vuelta al mundo en la Nu-*

mancia (1906); *Memoranda* (1906); *Prim* (1906); *La de los tristes destinos* (1907); *Zaragoza* (play, 1907); *España sin rey* (1908); *Pedro Minio* (1908); *El caballero encantado* (1909); *España trágica* (1909); *Amadeo I* (1910); *Casandra* (play, 1910); *De Cartago a Sagunto* (1911); *La primera república* (1911); *Celia en los infiernos* (1913); *Alceste* (1914); *La razón de la sinrazón* (1915); *Sor Simona* (1915); *El tacaño Salomón* (1916); *Santa Juana de Castilla* (1918); *Arte y crítica* (1923); *Fisonomías sociales* (1923); *Nuestro teatro* (1923); *Política española* (2 vols., 1923); *Crónica* (2 vols., 1924); *Toledo: Su historia y su leyenda* (1924); *Viajes y fantasías* (1928); *Memorias* (1930); *Crónica de Madrid* (1933); *La novela en el tranvía* (1936); *Crónica de la Quincera* (1948); *Obras completas* (6 vols., 1951–61)

BIBLIOGRAPHY: Berkowitz, H. C., *B. P. G.: Spanish Liberal Crusader* (1948); Casalduero, J., *Vida y obra de G.*, 2nd ed. (1951); Eoff, S. H., *The Novels of P. G.: The Concept of Life as Dynamic Process* (1954); Gullón, R., *G., novelista moderno* (1960); Schraibman, J., *Dreams in the Novels of G.* (1960); Nimetz, M., *Humor in G.* (1968); Roger, D., ed., *B. P. G.* (1973); Pattison, W. T., *B. P. G.* (1975); Engler, K., *The Structure of Realism: The "Novelas contemporáneas" of B. P. G.* (1977); Dendle, B. J., *G.: The Mature Thought* (1980); Gilman, S., *G. and the Art of the European Novel: 1867–1887* (1981)

MARSHALL J. SCHNEIDER

PERRON, Edgar du

(pseud.: Duco Perkens) Dutch novelist, poet, essayist, critic, and journalist, b. 2 Nov. 1899, Meester Cornelis, Java, Indonesia; d. 14 May 1940, Bergen

P. was descended from a well-to-do planter's family of French ancestry. He attended secondary school in Bandung, Java, but beyond that was largely self-educated. For a time he was employed on various Batavian newspapers and as a library assistant at the Royal Batavia Society of Arts and Sciences. Having left for Paris in 1921, he became a close friend of André Malraux (q.v.)—indeed Malraux dedicated his *Man's Fate* to him.

In 1930 P. went to the Netherlands, where he lived for brief periods in Amsterdam and The Hague, but most of the years 1921–36 were spent in Paris and Brussels. He collabo-

rated on several literary journals, most notably the influential *Forum* (Rotterdam, 1932–35), which he founded together with Menno ter Braak and Maurice Roelants (qq.v.). In 1936 P. returned to Indonesia, where he worked for a time as a journalist for the periodical *Kritiek en opbouw*. But his stay was a keen disappointment to him; he felt himself a stranger in what he considered a materialistically attuned Dutch society in the Indies. He also recognized the just cause of Indonesians who were seeking independence; expressions of his sentiments are to be found in the posthumously published *Indies memorandum* (1946; Indies memorandum). P. returned to the Netherlands for the last time in 1939. He died of a heart attack on the day the Dutch army surrendered to the Germans.

P.'s masterpiece, *Het land van herkomst* (1935; the country of origin), is an autobiographical novel in which the East Indies of the past and the Paris of the 1930s are juxtaposed. Quite unconventional in Dutch literature, the work consists of diaries, conversations, letters, memoirs, and narration, but without any plot and with little coherence. He called it an antinovel.

P. is regarded as one of the liveliest and most stimulating Dutch critics of the 1930s. His criticism was based on a highly individualistic approach. He never wished to be regarded as a critic in the traditional sense; that is, he did not wish his views to be binding upon the reader's own judgment. P. considered his opinions to be valid for himself alone.

P. quite consciously wrote for the few; his works have never enjoyed wide popularity. They did, however, exert great influence upon his contemporaries and upon later writers in the Netherlands and Belgium. He was a notable polemicist and fiercely combated all forms of insincerity and affectation. He did not suffer fools gladly and as an individualist he remained aloof from politics but was strongly and outspokenly antifascist. P.'s role as critic and as author of *Het land van herkomst* assures him of a prominent place in Dutch letters.

FURTHER WORKS: *Manuscrit trouvé dans une poche* (1923); *Het roerend bezit* (1924, as Duco Perkens); *De behouden prullemand* (1925, as Duco Perkens); *Bij gebrek aan ernst* (1926, as Duco Perkens); *Een voorbereiding* (1927); *Poging tot afstand* (1927); *Cahiers van een lezer* (5 vols., 1928–31);

Nutteloos verzet (1929); *Parlando* (1930); *Micro-chaos* (1932); *Uren met Dirk Coster* (1933); *De smalle mens* (1934); *Blocnote klein formaat* (1936); *De man van Lebak* (1937); *Multatuli, tweede pleidooi* (1938); *Schandaal in Holland* (1939); *Multatuli en de Luizen* (1940); *Een lettré uit de 18e eeuw: Willem van Hogendorp* (1940); *De bewijzen uit het pak van Sjaalman* (1940); *De grijze dashond* (1941); *Een groote stilte* (1942); *Scheepsjournal van Arthur Ducroo* (1943); *Over Stendhal* (1944); *In de grootse tijd* (1947); *Verzameld werk* (7 vols., 1954–59); *Briefwisseling Ter Braak–Du P.: 1930–1940* (4 vols., 1962–67)

BIBLIOGRAPHY: Meijer, R. P., *Literature of the Low Countries,* new ed. (1978), pp. 325–28.

JOHN M. ECHOLS

PERSIAN LITERATURE
See Iranian Literature; see also Afghan (Dari) Literature and Indian Literature

PERUVIAN LITERATURE

Fiction

Peruvian fiction in the 20th c.—short story and novel alike—has a readily discernible pattern. It has evolved from studiedly cosmopolitan work to writing oriented along national lines—with the distinctive rural areas of Peru providing the settings for the action—and finally to an emphasis on urban life and on the more universal problems of modern man. Throughout the first half of this century, the short story was the more cultivated and significant form of fiction, with the novel developing relatively slowly and irregularly. In the 1960s and 1970s, however, with the appearance of such gifted novelists as Mario Vargas Llosa, Julio Ribeyro (qq.v.), and Alfredo Bryce Echenique (b. 1939), a balance was achieved between the two genres.

The beginnings of 20th-c. Peruvian fiction coincide with the tardy influence of modernism (q.v.), a literary phenomenon that, although peculiarly Spanish American in its development, subsumes many major European artistic and philosophical preoccupations

of the second half of the 19th c. The Peruvian modernists, who were well aware of prevailing fin-de-siècle themes and forms, produced their major works from the last years of the 19th c. through the first decade of the 20th. Clemente Palma (1875–1946), the most significant exponent of modernist fiction, was instrumental in giving the Peruvian narrative a more universal orientation. He is also credited with initiating the modern short-story form in Peru. The content of most of his fiction is shocking and bizarre; its tone is ironic and pessimistic. Decadent, worldly-wise protagonists, cosmopolitan settings, and themes inspired by the disturbing implications of the scientific advances of the age characterize his best-known work, *Cuentos malévolos* (1904; malevolent stories).

Just before World War I Peruvian fiction began to lean toward national settings and characters. Abraham Valdelomar (1888–1919), Enrique López Albújar (1872–1966), and Ventura García Calderón (1886–1959) had begun writing fiction in the manner of Palma. That these three writers again coincided in the more mature phase of their careers is highly significant: their nationally oriented fiction, highlighting the coast, mountains, and jungle, marked the beginning of a rural-regional trend, which virtually dominated Peruvian fiction until the 1950s. Valdelomar's short-story collection *El caballero Carmelo* (1918; gentleman Carmelo), which beautifully depicts the landscape and inhabitants of the Peruvian seacoast, and López Albújar's *Cuentos andinos* (1920; Andean stories), a limited but unusual presentation of Indian customs and mentality, are notable examples of this period.

The novelists and short-story writers of the 1930s and 1940s continued the regional emphasis, and in general their focus was even sharper and more sensitive to surface detail as they strove to record, often with photographic accuracy, the topography, customs, speech habits, and racial types of Peru. Social protest was also an important element of many of these narratives: the Indian as a victim of cruel, unscrupulous oppressors was of particular concern to several writers.

During the 1930s two major writers, Ciro Alegría and José María Arguedas (qq.v.), emerged. They are pivotal figures, for while sharing their contemporaries' concern for the national scene and its problems, they strove for and achieved new, more transcendent modes of expressing those realities. Their novels and short stories are, in fact, a striking synthesis of the work of their predecessors and of their own innovations. Alegría's *El mundo es ancho y ajeno* (1941; *Broad and Alien Is the World,* 1941) and Arguedas's *Los ríos profundos* (1959; *Deep Rivers,* 1978) are novels that depict in an extraordinarily powerful and profound way the complexities of the Indian and his environment.

While not forsaking rural Peru, writers during the 1950s turned with marked interest to the social, economic, and psychological problems of city dwellers. But whether detailing urban or rural Peru, they were fully aware that they were also dealing with universal moral and spiritual problems. The rejection or loss of tradition and the quest for new values in Peruvian life are understood to be a reflection of modern civilization.

The novelists and short-story writers who have emerged since 1950 also give evidence of an increased concern for the principles of the art of modern fiction. Julio Ribeyro, Carlos Zavaleta (b. 1928), Enrique Congrains Martín (b. 1932), Alfredo Bryce Echenique, and Mario Vargas Llosa are just five of a large group of talented contemporary authors. Congrains Martín is especially attuned to the desperation of the lower classes struggling to survive in *barriadas,* the peripheral slum areas that have grown up around Lima since the end of World War II. Indeed, his first short-story collection, *Lima, hora cero* (1954; Lima, zero hour), predates by two years the publication of sociological studies of the *barriada* phenomenon. Ribeyro, likewise concerned about the deprivations suffered by the poor, also provides subtle insights into the psychology of the middle class, with its own deep sense of alienation. The confusion of values afflicting that class is presented sensitively in such works as the novel *Los geniecillos dominicales* (1965; Sunday temper). Perhaps better than any modern author, Bryce Echenique understands the so-called upper class of Lima. He portrays its value system with authenticity and irony in the novel *Un mundo para Julius* (1970; a world for Julius). Zavaleta is at his best when dealing with the implications of Peru's rural traditions: How have they shaped national identity, and how do they fit within the universal beliefs and preoccupations of man? His short-story collection *La batalla* (1954; the battle) illuminates the pervasiveness of violence within the cultural tradition.

These writers have in common a thorough knowledge of narrative technique, an uncanny ear for spoken language, and a special interest in narrative structure. Within this group, however, one figure, Mario Vargas Llosa, clearly stands out. He is a stylistic innovator, a provider of striking perspectives on human experience, and a writer who devotes himself tirelessly to his craft. His first novel, *La ciudad y los perros* (1962; *The Time of the Hero,* 1966), attracted critical acclaim, stirred bitter controversy, and catapulted him into international prominence. The work examines critically and forthrightly the lives of cadets in the Lima military academy Leoncio Prado. The novel's complex structure is achieved by an extraordinary manipulation of narrative point of view.

Poetry

Peruvian poetry in the 20th c. is not quite comparable to the fiction in terms of vitality and prestige, although the work of César Vallejo (q.v.), a prominent figure in world literature, is a notable exception to this generalization.

Like fiction, the beginnings of 20th-c. poetry coincide with modernism in Peru. Although Manuel González Prada's (q.v.) most significant publications are his essays, he was also important as an innovator of verse form. His poetry is generally associated with the very beginnings of the modernist movement. *Exóticas* (1911; exotics) evinces many characteristics of modernism.

José Santos Chocano (q.v.), whose works combine a preoccupation with modernist imagery and meter and also a desire to exalt the inhabitants and landscape of Latin America, is the best-known Peruvian poet of the early part of the century. His *Alma América—Poemas indo-españoles* (1906; America soul—Indo-Spanish poems) is somewhat reminiscent of the poetry of Walt Whitman.

The next phase of Peruvian poetry was postmodernism. Two literary magazines, *Colónida* and *Contemporáneos,* were primarily responsible for introducing the major new poets during the period 1910–20. The postmodernists, while continuing to cultivate the modernist interest in euphony, reacted strongly against many of its rhetorical adornments, seeking a purer form of expression and preferring to deal more intimately and subtly with the basic problems of man. José

María Eguren (1874–1942) was one of the most gifted, and until recently, underrated poets of the period.

César Vallejo must be ranked with the Chilean Pablo Neruda (q.v.) in importance. He resists easy classification, but his influence on poetry has been enormous. At the risk of oversimplification, one can characterize his first collection of poetry, *Los heraldos negros* (1918; the black messengers), as postmodernist. Even in these early poems the existential problem of suffering mankind, a theme that forms the essence of his later works, can be detected. It would not be inaccurate to classify *Trilce* (1922; *Trilce,* 1973), his second book, as vanguardist. His last two collections of poetry, *Poemas humanos* (1939; *Poemas humanos/Human Poems,* 1968) and *España, aparta de mí este cáliz* (1939; *Spain, Take This Cup from Me,* 1974), treat social themes with a deep pessimism, yet with a profound love for humanity.

During the 1930s and 1940s, surrealism (q.v.) and Indianism were the major influences, with the poets either tending toward abstract interests or nativistic concerns. Emilio Adolfo Westphalen (b. 1911) and César Moro (1903–1956) were the most prominent and productive of the surrealists. Alejandro Peralta (1896–1973), whose poetry contains much imagery associated with the Peruvian Andes, represents the nativistic vein.

Two poetic tendencies in Peru may be traced from the 1950s to the present. One is a social preoccupation, with subjects inspired by historical realities, including the mundane aspects of daily life; the other is more conceptual, even hermetic in nature. Washington Delgado (b. 1927), whose poetry ranges from a subtle lament about the alienation of modern man to strong protest, is a noteworthy example of the first tendency. Fine representatives of more conceptual poetry are Javier Sologuren (b. 1923), Francisco Bendezú (b. 1928), and Carlos Germán Belli (b. 1927).

Drama

Drama is of comparatively little significance within 20th-c. Peruvian literature. For the first three decades, the plays written and staged were mainly in the costumbristic (folkloric) vein. They were of little literary interest. Since the 1930s the influence of the theater of Europe and the U.S. has been more apparent.

Two playwrights, Sebastián Salazar Bondy (1924–1965) and Enrique Solari Swayne (b. 1915), whose works were presented with some success in the 1950s and 1960s, are worthy of mention. Salazar Bondy was intimately acquainted with and influenced by the plays of the French existentialists (q.v.) and the American drama of social concern. *Rodil* (1951; Rodil) is an excellent example of his existentialist production, and *No hay isla feliz* (1957; there is no happy island) is reminiscent of Arthur Miller's (q.v.) works. Solari Swayne is equally aware of European and North American trends in drama. In his two best-known plays, *Collacocha* (1959; Collacocha) and *La mazorca* (1965; the ear of corn), he seeks to infuse national themes with universal significance. The first play deals with the struggle of man against the Andes, and the second protrays man's efforts to accommodate himself to the jungle environment.

BIBLIOGRAPHY: Escobar, A., *La narración en el Perú* (1960); Nuñez, E., *La literatura peruana en el siglo XX* (1965); Aldrich, E., *The Modern Short Story in Peru* (1966); Luchting, W., "Recent Peruvian Fiction: Vargas Llosa, Ribeyro, and Arguedas," *RS,* No. 35 (1968), 271–90; Tamayo Vargas, A., *Literatura peruana* (1976); Luchting, W., *Escritores peruanos que piensan que dicen* (1977); Tipton, D., ed., Introduction to *Peru: The New Poetry* (1977), pp. 11–14

EARL M. ALDRICH, JR.

PESSOA, Fernando

Portuguese poet and critic (also writing in English), b. 13 June 1888, Lisbon; d. 30 Nov. 1935, Lisbon

After P.'s father's death in 1893, his mother married the Portuguese consul in Durban, South Africa, where P. lived from 1896 to 1905. He graduated from junior college in South Africa, winning the Queen Victoria Prize for English Composition, and went to Lisbon in 1905 to attend the university. The early British education that P. received was far different from the French culture then pervasive in Portuguese literature and made an everlasting impression on his views and his handling of language. Moreover, through his work he was to exert an anglicizing influence on subsequent poetic diction in Portugal and Brazil. Soon after 1905 he gave up his studies, using his knowledge of English to get employment as a business correspondent. For the rest of his life he lived alone in Lisbon, avoiding social life and the literary world.

At his debut in 1912—which was as a literary critic—he praised the *saudosismo* (nostalgia) movement in such extravagant terms that his articles provoked nationwide polemics. From that year on he proceeded uninterruptedly to comment on politics and literature by means of paradoxical and mystifying articles and pamphlets. He helped to launch the avant-garde movement in Portuguese literature and, through the reviews *Orpheu* and *Portugal futurista,* was its leading figure along with Mário de Sá-Carneiro (q.v.) and José de Almada-Negreiros (1893–1970).

But it is as a poet that P. has won eminence in modern world literature. He wrote poetry under his own name as well as under at least three other names. As Fernando Pessoa he wrote poems that are marked by their startling innovations of language, although he used traditional stanza and metrical patterns. As Alvaro de Campos he was a bold modernist, tragically minded, whose forte was for dour and majestic diction in free verse. As Alberto Caeiro he was a straightforward empiricist, a sensualist, whose free verse seems indifferent to technique. As Ricardo Reis he was a classicist, whose Horatian odes surpass the ambitions of most 18th-c. writers. These names were "heteronyms," as P. said of them, not pen names. Each persona had a distinct philosophy of life, wrote at a certain linguistic level, and worked in a distinctive style and form. P. even wrote literary discussions among them. He prepared their horoscopes to fit their lives and personalities—or he may have shaped a personality according to a horoscope. (Like other Western postsymbolist poets he had esoteric tendencies that show in his work.)

What is most impressive is that each of these "heteronyms" (and when he wrote poetry under his own name he was as much of a heteronym as when he "was" somebody else) is a great poet in his own right.

The bulk of P.'s work was published in literary magazines, especially in his own *Athena.* Editors did not begin to compile his work until 1942, and the wealth of his scattered or unpublished writings has still to be rescued, in spite of his having been recognized as a master as early as 1927.

Little of P.'s work was published in book

form during his lifetime. His English poems *were* collected in books: *35 Sonnets* (1917), *Antinous* (1918), *English Poems I–II* (1921), *English Poems III* (1921). Most of them were too "metaphysical" for the time and hence very much in advance of the change of taste that was to occur in English poetry. In addition, he published *Mensagem* (1934; message), a sequence of emblematic poems in Portuguese on the history of Portugal. Although a minor work, it is still controversial today, as it can be interpreted as "nationalist" and used to present P. as an apologist for the authoritarian regime that had come into power in 1926, which he was not.

P. is admirable for his terrifying lucidity, his linguistic virtuosity, and his inventive imagery. His deeply felt intellectualism was in the best Portuguese tradition of Luís Vaz de Camões (1524?–1580) and Antero de Quental (1842–1891). (One of his best-known lines states, "What in me feels is now thinking.") Today, P.'s poetry is still original and audacious. No one in Western literature has been more successful than he in realizing the modern dream of creating an antiromantic "objective correlative." All this qualifies him as one of the greatest poets in Portuguese, and as such he is admired in Portugal and Brazil. Translations of his poems in Spanish, French, English, German, and other languages have been appearing since the 1940s, thus opening the way for P. to be recognized as one of the most important and original masters of modern poetry.

FURTHER WORKS: *Poemas de F. P.* (1942); *Poemas de Álvaro de Campos* (1944); *A nova poesia portuguesa* (1944); *Poemas de Alberto Caeiro* (1946); *Poemas de Ricardo Reis* (1946); *Páginas de doutrina estética* (1946); *Poemas dramáticos* (1952); *Quadras ao gosto popular* (1955); *Poesias inéditas: 1919–1930* (1956); *Páginas íntimas e de auto-interpretação* (1966); *Páginas de estética e de teoria e crítica literária* (1966); *Textos filosóficos* (2 vols., 1968); *Novas poesias inéditas* (1973); *Cartas de amor de F. P.* (1978); *Sobre Portugal: Introdução ao problema nacional* 1979); *Livro do desassossego por Bernardo Soares* (1982). FURTHER VOLUMES IN ENGLISH: *Selected Poems by F. P.* (1971); *Selected Poems of F. P.* (1971)

BIBLIOGRAPHY: Biderman, S., "Mount Abiegnos and the Masks: Occult Imagery in Yeats and P.," *LBR*, 5 (1968), 59–74; Hamburger, M., "F. P.," *Agenda,* 6, 3–4 (1968), 104–12; Paz, O., Introduction to *Selected Poems by F. P.* (1971), pp. 1–21; Rickard, P., Introduction to *Selected Poems of F. P.* (1971), pp. 1–61; Jones, M. S., "P.'s Poetic Coterie: Three Heteronyms and an Orthonym," *LBR,* 14 (1977), 254–62; Bacarisse, P., "F. P.: Towards an Understanding of a Key Attitude," *LBR,* 17 (1980), 51–61; Sousa, R. W., "P.: The Messenger," *The Rediscoverers: Major Portuguese Writers in the Portuguese Literature of National Regeneration* (1981), pp. 131–60

JORGE DE SENA
UPDATED BY IRWIN STERN

PETERS, Lenrie

Gambian poet and novelist (writing in English), b. 1 Sept. 1932, Bathurst

In 1952 P. left Africa to study medicine at Cambridge, eventually going on to specialize in surgery. He now resides in Gambia.

P.'s one novel, *The Second Round* (1965), is important as one of the first African novels to turn from the theme of colonial protest and culture conflict to that of self-criticism— the African's criticism of his own country. In this book a doctor returns to his home in Freetown after studying and then practicing medicine for several years in England. He finds himself to be an objective observer, unable to engage himself fully in the lives of his friends, who are being torn apart as they fail to adjust to, or even to recognize, the values of their changing society. Despite several passages of a fine lyrical quality, the novel is marred by excessively sentimental scenes and a contrived plot.

P.'s forte is clearly his poetry. In *Satellites* (1967), his best collection to date, he draws together his experience of living in two worlds, the African and the Western, and analyzes both worlds in fine, almost microscopic detail. The particular confusion, frustration, and alienation he finds in his own soul is seen to be representative of Everyman's malaise in the face of technology and its suffocation of human values. P.'s medical training informs the poetry in this volume with a precision that the reader finds not only in his short, tight stanzas, but also in the incisive, at times surgical, images he employs.

This analytical introspection is continued in much of the poetry in *Katchikali* (1971),

but the collection as a whole lacks the vitality of *Satellites.* Nevertheless, in a few of the poems P. made some interesting experiments with form, breaking away from the tighter structures of his earlier verse.

P.'s total output has been small, and he has published nothing since *Katchikali.* He remains, however, one of the finest contemporary African poets. No other living African poet has, in fact, so consistently displayed such control of form or created such startling images. Concerned with the spirit no less than the flesh, P. has effectively married his concerns in a poetry that addresses the social and economic problems of contemporary Africa and reasserts the aesthetic principles he finds threatened in his society.

FURTHER WORKS: *Poems* (1964); *Selected Poetry* (1981)

BIBLIOGRAPHY: Moore, G., "The Imagery of Death in African Poetry," *AfricaL,* 38 (1968), 57–70; Theroux, P., "Six Poets," in Beier, U., ed., *Introduction to African Literature* (1970), pp. 110–31; Knipp, T. R., "L. P.: The Poet as Lonely African," *SBL,* 2, 3 (1971), 9–13; Larson, C. R., "L. P.'s *The Second Round:* West African Gothic," *The Emergence of African Fiction* (1972), pp. 227–41; Egudu, R. N., *Four Modern West African Poets* (1977), passim

RICHARD PRIEBE

PETERSEN, Nis

Danish poet, short-story writer, and novelist, b. 22 Jan. 1897, Vamdrup; d. 9 March 1943, Laven

After three years as a pharmacist's apprentice, P. worked as a journalist from 1918 until 1921, when he severed all ties with the bourgeois world. He spent the rest of his life as a casual laborer, beggar, and vagabond—and writer.

Because of his break with his pietistic upbringing and its view of life in which responsibility and sin play an important part, P. became burdened with a chronic sense of guilt and a fatal irresoluteness. Similarly, many of his fictional characters feel themselves lost: they are outcasts marked by skepticism and angst. The idyll of childhood and the experience of love as well as death itself and the hope for divine grace offered the possibility of an escape from this rootlessness. But P. feared death, too; a prevalent theme in his work is death as judgment rather than as a means of salvation.

P.'s existential insecurity is most distinctly expressed in his poetry, which he began writing as early as 1915. The early verse reflects the horror of the outbreak of World War I and his own rather pathetic suicidal thoughts. These poems, written around the time of World War I, were published posthumously in *For tromme og kastagnet* (1951; for drum and castanet). His official debut was with *Nattens pibere* (1926; the pipers of the night). Here P.'s expressions of disillusion are juxtaposed to a number of nature idylls; there is a persistent dwelling on man's capacity for love and fellowship. P.'s subsequent poetry collections, *En drift vers* (1933; a drove of verses), *Til en dronning* (1935; to a queen), and *Stykgods* (1940; mixed cargo), are variations on these themes with Rudyard Kipling (q.v.) as an increasingly dominant model not only in regard to verse technique—several of the poems are long ballad-like epics—but also in regard to the worship of the heroic.

Among P.'s works of fiction *Sandalmagernes gade* (1931; *The Street of the Sandalmakers,* 1932) ranks the highest. A historical novel set in Rome during the reign of Marcus Aurelius, it is based on exhaustive use of historical sources. His true subject, however, is interwar Europe and its rootless human beings, exemplified by the weak Marcellus, and it is written in a modern, anachronistic style. Through a love affair Marcellus comes into contact with Christians and is killed through pure chance.

Sandalmagernes gade became an international best seller and was translated into ten languages. Its narrative concentration, colorful character delineation, and universal perspective are lacking in P.'s second novel, *Spildt mælk* (1934; *Spilt Milk,* 1935), set in Ireland during the civil war of the 1920s. Also less successful were P.'s last writings, which apart from a collection of moralizing aphorisms, *99 bemærkninger* (1936; 99 remarks) consist of short stories, some composed in an imaginative and witty style inspired by P. G. Wodehouse (q.v.), and the later ones written in the fashion of modern hard-boiled American prose. They are based on P.'s own experiences in the Danish provinces and were usually first printed in popular magazines before they were published in the collections: *Engle blæser på trompet* (1937; angels play the

trumpet), *Dagtyve* (1941; day thieves), *Muleposen* (1942; the nose bag), and *Stynede popler* (1943; pollarded poplars), the last of which also contains a number of love poems. The subjects of P.'s short stories are often trivial and anecdotal and the characterizations deliberately sketchy. They are clearly meant to serve as expressions of P.'s own nihilism. This negative world view is a phenomenon commonly found in the writers of the chaotic interwar period, but with P. it was particularly desperate.

FURTHER WORKS: *Digte* (1942); *Brændende Europa* (1947); *Aftenbønnen* (1947); *Da seeren tav* (1947); *Memoirer: "Lad os leve i nuet"* (1948); *Samlede digte* (1949); *Mindeudgave* (8 vols., 1962)

BIBLIOGRAPHY: Claudi, J., *Contemporary Danish Authors* (1952), pp. 115–18

SVEN H. ROSSEL

PETRESCU, Camil

Romanian novelist, dramatist, and poet, b. 22 April 1894, Bucharest; d. 14 May 1957, Bucharest

P. studied literature and philosophy at the University of Bucharest and was later a secondary-school teacher, an influential journalist, critic, and polemicist, a director of the Bucharest National Theater (1939), and a member of the Romanian Academy.

In spite of recurrent personal differences, P. was throughout the 1930s and early 1940s close to Eugen Lovinescu's (q.v.) intellectual circle, which made a stand for an art independent of political influences, one that was modern, urban, and Western-oriented. Somewhat amateurish essays on the philosophy of Henri Bergson (q.v.) and on phenomenology, as well as critical essays, particularly those in *Teze și antiteze* (1936; theses and antitheses), are evidence of his adherence to such ideas.

P. was firmly committed to an analytical rationalism, the very mechanism of which, he believed, was productive of aesthetic satisfaction. This concept is equally reflected in the tough idealism of his poems, *Versuri* (1923; expanded ed., 1957; verse), and in the theme underlying his principal dramatic works— *Suflete tari* (1925; *Those Poor Stout Hearts,* 1960), *Danton* (1931; Danton), *Act venețian* (1931; Venetian act), and *Mioara* (1931;

Mioara)—the incompatibility of a power-hungry intellect with the surrounding world.

P.'s significance rests on his novels. *Ultima noapte de dragoste, întîia noapte de război* (1930; last night of love, first night of war) probes the consciousness of the World War I generation. With subtlety and precision, parallels are drawn between individual and social psychology on the one hand, between personal, erotic suffering and failure and the cruel experience of war on the other. Even more important is *Patul lui Procust* (2 vols., 1933; Procrustes' bed), in which the series of events leading to the breakdown in sexual and social communication of a lucid and sensitive intellectual is presented from the viewpoint of several characters.

While these novels are marked by the opposition between the individual and society, *Un om între oameni* (3 vols., 1953–57; *A Man amongst Men*, 1958) is devoted to a 19th-c. Romanian revolutionary intellectual who emerges from his solitude. Although marred by a sedulous projection of abstract sociological patterns, this novel is distinguished by finely worked-out historical imagery and seems to offer the outline of a solution through action of the intellectual's dilemmas.

P.'s main strength lies in his ability to describe the psychological dimensions of conflict in Romania's increasingly urbanized social structures. His substantial influence on later prose writers was due in part to his clean factual style and innovative techniques.

FURTHER WORKS: *Jocul ielelor* (1919); *Mitică Popescu* (1926); *Transcendentalia* (1931); *Eugen Lovinescu sub zodia seninătății imperturbabile* (1936); *Modalitatea estetică a teatrului* (1937); *Husserl* (1938); *Rapid Constantinopol–Bioram* (1939); *Teatru* (3 vols., 1946–47); *Bălcescu* (1949); *Turnul de fildeș* (1950); *Caragiale în vremea lui* (1957); *Teatru* (2 vols., 1957–58); *Note zilnice 1927–1940* (1975)

BIBLIOGRAPHY: Munteanu, B., *Modern Romanian Literature* (1939), pp. 242–44; Calin, V., "One of the Many," *RoR,* 9, 2 (1954), 107–19; Tertullian, N., "P.'s Plays," *RoR,* 14, 2 (1959), 138–44; Philippide, A., "The Spirit and Tradition of Modern Romanian Literature," *RoR,* 21, 2 (1967), 5–10; Alexandrescu, S., "Analyse structurelle des personnages et conflits dans le roman *Patul lui Procust* de C. P.," *Cahiers de linguistique théorique et appliqué,* No. 6 (1969), 209–24

VIRGIL NEMOIANU

PETROV, Yevgeny
See under Ilf, Ilya

PEUL LITERATURE
See Senegalese literature

PHENOMENOLOGY AND LITERATURE

The phenomenological movement has proliferated and diverged greatly since Edmund Husserl (1859–1938), the father of the movement, started it all with his *Logische Untersuchungen* (2 vols., 1900–1901; 2nd rev. ed., 1913; *Logical Investigations,* 1970). For example, there are the ontological phenomenology of Nicolai Hartmann (1882–1950) and Martin Heidegger (1889–1976); the phenomenological investigation of values by Max Scheler (1874–1928); the existentialist (q.v.) phenomenology of Jean-Paul Sartre (q.v.) and Maurice Merleau-Ponty (1908–1961); the religious phenomenology of Mircea Eliade (q.v.), Gerhard van der Leeuw (1890–1950), and Gabriel Marcel (q.v.); the work in aesthetics of Roman Ingarden (1893–1970), André Malraux (q.v.), and Michel Dufrenne (b. 1910); in psychology, the work of Ludwig Binswanger (1881–1966), R. D. Laing (b. 1927) and Rollo May (b. 1909); and in sociology, the work of Alfred Schutz (1899–1959). The reader who would like more background is referred to the standard history, Herbert Spiegelberg's *The Phenomenological Movement* (1960).

The objective of this essay is to handle these centrifugal developments so that an informative and meaningful relation can be established between phenomenology and literature. The procedure will be to describe those general features of phenomenology on which most adherents agree; to differentiate existential phenomenology from that of Husserl because its literary influence has been more pervasive; to discuss representative writers and critics influenced by phenomenological investigations; and finally to clarify phenomenology in its relationship to structuralism (q.v.), its near cousin and rival.

The concern of Husserl was to search out and establish the foundation of all knowledge. In *Logische Untersuchungen,* he sought the foundations of a pure logic and epistemology. In a series of lectures given in 1929 and first published in French as *Meditations cartésiennes* (1931; *Cartesian Meditations,* 1964), he wanted to provide the sciences with an absolute criterion of truth. But the novelty in his approach consisted in his finding this "objective" foundation in an analysis of subjective consciousness. Rather than trying to account for knowledge in the traditional ways of empiricism or idealism, Husserl analyzed consciousness phenomenologically. Empiricism had sought to account for knowledge by picturing consciousness as a *tabula rasa,* a passive receptor of sense data. Viewed as elementary units or building blocks, sense impressions were taken into the mind and then formed by "laws of association" into more complex edifices of knowledge. David Hume (1711–1776) had already demonstrated how questionable were the limits of knowledge built on such premises. Never acquiring the attribute of necessity, such knowledge remains only probable. Immanuel Kant (1724–1804), in trying to overcome this shortcoming, made consciousness constitutive and creative rather than a mere passive receiver. Because of universal categories within the human mind, Kant affirmed that some knowledge (the synthetic priori) could be established as necessarily true. His solution, however, gave to the mind static categories the operations of which were dependent on a world ruled by Euclidean geometry. These categories proved inadequate with the advent of non-Euclidean thinking. Husserl's phenomenology escaped the psychologism of empirical epistemology and the doctrine that objects of knowledge have no existence except in the mind of the perceiver. Husserl focused specifically on phenomena. His famous phrase "to the things themselves" (*"zu den Sachen selbst"*) is not to be interpreted in a naïve empirical way. It meant a return to objects as experienced by a subject. Phenomenology is a meditation on and description of experience understood always as a field wherein the subject and the object contribute equally. For Husserl, objects are given to the subject as a direct intuition, while simultaneously the subject constitutes that object in any meaning-giving act. Characterized this way, experience becomes a perceptual field, an "active receiving" that must include both the subject and the object as complementary poles. Husserl expressed this new understanding of experience in the term "intentionality." Consciousness is never an empty *I think,* a *cogito* without content. Consciousness always involves a something-thought-about, a *cogitatum.* This *consciousness-of* relationship, which posited the indissoluble union of the subject and object in experience, Husserl called intentionality and made it the starting point of his philosophy.

The various other methods he introduced, such as the *epoche* (neither affirming nor denying existence), the eidetic reduction, and the phenomenological reduction need not concern us except for a general comment. The purpose of these methods was to lay bare the intentionality of consciousness by serving as an antidote to our habitual natural responses. They were to displace the usual acceptances of things as existing independently in-themselves by making us aware that things do not so exist but come into existence by and for a subject. For an object to exist at all, it has to exist as a meaning for a subject.

Scientists, those redoubtable empiricists, have been coming to much the same conclusions. The ideal of a science that has complete objectivity (i.e., being completely independent of man) was seen to be an illusion. The physicist Werner Heisenberg (1901–1976) pointed out that the subject, man, can never be separated from the object he observes. Jacob Bronowski (1908–1974), in an essay in *Scientific American* entitled "The Logic of Mind" (1966), more recently concluded with almost Husserlian overtones that "logical theorems reach decisively into the systematization of empirical science. It follows in my view that the aim that the physical sciences have set themselves since Isaac Newton's time can not be attained. The laws of nature cannot be formulated as an axiomatic, deductive, formal, and unambiguous system, which is also complete."

Although Husserl considered his philosophy a radical empiricism, he began his career as a mathematician. This may account for the abstract idealistic tendency in some of his writing. Wishing to give his philosophy (and science) access to transcendental (necessary) truths, he aimed at elucidating universal essences that underlay every intentional act. This abstracted universal, Husserl named the "transcendental ego." Many of Husserl's students refused to follow him in this very Kantian, too narrowly schematic procedure. The existential phenomenologists were the foremost dissenters.

Heidegger, in *Sein und Zeit* (1927; *Being*

and Time, 1962), broadened Husserl's notion of intentionality to include the whole man, his feeling as well as his volitional and intellectual capacities. Husserl focused his analysis on reflecting consciousness; Heidegger turned more to the prereflective structures of consciousness. He defined human existence more generally as *Dasein,* or being-in-the-world. Because man is the only being who can and does ask questions about Being, this characteristic can serve to define his essential nature. Man is not another object among many but is the instrumental process whereby Being takes on meaning. Being reveals itself as meaning and culture in man's many and complex interrelations with the things-that-are. Being has no way of expressing itself other than through human existence (*Dasein*). Ultimately, what makes meaning-giving possible is temporality, the human orientation toward past, present, and future. Temporality is not to be identified with some externally measured time like that of the clock or calendar. It is lived time, or better, the process whereby the intentional relationship (now expressed as being-in-the-world) operates. Man originates or "founds" the world he occupies with other things by projecting a future on the basis of an inherited past, one that gives meaning to the things-that-are in the present. Such temporalizing of intentionality leads to more awareness of history. If meaning-giving is a temporal process, then truth itself (the meaning of Being) becomes an open-ended, unfinished, historical affair. If there is no escape from having to work at truth from within time and history, the quest may become an absolute, but the truths so found must remain partial and relative. However much it is desired, an absolute vantage, or God's point of view, becomes an impossibility. This insight was to have a direct influence on post-World War II literary themes and techniques.

Of the two French existential phenomenologists, Sartre and Merleau-Ponty, the former influenced literature through his description of human existence as "dreadful freedom." Such themes as nausea, anxiety, abandonment, nothingness, and Promethean heroism fill his literary works. The same themes, or variations thereof, dominate the works of such writers as Camus, Beckett, Ionesco and Genet (qq.v.).

Merleau-Ponty had more direct influence on critics than Sartre because he carried on the main epistemological concerns of pheno-menology and remained far more concrete and empirical than either Husserl or Heidegger. For Merleau-Ponty, "lived experience," from which all analysis must begin, is now centered in the body. While the body is not identical with the subject, it is the instrument whereby the subject situates itself in a real world. By the same token, the body cannot be taken merely as a thing because it is the only object experienced from within. So the body becomes the perfect mediator between the subjective and objective poles of experience. Here is the location of the prereflective and prethematic consciousness. Fully conceptualized, or thematic, meaning takes its sense from its figure-background relation to the horizons of a prior "incarnated experience." Said another way, our body provides us with an opaque "lived experience," which in turn provides the content for and always precedes any disciplined study, the aim of which is to clarify this "lived experience" from a particular point of view.

Meaning thus becomes a dialectical movement of making explicit (bringing to foreground) what is only potentially and latently present to the inarticulate, embodied "cogito" (background). Embodied consciousness is not transparently clear like intellectual conceptions but needs ensuing reflections to become thematic and conceptualized. Basically, all knowledge is conscious reflection on prereflective experience constituted by the "perceptual" body-world relationship. Human existence becomes an expressive activity, and its proper functioning will be to give meaning to the objects around itself. Culture results from the sedimentation and accumulation of man's past symbolic or interpretative acts. This historical process will be never-ending, because the instrumentality whereby man has a perspective on the world is partial and the truth or insight thus obtained will be limited by the physical and historical environs of the creative individual. History, properly understood, is the record of our self-awareness of this symbolization process in which man articulates the world and simultaneously gives himself an identity. What previously had been the special vocation of poets and artists—the creation of meaning—Merleau-Ponty (like Heidegger before him) presents as the generic function of human existence. As such, it constitutes a philosophic anthropology, a norm for existential psychoanalysis, and a guide to literary analysis.

From the perspective above, philosophy

becomes an external but foredoomed quest. If no human expression can ever completely formulate absolute truth; if every interpretative act conceals at the same time as it reveals; if truth can establish itself only in terms of a momentary functional adequacy—then a certain ambiguity will perpetually trouble the meaning-giving function. For creative writers, this predicament often translates into self-torment, into making the creative process itself the theme of their writing. Treatments range from the bleakly tragic to self-mockery. In certain writers, occupational futility has become so exacerbated that they can keep going only by making a game of the technique of writing. Other writers, not so severely afflicted, circle around the problem of how difficult it is to stay undeluded about ourselves or the external world.

The theme of most of Jorge Luis Borges's (q.v.) fiction, for example, is that there is no ordering principle given to the universe that is not arbitrary and open to doubt. All classification systems are provisional, and in order that their provisional character be kept in mind, Borges writes "self-destruct"stories. Because semblance tends to reduce the reader's disbelief, leading him to accept illusion for reality, Borges frequently exposes his fictions as a game. He quite deliberately postulates a state of affairs at the beginning of a story that the subsequent action shows to be completely impossible. With gentle, deft irony, Borges identifies total order with total disorientation. Since there is nothing of lasting value to reveal, the use of intelligence to create fictions becomes a nonserious game. To the skeptical Borges, meaning-giving provides an aesthetic pleasure, a playful exercise of the intellect that must never lose its provisional character.

A warm admirer of Borges, John Barth (q.v.), in his essay "The Literature of Exhaustion" (1967), has drawn parallels between his aims and the gameplaying of Borges. In place of Borges's lean intellectual style, however, Barth has developed a frivolous, baroque manner as thematically more suitable while also more protective of his sanity. Constantly interrupting his narrative, he destroys the reader's illusionary participation either by commenting on how badly the story is going or self-consciously calling attention to a technical point, usually a methodological inadequacy, raised by the content. In effect, the novel in his hands seems to be feeding on itself while entertaining the reader

and overcoming the "insuperable" obstacle of seemingly having nothing to say. A confirmed optimist writing on nihilistic themes, Barth describes his efforts in *Lost in the Funhouse* (1968) thus: "The final possibility is to turn ultimacy, exhaustion, paralyzing self-consciousness, and the adjective weight of accumulated history....To turn ultimacy against itself to make something new and valid, the essence whereof would be the impossibility of making something new."

With Borges and Barth, the style is most often satirical or ironical, in keeping with their playful-serious attitude. But when the dramatist Harold Pinter (q.v.) treats this epistemological theme, it becomes menacing. A world never totally amenable to human interpretation and control constantly threatens the security of his characters and sooner or later breaks down the feeble barriers they have raised in self-defense. In *A Slight Ache* (1959), Edward, a writer of theological and philosophical essays, believes he has the world and himself under control. But neither the objective nor the subjective areas in his formulated world retain the polished clear edges that his mind so cleverly imposes. Edward cannot keep objects in focus. His eyes give him "a slight ache." He feels threatened by a world that will not yield to his rational ordering. Silent nature weights like a heavy enigma on him; it undermines his integrative will and finally wears him down to hapless impotence. Such failure of the protagonist to control a momentarily secure position, be it physical or mental space, recurs as a fundamental motif in Pinter's plays. External contingencies or subconscious desires shatter the civilized proprieties erected by the ordering mind. To keep a grip on themselves and their shifting, unpredictable world, his characters hide behind familiar habits, clichéd language, and social rules. Unlike the effete and bloodless milieu of Beckett's plays, the characters of which talk compulsively to hide from a vacant universe, the destruction of verbal and social façades in Pinter's plays delivers his hero-victims to violence and animality.

Not all writers endure man's epistemological relations with reality with such bleak sufferance. Two representatives of a more positive attitude are Iris Murdoch and Alain Robbe-Grillet (qq.v.). Murdoch studied and taught philosophy in England. Not attracted to English analytic philosophy, she went through a brief flirtation with existentialism out of which came a good book, *Sartre, Ro-*

mantic Rationalist (1953). Murdoch's novels lack the innovative brilliance of Robbe-Grillet's, but she shares his phenomenologically inspired conviction of the difficulties (and necessity) of maintaining objectivity with people and things.

Husserl's basic principle, "back to the things themselves," has as its corollary a special method, the *epoche,* which was to insure the purity of the starting point. Why was such bracketing needed? Because man has an inveterate tendency to project extraneous elements on the object he sees that do not belong to the object at all. The origin of these projections most often are subjective emotional states but can also be commitments to prior theories, hypotheses, and traditions that refract and distort experience. Secondly, no object is graspable from one point of view or from a single system. Thus, the external world should be an inexhaustible resource for thematic study and explication. To freeze the meaning-giving process, to objectify and subordinate it to one particular theoretical construction, would be intellectual bad faith. It leads to stagnation, dogmatic error, and fantasizing. Both Murdoch and Robbe-Grillet stress the need to escape delusion, and their novels illustrate the problematic nature of the subject-object encounter. In Murdoch's novel *Under the Net* (1954), Jake Donaghue blunders through a series of faulty relationships because of his own self-obsessions. The novel ends only when Jake recognizes that other people do not always surrender themselves to familiarity and classification; that contingency should not be feared but, indeed, embraced as a rich and complicated mystery; and that one finds self-knowledge (i.e., becomes a moral person) only through social interaction. A self-absorbed consciousness forms the greatest obstacle to seeing the world as it really is. To act justly one must perceive correctly—that is the lesson encountered in Murdoch's novels.

A similar message may be found in Robbe-Grillet's novels—although stated more obliquely. Like other writers of the New Novel (q.v.), Robbe-Grillet experiments with inner lived time and dispenses with clock time. He writes in the present tense to communicate the immediacy of experience and presents the action rigorously through the sensibility of one protagonist. He has given up all authorial claims to omniscience and has publicly stated that as a literary device omniscience is outmoded and no longer be-lievable. A writer can no longer present plot, characters, motivations, setting, etc., as Balzac did, offering a world fully analyzed and understood to himself. Because there are no complete truths, no God, and no absolute standpoint, the reader must undergo the experience while it is happening to the protagonist. What the writer asks of the reader is that he expect not to "receive ready-made a world that is finished, full, and closed in on itself, but, on the contrary, to take part in a creation, to invent the work in his turn" (*Pour un nouveau roman* [1963; *For a New Novel,* 1965]).

To simulate the interior processes of thought or the latent desires of the subconscious, Robbe-Grillet juxtaposes and splices his protagonist's past memory, present reality, and future fantasies. As he never intrudes, it is up to the reader to follow these inner meanderings as best he can. Because the protagonists have abnormal sensibilities—for example, a sex pervert in *Le voyeur* (1955; *The Voyeur,* 1958); a jealous husband in *La jalousie* (1957; *Jealousy,* 1959); a wounded, feverish soldier in *Dans le labyrinthe* (1959; *In the Labyrinth,* 1960)—their interiority distorts the real world. It is precisely this abnormal subjectivizing of the external world that Robbe-Grillet alternates with his *choisisme* (a neutral geometrical description of surfaces). His method very deliberately accentuates the gap between things neutrally observed and the emotionally charged world of his central characters. In essays, he has stated his aim to be the freeing of man from "tragic complicity," from his need to humanize nature. Robbe-Grillet insists on maintaining the exteriority and independence of the object. His minute description of surfaces is a limitation and hedge against projecting any kind of depth or preestablished order between things and the perceiver. If we can allow the object to maintain its independence, to remain hard, dry, impenetrable, and alien to our wishful thinking (as he believes they always should be), then there is hope that we can finally escape tragedy. Rather than contaminate objects with our hopes and fears, and then allow them to operate upon us with these accrued forces while forgetting the true origin of their power—we must refuse all complicity with objects. Robbe-Grillet wishes to end the chapter of literary history preoccupied with existential despair, alienation, and unhappiness by diagnosing the malaise as self-inflicted. He believes tragedy to be a

519

conditioned response, and that the remedy lies in correct perception—"for once scraped clean, things relate only to themselves, with no chinks or crevices for us to slip into, and without causing us the least dizziness."

Phenomenology has influenced literary criticism in a variety of ways. In Europe it helped turn literary studies away from biographical and historical-background scholarship to a study of the creative process itself. Phenomenology had its profoundest effect on the criticism written by the Geneva School, which became prominent after World War II. Critics such as Marcel Raymond (1897–1956), Albert Béguin (1901–1957), Georges Poulet (b. 1902), Jean-Pierre Richard (b. 1922), and Jean Starobinski (b. 1920), all share the common methodology of viewing literature as an expression of a creative consciousness. Individual texts of one writer are analyzed as so many variants of a single subjectivity, whose controlling "project" may be abstracted and thematically rendered. The author's intentionality—the configuration of which can only be grasped by an examination of all his writing (literary and nonliterary)—becomes the object of analysis. Unlike American New Criticism (see Literary Criticism), which views the individual work as an autonomous and privileged object, the "critics of consciousness" impose no formal work-in-itself restriction upon their analyses. They may even move from considering the creative output of an individual author to speculating on the content of his historical subjectivity, which is akin to a *Zeitgeist*.

Georges Poulet, in his *Études sur le temps humain* (3 vols., 1949–64; Vol. 1 tr. as *Studies in Human Time,* 1956; Vol. 2, *La distance intérieure* [1952], tr. as *The Interior Distance,* 1959), employs such a wider framework to give organization to his discussion of individual writers. Using either approach, the critical analysis is not objective, but the result of a creative empathy that a critic achieves with a writer or with his age. "What must be reached," says Poulet, "is a subject, or a mental activity, that can be understood only by putting oneself in its place and perspective—by making it play again its role of subject in ourselves."

When Heidegger defined human existence as a being-in-the-world, he made possible an ontological realignment within humanistic studies that replaced a worn-out naturalism and idealism with a creative existentialism.

In psychology, being-in-the-world offered an alternative to the reductive mechanistic theories of Freud (q.v.) and the behaviorists. Man, in Heidegger's perspective, was not a mechanism controlled by his instincts. Life may be driven by psychobiological forces, but man utilizes these forces to create himself and history. With this new anthropology, existentialism developed its own psychoanalysis and therapy. Like its Freudian counterpart, it could and did analyze writers and their literary works. The Swiss psychologist Ludwig Binswanger appropriated from Heidegger the existentialia of temporality, spatiality, materiality, and so forth, and investigated how they are experienced by the patient. Psychoses and neuroses are not the effect of repressed instincts but are deviations of the a priori transcendental structure of *Dasein.* In his psychoanalysis of artists, that deviation most frequently occurring he called *Verstiegenheit* (eccentricity). Artists most often distort their spatial orientation by aiming too high, thereby losing their equilibrium; the result is a "tragic fall." Binswanger, in his monograph on Ibsen, saw the playwright successfully warding off this occupational hazard by bringing it to a catharsis via his tragic heroes.

Sartre applied existential psychoanalysis to a wide range of literary works and their writers. Invariably these critical writings are both application and substantiation of his own philosophy. Sartre wrote elaborate critical works on Baudelaire and Genet and published ten volumes of shorter essays from 1947 to 1976 under the general title *Situations.* In his philosophy, the prereflective consciousness is a pure nihilating power. Consciousness is not a thing—it is a continual projection into the future always breaking away or becoming unfastened from the solidified products and roles constituted by the creative process of the consciousness. Consciousness is, and should remain, an ongoing, spontaneous activity wholly self-transcending. Unfortunately it has a tendency to reify itself, to substantialize its activity and freeze itself into a role or object. Man, however, can never find rest as a thing or being. His essence is to be a continual nihilating movement over and beyond the limitations of any given situation.

Man is condemned to be free, but the exercise of this freedom will find its expression in and through the particularities of an individual's concrete historical situation. Sartre's critical essays present writers either as authentically questioning and moving beyond their situation, as a proper exercise of freedom in context, or as acting in bad faith, an example of botched opportunity and disobedience to the ethical imperative to be free and to make the right use of this freedom. His *Saint Genet: Comédien et martyr* (1952; *Saint Genet: Actor and Martyr,* 1963), without doubt, has been the most successful and brilliant phenomenological treatment of a writer's consciousness written to date.

Other phenomenological critics who should be mentioned are Gaston Bachelard (1884–1962), Emil Staiger (b. 1908), Johannes Pfeiffer (b. 1902), Paul Ricœur (b. 1913), and Serge Doubrovsky (b. 1928). Not many critics within the Anglo-American tradition have affinities with Continental criticism, but Geoffrey Hartman (b. 1929), J. Hillis Miller (b. 1928), and Ihab Hassan (b. 1925) do owe a debt to phenomenology. Hartman, particularly, would seem to be the most influential and prolific phenomenological critic writing in the U.S.

Whereas phenomenology views the meaning-giving process as perception, as the intentionality of a subject toward an object, structuralism (q.v.) replaces the subject-object relation with the unconscious ordering activity of the human mind. Although Claude Lévi-Strauss (q.v.) repudiated phenomenology in *Tristes tropiques* (1955; *Tristes Tropiques,* 1964), the unconscious "depth structure" he has formulated has the same aim as the "transcendental ego" formulated by Husserl: both men wish to erect universal laws to govern the meaning-giving process. Thus, Lévi-Strauss's symbolic order and Husserl's transcendental ego share the identical aim of giving a structure to the empirical acts of each individual consciousness.

When Heidegger expanded intentionality to include the whole man, to include his feelings and volitions as well as his intelligence, his starting point, although experiential, was neither clear not articulate. It needed little for such a preconceptual, prereflective, preconscious intentionality to assume some of the attributes and function of an unconscious. For psychoanalysis, the relationship of unconscious to conscious was archaeological and one of cause to effect. For non-Sartrian phenomenology, "lived experience" became a pregnant latency needing deliverance into the light of conscious revelation.

The midwife, or mediator, was the creative individual.

Structuralism changed this relationship with the unknown. Intentionality found itself displaced by a structured unconscious whose natural activity brings into equilibrium the contradictions and oppositions man encounters while interacting with the world. Structuralism may be said to have "naturalized" the reconciliation of opposites so prevalent in literary and religious discourse. Rather than locate this reconciliation in some transcendent unity, concrete universal, or supernatural personage, structuralism turns reconciliation into a natural attribute of how the mind unconsciously operates. Structuralism disregards all claims to a transcendent referent or presence that needs a consciousness to "speak" it. The ultimate realities of past philosophies, sciences, and literary visions have value not as truths but as various centers around which systems of meaning organized themselves. Now that we have become aware of the structuration that creates all meaning structures, these centers should be demythologized into their real function by ignoring their semantic reference (claims to truth). These claims only hide from view the structural activity that operates latently in all interpretative acts.

Existential phenomenology, on the other hand, still believed that human consciousness mediates an external otherness, or presence, and refused to subordinate intentionality to a timeless structured unconscious. While it did not object to language later being made the privileged model for understanding all our meaningful experiences, it upheld the preeminence of the speaking act (*parole*) over any semiological system (*langue*). Meaning-giving remained an original, individual act operating through human temporality and in need of the creative voice. For most phenomenologists, Orpheus, that ambiguous figure of success and failure, remained the archetypal representative of modern man in his precarious vocation.

The battle between the structuralists and phenomenologists over the "death of the subject" ended not because some universal unconscious mind eventually supplanted the conscious ego but because the individual ego was seen to be a historical consciousness made up of a matrix of social codes. The identity of any individual consciousness received its configuration from the number and range of the cultural codes in which it participated. The phenomenal world was no longer perceived as emerging from the interaction of an intentional subject with external neutral objects, but was described as a world that was always already interpreted, with its horizon rearranged and reorganized by those living within that horizon. In this dialogical process, individuals living in the present reinterpret the past, out of which comes the future—that is, new interpretations of world and self.

By the 1980s it had become clear that the most pervasive influence on the study of literature and culture in general was the later philosophy of Martin Heidegger. Instead of the temporal structures of human existence (*Dasein*) articulated in *Sein und Zeit*, language became the "house of Being," capable of bringing together Being with beings and providing man with authentic existence. The antithesis between subject and object is overcome in a language conceived not as an instrumentality operating upon the objects of the world but as the familiar horizon in which new worlds present themselves and allow Being to stand revealed. Language becomes both access and hindrance to Being, in any event an inescapable mediator. Whether positively or nihilistically, literary theorists followed this Heideggerian focus on language. As the French writer Julia Kristeva (b. 1941) put it in the collection of her essays published in English translation as *Desire in Language* (1980): "Following upon the phenomenological and existentialist shock of the post-war period, the sixties witnessed a theoretical ebullience that could roughly be summarized as leading to the discovery of the determinative role of *language* in all human sciences." That statement applies to the philosophical hermeneutics launched by Hans-Georg Gadamer (b. 1900), especially in his *Wahrheit und Methode* (1960; *Truth and Method*, 1975), and which was subsequently developed into *Rezeptionsästhetik* by Hans Robert Jauss (b. 1921) and Wolfgang Iser (b. 1926). It also applies to the "deconstructive philosophy" of Jacques Derrida (b. 1930), whose three books, *De la grammatologie* (1967; *Of Grammatology*, 1976), *La voix et la phénomène* (1967; *Speech and Phenomena*, 1973), and *L'écriture et la différence* (1967; *Writing and Difference*, 1978), helped turn "scientific" structuralism into poststructuralism, a semiology of historical consciousness.

Hans-Georg Gadamer, Michel Foucault (b. 1926), and Jacques Derrida all follow Hei-

degger in making language central to any understanding of human existence. All of the human sciences have become interpretive not of "phenomena" but of "meanings" seen as cultural products whose social existence have their beginnings and continuation in shared conventions or traditions. Thus, phenomenology as name or program is not often met with in current literary study; however, most of the diverging critical schools of hermeneutics, poststructuralism, *Rezeptionsästhetik*, semiotics, or reader-response operate in what can only be called a phenomenological ambience.

BIBLIOGRAPHY: Müller-Vollmer, K., *Towards a Phenomenological Theory of Literature* (1963); Duroche, L. L., *Aspects of Criticism* (1967); Lawall, S., *Critics of Consciousness* (1968); Hartman, G., *Beyond Formalism* (1970); Hassan, I., *The Dismemberment of Orpheus* (1971); Heidegger, M., *Poetry, Language, Thought* (1972); Ingarden, R., *The Literary Work of Art* (1973); Doubrovsky, S., *The New Criticism in France* (1973); Ricœur, P., *The Conflict of Interpretations* (1974); Spanos, W., ed., *Martin Heidegger and the Question of Literature* (1976); Magliola, R. R., *Phenomenology and Literature* (1977); Iser, W., *The Act of Reading* (1978); Amacher, R., and Lange, V., eds., *New Perspectives in German Literary Criticism* (1979); Tompkins, J. P., ed., *Reader-Response Criticism* (1980)

VERNON GRAS

PHILIPPIDE, Alexandru

Romanian poet, short-story writer, essayist, and translator, b. 1 April 1900, Iași; d. 8 Feb. 1979, Bucharest

Son and namesake of a well-known linguist, classmate and lifelong friend of the writer Barbu Fundoianu (1898–1944; also known as Benjamin Fondane), P. studied law at the University of Iași, and also studied in Berlin and Paris. In Paris, Fundoianu introduced him into avant-garde circles. Upon his return to Romania he served in the Ministries of Foreign Affairs and Propaganda, from 1929 to 1947.

P. began his career as a poet in 1919 with contributions to *Viața românească* in Iași and quickly became a principal in that circle. Through his friendship with Cezar Petrescu (1892–1961) he also collaborated with

Gândirea (or Gîndirea), the postwar literary and philosophical movement attempting to define and express the Romanian genius—until its break with the Iași group in 1929.

His first collection of verse, *Aur sterp* (1922; barren gold), showed the influence of symbolism (q.v.) and a fondness for the neoromantic dream motif. *Stînci fulgerate* (1930; lightning-struck rocks) expressed violent states of mind. *Visuri în vuietul vremii* (1939; dreams amid the roar of time), uninhibitedly lyrical but also increasingly cerebral, continued philosophical queries about life and death. After a long hiatus, during which he gave his attention to translation, a collection of earlier verse, *Poezii* (short poems) appeared in 1964. *Monolog în Babilon* (1967; monologue in Babylon), probably his masterpiece, introduced an original mythology with terrifying Dantesque landscapes and a luminous paradisiac space; it reflected an existential concern with pessimism, monstrosity, and decadence, with allegorical allusions to cultural and political conditions in Romania. In 1963 P. was elected to the Romanian Academy, and in 1977 awarded the Grand Prize in Poetry by the Writers' Union. The posthumously published *Vis și căutare* (1979; dream and search) presents eighteen poems from over a half century, including some recent verse.

A collection of tales, *Floarea de prăpastie* (1942; the flower of the precipice), blended realistic detail and the fantastic, fluctuating between infernal and paradisiac settings and Romanian townscapes.

P.'s translations and much of his criticism focused on writers who most affected his own work, principally German romantics, Poe, Baudelaire, and Rilke (q.v.). Other essays attempted to formulate a Romanian modernism. *Considerații confortabile* (2 vols., 1970, 1972; comfortable considerations) was a series of aphorisms.

All of P.'s work is distinguished by a classicist regard for artistic discipline; romantic idealism, pathos, and love of the fantastic; and modernist techniques. Essentially his work is a Faustian search for answers about the destiny and purpose of man. Its images are oneiric, often morbid or demonic, but never sordid or ugly.

FURTHER WORKS: *Studii și portrete literare* (1963); *Studii de literatură universală* (1966); *Scriitorul și arta lui* (1968); *Puncte cardinale europene: Orizont romantic* (1973); *Flori de poezie străină răsădite în româește* (1973); *Scrieri: Studii și eseuri* (1978)

BIBLIOGRAPHY: Eulert, D., and Avădanei, Ș., eds., *Modern Romanian Poetry* (1973), pp. 88–91; Gibescu, G., "A. P.," *Romanian Bulletin,* 5, 8 (1976), 6–7; Teodorescu, A., and Bantaș, A., eds., *Romanian Essayists of Today* (1979), pp. 59–61

THOMAS AMHERST PERRY

PHILIPPINE LITERATURE

For twenty years before the outbreak of the revolution of 1896, Filipinos who favored civil reform and freedom without independence published novels and newspapers in Spanish and directed them hopefully at liberals in Madrid and Barcelona. Among these were the essays of Marcelo H. del Pilar (1850–1896) and Graciano Lopez-Jaena (1856–1896), and the panoramic, accusatory novels of José Rizal (1861–1896), *Noli me tangere* (1887; *The Lost Eden,* 1961) and *El filibusterismo* (1891; *The Subversive,* 1962), which cast shadows of excellence far into the 20th c.

Yet, with the end of the Spanish-American War in 1898, virtually all Spanish literature as well as political influence ceased. Rearguard critics sometimes speak of the first half of the new century as the "golden age" of Philippine literature in Spanish. However, aside from Jesús Balmori's (pseud.: Batikuling, 1886–1948) nationalistic lyric poetry—*Rimas malayas* (1904; Malayan verses) and *Mi casa de nipa* (1941; my house made of palm leaves)—and the poems of Claro Recto (1890–1960) in *Bajo los cocoteros* (1911; under the coconut trees) and his play *Solo entre las sombras* (1917; alone among the shadows), Antonio M. Abad's (dates n.a.) Commonwealth Prize-winning novel, *El campeón* (1939; the champion), and occasional speeches left by Recto and President Manuel Quezon (1878–1944), little that is comparable with the end-of-century flowering can be discovered. Less biased historians record, instead, a prolonged cultural pause before general education in English, which replaced education of the elite in Spanish, could produce its own literature and, by example, elevate literature in the vernacular as well.

The beginning of commonwealth status in 1935, with anticipation of full independence after ten years, gave special urgency to the search for a national identity among people with varied cultural and linguistic backgrounds. Although this was also the year of the founding of the Institute of National Language, which made Tagalog the core of various composite vernaculars, at least temporarily Filipinos found in English rather than native languages and literary traditions the same creative challenge that Spanish once brought.

To assert some kind of continuity between otherwise alienated generations, the works of Nick Joaquin (q.v.) have attempted to recover the moral and religious orientation, which constitute the most enduring aspect of the Spanish heritage. Aside from several imitations of late-medieval saintly legends and random essays, his concern has been less with the past re-created than with its modern vestiges. Joaquin's short story "Three Generations," in *Prose and Poems* (1952), reveals irrevocable family resemblances—a rigorous Spanish sense of kinship—even in the midst of recurrent revolt against family pieties. Other stories, such as "The Summer Solstice," also in *Prose and Poems,* find in Filipinos counterparts of Spanish ambivalences: primitivistic sensuousness and Christian asceticism. His 1952 omnibus volume also contains the play *Portrait of the Artist as Filipino,* in which descendants of the declining Don Lorenzo finally confirm his inborn integrity by their own. Despite impoverishment, they refuse to sell the masterpiece which he has painted for them and which depicts Anchises being borne like a household god from burning Troy. The faces of son and father are identical. Joaquin has depicted the Filipino's need to take the burden of history on his back. However, Aeneas was not only deliverer of the past but founder of the future: and Joaquin's novel *The Woman Who Had Two Navels* (1961) respects but does not admire without qualification the ex-revolutionary, Monson, who hides in Hong Kong exile, afraid to face the trials of postwar independence.

The Spanish past is viewed with an equally discriminating eye in *The Peninsulars* (1964), Linda Ty-Casper's (b. 1931) novel of the confusion of loyalties that made possible British occupation of Manila in the mid-18th c. Each figure of colonial authority—even those with the highest concern for the ruled—has some imperfection of motive, some overriding personal ambition that maims his magistracy. However, the *indios* too (as Spaniards called the natives) are torn between national loyalties and self-interest. Only the dying governor-general and the *indio* priest Licaros achieve a sufficient understanding of the need for mutual dependence: on one level, love; on another, the social contract. Such a novel represents an increasingly selective salvaging, by the Philippine writer, of his various usable pasts. Similarly, Ty-Casper's novel *The Three-Cornered Sun* (1979) depicts the revolution of 1896 as a series of individually motivated acts rather than as an orchestrated uprising guided by national purpose.

The epic impulse, the concern with rendering history as meaningful fable, has shaped the writings of poets such as Ricaredo Demetillo (b. 1920) and Alejandrino Hufana (b. 1926). *Barter in Panay* (1961) represents the first portion of Demetillo's verse adaptation of the Visayan folktale *Maragtas,* about ten groups led by *datus* (chiefs) who, in 1212, fled tyranny in Brunei. Its twenty-one cantos explain the peaceful arrangement between *Datu* Puti and the pygmy Negrito inhabitants of Panay island; and begin to explore the lust of Guronggurong for *Datu* Sumakwel's young wife, which was to test intimately the new rules of social order. Demetillo's verse-play sequel, *The Heart of Emptiness Is Black* (1975) suggests how only love can reconcile personal desire and impersonal social codes.

Hufana's early volume *Sickle Season* (1959) deals with this same theme of the one and the many but is less restricted historically: for it, he invented Geron Munar, timeless Malayan wanderer and culture hero, mirrored in many facsimiles throughout Philippine history, legend, and myth. In *Poro Point: An Anthology of Lives* (1961), Hufana substituted for Munar personae from the author's tribal family, all Ilocanos, who, as the most migrant of Filipinos, epitomize both their countrymen's unity and their diversity.

The Philippine dream of a national identity compatible with an open, pluralistic society, evident in such adaptations from ethnohistory, has been tested severely even by Bienvenido N. Santos (b. 1911), sometimes considered a sentimentalist. The Philippine expatriates in his story collection *You Lovely People* (1956), caught in the U.S. by World War II, long passionately to return to their kinfolk. In the aftermath of war, however, many discover their homeland changed, their loved ones not inviolable; and, disillusioned, some retreat into exile once more. Similarly, his second collection, *Brother, My Brother* (1960), and his two novels, *Villa Magdalena* (1965) and *The Volcano* (1965), continue to rely on the imagery of rejection and return. However far ambition takes his characters from the ancestral home that once seemed to deprive them of personal potential, that home remains the place of least loneliness; and no satisfactory sense of self is found outside one's native community. How that problem is exacerbated among "overseas Filipinos" is encapsulated in his collection *Scent of Apples* (1979).

Although all major Philippine writers may be said to be searching for those constants that define their identity as a people, many have avoided the historical/epic modes and have confined themselves to fundamentally agrarian aspects that are continuous in their culture. Their fiction maintains a slowness of pace and cautious simplicity appropriate to the sacred, seasonal mysteries of timeless folkways, as well as to the patient, modern search for reassurance. That pace is represented in Francisco Arcellana's (b. 1916) peasant/working-class sketches, *15 Stories* (1973), characterized by Scriptural simplicity and cyclic repetition. Manuel Arguilla (1910–1944), in the rural tales collected in *How My Brother Leon Brought Home a Wife* (1940), undercuts folk romanticism with the realism of social protest as he engages the causes of the Sakdal uprisings among tenant farmers during the 1930s. Similarly, N. V. M. Gonzalez's (q.v.) tales of the frontier country, the *kaingin* (cultivated clearing burned out of forest land) ricelands—*Seven Hills Away* (1947); *Children of the Ash-Covered Loam* (1954)—as well as the novel *A Season of Grace* (1956), reveal both the hardships and enduring self-possession of his tradition-centered pioneers. In his collection *Look, Stranger, on This Island Now* (1963) the *kaingineroo* enjoys a kind of consoled loneliness when compared with the peasant who has migrated to the metropolis; and his restricted life is far more meaningful than that of the sophisticated *ilustrado* (a member of the "enlightened," intellectual elite) who is the protagonist of the novel *The Bamboo Dancers* (1959), a homeless international wanderer.

The provincial's life is a trial, even in Carlos Bulosan's (1914–1956) humorous tales in *The Laughter of My Father* (1941), which were intended as a satiric indictment of sharecropping penury. At the same time, Bu-

losan expresses admiration for the good humor, love, and other humane virtues that survive the peasant's near-penal conditions.

This capacity to endure marks each of the four major Philippine war novels—Stevan Javellana's (b. 1918) *Without Seeing the Dawn* (1947); Juan Laya's (1911–1952) *This Barangay* (1950); and Edilberto Tiempo's (b. 1917) *Watch in the Night* (1953) and *More than Conquerors* (1964)—all of them, appropriately, stories of small-scale, rural, guerrilla action supported by a kind of primitive communal interdependence.

When this close group identity is sacrificed by the ambitious provincial migrant to the city, he suffers from the anonymity of mass living without his poverty's lessening measurably. Only occasionally is adequate human warmth rediscovered among slumdwellers, as in the stories of Estrella Alfon (b. 1917)—*Magnificence* (1960)—and Andres Cristobal Cruz (b. 1929) and Pacifico Aprieto (b. 1929)—*Tondo by Two,* 1961); or in Alberto Florentino's (b. 1931) *The World Is an Apple, and Other Prize Plays* (1959).

Far less sympathy is directed toward other urban classes. The pretensions of the nouveaux riches are constantly satirized in Gilda Cordero-Fernando's (dates n.a.) collections of stories *The Butcher, the Baker, the Candlestick Maker* (1962) and *A Wilderness of Sweets* (1973); as well as Wilfrido Guerrero's (b. 1917) four volumes of plays (1947, 1952, 1962, 1976). Movement from a rural area to suburbia involves risking loss of character. The consequences of social mobility unaccompanied by maturing morality are more savagely exposed in the novels of Kerima Polotan-Tuvera (b. 1925)—*The Hand of the Enemy* (1962)—and of F. Sionil Jose (b. 1924)—*The Pretenders* (1962). In both instances, the mountaineer or uprooted rural peasant is corrupted by industrialism and the new self-seeking elite, just as the agrarian revolts at the turn of the century allegedly were betrayed by the *ilustrados,* first to the Spaniards and later to the Americans. This tension between classes is central in Jose's ongoing series of novels about Rosales, an imaginary northern town: *Tree* (1978) and *My Brother, My Executioner* (1979). Social discrimination finds its parallel in the oppression of women in Polotan-Tuvera's *Stories* (1968). Wilfrido Nolledo's (b. 1933) *But for the Lovers* (1970), a parable of wartime grotesques awaiting liberation, suggests a similar situation for the masses mutilated by the forces of leftist radicals and of government by martial law.

Because, like Rizal's novels before them, they constitute assessments of agrarian values during decades of challenging cultural transition, such works will always be of historical value regardless of what other Philippine literatures emerge in the vernaculars. Even Jose Garcia Villa's (q.v.) poetry, which, beginning with *Many Voices* (1939), has been criticized for not focusing on national concerns but rather offering disembodied Blakean encounters between God and the luminous poet, are in some ways relevant to the Philippine experience. Villa's dependence on devices of negation and rejection, the nearly solipsistic alienation of the protagonist, at least parallel the national passion for self-determination and the overcompensatory self-enlargement of a people reduced to colonial status for centuries.

For inventiveness and for dynamic selfhood in revolt, the counterpart of Villa in Pilipino (Tagalog) is A. G. Abadilla (1905–1969), whose volumes include *Piniling mga tula* (1965; selected poems). Sometimes as antagonist, sometimes as complement, his name is juxtaposed with the socialistically inclined Amado V. Hernandez (1903–1970), a labor leader and later premier writer in the vernacular. With his prize play *Muntinlupa* (1958; tight place; also the name of a national prison), his poems in *Isang dipang langit* (1961; a stretch of sky), and his novel *Mga ibong mandaragit* (1965; birds of prey), Hernandez revived the polemical tradition of the 19th c. and recapitulated the social protest evident in Lope K. Santos's (1879–1963) earlier novel *Banaag at sikat* (1906; false dawn and sunrise). Together with Andres Cristobal Cruz (b. 1929), author of the novel *Sa Tundo, may langit din* (1961; even in Tondo the sun shines) and the contributors to the short fiction collection *Agos sa diyerta* (1965; oasis in the desert), these writers, by avoiding the sentimentality and floridity of vernacular conventions, have made Pilipino equal to English as a reputable instrument for self-discovery.

Those conventions, derived from centuries of reducing literary function to either moral indoctrination or pure emotional expressiveness, have proven more resistant in the case of other vernacular literatures. Zarzuelas, for example, introduced as a form of concealed protest under the American occupation, deteriorated before 1930 into either musical com-

edies or melodramas. This predisposition toward literature as either instruction or entertainment, reinforced by the dearth of book publication and reliance on serialization of magazine fiction, has kept minimal the number of vernacular models equivalent in seriousness to their English counterparts. These would include, in the Bisayan languages, the novels of Magdalena Jalandoni (1893–1980) in the 1920s and 1930s, the political sketches of Vicente Sotto (1877–1950) throughout the 1920s, Buenaventura Rodriguez's (1893–1941) plays *Ang mini* (1921; counterfeit man) and *Pahiyum* (1935; a smile), and the prewar poetic experiments of Vicente Ranudo (1883–1930), as well as the sampling of breakthrough pieces in the 1967 anthology by the Lubasan group; and in Iloko, the early-20th-c. plays of Mena Pecson Crisologo (1844–19??), especially *Natakneng a panagsalisal* (n.d.; noble rivalry), which concerns the Philippine-American War (1898–1902), Marcelino Pena Crisologo's (1866–1923) novel *Pinang* (1915; Pinang), and Constante Casabar's (dates n.a.) sociopolitical novels (published serially), *Puris iti barukong* (1956–57; thorn in the side) and *Dagiti mariing iti parbongon* (1955–57; those awakened at dawn).

Like their Pilipino compatriots, contemporary writers in Bisayan and Iloko are, typically, bilingual and thus manage to enrich their work from many sources and to choose which readers they will address.

BIBLIOGRAPHY: Bernad, M., *Bamboo and the Greenwood Tree* (1963); Del Castillo, T., and Medina, B., Jr., *Philippine Literature* (1964); Casper, L., *New Writing from the Philippines: An Anthology and a Critique* (1966); Manuud, A., ed., *Brown Heritage: Essays on Philippine Cultural Tradition and Literature* (1967); Galdon, J., ed., *Philippine Fiction* (1972); Mojares, R., *Cebuano Literature* (1975); Galdon, J., ed., *Essays on the Philippine Novel in English* (1979)

LEONARD CASPER

PICCOLO, Lucio

Italian poet, b. 27 Oct. 1901, Palermo; d. 26 May 1969, Capo d'Orlando

P. was a member of one of the most distinguished Sicilian families and an accomplished musician and scholar. Little is known of his early life. He lived a rather cloistered life, reading extensively in classical and modern languages. His interest in the occult drew him to the works of W. B. Yeats (q.v.), with whom he corresponded regularly.

In 1954, in the company of his cousin, Prince Giuseppe Tomasi di Lampedusa (q.v.), he met Eugenio Montale (q.v.), who recognized P.'s talent as a poet and helped make him known. In 1956 he won the Chianciano Prize for poetry, and his reputation as a genuine and significant voice in Italian literature was established.

Religious belief, vast erudition, and an extraordinary musical sense are the hallmarks of P.'s artistry. Three thin, highly polished volumes constitute this accomplished poet's complete oeuvre: *Canti barocchi* (1956; baroque songs), *Gioco a nascondere* (1960; hide and seek), and *Plumelia* (1967; Plumelia). All his works could appropriately have been called "canti barocchi"—not "baroque" in the historical sense but as an eternal impulse of the human spirit, as an awareness of living in a world of contrasting realities—both atavistic instincts and ideas expressed through imagination and dreams.

P.'s persona is a "voice" recounting impressions, taking the multiplicity of experiences and reducing them to an undifferentiated unity of color and music. All images, all sensations are gradually transformed into incorporeal light and sound. His images, deriving from the depths of the unconscious, become visions of transfigured reality: wisps of smoke and sunbeams acquire human forms; playing cards set themselves in motion; gusts of wind become whispering voices. P.'s poetic creation is a fluctuating play between matter and spirit. Past and present coalesce. Just as the rose of June in one of his poems encompasses all the colors and fragrances that all Marches, Aprils, and Mays of the past have meticulously concocted, so, too, the poet sings with voices that come to him from past poetic experiences.

P.'s poetic instrument does not have many chords, but his voice has an extraordinary distinctiveness, and his presence in many anthologies of modern poetry is well deserved.

FURTHER VOLUME IN ENGLISH: *The Collected Poems of L. P.* (1972)

BIBLIOGRAPHY: Lopez, G., "The Leopard Nobody Saw," *TQ*, 14 (1971), 94–97; Cambon, G., Foreword, and Montale, E., Afterword to *The Collected Poems of L. P.* (1972), pp. 3–9, 197–205; Ricciardelli, M., "A Baroque Life: An Interview with L. P.," *BA*, 47 (1973), 39–50; Iannace, G. A., on *The Collected Poems of L. P., FI*, 9 (1974), 312–17; Barolini, H., "The Birth, Death, and Re-life of a Poet: L. P.," *YR*, 65 (1976), 194–202

GAETANO A. IANNACE

PIEYRE DE MANDIARGUES, André

French novelist, poet, essayist, dramatist, and art critic, b. 14 March 1909, Paris

P. de M.'s scholarly preparation includes literary studies at the Sorbonne and research in archaeology and Etruscan civilization at the University of Perugia, Italy. Extensive travels in Mexico, Europe, and the Mediterranean countries sustained P. de M.'s passion for the unconventional, the incongruous, the bizarre. Since poor health exempted him from military service during World War II, P. de M. spent that time writing in Monaco. After the war, he became associated with André Breton (q.v.) and other surrealist (q.v.) writers and painters, sharing their interest in eroticism and the fantastic. Painting has played an important role in his personal and literary life, and he has written numerous exhibition catalogues and introductions to art books, including those of his wife, Bona, an Italian painter.

The themes that appear throughout P. de M.'s work are present in his first collection of fiction, *Dans les années sordides* (1943; in the sordid years). He created seaside landscapes, artificial grottoes, and dreamlike caverns peopled with anthropomorphic insects. He pursued the idea of the macrocosm reflected in the microcosm by portraying miniaturized naked women performing erotic rituals, hands tied behind their backs. And he revealed his fascination with colors, rites of initiation, the four elements, and blood and violence as they relate to sexuality, death, and regeneration.

These motifs reappear not only in M.'s major collections of short stories, such as *Le musée noir* (1946; the dark museum) and *Feu de braise* (1959; *Blaze of Embers*, 1971), but in his poetry as well. His first volume of poems, written in the 1940s but published in 1961, *L'âge de craie* (the age of chalk), takes its title from the pockmarked chalk cliffs of the Normandy coast where he spent summers as a child.

The sea figures prominently in P. de M.'s fiction. In *Le lis de mer* (1956; *The Girl be-*

neath the Lion, 1958), a novella of passionate intensity in which two young women go on vacation to Sardinia, the island becomes a sanctuary for the god Pan. The heroine plans her own ritualistic deflowering in a clearing by the sea, and the young man who silently performs the rite introduces her to nature as a "Pan-ic" experience. Thus P. de M. consciously relates eroticism to communion with the physical universe.

Color symbolism, particularly as it refers to black, white, and red, appears frequently in P. de M.'s work. In addition to representing alchemical substances and processes, these colors are emblematic of the Nazi flag in the novel *La motocyclette* (1963; *The Motorcycle,* 1965), in which the protagonist makes a fatal trip from France to Germany to see her lover, who had given her a motorcycle as a gift.

P. de M. began to achieve wide recognition when he received the Goncourt Prize for *La marge* (1967; *The Margin,* 1969). In this novel he spins an intricate web of references and symbols around the themes of life, desire, and death. Although he is not conventionally religious, M. decries modern materialism and seeks to reestablish correspondences between the worlds of the flesh and the spirit. This he achieves by subtly evoking arcane rituals, tarot representations, numerology, alchemy, astrology, and other esoteric lore.

P. de M. has published two plays, *Isabella Morra* (1973; Isabella Morra), and *La nuit séculaire* (1979; the last night of the century), as well as a number of translations of drama and poetry. *Le belvédère* (1958; the belvedere), *Le deuxième belvédère* (1962; the second belvedere), and *Le troisième belvédère* (1971; the third belvedere) are collections of essays dedicated to places, poets, and painters. He also wrote a sado-erotic novel in 1951 but published it only in 1979: *L'anglais décrit dans le château fermé* (the Englishman described within the enclosed chateau).

P. de M. continues the "fantastic tale" tradition of the 18th and 19th cs. His quasi-baroque narratives, rich with recondite allusions, will continue to beguile readers with their beautiful style and their multiple levels of significance.

FURTHER WORKS: *Les masques de Léonor Fini* (1951); *Soleil des loups* (1951); *Marbre* (1953); *Les monstres de Bomarzo* (1957); *Le*

cadran lunaire (1958); *Sugaï* (1960); *L'âge de craie, suivi de Hédéra* (1961); *La marée* (1962); *Sabine* (1963); *Saint-John Perse: À l'honneur de la chair* (1963); *Astyanax, précédé de Les incongruités monumentales, et suivi de Cartolines et dédicaces* (1964); *Le point òu j'en suis, suivi de Dalila exaltée et de La nuit l'amour* (1964); *Porte dévergondée* (1965); *Beylamour* (1965); *Les corps illuminés,* photographies de Frédéric Barzilay (1965); *Larmes de généraux,* lithographies de Baj (1965); *Critiquettes,* eau-forte de Bona (1967); *Ruisseau des solitudes, suivi de Jacinthes et de Chapeaugaga* (1968); *Le marronier* (1968); *La magnanerie de La Ferrage,* gravures sur linoléum de Magnelli (1969); *Le lièvre de la lune,* eaux-fortes de Baj (1970); *Eros solaire,* dessins érotiques, lithographies d'André Masson (1970); *Bona l'amour et la peinture* (1971); *Mascarets* (1971); *La nuit de mil neuf cent quatorze* (1971); *Croiseur noir,* eaux-fortes de Wilfredo Lam (1972); *Miranda, suivi de La spirale,* eaux-fortes de Miró (1973); *Terre érotiques,* lithographies d'André Masson (1974); *Chagall* (1975); *Le désordre de la mémoire* (1975); *Parapapilloneries,* lithographies de Meret Oppenheim (1976); *Sous la lame* (1976); *Des jardins enchantés,* lithographies de Franco Gentilini (1977); *Arcimboldo le merveilleux* (1977); *Le trésor cruel de Hans Bellmer* (1979); *L'ivre œil, suivi de Croiseur noir et de Passage de l'Égyptienne (1979)*

BIBLIOGRAPHY: Temmer, M., "A. P. de M.," *YFS,* 31 (1964), 99–104; Haig, S., "A. P. de M. and 'Les pierreuses,'" *FR,* 39 (1965), 275–80; Robin, A., "A. P. de M.; ou, L'initiation panique," CS, 52 (1965), 138–50, 295–313; Campanini, S., "Alchemy in P. de M.'s 'Le diamant,'" *FR,* 50 (1977), 602–9; Bond, D., "A. P. de M.: Some Ideas on Art," *RR,* 70 (1979), 69–79; Lowrie, J., "The *Rota Fortunae* in P. de M.'s *La motocyclette,*" *FR,* 53, (1980), 378–88

JOYCE O. LOWRIE

PILINSZKY, János

Hungarian poet, b. 25 Nov. 1921, Budapest; d. 27 May 1981, Budapest

The event that had the most profound effect on P.'s creative life was World War II. P. grew up as the sheltered child of middle-class parents and studied law at the University of

Budapest, but in late 1944 he was drafted into the Hungarian army and with the retreating Axis forces taken to Germany, where he witnessed the ravages of war as well as the mental anguish of prisoners and concentration-camp inmates. He was the first—and for a long time the only—Hungarian poet who dealt insistently with the implications of the Holocaust, seeing it as a moral disaster, a failure of civilization.

P.'s wartime experiences and their reverberations are at the center of his first two volumes of poetry, *Trapéz és korlát* (1946; trapeze and parallel bars) and *Harmadnapon* (1959; on the third day), the latter published after a decade-long silence. In the 1960s P.'s literary horizon broadened somewhat; he wrote more, became more visible, and after a number of Western poets and intellectuals—Pierre Emmanuel and Ted Hughes (qq.v.), in particular—began taking note of his achievement, he traveled abroad, spending some time in Western Europe and America, although he remained on the staff of *Új ember,* a Catholic weekly, until his death.

A Catholic poet, P. also expressed the existential agony of modern man. The ardent quest for salvation in his poems is always accompanied by a perception of solitude and despair. With radical verbal economy, although in images that are often bizarre and surrealistic, the poet conveys a sense of immobility, of utter hopelessness. P. said that for him the main purpose of poetry is not to re-create human experience but to discover, painfully, the real nature of the human condition. Many of his longer poems—for example, the celebrated "Apokrif" (1959; "Apocrypha," 1976)—are biblical in tone; in them apocalyptic visions blend with the more familiar memory flashes of wartime horrors. His later volumes, *Szálkák* (1972; splinters) and *Végkifejlet* (1974; denouement), while still spare, are a little less somber, and in his prose works he mellowed even further. *Beszélgetések Sheryl Suttonnal* (1977; conversations with Sheryl Sutton), which he subtitled "The Novel of a Dialogue," is really a series of tender and tentative monologues by and about a black American actress P. befriended in Paris.

P.'s was a lonely, distant, self-abnegating voice in an otherwise richly polyphonic literature. By Hungarian standards his total output was unusually small (in addition to poems and short prose pieces he wrote a few

playlets, film scripts, and poetic oratorios), and his verse is in fact more akin to the austere objective poetry of some modern French and English poets than to the expansive, experiential lyric traditions of his native country. Yet the starkness and biblical weightiness of his poetic lines and his obsessive preoccupation with just a few themes had a stunning impact on the postwar generation of Hungarian poets. It is also true that in the 1950s Hungary's cultural leadership had no use for P.'s unwavering, self-tormenting pessimism: he became, and remained for years, an unpublishable poet. Nowadays, however, he is seen as an exemplary figure—a man of rare literary and moral sensibility.

FURTHER WORKS: *Rekviem* (1963); *Nagyvárosi ikonok* (1970); *Tér és forma* (1975); *Kráter* (1976). FURTHER VOLUMES IN ENGLISH: *Selected Poems* (1976); *Crater* (1978)

BIBLIOGRAPHY: Gömöri, G., "P.: The Lonely Poet," *HungQ,* 5 (1965), 43–47; Hughes, T., Introduction to J. P., *Selected Poems* (1976), pp. 7–14; Nemes Nagy, Á., "J. P.: A Very Different Poet," *NHQ,* No. 84 (1981), 54–59

IVAN SANDERS

PILIPINO LITERATURE
See Philippine Literature

PILLAT, Ion
Romanian poet, essayist, dramatist, and translator, b. 31 March 1891, Bucharest; d. 17 April 1945, Bucharest

Scion of an old aristocratic family, P. studied literature and law at the Sorbonne. Destined by family tradition for a career in politics (he was the nephew of the Brătianus, a prominent Romanian political family), he chose instead poetry and a quiet private life. Between 1926 and 1937 he traveled to Spain, Italy, and Greece. He was active in Romanian cultural life, editing several journals and anthologies of poetry, and frequenting literary circles, notably that of the symbolist (q.v.) poet Alexandru Macedonski (1854–1920). He also translated extensively from French and German poetry. After 1924 he became closely associated with the group around the influential journal *Gîndirea,* where he published many of his poems.

Often compared to Vasile Alecsandri (1821–1890), P. actually had little in common with that 19th-c. poet-revolutionary beyond such superficial similarities as an aristocratic background, a taste for quiet country life, and a certain ease and elegance in writing verse. He was much closer, both in poetic temperament and ideology, to the Parnassian and symbolist poets. In his collection of essays *Portrete lirice* (1936; lyrical portraits) P. advocated a "pure" poetry that had "algebra and music as its limits." His own early verse drew upon such Parnassian and hermetic sources as Greek mythology and Oriental poetry, and sought a cold and studied perfection of poetic form. Throughout his career P. remained interested in poetical modernism without actually engaging in experiments himself.

His volume of poems *Pe Argeş în sus* (1923; up the Argeş river) marked his return to his national roots and was strongly influenced by the traditionalist ideology of *Gîndirea*. However, P. cast the traditional, "naïve" themes of Romanian folklore in a highly refined symbolist and neoclassicist form. He brought this curious but effective poetic blend to perfection in such volumes as *Caietul verde* (1932; the green notebook) and *Împlinire* (1942; fulfillment).

P. also wrote two plays, in collaboration with Adrian Maniu (q.v.), which were adaptations from Romanian literature and folklore and which also bore a strong traditionalist mark. P. is also recognized as one of the best Romanian translators of poetry from French, English, German, Spanish, and Italian. It was P.'s poetry, however, especially the verse of his late period, that established him in Romanian literature as one of the most cerebral, cosmopolitan, and refined artistic personalities of this century.

FURTHER WORKS: *Povestea celui din urmă sfînt* (1911); *Visări păgîne* (1912); *Eternităţi de-o clipă* (1914); *Iubita de zăpadă* (1915); *Amăgiri* (1917); *Grădina între ziduri* (1919); *Satul meu* (1925); *Dinu Paturică* (1925, with Adrian Maniu); *Tinereţe fără bătrîneţe* (1926, with Adrian Maniu); *Biserica de altădată* (1926); *Florica* (1926); *Întoarcere (1908–1918)* (1927); *Limpezimi* (1928); *Scutul Minervei* (1933); *Pasărea de lut* (1934); *Poeme într-un vers* (1935); *Ţărm pierdut* (1937); *Umbra timpului* (1940); *Tradiţie şi literatură* (1943); *Asfodela* (1943); *Cumpăna dreaptă* (1965)

BIBLIOGRAPHY: Munteanu, B., *Panorama de la littérature roumaine contemporaine* (1938), pp. 284–87

MIHAI SPARIOSU

PILLECIJN, Filip de

Belgian novelist and essayist (writing in Flemish), b. 25 March 1891, Hamme; d. 7 Aug. 1962, Ghent

P. started his career as a teacher, biographer, and essayist. Early creative work, the novels *Pieter Fardé* (1926; Pieter Fardé) and *Blauwbaard* (1931; Bluebeard), relied on historical or legendary sources; but in the novellas *Monsieur Hawarden* (1935; Monsieur Hawarden), *Schaduwen* (1937; shadows), and *De aanwezigheid* (1938; the presence) P. established himself as a superb stylist who gained fame for his evocation of mood and landscape, and for his subtle exploration of the psychology of eroticism.

In his novellas and the novels *Hans van Malmédy* (1935; Hans of Malmédy), *De soldaat Johan* (1939; soldier John), and *Jan Tervaert* (1947; Jan Tervaert) P. set a new standard for Flemish prose and influenced a generation of writers with his delicate yet masculine romanticism. These are works of a poetic sensibility dealing with a melancholy that found its only solace in the peaceful perpetuity of nature. The autumnal mood and an oneiric imagination found its arcadian perfection in the novel *De veerman en de jonkvrouw* (1950; the ferryman and the lady)—practically a romantic fairy tale.

Experiences of violence, social unrest, and misery during two world wars embittered P., and social considerations came to replace his earlier romanticism. The negative ramifications of man as a social and political animal are portrayed in the story "De boodschap" (1946; the message), the novella *Rochus* (1951; Rochus), and the novels *Mensen achter de dijk* (1949; people behind the dike), *Vaandrig Antoon Serjacobs* (1951; ensign Antoon Serjacobs), and *Aanvaard het leven* (1956; accept life). In the last two novels, P. responds to life's pain with the resigned acceptance of an idealist purified by suffering.

Beginning with *De rit* (1927; the ride), the majority of P.'s heroes are soldiers. In conflict with conventional society and subjected to bureaucratic injustice, these outsiders—of a type that has come to dominate 20th-c. fiction—pay dearly (either by imprisonment or death) for their impotent rebellion. Only women provide solace and hope in this inhospitable and threatening world. But although physical passion is celebrated, P. insists on man's inability to establish a lasting and authentic relationship. Nature gradually emerges as mankind's only lasting joy. The farmer, in an otherwise anticlerical oeuvre, assumes the stature of a priest in P.'s telluric devotion.

P. perfected an economical prose style that is suggestive rather than explicit, lyrical rather than realistic; its melodic serenity strikes a fascinating balance between virility and refinement.

P.'s preference for historical settings—used exclusively to provide objectivity and a sense of timelessness—recalls German masters of shorter fiction such as Conrad Ferdinand Meyer (1825–1898), Gottfried Keller (1819–1890), and Adalbert Stifter (1805–1865), with all of whom he shares stylistic similarities and a preoccupation with the majesty of nature. The romantic and lyric side of P.'s work recalls the melancholy novels of the French authors Eugène Fromentin (1820–1876) and Alain-Fournier (q.v.). His unsentimental devotion to nature, a characteristic shared with so many Flemish and Dutch writers, is of special interest in an age newly concerned with ecology.

FURTHER WORKS: *Onder den hiel* (1920); *Hugo Verriest* (1926); *Stijn Streuvels en zijn werk* (1932); *Dona Mirabella* (1952); *Het boek van de man Job* (1956); *Verzameld werk* (4 vols., 1959–60); *Elizabeth* (1961)

E. M. BEEKMAN

PILNYAK, Boris

(pseud. of Boris Andreevich Vogau) Russian novelist and short-story writer, b. 12 Sept. 1894, Mozhaysk; d. 1938

The son of a veterinarian of Volga-German origin, P. published short stories before the Russian Revolution, but attained fame later with an avant-garde novel, *Goly god* (1922; *The Naked Year,* 1927), depicting the civil war and the famine of 1919. An exceptionally popular and influential writer, he angered the Soviet authorities with his romantic view of the revolution. He incurred official disfavor for "Povest o nepogashennoy lune" (1927; "The Tale of the Unextinguished Moon," 1967), a fictionalized account of the death,

believed to have been ordered by Stalin, of General Mikhail Frunze during an operation. He was expelled from the Writers' Union after the publication in Germany of *Krasnoe derevo* (1929; mahogany), which contained sympathetic portraits of old Bolsheviks. His Five-Year-Plan novel, *Volga vpadaet v Kaspyskoe more* (1930; *The Volga Falls to the Caspian Sea,* 1931), depicting the construction of a vast dam, did little to reestablish his reputation. His trips to China, Japan, and the U.S., undertaken in the late 1920s and early 1930s, resulted in the publication of several travel diaries. In 1937 he was arrested and convicted of "fascist" activities. It is believed that he died in 1938, but it is not generally known what fate he met after his arrest.

P.'s early short stories are set in rural areas and evoke the primitive, even biological, aspects of life in a lyrical style reminiscent of Chekhov, Bunin (qq.v.), and Turgenev. Throughout his career his admiration for the instinctual and natural influenced his psychological portrayals and his thinking on culture and history.

His popularity in the early 1920s derived partly from his reputation as the first novelist of the revolution. In episodic avant-gardist narratives he eulogized the revolution as the resurgence of a Russian peasant culture which had existed before the reign of Peter the Great and which remained unadulterated by debilitating Western traits. He was, like Andrey Bely and Aleksey Remizov (qq.v.), a 20th-c. Slavophile and depicted Western Europe as moribund. His use of the novel form for the examination of philosophical ideas is also reminiscent of Dostoyevsky.

P.'s portrayals of Russia in his novels are all studies of confrontations between the new and the old. In *Mashiny i volki* (1924; machines and wolves) the communal peasant culture he admired is shown in conflict with Marxism and technology. The complex and unconventional style of these novels, which was deplored as "Pilnyakism" by orthodox Soviet critics, features the liberal use of such devices as the frame story, the flashback, enigmatic narrative transitions, lyrical digressions, leitmotifs, symbols, insertions of documents, dialect renderings, wordplay, and typographical peculiarities. The style resembles Bely's in its musical traits and Remizov's in its antiquarianism, while its satire stems from Gogol.

In the late 1920s and 1930s P. ostensibly attempted to correct his ideology and to subdue his style, but with ambiguous results. He turned with sympathetic interest to non-European cultures. In *Rossia v polyote* (1926; Russia in flight) he depicted the Komis, a Finno-Ugric people living west of the Urals. In *Korni yaponskogo solntsa* (1927; roots of the Japanese sun) and *Kitayskaya povest* (1927; a Chinese story) he tried to capture the spirit of Oriental cultures, while in *Okey: Amerikansky roman* (1933; OK: an American novel) he denigrated capitalism. In some works of the 1930s, such as "Sozrevanie plodov" (1936; the ripening of fruit), whose subject is a craft industry, he created a new kind of mélange consisting of fiction, reportage, and autobiography. Between the late 1930s and the mid-1960s his name virtually disappeared from print in the Soviet Union. He was subsequently rehabilitated, but few of his works have been reprinted there.

Although P. defended the spontaneous and primitive, he was a bookish and derivative writer. His work was sometimes flawed by raw naturalism, shallow psychology, or an overweening didacticism. Nevertheless, his underlying compassion and intense concern for freedom associate him with the best traditions of Russian literature. His delight in the picturesque and his savoring of the eccentric rescue him from the realm of the platitudinous, and his pessimism is relieved by comic and ironic touches.

FURTHER WORKS: *Prostye rasskazy* (1923); *Ocherednye povesti* (1927); *Sobranie sochineny* (8 vols., 1930); *Izbrannye rasskazy* (1935); *Izbrannye proizvedenia* (1976). FURTHER VOLUMES IN ENGLISH: *Tales of the Wilderness* (1925); *The Tale of the Unextinguished Moon, and Other Stories* (1967); *Mother Earth, and Other Stories* (1968)

BIBLIOGRAPHY: Bristol, E., "B. P.," *SEER,* 41 (1963), 494–512; Wilson, P., "B. P.," *Survey,* No. 46 (1963), 134–42; Maloney, P., "Anarchism and Bolshevism in the Works of B. P.," *RusR,* 32 (1973), 43–53; Reck, V., *B. P.: A Soviet Writer in Conflict with the State* (1975); Brostrom, K., "P.'s *Naked Year:* The Problem of Faith," *RLT,* 16 (1979), 114–53; Browning, G. L., "Polyphony and the Accretive Refrain in B. P.'s *Naked Year,*" *RLT,* 16 (1979), 154–70; Falchikov, M., "Rerouting the Train of Time: B. P.'s *Krasnoye derevo,*" *MLR,* 75 (1980), 138–47

EVELYN BRISTOL

PINGET, Robert

French novelist and dramatist, b. 19 July 1919, Geneva, Switzerland

P. received a law degree in Switzerland before his interest in art led him to become a painter and an art teacher. In 1946, having made Paris his permanent residence, he studied painting at the Academy of Fine Arts, and exhibited at the Galerie du Siècle in 1949. He then turned to prose writing in an attempt to adapt the free expression of poetry to the novel form.

P. was first attracted by the verbal acrobatics of surrealism (q.v.) and by the unbridled imagination of the French poet Max Jacob (q.v.), who excelled in the spontaneous expression of his own sensibilities. The impetuous style and the burlesque ingenuity of Jacob's flights into fantasy led P. to write esoteric tales such as *Graal Flibuste* (1956; Graal Flibuste) and *Clope au dossier* (1961; Clope to the dossier), the latter dramatized as *Ici et ailleurs* (1961; *Clope,* 1963).

As early as 1957 P. also became attuned to the despairing quality of Samuel Beckett's (q.v.) nihilistic philosophy, when he translated into French Beckett's drama *All That Fall.* P. himself conveyed the same feeling for the emptiness and absurdity of the modern world, as expressed by the inanity of the spoken word, in his first radio scripts, such as *La manivelle* (1960; *The Old Tune,* 1963)—the English version of which was done by Beckett.

Since 1951 P. has written short stories, plays, dialogues, a film scenario, and several radio scripts, which have been produced in France and Germany, as well as numerous novels. His works have been published in translation in thirteen different countries.

L'inquisitoire (1962; *The Inquisitory,* 1966) was awarded the Critics' Grand Prize in 1963. In this lengthy novel, the experience of the past, the endless unfolding of lost time, is conveyed through a deluge of words. An aged, deaf, broken man utters bits of broken sentences. The mumbled recollections of his rambling monologue continue without a single semicolon or period. What begins to emerge is not only the underlying insecurity of an anguished humanity, but also the elusive, often irrational quality of reality itself.

The baroque, fablelike, at times dreamlike fantasies of P.'s early books have taken on, in later years, bizarre and pessimistic undertones. The same almost poignant cries of echo-voices appear in his short novel *Quelqu'un*

(1965; someone), which won the Fémina Prize. Here again we find the familiar setting of P.'s geography of the imaginary. The discourse meanders afresh; there is no coherent narrative. This is because for P., literature is exclusively language, exclusively free, "gratuitous" verbal communication. He is not interested in telling a story or in developing a plot; he is concerned only with the transcription of the spoken word.

P.'s stylistic experiments have linked him to the New Novel (q.v.). But his originality lies in the fact that unlike the avant-garde French novelists who perceive visually and try to render minutely, as objectively as possible, a world of things, P. listens acutely and patiently. He tries to distinguish between the textures of the many dialogues that he discerns within himself.

So, in *Le Libera* (1968; *The Libera Me Domine*, 1976), rejecting the old-fashioned stereotyped meaning of words and clichés and rigid syntax, P. searches for his own method of communication. He attempts what seems an impossible task—to pinpoint the everchanging aspect of a mobile language. The preface of *Le Libera* almost constitutes a manifesto. In it, P. defines each one of his novels as a separate quest for a particular mood, more precisely, a distinct tone of voice. He is seeking a certain inflection or a separate modulation, selected from among the many original vibrations that constitute P.'s own ways of expressing himself, each and all of them being representative of his true complex sensitivity. The right intonation for a particular novel, which he discerns within himself, is poured forth onto the page spontaneously at first. Then comes the painful labor of filtering, the conscientious effort of composing. The very process becomes a literary vein, a style; and the style in turn determines, automatically, the intrigue. The story could have been something else; the authenticity of the speech is what constitutes, for P., his own true creation.

The search for veracity automatically implies false starts, innumerable meanderings, reversals, and culs-de-sac. Dealing with the immense and complicated palimpsest of memory—scraping, rubbing, erasing P.'s tablets of time—the author painstakingly attempts to unscramble and re-create the past in a new, "spoken" form in *Cette voix* (1975; this voice). Finally, in an effort to project into the future, old age, and an ultimately looming death, he humbly submits to the reader his "obscure"

writings of "dubious" authenticity, crowning his quest with *L'apocryphe* (1980; the apocrypha). Ambiguously written in the conditional, *L'apocryphe*, with its occasional "gray humor" undertones, unfolds P.'s maddening world of nightmares and daydreams. The engrossed reader must penetrate the many layers of meaning of this contemporary Homerian-Vergilian-Montaignian opus.

FURTHER WORKS: *Entre Fantoine et Agapa* (1951); *Mahu; ou, Le matériau* (1952; *Mahu; or, The Material*, 1967); *Le renard et la boussole* (1955); *Baga* (1958; *Baga*, 1967); *Le fiston* (1959; *Monsieur Levert*, 1961); *Lettre morte* (1959; *Dead Letter*, 1963); *Architruc* (1961; *Architruc*, 1967); *L'hypothèse* (1961; *The Hypothesis*, 1967); *Autour de Mortin* (1965; *About Mortin*, 1967); *Passacaille* (1969); *Identité, suivi d'Abel et Bela, Nuit* (1971); *Fable* (1971; *Fable*, 1981); *Paralchimie* (1973); *Amorces* (1973); *Le rescapé* (1974); *Le mois d'août* (1975); *Le vautour; Attendre; Genèse de "Fable"* (1980); *Le bifteck* (1981); *Monsieur Songe* (1982)

BIBLIOGRAPHY: Steisel, M.-G., "P.'s Method in *L'inquisitoire*," *BA*, 40 (1966), 267–71; Robbe-Grillet, A., *For a New Novel* (1965), pp. 127–32; Steisel, M.-G., "Paroles de R. P.," *PSMLAB*, 45 (1966), 35–38; Mercier, V., *The New Novel from Queneau to P.* (1971), pp. 363–415; Meyer, F., "P., le livre disséminé comme fiction, narration, et object," in Ricardou, J., and Van Rossum-Guyon, F., eds., *Le nouveau roman: Hier, aujourd'hui* (1972), Vol. II, pp. 299–310, 325–50; Knapp, B., *French Novelists Speak Out* (1976), pp. 6–14; special P. issue, *Bas de casse*, No. 2 (1981)

MARIE-GEORGETTE STEISEL

PINTER, Harold
English dramatist and screenwriter, b. 10 Oct. 1930, London

P. was born in Hackney, a working-class section of London. The son of a Jewish tailor, he was at an impressionable age when he began hearing horror stories about Hitler's Germany, and was an evacuee during the blitz. In fact, he remembers seeing the family's garden in flames. After attending a local school on a scholarship, P. received a grant to study acting at the Royal Academy of Dramatic Art. He was temperamentally unsuited to the institution, however, and soon left. At about this time he also had encounters with broken-milk-bottle-wielding neofascists, declared himself a conscientious objector and stood trial for refusing to join the National Service, and published his first poems. By 1950 he had acted in BBC radio plays. He toured Ireland for eighteen months with Anew McMaster's Shakespearean repertory company and continued as a professional actor (stage name: David Baron) through the late 1950s, an experience that provided him with an important understanding of the production aspects of playwriting.

P.'s former wife, the actress Vivien Merchant, and his dramatist friend Samuel Beckett (q.v.) have also advised him on the performability of his plays. Essentially apolitical, P. occasionally works for various arts causes and sometimes directs for the National Theatre in London. His personal life generally does not enter into his works *per se,* but a six-year-long, well-publicized affair with the biographer Lady Antonia Fraser (b. 1932) ended in a divorce from Merchant in 1981 and marriage to Lady Antonia the same year. During this period, his output declined.

Over the years P. has been considered one of the most important English-language dramatists of this century. Recognition in the form of various awards and honors is one measure of how P.'s contemporaries appreciate his work. *The Caretaker* (1960) and *The Homecoming* (1965) won best-play designations on Broadway and in London, and major awards were gathered by several films for which P. wrote the screenplays. P. was made a Commander of the Order of the British Empire in 1966 and has received several other prizes and honorary degrees.

P.'s three early plays, *The Room* (1957), *The Birthday Party* (1958), and *The Dumb Waiter* (1959), have been labeled "comedies of menace." A likely outgrowth of his early experiences as a youth, the dramas are concerned with the themes of menace and dominance. The basic metaphor is of a room or some other sanctuary that is about to be invaded. The inhabitant of the room understands the existence of the menace outside, and in spite of terror and loneliness tries to communicate with the invader in an attempt to verify whether or not it is friendly. Fear of exposing a point of vulnerability, however, leads the inhabitant to be so wary that communication is impossible, even if the intruder were not so ambiguous. As a result, menace is heightened, as is the consequent need for further verification

and communication, but the ability to verify or communicate is broken down, creating more menace. In *The Room* an old woman's sanctuary cannot protect her from a menacer; in *The Birthday Party* the protagonist tries to run away but is tracked down; in *The Dumb Waiter* two hired killers find that even menacers can be menaced.

Stylistically, these plays are not at all traditional. Although the dialogue is extremely realistic, P. presents his material with little or no explanation, and many theatergoers were at a loss to understand plays that neither spelled out their meaning in great detail nor conformed to the audience's preconceptions of what drama should be.

Having established the pervasive existence of menace in the modern world, P. next focused on the source of the menace. Transitional elements are obvious in the radio play *A Slight Ache* (1959) when the presence of a tramp, who never speaks, leads to the emotional breakdown of a husband and to the wife's replacing her husband with the tramp. In the dramatist's first commercial success, *The Caretaker,* two brothers and another tramp become involved in establishing or maintaining their relationships with each other. By now audiences understood what P. was doing.

In both of these plays, and the shorter works that immediately followed them (radio and television scripts included), it is clear that menace does not derive from an external, physical source; it comes from within the individual and is psychological in nature. This idea is summed up in *The Homecoming*, one of P.'s two best plays, and his most honored work. In *The Homecoming*, Teddy returns to his father's home with his wife, Ruth, only to leave, rejected by his family, while his wife stays behind. Throughout, the characters attempt to establish relationships with each other, no matter how absurd the basis for that relationship may at first seem. Desperately they grasp at anything that might be used to satisfy their needs; nonchalantly they dismiss anything that fails to meet their requirements. Teddy can leave because no one needs him and he needs no one; Ruth stays because everyone needs her and she needs to be needed. Individual need thus is determined to be the source of the characters' terror and desperation—and they are willing to do anything and to accept everything that might fulfill their particular needs.

Completely new thematic and stylistic elements emerged in *Landscape* (1968). Given the psychological nature of the source of menace and its location—the human mind—P. began to examine how the mind functions. The intermixing of memory, time, and the nature of reality became the focal point of his interest. In *Landscape* Duff has wronged his wife, Beth, and she retreats into the world of her imagination, in which memories of the past and her romantic daydreams allow her to withdraw from reality to the extent that her husband can no longer communicate with her. In dealing with this very abstract concept, P. adopts a more lyrical style than was present in his earlier plays.

Old Times (1971), P.'s finest work to date, continues both the themes and style of *Landscape.* When Anna visits her former roommate, Kate, and Kate's husband, Deeley, a verbal battle develops between the visitor and the husband over the wife. Through a series of memories, created by the rememberer, each character tries to diminish the other in Kate's eyes. The nature of reality is such that the characters can invent tales to explain a past that will lead to a future in which their present needs and desires are fulfilled. Thus, reality, all time, and memory are shown to coexist simultaneously in the human mind and to be manipulable by it. The drama ends with Kate's deciding to remain with her husband when she remembers seeing Anna dead—and to all intents and purposes Anna ceases to exist.

P.'s screenwriting tends to parallel his playwriting: his film scripts include many of the themes that were occupying his attention in the plays written at the same time. P. has adapted several of his own works to the screen: *The Caretaker* (1963), released in the U.S. under the title *The Guest; The Birthday Party* (1969); and *The Homecoming* (1973). He has also adapted other writers' novels: *The Servant* (1963), from Robin Maugham (b. 1916); *The Pumpkin Eater* (1964), from Penelope Mortimer (b. 1918); *The Quiller Memorandum* (1966), from Adam Hall (pseud. of Elleston Trevor, b. 1920); *Accident* (1967), from Nicholas Mosley (b. 1923); *The Go-Between* (1971), from L. P. Hartley (q.v.); *The Last Tycoon* (1976), from F. Scott Fitzgerald (q.v.); *The Proust Screenplay* (pub. 1977, never filmed), from Marcel Proust (q.v.); and *The French Lieutenant's Woman* (1981; pub. 1981), from John Fowles (q.v.). (The first five of these screenplays from other writers were published together in *Five Screenplays* [1971].) Menace, interpersonal communications, psychological need, reality, and the nature of time are again his subjects. As with his radio and television writing, some of the techniques he used in the cinematic medium are carried over into his stage writing (the opening of *Old Times,* for example, incorporates a jump cut). P.'s screenplays, however, are often too wordy for the medium and on the whole are less successful than his dramas.

Throughout P.'s career, one thing has remained constant. A reader unfamiliar with the dramatist's canon would be hard pressed to conclude that *The Room* and *Landscape* were written by the same author, but an analysis of P.'s writing shows that there has been a steady thematic evolution and a concurrent and continual stylistic development from the very beginning of his career. Whereas many authors simply rewrite the same story, P. has progressed and constantly changed. The thematic movement from exposure of menace naturally led him to an investigation into the source of menace, which in turn stimulated his examination of the interconnections of memory and time and the nature of reality. Simultaneously, his form changed to reflect his content, so much so that at different times scholars have labeled him an absurdist (see Theater of the Absurd), an existentialist (q.v.), a Freudian, and a poetic dramatist.

The elements that will ensure P.'s lasting reputation are his contributions in the areas of language (realistic dialogue, including pauses and silences) and exposition (as in real life, characters' backgrounds and motivations may be clear to them while the audience remains uninformed and must determine backgrounds and motivations purely from the characters' actions). The importance of P.'s themes and the insights into human nature he provides (often in a humorous manner, despite the seriousness of his topics), the emotional impact combined with intellectual depth, and the influence he has already had on a generation of playwrights make him a pivotal figure in the history of English drama.

FURTHER WORKS: *The Hothouse* (written 1958, pub. 1980); *A Slight Ache, and Other Plays* (1961 [with *A Night Out* and *The Dwarfs*]); *The Collection and The Lover* (1963); *Dialogue for Three* (1963); *The Compartment* (1963); *The Dwarfs, and Eight Review Sketches* (1965); *The Lover; Tea Party; The Basement* (1967); *Poems* (1968); *Mac* (1968); *Night School* (1968); *Landscape and*

535

Silence, with Night (1970); *Monologue* (1973); *No Man's Land* (1975); *Complete Works* (4 vols., 1976–81); *Poems and Prose 1949–1977* (1978); *Betrayal* (1978); *Family Voices* (1981)

BIBLIOGRAPHY: Hinchliffe, A. P., *H. P.* (1967; rev. ed., 1981); Kerr, W., *H. P.* (1967); Taylor, J. R., *Anger and After,* rev. ed. (1969), pp. 321–59; Esslin, M., *The Peopled Wound: The Work of H. P.* (1970; 2nd ed., *P.: A Study of His Plays,* 1973); Hollis, J. R., *H. P.: The Poetics of Silence* (1970); Sykes, A., *H. P.* (1970); Burkman, K. H., *The Dramatic World of H. P.: Its Basis in Ritual* (1971); Lahr, J., ed., *A Casebook on H. P.'s "The Homecoming"* (1971); Ganz, A., ed., *P.: A Collection of Critical Essays* (1972); Hayman, R., *H. P.* (1973); special P. issue, *MD,* 17, 4 (1974); Quigley, A. E., *The P. Problem* (1975); Dukore, B. F., *Where Laughter Stops: P.'s Tragicomedy* (1976); Gabbard, L. P., *The Dream Structure of P.'s Plays: A Psychoanalytic Approach* (1976); Gale, S. H., *Butter's Going Up: A Critical Analysis of H. P.'s Work* (1977); Gale, S. H., *H. P.: An Annotated Bibliography* (1978)

STEVEN H. GALE

H. P.'s people are generally at cross-purposes with each other and sometimes tangled in a world of disconcerting objectivity. Mental discontinuities balance objective absurdities to arouse suspense and a sense of threat, bordering on insanity, as when in *The Dumb Waiter* mysterious orders for elaborate meals come down the lift from what had once been a restaurant to the basement kitchen where the two ambiguous ruffians are at their simultaneously flaccid and ominous talk; wherein perhaps a lucid symbolism may be felt flowering from a superficial absurdity. P.'s conversation is usually that of lower middle-class normality, and the disconcerting objects those of town life and human fabrication. In *The Caretaker* Mick reels off a speech about London districts and its various bus-routes and then one about the legal and financial conditions of letting his property, in such a way as to make one dizzy. Questions may be left unanswered: who is the negro in *The Room,* who comes up from the basement of the tenement house, striking terror? Much of this is in the manner of Eugene Ionesco. What is so strange is that we are nowadays given the experience of nightmare, almost of the supernatural, in terms not of devils or ghosts, but of ordinary, material objects and affairs; and of people at cross-purposes with each other and with the audience in a paradoxical and dangerous world.

G. Wilson Knight, "The Kitchen Sink," *Encounter,* Dec. 1963, 49

Language—that common to men and of common man—is employed to make us constantly aware of the essential loneliness of the human condition. In discussing or including remedies, P. rarely indulges in overt speculation. . . . He attempts to show the constant effort of human beings to impress, confuse, or simply refuse to give answers about the problems that beset them, a refusal P. demonstrates in his plays. . . . Where [N. F.] Simpson merely exploits cliché, P.'s usage of it fascinates and evolves; and this usage makes him of all contemporary British dramatists the most poetical—more so than either [Christopher] Fry or [T. S.] Eliot. P. has looked at the whole, not merely at the language. . . . Certainly, of all contemporary British dramatists only P. manages to be topical, local, and universal—to combine the European Absurd with native wit to create a record of common inevitability. P. says, modestly, of his own work: "I am very concerned with the shape and consistency of mood of my plays. I cannot write anything that appears to me to be loose and unfinished. I like a feeling of order in what I write." This sense of order is the key to his work in any medium, and his success rests on it. In a very precise sense, among his contemporaries P. is the *miglior fabbro.*

Arnold P. Hinchliffe, *H. P.* (1967), pp. 164–65

The technique of casting doubt upon everything by matching each apparently clear and unequivocal statement with an equally clear and unequivocal statement of its contrary—used rather crudely in some parts of [*The Room*], as when Rose Hudd actually comments on the discrepancy between the Sandses' initial statement that they were on their way up and their later statement that they were on their way down when they called on her—is one which we shall find used constantly in P.'s plays to create an air of mystery and uncertainty. The situations involved are always very simple and basic, the language which the characters use is an almost uncannily accurate reproduction of everyday speech (indeed, in this respect P., far from being the least realistic dramatist of his generation, is arguably the most realistic), and yet in these ordinary surroundings lurk mysterious terrors and uncertainties—and by extension the whole external world of everyday realities is thrown into question. Can we ever know the truth about anybody or anything? Is there an absolute truth to be known?

John Russell Taylor, *Anger and After,* rev. ed. (1969), pp. 325–26

A playwright so fascinated by the difficulty, the terror, the pitfalls of communication will inevitably be fascinated by words and their multifarious uses to disclose and to disguise meaning. P.'s theatre is a theatre of language; it is from the words and their rhythm that the suspense, the dramatic tension, the laughter, and the tragedy spring. Words, in P.'s plays, become weapons of domination and subservience, silences explode, nuances of vocabulary strip human beings to the skin. Not even his severest critics have ever cast doubt on P.'s virtuosity in the use of language. His "taperecorder" ear has often been praised. And rightly: few English playwrights before him have displayed so acute an observation of the mannerisms, repetitions, and nonsensicalities of the vernacular as it is actually spoken. But there is more to P.'s use of language than merely accurate observation. In fact, what sounds like tape-recorded speech is highly stylised, even artificial. It is his ability to combine the appearance of utter reality with complete control of rhythm and nuance of meaning that is the measure of P.'s stature as a poet. P.'s dialogue is as tightly—perhaps more tightly—controlled than verse. Every syllable, every inflection, the succession of long and short sounds, words and sentences, is calculated to a nicety. And precisely the repetitiousness, the discontinuity, the circularity of ordinary vernacular speech are here used as formal elements with which the poet can compose his linguistic ballet. And yet, because the ingredients from which he takes the recurring patterns and artfully broken rhythms *are* fragments of a brilliantly observed, and often hitherto overlooked, reality, he succeeds in creating the illusion of complete naturalness, of naturalism.

Martin Esslin, *The Peopled Wound: The Work of H. P.* (1970), pp. 28–29, 30, 42–43

P.'s particular achievement has been to sustain linguistically the sort of tensions which seem to drive his characters from within. The fragmentary sentence, the phrase left hanging, the awkward pause, become outer manifestations of the inner anxiety, the deeper uncertainty. The discordant clash of language in, say, *The Caretaker,* is indicative of the discord that arises not only between character and character but within each of the characters. The fumbling efforts at conversation which ensue indicate the desperate need the characters have to make themselves known. Paraphrasing von Clausewitz's definition of "war," language becomes *a continuation of tension by other means.* On such occasions, Heidegger reminds us, language seems not so much a faculty that man possesses as that which possesses man.

But the "continuation of tension" may not always have the exchange of information as its goal. Many of P.'s characters, on the contrary, go to some length to evade being known by others. The sounds these characters exchange are a holding action, a skirmish designed to avoid the larger confrontation. P. describes such a strategy, "communication itself between people is so frightening that rather than do that there is continual crosstalk, a continual talking about other things rather than what is at the root of their relationship." One source of this circumvention of communication may derive from opposing levels of knowledge or intelligence. In *The Birthday Party,* for example, Goldberg and McCann can badger Stanley to distraction because of their continued reference to unknown forces or significant but hidden events. Or, as in *The Caretaker,* Mick can keep ahead of Davies because of his superior intelligence and wit. But the more important source of evasion arises out of the character's fear that if he reveals himself, if he comes clean, he will be at the mercy of those who know him.

James R. Hollis, *H. P.: The Poetics of Silence* (1970), pp. 123–24

One way of looking at P.'s work is to say that it is a constant strategem to uncover nakedness. The behavior of his characters is so seldom a reflection of the way people normally behave and so often a reflection of the way they would like to, if they weren't afraid to. Sometimes this behavior is a refraction of fears and anxieties in the form of actions. Violence occurs because animality is unleashed and, unlike the Greeks who took a high view of human dignity and kept the violence offstage, P. peers in through the glass wall with no reverence for humanity, no belief in our lives being mapped out by divine powers. He has a keen eye for the cracks in the surface of normal conversation and normal behavior. He is always on the alert for the moments when his characters betray what is underneath and then he simply records what he sees and what he hears; but he does not do so in order to evolve theories or to warn us against ourselves. His vision and his hearing are both highly tuned instruments, invaluable in his one-man forays into the unarticulated and irrational no-man's-land inside the modern Everyman.

Ronald Hayman, *H. P.* (1973), p. 152

Attempts to categorize P.'s plays have given rise to two descriptive terms: "comedy of menace" and "Pinteresque." ... The great danger with such terms is that they tend to become institutionalized when they are not transcended. And as they interact only minimally with the details of the plays, they tend to obscure the sublety and variety of P.'s work and contribute to the impression that his experimentation reduces to the mere repetition of a consistent formula. At a certain level of abstraction, P.'s work does deal with recurring problems: the problem of interrelational adjustment being a major one. But to give stress to less central generalizations at the expense of an acknowledgement of the great variety of his work is to promote ... circularity of thought....The point which is basic to this approach to P. is that which should be basic to any approach to language. Far from being a monolithic unity, language is an essentially pluralistic activity. Even within a certain general function, such as its interrelational use, language is characterized by variety and adaptability as well as by recurring patterns. . . . If one approaches the plays with a belief that truth, reality and communication ought to conform to certain norms, then the plays will remain tantalizingly enigmatic. But once it is realized that all of these concepts are, like any others, moves in language games, the barrier to an understanding of P. is removed.

In striving to adjust to one another, P.'s characters are negotiating not only truth and reality but their very freedom to engage their preferred identities in the environments that surround them. Their linguistic battles are not the product of an arbitrary desire for dominance but crucial battles for control of the means by which personality is created in the social systems to which they belong. As they struggle to cope, their misunderstandings and miscalculations provide a great deal of amusement for any audience, but invariably desperation and terror are eventually revealed as the linguistic warfare becomes increasingly crucial.

Austin E. Quigley, *The P. Problem* (1975), pp. 274–77

PIONTEK, Heinz

West German poet, short-story writer, novelist, editor, and essayist, b. 15 Nov. 1925, Kreuzberg

Born and raised in Upper Silesia near the Polish frontier, P. served in the armed forces toward the end of World War II. He then briefly studied German literature and held a variety of jobs before becoming a full-time writer. Among his numerous awards and honors is the Georg Büchner Prize (1976).

On the basis of his first books, the poetry collections *Die Furt* (1952; the ford) and *Die Rauchfahne* (1953; the wisp of smoke), critics praised P.'s powers of observation and originality, qualities that were to remain the hallmarks of his later works. These early poems and those of *Wassermarken* (1957; watermarks) are characterized by a variety of forms, from rhymed verse reminiscent of the poetry of Wilhelm Lehmann (1882–1968) to longer, less regular narratives. Transience is a common theme, and the mood is generally elegiac, but not without an element of Christian hope. Descriptions of nature scenes al-

ternate with observations on human existence.

Vor Augen (1955; before our eyes) firmly established P.'s reputation as a master of short fiction. As the title suggests, the style and perspective are realistic. The war and its aftermath, the suffering of the past and its lingering presence are central to these stories, which owe their power and appeal to the interplay between past and present and between internal and external reality.

P.'s later works reflect the author's subtle and consistent development as well as his continuing respect for tradition. Some poems of *Mit einer Kranichfeder* (1962; with a crane feather) are written in the laconic, aphoristic style that characterizes *Klartext* (1966; clear text) and *Tot oder lebendig* (1971; abridged tr., *Alive or Dead,* 1975). Nature, memories of childhood, and transience remain pervasive themes, and in *Tot oder lebendig* a concern with poetic process becomes important. P.'s long-standing interest in narrative poetry, reflected in essays and an anthology he edited, *Neue deutsche Erzählgedichte* (1964; new German narrative poems), culminated in *Vorkriegszeit* (1980; prewar period), a book-length poem set in the present.

The novels *Die mittleren Jahre* (1967; the middle years) and *Dichterleben* (1976; a poet's life) combine introspective passages, realistic vignettes, and flashbacks. The artistic consciousness and the tension between the outsider and the establishment are important themes. The generation gap—an especially significant problem in Germany—is central to P.'s third novel, *Juttas Neffe* (1979; Jutta's nephew).

P. remains one of German's most outstanding and versatile writers. An opponent of the radical avant-garde, his literary works, as well as his numerous essays, including those of *Männer die Gedichte machen* (1970; men who make poems), reveal a concern for poetic form and the author's quest for human values in an inhuman age.

FURTHER WORKS: *Buchstab, Zauberstab* (1959); *Weißer Panther* (1962); *Die Zwischenlandung* (1963); *Kastanien aus dem Feuer (1963); Windrichtungen* (1963); *Randerscheinungen* (1965); *Außenaufnahmen* (1968); *Liebeserklärungen in Prosa* (1969); *Die Erzählungen* (1971); *Klarheit schaffen* (1972); *Helle Tage anderswo* (1973); *Leben mit Wörtern* (1975); *Gesammelte Gedichte* (1975); *Die Zeit der anderen Auslegung* (1976); *Wintertage, Sommernächte* (1977); *Das Schweigen überbrücken* (1977); *Träumen, wachen, widerstehen* (1978); *Dunkelkammerspiel* (1978); *Wie sich Musik durchschlug* (1978); *Das Handwerk des Lesens* (1979); *Was mich nicht losläßt* (1981)

BIBLIOGRAPHY: Middleton, C., "The Poetry of H. P.," *GL&L,* 13 (1959), 55–57; Kügler, H., "Spur und Fährte," *Weg und Weglosigkeit* (1970), pp. 161–86; Domandi, A. K., ed., *Modern German Literature* (1972), Vol. II, pp. 183–87; H. P., *Leben mit Wörten* (1975), pp. 133–224; Lubos, A., *Von Bezruč bis Bienek* (1977), pp. 82–99; Exner, R., "H. P.," in Weissenberger, K., ed., *Die deutsche Lyrik 1945–1975* (1981), pp. 186–97

JERRY GLENN

PIOVENE, Guido

Italian novelist, journalist, and critic, b. 27 July 1907, Vicenza; d. 12 Nov. 1974, London, England

P. was educated in private schools and at the University of Milan, where he earned a degree in philosophy. His lifelong career in journalism began in 1927; from 1935 to 1952 he worked for *Il corriere della sera,* traveling extensively in Europe, the Soviet Union, and the U.S. During the latter part of his life, he was associated with *La stampa* of Turin.

P.'s early fiction, through 1962, reflects an intense preoccupation with deviant behavior evidenced by spiritually flawed individuals prone to violence, crime, and self-destruction. Structurally, his early work consists of retrospective, first-person narratives whose confessional tone and sustained analytical focus on behavioral motivations illuminate the characters' psychological makeup.

La gazzetta nera (written 1939, pub. 1943; the black gazette) includes five novellas whose respective protagonists, unable to repress their aversion to life, seek liberation through a criminal act. The most popular of P.'s novels, *Lettere di una novizia* (1941; *Confession of a Novice,* 1950), portrays the inner struggle of a young woman driven to murder in a desperate effort to escape convent life. The epistolary form is effectively employed to explore the manifold ways in which truth and reality are distorted to achieve selfish aims. The characters move in a climate of moral ambiguity; their sincerity and duplicity, exhaustively diagnosed, shed much light on the darker side of human consciousness.

The second stage of P.'s creative career is marked by richer introspective analysis and metaphysical reflections on the human condition. In *Le Furie* (1963; the Furies) haunting visions of the past are drawn from the author's adolescent years and youthful attraction to Fascism—also recounted in *La coda di paglia* (1962; the tail of straw). In P.'s most important work, *Le stelle fredde* (1970; the cold stars), the protagonist abandons his urban life to seek solitude and meditation. In the seclusion of his country house he discovers his insignificance in a meaningless universe and, through a visionary encounter with Dostoevsky, confronts deep perplexities about God and the afterlife. Equally revealing of P.'s despairing view of contemporary man is his last, unfinished novel, *Verità e menzogna* (1975; truth and lies), published posthumously.

P.'s distinguished activity as a journalist is represented by *De America* (1953; on America), widely regarded as a penetrating study of the U.S.; *Viaggio in Italia* (1958; traveling through Italy), a subjective account of Italian life; and *Madame la France* (1967; Madame France), a collection of articles dealing with France in the aftermath of World War II.

An original writer deeply concerned with the spiritual crisis of our time, P. brought to contemporary Italian narrative an outlook on life rich in insight, intellectual acumen, and metaphysical probing.

FURTHER WORKS: *La vedova allegra* (1931); *Pietà contro pietà* (1946); *I falsi redentori* (1949); *Lo scrittore tra la tirannide e la libertà* (1952); *Processo dell'Islam alla civiltà occidentale* (1957); *La gente che perdè Ierusalemme* (1967); *Inverno d'un uomo felice* (1977)

BIBLIOGRAPHY: Heiney, D., *America in Modern Italian Literature* (1964), pp. 44–49; Kanduth, E., *Wesenzüge der modernen italienischen Erzählliteratur: Gehalte und Gestaltung bei Buzzati, P. und Moravia* (1968), pp. 82–136; Goudet, J., "P., la morale et la métaphysique," *REI,* 15 (1969), 148–97

AUGUSTUS PALLOTTA

PIRANDELLO, Luigi

Italian dramatist, novelist, short-story writer, and poet, b. 28 June 1867, Agrigento; d. 10 Dec. 1936, Rome

P. was the second of six children born to a well-to-do Sicilian family that had been deeply involved in the struggle for Italian unity. He was destined for the study of law, but from his teens showed strong literary leanings: two manuscript notebooks of poetry date back to 1883. In 1887 he transferred from the University of Palermo to the University of Rome, where his study of Italian literature proved as short-lived as his study of law had been. He earned his doctorate in romance philology at the University of Bonn (Germany) in 1891 with a dissertation written in German on the dialect of his native region, *Laute und Lautentwickelung der Mundart von Girgenti* (facsimile ed., 1973; the sounds and their formation in the dialect of Girgenti [i.e., Agrigento]). In 1893 he settled in Rome and, aided by an allowance from his family, turned his attention to writing. He married Antonietta Portulano, a fellow Sicilian, in 1894, and in 1898 began teaching Italian language and stylistics at a teachers' college for women, a post he held until 1922. Two sons and a daughter were born between 1895 and 1899. A disaster in the sulfur mine in which his father's capital and his wife's dowry were invested cut off his private income in 1903 and forced him to turn his writing into a financially profitable activity and to stabilize his position at the college.

His first great success, the novel *Il fu Mattia Pascal* (1904; *The Late Mattia Pascal*, 1923; new tr., 1964), and two volumes of essays, *Arte e scienza* (1908; art and science) and *L'umorismo* (1908; *On Humor*, 1974), were the products of these changed circumstances. He had by that time already published four collections of poetry, his translation of Goethe's *Roman Elegies*, a narrative poem in verse, four collections of short stories—later incorporated with the many others he was to write in the two volumes of *Novelle per un anno* (1937–38; a year's worth of stories)—a full-length novel and a novelette, his first play—the one-act *L'epilogo* (1898; later retitled *La morsa; The Vise*, 1928; new tr., 1964)—and many articles on linguistic and literary topics. He was to continue to write mainly novels and short stories until 1916, at which time he was

drawn to the theater.

The years of World War I were very difficult for P.: both his sons became prisoners of war and his wife's mental illness (which had first manifested itself at the time of the mine disaster) got worse to the point that she had to enter a nursing home in 1919. From the production of his first three-act play, *Se non così...* (1915; if not so...; later retitled *La ragione degli altri* [other people's reasons]) to 1921, the date first of the spectacular failure in Rome and then the phenomenal success in Milan of *Sei personaggi in cerca d'autore* (rev. ed., 1925; *Six Characters in Search of an Author,* 1922; new tr., 1954), P. wrote and had performed sixteen plays, four of them in Sicilian dialect.

In 1922 the London and New York performances of *Sei personaggi in cerca d'autore* and the Paris performance of *Il piacere dell' onestà* (1917; *The Pleasure of Honesty,* 1923; new tr., 1962) ushered in a new period in P.'s life. More frequent and intense contacts with the theater both in Italy and abroad made him eager to try his hand at directing and producing. In 1924 he founded his own company and in 1925 inaugurated the Art Theater of Rome, for which he had won government backing. He was awarded the Nobel Prize in 1934 for "his bold and brilliant renovation of the drama and the stage." Until the very end he remained a prolific short-story writer and dramatist, renewing himself in a trajectory that had passed from the regional realism of his early work to the antitraditionalism of *teatro del grottesco* (theater of the grotesque, so called to define its combination of fantasy and seriousness), the self-reflexiveness of the plays of the theater-within-the-theater, and the symbolism of the "myth" plays.

Of P.'s seven novels, the first, *L'esclusa* (1901; *The Outcast,* 1925), is significant thematically for its unconventional treatment of adultery and historically for its subtle undermining of the assumptions of naturalism on which it appears to be based. *I vecchi e i giovani* (1908; *The Old and the Young,* 1928) is a large-scale historical novel set in 1892–94, the period that corresponds to P.'s return from Germany and his encounter with the "bankruptcy" of the new regime of united Italy. Although there is much that is "Pirandellian" in it, it was judged from the beginning to be a throwback to an earlier stage in the development of the modern novel. More original because of its protagonist—the inept "stranger in life" Mattia—and its philosophical relativism—presented as a remedy for or mitigation of the ills of existence—is *Il fu Mattia Pascal,* in which P. already plays with the idea of the "character without an author."

From a formal point of view, P.'s most interesting novels are the fragmented, kaleidoscopic, first-person narratives, *Si gira* (1915; later retitled *Quaderni di Serafino Gubbio operatore; Shoot! The Notebooks of Serafino Gubbio, Cinematograph Operator,* 1926) and *Uno, nessuno e centomila* (1926; *One, None, and a Hundred Thousand,* 1933). In *Quaderni di Serafino Gubbio* the device of the plot-within-the-plot foreshadows the later dramatic works on the theater; as a matter of fact, *Ciascuno a suo modo* (1923; *Each in His Own Way,* 1923) is based on an episode from it. In its weaving back and forth to recapture moments of the past suddenly essential to the plot, *Si gira* creates vividly the feeling of life lived without the structuring effect of a unifying concept. In its attack on the "machine that mechanizes life"—concretized in the movie camera that its protagonist operates—and in its treatment of man's alienation from his fellow men, it has lost none of its freshness.

Uno, nessuno e centomila is, on P.'s own testimony, his most important novel, the work that, had he been able to complete it when it was first begun around 1915, would have contributed to a "more exact view of my theater," for it contains the "complete synthesis of everything I have done and the source of everything I shall do." The short, discontinuous chapters of *Uno, nessuno e centomila,* with their humorous, conversational titles, are the structural counterpart of the protagonist's step-by-step discovery of the multiplicity of the personality and his final rejection of all constricting social forms in the timeless universe of madness.

P.'s short stories, the most significant body of short prose fiction in Italian literature since Boccaccio and comparable in other respects to Maupassant's, belong in any international collection devoted to the genre. They are a neglected area of his work even though rated by some critics as superior to his plays. The earliest one, "Capannetta" (1884; "The Little Hut," 1965), is a Sicilian sketch in the manner of Giovanni Verga (q.v.). Many others use the same locale and are populated by intense, tragicomic types dominated by the need to argue and dispute

and embroiled in the most muddled situations: such are the crazed lawyer Zummo in "La casa del Granella" (1905; "The Haunted House," 1938), the contentious landowner Don Lollò Zirafa in "La giara" (1909; "The Jar," 1933), or Chiàrchiaro, the bearer of the "evil eye" in "La patente" (1911; the license).

Among the best known of P.'s stories are those that, like "La giara" and "La patente," were reworked as plays or are closely related to the plays: "La signora Frola e il signor Ponza, suo genero" (1915; "Signora Frola and Her Son-in-Law, Signor Ponza," 1965), for instance, in which the narrating voice prefigures the typical Pirandellian spokesman, Laudisi, in *Così è (se vi pare)* (1917; *Right You Are! (If You Think So),* 1922), or "La tragedia di un personaggio" (1911; "A Character in Distress," 1938), in which the author's persona refuses to portray the vain Dr. Fileno, much like a later author (and play director) will refuse to tell the story of the Father and his family in *Sei personaggi in cerca d'autore.*

There is also a whole group of urban stories, from "L'eresia catara" (1905; "Professor Lamis' Vengeance," 1938) about the nearsighted professor so obsessed with his esoteric research that he does not notice he is lecturing to an empty classroom, to "La carriola" (1916?; the wheelbarrow), in which a staid, respected lawyer guards against an impulse to madness by permitting himself one carefully dosed-out moment of irrationality each day, to "Il treno ha fischiato" (1914; the train whistled), in which a harried clerk finds his own private safety valve in from time to time escaping in the imagination, "between one set of figures and the other," to Siberia or the Congo.

There are, finally, the powerful, disquieting later stories, in which the major action, however violent what actually happens is, takes place in the psyche: "La distruzione dell'uomo" (1921; "Destruction of Man," 1956), whose protagonist, maddened by the horror of the overcrowded slum in which he lives, kills a pregnant woman; "Soffio" (1931; a breath of air), whose protagonist discovers that he has the power of life and death over other men; and "Cinci" (1932; "Cinci," 1959), the story of a boy who kills another boy and then simply forgets that he had ever done it.

P.'s earliest plays were one-acters reflecting distinct tendencies in the contemporary drama: *L'epilogo* and *Il dovere del medico* (1912; *The Doctor's Duty,* 1928) are classifiable as fin-de-siècle bourgeois problem plays; *Lumìe di Sicilia* (1911; *Sicilian Limes,* 1928) and *La giara* (1917; *The Jar,* 1928) belong to the regional theater and exist in dialect versions as well as in Italian; *All'uscita* (1916; *At the Gate,* 1928) is a "profane mystery" reminiscent of Maeterlinck's (q.v.) kind of symbolism (q.v.). In *Pensaci, Giacomino!* (1916; *Better Think Twice About It,* 1955), *Il berretto a sonagli* (1917; *Cap and Bells,* 1957), and *Liolà* (1917; *Liolà,* 1952), Sicilian motifs are combined with such basic Pirandellian themes as the triumph of the irrational, the destruction of the individual's self-constructed mask, and the conflict between appearance and reality.

But P.'s first play of fundamental importance is *Così è (se vi pare),* a parable that uses a provincial bureaucratic milieu as a setting in which to demonstrate the relativity of truth and to plead for each man's right to his "phantom"—that private illusion he creates for himself and by which he lives "in perfect harmony, pacified." *Il piacere dell'onestà, Il gioco delle parti* (1918; *The Rules of the Game,* 1959), and *Tutto per bene* (1920; *All for the Best,* 1960) continue the trend of disassociation between the realistic foundations of P.'s art—reflected in the elements of the plot of the story being told—and its "philosophical" superstructure—the "particular sense of life" that gives the stories universal value (see P.'s preface to the 1925 edition of *Sei personaggi in cerca d'autore;* Eng. tr., 1952).

Enrico IV (1922; *Henry IV,* 1923) is without doubt P.'s masterpiece. Here alienation reaches the dimensions of madness: actual madness at first, and feigned madness later, as the only possible solution, short of suicide, by which the nameless protagonist can protect his "phantom" from the corrupt, egotistical, foolish, and vicious world about him. In the play—often called a tragicomedy, although not by P. himself, who considered it a tragedy—the tremendous and unequivocal pressure of life "on stage," which is one of the distinguishing features of P.'s dramaturgy, is given its fullest, shattering impact. *Vestire gli ignudi* (1922; *Naked,* 1923; new tr., *To Clothe the Naked,* 1962), whose protagonist *is* driven to suicide, is in many ways a companion piece to *Enrico IV.* Its middle-class setting, however, and a few stock char-

acters from the comic repertoire account for its elegiac, rather than tragic, tone.

In the trilogy of theater-within-theater, *Sei personaggi in cerca d'autore, Ciascuno a suo modo,* and *Questa sera si recita a soggetto* (1930; *Tonight We Improvise,* 1932), the focus shifts from the existential anguish of the protagonist to the anguish of the character in search of being (compare the short story "La tragedia di un personaggio"). What these plays actually deal with is the problem of artistic creation. While ostensibly concerned with the interaction of character, actor, and spectators in achieving the illusion of life on stage—and as such they can be read as little more than amusing though brilliant theatrical experiments—within the broader framework of P.'s thought they are evidence that the theater itself was only one concretization of the concept of artistic form. This point of view is stated with uncommon cogency in the preface to *Sei personaggi in cerca d'autore.*

A second trilogy—*La nuova colonia* (1928; *The New Colony,* 1958), *Lazzaro* (1929; *Lazarus,* 1959), and *I giganti della montagna* (1937; *The Mountain Giants,* 1958), described by P. as "myths"—marks the final stage of his development. In them the frame of reference is no longer the individual whose experience is universalized, but society itself. The last play, although left unfinished at P.'s death, belongs with his masterpieces. In the figure of the magician Cotrone, who lives with his refugees from the real world in an abandoned villa that he has turned into the realm of fantasy, P. created the last projection of himself as the self-effacing artist perceiving the abundant life swirling in never-ending movement about him.

As in the case of other artists who originally struck their public as unique and revolutionary, the passing of time has served for P., also, to reveal characteristics of his age that he shared with others. In a changing play of perspectives he has become "historicized." Yet his world view, with its pessimism, irrationalism, rebellion against convention, sympathy for the downtrodden and the misunderstood, and, at the same time, its pitiless eye for the deformed and the grotesque, continues to elicit a direct, subjective response on the part of readers and spectators that translates itself into either warm partisanship or troubled repulsion, reactions not unlike those of his first public. The controversial nature of his work—exemplarily brought out by the simultaneous official recognition accorded him by the Fascist government of Italy, the Soviet Academy that authorized the translation of his works into Russian, and the jury of the Nobel Prize—has not yet been dulled with time, and his reputation, as is true for other writers of equal stature, has grown ever stronger over the years.

FURTHER WORKS: *Pasqua di Gea* (1891); *Amori senza amore* (1894); *Elegie renane* (1895); *Il turno* (1902; *The Merry-Go-Round of Love,* 1964); *Le beffe della vita e della morte* (1902); *Quand' ero matto* (1902); *Bianche e nere* (1904); *Erma bifronte* (1906); *La vita nuda* (1908); *Suo marito* (1911); *Terzetti* (1912); *Le due maschere* (1914); *La trappola* (1915); *Erba del nostro orto* (1915); *E domani, lunedì?...* (1917); *L'innesto* (1917); *Un cavallo nella luna* (1918); *Il carnevale dei morti* (1919); *Tu ridi* (1919); *Berecche e la guerra* (1919); *Come prima, meglio di prima* (1921); *La signora Morli una e due* (1922); *La vita che ti diedi* (1924; *The Life I Gave You,* 1959); *Diana e la Tuda* (1927; *Diana and Tuda,* 1960); *L'amica delle mogli* (1927; *The Wives' Friend,* 1960); *O di uno o di nessuno* (1929); *Come tu mi vuoi* (1930; *As You Desire Me,* 1931); *Trovarsi* (1930; *To Find Oneself,* 1960); *Quando si è qualcuno* (1933; *When Somebody Is Somebody,* 1958); *Non si sa come* (1935; *No One Knows How,* 1960); *Novelle per un anno* (2 vols., 1956–57); *Tutti i romanzi* (1957); *Maschere nude* (2 vols., 1958; new ed., 1973); *Saggi, poesie, scritti varii* (1960). FURTHER VOLUMES IN ENGLISH: *One-Act Plays* (1928); *A Horse in the Moon: Twelve Short Stories* (1932); *Better Think Twice About It!, and Twelve Other Stories* (1934); *The Naked Truth, and Eleven Other Stories* (1934); *The Medals, and Other Stories* (1938); *Four Tales* (1939); *Naked Masks* (1952); *Short Stories* (1959); *To Clothe the Naked, and Two Other Plays* (1962); *The Merry-Go-Round of Love, and Selected Stories* (1964); *P.'s One-Act Plays* (1964); *Short Stories* (1964)

BIBLIOGRAPHY: MacClintock, L., *The Age of P.* (1951); Bentley, E., Introduction to *Naked Masks* (1952), pp. vii–xxvii; Vittorini, D., *The Drama of L. P.,* 2nd ed. (1957); Bishop, T., *P. and the French Theater* (1960); Brustein, R., *The Theatre of Revolt* (1964), pp. 281–317; Poggioli, R., "P. in Retrospect," *The Spirit of the Letter* (1965), pp. 146–70; Starkie, W., *L. P.,* 3rd rev. ed. (1965); Büdel, O., *P.* (1966); special P. section, *TDR,* 10, 3 (1966), 30–111; Cambon, G., ed., *P.: A Collection of Critical Essays* (1967); Moestrup, J., *The Structural Patterns of P.'s Work* (1972); Matthaei, R., *L. P.* (1973); Gilman, R., *The Making of Modern Drama* (1974), pp. 157–89; Paolucci, A., *P.'s Theater: The Recovery of the Modern Stage for Dramatic Art* (1974); Giudice, G., *P.: A Biography* (1975); Oliver, R. W., *Dreams of Passion: The Theater of L. P.* (1979); Ragusa, O., *L. P.: An Approach to His Theatre* (1980); Valency, M., *The End of the World: An Introduction to Contemporary Drama* (1980), pp. 84–205

OLGA RAGUSA

. . . If the great human gift is that of words, by what diabolic plan does it happen that words multiply misunderstanding? The very humanity of man increases his isolation. Such is the idea "behind" one of P.'s most famous ideas. "Multiple personality" is a similar instance: Pirandellian man is isolated not only from his fellows but also from himself at other times. Further than this, isolation cannot go. This is a "nihilistic vision" with a vengeance.

Perhaps it would nowadays be called an existentialist vision: life is absurd, it fills one with nausea and dread and anguish, it gives one the metaphysical shudder, yet, without knowing why, perhaps just because one is *there,* in life, one faces it, one fights back, one cries out in pain, in rage, in defiance (if one is a Sicilian existentialist), and since all living, all life, is improvisation, one improvises some values. Their Form will last until Living destroys them and we have to improvise some more.

P.'s plays grew from his own torment (I overlook for the moment the few precious pages that grew from his joy) but through his genius they came to speak for all the tormented and, potentially, *to* all the tormented, that is, to all men. And they will speak with particular immediacy until the present crisis of mankind—a crisis which trembles, feverishly or ever so gently, through all his plays—is past.

Eric Bentley, Introduction to L. P., *Naked Masks* (1952), p. xxvii

P. is a realist. In his long and great career as a writer he has sought to portray individuals as such rather than to present them through the concept of man, stately but abstract. He has always molded his art after the individuals that he has met, known, and studied, who have touched both his sense of humor and his heart. His powerful imagination and his genius have done the rest in transporting them from the tumult of life into the serenity of his art.

We are not using the term "realist" in the usual sense of the word. P. is a realist in the sense that he tries to encompass within the scope of his art the basic, instinctive needs of man together with the secret torment of his soul and the mobile life of his intellect. Man is one in his various attributes, and P. has pictured to us the drama of humanity as he sees it and feels it. In so doing he has joined the ranks of the great who have from time to time appeared under all skies.

Domenico Vittorini, *The Drama of L. P.*, 2nd ed. (1957), p. 9

P.'s most original achievement in his experimental plays, then, is the dramatization of the very act of creation. If he has not made a statue that moves, he has made a statue which is the living signature of the artist, being both his product and his process. The concept of the face and the mask has become the basis for a totally new relationship between the artist and his work. Thus, P. completes that process of Romantic internalizing begun by Ibsen and Strindberg. Ibsen, for all his idealization of personality, still believed in an external reality available to all, and so did Chekhov, Brecht, and Shaw. Strindberg had more doubts about this reality, but believed it could be partially perceived by the inspired poet and seer. For P., however, objective reality has become virtually inaccessible, and all one can be sure of is the illusion-making faculty of the subjective mind. After P., no dramatist has been able to write with quite the same certainty as before. In P.'s plays, the messianic impulse spends itself, before it even fully develops, in doubts, uncertainties, and confusions.

Robert Brustein, *The Theatre of Revolt* (1964), pp. 315–16

When all the characters of the Pirandellian universe shall have faded into thin air, the author will nevertheless be remembered for his curious humour made up of contradiction. In an exceedingly interesting volume on *Humour* he analyses his ideas on the subject and makes them fit into the scheme of Italian literature. Every true humourist, according to P., is also a critic—a fantastic critic. For in the conception of a work of art reflection becomes a form of sentiment, as it were a mirror in which sentiment watches itself. And he gives many examples to show that reflection is like icy water in which the flame of sentiment quenches itself. Thus we can explain the frequent digressions which occur in the novels and plays, digressions which are always due to the disturbing effect caused by the active reflection of the author. The Pirandellian humour arises by antithesis. In the mind of a man a thought cannot arise

without at the same time causing a directly opposite and contrary one to appear, and so free, unfettered emotion or sentiment, instead of soaring aloft like the lark in the clear air, finds itself held back just at the moment that it stretches out its wings to fly.

Walter Starkie, *L. P., 1967–1936*, 3rd rev. ed. (1965), p. 270

If P. does explode the notion of a fixed personal identity, this by no means implies the moral annihilation of the individual self; on the contrary, the effect may be to dissuade human beings from taking themselves and one another for granted. In P.'s fictional world, the elusive reality of personal existence impinges on our awareness precisely because it is felt to be inaccessible to ready-made definitions. The capital question of whether his work is poetry or just abstract speculation will have to be settled case by case, and more attention to the physiognomy of his style than has generally been applied so far should prove very helpful here. As a result, instead of labeling him a dramatist or novelist of ideas, we can more aptly speak of his whole work as an exploration of consciousness. It is as a drama of consciousness that it retains relevance, to the extent that the ideas operate functionally in each formal embodiment. Once this focus is established, many critical problems will become clearer....

Glauco Cambon, ed., Introduction to *P.: A Collection of Critical Essays* (1967), p. 9

P.'s relativism stems from his antirationalist notions which aim at destroying any and every illusion or fiction of man and society, tearing off the mask man fashions for himself or society forces on him. Nowhere more than in the bleak environment P. has chosen as his domain is appearance more important. The lower we get in the animal world and its species, the more important and the more effective mimicry becomes, and the lower we get in terms of social conditions, the more important fictions, fronts, and appearances become in the struggle of life. Neither the peasants, who are still close to life, to the origin of things, nor the affluent need care about appearances; they, too, do have concerns and taboos, but of a different sort. It is the bleak social segment in between, that vegetates in tenement houses at the edge of cities . . . , that needs these appearances; the white collar worker who ekes out a measly existence . . ., the decrepit professional . . . , the small-time charlatan. . . . Indeed, no social group lends itself better to a demonstration of the relative value of human appearances; and that is what P. set out to do.

Oscar Büdel, *P.* (1969), p. 58

In his last plays, P. is in effect drawing the chief meridians of his theatrical world upward to con-

HAROLD PINTER

LUIGI PIRANDELLO

FRANCIS PONGE

KATHERINE ANNE PORTER

verge at a single pole. This whole business of life can be for us all no more than a tale told by an idiot unless we get deep enough below the surface of conventional values to the substantive core. What blind Oedipus "saw" at Colonus, what Orestes experienced in Athene's court of ultimate appeal, what Shakespeare reveals to us in the magic art of Prospero and in Cranmer's prophecy at the christening of the child destined to become Queen Elizabeth—such is the substance of P.'s myth plays. In them he gathers up all that he had already dramatized, into a new synthesis, to show us its social, religious, and artistic reality, in its rightness, its holiness, and its beauty.

P.'s theatrical world is planted deep in the common soil of human experience, with a sturdy weathered and twisted trunk of theatrical expertise that enables him to review for us dramatically the meaning of theater, and with marvelous branches of evergreen leaves that come and go imperceptibly, laden with seasonal fruit. Just before he died, P. had a vision of such a tree—the great Saracen olive of Sicily. He explained to his son, on the morning of the day before his death, that with that tree planted in the center of the stage, for the curtain to come down in the unwritten final act of *The Mountain Giants,* he would solve everything he meant to show. That great tree, whose roots he had revealed in his masterful *Liolà,* was meant to symbolize the completion of his theater.

Anne Paolucci, *P.'s Theater: The Recovery of the Modern Stage for Dramatic Art* (1974), pp. 20–21

. . . The genius of P.'s accomplishments lies in his ability to suggest the need for the movement from an *avvertimento* [awareness] to a *sentimento del contrario* [feeling of the opposite], not merely in content, but in the dramatic encapsulation of those ideas. He became a theatrical innovator in a much deeper and more important sense than the Futurists, Surrealists, and Dadaists, whose alternative vision was couched in terms that made it inaccessible to those very people who needed to be confronted with it. P.'s initial reception gives evidence that his work also met resistance. Yet his retention of aspects of conventional realism allowed him both to draw his audience into his world in order to frustrate their old expectations and, more important, to communicate the relationship of his new vision to their everyday reality.

Roger W. Oliver, *Dreams of Passion: The Theater of L. P.* (1979), p. 156

PIRES, José Cardoso

Portuguese novelist, short-story writer, essayist, and dramatist, b. 2 Oct. 1925, Pêso

P.'s birth was almost contemporaneous with that of the beginning of the dictatorship in Portugal (1926–74). After studying advanced mathematics in Lisbon, P. held a variety of jobs. He became involved in magazine publishing and has been the chief editor of several magazines and newspapers. His commitment to a sociopolitical literature resulted from his early literary contacts with the neorealist (q.v.) movement. His openly avowed political beliefs during the dictatorship years not only brought great attention to his writings, but also resulted in continual problems with the regime's censorship.

In the 1940s and early 1950s P. had difficulties in getting his short stories published because they vividly presented the bleaker aspects of everyday Portuguese life, such as widespread rural impoverishment, the demoralizing military life, political repression, and the mistreatment of the aged. Several of these stories were collected in *Jogos de azar* (1963; games of chance).

O anjo ancorado (1958; the anchored angel), P.'s first novel, presented a society enduring in a centuries-old state of chaotic numbness. Its victims—the wealthy, the cultured, and the impoverished—are no longer capable of reacting to common class confrontations except through deceit and physical violence. The great depths and extremes of this national malaise were further developed in P.'s prize-winning *O hóspede de Job* (1963; Job's guest), in which the recurrent metaphor for the Portuguese is that of beasts of burden, plodding along aimlessly, abusing and being abused. P.'s sophisticated use of cinematic techniques and his extremely penetrating characterizations resulted in his most dynamic stylistic achievement.

P.'s treatise *Cartilha do marialva* (1960; primer for the *marialva* [rural macho male]) delved into the historical origin of the common Portuguese "macho" type. The feudal life style that reigned in Portugal well into the 20th c. is viewed as the major catalyst for the creation of this negative, hedonistic kind of person. The novel *O delfim* (1968; the dauphin) is P.'s literary investigation into the nature of a *marialva.*

The life of the late dictator Salazar was parodied in *Dinossauro excelentíssimo* (1974; most excellent dinosaur). The parliamentary debate that accompanied the publication of this "fable" was caused by P.'s exaggerated and biting satire.

P.'s works have reflected the pulse of Portugal's sociopolitical change from a purely rural society to an insignificant industrial one. Although the style of his novels is simple and direct, he attains a profundity of thought and purpose that no other contemporary Portuguese writer has approached. His ultimate goal is to discover the key to the almost masochistic national soul. His most recent collection of essays, *E agora, José?* (1977; what next, José?), reaffirms this interest. It presents, however, a rather negative, doubting tone about Portugal's future in the post-1974 revolutionary period.

FURTHER WORKS: *Os caminheiros, e outros contos* (1946); *Histórias de amor* (1952); *O render dos heróis* (1960); *O corpo-delito na sala de espelhos* (1979); *O burro-em-pé (contos)* (1979)

BIBLIOGRAPHY: Ares Montes, J., on *O hóspede de Job, Ínsula,* 212 (1964), 16; on *O delfim, TLS,* 29 Jan. 1970, 115; Stern, I., on *E agora, José?, WLT,* 52 (1978), 611–12

IRWIN STERN

PITTER, Ruth
English poet, b. 7 Nov. 1897, Ilford

Oldest of three children born to two London elementary schoolteachers, P. started writing verse at five and published her first poem at thirteen, in A. R. Orage's *New Age* (later *New English Weekly*). She worked as a War Office clerk in World War I; after the war she mastered various crafts (especially woodworking and painting) and worked first for a large specialty firm and later in partnership in her own shop in London until 1945; she then retired to Aylesbury, where she still resides. Among the awards she has received are the Hawthornden Prize (1937), the Heinemann Award (1954), and the Queen's Gold Medal for Poetry (1955).

P.'s poetry is frequently identified as reflecting a 17th-c. mind, and comparisons have been made with the work of Henry Vaughan, Thomas Traherne, and Thomas Carew, as well as with such other poets as Edmund Spenser, William Blake, John Clare, and Gerard Manley Hopkins. She writes lyrical verse on a wide range of traditional subjects, notably the natural world and religion. Her combination of metaphysical passion and a vivid sensual awareness springs at least in part from her identification with and precise knowledge of the English countryside, gardening, and a life of physical labor. She thus

appeals to both the heart and the mind, and her "perfect ear and exact epithet" (to quote Hilaire Belloc [q.v.], one of her first major supporters) produces a balanced, deeply felt, and often deceptively simple lyric.

She herself believes that a poem "begins and ends in mystery . . . in that secret movement of the poet's being, in response to the secret dynamism of life," and many of her poems are contemplative celebrations, such as "The Fishers" (1939) and "The Cygnet" (1945); the latter poem, one of her longest, uses two swans on the Thames to represent the soul's victory over evil. Similar poems include "Urania" (1936), "The Eternal Image" (1936), and "The Downward-Pointing Muse" (1939). But she is also capable of writing sardonic, witty verse, such as the poems in *The Rude Potato* (1941) and *R. P. on Cats* (1947), the latter less "old-maidish" (P.'s term) and rollicking than the similar volume by her acquaintance T. S. Eliot (q.v.).

P. is neither experimental nor avant-garde, and her use of traditional meters and forms sets her apart from most modern poets. Nor does she reflect much topical interest in the hurried world around her (although her "The Military Harpist" [1939] is both serious and sardonic in its subdued commentary about war). Rather, her vivid, precise, always apt sensitivity celebrates silence and contemplation, especially in the contrast between ordinary life and the Christian hope, or in the personification of natural beauty and life as reflective of divine reality.

Although highly praised by some critics and many other poets, P. has never been a fashionable or popular writer, has never been identified with any "school" or movement, and has lived in comparative but wholly unjustified obscurity. Her talent, dedication, and virtuosity warrant much higher critical esteem.

FURTHER WORKS: *First Poems* (1920); *First and Second Poems* (1930); *Persephone in Hades* (1931); *A Mad Lady's Garland* (1934); *A Trophy of Arms* (1936); *The Spirit Watches* (1939); *Poem* (1943); *The Bridge* (1945); *Urania* (1951); *The Ermine* (1953); *Still by Choice* (1966); *Poems 1926–1966* (1968 Am., *Collected Poems,* 1969); *End of Drought* (1975)

BIBLIOGRAPHY: Bogan, L., "A Singular Talent," *Poetry,* 51 (1937), 43–45; Swartz, R. T., "The Spirit Watches," *Poetry,* 56 (1940),

334–37; Gilbert, R., *Four Living Poets* (1944), pp. 48–54; Watkin, E. I., *Poets & Mystics* (1953), pp. 301–18; special P. section, *Poetry Northwest*, 1, 3 (1960), 3–20; Wain, J., "A Note on R. P.'s Poetry," *Listener*, 81 (1969), 239–40; Russell, A., ed., *R. P.: Homage to a Poet* (1969)

PAUL SCHLUETER

PLATH, Sylvia

American poet, novelist, and short-story writer, b. 27 Oct. 1932, Winthrop, Mass.; d. 11 Feb. 1963, London, England

P. graduated from Smith College, and while on a Fulbright scholarship to Cambridge, met and married the English poet Ted Hughes (q.v.) in 1956. She had suffered a nervous breakdown in 1953 while at Harvard Summer School and had twice attempted suicide. In *Letters Home* (1975), the volume of correspondence edited by her mother, there emerges a self-portrait of a young woman driven by hopes for the highest success alternating with moods of deep depression. After marital difficulties and a period of physical and psychological strain, P. committed suicide.

P.'s early poetry was somewhat derivative and academic, based on the then current styles of refined and ironic verse. Then, under the influence of her husband and the work of Dylan Thomas (q.v.) and Gerard Manley Hopkins, the promise and depth of her talent developed rather suddenly and with great force. Often thought of as a "confessional" poet, since she studied with Anne Sexton (1928–1974) in Robert Lowell's (q.v.) Harvard class, P. became more and more a mythic poet. Her later work, especially the volume *Ariel* (1966), was remarkable for its tight syntactic pressures and its obsessive imagery. Resembling somewhat the work of the German poet Gottfried Benn (q.v.)—with its expressionist (q.v.) nihilism and atavistic urgings—P.'s lyric mode was dominated by a fierce commitment to the most exalted ideal of artistic intensity: "The blood jet is poetry,/There is no stopping it."

In her well-known poems "Lady Lazarus" (1963) and "Daddy" (1963) P. pushes the traditions of self-revelation and lyric intimacy in directions not often explored in the English or American idiom. One predecessor might be Emily Dickinson, but P. has no fund of biblical or hymnbook imagery to cre-

ate a sense of herself as a representative sufferer. Instead, many of the assumptions of Freudian psychology, especially with its paradigms of family conflict, self-disgust, and "split" awareness, underpin the poetry's dynamic surge toward revelation. The poetry apparently asks for no pity, and the deepest motives for its unveilings remain obscure, although clearly powerful.

P.'s poetry is not easily accessible, but she gained a considerable reputation when her novel, *The Bell Jar* (1971; English ed. published pseudonymously, 1962), appeared and won a readership drawn largely from college students. The novel is semiautobiographical, and its portraits of several characters are ripe with a controlled sense of invective (hence the use of a pseudonym). P.'s depiction of psychological disorder and the experience of recuperation in a mental hospital are especially affecting; in many ways this depiction parallels R. D. Laing's (b. 1927) account, in the popular *The Divided Self* (1960), of what he terms "ontological insecurity."

In addition to the novel, P. published several short stories, most of them in "slick" magazines. She was also occupied with writing feature stories and travel pieces, many of which were never published. *The Collected Poems* (1981) and *The Journals of S. P.* (1982), the latter with a preface by Ted Hughes, showed that her stature was still high—many reviewers praised both volumes. Unfortunately, the journals for the months immediately preceding her suicide were destroyed or lost. The questions surrounding her last, intensely creative period will still be posed, but may prove unanswerable.

Those who value P. highly see her as a starkly honest poet, often working with such contemporary themes as the woman-victim in a patriarchal society. Others find her reputation overblown, feeling that her emphasis on individual psychological disorders is finally narrow and stultifying. In part her reputation has risen and fallen with the fortunes of "confessional poetry." But her language continues to have an undeniable power, and her genius for exfoliating imagery to capture a sense of emotional distress is indeed distinctive. It will be increasingly difficult for readers and critics to separate the merits of the work from the lurid elements of the biography. But it will also be hard to ignore her considerable gift for verbalizing a certain extreme psychological reality that has been one of the chief concerns of modern literature.

FURTHER WORKS: *The Colossus, and Other Poems* (1962); *Crossing the Water* (1971); *Winter Trees* (1972); *Johnny Panic and the Bible of Dreams* (1979)

BIBLIOGRAPHY: Newman, C., ed., *The Art of S. P.* (1970); Alvarez, A., *The Savage God* (1972), pp. 3–42; Steiner, N., *A Closer Look at "Ariel"* (1973); Holbrook, D., *S. P.: Poetry and Existence* (1976); Kroll, J., *Chapters in a Mythology: The Poetry of S. P.* (1976); Lane, G., ed., *S. P.: New Views on the Poetry* (1979); Broe, M. L., *Protean Poet: The Poetry of S. P.* (1980)

CHARLES MOLESWORTH

PLATONOV, Andrey Platonovich

Russian novelist and short-story writer, b. 20 Aug. 1899, Yamskaya Sloboda (near Voronezh); d. 5 Jan. 1951, Moscow

P., the son of a metalworker, had his first job at the age of thirteen. In 1924 he finished polytechnical school with an engineering degree. After several years as a specialist in land reclamation (1923–26), he permanently abandoned engineering for writing.

P. began writing in the early 1920s, with some two hundred articles of a journalistic or essayistic nature, as well as his first stories and his only book of verse, the often bombastic and undistinguished *Golubaya glubina* (1922; blue depths). Initially, P. shared with many of his fellow writers a nearly messianic faith in the power of man to transform and *defeat* nature, to reshape the world, and ultimately the universe, to suit his own ends. Yet, in one of P.'s earliest stories, "Potomki solntsa" (1921; descendants of the sun), and in "Efirny trakt" (1927; the etheric way), he warned against both the potentially destructive evil inherent in technological advance and the hypertrophy of mind at the expense of feelings and scruples. While machines would remain dear to P. the engineer, by the end of the 1920s interest in technology became secondary in his work to a focus on man's restless quest for self-knowledge and meaning in life, his battle to overcome isolation and to survive in a hostile world.

In the late 1920s and early 1930s P. became increasingly skeptical of Soviet socioeconomic experimentation, with its tendency to place bureaucratic imperatives over both the individual and collective interests of workers and peasants. This attitude can be seen in stories like "Usomnivshiisya Makar" (1929; "Makar the Doubtful," 1974) and "Vprok" (1931; for future use) and in novels like *Chevengur* (1972; *Chevengur,* 1978) and *Kotlovan* (1969; *The Foundation Pit,* 1973). *Chevengur,* which has never been published in the Soviet Union, dates from 1929 and is a satirical, folkloristic account of naïve Communist visionaries leading the masses to destitution. *Kotlovan,* which dates from the early 1930s, was P.'s answer to the call to depict new socialist construction and collectivization—which he did in a grimly phantasmagorical, and at times, surrealistic way.

P.'s reservations about the course of Soviet development earned him severe reproval from critics and caused him difficulties in getting his fiction published during the 1930s. Some of his stories were printed in journals, but only one small collection appeared separately: *Reka Potudan* (1937; *The River Potudan,* 1978), which, besides the title story, included several of P.'s best stories, "Takyr" (1934; "The Takyr," 1978), "Fro" (1936; "Fro," 1967), and "Treti syn" (1937; "The Third Son," 1969). During the "great terror" of the late 1930s P. turned to literary criticism and stories for children.

World War II offered new opportunities to write, and P. responded with six separate collections of sketches between 1942 and 1945. After his return from the front, he was once more officially rebuked, this time for the story first published under the title "Semya Ivanova"—later changed to "Vozvrashchenie"—(1936; "The Homecoming," 1970). In broken health, P. spent his last years revamping folk literature, with which many of his own works had had much in common.

P.'s artistic craft was formed by the literary experimentation of the Soviet 1920s—extreme compositional diffusion, heavy emphasis on stylistic expressiveness. Although he shared in the gray, sobering development that marked Soviet literature overall from the early 1930s until many years after Stalin's death in 1953, certain constants remained in the best of his fiction: the depiction of restless vagabonds, for whom domestic life is either not satisfying or impossible; close attention to simple, usually inarticulate people whose experiences are given an inimitable poetic quality through P.'s highly creative manipulation of roughhewn, but expressive common speech. That these experiences were usually sorrowful, even tragic, did not help P. fit into a literature that expected optimism from its writers. Still, P.'s uncommon talent, social background, and education equipped him as few others to depict the life of Russians during a particularly momentous period in their country's history. The rediscovery of P. in his homeland and the growing awareness of him abroad are among the brightest developments in post-Stalinist Russian literature.

FURTHER WORKS: *Gorod Gradov* (1926; *The City of Gradov,* 1978); *Epifanskie shliuzy* (1927; *The Epifan Locks,* 1974); *Dzhan* (written 1933–35, pub. 1966; *Dzhan,* 1970); *Izbrannye rasskazy* (1958); *V prekrasnom i yarostnom mire: Povesti i rasskazy* (1965); *Izbrannoe* (1966); *V preskrasnom i yarostnom mire: Povesti i rasskazy* (1979). FURTHER VOLUME IN ENGLISH: *The Fierce and Beautiful World: Stories by A. P.* (1970)

BIBLIOGRAPHY: Yevtushenko, Y., "Without Me, the Country's Not Complete," in *The Fierce and Beautiful World: Stories by A. P.* (1970), pp. 7–18; Brodsky, J., Preface to *The Foundation Pit/Kotlovan* (1973), pp. ix–xii; Jordan, M., *A. P.* (1973); Jordan, M., "A. P.," *RLT,* No. 8 (1974), 363–72; Yahushev, H., "A. P.'s Artistic Model of the World," *RLT,* No. 16 (1979), 171–88; Teskey, A., "The Theme of Science in the Early Works of A. P.," *Irish Slavonic Series,* No. 1 (1980), 3–19

ROBERT L. BUSCH

PLOMER, William

South African novelist, poet, short-story writer, and librettist (writing in English), b. 10 Dec. 1903, Pietersburg; d. 22 Sept. 1973, London, England

After completing his education in South Africa and England, P. worked on a farm and on a trading station with his father. By the time he was nineteen, he was writing verse and had begun *Turbott Wolfe* (1925), his first novel. His writing brought him into contact with Roy Campbell (q.v.) and Laurens van der Post (b. 1906), with whom he cofounded the significant although short-lived literary magazine *Voorslag.* In 1926 P. went to Japan, where he lived until 1929. He returned to England, where he was to spend the larger part of his life. In 1963 he was

awarded the Queen's Gold Medal for Poetry; he was President of the Poetry Society from 1968 to 1971.

Of P.'s five novels, *Turbott Wolfe* is the most renowned; it has recently received renewed attention from South African and American critics. *Turbott Wolfe* shows an Africa capable of developing within its own civilization, despite the intervention of Western values. Its focus, as the eponymous narrator states, is on the "unavoidable question of colour." It is written with enormous force and descriptive power, but it is structurally uneven: there is an anecdotal quality to the events described, and the ineffectual narrator is incapable of serving as a unifying device. The novel flashes with understated wit, interspersed with a coarse humor, like the coarseness of the world he describes.

P. was a prolific poet; like his short stories, his verse is a reflection of personal experience. The strength of his poetry lies in its descriptive power, its economy of detail, and its symbolic imagery. He wrote of Africa from the colonial perspective, and in his poems written in Japan and Europe the point of view is that of a concerned foreigner. The phrase "Ballads Abroad," the title P. gave to a section of his *Collected Poems* (1960; expanded ed., 1973), suggests the position with which he was most comfortable, that of the tolerant outsider, generally observing with detached humor and ironic wit. He had a great love of landscape and used natural detail to capture impressions of local atmosphere. In two poems written in Japan, "The Aburaya" and "Hotel Magnificent," collectively labeled "Two Hotels" in the *Collected Poems,* a sense of nostalgia is expressed for a delicate and transient culture, contrasted with the hollowness of a "tradition" ready-made for foreigners.

A poem that expresses many of P.'s central concerns is "The Scorpion," one of the "African Poems" in the *Collected Poems.* It speaks of the drowning of an African culture: both the traditional domestic and magical elements have been swept away. The poem focuses on two images, the corpse of a black woman and a scorpion, which P. uses to convey the demise of an Africa that was dangerous, sensuous, and noble.

P. also worked as a librettist with Benjamin Britten: their collaborations include the opera *Gloriana* (1953) for the coronation of Queen Elizabeth II. P.'s autobiography *Double Lives* (1943) describes with wit and detachment the early part of his life, in South Africa.

P. can be regarded as representing the beginnings of the "protest novel" in South Africa; however, critics now generally see him as a writer whose outlook was shaped by his world view as a liberal humanist in the tradition of Joseph Conrad (q.v.). In his writings about Africa there is a sense of his alienation from the country he lived in and loved but never fully possessed.

FURTHER WORKS: *I Speak of Africa* (1927); *Notes for Poems* (1927); *The Family Tree* (1929); *Paper Houses* (1929); *Sado* (1931; Am., *They Never Came Back*); *The Fivefold Screen* (1932); *The Case Is Altered* (1932); *The Child of Queen Victoria* (1933); *Cecil Rhodes* (1933); *The Invaders* (1934); *Visiting the Caves* (1936); *Ali the Lion* (1936; rpt. as *The Diamond of Jannina: Ali Pasha 1741–1822,* 1970); *Selected Poems* (1940); *The Dorking Thigh, and Other Satires* (1945); *Curious Relations* (1945, under pseud. William D'Arfey); *Four Countries* (1949); *Museum Pieces* (1952); *A Shot in the Park* (1955); *Borderline Ballads* (1955); *At Home* (1958); *Curlew River* (libretto, 1965); *The Burning Fiery Furnace* (libretto, 1966); *Taste and Remember* (1966); *The Prodigal Son* (libretto, 1968); *Celebrations* (1972); *The Butterfly Ball and the Grasshopper Feast* (1973); *The Autobiography of W. P.* (1975); *Electric Delights* (1977)

BIBLIOGRAPHY: Margery, K., "The South African Novel and Race," *SoRA,* 1 (1963), 27–46; Doyle, J. R., Jr., *W. P.* (1969); Rabkin, D., "Race and Fiction: [Sarah Gertrude Milin's] *God's Stepchildren* and *Turbott Wolfe,*" in Parker, K., ed., *The South African Novel in English* (1978), pp. 77–94; Marquard, J., Introduction to *A Century of South African Short Stories* (1978), pp. 22–31; Hallet, R., "The Importance of *Voorslag:* Roy Campbell, W. P., and the Development of South African Literature," *Theoria,* 50 (1978), 29–39; Herbert, M., "The Early Writings of W. P.: Some New Material," *ESA,* 22 (1979), 13–26; Gray, S., ed., *W. P., Turbott Wolfe,* with background pieces by Laurens van der Post, Roy Campbell, Michael Herbert, Nadine Gordimer, Peter Wilhelm, David Brown, and Stephen Gray (1980)

GILLIAN L. G. NOERO

POLGAR, Alfred

(born Alfred Polak) Austrian theater critic, journalist, short-story writer, and satirical dramatist, b. 17 Oct. 1873, Vienna; d. 24 April 1955, Zurich, Switzerland

P. was born into a petit-bourgeois family of restricted means. His father was a piano teacher; of his mother little is known. From the beginning of his career he used the pseudonym Polgar, which became his legal name in 1914. A habitué of the now legendary Vienna literary coffeehouses Griensteidl and Central, he began his career as a reporter and drama critic. As Vienna theater correspondent, he was among the first contributors to Siegfried Jacobsohn's *Weltbühne,* published in Berlin. From the mid-1920s on P. lived mostly in Berlin, where he also wrote regularly for the literary weekly *Das Tagebuch* and for its successor, *Das neue Tagebuch.* Hitler's rise to power in 1933 forced him to return to Vienna.

After the 1938 Anschluss P. lived precariously as an exile in Prague, Zurich, and Paris, before emigrating to America in 1940. For two years he held an unproductive and unrewarding post as "literary adviser" to M-G-M in Hollywood. In 1943 he moved to New York, where he contributed to *Aufbau,* the German-Jewish émigré weekly. He returned to Europe in 1949 and settled in Zurich, resuming activity as a drama critic and correspondent. The experiences of emigration and return are depicted in *Anderseits: Erzählungen und Erwägungen* (1948; on the other hand: stories and considerations) and in *Im Lauf der Zeit* (1954; in the course of time), another collection of short prose pieces.

As a master of the short form, P. followed in the Viennese tradition of Peter Altenberg (1859–1919), whom he deeply admired and whose unpublished writings he edited in 1925. Although P.'s literary stature was lastingly confirmed with *An den Rand geschrieben* (1926; written in the margins), a collection of prose sketches, and *Orchester von oben* (1926; orchestra from above), a collection of short narratives, no one title, or combination of titles, among the many he published can be designated as his major or most characteristic work. His books are almost exclusively collections of theater reviews, sketches, and short satirical-critical essays. They are typified by their originality and lucidity of expression and by a seemingly effortless stylistic brilliance.

P.'s ethical and literary kinship to Karl Kraus (q.v.) is evidenced in *Kleine Zeit* (1919; small times), an anthology of sketches from the "home front" in which he exposes the "satanic imbecility" that nourishes and accompanies war. As a journalist he restored to the feuilleton a standard of excellence and responsibility it had not enjoyed in Vienna since Ludwig Speidel (1830–1906). His drama reviews and portraits of actors, first collected in the four volumes of *Ja und nein: Schriften des Kritikers* (1926–27; yes and no: the critic's papers), offer a panorama of the contemporary stage. Their strikingly artistic qualities, combined with an often biting wit, may actually work to obscure their critical substance. Of the satirical playlets he composed in collaboration with Egon Friedell (q.v.), the most successful was *Goethe: Eine Szene* (1908; Goethe: a scene).

The number of distinguished colleagues whose admiration P. gained during his long career testifies convincingly to his exceptional literary rank; it includes Franz Kafka, Kurt Tucholsky, Joseph Roth, and Walter Benjamin (qq.v.), in addition to Kraus. The qualities they esteemed in him—above all, his enlightening wit and, along with the brilliance, the integrity of his language—are not, however, entirely identical with the ones that fostered his broader popularity. Beguiled by the sparkle and buoyancy of his style, readers were prone to miss his trenchant insights into social abuses and the frailty of the human condition. The characterization "master of the short form," while incontestably apt, was applied in wholesale manner to describe a P. who makes for light, entertaining reading; his skepticism and his defense of humane values were largely unnoticed.

While the case for a "political" P. must be argued with caution—he was not an activist or adherent to any doctrine—to judge his work properly one must also take account of his social-critical themes, and of their provocative intent. More recent and discriminating P. editions, from Bernt Richter's *Auswahl* (1968; selected writings) to Ulrich Weinzierl's *Taschenspiegel* (1979; pocket mirror), promise to further such recognition and thereby reveal more clearly how P. employed his mastery of the "short form" to create an oeuvre that is both artistically and ethically compelling.

FURTHER WORKS: *Der Quell des Übels* (1908); *Der Petroleumkönig; oder, Donauzauber* (1908, with Egon Friedell); *Bewegung ist alles* (1909); *Brahms Ibsen* (1910); *Talmas Tod* (1910, with Armin Friedmann); *Soldatenleben im Frieden* (1910, with Egon Friedell); *Hiob* (1912); *Max Pallenberg* (1921); *Gestern und heute* (1922); *Ich bin Zeuge* (1928); *Schwarz auf weiß* (1928); *Hinterland* (1929); *Bei dieser Gelegenheit* (1930); *Auswahlband* (1930); *Die Defraudanten* (1931); *Ansichten* (1933); *In der Zwischenzeit* (1935); *Der Sekundenzeiger* (1937); *Handbuch des Kritikers* (1938); *Geschichten ohne Moral* (1943); *Im Vorübergehen* (1947); *Begegnung im Zwielicht* (1951); *Standpunkte* (1953); *Fensterplatz* (1959); *Im Vorüberfahren* (1960); *Bei Lichte betrachtet* (1970); *Die Mission des Luftballons* (1975); *Sperrsitz* (1980); *Lieber Freund!: Lebenszeichen aus der Fremde* (1981)

BIBLIOGRAPHY: Musil, R., *Tagebücher, Aphorismen, Essays und Reden* (1957), pp. 750–55; Schümann, K., *Im Bannkreis von Gesicht und Wirken* (1959), pp. 135–70; Pollak, F., "A. P.: An Introduction," *TriQ,* 2 (1959), 35–39; Greuner, R., *Gegenspieler: Profile linksbürgerlicher Publizisten aus Kaiserreich und Weimarer Republik* (1969), pp. 127–57; Warde, A., "A. P.," in Spalek, J. P., and Strelka, J., eds., *Deutsche Exilliteratur seit 1933* (1976), Vol. I, pp. 581–90; Weinzierl, U., *Er war Zeuge: A. P.* (1978); Philippoff, E., *A. P.: Ein moralischer Chronist seiner Zeit* (1980)

SIDNEY ROSENFELD

POLISH LITERATURE

1900–18

The second part of the 19th c. was the period of the realistic novel in Poland. In this respect Polish literature displayed a development very similar to that in other literatures in both western and eastern Europe, although in relationship to the West there was the usual delay of several decades. In the same way as the works of Balzac, Stendhal, and even Flaubert in France, Dickens and Thackeray in England, and Tolstoy, Turgenev, and Dostoevsky in Russia, had their sources in romanticism but developed a distinctly different, realistic method, a realistic vision of the world, so were Bolesław Prus (pseud. of Aleksander Głowacki, 1845–1912), Eliza Orzeszkowa (1842–1910), and Henryk Sienkiewicz (q.v.), representatives of a similar development of this genre in Poland. Since the creative activity of all three of them carried into the 20th c., they also absorbed some later ideas. All three became quite well known outside Poland, so much so that when Sienkiewicz was awarded the Nobel Prize in literature (1905), those literary critics, in Sweden and especially in France, who had hopes for their national artists, used Sienkiewicz's enormous popularity as a possible argument against the Polish artist. His novel *Quo Vadis* (1896; *Quo Vadis,* 1896), which in France alone reached millions of copies, was considered by some as "too popular for a work of a true artistic value."

Since several trends penetrated into Poland simultaneously, the picture of Polish literature at the turn of the century is rather difficult to present in terms of this or that dominating "ism." As elsewhere, realism in Poland first began to give way to naturalism, but by the end of the 19th c. the ideas of symbolism (q.v.) and impressionism were also felt, so that the same artists often reacted to both trends simultaneously. In fiction Adolf Dygasiński (1839–1902) created novels and short stories in which he performed naturalistic experiments based on principles of natural science; with time, however, his "objective" descriptions of nature and the world of animals acquired certain lyrical, impressionistic qualities that were at times elevated to an almost symbolic level. His novel *Gody życia* (1902; feast of life) was highly praised both by the adherents of realism and by adepts of the new "modernist" aesthetics. Antoni Sygietyński (1850–1923) in fiction and Gabriela Zapolska (1857–1921) in drama were above all continuators of the aesthetics of realism and naturalism, although some ingredients of the new trends found their way into their works. They were soon followed by a whole generation of artists whose creative activities began in the same vein but whose main achievements were a clear departure into the new aesthetics. It is the period popularly called "Młoda Polska" (Young Poland), embracing the last decade of the 19th c. and the first two decades of the 20th, that marks a departure from the models in which preoccupation with national or social themes and with traditional narrative structures pre-

vailed, and a shift toward more abstract, universal themes and toward modernistic modes of expression. While the main achievements of realism and naturalism were in the field of narrative prose, the ideas of modernism manifested themselves above all in poetry and in drama. This was a natural development, which paralleled developments in other literatures, notably in France and Russia, where the trend of symbolism especially manifested itself in lyrical poetry, in the works of Verlaine, Mallarmé, Rimbaud, and of the Russian poets Valery Bryusov and Konstantin Balmont (qq.v.), among many others.

The Polish poet who perhaps best embodies the spirit of fin de siècle, the spirit of aimless aestheticism, pessimism, frustration, punctuated with intermittent erotic extasis and expressed by means of impressionistic technique, intense "musicality," and highly emotional lyrical cadence, is Kazimierz Tetmajer (1865–1940). From the very first volume of his "series," *Poezje* (8 vols., 1891–1924; poetry), Tetmajer's fame grew rapidly, and he soon became Poland's favorite poet. His verses were known by heart, and were read and recited on every occasion, since they represented the moods and feelings of his generation. Tetmajer was also known as the author of less successful although once quite popular novels such as *Panna Mery* (1901; Miss Mery) and *Koniec epopei* (3 vols., 1913–17; end of the epic adventure). In fiction, his stories, especially the cycle *Na skalnym Podhalu* (5 vols., 1903–10; in the rocky Podhale highlands), are his really lasting achievements.

The other two important poets of the Young Poland period, although less representative of fin-de-siècle tendencies, were Jan Kasprowicz (1860–1926) and Leopold Staff (1878–1957). Kasprowicz's early poetry was conceived and couched in a realistic spirit and continued the tradition of speaking for the poor and the oppressed. Like his predecessor, Maria Konopnicka (1842–1910), he depicted in almost naturalistic style the misery of landless peasants, for example in the volume *Z chałupy* (1888; from the shanty). Gradually his poetic horizon expanded, embracing general social, moral, and philosophical themes. There is not much of the decadent spirit of the time in this poetry, but the style reflects the period quite well, with the obvious search for new modes of expression, typical archaisms, neologisms, hyperbolic metaphors and—what is rather unusual, even in modernist poetry in Po-land—free verse. All this can be perhaps best observed in the volume *Hymny* (1901; hymns), where tradition and innovation blend together in a fascinating way. Leopold Staff's poetry all clearly belongs chronologi-cally to the 20th c., since his first volume, *Sny o potędze* (dreams of power) appeared in 1901. Nevertheless, his early poetics displays most of the typical features of the Young Po-land period. On the whole, the beginning of the new century is in many respects a water-shed, since a number of significant literary events took place in those years, events that in some ways represented new developments, new not only in Poland but in a wider, inter-national perspective.

The most important was the staging in Cracow in March 1901 of a play by Stanisław Wyspiański (q.v.) called *Wesele* (the wed-ding). It is a curious, puzzling play in which the ideas of symbolist drama, operating with-in the primitivist basic structure of a popular Christmas play, or rather puppet show, are at the same time imbued with motifs and de-vices that anticipate surrealism (q.v.) and even the Theater of the Absurd (q.v.). The multilevel structure of this work, the inter-play of traditional realistic motifs and the "dream world" of the imaginary scenes rep-resenting the inner, deeper stream of the dra-ma—all this was a new, challenging kind of theater. A daring confrontation of the tyran-ny of romantic illusion and "squelching reali-ty" at first stunned the audiences and the critics, and many a wrong interpretation and even condemnation was made before it was realized that Wyspiański's theater simply represented certain new ideas, anticipating some of the 20th-c. experiments. In retro-spect, an aura of Samuel Beckett's (q.v.) *Waiting for Godot* seems to pervade this play in which national myths are exposed with a strange, ironic twist and with mastery of par-adox and scenic effect. In several other plays, too, especially in *Wyzwolenie* (1903; deliver-ance) and *Noc listopadowa* (1904; November night), Wyspiański managed to achieve strik-ing effect by blending historical motifs with modern and, indeed, modernistic dramatic ideas and techniques. Struggling against the romantic tradition that saw Poland as a kind of martyr, a "Christ" among European na-tions, he himself became a new, romantic bard. The national cause was still his obses-sion as it were, although at the same time he called for "deliverance" from its yoke. ("You

want to make me a slave of freedom, while I am free, free, free," exclaims his hero Kon-rad in *Wyzwolenie.*)

An important event in Polish literary life was the establishment in 1901 of the periodi-cal *Chimera* under the editorship of Zenon Przesmycki (pseud.: Miriam, 1861–1944). In his essays and translations in *Chimera* and in his earlier periodical *Życie,* Przesmycki ac-quainted Polish readers with trends and indi-vidual writers in the West. Of special importance was his study of Rimbaud and his translations and interpretations of the dramatic works of Maeterlinck (q.v.), in which he gave a profound analysis of the main tenets of symbolism.

But the man who managed to create the most intense artistic ferment in Poland at the turn of the century was Stanisław Przyby-szewski (q.v.). Przybyszewski was the most internationally recognized figure in Polish arts of that period, a writer who was active and known in modernist circles in Germany and Scandinavia before "descending" on the Polish literary scene in 1890 surrounded by an aura of a certain fame and considerable scandal. He was known as a "Satanist," a "Chopinist," an author of a number of works written in German: novels, plays, volumes of poetic prose, and a quite widely debated and not uninfluential study *Zur Psychologie des Individuums* (1891; on the psychology of the individual), containing certain ideas that an-ticipated expressionism (q.v.). Invited by a group of Young Poland artists active in Cra-cow, this member in good standing of the Young Germany and Young Scandinavia cir-cles became quite an influential force in Pol-ish literature, even though his leading role was rather short-lived. He became editor of the modernist periodical *Życie* (not to be confused with Miriam's *Życie* in Warsaw), which, however, did not last longer than about a decade (1890–1900). Przybyszewski's artistic manifesto in *Życie* was entitled "Confiteor" (Latin: I confess). It was a dec-laration of the absolute freedom of an artist to reject all the traditional notions of art's social, national, and moral obligations, and all the aesthetic conventions. At a time when for many groups in Poland the main preoccu-pation was the problem of regaining political independence, Przybyszewski's ideas were too abstract; moreover, they did not really amount to a well-thought-out, coherent aes-thetic program. (Przybyszewski's obsession with "sex-drive" [*chuć*] as the source of all art overshadowed more serious considerations). His demands for artistic integrity, however, anticipated some of the slogans that the poets of the *Skamander* group would voice after Poland's rebirth in 1918.

Przybyszewski's novels and quasi-symbolist plays did not prove to be of lasting value, although they were received with considerable interest at the time. His chief merit is that through his indefatigable activities as editor, creative writer, and extremely popular and effective speaker he spread ideas of modernism all over the Slavic world, perhaps more than any other writer or critic. His works were translated and his plays staged, he lectured widely (especially in Russia, where he became the chief prophet of modernism), he corresponded with artists and editors in capitals of the East and West, securing their contributions for his periodicals and informing the world of developments in Poland. From this point of view, his position in the development of Polish letters is probably more important than generally realized.

The leading writers of fiction at the turn of the century were Stefan Żeromski and Władysław Stanisław Reymont (qq.v.). In spite of the general tendency toward fragmentation of the traditional "large forms," both these writers succeeded in creating impressive works. Żeromski's novels were neoromantic in spirit (in that he took up the utopian romantic note of heroism, whether in patriotic struggle or in struggle against social injustice) and neorealistic or outright modernistic, lyrical, disjointed, often symbolist in style. Żeromski's chief novels during that period were *Ludzie bezdomni* (2 vols., 1900; homeless people), one of the first European novels depicting a physician (Dr. Judym, who sacrifices personal happiness for working for the poor and the oppressed); *Popioły* (3 vols., 1904; *Ashes,* 2 vols., 1928), a Polish *War and Peace,* and *Walka z szatanem* (3 vols., 1916–19; wrestling the devil). Reymont did not attain Żeromski's stature as a moral authority and "people's conscience," but his position as an artist of international importance was assured because of his two masterpieces, *Ziemia obiecana* (2 vols., 1899; *The Promised Land,* 1927) and *Chłopi* (4 vols., 1904–9; *The Peasants,* 4 vols., 1924–25). Reymont's style is not free from the Young Poland modernistic mannerisms. Nevertheless, he did succeed in creating two of the few truly epic novels of modern time, novels in which he managed to present a collective hero, as it were: the big

industrial city in the first and the backward peasant village in the second novel. While it was the general opinion in Poland that Żeromski was the writer most deserving of the Nobel Prize, it was Reymont who was awarded the prize in 1924 for his epic talent. A faithful reflection of the dilemmas of the generation torn between the traditional moral and social values and nihilistic skepticism can be found in Wacław Berent's (1873–1940) novels: *Próchno* (1901; rotten wood) and *Ozimina* (1911; winter crop).

1918–39

On the eve of World War I Polish letters and Polish arts in general experienced quite an intense ferment of ideas penetrating from both the West and from the East and finding fertile ground. Problems of revolution and underground struggle manifested themselves in a number of prose works by such writers as Andrzej Strug (1871–1937) and Władysław Orkan (1876–1930) and in Żeromski's play *Róża* (1905; the rose). In poetry ideas of expressionism, "formism," futurism (q.v.), and so forth initiated experiments with new forms and themes. World War I interrupted for a while these artistic activities, but after 1918 in the reborn Poland they continued with increased intensity.

The reestablishment of the independent state brought a veritable eruption of poetry. It was a group of fresh young talents centered around the periodical *Skamander* which was the most vocal in proclaiming freedom of expression and which soon gained the status of the leading group. They were Julian Tuwim, Antoni Słonimski, Kazimierz Wierzyński, Jarosław Iwaszkiewicz, and Jan Lechoń (qq.v.). Although they all started with very bold, seemingly antitraditional and antibourgeois declarations, their actual poetry amounted mostly to what can be called a colloquialized Young Poland tradition plus certain motifs and tropes associated with the new problems and mores in the reborn Poland. Tuwim tried to challenge the conventions in his poem "Wiosna" (1918; spring); Wierzyński exclaimed gaily: "It is green in my head and violets bloom inside it"; Lechoń demanded: "And in the spring let me see the spring, not Poland." But all this fervor and vitalism did not lead to any real changes in poetics, and subsequently the *Skamander* poets easily joined the political establishment and they themselves became the poetic establishment. Thanks to their genuine talents, they succeeded in creating a real interest for poetry, which thus dominated the literary scene in Poland, especially during the first postwar decade.

Within the orbit of the *Skamander* group, but more independent, were a number of other poets of considerable importance. The most outstanding and influential among them were Leopold Staff, who continued to produce lyrics of clarity and suggestiveness, and Bolesław Leśmian (q.v.), whose metaphysical, symbolist poetry became a source of inspiration to other poets because of the author's uncanny talent for introducing new semantic values by creative neology and metaphors. On a different level, an important place was occupied by the leader of the revolutionary "proletarian" poetry, Władysław Broniewski (q.v.), whose social message was highly effective because of the author's ability to couch it in a deeply lyrical idiom of personal experience.

The dominating, generally recognized position of the *Skamander* group, popularized by the most influential literary periodical, the weekly *Wiadomości literackie,* was not completely unchallenged. It was attacked on several fronts by younger poets who felt the need of a thorough revision of the traditional aesthetics, and who gradually formed a true artistic avant-garde.

The most radical avant-garde movement was futurism, led and most articulately formulated in Poland by Bruno Jasieński (1901–1939), one of the most intriguing international figures, who left his mark in three literatures—from his start as a militant futurist in Poland with his volume of poetry *But w butonierce* (1921; boot in a buttonhole) through a political novel written in French, *Je brûle Paris* (1928; I burn Paris), to his influential role in establishing Socialist Realism (q.v.) in the Soviet Union, where he was highly praised for his novel in Russian, *Chelovek menyaet kozhu* (1932; man changes skin) before he disappeared in Stalin's purges. In his early struggle for Polish futurism Jasieński was joined by a number of other young writers, among whom the most active and vocal were Aleksander Wat (1900–1967) and Anatol Stern (1899–1968). No less radical, and much more extensively and coherently argued in its program of antitraditional, "functional" poetry, was the so-called Cracow avant-garde initiated by Tadeusz Peiper (1891–1969) and represented mainly by Julian Przyboś (q.v.), Jalu Kurek (b. 1904), Jan Brzękowski (b. 1903) and Marian Czuchnowski (b. 1909).

In terms of popular appeal the position of *Skamander* poetry, with its eclectic character and undeniable artistic suggestiveness, remained unassailable. Nevertheless, the new avant-garde poetics gradually began to attract more and more genuine young talents, such as Józef Czechowicz, Czesław Miłosz (qq.v.), and Jerzy Zagórski (b. 1907), poets who not only were able to assert themselves as writers of integrity and originality but who in turn began to exert influence on other artists, both younger and older. Although often presented as sheer experimenters, in form many of the avant-garde poets showed deep concern with the growing social and political problems. The note of "catastrophism" was quite strong in their poems, and in certain cases one can speak of an almost prophetic quality, even in some works of a seemingly "frivolous" poet Konstanty Ildefons Gałczyński (q.v.), for example, his long poem *Koniec świata* (1929; the end of the world).

In prose the development was much slower, and traditional forms prevailed during most of this period. The ideological tensions were still most suggestively reflected in the works of Stefan Żeromski, who continued to be regarded as the most important writer. His novel *Przedwiośnie* (1925; before the spring) was one of the most courageous and honest attempts at depicting the social conflicts and frustrations of radical socialists and liberals who wanted progress and justice but also wanted to prevent the tragedies and cruelties that followed the revolution in Russia. Contemporary problems and frustrations were also depicted in works by Zofia Nałkowska (q.v.)—*Romans Teresy Hennert* (1924; Teresa Hennert's love affair) and *Granica* (1935; the boundary)—and Juliusz Kaden-Bandrowski (q.v.)—*Generał Barcz* (1923; General Barcz) and *Czarne skrzydła* (2 vols., 1928–29; black wings), both lengthy and rather tedious attempts at creating an original style that consisted of blending supposedly realistic vulgarity with quasi-expressionistic stream-of-consciousness (q.v.) passages. A writer who gained a moral stature once afforded Stefan Żeromski was Maria Dąbrowska (q.v.). Her volume of stories *Ludzie stamtąd* (1926; folks from over yonder) was followed by one of the few true epic novels in modern Polish literature, a tetralogy, *Noce i dnie* (1932–34; nights and days), a chronicle novel somewhat reminiscent of John Galsworthy's (q.v.) *The Forsyte Saga* and Thomas Mann's (q.v.) *Buddenbrooks* but basically an original, thoughtful depiction in what can be termed "modernized neorealistic style" of contemporary problems in the Polish countryside.

On the whole, literature in postwar Poland developed more and more into a "profession" rather than a "mission." There was a fast-growing number of popular and respectable belletristic writers whose works competed successfully with translations of foreign literature. A popular author of historical fiction was Zofia Kossak (q.v.). A steady stream of more or less successful prose works comes from Andrzej Strug, Ferdynand Goetel (q.v.), Maria Kuncewiczowa (b. 1899), Jarosław Iwaszkiewicz, and others. Works that for various reasons were most frequently and heatedly discussed in intellectual circles were *Sól ziemi* (1936; *Salt of the Earth,* 1939) by Józef Wittlin (q.v.), an indictment of all militaristic mentality; Leon Kruczkowski's (q.v.) Marxist analysis of the historical past, *Kordian i cham* (1932; Kordian and the boor); and *Niebo w płomieniach* (1936; heaven in flames) by Jan Parandowski (1895–1978), which explored the younger generation's attitudes toward religion.

In the field of theater, this was a period of steady production of professionally respectable plays by such writers as Zofia Nałkowska, Jerzy Szaniawski (1886–1970), Ludwik Hieronim Morstin (1886–1966), Karol Hubert Rostworowski (q.v.), and many others.

A special place in this general picture is occupied by a few individual artists who were far ahead of their time and whose full significance in Polish literature and, indeed, in world literature, did not become apparent for several decades. They were Stanisław Ignacy Witkiewicz, popularly called Witkacy, Bruno Schulz, and Witold Gombrowicz (qq.v.). Witkiewicz's main achievement was in the field of theater, where he was a precursor of the Theater of the Absurd. His original idea was that of the theater of "pure form," that is, a totally antirealistic concept, reaching further than the futurist experiments by Marinetti (q.v.) in Italy and Mayakovsky (q.v.) in Russia and striving for a "total freedom of formal elements." Bruno Schulz's strange, haunting tales in his collections *Sklepy cynamonowe* (1934; *The Street of Crocodiles,* 1963) and *Sanatorium pod klepsydrą* (1937;

The Sanatorium under the Sign of the Hourglass, 1978) have been quite recently "discovered" in the West as early existentialist (q.v.) prose par excellence. Witold Gombrowicz is today certainly one of the best-known names in world literature. Long ignored both in his country and abroad, Gombrowicz won international recognition after World War II, when his prewar and postwar works were translated and pronounced an important contribution to the development of avant-garde fiction and drama. His basic device is that of negating the conventional concept of descriptive narrative and instead seeing—somewhat as the futurists did—his characters undergoing constant deformation and transformation in their interaction. Gombrowicz's first novel, *Ferdydurke* (1938; *Ferdydurke,* 1961), and his first play, *Iwona, księżniczka* Burgunda (1938; *Ivona, Princess of Burgundia,* 1969), already contained these main premises.

1939–56

It has yet to be fully assessed what World War II meant for Poland, its people, and its art. It is certain that after all that the people went through, their life, including their culture and art, could never be the same. The shattering experience of the new total war and of genocide defied normal expression, and writers had to resort to the biblical style of Job and Jeremiah or to sober, brutal simplicity. Some of the best-known writers—Tuwim, Wierzyński, Lechoń, Słonimski, Wittlin—found themselves in exile in the West; their works, published freely in France, England, and the U.S., became the most visible part of the literature's continued fight for their country. Some younger ones—for example, Ksawery Pruszyński (1907–1950), Wacław Iwaniuk (b. 1915), Artur Miedzyrzecki (b. 1922)—fought as soldiers in the Polish army in the West. Of those who stayed in Poland, many were sent to German concentration camps, and only after the war those who survived gave witness to their experience: Zofia Kossak published her memoirs, *Z otchłani* (1946; from the abyss); Gustaw Morcinek (1891–1963) wrote his *Listy spod morwy* (1946; letters from under the mulberry tree); Stanisław Dygat (q.v.) gave a fictionalized reaction to some of the problems of *Jezioro Bodeńskie* (1946; Lake Constance). Ironically, some of the most vocal "revolutionary" poets—Broniewski,

Czuchnowski, Wat—who in prewar Poland were accused of communism and even imprisoned, were now, in turn, quickly jailed, when they found themselves in the Soviet-occupied territories.

Writers who stayed in Poland and managed to escape arrest, deportation, and concentration camps participated in the underground movement, publishing in underground presses poems, stories, and patriotic appeals and declarations, and on the whole assuming their new role as "soldiers of fighting literature." Among them were such well-known artists as Dąbrowska, Miłosz, Iwaszkiewicz and Jerzy Andrzejewski (q.v.). A number of poems and stories by Miłosz, Andrzejewski, Iwaszkiewicz, and other mostly anonymous writers were published in underground editions. A wave of the "condemned generation" poets (those born around 1920) emerged in response to the war, with most of them dying as members of the Polish Underground Army or in the Warsaw Uprising before reaching full maturity. Tadeusz Gajcy (1922–1944), Andrzej Trzebiński (1922–1943), Krzysztof K. Baczyński (1921–1944), and Zdzisław Stroiński (1920–1943) all died soldiers' deaths. Others perished in death camps or mass executions; a few survived to give testimony to the experience of crematoria, death commandos, burning ghettos, and total degradation of human values. Among them was Tadeusz Borowski (q.v.), who gave a faithful depiction of Auschwitz and on the whole of the fate of his generation, which he saw as destined to leave behind nothing but "scrap iron and hollow, jeering laughter of generations."

The first years in postwar Poland were a period of general uncertainty as to the direction of literature. It was quite clear from the beginning that the decisive voice in the lively and fairly free debates and confrontations belonged to those who took their inspiration from the U.S.S.R. Before the new directions were officially introduced, however, the field was quite wide open and writers searched for their individual solutions in trying to articulate their experiences. It was mostly felt that the traditional fabular forms of expression were no longer adequate, and that writers had to resort either to a documentary reportage form or to an antinarrative style of letting facts, thoughts, and emotions flow freely in constant interchange. Fairly conventional were Nałkowska's *Medaliony* (1946; medallions) and Andrzejewski's stories, since they

were indirect, secondhand descriptions. In more personal works the style and structure were much more "convulsive," since the events depicted defied normal narrative means. Such were tales of the Jewish tragedy by Adolf Rudnicki (b. 1912) and Leopold Buczkowski's (b. 1905) "antinovel" written in 1946, *Czarny potok* (1954; *Black Torrent*, 1969).

In poetry, too, the main preoccupation for some time after the war was to find an idiom capable of expressing the experience of these years. One of the first and most important books was the volume *Ocalenie* (1945; rescue) by Czesław Miłosz, in which the strongest and most profound feelings and reflections are expressed in the simplest poetic language without any aesthetic adornments or formal experimentation. It is almost frightening to realize what the years of war must have meant when one perceives the depth and the moral maturity of a poet still under thirty-five. The most striking achievements in the search for a new idiom that was free of rhetoric and exaggeration were probably those of the young poet Tadeusz Różewicz (q.v.), who started writing during the war and after the war published regularly—for example, *Niepokój* (1947; anxiety) and *Czerwona rękawiczka* (1948; red glove). Scores of other volumes appeared soon after the war by poets of such different artistic and political persuasions as Adam Ważyk, Mieczysław Jastrun (qq.v.), Julian Przyboś, Władysław Broniewski, Julian Tuwim, Antoni Słonimski, Jalu Kurek, and many others. In theater the wave of creative experiments was yet to come, although there were signs of the new idiom in Gałczyński's absurdist pieces in the weekly *Przekrój* called "Teatrzyk 'Zielona gęsi'" (the minitheater "Green Goose"). Two serious plays by older writers had the strongest reverberations: Leon Kruczkowski's *Niemcy* (perf. 1948, pub. 1950; the Germans), which questioned some of the popular myths about the enemy, and Jerzy Szaniawski's *Dwa teatry* (1966; two theaters), which challenged the validity of materialism and realism as the only guiding light in literature.

Gradually, the implications of the new political system were becoming apparent and the tasks expected from the artists were being defined. A number of works appeared in which the scheme was to depict the prewar reality in Poland realistically but with the emphasis on the negative aspects, and to pro-

ject optimism and faith in a better future under the new system. Such were the novels
like Zofia Nałkowska's *Węzły życia* (1948;
knots of life), Tadeusz Breza's (1905–1970)
Mury Jerycha (1946; the walls of Jericho),
and Kazimierz Brandys's (q.v.) *Drewniany
koń* (1946; the wooden horse). A prominent
place is occupied by a novel that better than
any other work catches the dilemmas of the
postwar situation in Poland: Andrzejewski's
Popiół i diament (1948; *Ashes and Diamonds,*
1962).

In 1949 Socialist Realism was proclaimed
as the only correct artistic "method." Those
unwilling to accept it had to refrain from
publishing or else resort to historical or exotic themes and/or translations. Czesław Miłosz made a difficult personal decision: in
1951, while in Paris, he renounced his citizenship. The requirement of ideologically
correct "socialist orientation" created a climate that proved not favorable to art. Few
works of that period had much artistic value,
although some of the so-called production
novels and stories were of a certain documentary interest.

The historical novel was in general less
subject to political interference than other
genres. The most productive authors in this
mode were Antoni Gołubiew (1907–1979),
with his huge cycle on medieval Polish history, *Bolesław Chrobry* (7 vols., 1947–55; Bolesław the Brave), and Teodor Parnicki
(q.v.), many of whose novels were devoted to
the same period, although they had a much
wider world perspective and were much more
ambitious and accomplished than Gołubiew's.

1956–the Present

Although the political and cultural "thaw"
of 1956 did not change the basic political system, it nevertheless led to quite a radical relaxation of the dogmatic "Stalinist" cultural
policies, and the results in the field of art and
in the entire cultural life of Poland were
quite spectacular. To be sure, the euphoria of
liberation did not last long, but a return to
the previous policies proved impossible.
There was a veritable eruption of original
and translated works that represented all
possible philosophical and aesthetic trends
and schools: from existentialist novels and
plays through Theater of the Absurd to New
Novels (q.v.) and concrete poetry. Witkiewicz, Schulz, and the émigré Gombrowicz

were rediscovered, and widely debated. Most
(although not all) of Gombrowicz's postwar
works that were brought out in Paris by the
Kultura publishing house were now reissued
in Poland. Other émigré writers, whose existence had been barely admitted before, were
now published and discussed. To be sure,
there were still restrictions, but the importance of the émigré writers as an organic part
of Polish literature was recognized. On the
other hand, the émigré writers—Wierzyński,
Lechoń, Wittlin—took into account in their
work the achievements of writers at home
and thus were not seen as anachronisms in
Poland. Miłosz, of course, never for a moment ceased being regarded by both young
and old as a leading artistic force; his volumes, published regularly by the Paris Kultura, found their way to readers in Poland
even when his name was banned. A real "second birth" could be seen in the case of poets
like Lechoń and especially Wierzyński. Wierzyński proved to be able to keep pace with
the postwar changes in the poetic idiom.
Such volumes as *Kufer na plecach* (1964;
with a trunk on my shoulders), *Tkanka
ziemi* (1968; tissue of the earth), and *Sen
mara* (1969; dream-phantom) were almost
unanimously pronounced masterpieces by
critics of various persuasions. Several editions of his selected poetry appeared in Poland within a short time and several studies
were devoted to his entire work. On the other
hand, some writers living in Poland, such as
Brandys and Andrzejewski, openly published
abroad.

On the whole, extremely lively activity
took place during the first years after 1956.
Poets, novelists, playwrights of all possible
convictions and temperaments wrote with a
real frenzy, undertaking a number of very
daring and innovative experiments, especially
in the theater. In poetry the search for new
forms had never actually stopped, but it now
got a new impetus. Tadeusz Różewicz published regularly: *Poemat otwarty* (1956; open
poem), *Formy* (1958; forms), *Rozmowa z
księciem* (1960; conversation with a prince).
Zbigniew Herbert (q.v.) appeared as one of
the most original new talents in his volumes:
Struna światła (1956; the chord of light),
Hermes, pies i gwiazda (1957; Hermes, dog
and star), *Studium przedmiotu* (1961; study
of the object). Miron Białoszewski (q.v.)
showed an uncanny linguistic inventiveness
in *Obroty rzeczy* (1956; *Revolutions of
Things,* 1974), *Mylne wzruszenia* (1961; mis-

taken emotions), and other volumes. A large number of other poets such as Tadeusz Nowak (b. 1930), Wisława Szymborska (q.v.), Stanisław Grochowiak (1934–1976), and Tymoteusz Karpowicz (b. 1921) all contributed original works. Adam Ważyk, who earlier assumed the role of a teacher in the "Marxist school of emotions," now wrote his *Poemat dla dorosłych* (1955; poem for adults), in which he seemed to rediscover the individual.

It is not a coincidence that many of the young poets participated in the spectacular development of a new theatrical idiom, that of the Theater of the Absurd. It started with the establishment in 1956 by Adam Tarn (1902–1972) of a monthly, *Dialog,* which became the forum for all that was new and creative in theater. It published translations (for example, Beckett's *Waiting for Godot*), original plays, scenarios, and theoretical discussions. The author best known at home and abroad was Sławomir Mrożek (q.v.), whose plays *Zabawa* (1962; *The Party,* 1967) and *Tango* (1964; *Tango,* 1968) were perhaps the best examples of this genre in Poland. Other well-known plays by some of the above mentioned poets were *Kartoteka* (1960; *The Card Index,* 1970) by Różewicz, *Dziwny pasażer* (1964; *The Strange Passenger,* 1969) by Karpowicz, and *Chłopcy* (1964; boys) by Grochowiak.

In prose, the changes were at first mainly thematic. Maria Dąbrowska, long silenced, published her *Gwiazda zaranna* (1955; the morning star), which indeed initiated a wave of works free from political strictures. A group of young writers, mostly born after 1930, gave vent to their personal feelings of anger and frustration in face of postwar reality. Marek Hłasko (q.v.), Marek Nowakowski (b. 1939), and Ireneusz Iredyński (b. 1939) represent this generation. Hłasko's ruthlessly realistic stories, in the collection *Pierwszy krok w chmurach* (1956; first step in the clouds), were perhaps the most vocal expression of these sentiments. The author proved too restless and unruly and soon left the country to live in the West; he committed suicide at the age of thirty-five.

While controls over the political and economic life in Poland were soon tightened again, the striving for cultural and artistic independence continued with unceasing vigor and at least partial success. Although Socialist Realism is still the officially prescribed "method," nobody seems to pay much attention to it—with the exception of a few self-

admitted "stragglers" such as the novelists Jerzy Putrament (b. 1911) or Roman Bratny (b. 1921). A steady stream of novels, short stories, and poetry, some of which experiment freely with the most daring, "formalist" artistic devices, is proof of creative integrity of Polish writers. Among the most interesting works of this period are such novels as Tadeusz Konwicki's (q.v.) *Sennik współczesny* (1963; *A Dreambook for Our Time,* 1969) and *Kronika wypadków miłosnych* (1974; chronicle of love events), and Tadeusz Nowak's *Obcoplemienna ballada* (1963; ballad of an alien tribe) and *A jak królem a jak katem będziesz* (1968; when you will be a king, when you will be a hangman). In all of them the basic structural pattern is the device of blending dreams and reality with a constantly changing mode of narration and swiftly shifting levels of symbolism and realism. Especially in the case of Konwicki the added element of suspense derives from the fact that some of his novels often deal with the politically sensitive theme of the Polish Underground Army's dilemma at the end of the war, when they were facing the Germans and the Communists at the same time.

An important and indeed unique development in the 1970s was the emergence of a number of independent presses—unlicensed but not openly prohibited—which put out uncensored journals, bulletins, literary magazines, and separate works in book form. The most active among them was NOWA—Niezależna Oficyna Wydawnicza (Independent Publishing House)—in Warsaw, but there were many others, such as ABC in Cracow and Młoda Polska (Young Poland) in Gdańsk. The most important literary magazine was *Zapis,* launched in 1977 by a group of mostly younger writers and critics. One of the initiators and later a true moving spirit of this and other enterprises was Stanisław Barańczak (b. 1946), a poetic and scholarly talent of high rank. Quite a few important works of Polish literature—important both artistically and ideologically—would have remained unpublished without these bold initiatives. Among them are such works as Tadeusz Konwicki's novels *Kompleks polski* (1977; *The Polish Complex,* 1981) and *Mała apokalipsa* (1979; small apocalypse), and Julian Stryjkowski's (b. 1905) *Wielki strach* (1980; great fear). The microcosm of both the governing circles and the opposition is explored in these novels with courage and integrity, characteristic in general of most works thus published. Further evidence of the changing mood and tone of literature can be seen in the recent works of Kazimierz Brandys. In a finely filtered but by no means ambiguous interplay of memory flashbacks and contemporary observations Brandys depicts an individual's anguish in coming to the realization of his country's "unreal" reality in his novel *Nierzeczywistość* (1977; *A Question of Reality,* 1980). More insights and narrative experiments follow in a kind of diary, *Miesiące* (1980; months).

Since August 1980 the situation in Poland has changed dramatically. Between then and the proclamation of martial law on December 13, 1981, an almost complete emancipation of Polish literature took place as the result of the astounding successes of the "Solidarity" struggle for basic social, economic, and cultural rights, which swept through the country like an avalanche. These almost revolutionary changes coincided with the award of the Nobel Prize to Czesław Miłosz. This event, of great international importance, in Poland turned out to be of truly cataclysmic consequence. Not only did Miłosz have to be restored to his rightful place as the most important creative force in Polish letters, but the event automatically created a much more favorable climate for Polish writers and publishers in general. Works previously banned were allowed to be published again, and most émigré writers were again publicly recognized. Independent publishing houses and more-or-less regularly issued magazines were thriving. NOWA and the Paris Kultura (or rather its publisher, Institut Littéraire) signed an agreement of the mutual exchange of copyrights; in *Zapis* and other magazines, poetry, short stories, and literary and political essays were published by previously banned authors and writers in exile.

By the spring of 1981 literary activities—those outside of official control and even those controlled—were marked by a complete freedom of expression. Practically every existing journal or magazine put out a special issue devoted to Miłosz; demands were made that the works of all the more important émigré writers—especially the novelist Zofia Romanowiczowa (b. 1922) and the short-story writer Tadeusz Nowakowski (b. 1918)—be published. Plans for publication of "practically all" the works of Miłosz and of some other writers were announced. Some critics

even raised the possibility of publishing the most militant writers in exile: Gustaw Herling Grudziński (b. 1919), whose short-story collection *Skrzydła ołtarza* (1960; the wings of the altar), first published in Paris, was now acknowledged as being of a high artistic value; and Józef Mackiewicz (b. 1902), who was recently nominated for the Nobel Prize by Russian émigré circles in the West for his sharply political novels *Droga donikąd* (1954; *Road to Nowhere,* 1955) and *Nie trzeba głośno mówić* (1969; one should not say it aloud). Unfortunately, before all these hopes and plans could materialize, the curtain again came down with the imposition of martial law. At the time of this writing, no exact information is available on either the official or unofficial publishing activities, no published materials are allowed to be sent abroad, and virtually all private presses are shut down. Thus, remarks on the present situation must be inconclusive.

BIBLIOGRAPHY: Dyboski, R., *Modern Polish Literature* (1924); Scherer-Virski, O., *The Modern Polish Short Story* (1955); Heyst, A., "Poland's Contemporary Literature," *Dublin Review,* 233 (1959), 171–78; Folejewski, Z., "Socialist Realism in Polish Literature and Criticism," *CL,* 13 (1961), 72–80; Kunstmann, H., *Die moderne polnische Literatur* (1962); Csato, E., *The Polish Theatre* (1963); Herman, M., *Histoire de la littérature polonaise* (1963); Kridl, M., *Survey of Polish Literature and Culture* (1965); Kunstmann, H., *Moderne polnische Dramatik* (1965); Wirth, A., *Modernes polnisches Theater* (1967); Miłosz, C., *The History of Polish Literature* (1969); Czerwiński, E. J., "Polish Dramatists in Search of Self," *CompD,* 3 (1969), 210–17; Folejewski, Z., "The Theatre of Ruthless Metaphor: Polish Theatre between Marxism and Existentialism," *CompD,* 3 (1969), 176–82; Folejewski, Z., "Notes on the Novel in Contemporary Poland," *CSP,* 13 (1971), 299–313; Gerould, D., *Twentieth-Century Polish Drama* (1977); Krzyżanowski, J., *A History of Polish Literature* (1978); Barańczak, S., "The Gag and the Word," *Survey,* 110 (1980), 58–79; Głowiński, M., "The Grotesque in Contemporary Polish Literature," in Birnbaum, H., and Eekman, T., eds., *Fiction and Drama in Eastern and Southeastern Europe: Evolution and Experiment in the Postwar Period* (1980), pp. 177–90; Czerwiński, E. J., "Quo Vadis? Polish Theatre and Drama in the 1980s," in Clayton, J. D., and Schaarschmidt, G., eds., *Poetica Slavica: Studies in Honour of Zbigniew Folejewski* (1981), pp. 13–20; Levine, M. G., *Contemporary Polish Poetry, 1925–1975* (1981)

ZBIGNIEW FOLEJEWSKI

Kashubian Literature

The Kashubs, a Slavic people living in the region of Gdańsk (formerly Danzig), possess a rich heritage of oral literature, which serves as a primary thematic source for their written literature, launched at the close of the 19th c. by the first Kashubian poet, Jan Hieronim Derdowski (1852–1902). The author of three humorous epics, Derdowski is best remembered for *O panu Czorlińscim co do Pucka po sece jachoł* (1880; concerning Mr. Czorliński, who drove to Puck for a fishing net).

Begun when the Kashubian homeland was German territory, Kashubian literary activity has continued in contemporary Poland, where it functions as dialect literature not subsidized by funds from the central government. Consequently, it is to be found in short-lived journals and in the small printings of works published by subscription or at the author's own expense. Alexander Majkowski (1876–1938) was the first to publish Kashubian lyric poetry—*Spiewe i frańtówci* (1905; songs and lyrics)—as well as the first Kashubian novel, *Zëcé i przigodë Remusa* (1938; the life and adventures of Remus), the best-known work in Kashubian literature. His greatest contribution was the founding, in 1909, of *Gryf*, a journal of Kashubian culture. It became the organ of the Young Kashubian movement, which included Jan Karnowski (1886–1939), the foremost Kashubian lyric poet; Leon Heyke (1885–1939) and Franciszek Sędzicki (1882–1957), lyric and epic poets; and Jan Patock (1886–1940), a folklorist. The most successful Kashubian dramatist is Bernard Sychta (b. 1907), whose *Hanka sę żeni* (1935; Hanka marries) is his most popular Kashubian play.

Although Kashubian writers have always championed their ethnicity, they have never, either singly or in concert, advocated political separatism. Prior to World War I their chief goal, especially among the Young Kashubs, was resistance to the encroachment of German language and culture. During the interwar period they flourished in the so-called Polish Corridor, forming several new literary groups and journals. Nazi invasion resulted

in an almost total liquidation of the Kashubian intelligentsia. Only after the end of Stalinism in the 1950s did Kashubian literature begin to flourish once again, led by the scholar Leon Roppel (b. 1912) and the poet and short-story writer Jan Piepka (b. 1926).

Although the greater part of their literary production has been poetry, the Kashubs have not produced a poet of such a stature that his language would serve as the basis for a unified literary language. Instead Kashubian writers continue in their regionalism, each writing in his own local dialect, using local themes. From its beginning Kashubian literature has been intimately tied to Kashubian folklore. Both in poetry and prose Kashubian writers sing the praise of their homeland with images of village maidens, fishermen in the perilous sea, and the exploits of local heroes during the two world wars. Aside from Majkowski's novel, only Alojzy Nagel's (b. 1930) poetry has had an impact beyond the ethnic borders.

There are now several dozen active Kashubian writers, some in their teens, who may insure the further development of Kashubian literature, at least for one more generation.

BIBLIOGRAPHY: Lorentz, F., et al., *The Cassubian Civilization* (1933); Stone, G., "The Language of Cassubian Literature and the Question of a Literary Standard," *SEER*, 1 (1972), 521–29; Neureiter, F., ed., "Übersicht über die kaschubische Literatur," *Kaschubische Anthologie* (1973), pp. 1–19; Perkowski, J., "Kashubian Émigré Literature," *Kurier Polsko-Kanadyjski,* 6 Feb. 1975, 33; Neureiter, F., *Geschichte der kaschubischen Literatur* (1978)

JAN L. PERKOWSKI

POLYNESIAN LITERATURE
See Pacific Islands Literatures

PONGE, Francis
French poet, essayist, and art critic, b. 27 March 1899, Montpellier

P. is a child of the Midi (Montpellier, Nîmes, Avignon) but also of Normandy (Caen), where his family moved when he was ten. He pursued his secondary studies in Caen and later in Paris, after which he began the study of law. In 1918, however, he was drafted into

561

the army, and his formal education came to an end. His earliest extant writings date from the immediate post-World War I period.

By 1923 P. had become friendly with the *Nouvelle revue française* group—Jacques Rivière (1886–1925), Jean Paulhan (q.v.)—who published several of his poems in their review. A few years later he was frequenting the surrealists (q.v.) and in 1929 signed their second manifesto. Throughout this period he continued to write, but published little until 1942, when *Le parti pris des choses* (taking the side of things) appeared, an event that brought him a certain renown in avant-garde circles. He worked at the Hachette publishing house in the 1930s, was a member of the Communist Party between 1937 and 1947, performed various writing (and other) duties for the Resistance in occupied France during World War II, and was employed as a teacher at the Alliance Française from 1952 to 1964. Since the mid-1960s he has lectured widely in Europe and the U.S., but now spends most of the year writing at his home in Le Bar-sur-Loup (Provence).

Although one can discern an evolution or, more precisely, a shift in his writings over the last six decades, essentially P. has been producing the same kind of text since 1919. On the other hand, during that time his oeuvre has attracted strongly favorable attention from rather disparate quarters. In the early 1920s, for example, the *NRF* group admired the satirical dimension of P.'s texts; Jean-Paul Sartre (q.v.), in his laudatory 1944 study of P., extolled the phenomenologist he found at work in *Le parti pris des choses;* and in the 1960s P.'s writings were praised for their semantic materialism by figures associated with the review *Tel Quel*—Philippe Sollers (q.v.), Jean Thibaudeau (b. 1935), Marcelin Pleynet (b. 1933). While all three views have their validity, in hindsight the *Tel Quel* approach to P.'s work seems closest to the mark. For P. is above all an explorer of the infinite resources of the French language. If he has often chosen to write of things, of objects, he has done so, as he observed in a 1969 interview, so that he "would always have a brake on [his] subjectivity." He is totally opposed to the goal of self-expression in poetry, as he is to the conception of the poet as a seeker of metaphysical truths. In his scheme of things, poets must seek out within their native language the endless interconnections (rhythmic, phonic, semantic, orthographic) that they alone are equipped to

discover and celebrate. Like François de Malherbe (1555–1628), whom P. reveres, he is concerned as a poet "only with his instrument."

P.'s texts are characterized by extreme self-consciousness, by an almost exacerbated lucidity regarding their own constituent elements. They fold back on themselves in puns and other ludic devices that stress the autonomy of the text as text rather than the text's fidelity to the thing being described. With his *objeux,* his object-wordgames, P. re-creates the world piecemeal; bit by bit he is building a thoroughly demystified but perfectly habitable universe, one of rooted discourse, of world-anchored words.

His first published texts, like the short prose pieces in *Le parti pris des choses,* were not only for the most part brief, but also highly polished and tightly organized as well. From the mid-1940s onward, however, P.'s published pieces suddenly grew longer, became more loosely structured, less finished than his early pieces had been—for example, the texts collected in *Le grand recueil* (3 vols., 1961; the great collection) and *Nouveau recueil* (1967; new collection). Also, around this same time P. began to publish what appeared to be rather casually fashioned essays on the work of some contemporary painters and sculptors, essays that have been collected in *L'atelier contemporain* (1977; the contemporary atelier). P.'s "second manner," his meandering later style, represents, in fact, a freer, more comodious, less composed version of his previous mode; with it he has managed to focus steadily for the first time on a notion that has always obsessed him: the birth of form, the procedures by which a poem or a painting comes into being. The poet's preliminary notes and the artist's sketches are now put in the foreground at the expense of the finished product.

Deploying within the work the traces of its own gestation—for instance, outlines, false starts, revisions, recapitulations—the signs of the productive process that culminates in the work's creation, has been the hallmark of P.'s writing since the beginning. In recent decades an increasingly dominant metapoetic orientation has opened his writing up to a point where all distinctions in it between theory and practice, notebook (or sketch pad) and completed work, have disappeared, yielding texts of dazzling complexity and elaborateness, not incomplete, only unclosed. Today P. has emerged as France's greatest metapoet and at the same time as one of that small band of truly original writers in our century.

FURTHER WORKS: *Douze petits écrits* (1926); *L'œilet; La guêpe; Le mimosa* (1946); *Dix courts sur la méthode* (1946); *Le carnet du bois de pins* (1947); *Proêmes* (1948); *Le peintre à l'étude* (1948); *La rage de l'expression* (1952); *Tome premier* (1965); *Pour un Malherbe* (1965); *Le savon* (1967; *Soap,* 1969); *Entretiens de F. P. avec Phillipe Sollers* (1970); *La fabrique du pré* (1971; *The Making of the "Pré,"* 1979); *L'écrit Beaubourg* (1977); *Comment une figue de paroles et pourquoi* (1977). FURTHER VOLUMES IN ENGLISH: *The Voice of Things* (1972); *The Power of Language* (1979)

BIBLIOGRAPHY: Sollers, P., *F. P.* (1963); Thibaudeau, J., *P.* (1967); Spada, M., *F. P.* (1974); Bonnefis, P., ed., *F. P.: Colloque de Cerisy* (1977); Higgins, I., *F. P.* (1979); Sorrell, M., *F. P.* (1981)

ROBERT W. GREENE

POPA, Vasko

Yugoslav poet (writing in Serbian), b. 29 July 1922, Grebenac

During World War II P. supported the side of the partisans. He studied literature at the universities of Vienna, Bucharest, and Belgrade and received his degree at Belgrade in 1949. Since then he has worked as an editor in publishing houses. His poetry has been translated into all major languages.

When his first collection, *Kora* (1953; tree bark) was published it was not well received by those readers and critics who resisted the modernization of Yugoslav poetry. P.'s poetry, together with that of Miodrag Pavlović (q.v.), contributed decisively to the victory of the modernists who were influenced by Western currents.

From the very first, P. showed a predilection for the concrete rather than the abstract. For him a thing is not just an inanimate object—it has a life of its own, which only the eye of a poet can discern. P. likes to use things such as quartz stone, the bark of a tree, bones, a small box as symbols for his own concepts and attitudes. His closeness to things was undoubtedly accentuated by his war experiences as a young man, when people were primarily concerned with material things in their struggle for survival and when the language they spoke was direct and concrete.

P. combines the grotesque and the fantastic, thus dramatizing what he sees as the senselessness of the human condition. Yet there is a certain playfulness in his poetry. In his approach to reality he often eradicates the boundary between sense perceptions and even violates logic. Often he uses proverbs, puns, and witticisms, underlining the meaningless and at the same time tragicomic nature of man's existence.

P.'s preferred mode is the cycle. Each one is a self-contained entity, in which the poems deal with a common topic and are written in the same vein. Each one is related to the others. From the small seemingly insignificant objects around him in *Kora* P. moved to the larger microcosm of his native land in *Nepočin-polje* (1956; the unrest field) and on to the macrocosm of the universe in *Sporedno nebo* (1968; the secondary sky), only to return to his native land in *Uspravna zemlja* (1972; *Earth Erect,* 1973) and to objects in *Mala kutija* (original unpub.; *The Little Box,* 1970).

P. does not use rhyme, traditional or experimental. Nor is he given to the excesses of free verse. His metrics follow a distinct, though by no means regular, pattern of groups of two or three lines, rarely four; generally it is a combination of these, interchanging freely. His style is terse, often aphoristic, even elliptic. His verse, which often resembles folk poetry, impresses by its strong rhythm.

P.'s poetry is modern in both theme and originality of expression. His concern with death, fate, the meaning of life, and love, gives his poetry universal scope. The English poet Ted Hughes (q.v.) has said of P. that his "total vision is vast and one understands why he has been called an epic poet. His Cosmos is more mysteriously active and dreadful but his affection for our life is closer than ever." P. is generally recognized as the leading contemporary Serbian poet.

FURTHER WORKS: *Od zlata jabuka* (1958; *The Golden Apple,* 1980); *Pesme* (1965); *Vučja so* (1975); *Živo meso* (1975); *Kuća nasred druma* (1975); *Rez* (1981). FURTHER VOLUMES IN ENGLISH: *Collected Poems 1943–1976* (1978); *The Blackbird's Field* (1979); *Homage to the Wolf: Selected Poems 1956–1975* (1979)

BIBLIOGRAPHY: Bosquet, A., "V. P.; ou, L'exorcisme populaire," *Verbe et vortige* (1961), pp. 193–200; Hughes, T., "The Poetry of V. P.," *TriQ,* No. 9 (1967), 201–5; Mihailovich, V. D., "V. P.: The Poetry of Things in a Void," *BA,* 43 (1969), 24–29; Hughes, T., Introduction to V. P., *Collected Poems 1943–1976* (1978), pp. 1–9

VASA D. MIHAILOVICH

POPESCU, Dumitru Radu

Romanian novelist, short-story writer, and dramatist, b. 19 Aug. 1935, Păușa-Bihor

P. studied medicine and the humanities in various Transylvanian colleges and obtained a degree in philology in 1961 from the University of Cluj. He became a journalist and since 1970 has been the editor of the literary weekly *Tribuna.* He is a member of the Central Committee of the Communist Party of Romania and a member of the National Assembly, and in 1981 was elected president of the Romanian Writers' Union.

P.'s first volumes of short stories were devoted to descriptions of the traumatic social changes in Romania after World War II, particularly urbanization and the collectivization of the villages. He depicted psychologically baffled types, humorous, tragic, and disoriented. The solemn dignity of the traditional rhythms of peasant life, intimately connected with love and death, are shown to remain at the center of a life otherwise full of comic chaos and naïve trickery in the stories in the collections *Dor* (1966; yearning) and *Duios Anastasia trecea* (1967; fondly passing Anastasia).

Gradually P. introduced two new elements in his writings. The first was the fantastic as derived from folklore and myth, but also from the traditions of the Romanian novel. The second was a moral theme: the search for an unnamed guilt by the younger generation who attempt to judge those who had effected the socialist modification of Romanian society. The main narrative section of the novel *Vînătoarea regală* (1973; the royal hunt) describes a strange drought and epidemic haunting a Danubian area. Suspicion and self-interest grow into mob terror and absurd crime. This gloomy atmosphere is lightened by the dogged search for truth by a young attorney, the son of one of the victims.

In *Ploile de dincolo de vreme* (1976; rains from beyond time) one of P.'s archvillains, a school superintendent who had formerly been a Party activist guilty of many abuses of power, is now investigated for the alleged drunken manslaughter of his common-law wife. The presumed victim (herself the former wife of an innocent purge victim) reappears, and the suspect is proved innocent. It is a grotesque and drab replay of what had been, some twenty years before, sheer pain and violence. These and other novels and short stories tend to organize themselves into a cycle, set in a specific "country," much like William Faulkner's (q.v.) work (which influenced P.) and that of Gabriel García Márquez (q.v.), which they resemble in their mixture of fantastic and satirical features. P.'s ultimate message is not pessimistic: good and truth are elusive and weak, but evil is sterile and ridiculous, while the spectacle of their inconclusive struggle is a source of joy and wisdom.

P. also wrote a number of plays in a lyrical and absurdist vein; they are somber and fantastic and have often been effective on stage.

FURTHER WORKS: *Fuga* (1958); *Zilele săptămînii* (1959); *Umbrela de soare* (1962); *Vara oltenilor* (1964; rev. ed., 1972); *Fata de la miazăzi* (1964); *Somnul pămîntului* (1965); *Prea mic pentru un război așa de mare* (1969); *F* (1969); *Acești îngeri triști* (1970); *Ploaia albă* (1971); *Cei doi din dreptul Tebei* (1973); *Teatru* (1974); *O bere pentru calul meu* (1974); *Împăratul norilor* (1976)

BIBLIOGRAPHY: Nemoianu, V., on *Vînătoarea regală, BA,* 48 (1974), 764; Nemoianu, V., on *Ploile de dincolo de vreme, WLT,* 51 (1977), 267; Kleininger, T., on *Vînătoarea regală, CREL,* 6, 4 (1978), 78–80

VIRGIL NEMOIANU

PORTER, Katherine Anne

American short-story writer and novelist, b. 15 May 1890, Indian Creek, Texas; d. 18 Sept. 1980, Silver Spring, Md.

Although her personal experience profoundly influenced P.'s art, many of the biographical facts, including the date of her birth, have not been established beyond question. On a few of the more obviously pertinent matters, however, the evidence is reasonably consistent. P. was third or fourth of a family of five children. Her mother died when P. was very young, perhaps no more than two years old, and the children's paternal grandmother, a Kentuckian who had moved to Texas shortly after the Civil War, assumed principal responsibility for their rearing. P.'s education was irregular. Rebelliously precocious as a child and adolescent, she ran away from school and was married at the age of sixteen. The first and two succeeding marriages all ended in divorce. As a young woman she made a precarious living—at occupations including those of journalist, movie extra, ballad singer, and book reviewer—in Chicago, Denver, New York City, and various places in Texas and Louisiana. Between World Wars I and II she sojourned twice in Mexico for extended periods and then in Europe, chiefly in Berlin and Paris. Later, on the strength of growing critical recognition of her work, she held appointments as lecturer and writer-in-residence at a number of colleges and universities. In old age she lived many years in College Park, Maryland. For a long time she was a fallen-away Catholic, but newspaper notices of her death referred to plans for celebration of a requiem mass.

Beyond noting her generally somber view of the human situation, which underlies even the richly comical effects of stories like "The Cracked Looking-Glass" (1932)—her recurrent emphasis upon the appalling burden of ignorant and sinful man's individual responsibility for his destiny—it is difficult to categorize P.'s work as a whole. Elements of regionalism are apparent in many of her stories; but, true to her mixed family heritage, she is not consistently classifiable as either Southerner or Southwesterner. She is propagandist for no cause or doctrine. Typically, as in "Flowering Judas" (1930), where the heroine, torn between two faiths, is loyal finally to neither, it is the psychology of apostasy and betrayal that most fascinates P. Her early and difficult experience of independent survival, artistic and financial, in the man's world of her generation, encouraged feminist leanings. Unflattering portraits of male chauvinists, feckless fools for the most part, but a few of them hideously cruel, appear often in her fiction. Yet no special sympathy for such men's female antagonists, strictly on the grounds of sex, is ever evoked.

As previously noted, much of her work is heavily autobiographical. Virtually all her fiction, from "María Concepción" (1922) to *Ship of Fools* (1962), even those stories centered upon the pained awakenings of childhood, involve in one way or another

situations of broken or strained marriages or unhappy love affairs. The climactic events of the tragic love story "Pale Horse, Pale Rider" (1938) are a fictional account of P.'s near-fatal illness in Denver during the influenza epidemic of 1918. The heroine named Miranda, who appears as child, adolescent, or woman in a number of stories, most obviously resembles the author. But aspects of P.'s personality are discoverable in many other characters, including not only the nunnish schoolteacher-revolutionary of "Flowering Judas" and at least three different women among the passengers of *Ship of Fools,* but even the male protagonist of "The Leaning Tower" (1941), which draws upon P.'s experience in Berlin during the early Nazi era.

Yet none of the stories is pure confession, of the self-therapeutic or any other design. Every persona, Miranda as much as any of the others, is fully realized as an independent dramatic agent, whose actions are explicable without necessary reference to the author's life. Always, there is a dimension of extrapersonal significance in the fiction. In some pieces—for example, "Flowering Judas" and "Hacienda" (1932) of the Mexican group, "The Leaning Tower," *Ship of Fools,* the stories of the sequence entitled (in the 1965 collected volume) "The Old Order"—there is a readily definable element of the "documentary." Nor can P. be convicted of any theoretical commitment to the necessary priority of personal values as opposed to public concerns. In all her work, however subtly, a profound consciousness of the larger cultural context of private affairs is discernible. And, finally, among P.'s many strategems for "coming to terms with herself" in fiction—which is largely, for her, a matter of transcendence rather than either triumph or reconciliation—her uncompromising dedication to artistic *form* is most important.

For the contents of the three earlier volumes, *Flowering Judas, and Other Stories* (1930), *Pale Horse, Pale Rider: Three Short Novels* (1939), and *The Leaning Tower, and Other Stories* (1944), which with a few additional pieces were brought together in *The Collected Stories of K. A. P.* (1965), she is recognized as one of the world's great modern masters of short fiction. Her numerous honors include Guggenheim and Ford Foundation fellowships, election to the National Institute of Arts and Letters, a Pulitzer Prize and a National Book Award (both 1966, for *The Collected Stories*), and various medals.

Critical opinion of her principal popular success, the long novel *Ship of Fools*, a fictional account of P.'s voyage from Mexico to Germany in 1932 aboard a German liner, has been sorely divided on a variety of issues. But the trouble may be simply that the critic is yet to appear who can satisfactorily define that book's formal principle.

FURTHER WORKS: *The Days Before* (1952); *The Collected Essays and Occasional Writings of K. A. P.* (1970); *The Never Ending Wrong* (1977)

BIBLIOGRAPHY: Mooney, H., *The Fiction and Criticism of K. A. P.* (1957); Nance, W., *K. A. P. and the Art of Rejection* (1964); Hendrick, G., *K. A. P.* (1965); Hartley, L., and Core, G., eds., *K. A. P.: A Critical Symposium* (1969); Liberman, M., *K. A. P.'s Fiction* (1971); Hardy, J., *K. A. P.: An Introduction* (1973); Kiernan, R., *K. A. P. and Carson McCullers: A Reference Guide* (1976); Warren, R., ed., *K. A. P.: A Collection of Critical Essays* (1979)

JOHN EDWARD HARDY

PORTUGUESE LITERATURE

The modern Portuguese intellectual's cultural inheritance from past centuries is a bizarre combination of insular ultrachauvinism and fatalism. Indeed, the writers of the much admired Portuguese Generation of 1870—José Maria Eça de Queiroz (1845–1900), Antero de Quental (1842–1891), and Joaquim Pedro de Oliveira Martins (1845–1894)—censured these national idiosyncrasies and suggested the complete "Europeanization" of Portugal to remedy them. Public events, however, superseded their desires.

A decaying monarchy was replaced in 1910 by an unmanageable republic, followed by a half-century of repressive dictatorship. The Portuguese empire was dismembered by the English Ultimatum of 1890, through which the British seized Portuguese territory in Africa for the construction of the Capetown-to-Cairo railroad. The empire gradually dwindled and finally disappeared after the 1974 revolution.

Portuguese literature was consistently ignored and/or repressed, but survived. Poetry, as throughout all of Portuguese literary history, has been dominant, but the novel and drama have also been strong and innovative. All genres have produced works of high quality and internationally respected writers.

Symbolist (q.v.) and Parnassian poetry prevailed during the first decades of the century. Eugénio de Castro (1869–1944) was the most notable Portuguese poet after the suicide of Quental and the death of António Nobre (1867–1900). In 1890 Castro published the major Portuguese symbolist treatise as a preface to his collection of poems, *Oaristos* (1890; intimacies). His poetry revealed the influence of Baudelaire and Verlaine, while it aspired to the revitalization of Portuguese poetry through the introduction of new, shocking imagery and unusual rhyme schemes. Castro was highly esteemed by Miguel de Unamuno, Rubén Darío (qq.v.), and Mallarmé. A small Decadent school of poets formed around Castro, but none of them approached his expressive powers.

The verse of Florbela Espanca (1894–1930) described the fate of a woman unable to achieve the perfect love. In *Charneca em flor* (1931; the heath in flower) she admitted the impossibility of pure love and accepted instead an inner peace.

Meantime, on the other side of the world in colonial Macau, Camilo Pessanha (1867–1926) was also writing symbolist poetry. The poems in *Clepsidra* (1920; clepsydra) reveal the author's emotional instability through passages preoccupied with rapid time movement, flowing currents, and changing seasons. Wenceslau de Moraes (1854–1929) had spent time with Pessanha in Macau, but took up permanent residence in Japan and became a practicing Buddhist. He chronicled life there, evoking the great age of Portuguese explorations, as in *Dai Nippon* (1897; the great Japan).

The founding of the Portuguese Republic in 1910 saw the initiation of the Portuguese Renascence movement, dedicated to a national cultural rebirth. Founded by the poet Teixeira de Pascoaes (q.v.), the movement's magazine *A águia* (1910–32) proffered *saudosismo*, a nebulous theory of mystical, pantheistic nostalgia, as the most adequate definition of Portuguese sociopolitical and cultural existence. Although *saudosismo* retained an influence on later Portuguese poetry—most notably in the works of Afonso Lopes Vieira (1878–1946)—it was debunked by an opposition group that had formed around the *Seara nova* review, including the historians António Sérgio de Sousa (1883–1968) and Jaime Cortesão (1884–1960).

Little literary and cultural reviews, like *A águia* and *Seara nova,* have traditionally kept the Portuguese abreast of European culture and also are publishing outlets for new writers. *Orpheu* (1915) was inspired by the concepts of futurism (q.v.) and was initially a Luso-Brazilian undertaking. Fernando Pessoa (q.v.), who had participated in *A águia,* and Mário de Sá-Carneiro (q.v.) were contributors to the first issue and the editors of the second and final number. Modernism (q.v.) was heralded by other ephemeral reviews—*Exílio* (1916), *Portugal futurista* (1917), and *Athena* (1924–25). José de Almada-Negreiros (1893–1970), a poet, novelist, and artist, was the most dashing figure of Portuguese modernism. Almada-Negreiros participated in all the literary reviews and organized the movement's most remembered scandal—the bitter attack on the highly touted "commercial literature" of the historical dramatist Júlio Dantas (1876–1962).

Portuguese drama of the period included symbolist tendencies, represented by João da Câmara (1852–1908); the Dostoevskyan atmospheres of the dramas of Raúl Brandão (q.v.); and the comedy of manners, which was the forte of Eduardo Schwalbach (1860–1946). Another fine dramatist was António Patrício (1875–1930), whose *O fim* (1909; the end) was recently revived owing to its presentation of the political intrigues that led to the downfall of the monarchy. Although Pessoa and Sá-Carneiro dabbled in theater, it was Almada-Negreiros who proposed a new existential concern for drama—thus attacking the historical exaggerations of Dantas. Alfredo Cortez (1880–1946) took up some aspects of Almada-Negreiros's doctrine and created a social drama. The rural themes of Carlos Selvagem (b. 1890) have both dramatic and documentary values. Both Cortez and Selvagem presented the conflict of the individual with society, à la Ibsen.

It was not until the founding in Coimbra of the critical review *Presença* (1927–40) that the modernist ideals gained stature within Portuguese culture. Choosing as their Portuguese masters Pessoa, Sá-Carneiro, and Almada-Negreiros—the so-called lunatics of *Orpheu*—the *presencistas* brought the newer figures of European literature—Apollinaire, Proust, Gide, Valéry, and Pirandello (qq.v.)—to the attention of Portuguese readers. They advocated a literature that relied on emotions rather than on intellect and rejected academic, nonartistic limits placed on culture.

The *presencistas* (like most Portuguese writers of our century) cultivated all genres, José Régio (q.v.) and João Gaspar Simões (b. 1903) were the founders of the review. António Botto (1897–1959), whose *Canções* (1921; songs) expressed his avowedly homosexual leanings in a light, proselike form, also tangentially participated in *Presença*.

Miguel Torga (q.v.) and Adolfo Casais Monteiro (1908–1972) joined the *Presença* group in the early 1930s. Monteiro's poetry, following the group's literary credo, rejected the formalities of structure. His work as a commentator and critic of literature is also significant, although it has been open to much dispute owing to its *presencista* reliance on personal judgment. The multitalented Vitorino Nemésio (1901–1978) also had his literary roots in *Presença*. His poetry expressed his sentimental attachment to his childhood in the Azores, his paradise lost. Nemésio's novel about the Azores, *Mau tempo no canal* (1944; hard times in the canal), and his role as a popularizer of Portuguese culture among the masses won him national renown. The *presencistas* also were dramatists; one of their recurrent themes (and indeed one of the most important themes in Luso-Brazilian literature) was the Sebastianic myth. Pessoa, Patrício, and Régio invoked the legend of the youthful King Sebastian, who died in battle in Africa in 1578, but who, tradition holds, would return to lead his nation on to new conquests and grandeur.

After the death of the realist Eça de Queiroz, new trends in fiction appeared, notably the symbolist novels of Raúl Brandão. When João Gaspar Simões published his novel *Eloi* (1932; Eloi), relating a common man's jealousies, he revolutionized Portuguese fiction by initiating a psychological trend, influenced by Joyce, Freud (qq.v.), and Proust. António Branquinho da Fonseca (1905–1974) wrote poetry and drama, but his thriller *O barão* (1943; the baron) and his short stories, which ever so gently remove the reader from reality, have given him an enviable place in Portuguese fiction.

Portuguese fiction was also thriving outside the *presencista* group. Aquilino Ribeiro (q.v.) revitalized regionalism. José Maria

Ferreira de Castro (q.v.) published his first novels on the Portuguese emigrant experiences in the 1920s, while Manuel Teixeira Gomes (1860–1941), who was the last president of the ill-fated republic, published *Gente singular* (1909; singular people), a collection of short stories presenting disturbed, unusual characters. Irene Lisboa (1892–1958) was a fine poet, but an even more masterful narrator of the daily problems of Lisbonites in *Solidão* (1939; solitude) and of the hard existence of rural people in *Crónicas da serra* (1961; hill tales). José Rodrigues Miguéis (1901–1980), who began his impressive career as a novelist with psychological fiction, wrote novels about his childhood in Lisbon, such as *Onde a noite acaba* (1946; where night ends). His later works dealt with Portuguese immigrants in North America. Joaquim Paço d'Arcos (b. 1908) and Tomás Ribas (b. 1918) have produced popular novels detailing the personal crises of Lisbon's bourgeoisie.

Under the influence of Brazilian and North American social realism and owing to a gradual rejection of the *presencista* aesthetic, the Portuguese neorealist (q.v.) movement was born. The Marxist orientation of the magazines *Diabo* (1934–40) and *Sol nascente* (1937–40), and others appearing between the period of the Spanish Civil War and the beginning of World War II, opened the way for doctrinal views of the social obligations of modern Portuguese literature by José Maria Ferreira de Castro, António Alves Redol (q.v.), and Mário Dionísio (b. 1916). The Salazar dictatorship's reaction to these writings was to institute a rigid censorship, which caused publication difficulties for many writers until the 1974 revolution.

Redol's novel *Gaibéus* (1939: gaibéus [field workers of the Ribatejo]) is considered to have initiated neorealism in Portuguese fiction. Joaquim Soeiro Pereira Gomes (1910–1949), who had been a member of the clandestine Portuguese Communist Party, pessimistically presented the conflict between factory owners and workers in the poor suburbs around Lisbon. For example, *Esteiros* (1941; inlets), his only novel published during his lifetime, is almost a poetic elegy on child exploitation. The fiction of Fernando Namora (q.v.) and José Marmelo e Silva (b. 1913) presented similar social questions. Carlos de Oliveira (1921–1981) attacked the complacent bourgeoisie as the cause of the nation's desolation, for example, in *Uma abelha na chuva* (1953; a bee in the rain).

Although Vergílio Ferreira (b. 1916) dealt with social preoccupations in his early writings, such as *Vagão J* (1942; car J), his interest in man's fate within a tradition-laden society led him to the existential themes of *Aparição* (1959; apparition) and *Nítido nulo* (1971; clear void). José Cardoso Pires (q.v.) passed through social and existential themes and most recently has analyzed the almost schizophrenic Portuguese soul.

Fiction of the late 1950s and the 1960s began indirectly to challenge the dictatorship. Augusto Abelaira's (b. 1926) impressive *A cidade das flores* (1959; the city of flowers) examined the plight of young Portuguese intellectuals using as a metaphorical backdrop Mussolini's Italy of the 1930s. He follows the continued depression of these intellectuals in *Sem tecto, entre ruínas* (1979; roofless, among ruins), as they vicariously participate in the worldwide upheavals of 1968. Fernando Castro Soromenho (q.v.) presented the lives of petty Portuguese officials in Angola, and Urbano Tavares Rodrigues (b. 1923) has written a score of novels detailing rural and urban social concerns. José Almeida Faria (b. 1943) was the major voice of the New Novel (q.v.). He has published a fictional trilogy about the last twenty years of Portuguese life, which encompasses the fall of the dictatorship and the confused, initial phase of the revolutionary government: *A paixão* (1965; the passion), *Cortes* (1978; cuttings), and *Lusitânia* (1980; Lusitania). *Lusitânia* is perhaps the most significant recent work of Portuguese fiction.

A number of women writers of great merit have appeared since the 1950s. Agustina Bessa Luís (b. 1921), using northern Portuguese locales, presents sociopsychological probings of her women characters in fiction about modern decadent rural aristocracy. Her *A sibila* (1953; the sibyl) and *O mosteiro* (1981; the cloister) are outstanding achievements. Maria da Graça Freire (b. 1918), Fernanda Botelho (b. 1926), and Maria Judite de Carvalho (b. 1921) also emphasize women and the woman's point of view in their fiction and short stories.

The ten volumes by different poets in the series called *Novo Cancioneiro* (1941–42; new songbook) constituted the apogee of the neorealist movement in Portuguese poetry. A lack of theoretical coherence, however, prevented the group from exerting extensive influence. Aside from Fernando Namora and Mário Dionísio, João José Cochofel (1919–1982) and Carlos de Oliveira were active participants. José Gomes Ferreira (b. 1900) has links with all the earlier Portuguese poetic movements of the 20th c. Nonetheless, his role as an "idealist militant poet" who denounces human oppression and injustice through presenting its stark reality, as in *Poeta militante* (3 vols., 1977–78; militant poet), places him ideologically closest to the neorealists.The poetry of Egito Gonçalves (b. 1922) written in the 1950s presented an outcry in code against dictatorial repression.

Surrealist (q.v.) ideas had occasionally surfaced in Portuguese culture since the time of André Breton's (q.v.) 1924 manifesto—for example, the poetry of António Pedro (1909–1966); it was only in 1947, however, that a group of surrealist poets appeared. Mário Cesariny de Vasconcelos (b. 1924) was the bulwark of Portuguese surrealism. His major volume, *Pena capital* (1957; capital punishment), reveals a chaotic, humorous, nonsense world. The poetry of António Maria Lisboa (1928–1953) was preoccupied with eroticism, which he viewed as the key to self-understanding and liberty. Alexandre O'Neill (b. 1924) presents everyday life through comic verse. The most notable work of Portuguese surrealist fiction was *A torre de Barbela* (1964; the tower of Barbela) by Ruben A[dresen Leitão] (1920–1975).

Lyric poets whose works were not directly characterized by specific sociopolitical or literary attitudes united around other little reviews. *Cadernos de poesia* was issued in three different phases between 1940 and 1953 and revealed the works of Tomaz Kim (pseud. of Joaquim Tomás Monteiro-Grillo, 1915–1967), José Blanc de Portugal (b. 1914), and Rui Cinatti (b. 1915). Sebastião de Gama (1924–1952), David Mourão-Ferreira (b. 1927), and Alberto de Lacerda (b. 1928) were associated with *Távola redonda*, which appeared between 1950 and 1954. Sophia de Mello Breyner Andresen (b. 1919) participated in both of these reviews. Her notable poetry presents maritime and aerial images suggesting a search for personal liberation, as in *O nome das coisas* (1977; the name of things). Eugénio de Andrade (b. 1923) is yet another distinguished poet whose verse achieves a musical quality. Jorge de Sena (q.v.), however, towers over all others since

Pessoa. Recent poetic groups have included the Poetry 61 vanguard movement, which developed from concretism: E. M. de Melo e Castro (b. 1932), Fiama Hasse Pais Brandão (b. 1938), and Maria Teresa Horta (b. 1937) are its notable figures. Horta was also one of the "Three Marias," along with Maria Isabel Barreno (b. 1939) and Maria Velho da Costa (b. 1938), who wrote the multigenre *Novas cartas portuguesas* (1973; *The New Portuguese Letters,* 1975), whose outspoken feminist viewpoint caused a worldwide sensation and resulted in its banning and the prosecution in court of its authors. Other important contemporary lyric poets include António Gedeão (b. 1906), Herberto Helder (b. 1930), and António Ramos Rosa (b. 1924).

Post-*Presença* drama has its roots in Lisbon's Salitre Studio Theater group, founded in 1946. The dramas of Bernardo Santareno (1924–1980) have a psychosexual orientation, while those of Luiz Francisco Rebello (b. 1924), a major theater critic, present the conflicts between the forces of life and death with little hope for the future, as, for example, in *Condenados à vida* (1963; condemned to life). The political criticism suggested in two plays by Luís de Sttau Monteiro (b. 1926) resulted in his imprisonment in 1967; his Brechtian drama *Felizmente há luar* (1961; luckily there's moonlight) and his novel *Angústia para o jantar* (1961; *A Man of Means,* 1965) are essential reading for the comprehension of Portuguese life during the last decades of the dictatorship.

With the collapse of the regime in April 1974, an avalanche of long-suppressed works by many of the above-cited writers and others began to appear. Literature by African-Portuguese writers was published more openly. Most notable is the fiction of the Angolan José Luandino Vieira (q.v.). His collection of short stories *Luuanda* (1964; *Luuanda: Short Stories of Angola,* 1980), which resulted in his incarceration, viewed life in Angola during the early years of the liberation movement. Recent Portuguese fiction has also included many accounts of life under Salazar and narrations of African war experiences. Olga Gonçalves (b. 1929) has produced perhaps the most original postrevolutionary body of fiction. With little of past glories to extol, Gonçalves, in *Este verão o emigrante là-bas* (1978; this summer the emigrant down there [i.e., in Portugal]) and in *Ora esguardae* (1982; hark ye now), views the sociopolitical and linguistic identity crises faced by the Portuguese in the postrevolutionary epoch.

Nuno Bragança (b. 1929) also expresses great interest in linguistic and technical aspects of narrative, as in *Directa* (1977; direct) and *Square Tolstoi* (1982; Tolstoy Square). The younger poets Gastão Cruz (b. 1941) and Nuno Júdice (b. 1949) have also attracted much attention. Carlos Coutinho's (b. 1943) postrevolutionary drama, published in his *Teatro de circunstância* (2 vols., 1976–77; theater of circumstance), evokes the social atmosphere that supported both repression and resistance. The Barraca Theater Group has become an important center of theatrical revival and growth.

Portuguese literature of the 1980s has been characterized by a search for a new identity. Literary critics and historians have reviewed the national past with great skepticism about the "national myths" that were propagated in literature down through the centuries. While António José Saraiva (b. 1917) has questioned the concept of the Portuguese identity—for example, the role as the "most Catholic country"—Eduardo Lourenço (b. 1923) has reexamined the recent past and its significance for the present and future of Portugal.

BIBLIOGRAPHY: Bell, A., *Portuguese Literature* (1922); Moser, G., "Portuguese Literature in Recent Years," *MLJ*, 44 (1960), 245–54; Sayers, R., "Twenty-Five Years of Portuguese Short Fiction," *SSF*, 3 (1966), 253–64; Moser, G., "Portuguese Writers of This Century," *Hispania*, 50 (1966), 947–54; Stern, I., "Suppressed Portuguese Fiction: 1926–1974," *BA*, 50 (1976), 54–60; Macedo, H., Introduction to *Contemporary Portuguese Poetry* (1978), pp. 1–18; Sayers, R., "The Impact of Symbolism in Portugal and Brazil," in Grass, R., and Risley, W. R., eds., *Waiting for Pegasus: Studies of the Presence of Symbolism and Decadence in Hispanic Letters* (1979), pp. 125–41

IRWIN STERN

PORTUGUESE CREOLE LITERATURE
See Cape Verdean, Guinea-Bissau, and São Tomé e Principe literatures

POSTREALISM

During the late 19th c. realism was a goal at which to arrive; in the 20th c. it has become a platform from which to take off. Realism was not dead, as the French writer Paul Alexis (1847–1901) urgently assured the reporter Jules Huret in 1893, but it was out of favor with writers and critics alike, or rather it had reached its zenith and an inevitable reaction would lead to new interests for literary endeavor, in a ferment that would produce works that can only be called postrealistic.

There have, to be sure, been resurgences of realism as an innovating force, especially where a reexamination of actuality seemed of paramount importance or where a body of writers wished to capitalize on the positive implications of the term. In Italy after the obfuscations of the Fascist regime, there was need for an opening into contemporary reality and neorealism (q.v.) emerged in both fiction and film. As Portugal in the 1940s showed signs of shaking off its intellectual and social torpor, a similar banner was raised. In France the Populists of the 1930s and the practitioners of the New Novel (q.v.) in the 1960s legitimized themselves as purveyors of a new and improved brand of realism. Such renewals of enthusiasm, however, have departed from basic doctrine and have been directed more at serving a partisan view about society or aesthetics than at forwarding what Hippolyte Taine (1828–1893) called "a great inquiry" into man and society. Indeed, the most widespread of these labels, Socialist Realism (q.v.), has come to be seen (outside the communist bloc) as no realism, as a denial of the central philosophic principles on which the 19th-c. movement rested.

When it comes to depiction of social institutions and their dynamics, however, the realistic mode continues to constitute the norm in this century (see Society and Literature). Such works are legion and have a bland respectability, but they bring no surprises and have no innovative force. They are variations on a hackneyed form, having a certain interest when they explore an area of society not previously brought into view or when, more rarely, an author of compelling vision gives them at least temporary impact. They are popular perhaps because they are in a familiar vein and make no urgent demands on the reader. They tend to blend with the strictly reportorial account of sociological or anthropological cast, to move from objective selection to indiscriminate tape recording. There are no significant new worlds to conquer in this repetitive genre, and aspiring writers turn elsewhere to find models for their own vision of reality.

The most lasting and widely diffused legacy of the older realism was the massive infusion of "modern and popular subjects" that have come to dominate the literature of our time. Whereas classical writers almost automatically turned to traditional tales or exercised untrammeled imagination in their devising of illustrative actions, the contemporary author as automatically turns to the here and now, to the observed scene, for his materials, such occasional tours de force as John Erskine's (1879–1951) once popular *The Private Life of Helen of Troy* (1925) or John Gardner's (b. 1933) *Grendel* (1971) notwithstanding. For better or worse, the stuff from which modern writers make their statement about the human condition is predominantly what they have observed, however filtered or transformed by their individual consciousness.

In large part these transformations are dictated by the very limitations imposed by realist orthodoxy. It embodied self-denying ordinances of such rigor as to proscribe for the writer much of his traditional function. He could no longer be *maker* or *seer*. He was confined to being observer and recorder, a machine, not a person. The tenet of objectivity, of an ostensibly complete authorial withdrawal, as enunciated by Gustave Flaubert (1821–1880)and reiterated even by James Joyce (q.v.) in *A Portrait of the Artist as a Young Man* (1916)—was one source of limitation. The tenet that data should be accessible to all observers was another. The aspiration to a style as colorless and impersonal as that of a court transcript (Stendhal, 1783–1842) was a third. If art is an assertion and perpetuation of self—the imposition of a unique, ordering consciousness upon the disorderly and confusing data of experience—then realism as dogmatically conceived and tentatively practiced denied the artist his rightful personal role.

There had always been resistance against these restrictions; and by the end of the 19th c., Joris-Karl Huysmans (1848–1907) had forsaken Emile Zola (1840–1902), Edmond Rostand (1868–1918) had revived the romantic drama à la Victor Hugo (1802–1885), Maurice Maeterlinck (q.v.), followed by J. M. Barrie (q.v.), had made capital of the fairy tale. The romance, set in a never-neverland (Graustark or Ruritania) of swashbuckling derring-do, flourished again. None of this activity carried any hope for the future; such worn-out soil could not nurture healthy plants. The signal of change would have to come from major talents reaching their full powers, at the turn of the century. As it happened, all of them, overtly or by implication, repudiated realism, or, more properly, took from it what they needed as they set themselves new goals.

Before turning to the transformations that writers like Marcel Proust, Thomas Mann, Hermann Hesse, Franz Kafka, William Faulkner (qq.v.), and James Joyce effected, it is instructive to consider how the realistic infusion was adapted in subliterary genres, such as the crime novel and the sex novel. Here the realist restriction had been one of sobriety, of refraining from use of the exceptional and the outré, whereas the unaligned purveyor of this kind of fare knew that the appetite of his readers was for sensationalism in increasingly hyperbolic doses. The realists had a legitimate interest in opening up the seamy side of life as part of the total human record. They fought a stubborn battle in defense of the presentation of violence and sex as part of that record, and the more responsible among them were careful not to present violence for the sake of violence or sex for the sake of sex. Predictably, however, sensation destroyed objective balance.

Zola, who always had a taste for the hyperbolic, opened the way even before the Rougon-Macquart cycle in *Thérèse Raquin* (1867; *Thérèse Raquin,* 1881; later tr., 1960), where sex *and* violence were placed together in a heady mixture. Such later writers as Dashiell Hammet (1894–1961), James M. Cain (1892–1977), and Mickey Spillane (b. 1918) are the continuators, not the originators, of this line. In his later works Zola often went overboard in his use of sensationalism: the multiple violences of *La terre* (1887; *Earth,* 1895; later tr., 1954); Jacques Lantier running amok in his locomotive in *La bête humaine* (1890; *The Human Beast,* 1954); the alcohol-sodden body of old Antoine Macquart reduced to a heap of blue ash in *Le docteur Pascal (1893; Doctor Pascal,* 1893). For those disposed to read in that way, his works were a titillating *psychopathia sexualis* and *criminalis.* And they were so read.

Sensationalism, a deliberate choice of only the most heightened data, has pervaded all popular literature, even the comic book. Its hero is the sadomasochistic private detective, who exceeds the knights of old in his capacity to inflict and endure physical punishment. His recuperative powers are phenomenal; he lives in order to be beaten up another day. He is also a sexual athlete of consummate skill.

On the borderline between popular and serious novels is the exposé, the work that pleads a case. Realist objectivity forbade an author to engage in special pleading: objectively assembled fact would make its own case. Authorial withdrawal was a more effective instrument of truth than personal, and therefore suspect, bias. Because the line between such special pleading and complete objectivity was never clear, realism, from the beginning, tended to be identified with social criticism. In any event, postrealistic writers have rediscovered the joys of partisanship. Since precise truth is less important than scoring a point, they too open the doors to a form of sensationalism and see their battles in the stark colors of black and white. They surround their fables with a convincing air of verisimilitude, a specious, because selective, documentation, but their excesses of heightening and emphasis and above all of omission eventually convict them of taking sides. Upton Sinclair (q.v.) is a particularly well-known example of this kind of writer. *The Jungle* (1906), which might have been a dispassionate and probing analysis of the life of the immigrant in the Chicago stockyards, became first a sensational exposé of meat-packing malpractices and then a gospel tract for socialism.

Less fractured but equally contrived is the whole body of Great Depression novels in the U.S. and elsewhere. Mobs do not respond to a reasoned analysis of the facts; they want to feel the bombardment of a heightened appeal in their guts.

It is in the assimilation of realist materials by serious literature that the significant transformations have taken place. The most dramatic change has been the return to expression of a unique personal vision, of a reality that is private and unduplicatable. Surrealism (q.v.) is a special embodiment of this effort, although basically antirealistic, since it repudiates realistic method and most

of realistic material. It was Marcel Proust, who, in his avowed intention to write the book of himself, led the main attack. He asserted that the only true reality is that which lies in the depths of memory uncorrupted by the deformations of analysis. It cannot be compared or measured against the reality that others perceive. He called into question the whole established idea of reality, finding it "not in the outward appearance of the subject," which is only "a sort of cinematographic parade." He denied that it was merely a "byproduct of existence, so to speak, approximately identical for everybody." He considered "the literature that is satisfied merely to 'describe things'" to be "the farthest removed from reality, the one that most impoverishes and saddens us . . ." by its superficiality.

Such a view may lead to a practical solipsism in which the author writes only for himself, since he is all that exists. More likely, the author attempts—but fails—to transmute personal signs and symbols into elements that convey meaning for other intelligences. What is unique and impressive in Proust is that he does not drift off into a private world of the imagination, does not revel in the chaos of the subconscious, but brings everything into the light of day by a rigorously analytical, if convoluted, method. His world is a social world. His perceptions are of people, places, and things, although he early makes the cardinal point that none of these is constant even to one observer, let alone uniform for all observers. Thus, what the mind of the narrator engages with is not a private refuge of dream removed from reality. On the contrary, it has hard, clear contours; it is apprehended by others; it exists in its own right. But that existence has no interest until it is illuminated by a unique consciousness. Space, time, and objects are elements of actuality, but only as givens. They take an inferior place to the mind that reassorts them. It is the mind that gives these elements a reality that is, prior to the ordering, only contingent. So real is the world Proust evokes, so sharp is his social analysis, that Harry Levin (b. 1912), in *The Gates of Horn: A Study of Five French Realists* (1963), makes him part of the continuum of traditional realists beginning with Balzac (1799–1850). Yet Proust's essence is different from that of his predecessors. For him outward reality is merely the inescapable material on which the mind feeds, since there can be nothing in the mind that has not previously been apprehended by the senses. He stands as the unequaled practitioner of the book of oneself. Perhaps the logical direction in which to go, after his example, is toward outright poetic autobiography. Elridge Cleaver's (b. 1935) *Soul on Ice* (1968) is in a way a successor of *À la recherche du temps perdu* (1913–27; *Remembrance of Things Past,* 1922–32) just as *The Education of Henry Adams* (1918, privately printed 1907) by Henry Adams (q.v.) is a predecessor. At any rate, the right of the author to personal testimony has been reestablished, not in a void, but in the real world.

The glaring self-exposure of the book of oneself is not for most authors. They wish to impose themselves on their material in a less overt way. They prefer to take shelter in a degree of anonymity by way of allegory, fable, symbolic framework—some sort of analogical format—through which they impose meaning, or cause the reader to discern meaning, without mounting a pulpit. This is the high road of great literature. The realists never quite succeeded in abandoning it—witness Zola's *Germinal* (1885; *Germinal,* 1895) or Dostoevsky's (1821–1881) great novels.

The process may be only suggestive (often with ironical intent) by way of a title, such as Jules Romains's (q.v.) *Les hommes de bonne volonté* (27 vols., 1932–46; *Men of Good Will,* 14 vols., 1933–46), in which men of good will do not prevail; John Steinbeck's (q.v.) appropriation of a Miltonic phrase for his *In Dubious Battle* (1936); or Robert Penn Warren's (q.v.) *All the King's Men* (1946). In such cases the novel is not shaped to conform with the suggested analogue; but the meaning is implied by the title, and the reader's options of interpretation are narrowed, if not closed. A further step, as in Faulkner's *Absalom, Absalom!* (1936), is actually to conduct the narrative in broad parallel with the traditional story, although with no detailed adherence to it. The result is that a densely detailed modern story takes on breadth and poignancy by reference to a suggested or lightly sketched literary analogue.

Beyond this minimal shaping for meaning is the imposition of an allegorical matrix, as a result of which the selection and position of materials of observation are determined by a preconceived idea. Realist induction gives way to a process of deduction, just as it does in traditional allegory, but with a vastly greater density of observed data. The author (and reader) can thus have it both ways:

there is the factual security of an apparent slice of life in the realist mode and the interpretive assistance of a doctrinal system that leaves no loophole of doubt as to what the author means. The most impressive writer in this vein is Thomas Mann. His first novel, *Buddenbrooks* (1901; *Buddenbrooks,* 1924) is more than a slice of life depicting existence in a German Hanseatic town, since it is dominated by the Hegelian dialectic system in its portrayal of the rise and fall of a middle-class family and, by extension, of a middle-class culture. This same Hegelian matrix is more sketchily applied to describe the nature and fate of the artist in *Tonio Kröger* (1903; *Tonio Kröger,* 1914) and *Der Tod in Venedig (1913; Death in Venice,* 1925). Then, in the major philosophical novel of our time, *Der Zauberberg* (1924; *The Magic Mountain,* 1927), Mann applies the dialectic on a vast scale to explain and project the history of European thought and culture. The milieu of a tuberculosis sanatorium is well documented, but both the disease and those suffering from it are pawns in a symbolic game where universal meanings are the goal. Although he abandoned the Hegelian framework in his later writings, Mann continued to use analogical devices, notably in *Doktor Faustus* (1947; *Doctor Faustus,* 1948), in which the fate of Adrian Leverkühn is in parallel with that of Nazi Germany, and the clinical metaphor of the work becomes syphilis instead of tuberculosis.

Another, although less successful, instance of this general tendency to shape by means of analogy is the work of Franz Kafka. Whatever the uncertainties about his novels in their unfinished state, the general formula is clear. *Der Prozeß* (1925; *The Trial,* 1937) is an allegory of contemporary man on three levels: religious, social, sexual. The arrest that occurs on the protagonist's thirtieth birthday is very like the sense of sin that falls upon John Bunyan (1628–1688) in *Grace Abounding to the Chief of Sinners* (1666). But it can also be read as an account of a general (and banal) sense of secular frustration or as a description of a Freudian instance of sexual inadequacy. If Kafka had carried it off, this would have been a remarkable work. As it is, it has been widely influential in showing the way to raise the individual data of everyday life to the constant universals of man's quest for meaning. Kafka, like Albert Camus (q.v.) and others, provides a wonderfully matter-of-fact texture of events, a deceptively casual and realistic narrative in pedestrian language, as a base from which to rise to cosmic questions.

The most important example of this tendency to employ analogues is James Joyce's *Ulysses* (1922), no doubt the most widely influential novel of the 20th c. His innovations, both stylistic and structural, boil down to the provision of multiple perspectives from which to view an ostensibly objective reality. The events and personalities in Dublin on June 16, 1904, are a dense assemblage of data of documentary cast. They add up to a picture of mediocrity, if not of frustration. Beyond this is the presence of the external referent of the story of Odysseus and Telemachus, which is, of course, an authorial intrusion, especially since contrivance rather than obvious similarity sustains the parallel. The result is that the all too mediocre present is to be viewed both in and for itself and *sub specie aeternitatis*. In addition to this major shaping element there are suggested parallels of Daedalus-Icarus, of Hamlet, of the Wandering Jew, and possibly of *The Divine Comedy*. As if the revisions of judgment demanded by these analogues were not enough, there are the parodic styles that begin about halfway through the novel. No major writer since Joyce has dared see reality plain. Each ingenious author has sought in his own way, by both external and internal devices, to pay tribute to the complexity, the ambiguity, and the paradoxicality of what the realists of the 19th c., in their simple faith, thought was the same for all observers.

Finally, major writers of this century have for the most part reasserted a personal style. There is a joy in language that has not been so fervent since the Renaissance. Different as they are, the styles of Joyce, Proust, Mann, and Faulkner have the indelible stamp of personality. Slang and neologism enrich the language of literature. Sentence structure after a century of radical realist pruning luxuriates once again. The heady intoxication of verbal play undoes some writers, such as Thomas Wolfe (q.v.), encourages turgidity and obscurity of statement among all but the most gifted, and spurs beginners to spend themselves in verbal pyrotechnics. No doubt a new efflorescence of language was the first sign of a postrealism, but by its very excess and inappositeness on occasion it will also be the first to be curbed.

BIBLIOGRAPHY: Baumbach, J., *The Landscape of Nightmare: Studies in the Contemporary American Novel* (1965); Galloway, D., *The Absurd Hero in American Fiction* (1966); Graff, G., *Poetic Statement and Critical Dogma* (1970); Hassan, I., *The Dismemberment of Orpheus: Toward a Post-Modern Literature* (1971); Barthes, R., *Mythologies* (1973); Glicksberg, C. I., *The Literature of Commitment* (1976); Korg, J., *Language in Modern Literature: Innovation and Experiment* (1979)

GEORGE J. BECKER

POULAR LITERATURE
See Guinean Literature

POUND, Ezra
American poet, translator, and literary critic, b. 30 Oct. 1885, Hailey, Idaho; d. 1 Nov. 1972, Venice, Italy

Specializing in Romance languages and literatures, P. graduated from Hamilton College in 1905. After postgraduate work at the University of Pennsylvania and extensive travel in the Mediterranean countries, he settled in London in 1908, where for the next twelve years he was involved in prodigious literary activities. He helped initiate the imagist (q.v.) and vorticist movements; and as foreign editor of *Poetry* (1912–18) and *The Little Review* (1917–18) he tirelessly promoted significant new work by such writers as T. S. Eliot, James Joyce, and William Carlos Williams (qq.v.). He published numerous music and art reviews and social and literary criticism as well as poetry in such journals as *The Egoist* and *The New Age*. Much of this criticism is reflected in the verse of *Hugh Selwyn Mauberley* (1920). He also began his magnum opus, *The Cantos* (1917–68). In 1920 he moved to Paris and in 1924 settled in Rapallo, Italy. For making broadcasts during World War II from Radio Rome espousing his idiosyncratic economic and social theories and defending some Fascist policies, he was charged with treason. Arrested in 1945, he was imprisoned in the American Disciplinary Training Center at Pisa. Here he wrote the *Pisan Cantos,* the most acclaimed section of *The Cantos,* for which, amid bitter controversy, he was awarded the Bollingen

Prize in 1949. P. was returned to the U.S. for trial in 1946 and was committed to St. Elizabeths Hospital for the insane in Washington, D.C., where he remained for the next twelve years. In 1958 charges against him were dismissed, and P. returned to Italy.

P.'s career was characterized by a selfless and ceaseless devotion to the art of poetry. He supported and encouraged his gifted contemporaries while endeavoring to discover and restore what he considered to be masterwork from the past. Studying the various forms and functions of poetry from other countries and other ages, P. assimilated poetic traditions from Italy, Greece, Spain, France, China, and Japan, as well as from England and America. He believed that poetry could fulfill essential functions for civilization: it provided a unique record of private sensibilities and communal values while transmitting the "tale of the tribe" (*Guide to Kulchur,* 1938). He insisted on poetry's potential importance as a linguistic and social document, a medium that could bring not only ideas and feelings, but language and historical events under scrutiny. Translation and criticism are important elements in his writing; both serve as essential guides to his poetry.

Early, major influences on P.'s work include Homer, Dante, and Confucius. From the work of these writers, P. drew techniques and themes that he developed throughout his early poetry and *The Cantos.* In the essay "Dante" in *The Spirit of Romance* (1910) P. interpreted the *Divine Comedy* both as a literal description of Dante's imagining a journey "through the realms inhabited by the spirits of men after death" and as the journey of "Dante's intelligence through the states of mind wherein dwell all sorts and conditions of men before death." P. envisaged his *Cantos* as a record of such a journey, the dramatization of individual exploration of past and present in an effort to understand our world. P. explained in *Introduzione alla natura economica degli S.U.A.* (1944; *An Introduction to the Economic Nature of the United States,* 1950; rpt., *Impact: Essays on Ignorance and the Decline of American Civilization,* 1960) that he had planned to write an epic poem that begins "in the Dark Forest, crosses the Purgatory of human error, and ends in the light." The journey in *The Cantos,* however, was "by no means an orderly Dantescan rising/but as the winds veer" (*Canto LXXIV*). *The Cantos'* structure is more like that of a musical fugue: themes are repeated in endless variation and woven into complex patterns. Major themes include (1) the journey into the world of the dead or the past that symbolizes mankind's struggle out of ignorance into understanding; (2) the "repeat in history," the discovery of parallel or analogous events through the ages; and (3) the "magic moment," the experience of transcendent vision.

Combining his perception of Dante's work as a dramatization of states of mind with Robert Browning's use of persona and dramatic monologue, P. developed a technique of using the shifting voices of self-revelatory characters to people *The Cantos.* Mythical, historical, and contemporary figures are presented, mirroring in words and deeds their states of mind. P. relies heavily on material extracted from personal letters and literary and historical documents in *The Cantos;* he is interested not just in describing events but in revealing the motives and temperaments of those who influenced events. Historical figures such as the 15th-c. soldier and patron of the arts Sigismundo Malatesta, the Elizabethan jurist Edward Coke, Elizabeth I, John Adams, and Thomas Jefferson speak through fragments of their own writings. Embodying the ideals of personal liberty as well as ethical and responsible behavior, they represent to P. heroic figures who tried to advance civilization. P. searched through history to find those who embodied the Confucian ideals of "sincerity" and "rectitude" in contrast to those who through greed, ignorance, and malevolence worked against the common good. *The Cantos* record an endless struggle between the creators and the destroyers.

Two journeys are dramatized in *The Cantos:* one, a spiritual quest for transcendence; the other, an intellectual search for worldly wisdom. The poet's goals are for the individual and the community: personal enlightenment combined with a vision of civic order. Just as Beatrice guided Dante's pilgrim, so classical goddesses appear in *The Cantos,* signaling the advent of visionary experience: Aphrodite, Diana, Persephone, Pomona, Artemis, and other goddesses represent manifestations of divine beauty, mercy, and love. The traveler through these *Cantos* also encounters the way to the Just City. Destroyed in the past through vanity, falsehood, greed, and dissension, the ideal city appears in various guises: Wagadu, "in the mind indestructible" (*Canto LXXVII*), or Dioce, "whose terraces are the color of stars" (*Canto LXXIV*), reminds us of continued human effort to create ordered and harmonious societies.

These themes, present throughout the *Cantos,* appear in miniature in *Canto I.* A translation of a Renaissance Latin translation of Book XI of the *Odyssey, Canto I* is itself a metaphor for renewing the poetry of the past. It recounts Odysseus' visit to the underworld to receive information that will enable him to return home. Calling the shades or spirits of the dead to life, Odysseus, like the poet, symbolically gives blood to the ghosts. The journey to the underworld parallels Dante's journey in the *Divine Comedy;* it is also analogous to the Eleusinian fertility myths, recounting the emergence of the goddess from the underworld or the sea to bring spring, the flowering of the earth.

A late section of *The Cantos,* published as *Thrones: 96–109 de los cantares* (1959), presents these themes and illustrates how P. integrated them with Confucian principles. Confucius, P. believed, represented an entire system of good government and moral order; and the dominant theme of "Thrones," conceived while P. was confined in St. Elizabeths, is Justice. Its title alludes to the seventh heaven of Dante's paradise: thrones are for the spirits of those who have been responsible for good government. Creating a mosaic of cryptic fragments extracted from various legal and philosophical documents ranging from China's *Sacred Edict* (1670) to the Magna Charta (1215) and the American Constitution, P. compares the governments, the legal and moral codes, and the linguistic systems of China, America-England, and Greece-Italy. He compares leaders who worked to establish judicious laws, encourage individual and civic responsibility, and clarify the language. Obfuscation and excessive abstraction in the language, P. believed, was one indication of corruption and tyranny in the society. A general rectification, then, had to begin with a concern with clear meanings, with the "precise definition of the word." Good laws were made by those who had respect not only for the language, but also for the processes of nature (Confucian taxes, for example, were based on a fair share of the harvest). Nature imagery forms an important part of *The Cantos,* linking Confucius, whose code leads to the Just City, with Eleusis, whose rituals lead to enlightenment. For P., the natural world is sacred, venerated in Eleusinian rites that celebrate the mysteries of nature (reproduction) and the Confucian ethos that honors the partnerships of men and nature (production).

P. has been called the "inventor" of Chinese poetry for our time. Beginning in 1913 with the notebooks of the Orientalist Ernest Fenollosa (1853–1903), P. pursued a lifelong study of ancient Chinese texts. Sinologists have disputed some of P.'s claims (for instance, that the ideogram was based on pictorial representations); nevertheless, his views are important for what they tell us about his own poetic practices. Initially, P. saw correspondences between his imagist principles and Oriental poetry. He admired the obscurity of its hidden meanings, the clarity of its directness and realism, its inclusion of mystical experiences, and its use of personae to portray states of mind. He also admired its use of nature imagery as a "metaphor by sympathy" for human emotions. His first translations appeared in *Cathay* (1915), a collection of poems by Rihaku (also known as Li Po, A.D. 701–762). Later, P. translated the writings of Confucius: *The Great Digest* (1928), *The Unwobbling Pivot* (1947), and *The Analects* (1950). His *Confucian Odes: The Classic Anthology Defined by Confucius* (1955) contains translations of over three hundred songs and narratives that represent the Confucian ethos. Often, P.'s work should not be regarded as a literal translation, but as an attempt to reproduce the ideas and the effects of the original in a modern idiom.

Of major importance to P. was the discovery of the ideogram, a more complex form of his "image." P.'s ideogrammatic method was an attempt to duplicate the graphic precision of the Chinese characters. Images and allusions were arranged in order to suggest some general concept. Names, fragments from literary and historical documents, phrases from various languages, and other references are juxtaposed as specific examples of an unstated, but unifying, idea. These examples P. called "luminous details," charged facts that supposedly illuminate an entire situation or figure. Such details arranged in a pattern become his ideograms. P. conceived of these patterns as dynamic structures that are drawn into a design by the mind perceiving the relationships between the parts. Like P.'s example of the rose formed from steel filings by the magnet, luminous details form concepts, intellectual patterns in the mind's eye. For the reader who suddenly recognizes the relationships that unify the details, the effect on the imagination can be startling and powerful. The difficulty with the method is that P. often fails to communicate because the reader does not have the information necessary to understand each reference. One name may represent a whole set of values; but it is often difficult, if not impossible, to determine its significance. This is especially true when P. cites evidence in order to challenge common opinion. Much recent scholarship has been directed toward establishing a context for *The Cantos* so that the reader will be able to interpret allusions more easily. P. believed that the ideogrammatic method allowed poetry a procedure analogous to scientific investigation: observation, collection of data, analysis, then conclusions. A theory or an abstract idea is thus always measured against observed examples. Ideas can be evaluated and qualified by how they "go into action."

Economics is another area of major importance throughout P.'s *Cantos* and in his social criticism. Influenced by the English social economist C. H. Douglas (1879–1952), P. urged monetary reforms in, for example, *Social Credit: An Impact* (1935). He railed against the evils of a private banking system that could withhold money and credit from the people and compel the government to borrow, creating a public debt. P. believed that the usurious and manipulative practices of international bankers led to scarcities for the general public, to fierce competition for foreign markets, and eventually to world war. His belief that Mussolini was instituting long-needed economic and social reforms led to his ill-advised support of Mussolini's policies. His anti-Semitic statements stemmed from his belief that the economic system was being exploited by Jewish financiers. P. proposed that the government should control the distribution of money. Congress, he maintained, had the right to determine the value of money, to regulate interest rates, and to set just prices. He opposed the gold standard, believing that money itself had no intrinsic value and should not be tied to the value of any single commodity. Rather, he believed money was merely a medium of exchange, a means to effect the orderly and equitable distribution of goods. The intrinsic wealth of the community, he believed, came from the yield of nature and human labor, and from our entire intellectual heritage. Production is affected by the enormous store of ideas and information, the invention of tools and processes, and the development of scientific formulas—all these contribute to our cultural and technological wealth: our social credit. The benefits from this heritage, P. believed, should be equitably shared among the citizens. Evidence of P.'s economic concerns, like his interest in just government, appears in condensed, often cryptic, fragments throughout *The Cantos*.

P. was one of the most influential and controversial literary figures of the 20th c. He challenged many of the political, aesthetic, and religious assumptions of his time, outraging many in the process. His criticism established some of the fundamental principles of what we now call "modernism" (q.v.); his translations have extended and redefined our cultural heritage. His work remains a major influence on today's writers.

FURTHER WORKS: *A Lume Spento* (1908); *A Quinzaine for This Yule* (1908); *Exultations* (1909); *Personae* (1909; rev. eds., 1926, 1949); *Provença* (1910); *Canzoni* (1911); *Ripostes* (1912); *The Sonnets and Ballate of Guido Cavalcanti* (1912, tr.); *Personae & Exultations* (1913); *Lustra* (1916); *Gaudier-Brzeska: A Memoir* (1916); *Certain Noble Plays of Japan* (1916, tr., with Ernest Fenollosa); *"Noh," or Accomplishment: A Study of the Classical Stage of Japan* (1916, with Ernest Fenollosa); *Dialogues of Fontenelle* (1917, tr.); *Pavannes and Divagations* (1918); *Quia Pauper Amavi* (1919); *Umbra* (1920); *Instigations* (1921); *Poems, 1918–1921* (1921); *The Natural Philosophy of Love* (1922, tr. of Remy de Gourmont); *Indiscretions* (1923); *Antheil and the Treatise on Harmony* (1924); *Selected Poems* (1928); *Ta Hio* (1928, tr.); *Imaginary Letters* (1930); *How to Read* (1931); *Prolegomena I* (1932); *ABC of Economics* (1933); *ABC of Reading* (1934); *Make It New* (1934); *Jefferson and/or Mussolini* (1935); *Polite Essays* (1937); *If This Be Treason* (1948); *Selected Poems* (1949); *Money Pamphlets* (6 pamphlets, 1950–51); *Patria Mia* (1950); *The Letters of E. P., 1907–1941* (1950); *The Translations of E. P.* (1953); *Literary Essays* (1954); *The Women of Trachis* (1956, tr. of Sophocles); *Love Poems of Ancient Egypt* (1962, tr. with Noel Stock); *Cavalcanti Poems* (1965, tr.); *P./Joyce Letters* (1967); *Drafts and Fragments of Cantos CX–CXVI* (1968); *Selected Prose 1909–1965* (1973); *Collected Early Po-*

ems of E. P. (1976); *E. P. and Music: The Complete Criticism* (1977); *E. P. Speaking: Radio Speeches of World War II* (1978); *E. P. and the Visual Arts* (1981)

BIBLIOGRAPHY: Kenner, H., *The Poetry of E. P.* (1951); Leary, L., ed., *Motive and Method in the Cantos of E. P.* (1954); Espey, J., *E. P.'s Mauberley: A Study in Composition* (1955); Edwards, J. H., and Vasse, W., *Annotated Index to the Cantos of E. P.* (1957); Emery, C., *Ideas into Action: A Study of P.'s Cantos* (1958); Dembo, L. S., *The Confucian Odes of E. P.: A Critical Appraisal* (1963); Davie, D., *E. P.: Poet as Sculptor* (1964); Sullivan, J. P., *E. P. and Sextus Propertius: A Study in Creative Translation* (1964); de Nagy, N. C., *E. P.'s Poetics and Literary Tradition: The Critical Decade* (1966); Hesse, E., ed., *New Approaches to E. P.* (1969); Pearlman, D., *The Barb of Time: On the Unity of E. P.'s Cantos* (1969); Witemeyer, H., *The Poetry of E. P.: Forms and Renewal, 1908–20* (1969); Stock, N., *The Life of E. P.* (1970); Brooke-Rose, C., *A ZBC of E. P.* (1971); Kenner, H., *The P. Era* (1971); Bush, R., *The Genesis of E. P.'s Cantos* (1976); Sieburth, R., *Instigations: E. P. and Remy de Gourmont* (1978); Makin, P., *Provence and P.* (1978); Bernstein, M., *The Tale of the Tribe: E. P. and the Modern Verse Epic* (1980); Terrell, C. F., *A Companion to the Cantos of E. P.* (1980); Woodward, A., *E. P. and the Pisan Cantos* (1980); Surette, L., *A Light from Eleusis: A Study of E. P.'s Cantos* (1980); Kearns, G., *Guide to E. P.'s Selected Cantos* (1980); Bell, I. A. F., *Critic as Scientist: The Modernist Poetics of E. P.* (1981); Read, F., *'76: One World and "The Cantos" of E. P.* (1981)

JO BRANTLEY BERRYMAN

The opinion has been voiced that P.'s eventual reputation will rest upon his criticism and not upon his poetry. (I have been paid the same compliment myself.) I disagree. It is on his total work for literature that he must be judged: on his poetry, and his criticism, and his influence on men and on events at a turning point in literature. In any case, his criticism takes its significance from the fact that it is the writing of a poet about poetry: it must be read in the light of his own poetry, as well as of poetry by other men whom he championed.... P.'s great contribution to the work of other poets (if they choose to accept what he offers) is his insistence upon the immensity of the amount of conscious labor to be performed by the poet.... He ... provides an example of devotion

to "the art of poetry" which I can only parallel in our time by the example of Valéry.

T. S. Eliot, "E. P.," *Poetry,* 68, 6 (1946), 331–38

P. was one of the most opinionated and unselfish men who ever lived, and he made friends and enemies everywhere by the simple exercise of the classic American constitutional right of free speech. His speech was free to outrageous license. He was completely reckless about making enemies. His so-called anti-Semitism was, hardly anyone has noted, only equaled by his anti-Christianism. It is true he hated most in the Catholic faith the elements of Judaism. It comes down squarely to anti-monotheism.... P. felt himself to be in the direct line of Mediterranean civilization, rooted in Greece.... He was a lover of the sublime, and a seeker after perfection, a true poet, of the kind born in a hair shirt—a God-sent disturber of the peace in the arts, the one department of human life where peace is fatal.

Katherine Anne Porter, on *The Letters of E. P., 1907–1941, NYTBR,* 29 Oct. 1950, 4

P. should be credited with having weighed the perils of the method he elected. It pays the reader the supreme compliment of supposing that he is seriously interested: interested, among other things, in learning how to deploy his curiosity without being a dilettante.... His utility enters its second phase when disparate materials acquire, if only by way of his personality, a unity of tone which makes them accessible to one another.... In his third phase of utility ... the poet instigates curiosity: how many people in the last thirty years have read the *Odyssey* on account of Joyce, or Donne at the encouragement of Mr. Eliot, or Dante and Confucius thanks to P.? ... And he would consider that he was performing his maximum service for the fourth kind of reader, the one with the patience to learn and observe, within the poem, how exactly everything fits together and what exactly, page by page and canto by canto, the fitting together enunciates.

Hugh Kenner, "Homage to Musonius," *Poetry,* 90, 4 (1957), 240–41

This claim for P.—that he recovered for English verse something lost to it since Campion or at least since Waller—may get more general agreement than any other. And Charles Olson is surely right to point to this achievement as rooted in something altogether more basic and less conspicuous than, for instance, the luxurious orchestration of the choruses in *Women of Trachis.* It is something that has to do with the reconstituting of the verse-line as the poetic unit, slowing down the surge from one line into the next in such a way that smaller components within the line (down to the very syllables) can recover weight and value. When P. is writing at his best we seem to have perceptions succeeding one another at unusual speed at the same time as the syllables succeed one another unusually slowly. But succession, in any case, is what is involved—succession, sequaciousness.

Donald Davie, *E. P.: Poet as Sculptor* (1964), p. 246

E. P.'s writings belong to the moment of experimental explosion—Stravinsky, Schoenberg, Picasso, Rilke, Joyce, Eliot, Proust. His work, like theirs, is alive with a radiant daring.... His *Cantos* are heroic, a poem as long as a long novel, written in a time when it seemed as if only prose fiction could bring off anything extended, important, and readable. And yet the *Cantos* are not metered fiction, nor do they go against the grain of what is possible in poetry.

Robert Lowell, "A Tribute," *Agenda,* 4, 2 (1965), 22

It's a shame he didn't get the Nobel and all the other awards at once—he was the greatest poet of the age! ... P. told me he felt that the Cantos were "stupidity and ignorance all the way through," and were a failure and a "mess," and that his "greatest stupidity was stupid suburban anti-Semitic prejudice," he thought—as of 1967, when I talked to him. So I told him I thought that since the Cantos were for the first time a single person registering over the course of a lifetime all of his major obsessions and thoughts and the entire rainbow arc of his images and clingings and attachments and discoveries and perceptions, that they were an accurate representation of his mind and so couldn't be thought of in terms of success or failure, but only in terms of the actuality of their representation, and that since for the first time a human being had taken the whole spiritual world of thought through fifty years and followed the thoughts out to the end—so that he built a model of his consciousness over a fifty-year time span—that they were a great human achievement. Mistakes and all, naturally. [1972]

Allen Ginsberg, *Allen Verbatim: Lectures on Poetry, Politics, Consciousness* (1974), pp. 180–81

There is a strong presence of gods and goddesses in *The Cantos* and yet P.'s poem is not "a vision." Instead, it is an attempt at an all-embracing historical and aesthetic synthesis, a poem that praises or attacks well-known men and institutions, that proposes an economic explanation of civilization's rise and fall, and contains an explicit series of specific recommendations to both ruler and ruled. Like Dante's *Divina Commedia, The Cantos* demand to be taken as literally and historically

true.... P. ... was equally determined to endow *The Cantos* with at least the same degree (which is not identical to the same *kind*) of authority as that possessed by a historian's text.

Michael Bernstein, *The Tale of the Tribe: E. P. and Modern Verse Epic* (1980), pp. 31–32

Although it is not possible now—nor will it ever be—to make a complete statement about all the themes in *The Cantos,* it is possible to posit a hypothesis that can help the reader, a hypothesis he can alter to his own bent as his experience dictates. To me, *The Cantos* is a great religious poem. The tale of the tribe is an account of man's progress from the darkness of hell to the light of paradise. Thus it is a revelation of how divinity is manifested in the universe: the process of the stars and planets, the dynamic energy of the seed in motion (*semina motuum*), and the kind of intelligence that makes the cherrystone become a cherry tree. Hell is darkness ("there is only the darkness of ignorance"); thus the highest manifestation of divinity flows from the mind and the spirit of man.

Carroll F. Terrell, *A Companion to the Cantos of E. P.* (1980), p. viii

POWELL, Anthony
English novelist, b. 21 Dec. 1905, London

P. attended Eton, then studied history at Balliol College, Oxford. He worked in London for a publisher, Duckworth, and briefly wrote film scripts. Between 1931 and 1939 he published five short novels, somewhat in the vein of the early satirical novels of his friend Evelyn Waugh (q.v.). He joined the British army in 1939, serving throughout the war and rising to the rank of major; much of his time was spent in London as a liaison officer with Belgian and Polish troops headquartered there. He wrote no fiction during and immediately after the war, working instead on a biography of John Aubrey, the 17th-c. antiquary and biographer; later he also published an edition of Aubrey's *Lives.*

P.'s early accomplishments deserve attention: five good novels, a readable and reliable biography of an important figure, six years of estimable as well as engrossing war service. Still, few would on the basis of his early works accord him a place among the major writers of the modern era. Somewhat inauspiciously, then, after the war, P. began work on a twelve-volume roman-fleuve, the first volume, *A Question of Upbringing,* appearing in 1951, successor volumes following at roughly two-year intervals until the series' completion in 1975. Reading the novels as a completed sequence, however, one discovers the work of a major writer: a comprehensive social historian, with a superb sense of historical change; a master of the intricate organization of a large form; a brilliant and versatile stylist; and the creator of a comic masterpiece.

P. takes the title of the sequence, *A Dance to the Music of Time*—or sometimes just *The Music of Time*—from a Poussin painting, in which, as he describes it near the beginning of *A Question of Upbringing,* "the Seasons, hand in hand and facing outward, tread in rhythm to the notes of the lyre that the winged and naked greybeard plays." This scene suggests the sense of life's continuities and changes that the entire sequence tries to present.

Any such sequence will depend for both its inner strength and its overall continuity on its means of narration. P. uses a central character, Nicholas Jenkins, whose life resembles his own, to tell the stories. The sequence begins when Jenkins is at school, at about the age of sixteen, and, with one major and important flashback (to August 1914 in *The Kindly Ones* [1962], the sixth novel), proceeds forward chronologically, ending in the early 1970s.

A reader might expect so long a novel, and one centering on a single character, to be intolerably narcissistic. But although we spend a good deal of time with Nicholas Jenkins by the time the sequence is finished, he is, about himself, a most reticent character: to spend time with him is not necessarily to know him. The indescribability of certain relationships partly accounts for Jenkins's reticence; but he is also quite fascinated by modes of indirection. Of a member of an earlier generation, he says that she "represented to a high degree that characteristic of her own generation that everything may be said, though nothing indecorous discussed openly." Jenkins, then, is anything but forthcoming about his own life, inner thoughts, and most personal relationships; the handling of his marriage, for example, is a marvelous tour de force: there is almost no description of it, and yet it is something we feel we are well acquainted with. More than anything else, such obliquity and unforthcomingness establish Jenkins primarily as an observer, rather

than as the object of our observation; but as an observer of a very complex sort.

Many readers at first find P.'s style a barrier to immediate involvement: elaborate and at times circumlocutory, often abstract in vocabulary, he particularly leans toward sudden contrasts of obliquity and directness. Among his favored constructions are those that, while displaying a certain elaborateness of description or modification, also employ an unusual economy of phrasing, especially ones in which a crucial connective is suppressed, giving the suggestion, probably accurate, of someone well trained in reading and writing Latin. P.'s stylistic range is large, made more so by the counterpointing of comically stylized dialogue with sections of narration and reflection. Several crucial characters—Charles Stringham, Ralph Barnby, Hugh Moreland—are natural epigrammists, their remarks underscored by frequent requotation.

Such stylizations, the means and varieties of which are too numerous to mention here, accumulate over the course of the long novel, and are part of the method by which action becomes myth. Among the compensations for growing old, Jenkins says, is "a keener perception for the authenticities of mythology, not only of the traditional sort, but—when such are any good—the latterday mythologies of poetry and the novel." Mythology is perhaps the major way by which the sequence is made to hold together. Important scenes occur in front of a painting, or in connection with a musical or dramatic production, often one depicting some bit of classical mythology. For example, an important scene in *Temporary Kings* (1973), the next to the last novel, occurs beneath an apocryphal Tiepolo ceiling in Venice that depicts the story, taken from Herodotus and Plato, of Candaules and Gyges. Several ironic connections exist between the mural and the characters below; the story of the whole novel echoes that told by the painting. At the same time, individual character is illuminated by seeing it in terms of "personal mythology": each of us has his own personal myth, the key to our consciousness and actions. As the entire sequence unfolds, personal mythologies, the various stories from the sequence's own earlier volumes, frequently included snatches of those latter-day mythologies of poetry and fiction, and the classical myths alluded to and represented in the sequence in various forms all weave together to create the work's largest patterns. Mutable time becomes subsumed within the patterns of eternally recurrent mythology.

Two characters most clearly dominate the sequence (indeed only these two appear in all twelve volumes): Jenkins, and his linked opposite, Kenneth Widmerpool. Widmerpool is a laughable but unlovable grotesque, an ambitious and self-serving egotist with a genius for showing up at the wrong time and saying the wrong thing; we can count on him for several major blunders in every novel. He also represents a social class that P. depicts in increasingly ominous terms, a bureaucratic pseudomeritocracy that the sequence depicts as coming more and more to rule England. We watch Widmerpool's ascent of the ladders of power, through various businesses, the military bureaucracy, Parliament, the postwar world of left-wing politics and journalism, progressive universities, television; it plays against the far more subtly portrayed growth of Jenkins's intellectual and moral awareness. Satirically the sequence offers us the "triumph of Widmerpool" as a version of the decline of Great Britain since the end of World War I; Widmerpoolism is what replaces the traditional institutions of government and culture. Finally P. affiliates Widmerpool with large mythic forces of misrule, and yet he remains a magnificent comic character, even while carrying the increasing weight of satirized social commentary.

Widmerpool marries, after various inconsequential, extraordinary liaisons. Pamela Widmerpool is both a more compelling and a more awful character than her husband. She is a figure of death, and particularly of beauty and sexuality become thanatotic, finally destroying herself in order to be able to offer herself to a necrophiliac American professor.

Between Jenkins, cool, reserved, melancholy, ironic, and increasingly reflective, and the Widmerpools, as brilliantly and comically dreadful a pair as exists in the fiction of this century, P. offers a small multitude of highly individualized characters. Among the strengths of the roman-fleuve is the opportunity it offers the novelist to deal with minor characters in a major way, and major characters in a minor way.

Somewhat obscure characters—Jenkins's uncle-in-law Alfred Tolland, Jenkins's housemaster La Bas, Sunny Farebrother, Dicky Umfraville or Jeavons or Odo Stevens, or the literati J. C. Quiggins and Mark Members—achieve prominence in our minds simply by reappearance, without their ever having been made major in the usual novelistic sense. Meanwhile, potentially major characters like Jenkins's school friends Peter Templar and even Charles Stringham begin to recede as others survive or as other concerns begin to occupy Jenkins. Perhaps the fullest appreciation of P.'s art would demand a thorough census, particularly of characters who perform a relatively minor role in a given novel but, through return engagements, themselves not particularly noteworthy, begin to exert a surprisingly large claim on our attention. By his creation of dozens of such characters P. transforms a relatively small base of population—school friends, relatives, various members besides Jenkins of London literary circles, fellow soldiers and other military acquaintances—into a fictional population both representative of society at large and capable of supporting a work of fiction of this size. Such a population, viewed through time, reconsidered, remembered, disappearing and occasionally reappearing, both instigates and illustrates Jenkins's increasingly frequent musings about time, mutability, recurrence, and permanence.

A case can be made for viewing this sequence as the single most important work of English fiction since World War II, and also the most important since the prewar era when the major works of modern English fiction were published—those of Lawrence, Joyce, Woolf, Conrad, and Ford (qq.v.). A rival of such masters of social comedy as Evelyn Waugh, Ronald Firbank, P. G. Wodehouse, Joyce Cary, and Henry Green (qq.v.), P., through his roman-fleuve, elevates that genre to a level of social comprehensiveness and large-scale artistry none of these writers except Waugh achieved. By this adaptation, influenced as it is by such diverse figures as Proust (q.v.) and Ariosto, P. has shown himself to be both a profound traditionalist and a brilliant innovator.

FURTHER WORKS: *Afternoon Men* (1931); *Venusberg* (1932); *From a View to a Death* (1933); *Agents and Patients* (1937); *What's Become of Waring* (1939); *John Aubrey and His Friends* (1949); *A Buyer's Market* (1952); *The Acceptance World* (1955); *At Lady Molly's* (1957); *Casanova's Chinese Restaurant* (1960); *The Valley of Bones* (1964); *The Sol-*

dier's Art (1966); *The Military Philosophers* (1968); *Books Do Furnish a Room* (1971); *Hearing Secret Harmonies* (1975); *To Keep the Ball Rolling: The Memoirs of A. P.:* Vol. I, *Infants of the Spring* (1976); Vol. II, *Messengers of the Day* (1978); Vol. III, *Faces in My Time* (1980); Vol. IV, *The Strangers All Are Gone* (1982)

BIBLIOGRAPHY: Mizener, A., *The Sense of Life in the Modern Novel* (1965), pp. 79–88; Pritchett, V. S., *The Living Novel and Later Appreciations* (1964), pp. 294–303; Morris, R., *The Novels of A. P.* (1968); Pritchard, W. H., "A. P.'s Serious Comedy," *MR,* 10 (1969), 812–19; Russell, J. D., *A. P.: A Quintet, Sextet, and War* (1970); Bergonzi, B., *A. P.,* rev. ed. (1972); Brennan, N., *A. P.* (1974); Tucker, J., *The Novels of A. P.* (1976); Jones, R., "A. P.'s *Music:* Swansong of the Metropolitan Romance," *VQR,* 52 (1976), 353–69; Wilcox, T., "A. P. and the Illusion of Possibility," *ConL,* 12 (1976), 223–39; Spurling, H., *Invitation to the Dance: A Guide to A. P.'s "Dance to the Music of Time"* (1977); Tapscott, S., "The Epistemology of Gossip: A. P.'s 'Dance to the Music of Time,'" *TQ,* 21 (1978), 104–16; Wiseman, T. P., "The Centaur's Hoof: A. P. and the Ancient World," *RRWL,* 2 (1980), 7–23

RICHARD A. JOHNSON

The effect of *The Music of Time* is a very remarkable one for the mid-twentieth century. It is as if we had come suddenly on an enormously intelligent but completely undogmatic mind with a vision of experience that is deeply penetrating and yet wholly recognizable, beautifully subtle in ordination and yet quite unostentatious in technique, and in every respect undistorted by doctrine. Great as the achievement of many twentieth-century novelists has been, they have been, almost to a man, novelists of ideas, in whose work experience is observed from the point of view of some more or less rationally conceived "philosophy" and functions essentially as illustration, and the writer's passion manifests itself as rhetoric rather than poetry. . . .

However powerful such novels may be—and most of the great novelists of our time have written such novels—there is something more immediately human and satisfying about an equally great novelist whose imagination apprehends all the dogmas of our time and the uses men make of them without itself being at the mercy of any of them. Such an imagination has the profound common sense, the unshakable awareness of other people, that has always given the great comic writer his sense of the discrepancies between motive and

theory and allowed him to see human affairs, not as an illustration of some social or philosophical generalization, but as some kind of dance to the music of Time.

Arthur Mizener, *The Sense of Life in the Modern Novel* (1964), pp. 102–3

But these novels constitute a *roman fleuve.* The same characters reappear, with new wives, husbands, careers, fortunes and fates; they are connected intimately in their social set. They live in a whispering gallery, in a mocking music of echoes from the past. They astonish one another by their unpredictable actions and their new chummings-up. Who would have thought, in *At Lady Molly's,* that Widmerpool would fall for that brassy ex-VAD, Mrs. Haycock? Or, in a later volume, that the grand Mrs. Foxe would take up with a ballet dancer and shower him with presents? Here a difficulty arises. After the deep spate of their early flow, such novels run into shallows. What began as a panorama begins to sound like a gossip column. One noticed this in *At Lady Molly's;* in *Casanova's Chinese Restaurant,* the habit of gossip has really set in and the central interest—the examination of two marriages—is not strong enough to stop it. One has the irritating impression that Jenkins, the narrator, has no other profession but to run about collecting the news; his stability has become fitful. The characters exchange too much hearsay. This is the danger with the *roman fleuve* when it lacks a strongly sustaining idea beyond the convenience of its own existence. I am not sure that the idea of the decadence of a class, anecdotally viewed, is strong enough. I think Mr. P. has now to guard against the risk that his characters will be so familiar and real to him that he will cease to make them important to us; that they will lose their true strength, *i.e.,* that they are obsessive fictions. The constant difficulty of the novelist is to avoid the engaging demi-monde that lies between art and life. Hearsay enfeebles, if Aubrey's brief emblematic lives become Aubrey's long ones.

V. S. Pritchett, *The Living Novel and Later Appreciations* (1964), pp. 301–2

For P., however, external time (clock time) is the flux. Time is actual; its very sheerness brings about events as it relentlessly pursues the dancers who, loving, marrying, dying, are reluctant to admit that they are changing at all. P. returns to the classical conception of time: the musical old greybeard who conducts the rounds of the seasons, or the cold goddess Mutability, altering people and events from day to day. Consequently, time functions critically, not mystically. Passing because it must, it is not mysterious, only at moments indefinable. P. is concerned with time, not obsessed by it; for while he sees it as blasting the hopes of some, wasting the promises of others, he knows that it is also the sole arbiter for shaping in the future the formless formulae of the past. It is this outlook that enables him to focus on the essential aim of the novel sequence: to play changing sensibilities against the continuum of human history.

This concept is at the center of *The Music of Time*. Stated with thematic force, it resounds as a note of resignation, often melancholy or sad, sometimes even tragic, but mostly pitched to the comic stoicism of the narrator, which keeps the sequence from growing tedious, oppressive, or unwieldy.

Robert K. Morris, *The Novels of A. P.* (1968), p. 108

Later in the thirties P.'s style changed; the sentences became longer and the syntax more elaborate, and in *The Music of Time* he writes in a way quite unlike *Afternoon Men*: a complicated, leisurely, reflective and analytical manner, which unsympathetic readers have found merely longwinded. Yet whereas the style of P.'s first two novels had effectively rendered the comic disparity and randomness of experience as it unfolds moment by moment, in *The Music of Time,* P. is attempting to make aesthetic sense of a lifetime of vanished experiences, to understand them and draw out the significances that were hidden at the time. P. seems no more convinced in the sequence than he was in the early novels that order and coherence are actually part of reality, but he is prepared to allow that they may appear in the verbal patterning that the novelist imposes on his material, so that style is a necessary principle of order.

The other major aspect of P.'s method that is already quite apparent in *Afternoon Men* is his preoccupation with anecdote and gossip. To some extent such an interest is an essential part of any novelist's equipment, for he is nothing if he is not both a collector and a teller of stories. But P.'s sense of anecdote is remarkably well developed.

Bernard Bergonzi, *A. P.,* rev. ed. (1971), p. 5

What, then, is P.'s stature? It can be unfair and dangerous to blame novelists for what they have left out: the critical focus has slipped on to infinity. All the same, one does feel conscious of large gaps in P.'s work. Without joining such of P.'s justifiably guyed figures as Guggenbühl—who heavily demands social commitment in literature ("No mere entertainment, please")—one would like to glimpse the presence now and then, or even the shadow, of that duller, poorer, grubbier world most of us inhabit. . . . Again, though P. believes in and extols feelings he is not good at igniting them on the page so that the reader feels the heat; it does happen, but the moments are exceptional. The books fall particularly short on the emotional lives of women, and a disproportionate number of his females seem brassy, shallow, restless. . . .

Possibly related to his failure to involve us in feelings is an inability, or disinclination, to deal with action as if it were taking place while we watch; the reader tends to view from afar, with the aid of first-class field-glasses, it is true, and an amusing commentary, but we are at times conscious of the distance. In P.'s work there is a general flight from immediacy, and notably in *A Dance to the Music of Time* where the narrative method is allowed to fuzz incident and situation. Often this is essential to P.'s intent, but the lack of definition and energy which can result is a disturbing weakness, just the same. . . .

What P. has is a powerful sense of life through character, caricature and period; fine humour and invention; a largely humane point of view; and unequalled competence at setting down the ways of a small, deeply interesting class of English society. Technically, he has remarkably extended what can be done through the first-person narrative; and he has the control to mix comfortably within one volume very different modes of novel writing: naturalism, fantasy, comedy, farce, occasional tragedy.

James Tucker, *The Novels of A. P.* (1976), pp. 3–5

It is paradoxical . . . that despite the great length of the novel sequence the reader is left with the impression of something small, rather delicate, a string of vignettes or miniatures, rather than a solid structure. This smallness, culminating in the refusal to end the sequence with a flourish, without valedictory passages, without giving the reader that sense of moral or spiritual growth he might have expected, finally suggests that the comparison should not be with Proust at all but with someone working on a much smaller scale: Noel Coward, whose theatrical historical pageant *Cavalcade* offered its audiences much the same pleasures as *The Music of Time*. The suggestion is not hostile (Coward was a great craftsman and entertainer) but is meant to pin down the essential quality of the sequence and to explain its hold over its devotees. P.'s ability to "hit off" the flavour of each period (up until the end of the 1940's) is celebrated justly, and readers enjoy this period detail, the popular songs, the modish paraphernalia, the new social types coming into being. And so a man with an antiquarian, rather than a historian's, feeling for the past has written a long novel that has elements in it of a parable about the decline of his class and is itself the swansong of the Metropolitan Romance. For a writer who has not believed in a general framework of ideas or historical theories, this is the greatest paradox of all.

Richard Jones, "A. P.'s *Music:* Swansong of the Metropolitan Romance," *VQR,* 52 (1976), 369

"Reading novels needs almost as much talent as writing them" is a favourite saying of X. Trapnel's [a character in the sequence], and one perhaps specially appropriate to the work in which he figures. For one could hardly find a work of fiction which more clearly demonstrates what Trapnel himself calls "the heresy of naturalism" than this sequence of novels in which, for the reader, the deepest satisfaction comes less from character and incident than from the structure that supports them both: a structure so contrived that, as it flows, straggles or jerks itself along, by turns farcical and grim, sombre, tumultous, absurd, reaching out through almost infinite varieties of egotism to embrace the furthest shores of crankiness and melancholia, it seems not so much to shape as to contain the disorderly process of life itself. It is not for nothing that Nicholas Jenkins takes his first name from that specialist in rhythm and design, Nicolas Poussin, whose painting provides both the title and the model for *A Dance to the Music of Time.*

Hilary Spurling, *Invitation to the Dance: A Guide to A. P.'s "Dance to the Music of Time"* (1977), p. xi

POWYS, John Cowper
English novelist, essayist, poet, and critic, b. 8 Oct. 1872, Shirley; d. 17 June 1963, Merionethshire, Wales

P. was the oldest son of a prolific literary family. Seven children of the Reverend Charles Francis and Mary Cowper Johnson P. published books, and an eighth was a book illustrator. Two of his brothers, T. F. Powys (q.v.) and Llewelyn Powys (1884–1939), also achieved substantial fame. Of Welsh descent, the Powyses have been in England since 1500.

P. grew up in vicarages in Derbyshire, Dorset, and Somerset, took his degree at Corpus Christi College, Cambridge, and became a lecturer on literature. He toured England for various university-extension series, then "transferred these recitative performances, which were more like those of an actor than a lecturer, to the new world [where I spent] thirty years of my life in American railways." Turning to full-time writing in 1929, P. lived five years in upstate New York before moving "home" to Wales.

Of his six volumes of poetry, P. named *Lucifer* (written 1905, pub. 1956) "the only poem I feel [tempted] to pray that posterity may read." P.'s nonfiction smacks of the podium. *Visions and Revisions* (1915) exhorts a general audience to read, to enjoy, to share his strong literary enthusiasms. His philo-

sophic writings, beginning with *The Complex Vision* (1920) and the best-selling *The Meaning of Culture* (1929), present a view of life consistent with his novels.

The novels center on two convictions: In P.'s words, "the deepest thing in life is the soul's individual struggle to reach an exultant peace in relation to . . . cosmic forces." And "below all the great systems of philosophic thought [and] mystical redemption stir these ultimate personal reactions to the terrible urge of sex." In "this irrational multiverse" P.'s "imaginative sensuality" is a prime tool, together with his introspective reaching for the "memories we inherit . . . from the world's remote Past." P.'s masterpieces are *A Glastonbury Romance* (1932) and *Porius* (1951). These incomparable novels and his *Autobiography* (1934), by exploring the human psyche with a deep and reckless probity, insure P.'s literary permanence.

P.'s fiction divides into three groups that engage, successively, the present, the past, and the future: the 20th-c. novels of southwestern England that culminate in the massive "Wessex novels" of 1929–35; the historical novels reaching back into ancient Wales; and the less substantial science fantasies written after 1952, when he turned eighty.

In the first Wessex novel, *Wolf Solent* (1929), the eponymous hero stops teaching history and edits pornography for an eccentric Somerset squire. He loves "androgynous" Christie, marries "voluptuous" Gerda, and finds himself, at story's end, halfway between the pigsty and the sun. The essence of the novel, P. writes, "is the necessity of opposites."

A Glastonbury Romance is of epic proportions—in time, in bulk, and in tale-telling vitality. Communists and industrialists clash in Glastonbury, but the Somerset town is a palimpsest with living traces of King Arthur and Merlin, Joseph of Arimathea, the Druids, the Fisher Kings, and "men older than the worship of gods." The novel's heroine is the Grail, P. says, and the search is for "the copulation-cry of Yes and No," and "the Self-Birth of Psyche."

Although his historical novels are as authentic as research into dark times permits, P.'s central concern in *Owen Glendower* (1941) and *Porius* (1951) remains the individual soul's quest. Prince Porius, preparing to take over the reign of his father in North

Wales one October week in A.D. 499, confronts the creeds, ethnic tenets, and primitive mysticism of a medley of forces. Only a truncated *Porius* has been published, cut by one third when publishers refused to gamble on another "eleven-hundred-pager like *Glastonbury*." Even so, the novel brilliantly shows P.'s ability to imbue high drama with finely shaded introspection, to move in a page from Porius's slaughter of fifteen men using a corpse as weapon to Porius's musings on the sanctity of gray clouds.

The *Autobiography* is, for P., "a sort of Faustian Pilgrimage of the Soul." It fully confirms a rare quality—P.'s willingness to be the fool in print, to be a "ninny." Religious mystics through the ages have shamelessly shown themselves as fools; some authors can laugh at themselves; P. dares, in the intensity of pursuing his deepest thoughts and sensations, to lay himself open to all ridicule. The "ninnyism" in his personal writings and the novels puts off many readers, but it has, as he says, "a deep and subtle irony." It is a "malicious challenge," a "protest against the shallow rationality of the hour," and, ultimately, "an arraignment of the unsympathetic First Cause" in which P. finds good and evil inextricably mixed.

In the last full-length novel, *All or Nothing* (1960), written as P. approached the age of ninety, an Arch-Druid escorts earthlings to the core of the sun and the limits of the Milky Way—and back to England. The Powysian quest continues. But the mystery—the Grail mystery—yet abides. P.'s genius is in his ability to dramatize imaginatively the pursuit of ultimate questions, to probe the very souls of his questers, and to convey the sheer urgency and excitement of the eternal quest.

FURTHER WORKS: *Odes, and Other Poems* (1896); *Poems* (1899); *The War and Culture* (1914; Br., *The Menace of German Culture,* 1915); *Wood and Stone* (1915); *Confessions of Two Brothers* (1916, with Llewelyn Powys); *Wolf's Bane: Rhymes* (1916); *One Hundred Best Books* (1916); *Rodmoor* (1916); *Suspended Judgments* (1916); *Mandragora* (1917); *Samphire* (1922); *Psychoanalysis and Morality* (1923); *The Art of Happiness* (1923); *The Religion of a Sceptic* (1925); *Ducdame* (1925); *The Secret of Self Development* (1926); *The Art of Forgetting the Unpleasant* (1928); *The Owl, the Duck, and Miss Rowe! Miss Rowe!* (1930); *Debate: Is*

Modern Marriage a Failure? (1930, with Bertrand Russell); *In Defence of Sensuality* (1930); *Dorothy M. Richardson* (1931); *A Philosophy of Solitude* (1933); *Weymouth Sands* (1934; Br., *Jobber Skald,* 1935); *The Art of Happiness* (1935); *Maiden Castle* (1936); *Morwyn* (1937); *The Pleasures of Literature* (1938; Br., *The Enjoyment of Literature,* 1938); *Mortal Strife* (1942); *The Art of Growing Old* (1944); *Dostoievsky* (1946); *Obstinate Cymric* (1947); *Rabelais* (1948); *The Inmates* (1952); *In Spite Of* (1953); *Atlantis* (1954); *The Brazen Head* (1956); *Up and Out* (1957; includes *The Mountains of the Moon*); *Letters of J. C. P. to Louis Wilkinson, 1935–1956* (1958); *Homer and the Aether* (1959); *Poems: A Selection* (1964); *Letters to Nicholas Ross* (1971); *Real Wraiths* (1974); *Two & Two* (1974); *You and Me* (1975); *Letters to His Brother Llewelyn* (1975); *Letters to C. Benson Roberts* (1975); *Letters to Henry Miller* (1975); *After My Fashion* (1980)

BIBLIOGRAPHY: Marlow, L., *Welsh Ambassadors: P. Lives and Letters* (1936); Knight, G. W., *The Saturnian Quest: A Chart of the Prose Works of J. C. P.* (1964); Langridge, D., *J. C. P.: A Record of Achievement* (1966); *The P. Newsletter* (1970 ff.); Humfrey, B., ed., *Essays on J. C. P.* (1972); Cavaliero, G., *J. C. P.: Novelist* (1973); Thomas, D., *A Bibliography of the Writings of P.* (1975); *The P. Review* (1977 ff.); Krissdottir, M., *P. and the Magical Quest* (1980)

R. L. BLACKMORE

POWYS, T(heodore) F(rancis)
English novelist and short-story writer, b. 20 Dec. 1875, Shirley; d. 27 Nov. 1953, Mappowder

P.'s novels, stories, and fables of rural southwestern England derive from a most circumscribed life. He did not follow his older brother, the novelist John Cowper Powys (q.v.), to university, but was educated at private schools and at Dorchester Grammar School. As a young man he attempted farming in Suffolk, then returned to isolated villages in the Dorset of his childhood to begin writing. He moved farther inland twice in fifty years as his first choices grew too populous.

Depending on a small paternal subsidy, he

first wrote two "meditations": *An Interpretation of Genesis* (1908) and *The Soliloquy of a Hermit* (1916). "Powys believes in monotony," P. said of himself. "Writes from 11 to 1:30. Walks nearly always the same path in the afternoon, goes by the Inn to the Hill." That hill—"Madder Hill"—looks down on the several farms and hamlets of P.'s fiction, on rapacious farmers and their sons, naïve vicars and their volatile wives, teasing girls and the men at the Inn who talk about them, gossiping women who sometimes act as pimps, and simple-minded lovers. These rustics care little for the world beyond, and rarely receive visitors—with the signal exception of God, in various guises. P.'s theme is death, and the loves, sacred and profane, that precede it. He broods deeply on religious mystery and man's fate—with realistic and ironic bitterness in the early tales, then with a gentler irony as the novels and stories become fabulistic, allegorical. His art looks back to the Bible, John Bunyan, and Thomas Hardy (q.v.), and foreshadows Dylan Thomas's (q.v.) *Under Milk Wood*.

Mr. Weston's Good Wine (1927) is P.'s acknowledged masterpiece. God, in the guise of Mr. Weston, a wine merchant, comes to the hamlet of Folly Down selling two vintages: a light wine (love) and a rarer dark wine of peaceful, eternal death that he, too, hopes one day to drink. Mr. Weston does business with easy dignity and humor, but can show an author's defensive pride whenever someone at the inn (which he prefers to the church) quotes from the Bible.

P.'s *Fables* (1929) are dialogues, trenchant and cryptic commentaries on profound matters by, among others, a stone, a crumb, a spittoon, a coat, a crow, a corpse, and a flea. Here, as in the novels, the humor is subtle and organic—a true yield of the topics.

P.'s last novel, *Unclay* (1931), gathers several people from the earlier novels and stories as John Death arrives, unable, at first, to carry out his duties because he has lost his list of those due to die—to be "unclayed."

Fable and allegory—ancient traditions that are patently false (a crow does not speak with courtly diction)—serve P. better than artful ambiguity. His tales are symbolically rich, but his symbols, like his humor and irony, grow naturally from his people and their actions. P.'s art is at once dark and innocent. Life in the cottages under Madder Hill is harsh; John Death is only briefly deterred from his duty. It is P.'s genius to cast a cool eye on these rural folk, and to trace their courses in unvarnished prose with deep, unsentimental compassion.

FURTHER WORKS: *The Left Leg* (1923); *Black Bryony* (1923); *Mark Only* (1924); *Mr. Tasker's Gods* (1925); *Mockery Gap* (1925); *A Stubborn Tree* (1926); *Innocent Birds* (1926); *Feed My Swine* (1926); *A Strong Girl, and The Bride* (1926); *What Lack I Yet?* (1927); *The Rival Pastors* (1927); *The House with the Echo* (1928); *The Dew Pond* (1928); *Christ in the Cupboard* (1930); *The Key of the Field* (1930); *Kindness in a Corner* (1930); *The White Paternoster* (1930); *Uriah on the Hill* (1930); *Uncle Dottery* (1930); *The Only Penitent* (1931); *When Thou Wast Naked* (1931); *The Tithe Barn, and The Dove and the Eagle* (1932); *The Two Thieves* (1932); *Captain Patch* (1935); *Make Thyself Many* (1935); *Goat Green* (1936); *Bottle's Path* (1936); *God's Eyes A-Twinkle* (1947); *Rosie Plum* (1966)

BIBLIOGRAPHY: Marlow, L., *Welsh Ambassadors: P. Lives and Letters* (1936); Coombes, H., *T. F. P.* (1960); Churchill, R., *The P. Brothers* (1962); Sewell, B., ed., *Theodore: Essays on T. F. P.* (1964); Hopkins, K., *The P. Brothers: A Biographical Appreciation* (1967); Riley, P., *A Bibliography of T. F. P.* (1967); Cavaliero, G., *The Rural Tradition in the English Novel 1900–1939* (1977), pp. 173–95; Humfrey, B., ed., *Recollections of the P. Brothers* (1980)

R. L. BLACKMORE

PRAMOEDYA Ananta Toer

Indonesian short-story writer, novelist, essayist, and critic, b. 6 Feb. 1925, Blora, Java

The works of P., generally recognized as the master prose writer of his country, have fundamentally been shaped by his painful experiences under Dutch colonialism, Japan's occupation of Indonesia during World War II, the subsequent armed revolutionary struggle against the returning Dutch, and the many disappointments of postindependence society. The son of an embittered nationalist schoolteacher who ruined the family by obsessive gambling, P. never completed high school. As an adolescent during the Japanese occupation he worked as a stenographer; and when the revolution broke out, he joined the Indonesian armed forces. Between 1950 and

1958 he published a stream of fine novels, novellas, and short stories. After 1958 he steadily moved politically to the left and largely abandoned fiction for critical essays and historical studies.

In the wake of the October 1, 1965, coup, P. was imprisoned without trial by the ascendant military regime and was not freed until the end of 1979. In 1973 he was given access to a typewriter and began writing down a series of historical novels originally narrated orally to his fellow prisoners. In 1980 *Bumi manusia* (*This Earth of Mankind,* 1982) and *Anak semua bangsa* (child of all nations), the first two volumes of a tetralogy on the dawn of Indonesia's struggle against colonial capitalism, were published to great critical and popular acclaim. The military authorities responded to this success by banning both books and ordering thousands of copies seized and publicly burned. Typescripts of the last two volumes, *Jejak langkah* (steps forward) and *Rumah kaca* (house of glass) have been smuggled out of the country and are scheduled for publication abroad.

Initially, P.'s fame rested on three novels composed largely while he was imprisoned by the returning Dutch colonial government after the war. *Perburuan* (1950; *The Fugitive,* 1975) is a haunting description of the homeward flight of a military rebel against the Japanese, written in terms deliberately evocative of traditional Javanese legend. *Keluarga gerilya* (1950; guerrilla family), his best-known novel, depicts the agonizing destruction of a Javanese family during the national revolution. The father, a soldier in the colonial army, is killed by his own sons, who have joined the revolutionaries. Two of the sons die in battle, while the eldest is executed by the Dutch and their mother goes mad with grief. *Mereka yang dilumpuhkan* (1951; the paralyzed) depicts the strange assortment of P.'s fellow prisoners. While all three texts show P.'s narrative virtuosity, they are still couched in a semirealist style which he later abandoned for a more surrealistic one. Their prestige derived partly from their direct portrayal of grand historical themes—war and revolution—and partly on the idea, derived from Western critics of that era, that the novel was the test and confirmation of any great writer's achievement.

The passage of time, however, has shown that P.'s greatness lies, like that of another modern Asian master, the Chinese Lu Hsün (q.v.), in his short stories. Most of the tales in *Subuh* (1950: dawn) and *Percikan revolusi* (1950; sparks of revolution) are set during the revolution. *Cerita dari Blora* (1952; tales of Blora) deals with provincial Javanese society in the late colonial period, as well as with the Japanese occupation and the revolution. *Cerita dari Jakarta* (1957; tales of Djakarta) depicts an extraordinary range of postrevolutionary catastrophes in Indonesia's capital. While the key figures in these tales—maimed veterans, child-brides, failed writers, tubercular maids, careerist politicians, deracinated nouveaux riches, and so forth—are recognizable products of the breakdown of feudal Javanese society and of Indonesia's tumultuous modern political history, the peculiar power of the tales derives not from "realism," but from P.'s mature style.

Characteristic of this style is the infusion of the Indonesian language with eerily transformed images from classical Javanese culture and the use of Indonesian to describe the lower depths of Javanese-speaking communities. A polylingual living in a polylingual society, P. essentially writes "between languages," playing languages and cultures off against one another. It is characteristic that some of his best later stories are really about the marginality of the writer in Indonesian society and the problematic nature of writing itself.

The two novels published after P.'s fourteen-year imprisonment differ markedly from his earlier work. They are vast canvases of all strata of colonial society at the turn of the century. But this social and cultural complexity is conveyed in a plain, fast-paced narrative style in striking contrast to the polyphonic allusiveness of his great short stories. P. has said that he deliberately adopted some of the conventions of contemporary popular literature in order to reach the younger generation of Indonesian readers.

FURTHER WORKS: *Kranji dan Bekasi jatuh* (1947); *Bukan pasar malam* (1951; *It's Not an All Night Fair,* 1973); *Gulat di Jakarta* (1953); *Korupsi* (1954); *Midah—simanis bergigi emas* (1954); *Ditepi Kali Bekasi* (1957); *Suatu peristiwa di Banten Selatan* (1958); *Hoa Kiau di Indonesia* (1960); *Panggil aku Kartini saja* (1962). FURTHER VOLUME IN ENGLISH: *A Heap of Ashes* (1975)

BIBLIOGRAPHY: Johns, A. H., "P. A. T.—The Writer as Outsider: An Indonesian Example," *Meanjin,* 22 (1963), 354–63; Johns,

A. J., "Genesis of a Modern Indonesian Literature," in McVey, R., ed., *Indonesia* (1963), pp. 410–37; Teeuw, A., "Silence at Life's Noon," *Papers of the Michigan Academy of Sciences, Arts and Letters,* 49 (1964), 245–50; Teeuw, A., *Modern Indonesian Literature* (1967), pp. 163–80; Siegel, J., "P.'s 'Things Vanished,' with a Commentary," *Glyph,* 1 (1977), 67–100

BENEDICT R. O'G. ANDERSON

PRATOLINI, Vasco

Italian novelist, short-story writer, and essayist, b. 19 Oct. 1913, Florence

From a working-class background and essentially an autodidact, P. held various jobs before becoming a professional writer. Under the influence of the confusion and widespread disillusionment that affected every segment of Italian society after World War I, the young P. embraced Fascism, contributing articles to *Il Bargello,* a Fascist periodical. Although he evinces considerable sympathy for the masses even in his fiction written in the 1930s he does not reveal any inner struggle for their advancement.

By the beginning of World War II P. had become strongly anti-Fascist, and in 1943 he joined the Resistance, quickly emerging as one of its leaders. His experience with the Resistance, coupled with the political freedom in Italy during the postwar years of reconstruction, helped him to shake off spiritual isolation and to achieve a new perspective. He advanced beyond the restricted dimensions of the autobiographical short story and delicate prose poem, giving a predominantly social character to his works from 1943 to 1950. Interweaving social and personal relationships with larger, historical events in *Il quartiere* (1944; *The Naked Streets,* 1952) and *Cronache di poveri amanti* (1947; *A Tale of Poor Lovers,* 1949), as well as in his minor works of this period, P. takes the reader into his native working-class quarters of Florence to show in concrete terms that life under the Mussolini dictatorship—while not as bad as life under Hitler—was full of suffering and evil. Yet because of the author's experience in the Resistance, he is able to convey a strong confidence in man's capacity to change and to shape his own destiny.

The characters of *Il quartiere* and *Cronache di poveri amanti* evidence a strong sense

of love and are motivated by principles of equality and the feeling of fellowship. They stand together not simply because they have learned about the value of solidarity from reading the *Communist Manifesto* but because the very condition of their lives forces them to close ranks behind barricades. Everything in these works—from the political and social attitudes to the profound sense of human solidarity—ultimately forms part of the natural rhythm and flow of life, which is itself a manifestation of things simple and eternal.

In 1950 P. began work on an ambitious trilogy entitled *Una storia italiana* (1955–66; an Italian story) whose aim was to represent various aspects of Italian life from 1879 to 1945. In it he sought to create social realism embedded in historically verifiable facts. *Metello* (1955; *Metello,* 1968), the first and the finest of the three parts, describes the awakening of class consciousness among the Italian proletariat at the end of the 19th c. As he does in the following two parts, *Lo scialo* (1960; the waste) and *Allegoria e derisione* (1966; allegory and derision), P., who draws many of his characters, episodes, and background material from real life, aims not at a mere reproduction of reality but at the creative and symbolic component underlying all literary realism.

P.'s commitment to the principles of realism and to political and moral dedication is also evident in *La costanza della ragione* (1963; *Bruno Santini,* 1964), the story of a worker set against the background of Italian society during the period from 1941 to 1960. As in all his major works, solidarity and interdependence in the struggle against exploitation are dominant themes. It is, indeed, primarily his moral and political commitment and the psychological insight with which he portrays his characters that distinguish P.'s work.

FURTHER WORKS: *Il tappeto verde* (1941); *Via de' Magazzini* (1942); *Le amiche* (1943); *Cronaca familiare* (1947; *Two Brothers,* 1962); *Mestiere da vagabondo* (1947); *Un eroe del nostro tempo* (1949; *A Hero of Our Time,* 1951); *Le ragazze di San Frediano* (1952; *The Girls of San Frediano,* 1954); *Diario sentimentale* (1956); *La costanza della ragione* (1963; *Bruno Santini,* 1964)

BIBLIOGRAPHY: Pacifici, S., *A Guide to Contemporary Italian Literature* (1962), pp. 57–

86; Rosengarten, F., *V. P.: The Development of a Social Novelist* (1965); Rosengarten, F., "The Italian Resistance Novel (1945–1962)," in Pacifici, S., ed., *From Verismo to Experimentalism: Essays on the Modern Italian Novel* (1969), pp. 212–38; Kozma, J. M., "Metaphor in P.'s Novels: *Il quartiere* and *Cronache di poveri amanti*," *RomN*, 20 (1980), 298–303

MARIO B. MIGNONE

PRATT, E(dwin) J(ohn)

Canadian poet (writing in English), b. 4 Feb. 1882, Western Bay, Newfoundland; d. 26 April 1964, Toronto, Ont.

After working with his father as a teacher and Methodist minister in the small fishing communities of Newfoundland, P. went to the University of Toronto, where he earned a Ph.D. in theology in 1917. Because of a crisis in his religious belief, he did not resume the ministry but joined the English Department at Toronto's Victoria College, where he was a much-loved teacher, poet, and raconteur until his retirement in 1953.

The central metaphor in P.'s work is evolution. He views wind, water, and rock as the sources of existence but recognizes that they can be equally destructive to life. He is particularly fascinated with primordial forms of life, with nature "red in tooth and claw," as represented by sharks, vultures, and wolves. But at the same time the poet marvels at the evolutionary process that produced man, with his fine emotions and intelligence, and above all Christ, who, for P., represents the highest point attained by evolution thus far. Man is torn between his primitive instincts to kill and the Christian ideal of compassion and self-sacrifice.

Although P. is best known for his long narrative poems on epic subjects, his evolutionary themes are central to his lyric poetry as well. His shorter poems, moreover, are often more appealing to a modern audience. In "The Shark," in *Newfoundland Verse* (1923), P. creates a symbol of something terrifying and malignant in nature, a creature more frightening than a vulture or wolf because its blood is cold. In "The Highway," in *Many Moods* (1932), P. asks whether the point of history and evolution has not been missed when man put Christ to death, but in "The Truant," in *Still Life, and Other Verse* (1943), he comes to man's defense when he

sees him pitted against an amoral, mechanistic principle in the universe. Man, he contends, has frequently erred, yet evolution has created in him an ethical impulse that raises him above his savage origins. But again in his finest lyric, "Come Away, Death" (also in *Still Life*), a reflection on the bombing of Britain, he describes the possibility of man being thrown back to a state of savagery through the holocaust of war.

In his epic narratives P. deals with specific phases of the evolutionary process. In "The Great Feud" (1926), which takes place just before the Ice Age and the emergence of early man, there is a great battle between land and sea creatures over territorial rights to the shoreline. In *The Titanic* (1935) man has evolved to a point of almost complete technical mastery over his environment, but the iceberg that sinks the ship reveals that man is still vulnerable, betrayed not only by his mechanical inventions but also by his pride. P.'s finest narrative, *Brébeuf and His Brethren* (1940), is the story of the 17th-c. Jesuit mission to the Indians of New France, and in the martyrdom of Father Brébeuf P. presents the conflict between civilized man and savagery. In all his narratives he focuses on man's potential for greatness through acts of courage and compassion. His last poem was *Towards the Last Spike* (1952), which records man's struggle to build a transcontinental railway in Canada. In this poem the enemy is the immense and formidable geography of Canada.

P. is virtually unknown outside of Canada. Technically he is an old-fashioned poet who worked outside the mainstream of modernism. Nonetheless he is a highly original, myth-making poet who wrote of the heroic phases in Canada's history with a vision of life's intractable hardness.

FURTHER WORKS: *The Witches' Brew* (1925); *Titans* (1926); *The Iron Door* (1927); *The Roosevelt and the Antinoe* (1930); *The Fable of the Goats, and Other Poems* (1937); *Dunkirk* (1941); *Collected Poems* (1944); *Behind the Log* (1947); *The Collected Poems of E. J. P.* (1958)

BIBLIOGRAPHY: Frye, N., Introduction to *The Collected Poems of E. J. P.* (1958), pp. xiii–xxviii; Pacey, D., *Ten Canadian Poets* (1958), pp. 165–93; Pitt, D. G., *E. J. P.* (1969); Wilson, M., *E. J. P.* (1969); Djwa, S., *E. J. P.: The Evolutionary Vision* (1974)

DAVID STOUCK

PREDA, Marin

Romanian novelist, short-story writer, and essayist, b. 5 Aug. 1922; Siliştea-Gumeşti, d. 16 May 1980, Mogoşoaia

P. was born into a peasant family. He graduated from a junior college in 1941 and worked as a proofreader and editor for journals such as *Timpul* and *România liberă.* He became the editor-in-chief of the monthly *Viaţa românească* in 1957 and was director of the publishing house Cartea Românească, until his death. He also held high positions in the Romanian Writers' Union. He is believed by some to have committed suicide.

P.'s talent was revealed in short stories written before 1944 as well as in his ability to maintain realistic integrity even in texts published during the repressive 1950s. His stature came to be recognized, however, in the cycle begun with *Moromeţii* (2 vols., 1955, 1967; first vol. tr. as *The Morometes,* 1957) and continued notably in *Marele singuratic* (1972; the lone wolf), although characters and situations linked to the cycle can be met in virtually all his other books. It is the saga of a peasant family from the Danubian plain; P. emphasizes their cunning and resilience in the face of changing historical circumstances. P. is an objective and unsentimental narrator who does not hide the instinctual brutality and cupidity of his characters; but he also shows how rough, redneck men react with sly wisdom and wide-awake irony to the decay of small holdings before World War II and to the simplistic cruelty of farm collectivization after it. P. pays particular attention to the complicated psychology of intellectuals who have come from and grown away from the village community, both in his novels and in the collection of essays *Imposibila întoarcere* (1971; the impossible return) and in his memoirs, *Viaţa ca o pradă* (1977; my life as a prey), which reveal some of the autobiographical sources of his works.

Eventually P. turned from peasant life to political problems. *Intrusul* (1968; the intruder) analyzes the defeat of an idealistic young worker who cannot adapt to the tough and pitiless rhythms of life in a new industrial urban township he had enthusiastically helped build. *Delirul* (1975; the delirium) describes the beginning of World War II and the accompanying disorders in Romania through the eyes of an offspring of the Moromete clan. The novel stirred political uneasi-ness because of its apparent sympathy for the military dictator who crushed the fascist uprising of 1940; subsequent editions appeared with many censored passages. P.'s last novel, *Cel mai iubit dintre pămînteni* (3 vols., 1980; the most beloved among earthlings), is a sweeping and scathing criticism of Romania's present-day society as a whole; it appeared two months before P.'s death and was soon suppressed.

FURTHER WORKS: *Întîlnirea din pămînturi* (1948); *Ana Roşculeţ* (1949); *Desfăşurarea* (1952); *Ferestre întunecate* (1956); *Risipitorii* (1962; rev. ed., 1972); *Friguri* (1963); *Martin Bormann* (1966)

BIBLIOGRAPHY: Iorgulescu, M., "A New Dimension in M. P.'s Literary Craftsmanship," *RoR,* 17, 4 (1972), 76–78; Nemoianu, V., on *Imposibila întoarcere, BA,* 46 (1972), 656; Crohmălniceanu, O. S., "M. P. et ses *Moromeţii,*" *CREL,* 3 (1976), 29–38; Nemoianu, V., "The Road to Bucharest," *TLS,* 2 April 1976, 402; Nemoianu, V., "The Innocent Abroad," *TLS,* 19 Feb. 1982, 199

VIRGIL NEMOIANU

PREMCHAND

(pseud. of Dhanpat Rai Srivastav) Indian short-story writer and novelist (writing in Urdu and Hindi), b. 1 July 1880, Lahmi; d. 8 Oct. 1936, Benares

P. was born in a town near Benares into a poor family of *kayasthas,* or scribes, who in this case served as village accountants. P. received his early education in Urdu and Persian, and also studied English. In 1899 he became a schoolteacher, a profession he pursued for over twenty years. In 1908 he published his first volume of Urdu short stories, *Soz-e vatan* (passion for the fatherland) under the pen name Navab Rai. Because of the unabashed patriotism of these pieces, the British colonial authorities proscribed the book and ordered the unsold copies burned. The author then took the name P. and continued to write.

By 1915 he started to switch from writing in Urdu to Hindi; they are essentially the same language, sharing the same grammar and vocabulary, but written in different scripts and drawing their intellectual vocabulary, imagery, and sensibility from different literary traditions: Urdu borrows from the Persian-Arabic tradition, Hindi from the Sanskrit. As a result of this change, P.'s reading audience increased appreciably, although he continued to have his works published in Urdu versions as well.

In 1921 P. resigned his teaching position with the civil service and joined Mahatma Gandhi's nonviolent Non-Cooperation Movement, which sought to oust the British from India. P.'s commitment to Gandhian ideology is marked in a number of his novels. He also edited two literary journals, neither of which was financially successful, and wrote a number of screenplays for film companies in Bombay. Toward the end of his life P. became sympathetic to Marxism, looking to it as a possible means of solving India's myriad ills. In 1936, just a few months before his death, he served as president of the first meeting of the Marxist-oriented All India Progressive Writers' Association, which, with the help of P.'s immense literary prestige, later grew into one of the most powerful forces in nearly every major literature of India.

P. wrote about a dozen novels; the first major one was *Premashram* (1922; love retreat). The last one, *Godan* (1936; *Godan*, 1957; also tr. as *The Gift of a Cow*, 1968), is considered his best. It is notable for its evocation of the rural world of the peasant Hori, his wife Dhaniya, and their children. Here the overwhelming vicissitudes that plague the poor of India are carefully chronicled in microcosm and delineated to their final moment of tragedy. In addition, he published over three hundred short stories, collected in eight volumes as *Manasarovar* (1962; holy lake), as well as criticism, essays, plays, and translations and adaptations from Indian and European literatures.

P. is best known for his short stories, where the influence of Western writers, notably Dickens, Tolstoy, and Maupassant, is readily discernible. P. is credited in both Urdu and Hindi literatures for having single-handedly shaped the short story into its modern form. Early pieces deal with patriotic and supernatural themes; later ones depict a wide variety of characters and types from all quarters of Indian society. The best stories concentrate on village life and characters, portraying them with realism, insight, and compassion. "Mukhti marg" (1924; "The Road to Salvation," 1969), for example, de-

picts the bitter feud between the well-to-do farmer Jhingur and the boastful shepherd Buddhu, which ends only when each is reduced to poverty. P.'s most famous, and last, short story is "Kafan" (1936; "The Shroud," 1969), in which the untouchable Ghisu and his son Madhav witness the death of the latter's wife in childbirth. The two men then go out and beg for money with which to purchase wood for her funeral pyre and a shroud. In a fit of venality they buy liquor instead of the shroud and drink themselves into a stupor.

In some instances, especially in the novels, P. exhibits an unconvincing streak of idealism whereby unsympathetic characters have an unexplainable "change of heart" and convert to goodness. At their best, however, P.'s stories are well wrought, succinct tours de force; they are remarkable in the power of their effect. For this reason P. is considered the major writer of fiction in both Urdu and Hindi during the first half of this century.

FURTHER WORKS: *Asrar-e mabid* (1903); *Kishna* (1907); *Prema* (1907); *Ruthi rani* (1907); *Jalva-e isar* (1912); *Mahatma shaikh sadi* (1918); *Seva sadan* (1918); *Sangram: Ek samajik natak* (1923); *Karbala* (1924); *Rangabhumi* (1925); *Kayakalp* (1926); *Nirmala* (1926); *Pratigya* (1927); *Ba kamalon ke darshan* (1928); *Ghaban* (1931); *Karmabhumi* (1932); *Durga das* (1938); *Ram carca* (1941); *Mangal sutra va anya racnayen* (1948); *Citthi patri* (1962); *Gupt dhan* (1962); *Vividh prasang* (1962); *Sahitya ka uddeshya* (1967); *Kuc vicar* (1973). FURTHER VOLUMES IN ENGLISH: *Short Stories of P.* (1946); *A Handful of Wheat, and Other Stories* (1955); *The Secret of Culture, and Other Stories* (1960); *The Chess-Players, and Other Stories* (1967); *The World of P.* (1969); *The Shroud, and Twenty Other Stories by P.* (1972); *Twenty-Four Stories* (1980)

BIBLIOGRAPHY: Coppola, C., "A Bibliography of English Sources for the Study of P.," *Mahfil*, 1, 2 (1963), 21–24; Gopal, M., *Munshi P.: A Literary Biography* (1964); Gupta, P., *P.* (1968); Swan, R., *Munshi P. of Lahmi Village* (1969); Sharma, G., *Munshi P.* (1978); Thomas, C., *L'ashram de l'amour: Le gandhisme et l'imaginaire* (1979); Naravane, V. S., *P.: His Life and Work* (1980)

CARLO COPPOLA

PRERADOVIĆ, Paula von

Austrian poet and novelist, b. 12 Oct. 1887, Vienna; d. 25 May 1951, Vienna

Granddaughter of the Austro-Croatian officer and poet Petar von Preradović (1818–1872), P. spent most of her childhood in Pola (now in Yugoslavia), to which she returned after graduating from the Institute of the English Ladies, a convent school in Sankt Pölten. In 1914 she went to Vienna, where, in 1916, she married Ernst Molden (1886–1953), the future publisher of the *Neue Freie Presse,* the most prestigious Vienna daily. Their home soon became an important center of Viennese intellectual life, with P. also taking a strong, active interest in the Catholic renewal movement. In 1938, after the Nazi annexation of Austria, a time of tribulation began for the entire family. Because of their ties to the resistance movement, their lives were in constant danger. After the war, as the author of the Second Republic's national anthem, P. gave voice to the strongly emerging new national consciousness.

In her early poetry, *Südlicher Sommer* (1929; southerly summer) and *Dalmatinische Sonette* (1933; Dalmatian sonnets), P. celebrates the beloved Adriatic landscape of her lost ancestral homeland. The poems, whose melodious rhythms infuse them with a quality akin to folk songs, display P.'s instinctive flair for language and tonal color. Their expressive power, cultivated diction, and intensity of feeling imbue them with an unmistakably distinctive tone.

In *Lob Gottes im Gebirge* (1936; praise of God in the mountains), P.'s poetic discovery of her adopted "home without sea" (that is, what was left of Austria after World War I), she pays homage to the awe-inspiring mountainscape of her second home. The essentially new aspect, however, is the religious experience that pervades these poems, a Christian faith extolling nature's beauty and majesty as a revelation of its creator. The lighter, folk-songlike character of her earlier poetry gives way, in keeping with the new, more reflective tone, to still melodious but more austere and contemplative lyrics.

From this point on, her work became deeply imbued with a firmly rooted religiousness. Her unshakable faith, the source of both her poetic inspiration and moral fortitude, is exemplarily expressed in *Ritter, Tod und Teufel* (1946; knight, death, and the devil), eight sonnets inspired by Albrecht Dürer's famous engraving. The true Christian, God's "pure knight," dauntlessly follows the right path, fearing neither death nor devil.

Christian motives and impulses also pervade her narrative work, especially the masterful novellas *Königslegende* (1950; legend of a king) and *Die Versuchung des Columba* (1951; Columba's temptation). Savatz, the Croatian king of *Königslegende,* whose abrupt fall from power deprives him of all he held dear, is seen not so much as a historical figure of the 11th c. but rather as a timeless poetic image of a fate experienced by many in those postwar years: the plight of the uprooted man driven from home and country. Only after bitterly quarreling with his fate does Savatz finally become reconciled to his new, humble life in exile. Accepting the inscrutable ways of the Lord—"Thy will be done"—he finds strength, comfort, and a new meaning in his existence.

In *Die Versuchung des Columba* P. dwells largely on the human side of the man who was to become the great Irish saint. Homesick and fearful of his missionary calling, he longs for the "human warmth of a life without mission." The encounter with Maurinn, to whom he was betrothed in his youth and who comes to claim him as her husband, precipitates the climactic struggle between the spirit and the flesh from which the apostle of the Picts emerges victoriously metamorphosed from man into saint. The spiritual calling proves stronger than any human ties.

P.'s poetic message is closely connected with her personal fate, making her work true "fragments of a great confession" in the Goethean sense—subjective experiences transformed into objective works of art. Although no formal innovator—song, romance, and sonnet were her preferred lyrical forms—she wrote poems that are powerfully original and display a masterful craftsmanship. The language, rich in striking imagery, is refined and melodious; some of her poems have been set to music.

FURTHER WORKS: *Pave und Pero* (1940); *Gesammelte Gedichte* (3 vols., 1951–52); *P. v. P.: Porträt einer Dichterin* (1955); *Gesammelte Werke* (1967)

BIBLIOGRAPHY: Schoolfield, G. C., "P. v. P.—An Introduction," *GL&L,* n. s., 7, 4 (1954), 285–92; Molden, E., "Skizzen zu einem Porträt," in Molden, E., ed., *P. v. P.: Porträt einer Dichterin* (1955), pp. 9–82;

Csokor, F. T., "P. v. P.," in *Neue österreichische Biographie* (1960), Vol. XIV, pp. 194–97; Vogelsang, H., "P. v. P.: Die Dichterin der Ehrfurcht, der Demut und des Glaubens," *ÖGL,* 10 (1965), 198–206
                                    FRIEDHELM RICKERT

PREVELAKIS, Pandelis

Greek poet, novelist, dramatist, and art historian, b. 18 Feb. 1909, Rethymnon, Crete

After graduating from the University of Athens, P. studied at the University of Paris. Receiving a doctorate from the University of Thessaloniki in 1933 for his work on his illustrious fellow-Cretan Dominikos Theotokopoulos (El Greco), he served for four years as Director of Fine Arts of the Greek Ministry of Education and for thirty-five years as a professor of art history at the Higher School of Fine Arts in Athens. The recipient of several Greek and foreign awards, including the Prize of Excellence in Letters of the Academy of Athens, he was elected a member of that Academy in 1978.

The descendant of distinguished educators, clergymen, fighters, and martyrs in the long battle for Crete's liberation from Ottoman rule, P. drew from his ancestry and from his country's heroic tradition a high sense of responsibility, dignity, and pride, as well as inspiration for most of his literary work. The pupil, lifelong close friend, and collaborator of his fellow-Cretan Nikos Kazantzakis (q.v.), in his *O piitis ke to piima tis "Odhyssias"* (1958; *Nikos Kazantzakis and His "Odyssey,"* 1961), an exemplary critical study of his master's personality and work, P. expressed, along with his admiration, his reservations about Kazantzakis's yielding to modern Western skepticism, Nietzschean philosophy, and nihilism at the expense of his Greek and Cretan cultural heritage. To that heritage he himself has remained faithful in his creative work. He has also been unswervingly committed to the poetic beauty of demotic Greek, enriched in his masterful work by use of the Cretan idiom.

P.'s first book of verse, *Stratiotes* (1928; soldiers), a "short epic," was inspired by the tragic state of the refugees of the Greek national disaster in Asia Minor in 1922. In the pure lyricism of his next two collections, *I yimni piisi* (1939; naked poetry) and *I pio yimni piisi* (more than naked poetry), P., as an idealized poet-lover, addresses his beloved, the complex personification of his fatherland, of poetry, of human virtue, and of natural and spiritual beauty, in the hope of a mutual transcendence, of a liberating rescue from the darkness of the ominous times—the eve of World War II.

P.'s first prose work, *To hroniko mias politias* (1930; *The Tale of a Town,* 1976), still the most popular of his works, is an affectionate, idealized, and poetic narrative about his native Rethymnon. It depicts the community when it still functioned like an industrious and harmonious beehive, shortly before that way of life succumbed to the disruptive and alienating influence of the West, which came as a result of Crete's liberation from Ottoman rule.

In order to counteract the despair of the years of war and German occupation, P. turned to studying and imaginatively chronicling the heroism of Crete's battle for freedom, more particularly the major uprising of 1866–69 that culminated in the sacrificial resistance at the Arkadhi monastery. Two "myth-histories," as he called them, *Pandermi Kriti* (1945; all-desolate Crete) and the trilogy *O Kritikos* (1948–50; the Cretan), as well as the later play *To ifestio* (1962; the volcano), all centered around this episode. *O Kritikos,* which blends real figures and events with imaginary ones, much in the manner of Tolstoy's *War and Peace,* besides giving expression to the Cretan spirit, traces the developments leading to the island's liberation from the Turks. Ironically enough, that final victory brought the disruption of the social harmony and the unity of spirit of the Cretan people. The resulting political conflicts and clashes of ideologies were symptomatic of what P. called the "disease of the century": man enters a "tragic stage" as an isolated, alienated individual, deprived of social and moral directives, and must face difficult choices alone.

"The disease of the century" was the theme of a trilogy of plays: *O thanatos tou Medhikou* (1939; the death of the Medici)—later revised as *To iero sfaghio* (1952; *The Last Tournament,* 1969)—*Lazaros* (1954; Lazarus), and *Ta heria tou zontanou Theou* (1955; the hands of the living God). It was followed by a novelistic trilogy, a *Bildungsroman* whose motif P. called "the paths of creation," consisting of *O ilios tou thanatou* (1959; *The Sun of Death,* 1964), *I kefali tis Medhousas* (1963; the head of Medusa), and *O artos ton angelon* (1963; the bread of the angels). Here P. used an autobiographical first-person narrator in order to give an imaginative yet true account of the three stages of his intellectual development. In the first volume the narrator, orphaned early in life, is nurtured by the spirit of his native soil, where the reality of death is omnipresent. In the second volume he is alienated by the impact of Western skepticism. In his despair he attempts a return to his roots in the last volume, in order to find himself again, and also possibly to rescue the traditions of his people and enlighten them about the value of the old ways. The result of his quest, however, is frustration and failure: the protagonist reaches the spiritual impasse of modern man.

A romance of love and heroism, *Erotokritos* (a name meaning "the one tested and judged by love") by Vitzentzos Kornaros, the poetic masterpiece of the 17th c. Cretan literary renascence; the ethics and lore of Byzantine Christianity; Cretan history; and P.'s personal experience all served as the mythical and spiritual foundations and framework for a lyrical, allegorical epic, *O neos Erotokritos* (1973; rev. ed., 1978; the new Erotokritos), which was to integrate and crown P.'s oeuvre by endowing his intellectual enterprise with the power of mythic universality. It is a highly complex work of great poetic beauty, moving in the realm of the spirit where suffering and death are accepted for their promise of transcendence and because of the possibility of resurrection: beauty, virtue, and love are transformed, through the tree of life, into freedom, man's supreme and eternal good, accomplishment, and reward.

FURTHER WORKS: *Dominikos Theotokopoulos* (1930); *Dhokimio yenikis isaghoyis stin istoria tis tehnis* (1934); *O Greco sti Romi* (1941); *Tetrakosia ghrammata tou Kazantzaki ston P.* (1965); *O angelos sto pighadhi* (1970; *The Angel in the Well,* 1974); *To heri tou skotomenou* (1971; *The Hand of the Slain,* 1974); *Mousafireï sto Stepantsikovo* (1972); *I antistrofi metrisi* (1974); *Dhio Kritika dhramata* (1974); *Arhea themata stin Italiki zoghraphiki tis Anayiennisis* (1975); *Mnimosino stous iroes ke tous martires tou meghalou sikomou tou 66* (1976); *To Rethemnos os ifos zois* (1977; *Rethymno as a Style of Life,* 1981); *O piitis Yiannis Ritsos* (1981); *Loghodhosia kritikou singhrafea stous sinpatriotes tou* (1981); *Monaxia* (1981)

BIBLIOGRAPHY: Chamson, A., "P. et la Crête," *Mercure de France,* April 1959, 577–88; Laourdas, B., "Introduction to P. P.," *Odyssey Review,* June 1962, 148–55; Coavoux, P., "Réflexions sur *La chronique d'une cité,*" *BalSt,* 9 (1968), 429–50; "P. P. Talks to Peter Mackridge: An Interview," *Omphalos,* 1, 1 (1972), 34–39; Decavalles, A., "P. P.: An Introduction," *The Charioteer,* 16–17 (1974–75), 10–40; Decavalles, A., *P. P. and the Value of a Heritage* (1981)

ANDONIS DECAVALLES

PRÉVERT, Jacques

French poet and screenwriter, b. 4 Feb. 1900, Neuilly-sur-Seine; d. 12 April 1977, Paris

P.'s father came from Brittany, his mother from the Auvergne. At fifteen he left school and tried various occupations. At twenty he did his military service, first in Lorraine, then in Turkey with the French occupation forces. In 1925 he was introduced by Raymond Queneau (q.v.) to the group of French surrealists (q.v.), including Louis Aragon, André Breton, Robert Desnos, and Michel Leiris (qq.v.). P.'s first published texts appeared in *Commerce,* a surrealist monthly. Starting in 1930 he went to work with a theatrical group, writing playlets in which he also performed. In 1933 the group, called October, went to Moscow, and one of P.'s playlets, *La bataille de Fontenoy* (the battle of Fontenoy) was premiered in an international workers' theater Olympiad. Besides film scripts, he also wrote songs. In 1948, while at the offices of the French national radio, P. fell out of a second-floor window onto the pavement and remained in a coma for several weeks. He spent months convalescing at Saint-Paul-de-Vence, where he was to stay, with his family, until 1955, when he moved back to Paris. He had a number of collages exhibited at the Galerie Maeght in 1957.

Surrealism had influenced the young P. but he soon broke away from its formulas to establish his own style. He did use some surrealist devices over the years, without, however, observing the nonpolitical stance of most surrealists. P.'s brand of surrealism, or what survived of it, strongly resembles the paintings of René Magritte: in an airy yet concrete way he thumbs his nose at society and defies logic and the laws of physics.

In his seemingly artless yet moving descriptions, P. communicates the immediacy of man's experience of everyday life. A radical anarchist, acutely critical of society and passionately opposed to authority and coercion, P. remained aloof from party politics even though he often espoused the causes of antimilitarism, anticlericalism, and social justice.

When *Paroles* (1946; *Paroles*, 1978) appeared, it was an immediate popular success. While academic critics remained indifferent or hostile toward much of P.'s writing, the initial success of *Paroles* was confirmed through dozens of subsequent editions, and P. is still the best known and most widely read poet in France. Although P.'s poems are usually a mating of laughter and tears, a few of them are indeed tragic. His humor, which is both subtle and ferocious, is at all times put at the service of serious social and human ideals. His endeavor to use laughter to combat many social and political evils as well as the absurd and degrading frailties man is heir to in such abundance may well stem from a desire to free himself of anguish.

P. scrupulously abides by the literal meaning of words, but he makes those words bear a meticulous responsibility. In these days when vagueness is rampant, this is an especially admirable quality. Like Christian Morgenstern (q.v.) he is alert to the absurdity of pompous language, and his merciless precision effectively underscores the insincerity of much that is uttered at solemn occasions. He punctures pretentious speech and caricatures those who misuse language to deceive others.

P. also exploded conventional word patterns and juggled with neologisms. He ridiculed meaningless clichés, but he also proved, by his ability to instill fresh meaning into stale expressions, that old adages still have significance for mankind. Many of his poems contain gruesome images; P. is obviously haunted by bloodshed. These images—used concretely, not symbolically—frequently depict animals (he shows a marked preference for donkeys and giraffes), birds of all kinds, flowers, and fruit. As P. shows the world through his lenses, animals can peacefully coexist, but as soon as man enters the picture, war breaks out, animals are mistreated, even murdered, and the balance of nature is upset.

In P.'s view, all men are not evil. Simple, nature-loving people are exempted from his condemnation. The political slant in his poems clearly is directed against capitalism, military commanders, the clergy, and the whole middle class in its rigid system of values. Artists, workers, children, innocent bystanders in the social struggle are viewed with friendly interest and sympathy. Oddballs and social outcasts are looked upon fondly, and the pathetic fight for daily bread is illustrated by the hopeless monotony of a lonely person's breakfast. P. looks on approvingly at every nonconformist's protest against the rules of bourgeois society.

P. created his own mythology around existing names. His great men may coincide with history's, but they usually turn out to represent the exact reverse of grandeur, as in *Histoires* (1946; stories), where an odd assortment of names familiar through literature or history threaten to step out of the book and start autonomous lives of their own. Mixed metaphors, in P.'s poetry, become tidbits of insane humor, but of an incisive, purposeful kind loaded with iconoclastic meaning and aimed at old taboos. His humor disintegrates age-old prejudice and creates a liberating atmosphere in which true humanism flourishes.

Although P. sometimes seems to be playing around with mere words loosely strung together, he is actually working in dead earnest to get his message across—a message of warmth and love of life, of delight in people, places, things, and beings, of faith in eventual progress. P.'s famous dunce in the poem "Le cancre" (1946; the dunce) shakes his head to say "no," but his heart says "yes," and "despite the teacher's threats . . . he draws on the board the face of happiness."

P. also wrote numerous widely acclaimed screenplays, some of the most notable being *Le crime de Monsieur Lange* (1935; the crime of Monsieur Lange), directed by Jean Renoir, and those for films directed by Marcel Carné: *Drôle de drame* (1937; pub. 1974; a peculiar drama; known in Eng. as *Bizarre, Bizarre*); *Quai des brumes* (1938; quay of fogs); *Le jour se lève* (1939; pub. 1965; day is dawning; pub. in Eng. as *Le Jour Se Lève*, 1970); *Les visiteurs du soir* (1942; pub. 1974; the night visitors); *Les enfants du paradis* (1944; pub. 1974; *Children of Paradise*, 1968); and *Les portes de la nuit* (1946; the gates of night).

FURTHER WORKS: *C'est à Saint-Paul-de-Vence* (1945); *Le cheval de Trois* (1946, with

André Verdet and André Virel); *L'ange garde-chiourme* (1946); *Contes pour enfants pas sages* (1947); *Le petit lion* (1947); *Des bêtes . . .* (1950); *Spectacle* (1951); *Vignette pour les vignerons* (1951); *Le grand bal du printemps* (1951); *Bim, le petit âne* (1952, with Albert Lamorisse); *Charmes de Londres* (1952); *Guignol* (1952); *Lettres des Îles Baladar* (1952); *Tour de chant* (1953); *L'opéra de la lune* (1953); *La pluie et le beau temps* (1955); *Lumière d'homme* (1955); *Miró* (1956); *Images* (1957); *P. vous parle* (1958); *Portraits de Picasso* (1959); *Couleur de Paris* (1961); *Diurnes* (1962); *Histoires et d'autres histoires* (1963); *Les chiens ont soif* (1964); *Fatras* (1966); *Arbres* (1967, with Georges Ribemont-Desaignes); *Imaginaires* (1970); *Fromanger* (1971, with Alain Jouffroy); *Hebdromadaires* (1972, with André Pozner); *Choses et autres* (1972); *Cinquante chansons* (1977, with Joe Kosma); *Soleil de nuit* (1980). FURTHER VOLUMES IN ENGLISH: *Selections from "Paroles"* (1958); *Poems I* (1967); *Poems II* (1968); *Words for All Seasons: Collected Poems of J. P.* (1979)

BIBLIOGRAPHY: Quéval, J., *J. P.* (1955); Guillot, G., *Les P.* (1966); Bergens, A., *J. P.* (1969); Baker, W. E., *J. P.* (1967); Sadeler, J., *À travers P.* (1975); Greet, A. H., Introduction to *Words for All Seasons: Collected Poems of J. P.* (1979), pp. 3–11; Mancini, M., "P.: Poetry in Motion Pictures," *Film Comment,* Nov.–Dec. 1981, 34–37

KONRAD BIEBER

PRIESTLEY, J(ohn) B(oynton)

English novelist, dramatist, essayist, and critic, b. 13 Sept. 1894, Bradford

Son of a schoolmaster, P. attended a local grammar school, and at seventeen began working as a clerk in a wool firm. World War I changed his life; after four years in the army, he went to Cambridge after demobilization, graduating in 1921. He then became a journalist in London; by 1925 he had published five books and established himself as a professional writer. He produced nine more books in the next three years.

P.'s early works included critical studies like *The English Comic Characters* (1925) and *George Meredith* (1926), together with several collections of essays. Kenneth Young has described his early essays as diverting and charming, the later ones as tough as old

boots. P. is sharply observant, and often polemical. In *English Journey* (1934) he showed an acute perception of social problems and social changes. In *Literature and Western Man* (1960) he saw not merely England but the whole Western world in crisis, and he tried to remind it of what it had created through its literature. Some fifty volumes of nonfiction, few of them negligible, constitute only one side of his remarkable output; they contain some of his best writing.

P.'s first novel, *Adam in Moonshine* (1927), was, in P.'s words, "all fine writing and nonsense, a little coloured trial balloon"; it was an experiment that failed. Resembling modernists like Virginia Woolf (q.v.) in looking deeply inside his characters, he still wanted to tell a straightforward story. With *The Good Companions* (1929) he achieved a major success; its warmheartedness and vitality won it favor, and it is still the single book by which he is best known. Centering his story around a group of traveling entertainers touring England, P. brings in a wide variety of characters, many of them portrayed with Dickensian humor and gusto, and illustrates a theme he had borrowed from H. G. Wells (q.v.): "You can change your life." Surprisingly, his next novel, *Angel Pavement* (1930), deals with people whose lives would never change, except for the worse; it tells of the impact the mysterious and predatory Mr. Golspie has on the lives of people working for a small veneer firm. Among many other humorous or satirical novels, *Festival at Farbridge* (1951) gives an amusing account of a Midland town responding to the Festival of Britain, and *Sir Michael and Sir George* (1964) tells of the rivalry between the heads of two government cultural agencies. The latter novel was a forerunner of the major work of P.'s later years, *The Image Men,* which appeared in two volumes—*Out of Town* (1968) and *London End* (1969)—an account of the effects of media on society told through the story of the founding of an "Institute of Social Imagistics."

While writing novels, P. was carving out a substantial reputation as a dramatist. His first play, *Dangerous Corner* (1932), he himself called an "ingenious box of tricks"; it cleverly exploited the device of George Bernard Shaw (q.v.) of turning half a dozen apparently pleasant people inside out. Several of his plays during the 1930s experimented with concepts of time, notably *Johnson over Jordan* (1939), the story of a man who has recently died. His dramatic works cover a very wide range, from farces like *When We Are Married* (1938) to plays in the manner of Chekhov (q.v.) like *Eden End* (1934) and *The Linden Tree* (1947). Critics who consider his novels diffuse sometimes think that the discipline of the theater has been good for him; a play like *An Inspector Calls* (1947) is enigmatic, tense, and tightly constructed.

Many English critics consider P. undervalued; they think of him as a thoroughly professional writer, who has done work of distinction in a number of fields, and whose oeuvre coheres into a unity marked by a strong and inimitable personality. In 1940, during the low point of the war for Britain, his radio broadcasts touched a national nerve; similarly, in his writing he has a strong sense of what the public will respond to. As he himself once said, he may not have been a genius but he had "a hell of a lot of talent."

FURTHER WORKS: *The Chapman of Rhymes* (1918); *Brief Diversions, Being Tales, Travesties and Epigrams* (1922); *Papers from Lilliput* (1922); *I for One* (1923); *Figures in Modern Literature* (1924); *Talking* (1926); *The English Novel* (1927); *Open House* (1927); *Benighted* (1927; Am., *The Old Dark House*, 1928); *Thomas Love Peacock* (1927); *Apes and Angels* (1928); *Too Many People* (1928); *Farthing Hall* (1929, with Hugh Walpole); *English Humour* (1929); *The Balconinny* (1929); *The Town Major of Miraucourt* (1930); *The Works of J. B. P.* (1931); *Faraway* (1932); *Self-Selected Essays* (1932); *I'll Tell you Everything: A Frolic* (1933, with Gerald Bullett); *The Roundabout* (1933); *Albert Goes Through* (1933); *Wonder Hero* (1933); *Laburnum Grove* (1934); *Four-in-Hand* (1934); *Cornelius* (1935); *Duet in Floodlight* (1935); *Spring Tide* (1936, with George Billam); *Bees on the Boat Deck* (1936); *They Walk in the City* (1936); *Midnight on the Desert: A Chapter of Autobiography* (1937); *Mystery at Greenfingers* (1937); *People at Sea* (1937); *Time and the Conways* (1937); *The Doomsday Men* (1938); *Let the People Sing* (1939); *Rain Upon Godshill: A Further Chapter of Autobiography* (1939); *Britain Speaks* (1940); *Out of the People* (1941); *Britain at War* (1942); *Black-Out in Gretley* (1942); *Britain Fights* (1943); *British Women Go to War* (1943); *Daylight on Saturday* (1943); *Desert Highway* (1944); *They Came to a City* (1944); *Three Men in New Suits* (1945); *How Are They at Home?* (1945); *The Secret Dream: An Essay on Britain, America, and Russia* (1946); *Bright Day* (1946); *Russian Journey* (1946); *Jenny Villiers* (1947); *The Long Mirror* (1947); *The Rose and Crown: A Morality Play* (1947); *The Plays of J. B. P.* (3 vols., 1948); *The Golden Fleece* (1948); *The High Toby: A Play for the Toy Theatre* (1948); *Ever Since Paradise* (1949); *Home Is Tomorrow* (1949); *Delight* (1949); *Bright Shadow* (1950); *Going Up, with Other Stories and Sketches* (1950); *Summer Day's Dream* (1950); *The P. Companion: A Selection* (1951); *Dragon's Mouth* (1952, with Jacquetta Hawkes); *Private Rooms* (1953); *Mother's Day* (1953); *The Other Place, and Other Stories of the Same Sort* (1953); *Try It Again* (1953); *Treasure on Pelican* (1953); *A Glass of Bitter* (1954); *Low Notes on a High Level* (1954); *The Magicians* (1954); *Journey Down a Rainbow* (1955, with Jacquetta Hawkes); *All About Ourselves* (1956); *The Scandalous Affair of Mr. Kettle and Mrs. Moon* (1956); *The Writer in a Changing Society* (1956); *The Art of the Dramatist* (1957); *Thoughts in the Wilderness* (1957); *Topside; or, The Future of England* (1958); *The Glass Cage* (1958); *The Story of Theatre* (1959); *William Hazlitt* (1960); *Saturn over the Water* (1961); *Charles Dickens* (1961); *The Thirty-First of June* (1961); *The Shapes of Sleep* (1962); *Margin Released* (1962); *Man and Time* (1964); *A Severed Head* (1964, with Iris Murdoch); *Lost Empires* (1965); *The Moment, and Other Pieces* (1966); *Salt Is Leaving* (1966); *It's an Old Country* (1967); *Essays of Five Decades* (1968); *Trumpets over the Sea* (1968); *All England Listened: The Wartime Broadcasts of J. B. P.* (1968); *The Prince of Pleasure and his Regency, 1811–1820* (1969); *Anton Chekhov* (1970); *The Edwardians* (1970); *Snoggle* (1971); *Victoria's Heyday* (1972); *Over the Long High Wall: Some Reflections and Speculations on Life, Death and Time* (1972); *The English* (1973); *A Visit to New Zealand* (1974); *Outcries and Asides* (1974); *Particular Pleasures* (1975); *The Carfitt Crisis, and Two Other Stories* (1975); *English Humour* (1976); *Found, Lost, Found; or, The English Way of Life* (1976); *The Happy Dream: An Essay* (1976); *Instead of the Trees: A Final Chapter of Autobiography* (1977); *The English Novel* (1977)

BIBLIOGRAPHY: Hughes, D., *J. B. P.: An Informal Study* (1958); Evans, G. L., *J. B. P., the Dramatist* (1964); Cooper, S., *J. B. P.: Portrait of an Author* (1970); Young, K., *J. B. P.* (1977); Braine, J., *J. B. P.* (1978); De Vitis, A., and Kalsen, A. E., *J. B. P.* (1980); Atkins, J., *J. B. P.: The Last of the Sages* (1981)

D. J. DOOLEY

PRISCO, Michele
Italian novelist and short-story writer, b. 18 Jan. 1920, Torre Annunziata

After graduating from law school in 1942, P. decided to follow his literary vocation and began to write for leading newspapers and reviews such as *Risorgimento, Il messaggero,* and *La fiera letteraria.* His first collection of short stories, *La provincia addormentata* (1949; the sleepy province), and his first novel, *Gli eredi del vento* (1950; *Heirs of the Wind,* 1953), were early indications of his major concerns as a writer, particularly of his keen perception of the human, social, psychological, and psychopathological makeup of the people he knew best, the middle class of the small towns of the Vesuvian hinterland.

While P.'s subsequent novels did show a gradual widening of the historical perspective, along with a new sense of the social reality of the postwar years, his main works of fiction—the novels *Una spirale di nebbia* (1966; a spiral of fog), which won the Strega Prize; *I cieli della sera* (1970; evening skies); and *Gli ermellini neri* (1975; black ermines)—focused again, with growing lucidity and slow but intense narrative pace, on the study of human nature as a consistent source for the portrayal of types and characters, on the complex world of family life, and on the moral decline of the provincial middle class. P.'s persistent and keenly analytical observations reveal the disturbing forces that motivate from within the actions and reactions that constitute human behavior. Cowardice and dissimulation, greed and ambition, hatred and violence are constant manifestations of the human condition, which are to be viewed within the wider spectrum of good and evil. The reader is invited to consider these observations in order to gain some understanding of the roots of the problems of contemporary history as reflected by provincial society: the disintegration of the traditional family structure, the continuing disarray in the social system, and the result-

ing displacement and degradation of the natural order of things and of the basic values of human existence.

The author himself has provided some valuable insights into the themes and issues of his writing in a book he is particularly fond of: *Punto franco* (1965; duty-free point), a collection of stories and narratives, substantially autobiographical in inspiration.

FURTHER WORKS: *Figli difficili* (1954); *Fuochi a mare* (1957); *La dama di piazza* (1961); *Il colore del cristallo* (1977)

A. ILLIANO

PRISHVIN, Mikhail Mikhailovich
Russian short-story writer, essayist, nature writer, and novelist, b. 4 Feb. 1873, Krushchevo; d. 16 Jan. 1954, Moscow

Born on the estate of his parents in the Orel district, P. studied agronomy in Riga and Leipzig. Finding work as a journalist in St. Petersburg, he published his first story in 1906. After brief service in World War I, he moved to the countryside, the setting for nearly all his subsequent works. Early in the 1930s P. made excursions to the Urals, to the northern regions of Russian and to the far east of the Soviet Union. He devoted the last years of his life largely to juvenile literature and his memoirs.

P.'s writings are marked by an optimism and idealism typical of 19th-c. Russian populism. Fascinated by nature, hunting, and rural life, which he knew from earliest childhood, P. can be compared with gentry writers such as Konstantin Aksakov (1817–1860), Turgenev, and Tolstoy. Unlike them, however, P. expanded his rural interests with systematic studies in agronomy and ethnography.

P.'s earliest books describing his journey to the White Sea region, *V krayu nepugannykh ptits* (1907; in the land of unfrightened birds) and *Za volshebnym kolobkom* (1908; following the gingerbread man), combine poetic, informed nature lore and a fascination with primitive peoples. After the revolution P. published what is perhaps his most characteristic work, *Kalendar prirody* (1939; *The Lake and the Woods; or, Nature's Calendar,* 1951), a collection of essays on natural history, hunting, and peasant life, in which he speaks with the voice of an educated, cosmopolitan artist isolated in the remote Russian countryside. Soviet exploitation of the country's natural resources is reflected in P.'s *Zhen-shen* (1933; *Jen Sheng: The Root of Life,* 1936), describing the establishment of a game farm in the Soviet far east.

Toward the end of his life P. published a charming juvenile tale, *Kladovaya solntsa* (1947; *The Treasure Trove of the Sun,* 1952), to great acclaim. From 1923 until his death P. labored intermittently over his fictionalized autobiography, *Kashcheeva tsep* (1956; Kashcheev's chain). The title refers to the monster in a Russian folktale who holds his victims in chains; P. saw this tale as a metaphor for the social and psychological limitations that restrain human potentialities.

Very popular in the Soviet Union, P.'s works are marked by a deft stylistic touch and fine poetic sensibility. Highly typical are his love and knowledge of the natural world and his earnest striving to fit man into the greater scheme of things.

FURTHER WORKS: *Adam i Yeva* (1909); *Cherny arab* (1910; *The Black Arab,* 1947); *Krutoyarsky zver* (1911); *Nikon Starokolenny* (1912); *Slavny bubny* (1913); *Okhotnichi byli* (1926); *Zhuravlinaya rodina* (1929); *Vesna sveta* (1938); *Fatselia* (1940); *Lesnaya kapel* (1940); *Korabelnaya chashcha* (1954; *Ship-Timber Grove,* 1957); *Sobranie sochineny* (6 vols., 1956–57); *Glaza zemli* (1957). FURTHER VOLUMES IN ENGLISH: *The Black Arab, and Other Stories* (1947); *The Sun's Storehouse: Short Stories* (1955)

BIBLIOGRAPHY: Huxley, J. S., Foreword to *Jen Sheng* (1936), pp. v–vii; Alexandrova, V., *A History of Soviet Literature* (1963), pp. 191–202; Struve, G., *Russian Literature under Lenin and Stalin* (1971), p. 146; Slonim, M., *Soviet Russian Literature* (1977), pp. 109–15; Parrott, R., "Evolution of a Critical Response: M. P.," *RLJ,* 109 (1977), 101–23; Parrott, R., "Questions of Art, Fact, and Genre in M. P.," *SlavR,* 36 (1977), 465–74

LELAND FETZER

PRITCHETT, V(ictor) S(awdon)

English critic, novelist, short-story writer, and journalist, b. 16 Dec. 1900, Ipswich

In two volumes of memoirs, *A Cab at the Door* (1968) and *Midnight Oil* (1971), P. has given a fascinating account of the middle-class suburban London atmosphere in which

he grew up. His father's life, he says, was blighted by Christian Science and extravagant ambition; the cab was often at the door, to move the family after a business failure. Although P. showed an aptitude for languages, he had to leave school at age fifteen to go into the leather trade. He found its mysteries fascinating, and through it he met a whole gallery of memorable eccentrics. Nevertheless, he had his vocation fixed in his mind: he wanted to pursue a writing career. From 1920 to 1927 he lived abroad. Back in England, he struggled to become a journalist; eventually he became a book reviewer for the *New Statesman,* for which he was to write a literary column over a period of several decades.

His first volume, *Marching Spain* (1928), was a travel book. Three works of fiction, described by one critic as "highly wrought tales of highly intellectualized passion," came in swift succession after it—the novel *Clare Drummer* (1929), *The Spanish Virgin, and Other Stories* (1930), and another novel, *Shirley Sanz* (1932; Am., *Elopement into Exile*). *Dead Man Leading* (1937), dealing with an expedition into the Brazilian jungle, was an ambitious combination of psychological novel and adventure story. But P. found the novel too ruminative and discursive, and too time-consuming. His best-known novel, *Mr. Beluncle* (1951), illustrates his difficulties with the form; despite its verbal brilliance, its successful capturing of atmosphere, and its memorable characters, especially its profound imaginative insight into an extreme puritan, it lacks the interior dynamics a good novel must have. P. was to put the same material—basically the story of his own father—to far better use in his autobiographical works.

During World War II he developed a considerable reputation in a form much more congenial to him—the short story. It has been said that he has a remarkable ability to convey a freighterful of implication in a skiff of words. A few strokes of the pen establish a setting; a few more, the people and their situation. Another fine short-story writer, Eudora Welty (q.v.), commends him for his ability to distill each story's truth through a pure concentration of human character. Often there is a note reminiscent of Chekhov (q.v.), emphasizing the place of illusion and obsession in life. In "The Camberwell Beauty" (1974) the world of antique dealers is vividly realized: their main aim, it becomes apparent, is not to sell but to possess. P. has always defended the short story as a distinct art form; it can no longer be viewed as the refuge of writers unequal to the demands of the novel.

His method in criticism is inductive: he wants to describe accurately "the new point in life from which any given novel started." Although he has written a biography, *Balzac* (1973), and a study of Turgenev, *The Gentle Barbarian* (1977), he prefers the short incisive essay to the long discursive work. His comment that literary criticism does not add to its stature by opening an intellectual hardware store reveals his opinion of academic criticism and theorizing. He is, however, anything but insular; in fact his book *The Myth Makers* (1979), a "plain man's guide to world fiction," contains essays on nineteen writers, none of whom wrote in English. Although he has not written the major work that would rank him among the leaders in an age of criticism, he has established a substantial reputation because of his ability to strike at the heart of a book and explain whether or not it should last, to set English novels against Continental ones and to produce striking capsule judgments.

In his travel books, he said, he took a lesson from D. H. Lawrence (q.v.) and selected the short, compact subject, made personal. Most of his writing shows a similar desire to get at the essence of a thing and describe it precisely, clearly, and economically. He also writes that in prose he found the common experience and the solid world in which he could firmly tread. He wants to describe the world around him, in all its solidity, but not to rise above it. Therefore some critics find him unduly limited in outlook: one complains that he fiddles while literature burns. His autobiography—that is, his two volumes of memoirs—has been called one of the best of our time, but about some incidents in his life he remains curiously reticent; he does not allow us very far inside himself. Still, if he gives us the impression of coming close to the highest reaches of art but not quite getting there, he has won distinction as a short-story writer, critic, and autobiographer. It is not surprising that he was knighted for his services to literature (1975).

FURTHER WORKS: *This England* (1930); *Nothing Like Leather* (1935); *In My Good Books* (1942); *It May Never Happen, and Other Stories* (1945); *Build the Ships* (1946);

The Living Novel (1946); *Why Do I Write? An Exchange of Views between Elizabeth Bowen, Graham Greene,* and *V. S. P.* (1948); *Books in General* (1953); *The Spanish Temper* (1954); *Collected Stories* (1956); *The Sailor, Sense of Humor, and Other Stories* (1956); *When My Girl Comes Home* (1961); *London Perceived* (1962); *The Key to My Heart: A Comedy in Three Parts* (1963); *Foreign Faces* (Am., *The Offensive Traveller,* 1964); *The Living Novel, and Later Appreciations* (1964); *New York Proclaimed* (1965); *The Working Novelist* (1965); *Shakespeare: The Comprehensive Soul* (1965, with others); *Blind Love, and Other Stories* (1969); *George Meredith and English Comedy* (1970); *The Camberwell Beauty, and Other Stories* (1974); *Autobiography* (Presidential Address to the English Association) (1977); *Selected Stories* (1978); *On the Edge of the Cliff* (1979); *The Tale Bearers: Literary Essays* (1980); *Collected Stories* (1982); *The Turn of the Years: As Old as the Century* (1982)

BIBLIOGRAPHY: "Mr. P.'s Novels," *TLS,* 19 Oct. 1951, 660; Mellors, J., "V. S. P.: Man on the Other Side of a Frontier," *London,* April–May 1975, 5–13; Reid, B. L., "Putting in the Self," *SR,* 75 (1977), 262–85; Welty, E., "A Family of Emotions," *NYTBR,* 25 June 1978, 1, 39–40; Theroux, P., "V. S. P.'s Stories: His Greatest Triumph" *SatR,* May 1982, 56–57; Raban, J., "Going Strong," *NYRB,* 24 June 1982, 8–12; Cunningham, V., "Coping with the Bigger Words," *TLS,* 25 June 1982, 687

D. J. DOOLEY

PROUST, Marcel

French novelist, b. 10 July 1871, Auteuil; d. 18 Nov. 1922, Paris

P. was born in what was then a suburb of Paris, although the family soon returned to Paris. P.'s father was a professor of medicine; his mother came from a prosperous Alsatian Jewish family. At the age of nine, P. suffered his first attack of asthma, and this affliction, aggravated by nervous disorders, would make of him a lifelong invalid. The death of his father in 1903, and particularly that of his mother two years later, left P. stricken with grief and obliged to undertake the first of several retreats to a sanatorium. Living virtually as a recluse from the age of thirty-four to his death at fifty-one, P. had constructed for himself the celebrated "cork-lined chamber" where he worked through long nights to complete the vast novel he had conceived. Occasionally he would make forays into the social world about which he was writing, and be seen at the opera, the new Russian ballet, or dining at the Ritz, wrapped in furs and looking like a waxen ghost.

As a young man, P. had sporadically contributed society notes and articles to the newspaper *Le Figaro,* but his first published literary work was a collection of bizarre tales called *Les plaisirs et les jours* (1896; *Pleasures and Regrets,* 1948; enlarged ed., *Pleasures and Days, and Other Writings,* 1957). Although the book received a polite critical reception, it was steeped in typically fin-de-siècle "hothouse" prose and bore little resemblance to the majestic style and sweep of his later masterpiece, *À la recherche du temps perdu* (1913–27; *Remembrance of Things Past,* 1922–32; rev. tr., 1981). Despite his uncertain English, P. next turned to translating the art criticism of John Ruskin. After P.'s death, it was discovered that during the first decade of the century he had already written a full-length novel bearing the title of its hero, *Jean Santeuil* (1952; *Jean Santeuil,* 1956) and also a substantial collection of literary criticism.

In 1913 the first volume of *À la recherche du temps perdu* was printed at P.'s own expense; it would take a decade for him to complete the seven-volume, four-thousand-page novel, and fifteen years before it was published in full: I, *Du côté de chez Swann* (1913; *Swann's Way,* 1922); II, *À l'ombre des jeunes filles en fleur* (1918; *Within a Budding Grove,* 1924); III, *Le côté de Guermantes* (1920–21; *The Guermantes Way,* 1925); IV, *Sodome et Gomorrhe* (1921–22; *Cities of the Plain,* 1927); V, *La prisonnière* (1923; *The Captive,* 1929); VI, *Albertine disparue* (1925; *The Sweet Cheat Gone,* 1930); VII, *Le temps retrouvé* (1927; *The Past Recaptured,* 1932).

The English phrase "remembrance of things past" (taken from a Shakespeare sonnet) does not convey the novel's central theme as expressed in the French title: "in search of lost time." Far more than writing a mere "remembrance," P. was profoundly concerned with the metaphysics of time and the function of human memory, and he developed the radical relativistic thesis that, contrary to common acceptance, it is not the fleeting present or the uncertain future that

has true reality for man but rather the *past,* and that the past is never "gone" but an accessibly present phenomenon. Writing in the first person throughout, P. demonstrates his theory by reproducing a narrative sequence that closely resembles his own life struggle to become a writer. It seems to him a wasted life, spent in a glittering but hollow social world; his personal and emotional pursuits he can only judge to be vain until he discovers that his very quest for understanding and meaning is in itself the theme and subject of a novel. He thus transcends time by deciding to "recapture the past" in words and endow it with the greater permanence of art. Readers are thus faced with the enticing conceit that the novel P. is about to start writing is the novel they have just finished reading!

The pivotal scene, one of the most memorable and literally evocative in Western fiction, is one in which P. dips a *madeleine* cake into a cup of tea and finds that the physical sensations evoked transport him back in time to an identical experience of childhood and enable him to experience the past completely as a simultaneous part of his present existence: " . . . the whole of Combray and its surroundings, all this came forth with shape and solidity, town, gardens and everything, from my cup of tea." We then follow the narrator as his universe expands from the provincial town of Combray to a seashore resort for the socially prominent to the most elegant and fashionable drawing rooms of Paris at the turn of the century, and even into the shadowy labyrinth of the homosexual world, where duke and workingman meet as peers.

The characters P. depicts are among the most vivid and complex in literature, rivaling those of Shakespeare and Balzac in their gigantic proportions. There is the Jewish bourgeois Charles Swann, who scales the Parisian social ladder, introduces the adolescent narrator to the arts, but loses his personal dignity and ruins his life through jealousy of a woman he does not really even love. In contrast, an uncouth but ambitious bourgeois couple named Verdurin successfully claw their way to the top and are not only accepted by, but ultimately supersede, the old nobility of France. That titled upper class, represented primarily by the Duke and Duchess de Guermantes, is portrayed by P. with both affection and satire; he conveys their human weaknesses and follies yet admires the traditions they embody. As a boy, he is "in love" with the duchess—meaning that he seeks to become a part of her world. P.'s most monumental portrait is the Baron de Charlus, another member of the illustrious Guermantes family, who is cultivated and socially powerful but leads the secret "double life" of a homosexual. Like Swann, he is a slave to passion; for love of a young musician of the lower classes, he frequents a level of society beneath his station, is consumed by jealousy, and courts disaster. At the novel's end, the aged and dying baron can still summon his powers to bow deeply to a "grande dame" in a passing carriage; ironically, she is a mere social climber who once insulted him.

À la recherche du temps perdu can be read simply as a compelling narrative, but also at a variety of other levels: sociohistorical, psychological, philosophical. With great insight and awareness of social change, P. traces the decline and fall of Parisian society and the rise of the bourgeoisie during the Third Republic. Many critics felt that this was his principal intention; P., however, also sought to demonstrate what he considered to be the governing laws of human behavior. Paramount among these is his concept of "successive selves." In keeping with his relativistic theory of time and memory, P. shows that no individual is a permanent reality but a series of different, changing persons throughout life, and that some of our apparent "selves" depend chiefly on how we are perceived by others.

The brilliant climax of the novel occurs at a great social gathering at which the narrator fails to recognize many of the people he has known for decades because the ravages of time have so transformed them physically. It is there that he realizes that he too is no longer young—no longer any *one* self from the past but the present accumulation of these. But he can still recapture the past and all past "selves" in a book, and thereby defy the metamorphoses of time through the metamorphosis of literature. Just as individuals and society may be transformed by time, P.'s quest for self-identity culminates in his discovery of his vocation as a writer—an artist who can transform life into the relatively more permanent reality of art.

À la recherche du temps perdu is not easy to classify. Although P. necessarily "paints from life," his novel is no roman à clef wherein real people are thinly disguised as fictional characters. Nor is it a roman-fleuve, a series of separate novels with continuing characters; this is a single cohesive work of fiction. Finally, it is not autobiography in the usual sense. P. himself was homosexual and part-Jewish; his first-person narrator is neither. What P. sought to communicate was not so much the *events* of his life but the essence of his spiritual quest.

Previously unpublished manuscripts found in the 1950s shed great light on the nature of that quest and on his method of composition. The novel *Jean Santeuil* had been written in the traditional third person, and the objective omniscient narrator clearly could not accommodate P.'s subjective need for interaction with the characters of his creation. The essays composed in 1908 and collected as *Contre Sainte-Beuve* (1954; *On Art and Literature,* 1958) yield another important clue. The 19th-c. critic Sainte-Beuve contended that thoroughly investigating a writer's personal life illuminates his work, and that notion held sway for many years. P. was among the first to attack this theory, claiming that the person and the artist are separate beings, that the writer becomes "another" when recreating experience in terms of fiction. It is believed that this conceptual breakthrough is the key to *À la recherche du temps perdu:* P. needed to speak not with his own voice but with the voice of P. the *artist*.

P. himself consciously set about writing with three very different models in mind. Just as the memoirs of Saint-Simon had pictured in minute detail the vast panorama of 17th-c. court life under Louis XIV, P. sought to re-create a social tapestry of his own era. He also wished to emulate Balzac, whose seventy-volume "Human Comedy" captures the sweep of Parisian and provincial life in the early 19th c. and conjures a total vision of mankind. Oddest of all, P. wanted to weave into his monumental work the color and the fantastic proportions of the legendary Arabian saga, *A Thousand and One Nights.*

One editor, little dreaming that P.'s novel was destined to become one of the classics of world literature, rejected the first volume, *Du côté de chez Swann,* as wordy, boring, wandering, and diffuse. However, the second volume, *À l'ombre des jeunes filles en fleurs,* won the prestigious Goncourt Prize in 1919. P.'s elaborate style, ideally suited to the complexity of his thought and to the sweep of his undertaking, is not an easy style. A single sentence may run to well over a page, yet each sentence, like the novel in its totality, is harmoniously balanced, frequently digressive but never meandering, and precisely structured to the idea or image conveyed. P. spoke often of the "architectural design" of his work, ambitiously likening it to a cathedral of prose. P.'s "digressions," whether on painting, music, psychology, or philosophy, actually illuminate his aesthetics and enable the reader more fully to appreciate the form and pattern of the novel.

Early critics and readers, for the most part, could not see, until the final volume appeared after P.'s death, the complete and complex design he had envisioned from the very start. Because of the richness of its texture, both stylistically and thematically, *À la recherche du temps perdu* has become one of the most abundantly analyzed literary achievements of all time. P. has been acclaimed as a master social historian and the creator of characters as memorable as those of Dickens, Balzac, and Dostoevsky. His serious presentation of homosexuality, however primitive and naïve it may seem today, was a pioneering accomplishment for its time. Ultimately, however, it is perhaps P.'s bold metaphysical concept of "time lost, time recaptured and transcended" that has earned for *À la recherche du temps perdu* not only enduring distinction among the great works of fiction but an important place in the realm of philosophical literature.

FURTHER WORKS: *Portraits de peintres* (1896); *Pastiches et mélanges* (1921); *Chroniques* (1927); *Morceaux choisis* (1928); *Comment parut "Du côté de chez Swann": Lettres de M. P.* (1930; repub. as *P. et la stratégie littéraire, avec des lettres de M. P. à René Blum, Bernard Grasset et Louis Brun*, 1954); *Correspondance générale* (6 vols., 1930–36); *À un ami: Correspondance inédite, 1903–1922* (1948; *Letters to a Friend*, 1949); *Lettres à André Gide, avec trois lettres et deux textes d'André Gide* (1949); *Lettres de M. P. à Antoine Bibesco* (1949; *Letters to Antoine Bibesco*, 1955); *Correspondance avec sa mère* (1954; *Letters to His Mother*, 1956); *Choix de lettres* (1965); *Lettres retrouvés* (1966); *Correspondance de M. P.* (1970 ff.); *Textes retrouvés* (1971). FURTHER VOLUMES IN ENGLISH: *The Maxims of M. P.* (1948); *M. P.: A Selection from His Miscellaneous Writings* (1948); *Letters* (1949)

BIBLIOGRAPHY: Beckett, S., *P.* (1931); Spagnoli, J. J., *The Social Attitudes of M. P.* (1931); March, H., *The Two Worlds of M. P.* (1948); Green, F. C., *The Mind of P.* (1949); Maurois, A., *P.: Portrait of a Genius* (1950); Hindus, M., *The Proustian Vision* (1954); Painter, G., *M. P.: A Biography* (2 vols., 1959–65); Girard, R., ed., *P.: A Collection of Critical Essays* (1962); Moss, H., *The Magic Lantern of M. P.* (1962); Shattuck, R., *P.'s Binoculars* (1963); Bersani, L., *M. P.: The Fictions of Life and Art* (1965); Brée, G., *M. P. and Deliverance from Time* (1969); Bucknall, B. J., *The Religion of Art in P.* (1969); Fowlie, W., *A Reading of P.* (1969); Kopp, R., *M. P. as a Social Critic* (1971); Wolitz, S., *The Proustian Community* (1971); Deleuze, G., *P. and Signs* (1972); Revel, J.-F., *On P.* (1972); Stambolian, G., *M. P. and the Creative Encounter* (1972); Rivers, J. E., *P. and the Art of Love* (1980)

JAMES ROBERT HEWITT

P. was both a realist and an idealist.

As a realist he observed carefully the world about him and with scientific accuracy noted the details which, according to the latest nineteenth-century thought, enter into the composition of the character. This compelled him to treat each of his characters as a social being, belonging to a particular class with distinctive traits which play an important part in his behavior. From such observation of individuals, P. charted the flux of late nineteenth-century French society and drew general conclusions regarding the different social classes.

However, his observation soon reaches a point where it ceases to be scientific and is colored by his abnormal temperament. Unattached to any social institution, he can criticize every one of them with the intransigeance of an idealist. He is sensitive to all of the faults of society and refuses to see any spiritual values in it. He therefore depicts a world in which the upper classes have no intellectual, artistic or moral principles, in which the middle classes are interested only in making money and in rising to the social position of the upper classes, and in which the lower classes have the same social ambition as the others and the greed that springs from such ambition.

John J. Spagnoli, *The Social Attitudes of M. P.* (1931), p. 157

P. has several conceptions of time—which are not contradictory but are merely different views of the same reality. These divergences may give the impression that his ideas are more complicated than they really are. Sometimes he considers Time as an enemy, eager to destroy everything that is dear and precious to us, perpetually changing each one of us into another being. It kills our affections, subtly undermines our health, slowly but surely ruins our minds, turns pretty maidens into decrepit old hags. A great part—perhaps the greatest part—of P.'s writings is intended to show the havoc wrought in and round us by Time; and he succeeded amazingly not only in suggesting to the reader, but in making him actually feel, the universal decay invincibly creeping over everything and everybody with a kind of epic and horrible power. This conception of Time is a reflection of P.'s own experience. His whole life was a fight against Time—an endless struggle to last out a few more moments in spite of tremendous physical odds. He felt, especially in the latter part of his existence, more than ever threatened by the danger of having his thread of life cut short before he could express all that he had to say. Then the idea of Time became like a haunting nightmare and all his writings of that period bear the stamp of the ever-present, hostile obsession.

Georges Lemaitre, *Four French Novelists* (1938), pp. 92–93

But a part of P.'s special savor comes from his invalidism and neuroticism. His world is that of the man in bed, seen at one remove, and this fact is his strength and his weakness. Imagination and memory play larger rôles than in the case of a more normal writer. He remembers and he imagines slights, deceptions, tricks; he projects his idiosyncrasies beyond his cork-lined walls and fastens them on to others. But from his claustration, too, he drew his extraordinary acuity of vision and the rich quality of his memory. "Never," he wrote, long before he could realize how fully the statement was to apply to himself, "was Noah able to see the world so well as from the Ark."

His great achievement as a psychologist is his description of himself. No one, not even Stendhal, has told himself so fully; and no one has probed more patiently and more exhaustively into the dark corners of the neurotic personality. To do this, it was not enough to be himself the neurotic introvert; he needed, and he had, a remarkable power of detachment and a strong analytic talent. The result is that from his own highly special psychology he was able to abstract a general truth.

Harold March, *The Two Worlds of M. P.* (1948), pp. 245–46

These memories [of his early childhood and youth] had lain undisturbed in the depths of his mind for a certain necessary gestative period of time, when they were delivered fresh and unretouched to the surface by a strong sensory impression like that made upon the narrator by the taste of the little madeleine dipped into a cup of tea, out of which, like the goddess Venus, Combray sprang in full bloom. Commonplace experiences and memories recalled after many years had

passed were commonplace no longer. Something magical had happened to them. They were transmuted as if by alchemy, and, simply from having lain imbedded for so long in the mysterious caves and recesses of the mind, they came forth once more into the light of an unfading day, completely emblazoned and covered over with the golden imagery of his genius.

Milton Hindus, *The Proustian Vision* (1954), pp. 277–78

The confrontation between Marcel and the world is thus re-created in the details of the narrator's style; the dramatic tensions of the Proustian sentence repeat stylistically the conflicts between the self and the world. It is easy to see the significance of certain characteristics of the narrator's style—for example, the seemingly endless proliferations around any starting point of description. It is as if this could do away with the memory of the world as distinct from the self, as if, under the melting pressure of analysis and comparison, objects could be thoroughly de-objectified and everything made to appear as a metaphor for everything else. The galleys of *À la recherche du temps perdu* came back to Gallimard covered with additions, and P.'s publishers understandably felt some panic when they saw how a job of correction inevitably became the occasion for uncontrollable elaboration. In looking over his text, P. apparently never found things sufficiently "digested"; the way to conquer their resistance, their opaqueness, was not to revise or cut out passages, but to inflate them, to "cover" every aspect of the elusive world with a continuously dense reflection on the world.

Leo Bersani, *M. P.: The Fictions of Life and Art* (1965), pp. 230–31

On tasting the crumbs of the *madeleine* in a spoonful of tea, the narrator is invaded by a powerful joy.... This rapture might be compared, if one wished, to that of a saint taking communion. The *madeleine* resembles the Host, in that a metaphysical ecstasy has been induced as a result of the physical act of eating, without the ecstasy's being limited to the taste of the food or of the same nature as that taste. We could say that like the ecstatic who goes so far as to doubt whether God is in him or whether he is not himself God, the narrator feels that the precious essence with which he has been filled is actually himself. But again, it might be safer to understand this statement about the "precious essence" with which the narrator has been filled as a warning not to confuse that essence with God or with the Infinite or any transcendental entity. P. goes on, after this, to speak of the tea as a "breuvage" whose "vertu" is diminishing. No longer would the reader be justified in thinking of the tea as a communion cup: these are rather the terms in which one speaks of a magic potion whose effects can wear off, like the love philter of Tristan and Yseult. Then the narrator says that the answer is not in the cup but in his mind: what he is seeking is something, as yet undiscovered, within his mind, which his mind, to discover, will have to create.

Barbara J. Bucknall, *The Religion of Art in P.* (1969), pp. 155–56

In his seemingly excessive preoccupation with the world: the worldliness of social groups, time, love, snobbism, painting, music, the prestige of names, P. never forgets the real subject of his novel: the literary vocation of his protagonist. This spiritual theme dominates all others and bears a relationship with all others. It is the framework of the novel and pervades the matinée scene at the end. Throughout the final pages, all the dramas announced and developed in the novel are transcended and fused into the one taking place in Marcel's mind. The struggle is that being waged by the esthete in Marcel, the artist, the potential novelist, and the terrified human observer of the immense changes brought about by time. More discreet than other themes in the novel, but never absent for long from any of the volumes, the two themes—Marcel's literary vocation and his obsession with death—assume the greatest importance and form both symbolically and in fact the conclusion of *À la recherche du temps perdu.*

Wallace Fowlie, *A Reading of P.* (1975), p. 288

How does the narrator's statement that homosexually oriented people are as numerous as "the sands of the earth" accord with his position that they are sick, mentally deranged, suffering from a hereditary affliction, and, in general, physically and psychologically different from the rest of the population—"[belonging] not to common humanity but to a strange race which mixes with it, hides within it, but never merges with it"? These ideas do not, of course, accord at all. When the narrator says people with homosexual tastes are found everywhere, in great numbers, and in all walks of life, he seems to forget that elsewhere he says they are grotesque anomalies who are radically, ontologically different from the general run of humanity. It may be that P. uses the former idea because he knows from personal experience it is true and the latter idea because it is the expected and the socially acceptable thing to say. In any case, the extremely high incidence of homosexuality depicted in *À la recherche* is one of the most original aspects of P.'s treatment of the theme, owing very little to—in fact, directly contradicting—both the scientific and the popular thinking of his era.

J. E. Rivers, *P. and the Art of Love* (1980), p. 177

PROVENÇAL LITERATURE
See French Literature: Occitan Literature

PRZYBOŚ, Julian
Polish poet and critic, b. 5 May 1901, Gwoźnica; d. 6 Oct. 1970, Warsaw

P. was raised in a provincial backwater of what was then the Austro-Hungarian Empire. During the 1920s and 1930s, while earning his living as a schoolteacher, he was affiliated with a number of avant-garde literary journals. From 1937 to 1939 he lived in Paris: this was his first sustained contact with life in a major cosmopolitan city. P. spent most of World War II in his native region, having assumed for his protection the identity of a peasant laborer. In 1944 he offered his services to the Soviet-backed Polish government; thus began a long career as a trusted member of the Communist literary establishment. From 1947 through 1951 P. served as Polish ambassador to Switzerland. The last two decades of his life were spent in Warsaw.

When P. came to Cracow—itself a rather sleepy medieval town, albeit an intellectual center—to pursue his university education after World War I, he was swept off his feet by the dynamics of city life. He enthusiastically endorsed the manifestos of the Polish futurist (q.v.) movement, especially the "three M's" proclaimed by Tadeusz Peiper (1891–1969): *miasto, masa, maszyna* (metropolis, masses, machinery). His earliest poetry collections, *Śruby* (1925; screws) and *Oburącz* (1926; with both hands), are aggressive celebrations of technology and urban life. They merge calls for social revolution with paeans of praise to dynamos, generators, and other manifestations of industrialized society. Rich sound instrumentation, insistent repetition, and the use of verbs dynamic in both meaning and form (for example, imperatives and active participles) combine with images of power and motion to create hymns to human and mechanical energy. In P.'s work of this time one can discern similarities to both Marinetti and Mayakovsky (qq.v.).

In the 1930s, beginning with the volume *W głąb las* (1932; into the forest depths), a private lyrical strain entered P.'s poetry, coexisting with the more strident political theme of revolution, which remained prominent throughout the decade. The lyrical poems merge contemplation of nature, particularly the rural landscape, with meditations on death and the meaning of life. Metaphors and language are designed to concentrate as many layers of meaning as possible into a single image. The majority of these poems are suffused with enthusiasm for life. Images of light, usually radiant and life-giving, although at times threatening destruction, are a characteristic feature. A series of annual poems in celebration of spring, beginning with spring 1934 and ending in 1970, exemplify P.'s delight in life coupled with his insatiable yearning for experience.

A new theme, which reveals as it were the terrors shoved aside in the dynamic poems of affirmation and revolution, appeared in the late 1950s. The poems of the last decade of P.'s life are more introspective than anything previous. They combine the insights of psychoanalysis with the poet's license to create his personal myth, and are attempts at probing the singular obsessions that had driven him for much of his life. The best of these poems, written under the cloud of serious illness, achieve a delicate balance between the expansiveness of the poet's response to nature's abundance and man's inventiveness, and the private grief attendant upon recognition of his mortality.

P.'s literary career of almost half a century was marked by paradox. His ideological stance and avant-garde poetic practices made him a rather marginal figure in prewar Poland, but his fortunes were reversed by the Communist accession to power. His virulent attacks on the avant-garde of the late 1950s and early 1960s defended both his own poetic values and the social needs of the state. Nonetheless, P. remained an aesthete whose difficult poetry demands a higher level of sophistication from its audience than is normally tolerated under even the loose Polish guidelines of Socialist Realism (q.v.).

FURTHER WORKS: *Sponad* (1930); *Równanie serca* (1938); *Póki my żyjemy* (1944); *Miejsce na ziemi* (1945); *Czytając Mickiewicza* (1950; rev. ed., 1956); *Rzut pionowy* (1952); *Najmniej słów* (1955); *Narzędzie ze światła* (1958); *Linia i gwar* (1959); *Poezje zebrane* (1959; 2nd ed., 1967); *Próba całości* (1961); *Więcej o manifest* (1962); *Sens poetycki* (1963); *Nike i słowik* (1964); *Na znak* (1965); *Liryki 1930–1964* (1966); *Kwiat nieznany* (1969); *Zapiski bez daty* (1970); *Wiersze i obrazki* (1970); *Utwory poetyckie* (1975)

BIBLIOGRAPHY: Miłosz, C., *The History of Polish Literature* (1969), pp. 401–4; Levine, M. G., *Contemporary Polish Poetry 1925–1975* (1981), pp. 21–35; Carpenter, B., "J. P.: The Double Image," *PolR,* 26, 2 (1981), 23–34

MADELINE G. LEVINE

PRZYBYSZEWSKI, Stanisław

Polish novelist, dramatist, and critic (also writing in German), b. 7 May 1868, Łojewo; d. 23 Nov. 1927, Jaronty

Until he was thirty years old, P. moved almost exclusively in German cultural circles. Born in the Prussian-ruled area of partitioned Poland, he went to Berlin to study architecture and medicine, but never finished. Extremely popular with the intelligentsia of that city as a pianist, writer, and bon vivant, P. quickly came to typify for them fin-de-siècle decadence: he was cosmopolitan, scandalous (alcohol, sex, and satanism were among his principal interests), refined (his renditions of Chopin brought him much fame), and cerebral (his novels in German were highly regarded). In 1898 he left Berlin to take a position as the editor of the literary journal *Życie* in Cracow, where he worked largely in Polish and even began to put his earlier German works into his native language. After a fruitful although brief period (until 1906), he returned once again to Germany, remaining there until the end of World War I. When Poland was reconstituted as a nation in 1918, he settled first in the Free City of Danzig (now Gdańsk) and then in Warsaw; no longer a professional littérateur, he served as a minor clerk in a government office. He died near Warsaw in relative obscurity.

Although hailed as a genius when he was at the height of his career (approximately 1893–1907), P. today is regarded more as a promoter of literature than a great writer. His novels, prose poems, and plays are all characterized by his insistence on the principle of art for art's sake. In this regard he became the most visible and vocal exponent of his time of the neoromantic movement in Polish literature known as Young Poland. As the editor of *Życie* from 1898 to 1900, he published many fine young poets and, albeit in exaggerated and excessive terms, outlined a literary program that postulated not only the absoluteness of art for its own sake but also the primacy of sexuality in determining human conduct, the superiority of the neurotic over the "healthy" psyche, and the bankruptcy of the older generation of utilitarian, positivist, and, to his mind, tendentious writers. Most of these notions he summarized in his manifesto *Confiteor* (1899; Latin: I confess), which many considered at the time a kind of charter of Polish neoromanticism. Even today his theoretical formulations are occasionally cited to underscore points in contemporary Polish literary controversies.

The practical result of P.'s beliefs as embodied in his fiction was a vehement style seemingly weighty with new ideas, but in the final analysis unoriginal. His three-part novel *Homo sapiens* (German original, 1895–96; Polish version, 1901; *Homo Sapiens,* 1915), for example, examines at great length the psychological states (P.'s famous "naked soul") of the hero, Eric Falk, as he destroys the lives of several women in order to assert his superiority over them. The details of mood and feeling, richly developed in the novel, contrast sharply with the work's colorless settings and plotless construction. P.'s goal here as elsewhere was to focus attention on his theories of art, sexuality, psychology, and the power of the will.

While his views were in vogue, his writings were both popular and influential. But as those theories became dated, P.'s fiction also suffered, for it had few literary qualities to offer audiences grown bored with his notions. Moreover, his indebtedness to other writers, particularly Schopenhauer, Nietzsche, Tolstoy, Dostoevsky, Ibsen, Maeterlinck (q.v.), and the French symbolists (q.v.), soon became obvious. Only a few essays on music—for example "Chopin und Nietzsche" (1891; Chopin and Nietzsche)—also included in the collection *Zur Psychologie des Individuums* (1892; on the psychology of the individual) and "Szopen a naród" (1910; Chopin and the nation)—in which he displays genuine sensitivity to the art; and memoiristic pieces like "Z gleby kujawskiej" (1902; from the soil of Kujawy) and *Moi współcześni wśród obcych* (1926; my contemporaries abroad) and the unfinished, posthumously published *Moi współcześni wśród swoich* (1930; my contemporaries at home), in which he vividly recalls the many literary and artistic personalities with whom he was intimate, are read with any frequency today.

On the whole, P.'s position in Polish literature is secure, if not outstanding, for he worked indefatigably to bring to the public eye the works of the best Young Poland writers, like Stanisław Wyspiański (q.v.) and Jan Kasprowicz (1860–1926). "A genius without portfolio," as Henryk Sienkiewicz (q.v.) called him, he was a powerful influence in his time. And although his bold theoretical statements and even bolder attempts to embody them in fiction have for the most part aged badly, nonetheless the charismatic hold he had on his generation makes him a figure to be reckoned with in Polish literary history to the present day.

SELECTED FURTHER WORKS: *Totenmesse* (1893; Polish, *Requiem aeternam,* 1901); *Vigilien* (1894; Polish, *Z cyklu Wigilii,* 1899); *De profundis* (German, 1895; Polish, 1899; rev. ed., 1922); *Pro domo mea* (German, 1895); *Die Synagoge des Satan* (1896; Polish, *Synagoga Szatana,* 1899); *Satans Kinder* (1897; Polish, *Dzieci Szatana,* 1899); *Das große Glück* (1897; Polish, *Dla szczęścia,* 1900; *For Happiness,* 1912); *Androgyne* (1899); *Na drogach duszy* (1900); *Nad morzem* (1901); *Złote runo* (1901); *Goście* (1901); *Synowie ziemi* (Part I, 1901; Part II, *Dzień sądu,* 1909; Part III, *Zmierzch,* 1910); *Die Mutter* (1902; Polish, *Matka,* 1903); *Śnieg* (1903; *Snow,* 1920); *Odwieczna baśń* (1906); *W godzinie cudu* (1906); *Gelübde* (1906; Polish, *Śluby,* 1907); *Dzieci nędzy* (Part I, 1913; Part II, *Adam Drzazga,* 1914); *Gody życia* (1910); *Mocny człowiek* (Part I, 1911; Part II, *Wyzwolenie,* 1912; Part III, *Święty gaj,* 1913); *Topiel* (1912); *Miasto* (1914); *Krzyk* (1914–15); *Polen und der heilige Krieg* (1915); *Von Polens Seele* (1917; Polish, *Szlakiem duszy polskiej,* 1917); *Il regno doloroso* (in Polish, 1924); *Mściciel* (1927); *Listy* (3 vols., 1937, 1938, 1954)

BIBLIOGRAPHY: Czaykowski, B., "Poetic Theories in Poland: Przesmycki and P.," *PolR,* 11 (1966), 45–55; Miłosz, C., *The History of Polish Literature* (1969), pp. 329–33; Schluchter, M., *S. P. und seine deutschsprachigen Prosawerke, 1892–1899* (1969); Stammler, H., "S. P. and Antonio Choloniewski: Two Interpreters of the Meaning of Polish History," *Jahrbücher für die Geschichte Osteuropas,* 20 (1972), 42–59; Jaworska, W., "Edvard Munch and S. P.," *Apollo,* 100 (1974), 312–17; Klim, G., "S. P.'s Expressionism: Between Philosophy and Mysticism," in Sussex, R., ed., *Polish Collo-*

quium of the University of Melbourne (1976), pp. 45–62

HENRY R. COOPER, JR.

PSAILA, Carmelo

(known as Dun Karm) Maltese poet (writing in Maltese and Italian), b. 18 Oct. 1871, Żebbuġ; d. 13 Oct. 1961, Sliema

P. received a classical and theological education at the Seminary of Malta. For over twenty-five years he was assistant librarian at the National Library and was director of the circulating libraries from 1923 to 1936. The second president of the Association of Maltese Authors, P. edited its journal, *Il-Malti* (1927–40). On his retirement in 1936, the Government of Malta entrusted him with the compilation of a Maltese-English Dictionary, which was completed in 1955. In recognition of his stature as a national poet writing in the people's language, he was awarded an honorary doctorate from the University of Malta in 1945 and the Ġużè Muscat-Azzopardi Medal in 1946.

P.'s early poetry, written in Italian, was published in *Foglie d'alloro* (1896; laurel leaves). His later Italian poetry shows increasing proficiency, including metrical experimentation. Nevertheless, he decided to turn to Maltese. His poetic work in the previously neglected language was later collected by the novelist Ġużé Bonnici (1907–1940) and published in three volumes: *X'ħabb u x'ħaseb il-poeta* (1939; the poet's love and thought); *X'emmen il-poeta* (1939; the poet's faith); *X'għamel iżjed il-poeta* (1940; the poet's other poems).

P.'s poetry is a remarkable fusion of Italian literary influences, particularly the techniques and subjects of Giacomo Zanella (1820–1888), and of Maltese themes and images. His ethnic identity emerges more forcefully in his Maltese poetry.

P. is the most significant poet in Maltese literature because, by his literary contributions and his open advocacy of the people's language against the prejudices of the upper class, he gave it a literary prestige it never enjoyed before. Several of the older Maltese poets followed in his footsteps. Younger poets have been moving away from his influence in their search for new, modern verse techniques and different intellectual horizons; they nevertheless still hold him in high regard.

FURTHER WORKS: *Liriche* (1954); *Antoloġija* (1969); *Dun Karm: Il-poeżiji miġbura* (1980)

BIBLIOGRAPHY: Arberry, A. J., *Dun Karm: Poet of Malta* (1961)

JOSEPH AQUILINA

PUERTO RICAN LITERATURE
See Spanish-Caribbean Literature

PUIG, Manuel
Argentine novelist, b. 1932, General Villegas

P.'s youthful experiences left an indelible mark on his work. The drab existence of a typical middle-class family in a small town in the province of Buenos Aires—offset by the glamour of distant urban life, embodied in American films—has been the core of much of his fiction. In 1951 he began studies at the University of Buenos Aires. Unable to define a career for himself, he went to Rome in 1957 with a scholarship to study at the Experimental Film Center. For the next ten years he lived abroad, collaborating in the direction of several films and beginning to write. He returned to Buenos Aires briefly in 1967 but has lived abroad since then, mostly in Rome and New York. Since the publication of his first novel he has dedicated himself exclusively to writing fiction and to teaching writing.

With the publication of his first novel, *La traición de Rita Hayworth* (1968; *Betrayed by Rita Hayworth*, 1971), P. was immediately acclaimed as one of Latin America's most talented writers. Although the quality of P.'s fiction is remarkably even, most critics consider this first novel his masterpiece. It was followed by *Boquitas pintadas* (1969; *Heartbreak Tango*, 1973), a story of two love triangles written in the form of a serialized novel. The structural model for *The Buenos Aires Affair* (1973 [title in English]; *The Buenos Aires Affair*, 1976) is the detective story. *El beso de la mujer araña* (1976; *Kiss of the Spider Woman*, 1979) deals with a political prisoner and a homosexual who share a cell in a prison. Politics and sexuality, and their mutual relationship, are also evident in two recent novels, *Pubis angélical* (1979; angelic pubis) and *Maldición eterna a quienes lean estas páginas* (1981; *Eternal Curse on the Reader of These Pages*, 1982), the latter written first in English and translated into Spanish by the author.

P. has been called the chronicler of middle-class Argentina. His fiction describes the devastating emptiness of this life, the frustrations of those who desire to get beyond it, and the disappointments of failure. His novels, however, are far more than social documents portraying everyday reality. They penetrate and probe the complexities of human emotion and psychology. A pattern emerges among these complexities: although P.'s characters suffer from their empty daily existence, they live rich and full inner lives, often through fantasy. This creative aspect of existence is commonly expressed through cinematic metaphors.

In *La traición de Rita Hayworth* much of the mundane reality is filtered through the young protagonist, Toto Casals. It relates his story from infancy in 1933 to adolescence in 1948. The structure is typical of P.'s novels: it features eight chapters in each of the work's two parts, and the order of the chapters is not completely chronological. Rather than understanding all the circumstances surrounding Toto's life from the outset, the reader gradually fits the pieces of the puzzle together. It becomes apparent that Toto is a sensitive and intelligent person surrounded by mediocrity. Argentine society obviously does not accommodate those who do not fit into its structures and conform to its traditional values.

La traición de Rita Hayworth offers a variety of changing narrative situations with different narrators, written documents, and extensive dialogue. P. is a master of diverse writing styles, using several of them in each of his works. Some of the technical devices he employs are adopted from films, such as close-ups and the presentation of one-sided conversations. Among his other techniques are the use of shifting points of view and streams of sensory impressions.

The problems P.'s characters confront follow a chronological trajectory in the first three novels: *La traición de Rita Hayworth* deals with youth, *Boquitas pintadas* with late adolescence and early adulthood, and *The Buenos Aires Affair* with adulthood. In each of these novels sexual frustration and the ways a dominating society can limit human potential are major themes.

P. is one of Latin America's major writers and one of the most widely read. He has created a body of fiction that is highly sophisti-cated technically and thematically, yet at the same time quite accessible.

FURTHER WORK: *Sangre de amor correspondido* (1982)

BIBLIOGRAPHY: Rodríguez Monegal, E., "A Literary Myth Exploded," *Review*, 4–5 (1971–72), 56–64; Hazera, L., "Narrative Technique in M. P.'s *Boquitas pintadas*," *LALR*, 2, 3 (1973), 45–51; Brushwood, J., *The Spanish American Novel* (1975), pp. 305–8; Christ, R., "An Interview with M. P.," *PR*, 44 (1977), 52–61; Luchting, W. A., "Betrayed by Education: M. P.'s *La traición de Rita Hayworth*," *PPNCFL*, 28, 1 (1977), 134–37; Lindstrom, N., "The Problem of Pop Culture in the Novels of M. P.," *TAH*, 4, 30–31 (1978), 28–31

RAYMOND L. WILLIAMS

PUNJABI LITERATURE

See Indian Literature and Pakistani Literature

PURDY, James

American novelist, short-story writer, dramatist, and poet, b. 14 July 1923, near Fremont, Ohio

P., a child of divorced parents, spent his formative years moving about his native state. Finally graduating from a Chicago high school, P. attended the University of Chicago and the University of Puebla in Mexico. His linguistic abilities earned him a position teaching English in a private boys' school in Havana, Cuba. In 1953, after graduate study, traveling abroad, and four years on the faculty at Lawrence College in Wisconsin, he devoted himself to writing full-time. Rejected for years by American publishers, P.'s early stories were printed privately in 1956 and publicly, thanks to the support of Dame Edith Sitwell (q.v.), in England in 1957 under the title *63: Dream Palace*. The collection was then published in the U.S. under the title *Color of Darkness* (1957). A recipient of Guggenheim and Ford Foundation grants, P. now lives in New York.

P.'s first collection of macabre tales, *Color of Darkness*, signals the major themes, characteristics, and discernments of American society that permeate his later works and properly link him to a Southern Gothic tradition. Loveless, barren marriages and family lives abound in the stories, estranged children strive to communicate and find identity, while the spiritually deprived seek fulfillment through perverse love and violent sexuality. These subjects find their fullest expression in P.'s first and most popular novel, *Malcolm* (1959), an elusive allegory/fable/parable of Black Humor (q.v.) structured as a picaresque tale through which an innocent boy in search of his father moves progressively toward his own death, encountering the false, empty values of America that are emblematized in marriages, sexual attitudes, science, wealth, and art.

Satire functions as the dominant mode in two major novels. *The Nephew* (1961) turns to traditional realism to expose gently the small-town life of the Middle West and its underlying human darkness. More vitriolic and savage, *Cabot Wright Begins* (1964) scathingly portrays the brutal, immoral heart of American culture, where rape becomes a release from boredom and ennui, where the institutions of Wall Street and the New York publishing industry alienate and dehumanize; thus the corrupting ethos of commerce and the failure of art to engage reality are revealed.

P.'s works often explore the theme of homosexuality in order to show the anguish and suffering of the human condition, the dual curse of love as healer and betrayer. In *Eustace Chisholm and the Works* (1967) the hero, unable to accept his love for another man, escapes to the army, where he meets his human nemesis. The sadomasochistic relationship of hero and nemesis culminates in a horrific, ferocious scene of disembowelment and suicide.

P. regularly employs bizarre incident to underscore his ideas. The maimed soldier of *In a Shallow Grave* (1976) attempts to heal psychic wounds through love, for example, by drinking his lover's blood, spilled in a Christlike act by his lover's own hand. Similarly, *Narrow Rooms* (1978) concerns the love-hate, fear-submission bonds that bring four men to mystical absolution and murder. The protagonist purifies himself at the end by being crucified on a barn door as the disinterred body of his lover lies before him.

Jeremy's Version (1970) and *The House of the Solitary Maggot* (1974), parts of the incomplete trilogy *Sleepers in Moon-Crowded Valleys,* are regional in character and evoke a

nostalgia for the Midwest of the 1920s and 1930s, but they also focus on a final and familiar P. theme: metaphysical preoccupation with the relation of language to reality. Through layers of narrative, stories within stories, memoirists feeding on memoirists, these novels imply a madness in the American psyche that substitutes dreams for life itself.

Despite the eccentric nature of P.'s works, the originality and power of his dour vision into the blackness of the human soul, as well as his highly wrought style and unique symbolist techniques, will secure his position as an outstanding American craftsman.

FURTHER WORKS: *Children Is All* (1962); *An Oyster Is a Wealthy Beast* (1967); *Mr. Evening: A Story and Nine Poems* (1968); *On the Rebound: A Story and Nine Poems* (1970); *The Running Sun* (1971); *I Am Elijah Thrush* (1972); *Two Plays* (1979); *Mourners Below* (1981)

BIBLIOGRAPHY: Pomeranz, R., "The Hell of Not Loving: P.'s Modern Tragedy," *Renascence,* 15 (1963), 149–53; Skerrett, T., "J. P. and the Works: Love and Tragedy in Five Novels," *TCL,* 15 (1969), 25–53; Baldanza, F., "Playing House for Keeps with J. P.," *ConL,* 11 (1970), 489–510; Tanner, T., *City of Words* (1971), pp. 85–108; Chupack, H., *J. P.* (1975); Adams, S., *J. P.* (1976)

LYNN DEVORE

PUTINAS, Vincas

See Mykolaitis, Vincas

PYNCHON, Thomas

American novelist, b. 8 May 1937, Glen Cove, N.Y.

P.'s family traces back to a colonial magistrate who presided over a witchcraft trial and who wrote a theological tract that was burned on Boston Common. Like Hawthorne, P. has made literary capital out of his Puritan antecedents. He also has mined the vast resources of Western culture, particularly its recent history, science, and technology.

P. began writing while an undergraduate at Cornell University, where he studied engineering and English, receiving a B.A. degree in 1959 after a two-year interval in the Navy.

While working at an aircraft company in Seattle, and later living in Mexico, he wrote *V.* (1963), which won the William Faulkner Prize for the best first novel of the year. For his second novel, *The Crying of Lot 49* (1966), he received the Rosenthal Foundation Award of the National Institute of Arts and Letters. *Gravity's Rainbow* (1973) was denied the Pulitzer Prize for its alleged obscenity and obscurity, despite the unanimous recommendation of the committee's judges. In 1975 P. declined the William Dean Howells gold medal for the best fiction of the previous five years. P. today lives a reclusive life, refusing to be interviewed or photographed.

Meanwhile, critical interest in P.'s work accelerates. Reviewers have been succeeded by scholars who log into the vast data bank that comprises P.'s three novels and a few short stories, each critic attempting to extract new meanings from the profusion and confusion of signals input by the author.

P.'s stylistic virtuosity has been both praised as awesome and damned as tedious. Unquestionably, he has exploited, with brilliance and originality, the entire range of the novelistic tradition, drawing inspiration from Sterne and Voltaire, from Melville and Mark Twain, and from 20th-c. masters like Conrad, Joyce, Nabokov, and Borges (qq.v.). No doubt he owes something to the example of works like William Gaddis's (q.v.) *The Recognitions* (1955).

P. changes modes and moods with disconcerting speed—shifting from romance to satire, from burlesque and slapstick to poignant lyricism. He seems to have overlooked no literary precedent—Anatole France's (q.v.) missionary to the penguins, for example, is matched by Father Fairing and his parish of rats in the sewers of Manhattan in *V.* His pages abound with mandalas, carbon rings, limericks, and notes on art history and musicology. With a wildness of tone and taste, he applies the tricks of cinematography, comic books, and other forms of pop culture. His most powerful and subversive weapon is parody.

P.'s work bears evidence of his substantial knowledge of Egyptian and classical myth, the thought of Max Weber (1864–1920), Henry Adams (q.v.), and Ludwig Wittgenstein (1889–1951) and the poetry of Rilke and Eliot (qq.v.). His offbeat erudition enables him to utilize history and anthropology in startling ways (the 1898 Fashoda Crisis in the Sudan, the death of the composer Anton von Webern, Ojibwa customs, the Kirgiz language), although readers must remain on guard against invented peoples, persons and places, and institutions.

Perhaps P.'s most stunning achievement is the use he makes of science and technology in the creation of his metaphors. An early short story, "Entropy" (1960), revealed P.'s fascination with the Second Law of Thermodynamics. The entropy concept, in its dual application in physics and in information theory, pervades all three novels—iterating a theme of the general breakdown of the contemporary sociocultural order.

P.'s prose is strewn with scientific and mathematical allusions—Gödel's Theorem, Maxwell's Demon, Poisson's Distribution. Such concepts, together with discourses on cybernetics, chemistry, and rocketry, are implanted in the very tissue of the fiction, and they grow into symbolic significance that sets P. apart from practitioners of science fiction and fantasy. Equipped as he is with the latest and most specialized scientific and technical lore and the most innovative literary techniques, P. seems fitted to provide his readers with a complete Baedeker's guide through the 20th c.

The novel *V.*, set in the 1950s, traverses the previous half dozen decades in a bewildering itinerary across continents and cultures, to the frontiers of reality and beyond. The novel's overriding form is a doubling of the ancient quest motif. One plot focuses on Herbert Stencil and his obsessive search for the identity of the title symbol: V. is at once a person, a place, and a mental construct—she/he metamorphoses through several identities, ending finally in an assortment of prosthetic attachments. Stencil's career is counterpointed by the aimless peregrinations of Benny Profane, whose freedom dissipates into the mechanical motions of a human yo-yo.

The protagonist of *The Crying of Lot 49* is a California housewife named Oedipa Maas who is doomed as the pursuer pursued through Kafkaesque horrors of contemporary American civilization.

The paranoia of this slim book spills over into *Gravity's Rainbow,* a novel of enormous proportions populated by over three hundred characters who operate on an international scale near the close of World War II and in the Allied Zones of Occupation in 1945. Among these characters is an American lieutenant named Tyrone Slothrop, comically and ironically both quester and quarry. Slothrop, it turns out, was the unwitting subject of scientific manipulation during childhood and now he is the experimental target of competing military factions, one of which attempts to correlate a Poisson distribution of the lieutenant's sex encounters with the pattern of V-2 bombs that fall on London. As the book progresses, Slothrop is the victim of multiple intrigues from all directions. His paranoia is paradigmatic of the hostility and suspicion in all ranks. The rage to control and the terror of being controlled are doubled and redoubled on both sides of the Channel. Over and over again we are brought to the threshold of cosmic conspiracy.

Underneath a metaphysical cloud of doubt and suspicion, P.'s multitudes of men and women move in and out of the Zone, dabbling in their own puddles of purpose, puddles which are iridescent with the slime of humanity. And over all—beyond good and evil?—arches the trajectory of the rocket: the vapor trail of the V-2, caught in the light of the sun whose image dominates the pages of *Gravity's Rainbow*. The rocket is P.'s candidate for an apocalyptic successor and synthesizer of Henry Adams's Virgin and Dynamo.

One critic, Edward Mendelson, has proposed a new genre, the encyclopedic narrative; and into this exclusive category *Gravity's Rainbow* has been admitted along with works of Dante, Rabelais, Cervantes, Goethe, Melville, and Joyce. It is astonishing how often the book has been compared to *Moby-Dick* and *Ulysses*.

All art is a matter of the artist's selecting and arranging what he finds in his world. P.'s powers of assimilation are prodigious: his world is fabulous, his fabrications are splendid. In the process of creating his fables, he has teased the old questions, especially those of freedom and determinism (his is not a binary view), and enlarged our view of human nature.

BIBLIOGRAPHY: Slade, J., *T. P.* (1974); Levine, G., and Leverenz, D., eds., *Mindful Pleasures: Essays on T. P.* (1976); Mendelson, E., ed., *P.: A Collection of Critical Essays* (1978); Siegel, M. R., *P.: Creative Paranoia in "Gravity's Rainbow"* (1978); Cowart, D., *T. P.: The Art of Illusion* (1980); Fowler, D., *A Reader's Guide to "Gravity's Rainbow"* (1980); Mackey, D. A., *The Rainbow Quest of T. P.* (1980); Stark, J. O., *P.'s Fictions: T. P. and the Literature of Information* (1980); Pearce, R., ed., *Critical Essays on T. P.* (1981); Schaub, T. H., *P.: The Voice of Ambiguity* (1981)

CARL D. BENNETT

MARCEL PROUST

EZRA POUND

SALVATORE QUASIMODO

QABBĀNĪ, Nizār

Syrian poet, b. 21 March 1923, Damascus

Son of a rich merchant, Q. joined the Syrian foreign service after finishing his law studies in 1945. As a diplomat he was posted successively to Egypt, Turkey, the United Kingdom, Lebanon, Spain, and China, and he traveled widely. He resigned from the foreign service in 1966 and settled in Beirut, Lebanon, where he worked in literary journalism and eventually started a publishing house.

Q. is perhaps the most popular poet in the Arab world, his collections having run into several printings. Since the early 1940s, when he began writing poetry, to the present day, love and women have continued to be his major themes. Whether or not he is an irresponsible intellectual locked up in an adolescent sensuality that wastes his talent, as some critics think, his achievement is astounding in that for over thirty-five years his creativity has never ceased exploring ever new ways of expressing his love for woman's beauty and portraying women in ever different love situations.

His early poems, such as those in *Qālat lī al-samrā'* (1944; the brunette said to me) and *Anti lī* (1950; you are mine), exhibit a stark physical craving for woman, as he dwells on parts of her body, which he paints in thrilling, evocative images of great beauty. In later poems, as in *Qasā'id* (1956; poems), *Habībatī* (1961; my sweetheart), and *Al-Rasm bi-al-kalimāt* (1966; painting in words), his sensuality becomes refined as he portrays the elegance of high-society women. But Q. has become increasingly aware of the complexities of love relations, especially of woman's vulnerability in man's world, and he has

written several poems expressing woman's disgust with man's crass insensitivity to her. The love poems of his more mature years, as in *Qasā'id mutawahhisha* (1970; wild poems) and *Ash'ār khārija 'alā al-qānūn* (1972; law-breaking poems), treat the experience of love and see it ideally as an honest relation of two reciprocating equals free from social taboos.

Q. has occasionally dealt with other social themes, as in his poem "Khubz wa hashīsh wa qamar" (1955; "Bread, Hashish, and Moon," 1972), in which he castigated Arab society for its languor, superstitiousness, and quiescence. But it was not until 1967, after the humiliating defeat of the Arabs by Israel in the Six Day War, that Q. produced a series of politically motivated poems criticizing repressive Arab regimes and their submissive citizenry, and supported the Palestine Liberation Movement as a hope for wider Arab liberation and transformation. These poems, mostly collected in his *Al-A'māl al-siyāsiyya* (1974; political works), are characterized by the same naturalness and spontaneity that mark his love poems.

FURTHER WORKS: *Tufūlat nahd* (1948); *Sāmbā* (1949); *Al-Shi'r qindīl akhdar* (1964); *Yawmiyyāt imra'a lā-mubāliya* (1969); *Kitāb al-hubb* (1970); *Lā* (1970); *Al-Kitāba 'amal inqilābī* (1978)

BIBLIOGRAPHY: Loya, A., "Poetry as a Social Document: The Social Position of the Arab Woman as Reflected in the Poetry of N. Q.," *MW,* 63, 1 (1973), 39–52; Gabay, Z., "N. Q., the Poet and His Poetry," *MES,* 9, 2 (1973), 207–22; Badawi, M. M., *A Critical Introduction to Modern Arabic Poetry* (1975), pp. 221–22; Jayyusi, S. K., *Trends and Movements in Modern Arabic Poetry* (1977), Vol. II, pp. 563, 664–65

ISSA J. BOULLATA

QADIRIY, Abdullah

(pseud.: Julqunbay) Uzbek novelist, short-story writer, dramatist, and satirist, b. 1894, Tashkent; d. 1940

Q.'s Muslim education combined Persian, Arabic, and Chaghatay (a Turkic literary language) classics with post-1900 "new-method" instruction introduced into Turkistan by the modernizing reformers known as the Jadids. His father, a bankrupt merchant turned winegrower, was a firsthand source

for the 19th-c. history of the khanate of Qo-
qan, the setting for Q.'s novels. Q., arrested
in 1939 as an "enemy of the people," died in
prison; since his 1956 rehabilitation some of
his works have been republished, although in
altered form.

Q. began writing as early as 1910. He produced some poetry and won early success
with his innovative prose: satires, sketches,
short stories like "Ulaqdä" (1916; at a horse-
men's goat-snatching contest) and "Juwan-
baz" (1915; the pederast), and plays,
including the much-performed *Bäkhtsiz
kuyaw* (1915; the unlucky son-in-law).

Q. brought his dramatist's skills—lively dialogue and vivid episodic style—to his major
venture: replacing Central Asian folk epics
with the first Uzbek novel. Q., who was acquainted with works of Jurjī Zaydān (1861–
1914), an Arab historical novelist, used court
intrigues, harem politics, and merchant and
clerical households as backdrop for his novels: *Otgän kunlär* (1925–26; days gone by), a
tragedy of an arranged polygamous marriage,
and *Mehrabdän chäyan* (1929; scorpion from
the pulpit), the true story of a poor orphan
who rose to be chief secretary to the khan.
Both books, written in modern literary language laced with folk humor, were best sellers, reprinted often, and later translated into
other Central Asian languages and Russian.
Avoiding both the stereotyped beautiful
women of Oriental literature and the tractor-
driving heroines of much Soviet fiction, Q.
presents subtle characterizations, psychologically motivated, of both sexes.

In satirical story cycles published between
1923 and 1927 in *Mushtum,* one of several
periodicals with which Q. was associated, the
comical portraits of the self-important characters Kälwäk Mähzum and Aunty Shärwan
were popular.

Q.'s belated recognition as creator of the
Uzbek novel filled an awkward void in Soviet
Uzbek literary history, for except for his
work there was little of note in this genre by
Uzbeks before Aybek's (q.v.) novel *Näwaiy*
in 1944. Q.'s influence on succeeding writers
as mentor and model has been gratefully and
openly acknowledged by Aybek, by the Ka-
zakh author Mukhtar Omarkhan-uli Auezov
(q.v.), by the Turkmen novelist Berdi Kerba-
bay-oghli (1894–1974), and by many others.

FURTHER WORKS: *Abid ketman* (1934)

BIBLIOGRAPHY: Hayit, B., "Die jüngste özbe-
kische Literatur," *CAsJ,* 7 (1962), 119–52;

Allworth, E., *Uzbek Literary Politics* (1964),
passim; Benzing, J., "Die usbekische und
neu-uigurische Literatur," *Philologiae Turcicae Fundamenta,* 2 (1965), 700–20; "Kadyri,
Abdulla," *Great Soviet Encyclopedia,* 3rd ed.
(1976), Vol. XI, p. 334

SUSANNA S. NETTLETON

QUASIMODO, Salvatore

Italian poet, translator, and essayist, b. 20
Aug. 1901, Modica, Sicily; d. 14 June 1968,
Naples

Q. was born into a family of modest means.
His father was a stationmaster whose trans-
fers allowed the boy to know various Sicilian
scenes, which were later to appear in his poetry. He pursued technical studies in Palermo and Rome, and became a civil engineer
with the Ministry of Public Works (1926–
38). Thereafter he moved into the more congenial field of letters, contributing to literary
journals, serving as editor of the weekly *Il
tempo* several times, and from 1940 on teaching Italian literature at the Milan Conserva-
tory of Music. He was always an assiduous
student of ancient and modern languages and
literatures. His poetry brought him several
literary awards, including the Etna-Taormina
Prize for Poetry (1953, shared with Dylan
Thomas [q.v.]), the Viareggio Prize (1958),
and the Nobel Prize for literature (1959).

Q.'s literary production consists of a dozen
slender volumes of poetry; fifteen or more
volumes of excellent translations of Greek
and Latin classics, Shakespeare, and modern
poets of various nationalities; two volumes of
critical essays; numerous (partly uncollected)
articles and reviews; and several librettos for
music.

His first volume of verse, *Acque e terre*
(1930; water and land), contains features that
were to recur throughout his work: vivid
memories of his youth, compassion and concern for the humble folk from whom he
came, a deep sense of the solitude of the individual, a personal seriousness and melancholy, a generally negative view of life. This
early collection contains at least one authentic masterpiece, "Vento a Tíndari" ("Wind at
Tíndari," 1960). Q.'s forceful and evocative
style was immensely attractive despite its initial "difficulty," and was quickly acclaimed
by the public and the critics. Several other
volumes appeared in quick succession. His
whole prewar output was pruned, revised,

and republished in the volume *Ed è subito sera* (1942; and suddenly it is evening), which remains his most widely read book.

World War II broadened Q.'s human sympathy and the horizon of his poetry. *Giorno dopo giorno* (1947; day after day) reflects his country's hardships. The poems in it are intense, deeply felt; their eloquence is achieved less through rhetoric than through a precise directness of language, brief realistic notations, a humane commentary. A less closed and less intimate style, a more "public" utterance, are appropriately used here to deal with Italy's woes, in poems such as "Alle fronde dei salici" ("On the Willow Branches," 1960) and "Uomo del mio tempo" ("Man of My Time," 1960). This may be Q.'s best work, and perhaps the best volume of poetry to come out of World War II in any country.

Q.'s last four volumes of verse show a continuing concern for social justice, fond memories of past friends and past loves, probings into the meaning of life, and ponderings on illness and death. They are somewhat uneven collections, but with a preponderance of fine poems.

Q.'s overall production is impressive in its uncommon originality and its high quality. One of its most attractive features is the great sensitivity to the look and feel of the poet's native Sicily and a constant awareness of its cultural heritage from Greeks, Romans, Arabs, and other invaders. He recalls certain landscapes, his experience of them, what they meant to him; he notes literary associations ("my Homeric childhood," "Ulysses' isle,"), historical relics, the physical environment— its harshness and its Mediterranean beauty ("earth and sky and gentle gift of water"). The voluntary exile in the northern metropolis remembers his island as a brave, bright Eden, situated on storied ground; he inevitably poetizes it, viewing it through the prisms of love, memory, time and distance. The "myth" of Sicily that he creates adds much to the richness and flavor of Q.'s poetry. He is also keenly interested in the island's present-day economic and political problems; these he notes with harsh realism.

In style and language Q. avoids the "classical" and the ornate in favor of a condensed, lean, and forceful utterance that is nonetheless flexible and varied. He is sober in the expression of feeling. He manages a fine affectionate poem to his mother, and another to his father, that have none of the usual sentimental effusions. Everywhere the superfluous or vague is pared away, and the word is given its essential meaning in an essential role. This is the mark of Q.'s modernity and places him in the current of hermeticism (q.v.) that dominated his time. The critics speak of the "tension" and "intensity" of the word, of his "poetics of the word," of a process of "essentialization" resulting in a spare and "naked" language. His poems are brief; the short lines conform only loosely, if at all, to traditional meters. They have a natural harmony and a sustained literary dignity. Q. has assumed his rightful place among the three or four best Italian poets of the century.

FURTHER WORKS: *Oboe sommerso* (1932); *Odore di eucalyptus* (1933); *Erato e Apòllion* (1936); *Poesie* (1938); *Con il piede straniero sopra il cuore* (1946); *La vita non è sogno* (1949); *Il falso e vero verde* (1956); *La terra impareggiabile* (1958; *The Incomparable Earth*, 1958); *Il poeta e il politico, e altri saggi* (1960; *The Poet and the Politician, and Other Essays*, 1964); *Tutte le poesie* (1960); *Dare e avere* (1966; *To Give and to Have, and Other Poems*, 1969); *Poesie e discorsi sulla poesia* (1971). FURTHER VOLUMES IN ENGLISH: *The Selected Writings of S. Q.* (1960); *Selected Poems* (1965); *To Give and to Have, and Other Poems* (1969)

BIBLIOGRAPHY: Cambon, G., "A Deep Wind: Q.'s Tíndari," *IQ*, 3 (1959), 16–28; Rossi, L. R., "S. Q.: A Presentation," *ChiR*, 14 (1960), 1–21; Cambon, G., "Q.," *Chelsea*, 6 (1960), 60–67; Pacifici, S., "S. Q.," *Cesare Barbieri Courier*, 3 (1960), 10–16; Jones, F. J., "Poetry of S. Q.," *IS*, 16 (1961), 60–77; Beall, C. B., "Q. and Modern Italian Poetry," *NorthwestR*, 4 (1961), 41–48; Dutschke, D., "S. Q.," *IQ*, 12 (1969), 91–103; Molinaro, J. A., "Q. and the Theme of the Willow Trees," *RomN*, 18 (1977), 32–37; Danesi, M., "Some Observations on Information Theory and Poetic Language, with Illustrations from the Poetry of S. Q.," *CJItS*, 1 (1978), 224–30

CHANDLER B. BEALL

QUEIROZ, Rachel de

Brazilian novelist, dramatist, and journalist, b. 17 Nov. 1910, Fortaleza

Q. started her literary career in 1927 as a journalist in her native city. She made a sen-

615

sational debut as a novelist with *O quinze* (1930; 'fifteen [i.e., 1915]), which was received with enthusiastic critical acclaim throughout Brazil. The fact of her youth contributed to this success, but more important was the fact that the novel was one of the first, after *A bagaceira* (1928; sugar mill) by José Américo de Almeida (1887–1980), to introduce to Brazil a new social-minded literature of the 1930s. Although the periodic droughts in northeastern Brazil had been the theme of a few earlier novels, the literary school initiated with the books of Almeida and Q. substituted social and even socialist intentions and preoccupations for the traditional sentimental approach to that tragedy. The novel's title refers to the year of 1915, in which one of the most catastrophic droughts occurred. All these circumstances explain the immense interest awakened by *O quinze,* which was awarded the Graça Aranha Foundation literary prize in 1931.

Q.'s second novel, *João Miguel* (1932; João Miguel), was a tentative effort toward a proletarian novel. Its hero is in fact an antihero, the common man of northeast Brazil. In terms of Q.'s development as a novelist, it marks a transition from a social to a psychological approach.

Indeed, after a five-year period of silence, Q. published *Caminho de pedras* (1937; road of stones), which was followed by *As três Marias* (1939; *The Three Marias,* 1963). Both are clearly individualist in accent and purpose. With the exception of *O galo de ouro* (the golden rooster)—not yet published in book form—which appeared in installments in 1950 in a Rio de Janeiro publication, Q. stopped writing narratives until 1975, when the novel *Dôra Doralina* (Dôra Doralina) was published.

In the 1940s Q. began to write columns for several newspapers and particularly for the periodical *O cruzeiro.* Her *crônicas* gained widespread popularity in Brazil and assured her reputation as one of Brazil's outstanding writers. Many of those *crônicas* were subsequently collected into books—for example, *100 crônicas escolhidas* (1958; 100 selected chronicles).

In the 1950s she became interested in the theater. Her first play, *Lampião* (1953; Lampião), is about the life and deeds of the famous rural outlaw nicknamed Lampião. It was well received in Rio de Janeiro and São Paulo, where it was awarded the Saci Prize as the year's best play. Five years later, another play, *A beata Maria do Egito* (1958; blessed Mary of Egypt), was awarded two other prizes.

In addition, Q. is a highly respected translator, having brought out in Portuguese works by Dostoevsky, Jane Austen, Emily Brontë, and John Galsworthy (q.v.).

What can be said about Q. without hesitation is that she is to be credited with writing a Portuguese that is highly expressive and that she handles colloquial Portuguese masterfully. In 1957 she was awarded the Brazilian Academy of Letters prize for her total work, and was elected to this academy in 1977.

FURTHER WORKS: *Três romances* (1948); *A donzela e a moura torta* (1948); *Quatro romances* (1960); *O Brasileiro perplexo* (1964); *O caçador de tatu* (1967); *O menino mágico* (1969)

BIBLIOGRAPHY: Ellison, F. P., *Brazil's New Novel: Four Northeastern Writers* (1954), pp. 135–54; Schade, G. D., "Three Contemporary Brazilian Novels: Some Comparisons and Contrasts," *Hispania,* 39 (1956), 391–96; Woodbridge, B. M., Jr., "The Art of R. de Q.," *Hispania,* 40 (1957), 139–48; Reynolds, C. R., "The Santa María Egipciaca Motif in Modern Brazilian Letters," *RomN,* 13 (1971), 71–76

WILSON MARTINS

QUENEAU, Raymond

French novelist and poet, b. 21 Feb. 1903, Le Havre; d. 25 Oct. 1976, Paris

As a young writer, Q. was attracted to surrealism (q.v.) and participated actively in the movement between 1924 and 1929. He became a reader for Gallimard in 1938 and was the principal editor of their encyclopedias and histories of literature published in the Pléiade series beginning in the late 1940s. Q. engaged in a broad range of activities, including painting and film, and he wrote of these as well as on literature and many other subjects, including mathematics. He was elected to the Goncourt Academy in 1951.

Q.'s first novel, and perhaps his best, was *Le chiendent* (1933; *The Bark-Tree,* 1968). It was one of the first books to reveal, through the use of slangy speech, a crisis in the language of the novel. Q., who was at that time still close to surrealism, seems to have reenacted the surrealist rebellion here, insisting that the real subject of his work is language itself, language that is being endlessly created.

Pierrot mon ami (1942; *Pierrot,* 1950), whose hero moves about an amusement park in a manner reminiscent of Charlie Chaplin, is also a clever exercise in words, a detective story in which one can never be sure whether a crime has been committed.

Loin de Rueil (1944; *The Skin of Dreams,* 1948) is very much admired by sophisticated readers. The protagonist, Jacques L'Aumône, leads a complex fantasy life as well as a mundane existence; he becomes the hero of films he sees, a boxing champion, a bishop, a nobleman, until finally neither he nor the reader is sure who he is. *Loin de Rueil* presents a half-mad, half-poetic vision of the world.

Zazie dans le métro (1959; *Zazie,* 1960) was an immediate popular success, perhaps because Zazie is a sort of farcical French Lolita, but its ultimate value lies in Q.'s use of a popular, if salacious, style of dialogue, often reproduced phonetically. As in his earlier novels, he thus questions the nature and value of language itself, and here the banal setting stresses the meaninglessness of action and speech.

Q. had already experimented explicitly with language in *Exercices de style* (1947; *Exercises in Style,* 1958), in which he presents ninety-nine different versions of the same totally insignificant anecdote. In fact, Q.'s entire work could be characterized as an exercise in style intended to reveal the absurdity of human activity.

This expression of the gratuitousness of life through experimentation with language is especially apparent in his poems. They are often built on plays on words and on the repetition of key words, as in the collection with the meaningless title of *Les ziaux* (1943; the ziaux). *Cent mille milliards de poèmes* (1961; one hundred trillion poems) carries this tendency several steps further, and also reflects Q.'s mathematical bent, by presenting ten sonnets in which any line can be substituted for any other line, thereby creating the number of poems in the title.

In his efforts to rejuvenate literary forms and to develop new means of literary communication, Q. often employed traditional forms—the novel, the sonnet, the alexandrine—but always parodying them, using the vocabulary and tempo of popular speech. He does not attempt to provide an exact transcription of contemporary life and society; rather, he creates a new view of it based on the language forged from his observations.

Q.'s view of language shows his affiliation with surrealism; yet he was also close to existentialism (q.v.) in his creation of a sense of the absurd, of the hopelessness and ridiculousness of the contemporary world. Q. has not reached the vast public of Sartre and Camus (qq.v.), however, because he did not attempt to go beyond the meaninglessness he expressed, but, rather, enjoyed it. His readership will remain those who can share his joy without demanding more.

Many writers, including Henry Miller and Boris Vian (qq.v.), have found affinities with Q. and admitted his influence. Perhaps Q., of all modern French writers, comes closest to James Joyce (q.v.), in the breadth of his learning and his creation of new literary structures through his linguistic virtuosity. But again, his seemingly frivolous attitude toward literature and life precludes his being treated critically with as much seriousness as his Irish predecessor.

FURTHER WORKS: *Gueule de Pierre* (1934); *Les derniers jours* (1936); *Odile* (1937); *Chêne et chien* (1937); *Les enfants du limon* (1938); *Un rude hiver* (1939; *A Hard Winter,* 1948); *Les temps mêlés* (1941); *En passant* (1944); *Foutaises* (1944); *L'instant fatal* (1946); *Pictogrammes* (1946); *À la limite de la forêt* (1947; *At the Edge of the Forest,* 1954); *Bucoliques* (1947); *Une trouille verte* (1947); *On est toujours trop bon avec les femmes* (1947, under pseud. Sally Mara; *We Always Treat Women Too Well,* 1981); *Monuments* (1948); *Saint Glinglin* (1948); *Bâtons, chiffres et lettres* (1950); *Petite cosmogonie portative* (1950); *Journal intime* (1950, under pseud. Sally Mara); *Si tu t'imagines* (1952); *Le dimanche de la vie* (1952); *Le chien à la mandoline* (1958); *Sonnets* (1958); *Texticules* (1961); *Entretiens avec Georges Charbonnier* (1962); *Les œuvres complètes de Sally Mara* (1962; reprint of *On est toujours trop bon avec les femmes* and *Journal intime*); *Bords* (1963); *Les fleurs bleues* (1965; *Blue Flowers,* 1967); *Une histoire modèle* (1966); *Courir les rues* (1967); *Battre la campagne* (1968); *Le vol d'Icare* (1968; *The Flight of Icarus,* 1973); *Fendre les flots* (1969); *Morale élémentaire* (1975)

BIBLIOGRAPHY: Bens, J., *R. Q.* (1962); Bergens, A., *R. Q.* (1963); Guicharnaud, J., *R.*

Q. (1965); Gayot, P., *R. Q.* (1966); Klinkesberg, J.-M., *Jeu et profondeur chez R. Q.* (1967); Queval, J., *R. Q.* (1971); Baligand, R., *Les poèmes de R. Q.* (1972)

CHARLES G. HILL

QUIROGA, Horacio

Uruguayan short-story writer, b. 31 Dec. 1878, Salto; d. 19 Feb. 1937, Buenos Aires, Argentina

Certain thematic designs run through Q.'s life and work. His life was crammed with adventure, hazardous enterprise, and recurrent tragedy. When he was an infant, his father was accidentally killed when a shotgun went off; later, his stepfather shot himself. His first wife, unable to endure the hardships in the jungle where Q. insisted on living, committed suicide by taking poison. The singular amount of violence marring Q.'s personal life doubtless explains a great deal about the obsession with death so marked in his stories.

Q.'s zest for adventure and the magnetic attraction the jungle hinterland of northern Argentina held for him are also biographical details that have great impact on his work. His first trip to Misiones province occurred in 1903, and in 1906 he bought land there and from then on divided his time between Misiones and Buenos Aires. (Although born and raised in Uruguay, he spent most of his years in Argentina.)

Q. began writing under the aegis of modernism (q.v.), which dominated Spanish American literary life at the turn of the century. Soon, however, he reacted against the highly artificial mode of his first book, *Los arrecifes de coral* (1901; coral reefs), a collection of prose poems and poetry, and turned to writing tales firmly rooted in reality, although they often emphasized the bizarre or the monstrous. Many of these early stories are reminiscent of Poe and show a skillful handling of gothic elements.

For three decades Q. continued publishing short stories in great quantity, many of them also of impressive quality. (His few attempts at the novel were failures.) Two collections should be singled out as high points: *Los desterrados* (1926; the exiled) and *Cuentos de amor, de locura, y de muerte* (1917; stories of love, madness, and death). The latter title sets forth Q.'s major themes and could properly be the heading for his entire work.

He also achieved renown with *Cuentos de la selva* (1918: *South American Jungle Tales*, 1959), a volume cast in fable mold, with talking animals, for children of all ages, which is permeated with tenderness and humor; and with *Anaconda* (1921; anaconda), whose title story describes a world of snakes and how they battle men and also one another. This long tale moves at a leisurely pace, with a spun-out plot. Its ophidian characters are more compelling than believable, and the animal characterization is not as striking as that of his shorter narratives.

If we examine Q.'s stories closely, we will find moments full of vision concerning mankind. He has an astute awareness of the problems besetting man on every side—not only the pitfalls of savage nature but also those pertaining to human relationships. His comments on illusions can be withering. Although he never palliates man's faults and weaknesses, the heroic virtues of courage, generosity, and compassion also emerge in many of his stories.

Q. at his best was a master craftsman. He described his technique in "Manual del cuentista perfecto" (1927; manual for the perfect short-story writer), a succinct decalogue filled with cogent advice. Usually Q. practiced the economy he preaches in this short-story manual. Wonderful feats of condensation are common, as in "El hombre muerto" (1934; the dead man), where he shows his powers in dramatic focus on a single scene, or in "A la deriva" (1917; drifting), a stark story in which everything seems reduced to the essential, where the brief opening scene of a man bitten by a viper contains the germs of all that comes afterward. The language is terse and pointed, the situation of tremendous intensity, the action straightforward and lineal.

Q. does not have a social axe to grind, but some of the most trenchant social commentary in Spanish American fiction can be perceived in his stories, particularly those concerned with the exploitation of Misiones lumberjacks, like "Los mensú" (1917; "The Contract Workers," 1962). Setting, as well as narrative technique, is vitally important to Q., because it is inseparable from the real, day-to-day experience of human existence. Q.'s feelings are bound up in place, especially in Misiones, where the majority of his best stories take place. He makes us feel the significance of this setting, the symbolic strength of the rivers, and the hypnotic force of its snake-infested jungles.

Q. continues to rank as one of Latin America's finest short-story writers. He knew his trade in and out, and was universal in scope. He subjected his themes to dramatic form, transmitting to his readers all their virtues and ferment. He wrote tautly and described with intensity so that the story would make its mark on the reader.

FURTHER WORKS: *El crimen del otro* (1904); *Los perseguidos* (1905); *Historia de un amor turbio* (1908); *El salvaje* (1920); *El desierto* (1924); *Pasado amor* (1929); *El más allá* (1934); *Cuentos* (7 vols., 1937); *Diario de viaje a París* (1950); *Obras inéditas y desconocidas* (7 vols., 1967–68). FURTHER VOLUME IN ENGLISH: *The Decapitated Chicken, and Other Stories* (1976)

BIBLIOGRAPHY: Delgado, J., *H. Q.* (1939); Etcheverry, J., *H. Q.* (1957); Martínez Estrada, E., *El hermano Q.* (1957); Rodríguez Monegal, E., *El desterrado: Vida y obra de H. Q.* (1968); Bratosevich, N., *El estilo de H. Q. en sus cuentos* (1973); Schade, G., Introduction to *The Decapitated Chicken, and Other Stories* (1976), pp. ix–xviii; Flores, Á., et al., *Aproximaciones a H. Q.* (1976)

GEORGE D. SCHADE